The Reformation in England

Volume Two

History should be made to live with its own proper life.
God is this life. God must be acknowledged—
God proclaimed—in history.

J. H. MERLE D'AUBIGNÉ

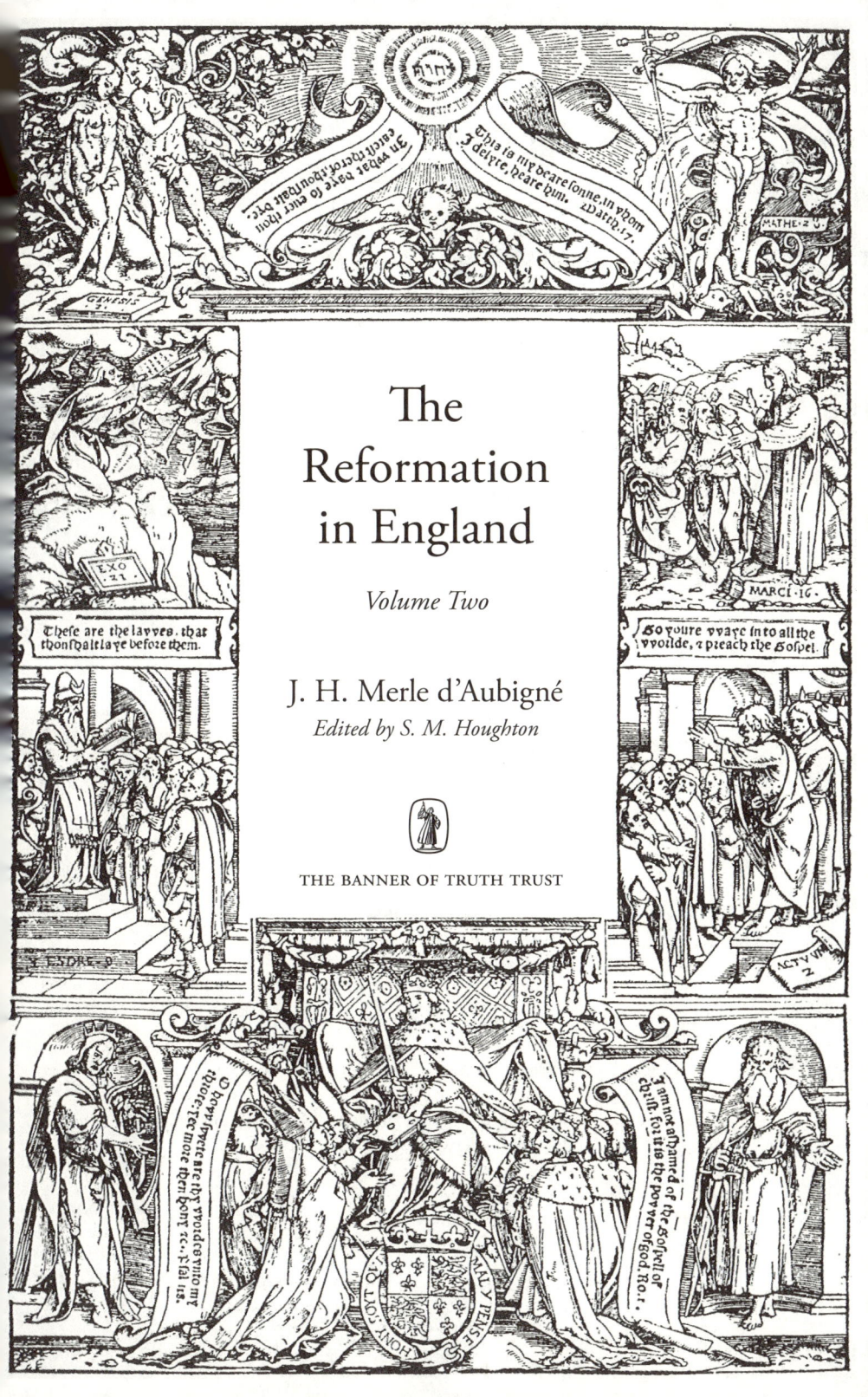

The Reformation in England

Volume Two

J. H. Merle d'Aubigné

Edited by S. M. Houghton

THE BANNER OF TRUTH TRUST

THE BANNER OF TRUTH TRUST

Head Office	*North America Office*
3 Murrayfield Road	PO Box 621
Edinburgh	Carlisle
EH12 6EL	PA 17013
UK	USA

banneroftruth.org

First published in 1866-78 as Vol. VI, VIII, and XV of of
The History of the Reformation in Europe in the Time of Calvin

First Banner of Truth Trust edition 1963
Reprinted 1972, 1977, 1985, 1994
This revised and re-typeset edition 2015

© Banner of Truth Trust 2015
Reprinted 2020

*

ISBN (Volume 2)
Print: 978 1 84871 646 9
Epub: 978 1 84871 647 6
Kindle: 978 1 84871 649 0

2-Volume Set: 978 1 84871 650 6

*

Typeset in 10.5/13.5 Adobe Garamond Pro
at The Banner of Truth Trust, Edinburgh

Printed in the USA by
Versa Press Inc.,
East Peoria, IL.

Contents

BOOK ONE
England Begins to Cast Off the Papacy

BOOK TWO
England Breaks with Rome

CHAPTER EIGHT

HENRY NEGOTIATES WITH GERMAN LUTHERANS

(1534 to 1535)

CHAPTER NINE

THE ACCUSATION OF THE QUEEN

(1535 to May 1536)

BOOK THREE
Reformation, Reaction, Relief

CHAPTER FOUR
A Bitter Cup for Henry VIII
(1539–1540)

CHAPTER FIVE
The Disgrace and Death of Thomas Cromwell
(1540)

CHAPTER SIX
The Divorce of Anne of Cleves
(1540)

CHAPTER SEVEN
Catherine Howard, the Fifth Queen
(1540)

CHAPTER EIGHT
CRANMER PURSUES HIS TASK

(1542)

CHAPTER NINE
THE LAST MARTYRS OF HENRY'S REIGN

(1545)

CHAPTER TEN
DEATH CASTS ITS SHADOW OVER CATHERINE PARR

(1546)

CHAPTER ELEVEN

The Last Days of Henry VIII

(1546–January 1547)

BOOK ONE

England Begins to Cast Off the Papacy

Thomas Bilney on his way to the stake

CHAPTER ONE

The Nation and Its Parties

(Autumn 1529)

England, during the period of which we are about to treat, began to separate from the pope and to reform her church. The fall of Wolsey divides the old times from the new.

The level of the laity was gradually rising. A certain amount of instruction was given to the children of the poor; the universities were frequented by the upper classes, and the king was probably the most learned prince in Christendom. At the same time the clerical level was falling. The clergy had been weakened and corrupted by its triumphs, and the English, awakening with the age and opening their eyes at last, were disgusted with the pride, ignorance, and disorders of the priests.

While France, flattered by Rome calling her its eldest daughter, desired even when reforming her doctrine to preserve union with the papacy, the Anglo-Saxon race, jealous of their liberties, desired to form a church at once national and independent, yet remaining faithful to the doctrines of Catholicism. Henry VIII is the personification of that tendency, which did not disappear with him, and of which it would not be difficult to discover traces even in later days.

Other elements calculated to produce a better reformation existed at that time in England. The Holy Scriptures, translated, studied, circulated, and preached since the fourteenth century by Wycliffe and his disciples, became in the sixteenth century, by the publication of Erasmus' Testament and the translations of Tyndale and Coverdale, the powerful instrument of a real evangelical revival, and created the scriptural reformation.

These early developments did not proceed from Calvin; he was too young at that time; but Tyndale, Fryth, Latimer, and the other evangelists of the reign of Henry VIII, taught by the same word as the reformer of Geneva, were his brethren and his precursors. Somewhat later, his books and his letters to Edward VI, to the regent, to the primate, to Sir William Cecil and others, exercised an indisputable influence over the reformation of England. We find in those letters proofs of the esteem which the most intelligent persons of the kingdom felt for that simple and strong man, whom even non-Protestant voices in France have declared to be 'the greatest Christian of his age'.

A religious reformation may be of two kinds: internal or evangelical, external or legal. The evangelical reformation began at Oxford and Cambridge almost at the same time as in Germany. The legal reformation was making a beginning at Westminster and Whitehall. Students, priests, and laymen, moved by inspiration from on high, had inaugurated the first; Henry VIII and his Parliament were about to inaugurate the second, with hands occasionally somewhat rough. England began with the spiritual reformation, but the other had its motives too. Those who are charmed by the reformation of Germany sometimes affect contempt for that of England. 'A king impelled by his passions was its author', they say. We have placed the scriptural part of this great transformation in the first rank; but we confess that for it to lay hold upon the people in the sixteenth century, it was necessary, as the prophet declared, that kings should be its nursing fathers, and queens its nursing mothers. If diverse reforms were necessary, if by the side of German cordiality, Swiss simplicity, and other characteristics, God willed to found a Protestantism possessing a strong hand and an outstretched arm; if a nation was to exist which with great freedom and power should carry the gospel to the ends of the world, special tools were required to form that robust organization, and the leaders of the people – the commons, lords, and king – were each to play their part. France had nothing like this: both princes and parliaments opposed the reform; and thence partly arises the difference between those two great nations, for France had in Calvin a mightier reformer than any of those whom England possessed. But let us not forget that we are speaking of the sixteenth century. Since then the work has advanced; important changes have been wrought in Christendom; political society is growing daily more distinct from religious society, and more independent; and we willingly say with Pascal, 'Glorious is the state of the church when it is supported by God alone!'

Two opposing elements – the reforming liberalism of the people, and the almost absolute power of the king – combined in England to accomplish the legal reformation. In that singular island these two rival forces were often seen acting together; the liberalism of the nation gaining certain victories, the despotism of the prince gaining others; king and people agreeing to make mutual concessions. In the midst of these compromises, the little evangelical flock, which had no voice in such matters, religiously preserved the treasure entrusted to it: the word of God, truth, liberty, and Christian virtue. From all these elements sprang the Church of England. A strange church some call it. Strange indeed, for there is none which corresponds so imperfectly in theory with the ideal of the church, and, perhaps, none whose members work out with more power and grandeur the ends for which Christ has formed his kingdom.

Scarcely had Henry VIII refused to go to Rome to plead his cause, when he issued writs for a new Parliament (25 September 1529). Wolsey's unpopularity had hitherto prevented its meeting: now the force of circumstances constrained the king to summon it. When he was on the eve of separating from the pope, he felt the necessity of leaning on the people. Liberty is always the gainer where a country performs an act of independence with regard to Rome. It was natural that in England, possessing as it did from of old time a body of elected representatives, the king should seek the nation's co-operation in the work of reform: and certainly the House of Commons gained power and prestige during this period. At the same time, the whole kingdom being astir, the different parties became more distinct.

The papal party was alarmed. Fisher, Bishop of Rochester, already very uneasy, became disturbed at seeing laymen called upon to give their advice on religious matters. Men's minds were in a ferment in the bishop's palace, the rural parsonage, and the monk's cell. The partisans of Rome met and consulted about what was to be done, and retired from their conferences foreseeing and imagining nothing but defeat.

Du Bellay, at that time Bishop of Bayonne, and afterwards of Paris, envoy from the King of France, and eye-witness of all this agitation, wrote to Montmorency (Grand Master of France): 'I fancy that in this Parliament the priests will have a terrible fright.' Ambitious ecclesiastics were beginning to understand that the clerical character, hitherto so favourable to their advancement in a political career, would now be an obstacle to them. 'Alas!' exclaimed one of them, 'we must off with our frocks.'

Such of the clergy, however, as determined to remain faithful to Rome gradually roused themselves. A prelate put himself at their head. Fisher, Bishop of Rochester, was learned, intelligent, bold, and slightly fanatical; but his convictions were sincere, and he was determined to sacrifice everything for the maintenance of Roman Catholicism in England. Though discontented with the path upon which his august pupil King Henry had entered, he did not despair of the future, and candidly applied to the papacy our Saviour's words, *The gates of hell shall not prevail against it.*

A recent act of the king's increased Fisher's hopes: Sir Thomas More had been appointed chancellor. The Bishop of Rochester regretted indeed that the king had not given that office to an ecclesiastic, as was customary; but he thought to himself that a layman wholly devoted to the church, as the new chancellor was, might possibly in those strange times be more useful to it than a priest. With Fisher in the church, and More in the state (for Sir Thomas, in spite of his gentle *Utopia*, was more papistical and more violent than Wolsey), had the papacy anything to fear? The whole Romish party rallied round these two men, and with them prepared to fight against the reformation.

Opposed to this hierarchical party was the political party, in whose eyes the king's will was the supreme rule. The dukes of Norfolk and Suffolk, president and vice-president of the council, Sir William Fitz-William, comptroller of the household, and those who agreed with them, were opposed to the ecclesiastical domination, not from the love of true religion, but because they believed the prerogatives of the state were endangered by the ambition of the priests, or else because, seeking honour and power for themselves, they were impatient at always encountering insatiable clerics on their path.

Between these two parties a third appeared, on whom the bishops and nobles looked with disdain, but with whom the victory was to rest at last. In the towns and villages of England, and especially in London, were to be found many lowly men, animated with a new life – poor artisans, weavers, cobblers, painters, shopkeepers – who believed in the word of God and had received moral liberty from it. During the day they toiled at their respective occupations; but at night they stole along some narrow lane, slipped into a court, and ascended to some upper room in which other persons had already assembled. There they read the Scriptures and prayed. At times even during the day, they might be seen carrying to well-disposed citizens certain books strictly prohibited by the late cardinal. Organized under the name of 'The Society of Christian Brethren', they had a central committee in London and missionaries everywhere, who distributed the Holy Scriptures and explained their lessons in simple language. Several priests, both in the city and country, belonged to their society.

This Christian brotherhood exercised a powerful influence over the people, and was beginning to substitute the spiritual and life-giving principles of the gospel for the legal and theocratic ideas of popery. These pious men required a moral regeneration in their hearers, and entreated them to enter, through faith in the Saviour, into an intimate relation with God, without having recourse to the mediation of the clergy; and many of those who listened to them, enraptured at hearing of truth, grace, morality, liberty, and of the word of God, took the teachings to heart. Thus began a new era. It has been asserted that the reformation entered England by a back door. Not so; it was the true door these missionaries opened, having even prior to the rupture with Rome preached the doctrine of Christ. Idly do men speak of Henry's passions, the intrigues of his courtiers, the parade of his ambassadors, the skill of his ministers, the complaisance of the clergy, and the vacillations of Parliament: we too shall speak of these things; but above them all there was something else, something better – the thirst exhibited in this island for the word of God, and the internal transformation accomplished in the convictions of a great number of its inhabitants. This it was that worked such a powerful revolution in English society.

In the interval between the issuing of the writs and the meeting of Parliament, the most antagonistic opinions came out. Conversation everywhere turned on present and future events, and there was a general feeling that the country was on the eve of great changes. The members of Parliament who arrived in London gathered round the same table to discuss the questions of the day. The great lords gave sumptuous banquets, at which the guests talked about the abuses of the church, of the approaching session of Parliament, and of what might result from it. One would mention some striking instance of the avarice of the priests; another slyly called to mind the strange privilege which permitted them to commit with impunity certain sins which they punished severely in others. 'There are, even in London, houses of ill-fame for the use of priests, monks, and canons.' 'And', added others, 'they would force us to take such men as these for our guides to heaven.' Du Bellay, the French ambassador, a man of letters, who, although a bishop, had attached Rabelais to his person in the capacity of secretary, was frequently invited to parties given by the great lords. He lent an attentive ear, and was astonished at the witty and often very biting remarks uttered by the guests against the disorders of the priests. One day a voice exclaimed: 'Since Wolsey has fallen, we must forthwith regulate the condition of the church and of its ministers. We will seize their property.' Du Bellay on his return home did not fail to communicate these things to Montmorency: 'I have no need', he says, 'to write this strange language in cipher; for the noble lords utter it at open table. I think they will do something to be talked about.'

The leading members of the commons held more serious meetings with one another. They said they had spoken enough, and that now they must act. They specified the abuses they would claim to have redressed, and prepared petitions for reform to be presented to the king.

Before long the movement descended from the sphere of the nobility to that of the people: a sphere always important, and particularly when a social revolution is in progress. Petty tradesmen and artisans spoke more energetically than the lords. They did more than speak. The apparitor of the Bishop of London having entered the shop of a mercer in the ward of St Bride, and left a summons on the counter calling upon him to pay a certain clerical tax, the indignant tradesman took up his yard-measure, whereupon the officer drew his sword, and then, either from fear or an evil conscience, ran away. The mercer followed him, assaulted him in the street, and broke his head. The London shopkeepers did not yet quite understand the representative system; they used their staves when they should have waited for the speeches of the members of Parliament.

The king tolerated this agitation because it forwarded his purposes. There were advisers who insinuated that it was dangerous to give free course to the passions of the people; and that the English, combining great physical strength with a decided character, might go too far in the way of reform, if their prince gave them the rein. But Henry VIII, possessing an energetic will, thought it would be easy for him to check the popular ebullition whenever he pleased. When Jupiter frowned, all Olympus trembled.

CHAPTER TWO

Parliament and Its Grievances

(November 1529)

On the morning of 3 November, Henry went in his barge to the palace of Bridewell; and, having put on the magnificent robes employed on great ceremonies, and followed by the lords of his train, he proceeded to the Blackfriars Church, in which the members of the new Parliament had assembled. After hearing the mass of the Holy Ghost, king, lords, and commons met in Parliament; when, as soon as the king had taken his seat on the throne, the new chancellor, Sir Thomas More, explained the reason of their being summoned. Thomas Audley, chancellor of the Duchy of Lancaster, was appointed Speaker of the lower house.

Generally speaking, Parliament confined itself to passing the resolutions of the government. The Great Charter had, indeed, been long in existence, but until now it had been little more than a dead letter. The reformation gave it life. 'Christ brings us out of bondage into liberty by means of the gospel', said Calvin. This emancipation, which was essentially spiritual, soon extended to other spheres, and gave an impulse to liberty throughout all Christendom. Even in England such an impulse was needed. Under the Plantagenets and the Tudors the constitutional machine existed, but it worked only as it was directed by the strong hand of the master. Without the reformation, England might have slumbered long.

The impulse given by religious truth to the latent liberties of the people was felt for the first time in the Parliament of 1529. The representatives shared the lively feelings of their constituents, and took their seats with the firm resolve to introduce the necessary reforms in the affairs of both church and state. Indeed, on the very first day several members pointed out the abuses of the clerical domination, and proposed to lay the desires of the people before the king.

The commons might of their own accord have applied to the task, and by proposing rash changes have given the reform a character of violence that might have worked confusion in the state; but they preferred petitioning the king to take the necessary measures to carry out the wishes of the nation; and accordingly a petition respectfully worded, but in clear and strong language, was agreed to. The reformation began in England, as in Switzerland and in Germany, with personal conversions. The individual was reformed first; but it was necessary for the people to reform afterwards, and the measures requisite to success could not be taken in the sixteenth century without the participation of the governing powers. Freely therefore and nobly a whole nation was about to express to their ruler their grievances and wishes.

On one of the first days of the session, the Speaker and certain members who had been ordered to accompany him proceeded to the palace. 'Your Highness', they began, 'of late much discord, variance, and debate hath arisen and more and more daily is likely to increase and ensue amongst your subjects, to the great inquietation, vexation, and breach of your peace, of which the chief causes followingly do ensue.'

This opening could not fail to excite the king's attention, and the Speaker of the House of Commons began boldly to unroll the long list of the grievances of England. 'First, the prelates of your most excellent realm, and the clergy of the same, have in their convocations made many and divers laws without your most royal assent, and without the assent of any of your lay subjects.

'And also many of your said subjects, and specially those that be of the poorest sort, be daily called before the said spiritual ordinaries or their commissaries, on the accusement of light and indiscreet persons, and be excommunicated and put to excessive and impostable charges.

'The prelates suffer the priests to exact divers sums of money for the sacraments, and sometimes deny the same without the money be first paid.

'Also the said spiritual ordinaries do daily confer and give sundry benefices unto certain young folks, calling them their nephews or kinsfolk, being in their minority and within age, not apt nor able to serve the cure of any such benefice … whereby the said ordinaries accumulate to themselves large sums of money, and the poor silly souls of your people perish without doctrine or any good teaching.

'Also a great number of holy days be kept throughout this your realm, upon the which many great, abominable, and execrable vices, idle and wanton sports be used, which holy days might by Your Majesty be made fewer in number.

'And also the said spiritual ordinaries commit divers of your subjects to ward, before they know either the cause of their imprisonment, or the name of their accuser.'

Thus far the commons had confined themselves to questions that had been discussed more than once; they feared to touch upon the subject of heresy before the Defender of the [Roman] Faith. But there were evangelical men among their number who had been eye-witnesses of the sufferings of the reformed. At the peril, therefore, of offending the king, the Speaker boldly took up the defence of the pretended heretics.

'If heresy be ordinarily laid unto the charge of the person accused, the said ordinaries put to them such subtle interrogatories concerning the high mysteries of our faith, as are able quickly to trap a simple unlearned layman. And if any heresy be so confessed in word, yet never committed in thought or deed, they put the said person to make his purgation. And if the party so accused deny the accusation, witnesses of little truth or credence are brought forth for the same, and deliver the party so accused to secular hands.'

The Speaker was not satisfied with merely pointing out the disease: 'We most humbly beseech Your Grace, in whom the only remedy resteth, of your goodness to consent, so that besides the fervent love Your Highness shall thereby engender in the hearts of all your commons towards Your Grace, ye shall do the most princely feat, and show the most charitable precedent that ever did sovereign lord upon his subjects.'

The king listened to the petition with his characteristic dignity, and also with a certain kindliness. He recognized the just demands in the petition of the commons, and saw how far they would support the religious independence to which he aspired. Still, unwilling to take the part of heresy, he selected only the most crying abuses, and desired his faithful commons to take their correction upon themselves. He then sent the petition to the bishops, requiring them to answer the charges brought against them, and added that henceforward his consent would be necessary to give the force of law to the acts of convocation.

This royal communication was a thunderbolt to the prelates. What! the bishops, the successors of the apostles, accused by the representatives of the nation, and requested by the king to justify themselves like criminals! ... Had the commons of England forgotten what a priest was? These proud ecclesiastics thought only of the indelible virtues which, in their view, ordination had conferred upon them, and shut their eyes to the vices of their fallible human nature. We can understand their emotion, their embarrassment, and their anger. The reformation which had made the tour of the Continent was at the gates of England; the king was knocking at their doors. What was to be done? they could not tell. They assembled, and read the petition again and again. The Archbishop of Canterbury, and the bishops of London, Lincoln, St Asaph, and Rochester carped at it and replied to it. They would willingly have thrown it into the fire – the best of answers in their opinion; but the king was waiting, and the Archbishop of Canterbury was commissioned to enlighten him.

Warham did not belong to the most fanatical party; he was a prudent man, and the wish for reform had hardly taken shape in England when, being uneasy and timid, he had hastened to give a certain satisfaction to his flock by reforming abuses which he had sanctioned for thirty years. But he was a priest, a Romish priest; he represented an inflexible hierarchy. Strengthened by the clamours of his colleagues, he resolved to utter the famous *non possumus*, less powerful, however, in England than in Rome. 'Sire', he said, 'Your Majesty's commons reproach us with uncharitable behaviour. ... On the contrary, we love them with hearty affection, and have only exercised the spiritual jurisdiction of the church upon persons infected with the pestilent poison of heresy. To have peace with such had been against the gospel of our Saviour Christ, wherein he saith, *I came not to send peace, but a sword.*

'Your Grace's commons complain that the clergy daily do make laws repugnant to the statutes of your realm. We take our authority from the Scriptures of God, and shall always diligently apply to conform our statutes thereto; and we pray that Your Highness will, with the assent of your people, temper Your Grace's laws accordingly; whereby shall ensue a most sure and hearty conjunction and agreement.

'They accuse us of committing to prison before conviction such as be suspected of heresy. ... Truth it is that certain apostates, friars, monks, lewd priests, bankrupt merchants, vagabonds, and idle fellows of corrupt intent have embraced the abominable opinions lately sprung up in Germany; and by them some have been seduced in simplicity and ignorance. Against these, if judgment has been exercised according to the laws of the church, we be without blame.

'They complain that two witnesses be admitted, be they never so defamed, to vex and trouble your subjects to the peril of their lives, shames, costs, and expenses. ... To this we reply, the judge must esteem the quality of the witness, but in heresy no exception is necessary to be considered, if their tale be likely. This is the universal law of Christendom, and hath universally done good.

'They say that we give benefices to our nephews and kinsfolk, being in young age or infants, and that we take the profit of such benefices for the time of the minority of our said kinsfolk. If it be done to our own use and profit, it is not well; but if it be bestowed to the bringing up and use of the same parties, or applied to the maintenance of God's service, we do not see but that it may be allowed.'

As for the irregular lives of the priests, the prelates remarked that they were condemned by the laws of the church, and consequently there was nothing to be said on that point.

Lastly, the bishops seized the opportunity of taking the offensive: 'We entreat Your Grace to repress heresy. This we beg of you, lowly upon our knees, so entirely as we can.'

Such was the brief of Roman Catholicism in England. Its defence would have sufficed to condemn it.

CHAPTER THREE

Early Reforms

(End of 1529)

T he answer of the bishops was criticized in the royal residence, in the House of Commons, at the meetings of the burgesses, in the streets of the capital, and in the provinces, everywhere exciting a lively indignation. 'What!' said they, 'the bishops accuse the most pious and active Christians of England – men like Bilney, Fryth, Tyndale, and Latimer – of that idleness and irregularity of which their monks and priests are continually showing us examples. To no purpose have the commons indisputably proved their grievances, if the bishops reply to notorious facts by putting forward their scholastic system. We condemn their practice, and they take shelter behind their theories; as if the reproach laid against them was not precisely that their lives are in opposition to their laws. "The fault is not in the church", they say. But it is its ministers that we accuse.'

The indignant Parliament boldly took up the axe, attacked the tree, and cut off the withered and rotten branches. One bill followed another, irritating the clergy, but filling the people with joy. When the legacy dues were under discussion, one of the members drew a touching picture of the avarice and cruelty of the priests. 'They have no compassion', he said; 'the children of the dead should all die of hunger and go begging, rather than they would of charity give to them the silly cow which the dead man owed, if he had only one.' There was a movement of indignation in the house, and they forbade the clergy to take any mortuary fees when the effects were small.

'And that is not all', said another; 'the clergy monopolize large tracts of land, and the poor are compelled to pay an extravagant price for whatever they buy. They are everything in the world but preachers of God's word and shepherds of souls. They buy and sell wool, cloth, and other merchandise; they keep tanneries and breweries. ... How can they attend to their spiritual duties in the midst of such occupations?' The clergy were consequently prohibited from holding large estates or carrying on the business of merchant, tanner, brewer, *etc.* At the same time plurality of benefices (some ignorant priests holding as many as ten or twelve) was forbidden, and residence was enforced. The commons further enacted that anyone seeking a dispensation for non-residence (even were the application made to the pope himself) should be liable to a heavy fine.

The clergy saw at last that they must reform. They forbade priests from keeping shops and taverns, playing at dice or other games of chance, passing through towns and villages with hawks and hounds, being present at unbecoming entertainments, and spending the night in suspected houses. Convocation proceeded to enact severe penalties against these disorders, doubling them for adultery, and tripling them for incest. The laity asked how it was that the church had waited so long before coming to this resolution; and whether these scandals had become criminal only because the commons condemned them?

But the bishops who reformed the lower clergy did not intend to resign their own privileges. One day when a bill relating to wills was laid before the upper house, the Archbishop of Canterbury and all the other prelates frowned, murmured, and looked uneasily around them. They exclaimed that the commons were heretics and schismatics, and almost called them infidels and atheists. In all places, good men required that morality should again be united with religion, and that piety should not be made to consist merely in certain ceremonies, but in the awakening of the conscience, a lively faith, and holy conduct. The bishops, not discerning that God's work was then being accomplished in the world, determined to maintain the ancient order of things at all risks.

Their efforts had some chance of success, for the House of Lords was essentially conservative. The Bishop of Rochester, a sincere but narrow-minded man, presuming on the respect inspired by his age and character, boldly came forward as the defender of the church. 'My lords', he said, 'these bills have no other object than the destruction of the church; and if the church goes down, all the glory of the kingdom will fall with it. Remember what happened to the Bohemians. Like them, our commons cry out, 'Down with the church!' Whence cometh that cry? Simply from lack of faith. … My lords, save the country, save the church.'

This speech made the commons very indignant; some members thought the bishop denied that they were Christians. They sent thirty of their leading men to the king. 'Sire', said the Speaker, 'it is an attaint upon the honour of Your Majesty to calumniate before the upper house those whom your subjects have elected. They are accused of lack of faith, that is to say, they are no better than Turks, Saracens, and heathens. Be pleased to call before you the bishop who has insulted your commons.'

The king made a gracious reply, and immediately sent one of his officers to invite the Archbishop of Canterbury, the Bishop of Rochester, and six other prelates to appear before him. They came quite uneasy as to what the prince might have to say to them. They knew that, like all the Plantagenets, Henry VIII would not suffer his clergy to resist him. Immediately the king informed them of the complaint made by the commons their hearts sank and they lost courage. They thought only how to escape the prince's anger, and the most venerated among them, Fisher, asserted that when speaking about 'lack of faith', he had not thought of the commons of England, but of the Bohemians only. The other prelates confirmed this inadmissible interpretation. This was a graver fault than the fault itself, and the unbecoming evasion was a defeat to the clerical party from which they never recovered. The king allowed the excuse, but he afterwards made the bishops feel the little esteem he entertained for them. As for the House of Commons, it loudly expressed the disdain aroused in them by the bishop's subterfuge.

One chance of safety still remained to them. Mixed committees of the two houses examined the resolutions of the commons. The peers, especially the ecclesiastical peers, opposed the reform by appealing to usage. 'Usage!' ironically observed a Gray's Inn lawyer; 'the usage hath ever been of thieves to rob on Shooter's Hill, *ergo* it is lawful and ought to be kept up!' This remark sorely irritated the prelates; 'What! our acts are compared to robberies!' But the lawyer, addressing the Archbishop of

Canterbury, seriously endeavoured to prove to him that the exactions of the clergy in the matter of probates and mortuaries were open robbery. The temporal lords gradually adopted the opinions of the commons.

In the midst of these debates, the king did not lose sight of his own interests. Six years before, he had raised a loan among his subjects; he thought Parliament ought to relieve him of this debt. This demand was opposed by the members most devoted to the principle of the reformation; John Petit, in particular, the friend of Bilney and Tyndale, said in Parliament: 'I give the king all I lent him; but I cannot give him what others have lent him.' Henry was not however discouraged, and finally obtained the act required.

The king soon showed that he was pleased with the commons. Two bills met with a stern opposition from the lords; they were those abolishing pluralism and non-residence. These two customs were so convenient and advantageous that the clergy determined not to give them up. Henry, seeing that the two houses would never agree, resolved to cut the difficulty. At his desire eight members from each met one afternoon in the Star Chamber. There was an animated discussion; but the lay lords, who were in the conference, taking part with the commons, the bishops were forced to yield. The two bills passed the lords the next day, and received the king's assent. After this triumph the king adjourned Parliament in the middle of December.

The different reforms that had been carried through were important, but they were not the reformation. Many abuses were corrected, but the doctrines remained unaltered; the power of the clergy was restricted, but the authority of Christ was not increased; the dry branches of the tree had been lopped off, but a scion calculated to bear good fruit had not been grafted on the wild stock. Had matters stopped here, England might perhaps have obtained a church with morals less repulsive, but not with a holy doctrine and a new life. But the reformation was not contented with more decorous forms; it required a second creation.

At the same time Parliament had taken a great stride towards the revolution that was to transform the church. A new power had taken its place in the world: the laity had triumphed over the clergy. No doubt there were upright Catholics who gave their assent to the laws passed in

1529; but these laws were nevertheless a product of the reformation. This it was that had inspired the laity with that new energy, Parliament with that bold action, and given the liberties of the nation that impulse which they had lacked hitherto. The joy was great throughout the kingdom; and while the king removed to Greenwich to keep Christmas there 'with great plenty of viands, and disguisings and interludes', the members of the commons were welcomed in the towns and villages with great rejoicings. In the people's eyes their representatives were like soldiers who had just gained a brilliant victory. The clergy, alone in all England, were downcast and exasperated. On returning to their residences the bishops could not conceal their anguish at the danger to the church. The priests, who had been the first victims offered up on the altar of reform, bent their heads. But if the clergy foresaw days of mourning, the laity hailed with joy the glorious era of the liberties of the people, and of the greatness of England. The friends of the reformation went further still: they believed that the gospel would work a complete change in the world, and talked, as Tyndale informs us, 'as though the golden age would come again'.

CHAPTER FOUR

Anne Boleyn's Father Meets the Emperor and the Pope

(Winter 1530)

Before such glorious hopes could be realized, it was necessary to emancipate Great Britain from the yoke of Romish supremacy. This was the end to which all generous minds aspired; but would the king assist them?

Henry VIII united strength of body with strength of will: both were marked on his manly form. Lively, active, eager, vehement, impatient, and voluptuous – whatever he was, he was with his whole soul. He was at first all heart for the Church of Rome; he went barefoot on pilgrimages, wrote against Luther, and flattered the pope. But before long he grew tired of Rome without desiring the reformation: profoundly selfish, he cared for himself alone. If the papal domination offended him, evangelical liberty annoyed him. He meant to remain master in his own house, the only master, and master of all. Even without the divorce, Henry would possibly have separated from Rome. Rather than endure any contradiction, he put to death friends and enemies, bishops and missionaries, ministers of state and favourites – even his wives. Such was the prince whom the reformation found King of England.

History would be unjust, however, were it to maintain that passion alone urged him to action. The question of the succession to the throne had for a century filled the country with confusion and blood. This Henry could not forget. Would the struggles of the two Roses be renewed after his death, occasioning perhaps the destruction of an ancient monarchy? If Mary, a princess of delicate health, should die, Scotland, France, the party of the White Rose, the Duke of Suffolk, whose wife was Henry's sister, might drag the kingdom into endless wars. And even if Mary's days were prolonged, her title to the crown might be disputed, no female sovereign having as yet sat upon the throne. Another train of ideas also occupied the king's mind. He enquired sincerely whether his marriage with the widow of his brother was lawful. Even before its consummation, as we have seen, he had felt doubts about it. But even his defenders, if there are any, must acknowledge that one circumstance contributed at this time to give unusual force to these scruples: his love for Anne Boleyn.

Catholic writers imagine that this guilty motive was the only one: it is a mistake, for the two former indisputably occupied Henry's mind. As for Parliament and people, the king's love for Anne Boleyn affected them very little: it was the reason of state which made them regard the divorce as just and necessary.

A congress was at that time sitting at Bologna with great pomp. On 5 November 1530, Charles V, having arrived from Spain, had entered the city, attended by a magnificent suite, and followed by 20,000 soldiers. He was covered with gold, and shone with grace and majesty. The pope waited for him in front of the Church of San Petronio, seated on a throne and wearing the triple crown. The emperor, master of Italy, which his soldiers had reduced to the last desolation, fell prostrate before the pontiff, but lately his prisoner. The union of these two monarchs, both enemies of Henry VIII, seemed destined to ruin the King of England and thwart his great affair.

And yet not long before, an ambassador from Charles V had been received at Whitehall: it was Master Eustace Chapuys. He came to solicit aid against the Turks. Henry caught at the chance: he imagined the moment to be favourable, and that he ought to despatch an embassy to the head of the empire and the head of the church. He sent for the Earl of Wiltshire, Anne Boleyn's father; Edward Lee, afterwards Archbishop of York; John Stokesley, afterwards Bishop of London, and some others. He told them that the emperor desired his alliance, and commissioned them to proceed to Italy and explain to Charles V the serious motives that induced him to separate from Catherine. 'If he persists in his opposition to the divorce', continued Henry, 'threaten him, but in covert terms.

If the threats prove useless, tell him plainly that, in accord with my friends, I will do all I can to restore peace to my troubled conscience.' He added with more calmness: 'I am resolved to fear God rather than man, and to place full reliance on comfort from the Saviour.' Was Henry sincere when he spoke thus? No one can doubt of his sensuality, his scholastic Catholicism, and his cruel violence: must we also believe in his hypocrisy? He was no doubt under a delusion, and deceived himself on the state of his soul.

An important member was added to the deputation. One day when the king was occupied with this affair, Thomas Cranmer appeared at the door of his room with a manuscript in his hand. Cranmer had a fine understanding, a warm heart, a character perhaps too weak,[1] but extensive learning. Captivated by the Holy Scriptures, he desired to seek for truth nowhere else. He had suggested a new point of view to Henry VIII. 'The essential thing', he said, 'is to know what the word of God teaches on the matter in question.' 'Show me that', exclaimed the king. Cranmer brought him his treatise, in which he proved that the word of God is above all human jurisdiction, and that it forbids marriage with a brother's widow. Henry took the work in his hand, read it again and again, and praised its excellence. A bright idea occurred to him. 'Are you strong enough to maintain before the Bishop of Rome the propositions laid down in this treatise?' said the king. Cranmer was timid, but convinced and devoted. 'Yes', he made answer, 'with God's grace, and if Your Majesty commands it.' 'Marry, then!' exclaimed Henry with delight, 'I will send you.' Cranmer departed with the others in January 1530.

While Henry's ambassadors were journeying slowly, Charles V, more exasperated than ever against the divorce, endeavoured to gain the pope. Clement VII, who was a clever man, and possessed a certain kindly humour, but was at heart cunning, false, and cowardly, amused the puissant emperor with words. When he learnt that the King of England was sending an embassy to him, he gave way to the keenest sorrow. What

---

[1] [G. W. Bromiley argues that Cranmer was more than a weak puppet and that he influenced the king behind the scenes: *Thomas Cranmer, Theologian* (Lutterworth Press, 1956); *Thomas Cranmer, Archbishop and Martyr* (Church Book Room Press, 1956).]

was he to do? which way could he turn? To irritate the emperor was dangerous; to separate England from Rome would be to endure a great loss. Caught between Charles V and Henry VIII, he groaned aloud: he paced up and down his chamber gesticulating; then suddenly stopping, sank into a chair and burst into tears. Nothing succeeded with him: it was, he thought, as if he had been bewitched. What need was there for the King of England to send him an embassy? Had not Clement told Henry through the Bishop of Tarbes: 'I am content the marriage should take place, provided it be without my authorization.' It was of no use: the pope asked him to do without the papacy, and the king would only act with it. He was more popish than the pope.

To add to his misfortunes, Charles began to press the pontiff more seriously, and yielding to his importunities, Clement drew up a brief on 7 March, in which he commanded Henry 'to receive Catherine with love, and to treat her in all things with the affection of a husband'. But the brief was scarcely written when the arrival of the English embassy was announced. The pope in alarm immediately put the document back into his portfolio, promising himself that it would be long before he published it.

As soon as the English envoys had taken up their quarters at Bologna, the ambassadors of France called to pay their respects. De Gramont, Bishop of Tarbes, was overflowing with politeness, especially to the Earl of Wiltshire. 'I have shown much honour to M. de Rochford', he wrote to his master on 28 March. 'I went out to meet him. I have visited him often at his lodging. I have feted him, and offered him my solicitations and services, telling him that such were your orders.' Not thus did Clement VII act: the arrival of the Earl of Wiltshire and his colleagues was a cause of alarm to him. Yet he must make up his mind to receive them: he appointed the day and the hour for the audience.

Henry VIII desired that his representatives should appear with great pomp, and accordingly the ambassador and his colleagues went to great expense with that intent. Wiltshire entered first into the audience-hall: being father of Anne Boleyn, he had been appointed by the king as the man in all England most interested in the success of his plans. But Henry had calculated badly: the personal interest which the earl felt in the divorce made him odious both to Charles and Clement. The pope, wearing his pontifical robes, was seated on the throne, surrounded by his cardinals. The ambassadors approached, made the customary salutations, and stood before him. The pontiff, wishing to show his kindly feelings towards the envoys of the *'Defender of the Faith'*, put out his slipper according to custom, presenting it graciously to the kisses of the proud Englishmen. The revolt was about to begin. The earl, remaining motionless, refused to kiss His Holiness's slipper. But that was not all: a fine spaniel, with long silky hair, which Wiltshire had brought from England, had followed him to the episcopal palace. When the Bishop of Rome put out his foot, the dog did what other dogs would have done under similar circumstances: he flew at the foot, and caught the pope by the big toe. Clement hastily drew it back. The sublime borders on the ridiculous: the ambassadors, bursting with laughter, raised their arms and hid their faces behind their long rich sleeves. 'That dog was a *Protestant*', said a reverend father. 'Whatever he was', said an Englishman, 'he taught us that a pope's foot was more meet to be bitten by dogs than kissed by Christian men.' The pope, recovering from his emotion, prepared to listen, and the earl, regaining his seriousness, explained to the pontiff that as Holy Scripture forbade a man to marry his brother's wife, Henry VIII required him to annul as unlawful his union with Catherine of Aragon. As Clement did not seem convinced, the ambassador skilfully insinuated that the king might possibly declare himself independent of Rome, and place the English Church under the direction of a patriarch. 'The example', added the ambassador, 'will not fail to be imitated by other kingdoms of Christendom.'

The agitated pope promised not to remove the suit to Rome, provided the king would give up the idea of reforming England. Then, putting on a most gracious air, he proposed to introduce the ambassador to Charles V. This was giving Wiltshire the chance of receiving a harsh rebuff. The earl saw it; but his duty obliging him to confer with the emperor, he accepted the offer.

The father of Anne Boleyn proceeded to an audience with the nephew of Catherine of Aragon. Representatives of two women whose rival causes agitated Europe, these two men could not meet without a collision. True, the earl flattered himself that as it was Charles' interest to detach Henry from Francis I, that phlegmatic and politic prince would certainly not sacrifice the gravest interests of his reign for a matter of sentiment; but he was deceived. The emperor received him with a calm and reserved air, but unaccompanied by any kindly demonstration. The ambassador skilfully began by speaking of the Turkish war; then ingeniously passing to the condition of the kingdom of England, he pointed out the reasons of state which rendered the divorce necessary. Here Charles stopped him short: 'Sir Count, you are not to be trusted in this matter; you are a party to it; let your colleagues speak.' The earl replied with respectful coldness: 'Sire, I do not speak here as a father, but as my master's servant, and I am commissioned to inform you that his conscience condemns a union contrary to the law of God.' He then offered Charles the immediate restitution of Catherine's dowry. The emperor coldly replied that he would support his aunt in her rights, and then abruptly turning his back on the ambassador, refused to hear him any longer.

Thus did Charles, who had been all his life a crafty politician, place in this matter the cause of justice above the interests of his ambition. Perhaps he might lose an important ally; it mattered not; before everything he would protect a woman unworthily treated. On this occasion we feel more sympathy for Charles than for Henry. The indignant emperor hastily quitted Bologna on 22 or 24 February.

The earl hastened to his friend M. de Gramont, and, relating how he had been treated, proposed that the kings of France and England should unite in the closest bonds. He added that Henry could not accept Clement as his judge, since he had himself declared that he was ignorant of the law of God. 'England', he said, 'will be quiet for three or four months. Sitting in the ballroom, she will watch the dancers, and will form her resolution according as they dance well or ill.' A rule of policy that has often been followed.

Gramont was prepared to make common cause with Henry against the emperor; but, like his master, he could not make up his mind to do without the pope. He strove to induce Clement to join the two kings and abandon Charles; or else – he insinuated in his turn – England would separate from the Romish Church. This was to incur the risk of losing Western Europe, and accordingly the pope answered with much concern: 'I will do what you ask.' There was, however, a reserve; namely, that the steps taken overtly by the pope would absolutely decide nothing.

Clement once more received the ambassador of Henry VIII. The earl carried with him the book wherein Cranmer proved that the pope cannot dispense anyone from obeying the law of God, and presented it to the pope. The latter took it and glanced over it, his looks showing that a prison could not have been more disagreeable to him than this impertinent volume. The Earl of Wiltshire soon discovered that there was nothing for him to do in Italy. Charles V, usually so reserved, had made the bitterest remarks before his departure. His chancellor, with an air of triumph, enumerated to the English ambassador all the divines of Italy and France who were opposed to the king's wishes. The pope seemed to be a puppet which the emperor moved as he liked; and the cardinals had but one idea, that of exalting the Romish power. Wearied and disgusted, the earl departed for France and England with the greater portion of his colleagues.

Cranmer was left behind. Having been sent to show Clement that Holy Scripture is above all Roman pontiffs, and speaks in a language quite opposed to that of the popes, he had asked more than once for an audience at which to discharge his mission. The wily pontiff had replied that he would hear him at Rome, believing he was thus putting him off until the Greek calends. But Clement was deceived: the English doctor, determining to do his duty, refused to depart for London with the rest of the embassy, and repaired to the metropolis of Catholicism.

CHAPTER FIVE

Oxford and Cambridge Debate the Divorce

(Winter 1530)

At the same time that Henry sent ambassadors to Italy to obtain the pope's consent, he invited all the universities of Christendom to declare that the question of divorce was of divine right, and that the pope had nothing to say about it. It was his opinion that the universal voice of the church ought to decide, and not the voice of one man.

First he attempted to canvass Cambridge, and as he wanted a skilful man for that purpose, he applied to Wolsey's old servant, Stephen Gardiner, an intelligent, active, wily churchman and a good Catholic. One thing alone was superior to his Catholicism – his desire to win the king's favour. He aspired to rise like the cardinal to the summit of greatness. Henry named the chief almoner, Edward Fox, as his colleague.

Arriving at Cambridge one Saturday about noon in the latter half of February, the royal commissioners held a conference in the evening with the vice-chancellor (Dr Buckmaster), Dr Edmunds, and other influential men who had resolved to go with the court. But these doctors, members of the political party, soon found themselves checked by an embarrassing support on which they had not calculated: it was that of the friends of the gospel. They had been convinced by the writing which Cranmer had published on the divorce. Gardiner and the members of the conference, hearing of the assistance which the evangelicals desired to give them, were annoyed at first. On the other hand, the champions of the court of Rome, alarmed at the alliance of the two parties who were opposed to them, began that very night to visit college after college, leaving no stone unturned that the peril might be averted. Gardiner, uneasy at their zeal, wrote to Henry VIII: 'As we assembled they assembled; as we made friends they made friends.' Dr Watson, Dr Tomson, and other papal supporters at one time shouted very loudly, at another spoke in whispers. They said that Anne Boleyn was a heretic, that her marriage with Henry would hand England over to Luther; and they related to those whom they desired to gain – wrote Gardiner to the king – 'many fables, too tedious to repeat to Your Grace.' These 'fables' would not only have bored Henry, but greatly irritated him.

The vice-chancellor, flattering himself that he had a majority, notwithstanding these clamours, called a meeting of the doctors, bachelors of divinity, and masters of arts, for Sunday afternoon. About two hundred persons assembled, and the three parties were distinctly marked out. The most numerous and the most excited were those who held for the pope against the king. The evangelicals were in a minority, but were quite as decided as their adversaries, and much calmer. The politicians, uneasy at seeing the friends of Latimer and Cranmer disposed to vote with them, would have, however, to accept of their support, if they wished to gain the victory. They resolved to seize the opportunity offered them. 'Most learned senators', said the vice-chancellor, 'I have called you together because the great love which the king bears you engages me to consult your wisdom.' Thereupon Gardiner and Fox handed in the letter which Henry had given them, and the vice-chancellor read it to the meeting. In it the king set forth his hopes of seeing the doctors unanimous to do what was agreeable to him. The deliberations commenced, and the question of a rupture with Rome soon began to appear distinctly beneath the question of the divorce. Edmunds spoke for the king, Tomson for the pope. There was an interchange of antagonistic opinions, and a disorder of ideas among many; the speakers grew warm; one voice drowned another, and the confusion became extreme.

The vice-chancellor, desirous of putting an end to the clamour, proposed referring the matter to a committee, whose decision should be regarded as that of the whole university, which was agreed to. Then seeing more clearly that the royal cause could not succeed without the help of the evangelical party, he proposed some of its leaders – Doctors Salcot, Reps, Crome, Shaxton, and Latimer – as members of the committee. On hearing these names, there was an explosion of murmurs in the meeting. Salcot, Abbot of St Benet's, was particularly offensive to the doctors of the Romish party. 'We protest', they said, 'against the presence in the committee of those who have approved of Cranmer's book, and thus declared their opinion already.' 'When any matter is talked of all over the kingdom', answered Gardiner, 'there is not a sensible man who does not tell his friends what he thinks about it.' The whole afternoon was spent in lively altercation. The vice-chancellor, wishing to bring it to an end, said: 'Gentlemen, it is getting late, and I invite everyone to take his seat, and declare his mind by a secret vote.' It was useless; no one took his seat; the confusion, reproaches, and declamations continued. At dark, the vice-chancellor adjourned the meeting until the next day. The doctors separated in great excitement, but with different feelings. While the politicians saw nothing else to discuss but the question of the king's marriage, the evangelicals and the papists considered that the real question was this: Which shall rule in England – the reformation or popery?

The next day, the names of the members of the proposed committee having been put to the vote, the meeting was found to be divided into two equal parties. In order to obtain a majority Gardiner undertook to get some of his adversaries out of the way. Going up and down the senate house, he began to whisper in the ears of some of the less decided; and inspiring them either with hope or fear, he prevailed upon several to leave the meeting.

The grace [act] was then put to the vote a third time and passed. Gardiner triumphed. Returning to his room, he sent the list to the king. Sixteen of the committee, indicated by the letter A, were favourable to His Majesty. 'As for the twelve others', he wrote, 'we hope to win most of them by *good means*.' The committee met and considered the royal demand. They carefully examined the passages of Holy Scripture, the explanations of translators, and gave their opinion. Then followed the public discussion. Gardiner was not without fear: as there might be skilful assailants and awkward defenders, he looked out for men qualified to defend the royal cause worthily. It was a remarkable circumstance that, passing over the traditional doctors, he added to the defence

– of which he and Fox were the leaders – two evangelical doctors, Salcot, Abbot of St Benet's, and Reps. He reserved to his colleague and himself the political part of the question; but notwithstanding all his Catholicism, he desired that the scriptural reasons should be placed foremost. The discussion was conducted with great thoroughness, and the victory remained with the king's champions.

On 9 March, the doctors, professors, and masters having met after vespers in the priory hall, the vice-chancellor said: 'It has appeared to us as most certain, most in accord with Holy Scripture, and most conformable to the opinions of commentators, that it is contrary to divine and natural law for a man to marry the widow of his brother dying childless.' Thus the Scriptures were really, if not explicitly, declared by the University of Cambridge to be the supreme and only rule of Christians, and the contrary decisions of Rome were held to be not binding. The word of God was avenged of the long contempt it had endured, and after having been long put below the pope's word, was now restored to its lawful place. In this matter Cambridge was right.

It was necessary to try Oxford next. Here the opposition was stronger, and the popish party looked forward to a victory. Longland, Bishop of Lincoln and chancellor of the university, was commissioned by Henry to undertake the matter, Dr Bell, and afterwards Edward Fox, the chief almoner, being joined with him. The king, uneasy at the results of the negotiation, and wishing for a favourable decision at any cost, gave Longland a letter for the university, through every word of which an undisguised despotism was visible. 'We will and command you', he said, 'that ye, not leaning to wilful and sinister opinions of your own several minds, considering that we be your sovereign liege lord, and totally giving your affections to the true overtures of divine learning in this behalf, do show and declare your true and just learning in the said cause. … And we, for your so doing, shall be to you and to our university there so good and gracious a lord for the same, as ye shall perceive it well done in your well fortune to come. And in case you do not uprightly handle yourselves herein, we shall so quickly and sharply look to your unnatural misdemeanour herein, that it shall not be to your quietness and ease hereafter. … Accommodate yourselves to the mere truth; assuring you that those who do shall be esteemed and set forth, and the contrary neglected and little set by. ... We doubt not that your resolution shall be our high contentation and pleasure.'

This royal missive caused a great commotion in the university. Some slavishly bent their heads, for the king spoke rod in hand. Others declared themselves convinced by the political reasons, and said that Henry must have an heir whose right to the throne could not be disputed. And, lastly, some were convinced that Holy Scripture was favourable to the royal cause. All men of age and learning, as well as all who had either capacity or ambition, declared in favour of the divorce. Nevertheless a formidable opposition soon showed itself.

The younger members of the senate were enthusiastic for Catherine, the church, and the pope. Their theological education was imperfect; they could not go to the bottom of the question, but they judged by the heart. To see a Catholic lady oppressed, to see Rome despised, inflamed their anger; and if the elder members maintained that their view was the more reasonable, the younger ones believed theirs to be the more noble. Unhappily, when the choice lies between the useful and the generous, the useful commonly triumphs. Still, the young doctors were not prepared to yield. They said – and they were not wrong – that religion and morality ought not to be sacrificed to reasons of state, or to the passions of princes. And seeing the spectre of reform hidden behind that of the divorce, they regarded themselves as called upon to save the church. 'Alas!' said the royal delegates, the Bishop of Lincoln and Dr Bell, 'Alas! we are in continual perplexity, and we cannot foresee with any certainty what will be the issue of this business.'

They agreed with the heads of houses that, in order to prepare the university, three public disputations should be solemnly held in the divinity schools. By this means they hoped to gain time. 'Such disputations', they said, 'are a very honourable means of amusing the multitude until we are sure of the consent of the majority.' The discussions took place, and the younger masters, arranging each day what was to be done or said, gave utterance to all the warmth of their feelings.

When the news of these animated discussions reached Henry, his displeasure broke out, and those immediately around him fanned his indignation. 'A great part of the youth of our university', said the king, 'with contentious and factious manners, daily combine together.' The courtiers, instead of moderating, excited his anger. Every day, they told him, these young men, regardless of their duty towards their sovereign, and not conforming to the opinions of the most virtuous and learned men of the university, meet together to deliberate and oppose His Majesty's views. 'Has it ever been seen', exclaimed the king, 'that such a number of right small learning should stay their seniors in so weighty a cause?' Henry, in exasperation, wrote to the heads of the houses: 'It is not good to stir a hornet's nest.' This threat excited the younger party still more: if the term 'hornet' amused some, it irritated others. In hot weather, the hornet (the king) chases the weaker insects; but the noise he makes in flying forewarns them, and the little ones escape him. Henry could not hide his vexation; he feared lest the little flies should prove stronger than the big hornet. He was uneasy in his castle of Windsor; and the insolent opposition of Oxford pursued him wherever he turned his steps – on the terrace, in the wide park, and even in the royal chapel. 'What!' he exclaimed, 'shall this university dare show itself more unkind and wilful than all other universities, abroad or at home?' Cambridge had recognized the king's right, and Oxford refused.

Wishing to end the matter, Henry summoned High-Almoner Fox to Windsor, and ordered him to repeat at Oxford the victory he had gained at Cambridge. He then dictated to his secretary a letter to the recalcitrants: 'We cannot a little marvel that you, neither having respect to our estate, being your prince and sovereign lord, nor yet remembering such benefits as we have always showed unto you, have hitherto refused the accomplishment of our desire. Permit no longer the private suffrages of light and wilful heads to prevail over the learned. By your diligence redeem the errors and delays past.

'Given under our signet, at our castle of Windsor.'

Fox was entrusted with this letter.

The lord high-almoner and the Bishop of Lincoln immediately called together the younger masters of the university, and declared that a longer resistance might lead to their ruin. But the youth of Oxford were not to be overawed by threats of violence. Lincoln had hardly finished, when several masters of arts protested loudly; some even spoke 'very wickedly'. Not permitting himself to be checked by such rebellion, the bishop ordered the poll to be taken; twenty-seven voted for the king, and twenty-two against. The royal commissioners were not yet satisfied; they assembled all the faculties, and invited the members to give their opinion in turn. This intimidated many, and only eight or ten had courage enough to declare their opposition frankly. The bishop, encouraged by such a result, ordered that the final vote should be taken by ballot. Secrecy emboldened many of those who had not dared to speak; and while thirty-one voted in favour of the divorce, twenty-five opposed it. That was of little consequence, as the two prelates had the majority. They immediately drew up the statute in the name of the university, and sent it to the king; after which the bishop, proud of his success, celebrated a solemn mass of the Holy Ghost. The Holy Ghost had not, however, been much attended to in the business. Some had obeyed the prince, others the pope; and if we desire to find those who obeyed Christ, we must look for them elsewhere.

The University of Cambridge was the first to send in its submission to Henry. The Sunday before Easter (1530), Vice-Chancellor Buckmaster arrived at Windsor in the forenoon. The court was at chapel, where Latimer, recently appointed one of the king's chaplains, was preaching. The vice-chancellor came in during the service and heard part of the sermon. Latimer was a very different man from Henry's servile courtiers. He did not fear even to attack such of his colleagues as did not do their duty: 'That is no godly preacher that will hold his peace, and not strike you with his sword that you smoke again. … Chaplains will not do their duties, but rather flatter. But what shall follow? They shall have God's curse upon their heads for their labour. The minister must reprove without fearing any man, even if he be threatened with death.' Latimer was particularly bold in all that concerned the errors of Rome, which Henry VIII desired to maintain in the English Church. 'Wicked persons', he said, 'men, who despise God, call out, we are christened, therefore we are saved. Make no mistake, to be christened and not obey God's commandments is to be worse than the Turks! Regeneration cometh from the word of God; it is by hearing and believing this word that we are born again.'

Thus spoke one of the fathers of the English reformation: such is the real doctrine of the Church of England; the contrary doctrine is a mere relic of popery.

As the congregation were leaving the chapel, the vice-chancellor spoke to the secretary (Cromwell) and the provost, and told them the occasion of his visit. The king sent a message that he would receive the deputation after evening service. Desirous of giving a certain distinction to the decision of the universities, Henry ordered all the court to assemble in the audience chamber. The vice-chancellor presented the letter to the king, who was much pleased with it. 'Thanks, Mr Vice-Chancellor', he said, 'I very much approve the way in which you have managed this matter. I shall give your university tokens of my satisfaction. ... You heard Mr Latimer's sermon', he added, which he greatly praised and then withdrew. The Duke of Norfolk, going up to the vice-chancellor, told him that the king desired to see him the following day.

The next day, Dr Buckmaster, faithful to the appointment, waited all the morning; but the king had changed his mind, and sent orders to the deputy from Cambridge that he might depart as soon as he pleased. The message had scarcely been delivered before the king entered the gallery. An idea which quite engrossed his mind urged him on: he wanted to speak with the doctor about the principle put forward by Cranmer. Henry detained Buckmaster from one o'clock until six, repeating in every possible form, 'Can the pope grant a dispensation when the law of God has spoken?' He even displayed much ill-humour before the vice-chancellor, because this point had not been decided at Cambridge. At last he quitted the gallery; and, to counterbalance the sharpness of his reproaches, he spoke very graciously to the doctor, who hurried away as fast as he could.

CHAPTER SIX

Henry Appeals to Foreign Opinion

(January to September 1530)

T he king did not limit himself to asking the opinions of England: he appealed to the universal teaching of the church, represented according to his views by the universities and not by the pope. The element of individual conviction, so strongly marked in Tyndale, Fryth, and Latimer, was wanting in the official reformation that proceeded from the prince. To know what Scripture said, Henry was about to send delegates to Paris, Bologna, Padua, and Wittenberg: he would have sent even to the East, if such a journey had been easy. That false Catholicism which looked for the interpretation of the Bible to churches and declining schools where traditionalism, ritualism, and hierarchism were magnified, was a counterfeit popery. Happily the supreme voice of the word of God surmounted this fatal tendency in England.

Henry VIII, full of confidence in the friendship of the King of France, applied first to the University of Paris; but Dr Pedro Garray, a Spanish priest, as ignorant as he was fanatical (according to the English agents), eagerly took up the cause of Catherine of Aragon. Aided by the impetuous Beda, he obtained an opinion adverse to Henry's wishes.

When he heard of it, the alarmed prince summoned Du Bellay, the French ambassador, to the palace, gave him for Francis I a famous diamond *fleur-de-lis* valued at £10,000 sterling, also the acknowledgments for 100,000 livres which Francis owed Henry for war expenses, and added a gift of 400,000 crowns for the ransom of the king's sons. Unable to resist such strong arguments, Francis charged Du Bellay to represent to the faculty of Paris 'the great scruples of Henry's conscience';

whereupon the Sorbonne deliberated, and several doctors exclaimed that it would be an attaint upon the pope's honour to suppose him capable of refusing consolation to the wounded conscience of a Christian. During these debates, the secretary took the names, received the votes, and entered them on the minutes. A fiery papist, observing that the majority would be against the Roman opinion, jumped up, sprang upon the secretary, snatched the list from his hands, and tore it up. All started from their seats, and 'there was great disorder and tumult'. They all spoke together, each trying to assert his own opinion; but as no one could make himself heard amid the general clamour, the doctors hurried out of the room in a great rage. 'Beda acted like one possessed', wrote Du Bellay.

Meanwhile the ambassadors of the King of England were walking up and down an adjoining gallery, waiting for the division. Attracted by the shouts, they ran forward, and seeing the strange spectacle presented by the theologians, and 'hearing the language they used to one another', they retired in great irritation. Du Bellay, who had at heart the alliance of the two countries, conjured Francis I to put an end to such 'impertinences'. The president of the Parlement of Paris consequently ordered Beda to appear before him, and told him that it was not for a person of his sort to meddle with the affairs of princes, and that if he did not cease his opposition, he would be punished in a way he would not soon forget. The Sorbonne profited by the lesson given to the most influential of its members, and on 2 July declared in favour of the divorce by a large majority. The universities of Orleans, Angers, and Bourges had already done so, and that of Toulouse did the same shortly after. Henry VIII had France and England with him.

This was not enough: he must have Italy also. He filled that peninsula with his agents, who had orders to obtain from the bishops and universities the declaration refused by the pope. A rich and powerful despot is never in want of devoted men to carry out his designs.

The University of Bologna, in the states of the church, was, after Paris, the most important in the Catholic world. A monk was in great repute there at this time. Noble by birth and an eloquent preacher, Battista Pallavicini was one of those independent thinkers often met with in Italy. The English agents applied to him; he declared that he and his colleagues were ready to prove the unlawfulness of Henry's marriage, and when Stokesley spoke of remuneration, they replied: 'No, no! what we have received freely, we give freely.' Henry's agents could not contain themselves for joy: the university of the pope declares against the pope! Those among them who had an inkling for the reformation were especially delighted. On 10 June the eloquent monk appeared before the ambassadors with the judgment of the faculty, which surpassed all they had imagined. Henry's marriage was declared 'horrible, execrable, detestable, abominable for a Christian and even for an infidel, forbidden by divine and human law under pain of the severest punishment. ... The Holy Father, who can do almost everything', innocently continued the university, 'has not the right to permit such a union.' The universities of Padua and Ferrara hastened to add their votes to those of Bologna, and declared the marriage with a brother's widow to be 'null, detestable, profane, and abominable'. Henry was conqueror all along the line. He had with him that universal consent which, according to certain illustrious doctors, is the very essence of Catholicism. Crooke, one of Henry's agents, and a distinguished Greek scholar, who discharged his mission with indefatigable ardour, exclaimed that 'the just cause of the king was approved by all the doctors of Italy'.

In the midst of this harmony of catholicity, there was one exception of which no one had dreamt. That divorce which, according to the frivolous language of a certain party, was the cause of the reformation in England, found opponents among the fathers and the children of the reformation. Henry's envoys were staggered. 'My fidelity bindeth me to advertise Your Highness', wrote Crooke to the king, 'that all Lutherans be utterly against Your Highness in this cause, and have letted [hindered] as much with their wretched poor malice, without reason or authority, as they could and might, as well here as in Padua and Ferrara, where be no small companies of them.' The Swiss and German reformers having been summoned to give an opinion on this point, Luther, Œcolampadius, Zwingli, Bucer, Grynæus, and even Calvin,[1] all expressed the same

---

[1] Calvin's letter or dissertation (*Calvini Epistolæ*, p. 384) harmonizes the apparently contradictory passages of Leviticus and Deuteronomy; but I much doubt if it belongs to this period.

opinion. 'Certainly', said Luther, 'the king has sinned by marrying his brother's wife; that sin belongs to the past; let repentance, therefore, blot it out, as it must blot out all our past sins. But the marriage must not be dissolved; such a great sin, which is future, must not be permitted. There are thousands of marriages in the world in which sin has a part, and yet we may not dissolve them. *A man shall cleave unto his wife, and they shall be one flesh.* This law is superior to the other, and overrules the lesser one.' The collective opinion of the Lutheran doctors was in conformity with the just and Christian sentiments of Luther. Thus (we repeat) the event which, according to Catholic writers, was the cause of the religious transformation of England, was approved by the Romanists and condemned by the evangelicals. Besides, the latter knew very well that a reformation must proceed, not from a divorce or a marriage, not from diplomatic negotiations or university statutes, but from the power of the word of God and the free conviction of Christians.

While these matters were going on, Cranmer was at Rome, asking the pope for that discussion which the pontiff had promised him at their conference in Bologna. Clement VII had never intended to grant it: he had thought that, once at Rome, it would be easy to elude his promise; it was that which occupied his attention just now. Among the means which popes have sometimes employed in their difficulties with kings, one of the most common was to gain the agents of those princes. It was the first employed by Clement; he nominated Cranmer grand penitentiary for all the states of the King of England, some even say for all the Catholic world. It was little more than a title, and 'was only to stay his stomach for that time, in hope of a more plentiful feast hereafter, if he had been pleased to take his repast on any popish preferment'. But Cranmer was influenced by purer motives; and without refusing the title the pope gave him – since, having the task of winning him to the king's side, he would thus have compromised his mission – he made no account of it, and showed all the more zeal for the accomplishment of his charge.

The embassy had not succeeded, and they were getting uneasy about it in England. Some of the pope's best friends could not understand his blindness. The two archbishops, the dukes of Norfolk and Suffolk, the marquises of Dorset and Exeter, thirteen earls, four bishops, twenty-five barons, twenty-two abbots, and eleven members of the lower house determined to send an address to Clement VII. 'Most Blessed Father', they began, 'the king, who is our head and the life of us all, has ever stood by the see of Rome amidst the attacks of your many and powerful enemies, and yet he alone is to reap no benefit from his labours. ... Meanwhile we perceive a flood of miseries impending over the common-wealth. If Your Holiness, who ought to be our father, have determined to leave us as orphans, we shall seek our remedy elsewhere. ... He that is sick will by any means be rid of his distemper; and there is hope in the exchange of miseries, when, if we cannot obtain what is good, we may obtain a lesser evil. ... We beseech Your Holiness to consider with yourself: you profess that on earth you are Christ's vicar. Endeavour then to show yourself so to be by pronouncing your sentence to the glory and praise of God.' Clement gained time: he remained two months and a half without answering, thinking about the matter, turning it over and over in his mind. The great difficulty was to harmonize the will of Henry VIII, who desired another wife, and that of Charles V, who insisted that he ought to keep the old one. There was only one mode of satisfying both these princes at once, and that was by the king's having the two wives together. Wolsey had already entertained this idea. More than two years before, the pope had hinted as much to da Casale: 'Let him take another wife', he had said, speaking of Henry. Clement now recurred to it, and having sent privately for da Casale, he said to him: 'This is what we have hit upon: we permit His Majesty to have two wives.' The infallible pontiff proposed bigamy to a king. Da Casale was still more astonished than he had been at the time of Clement's first communication. 'Holy Father', he said to the pope, 'I doubt whether such a mode will satisfy His Majesty, for he desires above all things to have the burden removed from his conscience.'

This guilty proposal led to nothing; the king, sure of the lords and of the people, advanced rapidly in the path of independence. The day after that on which the pope authorized him to take two wives, Henry issued a bold proclamation, pronouncing against all who should ask for or bring in a papal bull contrary to the royal prerogative 'imprisonment and further punishment of their bodies according to His Majesty's good pleasure'. Clement, becoming alarmed, replied to the address: 'We desire as much as you do that the king should have male children; but, alas! we are not God to give him sons.'

Men were beginning to stifle under these manoeuvres and tergiversations of the papacy: they called for air, and some went so far as to say that if air was not given them, they must snap their fetters and break open the doors.

CHAPTER SEVEN

Latimer at Court

(January to September 1530)

H enry, seeing that he could not obtain what he asked from the pope, drew nearer the evangelical party in his kingdom. In the ranks of the reformation he found intelligent, pious, bold, and eloquent men, who possessed the confidence of a portion of the people. Why should not the prince try to conciliate them? They protest against the authority of the pope: good! he will relieve them from it; but on one condition, however – that if they reject the papal jurisdiction they recognize his own.

The first of the evangelical leaders whom Henry tried to gain was Latimer. He had placed him, as we have seen, on the list of his chaplains. 'Beware of contradicting the king', said a courtier to him one day, mistrusting his frankness. 'Speak as he speaks, and instead of presuming to lead him, strive to follow him.' 'Away with your counsel!' replied Latimer; 'Shall I say as he says? Say what your conscience bids you. … Still, I know that prudence is necessary. The drop of rain maketh a hole in the stone, not by violence, but by oft falling. Likewise a prince must be won by a little and a little.'

This conversation was not useless to the chaplain, who set to work seriously amid all the tumult of the court. He studied the Holy Scriptures and the Fathers, and frankly proclaimed the truth from the pulpit. But he had no private conversation with the king, who filled him with a certain fear. The thought that he did not speak to Henry about the state of his soul troubled him. One day, in the month of November, the chaplain was in his room, and in the volume of St Augustine which lay before him he read these words: 'He who for fear of any power *hides the truth*, provokes the wrath of God to come upon him, for he fears men more than God.' At another time, while studying St Chrysostom, these words struck him: 'He is not only a traitor to the truth who openly for truth teaches a lie; but he also who *does not pronounce and show the truth that he knoweth.*' These two sentences sank deeply into his heart. 'They made me sore afraid', he continued, 'troubled and vexed me grievously in my conscience.' He resolved to declare what God had taught him in Scripture. His frankness might cost him his life (lives were lost easily in Henry's time); it mattered not. 'I had rather suffer extreme punishment', he said, 'than be a traitor unto the truth.'

Latimer reflected that the ecclesiastical law, which for ages had been the very essence of religion, must give way to evangelical faith – that the form must yield to the life. The members of the church (calling themselves regenerate by baptism) used to attend catechism, be confirmed, join in worship, and take part in the communion without any real individual transformation; and then finally rest all together in the churchyard. But the church, in Latimer's opinion, ought to begin with the conversion of its members. Lively stones are needed to build up the temple of God. Christian individualism, which Rome opposed from her theocratic point of view, was about to be revived in Christian society.

The noble Latimer formed the resolution to make the king understand that all real reformation must begin at home. This was no trifling matter. Henry, who was a man of varied information and lively understanding, but also imperious, passionate, fiery, and obstinate, knew no other rule than the promptings of his strong nature; and although quite prepared to separate from the pope, he detested all innovations in doctrine. Latimer did not allow himself to be stopped by such obstacles, and resolved to attack this difficult position openly.

'Your Grace', he wrote to Henry, 'I must show forth such things as I have learned in Scripture, or else deny Jesus Christ. The which denying ought more to be dreaded than the loss of all temporal goods, honour, promotion, fame, prison, slander, hurts, banishment, and all manner of torments and cruelties, yea, and death itself, be it never so shameful and painful. ... There is as great distance between you and me as between God and man; for you are here to me and to all your subjects in God's stead; and so I should quake to speak to Your Grace. But as you are a mortal man having in you the corrupt nature of Adam, so you have no less need of the merits of Christ's passion for your salvation than I and others of your subjects have.'

Latimer feared to see a church founded under Henry's patronage, which would seek after riches, power, and pomp; and he was not mistaken. 'Our Saviour's life was very poor. In how vile and abject a place was the mother of Jesus Christ brought to bed! And according to this beginning was the process and end of his life in this world. ... But this he did to show us that his followers and vicars should not regard the treasures of this world. ... Your Grace may see what means and craft the clergy imagine to break and withstand the acts which were made in the last Parliament against their superfluities.'

Latimer desired to make the king understand who were the true Christians. 'Our Saviour showed his disciples', continued he, 'that they should be brought before kings. Wherefore take this for a sure conclusion, that where the word of God is truly preached, there is persecution as well of the hearers as of the teachers; and where quietness and rest in worldly pleasure, there is not the truth.'

Latimer next proceeded to declare what would give real riches to England. 'Your Grace promised by your last proclamation that we should have the Scripture in English. Let not the wickedness of worldly men divert you from your godly purpose and promise. There are prelates who, under pretence of insurrection and heresy, hinder the gospel of Christ from having free course. ... They would send a thousand men to hell ere they send one to God.'

Latimer had reserved for the last the appeal he had determined to make to his master's conscience: 'I pray to God that Your Grace may do what God commandeth, and not what seemeth good in your own sight; that you may be found one of the members of his church, and a faithful minister of his gifts, and not', he added, showing contempt for a title of which Henry was very proud, 'and not a defender of his faith; for he will not have it defended by man's power, but by his word only.

'Wherefore, Gracious King, remember yourself. Have pity on your soul, and think that the day is even at hand when you shall give account of your office, and of the blood that hath been shed with your sword. In the which day that Your Grace may stand steadfastly, and not be ashamed, but be clear and ready in your reckoning, and to have (as they say) your *quietus est* sealed with the blood of our Saviour Christ, which only serveth at that day, is my daily prayer to him that suffered death for our sins, which also prayeth to his Father for grace for us continually.'[1]

Thus wrote the bold chaplain. Such a letter from Latimer to Henry VIII deserves to be pointed out. The king does not appear to have been offended at it: he was an absolute prince, but there was occasionally some generosity in his character. He therefore continued to extend his kindness to Latimer, but did not answer his appeal.

Latimer preached frequently before the court and in the city. Many noble lords and old families still clung to the prejudices of the Middle Ages; but some had a certain liking for the reformation, and listened to the chaplain's preaching, which was so superior to ordinary sermons. His art of oratory was summed up in one precept: 'Christ is the preacher of all preachers.' 'Christ', he exclaimed, 'took upon him our sins: not the work of sin – not to do it – not to commit it, but to purge it, to bear the stipend [wages] of it, and that way he was the greatest sinner of the world.[2] ... It is much like as if I owed another man £20,000, and must pay it out of hand, or else go to the dungeon of Ludgate; and when I am going to prison, one of my friends should come and ask, Whither goeth this man? I will answer for him; I will pay all for him. Such a part played our Saviour Christ with us.'

Preaching before a king, he declared that the authority of Holy Scripture was above all the powers of the earth.[3] 'God', he said, 'is great, eternal, almighty, everlasting; and the Scripture, because of him, is also great, eternal, most mighty, and holy. ... There is no king, emperor, magistrate, or ruler, but is bound to give credence unto God's holy word.' He was cautious not to put 'the two swords' into the same hand. 'In this world God hath two swords', he said; 'the temporal sword resteth in the hands of kings, whereunto all subjects – as well the clergy as the laity – be subject. The spiritual sword is in the hands of the ministers

---

[1] Latimer, *Remains* (Parker Society), pp. 297-309.
[2] *Ibid.*, p. 223.
[3] *Ibid.*, p. 85 (First Sermon preached before King Edward VI, 8 March 1549).

and preachers of God's word to correct and reprove. Make not a mingle-mangle of them. To God give thy soul, thy faith; ... to the king, tribute and reverence. Therefore let the preacher amend with the spiritual sword, fearing no man, though death should ensue.' Such language astonished the court. 'Were you at the sermon today?' said one of his hearers to a zealous courtier one day. 'Yes', replied the latter. 'And how did you like the new chaplain?' 'Oh, even as I liked him always – a seditious fellow.'

Latimer did not permit himself to be intimidated. Firm in doctrine, he was at the same time eminently practical. He was a moralist; and this may explain how he was able to remain any time at court. Men of the world, who soon grow impatient when you preach to them of the cross, repentance, and change of heart, cannot help approving of those who insist on certain rules of conduct. King Henry found it convenient to keep a great number of horses in abbeys founded for the support of the poor. One day when Latimer was preaching before him, he said, 'A prince ought not to prefer his horses above poor men. Abbeys were ordained for the comfort of the poor, and not for kings' horses to be kept in them.'

There was a dead silence in the congregation – no one dared turn his eyes towards Henry – and many showed symptoms of anger. The chaplain had hardly left the pulpit, when a gentleman of the court, the Lord Chamberlain apparently, went up to him and asked, 'What hast thou to do with the king's horses? They are the maintenances and part of a king's honour, and also of his realm; wherefore, in speaking against them, ye are against the king's honour.' 'To take away the right of the poor', answered Latimer, 'is against the honour of the king. ... God is the grand master of the king's house, and will take account of everyone that beareth rule therein.'

Thus the reformation undertook to re-establish the rule of conscience even in the courts of princes. Latimer knowing, like Calvin, that 'the ears of the princes of this world are accustomed to be pampered and flattered', armed himself with invincible courage.

The murmurs grew louder. While the old chaplains let things take their course, the other wanted to restore morality among Christians. The reformer was alive to the accusations brought against him, for his was not a heart of steel. Reproaches and calumnies appeared to him sometimes like those impetuous winds which force the husbandman to fly hurriedly for shelter to some covered place. 'O Lord!' he exclaimed on one occasion, 'these people pinch me; nay, they have a full bite at me.' He would have desired to flee away to the wilderness, but he called to mind what had been done to his Master; 'I comfort myself', he said, 'that Christ himself was noted to be a stirrer up of the people against the emperor and was content to be called seditious.'

The priests, delighted that Latimer censured the king, resolved to take advantage of it to ruin him. One day, when there was a grand reception, and the king was surrounded by his councillors and courtiers, a monk slipped into the midst of the crowd, and, falling on his knees before the monarch, said, 'Sire, your new chaplain preaches sedition.' Henry turned to Latimer: 'What say you to that, sir?' The chaplain bent his knee before the prince; and, turning to his accusers, said to them, 'Would you have me preach nothing concerning a king in the king's sermon? Have you any commission to appoint me what I shall preach?' His friends trembled lest he should be arrested. 'Your Grace', he continued, 'I put myself in your hands: appoint other doctors to preach in my place before Your Majesty. There are many more worthy of the room than I am. If it be Your Grace's pleasure, I could be content to be their servant, and bear their books after them. But if Your Grace allow me for a preacher, I would desire you give me leave to discharge my conscience. Permit me to frame my teaching for my audience.'

Henry, who always liked Latimer, took his part, and the chaplain retired with a low bow. When he left the audience, his friends, who had watched this scene with the keenest emotion, surrounded him, saying, with tears in their eyes, 'We were convinced that you would sleep tonight in the Tower.' '*The king's heart is in the hand of the Lord*', he answered, calmly.

The evangelical reformers of England nobly maintained their independence in the presence of a Catholic and despotic king. Firmly convinced, free, strong men, they yielded neither to the seductions of the court nor to those of Rome. We shall see still more striking examples of their resolution, bequeathed by them to their successors.

CHAPTER EIGHT

The King Seeks Tyndale

(January to May 1531)

Henry VIII, finding that he wanted men like Latimer to resist the pope, sought to win over others of the same stamp. He found one, whose lofty range he understood immediately. Thomas Cromwell had laid before him a book then very eagerly read all over England, namely, the *Practice of Prelates*. It was found in the houses not only of the citizens of London, but of the farmers of Essex, Suffolk, and other counties. The king read it quite as eagerly as his subjects. Nothing interested him like the history of the slow but formidable progress of the priesthood and prelacy. One parable in particular struck him, in which the oak represented royalty, and the ivy the papacy. 'First, the ivy springeth out of the earth, and then awhile creepeth along by the ground till it find a great tree. There it joineth itself beneath alow unto the body of the tree, and creepeth up a little and a little, fair and softly. And at the beginning, while it is yet thin and small, that the burden is not perceived, it seemeth glorious to garnish the tree in the winter, and to bear off the tempests of the weather. But in the mean season it thrusteth roots into the bark of the tree to hold fast withal; and ceaseth not to climb up till it be at the top and above all. And then it sendeth its branches along by the branches of the tree, and overgroweth all, and waxeth great, heavy, and thick; and sucketh the moisture so sore out of the tree and his branches, that it choaketh and stifleth them. And then the foul stinking ivy waxeth mighty in the stump of the tree, and becometh a seat and a nest for all unclean birds and for blind owls, which hawk in the dark and dare not come at the light. Even so the Bishop of Rome, now called pope, at the beginning crept along upon the earth. ... He crept up and fastened his roots in the heart of the emperor, and by subtlety climbed above the emperor, and subdued him, and made him stoop unto his feet and kiss them another while. Yea, when he had put the crown on the emperor's head, he smote it off with his feet again, saying that he had might to make emperors and to put them down again.'[1]

Henry would willingly have clapped his hand on his sword to demand satisfaction of the pope for this outrage. The book was by Tyndale. Laying it down, the king reflected on what he had just read, and thought to himself that the author had some striking ideas 'on the accursed power of the pope', and that he was besides gifted with talent and zeal, and might render excellent service towards abolishing the papacy in England.

Tyndale, from the time of his conversion at Oxford, set Christ above everything: he boldly threw off the yoke of human traditions, and would take no other guide but Scripture only. Full of imagination and eloquence, active and ready to endure fatigue, he exposed himself to every danger in the fulfilment of his mission. Henry ordered Stephen Vaughan, one of his agents, then at Antwerp, to try to find the reformer in Brabant, Flanders, on the banks of the Rhine, in Holland, wherever he might chance to be; to offer him a safe-conduct under the sign-manual,[2] to prevail on him to return to England, and to add the most gracious promises in behalf of His Majesty.

To gain over Tyndale seemed even more important than to have gained Latimer. Vaughan immediately undertook to seek him in Antwerp, where he was said to be, but could not find him. 'He is at Marburg', said one; 'at Frankfurt', said another; 'at Hamburg', declared a third. Tyndale was invisible now as before. To make more certain, Vaughan determined to write three letters directed to those three places, conjuring him to return to England. 'I have great hopes', said the English agent to his friends, 'of having done something that will please His Majesty.' Tyndale, the most scriptural of English reformers, the most inflexible in his faith, labouring at the reformation with the cordial approbation of the monarch, would truly have been something extraordinary.

[1] Tyndale, *Expositions and The Practice of Prelates* (Parker Society), p. 270.
[2] [The king's signature.]

Scarcely had the three letters been despatched when Vaughan heard of the ignominious chastisement inflicted by Sir Thomas More on Tyndale's brother. Was it by such indignities that Henry expected to attract the reformer? Vaughan, much annoyed, wrote to the king (26 January 1531) that this event would make Tyndale think they wanted to entrap him, and he gave up looking for him.

Three months later (17 April), as Vaughan was busy copying one of Tyndale's manuscripts in order to send it to Henry (it was his answer to the *Dialogue* of Sir Thomas More), a man knocked at his door. 'Someone, who calls himself a friend of yours, desires very much to speak with you', said the stranger, 'and begs you to follow me.' – 'Who is this friend? where is he?' asked Vaughan. – 'I do not know him', replied the messenger, 'but come along, and you will see for yourself.' Vaughan doubted whether it was prudent to follow this person to a strange place. He made up his mind, however, to accompany him. The agent of Henry VIII and the messenger threaded the streets of Antwerp, went out of the city, and at last reached a lonely field, by the side of which the Scheldt flowed sluggishly through the level country. As he advanced, Vaughan saw a man of noble bearing awaiting him. 'Do you not recognize me?' he asked Vaughan. 'I cannot call to mind your features', answered the latter. 'My name is Tyndale', said the stranger. 'Tyndale!' exclaimed Vaughan with delight. 'Tyndale! what a happy meeting!'

Tyndale, who had heard of Henry's new plans, had no confidence either in the prince or in his pretended reformation. The king's endless negotiations with the pope, his worldliness, his amours, his persecution of evangelical Christians, and especially the ignominious punishment inflicted on John Tyndale: all these matters disgusted him. However, having been informed of the nature of Vaughan's mission, he desired to turn it to advantage by addressing a few warnings to the prince. 'I have written certain books', he said, 'to warn His Majesty of the subtle demeanour of the clergy of his realm towards his person, in which doing I showed the heart of a true subject; to the intent that His Grace might prepare remedies against their subtle dreams. An exile from my native country, I suffer hunger, thirst, cold, absence of friends, everywhere encompassed with great danger; in innumerable hard and sharp fightings, I do not feel their asperity, by reason that I hope with my labours to do honour to God, true service to my prince, and pleasure to his commons.'

'Cheer up', said Vaughan, 'your exile, poverty, fightings, all are at an end; you can return to England.' 'What matters it', said Tyndale, 'if my exile finishes, so long as the Bible is banished? Has the king forgotten that God has commanded his word to be spread throughout the world? If it continues to be forbidden to his subjects, very death were more pleasant to me than life.'

Vaughan did not consider himself worsted. The messenger, who remained at a distance and could hear nothing, was astonished at seeing the two men in that solitary field conversing together so long, and with so much animation. 'Tell me what guarantees you desire', said Vaughan: 'the king will grant them you.' 'Of course the king would give me a safe-conduct', answered Tyndale, 'but the clergy would persuade him that promises made to heretics are not binding.' Night was coming on, Henry's agent might have had Tyndale followed and seized. The idea occurred to Vaughan, but he rejected it. Tyndale began, however, to feel himself ill at ease. 'Farewell', he said; 'you shall see me again before long, or hear news of me.' He then departed, walking away from Antwerp. Vaughan, who re-entered the city, was surprised to see Tyndale make for the open country. He supposed it to be a stratagem, and once more doubted whether he ought not to have seized the reformer to please his master. 'I might have failed of my purpose', he said; besides it was now too late, for Tyndale had disappeared.

As soon as Vaughan reached home he hastened to send to London an account of this singular conference. Cromwell immediately proceeded to court and laid before the king the envoy's letter and the reformer's book. 'Good!' said Henry, 'as soon as I have leisure I will read them both.' He did so, and was exasperated against Tyndale, who refused his invitation, mistrusted his word, and even dared to give him advice. In his passion the king in all probability tore off the latter part of Vaughan's letter, flung it in the fire, and entirely gave up his idea of bringing the reformer into England to make use of him against the pope, fearing that such a torch would set the whole kingdom in a blaze. He thought only how he could seize him and punish him for his arrogance.

He sent for Cromwell; before him on the table lay the treatise by Tyndale, which Vaughan had copied and sent. 'These pages', said Henry to his minister, while pointing to the manuscript, 'these pages are the work of a visionary: they are full of lies, sedition, and calumny. Vaughan shows too much affection for Tyndale. Let him beware of inviting him to come into the kingdom. He is a perverse and hardened character who cannot be changed. I am too happy that he is out of England.'

Cromwell retired in vexation. He wrote to Vaughan, but the king found the letter too weak, and Cromwell had to correct it, to make it harmonize with the wrath of the prince.[1] An ambitious man, he bent before the obstinate will of his master; but the loss of Tyndale seemed irreparable. Accordingly, while informing Vaughan of the king's anger, he added that if wholesome reflection should bring Tyndale to reason, the king was 'so inclined to mercy, pity, and compassion', that he would doubtless see him with pleasure. Vaughan, whose heart Tyndale had gained, began to hunt after him again, and had a second interview with him. He gave him Cromwell's letter to read, and when the reformer came to the words we have just quoted about Henry's compassion, his eyes filled with tears. 'What gracious words!' he exclaimed. 'Yes', said Vaughan, 'they have such sweetness, that they would break the hardest heart in the world.' Tyndale, deeply moved, tried to find some mode of fulfilling his duty towards God and towards the king. 'If His Majesty', he said, 'would condescend to permit only a bare text of the Scriptures to circulate among the people, as they do in the states of the emperor and in other Christian countries, I would bind myself never to write again; I would throw myself at his feet, offering my body as a sacrifice, ready to submit if necessary to torture and to death.'

But a gulf lay between the monarch and the reformer. Henry VIII saw the seeds of heresy in the Scriptures; and Tyndale rejected every reformation which they wished to carry out by proscribing the Bible. 'Heresy springeth not from the Scriptures', he said, 'no more than darkness from the sun.' Tyndale disappeared again, and the name of his hiding place is unknown.

---

[1] The corrections are still to be seen in the original draft, and are indicated in the biographical notice of Tyndale printed in *Doctrinal Treatises, etc.* (Parker Society).

The King of England was not discouraged by the check he had received. He wanted men possessed of talent and zeal, men resolved to attack the pope. Cambridge had given England a teacher who might be placed beside, and perhaps even above, Latimer and Tyndale; this was John Fryth. He thirsted for the truth; he sought God, and was determined to give himself wholly to Jesus Christ. One day Cromwell said to the king, 'What a pity it is, Your Highness, that a man so distinguished as Fryth in letters and sciences, should be among the sectarians!' Like Tyndale, he had quitted England. Cromwell, with Henry's consent, wrote to Vaughan: 'His Majesty strongly desires the reconciliation of Fryth, who (he firmly believes) is not so far advanced as Tyndale in the evil way. Always full of mercy, the king is ready to receive him to favour; try to attract him charitably, politically.' Vaughan immediately began his inquiries; it was May 1531, but the first news he received was that Fryth, a minister of the gospel, was just married in Holland. 'This marriage', he wrote to the king, 'may by chance hinder my persuasion.' This was not all; Fryth was boldly printing, at Amsterdam, Tyndale's answer to Sir Thomas More. Henry was forced to give him up, as he had given up his friend. He succeeded with none but Latimer, and even the chaplain told him many harsh truths. There was a decided incompatibility between the spiritual reform and the political reform; the work of God refused to ally itself with the work of the throne. The Christian faith and the visible church are two distinct things. Some (and among them the reformers) require Christianity – a living Christianity; others (and it was the case of Henry and his prelates) look for the church and its hierarchy, and care little whether a living faith be found there or not. This is a capital error. Real religion must exist first; and then this religion must produce a true religious society. Tyndale, Fryth, and their friends desired to begin with religion; Henry and his followers with an ecclesiastical society, hostile to faith. The king and the reformers could not, therefore, come to an understanding. Henry, profoundly hurt by the boldness of those evangelical men, swore that as they would not have peace they should have war – war to the knife.

CHAPTER NINE

The King of England – 'Head of the Church'

(January to March 1531)

Henry VIII desired to introduce great changes into the ecclesiastical corporation of his kingdom. His royal power had
much to bear from the power of the clergy. It was the same
in all Catholic monarchies; but England had more to complain of than
others. Of the three estates, clergy, nobility, and commons, the first was
the most powerful. The nobility had been weakened by the civil wars;
the commons had long been without authority and energy; the prelates
thus occupied the first rank, so that in 1529 an archbishop and cardinal
(Wolsey) was the most powerful man in England, not even the king
excepted. Henry had felt the yoke, and wished to free himself, not only
from the domination of the pope, but also from the influence of the
higher clergy. If he had only intended to be avenged of the pontiff, it
would have been enough to allow the reformation to act; when a mighty
wind blows from heaven, it sweeps away all the contrivances of men. But
Henry was deficient neither in prudence nor calculation. He feared lest
a diversity of doctrine should engender disturbances in his kingdom. He
wished to free himself from the pope and the prelates, without throwing
himself into the arms of Tyndale or of Latimer.

Kings and people had observed that the domination of the papacy,
and its authority over the clergy, were an insurmountable obstacle to the
autonomy of the state. As far back as 1268, St Louis had declared that
France owed allegiance to God alone; and other princes had followed his
example. Henry VIII determined to do more – to break the chains which
bound the clergy to the Romish throne, and fasten them to the Crown.
The power of England, delivered from the papacy, which had been

its canker-worm, would then be developed with freedom and energy, and would place the country in the foremost rank among nations. The renovating spirit of the age was favourable to Henry's plans; without delay he must put into execution the bold plan which Cromwell had unrolled before his eyes in Whitehall Park. Henry concentrated upon having himself recognized as head of the church.

This important revolution could not be accomplished by a simple act of royal authority – in England particularly, where constitutional principles already possessed an incontestable influence. It was necessary to prevail upon the clergy to cross the Rubicon by emancipating themselves from Rome. But how to bring it about? This was the subject of the meditations of the sagacious Cromwell, who, gradually rising in the king's confidence to the place formerly held by Wolsey, made a different use of it. Urged by ambition, possessing an energetic character, a sound judgment, unshaken firmness, no obstacle could arrest his activity. He sought how he could give the king the spiritual sceptre, and this was the plan on which he fixed. The kings of England had been known occasionally to revive old laws fallen into desuetude, and visit with heavy penalties those who had violated them. Cromwell represented to the king that the statutes made punishable any man who should recognize a dignity established by the pope in the English Church; that Wolsey, by exercising the functions of papal legate, had encroached upon the rights of the Crown and been condemned, which was but justice; while the members of the clergy – who had recognized the unlawful jurisdiction of the pretended legate – had thereby become as guilty as he had been. 'The statute of *Præmunire*', he said, 'condemns them as well as their chief.' Henry, who listened attentively, found that the expedient of his Secretary of State was in conformity with the letter of the law, and that it put all the clergy in his power. He did not hesitate to give full power to his ministers. Under such a state of things there was not one innocent person in England; the two houses of Parliament, the Privy Council, all the nation must be brought to the bar. Henry, full of 'condescension', was pleased to confine himself to the clergy.

The convocation of the province of Canterbury having met on 7 January 1531, Cromwell entered the hall and quietly took his seat among the bishops; then rising, he informed them that their property and benefices were to be confiscated for the good of His Majesty, because they had submitted to the unconstitutional power of the cardinal. What terrible news! It was a thunderbolt to those selfish prelates; they were amazed. At length some of them plucked up a little courage. 'The king himself had sanctioned the authority of the cardinal-legate', they said. 'We merely obeyed his supreme will. Our resistance to His Majesty's proclamations would infallibly have ruined us.' – 'That is of no consequence', was the reply; 'there was the law: you should obey the constitution of the country even at the peril of your lives.' The terrified bishops laid at the foot of the throne a magnificent sum by which they hoped to redeem their offences and their benefices. But that was not what Henry desired: he pretended to set little store by their money. The threat of confiscation must constrain them to pay a ransom of still greater value. 'My lords', said Cromwell, 'in a petition that some of you presented to the pope not long ago, you called the king your *soul* and your *head*. Come, then, expressly recognize the supremacy of the king over the church, and His Majesty, of his great goodness, will grant you your pardon.' What a demand! The distracted clergy assembled, and a deliberation of extreme importance began. 'The words in the address to the pope', said some, 'were a mere form, and had not the meaning ascribed to them.' – 'The king being unable to untie the Gordian knot at Rome', said others, alluding to the divorce, 'intends to cut it with his sword.' – 'The secular power', exclaimed the most zealous, 'has no voice in ecclesiastical matters. To recognize the king as head of the church would be to overthrow the Catholic faith. … The head of the church is the pope.' The debate lasted three days, and as Henry's ministers pointed to the theocratic government of Israel, a priest exclaimed: 'We oppose the New Testament to the Old; according to the gospel, Christ is head of the church.' When this was told the king, he said: 'Very well, I consent. If you declare me *head of the church* you may add *under God.'* In this way the papal claims were compromised all the more. 'We will expose ourselves to everything', they said, 'rather than dethrone the Roman pontiff.'

The bishops of Lincoln and Exeter were deputed to beseech the king to withdraw his demand: they could not so much as obtain an audience.

Henry had made up his mind: the priests must yield. The only means of their obtaining pardon (they were told) was by their renouncing the papal supremacy. The bishops made a fresh attempt to satisfy both the requirements of the king and those of their own conscience. 'Shrink before the clergy and they are lions', the courtiers said; 'withstand them and they are sheep.' – 'Your fate is in your own hands. If you refuse the king's demand, the disgrace of Wolsey may show you what you may expect.' Archbishop Warham, president of the convocation, a prudent man, far advanced in years and near his end, tried to hit upon some compromise. The great movements which agitated the church all over Europe disturbed him. He had in times past complained to the king of Wolsey's usurpations, and was not far from recognizing the royal supremacy. He proposed to insert a simple clause in the act conferring the required jurisdiction on the king, namely, *Quantum per legem Christi licet* (so far as the law of Christ permits). 'You have played me a shrewd turn', exclaimed the king. 'I thought to have made fools of those prelates, and now you have so ordered the business that they are likely to make a fool of me. Go to them again, and let me have the business passed without any *quantums* or *tantums*. ... So far as the law of Christ permits! Such a reserve would make one believe that my authority was disputable.'

Henry's ministers ventured on this occasion to resist him: they showed him that this clause would prevent an immediate rupture with Rome, and it might be repealed hereafter. He yielded at last, and the archbishop submitted the clause with the amendment to convocation. It was a solemn moment for England. The bishops were convinced that the king was asking them to do what was wrong, the end of which would be a rupture with Rome. In the time of Hildebrand the prelates would have answered 'No', and found a sympathetic support in the laity. But things had changed; the people were weary of the long domination of the priests. The primate, desirous of ending the matter, said to his colleagues: 'Do you recognize the king as sole protector of the church and clergy of England, and, so far as is allowed by the law of Christ, also as your supreme head?' All remained speechless. 'Will you let me know your opinions?' resumed the archbishop. There was a dead silence.

'Whoever is silent seems to consent', said the primate. – 'Then we are all silent', answered one of the members. Were these words inspired by courage or by cowardice? Were they an assent or a protest? We cannot say. In this matter we cannot side either with the king or with the priests. The heart of man easily takes the part of those who are oppressed; but here the oppressed were also oppressors. Convocation next gave its support to the opinion of the universities respecting the divorce, and thus Henry gained his first victory.

For breach of *præmunire* the convocation of Canterbury was permitted by the king to purchase his pardon by rendering to the royal exchequer £100,000 sterling, an enormous sum for those times. This was in February 1531. Later in the year the convocation of York followed suit with a payment of a little less than £19,000. Thus at one stroke the clergy of England were deprived of both riches and honour.

Animated discussion took place in the northern convocation. 'If you proclaim the king supreme head', said Bishop Tunstall, 'it can only be in temporal matters.' – 'Indeed!' retorted Henry's minister, 'is an act of convocation necessary to determine that the king reigns?' – 'If spiritual things are meant', answered the bishop, 'I withdraw from convocation that I may not withdraw from the church.'

'My lords', said Henry, 'no one disputes your right to preach and administer the sacraments. Did not Paul submit to Caesar's tribunal, and our Saviour himself to Pilate's?' Henry's ecclesiastical theories prevailed also at York. A great revolution was effected in England, and fresh compromises were to consolidate it.

The king, having obtained what he desired, condescended in his great mercy to pardon the clergy for their unpardonable offence of having recognized Wolsey as papal legate. At the request of the commons this amnesty was extended to all England. The nation, which at first saw nothing in this affair but an act enfranchising themselves from the usurped power of the popes, showed their gratitude to Henry; but there was a reverse to the medal. If the pope was despoiled, the king was invested. Was not the function ascribed to him contrary to the gospel? Would not this act impress upon the Anglican reformation a territorial and aristocratic character, which would introduce into the

Reformed Church the world with all its splendour and wealth? If the royal pre-eminence endows the Anglican Church with the pomps of worship, of classical studies, of high dignities, will it not also carry along with it luxury, sinecures, and worldliness among the prelates? Shall we not see the royal authority pronounce on questions of dogma, and declare the most sacred doctrines indifferent? A little later an attempt was made to limit the power of the king in religious matters. 'We give not to our princes the ministry of God's word or the sacraments', says the Thirty-seventh Article of Religion.

CHAPTER TEN

The King Puts Catherine Away

(March to June 1531)

The king, having obtained so important a concession from the clergy, turned to his Parliament to ask a service of another kind – one in his eyes still more urgent. On 30 March 1531, the session being about to terminate, Sir Thomas More, the chancellor, went to the House of Commons, and submitted to them the decision of the various universities on the king's marriage and the power of the pope. The commons looked at the affair essentially from a political point of view; they did not understand that because the king had lived twenty years with the queen, he ought not to be separated from her. The documents placed before their eyes 'made them detest the marriage' of Henry and Catherine. The chancellor desired the members to report in their respective counties and towns that the king had not asked for this divorce of his own will or pleasure, but 'only for the discharge of his conscience and surety of the succession of his crown'. 'Enlighten the people', he said, 'and preserve peace in the nation with the sentiments of loyalty due to the monarch.'

The king hastened to use the powers which universities, clergy, and Parliament had placed in his hands. Immediately after the prorogation, certain lords went down to Greenwich and laid before the queen the decisions which condemned her marriage, and urged her to accept the arbitration of four bishops and four lay peers. Catherine replied sadly but firmly: 'I pray you, tell the king I say I am his lawful wife, and in that point I will abide until the court of Rome determine to the contrary.'

The divorce which, notwithstanding Catherine's refusal, was approaching, caused great agitation among the people, and the members of Parliament had some trouble to preserve order, as Sir Thomas More had desired them. Priests proclaimed from their pulpits the downfall of the church and the coming of Antichrist; the mendicant friars scattered discontent in every house which they entered, the most fanatical of them not fearing to insinuate that the wrath of God would soon hurl the impious prince from his throne. In towns and villages, in castles and alehouses, men talked of nothing but the divorce and the primacy claimed by the king. Women standing at their doors, men gathering round the blacksmith's forge, spoke more or less disrespectfully of Parliament, the bishops, the dangers of the Romish Church, and the prospects of the reformation. If a few friends met at night around the hearth, they told strange tales to one another. The king, queen, pope, devil, saints, Cromwell, and the higher clergy formed the subject of their conversation. The gypsies at that time strolling through the country added to the confusion. Sometimes they would appear in the midst of these animated discussions, and prophesy lamentable events, at times calling up the dead to make them speak of the future. The terrible calamities they predicted froze their hearers with affright, and their sinister prophecies were the cause of disorders and even of crimes. Accordingly an act was passed pronouncing the penalty of banishment against them.

An unfortunate event tended still more to strike men's imaginations. It was reported that the Bishop of Rochester, that prelate so terrible to the reformers and so good to the poor, had narrowly escaped being poisoned by his cook. Seventeen persons were taken ill after eating porridge at the episcopal palace; one of the bishop's gentlemen died, as well as a poor woman to whom the remains of the food had been given. It was maliciously remarked that the bishop was the only one who frankly opposed the divorce and the royal supremacy. Calumny even aimed at the throne. When Henry heard of this, he resolved to make short work of all such nonsense; he ordered the offence to be deemed as high treason, and the wretched cook was taken to Smithfield, there to be boiled to death. This was a variation of the penalty pronounced upon the evangelicals. Such was the cruel justice of the sixteenth century.

While the universities, Parliament, Convocation, and the nation appeared to support Henry VIII, one voice was raised against the divorce. It was that of a young man, brought up by the king, and that voice moved him deeply. There still remained in England some scions of the house of York, and among them a nephew of that unhappy Warwick whom Henry VII had cruelly put to death. Warwick's sister, Margaret, had been married to Sir Richard Pole, a knight of Buckinghamshire. In 1505 she was left a widow with two daughters and three sons – the youngest, Reginald, became a favourite with Henry VIII, who destined him for the archiepiscopal see of Canterbury. 'Your kindnesses are such', said Pole to him, 'that a king could grant no more, even to a son.' But Reginald, to whom his mother had told the story of the execution of the unhappy Warwick, had contracted an invincible hatred against the Tudors. Accordingly, in despite of certain evangelical tendencies, Pole, seeing Henry separating from the pope, resolved to throw himself into the arms of the pontiff. Reginald, invested with the Roman purple, rose to be president of the council and primate of all England under Queen Mary. Elegant in his manners, with a fine intellect, and sincere in his religious convictions, he was selfish, irritable, and ambitious: desires of elevation and revenge led a noble nature astray. If the branch of which he was the representative was ever to recover the crown, it could only be by the help of the Roman pontiffs: henceforward their cause was his. Loaded with benefits by Henry VIII, he was incessantly pursued by the recollection of the rights of Rome and of the White Rose; and he went so far as to insult before all Europe the prince who had been his first friend.

At this time Pole was living at a house in the country which Henry had given him. One day he received at this charming retreat a communication from the Duke of Norfolk. 'The king destines you for the highest honours of the English Church', wrote this nobleman, 'and offers you at once the important sees of York and Winchester, left vacant by the death of Cardinal Wolsey.' At the same time the duke asked Pole's opinion about the divorce. Reginald's brothers, and particularly the eldest, Lord Montague, entreated him to answer as all the Catholic world had answered, and not irritate a prince whose anger would ruin them all. The blood of Warwick and the king's revolt against Rome induced Pole to reject with horror all the honours which Henry offered; and yet that prince was his benefactor. He fancied he had discovered a middle course which would permit him to satisfy alike his conscience and his king.

He went to Whitehall, where Henry received him like a friend. Pole hesitated in distress; he wished to let the king know his thoughts, but the words would not come to his lips. At last, encouraged by the prince's affability, he summoned up his resolution, and in a voice trembling with emotion, said: 'You must not separate from the queen.' Henry had expected something different. Was it thus that his kindnesses were to be repaid? His eyes flashed with anger, and he laid his hand on his sword. Pole humbled himself: 'If I possess any knowledge, to whom do I owe it, unless to Your Majesty? In listening to me, you are listening to your own pupil.' The king recovered himself, and said, 'I will consider your opinion, and send you my answer.' Pole withdrew. 'He put me in such a passion', said the king to one of his gentlemen, 'that I nearly struck him. … But there is something in the man that wins my heart.'

Montague and Reginald's other brother again conjured him to accept the high position which the king reserved for him; but his soul revolted at being subordinate to a Tudor. He therefore wrote a memoir, which he presented to Henry, and in which he entreated him implicitly to submit the divorce question to the court of Rome. 'How could I speak against your marriage with the queen?' he said. 'Should I not accuse Your Majesty of having lived for more than twenty years in an unlawful union? By the divorce, you will array all the powers against you – the pope, the emperor; and as for the French … we can never find in our hearts to trust them. You are at this moment on the verge of an abyss. … One step more, and all is over. There is only one way of safety left Your Grace, and that is submission to the pope.'

Henry was moved. The boldness with which this young nobleman dared accuse him irritated his pride; still his friendship prevailed, and he forgave it. Pole received the permission he had asked to leave England, and to continue to draw his revenues as Dean of Exeter.

Reginald Pole was, as it were, the last link that united the royal pair. Thus far the king had continued to show the queen every respect; their mutual affection seemed the same, only they occupied separate rooms. Henry now decided to take an important step. On 14 July 1531, a new deputation entered the queen's apartment at Windsor, one of whom informed her that as her marriage with Prince Arthur had been duly consummated she could not be the wife of her husband's brother. Then after reproaching her with having, contrary to the laws of England and the dignity of the Crown, cited His Majesty before the pope's tribunal, he desired her to choose for her residence either the Castle of Oking or of Estamsteed, or the monastery of Bisham. Catherine remained calm, and replied: 'Wheresoever I retire, nothing can deprive me of the title which belongs to me. I shall always be His Majesty's wife.' She left Windsor the same day, and removed to the More in Hertfordshire, a splendid mansion which Wolsey had surrounded with beautiful gardens; then to Estamsteed, and finally to Ampthill in Bedfordshire. The king never saw her again; but all the papists and discontented rallied round her. She entered into correspondence with the sovereigns of Europe, and became the centre of a party opposed to the emancipation of England.

CHAPTER ELEVEN

'Not Sparing the Flock'

(September 1531 to 1532)

As Henry, by breaking with Catherine, had broken with the pope, he felt the necessity of uniting more closely with his clergy. Wishing to proceed to the establishment of his new dignity, he required bishops, and particularly dexterous bishops. He therefore made Edward Lee Archbishop of York, and Stephen Gardiner Bishop of Winchester; and these two men, devoted to scholastic doctrines, ambitious and servile, were commissioned to inaugurate the new ecclesiastical monarchy of the King of England. Although the pope had hastened to send off their bulls, they declared they held their dignity 'immediately and only' of the king, and began without delay to organize a strange league. If the king needed the bishops against the pope, the bishops needed the king against the reformers. It was not long before this alliance received its baptism of blood.

But before proceeding so far, the prelates deliberated about the means of raising the £119,000 they had bound themselves to pay the king. Each wished to make his own share as small as possible, and throw the largest part of the burden upon his colleagues. The bishops determined to place it in great measure on the shoulders of the parochial clergy.

Stokesley, Bishop of London, began the battle. An able, greedy, violent man, and jealous of his prerogatives, he called a meeting of six or eight priests on whom he believed he could depend, in order to draw up with their assistance such resolutions as he could afterwards impose more easily upon their brethren. These picked ecclesiastics were desired to meet on 1 September 1531, in the chapter house of St Paul's.

The bishop's plan had got wind, and excited general indignation in the city. Was it just that the victims should pay the fine? Some of the laity, delighted at seeing the clergy quarrelling, sought to fan the flame instead of extinguishing it.

When 1 September arrived the bishop entered the chapter house with his officers, where the conference with the priests was to be held. Presently an unusual noise was heard round St Paul's: not only the six or eight priests, but six hundred, accompanied by a great number of citizens and common people, made their appearance. The crowd swayed to and fro before the cathedral gates, shouting and clamouring to be admitted into the chapter house on the same footing as the select few. What was to be done? The prelate's councillors advised him to add a few of the less violent priests to those he had already chosen. Stokesley adopted their advice, hoping that the gates and bolts would be strong enough to keep out the rest. Accordingly he drew up a list of new members, and one of his officers, going out to the angry crowd, read the names of those whom the bishop had selected. The latter came forward, not without trouble; but at the same time the excluded priests made a vigorous attempt to enter. There was a fierce struggle of men pushing and shouting, but the bishop's officials having passed in quickly, those who had been nominated hurriedly closed the doors. So far the victory seemed to rest with the bishop, and he was about to speak, when the uproar became deafening. The priests outside, exasperated because their financial matters were to be settled without them, protested that they ought to hold their own purse-strings. Laying hands on whatever they could find, and aided by the laity, they began to batter the door of the chapter house. They succeeded: the door gave way, and all, priests and citizens, rushed in together. The bishop's officials tried in vain to stop them; they were roughly pushed aside. Their gowns were torn, their faces streamed with perspiration, their features were disfigured, and some even were wounded. The furious priests entered the room at last, storming and shouting. It was more like a pack of hounds rushing on a stag than the reverend clergy of the metropolis of England appearing before their bishop. The prelate, who had tact, showed no anger, but sought rather to calm the rioters. 'My brethren', he said, 'I marvel not a little why ye be so heady. Ye know not what shall be said to you, therefore I pray you hear me patiently. Ye all know that we be men frail of condition, and by our lack of wisdom have misdemeaned ourselves towards the king and fallen in a *præmunire*, by reason whereof all our lands, goods, and chattels were to him forfeit, and our bodies ready to be imprisoned. Yet His Grace of his great clemency is pleased to pardon us, and to accept of a little instead of the whole of our benefices, to be paid in five years. I exhort you to bear your parts towards payment of this sum granted.'

This was just what the priests did not want. They thought it strange to be asked for money for an offence they had not committed. 'My lord', answered one, 'we have never offended against the *præmunire*, we have never meddled with cardinal's faculties. Let the bishops and abbots pay; they committed the offence, and they have good places.' – 'My lord', added another, 'twenty nobles[1] a year is but a bare living for a priest, and yet it is all we have. Everything is now so dear that poverty compels us to say "No." Having no need of the king's pardon we have no desire to pay.' These words were drowned in applause. 'No', exclaimed the crowd, which was getting noisy again, 'we will pay nothing.' The bishop's officers grew angry and came to high words; the priests returned abuse for abuse; and the citizens, delighted to see their 'masters' quarrelling, fanned the strife. From words they soon came to blows. The episcopal ushers, who tried to restore order, were 'buffeted and stricken', and even the bishop's life was in danger. At last the meeting broke up in great confusion. Stokesley hastened to complain to the chancellor, Sir Thomas More, who, being a great friend of the prelate's, sent fifteen priests and five laymen to prison. They deserved it, no doubt; but the bishops, who, to spare their superfluity, robbed poor curates of their necessaries, were more guilty still.

Such was the unity that existed between the bishops and the priests of England at the very time the reformation was appearing at the doors. The prelates understood the danger to which they were exposed through that evangelical doctrine, the source of light and life. They knew that all their ecclesiastical pretensions would crumble away before the breath of the divine word. Accordingly, not content with robbing of their little

---

[1] The noble was worth six shillings and eightpence.

substance the poor pastors to whom they should have been as fathers, they determined to deprive those whom they called *heretics*, not only of their money, but of their liberty and life. Would Henry permit this?

The king did not wish to withdraw England from the papal jurisdiction without the assent of the clergy. If he did so of his own authority, the priests would rise against him and compare him to Luther. There were at that time three great parties in Christendom: the evangelical, the Catholic, and the popish. Henry purposed to overthrow popery, but without going so far as evangelicalism: he desired to remain in Catholicism. One means occurred of satisfying the clergy. Although they were fanatical partisans of the church, they had sacrificed the pope; they now imagined that, by sacrificing a few heretics, they would atone for their cowardly submission. In a later age Louis XIV did the same to make up for errors of another kind. The provincial synod of Canterbury met and addressed the king: 'Your Highness one time defended the church with your pen, when you were only a member of it; now that you are its supreme head, Your Majesty should crush its enemies, and so shall your merits exceed all praise.'

In order to prove that he was not another Luther, Henry VIII consented to hand over the disciples of that heretic to the priests; and gave them authority to imprison and burn them, provided they would aid the king to resume the power usurped by the pope. The bishops immediately began to hunt down the friends of the gospel.

A will had given rise to much talk in the county of Gloucester. William Tracy, a gentleman of irreproachable conduct and 'full of good works, equally generous to the clergy and the laity', had died praying God to save his soul through the merits of Jesus Christ, but leaving no money to the priests for masses. The primate of England had his bones dug up and burnt.[1] But this was not enough: they must also burn the living.

---

[1] [The 'testament and last will' of William Tracy is worthy of notice as showing how far reformed doctrine had penetrated into England by the year 1530. Tracy belonged to Toddington, eight miles south of Evesham, and was at one time high sheriff of his county. His will ran as follows: 'First and before all other things, I commit myself to God and to his mercy, believing, without any doubt or mistrust, that by his grace, and the merits of Jesus Christ, and by the virtue of his passion and of his resurrection, I have and shall have remission of all my sins, and resurrection of body

and soul, according as it is written, I believe that my Redeemer liveth, and that in the last day I shall rise out of the earth, and in my flesh shall see my Saviour: this my hope is laid up in my bosom. And touching the wealth of my soul, the faith that I have taken and rehearsed is sufficient (as I suppose) without any other man's works or merits. My ground of belief is, that there is but one God and one Mediator between God and man, which is Jesus Christ; so that I accept none in heaven or in earth to be mediator between me and God, but only Jesus Christ: and therefore will I bestow no part of my goods for that intent that any man should say or do to help my soul: for therein I trust only to the promises of Christ: 'He that believeth and is baptized shall be saved, and he that believeth not shall be damned.' As touching the burying of my body, it availeth me not whatsoever be done thereto; for ... the funeral pomps are rather the solace of them that live, than the wealth and comfort of them that are dead. And touching the distribution of my temporal goods, my purpose is, by the grace of God, to bestow them to be accepted as the fruits of faith; so that I do not suppose that my merit shall be by the good bestowing of them, but my merit is the faith of Jesus Christ only, by whom such works are good ... and ever we should consider that true saying, that a good work maketh not a good man, but a good man maketh a good work; for faith maketh a man both good and righteous; for a righteous man liveth by faith, and whatsoever springeth not of faith is sin. Witness mine own hand the tenth of October in the twenty-second year of the reign of King Henry the Eighth.'

It was for such a clear testimony as this that the dead body of this worthy successor of Wycliffe was exhumed and burnt nearly two years after his death. The will was likewise condemned under the common seal of the University of Oxford on 28 January 1531.]

CHAPTER TWELVE

The Martyrs

(1531)

The first blows were aimed at the court chaplain. The bishops, finding it dangerous to have such a man near the king, would have liked (Latimer tells us) to place him on burning coals. But Henry loved him, the blow failed, and the priests had to turn to those who were not so well favoured at court.

Thomas Bilney, whose conversion had begun the reformation in England, had been compelled to do penance at St Paul's Cross; but from that time he became the prey of the direst terror. His backsliding had manifested the weakness of his faith. Bilney possessed a sincere and lively piety, but a judgment less sound than many of his friends. He had not got rid of certain scruples which in Luther and Calvin had yielded to the supreme authority of God's word. In his opinion none but priests consecrated by bishops had the power to bind and loose. This mixture of truth and error had caused his fall. Such sincere but imperfectly enlightened persons are always to be met with – persons who, agitated by the scruples of their conscience, waver between Rome and the word of God.

At last faith gained the upper hand in Bilney. Leaving his Cambridge friends, he had gone into the Eastern counties to meet his martyrdom. One day, arriving at a hermitage in the vicinity of Norwich, where a pious woman[1] dwelt, his words converted her to Christ. He then began to preach 'openly in the fields' to great crowds. His voice was heard in all the county; weeping over his former fall, he said: 'That doctrine which I once abjured is the truth. Let my example be a lesson to all who hear me.'

[1] [Described by John Foxe as 'an anachoress'.]

Before long he turned his steps in the direction of London, and, stopping at Ipswich, was not content to preach the gospel only, but violently attacked the errors of Rome before an astonished audience. Some friars had crept among his hearers, and Bilney perceiving them called out: '*The Lamb of God taketh away the sins of the world*. If the Bishop of Rome dares say that the hood of St Francis saves, he blasphemes the blood of the Saviour.' John Huggen, one of the friars, immediately made a note of the words. Bilney continued: 'To invoke the saints and not Christ, is to put the head under the feet and the feet above the head.' Richard Seman took down these words. 'Men will come after me', continued Bilney, 'who will teach the same faith and manner of living that I do, the true gospel of our Saviour, and will disentangle you from the errors in which deceivers have bound you so long.' Friar Julles hastened to write down the bold prediction.

Latimer, surrounded by the favours of the king and the luxury of the great, watched his friend from afar. He called to mind their walks in the fields round Cambridge, their serious conversation as they climbed the hill afterwards called after them 'the Heretics' Hill', and the visits they had paid together to the poor and to the prisoners. Latimer had seen Bilney very recently at Cambridge in fear and anguish, and had tried in vain to restore him to peace. 'He now rejoiced that God had endued him with such strength of faith, that he was ready to be burnt for Christ's sake.'

Bilney, drawing still nearer to London, arrived at Greenwich about the middle of July. He procured some New Testaments, and hiding them carefully under his clothes, called upon a humble Christian named Lawrence Staples. Taking them 'out of his sleeves', he desired Staples to distribute them among his friends. Then, as if impelled by a thirst for martyrdom, and saying that 'he would go up to Jerusalem', he turned again toward Norwich, whose bishop, Richard Nix, a blind octogenarian, was in the front rank of the persecutors. Arriving at the solitary place where the pious 'anachoress' lived, he left one of the precious volumes with her. This visit cost Bilney his life. The poor solitary read the New Testament, and lent it to the people who came to see her. The bishop, hearing of it, informed Sir Thomas More, who had Bilney arrested, brought to London, and shut up in the Tower.

Bilney began to breathe again: a load was taken off him; he was about to suffer the penalty his fall deserved. In the room next to his was John Petit, a member of Parliament of some eloquence, who had distributed his books and his alms in England and beyond the seas. Philips, the under-gaoler of the Tower, who was a good man, told the two prisoners that only a wooden partition separated them, which was a source of great joy to both. He would often remove a panel, and permit them to converse and take their frugal meals together.

This happiness did not last long. Bilney's trial was to take place at Norwich, where he had been captured: the aged Bishop Nix wanted to make an example in his diocese. A crowd of monks and friars – Augustins, Dominicans, Franciscans, and Carmelites – visited the prison of the evangelist to convert him. Dr Call, provincial of the Franciscans, having consented that the prisoner should make use of Scripture, was shaken in his faith; but, on the other hand, Stokes, an Augustin and a determined papist, repeated to Bilney: 'If you die in your opinions, you will be lost.'

The trial commenced, and the witnesses gave their evidence. 'He said', deposed William Cade, 'that the Jews and Saracens would have been converted long since, if the idolatry of the Christians had not disgusted them with Christianity.' – 'I heard him say', added Richard Neale: 'down with your gods of gold, silver, and stone.' – 'He stated', resumed Cade, 'that the priests take away the offerings from the saints and hang them about their women's necks; and then, if the offerings do not prove fine enough, they are put upon the images again.'

Everyone foresaw the end of this piteous trial. One of Bilney's friends endeavoured to save him. Latimer took the matter into the pulpit, and conjured the judges to decide according to justice. Although Bilney's name was not uttered, they all knew who was meant. The Bishop of London went and complained to the king that his chaplain had the audacity to defend the heretic against the bishop and his judges. Said Latimer later: 'It might have become a preacher to say as I said, though Bilney had never been born.' The chaplain escaped once more, thanks to the favour he enjoyed with Henry.

Bilney was condemned, and after being degraded by the priests, was handed over to the two sheriffs of Norwich, one of whom, having great respect for his virtues, begged pardon for discharging his duty. The prudent bishop wrote to the chancellor, asking for an order to burn the heretic. 'Burn him first', rudely answered More, 'and then ask me for a bill of indemnity.'

A few of Bilney's friends went to Norwich to bid him farewell: among them was Matthew Parker, later Archbishop of Canterbury. It was in the evening, and Bilney was taking his last meal. On the table stood some frugal fare (ale brew), and on his countenance beamed the joy that filled his soul. 'I am surprised', said one of his friends, 'that you can eat so cheerfully.' – 'I only follow the example of the husbandmen of the country', answered Bilney, 'who having a ruinous house to dwell in, yet bestow cost so long as they may hold it up and so do I now with this ruinous house of my body.' With these words he rose from the table, and sat down near his friends, one of whom said to him: 'Tomorrow the fire will make you feel its devouring fierceness, but the comfort of God's Holy Spirit will cool it for your everlasting refreshing.' Bilney, appearing to reflect upon what had been said, stretched out his hand towards the lamp that was burning on the table and placed his finger in the flame. 'What are you doing?' they exclaimed. – 'Nothing', he replied; 'I am only trying my flesh; tomorrow God's rods shall burn my whole body in the fire.' And still keeping his finger in the flame, as if he were making a curious experiment, he continued: 'I feel that fire by God's ordinance is naturally hot; but yet I am persuaded, by God's holy word and the experience of the martyrs, that when the flames consume me, I shall not feel them. Howsoever this stubble of my body shall be wasted by it, a pain for the time is followed by joy unspeakable.' He then withdrew his finger, the first joint of which was burnt. He added, *When thou walkest through the fire, thou shalt not be burned.'*[1] These words remained imprinted on the hearts of some who heard them, until the day of their death, says a chronicler.

Beyond the city gate – that known as the *Bishop's Gate* – was a low valley, called the *Lollards' Pit:* it was surrounded by rising ground, forming a sort of amphitheatre. On Saturday, 19 August, a body of

[1] Isaiah 43:2. In Bilney's Bible, which is preserved in the library of Corpus Christi College, Cambridge, this passage (verses 1-3) is marked in the margin with a pen. [The book also contains many annotations in Bilney's own hand.]

javelin-men came to fetch Bilney, who met them at the prison gate. One of his friends approaching and exhorting him to be firm, Bilney replied: 'When the sailor goes on board his ship and launches out into the stormy sea, he is tossed to and fro by the waves; but the hope of reaching a peaceful haven makes him bear the danger. My voyage is beginning, but whatever storms I shall feel, my ship will soon reach the port.'

Bilney passed through the streets of Norwich in the midst of a dense crowd: his demeanour was grave, his features calm. His head had been shaved, and he wore a layman's gown. Dr Warner, one of his friends, accompanied him; another distributed liberal alms all along the route. The procession descended into the Lollards' Pit, while the spectators covered the surrounding slopes. On arriving at the place of punishment, Bilney fell on his knees and prayed, and then rising up, warmly embraced the stake and kissed it. Turning his eyes towards heaven, he next repeated the Apostles' Creed, and when he confessed the incarnation and cruci-fixion of the Saviour his emotion was such that even the spectators were moved. Recovering himself, he took off his gown, and ascended the pile, reciting the hundred and forty-third psalm. Thrice he repeated the second verse: *'Enter not into judgment with thy servant, for in thy sight shall no man living be justified.'* And then he added: *'I stretch forth my hands unto thee; my soul thirsteth after thee.'* Turning towards the officers, he said: 'Are you ready?' – 'Yes', was their reply. Bilney placed himself against the post, and held up the chain which bound him to it. His friend Warner, with eyes filled with tears, took a last farewell. Bilney smiled kindly at him and said: 'Doctor, *pasce gregem tuum* [feed your flock], that when the Lord cometh he may find you so doing.' Several monks who had given evidence against him, perceiving the emotion of the spectators, began to tremble, and whispered to the martyr: 'These people will believe that we are the cause of your death, and will withhold their alms.' Upon which Bilney said to them: 'Good folks, be not angry against these men for my sake; as though they be the authors of my death; *it is not they*.' He knew that his death proceeded from the will of God. The torch was applied to the pile: the fire smouldered for a few minutes, and then suddenly burning up fiercely, the martyr was heard to utter the name of Jesus several times, and sometimes the word *'Credo'* ('I believe'). A strong wind which blew the flames on one side prolonged his agony; thrice they seemed to retire from him, and thrice they returned, until at length, the whole pile being kindled, he expired.

A strange revolution took place in men's minds after this death: they praised Bilney, and even his persecutors acknowledged his virtues. The Bishop of Norwich was heard to exclaim, 'I fear I have burnt Abel and let Cain go.' Latimer was inconsolable; twenty years later he still lamented his friend, and one day preaching before Edward VI he called to mind that Bilney was always doing good, even to his enemies, and styled him 'that blessed martyr of God'.

One martyrdom was not sufficient for the enemies of the reformation. Stokesley, Lee, Gardiner, and other prelates and priests, feeling themselves guilty towards Rome, which they had sacrificed to their personal ambition, desired to expiate their faults by sacrificing the reformers. Seeing at their feet a fatal gulf, dug between them and the Roman pontiff by their faithlessness, they desired to fill it up with corpses. The persecution continued.

There was at that time a pious evangelist in the dungeons of the Bishop of London. He was fastened upright to the wall, with chains round his neck, waist, and legs. Usually the most guilty prisoners were permitted to sit down, and even to lie on the floor; but for this man there was no rest. It was Richard Bayfield, accused of bringing from the Continent a number of New Testaments translated by Tyndale.[1] When one of his gaolers told him of Bilney's martyrdom, he exclaimed: 'And I too, and hundreds of men with me, will die for the faith he has confessed.' He was brought shortly afterwards before the episcopal court. 'With what intent', asked Bishop Stokesley, 'did you bring into the country the errors of Luther, Œcolampadius the great heretic, and others of that damnable sect?' – 'To make the gospel known', answered Bayfield, 'and to glorify God before the people.' Accordingly, the bishop, having condemned and then degraded him, summoned the lord mayor and sheriffs of London, 'by the bowels of Jesus Christ' (he had the presumption to say), to do to Bayfield 'according to the *laudable custom*

[1] See Volume I, pp. 258-259, 459-460.

of the famous realm of England'. 'O ye priests', said the gospeller, as if inspired by the Spirit of God, 'is it not enough that your lives are wicked, but you must prevent the life according to the gospel from spreading among the people?' The bishop took up his crosier and struck Bayfield so violently on the chest that he fell backwards and fainted. He revived by degrees, and said, on regaining his consciousness: 'I thank God that I am delivered from the wicked church of Antichrist, and am going to be a member of the true church which reigns triumphant in heaven.' He mounted the pile; the flames, touching him only on one side, consumed his left arm. With his right hand Bayfield separated it from his body, and the arm fell. After enduring the flames for three quarters of an hour, he ceased to pray, because he had ceased to live.

John Tewkesbury,[1] one of the most respected merchants in London, whom the bishops had put twice to the rack already, and whose limbs they had broken, felt his courage revived by the martyrdom of his friend. CHRIST ALONE, he said habitually: these two words were all his theology. He was arrested, taken to the house of Sir Thomas More at Chelsea, shut up in the porter's lodge, his hands, feet, and head being held in the stocks; but they could not obtain from him the recantation they desired. The officers took him into the chancellor's garden, and bound him so tightly to the tree of truth, as the renowned scholar called it, that the blood started out of his eyes; after which they scourged him. Tewkesbury remained firm.

On 16 December the Bishop of London went to Chelsea and held a court at the house of Sir Thomas More. 'Thou art a heretic', said Stokesley, 'a backslider; thou hast incurred the great excommunication. We shall deliver thee up to the secular power.' He was burnt alive at Smithfield on 20 December 1531.

Such were at this period the cruel *utopias* of the bishops and of the witty Sir Thomas More. Other evangelical Christians were thrown into prison. In vain did one of them exclaim: 'The more they persecute this sect, the more will it increase.' That opinion did not check the persecution. 'It is impossible', says Foxe (doubtless with some exaggeration), 'to name all who were persecuted before the time of Queen Anne Boleyn. As well try to count the grains of sand on the seashore!'

[1] See Volume I, pp. 388-389.

Thus did the real reformation show by the blood of its martyrs that it had nothing to do with the policy, the tyranny, the intrigues, and the divorce of Henry VIII. If these men of God had not been burnt by that prince, it might possibly have been imagined that he was the author of the transformation of England; but the blood of the reformers cried to heaven that he was its executioner.

CHAPTER THIRTEEN

The King Despoils the Pope and Clergy

(March to May 1532)

Henry VIII, having permitted the bishops to execute their task of persecution, proceeded to carry out his own, that of making the papacy disgorge. Unhappily for the clergy, the king could not attack the pope and leave them unscathed. The duel between Henry and Clement was about to become more violent, and in the space of three months (March, April, and May, 1532) the Romish Church, stripped of important prerogatives, would learn that, after so many ages of wealth and honour, the hour of its humiliation in England had come at last.

Henry was determined, above all things, not to permit his cause to be tried at Rome. What would be thought if he yielded? 'Could the pope', wrote Henry to his envoys, 'constrain kings to leave the charge God had entrusted to them, in order to humble themselves before him? That would be to tread under foot the glory of our person and the privileges of our kingdom. If the pope persists, take your leave of the pontiff and return to us immediately.' – 'The pope', added Norfolk, 'would do well to reflect if he intend the continuance of good obedience of England to the see apostolic.'

Catherine on her part did not remain inactive: she wrote a pathetic letter to the pope, informing him that her husband had banished her from the palace. Clement, in the depths of his perplexity, behaved, however, very properly: he called upon the king (25 January) to take back the queen, and to dismiss Anne Boleyn from court. Henry spiritedly rejected the pontiff's demand. 'Never was prince treated by a pope as Your Holiness has treated me', he said; 'not painted reason, but the truth alone, must be our guide.' The king prepared to begin the emancipation of England.

Thomas Cromwell is the representative of the political reform achieved by that prince. He was one of those powerful natures which God creates to work important things. His prompt and sure judgment taught him what it would be possible to do under a Tudor king, and his intrepid energy put him in a position to accomplish it. He had an instinctive horror of superstitions and abuses, tracked them to their remotest corner, and threw them down with a vigorous arm. Every obstacle was shattered under the wheels of his car. He even defended the evangelicals against their persecutors, without committing himself, however, and encouraged the reading of Holy Scripture; but the royal supremacy, of which he was the staunch advocate, if not (as some claim) the originator, was his idol.

The events of 1532, involving as they did the royal supremacy, the impact upon the political and ecclesiastical scene of the new secretary Cromwell, the vigorous work of the commons, and the position and authority of convocation in a world of change, were of primary importance for both church and state. In the outcome the constitutional independence of the church in England was terminated.

The struggles of the Parliamentary session of 1532 commenced with a petition of the commons against church courts originally presented in 1529. At that time the matter had been allowed to fall into the background, but under Cromwell's energetic direction it was now revived and focussed on one special issue – the freedom of the church to legislate for itself. This freedom was no longer acceptable to the king. By the secretary's skilful strategy the commons were moved to present to Henry their 'Supplications against the Ordinaries', a document stressing their orthodoxy, reciting their complaints against the church courts, and urging the desirability of taking from the church its powers of independent legislation. This was precisely what Henry desired. He presented the Supplication to convocation and required it to produce its observations. To Gardiner, now Bishop of Winchester, fell the distasteful task of drawing up the reply. Its principal feature was a compromise proposal that while convocation should continue to legislate for the church, the laws it made should not become operative without royal sanction. This proved unacceptable to the king, and Cromwell and he craftily suggested that the commons would doubtless like to adopt the same attitude as the Crown. Their willingness to do so led the king to press his demands, and in a short time an overawed convocation accepted them in their completeness.

Henry's final argument proved more potent than all others. Cromwell drew his master's attention to the oaths which the bishops took at their consecration, both to the king and to the pope. Henry first read the oath to the pope. 'I swear', said the bishop, 'to defend the papacy of Rome, the regality of St Peter, against all men. If I know of any plot against the pope, I will resist it with all my might, and will give him warning. Heretics, schismatics, and rebels to our Holy Father I shall resist and persecute with all my power.' On the other hand, the bishops took an oath to the king at the same time, wherein they renounced every clause or grant which, coming from the pope, might be in any way detrimental to His Majesty. In one breath they must obey the pope and disobey him.

Such contradictions could not last: the king wanted the English to be not with Rome but with England. Accordingly he sent for the Speaker of the Commons, and said to him: 'On examining the matter closely, I find that the bishops, instead of being wholly my subjects, are only so by halves. They swear an oath to the pope quite contrary to that they swear to the Crown; so that they are the pope's subjects rather than mine. I refer the matter to your care.' Parliament was prorogued three days later on account of the plague; but the king did not allow the matter to rest.

The prelates felt that all their defences against the throne had been completely broken down. They knew well that it was their union with powerful pontiffs, always ready to defend them against kings, which had given them so much strength in the Middle Ages, and that now they must yield. They therefore lowered their flag before the authority which they had themselves set up. Convocation did, indeed, make a last effort. It represented that 'the authority of bishops proceeds immediately from God, and from no power of any secular prince, as *your Highness hath shown in your own book most excellently written against Martin Luther.*' But the king was firm, and made the prelates yield at last. As for

Gardiner, he lost the king's favour and any hopes he had of succeeding to the see of Canterbury when the aged Warham died were shattered.

The 15th May was fateful for the church. On that day convocation made its surrender in a document known as the Submission of the Clergy. As in 1531 the clergy had, with reservations, acknowledged Henry as their supreme head, so now they accepted him, without reservations, as their supreme legislator. The days of papal power in England were numbered. Thus a great revolution was accomplished: the spiritual power was taken away from the arrogant priests who had so long usurped the rights of the members of the church. It was only justice: but it ought to have been placed in better hands than those of Henry VIII.

The 16th May witnessed another notable event. To the last the English priests had hoped in Sir Thomas More. That disciple of Erasmus had acted like his master. After assailing the Romish superstitions with biting jests, he had turned round, and seeing the reformation attack them with weapons still more powerful, he had fought against the evangelicals with fire and scourge. For two years he had filled the office of Lord Chancellor with unequalled activity and integrity. Convocation having offered him £4,000 sterling 'for the pains he had taken in God's quarrel', he answered: 'I will receive no recompense save from God alone'; and when the priests urged him to accept the money, he said: 'I would sooner throw it into the Thames.' He did not persecute from any mercenary motives; but the more he advanced, the more bigoted and fanatical he became. Every Sunday he put on a surplice and sang mass at Chelsea. The Duke of Norfolk surprised him one day in this equipment. 'What do I see?' he exclaimed. 'My Lord Chancellor acting the parish clerk … you dishonour your office and your king.' – 'Not so', answered Sir Thomas seriously, 'for I am honouring his Master and ours.'

The great question of the bishop's oath warned him that he could not serve both the king and the pope. His mind was soon made up. In the afternoon of 16 May he went to Whitehall Gardens, where the king awaited him, and in the presence of the Duke of Norfolk resigned the seals. On his return home, he cheerfully told his wife and daughters of his resignation, but they were much disturbed by it. As for Sir Thomas, delighted at being freed from his charge, he indulged more than ever in his flagellations, without renouncing his witty sayings – Erasmus and Loyola combined in one.

Henry gave the seals to Sir Thomas Audley, a man well disposed towards the gospel: this was preparing the emancipation of England. Yet the reformation was still exposed to great danger.

Henry struck another blow against the papacy in 1532. It was being prepared while the struggle between the Crown and the clergy was causing deep and bitter searchings of heart. Annates were the payments made by the bishops to the pope when they entered into possession of their sees. A bill was introduced into Parliament – it became the famous First Act of Annates – which proposed to abolish these payments. Lest the pope should retaliate by refusing consecration to bishops-elect, the bill further proposed arrangements for their consecration at the hands of their fellow bishops, apart from his authority. Actually the bill was intended as a weapon to cause the pope to yield to Henry's wishes, for one of the clauses suspended its operation until the king was pleased to issue confirmatory letters patent. The bill therefore had the nature of a Damocles' sword suspended over the tiara-crowned head of the pope.

Clearly the work of reformation was gathering momentum. Henry VIII wished to abolish popery and set Catholicism in its place – maintain the doctrine of Rome, but substitute the authority of the king for that of the pontiff. He was wrong in keeping the Catholic doctrine; he was wrong in establishing the jurisdiction of the prince in the church. Evangelical Christians had to contend against these two evils in England, and to establish the supreme and exclusive sovereignty of the word of God. Can we blame them if they have not entirely succeeded? To attain their object they willingly have poured out their blood.

CHAPTER FOURTEEN

Liberty of Inquiry and Preaching

(1532)

There are writers who seriously ascribe the reformation in England to the divorce of Henry VIII, and thus silently pass over the word of God and the labours of the evangelical men who really founded English Protestant Christianity, some of whom loved not their lives unto the death. As well forget that light proceeds from the sun. But for the faith of such men as Bilney, Latimer, and Tyndale, the Church of England, with its king, ministers of state, Parliament, bishops, cathedrals, liturgy, hierarchy, and ceremonies, would have been a gallant bark, well supplied with masts, sails, and rigging, and manned by able sailors, but acted on by no breath from heaven. The church would have stood still. It is in the humble members of the kingdom of God that its real strength lies. 'Those whom the Lord has exalted to high estate', says Calvin, 'most often fall back little by little, or are ruined at one blow.' England, with its wealth and grandeur, needed a counterpoise: the living faith of the poor in spirit. If a people attain a high degree of material prosperity; if they conquer by their energy the powers of nature; if they compel industry to lavish its stores on them; if they cover the seas with their ships, the more distant countries with their colonies and marts, and fill their warehouses and their dwellings with the produce of the whole earth, then great dangers encompass them. Material things threaten to extinguish the sacred fire in their bosoms; and unless the Holy Ghost raises up a salutary opposition against such snares, that people, instead of acting a moralizing and civilizing part, may turn out nothing better than a huge noisy machine, fitted only to satisfy vulgar appetites. For a nation to do justice to a high and glorious calling, it must have within itself the life of faith, holiness of conscience, and the hope of incorruptible riches. At this time there were men in England in whose hearts God had kindled a holy flame, and who were to become the most important instruments of its moral transformation.

About the end of 1531, a young minister, John Nicholson, surnamed Lambert, was on board one of the ships that traded between London and Antwerp. He was chaplain to the merchants in the English house at the latter place, well versed in the writings of Luther and other reformers, intimate with Tyndale, and had preached the gospel with power. Being accused of heresy by a certain Barlow, he was seized, put in irons, and sent to London. Alone in the ship, he retraced in his memory the principal events of his life – how he had studied in the University of Cambridge and had been converted by Bilney's ministry; how, mingling with the crowd round St Paul's Cross, he had heard the Bishop of Rochester preach against the New Testament; and how, terrified by the impiety of the priests, and burning with desire to gain the knowledge of God, he had crossed the sea to the Netherlands. When he reached England, he was taken to Lambeth, where he underwent a preliminary examination. He was then taken to Otford, near Sevenoaks, Kent, where Archbishop Warham had a fine palace, and was brought before the archbishop, and called upon to reply to forty-five different articles.

Lambert, during his residence on the Continent, had become thoroughly imbued with the principles of the reformation. He believed that it was only by entire freedom of inquiry that men could be convinced of the truth. But he had not wandered without a compass over the vast ocean of human opinions: he had taken the Bible in his hand, believing firmly that every doctrine found therein is true, and everything that contradicts it is false. On the one hand he saw the papal system which opposes religious freedom, freedom of the press, and even freedom of reading; on the other hand Protestantism, which declares that every man ought to be free to examine Scripture and submit to its teachings.

The archbishop, attended by his officers, having taken his seat in the palace chapel, Lambert was brought in, and the examination began.

'Have you read Luther's books?' asked the prelate.

'Yes', replied Lambert, 'and I thank God that ever I did so, for by them hath God shown me, and a vast multitude of others also, such light as the darkness cannot abide.' Then testifying to the freedom of inquiry, he added: 'Luther desires above all things that his writings and the writings of all his adversaries might be translated into all languages, to the intent that all people might see and know what is said on each side, whereby they might better judge what is the truth. And this is done not only by hundreds and thousands, but by whole cities and countries, both high and low. But [he continued] in England our prelates are so drowned in voluptuous living that they have no leisure to study God's Scripture; they abhor it, no less than they abhor death, giving no other reason than the tyrannical saying of Sardanapalus: *Sic volo, sic jubeo: sit pro ratione voluntas,* So I will, so do I command, and let my will for reason stand. Moreover they curse as black as pitch men who keep and read the books written by Luther.'

Lambert, wishing to make these matters intelligible to the people, said: 'When you desire to buy cloth, you will not be satisfied with seeing one merchant's wares, but go from the first to the second, from the second to the third, to find who has the best cloth. Will you be more remiss about your soul's health? … When you go a journey, not knowing perfectly the way, you will inquire of one man after another; so ought we likewise to seek about entering the kingdom of heaven. Chrysostom himself in his commentary on Matthew, teaches you this. … Read the works not only of Luther, but also of all others, be they ever so ill or good. No good law forbids it, but only constitutions pharisaical.'

Warham, who was as much opposed then to the liberty of the press as the popes are now, could see nothing but a boundless chaos in this freedom of inquiry. 'Images are sufficient', he said, 'to keep Christ and his saints in our remembrance.' But Lambert exclaimed: 'What have we to do with senseless stones or wood carved by the hand of man? That word which came from the breast of Christ himself showeth us perfectly his blessed will.'

Warham having questioned Lambert as to the number of his followers, he answered: 'A great multitude through all regions and realms of Christendom think in like wise as I have showed. I ween [think] the multitude mounteth nigh unto the one half of Christendom.' Lambert was taken back to prison; but More having resigned the seals, and Warham dying, this herald of liberty and truth saw his chains fall off. One day, however, he was to die by fire, and, forgetting all controversy, to exclaim in the midst of the flames: 'None but Jesus Christ.'

There was a minister of the word in London who exasperated the friends of Rome more than all the rest; this man was Latimer. The court of Henry VIII, which was worldly, magnificent, fond of pleasures, intrigue, the elegances of dress, furniture, banquets, and refinement of language and manners, was not a favourable field for the gospel. 'It is very difficult', said a reformer, 'that costly trappings, solemn banquets, the excesses of pride, a flood of pleasure and debauchery should not bring many evils in their train.' Thus the priests and courtiers could not endure Latimer's sermons. If Lambert was for freedom of inquiry, the king's chaplain was for freedom of preaching: his zeal sometimes touched upon imprudence, and his biting wit, and extreme frankness did not spare his superiors. One day, some honest merchants, who hungered and thirsted for the word of God, begged him to come and preach in one of the city churches. Thrice he refused, but yielded to their prayers at last. The death of Bilney and of the other martyrs had wounded him deeply. He knew that wild beasts, when they have once tasted blood, thirst for more, and feared that these murders, these butcheries, would only make his adversaries fiercer. He determined to lash the persecuting prelates with his sarcasms. Having entered the pulpit, he preached from these words in the epistle of the day: *Ye are not under the law, but under grace.* 'What!' he exclaimed, 'St Paul teaches Christians that they are not under the law. ... What does he mean? ... No more law! St Paul invites Christians to break the law. ... Quick! inform against St Paul, seize him and take him before my lord Bishop of London! ... The good apostle must be condemned to bear a faggot at St Paul's Cross. What a goodly sight to see St Paul with a faggot on his back, before my Lord of London, Bishop of the same, sitting under the cross! Nay, verily, I dare say, my lord should sooner have burned him!'

This ironical language was to cost Latimer dear. To no purpose had he spoken in one of those churches which, being dependencies of a monastery, were not under episcopal jurisdiction: everybody about him condemned him and embittered his life. The courtiers talked of his sermons, shrugged their shoulders, pointed their fingers at him when he approached them, and turned their backs on him. The favour of the king, who had perhaps smiled at that burst of pulpit oratory, had some trouble to protect him. The court became more intolerable to him every day, and Latimer, withdrawing to his room, gave vent to many a heavy sigh. 'What tortures I endure!' he said; 'in what a world I live! Hatred ever at work; factions fighting one against the other; folly and vanity leading the dance; dissimulation, irreligion, debauchery, all the vices stalking abroad in open day. ... It is too much. If I were able to do something ... but I have neither the talent nor the industry required to fight against these monsters... I am weary of the court.'

On 14 January 1531, Latimer was presented to the living of West Kington, fourteen miles from Bristol.[1] Wishing to uphold the liberty of the Christian church, and seeing that it existed no longer in London, he resolved to seek it elsewhere. 'I am leaving', he said to one of his friends: 'I shall go and live in my parish.' – 'What is that you say?' exclaimed the other; 'Cromwell, who is at the pinnacle of honours, and has profound designs, intends to do great things for you. ... If you leave the court, you will be forgotten, and your rivals will rise to your place.' – 'The only fortune I desire', said Latimer, 'is to be useful.' He departed, turning his back on the episcopal crosier to which his friend had alluded.

Latimer began to preach with zeal in Wiltshire, and not only in his own parish, but in the parishes around him. His diligence was so great, his preaching so mighty, says Foxe, that his hearers must either believe the doctrine he preached or rise against it. 'Whosoever entereth not into the fold by the door, which is Christ, be he priest, bishop, or pope, is a robber', said he. 'In the church there are more thieves than shepherds, and more goats than sheep.' His hearers were astounded. One of them (Dr William Sherwood) said to him: 'What a sermon, or rather what a satire! If we believe you, all the hemp in England would not be enough to hang those thieves of bishops, priests, and curates. ... It is all exaggeration, no doubt, but such exaggeration is rash, audacious, and impious.' The priests looked about for some valiant champion of Rome, ready to fight with him the quarrel of the church.

---

[1] [The parish of West Kington was in the diocese of Salisbury, whose bishop was none other than Cardinal Campeggio who had presided over the legatine court which dealt with Henry's divorce suit. He had never visited his diocese and Latimer was instituted by his vicar-general, Richard Hiley.]

One day there rode into the village an old doctor of strange aspect; he wore no shirt, but was covered with a long gown that reached down to the horse's heels, 'all bedirted like a slobber', says a chronicler. He took no care for the things of the body, in order that people should believe he was the more given up to the contemplation of the interests of the soul. He dismounted gravely from his horse, proclaimed his intention of fasting, and began a series of long prayers. This person, by name Hubbardin, the Don Quixote of Roman Catholicism, went wandering all over the kingdom, extolling the pope at the expense of kings and even of Jesus Christ, and declaiming against Luther, Zwingli, Tyndale, and Latimer.

On a feast day Hubbardin put on a clerical gown rather cleaner than the one he generally wore, and went into the pulpit, where he undertook to prove that the new doctrine came from the devil – which he demonstrated by stories, fables, dreams, and amusing dialogues. He danced and hopped and leaped about, and gesticulated, as if he were a stage-player, and his sermon a sort of interlude. His hearers were surprised and diverted; Latimer was disgusted. 'You lie', he said, 'when you call the faith of Scripture a new doctrine, unless you mean to say that it makes new creatures of those who receive it.'

Hubbardin being unable to shut the mouth of the eloquent chaplain with his mountebank tricks, the bishops and nobility of the neighbourhood resolved to denounce Latimer. A messenger handed him a writ, summoning him to appear personally before the Bishop of London to answer touching certain excesses and crimes committed by him. Putting down the paper which contained this threatening message, Latimer began to reflect. His position was critical. He was at that time suffering from the stone, with pains in the head and bowels. It was in the dead of winter, and moreover he was alone at West Kington, with no friend to advise him. Being of a generous and daring temperament, he rushed hastily into the heat of the combat, but was easily dejected. 'Jesu mercy! what a world is this', he exclaimed, 'that I shall be put to so great labour and pains above my power for preaching of a poor simple sermon! But we must needs suffer, and so enter into the kingdom of Christ.'

The terrible summons lay on the table. Latimer took it up and read it. He was no longer the brilliant court chaplain who charmed fashionable congregations by his eloquence; he was a poor country minister, forsaken by all. He was sorrowful. 'I am surprised', he said, 'that my Lord of London, who has so large a diocese in which he ought to preach the word in season and out of season, should have leisure enough to come and trouble me in my little parish ... wretched me, who am quite a stranger to him.' He appealed to Richard Hiley, chancellor of the Salisbury diocese; but Bishop Stokesley did not intend to let him go, and being as able as he was violent, he prayed the archbishop, as primate of all England, to summon Latimer before his court, and to commission himself (the Bishop of London) to examine him. The chaplain's friends were terrified, and entreated him to leave England; but he began his journey to London.

On 29 January 1532, a court composed of bishops and doctors of the canon law assembled, under the presidency of Primate Warham, in St Paul's Cathedral. Latimer having appeared, the Bishop of London presented him a paper, and ordered him to sign it. The reformer took the paper and read it through. There were sixteen articles on belief in purgatory, the invocation of saints, the merit of pilgrimages, and lastly on the power of the keys which (said the document) belonged to the bishops of Rome, 'even should their lives be wicked', and other such topics. Latimer returned the paper to Stokesley, saying: 'I cannot sign it.' Three times in one week he had to appear before his judges, and each time the same scene was repeated: both sides were inflexible. The priests then changed their tactics: they began to tease and embarrass Latimer with innumerable questions. As soon as one had finished, another began with sophistry and plausibility, and interminable subterfuges. Latimer tried to make his adversaries keep within the circle from which they were straying, but they would not hear him.

One day, as Latimer entered the hall, he noticed a change in the arrangement of the furniture. There was a chimney, in which there had been a fire before: on this day there was no fire, and the fireplace was invisible. Some tapestry hung down over it, and the table round which the judges sat was in the middle of the room. The accused was seated between the table and the chimney. 'Master Latimer', said an aged bishop, whom he believed to be one of his friends, 'pray speak a little louder: I am hard of hearing, as you know.' Latimer, surprised at this remark, pricked up his ears, and fancied he heard in the fireplace the noise of a pen upon paper; in his own vivid words, 'I heard a pen walking in the chimney, behind the cloth.' 'Ho ho!' thought he, 'they have hidden someone behind there to take down my answers.' He replied cautiously to captious questions, much to the embarrassment of the judges.

Latimer was disgusted, not only with the tricks of his enemies, but still more with their 'troublesome unquietness': because by keeping him in London they obliged him to neglect his duties, and especially because they made it a crime to preach the truth. The archbishop, wishing to gain him over by marks of esteem and affection, invited him to come and see him; but Latimer declined, being unwilling at any price to renounce the freedom of the pulpit. The reformers of the sixteenth century did not contend that all doctrines should be preached from the same pulpit, but that evangelical truth should be freely preached everywhere. 'I have desired and still desire', wrote Latimer to the archbishop, 'that our people should learn the difference between the doctrines which God has taught and those which proceed only from ourselves. Go, said Jesus, and teach all things. ... What things? ... *all things whatsoever I have commanded you, and not whatsoever you think fit to preach*. Let us all then make an effort to preach with one voice the things of God. I have sought not my gain, but Christ's gain; not my glory, but God's glory. And so long as I have a breath of life remaining, I will continue to do so.'

Thus spoke the bold preacher. It is by such unshakable fidelity that great revolutions are accomplished.

As Latimer was deaf to all their persuasion, there was nothing to be done but to threaten the stake. The charge was transferred to the convocation of Canterbury, and on 11 March 1532, he was summoned to appear before that body at Westminster. The fifteen articles were set before him.[1]

[1] [They included the following:
  1. that there is a purgatory to purge the souls of the dead,
  2. that the souls in purgatory are holpen by the masses, prayers, and alms of the living,
  3. that the saints in heaven pray for us as mediators,
  5. that the invocation of saints is profitable,
  6. that pilgrimages and oblations to the relics and sepulchres of saints are meritorious,

'Master Latimer', said the archbishop, 'the synod calls upon you to sign these articles.' – 'I refuse', he answered. All the bishops pressed him earnestly. 'I refuse absolutely', he answered a second time. Warham, the friend of learning, could not make up his mind to condemn one of the finest geniuses of England. 'Have pity on yourself', he said. 'A third and last time we entreat you to sign these articles.' Although Latimer knew that a negative would probably consign him to the stake, he still answered, 'I refuse absolutely.'

The patience of convocation was now exhausted. 'Heretic! obstinate heretic!' exclaimed the bishops. 'We have heard it from his own mouth. Let him be excommunicated.' The sentence of excommunication was pronounced, and Latimer was taken to the Lollards' Tower.

Great was the agitation both in city and court. The creatures of the priests were already singing in the streets songs with a burden like this:

Wherefore it were pity thou shouldst die for cold.

'Ah!' said Latimer in the Tower, 'if they had asked me to confess that I have been too prompt to use sarcasm, I should have been ready to do so, for sin is a heavy load. O God! unto thee I cry; wash me in the blood of Jesus Christ.' He looked for death, knowing well that few left that tower except for the scaffold. 'What is to be done?' said Warham and the bishops. Many of them would have handed the prisoner over to the magistrate to do what was customary, but the rule of the papacy was coming to an end in England, and Latimer was the king's chaplain. One dexterous prelate suggested a means of reconciling everything. 'We must obtain something from him, be it ever so little, and then report everywhere that he has recanted.'

Some priests went to see the prisoner: 'Will you not yield anything?' they asked. – 'I have been too violent', said Latimer, 'and I humble myself accordingly.' – 'But will you not recognize the merit of works?' –

---

9. that fasting, prayer, and other good works merit favour at God's hands,

11. that Lent and other fasts should be observed,

14. that the crucifix and other images of saints should be kept in churches as memorials, and to the honour and worship of Jesus Christ and his saints,

15. that it is laudable to deck those images and to burn candles before them.]

'No!' – 'Prayers to the saints?' – 'No!' – 'Purgatory?' – 'No!' – 'The power of the keys given to the pope?' – 'No! I tell you.' – A bright idea occurred to one of the priests. Luther taught that it was not only permitted, but praiseworthy, to have the crucifix and the images of the saints, provided that it was merely to remind us of them and not to invoke them. He had added that the reformation ought not to abolish fast days, but to strive to make them realities. Latimer declared that he was of the same opinion.

The deputation hastened to carry this news to the bishops. The more fanatical of them could not make up their minds to be satisfied with so little. What! no purgatory, no virtue in the mass, no prayers to saints, no power of the keys, no meritorious works! It was a signal defeat; but the bishops knew that the king would not suffer the condemnation of his chaplain. Doubtless, Cromwell, too, worked hard to achieve a compromise. Convocation decided, after a long discussion, that if Master Latimer would sign the two articles, eleven and fourteen, he should be absolved from the sentence of excommunication. In fact, on 10 April the church withdrew the condemnation it had already pronounced.[1]

[1] [The original documents that bear on these matters are incomplete, and in at least one instance 'tantalizingly mutilated'. According to the records of convocation (lost for this period, but reconstructed from a variety of sources) Latimer, having first assented to the two articles, shortly, of his own accord, assented to the remainder.

Even so, difficulties persisted. On 15 April he was again examined by convocation, and, probably on the strongly-expressed advice of Cromwell, he appealed from convocation to the king. It seems likely that the king received Latimer in audience, and gave him the counsel which proved too strong for his wearied conscience to resist. He must submit himself unreservedly to his fellow clergy. Their doctrine must be his doctrine, their practices his practices. Latimer yielded to the royal mandate. At great cost to his comfort, though it was comfort he sought, he obtained his freedom. 'This', says his biographer, 'is the darkest page in Latimer's history.' It must have been with a vastly-troubled breast that the would-be reformer hastened back to his remote rural parish.]

CHAPTER FIFTEEN

Henry VIII Attacks Romanists and Protestants

(1532)

The vital principle of the reformation of Henry VIII was its opposition both to Rome and the gospel. He did not hesitate, like many, between these two doctrines: he punished alike, by exile or by fire, the disciples of the Vatican and those of Holy Scripture.

Desiring to show that the resolution he had taken to separate from Catherine was immutable, the king had lodged Anne Boleyn in the palace at Greenwich, even when the queen was still there, and had given her a reception room and a royal state. The crowd of courtiers, abandoning the setting star, turned towards that which was appearing above the horizon. Henry respected Anne's person, and was eager that all the world should know that if she was not actually queen, she would be so one day. There was a want of delicacy and principle in the king's conduct, at which the Catholic party were much irritated, and not without a cause.

The monks of St Francis who officiated in the royal chapel at Greenwich took every opportunity of asserting their attachment to Catherine and to the pope. Anne vainly tried to gain them over by her charms; if she succeeded with a few, she failed with the greater number. Their superior, Father Forest, Catherine's confessor, warmly defended the rights of that unhappy princess. Preaching at St Paul's Cross, he delivered a sermon in which Henry was violently attacked, although he was not named. Those who had heard it made a great noise about it, and Forest was summoned to the court. 'What will be done to him?' people asked; but instead of sending him to prison, as many expected, the king received him well, spoke with him for half an hour, and 'sent him a great piece of beef from his own table.'

On returning to his convent, Forest described with triumph this flattering reception; but the king did not attain his object. Among these monks there were men of independent, perhaps of fanatical character, whom no favours could gain over.

One of them, by name Peto, until then unknown, but afterwards of great repute in the Catholic world as cardinal-legate from the pope in England, thinking that Forest had not said enough, determined to go further. Anne Boleyn's elevation filled him with anger: he longed to speak out, and as the king and all the court would be present in the chapel on 1 May, he chose for his text the words of the prophet Elijah to King Ahab: *The dogs shall lick thy blood.* He drew a portrait of Ahab, described his malice and wickedness, and although he did not name Henry VIII, certain passages made the hearers feel uncomfortable. At the peroration, turning towards the king, he said: 'Now hear, O King, what I have to say unto thee, as of old time Micaiah spoke to Ahab. This new marriage is unlawful. There are other preachers who, to become rich abbots or mighty bishops, betray thy soul, thy honour, and thy posterity. Take heed lest thou, being seduced like Ahab, find Ahab's punishment … who had his blood licked up by the dogs.'

The court was astounded; but the king, whose features were unmoved during this apostrophe, waited until the end of the service, left the chapel as if nothing had happened, and allowed Peto to depart for Canterbury. But Henry could not permit such invectives to pass unnoticed. A clergyman named Kirwan was commissioned to preach in the same chapel on the following Sunday. The congregation was still more numerous than before, and more curious also. Some monks of the order of Observants, friends of Peto, got into the rood-loft, determined to defend him. The doctor began his sermon. After establishing the lawfulness of Henry's intended marriage, he came to the sermon of the preceding Sunday and the insults of the preacher. 'I speak to thee, Peto', he exclaimed, 'who makest thyself Micaiah; we look for thee, but thou art not to be found, having fled for fear and shame.' There was a noise in the rood-loft, and one of the Observants named Elstow rose and called out: 'You know that Father Peto is gone to Canterbury to a provincial council, but I am here to answer you. And to this combat I challenge thee, Kirwan, prophet of lies, who for thine own vain-glory art betraying thy king into endless perdition.'

The chapel was instantly one scene of confusion: nothing could be heard. Then the king rose: his princely stature, his royal air, his majestic manners overawed the crowd. All were silent, and the agitated congregation left the chapel respectfully. Peto and his friend were summoned before the council. 'You deserve to be sewn in a sack and thrown into the Thames', said one. 'We fear nothing', answered Elstow; 'the way to heaven is as short by water as by land.'

Henry, having thus made war on the partisans of the pope, turned to those of the reformation. Like a child, he see-sawed to and fro, first on one side, then on the other; but his sport was a more terrible one, for every time he touched the ground the blood spurted forth.

At that time there were many Christians in England to whom the Roman worship brought no edification. Having procured Tyndale's translation of the word of God, they felt that they possessed it not only for themselves but for others. They sought one another's company, and met together to read the Bible and receive spiritual graces from God. Several Christian assemblies of this kind had been formed in London, in garrets, in warehouses, schools, and shops, and one of them was held in a warehouse in Bow Lane. Among its frequenters was the son of a Gloucestershire knight, James Bainham by name, a man well read in the classics, and a distinguished lawyer, respected by all for his piety and works of charity. To give advice freely to widows and orphans, to see justice done to the oppressed, to aid poor students, protect pious persons, and visit the prisons were his daily occupations. 'He was an earnest reader of Scripture, and mightily addicted to prayer.' His marriage brought him under suspicion, for his wife was the widow of Simon Fish whose book previously mentioned had aroused a great storm of Catholic opposition. He was asked where his books were to be found but would not divulge. When his wife denied that they were in his house she was sent to the Fleet prison, and their goods were confiscated. When he entered the meeting, everyone could see that his countenance expressed a calm joy; but for a month past his Bow Lane friends noticed him to be agitated and cast down, and heard him sighing heavily. The cause was this. Some time before (in 1531), when he was engaged about his business in the Middle Temple, this 'model of lawyers' had been arrested by order of More, who was still chancellor, and taken like a criminal to the house of the celebrated humanist at Chelsea. Sir Thomas, quite distressed at seeing a man so distinguished leave the Church of Rome, had employed all his eloquence to bring him back; but finding his efforts useless, he had ordered Bainham to be taken into his garden and tied to 'the tree of truth'. There the chancellor whipped him, or caused him to be whipped: we adopt the latter version, which is more probable. Bainham having refused to give the names of the gentlemen of the Temple tainted with heresy, he was taken to the Tower. 'Put him on the rack', cried the learned chancellor, now become a fanatical persecutor. The order was obeyed in his presence. The arms and legs of the unfortunate Protestant were fastened to the instrument and pulled in opposite directions: his limbs were dislocated, and he went lame out of the torture chamber.[1]

Sir Thomas had broken his victim's limbs, but not his courage; and accordingly when Bainham was summoned before the Bishop of London, he went to the palace rejoicing to have to confess his Master once more. 'Do you believe in purgatory?' said Stokesley to him sternly. Bainham answered: *'The blood of Jesus Christ cleanseth us from all sin.'* 'Do you believe that we ought to call upon the saints to pray for us?' He again answered: *'If any man sin, we have an advocate with the Father – Jesus Christ the righteous.'*

A man who answered only by texts from Scripture was embarrassing. More and Stokesley made the most alluring promises, and no means were spared to bend him. Before long they resorted to more serious representation: 'The arms of the church your mother are still open to you', they said; 'but if you continue stubborn, they will close against you for ever. It is now or never!' For a whole month the bishop and the chancellor persevered in their entreaties; Bainham replied: 'My faith is that of the holy church.' Hearing these words, Foxford, the bishop's secretary, took out a paper. 'Here is the abjuration', he said; 'read it over.' Bainham began: 'I voluntarily, as a true penitent returned from my heresy, utterly abjure ...' At these words he stopped, and glancing over what followed, he continued: 'No, these articles are not heretical,

[1] Foxe, *Acts*, iv, p. 698.

and I cannot retract them.' Other springs were now set in motion to
shake Bainham. The prayers of his friends, the threats of his enemies,
especially the thought of his wife, whom he loved, and who would be
left alone in destitution, exposed to the anger of the world: these things
troubled his soul. He lost sight of the narrow path he ought to follow,
and five days later he read his abjuration with a faint voice. But he had
hardly got to the end before he burst into tears, and said, struggling with
his emotion: 'I reserve the doctrines.' He consented to remain in the
Roman Church, still preserving his evangelical faith. But this was not
what the bishop and his officers meant. 'Kiss that book', they said to him
threateningly. Bainham, like one stunned, kissed the book; that was the
sign; the abjuration was looked upon as completed. He was condemned
to pay a fine of twenty pounds sterling, and to do penance at St Paul's
Cross. After that he was set at liberty, on 17 February.

Bainham returned to the midst of his brethren: they looked sorrowfully at him, but did not reproach him with his fault. That was quite
unnecessary. The worm of remorse was preying on him; he abhorred the
fatal kiss by which he had sealed his fall; his conscience was never quiet;
he could neither eat nor sleep, and trembled at the thought of death.
At one time he would hide his anguish and stifle it within his breast; at
another his grief would break forth, and he would try to relieve his pain
by groans of sorrow. The thought of appearing before the tribunal of
God made him faint. The restoration of conscience to all its rights was
the foremost work of the reformation. Luther, Calvin, and an endless
number of lesser reformers had reached the haven of safety through
the midst of such tempests. 'A tragedy was being acted in all Protestant
souls', says a writer who does not belong to the reformation – the eternal
tragedy of conscience.

Bainham felt that the only means of recovering peace was to accuse
himself openly before God and man. Taking Tyndale's New Testament
in his hand, which was at once his joy and his strength, he went to St
Austin's church, sat down quietly in the midst of the congregation, and
then at a certain moment stood up and said: 'I have denied the truth.'
He could not continue for his tears. On recovering, he said: 'If I were
not to return again to the doctrine I have abjured, this word of Scripture

would condemn me both body and soul at the day of judgment.' And he lifted up the New Testament before all the congregation. 'O my friends', he continued, 'rather die than sin as I have done. The fires of hell have consumed me, and I would not feel them again for all the gold and glory of the world.' He wrote in a similar strain to the bishop.

Then his enemies seized him again and shut him up in the bishop's coal house, where, after putting him in the stocks, with his legs in irons, they left him for almost fourteen days. He was afterwards taken to the Tower, where he was scourged every day for a fortnight, and at last condemned as a relapsed heretic.

On the eve of the execution four distinguished men, one of whom was Latimer, were dining together in London. It was commonly reported that Bainham was to be put to death for saying that Thomas Becket was a traitor. 'Is it worth a man's while to sacrifice his life for such a trifle?' said the four friends. 'Let us go to Newgate and save him if possible.' They were taken along several gloomy passages, and found themselves at last in the presence of a man sitting on a little straw, holding a book in one hand and a candle in the other. He was reading; it was Bainham. Latimer drew near him: 'Take care', he said, 'that no vain-glory make you sacrifice your life for motives which are not worth the cost.' 'I am condemned', answered Bainham, 'for trusting in Scripture and rejecting purgatory, masses, and meritorious works.' – 'I acknowledge that for such truths a man must be ready to die.' Bainham was ready; and yet he burst into tears. 'Why do you weep?' asked Latimer. 'I have a wife', answered the prisoner, 'the best that man ever had. A widow, destitute of everything and without a supporter, everybody will point at her and say, That is the heretic's wife.' Latimer and his friends tried to console him, and then they departed from the gloomy dungeon.

The next day (30 April 1532) Bainham was taken to the scaffold. Soldiers on horseback surrounded the pile: Master Pave, the city clerk, directed the execution. Bainham, after a prayer, rose up, embraced the stake, and was fastened to it with a chain. 'Good people', he said to the persons who stood round him, 'I die for having said it is lawful for every man and woman to have God's book. I die for having said that the true key of heaven is not that of the Bishop of Rome, but the preaching of the gospel. I die for having said that there is no other purgatory than the cross of Christ, with its consequent persecutions and afflictions.' – 'Thou liest, thou heretic', exclaimed Pave; 'thou hast denied the blessed sacrament of the altar.' – 'I do not deny the sacrament of Christ's body', resumed Bainham, 'but I do deny your transubstantiation and your idolatry to a piece of bread.' – 'Light the fire', shouted Pave. The executioners set fire to a train of gunpowder, and as the flame approached him, Bainham lifted up his eyes towards heaven, and said to the city clerk: 'God forgive thee! and shew thee more mercy than thou showst to me! the Lord forgive Sir Thomas More ... pray for me, all good people!' The arms and legs of the martyr were soon consumed, and thinking only how to glorify his Saviour, he exclaimed: 'Behold! you look for miracles, you may see one here; for in this fire I feel no more pain than if I were on a bed of down, but it is to me as sweet as a bed of roses.' The primitive church hardly had a more glorious martyr.

Pave had Bainham's image continually before his eyes, and his last prayer rang day and night in his heart. In the garret of his house, far removed from noise, he had fitted up a kind of oratory, where he had placed a crucifix, before which he used to pray and shed bitter tears. He abhorred himself: half mad, he suffered indescribable sorrow, and struggled under great anguish. The dying Bainham had said to him: 'May God show thee more mercy than thou hast shown to me!' But Pave could not believe in mercy: he saw no other remedy for his despair than death. About a year after Bainham's martyrdom, he sent his domestics and clerks on different errands, keeping only one maidservant in the house. As soon as his wife had gone to church, he went out himself, bought a rope, and hiding it carefully under his gown, went up into the garret. He stopped before the crucifix, and began to groan and weep. The servant ran upstairs. 'Take this rusty sword', he said, 'clean it well, and do not disturb me.' She had scarcely left the room when he fastened the rope to a beam and hanged himself.

The maid, hearing no sound, again grew alarmed, went up to the garret, and seeing her master hanging, was struck with terror. She ran crying to the church to fetch her mistress home; but it was too late: the wretched man could not be recalled to life.

If the deaths of the martyrs plunged the wicked into the depths of despair, it often gave life to earnest souls. The crowd which had surrounded the scaffold of these men of God dispersed in profound emotion. Some returned to their fields, others to their shops or workrooms; but the pale faces of the martyrs followed them, their words sounded in their souls, their virtues softened many hearts most averse to the gospel. 'Oh! that I were with Bainham!' exclaimed one. These people continued for some time to frequent the Romish churches, but ere long their consciences cried aloud to them: 'It is Christ alone who saves us'; and they forsook the rites in which they could find no consolation. They courted solitude; they procured the writings of Wycliffe and of Tyndale, and especially the New Testament, which they read in secret, and if anyone came near, hid them hastily under a bed, at the bottom of a chest, in the hollow of a tree, or even under stones, until the enemy had retired and they could take the books up again. Then they whispered about them to their neighbours, and often had the joy of meeting with men who thought as they did. A surprising change was taking place. While the priests were loudly chanting in the cathedrals the praises of the saints, of the Virgin, and of the *Corpus Domini,* the people were whispering together about the Saviour *meek and lowly in heart.* All over England was heard a still, small voice such as Elijah heard, and on hearing it wrapped his face in his mantle and stood silent and motionless, because the Lord was there. Great changes were about to take place.

It is not without a reason that we describe in some detail in this history the lives and deaths of these evangelical men. We desire to show that the church in England, as in all the world, is not a mere ecclesiastical hierarchy, in which prelates exercise dominion over the inheritance of the Lord; nor a confused assemblage of men, whose spirit imagines about religion all kinds of doctrines contrary to the revelation from heaven, and whose profession of faith comprehends all the opinions that are found in the nation from Catholic scholasticism to pantheistic materialism. The church of God, raised above the human systems of the superstitious and the incredulous alike, is the assembly of those who by a living faith are partakers of the righteousness of Christ, and of the new life of which the Holy Ghost is the creator – of those in whom selfishness is vanquished, and who give themselves up to the Saviour to achieve with their brethren the conquest of the world. Such is the true church of God; very different, it will be seen, from all those invented by man.

CHAPTER SIXTEEN

The New Primate of All England

(February 1532 to March 1533)

Aman who for more than thirty years had had an important voice in the management of the ecclesiastical affairs of the kingdom now disappeared from the scene to give place to the most influential of the reformers of England. Warham, Archbishop of Canterbury, a learned canonist, a skilful politician, a dexterous courtier, and the friend of letters, had made it his special work to exalt the sacerdotal prerogative, and to that end had had recourse to the surest means, by fighting against the idleness, ignorance, and corruption of the priests. He had even hoped for a reform of the clergy, provided it emanated from episcopal authority. But when he saw another reformation accomplished in the name of God's word, without priests and against the priests, he turned round and began to persecute the reformers and to strengthen the papal authority. Alarmed at the proceedings of the commons, he sent for three notaries, on 24 February 1532, and protested in their presence against every act of Parliament derogatory to the authority of the Roman pontiff.

On 22 August of the same year, just at the very height of the crisis, 'the second pope', as he was sometimes called, was removed from his see by death, and the people anxiously wondered who would be appointed to his vacant place.

The choice was important, for the nomination might be the symbol of what the Church of England was to be. Would he be a prelate devoted to the pope, like Fisher; or a Catholic favourable to the divorce, like Gardiner; or a moderate evangelical attached to the king, like Cranmer; or a decided reformer, like Latimer? At this moment, when a new era was beginning for Christendom, it was of consequence to know whom England would take for her guide; whether she would march at the head of civil and religious progress, like Germany; or bring up the rear, like Spain and Italy. The king did not favour either extreme, and hesitated between the two other candidates. All things considered, he had no confidence in such bishops as Longland of Lincoln, and Gardiner of Winchester, who might promise and not fulfil. He wanted somebody less political than the one, and less fanatical than the other – a man separated from the pope on principle, and not merely for convenience.

Cranmer, after passing a few months at Rome, had returned to England. Then departing again for Germany on a mission from the king, he had arrived at Nuremberg, probably in the autumn of 1531. He examined with interest that ancient city, its beautiful churches, its monumental fountains, its old and picturesque castle; but there was something that attracted him more than all these things. Being present at the celebration of the sacrament, he noticed that while the priest was muttering the gospel in Latin at the altar, the deacon went up into the pulpit and read it aloud in German. He saw that, although there was still some appearance of Catholicism in Nuremberg, in reality the gospel reigned there. One man's name often came up in the conversations he had with the principal persons in the city. They spoke to him of Andreas Osiander as of a man of great eloquence. Cranmer followed the crowd which poured into the church of St Lawrence, and was struck with the minister's talents and piety. He sought his acquaintance, and the two doctors had many a conversation together, either in Cranmer's house or in Osiander's study; and the German divine, being gained over to the cause of Henry VIII, published shortly after a book on unlawful marriages.

Cranmer, who had an affectionate heart, loved to join the simple meals, the pious devotions, and the friendly conversations at Osiander's house; he was soon almost like a member of the family. But although his intimacy with the Nuremberg pastor grew stronger every day, he did not adopt all his opinions. When Osiander told him that he must substitute the authority of Holy Scripture for that of Rome, Cranmer gave his full assent; but the Englishman perceived that the German entertained views different from Luther's on the justification of the sinner. 'What justifies us', said Osiander, 'is not the imputation of the merits of Christ by faith, but the inward communication of his righteousness.' 'On the contrary', said Cranmer, 'Christ has paid the price of our redemption by the sacrifice of his body and the fulfilling of the law; and if we heartily believe in this work which he has perfected, we are justified. The justified man must be sanctified, and must work good works; but it is not the works that justify him.' The conversation of the two friends turned also upon the Lord's Supper. Whatever may have been Cranmer's doctrine before, he soon came (like Calvin) to place the real presence of Christ not in the wafer which the priest holds between his fingers, but in the heart of the believer.[1]

In June 1532 Protestant and Roman Catholic delegates arrived at Nuremberg to arrange the religious peace. The celibacy of the clergy immediately became one of the points discussed. It appeared to the chiefs of the papacy impossible to concede that article. 'Rather abolish the mass entirely', exclaimed the Archbishop of Mayence, 'than permit the marriage of priests.' 'They must come to that at last', said Luther; 'God is overthrowing the mighty from their seat.' Cranmer was of his opinion: 'It is better', he said, 'for a minister to have his own wife, than to have other men's wives, like the priests.' 'What services may not a pious wife do for the pastor her husband', added Osiander, 'among the poor, the women, and the children?'

Cranmer had lost his wife at Cambridge, and his heart yearned for affection. Osiander's family presented him a touching picture of domestic happiness. One of its members was a certain Margaret, a niece of Osiander's wife. Cranmer, charmed with her piety and candour, and hoping to find in her the virtuous woman who is a crown to her husband, asked her hand and married her, not heeding the unlawful command of those who 'forbid to marry.'

[1] ['Although Christ be not corporally in the bread and wine, yet Christ used not so many words in the mystery of his holy Supper, without effectual signification: for he is effectually present, and effectually worketh not in the bread and wine, but in the godly receivers of them, to whom he giveth his own flesh spiritually to feed upon, and his own blood to quench their great inward thirst.' Cranmer, *On the Lord's Supper* (Parker Society), pp. 34-5.]

Still Cranmer did not forget his mission. The King of England was desirous of forming an alliance with the German Protestants, and his agent made overtures to the electoral prince of Saxony. 'First of all', answered the pious John Frederick, 'the king must be in harmony with us as to the articles of faith.' The alliance failed, but, at the same moment, affairs took an unexpected turn. The emperor Charles V who was marching against Solyman the Magnificent, the greatest of all the Ottoman sultans, desired the help of the King of England, and Granvella, his minister, had some talk with Cranmer on the subject. The latter was procuring carriages, horses, boats, tents, and other things necessary for his journey, with the intention of rejoining the emperor at Linz, when a courier suddenly brought him orders to return to London. It was very vexatious. Just as he was on the point of concluding an alliance with the nephew of Queen Catherine, in which the matter of the divorce would consequently be arranged, Henry's envoy had to give up everything. He wondered anxiously what could be the motive of this sudden and extraordinary recall: the letters of his friends explained it.

Warham was dead, and the king thought of Cranmer to succeed him as Archbishop of Canterbury and primate of all England. The reformer was greatly moved. 'Alas!' he exclaimed, 'no man has ever desired a bishopric less than myself. If I accept it, I must resign the delights of study and the calm sweetness of an obscure condition.' Knowing Henry's domineering character and his peculiar religious principles, Cranmer thought that with him the reformation of England was impossible. He saw himself exposed to disputes without end: there would be no more peace for the most peaceable of men. A brilliant career, an exalted position – he was terrified. 'My conscience', he said, 'rebels against this call. Wretch that I am! I see nothing but troubles, and conflicts, and insurmountable dangers in my path.'

Upon mature reflection, Cranmer thought he might get out of his difficulty by gaining time, hoping that the king, who did not like delays, would doubtless give the see to another. He sent an answer that important affairs prevented his return to England. Solyman had retreated before the emperor; the latter had determined to pass through

Italy to Spain, and had appointed a meeting with the pope at Piacenza or Genoa. Henry's ambassador thought it his duty to neutralize the fatal consequences of this interview; and Charles having left Vienna on 4 October, Cranmer followed him two days later. The exalted dignity that awaited him oppressed him like a nightmare. On his road he found neither inhabitants nor food, and hay was his only bed. Sometimes he crossed battle fields covered with the carcasses of Turks and Christians. A comet appeared in the east foreboding some tragic event. Many declared they had seen a flaming sword in the heavens. 'These strange signs', he wrote to Henry, 'announce some great mutation.' Cranmer and his colleagues could not gain the pope to their side. Several months passed away, during which men's minds became so excited, that the cardinals forgot all decorum. 'Alas!' says a Catholic historian, 'all the time this affair continued, they went to the consistory as if they were going to a play.' Charles V prevailed at last.

A report having circulated in Italy that the king was about to place Cranmer at the head of the English Church, the imperial court treated him with unusual consideration. Charles V, his ministers, and the foreign ambassadors said openly that such a man richly deserved to hold a high place in the favour and government of the king his master. In November, the emperor gave Cranmer his farewell audience; and the latter returned to England not long after. But he did so reluctantly enough, knowing what awaited him and prolonging to seven weeks a journey which could easily have been accomplished in three. Not wishing to act in opposition to general usage and clerical opinion, he thought it more prudent to leave his wife for a time with Osiander. He sent for her somewhat later, but she was never presented at court. It was not necessary, and it might only have embarrassed the pious German lady.

As soon as Cranmer reached London, he waited upon the king, being quite engrossed in thinking of what was about to take place between his sovereign and himself. Henry went straight to the point: he told him that he had nominated him Archbishop of Canterbury. Cranmer objected, but the king would take no refusal. In vain did the divine urge his reasons: the monarch was firm. It was no slight matter to contend with Henry VIII. Cranmer was alarmed at the effect produced by his resistance. 'Your Highness', he said, 'I most humbly implore your Grace's pardon.'

When he left the king, he hurried off to his friends, particularly to Cromwell. The burden which Henry was laying upon him seemed more insupportable than ever. Knowing how difficult it is to resist a prince of despotic character, he foresaw conflicts and perhaps compromises, which would embitter his life, and he could not make up his mind to sacrifice his happiness to the imperious will of the monarch. 'Take care', said his friends, 'it is as dangerous to refuse a favour from so absolute a prince as to insult him.' But Cranmer's conscience was concerned in his refusal. 'I feel something within me', he said, 'which rebels against the supremacy of the pope, and all the superstitions to which I should have to submit as primate of England. No, I will not be a bishop!' He might sacrifice his repose and his happiness, expose himself to painful struggles; but to recognize the pope and submit to his jurisdiction was an insurmountable obstacle. His friends shook their heads. 'Your *nolo episcopari*', they said, 'will not hold against our master's *volo te episcopum esse.*[1] And after all what is it? Permitting the king to place you at the summit of honours and power. ... You refuse all that men desire.' 'I would sooner forfeit my life', answered Cranmer, 'than do anything against my conscience to gratify my ambition.'

Henry, vexed at all these delays, again summoned Cranmer to the palace, and bade him speak without fear. 'If I accept this office', replied that sincere man, 'I must receive it from the hands of the pope, and this my conscience will not permit me to do. ... Neither the pope nor any other foreign prince has authority in this realm.' Such a reason as this had great weight with Henry. He was silent for a little while, as if reflecting, and then said to Cranmer: 'Can you prove what you have just said?' 'Certainly I can', answered the doctor; 'Holy Scripture and the Fathers support the supreme authority of kings in their kingdoms, and thus prove the claims of the pope to be a miserable usurpation.'

Such a statement bound Henry to take another step in his reforms. As he had not yet thought of establishing bishops and archbishops without

---

[1] 'I am unwilling to be made a bishop.' 'I desire you to be a bishop.' (Fuller, *Church History*, v, p. 184.)

the pope, he sent for some learned lawyers, and asked them how he could confer the episcopal dignity on Cranmer without wounding the conscience of the future primate. The lawyers proposed, that as Cranmer refused to submit to the Roman primacy, someone should be sent to Rome to do in his stead all that the law required. 'Let another do it, if he likes', said Cranmer, 'but *super animam suam,* at the risk of his soul. As for me, I declare I will not acknowledge the authority of the pope any further than it agrees with the word of God; and that I reserve the right of speaking against him and of attacking his errors.'

The lawyers found bad precedents to justify a bad measure. 'Archbishop Warham', they said, 'while preserving the advantages he derived from the state, protested against everything the state did prejudicial to Rome. If the deceased archbishop preserved the rights of the papacy, why should not the new one preserve those of the kingdom? … Besides [they added] the pope knows very well that when they make oath to him, every bishop does so *salvo ordine mea,* without prejudice to the rights of his order.'

It having been conceded that in the act of consecration 'the rights of the word of God' should be reserved, Cranmer consented to become primate of England. Henry VIII, who was less advanced in practice than in theory, all the same demanded of Clement VII the bulls necessary for the inauguration of the new archbishop. The pontiff, only too happy still to have something to say to England, hastened to despatch them, addressing them directly to Cranmer himself. But the latter, who would accept nothing from the pope, sent them to the king, declaring that he would not receive his appointment from Rome.

By accepting the call that was addressed to him, Cranmer meant to break with the order of the Middle Ages, and re-establish, so far as was in his power, that of the gospel. But he would not conceal his intentions: all must be done in the light of day. On 30 March 1533, he summoned to the chapter house of Westminster Watkins, the king's prothonotary,[1] with other dignitaries of the church and state. On entering, he took up a paper, and read aloud and distinctly: 'I, Thomas, Archbishop of Canterbury, protest openly, publicly, and expressly, that I will not bind

[1] [A chief clerk in certain courts of law.]

myself by oath to anything contrary to the law of God, the rights of the King of England, and the laws of the realm; and that I will not be bound in aught that concerns liberty of speech, the government of the Church of England, and the reformation of all things that may seem to be necessary to be reformed therein. If my representative with the pope has taken in my name an oath contrary to my duty, I declare that he has done so without my knowledge, and that the said oath shall be null. I desire this protest to be repeated at each period of the present ceremony.' Then turning to the prothonotary: 'I beg you to prepare as many copies as may be necessary of this my protest.'

Cranmer left the chapter house and entered the abbey, where the clergy and a numerous crowd awaited him. He was not satisfied with once declaring his independence of the papacy; he desired to do it several times. The greater the antiquity of the Romish power in Britain, the more he felt the necessity of proclaiming the supremacy of the divine word. Having put on his sacerdotal robes, Cranmer stood at the top of the steps of the high altar, and said, turning towards the assembly: 'I declare that I take the oath required of me only under the reserve contained in the protest I have made this day in the chapter house.' Then bending his knees before the altar, he read it a second time in presence of the bishops, priests, and people; after which the bishops of Lincoln, Exeter, and St Asaph consecrated him to the episcopate.

The archbishop, standing before the altar, prepared to receive the pallium, but first he had a duty to fulfil: if he sacrificed his repose, he did not intend to sacrifice his convictions. For the third time he took up the protest, and again read it before the immense crowd that filled the cathedral. The accustomed order of the ceremony having been twice interrupted by an extraordinary declaration, all were at liberty to praise or blame the action of the prelate as they pleased. Cranmer, having thus thrice published his reserves, read at last the oath which the archbishops of Canterbury were accustomed to make to St Peter and to the holy apostolic Church of Rome, with the usual protest: *salvo meo ordine* (without prejudice to my order).

Cranmer's triple protest was an act of Christian decision. Some time afterwards he said: 'I made that protest in good faith: I always loved simplicity and hated falseness.' But it was wrong of him to use after it the formula ordinarily employed in consecrations. Doubtless it was nothing more than a form; a form that was imposed by the king, and Cranmer protested against all the bad it might contain: still 'it is necessary to walk consistently in all things', as Calvin says; and we here meet with one of those weaknesses which sometimes appear in the life of the pious reformer of England. He ought at no price to have made oath to the pope; that oath was a stain which in some measure tinged the whole of his episcopate. Yet if we were to condemn him severely, we should be forgetting that striking truth – *in many things we offend all.* Cranmer was the first in the breach, and he has claims to the consideration of those who are comfortably established in a position gained by him with so much suffering. The energy with which he thrice proclaimed his independence deserves our admiration. Nevertheless all weakness is a fault, and when that fault is committed in high station it may lead to fatal consequences. The sanctity of the oath taken by churchmen was compromised by Cranmer's act, and we have seen in later times other divines secretly communing with Romish doctrines while appearing to reject popery. There have sometimes been disguised papists in the Protestant Church of England.

After the ceremony the new archbishop returned to his palace at Lambeth. From that hour this patron of letters, a scholar himself, a truly pious man, a distinguished preacher, and of indefatigable industry, never ceased to labour for the good of the church. He was able to introduce Christian faith into many hearts, and sometimes to defend it against the king's ill-humour. He constantly endeavoured to spread around him moderation, charity, truth, piety, and peace. When Cranmer became primate of all England, on 30 March 1533, in St Stephen's, Westminster, the papal order was interred, and it might be foreseen that the apostolic order would be revived. England preserved episcopacy but she rejected that Roman superstition which makes bishops the sole successors of the apostles and maintains (as at the Council of Trent) that they are invested with an indelible character and a spiritual power which no other minister possesses. 'Most assuredly', said Cranmer, 'at the beginning of the religion of Christ, bishops and presbyters [priests] were not two things, but one only.' He declared that a bishop was not necessary to make a pastor; that not only presbyters possessed this right, but *'the people also by their election.'* 'Before there were Christian princes, it was the people', he said, 'who generally elected the bishops and priests.' Cranmer was not the only man who professed these principles, which make of the episcopalian and the presbyterian constitution two varieties, having many things in common. The most venerable fathers of the Anglican Church – Pilkington, Coverdale, Whitgift, Fulke, Tyndale, Jewel, Bradford, Becon, and others – have acknowledged the identity of bishops and presbyters. By the reformation, England belongs not to the papistical system of episcopacy, but to the evangelical system. A public act which would bring back that church to her holy origin, would be a source of great prosperity to her.

The great reformers of England did not separate from Rome only, but also from the semi-Catholicism that was intended to be substituted for it. To them the spirit and the life were in the ministry of the word of God, and not in rites and ceremonies. By their noble example they have called all men of God to follow them.

Catherine of Aragon Descends from the Throne and Anne Boleyn Ascends It

(November 1532 to July 1533)

C ranmer was on the archiepiscopal throne: if Anne Boleyn were now to take her seat on the royal throne by the side of Henry, it was the pope's opinion that everything would be lost. Clement recurred once more to his favourite suggestion of bigamy, already advised by him in 1528 and 1530. True, this suggestion could not be acceptable either to Henry or to Charles V, but that made it all the better in the eyes of the pontiff: he would then have the appearance of assenting to the king's plans without running the least risk of seeing them realized. 'Rather than do what His Majesty asks', he said to one of the English envoys, 'I would prefer granting him the necessary dispensation to have two wives: that would be a smaller scandal.'

The tenacity with which the pope advised Henry again and again to commit the crime of bigamy has not prevented the most illustrious advocates of Catholicism from exclaiming that 'to have two wives at once is a mystery of iniquity, of which there is no example in Christendom'. A singular assertion after a cardinal and then a pope had on several occasions advised what they call 'a mystery of iniquity'. Again, for the third time, the king refused a remedy that was worse than the disease.

The pope wished at any price to prevent Rome from losing England; and turning to the other side, he resolved to try to gain over Charles V and prevail upon him not to oppose the divorce. In order to succeed, Clement determined to undertake a journey to Bologna in the worst season of the year. He started on 18 November with six cardinals and a certain number of attendants, and took twenty days to reach that city by way of Perugia. Most of his officers had done everything to dissuade him from this painful expedition, but in vain. The rain fell in torrents; the rivers were swollen and unfordable; the roads muddy and broken up; the mules sank of fatigue one after another; the couriers who preceded him solicited the pope to travel on foot; and at last His Holiness' favourite mule broke its leg. It mattered not: he must oppose the reformation of England. But the discomforts of the journey increased: the pope often arrived at inns where there was no bed, and had to sleep among the straw. At last he reached Bologna on 7 December, but in such a plight that, notwithstanding his love for ceremonies, he entered the city furtively.

Another disappointment awaited him. The Cardinal of Ancona died, the most influential member of the sacred college, and on whom Clement relied to gain over the emperor, who greatly respected him. But this did not cool the pontiff's zeal: 'I am thoroughly decided to please the king in this great matter', he said to Henry's envoys, and added: 'To have universal concord between all the princes of Christendom, I would give a joint of my hand.' In fact Clement set to work and went so far as to tell Charles that, according to the theologians, the pope had no right to grant a dispensation for a marriage between brother and sister; but the emperor was immovable. The pope then proposed a truce of three or four years between Henry, Francis, and Charles, during which he would convoke a general council, to whom he would remit the whole affair. Francis informed Henry that all this was nothing but a trick.

The king, convinced that the pope was trifling with him, no longer hesitated to follow the course which the interests of his people and his own happiness seemed to point out. He determined that Anne Boleyn should be his wife and Queen of England also. It was now that the marriage took place. Cranmer states in a letter written on 17 June 1533, that he did not perform the ceremony, that he did not hear of it until a fortnight after, and that it was celebrated privately 'much about St Paul's day last' (25 January 1533).

Whatever may have been the exact date of the marriage,[1] it became the universal topic of conversation in the early months of 1533; people did not speak of it publicly, but in private, some attacking and others defending it. If the members of the Romish party circulated ridiculous stories and outrageous calumnies against Anne, the members of the national party replied that the purity of her life, her moderation, her chastity, her mildness, her discretion, her noble and exalted parentage, her pleasing manners, and (they added somewhat later) her fitness to give a successor to the crown of England, made her worthy of the royal favour. Men are apt to go too far in reproaches as well as in eulogies.

This important step on the part of Henry VIII was accompanied with an explosion of murmurs against Clement VII. 'The pope', he said, 'wanders from the path of the Redeemer, who was obedient in this world to princes. What! must a prince submit to the arrogance of a human being whom God has put under him? Must a king humble himself before that man above whom he stands by the will of God? No! that would be a perversion of the order God has established.' This is what Henry represented to Francis through Lord Rochford; but the words did not touch the King of France, for the emperor was just then making several concessions to him, and the evangelicals of Paris were annoying him. From that hour the cordial feeling between the two monarchs gradually decreased. England turned her eyes more and more towards the gospel, and France towards Rome. Just at the time when Anne Boleyn was about to reign in the palaces of Whitehall and Windsor, Catherine de Medici was entering those of St Germain and Fontainebleau. The contrast between the two nations became ever more distinct and striking: England was advancing towards liberty, and France towards the dragonnades.[2]

The divorce between Rome and Whitehall soon became manifest. A brief of Clement VII posted in February on the doors of all the churches in Flanders, in the states of the king's enemy, and as near to England as possible, attracted a great number of readers. 'What shall we do?' said the

---

[1] [Evidence for the exact date of the marriage is conflicting, but it is difficult to refuse credence to Cranmer's testimony. As Elizabeth, Anne's child, was born on 7 September of the same year, it is clear that Henry had urgent reasons for speeding up all matters connected with the marriage.]

[2] [Persecutions of Huguenots under Louis XIV at the hands of dragoons.]

pontiff to Henry. 'Shall we neglect thy soul's safety? ... We exhort thee, our son, under pain of excommunication, to restore Queen Catherine to the royal honours which are due to her, to cohabit with her, and to cease to associate publicly with Anne; and that within a month from the day on which this brief shall be presented to thee. Otherwise, when the said term shall have elapsed, we pronounce thee and the said Anne to be *ipso facto* excommunicate, and command all men to shun and avoid your presence.' It would appear that this document, demanded by the imperialists, had been posted throughout Flanders without the pope's knowledge.

A copy was immediately forwarded to the king by his agents. He was surprised and agitated, but believed at last that it was forged by his enemies. How could he imagine that the pope, just at the very time he was showing the king especial marks of his affection, would (even conditionally) have anathematized and isolated him in the midst of his people? Henry sent a copy of the document to Benet, his agent at Rome, and desired him to ascertain carefully whether it did really proceed from the pope or not.

Benet presented the document to Clement as a paper forwarded to him by his friend in Flanders. The latter was 'ashamed and in great perplexity', wrote the envoy. He then read it again more attentively, stopped at certain passages, and seemed as if he were choking. Having come to the end, he expressed his surprise, and pretended that the copy differed from the original. 'There is one mistake in particular which almost chokes the pope every time it is mentioned', wrote Benet to Cromwell. This mistake was the inclusion of Queen Anne Boleyn in the censure, without giving her previous warning, which (they said) was contrary to all the commandments of God. Accordingly Dr Benet received orders to bring up this mistake frequently in his audiences with the pope; and he did not fail to do so. At this moment, in which he was about to lose England, the pope was more uneasy at having committed an error of form with regard to Anne Boleyn, than with having struck the monarch of a powerful kingdom with an interdict. There is, besides, no doubt that he dictated the unhappy phrase himself.

Benet and his friends took advantage of the pope's vexation, and even increased it: they communicated the brief to the dignitaries of the church in Clement's household, and the latter acknowledged that the document must be offensive to His Majesty of England, and that 'the pope was much to blame'. Benet transmitted the pontiff's *errata* to the king, but it was too late: the blow had taken effect. The indignant Henry was about to proceed ostentatiously to the very acts which Rome threatened with her thunders.

Whilst the pope was hesitating, England firmly pursued her emancipation. Parliament met on 4 February, and the boldest language was uttered. 'The people of England, in accord with their king', said eloquent speakers, 'have the right to decide supremely on all things both temporal and spiritual; and certainly the English possess intelligence enough for that. And yet, in spite of the prohibitions issued by so many of our princes, we see bulls arriving every moment from Rome to regulate wills, marriages, divorces, everything, in short. We propose that henceforward these matters be decided solely before the national tribunals.' The law passed. It was Cromwell's legislative masterpiece. Appeals, instead of being made to Rome, were to be made in the first instance to the bishop, then to the archbishop, and, if the king was interested in the cause, to the upper chamber of the ecclesiastical convocation.

The king took immediate advantage of this law to inquire of convocation whether the pope could authorize a man to marry his brother's widow. Out of sixty-six present, and one hundred and ninety-seven who voted by proxy, there were only nineteen in the upper house who voted against the king. The opposition was stronger in the lower house; but even this agreed with the other house in declaring that Pope Julius II had exceeded his authority in giving Henry a dispensation, and that the marriage was consequently null from the very first.

Nothing remained now but to proceed to the divorce. On 11 April, two days before Easter, Cranmer, as archbishop, wrote a letter to the king, in which he set forth, that desiring to fill the office of Archbishop of Canterbury, 'according to the laws of God and holy church, for the relief of the grievances and infirmities of the people, God's subjects and yours in spiritual causes', he prayed His Majesty's favour for that office. Cranmer did not decline the royal intervention, but he avoided confounding spiritual with temporal affairs.

Henry, who was doubtless waiting impatiently for this letter, was alarmed as he read the words, 'according to the laws of God and holy church'. God and the church. Well! but what of the king and the royal supremacy? The primate seemed to assert the right of acting *proprio motu,* and, while asking the king's favour, to be doing a simple act of courtesy. Did the Church of England claim to take the pontiff's place and station, and leave the king aside? That was not what Henry meant. Tired of the pretensions of the pope of Rome, would he suffer a pope on a small scale at his side? He intended to be master in his own kingdom – master of everything. The letter must be modified, and this Henry intimated to Cranmer.

That day, or the next after the one on which this letter had been written, there was a great festival at the court in honour of Anne Boleyn. 'Queen Anne that evening went in state to her apartments openly as queen', says Hall. It was probably during this festival that the king, taking the prelate aside, desired him to suppress the unwelcome passage. The idea suggested by an eminent historian, that Cranmer sent both the letters together to Henry, that he might choose which he would prefer, seems to me inadmissible. Cranmer, as it would appear, submitted, waiting for better days. On returning to Lambeth, he recopied his letter, omitting the words which had been pointed out. Not content with asking the king's *favour,* he desired his *licence,* his authorization to proceed. (Actually, appropriate resolutions of convocation had already virtually decided the issues, and Cranmer knew that he could take action with the church supporting him.) He dated his second letter the same day, and sent it to his master, who was satisfied with it.

This alone did not satisfy Henry: in his reply to the archbishop, he marked still more strongly his intention not to have in England a primate independent of the crown: 'Ye therefore duly recognizing that it becometh you not, being our subject, to enterprise any part of your said office *without our licence obtained so to do.* ... In consideration of these things, albeit we being your king and sovereign, do recognize no superior upon earth but only God; yet because ye be under us, by God's calling and ours, the most principal minister of our spiritual jurisdiction, we will not refuse your humble request.'

This language was clear. Henry VIII did not, however, claim the arbitrary authority to which the pope pretended: human and divine laws were to be the supreme rule in England, but he, the king, was to be their chief interpreter. Cranmer must understand that. 'To these laws we, as a Christian king', wrote Henry, 'have always heretofore submitted, and shall ever most obediently submit ourselves.' The ecclesiastical system which Henry VIII established in England in 1533 was not a free church in a free state, and there is no reason to be surprised at it.

Cranmer, having received the royal licence, now prepared the measure for disposing of the problem which, for six years, had kept England and the Continent in suspense. Taking the bishops of Lincoln and Winchester and some lawyers with him, he proceeded quietly, and without ostentation, to the priory of Dunstable, five miles from Ampthill in Bedfordshire, where Queen Catherine was staying. He wished to avoid the notoriety of a trial held in London.

The ecclesiastical court being duly formed, Henry and Catherine were summoned to appear before it on 10 May. The king was present by attorney: but the queen replied: 'My cause is before the pope; I accept no other judge.' A fresh summons was immediately made out for 12 May, and as the queen appeared neither in person nor by any of her servants, she was pronounced contumacious, and the trial went forward. The king was informed every night of each day's proceedings, and he was often in great anxiety. Some unexpected event, an appeal from Catherine, the sudden intervention of the pope or of the emperor, might stop everything. His courtiers were on the watch for news. Anne said nothing, but her heart beat quick, and the ambitious Cromwell, whose fortunes depended on the success of the matter, was sometimes in great alarm. Cranmer rested on the declarations of Scripture, and showed much equity and uprightness during the trial. 'I have willingly injured no human being', he said. But he knew the queen had numerous partisans; they would conjure her, perhaps, to appear before her judges; there would then be a great stir, and the voice of the people would be heard. The archbishop could hardly restrain his emotion as he thought of this. He must indeed expect an inflexible resistance on the part of the queen; but in the midst of all the agitation around her, she alone remained calm and resolute. Her hand had grasped the pope's robe, and nothing could make her let it go. 'I am the king's lawful wife', she repeated; 'I am Queen of England. My daughter is the king's child: I place her in her father's hands.'

On Wednesday 23 May, the primate, attended by all the archiepiscopal court, proceeded to the church of St Peter's Priory at Dunstable, in order to deliver the final judgment of divorce. A few persons attracted by curiosity were present; but, although Dunstable was near Ampthill, all of Catherine's household kept themselves respectfully aloof from an act which was to deal their mistress such a grievous blow. The primate, after reciting the decisions of the several universities, provincial councils, and other premises, continued: 'Therefore we, Thomas, archbishop, primate, and legate, having first called upon the name of Christ, and having God altogether before our eyes, do pronounce and declare that the marriage between our sovereign lord King Henry and the most serene Lady Catherine, widow of his brother, having been contracted contrary to the law of God, is null and void; and therefore we sentence that it is not lawful for the said most illustrious Prince Henry and the said most serene Lady Catherine to remain in the said pretended marriage.' The announcement, drawn up very carefully by two notaries, was immediately sent to the king.

The divorce was pronounced, and Henry was free. Many persons gave way to feelings of alarm: they thought that all Europe would combine against England. 'The pope will excommunicate the English', said some; 'and then the emperor will destroy them.' But, on the other hand, the majority of the nation desired to have done with a subject which had been agitating their minds during the last seven years. England, getting out of a labyrinth from which she had never expected to find an issue, began to breathe again.

Catherine's marriage was declared to be null: it only remained now to recognize Anne Boleyn's. On 28 May, an archiepiscopal court held at Lambeth, in the primate's palace, officially declared that Henry and Anne had been lawfully wedded, and the king had now no thought but how to seal his union by the pomp of a coronation. It would certainly have been preferable had the new queen taken her seat quietly on the throne; but slanderous reports made it necessary for the king to present his wife to the people in all the splendour of royalty.

At three o'clock in the afternoon of Thursday before Whitsuntide, a magnificent procession started from Greenwich. Fifty barges, adorned with rich banners, conveyed the representatives of the different city companies, and the metropolis joyfully hailed a union that promised to inaugurate a future of light and faith: it was almost a religious festival. On the banner of the Fishmongers was the inscription, *All worship belongs to God alone;* on that of the Haberdashers, *My trust is in God only;* on that of the Grocers, *God gives grace;* and on that of the Goldsmiths, *To God alone be all the glory.* The city of London thus asserted, in the presence of the immense crowd, the principles of the reformation. The lord mayor's barge immediately preceded the galley, all hung with cloth of gold, in which Anne was seated. Near it floated another colourful barge, on which a little mountain was contrived, planted with red and white roses, in the midst of which sat a number of young maidens singing to the accompaniment of sweet music. A hundred richly ornamented barques, carrying the nobility of England, brought up the magnificent procession, and a countless number of boats and skiffs covered the river. The moment Anne set her foot on shore at the Tower, a thousand trumpets sounded notes of triumph, and all the guns of the fortress fired such a peal as had seldom been heard before.

Henry, who liked the sound of cannon, met Anne at the gate and kissed her, and the new queen entered in triumph that vast fortress from which, three years later, she was to issue, by order of the same prince, to mount, an innocent victim, the cruel scaffold. She smiled courteously on all around; and yet, seized with a sudden emotion, she sometimes trembled, as if, instead of the joyous flowers on which she trod with light and graceful foot, she saw a deep gulf yawning beneath her.

The king and queen passed the whole of the next day (Friday) at the Tower. On Saturday Anne left it for Westminster. The streets were bright with banners, and the houses were hung with velvet and cloth of gold. All the orders of the state and church, the ambassadors of France and Venice, and the officers of the court opened the procession. The queen was carried in a magnificent litter covered with white cloth shot with gold, her head, which she had modestly inclined, being encircled with a wreath of precious stones. The people who crowded the streets were full of enthusiasm, and seemed to triumph more than she did herself.

The next day, Whitsunday, she proceeded for the coronation to the ancient Abbey of Westminster, where the bishops and the court had been summoned to meet her. She took her seat in a rich chair, whence she presently descended to the high altar and knelt down. After the prescribed prayers she rose, and the archbishop placed the crown of St Edward upon her head. She then took the sacrament and retired; the Earl of Wiltshire, her father, trembling with emotion, took her right hand ... he was at the pinnacle of happiness, and yet he was uneasy. Alas! a caprice of the man who had raised his daughter to the throne might be sufficient to hurl her from it! Anne herself, in the midst of all these pomps, greater than any ever seen before at the coronation of an English queen, could not entirely forget the princess whose place she had now taken. Might not she be rejected in her turn? ... In such a thought there was enough to make her shudder.

Anne did not find in her marriage with Henry the happiness she had dreamt, and a cloud was often seen passing across those features once so radiant. The idol to which this young woman had sacrificed everything – the splendour of a throne – did not satisfy her longings for happiness: she looked within herself, and found once more, as queen, that attraction towards the doctrine of the gospel which she had felt in the society of Margaret of Valois, and which, amid her ambitious pursuits, had been almost extinguished in her heart. She discovered that for those who have everything, as well as for those who have nothing, there is only one single good – God himself. She did not probably give herself up entirely to him, for her best impressions were often fugitive; but there are occasional indications that she took advantage of her power to assist those who she knew were devoted to the gospel. Foxe intimates that the pardon granted to John Lambert, who was still in prison, was in part the result of 'the coming of Queen Anne'. That faithful confessor of Jesus Christ settled in London, where he began to teach children Latin and Greek, without however neglecting the defence of truth.

The king, who had informed Catherine through Lord Mountjoy of the archiepiscopal sentence, officially communicated his divorce and marriage to the various crowned heads of Europe, and particularly to the King of France, the emperor, and the pope. The pope on 11 July annulled the sentence of the Archbishop of Canterbury, declared the king's marriage with Anne Boleyn unlawful, and threatened to excommunicate both, unless they separated before the end of September. Henry angrily commanded his theologians to demonstrate that the bull was a nullity, recalled his ambassador, the Duke of Norfolk, and said that the moment was come for all monarchs and all Christian people to withdraw from under the yoke of the Bishop of Rome. 'The pope and his cardinals', he wrote to Francis I, 'pretend to have princes, who are free persons, at their beck and commandment. Sire, you and I and all the princes of Christendom must unite for the preservation of our rights, liberties, and privileges; we must alienate the greatest part of Christendom from the see of Rome.'

But Henry had scholastic prejudices which made him fall into the strangest contradictions. While he was employing his diplomacy to isolate the pope, he still prayed him to declare the nullity of his marriage with Catherine. It is not at the court of this prince that we must look for the real reformation: we must go in search of it elsewhere.

CHAPTER EIGHTEEN

Fryth in the Tower

(August 1532 to May 1533)

One of the leading scholars of England was about to seal the testimony of his faith with his blood. John Fryth had been one of the most brilliant stars of the University of Cambridge. 'It would hardly be possible to find his equal in learning', said many. Accordingly Wolsey had invited him to his college at Oxford, and Henry VIII had desired to place him among the number of his theologians. But the mysteries of the word of God had more attraction for Fryth than mere scholastic renown: the claims of conscience prevailed in him over those of the intellect, and neglecting his own glory, he sought only to be useful to mankind. A sincere, decided, and yet moderate Christian, preaching the gospel with great purity and love, this man of thirty seemed destined to become one of the most influential reformers of England. Nothing could have prevented his playing the foremost part, if he had had Luther's enthusiastic energy or Calvin's indomitable will. There were less strong, but perhaps more amiable features in his character; he taught with gentleness those who were opposed to the truth, and while many, as Foxe says, 'take the bellows in hand to blow the fire, but few there are that will seek to quench it', Fryth sought after peace. Controversies between Protestants distressed him. 'The opinions for which men go to war', he said, 'do not deserve those great tragedies of which they make us spectators. Let there be no longer any question among us of Zwinglians or Lutherans, for neither Zwingli nor Luther died for us, and we must be one in Christ Jesus.' This servant of Christ, meek and lowly of heart like his Master, never disputed even with papists, unless obliged to do so.

A true catholicism which embraced all Christians was Fryth's distinctive feature as a reformer. He was not one of those who imagine that a national church ought to think only of its own nation; but of those who believe that if a church is the depositary of the truth, she is so for all the earth; and that a religion is not good, if it has no longing to extend itself to all the races of mankind. There were some strongly marked national elements in the English reformation – the activity of the king and the Parliament, but there was also a universal element – a lively faith in the Saviour of the world. No one in the sixteenth century represented this truly catholic element better than Fryth. 'I understand the church of God in a wide sense', he said. 'It contains all those whom we regard as members of Christ. It is a net thrown into the sea.' This principle, sown at that time as a seed in the English reformation, was one day to cover the world with missionaries.

Fryth, having declined the brilliant offers the king had made to him through Cromwell and Vaughan, joined Tyndale in translating and publishing the Holy Scriptures in English. While labouring thus for England, an irresistible desire came over him to circulate the gospel there in person. He therefore quitted the Low Countries, returned to London, and directed his course to Reading, where the prior had been his friend. Exile had not used him well, and he entered that town miserably clothed, and more like a beggar than one whom Henry VIII had desired to place near himself. This was in August 1532.

His writings had preceded him. Having received, when in the Netherlands, three works composed in defence of purgatory by three distinguished men – Rastell, Sir Thomas More's brother-in-law, More himself, and Fisher, Bishop of Rochester – Fryth had replied to them: 'A purgatory! there is not one only, there are two. The first is the *word of God,* the second is the *cross of Christ:* I do not mean the cross of wood, but the cross of tribulation. But the lives of the papists are so wicked that they have invented a third.'

Sir Thomas, exasperated by Fryth's reply, said with that humorous tone he often affected, 'I propose to answer the good young Father Fryth, whose wisdom is such that three old men like my brother Rastell, the Bishop of Rochester, and myself are mere babies when confronted with Father Fryth alone.' The exile having returned to England, More had now the opportunity of avenging himself more effectually than by his jokes.

At Reading, Fryth's strange air and his look as of a foreigner arriving from a distant country attracted attention, and he was taken up for a vagabond. 'Who are you?' asked the magistrate. Fryth, suspecting that he was in the hands of enemies of the gospel, refused to give his name, which increased the suspicion, and he was set in the stocks. As they gave him but little to eat, with the intent of forcing him to tell his name, his hunger soon became insupportable. Knowing the name of the master of the grammar school, he asked to speak with him. Leonard Coxe had scarcely entered the prison, when the pretended vagabond all in rags addressed him in correct Latin, and began to deplore his miserable captivity. Never had words more noble been uttered in a dungeon so vile. The school master, astonished at so much eloquence, compassionately drew near the unhappy man and inquired how it came to pass that such a learned scholar was in such profound wretchedness. Presently he sat down, and the two men began to talk in Greek about the universities and languages. Coxe could not make it out: it was no longer simple pity that he felt, but love, which turned to admiration when he heard the prisoner recite with the purest accent those noble lines of the *Iliad* which were so applicable to his own case: –

> Sing, O Muse,
> The vengeance deep and deadly, whence to Greece
> Unnumbered ills arose; which many a soul
> Of mighty warriors to the viewless shades
> Untimely sent.

Filled with respect, Coxe hurried off to the mayor, complained bitterly of the wrong done to so remarkable a man, and obtained his liberation. Homer saved the life of a reformer.

Fryth departed for London and hastened to join the worshippers who were accustomed to meet in Bow Lane. He conversed with them and exclaimed: 'Oh! what consolation to see such a great number of believers walking in the way of the Lord!' These Christians asked him to expound the Scriptures to them, and, delighted with his exhortations, they exclaimed in their turn: 'If the rule of St Paul were followed, this man would certainly make a better bishop than many of those who wear the mitre.' Instead of the crosier he was to bear the cross.

One of those who listened was in great doubt relative to the doctrine of the Lord's Supper; and one day, after Fryth had been setting Christ before them as the food of the Christian soul through faith, this person followed him and said: 'Our prelates think differently: they believe that the bread transformed by consecration becomes the flesh, blood, and bones of Christ; that even the wicked eat this flesh with their teeth, and that we must adore the host. ... What you have just said refutes their errors, but I fear that I cannot remember it. Pray commit it to writing.' Fryth, who did not like discussions, was alarmed at the request, and answered: 'I do not care to touch that terrible tragedy'; for so he called the dispute about the Supper. The man having repeated his request, and promised that he would not communicate the paper to anybody, Fryth wrote an explanation of the doctrine of the sacrament and gave it to this London Christian, saying: 'We must eat and drink the body and blood of Christ, not with the teeth, but with the hearing and through faith.' The brother took the treatise, and, hurrying home with it, read it carefully.

In a short time everyone at the Bow Lane meeting spoke about this writing. One man, a false brother, named William Holt, listened attentively to what was said, and thought he had found an opportunity of destroying Fryth. Assuming a hypocritical look, he spoke in a pious strain to the individual who had the manuscript, as if he had desired to enlighten his faith, and finally asked him for it. Having obtained it, he hastened to make a copy, which he carried to Sir Thomas More, who was still chancellor.

Fryth soon perceived that he had tried in vain to remain unknown: he called with so much power those who thirsted for righteousness to come to Christ for the waters of life, that friends and enemies were struck with his eloquence. Observing that his name began to be talked of in various places, he quitted the capital and travelled unnoticed through several counties, where he found some little Christian congregations whom he tried to strengthen in the faith.

Tyndale, who remained on the Continent, having heard of Fryth's labours, began to feel great anxiety about him. He knew but too well the cruel disposition of the bishops and of More. 'I will make the serpent come out of his dark den', Sir Thomas had said, speaking of Tyndale, 'as Hercules forced Cerberus, the watchdog of hell, to come out to the light of day. ... I will not leave Tyndale the darkest corner in which to hide his head.'[1] In Tyndale's eyes Fryth was the great hope of the church in England; he trembled lest the redoubtable Hercules should seize him. 'Dearly beloved brother Jacob', he wrote, calling him Jacob to mislead his enemies, 'be cold, sober, wise, and circumspect, and keep you low by the ground, avoiding high questions that pass the common capacity. But expound the law truly, and open the veil of Moses to condemn all flesh and prove all men sinners. Then set abroach[2] the mercy of our Lord Jesus, and let the wounded consciences drink of him. ... All doctrine that casteth a mist on these two to shadow and hide them, resist with all your power. ... Beloved in my heart, there liveth not one in whom I have so great hope and trust, and in whom my heart rejoiceth, not so much for your learning and what other gifts else you may have, as because you walk in those things that the conscience may feel, and not in the imagination of the brain. Cleave fast to the rock of the help of God; and if aught be required of you contrary to the glory of God and his Christ, then stand fast and commit yourself to God. He is our God and his is the glory. I hope our redemption is nigh.'

Tyndale's fears were but too well founded. Sir Thomas More held Fryth's new treatise in his hand: he read it and gave way by turns to anger and sarcasm. 'Whetting his wits, calling his spirits together, and sharpening his pen', to use the words of the chronicler, he answered Fryth, and described his doctrine under the image of a cancer. This did not satisfy him. Although he had returned the seals to the king in May, he continued to hold office until the end of the year. He ordered search to be made for Fryth, and set all his bloodhounds on the track. If the reformer was discovered he was lost: when Sir Thomas More had once caught his man, nothing could save him – nothing but a merry

---

[1] *Confutation of Tyndale's Answer,* by Sir Thomas More, Lord Chancellor of England (1532).

[2] [Used of a cask being pierced to let the wine run out.]

jest, perhaps. For instance, one day when he was examining a gospeller named Silver: 'You know', he said with a smile, 'that silver must be tried in the fire.' 'Yes', retorted the accused instantly, 'but not quicksilver.' More, delighted with the repartee, set the poor wretch at liberty. But Fryth was no jester: he could not hope, therefore, to find favour with the ex-chancellor of England.

Sir Thomas hunted the reformer by sea and by land, promising a great reward to anyone who should deliver him up. There was no county where More did not look for him, no sheriff or justice of the peace to whom he did not apply, no harbour where he did not post some officer to catch him. But the answer from every quarter was: 'He is not here.' Indeed, Fryth, having been informed of the great exertions of his enemy, was fleeing from place to place, often changing his dress, and finding a safe retreat nowhere. Determining to leave England and return to Tyndale, he went to Milton Shone in Essex with the intention of embarking. A ship was ready to sail, and quitting his hiding place he went down to the shore with all precaution. But he had been betrayed. More's agents, who were on the watch, seized him as he was stepping on board, and carried him to the Tower. This occurred in October 1532.

Sir Thomas More was uneasy and soured. He beheld a new power lifting its head in England and all Christendom, and he felt that in despite of his wit and his influence he was unable to check it. That man so amiable, that writer of a style so pure and elegant, did not so much dread the anger of the king; what exasperated him was to see the Scriptures circulating more widely every day, and a continually increasing number of his fellow citizens converted to the evangelical faith. These new men, who seemed to have more piety than himself – he an old follower of the old papacy! – irritated him sorely. He claimed to have alone – he and his friends – the privilege of being Christians. The zeal of the partisans of the reformation, the sacrifice they made of their repose, their money, and their lives confounded him. 'These diabolical people', he said, 'print their books at great expense, notwithstanding the great danger; not looking for any gain, they give them away to everybody, and even scatter them abroad by night. They fear no labour, no journey, no expense, no pain, no danger, no blows, no injury. They take a malicious

pleasure in seeking the destruction of others, and these disciples of the
devil think only how they may cast the souls of the simple into hell fire.'
In such a strain as this did the elegant utopist give vent to his anger – the
man who had dreamt all his life of the plan of an imaginary world for the
perfect happiness of everyone. At last he had caught one of the chief of
these disciples of Satan, and hoped to put him to death by fire.

The news soon spread through London that Fryth was in the Tower,
and several priests and bishops immediately went thither to try to bring
him back to the pope. Their great argument was that More had confuted
his treatise on the Lord's Supper. Fryth asked to see the confutation, but
it was refused him. One day the Bishop of Winchester, having called
upon the prisoner, showed it to Fryth, and, holding it up, asserted that
the book quite shut his mouth: Fryth put out his hand, but the bishop
hastily withdrew the volume. More himself was ashamed of the apology,
and did all he could to prevent its circulation. Fryth could only obtain
a written copy, but he resolved to answer it immediately. There was no
one with whom he could confer, not a book he could consult, and the
chains with which he was loaded scarcely allowed him to sit and write.
But reading in his dungeon by the light of a small candle the insults of
More, and finding himself charged with having collected all the poison
that could be found in the writings of Wycliffe, Luther, Œcolampadius,
Tyndale, and Zwingli, this humble servant of God exclaimed: 'No!
Luther and his doctrine are not the mark I aim at, but the Scriptures
of God.' 'He shall pay for his heresy with the best blood in his body',
said his enemies; and the pious disciple replied: 'As the sheep bound by
the hand of the butcher with timid look beseeches that his blood may
soon be shed, even so do I pray my judges that my blood may be shed
tomorrow, if by my death the king's eyes should be opened.'

Before he died, Fryth desired to save, if it were God's will, one of his
adversaries. There was one of them who had no obstinacy, no malice: it
was John Rastell, More's brother-in-law. Being unable to speak to him or
to any of the enemies of the reformation, he formed the design of writing
in prison a treatise which should be called the *Bulwark*. But strict orders
had recently arrived that he should have neither pen, ink, nor paper.
However, some evangelical Christians of London, who succeeded in

getting access to him, secretly furnished him with the means of writing, and Fryth began. He wrote, but at every moment he listened for fear the lieutenant of the Tower or the warders should come upon him suddenly and find the pen in his hand. Often a bright thought would occur to him, but some sudden alarm drove it out of his mind, and he could not recall it. He took courage, however: he had been accused of asserting that good works were of no service: he proceeded to explain with much eloquence all their utility, and every time he repeated: 'Is that nothing? is that still nothing? Truly, Rastell', he added, 'if you only regard that as useful which justifies us, the sun is not useful, because it justifieth not.'

As he was finishing these words he heard the keys rattling at the door, and, being alarmed, immediately threw paper, ink, and pen into a hiding place. However, he was able to complete the treatise and send it to Rastell. More's brother-in-law read it; his heart was touched, his understanding enlightened, his prejudices cleared away; and from that hour this choice spirit was gained over to the gospel of Christ. God had given him new eyes and new ears. A pure joy filled the prisoner's heart. 'Rastell now looks upon his natural reason as foolishness', he said. 'Rastell, become a child, drinks the wisdom that cometh from on high.'

The conversion of Sir Thomas More's brother-in-law made a great sensation, and the visits to Fryth's cell became every day more numerous. Although separated from his wife and from Tyndale, whom he had been forced to leave in the Low Countries, he had never had so many friends, brothers, mothers, and fathers; he wept for very joy. He took his pen and paper from their hiding place, and, always indefatigable, began to write first the *Looking-glass of Self-knowledge,* and next a *Letter to the Faithful Followers of the Gospel of Christ.* 'Imitators of the Lord', he said to them, 'mark yourselves with the sign of the cross, not as the superstitious crowd does, in order to worship it, but as a testimony that you are ready to bear that cross as soon as God shall please to send it. Fear not when you have it, for you will also have a hundred fathers instead of one, a hundred mothers instead of one, a hundred mansions already in this life (for I have made the trial), and after this life, joy everlasting.'

At the beginning of 1533, Anne Boleyn having been married to the King of England, Fryth saw his chains fall off: he was allowed to have all he asked for, and even permitted to leave the Tower at night on parole. He took advantage of this liberty to visit the friends of the gospel, and consult with them about what was to be done. One evening in particular, after leaving the Tower, Fryth went to Petit's house, anxious to embrace once more that great friend of the reformation, that firm member of Parliament, who had been thrown into prison as we have seen, and at last set free. Petit, weakened by his long confinement, was near his end; the persecution agitated and pained him, and it would appear that his emotion sometimes ended in delirium. As he was groaning over the captivity of the young and noble reformer, Fryth appeared. Petit was confused, his mind wandered. Is it Fryth or his ghost? He was like the believers, when Rhoda came to tell them that Peter was at the gate waiting to see them. But gradually recovering himself, Petit said: 'You here! how have you escaped the vigilance of the warders?' 'God himself', answered Fryth, 'gave me this liberty by touching their hearts.' The two friends then conversed about the true reformation of England, which in their eyes had nothing to do with the diplomatic proceedings of the king. In their opinion it was not a matter of loading the external church with new frippery, but 'to increase that elect, sanctified, and invisible congregation, elect before the foundation of the world'. Fryth did not conceal from Petit the conviction he felt that he would be called upon to die for the gospel. The night was spent in such Christian conversation, and the day began to dawn before the prisoner hastened to return to the Tower.

The evangelist's friends did not think as he did. Anne Boleyn's accession seemed as if it ought to open the doors of Fryth's prison, and in imagination they saw him at liberty, and labouring either on the Continent or at home at that real reformation which is accomplished by the Scriptures of God.

But it was not to be so. Most of the evangelical men raised up by God in England during the reign of Henry VIII found – not the influence which they should have exercised, but – death. Yet their blood has weighed in the divine balance; it has sanctified the reformation of England, and been a spiritual seed for future ages. If the church in England has witnessed the development of a powerful evangelical life in its bosom, it must not forget the cause, but understand, with Tertullian, that the blood of the martyrs is the seed of the church.

CHAPTER NINETEEN

A Reformer Chooses Rather to Lose
His Life than Save It

(May to July 1533)

T he enemy was on the watch: the second period of Fryth's
captivity, that which was to terminate in martyrdom, was
beginning. Henry's bishops, who, while casting off the pope
to please the king, had remained devoted to scholastic doctrines, feared
lest the reformer should escape them: they therefore undertook to solicit
Henry to put him to death. Fryth had on his side the queen, Cromwell,
and Cranmer. This did not discourage them, and they represented to the
king that although the man was shut up in the Tower of London, he did
not cease to write and act in defence of heresy. It was the season of Lent,
and Fryth's enemies came to an understanding with Dr Curwin, the
king's chaplain, who was to preach before the court. He had no sooner
got into the pulpit than he began to declaim against those who denied
the material presence of Christ in the host. Having struck his hearers
with horror, he continued: 'It is not surprising that this abominable
heresy makes such great progress among us. A man now in the Tower of
London has the audacity to defend it, and no one thinks of punishing
him.'

When the service was over, the brilliant congregation left the chapel,
and each as he went out asked what was the man's name. 'Fryth' was
the reply, and loud were the exclamations on hearing it. The blow took
effect, the scholastic prejudices of the king were revived, and he sent
for Cromwell and Cranmer. 'I am very much surprised', he said, 'that
John Fryth has been kept so long in the Tower without examination. I
desire his trial to take place without delay; and if he does not retract, let

him suffer the penalty he deserves.' He then nominated six of the chief spiritual and temporal peers of England to examine him: they were the Archbishop of Canterbury, the bishops of London and Winchester, the Lord Chancellor, the Duke of Suffolk, and the Earl of Wiltshire. This demonstrated the importance which Henry attached to the affair. Until now, all the martyrs had fallen beneath the blows either of the bishops or of More; but in this case it was the king himself who stretched out his strong hand against the servant of God.

Henry's order plunged Cranmer into the cruellest anxiety. On the one hand, Fryth was in his eyes a disciple of the gospel; but on the other, he attacked a doctrine which the archbishop then held to be Christian; for, like Luther and Osiander, he still believed in consubstantiation. 'Alas!' he wrote to Archdeacon Hawkins, 'he professes the doctrine of Œcolampadius.' He resolved, however, to do everything in his power to save Fryth.

The best friends of the young reformer saw that a pile was being raised to consume the most faithful Christian in England. 'Dearly beloved', wrote Tyndale from Antwerp, 'fear not men that threat, nor trust men that speak fair. Your cause is Christ's gospel, a light that must be fed with the blood of faith. The lamp must be trimmed daily, that the light go not out.' There was no lack of examples to confirm these words. 'Two have suffered in Antwerp unto the great glory of the gospel; four at Ryselles in Flanders. At Rouen in France they persecute, and at Paris are five doctors taken for the gospel. See, you are not alone: follow the example of all your other dear brethren, who choose to suffer in hope of a better resurrection. Bear the image of Christ in your mortal body, and keep your conscience pure and undefiled. … *Una salus victis, nullam sperare salutem:* the only safety of the conquered is to hope for no safety. If you may write, tell us how it goes with you.' In this letter from a martyr to a martyr there was one sentence honourable to a Christian woman: 'Your wife is well content with the will of God, and would not for her sake have the glory of God hindered.'

If friends were thinking of Fryth on the banks of the Scheldt, they were equally anxious about him on the banks of the Thames. Worthy citizens of London asked what was the use of England's quitting the pope to cling to Christ, if she burnt the servants of Christ? The little church had recourse to prayer. Archbishop Cranmer wished to save Fryth: he loved the man and admired his piety. If the accused appeared before the commission appointed by the king, he was lost: some means must be devised without delay to rescue him from an inevitable death. The archbishop declared that, before proceeding to trial, he wished to have a conference with the prisoner, and to endeavour to convince him, which was very natural. But at the same time the primate appeared to fear that if the conference took place in London the people would disturb the public peace, as in the time of Wycliffe. He settled therefore that it should be held at Croydon, where he had a palace. The primate's fear seems rather strange. A riot on account of Fryth, at a time when king, commons, and people were in harmony, appeared hardly probable. Cranmer had another motive.

Among the persons composing his household was a gentleman of benevolent character, and with a leaning towards the gospel, who was distressed at the cruelty of the bishops, and looked upon it as a lawful and Christian act to rob them, if possible, of their victims. Giving him one of the porters of Lambeth Palace as a companion, Cranmer committed Fryth to his care to bring him to Croydon. They were to take the prisoner a journey of four or five hours on foot through fields and woods, without any constables or soldiers. A strange walk and a strange escort!

Lord Fitzwilliam, first Earl of Southampton and governor of the Tower, at the time lay sick in his house at Westminster, suffering such severe pain as to force loud groans from him. On 10 June, at the desire of my Lord of Canterbury, the archbishop's gentleman, and the Lambeth porter, Gallois, surnamed Perlebeane, were introduced into the nobleman's bedchamber, where they found him lying upon his bed in extreme agony. Fitzwilliam, a man of the world, was greatly enraged against the evangelicals, who were the cause, in his opinion, of all the difficulties of England. The gentleman respectfully presented to him the primate's letter and the king's ring. 'What do you want?' he asked sharply, without opening the letter. 'His Grace desires your lordship to deliver Master Fryth to us.' The impatient Southampton flew into a passion at the name, and cursed Fryth and all the heretics. He thought it strange that a gentleman and a porter should have to convey a prisoner of such importance to the episcopal court: were there no soldiers in the Tower? Had Fitzwilliam any suspicion, or did he regret to see the reformer leave the walls within which he had been kept so long? We cannot tell: but he must obey, for they brought him the king's signet. Accordingly, taking his own ring hastily from his finger: 'Fryth', he said, 'Fryth. ... Here, show this to the lieutenant of the Tower, and take away your heretic quickly. I am but too happy to get rid of him.'

A few hours later Fryth, the gentleman, and Perlebeane entered a boat moored near the Tower, and were rowed speedily to the archbishop's palace at Lambeth. At first the three persons preserved a strict silence, only interrupted from time to time by the deep sighs of the gentleman. Being charged to begin by trying to induce Fryth to make some compromise, he broke the silence at last. 'Master Fryth', he said, 'if you are not prudent you are lost. What a pity! you that are so learned in Latin and Greek and in the Holy Scriptures, the ancient doctors, and all kinds of knowledge, you will perish, and all your admirable gifts will perish with you, with little profit to the world, and less comfort to your wife and children, your kinsfolk and friends.' ... The gentleman was silent a minute, and then began again: 'Your position is dangerous, Master Fryth, but not desperate: you have many friends who will do all they can in your favour. On your part do something for them, make some concession, and you will be safe. Your opinion on the merely spiritual presence of the body and blood of the Saviour is premature: it is too soon for us in England; wait until a better time comes!'

Fryth did not say a word: no sound was heard but the plash of the water and the noise of the oars. The gentleman thought he had shaken the young doctor, and after a moment's silence he resumed: 'My lord Cromwell and my Lord of Canterbury feel great affection for you; they know that if you are young in years you are old in knowledge, and may become a most profitable citizen of this realm. ... If you will be somewhat advised by their counsel, they will never permit you to be harmed; but if you stand stiff to your opinion, it is not possible to save your life, for as you have good friends so have you mortal enemies.'

The gentleman stopped and looked at the prisoner. It was by such language that Bilney had been seduced; but Fryth kept himself in the presence of God, ready to lose his life that he might save it. He thanked the gentleman for his kindness, and said that his conscience would not permit him to recede, out of respect to man, from the true doctrine of the Lord's Supper. 'If I am questioned on that point, I must answer according to my conscience, though I should lose twenty lives if I had so many. I can support it by a great number of passages from the Holy Scriptures and the ancient doctors, and if I am fairly tried I shall have nothing to fear.' – 'Indeed!' quoth the gentleman, 'if you be fairly tried, you would be safe, but that is what I very much doubt. Our Master Christ was not fairly tried, nor would he be, as I think, if he were now present again in the world. How then should you be, when your opinions are so little understood and are so odious?' – 'I know', answered Fryth, 'that the doctrine which I hold is very hard meat to be digested just now; but listen to me.' As he spoke, he took the gentleman by the hand: 'If you live twenty years more, you will see this whole realm of my opinion concerning this sacrament of the altar – all, except a certain class of men. My death, you say, would be sorrowful to my friends, but it will be only for a short time. But, all things considered, my death will be better unto me and all mine than life in continual bondage. God knoweth what he hath to do with his poor servant, whose cause I now defend. He will help me, and no man shall prevail on me to step backwards.'

The boat reached Lambeth. The travellers landed, entered the archbishop's palace, and, after taking some refreshment, started on foot for Croydon, ten miles south of London.

The three travellers proceeded over the hills and through the plains of Surrey: here and there flocks of sheep were grazing in the scanty pastures, and to the east stretched vast woods. The gentleman walked mournfully by the side of Fryth. It was useless to ask him again to retract, but another idea engrossed Cranmer's officer: that of letting Fryth escape. The country was then thinly inhabited: the woods which covered it on the east and the chalky hills might serve as a hiding place for the fugitive. The difficulty was to persuade Perlebeane. The gentleman slackened his pace, called to the porter, and they walked by themselves behind the prisoner. When they were so far off that he could not hear their conversation, the gentleman said: 'You have heard this man, I am sure, and noted his talk since he came from the Tower.' – 'I never heard so constant a man', Perlebeane answered, 'nor so eloquent a person.' – 'You have heard nothing', resumed the gentleman, 'in respect both of his knowledge and his eloquence. If you could hear him at the university or in the pulpit, you would admire him still more. England has never had such a one of his age with so much learning. And yet our bishops treat him as if he were a very dolt or an idiot. ... They abhor him as the devil himself, and want to get rid of him by any means.' – 'Surely', said the porter, 'if there were nothing else in him but the consideration of his person both comely and amiable, his disposition so gentle, meek, and humble, it were pity he should be cast away.' – 'Cast away', interrupted the gentleman, 'he will certainly be cast away if we once bring him to Croydon.' And lowering his voice, he continued: 'Surely before God I speak it, if thou, Perlebeane, wert of my mind, we should never bring him thither.' – 'What do you mean?' asked the astonished porter. Then, after a moment's silence, he added: 'I know that you have a great deal more responsibility in this matter than I have; and therefore if you can honestly save this man I will yield to your proposal with all my heart.' The gentleman breathed again.

Cranmer had desired that all possible efforts should be made to change Fryth's sentiments; and these failing, he wished to save him in another way. It was his desire that the reformer should go on foot to Croydon, that he should be accompanied by only two of his servants, selected from those best disposed towards the new doctrine. The primate's gentleman would never have dared take upon himself, except by his master's desire, the responsibility of conniving at the escape of a prisoner who was to be tried by the first personages of the realm, appointed by the king himself. Happy at having gained the porter to his enterprise, he began to discuss with him the ways and means. He knew the country well, and his plan was arranged.

'You see yonder hill before us', he said to Perlebeane; 'it is Brixton Causeway, two miles from London. There are great woods on both sides. When we come to the top we will permit Fryth to escape into the woods on the left hand, whence he may easily get into Kent, where he was born, and where he has many friends. We will linger an hour or two on the road, after his flight, to give him time to reach a place of safety, and when night approaches we will go to Streatham, which is a mile and a half off, and make an outcry in the town that our prisoner has escaped into the woods on the right hand towards Wandsworth, that we followed him for more than a mile, and at length lost him because we were not many enough. At the same time we will take with us as many people as we can, to search for him in that direction; if necessary, we will be all night about it; and before we can send the news to Croydon of what has happened, Fryth will be in safety, and the bishops will be disappointed.'

The gentleman, we see, was not very scrupulous about the means of rescuing a victim from the Roman priests. Perlebeane thought as he did. 'Your plan pleases me', he answered; 'now go and tell the prisoner, for we are already at the foot of the hill.'

The delighted gentleman hurried forward: 'Master Fryth', he said, 'let us talk together a little. I cannot hide from you that the task I have undertaken, to bring you to Croydon, as a sheep to the slaughter, grieves me exceedingly, and there is no danger I would not brave to deliver you out of the lion's mouth. Yonder good fellow and I have devised a plan whereby you may escape: listen to me.' The gentleman having described his plan, Fryth smiled amiably and said: 'This then is the result of your long consultation together. You have wasted your time. If you were both to leave me here and go to Croydon, declaring to the bishops you had lost me, I should follow after as fast as I could, and bring them news that I had found and brought Fryth again.'

The gentleman had not expected such an answer. A prisoner refuse his liberty! ... 'You are mad', he said: 'do you think your reasoning will convert the bishops? At Milton Shone you tried to escape beyond the sea, and now you refuse to save yourself!' – 'The two cases are different', answered Fryth; 'then I was at liberty, and according to the advice of St Paul I would fain have enjoyed my liberty for the continuance of my studies. But now the higher power, as it were by Almighty God's permission, has seized me, and my conscience binds me to defend the doctrine for which I am persecuted, if I would not incur our Lord's condemnation. If I should now run away, I should run from my God; if I should fly, I should fly from the testimony I am bound to bear to his holy word, and I should deserve a thousand hells. I most heartily thank you both for your good will towards me, but I beseech you to bring me where I was appointed to be brought, for else I will go thither all alone.'

Those who desired to save Fryth had not counted upon so much integrity. Such were, however, the martyrs of Protestantism. The archbishop's two servants continued their journey along with their strange prisoner. Fryth had a calm eye and cheerful look, and the rest of the journey was accomplished in pious and agreeable conversation. When they reached Croydon, he was delivered to the officers of the episcopal court, and passed the night in the porter's lodge.

The next morning he appeared before the bishops and peers appointed to examine him. Cranmer and Lord Chancellor Audley desired his acquittal, but some of the other judges were men without pity.

The examination began:

'Do you believe', they said, 'that the sacrament of the altar is or is not the real body of Christ?'

Fryth answered simply and firmly: 'I believe that the bread is the body of Christ in that it is broken, and thus teaches us that the body of Christ was to be *broken* and delivered unto death to redeem us from our iniquities. I believe the bread is the body of Christ in that it is *distributed,* and thus teaches us that the body of Christ and the fruits of his passion are distributed unto all faithful people. I believe that the bread is the body of Christ so far as it is *received,* and thus it teaches us that even as the outward man receiveth the sacrament with his teeth and mouth, so doth the inward man truly receive through faith the body of Christ and the fruits of his passion.'

The judges were not satisfied: they wanted a formal and complete retraction. 'Do you not think', asked one of them, 'that the natural body of Christ, his flesh, blood, and bones, are contained under the sacrament and are there present without any figure of speech?'

'No', he answered; 'I do not think so'; adding with much humility and charity: 'notwithstanding I would not have that any should count my saying to be an article of faith. For even as I say, that you ought not to make any necessary article of the faith of your part; so I say again, that we make no necessary article of the faith of our part, but leave it indifferent for all men to judge therein, as God shall open their hearts, and no side to condemn or despise the other, but to nourish in all things brotherly love, and to bear one another's infirmities.'

The commissioners then undertook to convince Fryth of the truth of transubstantiation; but he quoted Scripture, St Augustine, and Chrysostom, and eloquently defended the doctrine of the spiritual eating. The court rose. Cranmer had been moved, although he was still under the influence of Luther's teaching. 'The man spoke admirably', he said to Dr Heath as they went out, 'and yet in my opinion he is wrong.' Not many years later he devoted one of the most important of his writings to an explanation of the doctrine now professed by the young reformer; it may be that Fryth's words had begun to shake him.

Full of love for him, Cranmer desired to save him. Four times during the course of the examination he sent for Fryth and conversed with him privately, always asserting the Lutheran opinion. Fryth offered to maintain his doctrine in a public discussion against anyone who was willing to attack it, but nobody accepted his challenge. Cranmer, distressed at seeing all his efforts useless, found there was nothing more for him to do; the cause was transferred to the ordinary, the Bishop of London, and on 17 June the prisoner was once more committed to the Tower. The bishop selected as his assessors for the trial, Longland, Bishop of Lincoln, and Gardiner, Bishop of Winchester: there were no severer judges to be found on the episcopal bench. At Cambridge Fryth had been the most distinguished pupil of the clever and ambitious Gardiner; but this, instead of exciting the compassion of that hard man, did but increase his anger, 'Fryth and his friends', he said, 'are villains, blasphemers, and limbs of the devil.'

On 20 June Fryth was taken to St Paul's before the three bishops, and though of a humble disposition and almost timid character, he answered boldly. A clerk took down all his replies, and Fryth, snatching up the pen, wrote: 'I Fryth think thus. Thus have I spoken, written, defended, affirmed, and published in my writings.' The bishops having asked him if he would retract his errors, Fryth replied: 'Let justice have its course and the sentence be pronounced.' Stokesley did not keep him waiting long. 'Not willing that thou, Fryth, who art wicked', he said, 'shouldest become more wicked, and infect the Lord's flock with thy heresies, we declare thee excommunicate and cast out from the church, and leave thee unto the secular powers, most earnestly requiring them in the truth of our Lord Jesus Christ that thy execution and punishment be not too extreme, *nor yet the gentleness too much mitigated.'*

Fryth was taken to Newgate and shut up in a dark cell, where he was bound with chains on the hands and feet as heavy as he could bear, and round his neck was a collar of iron, which fastened him to a post, so that he could neither stand upright nor sit down. Truly the 'gentleness' was not 'too much mitigated'. His charity never failed him. 'I am going to die', he said, 'but I condemn neither those who follow Luther nor those who follow Œcolampadius, since both reject transubstantiation.' A tailor's apprentice, twenty-four years of age, Andrew Hewet by name, was placed in his cell. Fryth asked him for what crime he was sent to prison. 'The bishops', he replied, 'asked me what I thought of the sacrament, and I answered, 'I think as Fryth does.' Then one of them smiled, and the Bishop of London said: 'Why, Fryth is a heretic, and already condemned to be burnt, and if you do not retract your opinion you shall be burnt with him.' 'Very well', I answered, 'I am content.' So they sent me here to be burnt along with you.'

On 4 July they were both taken to Smithfield: the executioners fastened them to the post, back to back; the torch was applied, the flame rose in the air, and Fryth, stretching out his hands, embraced it as if it were a dear friend whom he would welcome. The spectators were touched, and showed marks of lively sympathy. 'Of a truth', said an evangelical Christian in after-days, 'he was one of those prophets whom God, having pity on this realm of England, raised up to call us to repentance.' His enemies were there. Dr Cooke, a fanatic priest, observing some persons praying, called out: 'Do not pray for such folks, any more than you would for a dog.' At this moment a sweet light shone on Fryth's face, and he was heard beseeching the Lord to pardon his enemies. Hewet died first, and Fryth thanked God that the sufferings of his young brother were over. Committing his soul into the Lord's hands, he expired. 'Truly', exclaimed many, 'great are the victories Christ gains in his saints.'

So many souls were enlightened by Fryth's writings, that this reformer contributed powerfully to the reformation in England. 'One day, an Englishman', says Thomas Becon, prebendary of Canterbury and chaplain to Archbishop Cranmer, 'having taken leave of his mother and friends, travelled into Derbyshire, and from thence to the Peak, a marvellous barren country', and where there was then 'neither learning nor yet no spark of godliness.' Coming into a little village named Alsop in the Dale, he chanced upon a certain gentleman also named Alsop, lord of that village, a man not only ancient in years, but also ripe in the knowledge of Christ's doctrine. After they had taken 'a sufficient repast', the gentleman showed his guest certain books which he called his *jewels* and *principal treasures:* these were the New Testament and some books of Fryth's. In these godly treatises this ancient gentleman occupied himself among his rocks and mountains both diligently and virtuously. 'He did not only love the gospel', adds Cranmer's chaplain, 'he *lived it also.*'[1]

Fryth's writings were not destined to be read always with the same avidity: the truth they contain is, however, good for all times. The books of the apostles and of the reformers which that gentleman of Alsop read in the sixteenth century are better calculated to bring joy and peace to the soul than the light works read with such avidity in the modern world.

---

[1] Becon, *The Jewel of Joy* (Parker Society), p. 420.

CHAPTER TWENTY

The Isolation of England

(1533)

W hen Fryth was consigned to the flames, Anne Boleyn had been seated a month on the throne of England. The salvoes of artillery which had saluted the new queen had re-echoed all over Europe. There could be no more doubt: the Earl of Wiltshire's daughter, radiant with grace and beauty, wore the Tudor crown; everyone, especially the imperial family, must bear the consequences of the act. One day Sir John Hacket, English envoy at Brussels, arrived at court just as Mary of Hungary, regent of the Low Countries, was about to mount her horse. 'Have you any news from England?' she asked him in French. – 'None', he replied. Mary gave him a look of surprise, and added: 'Then I have, and not over-good, methinks.' She then told him of the king's marriage, and Hacket rejoined with an unembarrassed air: 'Madam, I know not if it has taken place, but everybody who considers it coolly and without family prejudice will agree that it is a lawful and a conscientious marriage.' Mary, who was niece of the unhappy Catherine, replied: 'Mr Ambassador, God knows I wish all may go well; but I do not know how the emperor and the king my brother will take it, for it touches them as well as me.' – 'I think I may be certain', returned Sir John, 'that they will take it in good part.' – 'That I do not know, Mr Ambassador', said the regent, who doubted it much; and then, mounting her horse, she rode out for the chase.

Charles V was exasperated: he immediately pressed the pope to intervene, and on 12 May Clement cited the king to appear at Rome. The pontiff was greatly embarrassed: having a particular liking for Benet, Henry's agent, he took him aside, and said to him privately: 'It is an affair of such importance that there has been none like it for many years. I fear to kindle a fire that neither pope nor emperor will be able to quench.' And then he added unaffectedly: 'Besides, I cannot pronounce the king's excommunication before the emperor has an army ready to constrain him.' Henry being told of this *aside* made answer: 'Having the justice of our cause for us, with the entire consent of our nobility, commons, and subjects, we do not care for what the pope may do.' Accordingly, he appealed from the pope to a general council.

The pope was now more embarrassed than ever: 'I cannot stand still and do nothing', he said. On 12 July he revoked all the English proceedings and excommunicated the king, but suspended the effects of his sentence until the end of September. 'I hope', said Henry contemptuously, 'that before then the pope will understand his folly.'

He reckoned on Francis I to help him to understand it; but that prince was about to receive the pope's niece into his family. The King of England, who had already against him the Netherlands, the Empire, Rome, and Spain, saw France also slipping from him. He was isolated in Europe, and that became a serious matter. Agitated and indignant, he came to an extraordinary resolution, namely, to turn to the disciples and friends of that very Luther whom he had formerly so disdainfully treated.

Stephen Vaughan and Christopher Mann were despatched, the former to Saxony, the other to Bavaria. Vaughan reached Weimar on 1 September, where he had to wait five days for the Elector of Saxony, who was away hunting. On 5 September he had an audience of the prince, and spoke to him first in French and then in Latin. Seeing that the elector, who spoke neither French, English, nor Latin, answered him only with nods, he begged the chancellor to be his interpreter. A written answer was sent to Vaughan at seven in the evening: the Elector of Saxony turned his back on the powerful King of England. He was unworthy, he said, to have at his court ambassadors from His Royal Majesty; and besides, the emperor, who was his only master, might be displeased. Vaughan's annoyance was extreme. 'Strange rudeness!' he exclaimed. 'A more uncourteous refusal has never been made to such a gracious proposition. And to my greater misfortune, it is the first mission of this kind

with which I have ever been entrusted.' He left Weimar, determined not
to deliver his credentials either to the Landgrave of Hesse or to the Duke
of Lauenberg, whom he was instructed to visit: he did not wish to run
the chance of receiving fresh affronts.

A strange lot was that of the King of England, the pope excommunicating him, and the heretics desiring to have nothing to do with him! No
more allies, no more friends! Be it so: if the nation and the monarch are
agreed, what is there to fear? Besides, at the very moment this affront was
offered him, his joy was at its height: the hope of soon possessing that
heir, for whom he had longed so many years, quite transported him. He
ordered an official letter to be prepared announcing the birth of a prince,
'to the great joy of the king', it ran, 'and of all his loving subjects'. Only
the date of the letter was left blank.

On 7 September, two days after the elector's refusal, Anne, then
residing in the palace at Greenwich, gave birth to a fine well-formed
child, reminding the gossips of the features of both parents; but alas!
it was a girl. Henry, agitated by two strong affections, love for Anne
and desire for a son, had been kept in great anxiety during the time of
labour. When he was told that the child was a girl, the love he bore for
the mother prevailed, and though disappointed in his fondest wishes, he
received the babe with joy. But the famous letter announcing the birth of
a prince ... what must be done with it now? Henry ordered the queen's
secretary to add an *s* to the word *prince,* and despatched the circular
without making any change in the expression of his satisfaction. The
christening was celebrated with great pomp; two hundred torches were
carried before the princess, a fit emblem of the light which her reign
would shed abroad. The child was named Elizabeth, and Henry declared
her his successor in case he should have no male offspring. In London
the excitement was great: *Te Deums,* bells, and music filled the air. The
adepts of judicial astrology declared that the stars announced a glorious
future. A bright star was indeed rising over England; and the English
people, throwing off the yoke of Rome, were about to start on a career
of freedom, morality, and greatness. Elizabeth was not destined to shine
by the amiability which distinguished her mother, and the restrictions
she placed upon liberty tend rather to remind us of her father. Yet while

on the Continent kings were trampling under foot the independence of their subjects, the English people, under Anne Boleyn's daughter, were to develop themselves, to flourish in letters and in arts, to extend navigation and commerce, to reform abuses, to exercise their liberties, to watch energetically over the public good, and to set up the torch of the gospel of Christ.

The King of France, very adverse to England's becoming independent of Rome, at last prevailed upon Henry to send two English agents (Gardiner and Bryan) to Marseilles. 'You will keep your eyes open', said Henry VIII to them, 'and lend an attentive ear, but you will keep your mouths shut.' The English envoys, being invited to a conference with Pope Clement and Francis I, and solicited by those great personages to speak, declared that they had no powers. 'Why then were you sent?' exclaimed the king, unable to conceal his vexation. The ambassadors only answered with a smile. Francis, who meant to uphold the authority of the pope in France, was unwilling that England should be free. Accordingly he took the ambassadors aside, and prayed them to enter immediately on business with the pontiff. 'We are not here for His Holiness', dryly answered Gardiner, 'or to negotiate anything with him, but only to do what the King of England commands us.' The tricks of the papacy had ruined it in the minds of the English people. Francis I, displeased at Gardiner's silence and irritated by his stiffness, intimated to the King of England that he would be pleased to see 'better instruments' sent. Henry did send another instrument to Marseilles, but he took care to choose one sharper still.

Edmund Bonner, late chaplain to Wolsey, and future Bishop of London, was a clever, active man, but ambitious, coarse, and rude, wanting in delicacy and consideration towards those with whom he had to deal, violent, and, as he showed himself later to the Protestants, a cruel persecutor. For some time he had got into Cromwell's good graces, and as the wind was against popery, Bonner was against the pope. Henry gave him his appeal to a general council, and charged him to present it to Clement VII: it was the 'bill of divorcement' between the pope and England. Bonner, proud of being the bearer of so important a message, arrived at Marseilles, firmly resolved to give Henry a proof of his zeal.

If Luther had burnt the pope's bull at Wittenberg, Bonner would do as much; but while Luther had acted as a free man, Bonner was only a slave, pushing to fanaticism his submission to the orders of his despotic master.

Gardiner was astounded when he heard of Bonner's arrival. What a humiliation for him! He hung his head, 'making a plaicemouth with his lip' (says Foxe), and then lifted up his eyes and hands, as if cursing the day and hour when Bonner appeared. Never were two men more discordant to one another. Gardiner could not believe the news. A scheme contrived without him! A bishop to see one of his inferiors charged with a mission more important than his own! Bonner having paid him a visit, Gardiner affected great coldness, and brought forward every reason calculated to dissuade him from executing his commission. – 'But I have a letter from the king', answered Bonner, 'sealed with his seal, and dated from Windsor: here it is.' And he took from his satchel the letter in which Henry VIII intimated that he had appealed from the sentence of the pope recently delivered against him. 'Good', answered Gardiner, and taking the letter he read: 'Our good pleasure is that if you deem it *good* and *serviceable* [Gardiner dwelt upon those two words] you will give the pope notice of the said appeal, according to the forms required by law; if not, you will acquaint us with your opinion in that respect.' – 'That is clear', said Gardiner; 'you should advise the king to abstain, for that notice just now will be neither good nor serviceable.' – 'And I say that it is both', rejoined Bonner.

One circumstance brought the two Englishmen into harmony, at least for a time. Catherine de Medici, the pope's niece, had been married to the son of Francis I, and Clement made four French prelates cardinals. But not one Englishman, not even Gardiner! That changed the question: there could be no more doubt. Francis is sacrificing Henry to the pope, and the pope insults England. Gardiner himself desired Bonner to give the pontiff notice of the appeal, and the English envoy, fearing refusal if he asked for an audience of Clement, determined to overleap the usual formalities, and take the place by assault.

On 7 November, Bonner, accompanied by Penniston, a gentleman who had brought him the king's last orders, went early to the pontifical palace, preparing to let fall from the folds of his mantle war between England and the papacy. As he was not expected, the pontifical officers stopped him at the door; but the Englishman forced his way in, and entered a hall through which the pope must pass on his way to the consistory.

Ere long the pontiff appeared, wearing his stole, and walking between the cardinals of Lorraine and Medicis, his train following behind. His eyes, which were of remarkable quickness, immediately fell upon the distant Bonner, and as he advanced he did not take them off the stranger, as if astonished and uneasy at seeing him. At length he stopped in the middle of the hall, and Bonner, approaching the datary, said to him: 'Be pleased to inform His Holiness that I desire to speak to him.' The officer refusing, the intrepid Bonner made as if he would go towards the pope. Clement, wishing to know the meaning of these indiscreet proceedings, bade the cardinals stand aside, took off the stole, and going to a window recess, called Bonner to him. The latter, without any formality, informed the pope that the King of England appealed from his decision to a general council, and that he (Bonner), His Majesty's envoy, was prepared to hand him the authentic documents of the said appeal, taking them (as he spoke) from his portfolio. Clement, who expected nothing like this, was greatly surprised: 'it was a terrible breakfast for him', says a contemporary document. Not knowing what to answer, he shrugged his shoulders, 'after the Italian fashion'; and at last, recovering himself a little, he told Bonner that he was going to the consistory, and desired him to return in the afternoon. Then beckoning the cardinals, he left the hall.

Henry's envoy was punctual to the appointment, but had to wait for an hour and a half, His Holiness being engaged in giving audience. At length he and Penniston were conducted to the pope's chamber. Clement fixed his eyes on the latter, and Bonner having introduced him, the pope remarked with a mistrustful air: 'It is well, but I also must have some members of my council'; and he ordered Simonetta, Capisuchi, and the datary to be sent for. While awaiting their arrival, Clement leant at the window, and appeared absorbed in thought. At last, unable to contain himself any longer, he exclaimed: 'I am greatly surprised that

His Majesty should behave as he does towards me.' The intrepid Bonner replied: 'His Majesty is not less surprised that Your Holiness, who has received so many services from him, repays him with ingratitude.' Clement started, but restrained himself on seeing the datary enter, and ordered that officer to read the appeal which Bonner had just delivered to him.

The datary began: 'Considering that we have endured from the pope many wrongs and injuries [*gravaminibus et injuriis*]', ... Clasping his hands and nodding dissent, Clement exclaimed ironically: '*O questo è molto vero!*' meaning to say that it was false, remarks Bonner. The datary continued: 'Considering that His Most Holy Lordship strikes us with his spiritual sword, and wishes to separate us from the unity of the church; we, desiring to protect with a lawful shield the kingdom which God has given us, appeal by these presents, for ourselves and for all our subjects, to a holy universal council.'

At these words, the pope burst into a transport of passion, and the datary stopped. Clement's gestures and broken words, uttered with vehemence, showed the horror he entertained of a council. A council would set itself above the pope, a council might perhaps say that the Germans and the King of England were right.

The pope gave way to convulsive movements, folding and unfolding his handkerchief, which was always a sign of great anger in him. At last, as if to hide his passion, he said: 'Continue, I am listening.' When the datary had ended, the pope said coldly to his officers: 'It is well written!'

Then turning to Bonner he asked: 'Have you anything more to say to me?' Bonner was not in the humour to show the least consideration. A man of the north, he took a pleasure in displaying his roughness and inflexibility in the elegant, crafty, and corrupt society of Rome. He boldly repeated the protest, and delivered the king's 'provocation' to the pope, who broke out into fresh lamentations. 'Ha!' he exclaimed vehemently, 'His Majesty affects much respect for the church, but does not show the least to me.'... Just at this moment, one of his officers announced the King of France. Francis could not have arrived at a more seasonable moment. Clement rose and went to the door to meet him. The king respectfully took off his hat, and holding it in his hand made a low bow, after which he enquired what His Holiness was doing. 'These English gentlemen', said the pontiff, 'are here to notify me of certain provocations and appeals … and for other matters', he added, displaying much ill-humour. Francis sat down near the table at which the pope was seated; and turning their backs to Henry's envoy, who had retired into an adjoining room, they began a conversation in a low tone, which Bonner, notwithstanding all his efforts, could not hear.

That conversation possibly decided the separation between England and France. The king showed that he was offended at a course of proceeding which he characterized as unbecoming; and Clement learnt, to his immense satisfaction, that the English had not spoken to Francis about the council. 'If you will leave me and the emperor free to act against England', he said to the king, 'I will ensure you possession of the Duchy of Milan.' Bonner, who had not lost sight of the two speakers, remarked that at this moment the king and the pope 'laughed merrily together', and appeared to be the best friends in the world.

The king having withdrawn, Bonner again approached the pope, and the datary finished the reading. The Englishman had not been softened by the mysterious conversation and laughter of Clement and Francis: he was as rough and abrupt as the Frenchman had been smooth and amiable. It was long since the papacy had suffered such insults openly, and even the German reformation had not put it to such torture. The Cardinal de Medici, chief of the malcontents, who had come in, listened to Bonner, with head bent down and eyes fixed upon the floor: he was humiliated and indignant. 'This is a matter of great importance', said Clement; 'I will consult the consistory and let you know my answer.'

In the afternoon of Monday, 10 November, Bonner returned to the palace to learn the pope's pleasure: but there was a grand reception that day. The lords and ladies of the court of Francis I were presented to Clement, who did nothing for two hours but bless chaplets, bless the spectators, and put out his foot for the nobles and dames to kiss.

At last Bonner was introduced: *Domine Doctor, quid vultis?* [Sir Doctor, what do you want?]' said the pope. 'I desire the answer which Your Holiness promised me.' Clement, who had had time to recover himself, replied: 'A constitution of Pope Pius, my predecessor, condemns all appeals to a general council. I therefore reject His Majesty's appeal as unlawful.' The pope had pronounced these words with calmness and dignity, but an incident occurred to put him out of temper. Bonner, hurt at the little respect paid to his sovereign, bluntly informed the pope that the Archbishop of Canterbury – that Cranmer – desired also to appeal to a council. This was going too far: Clement, restraining himself no longer, rose, and approaching Henry's envoy, said to him: 'If you do not leave the room instantly, I will have you thrown into a caldron of molten lead.' – 'Truly', remarked Bonner, 'if the pope is a shepherd, he is, as the king my master says, a violent and cruel shepherd.' And not caring to take a leaden bath, he departed for Lyons. Such is the story told by the historian Burnet.

Clement was delighted not only at the departure, but still more at the conduct of Bonner: the insolence of the English envoy helped him wonderfully; and accordingly he made a great noise about it, complaining to everybody, and particularly to Francis. 'I am wearied, vexed, disgusted with all this', said that prince to his courtiers. 'What I do with great difficulty in a week for my good brother [Henry VIII], his own ministers undo in an hour.' Clement endeavoured in secret interviews to increase this discontent, and he succeeded. The mysterious understanding was apparent to everyone, and Vannes, the English agent, who never lost sight either of the pope or the king, informed Cromwell of the close union of their minds.

When Henry VIII learnt that the King of France was slipping from him, he was both irritated and alarmed. Abandoned by that prince, he saw the pope launching an interdict against his kingdom, the emperor invading England, and the people in insurrection. He had no repose by night or day: his anger against the pope continued to increase. Wishing to prevent at least the revolts which the partisans of the papacy might excite among his subjects, he dictated a strange proclamation to his secretary: 'Let no Englishman forget the most noble and loving prince of this realm', he said, 'who is most wrongfully judged by the great idol and most cruel enemy to Christ's religion, which calleth himself pope. Princes have two ways to attain right – the general council and the sword. Now the king, having appealed from the unlawful sentence of the Bishop of Rome to a general council lawfully congregated, the said usurper hath rejected the appeal, and is thus outlawed. By Holy Scripture, there is no more jurisdiction granted to the Bishop of Rome than to any other bishop. Henceforth honour him not as an idol, who is but a man usurping God's power and authority; and a man neither in life, learning, nor conversation like Christ's minister or disciple.'

Henry, having given vent to his irritation, bethought himself, and judged it more prudent not to publish the proclamation. But to the subjects of Henry it was becoming increasingly clear that between the English throne and the papacy there was a great gulf fixed, and there seemed good reason to think that it would yet grow wider and deeper.

Parliament Abolishes Papal Usurpations in England

(January to March 1534)

While the papacy was intriguing with France and the Empire, England was energetically working at the utter abolition of the Roman authority. 'One loud cry must be raised in England against the papacy', said Cromwell to the council. 'It is time that the question was laid before the people. Bishops, parsons, curates, priors, abbots, and preachers of the religious orders should all declare from their pulpits that the Bishop of Rome, styled the pope, is subordinate, like the rest of the bishops, to a general council, and that he has no more rights in this kingdom than any other foreign bishop.'

It was necessary to pursue the same course abroad. Henry resolved to send ambassadors to Poland, Hungary, Saxony, Bavaria, Pomerania, Prussia, Hesse, and other German states, to inform them that he was touched with the zeal they had shown in defence of the word of God and the extirpation of ancient errors, and to acquaint all men that he was himself 'utterly determined to reduce the pope's power to the just and lawful bounds of his mediocrity'.

He did not stop here. Keenly desiring to withdraw France from under the influence of Rome, he instructed his ambassadors to tell Francis I in his name and in the name of the people: 'We shall shortly be able to give unto the pope such a buffet as he never had before.' This was quite in Henry's style. 'Things are going at such a rate here', wrote the Duke of Norfolk to Montmorency, 'that the pope will soon lose the obedience of England; and other nations, perceiving the great fruits, advantage, and profit that will result from it, will also separate from Rome.'

All this was serious: there was some chance that Norfolk's prophecy would be fulfilled. The pontiff could think of nothing else, and began to believe that the idea of a council was not so unreasonable after all, since the place and time of meeting and mode of proceeding would lead to endless discussions; and if the meeting ever took place, he would thus be relieved of a responsibility which became more oppressive to him every day. He therefore bade Henry VIII be informed that he agreed to call a general council. But events had not stood still: the position was not the same. 'It is no longer necessary', the king answered coldly. In his opinion, the Church of England was sufficient of herself, and could do without the Church of Rome.

The King of France, in the interests of the pope, immediately resumed his part of mediator. Du Bellay, his ambassador at Rome, made indefatigable efforts to inspire the consistory with an opinion favourable to Henry VIII. According to that diplomatist, the King of England was ready to re-establish friendly relations with Clement VII, and it was Parliament alone that desired to break with the papacy for ever: it was the people who wished for reform, it was the king who opposed it. 'Make your choice', he exclaimed with eloquence. 'All that the king desires is peace with Rome; all that the commonalty demands is war. With whom will you go – with your enemies or with your friend?' Du Bellay's assertions, though strange, were based upon a truth that cannot be denied. It was the best of the people who wanted Protestantism in England, and not the king.

The court of Rome felt that the last hour had come, and determined to despatch to London the papers necessary to reconcile Henry. It was believed on the Continent that the King of England was going to gain his cause at last, and people ascribed it to the ascendancy of French policy at Rome since the marriage of Catherine de Medici with Henry of Orleans. But the more the French triumphed, the more indignant became the imperialists. To no purpose did the pope say to them: 'You do not understand the state of affairs: the thing is done. ... The King of England is married to Anne Boleyn. If I annulled the marriage, who would undertake to execute my sentence?' – 'Who?' exclaimed the ambassadors of Charles V, 'Who? ... The emperor.' The weak pontiff knew not which way to turn: he had but one hope left – if Henry VIII were to re-establish Roman Catholicism in his kingdom, a fact so important would silence Charles V.

This fact was not to be feared: a movement had begun in the minds of the people of England which it was no longer possible to stop. While many pious souls received the word of God in their hearts, the king and the most enlightened part of the nation were agreed to put an end to the intolerable usurpations of the Roman pontiff. 'We have looked in the Holy Scriptures for the rights of the papacy', said the members of the Commons House of Parliament, 'but instead of finding therein the institution of popes, we have found that of kings and, according to God's commandments, the priests ought to be subject to them as much as the laity.' – 'We have reflected upon the wants of the realm', said the royal council, 'and have come to the conclusion that the nation ought to form one body; that one body can have but one head, and that head must be the king.' The Parliament which met in January 1534 was to give the death-blow to the supremacy of the pope.

This blow came strictly neither from Henry nor from Cranmer, but from Thomas Cromwell. Without possessing Cranmer's lively faith, Cromwell desired that the preachers should open the word of God and preach it 'with pure sincereness' before the people, and he afterwards procured for every Englishman the right to read it. Being pre-eminently a statesman of sure judgment and energetic action, he was in advance of his generation; and it was his fate, like those generals who march boldly at the head of the army, to procure victory to the cause for which he fought; but, persecuted by the traitors concealed among his soldiers, to be sacrificed by the prince he had served, and to meet a tragical death before the hour of his triumph.

The commons, wishing to put an end to the persecutions practised by the clergy against the evangelical Christians, summoned – it was a thing unprecedented – the lord Bishop of London to appear at their bar to answer the complaint made against him by Thomas Philips, one of the disciples of the reformation. The latter had been lying in prison three years under a charge of heresy. The Parliament, unwilling that a bishop should be able at his own fancy to transform one of His

Majesty's subjects into a heretic, brought in a bill for the repression of doctrines condemned by the church. They declared that, the authority of the Bishop of Rome being opposed to Holy Scripture and the laws of the realm, the words and acts that were contrary to the decisions of the pontiff could not be regarded as heresies. Then turning to the particular case which had given rise to the grievance, Parliament declared Philips innocent and discharged him from prison.

After having thus upheld the cause of religious liberty, the commons proceeded to the definitive abolition of the privileges which the bishops of Rome had successively usurped to the great detriment of both church and people. They restored to England the rights of which Rome had despoiled her. They prohibited all appeals to the pope, of what kind so ever they might be, and substituted for them an appeal to the king in chancery. They voted that the election of bishops did not concern the court of Rome, but belonged to the chief ecclesiastical body in the diocese, to the chapter, at least in appearance; for it really appertained to the crown, the king designating the person whom the chapter was to elect. This strange constitution was abolished under Edward VI, when the nomination of the bishops was conferred purely and simply on the king. If this was not better, it was at least more sincere; but the singular *congé d'élire*[1] was restored under Elizabeth.

At the same time new and loud complaints of the Romish exactions were heard in Parliament. 'For centuries the Roman bishops have been deceiving us', said the eloquent speakers, 'making us believe that they have the power of dispensing with everything, even with God's commandments. We send to Rome the treasures of England, and Rome sends us back in return ... a piece of paper. The monster which has fattened on the substance of our people bears a hundred different names. They call it reliefs, dues, pensions, provisions, procurations, delegation, rescript, appeal, abolition, rehabilitation, relaxation of canonical penalties, licences, Peter's pence, and many other names besides. And after having thus caught our money by all sorts of tricks, the Romans laugh at us in their sleeves.' Parliament forbade all Englishmen, even the king himself, to apply to Rome for any dispensation or delegation

[1] [leave to elect.]

whatsoever, and ordered them, in case of need, to have recourse to the Archbishop of Canterbury. Then, immediately putting these principles into practice, they declared the king's marriage with Catherine to be null, for 'no man has power to dispense with God's laws', and ratified the marriage between Henry and Anne, proclaiming their children heirs to the crown. At the same time, wishing England to become entirely English, they deprived two Italians, Campeggio and Ghinucci, of the sees of Salisbury and Worcester, which they held.

It was during the month of March, 1534 – an important date for England – that the main branches of the tree of popery were thus lopped off one after another. The trunk indeed remained, although stripped; but yet a few months, and that too was to strew the earth with its fall. Still the commons showed a certain degree of consideration. When Clement had threatened the king with excommunication, he had given him three months' grace; England, desiring to return his politeness, informed the pope that he might receive some compensation. At the same time she made an important declaration: 'We do not separate from the Christian church', said the commons, 'but merely from the usurped authority of the pope of Rome; and we preserve the catholic faith, as *it is set forth in the Holy Scriptures.*' All these reforms were effected with great unanimity, at least in appearance. The bishops, even the most scholastic, such as Stokesley of London, Tunstall of Durham, Gardiner of Winchester, and Rowland Lee of Coventry, declared the Roman papacy to be of human invention, and that the pope was, in regard to them, only a *bishop,* a *brother,* as his predecessors had been to the bishops of antiquity. Every Sunday during the session of Parliament a prelate preached at St Paul's Cross 'that the pope was not the head of the church', and all the people said Amen.

Meanwhile Du Bellay, the French ambassador at Rome, was waiting for the act by which the King of England was to bind himself once more to the pope – an act which Francis I still gave him reason to expect. Every morning he fancied it would arrive, and every evening his expectations were disappointed. He called upon the English envoys, and afterwards at the Roman chancery, to hear if there was any news; but everywhere the answer was the same – nothing.

The term fixed by Clement VII having elapsed, he summoned the consistory for Monday 23 March. Du Bellay attended it, still hoping to prevent anything being done that might separate England from the papacy. The cardinals represented to him, that as the submission of Henry VIII had not arrived, nothing remained but for the pope to fulminate the sentence. 'Do you not know', exclaimed Du Bellay in alarm, 'that the courier charged with that prince's despatches has seas to cross, and the winds may be contrary? The King of England waited your decision for six years, and cannot you wait six days?' 'Delay is quite useless', said a cardinal of the imperial faction; 'we know what is taking place in England. Instead of thinking of reparation, the king is widening the schism every day. He goes so far as to permit the representation of dramas at his court, in which the holy conclave, and some of your most illustrious selves in particular, are held up to ridicule.' The last blow, although a heavy one, was unnecessary. The priests could no longer contain their vexation; the rebellious prince must be punished. Nineteen out of twenty-two cardinals voted against Henry VIII; the remaining three only asked for further enquiry. Clement could not conceal his surprise and annoyance. To no purpose did he demand another meeting, in conformity with the custom which requires two, and even three, consultations: overwhelmed by an imposing and unexpected majority, he gave way.

Simonetta then handed him the sentence, which the unhappy pope took and read with the voice of a criminal rather than of a judge. 'Having invoked the name of Christ, and sitting on the throne of justice, we decree that the marriage between Catherine of Aragon and Henry King of England was and is valid and canonical; that the said King Henry is bound to cohabit with the said queen; to pay her royal honours; and that he must be constrained to discharge these duties.' After pronouncing these words, the pontiff, alarmed at the bold act he had just performed, turned to the envoys of Charles V and said to them: 'I have done my duty; it is now for the emperor to do his, and to carry the sentence into execution.' 'The emperor will not hold back', answered the ambassadors; but the thing was not so easily done as said.

Thus the great affair was ended; the King of England was condemned. It was dark when the pope quitted the consistory; the news so long expected spread immediately through the city; the emperor's partisans, transported with joy, lit bonfires in all the open places, and cannons fired repeated salvoes. Bands of Ghibelines paraded the streets, shouting, *Imperio e Espagna* (the Empire and Spain). The whole city was in commotion. The pope's disquietude was still further increased by these demonstrations. 'He is tormented', wrote Du Bellay to his master. Clement spent the whole night in conversation with his theologians. 'What must be done? England is lost to us. How can I avert the king's anger?' Clement VII never recovered from this blow: the thought that under his pontificate Rome lost England made him shudder. The slightest mention of it renewed his anguish, and sorrow soon brought him to the tomb.

Yet he did not know all. The evil with which Rome was threatened was greater than he had imagined. If in this matter there had been nothing more than the decision of a prince discontented with the court of Rome, a contrary decision of one of his successors might again place England under the dominion of the pontiffs; and these would be sure to spare no pains to recover the good graces of the English kings. But in despite of Henry VIII, a pure doctrine, similar to that of the apostolic times, was spreading over the different parts of the nation; a doctrine which was not only to wrest England from the pope, but to establish in that island a true Christianity – a vast evangelical propaganda which should ultimately plant the standard of God's word even at the ends of the world. The empire of Christendom was thus to be taken from a church led astray by pride, and which bade mankind unite with it that they might be saved; and to be given to those who taught that, according to the divine declarations, none could be saved except by uniting with Jesus Christ.

BOOK TWO

England Breaks with Rome

Henry VIII

CHAPTER ONE

A Conspiracy against the Reformation

(March and April 1534)

T he Parliament of 1534 had greatly advanced the cause of the reformation. The voices of the most enlightened men of England
had been heard in it with still greater power than in 1529;
and accordingly an historian,[1] referring to the meeting of 1534, speaks
of it as 'that great session'. These enlightened men, however, formed
but a small minority, and among them were many who, from a want
of independence, never voted on the side of liberty but when the king
authorized them. The epoch was a critical one for the nation. It might
as easily fall back to the pope as advance towards the gospel. Hesitating
between the Middle Ages and modern times, it had to choose either
life or death. Would it make a vigorous effort and reach those bracing
heights, like travellers scaling the rugged sides of the Alps? England
appeared too weak for so daring a flight. The mass of the people seemed
chained by time-worn prejudices to the errors and practices of Rome.
The king no doubt had political views which raised him above his age;
but, a slave to his passions, and the docile disciple of the old ways, he
detested a real reformation and real liberty. The clergy were superstitious,
selfish, and excitable; and the advisers of the Crown knew no other rule
than the will of their master. By none of these powers, therefore, could
a transformation be accomplished. The safety of England came from
that sovereign hand, that mysterious power, which was already stirring
the Western world. The nation began to feel its energetic impulse. A
strange breeze seemed to be filling the sails and driving the bark of the
state towards the harbour, notwithstanding the numerous shoals that lay
around it.

[1] Bishop Burnet.

173

The thought which at that time mainly engrossed the minds of the most intelligent men of England – men like Cranmer, Cromwell, and their friends – was the necessity of throwing off the papal authority. They believed that it was necessary to root out the foreign and unwholesome weed, which had spread over the soil of Britain, and tear it up so thoroughly that it could never grow again. Parliament had declared that all the powers exercised by the Bishop of Rome in England must cease and be transferred to the Crown; and that no one, not even the king, should apply to Rome for any dispensation whatsoever. A prelate had preached every Sunday at St Paul's Cross that the pope was not the head of the church. On the other hand, the pontiff, who was reckoning on Henry's promised explanations and satisfactory propositions, seeing that the messenger whom he expected from London did not arrive, had solemnly condemned that prince on 23 March 1534. But immediately startled at his own boldness, Clement asked himself with agony how he could repair this wrong and appease the king. He saw it was impossible, and in the bitterness of his heart exclaimed: 'Alas! England is lost to us!'

Two days after the famous consistory in which Henry's condemnation had been pronounced, an English courier entered Rome, still in a state of agitation and trouble, and went straight to the papal palace. 'What is his business?' people said; 'and what can give him such boldness?' The Englishman was bringing to the ministers of the Vatican the long-expected act by which the King of England declared himself prepared to enter into an arrangement with the pope, provided the cardinals of the imperial faction were excluded. The messenger at the same time announced that Sir Edward Carne and William Revett, two envoys from Henry VIII, would soon arrive to conclude the business. Cardinal Farnese, who erelong succeeded Clement under the title of Paul III, and the more moderate prelates of the sacred college waited upon the pope at once, and begged him to summon the consistory without delay. It was just what Clement desired; but the imperialists, more furious than ever, insisted on the confirmation of the sentence condemning Henry, and spared no means to ensure success. Monks went about repeating certain stories which their English brethren sent them, and which they furthermore exaggerated. They asserted that the English people were about to rise in a body against the king and throw themselves at the feet of the Holy Father. The pope ratified the sentence, and the consistory, taking one more step, urged the emperor to carry it out.

It has been said that a delay of two days was the cause of the reformation of England. That is a mistake. The reformation came from the Holy Scriptures, from God, from his mighty grace, and not from princes, their passions, or delays. Even had the pontifical court at last conceded to Henry the divorce he asked for, that prince would probably not have renounced the rights he had acquired, and which made him sole and true monarch of England. Had he done so, it is doubtful whether he was strong enough to check the reformation. The people were in motion, Christian truth had reappeared among them: neither pontifical agitations nor concessions could stop the rapid current that was carrying them to the pure and living waters of the gospel.

However, Sir Edward Carne and William Revett, Henry's envoys, arrived in Italy full of hope, and pledged themselves (as they wrote to the king) to reconcile England and the papacy 'in conformity to His Highness' purpose'. Having learnt on reaching Bologna that Du Bellay, the Bishop of Paris, who was instructed to support them, was in that city, they hurried to him to learn the exact state of affairs. The bishop was one of those enlightened Catholics who believed that the extreme papal party was exposing the papacy to great danger, and who would have prevented schism in the church by giving some satisfaction to Germany and England. Hence the envoys from Henry VIII found the prelate dejected and embarrassed. 'All is over', he told them. 'The pope has pronounced sentence against His Majesty.' Carne and Revett were thunder-struck; the burden was too heavy for them. 'All our hopes have vanished in a moment', they said. Du Bellay assured them that he had spared no pains likely to prevent so precipitate and imprudent an act on the part of a pope. 'But the imperialists', he said, 'moved heaven and earth, and constrained Clement VII to deliver a sentence in opposition to his own convictions.' The ambassador of Francis I added that there was still one gleam of hope. 'Raincé, secretary to the French embassy at Rome, with an oath, wished himself at perdition', said Du Bellay rather coarsely, 'if our Holy Father does not patch up all that has been damaged.' The Englishmen desired to go to the pope forthwith, in order to prevent the execution of the sentence. 'Do nothing of the kind', said the French bishop. 'Do not go to Rome on any pretext whatsoever.'

Perhaps Du Bellay wanted first to know what his master thought of the matter. Carne, undecided what to do, despatched a messenger to Henry VIII to ask for orders; and then, ten days later, wishing to do something, he appealed from the Bishop of Rome ill-informed to the Bishop of Rome better-informed.

When the King of England received his ambassador's message, he could hardly restrain his anger. At the very moment when he had made a concession which appeared to him the height of condescension, Rome treated him with contempt and sacrificed him to Charles V. Even the nation was aroused. The pope, it was said, commissions a foreign prince to execute his decrees; soldiers, newly raised in Germany, and brimful of insults and threats, are preparing to land in England. National pride arrayed the people on the king's side. Henry no longer hesitated; his offended honour demanded reparation: a complete rupture alone could satisfy it. Many writers supported him. 'The pope', said Dr Sampson, Dean of the Chapel Royal, 'has no more power in England than the Archbishop of Canterbury in Rome. It was only by tacit consent that the pope crept into the kingdom, but we intend to drive him out now by express consent.' The two Houses of Parliament were almost unanimously of that opinion. The Privy Council proposed to call upon the lord mayor to see that anti-Romish doctrines were taught in every house in London. Lastly, the people showed their opposition after their fashion, indulging in games and masquerades, in which a cardinal at one time, the pope at another, were represented. To call a man a 'papist' or 'a priest of the pope' was one of the greatest insults. Even the clergy declared against Rome. On 31 March the lower house of convocation discussed whether the Roman pontiff had in England, according to Scripture, a higher jurisdiction than any other foreign bishop. Thirty-three voted in the negative, only four in the affirmative. The king immediately forwarded the same question to all the ecclesiastical corporations of the kingdom. The friends of the gospel were filled with joy. The pope had made a great mistake when, imitating the style of ancient Rome, he had hurled the bolts of the Vatican, as Jupiter had in days of old launched the thunders of the Capitol. A great revolution seemed to be working itself out unopposed in this island, so long the slave of the Roman pontiffs. There was just at this time nothing to be feared from without: Charles V was overwhelmed with business; the King of Scotland was on better terms with his uncle of England, and Francis I was preparing for a friendly interview with Henry VIII. And yet the danger had never been greater; but the mine was discovered in March 1534, before the match could be applied to it.

A dangerous political and clerical conspiracy had been for some time silently organizing in the monasteries. It was possible, no doubt, to find here and there in the cloisters monks who were learned, pious, and loyal; but the greater number were ignorant and fanatical, and terribly alarmed at the dangers which threatened their order. Their arrogance, grossness, and loose manners irritated the most enlightened part of the nation; their wealth, endowments, and luxury aroused the envy of the nobility. A religious and social transformation was taking place at this memorable epoch, and the monks foresaw that they would be the first victims of the revolution. Accordingly they were resolved to fight to the uttermost for their altars and homes. But who was to take the first step in the perilous enterprise – who to give the signal?

As in the days of the Maid of Orleans, it was a young woman who grasped the trumpet and sounded the charge. But if the first was a heroine, the other was an ecstatic – nay, a fanatic.

There lived in the village of Aldington in Kent a young woman of singular appearance. Although of an age which is usually distinguished by a fresh and clear complexion, her face was sallow and her eyes haggard. All of a sudden she would be seized with a trembling of the whole body; she lost the use of her limbs and of her understanding, uttered strange and incoherent phrases, and fell at last stiff and lifeless to the ground. She was, moreover, exemplary in her conduct. The people declared her state to be miraculous, and Richard Masters, the rector of the parish, a cunning and grasping priest, noticing these epileptic attacks, resolved to take advantage of them to acquire money and reputation. He suggested to the poor sufferer that the extraordinary words she uttered proceeded from the inspiration of heaven, and declared that she would be guilty if she kept secret this wonderful work of God. An official of Canterbury, Dr Edward Bocking, joined the priest with the intention of turning the girl's disease to the profit of the Romish party. They represented to Elizabeth Barton – such was the name of the Kentish maiden – that the cause of religion was exposed to great danger in England; that it was intended to turn out the monks and priests; but that God, whose hand defends his church by the humblest instruments, had raised her up in these inauspicious days to uphold that holy ark, which king, ministers, and Parliament desired to throw down. Such language pleased the girl: on the faith of the priests, she regarded her attacks as divine transports; a feeling of pride came over her; she accepted the part assigned her. On a sudden her imagination kindled; she announced that she had held communications with saints and angels, even with Satan himself. Was this sheer imposture or enthusiasm? There was, perhaps, a little of both; but, in her eyes, the end justified the means. When speaking, she affected strange turns, unintelligible figures, poetical language, and clothed her visions in simple rhymes, which made the educated smile, but helped to circulate her oracles among the people. Erelong she set herself unscrupulously above the truth, and, inspired by a feverish energy, did not fear to excite the people to bloodshed.

There was somewhere out in the fields, in one part of the parish, a wretched old chapel that had been long deserted, and where a coarse image of the Virgin still remained. Masters determined to make it the scene of a lucrative pilgrimage. He suggested the notion to Elizabeth Barton, and erelong she gave out that the Virgin would cure her of her disorder in that holy consecrated edifice. She was carried thither with a certain pomp, and placed devoutly before the image. Then a crisis came upon her. Her tongue hung out of her mouth, her eyes seemed starting from their sockets, and a hoarse sepulchral voice was heard speaking of the terrors of hell; and then, by a singular transformation, a sweet and insinuating voice described the joys of paradise.[1] At last the ecstasy ended, Elizabeth came to herself, declared that she was perfectly cured,

---

[1] 'A voice speaking within her belly.' – Cranmer, *Letters and Remains* (Parker Society), p. 273.

and announced that God had ordered her to become a nun and to take Dr Bocking as her confessor. The prophecy of the Kentish maiden touching her own disease being thus verified, her reputation increased.

Elizabeth Barton's accomplices imagined that the new prophetess required a wider stage than the fields of Aldington, and hoped that, once established in the ecclesiastical metropolis of England, she would see her followers increase throughout the kingdom. Immediately after her cure, the ventriloquist entered the convent of St Sepulchre at Canterbury, to which Dr Bocking belonged. Once in this primatial city, her oracles and her miracles were multiplied. Sometimes in the middle of the night, the door of her cell opened miraculously: it was a call from God, inviting her to the chapel to converse with him. Sometimes a letter in golden characters was brought to her by an angel from heaven. The monks kept a record of these wonders, these oracles; and, selecting some of them, Masters laid the miraculous collection, this bible of the fanatics, before Archbishop Warham. The prelate, who appeared to believe in the nun's inspiration, presented the document to the king, who handed it to Sir Thomas More, and ordered the words of the Kentish maiden to be carefully taken down and communicated to him. In this Henry VIII showed probably more curiosity and distrust than credulity.

Elizabeth and her advisers were deceived, and thought they might enter into a new phase, in which they hoped to reap the reward of their imposture. The Aldington girl passed from a purely religious to a political mission. This is what her advisers were aiming at. All, and especially Dr Bocking, who contemplated restoring the authority of the papacy – even were it necessary to their end to take the king's life – began to denounce in her presence Henry's tolerance of heresy and the new marriage he desired to contract. Elizabeth eagerly joined this factious opposition. 'If Henry marries Anne Boleyn', she told Bishop Fisher, 'in seven months' time there will be no king in England.' The circle of her influence at once grew wider. The Romish party united with her. Abell, Queen Catherine's agent, entered into the conspiracy; twice Elizabeth Barton appeared before the pope's legates; Fisher supported her, and Sir Thomas More, one of the most cultivated men of his day, though at first little impressed in her favour, admitted afterwards the truth of some of her foolish and guilty revelations.

One thing was yet wanting, and that was very essential in the eyes of the supporters of the movement: Elizabeth must appear before Henry VIII as Elijah appeared before Ahab: they expected great results from such an interview. At length they obtained permission, and the Kentish maiden prepared herself for it by exercises which over-excited her. When brought into the presence of the prince, she was at first silent and motionless, but in a moment her eyes brightened and seemed to flash fire; her mouth was drawn aside and stretched, while from her trembling lips there fell a string of incoherent phrases. 'Satan is tormenting me for the sins of my people', she exclaimed, 'but our blessed Lady shall deliver me by her mighty hand. ... O times! O manners! ... Abominable heresies, impious innovations! ... King of England, beware that you touch not the power of the Holy Father. ... Root out the new doctrines. ... Burn all over your kingdom the New Testament in the vulgar tongue. Henry, forsake Anne Boleyn and take back your wife Catherine. ... If you neglect these things, you shall not be king longer than a month, and in God's eyes you will not be so even for an hour. You shall die the death of a villain, and Mary, the daughter of Catherine, shall wear your crown.'

This noisy scene produced no effect on the king. Henry, though prompt to punish, would not reply to Elizabeth's nonsense, and was content to shrug his shoulders. But the fanatical young woman was not discouraged: if the king could not be converted, the people must be roused. She repeated her threats in the convents, castles, and villages of Kent, the theatre of her frequent excursions. She varied them according to circumstances. The king must fall: but at one time she announced it would be by the hands of his subjects; at another, of the priests; and at a third, by the judgment of God. One point alone was unchanged in her utterances: Henry Tudor must perish. Erelong, like a prophetess lifted above the ordinary ministers of God, she reprimanded even the sovereign pontiff himself. She thought him too timid, and, taking him to task, declared that if he did not bring Henry's plans to naught, 'the great stroke of God which then hung over his head' would inevitably fall upon him.[1]

This boldness added to the number of her partisans. Monks, nuns, and priests, knights, gentlemen, and scholars, were carried away by her.

[1] Cranmer, *Letters and Remains* (Parker Society), p. 273.

Young folks especially and men of no culture eagerly embraced this mad cause. There were also men of distinction who did not fear to become her defenders. Bishop Fisher was gained over: he believed himself certain of the young woman's piety. Being a man of melancholy temperament and mystic tendency, a lover of the marvellous, he thought that the soul of Elizabeth might well have a supernatural intercourse with the Infinite Being. He said in the House of Lords: 'How could I anticipate deceit in a nun, to whose holiness so many priests bore witness?' The Roman Catholics triumphed. A prophetess had risen up in England, like Deborah in Israel.

One eminent and large-hearted Catholic, Sir Thomas More, had however some doubts; and the monks who were Elizabeth's advisers set every engine at work to win him over. During the Christmas of 1532, Father Risby, a Franciscan of Canterbury, arrived at Chelsea to pass the night there. After supper, he said: 'What a holy woman this nun of Kent is! It is wonderful to see all that God is doing through her.' – 'I thank God for it', answered More coldly. – 'By her mediation she saved the cardinal's soul', added the monk. The conversation went no farther. Some time later a fresh attempt was made: Father Rich, a Franciscan of Richmond, came and told More the story of the letter written in letters of gold and brought by an angel. 'Well, Father', said the chancellor, 'I believe the nun of Kent to be a virtuous woman, and that God is working great things by her; but stories like that you have told me are not part of our *Credo*, and before repeating them, one should be very sure about them.' However, as the clergy generally countenanced Elizabeth, More could not bear the idea of forming a sect apart, and went to see the prophetess at Sion monastery. She told him a silly story of the devil turned into a bird. More was satisfied to give her a double ducat and commend himself to her prayers. The chancellor, like other noble intellects among the Catholics, was prepared to admit certain superstitions; but he would have had the nun keep in her religious sphere; he feared to see her touch upon politics. 'Do not speak of the affairs of princes', he said to her. 'The relations which the late Duke of Buckingham had with a holy monk were in great part the cause of his death.' More had been chancellor of England, and perhaps feared the duke's fate.

Elizabeth Barton did not profit by this lesson. She again declared that, according to the revelations from God, no one should deprive the Princess Mary of the rights she derived through her birth, and predicted her early accession. Father Goold immediately carried the news to Catherine. The nun and her advisers, who chided the pope only through their zeal for the papacy, had communications with the nuncio; they thought it necessary for him to join the conspiracy. They agreed upon the course to be adopted: at a given time, monks were to mingle with the people and excite a seditious movement. Elizabeth and her accomplices called together such as were to be the instruments of their criminal design. 'God has chosen you', said the nun to them, 'to restore the power of the Roman pontiff in England.' The monks prepared for this meritorious work by devout practices: they wore sackcloth next to their skin; they fastened iron chains round their bodies, fasted, watched, and made long prayers. They were seriously intent on disturbing the social order and banishing the word of God.

The violent Henry VIII – easy-tempered for once in his life – persisted in his indifference. The seven months named by the prophetess had gone by, and the dagger with which she had threatened him had not touched him. He was in good health, had the approbation of Parliament, saw the nation prosper under his government, and possessed the wife he had so passionately desired. Everything appeared to succeed with him, which disconcerted the fanatics. To encourage them Elizabeth said: 'Do not be deceived. Henry is no longer really king, and his subjects are already released from every obligation towards him. But he is like King John, who, though rejected by God, seemed still to be a king in the eyes of the world.'

The conspirators intrigued more than ever: not content with Catherine's alliance, they opened a communication with Margaret Plantagenet, Countess of Salisbury, niece of Edward IV, and with her children, the representatives of the party of the White Rose. Hitherto this lady had refrained from politics; but, her son Reginald Pole having united with the pope and quarrelled with Henry VIII, they prevailed upon her to carry over to the Princess Mary, whose household she directed, the forces of the party of which she was the head.

The conspirators believed themselves sure of victory; but at the very moment when they imagined themselves on the point of restoring the papacy in England, their whole scheme suddenly fell to the ground. The country was in danger: the state must interfere. Cranmer and Cromwell were the first to discover the approaching storm. Canterbury, the primate's archiepiscopal city, was the centre of the criminal practices of the Kentish woman. One day the prioress of St Sepulchre received the following note from Cranmer: 'Come to my palace next Friday; bring your nun with you. Do not fail.' The two women duly came; Elizabeth's head was so turned that she saw in everything that happened the opportunity of a new triumph. This time she was deceived. The prelate questioned her; she obstinately maintained the truth of her revelations, but did not convince the archbishop, who had her taken to Cromwell, by whom she was sent to the Tower with five other nuns of her party. At first Elizabeth proudly stuck to her character of prophetess; but imprisonment, the searching questions of the judges, and the grief she felt on seeing her falsehoods discovered, made her give way at last. The unhappy creature, a blind tool of the priests, was not entirely wanting in proper feeling. She began to understand her offence and to repent of it: she confessed everything. 'I never had a vision in all my life', she declared; 'whatever I said was of my own imagination; I invented it to please the people about me and to attract the homage of the world.' The disorder which had weakened her head had much to do with her aberrations. Masters, Bocking, Goold, Deering, and others more guilty than she appeared before the Star Chamber. Elizabeth's confession rendered their denials impossible, and they acknowledged having attempted to get up an insurrection with a view of re-establishing the papacy. They were condemned to make a public disavowal of their impostures, and the following Sunday at St Paul's was appointed for that purpose. The Bishop of Bangor preached; the nun and her accomplices, who were exposed on a platform in front of him, confessed their crimes before the people, and were then led back to the Tower.

Personages far more illustrious than these were involved. Besides an epileptic woman and a few monks, the names of Fisher and of More were in the indictment. Cromwell urged both the bishop and the statesman to petition the king for pardon, assuring them they would obtain it. 'Good Master Cromwell', exclaimed Sir Thomas More, who was much excited and ashamed of his credulity, 'my poor heart is pierced at the idea that His Majesty should think me guilty. I confess that I did believe the nun to be inspired; but I put away far from me every thought of treason. For the future, neither monk nor nun shall have power to make me faithless to my God and my king.' Cranmer, Cromwell, and the chancellor prevailed on Henry VIII to strike More's name out of the bill. The illustrious scholar escaped the capital punishment with which he was threatened. His daughter, Margaret Roper, came in a transport of joy to tell him the news: 'In faith, Meg', said More with a smile, '*quod differtur non aufertur*', (what is postponed is not dropped).

The case of the Bishop of Rochester was more serious: he had been in close communication with all those knaves, and the honest but proud and superstitious churchman would not acknowledge any fault. Cromwell, who desired to save the old man, conjured him to give up all idea of defending himself; but Fisher obstinately wrote to the House of Lords that he had seen no deception in the nun. The name of the king's old tutor was left, therefore, in the bill of attainder, but he was charged with misprision, *i.e.* failure of duty in respect to the crime of another, and not with treason. In the outcome he was condemned to the loss of his goods and to imprisonment at the king's pleasure, penalties from which he escaped by the payment to the king of a fine of £300.

The bill was introduced into the House of Lords on 21 February, and received the royal assent on 21 March. The prisoners charged with treason were brought together in the Star Chamber to hear their sentence. Their friends had still some hope; but the bull which the pope had issued against Henry VIII on 23 March, endangering the order of succession, made indulgence difficult. The king and his ministers felt it their duty to anticipate, by a severe example, the rebellion which the partisans of the pontiff were fomenting in the kingdom. Sentence of death was pronounced upon all the criminals.

During this time the unfortunate Elizabeth Barton saw all the evils she had caused rise up before her eyes: she was grieved and agitated, she was angry with herself and trembled at the idea of the temporal and eternal penalties she had deserved. Death was about to end this drama of fanaticism. On 20 April the false prophetess was carried to Tyburn with her accomplices, in the midst of a great crowd of people. On reaching the scaffold, she said: 'I am the cause not only of my own death, which I have richly deserved, but of the death of all those who are going to suffer with me. Alas! I was a poor wretch without learning, but the praises of the priests about me turned my brain, and I thought I might say anything that came into my head. Now I cry to God and implore the king's pardon.' These were her last words. She fell – she and her accomplices – under the stroke of the law.

These were the means to which fervent disciples of Rome had recourse to combat the reformation in England. Such weapons recoil against those who employ them. The blindest partisans of the church of the popes continued to look upon this woman as a prophetess, and her name was in great favour during the reign of Mary. But the most enlightened Roman Catholics are now careful not to defend the imposture.[1] The fanatical episode was not without its use: it made the people understand what these pretended visions and false miracles were, through which the religious orders had acquired so much influence; and so far contributed to the suppression of the monasteries within whose walls such a miserable deception had been concocted.

---

[1] Lingard, the Roman Catholic historian, acknowledges the deception, as do almost all other historians.

CHAPTER TWO

The Church Becomes a Department of State

(Christmas 1533 to June 1534)

T he maid of Kent having been executed, her partisans rallied round another woman, who represented the Romish system in its highest features, as Elizabeth Barton had represented it in its more vulgar phase. After the nun came the queen.

Catherine had always claimed the honours due to the Queen of England, and her attendants yielded them to her. 'We made oath to her as queen', they said, 'and the king cannot discharge our consciences.' Whenever Lord Mountjoy, royal commissioner to the daughter of Ferdinand and Isabella, called her *princess*, she raised her head haughtily and said to him: 'You shall answer for this before God.' 'Ah!' exclaimed Mountjoy, fretted by the vexations of his office, 'I would a thousand times rather serve the king in the most dangerous cause!' Mary, having also received an injunction to drop her title of princess, made answer: 'I shall believe no such order, unless I see His Majesty's signature.' The most notable partisans of Roman Catholicism, and even the ambassador of Charles V, paid the queen frequent visits. Henry became uneasy, and shortly before Christmas 1533 he took measures to remove her from her friends. Catherine opposed everything. Suffolk wrote to the king: 'I have never seen such an obstinate woman.' But there was a man quite as obstinate, and that was Henry.

His most cherished desires had not been satisfied: he had no son. Should he chance to die, he would leave two daughters, Mary and Elizabeth; the former supported by the partisans of the old times, the latter by those of the new. Civil war would probably decide to whom the crown should belong. It was necessary to prevent such a misfortune. The

lords and commons, therefore, petitioned the king, no doubt at his instigation, that his marriage with Lady Catherine should be declared null,
and her child illegitimate; that his marriage with Queen Anne should
be recognized as valid, and the children issuing from it alone entitled to
succeed. All classes of people immediately took the statutory oath; even
the monks bowed their heads. They said: 'Bound to render to our King
Henry VIII, and to him alone after Jesus Christ, fidelity and worship,
we promise inviolable obedience to our said lord as well as to our most
serene Queen Anne, his wife, and to their children; and we profess
perpetual respect for the holy and chaste marriage which they have
legitimately contracted.'[1] This forced testimony, borne to Anne by the
monastic orders, is one of the numerous monuments of the despotism
of Henry VIII and of the moral weakness of the monks.

But in this oath of allegiance the king had meditated a more important
object – to banish the papacy from England. The monks bound
themselves not only to recognize the prescribed order of succession, but
further to substitute the primacy of the king for that of the pope. 'We
affirm', they said, 'that King Henry is the head of the Anglican Church,
that the Roman bishop, falsely styled pope and sovereign pontiff, has
no more authority than any other bishop; and we promise to preach
Christ simply and openly according to the rule of Scripture and of the
orthodox and catholic doctors.' A sign, a word from the state was sufficient to make the papal army pass from the camp of Rome to the camp
of the king.

The 'famous question', that of the Romish jurisdiction, was also put
before the two universities. On 2 May 1534, Cambridge declared that
'all its doctors, having carefully examined the Holy Scriptures, had not
discovered the primacy of the pope in them'. The clergy of the province
of York, led by the archbishop, Edward Lee, a churchman full of talent,
activity, and vanity, stoutly resisted at first; but eventually the prelate
wrote to the king on 2 June that 'according to the unanimous opinion
of his clergy, the pope in conformity with the Holy Scriptures had no
more authority in England than any other foreign ecclesiastic'. Henry,
not content with the proclamations of his council and the declarations

[1] Rymer, *Acta,* p. 192.

of Parliament, required for his separation from Rome the suffrage of the church; and the church, probably more from weakness than conviction, gave it. However, without reckoning the members of the clergy who, like the primate, wanted no pope, there were many bishops who, at heart, were not sorry to be liberated from the perpetual encroachments of the Roman court.

A rumour from the Continent suddenly alarmed the king among all his easy triumphs; a more formidable enemy than monks and bishops was rising against him. It was reported that the emperor was not only recruiting soldiers in Flanders, but was preparing considerable numbers from Bohemia, Germany, Italy, and Spain for the invasion of England. Francis I could not permit this kingdom, so close to his own, to be occupied by the armies of Charles V, his constant enemy; he determined therefore to have an interview with Henry, and to that intent sent over the Seigneur de la Guiche, his chamberlain and counsellor. Henry replied that it would be difficult to leave England just at a time when pope and emperor spoke of invading him; the more so as he must leave his 'most dearly beloved queen' (Anne Boleyn) and his young daughter, the Princess Elizabeth; as well as another daughter and her mother, the aunt of Charles V, whose partisans were conspiring against him. 'Ask my good brother the king', said Henry to de la Guiche, 'to collect a fleet of ships, galleys, and barks to prevent the emperor's landing. And in case that prince should invade either France or England, let us agree that the one who is not called upon to defend his own kingdom shall march into Charles' territories.' However, Henry consented to go as far as Calais.

There was another invasion which, in Henry's eyes, was much more to be dreaded. That king – a greater king perhaps than is ordinarily supposed – maintained that no prince, whether his name was Charles or Clement, had any business to meddle with his kingdom. The act of 23 March, by which the pope had condemned him, had terminated his long endurance: Clement VII had declared war against him and Henry VIII accepted it. A man, though he be ordinarily the slave of his passions, has sometimes impulses which belong to great characters. Henry determined to finish with the pope as the pope had finished with him. He will declare himself master in his own island; dauntlessly he will brave Rome and the imperial power ready to assail him. Erelong the fire which consumed him appeared to kindle his subjects. The political party, at the head of which were Suffolk and Gardiner, was ready to give up the papacy, even while maintaining the dogmas of Catholicism. The evangelical party desired to go farther, and drive the Catholic doctrines out of England. These two hostile sections united their forces against the common enemy.

At the head of the evangelicals, who were eventually to prevail under the son of Henry VIII, were two men of great intelligence, destined to be powerful instruments in the enfranchisement of England. Cranmer, the ecclesiastical leader of the party, gave way too easily to the royal pressure; but, being a moderate theologian, a conscientious Christian, a skilful administrator, and indefatigable worker, he carefully studied the Scriptures, the Fathers, and even the schoolmen; he took note of their sayings and, strengthened by their opinions, continued the work of the reformation with calmness and perseverance. Beside him stood Cromwell, the lay leader of Protestant feeling. Gifted in certain respects with a generous character, he loved to benefit those who had helped him in adversity; but too attentive to his own interests, he profited by the reformation to increase his riches and honours. Inferior to Cranmer in moral qualities, he had a surer and a wider glance than the primate; he saw clearly the end for which he must strive and the means necessary to be employed, and combined much activity with his talents. These leaders were strongly supported. A certain number of ministers and lay members of the church desired an evangelical reform in England. Latimer, a popular orator, was the tribune commissioned to scatter through the nation the principles whose triumph Cranmer and Cromwell sought. He preached throughout the whole extent of the province of Canterbury; but if his bold language enlightened the well-disposed, it irritated the priests and monks. His great reputation led to his being invited to preach before the king and queen. Cranmer, fearing his incisive language and sarcastic tone, begged him to say nothing in the pulpit that would indicate any soreness about his late disgrace. 'In your sermon let not any sparkle or suspicion of grudge appear to remain in you. If you feel authorized by the word of God to attack any sin or superstition, let not the reproof be given without affection.'¹ Latimer preached, and Anne Boleyn was so charmed by his evangelical simplicity, Christian eloquence, and apostolic zeal, that shortly she used her influence with the king to have the preacher elevated to the see of Worcester. Latimer takes his place by the side of Cranmer among the reformers of the English Church.

The evangelical and the political parties being thus agreed to support the prince, Henry determined to strike the decisive blow. On 9 June 1534, about three months after he had been condemned at Rome, he signed at Westminster the proclamation 'for the abolishing of the usurped power of the pope'. The king declared: 'That having been acknowledged next after God, supreme head of the Church of England, he abolished the authority of the Bishop of Rome throughout his realm, and commanded all bishops to preach and have preached, every Sunday and holy day, the true and sincere word of the Lord; to teach that the jurisdiction of the church belongs to him alone, and to blot out of all canons, liturgies, and other works the name of the Bishop of Rome and his pompous titles, so that his name and memory be never more remembered in the kingdom of England, except to his contumely and reproach.² By so doing you will advance the honour of God Almighty, manifest the imperial majesty of your sovereign lord, and procure for the people unity, tranquillity, and prosperity.'

Would these orders be executed? If there remained in any university, monastery, parish, or even in any wretched presbytery, a breviary in which the name of the *pope* was written; if on the altar of any poor country church a missal was found with these four letters un-erased – it was a crime. If every weed be not plucked up, thought the king's counsellors, the garden will soon be entirely overrun. The obstinacy of the clergy, their stratagems, their pious frauds were a mystery to nobody. Henry was persuaded, and his counsellors still more so, that the bishops would make no opposition; they resolved therefore to direct the sheriffs to see that the king's orders were strictly carried out. 'We command you', said that prince, 'under pain of our high indignation, to put aside

---

¹ [Harleian MSS., 6148 (probably to be dated in the first week of January, 1534).]
² 'And his name and memory to be never more remembered except to his contumely and reproach.' – Wilkins, *Concilia*, p. 773.

all human respect, to place God's glory solely before you, and, at the risk of exposing yourselves to the greatest perils, to make and order diligent search to be made. Inform yourselves whether in every part of your county the bishop executes our commands without veil or dissimulation. And in case you should observe that he neglects some portion, or carries out our orders coldly, or presents this measure in a bad light, we command you strictly to inform us and our council with all haste.

'If you hesitate or falter in the commission we give you, rest assured that being a prince who loves justice, we will punish you with such severity that all our subjects will take care for the future not to disobey our commands.'

Everybody could see that Henry was in earnest, and, immediately after this energetic proclamation, those who were backward hastened to make their submission. The dean and chapter of St Paul's made their protest against the pope on 20 June. On the 27th the University of Oxford, in an act where they described the king as 'that most wise Solomon', declared unanimously that it was contrary to the word of God to acknowledge any superiority whatsoever in the Bishop of Rome. A great number of churches and monasteries set their seals to similar declarations.

Such was the first pastoral of the prince who claimed now to govern the church. He seemed desirous of making it a mere department of the state. Henry allowed the bishops to remain, but he employed the functionaries of police and justice to overlook their episcopate; and that office was imposed upon them in such terms that they must necessarily look sharp after the transgressors. First and foremost the king wanted his own way in his family, in the state, and in the church. The last-named was to him as a ship which he had just captured: the captain was driven out, but for fear lest he should return, he threw overboard all who he thought might betray him. With haughty head and naked sword Henry VIII entered the new realm which he had conquered. He was far from resembling him whom the prophets had announced: *Behold thy king cometh unto thee, meek and lowly.*

The power in the church having been taken from the pope, to whom should it have been committed?

Scripture calls the totality of Christian people a holy nation, a royal priesthood;[1] words which show that, after God, the authority belongs to them. And, in fact, the first act of the church, the election of an apostle in the place of Judas, was performed by the brethren assembled in one place.[2] When it became necessary to appoint deacons, the twelve apostles once more summoned 'the multitude of the disciples'.[3] And later still, the evangelists, the delegates of the flocks, were selected by the voice of the churches.[4]

It is a principle of reason, that authority, where a corporate body is concerned, resides in the totality of its members. This principle of reason is also that of the word of God.

When the church became more numerous it was called upon to delegate (at least partially) a power that it could no longer exercise wholly of itself. In the apostolic age the Christians, called to form this delegation, adopted the forms with which they were familiar. After the pattern of the council of elders, which existed in the Jewish synagogues, and of the assembly of decurions, which exercised municipal functions in the cities of the pagans, the Christian church had in every town a council, composed of men of irreproachable life, vigilant, prudent, apt to teach,[5] but distinct from those who were called doctors, evangelists, or ministers of the word.[6] Still the Christians never entertained the idea of giving themselves a universal chief, after the image of the emperor. Jesus Christ and his word were amply sufficient. It was not until many centuries later that this anti-Christian institution appeared in history.

The authority, which in England had been taken away from the pope, should return in accordance with scriptural principles to the members of the church; and if, following the example of the primitive Christians, they had adopted the forms existing in their own country in the sixteenth century, they would have placed as directors of the church – Christ remaining their sole king – one or two houses or assemblies, authorized

[1] 1 Pet. 2:9.
[2] Acts 1:15-26.
[3] Acts 6:2.
[4] 2 Cor. 8:19.
[5] 1 Tim. 3; Titus 1.
[6] Eph. 4:11; 6:21; Col. 1:7; 1 Tim. 4:6.

to provide for the ecclesiastical administration, the maintenance of a pure faith, and the spiritual prosperity of that vast body. These assemblies would have been composed, as in the primitive times, of a majority of Christian laymen, with the addition of ministers; and both would have been elected by believers whose faith was in conformity with that of the church.

But was there at that time in England a sufficient number of enlightened Christians to become members of these assemblies, and even to hold the elections which were to appoint them? It is doubtful. They were not to be found even in Germany. 'I have nobody to put in them', said Luther; 'but if the thing becomes feasible, I shall not be wanting in my duty.'

This form of government not being possible in England then, according to the reformer's expression, two other forms offered themselves. If the first were adopted, the authority would be remitted to the clergy; but that would have been to perpetuate the doctrines and rites of popery and to lead back infallibly to the domination of Rome. The most dangerous government for the church is the government of priests: they commonly rob it of liberty, spontaneousness, evangelical faith, and life.

There remained no alternative then but to confide the supreme authority in the church to the state; and this is what was generally done in the sixteenth century. But men of the greatest experience in these matters have agreed that the government of the religious society by the civil power can only be a temporary expedient, and have universally proclaimed the great principle 'that the essence of all society is to be governed by itself' (Grotius). To deny this axiom would be utterly contrary not only to liberty, but, further still, contrary to justice.

We must not forget, when we speak of the relations between church and state, that there are three different systems: the government of the church by the state; the union of the church, governing itself, with the state; and their complete separation. There is no reason for pronouncing here upon the relative value of the two last systems.

CHAPTER THREE

Tyndale and His Enemies

(1534 to August 1535)

T wo persons were at this time specially dreaded by the Roman party: one was at the summit of the grandeurs of the world, the other at the summit of the grandeurs of faith – the queen and Tyndale. The hour of trial was approaching for both of them.

There existed another reformation than that of which the sheriffs were to be the agents; there were other reformers than Henry VIII. One man, desirous of reviving the Church of England, had made the translation of the Holy Scriptures the work of his life. Tyndale had been forced to leave his country; but he had left it only to prepare a seed which, borne on the wings of the wind, was to change the wildernesses of his native land into a fruitful garden.

The retired tutor from the vale of the Severn was living in 1534 as near as possible to England – at Antwerp, whence ships departed frequently for British harbours. The English merchants, of whom there were many in that city, welcomed him with fraternal cordiality. Among them was a friend of the gospel, Thomas Poyntz, a member of the grocers' company and distantly related to Lady Walsh of Little Sodbury. This warmhearted Christian had received Tyndale into his house, and the latter was unremittingly occupied in translating the Old Testament, when an English ship brought the news of the martyrdom of Fryth, his faithful colleague. Tyndale shed many tears, and could not make up his mind to continue his work alone. But the reflection that Fryth had glorified Jesus Christ in his prison aroused him: he felt it his duty to glorify God in his exile. The loss of his friend made his Saviour still more precious to him, and in Jesus he found comfort for his mind. 'I have lost my brother', he said, 'but in Christ, all Christians and even all the angels are father and mother, sister and brother, and God himself takes care of me. O Christ, my Redeemer and my shield! Thy blood, thy death, all that thou art and all that thou hast done – thou thyself art mine!'[1]

Tyndale, strengthened by faith, redoubled his zeal in his Master's service. While pursuing his study of the Scriptures with intense eagerness, he combined with learning the charity that maintains good works. The English merchants of Antwerp having made him an annual allowance, he consecrated it to the poor; but he was not content with mere giving. Besides Sunday he reserved two days in the week, which he called his 'days of recreation'. On Monday he visited the most out-of-the-way streets of Antwerp, hunting in garrets for the poor English refugees who had been driven from their country on account of the gospel; he taught them to bear Christ's burden, and carefully tended their sick. On Saturday, he went about the city, seeking out the poor in 'every hole and corner'. Should he happen to meet some hard-working parents burdened with children, or some aged or infirm man, he hastened to share his substance with the poor creatures. 'We ought to be for our neighbour', he said, 'what Christ has been for us.' This is what Tyndale called his 'pastime'. On Sunday morning he met with the merchants in a room prepared for evangelical worship, and read and explained the Scriptures with so much sweetness and unction and in such a practical spirit that the congregation (it was said) fancied they were listening to John the Evangelist. During the remainder of the week the laborious scholar gave himself entirely to his translation. He was not one of those who remain idle in the hope that grace may abound. 'If we are justified by faith', he said, 'it is in order that we may do Christian works.'

There came good news from London to console him for the death of Fryth. In every direction people were asking for the New Testament; several Flemish printers began to reprint it, saying: 'If Tyndale should print 2,000 copies, and we as many, they would be few enough for all England.' Four new editions of the sacred book issued from the Antwerp presses in 1534.

There was at that time living in the city a man little fitted to be Tyndale's associate. George Joye, a Fellow of Cambridge, was one of those

---

[1] Tyndale, *Doctrinal Treatises* (Parker Society), pp. 19, 110.

active but superficial persons, with little learning and less judgment, who are never afraid to launch out into works beyond their powers.[1] Joye, who had left England in 1527, noticing the consideration which Tyndale's labours brought to their author, and being also desirous of acquiring glory for himself, began, though he knew neither Hebrew nor Greek, to correct Tyndale's New Testament according to the Vulgate and his own imagination. One day when Tyndale had refused to adopt one of his extravagant corrections, Joye was touched to the quick: 'I am not afraid to cope with him in this matter', he said, 'for all his high learning in Hebrew, Greek, and Latin.' Tyndale knew more than these. 'He is master of seven languages', said Busche, Reuchlin's disciple: 'Hebrew, Greek, Latin, Italian, Spanish, English, French, and so thoroughly that, whichever he is speaking, one might believe it to be his mother-tongue.'

In the month of August Joye's translation appeared at Antwerp: he had advertised it as 'clearer and more faithful'. Tyndale glanced over the leaves of the work that had been so praised by its author, and was vexed to find himself so unskilfully 'corrected'. He pointed out some of Joye's errors, and made this touching and solemn declaration: 'Moreover, I take God, which alone seeth the heart, to record to my conscience, beseeching him that my part be not in the blood of Christ, if I wrote of all that I have written, throughout all my books, aught of an evil purpose, of envy or malice to any man, or to stir up any false doctrine or opinion in the church of Christ; or to be author of any sect; or to draw disciples after me. ... Also, my part be not in Christ, if mine heart be not to follow and live according as I teach; and also, if mine heart weep not night and day for mine own sin, and other men's. ... As concerning all I have translated, or otherwise written, I beseech all men to read it for that purpose I wrote it; even to bring them to the knowledge of the Scripture. And as far as the Scripture approveth it, so far to allow it; and if in any place the word of God disallow it, then to refuse it, as I do before our Saviour Christ and his congregation.'[2]

---

[1] [For a more sympathetic appraisal of Joye's work, see D. B. Knox, *The Doctrine of Faith* (James Clarke, 1961), especially pp. 55-63, 228-37.]

[2] [Quoted from the Second Preface to Tyndale's New Testament Revision of 1534, and dated August of that year. It appeared in print in the following November.]

While Joye was waging this petty war against Tyndale, every ship that came from London to Antwerp brought the cheering news that the great conflict seemed to be dying out in England, and that the king and those around him were drawing towards Protestantism. A change had been worked in Anne's mind analogous to that which had been wrought in her position. She had been ambitious and worldly, but, from the moment she ascended the throne, her character had expanded; she had become queen, she wished to be the mother of her people, especially of those who trod in the paths of Holy Scripture. In the first transports of his affection, Henry had desired to share all the honours of sovereignty with her, and she had taken this high position more seriously than Henry had intended. When he saw her whom he had placed by his side imagine that she had any power, the selfish and jealous monarch knit his brows: this was the beginning of the storm that drove Anne Boleyn from the throne to the scaffold. She ventured to order Cromwell to indemnify the merchants who had suffered loss for having introduced the New Testament into England. 'If a day passes', people said, 'without her having an opportunity of doing a service to a friend of the gospel, she is accustomed to say with Titus, "I have lost a day."' Harman, a merchant of Antwerp and a man of courage, who had helped Tyndale to publish the gospel in English, had been kept seven months in prison by Wolsey and Hacket. Although set at liberty, he was still deprived of his privileges and compelled to suspend business. He came over to England, but instead of applying either to the Lord Chancellor or to Cromwell for the restoration of his rights, he went straight to the queen. Anne, who was then at Greenwich Palace, was touched by his piety and sufferings, and, probably without taking counsel of the king, she dictated the following message to the chief minister, which we think worth quoting in full.

BY THE QUEEN

Anne the Queen. Trusty and right well-beloved, we greet you well. And whereas we be credibly informed that the bearer hereof, Richard Harman, merchant and citizen of Antwerp in Brabant, was in the time of the late Lord Cardinal put and expelled from his freedom and fellowship of and in the English house there, for nothing else, as he affirmeth like a good Christian man, but only for that, that he did, both with his goods and policy to his great hurt and hindrance in this world, help to the setting forth of the New Testament in English. We therefore desire and instantly pray you, that with all speed and favour convenient, you will cause this good and honest merchant, being my lord's true, faithful, and loving subject, to be restored to his pristine freedom, liberty, and fellowship aforesaid. And the sooner at this our request: and at your good pleasure to hear him in such things as he hath to make further relation unto you in this behalf.

Given under our signet at my lord's manor of Greenwich, the xiv day of May.

To our trusty and right well-beloved Thomas Cromwell, principal secretary to His Majesty, the king my lord.

This intervention of the queen in favour of a persecuted evangelical was much talked about. Some ascribed her conduct to the interests of her own cause, others to humanity: most of the friends of the reformation regarded it as a proof that Anne was gained over to their convictions, and Tyndale manifested his gratitude to the queen by presenting her with a handsome copy of his New Testament.[1]

What gave such joy to Tyndale annoyed the king greatly. Such a private order as this coming from the queen singularly displeased a monarch whose will it was that no business should be discussed except in his council. There was also in this order, at least in Henry's eyes, a still greater evil. The evangelical reformation, which Henry had so stoutly combated and which he detested to the last, was making great progress in England. On 4 July 1533, Fryth, the friend of Harman and Tyndale, was burnt at Smithfield, as being one of its followers; and ten months later, on 14 May 1534, Harman, the friend of Tyndale and Fryth, had been declared 'a good Christian' by the queen. Anne dared profess herself the friend of those whom the king hated. Did she design to make a revolution – to oppose the opinions of her lord the king? That letter did not remain without effect: it was reported that the friends of the word of God, taking advantage of these favourable dispositions, were

---

[1] [It was printed on vellum with illuminations; the prefatory matter was omitted; and the fore-edges bore the words, 'Anna, Regina Angliæ.']

printing at Antwerp six separate editions of the New Testament, and were introducing them into England.

It was not only the king who was irritated: the anger of the Romish party was greater still; but as they dared not strike the queen, they looked about for another victim. Neither Bishop Fisher, Sir Thomas More, nor Henry VIII appear to have had any part in this new crime. Gardiner, now Bishop of Winchester, gave a force to the episcopal body of which it had long been deprived; and several prelates, 'incensed and inflamed in their minds', says Foxe, called to remembrance that the best means of drying up the waters of a river is to cut off its springs. It was from Tyndale that all those writings proceeded – those Gospels which, in their opinion, were leading England astray. The moment seemed favourable for getting rid of him: he was actually in the territory of Charles V, that great enemy of the reformation. Gardiner and his allies, the chief of whom was probably Stokesley, Bishop of London, determined to send into the Low Countries two persons with instructions to keep an eye upon the reformer, to take him unawares, and have him put to death. For this purpose they selected a very clever monk of Stratford-le-Bow Abbey and a zealous young papist, who had the look of a gentleman, and who (they hoped) would soon gain Tyndale's heart by his amiability.

It was about the end of the year 1534, while the reformer was still living at Antwerp in the house of Thomas Poyntz, when one day, dining with another merchant, he observed among the guests a tall young man of good appearance whom he did not know. 'He is a fellow countryman', said the master of the house, 'Mr Harry Philips, a person of very agreeable manners.' Tyndale drew near the stranger and was charmed with his conversation. After dinner, just as they were about to separate, he observed another person near Philips, whose countenance from being less open pleaded little in his favour. It was 'Gabriel, his servant', he was told. Tyndale invited Philips to come and see him: the young layman accepted the invitation, and the candid reformer was so taken with him, that he could not pass a day without him – inviting him at one time to dinner, at another to supper. At length Philips became so necessary to him that he prevailed upon him, with Poyntz's consent, to come and live in the same house with him. For some time they had lost sight of Gabriel, and on Tyndale's asking what had become of him, he was informed that he had gone to Louvain, the centre of Roman clericalism in Belgium. When Tyndale and Philips were once lodged beneath the same roof, their intimacy increased: Tyndale kept no secrets from his fellow countryman. The latter spent hours in the library of the Hellenist, who showed him his books and manuscripts, and conversed with him about his past and future labours, and the means that he possessed for circulating the New Testament throughout England. The translator of the Bible, all candour and simplicity, supposing no evil, thinking nothing but good of his neighbour, unbosomed himself to him like a child.

Philips, less of a gentleman than he appeared, was the son of a tax collector in Dorsetshire and had disgraced himself by robbing his father of money. In 1534, he was living in London and seeking employment. The pretended domestic, a disguised monk, was a crafty and vicious churchman, who had been brought from Stratford-le-Bow and given to the so-called gentleman – apparently as a servant, but really as his counsellor and master. Neither Wolsey, More, nor Racket had succeeded in getting hold of Tyndale; but Gardiner and Stokesley, men of innate malice and indirect measures, familiar with all holes and corners, all circumstances and persons, knew how to go to work without noise, to watch their prey in silence, and fall upon it at the very moment when they were least expected. Two things were required in order to catch Tyndale: a bait to attract him, and a bird of prey to seize him. Philips was the bait, and the monk Gabriel Donne the bird of prey.[1] The noble-hearted Poyntz, a man of greater experience than the reformer, had been for some time watching with inquisitive eye the new guest introduced into his house. It was of no use for Philips to try to be agreeable, there was something in him which displeased the worthy merchant. 'Master Tyndale', he said one day to the reformer, 'when did you make that person's acquaintance?' – 'Oh! he is a very worthy fellow', replied Tyndale, 'well-educated and a thorough gentleman.' Poyntz said no more.

Meanwhile the monk had returned from Louvain, where he had

[1] [J. F. Mozley in his *William Tyndale* (pub. in 1937) considers it possible that although Gabriel Donne was made use of by Philips, he may have been ignorant of his sinister designs against the reformer. The evidence is not entirely conclusive.]

gone to consult with some of the most fanatical papal leaders. If he and his companion could gain Mr Poyntz, it would be easy to lay hold of Tyndale. They thought it would be sufficient to show the merchant that they had money, imagining that every man was to be bought. One day Philips said to Poyntz: 'I am a stranger here, and should feel much obliged if you would show me Antwerp.' They went out together. Philips thought the moment had come to let Poyntz know that he was well supplied with gold, and even had some to give to others. 'I want to make several purchases', he said, 'and you would greatly oblige me by directing me. I want the best goods. I have plenty of money', he added. He then took a step farther, and sounded his man to try whether he would aid him in his designs. As Poyntz did not seem to understand him, Philips went no farther.

As stratagem did not succeed, it was necessary to resort to force. Philips by Gabriel's advice set out for Brussels in order to prepare the blow that was to strike Tyndale. The emperor and his ministers had never been so irritated against England and the reformation. The troops of Charles V were in readiness, and people expected to hear every moment that war had broken out between the emperor and the king. On arriving at Brussels, the young Englishman appeared at court and waited on the government: he declared that he was a Roman Catholic disgusted with the religious reforms in England and devoted to the cause of Catherine. He explained to the ministers of Charles V that they had in the Low Countries the man who was poisoning the kingdom; and that, if they put Tyndale to death, they would save the papacy in England. The emperor's ministers, delighted to see Englishmen making common cause with them against Henry VIII, conceded to him all that he asked. Philips, sparing no expense to attain his end, returned to Antwerp, accompanied by the imperial prosecutor and other officers of the emperor.

It was important to arrest Tyndale without having recourse to the city authorities, and even without their knowledge. Had not the Hanseatic judges the strange audacity to declare, in Harman's case, that they could not condemn a man without positive proof? The monk, who probably had not gone to Brussels, undertook to reconnoitre the ground. One day, when Poyntz was sitting at his door, Gabriel went up to him and

said: 'Is Master Tyndale at home? My master desires to call upon him.'
They entered into conversation. Everything seemed to favour the monk's
designs: he learnt that in three or four days Poyntz would be going to
Bergen-op-Zoom, where he would remain about six weeks. It was just
what Gabriel wanted, for he dreaded the piercing eye of the English
merchant.

Shortly after this, Philips arrived in Antwerp with the prosecutor and
his officers. The former went immediately to Poyntz's house, where he
found only the wife at home. 'Does Master Tyndale dine at home today?'
he said. 'I have a great desire to dine with him. Have you anything good
to give us?' 'What we can get in the market', she replied laconically.

The new Judas hurried to meet the officers, and agreed with them
upon the course to be adopted. When the dinner hour drew near, he
said: 'Come along, I will deliver him to you.' The imperial prosecutor
and his followers, with Philips and the monk, proceeded towards
Poyntz's house, carefully noting everything and taking the necessary
measures not to attract observation. The entrance to the house was by a
long narrow passage. Philips placed some of the agents a little way down
the street; others, near the entrance of the alley. 'I shall come out with
Tyndale', he told the agents; 'and the man I point out with my finger is
the one you will seize.' With these words Philips entered the house; it
was about noon.

The creature was exceedingly fond of money; he had received a great
deal from the priests in England for the payment of his mission; but
he thought it would be only right to plunder his victim, before giving
him up to death. Finding Tyndale at home, he said to him after a few
compliments: 'I must tell you my misfortune. This morning I lost my
purse between here and Mechlin, and I am penniless. Could you lend
me some money?' Tyndale, simple and inexperienced in the tricks of
the world, went to fetch the required sum, and lent him forty shillings.
The delighted Philips put the money carefully in his pocket, and
then thought only of betraying his kind-hearted friend. 'Well, Master
Tyndale', he said, 'we are going to dine together.' 'No', replied Tyndale,
'I am going to dine out today; come along with me, I will answer for it
that you will be welcome.' Philips joyfully consented; promptitude of

execution was one element of success in his business. The two friends prepared to start. The alley by which they had to go out was (as we have said) so narrow that two persons could not walk abreast. Tyndale, wishing to do the honours to Philips, desired him to go first. 'I will never consent', replied the latter, pretending to be very polite. 'I know the respect due to you – it is for you to lead the way.' Thus Tyndale, who was of moderate height, went first, while Philips, who was very tall, came behind him. He had placed two agents at the entrance, who were sitting at each side of the alley. Hearing footsteps they looked up and saw the innocent Tyndale approaching them without suspicion, and over his shoulders the head of Philips. He was a lamb led to slaughter by the man who was about to sell him. The officers of justice, frequently so hard-hearted, experienced a feeling of compassion at the sight. But the traitor, raising himself behind the reformer, who was about to enter the street, placed his forefinger over Tyndale's head, according to the signal which had been agreed upon, and gave the men a significant look, as if to say to them, 'This is he!' The men at once laid hands upon Tyndale, who, in his holy simplicity, did not at first understand what they intended doing. He soon found out; for they ordered him to move on, the officers following him, and he was thus taken before the imperial prosecutor. The latter who was at dinner invited Tyndale to sit down with him. Then ordering his servants to watch him carefully, the magistrate set off for Poyntz's house. He seized the papers, books, and all that had belonged to the reformer; and returning home, placed him with the booty in a carriage, and departed. The night came on, and after a drive of about three hours they arrived in front of the strong castle of Vilvorde, built in 1374 by Duke Wenceslaus, situated two leagues north of Brussels, on the banks of the Senne, surrounded on all sides by water and flanked by seven towers. One of the three drawbridges was lowered, and Tyndale was delivered into the hands of the governor, who put him into a safe place. The reformer of England was not to leave Vilvorde as Luther left the Wartburg.[1]

The object of his mission once attained, Philips, fearing the indig-

---

[1] [The arrest occurred, as we now know from the Archives of Brussels, on 23 or 24 May 1535. In all, the reformer was a prisoner for a hundred and thirty-five days.]

nation of the English merchants, escaped to Louvain. Sitting in taverns or at the tables of monks, professors, and prelates – sometimes even at the court of Brussels, he would boast of his exploit, and desiring to win the favour of the imperialists would call Henry VIII a tyrant and a robber of the state.

Shortly Poyntz returned from Bergen-op-Zoom, and he and his fellow merchants, deeply offended by the loss of their friend and by the prosecutor's encroachment upon their rights and privileges, addressed a letter to Mary of Hungary, at that time queen regent of the Netherlands, urging her to agree to the speedy release of Tyndale, but their protest proved unavailing. Her officials objected strongly to the release of a man who had, in their opinion, done such great harm to the papal cause in England.

Tyndale, deprived of all hope, sought consolation in God. 'Oh! what a happy thing it is to suffer for righteousness' sake', he said. 'If I am afflicted on earth with Christ, I have joy in the hope that I shall be glorified with him in heaven. Trials are a most wholesome medicine, and I will endure them with patience. My enemies destine me for the stake, but I am as innocent as a new-born child of the crimes of which they accuse me. My God will not forsake me. O Christ, thy blood saves me, as if it had been mine own that was shed upon the cross. God, as great as he is, is mine with all that he hath.' And again: 'There is none other way into the kingdom of life than through persecution and suffering of pain and of very death, after the example of Christ.'

Tyndale in his prison at Vilvorde was happier than Philips at court. If we carefully study the history of the reformers, we recognize at once that they were not simply masters of a pure doctrine, but also men of lofty soul, Christians of great morality and exalted spirituality. We cannot say as much of their adversaries: what a contrast here between the traitor and his victim! The calumnies and insults of the enemies of Protestantism will deceive nobody. If it is sufficient to read the Bible with a sincere heart in order to believe it, it is sufficient also to know the lives of the reformers in order to honour them.

CHAPTER FOUR

Henry VIII as King-Pontiff

(1534 and 1535)

While the Roman papacy was triumphing in the Low Countries, a lay papacy was being established in England. Henry VIII gave his orders like a sovereign bishop, *summus episcopus,* and the majority of the priests obeyed him. They believed that such an extraordinary state of things would be but of short duration, and thought that it was not worth the trouble of dying in battle against what would perish of itself. They muttered with their lips what the king ordered them, and waited for the coming deliverance.

Every preacher was bound to preach once at least against the usurpations of the papacy; to explain on that occasion the engagements made by the pope with the King of England, the duplicity shown by Clement, and the obligation by which the monarch was bound to thwart so much falsehood and trickery. The ministers of the church were ordered to proclaim the word of Christ purely, but to say nothing about the adoration of saints, the marriage of priests, justification by works, and other doctrines rejected by the reformers, which the king intended to preserve. The secular clergy generally obeyed.

There were however numerous exceptions, particularly in the north of England, and the execution of Henry's orders gave rise to scenes more or less riotous. Due credit must be given to those who ventured to resist a formidable power in obedience to conscientious principles. There were here and there a few signs of opposition. On 24 August 1534, Father Ricot, when preaching at Sion Monastery, called the king, according to his orders, 'the head of the church'; but added immediately after, that he who had given the order was alone responsible before God, and that he 'ought to take steps for the discharge of his conscience'. The other monks went farther still: as soon as they heard Henry's new title proclaimed, there was a movement among them. Father Lache, who, far from resembling his name (meaning 'lax'), was inflexible even to impudence, got up; eight other monks rose with him and left the chapel 'contrary to the rule of their religion' and to the great scandal of all the audience. These nine, boldly quitting the church one after another, were the living protest of the monks of England. They wanted to maintain the dominion of the pope in the church, and in the state also. The king-pope would have none of these freaks of independence. Dr Bedyll, a Fellow of New College, Oxford, who had received Cromwell's order to inspect this monastery, proposed to send the nine monks to prison, 'to the terrible example of their adherents'.

The priests, finding that they must act with prudence, avoided a repetition of such outbreaks and began secretly to school their penitents in the confessional, bidding them employ mental reservations, in order to conciliate everything. They set the example themselves: 'I have abjured the pope *in the outward man,* but not in *the inward man',* said one of them to some of his parishioners. The confessor at Sion Monastery had proclaimed the king's new title and even preached upon it; yet when one of his penitents showed much uneasiness because he had heard Latimer say that the pope himself could not pardon sin: 'Do not be afraid', said the confessor; 'the pope is assuredly the head of the church. True, king and Parliament have turned him out of office here in England; but that will not last long. The world will change again, you will see, and that too before long.' – 'But we have made oath to the king as head of the church', said some persons to a priest. 'What matters!' replied he. 'An oath that is not very strictly made may be broken the same way.'

These mental reservations, however, made many ecclesiastics and laymen too feel uneasy. They longed for deliverance: they were on the look-out; they turned their eyes successively towards Ireland, which had risen for the pope, and towards the Low Countries, whence they hoped an imperial fleet would sail for the subjugation of England. Men grew excited. In the monasteries there were fanatical and visionary monks who, maddened by the abuses of power under which they suffered, and fired by persecution, dreamt of nothing but reaction and vengeance, and expressed their cruel wishes in daring language. One of them named Maitland, belonging to the Dominican order in London, exclaimed presumptuously, as if he were a prophet: 'Soon I shall behold a scaffold erected. … On that scaffold will pass in turn the heads of all those who profess the new doctrine, and Cranmer will be one of them. … The king will die a violent and shameful death, and the queen will be burnt.' Being addicted to the black art, Maitland pretended to read the future by the help of satanic beings. All were not so bold: there were the timid and fearful. Several monks of Sion House, despairing of the papacy, were making preparations to escape and hide themselves in some wilderness or foreign cloister. 'If we succeed', they said, 'we shall be heard of no more, and nobody will know where we are.' This being told to Bedyll, Cromwell's agent, he was content to say: 'Let them go; the loss will not be great.' Roman Catholicism was, however, to find more honourable champions.

Two men, a bishop and a layman, celebrated throughout Christendom, John Fisher and Sir Thomas More, were about to present an opposition to the king which probably he had not expected. Since More had fathomed the king's intentions, and resigned the office of chancellor, he often passed whole nights without sleep, shuddering at the future which threatened him, and watering his bed with tears. He feared that he was not firm enough to brave death. 'O God!' he exclaimed during his agitated vigils, 'come and help me. I am so weak I could not endure a fillip' (*i.e.* even a trifling blow). His children wept, his wife stormed against her husband's enemies, and he himself employed a singular mode of preparing his family for the fate that awaited him. One day, when they were all at table, a sergeant entered the room and summoned him to appear before the king's commissioners. 'Be of good cheer', said More; 'the time is not yet come. I paid this man in order to prepare you for the calamity that hangs over you.' It was not long delayed.

Shortly after the condemnation of Elizabeth Barton the nun, Sir Thomas More, Fisher, and many other influential men were summoned to the archbishop's palace to take the oath prescribed in the Act of Succession. More confessed, received the sacrament, and, forbidding his wife and children to accompany him, as was their custom, to the boat which was to carry him to Lambeth, he proceeded in great emotion towards the place where his future would be decided. His startled family watched him depart. The ex-chancellor, taking his seat in the boat along with his son-in-law William Roper, endeavoured to restrain his tears and struggled but without success against his sorrow. At length his face became more serene, and, turning to Roper, he whispered in his ear, 'I thank our Lord, my son; the field is won.' On his arrival at Lambeth Palace, where Bishop Fisher (of Rochester) and a great number of ecclesiastics were assembled, More, who was the only layman, was introduced first. The chancellor read the form to him: it stated in the preamble that the troubles of England, the oceans of blood that had been shed in it, and many other afflictions, originated in the usurped power of the popes; that the king was the head of the Anglican Church, and that the Bishop of Rome possessed no authority out of his own diocese. 'I cannot subscribe that form', said More, 'without exposing my soul to everlasting damnation. I am ready to give my adhesion to the Act of Succession which is a political act – but without the preamble.' 'You are the first man who has refused', said the chancellor. 'Think upon it.' A great number of bishops, doctors, and priests who were successively introduced took the required oath. But More remained firm, and so did Bishop Fisher.[1]

Cranmer, who earnestly desired to save these two conscientious men, asked Cromwell to accept the oath they proposed, and the latter consulted the king upon it. 'They must give way', exclaimed Henry, 'or I will make an example of them that shall frighten others.' As the king was inexorable, they were attainted by act of Parliament for refusing to take the required oath, and sent to the Tower.

The family of Sir Thomas More was plunged in affliction. His daughter Margaret, having obtained permission to see him, hurried to the Tower, penetrated to his cell, and, incapable of speaking, fell weeping into his arms. 'Daughter', said More, restraining himself with an effort, 'let us kneel down.' He repeated the seven penitential Psalms, and then, rising up, said: 'Dear Meg, those who have put me here think they

---

[1] 17 April 1534. Cranmer, *Letters and Remains* (Parker Society), p. 286.

have done me a high displeasure, but God treats me as he treats his best friends.' Margaret, who thought of nothing but to save her father, exclaimed: 'Take the oath! death is hanging over your head.' 'Nothing will happen to me but what pleases God', replied Sir Thomas More. His daughter left the Tower, overwhelmed with grief. His wife, who also went to see him, Chancellor Audley, the dukes of Norfolk and Suffolk, Cromwell, and other of the king's counsellors were not more successful than Margaret. Bishop Fisher met similar solicitations with a similar refusal.

As the king's government did not wish to hurry on the trial of these illustrious men, they turned from the chiefs to the followers. The Carthusians of London were in great odour of sanctity; they never spoke except at certain times, ate no meat, and affirmed that God had visited them in visions and miracles. Their house was not free from disorders, but many of the monks took their vocation seriously. When the royal commissioners visited them to tender the oath of succession, Prior Haughton, a man of small stature but agreeable appearance and noble carriage, appeared before them. The commissioners required him to acknowledge Henry's second marriage to be lawful; Haughton at first sought a loophole, and answered that the king might be divorced and married without him or his monks having anything to say to it. 'It is the king's command', answered the commissioners, 'that you and your brethren acknowledge by oath the lawfulness of his union. Call the monks together.' The Carthusians appeared, and all refused to take the oath. The prior and proctor were consequently sent to the Tower. The Bishop of London used all his influence to make them change their opinions, and succeeded in persuading them that they might take the oath, by making several reservations. They therefore returned to the charter house and prevailed upon their brethren to do as they had done.

Immediately all was confusion in the monastery. Several monks in deep distress could not tell which course to follow: others, more decided, exclaimed that they would not yield at any price. 'They are minded to offer themselves in sacrifice to the great idol of Rome', wrote Bedyll to Cromwell. At last, when the soldiers appeared to take the rebels to the Tower, the terrified monks lost heart, and took the oath to the new marriage of Henry VIII 'so far as it was lawful'. The bitter cup was removed, but not for long.

Whilst England was separating from Rome, Clement VII was dying of vexation. The hatred felt by the Romans towards him was only equalled by the joy they experienced at the election of his successor. Alexander Farnese, the choice of the French party, was a man of the world, desirous of putting down the Protestants, recovering England, reforming the church, and above all enriching his own family. When da Casale, Henry's envoy, presented his homage: 'There is nothing in the world', said Paul III to him, 'that I have more at heart than to satisfy your master.' It was too late.

Clement's behaviour had produced an evil influence on the character of the Tudor king. The services rendered by this prince to the papacy had been overlooked, his long patience had not been rewarded: he fancied himself despised and deceived. His pride was irritated, his temper grew fiercer, his violence, for some time restrained, broke out, and, unable to reach the pope, he revenged himself on the papacy. Until now, he had scarcely been worse than most of the sovereigns of Christendom: from this moment, when he proclaimed himself head of the church, he became harsh, and cared for nothing but gratifying his evil inclinations, his despotic humours, his bloodthirsty cruelty. As a *prince,* he had at times shown a few amiable qualities; as a *pope,* he was nothing but a tyrant.

Henry VIII, observing the agitation his pretensions caused in England, and wishing to strengthen his new authority, had caused several bills concerning the church to be brought into the Parliament, which met on 3 November 1534, and continued in session until 18 December. The ministers who had drafted them, far from being Protestants, were zealous partisans of scholastic orthodoxy. They included the cunning Gardiner, a furious Catholic; the Duke of Norfolk, who assisted in the king's movements against Rome only to prevent him from falling into the arms of the reformers; and the politic Cromwell, who, despite his zeal against the pope, declared at his death, possibly giving a particular meaning to the words, that he died in the catholic faith.[1]

[1] 'I die in the catholic faith, not doubting in any article of my faith.' – Foxe, *Acts,* v, p. 402.

The first act passed by Parliament was the ratification of the king's new title, already officially recognized by the clergy. Henry's ministers knew how to make the law strict and rigorous. 'It is enacted', so ran the act, 'that our lord the king be acknowledged sole and supreme head on earth of the Church of England; that he shall possess not only the honours, jurisdictions, and profits attached to that dignity, but also full authority to put down all heresies and enormities, whatever be the customs and the laws that may be opposed to it.'[1] Parliament also enacted that 'whoever should do anything tending to deprive the king or his heirs of any of their titles, or should call him heretic, schismatic, usurper, *etc.*, should be guilty of high treason.'[2]

Thus Henry VIII united the two swords in his hand, and virtually became a pope in his own dominions. Whether a pope claims to be king, or a king claims to be pope, it comes to nearly the same thing. At the time when the reformation was emancipating the long-enslaved church, a new master was given it, and what a master! The consciences of Christians revolted against this order of things. One day – it was some time later – Cranmer was asked: 'Who is the supreme head of the Church of England?' – 'Christ', was the reply, 'as he is of the universal church.' – 'But did you not recognize the king as supreme head of the church?' – 'We recognized him as head of *all the people of England*', answered Cranmer, 'of churchmen as well as of *laymen*.'[3] – 'What! not of the church?' 'No! *Supreme head of the church* never had any other meaning than what I tell you.' This is explicit. If the title given to Henry only signified that he was king of the clergy as well as of the laity, and that the former were under the jurisdiction of the royal courts as well as the latter, in all matters of common law, there can be nothing fairer. But how was it that Cranmer did not find as much courage in Henry's lifetime to speak according to his conscience, as when examined in 1555 by Brokes, the papal sub-delegate? An interpretative document drawn up by the government at almost the same time as the act of Parliament, corroborates however the explanation made by Cranmer; it said: 'The

[1] Act of Supremacy: 26 Henry VIII, c. 1.

[2] *Ibid.*, c. 13.

[3] 'Of all the people of England, as well ecclesiastical as temporal.' – Cranmer, *Letters and Remains* (Parker Society), p. 224.

title of supreme head of the church gives the king no new authority: it does not signify that he can assume any spiritual power.' This document declares that the words *reform abuses and heresies* indicate the authority which the king possesses to suppress the powers which the Bishop of Rome or other bishops have usurped in his realm. 'We heartily detest', said William Fulke, Master of Pembroke Hall, Cambridge, 'the notion that the king can do what he likes in matters of religion.'[1] Even Elizabeth refused the title of head of the church.[2] Probably these are facts which are not generally known.

---

[1] Fulke's *Defence* (Parker Society), p. 489.
[2] Jewel's *Works* (Parker Society), iv, p. 1144.

CHAPTER FIVE

Henry Destroys His Opponents

(1534–1535)

I n England it was reserved for Catholics as well as for evangelicals to
give the world, amid great misery, remarkable examples of Christian
virtues. Latimer and others preached the truth courageously;
martyrs like Bilney, Tewkesbury, and Fryth had laid down their lives for
the gospel. Now in the other party, laymen, monks, and priests, with
unquestionably a less enlightened piety, were about to furnish proofs
of their sincerity. There were Roman martyrs also. Two armies were in
presence; many fell on both sides; but there was a sensible difference
between this spiritual war and the wars of nations. Those who bit the
dust did not fall under the weapons of a hostile army: there was a third
power, the king-pope, who took his station between the two lines, and
dealt his blows now to the right, now to the left. Leaders of the pontifical
army were to be smitten in the struggle in which so many evangelicals
had already fallen.

Sir Thomas More, while in prison, strove to banish afflicting thoughts
by writing a history of Christ's passion. One day when he came to these
words of the gospel: *Then came they and laid hands on Jesus, and took him,*
the door opened, and Sir William Kingston, the constable of the Tower,
accompanied by Sir Richard Rich, the solicitor-general, appeared. 'Sir
Thomas', said Rich, 'if an act of Parliament ordered all Englishmen to
acknowledge me as their king, would you acknowledge me?' – 'Yes, sir.'
– 'And if an act of Parliament ordered all Englishmen to recognize me
as pope?' 'Parliament has no authority to do it', answered More. Sir
Thomas held that an act of Parliament was sufficient to dethrone a King
of England: it is to a great-grandson of More that we are indebted for

this opinion, which a grand-nephew of Cromwell put into practice a hundred years later. Was Henry VIII exasperated because More disposed so freely of his crown? It is possible, but be that as it may, the harshness of his imprisonment was increased. Suffering preceded martyrdom. The illustrious scholar was forced to pick up little scraps of paper on which to write a few scattered thoughts with a coal. This was not the worst. 'I have neither shirt nor sute', he wrote to the chief Secretary of State, 'nor yet other clothes that are necessary for me to wear, but that be ragged and rent too shamefully. Notwithstanding, I might easily suffer that if that would keep my body warm. And now in my age my stomach may not away but with a few kind of meats; which, if I want, I decay forthwith, and fall into crases and diseases of my body, and cannot keep myself in health. ... I beseech you be a good master unto me in my necessity, and let me have such things as are necessary for me in mine age. Restore me to my liberty out of this cold and painful imprisonment. Let me have some priest to hear my confession against this holy time, and some books to say my devotions more effectually. The Lord send you a merry Christmas.

'At the Tower, 23 December.'

It is a relief to hope that this scandalous neglect proceeded from heedlessness and not from cruelty. His requests were granted.

While these sad scenes were enacted in the Tower, there was great confusion in all England, where the most opposite parties were in commotion. When the traditional yoke was broken, every man raised up his own banner. The friends of More and Fisher wished to restore the papacy of the Roman bishop; Henry VIII, Cromwell, and the court thought how to establish the supremacy of the king; Cranmer and a few men of the same stamp endeavoured to steer between these quicksands, and aspired to introduce the reign of Holy Scripture under the banner of royalty. This contest between forces so different, complicated too by the passions of the sovereign, was a terrible drama destined to wind up not in a single catastrophe, but in many. Illustrious victims, taken indiscriminately from all parties, were to fall beneath the oft-repeated blows and be buried in one common grave.

The prudent Cranmer lived in painful anxiety. Surrounded by enemies who watched every step, he feared to destroy the cause of truth by undertaking reforms as extensive as those on the Continent. The natural timidity of his character, the compromises he thought it his duty to make with regard to the hierarchy, his fear of Henry VIII, his moderation, gentleness, and plasticity of character and in some respects of principle, prevented his applying to the work with the decision of a Luther, a Calvin, or a Knox. Tyndale, if he had possessed the influence that was his due, would have accomplished a reform similar to that of those great leaders. To have had him for a reformer would, in Wycliffe's native land, have been the source of great prosperity; but such a thing was impossible: his country gave him – not a professor's chair but exile. Cranmer moved forward slowly: he modified an evangelical movement by a clerical concession. When he had taken a step forward, he stopped suddenly, and apparently drew back; not from cowardice, but because his extreme prudence so urged him. The boldness of a Farel or a Knox is in our opinion far more noble; and yet this extreme moderation saved Cranmer and English Protestantism with him. Near a throne like that of Henry's, it was only a man of extreme caution who could have retained his position in the see of Canterbury. Cranmer knew that if he came into collision with the Tudor's sceptre, he would find it a sword. God gives to every people and to every epoch the man necessary to it. Cranmer was this man for England, at the time of her separation from the papacy. Notwithstanding his compromises, he never abandoned the great principles of the reformation; notwithstanding his concessions, he took advantage of every opportunity to encourage those who shared his faith to march towards a better future. The primate of England held a torch in his hand which had not the brilliancy of that borne by Luther and Calvin, but the tempest that blew upon it for fifteen or twenty years could not extinguish it. Sometimes he was seized with terror: as he heard the lion roar, he bent his head, kept in the background, and concealed the truth in his bosom; but again he rose and again held out to the church the light he had saved from the fury of the tyrant. He was a reed and not an oak – a reed that bent too easily, but through this very weakness he was able to do what an oak with all its strength would never have accomplished. The truth triumphed.

At this time Cranmer thought himself in a position to take a step – the most important step of all: he undertook to give the Bible to the laity. When the convocation of clergy and Parliament had assembled, he made a proposition that the Holy Scriptures should be translated into English by certain honourable and learned men, and be circulated among the people. To present Holy Scripture as the supreme rule instead of the pope was the bold act that decided the evangelical reformation. Stokesley, Gardiner, and the other bishops of the Catholic party cried out against such a monstrous design: 'The teaching of the church is sufficient', they said; 'we must prohibit Tyndale's Testament and the heretical books which come to us from beyond the sea.' The archbishop saw that he could only carry his point by giving up something: he consented to a compromise. Convocation resolved on 19 December 1534, to lay Cranmer's proposal before the king, but with the addition that the Scriptures translated into the vulgar tongue should only be circulated among the king's subjects in proportion to their knowledge, and that all who possessed suspected books should be bound to give them up to the royal commissioners: others might have called this resolution a defeat; Cranmer looked upon it as a victory. The Scriptures would no longer be admitted stealthily into the kingdom, like contraband goods: they would appear in broad daylight with the royal sanction. This was something.

Henry granted the petition of convocation, but hastened to profit by it. His great fixed idea was to destroy the Roman papacy in England, not because of its errors, but because he felt that it robbed princes of the affection and often of the obedience of their subjects. 'If I grant my bishops what they ask for', he said, 'in my turn I ask them to make oath never to permit any jurisdiction to be restored to the Roman bishop in my kingdom; never to call him *pope,* universal *bishop,* or most holy lord, but only Bishop of Rome, colleague and brother, according to the ancient custom of the oldest bishops.' All the prelates were eager to obey the king; but the Archbishop of York, secretly devoted to the Roman Church, added, to acquit his conscience, 'that he took the oath in order to preserve the unity of the faith and of the Catholic Church'.

Cranmer was filled with joy by the victory he had won. 'If we possess the Holy Scriptures', he said, 'we have at hand a remedy for every disease. Beset as we are with tribulations and temptations, where can we find arms to overcome them? In Scripture. It is the balm that will heal our wounds, and will be a more precious jewel in our houses than either gold or silver.' He therefore turned his mind at once to the realization of the plan he had so much at heart. Taking for groundwork an existing translation (doubtless that by Tyndale) he divided the New Testament into ten portions, had each transcribed separately, and transmitted them to the most learned of the bishops, praying that they might be returned to him with their remarks. He even thought it his duty not to omit such decided Catholics as Stokesley and Gardiner.

The day appointed for the return and examination of these various portions having arrived (June 1535) Cranmer set to work, and found that the *Acts of the Apostles* were wanting: they had fallen to the lot of the Bishop of London. When the primate's secretary went to ask for the manuscript, Stokesley replied in a very bad humour: 'I do not understand my Lord of Canterbury. By giving the people the Holy Scriptures, he will plunge them into heresy. I certainly will not give an hour to such a task. Here, take the book back to my lord.' When the secretary delivered his message, Thomas Lawney, one of Cranmer's friends, said with a smile: 'My Lord of London will not take the trouble to examine the Scriptures, persuaded that there is nothing for him in the Testament of Jesus Christ.' Many of the portions returned by the other bishops were pitiable. The archbishop saw that he must find colleagues better disposed.

Cranmer had soon to discharge another function. As popery and rebellion were openly preached in the dioceses of Winchester and London, the metropolitan announced his intention to visit them. The two bishops cried out vehemently, and Gardiner hurried to the king: 'Your Grace', he said, 'here is a new pope!' All who had anything to fear began to reproach the primate with aspiring to honours and dominion. 'God forgive me', he said with simplicity, 'if there is any title in the world I care for more than *the paring of an apple.*[1] Neither paper, parchment, lead, nor wax, but the very Christian conversation of the people, are the letters and seals of our office.' The king supported Cranmer, knowing that certain of the clergy preached submission to the pope. The visitation took place. Even in London priests were found who

---

[1] Cranmer, *Letters and Remains* (Parker Society), p. 305.

had taken the oath prescribed by Henry VIII, and who yet 'made a god of the Roman pontiff, setting his power and his laws above those of our Lord.' 'I command you', said the king, 'to lay hold of all who circulate those pernicious doctrines.'

Francis I watched these severities from afar. He feared they would render an alliance between France and England impossible. He therefore sent Bryon, High Admiral of France, to London, to reconcile the king with the pope, to strengthen the bonds that united the two countries, and at the same time, he prevailed upon Paul III to withdraw the decree of Clement VII against Henry VIII. But success did not crown his efforts: the King of England had no great confidence in the sincerity of the pope or of the French king. He was well pleased to be no longer confronted by a foreign authority in his own dominions, and thought that his people would never give up the reformation. Instead of being reconciled with the Roman pontiff, he found it more convenient to imitate the pope, and to break out against those subjects who refused to recognize him, the king, as head of the church.

He first attacked the Carthusians, the most respectable of the religious orders in England, and whom he considered as the most dangerous. Where there was the most goodness, there was also the most strength; and that strength gave umbrage to the despotic Tudor king.

Monastic life, abominable in its abuses, was, even in principle, contrary to the gospel. But we must confess that there was a certain harmony between the wants of society in the Middle Ages and monastic establishments. Many and various motives drove into the cloisters the men that filled them; and if some were condemnable, there were others whose value deserves to be appreciated. It was these earnest monks who, even while defending the royalty of the pope rejected most energetically the papacy of the king: this was enough to draw down upon them the royal vengeance. One day a messenger from the court brought to the charter house of London an order to reject the Roman authority. The monks, summoned by their prior, remained silent when they heard the message, and their features alone betrayed the trouble of their minds. 'My heart is full of sorrow', said Prior Haughton. 'What are we to do? If we resist the king, our house will be shut up, and you young men will be cast into the midst of the world, so that after commencing here in the spirit you will end there in the flesh. But, on the other hand, how can we obey? Alas! I am helpless to save those whom God has entrusted to my care!' At these words the Carthusians 'fell all a-weeping'; and then, taking courage from the presence of danger, they said: 'We will perish together in our integrity; and heaven and earth shall cry out against the injustice that oppresses us.' – 'Would to God it might be so', exclaimed the superior; 'but this is what they will do. They will put me to death – me and the oldest of us – and they will turn the younger ones into the world, which will teach them its wicked works. I am ready to give up my life to save you; but if one death does not satisfy the king, then let us all die!' – 'Yes, we will all die', answered the brethren. – 'And now let us make preparation by a general confession', said the prior, 'so that the Lord may find us ready.'

Next morning the chapel doors opened and all the monks marched in. Their serious looks, their pale countenances, their fixed eyes seemed to betoken men who were awaiting their last moments. The prior went into the pulpit and read the sixtieth Psalm: *'O God, thou hast cast us off.'* On coming to the end, he said: 'My brethren, we must die in charity. Let us pardon one another.' At these words Haughton came down from the pulpit, and knelt in succession before every brother, saying: 'O my brother, I beg your forgiveness of all my offences!' The other monks, each in his turn, made this last confession.

Two days afterwards they celebrated the mass of the Holy Ghost. Immediately after the elevation, the monks fancied they heard 'a small hissing wind'. Their hearts were filled with a tender affection: they believed that the Holy Ghost was descending upon them, and the prior, touched by this surprising grace, burst into tears. Enthusiasm mingled extraordinary fantasies with their pious emotions.

The king had evidently not much to fear in this quarter. His crown was threatened by more formidable enemies. In various parts, especially in Lincolnshire and Yorkshire, there were daring partisans of the papacy to be found who endeavoured to stir up the people to revolt; and thousands of Englishmen in the North were ready to help them by force of arms. At the same time Ireland wished to transport her soldiers across St George's Channel and hurl the king from his throne. The decision with which Fisher, Sir Thomas More, and the Carthusians resisted

Henry had not immediate insurrection for its object, but it encouraged the multitude to revolt. The government, thinking, therefore, that it was time to strike, sent the Carthusians an absolute order to acknowledge the royal supremacy.

At this time there was in reality no liberty on one side or the other. Rome, by not granting it, was consistent with herself; but not so the Protestantism that denies it. The reformation, acknowledging no other sovereign lord and teacher than God, must of necessity leave the conscience to the supreme Master, man having nothing to do with it. But the Roman Church, acknowledging a man as its head, and honouring the pope as the representative of God on earth, claims authority over the soul. Men may say in vain that they are in harmony with God and his word: that is not the question. The great business is to be in accord with the pope. That old man, throned in the Vatican on the traditions of the church and the bulls of his predecessors, is their judge: they are bound to follow exactly his line, without wavering either to the right or the left. If they reject an article, a jot of a papal constitution, they must be cast away. Such a system, the enemy of every liberty, even of the most legitimate, rose in the sixteenth century like a high wall to separate Rome and the new generation. It threatened to destroy in the future that power which had triumphed in the past.

After the festival of Easter 1535, the heads of two other Carthusian houses – Robert Laurence, Prior of Belleval, and Augustine Webster, Prior of Axholm – arrived in London in obedience to an order they had received, and, in company with Prior Haughton, waited upon Cromwell. As they refused to acknowledge the royal supremacy, they were sent to the Tower. A week later, they consented to take the oath, adding: 'So far as God's law permits.' – 'No restrictions', answered Cromwell. On 29 April they were placed on their trial, when they said: 'We will never believe anything contrary to the law of God and the teaching of our holy mother church.' At first the jury expressed some interest in their behalf; but Haughton uselessly embittered his position. 'You can only produce in favour of your opinion', he said, 'the parliament of one single kingdom; for mine, I can produce all Christendom.' The jury found the three prisoners guilty of high treason. Thence the government proceeded to more eminent victims.

Fisher and More, confined in the same prison, were now treated with more consideration. It was said, however, that these illustrious captives were endeavouring, even in the Tower, to excite the people to revolt. The king and Cromwell could hardly have believed it, but they imagined that if these two leading men gave way, their example would carry the recalcitrants with them: they were therefore exposed to a new examination. But they proved as obstinate as their adversaries, and perhaps more skilful. 'I have no more to do with the titles to be given to popes and princes', said Sir Thomas; 'my thoughts are with God alone.'

The court hoped to intimidate these eminent personages by the execution of the three priors, which took place on 4 May 1535. Margaret hurried to her father's side. Before long the procession passed under his window, and the affectionate young woman used every means to draw Sir Thomas away from the sight; but he would not avert his eyes. When all was over, he turned to his daughter: 'Meg', he said, 'you saw those saintly fathers; they went as cheerfully to death as if they were bridegrooms going to be married.'

The prisoners walked calmly along: they wore their clerical robes, the ceremony of degradation not having been performed, no doubt to show that a papal consecration could not protect offenders. Haughton, Prior of the London charter house, mounted the ladder first. 'I pray all who hear me', he said, 'to bear witness for me in the terrible day of judgment, that it is not out of obstinate malice or rebellion that I disobey the king, but only for the fear of God.' The rope was now placed round his neck. 'Holy Jesus!' he exclaimed, 'have mercy on me', and he gave up the ghost. The other priors then stepped forward. 'God has manifested great grace to us', they said, 'by calling us to die in defence of the Catholic faith. No, the king is not head of the Church in England.' A few minutes later and these monks, dressed in the robes of their order, were swinging in the air. This was one of the crimes committed when the unlawful tiara of the pontiffs was placed unlawfully on the head of a King of England. Other Carthusians were put to death somewhat later.

Meanwhile Henry VIII desired to preserve a balance between papists and heretics. The Roman tribunals struck one side only, but this strange prince gloried in striking both sides at once. An opportunity of doing so occurred. Some Anabaptists from the Low Countries were convicted on

25 May: two of them were taken to Smithfield and twelve others sent to different cities, where they suffered the punishment by fire. All of them went to death with cheerful hearts.

The turn of the illustrious captives was at hand.

CHAPTER SIX

Two Notable Executions

(May to September 1535)

Not long after the death of the Carthusians, Cromwell paid More a visit. Henry VIII loved his former chancellor, and desired to save his life. 'I am your friend', said Cromwell, 'and the king is a good and gracious lord towards you.' He then once again invited More to accept the act of Parliament which proclaimed the king's supremacy; and the same steps were taken with Fisher. Both refused what was asked. From that moment the execution of the sentence could not be long delayed. More felt this, and, as soon as the Secretary of State had left him, he took a piece of coal and wrote some verses upon the wall, expressive of the peace of his soul.

Henry and his minister seemed however to hesitate. It had not troubled them much to punish a few papists and obscure Anabaptists; but to put to death an ex-chancellor of the realm and an old tutor of the king – both personages so illustrious and so esteemed throughout Christendom – was another thing. Several weeks passed away. It was an act of the pope that hastened the death of these two men. On 20 May, Paul III created a certain number of cardinals: John Du Bellay, Contarini, Caracciolo, and lastly, Fisher, Bishop of Rochester. The news of this creation burst upon Rome and London like a clap of thunder. Da Casale, Henry's agent at the papal court, exclaimed that it was offering his master the greatest affront possible: the matter was the talk of the whole city. 'Your Holiness has never committed a more serious mistake than this', said da Casale to the pope. Paul tried to justify himself. As England desired to become reconciled with the Vatican, he said, it seemed to him that he could not do better than nominate an English cardinal. When Fisher heard the news, he said piously: 'If the cardinal's hat were at my feet, I would not stoop to pick it up.' But Henry did not take the matter so calmly: he considered the pope's proceedings as an insolent challenge. Confer the highest honours on a man convicted of treason – is it not encouraging subjects to revolt? Henry seemed to have thought that it would be unnecessary to take away the life of an old man whose end could not be far off; but the pope exasperated him. Since they place Fisher among the cardinals in Rome, in England he shall be counted among the dead. Pope Paul may, as long as he likes, send him the hat; but when the hat arrives, there shall be no head on which to place it.

On 14 June 1535, Thomas Bedyll and other officers of justice proceeded to the Tower. The bishop would give no answer to the demand that he should recognize the king as head of the church. Sir Thomas More, when questioned in his turn, replied: 'My only study is to meditate on Christ's passion.' 'Do you acknowledge the king as supreme head of the church?' asked Bedyll. 'The royal supremacy is established by law.' – 'That law is a two-edged sword', returned the ex-chancellor. 'If I accept it, it kills my soul; if I reject it, it kills my body.'

Three days later the bishop was condemned to be beheaded. When the order for his execution arrived, the prisoner was asleep: they respected his slumber. At five o'clock the next morning, 22 June 1535, Kingston, entering his cell, aroused him and told him that it was the king's good pleasure he should be executed that morning. 'I most humbly thank His Majesty', said the old man, 'that he is pleased to relieve me from all the affairs of this world. Grant me only an hour or two more, for I slept very badly last night.' Then turning towards the wall, he fell asleep again. Between seven and eight o'clock he called his servant, took off the hair shirt which he wore next his skin to mortify the flesh, and gave it to the man. 'Let no one see it', he said. 'And now bring me my best clothes.' – 'My lord', said the astonished servant, 'does not your lordship know that in two hours you will take them off never to put them on again?' – 'Exactly so', answered Fisher; 'this is my wedding day, and I ought to dress as if for a holiday.'

At nine o'clock the lieutenant appeared. The old man – he was about seventy-six years old – took up his New Testament, made the sign of the cross, and left the cell. He was tall, being six feet high, but his body was bent with age, and his weakness so great that he could hardly get down the stairs. He was placed in an armchair. When the porters stopped near the gate of the Tower to know if the sheriffs were ready, Fisher stood up, and, leaning against the wall, opened his Testament, and, lifting his eyes to heaven, said: 'O Lord! I open it for the last time. Grant that I may find some word of comfort to the end that I may glorify thee in my last hour.' The first words he saw were these: *And this is life eternal, that they might know thee the only true God, and Jesus Christ whom thou hast sent.*[1] Fisher closed the book and said: 'That will do. Here is learning enough to last me to my life's end.'

The funeral procession was set in motion. Clouds hid the face of the sun; the day was gloomy; the streets through which they passed seemed dull and in harmony with men's hearts. A large body of armed men surrounded the pious old man, who kept repeating in a low tone the words of his Testament: *Hæc est autem vita æterna, ut cognoscant te solum verum Deum et quem misisti Jesum Christum* (John 17:3). They reached Smithfield. 'We will help you to ascend', said his bearers at the foot of the scaffold. 'No, sirs', he replied, and then added in a cheerful tone: 'Come, feet! do your duty, you have not far to go.' Just as he mounted the scaffold, the sun burst out and shone upon his face: *They looked unto him and were lightened,* he cried, *and their faces were not ashamed.* It was ten o'clock. The noble bearing and piety of the aged bishop inspired all around him with respect. The executioner knelt before him and begged his forgiveness. 'With all my heart', he made answer. Having laid aside his robe and furred gown, he turned to the people, and said with gravity and joy: 'Christians, I give my life for my faith in the holy Catholic Church of Christ. I do not fear death. Assist me, however, with your prayers, so that when the axe falls I may remain firm. God save the king and the kingdom!' The brightness of his face at this moment struck the spectators. He fell on his knees and said: 'Eternal God, my hope is in thy deliverance.' The executioner approached and bound his eyes. The bishop raised his hands, uttered a cry towards heaven, and laid his head on the block. The doomsman seized his heavy axe, and cut off the head

[1] John 17:3. The Testament was in Latin.

at one blow. It was exposed for a time by Henry's orders on London Bridge and then thrown into the river; but soldiers carried the body to Barking churchyard, where they dug a lowly grave for it with their halberds. Later, it was removed to St Peter's Ad Vincula in the Tower, where it lies beside that of Sir Thomas More. Doubts have been thrown upon the details of this death; we believe them to be authentic, and it is a pleasure by reporting them to place a crown on the tomb of a Roman Catholic bishop whose end was that of a pious man.

It was now the turn of Sir Thomas More. On 1 July 1535, he was summoned before a special commission and a packed jury. The former chancellor of England quitted his prison in a frieze cloak, which had grown foul in the dungeon, and proceeded on foot through the most frequented streets of London on his road to Westminster. His thin pale face; his white hair, the effect not of time but of sorrow and imprisonment; the staff on which he leant, for he walked with difficulty, made a deep impression on the people. When he arrived at the bar of the tribunal, and looked around him, though weakened by suffering, with a countenance full of mildness, all the spectators were moved. The indictment was long and involved: he was accused of high treason. Sir Thomas, endeavouring to keep on his feet, said: 'My lords, the charges brought against me are so numerous, that I fear, considering my great weakness, I shall be unable to remember them all.' He stopped: his body trembled and he was near falling. A chair was brought him, and after taking his seat, he continued: 'I have never uttered a single word in opposition to the statute which proclaims the king head of the church.' – 'If we cannot produce your words', said the king's attorney, 'we can produce your silence.' – 'No one can be condemned for his silence', nobly answered More. '*Qui tacet consentire videtur* [Silence gives consent] according to the lawyers.'

Nothing could save him: the jury returned a verdict of guilty. 'Now that all is over', said the prisoner, 'I will speak. Yes, the oath of supremacy is illegal. The Great Charter laid down that *the Church of England is free,* so that its rights and liberties might be equally preserved.' – 'The church must be *free*', said the lawyers; 'it is not therefore the slave of the pope.' – 'Yes, *free*', retorted More; 'it is not therefore the slave of the king.' The chancellor then pronounced sentence, condemning him to be hanged and quartered. Henry spared his illustrious subject and old friend from this degrading treatment, and instead ordered that he should be beheaded. 'God save all my friends from His Majesty's favour', said Sir Thomas, 'and spare my children from similar indulgences. ... I hope, my lords', said the ex-chancellor, turning meekly towards his judges, 'that though you have condemned me on earth, we may all meet hereafter in heaven.'

Sir William Kingston approached; armed guards surrounded the condemned man, and the sad procession moved forward. One of the Tower wardens marched in front, bearing an axe with the edge turned towards More; it was a token to the people of the prisoner's fate. As soon as he crossed the threshold of the court, his son, who was waiting for him, fell at his feet distracted and in tears: 'Your blessing, father', he exclaimed, 'your blessing!' More raised him up, kissed him tenderly, and blessed him. His daughter Margaret was not there: she had fainted immediately on hearing of her father's condemnation. He was taken back to prison in a boat, perhaps to withdraw this innocent and illustrious man, treated like a criminal, from the eyes of the citizens of London. When they got near the Tower, the governor, who had until then kept his emotion under, turned to More and bade him farewell, the tears running down his cheeks. 'My dear Kingston', said the noble prisoner, 'do not weep; we shall meet again in heaven.' – 'Yes!' said the lieutenant of the Tower, adding: 'you are consoling me, when I ought to console you.' An immense crowd covered the wharf at which the boat was to land. Among this crowd, so eager for the mournful spectacle, was a young woman, trembling with emotion and silently waiting for the procession: it was Margaret. At length she heard the steps of the approaching guards, and saw her father appear. She could not move, her strength failed her; she fell on her knees just where she had stood. Her father, who recognized her at a distance, giving way to the keenest emotions, lifted up his hands and blessed her. This was not enough for Margaret. The blessing had caused a strong emotion in her, and had restored life to her soul. Regardless of her sex, her age, and the surrounding crowd, that feeble woman, to whom at this supreme moment filial piety gave the strength of many men, says a contemporary, rushed towards her father, and bursting through the officers and halberdiers by whom he was surrounded, fell on his neck and embraced him, exclaiming: 'Father, father!' She could say no more; grief stopped her voice: she could only weep, and her tears fell on her father's bosom. The soldiers halted in emotion; Sir Thomas, the prey at once of the tenderest love and inexpressible grief, felt as if a sword had pierced his heart. Recovering himself, however, he blessed his child, and said to her in a voice whose emotion he strove to conceal: 'Daughter, I am innocent; but remember that however hard the blow with which I am struck, it comes from God. Submit thy will to the good pleasure of the Lord.'

The captain of the escort, wishing to put an end to a scene that might agitate the people, bade two soldiers take Margaret away; but she clung to her father with arms that were like bars of iron, and it was with difficulty that she could be removed. She had been hardly set on the ground a few steps off, when she sprang up again, and thrusting those who had separated her from him she so loved, she broke through the crowd once more, fell upon his neck, and kissed him several times with a convulsive effort. In her, filial love had all the vehemence of passion. More, whom the sentence of death had not been able to move, lost all energy, and the tears poured down his cheeks. The crowd watched this touching scene with deep excitement and 'they were very few in all the troop who could refrain from weeping; no, not the guards themselves'. Even the soldiers wept, and refused to tear the daughter again from her father's arms. Two or three, however, of the less agitated stepped forward and carried Margaret away. The women of her household, who had accompanied her, immediately surrounded her and bore her away from a sight of such inexpressible sadness. The prisoner entered the Tower.

Sir Thomas spent six more days and nights in prison. We hear certainly of his pious words, but the petty practices of an ascetic seemed to engross him. His macerations were increased: he walked up and down his cell, wearing only a winding-sheet, as if he were already a corpse waiting to be buried. He often scourged himself for a long time together, and with extraordinary violence. Yet at the same time he indulged in Christian meditations. 'I am afflicted', he wrote to one of his friends, 'shut up in a dungeon; but God in his mercy will soon deliver me from this world of tribulation. Walls will no longer separate us, and we shall have holy conversations together, which no gaoler will interrupt.' On 5 July, desiring to bid his daughter a last farewell, More took a piece of charcoal (he had nothing else) and wrote to her: 'Tomorrow is St Thomas's day, and my saint's day; accordingly, I desire extremely that it may be the day of my departure. My child, I never loved you so dearly as when last you kissed me. I like when daughterly love has no leisure to look unto worldly courtesy. ... Farewell my dearly beloved daughter; pray for me. I pray for you all, to the end that we may meet in heaven.'

Thus one of the closest and holiest affections, that of a father for his daughter, and of a daughter for her father, softened the last moments of this distinguished man. Sir Thomas sent Margaret his hair shirt and scourge, which he desired to conceal from the eyes of the indifferent. What an inheritance!

That night he slept quietly, and the next morning early (6 July 1535) a fortnight after the death of Bishop Fisher, Sir Thomas Pope, one of his familiar friends, came to inform him that he must hold himself in readiness. 'I thank the king', said More, 'for shutting me up in this prison, whereby he has put me in a condition to make suitable preparation for death. The only favour I beg of him is, that my daughter may be present at my burial.' Pope left the cell in tears. Then the prisoner put on a fine silk robe which his wealthy friend Bonvisi, the merchant of Lucca, had given him. 'Leave that dress here', said Kingston, 'for the man to whom it falls by custom is only a gaoler.' – 'I cannot look upon that man as a gaoler', answered More, 'who opens the gates of heaven for me.'

At nine o'clock the procession quitted the Tower. More was calm, his face pale, his beard long and curly; he carried a crucifix in his hand, and his eyes were often turned towards heaven. A numerous and sympathetic crowd watched him pass along – a man one time so honoured, privy councillor, Speaker of the House of Commons, President of the House of Lords – whom armed men were now leading to the scaffold. Just as he was passing in front of a house of mean appearance, a poor woman standing at the door, went up to him and offered him a cup of wine to strengthen him: 'Thank you', he said gently, 'thank you, Christ drank vinegar only.' On arriving at the place of execution: 'Give me your hand to help me up', he said to Kingston, adding: 'As for my coming down, you may let me shift for myself.' He mounted the scaffold. Sir Thomas Pope, at the king's request, had begged him to make no speech, fearing the effect this illustrious man might produce upon the people. More desired however to say a few words, but the sheriff stopped him. 'I die', he was content to say, 'in the faith of the Catholic Church, and a faithful servant of God and the king.' He then knelt down and repeated the fifty-first Psalm:[1] *Have mercy upon me, O God, according to thy loving-kindness: according unto the multitude of thy tender mercies blot out my transgressions.* When he rose up, the executioner begged his forgiveness: 'Why do you talk of forgiveness?' replied More; 'you are doing me the greatest kindness I ever received from man.' He desired the man not to be afraid to do his office, and remarked that his neck was very short. With his own hands he fastened a bandage over his eyes, and then laid his head on the block. The executioner, holding the axe, was preparing to strike, when More stopped him, and, putting his beard carefully on one side, said: 'This at least has not committed treason.' Such words, almost jesting, no doubt startle us at such a moment; but strong men have often been observed to manifest the calmness of their souls in such a manner. More probably feared that his long beard would embarrass the executioner, and deaden the blow. At length that head fell through which so many noble thoughts had passed; that keen clear eye was closed; those eloquent lips were the lips of a corpse. The head was exposed on London Bridge, and Margaret discharged the painful duty her father had bequeathed her, by piously burying his body.[2]

Thus, at the cost of his life, this eminent man protested against the aberrations of a cruel prince, who usurped the title given by the Bible to Jesus Christ alone. The many evangelical martyrs who had been sacrificed in different countries and who were yet to be sacrificed, showed in general, to a greater extent than Fisher and More, an ardent love for the Saviour, a lively hope of eternal life; but none showed greater

[1] The fiftieth of the Vulgate: *Miserere mei, Deus.*
[2] [When Margaret died, by her wish her father's head, which she had herself preserved, was buried with her, in her arms.]

calmness than they. These two good men wanted discernment as to what constitutes the pure gospel; their piety bound them too much, as we have said, to monastic practices; they had (and More especially) in the days of their power persecuted the disciples of the Lord, and though they rejected the usurpations of the king, had acted as fanatical defenders of those of the pope. But at a time when there were so many cringing bishops and servile nobles – when almost everyone bent the head timidly before the mad popery of Henry VIII, these two firmly held up theirs. More and Fisher were companions in misfortune with Bilney and Fryth: the same royal hand struck them all. Our sympathies are for the victims, our aversion for the executioner.

The death of these two celebrated men caused an immense sensation. In England, the people and even the nobility were struck with astonishment. Could it be true, men asked, that Thomas More, whom Henry had known since he was nine years old, with whom he used to hold friendly conversations by night on the terrace of his country house, at whose table he used to love to sit down familiarly, whom he had chosen, although a layman and a knight only, to succeed the powerful Wolsey – could it be true that by the king's orders he had perished by the axe? Could it be true that Fisher had met with the same fate – that venerable old man of almost fourscore years, who had been his preceptor, the trusty friend of his grandmother, and to whose teaching he owed the progress he had made in learning? Men began to see that resistance to a Tudor meant the scaffold. Everyone trembled, and even those who had not known the two victims could not restrain their tears.

The horror which these executions caused among the enlightened men of the Continent was displayed with more liberty and energy. 'I am dead', exclaimed Erasmus, 'since More is dead; for, as Pythagoras says, we had but one soul between us.' – 'O England! O dearly beloved country', said Reginald Pole; 'he was not only Margaret's father, but thine also!' – 'This year is fatal to our order', said Melanchthon the reformer;[1] 'I hear that More has been killed and others also. You know how such things wring my heart.' – 'We banish such criminals', said Francis I sharply to the English ambassador, 'but we do not put them to death.' – 'If I

---

[1] The 'order' means that of men of letters.

had two such lights in my kingdom', said Charles V, 'I would sooner give two of my strongest cities than suffer them to be extinguished.' At Rome in particular the anger was extreme. They were still flattering themselves that Henry VIII would return to his old sympathies; but now there was no more hope! The king had put to death a prince of the church, and as he had sworn, the cardinal's hat could find no head to wear it. A consistory was immediately summoned: the French Cardinal de Tournon's touching letter was read, and all who heard it were moved even to tears. The embarrassed and speechless agents of England knew not what to do; and as they reported, there was everything to be feared.

Perhaps nobody was so much confounded as the pontiff himself. Paul III was circumspect, prudent, deliberative, and temporizing; but when he thought the moment arrived, when he believed further manoeuvring was not required, he no longer hesitated, but struck forcibly. It is known that he had two young relations whom, in his blind tenderness, he had created cardinals, notwithstanding their youth and the emperor's representations. 'Alas!' he exclaimed, 'I feel as mortally injured as if my two nephews had been killed before my eyes.' His most devoted partisans, and above all a cardinal of his creation put to death! There was a violent movement in his heart; he worked himself into a fury; he desired to strike the prince whose cruel deeds had wounded him so deeply. His anger burst out in a thunder-clap. On 30 August he sanctioned a bull worthy of Gregory VII, which the more zealous partisans of the papacy would like to remove from the papal records.[1] 'Let King Henry repent of his crimes', said the pontiff; 'we give him ninety days and his accomplices sixty to appear at Rome. In case of default, we strike him with the sword of anathema, of malediction, and of eternal damnation; we take away his kingdom from him: we declare that his body shall be deprived of ecclesiastical burial; we launch an interdict against his states; we release his subjects from their oath of fidelity; we call upon all dukes, marquises, and earls to expel him and his accomplices from England; we unbind all Christian princes from their oaths towards him, command them to march against him and constrain him to return to the obedience due to

[1] Lingard's *History*, iii, ch. iv.

the holy apostolic see, giving them all his goods for their reward, and he and his to be their slaves.'

Anger had the same effect upon the pontiff as inebriety; he had lost the use of his reason, and allowed himself to be carried away to threats and excesses of which he would have been ashamed, had he been sober. Accordingly the drunkenness was hardly over before the unfortunate Paul hastened to hide his bull, and carefully laid aside his thunderbolts in the arsenal, free to bring them out later.

Henry VIII, more calm than the pope, having heard of his discontent, feared to push him to extremities; and Cromwell, a month after the date of the bull, instructed da Casale to justify the king to the Vatican. 'Fisher and More', he was to say, 'had on all points of the internal policy of England come to conclusions diametrically opposed to the quiet and prosperity of the kingdom. They had held secret conversations with certain men notorious for their audacity, and had poured into the hearts of these wretches the poison which they had first prepared in their own. Could we permit their crime, spreading wider and wider, to give a death-blow to the state? Fisher and More alone opposed laws which had been accepted by the general consent of the people, and were necessary to the prosperity of the kingdom. Our *mildest* of sovereigns could not longer tolerate an offence so atrocious.'[1]

Even these excuses accuse and condemn Henry. Neither More nor Fisher had entered into a plot against the state; their resistance had been purely religious; they were free to act according to their consciences. It might have been necessary to take some prudential measures in an age as yet little fitted for liberty; but nothing could excuse the scaffold, erected by the king's orders, for men who were regarded with universal respect.

---

[1] State Papers, vii, pp. 634-5.

CHAPTER SEVEN

The Dissolution of the Smaller Monasteries

(September 1535 to 1536)

The death of the late tutor and friend of the prince was to be followed by a measure less cruel but far more general. The pope who treated kings so rudely should not be surprised if kings treated the monks severely. Henry knew – had indeed been a close witness – of their lazy and often irregular lives. One day, when he was hunting in the forest of Windsor, he lost his way, perhaps intentionally, and about the dinner hour knocked at the gate of Reading Abbey. As he represented himself to be one of His Majesty's guards, the abbot said: 'You will dine with me'; and the king sat down to a table covered with abundant and delicate dishes. After examining everything carefully: 'I will stick to this sir-loin', said he, pointing to a piece of beef of which he ate heartily.[1] The abbot looked on with admiration. 'I would give a hundred pounds', he exclaimed, 'to eat with as much appetite as you; but alas! my weak and squeazie [qualmish] stomach can hardly digest the wing of a chicken.' – 'I know how to bring back your appetite', thought the king. A few days later some soldiers appeared at the abbey, took away the abbot, and shut him up in the Tower, where he was put upon bread and water. 'What have I done', he kept asking, 'to incur His Majesty's displeasure to such a degree?' After a few weeks, Henry went to the state prison, and, concealing himself in an ante-room whence he could see the abbot, ordered a sirloin of beef to be set before him. The famished monk in his turn fell upon the joint, and (according to tradition) ate it all. The king now showed himself: 'Sir Abbot', he said, 'I have cured you of your

---

[1] 'A Sir Loyne of beaf, so knighted by this King Henry.' – Fuller, p. 299. [Other traditions attribute the 'Sir Loyne' joke to James I and Charles II.]

qualms; now pay me my wages. It is a hundred pounds, you know.' The abbot paid and returned to Reading; but Henry never after forgot the monks' kitchen.

The state of the monasteries was an occasion of scandal: all religious life had largely died out in most of those establishments. The monks lived, generally, in idleness, gluttony, and licentiousness, and what should have been houses of saints had become in many cases mere sties of lazy gormandizers and impure sensualists. 'The only law they recognize', said Luther, speaking of these cloisters, 'is that of the seven deadly sins.' History encounters here a twofold danger: one is that of keeping back what is essential, the scandalous facts that justified the suppression of monasteries; the other is that of saying things that cannot be named. We must strive to steer between these two quicksands.

All classes of society had become disgusted with the monasteries: the common people would say to the monks: 'We labour painfully, while you lead easy and comfortable lives.' The nobility regarded them with looks of envy and irony which threatened their wealth. The lawyers considered them as parasitical plants which drew away from others the nutriment they required. These things made the religious orders cry out with alarm: 'If we no longer have the pope to protect us, it is all over with us and our monasteries.' And they set to work to prevent Henry from separating from the pope: they circulated anonymous stories, seditious songs, trivial lampoons, frightful prophecies, and biting satires against the king, Anne Boleyn, and the friends of the reformation. They held mysterious interviews with the discontented, and took advantage of the confessional to alarm the weak-minded. 'The supremacy of the pope', they said, 'is a fundamental article of the faith: none who reject it can be saved.' People began to fear a general revolt.

When Luther was informed that Henry VIII had abolished the authority of the pope in his kingdom, but had suffered the religious orders to remain, he smiled at the blunder: 'The King of England', he said, 'weakens the body of the papacy but at the same time strengthens the soul.' That could not endure for long.

Cromwell had now attained high honours and was to mount higher still. He thought with Luther that the pope and the monks could not exist or fall one without the other. After the abolition of the rule of the Roman pontiff, it became necessary to abolish the monasteries. It was he who had prevailed on the king to take the place of head of the church; and now he wished him to be so really. 'Sire', he said to Henry, 'cleanse the Lord's field from all the weeds that stifle the good corn, and scatter everywhere the seeds of virtue. In 1525, 1528, 1531, and 1534 the popes themselves lent you their help in the suppression of monasteries; now you no longer require their aid. Do not hesitate, sire: the most fanatical enemies of your supreme authority are to be found in the religious houses. There is buried the wealth necessary to the prosperity of the nation. The revenues of the religious orders are far greater than those of all the nobility of England. The cloister schools have fallen into decay, and the wants of the age require better ones. To suppress the pope and to keep the monks is like deposing the general and delivering the fortresses of the country up to his army. Sire, imitate the example of the Protestants and suppress the monasteries.'

Such language alarmed the friends of the papacy, who stoutly opposed a scheme which they believed to be sacrilegious. 'These foundations were consecrated to Almighty God', they told the king; 'respect therefore those retreats where pious souls live in contemplation.' 'Contemplation!' said Sir Henry Colt, smiling; 'tomorrow, sire, I undertake to produce proofs of the kind of contemplation in which these monks indulge.' Whereupon, says an historian, Colt, knowing that a certain number of the monks of Waltham Abbey had a fondness for the conversation of ladies, and used to pass the night with the nuns of Chesham Convent, went to a narrow path through which the monks would have to pass on their return, and stretched across it one of the stout nets used in stag hunting. Towards daybreak, as the monks, lantern in hand, were making their way through the wood, they suddenly heard a loud noise behind them – it was caused by men whom Colt had stationed for the purpose – and instantly blowing out their lights they were hurrying away, when they fell into the toils prepared for them.[1] The next morning, he presented them to the king, who laughed heartily at their piteous looks. 'I have often seen better game', he said, 'but never fatter. Certainly', he added,

---

[1] Fuller, *Church History* (1655), p. 317.

'I can make a better use of the money which the monks waste in their debaucheries. The coast of England requires to be fortified, my fleet and army to be increased, and harbours to be built for the commerce which is extending every day. All that is well worth the trouble of suppressing houses of impurity.'

The protectors of the religious orders were not discouraged, and maintained that it was not necessary to shut all the monasteries, because of a few guilty houses.

Dr Layton, a former officer of Wolsey, proposed a middle course: 'Let the king order a general visitation of monasteries', he said, 'and in this way he will learn whether he ought to secularize them or not. Perhaps the mere fear of this inspection will incline the monks to yield to His Majesty's desires.' Henry charged Cromwell with the execution of this measure, and for that purpose he at once used him as his vicar-general, conferring on him all the ecclesiastical authority which belonged to the king. 'You will visit all the churches', he said, 'even the metropolitan, whether the see be vacant or not; all the monasteries both of men and women; and you will correct and punish whoever may be found guilty.' Henry gave to his vicar precedence over all the peers, and decided that the layman should preside over the assembly of the clergy instead of the primate; oversee the administration not only of the bishops but also of the archbishops; confirm or annul the election of prelates, deprive or suspend them, and assemble synods. This was at the beginning of September 1535. The influence of the laity thus re-entered the church, but not through the proper door. They came forward in the name of the king and his proclamations, whilst they ought to have appeared in the name of Christ and of his word. The king informed the primate, and through him all the bishops and archdeacons, that as the general visitation was about to commence, they should no longer exercise their jurisdiction. The astonished prelates made representations, but they were unavailing: they and their sees were to be inspected by laymen.

The monks began to tremble. Faith in the religious houses no longer existed – not even in the houses themselves. Confidence in monastic practices, relics, and pilgrimages had grown weaker; the timbers of the monasteries were worm-eaten, their walls were just ready to fall, and the edifice of the Middle Ages, tottering on its foundations, was unable to withstand the hearty blows dealt against it. When an antiquary explores some ancient sepulchre, he often comes upon a skeleton, apparently well preserved, but crumbling into dust at the slightest touch of the finger; in like manner the puissant hand of the sixteenth century had only to touch most of these monastic institutions to reduce them to powder. The real dissolver of the religious orders was neither Henry VIII nor Cromwell: it was the devouring worm which, for years and centuries, they had carried in their bosom.

The vicar-general appointed his commissioners and then assembled them as a commander-in-chief calls his generals together. In the front rank was Dr Richard Layton, his old comrade in Wolsey's household, a skilful man who knew the ground well and did not forget his own interests. After him came Dr John London, Warden of New College, a man of unparalleled activity, but without character and a weather-cock, turning to every wind. With him was Sir Richard Cromwell, nephew of the vicar-general, an upright man, though desirous of making his way through his uncle's influence. He was the ancestor of another Cromwell, far more celebrated than Henry VIII's vice-gerent. Other two were Dr Thomas Legh and Dr John ap Rice, the most daring of the colleagues of the king's ministers; besides other individuals of well-known ability. The vice-gerent handed to them the instructions for their guidance, the questions they were to put to the monks, and the injunctions they were to impose on the abbots and priors; after which they separated on their mission.

The universities, which sadly needed a reform, were not overlooked by Henry and his representative. Since the time when Garret, the priest of a London parish, circulated the New Testament at Oxford, the sacred volume had been banished from that city, as well as the *Beggars' Supplication* and other evangelical writings. Slumber had followed the awakening. The members of the university, especially certain ecclesiastics who, forsaking their parishes, had come and settled at Oxford, 'to enjoy the delights of Capua', passed their lives in idleness and sensuality. The royal commissioners aroused them from this torpor. They dethroned Duns Scotus, 'the subtle doctor', who had reigned there for three hundred years, and the leaves of his books were scattered to the winds. Scholasticism fell; new lectures were established; philosophical teaching, the natural sciences, Latin, Greek, and divinity were extended and developed. The students were forbidden to haunt taverns, and the priests who had come to Oxford to enjoy life were sent back to their parishes.

The visitation of the monasteries began with those of Canterbury, the primatial church of England. In October 1535, shortly after Michaelmas, Dr Layton, the visitor, entered the cathedral, and Archbishop Cranmer went up into the pulpit. He had seen Rome: he had an intimate conviction that that city exerted a mischievous influence over all Christendom; he desired, as primate, to take advantage of this important opportunity to break publicly with her. 'No', he said, 'the Bishop of Rome is not God's vicar. In vain you will tell me that the see of Rome is called *Sancta Sedes,* and its bishop entitled *Sanctissimus Papa:* the pope's holiness is but a holiness in name.'[1] Vain-glory, worldly pomp, unchaste living and vices innumerable prevail in Rome. I have seen it with my own eyes. The pope claims by his ceremonies to forgive men their sins: it is a serious error. One work only blots them out, namely, the death of our Lord Jesus Christ. So long as the see of Rome endures, there will be no remedy for the evils which overwhelm us. These many years I have daily prayed unto God that I might see the power of Rome destroyed.'[2] Language so frank necessarily displeased the adherents of the pope, and accordingly, when Cranmer alluded to his energetic daily prayer, the superior of the Dominicans, trembling with excitement, exclaimed: 'What a want of charity!'

He was not the only person struck with indignation and fear. As soon as the sermon was over, the Dominicans assembled to prevent the archbishop from carrying out his intentions. 'We must support the papacy', they said, 'but do it prudently.' The prior was selected, as being the most eloquent of the brothers, to reply to Cranmer. Going into the pulpit, he said: 'The church of Christ has never erred. The laws which it makes are equal in authority to the laws of God himself. I do not know

[1] Cranmer's *Letters and Remains* (Parker Society), p. 326.
[2] *Ibid.*, p. 327.

a single Bishop of Rome who can be reproached with vice.' Evidently the prior, however eloquent he might be, was not learned in the history of the church.

The visitation of the Canterbury monasteries began. The immorality of most of these houses was manifested by scandalous scenes, and gave rise to questions which we are forced to suppress. The abominable vices that prevailed in them are mentioned by St Paul in his description of the pagan corruptions (Rom. 1). The commissioners having taken their seats in one of the halls of the Augustine monastery, all the monks came before them, some embarrassed, others bold, but most of them careless. Strange questions were then put to men who declared themselves consecrated to a devout and contemplative life: 'Are there any among you', asked the commissioners, 'who, disguising themselves, leave the convent and go vagabondizing about? Do you observe the vow of chastity, and has anyone been convicted of incontinence? Do women enter the monastery, or live in it habitually?' We omit the questions that followed. The result was scandalous: eight of the brothers were convicted of abominable vices. The black sheep having been set apart for punishment, Layton called the other monks together, and said to them: 'True religion does not consist in shaving the head, silence, fasting, and other observances; but in uprightness of soul, purity of life, sincere faith in Christ, brotherly love, and the worship of God in spirit and in truth. Do not rest content with ceremonies, but rise to sublimer things, and be converted from all these outward practices to inward and deep considerations.'

One visitation still more distressing followed this. The Carthusian monastery at Canterbury, four monks of which had died piously, contained several rotten members. Some of them used to put on lay clothes, and leave the convent during the night. There was one house for monks and another for nuns, and the blacksmith of the monastery confessed that a monk had asked him to file away a bar of the window which separated the two cloisters. It was the duty of the monks to confess the nuns; but by one of those refinements of corruption which mark the lowest degree of vice, the sin and absolution often followed close upon each other. Some nuns begged the visitors not to permit certain monks to enter their house again.

The visitation being continued through Kent, the visitors came on 22 October to Langdon Abbey, near Dover. William Dyck, Abbot of the Monastery of the Holy Virgin, possessed a very bad reputation. Layton, who was determined to surprise him, ordered his attendants to surround the abbey in such a manner that no one could leave it. He then went to the abbot's house, which looked upon the fields, and was full of doors and windows by which anyone could escape. Layton began to knock loudly, but no one answered. Observing an axe, he took it up, dashed in the door with it, and entered. He found a woman with the monk, and the visitors discovered in a chest the men's clothes which she put on when she wished to pass for one of the younger brethren. She escaped, but one of Cromwell's servants caught her and took her before the mayor at Dover, where she was placed in the cage. As for the holy father abbot, says Layton, he was put in prison. A few of the monks signed an act by which they declared that their house being threatened with utter ruin, temporal and spiritual, the king alone could find a remedy, and they consequently surrendered it to His Majesty.

The Abbot of Fountains had ruined his abbey by publicly keeping six women. One night he took away the golden crosses and jewels belonging to the monastery, and sold them to a jeweller for a small sum. At Mayden-Bradley, Layton found another father prior, one Richard, who had five women, six sons, and a daughter pensioned on the property of the monastery: his sons, tall, stout young men, lived with him and waited on him. Seeing that the Roman Church prohibited the clergy from obeying the commandment of Scripture, which says: *A bishop must be the husband of one wife,* these wretched men took five or six. The impositions of the monks to extort money injured them in public opinion far more than their debauchery. Layton found in St Anthony's house at Bristol a tunic of our Lord, a petticoat of the Virgin, a part of the Last Supper, and a fragment of the stone upon which Jesus was born at Bethlehem. All these brought in money.

Every religious and moral sentiment is disgusted at hearing of the disorders and frauds of the monks, and yet the truth of history requires that they should be made known. Here is one of the means – of the blasphemous means – they employed to deceive the people. At Hales in Gloucestershire, the monks pretended that they had some of Christ's blood preserved in a bottle. The man whose deadly sins God had not yet pardoned could not see it, they said; while the absolved sinner saw it instantaneously. Thousands of penitents crowded thither from all parts. If a rich man confessed to the priest and laid his gift on the altar, he was conducted into the mysterious chapel, where the precious vessel stood in a magnificent case. The penitent knelt down and looked, but saw nothing. 'Your sin is not yet forgiven', said the priest. Then came another confession, another offering, another introduction into the sanctuary; but the unfortunate man opened his eyes in vain, he could see nothing until his contribution satisfied the monks. The commissioners, having sent for the vessel, found it to be 'a crystal very thick on one side and very transparent on the other.' 'You see, my lords', said a candid monk, 'when a rich penitent appears, we turn the vessel on the thick side; that, you know, opens his heart and his purse.' The transparent side did not appear until he had placed a large donation on the altar.

No discovery produced a greater sensation in England than that of the practices employed at Boxley in Kent. It possessed a famous crucifix, the image on which, carved in wood, gave an affirmative nod with the head if the offering was accepted, winked the eyes, and bent the body. If the offering was too small, the indignant figure turned away its head and made a sign of disapproval. One of the commissioners took down the crucifix from the wall, and discovered the pipes which carried the wires that the priestly conjuror was wont to pull. Having put the machine in motion, he said: 'You see what little account the monks have made of us and our forefathers.' The monks trembled with shame and alarm, while the spectators, says the record, roared with laughter, like Ajax. The king sent for the machine, and had it worked in the presence of the court. The figure rolled its eyes, opened its mouth, turned up its nose, let its head fall, and bent its back.

'Upon my word', said the king, 'I do not know whether I ought not to weep rather than laugh, on seeing how the poor people of England have been fooled for so many centuries.'

These vile tricks were the least of the sins of the monks. In several monasteries the visitors found implements for coining base money. In others they discovered traces of the horrible cruelties practised by the monks of one faction against those of another. Descending into the gloomy dungeons, they perceived, by the help of their torches, the bones of a great number of wretched people, some of whom had died of hunger and others had been crucified. But debauchery was the most frequent offence. Those pretended priests of a God who has said: *Be ye holy, for I the Lord am holy,* covered themselves with the hypocritical mantle of their priesthood, and indulged in infamous impurities. They discovered one monk, who, turning auricular confession to an abominable purpose, had carried adultery into two or three hundred families. The list was exhibited, and some of the commissioners, to their great astonishment, says a contemporary writer, found the names of their own wives upon it.

There were sometimes riots, sieges, and battles. The royal commissioners arrived at Norton Abbey in Cheshire, the abbots of which were notorious for having carried on a scandalous traffic with the monastic plate. On the last day of their visit, the abbot sent out his monks to muster his supporters, and collected a band of two or three hundred men, who surrounded the monastery to prevent the commissioners from carrying anything away. The latter took refuge in a tower, which they barricaded. It was two hours past midnight: the abbot had ordered an ox to be killed to feed his rabble, seated round the fires in front of the monastery, and even in the courtyard. On a sudden Sir Piers Dulton, a justice of the peace, arrived, and fell with his posse upon the monks and their defenders. The besiegers were struck with terror, and ran off as fast as they could, hiding themselves among the fish ponds and in the out-houses. The abbot and three canons, the instigators of the riot, were imprisoned in Halton Castle.

Be it said that the king's commissioners met with houses of another character. When George Gifford was visiting the monasteries of Lincolnshire, he came to a lonely district, abounding in water but very poor, where the abbey of Woolstrop was situated. The inhabitants of the neighbourhood, notwithstanding their destitution, praised the charity of the recluses. Entering the house, Gifford found an honest prior and some pious monks, who copied books, made their own clothes, and practised the arts of embroidering, carving, painting, and engraving. The visitor petitioned the king for the preservation of this monastery.

The commissioners had particular instructions for the women's convents. 'Is your house perfectly closed?' they asked the abbess and the nuns. 'Can a man get into it? Are you in the habit of writing love letters?' At Lichfield the nuns declared that there was no disorder in the convent; but one good old woman told everything, and when Layton reproached the prioress for her falsehood, she replied: 'Our religion compels us to it. At our admission we swore never to reveal the secret sins that were committed among us.' There were some houses in which nearly all the nuns trampled under foot the most sacred duties of their sex, and were without mercy for the unhappy fruits of their disorders.

Such were frequently in those times the monastic orders of the West. The eloquent apologists who eulogize their virtues without distinction, and the exaggerating critics who pronounce the same sentence of condemnation against all are both mistaken. We have rendered homage to the monks who were upright; we may blame those who were guilty. The scandals, let us say, did not proceed from the founders of these orders. Sentiments, opposed beyond a doubt to the principles of the gospel, although they were well intentioned, had presided over the formation of the monasteries. The hermits Paul, Anthony, and others of the third and fourth centuries gave themselves up to an anti-evangelical asceticism, but still they struggled courageously against temptation. However, one must be very ignorant not to see that corruption must eventually issue from monastic institutions. *Every plant which my heavenly Father hath not planted shall be rooted up,* is the language of the gospel.

We do not exaggerate. The monasteries were sometimes an asylum in which men and women, whose hearts had been wrecked in the tempests of life, sought a repose which the world did not offer. They were mistaken; they ought to have lived with God, but in the midst of society. And yet there is a pleasure in believing that behind those walls, which hid so much corruption, there were some elect souls who loved God. Such were found at Catesby, at Godstow, near Oxford, and in other places. The visitors asked for the preservation of these houses.

If the visitation of the religious houses was a bitter draught to many of the inmates, it was a cup of joy to the greater number. Many monks and nuns had been put into them during their infancy, and were detained in them against their will. No one ought to be forced, according to Cromwell's principles. When the visitation took place, the visitors announced to every monk under twenty-four years of age, and to every nun under twenty-one, that they might go free. Almost all to whom the doors were thus opened hastened to profit by it. A secular dress was given them, with some money, and they departed with pleasure. But great was the sorrow among many whose age exceeded the limit. Falling on their knees, they entreated the commissioners to obtain a similar favour for them. 'The life we lead here', they said, 'is contrary to our conscience.'

The commissioners returned to London, and made their report to the council. They were distressed and disgusted. 'We have discovered', they said, 'not seven, but more than seven hundred thousand deadly sins. ... These abominable monks are the *ravening wolves* whose coming Christ has announced, and who under sheep's clothing devour the flock. Here are the confessions of the monks and nuns, subscribed with their own hands. This book may well be called *The Book of God's Judgment*. The monasteries are so full of iniquity that they ought to fall down under such a weight. If there be here and there any innocent cloister, they are so few in number that they cannot save the others. Our hearts melt and all our limbs tremble at the thought of the abominations we have witnessed. O Lord! what wilt thou answer to the five cities which thou didst consume by fire, when they remind thee of the iniquities of those monks, with whom thou hast so long borne? The eloquence of Ptolemy, the memory of Pliny, and the pen of St Augustine would not be able to give us the detestable history of these abominations.'

The council began to deliberate, and many of the members called for the secularization of a part of the monasteries. The partisans of the religious orders took up their defence, and acknowledged that there was room for reform. 'But', they added, 'will you deprive of all asylum the pious souls who desire to quit the world, and lead a devout life to the glory of their Maker?' They tried even to invalidate in some points the testimony of the visitors; but the latter declared that, far from having recorded lightly those scandalous facts, they had excluded many.

Men of influence supported the commissioners' conclusions; a few members of the council were inclined to indulgence; even Cromwell seemed disposed to attempt the reform of whatever was susceptible of improvement; but many believed that all amendment was impossible. 'We must, above all things, diminish the wealth of the clergy', said Dr Cox; 'for so long as they do not imitate the poverty of Christ, the people will not follow their teaching. I have no doubt', he added, with a touch of irony, 'that the bishops, priests, and monks will readily free themselves from the heavy burden of wealth of every kind, which renders the fulfilment of their spiritual duties impossible.' Other reasons were alleged. 'The income of the monasteries', said one of the privy councillors, 'amounts to 500,000 ducats, while that of all the nobility of England is only 380,000. This disproportion is intolerable, and must be put an end to. For the welfare of his subjects and of the church, the king should increase the number of bishoprics, parishes, and hospitals. He must augment the forces of the state, and prepare to resist the emperor, whose fleets and armies threaten us. Shall we ask the people for taxes, who have already so much trouble to get a living, while the monks continue to consume their wealth in laziness and debauchery? It would be monstrous injustice. The treasures which the religious houses derive from the nation ought no longer to be useless to the nation.'[1]

In February 1536, this serious matter was laid before Parliament. It was Thomas Cromwell whose heavy hand struck these receptacles of impurity, and whom men called 'the hammer of the monks', who proposed this great reform. He laid on the table of the commons that famous *Black Book*, in which were inscribed the misdeeds of the religious orders, and desired that it should be read to the house. The book is no longer in existence; it was destroyed in the reign of Queen Mary by those who had an interest in its suppression.[2] But it was then opened before the Parliament of England. There had never before been such a reading in any assembly. The facts were clearly recorded – the most detestable enormities were not veiled: the horrible confessions of the monks, signed

[1] [In *English Monasteries on the Eve of the Dissolution* (Oxford Studies, 1919), A. Savine estimates the gross income of the religious houses to have been about £163,000. The ordinary annual income of the government was slightly more than £100,000.]

[2] [It was alleged by the Protestant historians of Elizabeth's reign that the *Black Book* was destroyed by Bishop Bonner. The Romanists affirmed that it was destroyed by the reforming party, who wished to destroy the evidence on which they acted.]

with their own hands, were exhibited to the members of the commons. The recital produced an extraordinary effect. Men had had no idea of such abominable scandals. The house was horror-stricken, and 'Down with them – down with them!' was shouted on every side.

The debate commenced. Personally, the members were generally interested in the preservation of the monasteries; most of them had some connection with one cloister or another; priors and other heads had relations and friends in Parliament. Nevertheless the condemnation was general, and men spoke of those monkish sanctuaries as, in former times, men had spoken of the priests of Jezebel – 'Let us pull down their houses, and overturn their altars.' There were, however, some objections. Twenty-eight abbots, heads of the great monasteries, were entitled to sit as barons in the upper house: these were respected. Besides, the great monasteries were less disorderly than the small ones. Cromwell restricted himself for the moment to the suppression of 372 cloisters, in each of which the annual income was less than £200.[1] The abbots, flattered by the exception made in their favour, were silent, and even the bishops hardly cared to defend institutions which had long been withdrawn from their authority. 'These monasteries', said Cromwell, 'being the dishonour of religion, and all the attempts, repeated through more than two centuries, having shown that their reformation is impossible, the king, as supreme head of the church under God, proposes to the lords and commons, and these agree, that the possessions of the said houses shall cease to be wasted for the maintenance of sin, and shall be converted to better uses.'

There was immediately a great commotion throughout England. Some rejoiced, while others wept: superstition became active, and weak minds believed everything that was told them. 'The Virgin', they were assured, 'had appeared to certain monks, and ordered them to serve her as they had hitherto done.' 'What! no more religious houses', exclaimed others, through their tears. 'On the contrary', said Latimer; 'look at that man and woman living together piously, tranquilly, in the fear of God, keeping his word and active in the duties of their calling: they form a

[1] [G. Baskerville in his *English Monks and the Suppression of the Monasteries* (1937) calculates that immediate suppression came to only about 220 houses, the remainder gaining a brief respite.]

religious house, one that is truly acceptable to God. Pure religion consists not in wearing a hood, but in visiting the fatherless and the widows, and keeping ourselves unspotted from the world. What has hitherto been called a religious life was an unreligious life; yea, rather an hypocrisy.' 'And yet', said the devout, 'the monks had more holiness than those who live in the world.' To this Latimer replied: 'When St Anthony lived in the desert on bread and water, and thought himself the most holy of men, he asked God who should be his companion in heaven, if it were possible for him to have one. 'Go to Alexandria', said the Lord; 'in such a street and house you will find him.' Anthony left the desert, sought the house, and found a poor cobbler in his shop mending old shoes. The saint took up his abode with him, that he might learn by what mortifications the cobbler had made himself worthy of such great celestial honour. Every morning the poor man knelt down in prayer with his wife, and then went to work. When the dinner hour arrived, he sat down at a table on which were bread and cheese; he gave thanks, ate his meal with joy, brought up his children in the fear of God, and faithfully discharged all his duties. At this sight, St Anthony looked inwards, became contrite of heart, and put away his pride. Such is the new sort of *religious houses',* added Latimer, 'that we desire to have now.'[1]

And yet, strange to say, Latimer, now Bishop of Worcester, was almost the only person among the evangelicals who raised his voice in favour of the religious bodies. He feared that if the property of the monasteries passed into the greedy hands of Henry's courtiers, the tenants, accustomed to the mild treatment of the abbots, would be oppressed by the lay landlords, desirous of realizing the fruits of their estate unto the very last drop. Hence he was anxious that a few monasteries should be preserved as houses of study, prayer, hospitality, charity, and preaching. Cranmer, who had more discernment and a more practical spirit, had no hope of the monks. 'Satan', he said, 'lives in the monasteries; he is satisfied and at his ease, like a gentleman in his inn, and the monks and nuns are his very humble servants.'[2] The primate, however, took little if any part in this great measure. His episcopal jurisdiction was suspended

---

[1] Latimer's *Sermons* (Parker Society), pp. 391-3.
[2] Cranmer's *Letters and Remains* (Parker Society), p. 64.

while the business was in hand, and he could do no other than acquiesce in the work of the vicar-general.

The bill for the suppression of the monasteries was introduced into the House of Commons on 11 March 1536. The confiscated wealth of the monasteries was taken by the Crown. The possessions hitherto employed by a few to gratify their carnal appetites seemed destined to contribute to the prosperity of the whole nation.

Unhappily, the shameless cupidity of the monks was replaced by a cupidity of a different nature. Petitions poured in to Cromwell from every quarter. The saying of Scripture was fulfilled, *Wheresoever the carcase is, there will the eagles be gathered together.* Thomas Cobham, brother of Lord Cobham, represented that the Grey Friars' house at Canterbury was in a convenient position for him; that it was the city where he was born, and where all his friends lived. He consequently asked that it should be given him, and Cranmer, whose niece he had married, supported the prayer. 'My good lord', said Lord Chancellor Audley, 'my only salary is that of the chancellorship; give me a few good houses; I will give you my friendship during my life, and twenty pounds sterling for your trouble.' 'My specially dear lord', said Sir Thomas Eliot, 'I have been the king's ambassador at Rome; my services deserve some recompense. Pray His Majesty to grant me some of the suppressed monastic lands. I will give your lordship the income of the first year.'

History has to record evils of another nature. Some of the finest libraries in England were destroyed, and works of great value sold for a trifle. Friends of learning on the Continent bought many of them, and carried away whole ship-loads. One man changed his religion for the sake of a piece of abbey land. Some persons had imagined that the suppression of the monasteries would lead to the abolition of taxes and subsidies; but it was not so, and the nation found itself burdened with a new need to make provision for the poor, in addition to the ordinary taxes. There were, however, more worthy cases than those of the king and his courtiers. 'Most dread, mighty, and noble prince', wrote the lord mayor of London to the king, 'give orders that the three city hospitals shall henceforward subserve not the pleasures of those canons, priests, and monks, whose dirty and disgusting bodies encumber our streets; but be used for the comfort of the sick and blind, the aged and crippled.'

The act of Parliament suppressing the poorer religious houses was immediately carried out. The Earl of Sussex, Sir John St Clair, Anthony Fitzherbert, Richard Cromwell, and several other commissioners, travelled through England and made known to the religious communities the statutory dissolution. The voice of truth was heard from a small number of monasteries. 'Assuredly', said the Lincolnshire Franciscans, 'the perfection of Christian life does not consist in wearing a grey frock, in disguising ourselves in strange fashion, in bending the body and nodding the head, and in wearing a girdle full of knots. The true Christian life has been divinely manifested to us in Christ; and for that reason we submit with one consent to the king's orders.' The monks of the house of St Andrew at Northampton acknowledged to the commissioners that they had taken the habit of the order to live in comfortable idleness and not by virtuous labour, and had indulged in continual drunkenness, and in carnal and voluptuous appetites. 'We have covered the gospel of Christ with shame', they said. 'Now, seeing the gulf of everlasting fire gaping to swallow us up and impelled by the stings of our conscience, we humble ourselves with lowly repentance, and pray for pardon, giving up ourselves and our monastery to our sovereign king and lord.'

But they did not all use the same language. There was a ceaseless movement in the cloisters; bursts of sorrow and fear, of anger and despair. What! No more monasteries! no more religious pomps! no more gossip! no more refectory! Those halls, wherein their predecessors had paced for centuries; those chapels in which they had worshipped kneeling on the pavement were to be converted to common uses. A few monasteries endeavoured to bribe Cromwell: 'If you save our house', said the Abbot of Peterborough, 'I will reward the king and you well.' But Cromwell had conceived a great national measure, and wished to carry it out. Neither the eloquence of the monks, their prayers, their promises, nor their money could move him.

Some of the abbots set themselves in open revolt against the king, but were forced to submit at last. The old halls, the long galleries, the narrow cells of the religious houses became emptier from day to day. The monks received a pension in proportion to their age. Those who desired to continue in the religious life were sent to the large monasteries. Many were dismissed with a few shillings for their journey and a new gown. 'As for you', said the commissioners to the young monks under twenty-five, 'you must earn a living by the work of your hands.' The same rule was applied to the nuns.

There was great suffering at this period. The inhabitants of the cloisters were strangers in the world: England was to them an unknown land. Monks and nuns might be seen wandering from door to door, seeking an asylum for the night. Many, who were young then, grew old in beggary. Their sin had been great, and so was their chastisement. Some of the monks fell into a gloomy melancholy, even into frightful despair: the remembrance of their faults pursued them; God's judgment terrified them; the sight of their miseries infuriated them. 'I am like Esau', said one of them, 'I shall be eternally damned.' And he strangled himself with his collar. Another stabbed himself with a penknife. Some compassionate people having deprived him of the power of injuring himself, he exclaimed with rage, 'If I cannot die in this manner, I shall easily find another'; and taking a piece of paper, he wrote on it: 'The king oppresses his people like a tyrant.' This he placed in one of the church books, where it was found by a parishioner, who in great alarm called out to the persons around him. The monk, full of hope that he would be brought to trial, drew near and said, 'It was I who did it: here I am; let them put me to death.'

Erelong those gloomy clouds, which seemed to announce a day of storms, appeared to break. There were tempests afterwards, but, speaking generally, England found in this energetic act one of the sources of her greatness, instead of the misfortunes with which she was threatened. At the moment when greedy eyes began to covet the revenues of Cambridge and Oxford, a recollection of the pleasant days of his youth was awakened in Henry's mind. 'I will not permit the wolves around me', he said, 'to fall upon the universities.' Indeed, the wealth of a few monasteries was employed in the foundation of new schools, and particularly of Trinity College, Cambridge; and these institutions helped to spread throughout England the lights of the Renaissance and of the reformation. An eloquent voice was heard from those antique halls, saying: 'O Most Invincible Prince, great is the work that you have begun. Christ had laid the foundation; the apostles raised the building. But alas! barren weeds had overrun it; the papal tyranny had bowed all heads beneath its yoke. Now, you have rejected the pope; you have banished the race of monks. What more can we ask for? We pray that those houses of cenobites, where an ignorant swarm of drones was wont to buzz, should behold in their academic halls a generous youth, eager to be taught, and learned men to teach them. Let the light which has been restored to us spread its rays far and wide and kindle other torches, so that the darkness may be put to flight by the dawn of a new day.'

It was not learning alone that gained by the suppression of the monasteries. Monastic wealth, hitherto useless, helped to strengthen England's defences and to build up her navy. At the same time, by the reformation the moral force of the nation gained even more than the material force. The abolition of the papacy restored to the people that national unity which Rome had taken away; and England, freed from subjection to a foreign power, could oppose her enemies with a sword of might and a front of iron.

Political economy, rural economy, all that concerns the collection and distribution of wealth then took a start that nothing has been able to check. The estates, taken from the easy-going monks, produced riches. The king and the nobility, desirous of deriving the greatest gain possible from the domains that had fallen to them, endeavoured to improve agriculture. Many men, until that time useless, electrified by the movement of minds, sought the means of existence. The reformation, from which the nation expected only purity of doctrine, helped to increase the general prosperity, industry, commerce, and navigation. The poor remembered that God had commanded man to eat his bread, not in the shade of the monasteries, but *in the sweat of his brow*. To this epoch we must ascribe the origin of those mercantile enterprises, of those long and distant voyages which were to be one day the strength of Great Britain. Henry VIII was truly the father of Elizabeth.

Moral, social, and political development was no less a gainer by the order that was established. At the first moment, no doubt, England presented the appearance of a vast chaos: but from that chaos there sprang a new world. Forces which had hitherto been buried in obscure cells were employed for the good of society. The men who had been dwelling carelessly within or without the cloister walls, and had expended all their activity in listlessly giving or listlessly receiving alms, were violently shaken by the blows from the *Malleus monachorum* (the hammer of the monks): they aroused themselves, and made exertions which turned to the public good. Their children, and especially their grandchildren, became useful citizens. The third estate appeared. The population of the cloisters was transformed into an active and intelligent middle class. The very wealth acquired, it is true greedily, by the nobility, secured them an independence, which enabled them to oppose a salutary counterpoise to the pretensions of the Crown. The upper house, where the ecclesiastical element had predominated, became essentially a lay house by the absence of the abbots and priors. A new life animated antique institutions that had remained almost useless. It was not, in truth, until later that England, having become decidedly evangelical and constitutional, emerged in greatness from the ruins of feudalism and popery; but an important step was taken under Henry VIII. That great transformation extended its influence even beyond the shores of Britain. The blow aimed at the system of the Middle Ages re-echoed throughout Europe, and everywhere shook the artificial scaffolding. Spain and Italy alone remained almost motionless in the midst of their ancient darkness.

The suppression of the monasteries, begun in 1535, was brought to a conclusion in 1539 by a second act of Parliament.

A voice was heard from these ruined houses exclaiming: 'Praise and thanksgiving to God! *For other foundation can no man lay than Jesus Christ.* Whoever believes that Jesus Christ is the *pacifier* who turneth away from our heads the strokes of God's wrath, lays the true foundation; and on that firm base he shall raise a better building than that which had the monks for its pillars!' This prophecy of Sir William Overbury did not fail of accomplishment.

CHAPTER EIGHT

Henry Negotiates with German Lutherans

(1534 to 1535)

H enry VIII, having thrown down the *chief pillar of the papacy* in England – the monks – felt the necessity of strengthening the work he had begun by alliances with the continental Protestants. He did not turn to the Swiss or the French reformers: their small political importance, as well as the decided character of their reform, alienated him from them. 'What inconsiderate men they are', said Calvin, 'who exalt the King of England. To ascribe sovereign authority to the prince in everything, to call him supreme head of the church under Christ, is blasphemy.'[1]

Henry hoped more from Germany than from Switzerland. As early as 1534 three senators of Lubeck had presented to him the Lutheran Confession of Augsburg of 1530, and proposed an alliance against the Roman pontiff.[2] Anne Boleyn pressed the king to unite with the Protestants, and in the spring of 1535 Henry's chaplain, Dr Anthony Barnes,

---

[1] [The words of Calvin which precede this quotation from his commentary on Amos 7:13 (Calvin Translation Society: *Minor Prophets,* ii, p. 349) are worth quoting as further illustrative of the strong feelings which the reformer entertained on this subject: '"Prophesy not again any more at Bethel, for it is the king's sanctuary and it is his court." Amaziah wished here to prove by the king's authority that the received worship at Bethel was legitimate. How so? "The king has established it; it is not then lawful for anyone to say a word to the contrary; the king could do this by his own right; for his majesty is sacred." We see the object in view. And how many are there at this day under the papacy who accumulate on kings all the authority and power they can, in order that no dispute may be made about religion; but power is to be vested in one king to determine according to his own will whatever he pleases, and this is to remain fixed without any dispute.']

[2] Rymer, *Fœdera,* VI, ii, p. 214.

was sent to Wittenberg, where he endeavoured to induce the reformers to claim his master's protection. Melanchthon, who was more inclined than Luther to have recourse to princes, did not reject the advances of Henry VIII. 'Sire', he wrote in March 1535, 'this is now the golden age for Britain. In times of old, when the armies of the Goths had stifled letters in Europe, your island restored them to the universe. I entreat you in the name of Jesus Christ to plead for us before kings.' The illustrious doctor dedicated to this prince the new edition of his *Common-Places,* and commissioned Alexander Alesius, a Scot, to present it with the hope that he should see England become the salvation of many nations, and even of the whole church of Christ. Alesius, who had taken refuge in Saxony, was happy to return to that island from which the fanaticism of the Scottish clergy had compelled him to flee. He was presented to the uncle of his king, and Henry, delighted with the Scot, said to him: 'I name you my scholar', and directed Cranmer to send Melanchthon two hundred florins. They were accompanied by a letter for the illustrious professor, in which the king signed himself: *Your friend Henry.*

But it was not long before the hopes of a union between Germany and England seemed to vanish. Scarcely had Melanchthon vaunted in his dedication to Henry VIII the moderation of the king – a moderation worthy (he had said) of a wise prince – when he heard of the execution of Fisher and More. He shrank back with terror. 'More', he exclaimed, 'has been put to death, and others with him.' The cruelties of the king tortured the gentle Philip. The idea that a man of letters like More should fall by the hands of the executioner scandalized him. He began to fear for his own life. 'I am myself', he said, 'in great peril.'

Henry did not suspect the horror which his crime would excite on the Continent, and had just read with delight a passage of Melanchthon in which the latter compared him to Ptolemy Philadelphus! He therefore said to Barnes: 'Go and bring him back with you.' Barnes returned to Wittenberg in September and delivered his message. But the doctor of Germany had never received so alarming an invitation before. He imagined it to be a treacherous scheme. 'The mere thought of the journey', he said, 'overwhelms me with distress.' Barnes tried to encourage him. 'The king will give you a magnificent escort', he said, 'and even hostages, if you desire it.' Melanchthon, who had More's bleeding head continually before him, was immovable. Luther also regarded Barnes with an unfavourable eye, and called him *the dark Englishman.*

The envoy was more fortunate with the Elector of Saxony. John Frederick, hearing that the King of England was desirous of forming an alliance with the princes of Germany, replied that he would communicate this important demand to them. He then entertained Barnes at a sumptuous breakfast, made him handsome presents, and wrote to Henry VIII that the desire manifested by him to reform religious doctrine augmented his love for him, 'for', he added, 'it belongs to kings to propagate Christ's gospel far and wide.'

Luther also, but from other motives than those of the elector, did not look so closely as Melanchthon; the suppression of the monasteries prepossessed him in favour of his ancient adversary. The penalties with which the Carthusians and others had been visited did not alarm him. Vergerio, the papal legate, who was at Wittenberg at the beginning of November, invited Luther to breakfast with him. 'I know', he said, 'that King Henry kills cardinals and bishops, but …' and biting his lips, he made a significant movement with his hand, as if he wished to cut off the king's head. When relating this anecdote to Melanchthon, who was then at Jena, Luther added: 'Would to God that we possessed several kings of England to put to death those bishops, cardinals, legates, and popes who are nothing but robbers, traitors, and devils!' Luther was less tender than he is represented when contrasted with Calvin. Those hasty words expressed really the thoughts of all parties. The spiritual leaven of the gospel had to work for a century or more upon the hard material of which the heart of man is made, before the errors of Romish teachings, a thousand years old, were banished. No doubt there was an immediate mitigation produced by the reformation; but if anyone had told the men of the sixteenth century that it was wrong to put men to death for acts of impiety, they would have been as astonished, and perhaps more so, than our judges, if they were abused because, in conformity with the law, they visited murder with capital punishment. It is strange, however, that it required so many centuries to understand those glorious words of our Saviour: *The Son of man is not come to destroy men's lives, but to save them* (Luke 9:56).

The condition which the German Protestants placed on their union with Henry VIII rendered the alliance difficult. 'We only ask one thing', said the reformers to Barnes, 'that the doctrine which is *in conformity with Scripture* be restored to the *whole world*'; but Henry still observed the Catholic doctrine. He was told, however, that the Lutherans and Francis I, thanks to Melanchthon's mediation, were probably coming to an agreement, and that a general council would be summoned. What treatment could he expect from such an assembly, he who had so grievously offended the papacy! Desirous of preventing a council at any price, the king determined in September 1535, to send a more important embassy to the Lutherans, in order to persuade them to renounce the idea of coming to terms with the pope, and rather to form an alliance with England.

Consequently Edward Fox, Bishop of Hereford, a proud and insolent courtier, and Nicholas Heath, archdeacon of Stafford, an amiable and enlightened man, with some others, started for Germany and joined Barnes, who had preceded them. On 24 December they were admitted into the presence of the Elector of Saxony, the Landgrave of Hesse, and other Protestant deputies and princes: 'The king our master', they said, 'has abolished the power of the Roman bishop throughout his dominions, and rejected his pretended pardons and his old wives' stories. Accordingly the pope, in a transport of fury, has summoned all the kings of the earth to take arms against him. But neither pope nor papists alarm our prince. He offers you his person, his wealth, and his sceptre to combat the Roman power. Let us unite against it, and the Spirit of God will bind our confederation together.' The princes replied to this eloquent harangue, 'that if the king engaged to propagate the pure doctrine of the faith as it had been confessed at the Diet of Augsburg; if he engaged, like them, never to concede to the Roman bishop any jurisdiction in his states, they would name him defender and protector of their confederation.' They added that they would send a deputation, including one man of excellent learning (meaning Melanchthon), to confer with the king upon the changes to be made in the church. The Englishmen could not conceal their joy, but the theologian had lost all confidence in Henry VIII. 'The death of More distresses me: I will have nothing to do with the business.' On 25 December 1535, the German princes at Schmalkald presented Fox with detailed propositions for a league with England. Henry VIII consulted Bishop Gardiner, at that time his ambassador in France, and then declined the terms, Gardiner having advised that the outcome of a league would be the establishment of Protestantism in England.

Meanwhile, at home, Henry's relations with the most decided partisans of the papacy were far from improving. His daughter Mary, whose temper was melancholy and irritable, observed no bounds as regards her father's friends or acts, and refused to submit to his orders. 'I bid her renounce the title of princess', said Henry in a passion. – 'If I consented not to be regarded as such', she answered, 'I should go against my conscience and incur God's displeasure.' Henry, no friend of half measures, talked of putting his daughter to death, and thus frightening the rebels. That wretched prince had a remarkable tendency for killing those who were nearest to him. We may see a father correct his child with a stripe; but with this man, a blow from his hand was fatal. There was already some talk of sending the princess to the Tower, when the evangelical Cranmer ventured to intercede in behalf of the Catholic Mary. He reminded Henry that he was her father, and that if he took away her life, he would incur universal reprobation. The king gave way to these representations, predicting to the archbishop that this intervention would some day cost him dear. In fact, when Mary became queen she put to death the man who had saved her life. Henry was content to order his daughter to be separated from her mother. On the other hand, the terrified Catherine endeavoured to mollify the princess. 'Obey the king in all things', she wrote from Buckden,[1] where she was living, 'except in those which would destroy your soul. Speak little; trouble yourself about nothing, play on the spinet or lute.' This unhappy woman, who had found so much bitterness in the conjugal estate, added: 'Above all, do not desire a husband, nor even think of it, I beg you in the name of Christ's passion. Your loving mother, CATHERINE THE QUEEN.'

But the mother was not less decided than the daughter in maintaining her rights, and would not renounce her title of queen, notwithstanding

---

[1] [Four miles from Huntingdon: formerly known as Bugden, where was a palace belonging to the Bishop of Lincoln.]

Henry's orders. A commission composed of the Duke of Suffolk, lord Sussex, and others arrived at Buckden to try to induce her to do so, and all the household of the princess was called together. The intrepid daughter of Ferdinand and Isabella said with a firm voice: 'I am the queen, the king's true wife.' Being informed that it was intended to remove her to Somersham and separate her from some of her best friends, she answered: 'I will not go unless you bind me with ropes.' And to prevent this she took to her bed and refused to dress, saying she was ill. The king sent two Catholic prelates, the Archbishop of York and the Bishop of Durham, hoping to soften her. 'Madam', said the archbishop, 'your marriage being invalid.' – 'It is a lawful marriage', she exclaimed with passionate vehemence. 'Until death I shall be His Majesty's wife.' – 'Members of your own council', continued the archbishop, 'acknowledge that your marriage with Prince Arthur was actually consummated.' – 'It is all false!' she exclaimed in a loud tone. – 'The divorce was consequently pronounced.' – 'By whom?' she asked. – 'By my Lord of Canterbury.' – 'And who is he?' returned the queen. 'A shadow! The pope has declared in my favour, and he is Christ's vicar.' – 'The king will treat you like a dear sister', said Bishop Tunstall. – 'Nothing in the world', answered Catherine, 'neither the loss of my possessions nor the prospect of death, will make me give up my rights.'

In October, 1535, Catherine was still at Buckden. That noble but fanatical woman increased her austerity, indulged in the harshest practices of an ascetic life, prayed frequently bare-kneed on the floor, while at the same time a deadly sorrow was undermining her health. At last consumption declared itself; and as it was judged that her condition required a change of air, she was removed to Kimbolton Castle, some eight miles to the west. She longed for the society of her daughter, which would no doubt have alleviated her sufferings; but she asked in vain with tears to see her. Mary also entreated the king to let her visit her mother: he was inflexible.

Henry's harshness towards the aunt of Charles V excited the wrath of that monarch to the highest degree. He was then returning victorious from his expedition against the corsair Barbarossa, whom he had driven out of Tunis, and determined to delay no longer in carrying out the mission he had received from the pope. To that end it was necessary to obtain, if not the co-operation, at least the neutrality of Francis I. That was not easy. The King of France had always courted the alliance of England: he had signed a treaty with Henry against the emperor and against the pope, and had just sought an alliance with the Lutheran princes. But the emperor knew that the acquisition of Italy, or at least of Lombardy, was the favourite idea of Francis I. Charles was equally desirous of it, but he was so impatient to re-establish Catherine of Aragon on the throne, and bring England again under the dominion of the pope, that he determined to sacrifice Italy, if only in appearance. Sforza, Duke of Milan, having just died without children, the emperor offered Francis I the Duchy of Milan for his second son, the Duke of Orleans, if he would not oppose his designs against England. The King of France eagerly accepted the proposal, and wishing to give a proof of his zeal, he even proposed that the pope should summon all the princes of Christendom to force the King of England to submit to the see of Rome. The love he had for Milan went so far as to make him propose a crusade against his natural ally, Henry VIII.

The matter was becoming serious: rarely had a greater danger threatened England, when an important event suddenly removed it. At the very time when Charles V, aided by Francis I, desired to rouse Europe in order to restore his aunt on the throne, she died. About the end of December 1535, Catherine became seriously ill, and felt that God was bringing her great sorrows to an end. The king, wishing to keep up appearances, sent to enquire after her. The queen, firm to the last in her principles, sent for her lawyers and dictated her will to them. 'I am ready', she said, 'to yield up my soul unto God. ... I supplicate that five hundred masses be said for my soul; and that some personage go in pilgrimage for me to Our Lady of Walsingham. I bequeath my gowns to the convent, and the furs of the same I give to my daughter.' Then Catherine thought of the king: to her he was always her husband, and despite his injustice, she would not address him but with respect. Feeling that the end was not far off, she dictated the following letter, at once so simple and so noble:

My most dear lord, king, and husband,

The hour of my death now approaching, I cannot choose but, out of the love I bear you, advise you of your soul's health. You have cast me into many calamities and yourself into many troubles; but I forgive you all, and pray God to do likewise. I commend unto you Mary our daughter, beseeching you to be a good father to her. Lastly, I make this vow, that mine eyes desire you above all things.

The queen, therefore, sought to bid farewell to him who had wrought her so much evil. Henry was moved, and even shed tears, but did not comply with the queen's wish: his conscience reproached him with his faults. On 7 January Catherine received the last sacraments, and at two o'clock she expired.

Anne felt at the bottom of her heart the rights of this princess. She had yielded to her imagination, and to the absolute will of the king; her marriage had given her some moments of happiness, but her soul was often troubled. She thought to herself that the proud Spanish woman was the one to whom Henry had given his faith; and doubted whether the crown did not belong to the daughter of Isabella. Catherine's death removed her anxieties. 'Now', she said, 'now I am indeed a queen.' The tears of the people accompanied to the tomb that unhappy and (to say truth) superstitious woman; but she was an affectionate mother, a high-spirited wife, and a queen of indomitable pride.

This decease was destined to effect great changes in Europe. The emperor, who was forming a holy alliance to restore his aunt to the throne, and who, to succeed, had gone so far as to sacrifice the northern part of Italy, having nothing more to do with Catherine, sheathed his sword and kept Milan. Francis I, vexed at seeing the prey slip from him which he had so eagerly coveted, and fancied already in his hands, went into a furious passion, and prepared for a war to the death. The emperor and the King of France, instead of marching together against Henry, began each of them to court him, desiring to have him for an ally in the fierce struggle that was about to begin.

At the same time Catherine's death facilitated, as we have said, the alliance of the king with the Protestants of Germany, who had maintained the validity of his marriage with the princess of Aragon. One of their chief grievances against Henry VIII had thus disappeared. Both sides now thought they could take a step forward and strive to come to an understanding theologically. The points on which they differed were important. 'The King of England', they said at Wittenberg, 'wishes to be pope in the place of the pope, and maintains most of the errors of the old popery, such as monasteries,[1] indulgences, the mass, prayers for the dead, and other Romish fables.'

The discussion began at Wittenberg. The champions in the theological tournament were Bishop Fox and Archdeacon Heath on one side; Melanchthon and Luther on the other. Heath, one of the young doctors whom Queen Anne had maintained at Cambridge University, charmed Melanchthon exceedingly. 'He excels in urbanity and sound doctrine', said the latter. Fox, on the other hand, who was the king's man, showed, in Philip's opinion, no taste either for philosophy or for agreeable and graceful conversation. The doctrine of the mass was the principal point of the discussion. They could not come to an understanding. Luther, who thought it would be only a three days' matter, seeing the time slip away, said to the elector: 'I have done more in four weeks than these Englishmen in twelve years. If they continue reforming in that style, England will never be *inside* or *out*.' This definition of the English reformation amused the Germans. They did not discuss, they disputed: it became a regular quarrel. 'I am disgusted with these debates', said Luther to Vice-Chancellor Burkhard, 'they make me sick.' Even the gentle Melanchthon exclaimed: 'All the world seems to me to be burning with hatred and anger.'

Accordingly the theological discussions were broken off, and the ambassadors of Henry VIII were admitted on 12 March into the presence of the elector. 'England is tranquil now', said the Bishop of Hereford; 'the death of a woman has for ever terminated all wrangling. At this moment the creed of Jesus Christ alone is the concern of His Majesty. The king therefore prays you to make an alliance between you and him possible, by modifying a few points of your Confession.' Whereupon the vice-chancellor of Saxony addressed Luther: 'What can we concede to the King of England?' – 'Nothing', answered the reformer. 'If we

---

[1] The great monasteries were not yet suppressed.

had been willing to concede anything, we might just as well have come to terms with the pope.' After this very positive declaration, Luther softened down a little. He knew well, as Calvin has said, 'that some men are weaker than others, and if we do not treat them very mildly, they lose their courage and turn away from religion; and that Christians who are more advanced in doctrine are bound to comfort the infirmities of the ignorant.' The Saxon reformer, retracing his steps a little, wrote to the vice-chancellor: 'It is true that England cannot embrace the whole truth all at once.' He thought it possible in certain cases to adopt other expressions, and tolerate some diversity of usages. 'But', he said, always firm in the faith, 'the great doctrines can neither be given up nor modified. Whether to make an alliance or not with the king is for my most gracious lord to decide: it is a secular matter. Only it is dangerous to unite outwardly, when the hearts are not in harmony.' The Protestant states, assembled on 24 April 1536, at Frankfurt on the Main, required Henry VIII to receive *the faith confessed at Augsburg,* and in that case expressed themselves ready to acknowledge him as protector of the evangelical alliance. The elector, who was much displeased with certain English ceremonies, added: 'Let Your Majesty thoroughly reform the *pontifical idolomania* in England.' It was agreed that Melanchthon, Sturm, Bucer, and Dracon should go to London to complete this great work of union. England and evangelical Germany were about to join hands.

This proposed alliance of the king with the Lutherans deeply chafed the Catholics of the kingdom, already so seriously offended by the suppression of the monasteries and the punishment of the two men to whom Henry (they said) was most indebted. While the Roman party was filled with anger, the political party was surprised by the bold step the prince had taken. But the blow which had struck two great victims had taught them that they must submit to the will of the monarch or perish. The scaffolds of Fisher and More had read them a great lesson of docility, and moulded all those around Henry to that servile spirit which leaves in the palace of a king nothing but a master and slaves.

They were about to see an illustrious instance in the trial of Anne Boleyn.

CHAPTER NINE

The Accusation of the Queen

(1535 to May 1536)

I f feeble minds did not shrink from bending beneath the royal despotism, men of fanatical mould cherished vengeance in their hearts. Great wounds had been inflicted on the papacy, and they burnt to strike some signal blow against the cause of reform. That also, they said, must have its victim. For all these monasteries sacrificed, one person must be immolated: one only, but taken from the most illustrious station. The king having, on the one side, struck his tutor and his friend, must now, to maintain the balance, strike his wife on the other. A tragedy was about to begin which would terminate in a frightful catastrophe. Anne Boleyn had not been brought up, as some have said, 'in the worst school in Europe', but in one of the best – in the household of the pious Margaret of Angoulême, who was the enlightened protectress not only of the learned, but of all friends of the gospel. Anne certainly seems to have had strong leanings towards the reformation and the reformers. And accordingly she was in the eyes of the papal partisans the principal cause of the change that had been wrought in the king's mind, and by him throughout the kingdom. The reformation, as we have seen, began in England about 1517 with the reading of the Holy Scriptures in the universities; but the most accredited Roman doctors have preferred to assign it another origin, and, speaking of Cranmer's connexion with Anne Boleyn, thirteen years later, have said, 'Such is the beginning of the reformation in England.'[1] In this assertion there is an error both of chronology and history.

Since her coronation, the queen had been in almost daily communication with the Archbishop of Canterbury, and habitually – even her

---

[1] Bossuet, *Histoire des Variations,* vii, art. 8.

enemies affirmed it – the interests of the evangelical cause were treated of. At one time Anne prayed Cranmer to come to the assistance of the persecuted Protestants. At another, full of the necessity of sending reapers into the harvest, she interested herself about such young persons as were poor, but whose pure morals and clear intellect seemed to qualify them for the practice of virtue and the study of letters;[1] these she assisted with great generosity. The queen did not encourage these students heedlessly: she required testimonials certifying as to the purity of their morals and the capacity of their intellect. If she was satisfied, she placed them at Oxford or Cambridge, and required them to spread around them, even while studying, the New Testament and the writings of the reformers. Many of the queen's pensioners did great service to the church and state in after-years. With these queenly qualities Anne combined more domestic ones. Cranmer saw her, like good Queen Claude, gathering round her a number of young ladies distinguished by their birth and their virtues, and working with them at tapestry of admirable perfection for the palace of Hampton Court, or at garments for the indigent. She established in certain poor parishes warehouses, filled with such things as the needy wanted. 'Her eye of charity, her hand of bounty', says a biographer, 'passed through the whole land.' 'She is said in three quarters of a year', adds Lord Herbert of Cherbury, the celebrated seventeenth-century philosopher and historian, 'to have bestowed fourteen or fifteen thousand pounds in this way', that is, in alms. And this distinguished writer, ambassador of England at the court of Louis XIII, and known in France by the exertions he made in behalf of the Protestants, adds: 'She had besides established a stock for poor artificers in the realm.' Such were the works of Queen Anne. Cranmer, who had great discernment of men and things, being touched by the regard which the queen had for those who professed the gospel, and seeing all that she did for the reformation and the consolation of the wretched, declared that next to the king, Anne was of all creatures living 'the one to whom he was most bound'.

Cranmer was not the only person among the evangelicals with whom Anne Boleyn maintained relations. From the first day she had seen

---

[1] Letter of Sir John Cheke, 1535. Parker's *Correspondence* (Parker Society), pp. 2-3.

Latimer, the Christian simplicity and apostolic manners of the reformer had touched her. When she heard him preach, she was delighted. The enthusiasm for that bold Christian preacher was universal. 'It is as impossible', said his hearers, 'for us to receive into our minds all the treasures of eloquence and knowledge which fall from his lips, as it would be for a little river to contain the waters of the ocean in its bed.' From the period (1535) when Latimer preached the Lent Sermons before the king, he was one of the most regular instruments of the queen's active charity.

A still more decided reformer had a high esteem for Anne Boleyn: this was Tyndale. No one, in his opinion, had declared with so much decision as the queen in favour of the New Testament and its circulation in English: and mention has already been made of the specially bound copy of his translation of the New Testament which he sent to England for the queen's acceptance in 1534.[1] This remarkable volume, now preserved in the library of the British Museum, is a monument of the veneration of the prisoner of Vilvorde for Anne Boleyn. A manuscript manual of devotion for the use of this princess has also been preserved: she used to present copies of it to her maids of honour. We see in it the value she attached to the Holy Scriptures: 'Give us, O Father of mercies', we read, 'the greatest of all gifts thou hast ever conferred on man – the knowledge of thy holy will, and the glad tidings of our salvation. Roman tyranny has long hidden it from us under Latin letters; but now it is promulgated, published, and freely circulated.'

Anne, having in 1535 lost Dr Betts, one of her chaplains, looked out for a man devoted to the gospel to take his place, for she loved to be surrounded by the most pious persons in England. She cast her eyes upon Matthew Parker, a native of Norwich, Fellow of Corpus Christi College, Cambridge, and a man who for two years had been preaching the truth with fervour. Parker loved retirement and obscurity; accordingly, when he received shortly after Palm Sunday two letters summoning him to court 'because the queen wished to see him', he was amazed and confounded. At first he wanted to refuse so brilliant a call; but Latimer wrote to him: 'Show yourself to the world; hide yourself no longer; work good while it is day, the night comes when no man

---

[1] Tyndale, *Doctrinal Treatises,* p. lxiv.

can work. We know what you can do; let not your will be less than your power.' Parker went to London, and in a short time his knowledge, piety, and prudence gained the entire esteem of the queen. That modest, intelligent, active man was just the person Anne wanted, and she took pleasure thenceforward in bestowing on him marks of her consideration. Parker was from this time one of those employed by Anne to distribute her benevolence. He had hardly arrived at court, when he presented to the queen one William Bill, a very young and very poor man, but by no means wanting in talent. Anne, rich in discernment, placed him in the number of students whom she was preparing for the ministry: he afterwards became Dean of Westminster. Parker, who began his career with Anne, was to finish it with Elizabeth. When he was deprived of all his offices by Queen Mary in 1554, he exclaimed: 'Now that I am stripped of everything, I live in God's presence, and am full of joy in my conscience. In this charming leisure I find greater pleasures than those supplied by the busy and perilous life I led at the court.' Forced to hide himself, often to flee by night, to escape the pursuit of his persecutors, the peace which he enjoyed was never troubled. He looked upon trials as the privilege of the child of God. All of a sudden a strange and unexpected calamity befell him. The daughter of Anne Boleyn, having ascended the throne, desired to have her mother's chaplain for Archbishop of Canterbury and primate of all England. 'I kneel before Your Majesty', he said to Queen Elizabeth, 'and pray you not to burden me with an office which requires a man of much more talent, knowledge, virtue, and experience than I possess.' A second letter from Nicholas Bacon, Lord Keeper of the Great Seal, repeated the summons. Then the unhappy Parker exclaimed in the depth of his sorrow: 'Alas! alas! Lord God! for what times hast thou preserved me! I am come into deep waters, where the floods overflow me. O Lord, I am oppressed: undertake for me. O Lord! strengthen me by thy mighty Spirit!' Parker was at the head of the Church of England for sixteen years, and dignified the elevated seat on which he had been constrained to sit. Such were the men whom Anne Boleyn gathered round her.

We should be mistaken, however, if we represented the young queen as a bigot, living like Catherine in the practices of a rigid austerity.

It appears even doubtful whether she knew by experience that inner, spiritual, and living Christianity which was found in Latimer, Tyndale, Cranmer, and Parker. She was a virtuous wife, a good Protestant, attached to the Bible, opposed to the pope, fond of good works, esteeming men of God more than courtiers; but she had not renounced the world and its pomps. A woman of the world, upright, religious, loving to do good, a class of which there is always a large number, she was unacquainted with the pious aspirations of a soul that lives in communion with God. Her position as queen and wife of Henry VIII may have hindered her from advancing in the path of a Christian life. She thought it possible to love God without renouncing the enjoyments of the age, and looked upon worldly things as an innocent recreation. Desiring to keep her husband's heart, she endeavoured to please him by cheerful conversation, by organizing pleasure parties of which she was the life, and by receiving all his courtiers gracefully. Placed on slippery ground and watched by prejudiced eyes, she may occasionally have let fall some imprudent expression. Her sprightliness and gaiety, her amiable freedom were in strong contrast with the graver and stiffer formalities of the English ladies. Latimer, who saw her closely, sometimes admonished her respectfully, when he was alone with her, and the grateful Anne would exclaim unaffectedly: 'You do me so much good! Pray never pass over a single fault.'

It is not from the writings of the pamphleteers that we must learn to know Anne Boleyn. Towards the end of the sixteenth century, opposite parties, in their extreme excitement, have painted her at one time in colours too dark, at another in colours too flattering. We must in this matter especially listen to men whose testimony is sanctioned by universal respect. There are not many princesses in history who have enjoyed, like Anne, the esteem of the most elevated minds – of Cranmer and Latimer, of Tyndale and Parker, and other Christians less illustrious, perhaps, but not less respectable. In the eyes of the papal partisans, however, she had committed an unpardonable crime: *she had separated England from the papacy:* and accordingly their savage hatred has known no bounds, and they have never ceased to blacken her memory with their vile calumnies. Of all the misdeeds that history can commit, the greatest consists in representing the innocent as if they were guilty. Many writers have forged and still forge base imputations against the reformers Luther, Calvin, and others. Anne Boleyn has had her full share of slander in this huge conspiracy of falsehood.[1]

The grandeur with which Anne was surrounded had opened her heart to the tenderest sympathies. To be the joy of her husband and the delight of her relations; to protect the friends of the gospel and to be loved by England – these were for some time the dreams of her young imagination. But ere long the crown of St Edward pressed heavily on her brow. The members of her own family became her enemies. Her uncle, the proud Duke of Norfolk, the chief along with Gardiner of the papal party, was animated by a secret hatred against the young woman who was the support of the evangelical party. Her father, the Earl of Wiltshire, imagining he saw that the king was not flattered at being his son-in-law, had quitted London, regretting a union which his ambition had so much desired. Lady Rochford, wife of Anne's brother, a woman of despicable character, whose former perfidies the queen had pardoned, and whom she had attached to the court, repaid this generous magnanimity by secretly plotting the ruin of a sister-in-law whose elevation had filled her with jealousy. At length, one of those who ate her bread and received favours from her was about to show her ingratitude to the unfortunate queen.

Among her ladies of honour was Jane Seymour, who united all the attractions of youth and beauty, and whose disposition held a certain mean between the severe gravity of Queen Catherine and the fascinating sprightliness of Queen Anne. Constancy in affection was not a feature of Henry's character; his heart was easily inflamed; his eye rested on the youthful Jane, and no sooner had he become sensible of her graces

---

[1] This sort of conspiracy extends from the publication of the work entitled, *De origine ac progressu schismatis Anglicani,* 1585, by Sanders – 'a book', says Bayle, 'in which there is much passion and very little accuracy' – down to the *Histoire de Henri VIII,* by Audin, a worthy successor of Sanders, and whose work is in high favour in all papal coteries. This miserable manufacture of outrageous fictions began even before Sanders, and is not yet ended. [The most easily accessible life of Anne Boleyn for the general reader is that to be found in Agnes Strickland's *Lives of the Queens of England,* vol. ii.]

than the charms of Anne Boleyn, which had formerly captivated him, became unendurable. The genial gaiety of the queen fatigued him; the accomplishments which are ordinarily the means of pleasing gave him umbrage; the zeal she manifested for Protestantism alienated him. Anne's enemies, especially the Duke of Norfolk and Lady Rochford, observed this, and resolved to take advantage of it to ruin the woman who overshadowed them.

One circumstance, innocent enough of itself, favoured the designs of the queen's enemies. Anne, who had been brought up in France, among a people distinguished for their inexhaustible stores of gaiety, easy conversation, witty and ingenious sallies, ironical phrases, and amiable hearts, had brought something of all this to London. Frank and prepossessing, she loved society; and her ordinary manners seemed too easy among a nation which, with deep affections, possesses much gravity and external coldness. Anne had found a certain freedom of speech in the court of France – it does not appear that she imitated it; but in a moment of gaiety she might have let slip some keen railleries, some imprudent words, and thus furnished her enemies with weapons. She had some difficulty in conforming with the strict etiquette of the court of England, and had not been trained to the circumspection so necessary with a husband like Henry VIII.

Anne was not understood. Her gaiety did not degenerate into frivolity: she did not possess that love of pleasure which, carried to excess, engenders corruption of manners; we have named the truly pious men whom she loved to gather round her. But it was quite enough for some persons that Anne was agreeable, like the ladies of St Germains and Fontainebleau, to suspect her of being a flirt, like many of them. Moreover, she had married above her station. Having lived at court as the equal of the young nobles belonging to it, she was not always able, after she ascended the throne, to keep herself on the footing of a queen. From that time her enemies interpreted unfavourably the innocent amiability with which she received them. The mistrustful Henry VIII began to indulge in suspicions, and Lady Rochford endeavoured to feed that prince's jealousy by crafty and perfidious insinuations.

Anne soon noticed the king's inclination for Jane Seymour; a thousand trifles, apparently indifferent, had struck her. She often watched the maid of honour; her pride was offended, and jealousy tortured her heart night and day. She endeavoured to win back the king's love; but Henry, who perceived her suspicions, grew more angry with her every hour. The queen was not far from her confinement; and it was at the very moment when she hoped to give Henry the heir he had longed for during so many years, that the king withdrew from her his conjugal affection. Her heart was wrung, and, foreseeing a mournful future, she wondered whether a blow similar to that which had struck Catherine might not soon be aimed at her. Jane Seymour did not reject the king's advances. Historians of the most opposite parties relate that one day, towards the end of January 1536, the queen, unexpectedly entering a room in the palace, found the king paying his court to the young maid of honour in too marked a manner. They may possibly exaggerate, but there is no doubt that Henry gave cause for very serious complaints on the part of his wife. It was as if a sword had pierced the heart of the unfortunate Anne Boleyn: she could not bear up against so cruel a blow, and prematurely gave birth to a dead son. God had at length granted Henry that long-desired heir, but the grief of the mother had cost the child's life. What an affliction for her! For some time her recovery was despaired of. When the king entered her room, she burst into tears. That selfish prince, soured at the thought that she had borne him a dead son, cruelly upbraided her misfortune, instead of consoling her. It was too much: the grief-stricken mother could not restrain herself. 'You have no one to blame but yourself', she exclaimed. Henry, still more angry, answered her harshly and left the apartment. These details are preserved by a well-informed writer of the time of Elizabeth. To present Henry under so unfavourable a light, if it were untrue, could hardly have been an agreeable mode of paying court, as some have insinuated, to a queen who took more after her father than her mother.

Anne now foresaw the misfortunes awaiting her: she recovered indeed after this storm, and exerted herself by taking part once more in social gatherings and fêtes; but she was melancholy and uneasy, like a foundering ship, which reappears on the waves of the sea after the storm, and still keeps afloat for a time, only to be swallowed up at last. All her attempts to regain her husband's affections were useless, and frightful dreams disturbed her during the slumbers of the night. This agony lasted three months.

The wind had changed: everybody noticed it, and it was, to certain heartless courtiers, like the signal given to an impatient pack of hounds. They set themselves to hunt down the prey, which they felt they could rend without danger. The extreme Catholics regained their courage. They had feared that, owing to Anne's intervention, the cause of Rome was lost in England, and their alarm was not unreasonable. Cranmer, realizing that he possessed the goodwill of the queen, never ceased pushing forward the reformation. When someone spoke in the House of Lords about a general council in Italy, he exclaimed: 'It is the word of God alone that we must listen to in religious controversies.' At the same time, in concert with Anne, he circulated all over England a new Prayer-book, *the Primer,* intended to counter the dangerous books of the priests.[1] The people used it. A pious and spiritual reader of that book exclaimed one day, after meditating upon it: 'O bountiful Jesu! O sweet Saviour! despise not him whom thou hast ransomed at the price of such a treasure – with thy blood! I look with confidence to the throne of mercy.' Religion was becoming personal with Anne Boleyn.

The queen and the archbishop had not stopped there: they had attempted, so far as Henry would permit, to place true shepherds over the flocks, instead of merchants who traded with their wool. The bishopric of Worcester, which had been taken from Jerome de Ghinucci, was given (as we have seen) to Latimer; so that the valley of the Severn, which four Italian bishops had plundered for fifty years, possessed at last a pastor who 'planted there the plenteousness of all spiritual blessings in Jesus Christ'.[2] Shaxton, one of Anne's chaplains, who at this time professed a great attachment to Holy Scripture, had been appointed Bishop of Salisbury, in place of the famous Cardinal Campeggio. Hilderly, formerly a Dominican prior – who had at one time defended the immaculate conception of the Virgin, but had afterwards acknowledged and worshipped Jesus Christ as the only Mediator – had been nominated to the see of Rochester, in place of the unfortunate Bishop Fisher. Finally,

---

[1] 'Pestilent and infectious books.' – Preface to the *Primer*.
[2] Latimer's *Sermons* (Parker Society), p. 82.

George Brown, ex-provincial of the Augustines in England – an upright man, a friend of the poor, and who, caught by the truth, had exclaimed from the pulpit, 'Go to Christ and not to the saints!' – had been elected Archbishop of Dublin, and thus became the first evangelical prelate of Ireland, a difficult post, which he occupied at the peril of his life.[1] Other prelates, like Fox, Bishop of Hereford, although not true Protestants, proved themselves to be anti-papists.

The members of the papal party saw the influence of the queen in all these nominations. Who resisted the proposal that the English Church should be represented at the general council? Who endeavoured to make the king advance in the direction of the reformation? Who threw England into the arms of the princes of Germany? The queen, none but the queen. She felt unhappy, it was said, when she saw a day pass without having obtained some favour for the reformation. Men knew that the pope was ready to forgive everything, and even to unite with Henry against Charles V, if the king would submit to the conditions laid down in the bull – that is to say, if he would put away Anne Boleyn.

The condition required by the pontiff was not an impossible one, for Henry liked to change his wives: he had six. Marriage was not to him a oneness of life. At the end of 1535, Anne had been his wife for three years; it was a long time for him, and he began to turn his eyes upon others. Jane Seymour's youth eclipsed the queen's. Unfortunate Boleyn! Sorrow had gradually diminished her freshness. Jane had natural allies, who might help her to ascend the throne. Her two brothers, Edward and Thomas – the elder more moderate, the younger more arrogant – each possessing great ambition and remarkable capacity, thought that a Seymour was as worthy as a Boleyn to wear the English crown. The first blow did not however proceed from them, but from a member of the queen's family – from her sister-in-law. There is no room for indifference between near relations: they love or, if they do not love, they hate. Lady Rochford, so closely allied to the queen, felt continually piqued at her. Jealousy had engendered a deep dislike in her heart, and this dislike was destined to lead her on to contrive the death of the detested object. Rendered desperate by the happiness and especially by the greatness of

[1] 'It was to the hazard of his life.' – Strype's *Memorials of Thomas Cranmer,* p. 38.

Anne Boleyn, it became her ruling passion to destroy them. One obstacle, however, rose up before her. Lord Rochford, her husband and Anne's brother, would not enter into her perfidious schemes. That depraved woman, who afterwards suffered capital punishment for conniving at crime, determined to ruin her sister-in-law and her husband together. It was arranged that three of the courtiers should give Henry the first hints. 'Thus began', says an author of that day, 'a comedy which was changed into a sorrowful tragedy.'[1] Nothing was omitted that tended to the success of one of the most infamous court intrigues recorded in history.

Anne became cognizant almost at the same time of her sister-in-law's hatred of her and of her husband's love for Jane Seymour. From that moment she foreboded an early death, and her most anxious thoughts were for her daughter. She wondered what would become of the child, and, desirous of having her brought up in the knowledge of the gospel, she sent for the pious, simple-minded Parker, told him of her apprehensions and her wishes, and commended Elizabeth to him with all a mother's love. Anne's words sank so deep into his heart that he never forgot them; and twenty-three years later, when that child, who had become queen, raised him to the primacy, he declared to Lord Burghley that if he were not under such great obligations to her mother, he would never have consented to serve the daughter in such an elevated station. After consigning the youthful Elizabeth to the care of a man of God, the unhappy queen was more at ease.

Meantime the plot was forming in silence, and two or three circumstances, such as occur in the most innocent life, were the pretext for Anne's destruction. One day, when she was with the king at Winchester, she sent for one of the court-musicians, named Mark Smeaton, 'to play on the virginals'. This was the first count in the indictment.

Norris, a gentleman of the king's chamber, was engaged to Margaret, one of Anne's maids of honour, and consequently was often in the queen's apartments. Slanderous tongues affirmed that he went more for the sake of his sovereign than for his betrothed. The queen, hearing of

[1] *Histoire d'Anne de Boleyn, Royne d'Angleterre*, p. 181. – This *History*, written in French verse of the sixteenth century, is from the pen of Crespin, Lord of Milherve, who was in London at the time of which he speaks.

it, and desiring to stop the scandal, determined to bind Norris to marry Margaret. 'Why do you not go on with your marriage?' she asked him. 'I desire to wait a little longer', answered the gentleman. Anne, with the intent of making him understand that there were serious reasons for not putting it off any longer, added: 'It is said at court that you are waiting for a dead man's shoes, and that if any misfortune befell the king, you would look to have me for your wife.' 'God forbid!' exclaimed Norris, in alarm; 'if I had such an idea, it would be my destruction.' 'Mind what you are about', resumed the queen, with severity. Norris, in great emotion, went immediately to Anne Boleyn's almoner. 'The queen is a virtuous woman', he said; 'I am willing to affirm it upon oath.' This was the second count in the indictment.

Sir Francis Weston, a bold frivolous man, was (although married) very attentive to a young lady of the court, a relative of the queen. 'Sir Francis', said Anne, who was distressed at his behaviour, 'you love Mistress Skelton, and neglect your wife.' 'Madam', answered the audacious courtier, 'there is one person in your house whom I love better than both.' 'And who is that?' said the queen. 'Yourself', answered Weston. Offended by such insolence, Anne ordered him, with scorn and displeasure, to leave her presence. This was the third count of the indictment.

Lord Rochford, a man of noble and chivalrous character, indignant at the calumnies which were beginning to circulate against his sister, endeavoured to avert the storm. One day, when she kept her bed, he entered her room to speak to her; and, the maids of honour being present, he leant towards the queen to say something on this matter which was not fit for the ears of strangers to the family. The infamous Lady Rochford made use of this innocent circumstance to accuse her husband and sister-in-law of an abominable crime.

Such are the four charges that were to cost Anne Boleyn her life. Futile observations, malicious remarks to which persons are exposed in the world, and especially at court, reached the ears of the king, and inspired him with jealousy, reproaches, angry words, and coldness. There was no more happiness for Anne.

There was enough in these stories to induce Henry VIII to reject his second wife, and take a third. This prince – and it was the case generally with the Tudors – had a temper at once decided and changeable, a heart susceptible and distrustful, an energetic character, and passions eager to be satisfied at any price. Very mistrustful, he did not easily get the better of his suspicions, and when any person had vexed him, he was not appeased until he had got rid of him. Common-sense generally appreciates at their true worth such stories as those we have reported; but the characters now on the stage were more rancorous than those usually to be found in the world. 'A tempest', says Lord Herbert of Cherbury on this subject, 'though it scarce stir low and shallow waters, when it meets a sea, both vexeth it, and makes it toss all that comes thereon.'

Henry, happy to have found the pretext which his new passion made him long for, investigated nothing; he appeared to believe everything he was told. He swore to prove Anne's guilt to others by the greatness of his revenge. Of his six wives, he got rid of two by divorce, and two by the scaffold; only two escaped his criminal humour. This time he was unwilling to proceed by divorce; the tediousness of Catherine's affair had wearied him. He preferred a more expeditious mode – the axe.

On 25 April the king appointed a commission to enquire into Anne's conduct, and placed on it the Duke of Norfolk, a maternal uncle but (as we have said) an implacable enemy of the unfortunate queen; the Duke of Suffolk, who, as Henry's brother-in-law, served him in his least desires; the Earl of Oxford, a skilful courtier; William Paulet, comptroller of the royal household, whose motto was, 'To be a willow and not an oak'; Audley, the most honest of all, but still his master's humble servant; Lord Delawarr, and several other lords and gentlemen, to the number of twenty-six. It has been said, by Burnet and others, that the king named Anne's father, the Earl of Wiltshire, one of the judges. It would, no doubt, have been the most striking trait of cruelty, of which Henry gave so many proofs; but we must in justice declare that the wretched prince did not perpetrate such a monstrosity. Burnet, after the most searching investigations, retracted his error.[1] On Thursday, 27 April, the king, understanding the necessity of a Parliament to repeal the laws made in favour of Anne and her children, issued writs for its assembling. He was

---

[1] Addenda to the Third Book of his History. – He acknowledges that this *mistake,* as he calls it, was an invention of Sanders.

resolved to hurry on the business – equally impatient to hear no more of his wife, and to possess her who was the object of his desires.

Anne, who was ignorant of what was going on, had gradually recovered a little serenity, but it was not so with those around her. The court was agitated and uneasy. The names of the commissioners were canvassed, and people wondered where the terrible blows of the king would fall. Would the storm burst on Sir Thomas Wyatt, who wrote verses in Anne's honour? or on Lord Northumberland, whom the queen had loved before Henry cast his eyes upon her? The king did not intend to go so high.

The indecision did not last long. At two o'clock on 27 April – the very day when the writs for the new Parliament were issued – William Brereton, one of the gentlemen of the king's household pointed out by the queen's enemies, was arrested and taken to the Tower. Two days later, on 29 April, Anne was crossing the presence chamber, where a miserable creature happened to be present at that moment. It was Mark Smeaton, the court musician – a vain, cowardly, corrupt man, who had felt hurt because, since the day when he had played before the queen at Winchester, that princess had never even looked at him. He was standing, in a dejected attitude, leaning against a window. It is possible that, having heard of the disgrace that threatened the queen, he hoped, by showing his sorrow, to obtain from her some mark of interest. Be that as it may, his unusual presence in that room, the posture he had assumed, the appearance of sorrow which he had put on, were evidently intended to attract her attention. The trick succeeded. Anne noticed him as she passed by. 'Why are you sad?' she asked. – 'It is no matter, madam.' The queen fancied that Smeaton was grieved because she had never spoken to him. 'You may not look to have me speak to you', she added, 'as if you were a nobleman, because you are an inferior person.' 'No, madam', replied the musician, 'I need no words; a look sufficeth me.' He did not receive the look he asked for, and his wounded vanity urged him from that moment to ruin the princess, by whom he had the insolence to wish to be remarked. Smeaton's words were reported to the king, and next day (30 April) the musician was arrested, examined at Stepney, and sent to the Tower.

A magnificent festival was preparing at Greenwich, to celebrate the first day of May in the usual manner. This was the strange moment which Henry had chosen for unveiling his plans. In certain minds there appears to be a mysterious connection between festivities and bloodshed; another prince (Nero) had shown it in old times, and some years later Charles IX was to celebrate the marriage of his sister Margaret by the massacres of St Bartholomew. Henry VIII gave to two of the victims he was about to immolate the foremost places in the brilliant tournament he had prepared. Lord Rochford, the queen's brother, was the principal challenger, and Henry Norris was chief of the defenders. Sir Francis Weston was also to take part in these jousts. Henry showed himself very gracious to them, and hid with smiles their approaching destruction. The king having taken his place, and the queen, in a magnificent costume, being seated by his side, Rochford and Norris passed before him, lowering their spears. The jousting began immediately after. The circumstances of the court gave a gloomy solemnity to the festival. The king, who was watching with fixed eyes the struggles of his courtiers, started up all of a sudden, with every appearance of anger, and hastily quitted the balcony. What had happened? The historian Sanders, notorious as being a most malicious and fabulous writer, mentions that the queen had dropped her handkerchief into the lists, and that Norris took it up and wiped his face with it. Lord Herbert, Burnet, and others affirm that there is nothing to corroborate the story, which, were it true, might be very innocent. However, the festivities were interrupted by the king's departure. The confusion was universal, and the alarmed queen withdrew, eager to know the cause of the strange procedure. Thus ended the rejoicings of the First of May.

Henry, who had gone back to the palace, hearing of the queen's return, refused to see her, ordered her to keep her room, mounted his horse, and, accompanied by six gentlemen, galloped back to London. Slackening his pace for a time, he took Norris aside, and, telling him the occasion of his anger, promised to pardon him if he would confess. Norris answered, with firmness and respect: 'Sire, if you were to cut me open and take out my heart, I could only tell you what I know.' On reaching Whitehall, Henry said to his ministers: 'Tomorrow morning you will take Rochford, Norris, and Weston to the Tower; you will then proceed to Greenwich, arrest the queen, and put her in prison. Finally, you will write to Cranmer and bid him go immediately to Lambeth, and there await my orders.' The victims were seized, and the high priest summoned for the sacrifice.

The night was full of anguish to Anne Boleyn, and the next day, when she was surrounded by her ladies, their consternation increased her terror. It seemed to her impossible that a word from her would not convince her husband of her innocence. 'I will positively see the king', she exclaimed. She ordered her barge to be prepared, but, just as she was about to set out, another barge arrived from London, bringing Cromwell, Audley, and the terrible Kingston, lieutenant of the Tower. That ominous presence was a death warrant: on seeing him the queen screamed aloud.

They did not, however, remove her at once: the council, on which sat her most violent adversaries, assembled in the palace, and Anne was summoned to appear before it. The Duke of Norfolk, the president, informed her coldly of what she was accused, and named her pretended accomplices. At these words, the queen, struck with astonishment and sorrow, fell on her knees and cried out: 'O Lord, if I am guilty, may I never be forgiven!' Then, recovering a little from her emotion, she replied to the calumnious charges brought against her, to which Norfolk answered carelessly and contemptuously, as if he were still speaking to the little girl whom he had seen born, 'Tut, tut, tut', and shook his head disdainfully. 'I desire to see the king', said Anne. 'Impossible', answered the duke; 'that is not included in our commission.' 'I have been very cruelly treated', said Anne Boleyn, later, when speaking of this horrible conversation with her uncle. 'It is His Majesty's good pleasure that we conduct you to the Tower', added Norfolk. 'I am ready to obey', said the queen, and all went in the same barge. When they reached the Tower, Anne landed. The governor was there to receive her. Norfolk and the other members of the council committed her into his charge and departed. It was five in the afternoon.

Then the gates of the fortress opened; and at this moment, when she was crossing the threshold under the charge of heinous crimes, Anne remembered how, three years before, she had entered it in triumph for the ceremony of her coronation, in the midst of the general acclamations of the people. Struck by the fearful contrast, she fell on her knees, 'as a ball' and exclaimed, 'O Lord, help me, as I am guiltless of that whereof I am accused!' The governor raised her up, and they entered. She expected to be put into close confinement. 'Mr Kingston', she said, 'do I go into a dungeon?' 'No, madam', answered the governor; 'you will be in your own lodging, where you lay at your coronation.' 'It is too good for me', she exclaimed. She entered, however, and on reaching those royal chambers, which occasioned such different recollections, she knelt again and burst into tears. The violence of her grief presently brought on convulsive movements, and her tears were succeeded by hysterical laughter. Gradually she came to herself, and tried to collect her thoughts. Feeling the need of strengthening herself by the evidences of the Lord's love, she said to Kingston, 'Entreat His Majesty to let me have the sacrament.' Then, in the consciousness of innocence, she added, 'Sir, I am as clear from the company of man as I am of you. I am the king's true wedded wife.'

She was not absorbed in her own misfortunes: she was moved by the sufferings of the others, and uneasy about her brother. 'Can you tell me where Lord Rochford is?' she asked. Kingston replied that he had seen him at Whitehall. She was not tranquillized by this evasive answer. 'Oh, where is my sweet brother?' she exclaimed. There was no reply. 'Mr Kingston', resumed Anne, after a few moments, 'do you know why I am here?' – 'No, madam.' 'I hear say that I am to be accused of criminal familiarities.' (Norfolk had told her so in the barge.) 'I can say no more than – Nay!' Suddenly tearing one of her garments, she exclaimed, as if distracted: 'If they were to open my body, I should still say – No.' After this her mind wandered. She thought of her step-mother, and the love she felt for the Countess of Wiltshire made her feel more than anything else the bitterness of her situation: she imagined the proud lady was before her, and cried, with unutterable agony, 'O my mother, my mother, thou wilt die for sorrow!' Then her gloomy thoughts were turned to other objects. She remembered that, while in the barge, the Duke of Norfolk had named Norris and Smeaton as her accusers, which was partly false. The miserable musician was not grieved at being wrongfully accused of a crime likely to make him notorious, but Norris had stoutly rejected the idea that the queen could be guilty. 'O Norris, hast thou accused me!' she ejaculated; 'and thou too, Smeaton!' After a few moments' silence, Anne fixed her eyes on the governor. 'Mr Kingston', she asked, 'shall I die without justice?' 'Madam', answered the governor, 'the meanest subject of the king has that.' At these words the queen again laughed hysterically. 'Justice – justice!' she exclaimed, with disdainful incredulity. She counted less upon justice than the humblest of her subjects. Gradually the tempest calmed down, and the silence of the night brought relief to her sorrow.

The same day (2 May) the news spread through London that the queen was arrested. Cranmer, who had received the royal intimation to go to his palace at Lambeth, and wait there until further orders, had arrived, and was thunder-struck on hearing what had happened. 'What! the queen in prison! the queen an adulteress!' ... A struggle took place in his bosom. He was indebted to the queen for much; he had always found her irreproachable – the refuge of the unhappy, the upholder of the truth. He had loved her like a daughter, respected her as his sovereign. That she was innocent, he had no doubt; but how to account for the behaviour of the king? The unhappy prelate was distracted by the most painful thoughts. This truly pious man showed excessive indulgence towards Henry VIII, and bent easily beneath his powerful hand; but his path was clearly traced – to maintain unhesitatingly the innocence of her whom he had always honoured. And yet he was to be an example of the fascination exerted by a despot over such characters – of the cowardice of which a good man may be guilty through human respect. Doubtless there are extenuating circumstances in his case. It was not only the queen's fate that made the prelate uneasy, but also the future of the reformation. If love for Anne had helped to make Henry incline to the side of the reformation, the hatred which he now felt against his unhappy wife might easily drive him in the other direction. Cranmer desired to prevent this at any price, and accordingly thought himself obliged to use extreme caution. But these circumstances are really no extenuation. No motive in the world can excuse a man from not frankly defending his friends when they are falsely accused – from not vindicating an innocent woman when she is declared to be guilty. Cranmer wrote to the king: 'I cannot without Your Majesty's command appear in your presence; but I can at least desire most humbly, as is my duty, that your great wisdom and God's help may remove the deep sorrow of your heart.

'I cannot deny that Your Majesty has great cause to be overwhelmed with sorrow. In fact, whether the things of which men speak be true or not, your honour, sire, according to the false appreciation of the world, has suffered; and I do not remember that Almighty God has ever before put Your Majesty's firmness to so severe a test.

'Sire, I am in such a perplexity that I am clean amazed; for I never had a better opinion in woman than I had in her, which maketh me think that she cannot be culpable.'[1]

This was tolerably bold, and accordingly Cranmer hastened to tone down his boldness. 'And yet, sire', he added, 'would you have gone so far, if you had not been sure of her crime? … Your Grace best knoweth that, next unto Your Grace, I was most bound unto her of all creatures living. Wherefore I must humbly beseech Your Grace to suffer me in that which both God's law, nature, and her kindness bindeth me unto, that I may (with Your Grace's favour) wish and pray for her. And from what condition Your Grace, of your only mere goodness, took her, and set the crown upon her head, I repute him not Your Grace's faithful servant and subject, nor true to the realm, that would not desire the offence to be without mercy punished, to the example of all others. And as I loved her not a little, for the love I judged her to bear towards God and his gospel; so, if she be proved guilty, there is not one that loveth God and his gospel that will ever favour her … for then there never was creature in our time that so much slandered the gospel.

'However', he added, appearing to recover his courage, 'forget not that God has shown his goodness to Your Grace in many ways, and has never offended you; whilst Your Grace, I am sure, acknowledgeth that you have offended him. Extend, therefore, to the gospel the precious favour you have always shown it, and which proceedeth not from your

[1] Cranmer's *Letters and Remains* (Parker Society), letter clxxiv to King Henry VIII, pp. 323-4.

love for the queen your wife, but from your zeal for the truth.

'From Lambeth, 3rd of May, 1536.'

When Cranmer addressed these soothing words to the king, it was doubtless on the supposition (on which he gives no opinion) that Anne was guilty. But, even admitting this hypothesis, is it not carrying flattery of the terrible autocrat very far, to compare him with Job as the prelate does, for in another part of this letter he says: 'By accepting all adversity, without despair and without murmuring, Your Grace will give opportunity to God to multiply his blessings, as he did to his faithful servant Job, to whom, after his great calamity, and to reward his patience, he restored the double of what he had possessed.' As regards the king, Cranmer had found for himself a false conscience, which led him into deceitful ways: his letter, although he still tries to defend Anne, cannot be justified.

He was about to despatch the letter, when he received a message from the Lord Chancellor, desiring him to go to the Star Chamber. The archbishop hastened across the Thames, and found at the appointed place not only Audley, but the lords Oxford and Sussex, and the Lord Chamberlain. These noblemen laid before him the charges brought against Anne Boleyn, adding that they could be proved, though they did not themselves produce any proof. On his return to Lambeth, Cranmer added a postscript to his letter, in which he expressed his extreme sorrow at the report that had just been made to him.

The morning of the same day (3 May) was a sad one in the Tower. By a refinement of cruelty, the king had ordered two of the queen's enemies – Lady Boleyn and Mistress Cosyns – to be always near her; to which end they slept in her room, while Kingston and his wife slept outside against her chamber door. What could be the object of these strange precautions? We can only see one. Every word that fell from Anne, even in her convulsions or in her dreams, would be perfidiously caught up, and reported to the king's agents with malicious interpretations. Anne, pardoning the former conduct of these ladies, and wholly engrossed with her father's sorrow, thought she might ask for news about him from the persons who had been given her for companions; but the two women, who never spoke to her without rudeness, refused to give her any information. 'The king knew what he was doing', said Anne to Kingston, 'when he put these two women about me. I could have desired to have two ladies of my chamber, persons whom I love; but His Majesty has had the cruelty to give me those whom I could never endure.'

The punishment continued. Lady Boleyn, hoping to detect some confusion in her niece's face, told her that her brother, Lord Rochford, was also in the Tower. Anne, who had somewhat recovered her strength, answered calmly, 'I am glad to learn that he is so near me.' 'Madam', added Kingston, 'Weston and Brereton are also under my charge.' The queen remained calm.

She purposed, however, to vindicate herself, and her first thought turned towards two of the most pious men in England: 'Oh, if God permitted me', she said, 'to have my bishops [meaning Cranmer and Latimer], they would plead to the king for me.' She then remained silent for a few minutes. A sweet reflection passed through her mind and consoled her. Since she had undertaken the defence of the persecuted evangelicals, gratitude would doubtless impel them to pray for her. 'I think', she said, 'that the greater part of England is praying for me.'

Anne had asked for her almoner, and, as some hours had elapsed without his arrival, gloomy images once more arose to sadden her mind. 'To be a queen', she said, 'and to be treated so cruelly – treated as queen never was before!' Then, as if a ray of sunshine had scattered the clouds, she exclaimed: 'No, I shall not die – no, I will not die! ... The king has put me in prison only to prove me.' The terrible struggle was too great for the young woman: distressed in her feelings beyond the bounds of endurance, she almost lost her senses. Then, attacked by a fresh hysterical paroxysm, the unfortunate lady burst into laughter. On coming to herself after a while, she cried: 'I will have justice ... justice ... justice!' Kingston, who was present, bowed and said: 'Assuredly, madam.' 'If any man accuses me', she continued, 'I can only say – No. They can bring no witness against me.' Then she had, all at once, an extraordinary attack: she fell down in delirium, and with eyes starting, as if she were looking into the future, and could foresee the chastisement with which God would punish the infamous wickedness of which she was the victim, she exclaimed: 'If I am put to death, there will be great judgments upon

England for seven years. ... And I ... I shall be in heaven ... for I have done many good deeds during my life.'

CHAPTER TEN

The Execution of Anne Boleyn

(May 1536)

E verything was preparing for the unjust judgment which was to have so cruel a termination. Justice is bound to watch that the laws are observed, and to punish the guilty; but if law is to be just law, the judges must listen fairly to the accused, diligently discharge all the duties to which their office calls them, and not permit themselves to be influenced either by the presents or the solicitations, the threats or the favours, or the rank (even should it be royal) of the prosecutor. Their decisions should be inspired only by such motives as they can give an account of to the Supreme Judge; their sentences must be arrived at through attentive consideration and serious reflection. For them there are no other guides than impartiality, conscience, and law. But the queen was not to appear before such judges: those who were about to dispose of her life set themselves in opposition to these imperious conditions.

Henry's agents redoubled their exertions to obtain, either from the ladies of the court or from the accused men, some deposition against Anne; but it was in vain. Even the women whom her elevation had eclipsed could allege nothing against her. Henry Norris, William Brereton, and Sir Francis Weston were carefully interrogated, one after the other: the examiners tried to make them confess to adultery, but they stoutly denied it; whereupon the king's agents, who were determined to get at something, began a fresh enquiry, and cross-examined the prisoners. It is believed that the gentlemen of the court were exempted from torture, but that the rack was applied to Mark Smeaton, who was thus made to confess all they wanted. It is more probable that the vile musician, a man of weak head and extreme vanity, being offended that his sovereign had not condescended even to look at him, yielded to the vengeance of irritated self-esteem. The queen had not been willing to give him the honour of a look – he boasted of adultery. The three gentlemen persevered in their declaration touching the queen's innocence: Lord Rochford did the same. The disheartened prosecutor wrote to the Lord Treasurer: 'This is to inform you that no one, except Mark, will confess anything against her; wherefore I imagine, if there be no other evidence, the business will be injurious to the king's honour.' The lawyers knew the value to be given to the musician's words. If the verdict was left to the equitable interpretation of the law – if the king did not bring his sovereign influence to bear upon the decisions of the judges, there could be no doubt as to the issue of the hateful trial.

But every passion was at work to paralyse the power of right. Vainly the queen's innocence shone forth on every side – the conspiracy formed against her grew stronger every day. To the wickedness of Lady Rochford, the jealousies of an intriguing *camarilla,* the hatred of the papal party, the unbridled ambition aroused in certain families by the prospects of the despot's couch soon to be empty though stained with blood, and to the instability of weak men was added the strong will of Henry VIII, as determined to get rid of Anne by death as he had been to separate from Catherine by divorce. The queen understood that she must die; and, wishing to be prepared, she sought to wean herself from that life which had so many attractions for her. She felt that the pleasures she had so much enjoyed were vain; the knowledge that she had endeavoured to acquire, superficial; the virtue to which she had aspired, imperfect; and the active life she had desired, without decisive results. The vanity of all created things, once proclaimed by one who also had occupied a throne, struck her heart. Everything being taken from her, she renounced

Le vain espoir de ce muable monde.[1]

Anne, giving up everything, turned towards a better life, and sought to strengthen herself in God.[2]

---

[1] 'The vain hope of this changeable world.' – *Histoire d'Anne de Boleyn* by Crespin, p. 140.
[2] *Ibid.*, p. 190.

Such were her affecting dispositions when the Duke of Norfolk, accompanied by other noblemen, came in the king's name to set before her the charges brought against her, to summon her to speak the truth, and to assure her that, if she confessed her fault, the king might pardon her. Anne replied with the dignity of a queen still upon the throne, and with the calmness of a Christian at the gates of eternity. She threw back with noble indignation the vile accusations of which the royal commissioners were the channel.

'You call upon me to speak the truth', she said to Norfolk. 'Well then, the king shall know it', and she dismissed the lords. It was beneath her to plead her cause before these malicious courtiers, but she would tell her husband the truth. Left alone, she sat down to write that celebrated letter, a noble monument of the elevation of her soul; a letter full of the tenderest complaints and the sharpest protests, in which her innocence shines forth, and which combines at once so much nature and eloquence that in the opinion of the most competent judges it deserves to be handed down to posterity.

It ran as follows:

> Your Grace's displeasure and my imprisonment are things so strange unto me, that what to write, or what to excuse, I am altogether ignorant. Whereas you sent to me (willing me to confess a truth and so obtain your favour), by such a one whom you know to be my ancient professed enemy; I no sooner received this message by him,[1] than I rightly conceived your meaning; and if, as you say, confessing a truth indeed may procure my safety, I shall with all willingness and duty perform your command.
>
> But let not Your Grace ever imagine that your poor wife will ever be brought to acknowledge a fault, where not so much as a thought thereof ever proceeded. And, to speak truth, never a prince had wife more loyal in all duty and in all true affection, than you have ever found in Anne Boleyn – with which name and place I could willingly have contented myself, if God and Your Grace's pleasure had so pleased. Neither did I at any time so far forget myself in my exaltation or received queenship, but that I always looked for such

---

[1] [It is probable that Anne means the Duke of Suffolk.]

alteration as I now find; for the ground of my preferment being on no surer foundation than Your Grace's fancy, the least alteration was fit and sufficient (I knew) to draw that fancy to some other subject.

You have chosen me from a low estate to be your queen and companion, far beyond my desert or desire. If then you found me worthy of such honour, good Your Grace, let not any light fancy or bad counsel of my enemies withdraw your princely favour from me; neither let that stain – that unworthy stain – of a disloyal heart towards Your Good Grace ever cast so foul a blot on me and on the infant princess, your daughter.

Try me, Good King, but let me have a lawful trial, and let not my sworn enemies sit as my accusers and as my judges; yea, let me receive an open trial, for my truth shall fear no open shames. Then shall you see either mine innocence cleared, your suspicions and conscience satisfied, the ignominy and slander of the world stopped – or my guilt openly declared; so that whatever God and you may determine of, Your Grace may be freed from an open censure, and mine offence being so lawfully proved, Your Grace may be at liberty, both before God and man, not only to execute worthy punishment on me, as an unfaithful wife, but to follow your affection already settled on that party, for whose sake I am now as I am; whose name I could, some good while since, have pointed unto, Your Grace being not ignorant of my suspicion therein. But if you have already determined of me, and that not only my death but an infamous slander must bring you the joying of your desired happiness, then I desire of God that he will pardon your great sin herein, and likewise my enemies, the instruments thereof; and that he will not call you to a strict account for your unprincely and cruel usage of me at his general judgment seat, where both you and myself must shortly appear; and in whose just judgment, I doubt not (whatsoever the world may think of me), mine innocency shall be openly known and sufficiently cleared.

My last and only request shall be, that myself may only bear the burden of Your Grace's displeasure, and that it may not touch the innocent souls of those poor gentlemen, who, as I understand, are likewise in strait imprisonment for my sake. If ever I have found favour in your sight – if ever the name of Anne Boleyn have been pleasing in your ears – then let me obtain this request; and so I will

leave to trouble Your Grace any further; with mine earnest prayer to
the Trinity to have Your Grace in his good keeping, and to direct you
in all your actions.

From my doleful prison in the Tower, the 6th of May.

ANNE BOLEYN.

We see Anne thoroughly in this letter, one of the most touching
that was ever written. Injured in her honour, she speaks without fear,
as one on the threshold of eternity. If there were no other proofs of her
innocence, this document alone would suffice to gain her cause in the
eyes of an impartial and intelligent posterity.[1]

This noble letter aroused a tempest in the king's heart. The firm
innocence stamped on it; the mention of Henry's tastes, and especially
of his inclination for Jane Seymour; Anne's declaration that she had
anticipated her husband's infidelity; the solemn appeal to the day of
judgment; and the thought of the injury which such noble language
would do to his reputation – all combined to fill that haughty prince
with vexation, hatred, and wrath. The letter gives the real solution of the
enigma. A guilty caprice had inclined Henry to Anne Boleyn; another
caprice inclined him now to Jane Seymour. This explanation is so patent
that no one need look for another.

Henry determined to inflict a great humiliation upon this daring
woman. He would strip her of the name of wife, and pretend that she
had only been his concubine. As his marriage with Catherine of Aragon
had been declared null because of her union with his brother Arthur,
Henry imagined that his marriage with Anne Boleyn might be annulled
because of an attachment once entertained for her by Percy, afterwards
Duke of Northumberland. When that nobleman was summoned before
Cromwell, he thought that he also was to be thrown into the Tower as
the queen's lover; but the summons had reference to quite a different
matter. 'There was a pre-contract of marriage between you and Anne
Boleyn?' asked the king's vicar-general. 'None at all', he answered; and

---

[1] A copy of this letter was found among the papers of Thomas Cromwell, at that
time the king's chief minister. 'It is universally known', says Sir Henry Ellis, 'as one
of the finest compositions in the English language.' [The original must have been
sent by Cromwell to the king. Although its authenticity has been called in question,
it is undoubtedly genuine. It is impossible to regard it as 'an Elizabethan forgery'.]

in order that his declaration might be recorded, he wrote it down and sent it to Cromwell. In it he said: 'Referring to the oath I made in this matter before the archbishops of Canterbury and York, and before the blessed body of our Saviour, which I received in the presence of the Duke of Norfolk and others of His Majesty's counsellors, I acknowledge to have eaten the holy sacrament to my condemnation, if there was any contract or promise of marriage between the queen and me. This 13th of May, in the twenty-eighth year of His Majesty King Henry VIII.' This declaration was clear, but the barbarous monarch did not relinquish his idea.

A special commission had been appointed, on 24 April, 'to judge of certain offences committed at London, Hampton Court, and Greenwich'. They desired to give to this trial the appearance at least of justice; and as the alleged offences were committed in the counties of Middlesex and Kent, the indictment was laid before the grand juries of both counties. On 10 May they found a true bill. The writers favourable to Henry VIII in this business – and they are few – have acknowledged that these 'hideous charges' (to use the words of one of them) were but fables invented at pleasure, and which 'overstepped all ordinary bounds of credulity'. Various explanations have been given of the conduct of these juries; the most natural appears to be that they accommodated themselves, according to the servile manner of the times, to the king's despotic will, which was always to be feared, but more especially in matters that concerned his own person.

The acts that followed were as prompt as they were cruel. Two days later (on 12 May) Norris, Weston, Brereton, and the musician were taken to Westminster, and brought before a commission composed of the dukes of Norfolk and Suffolk, Henry's two intimates, and other lords; it is even said that the Earl of Wiltshire was present. The three gentlemen repelled the charge with unshakable firmness. 'I would endure a thousand deaths', said Norris, 'sooner than betray the innocent. I declare, upon my honour, that the queen is innocent, and am ready to support my testimony in arms against all the world.' When this language of Henry VIII's favourite was reported to that prince, he cried out: 'Hang

him up, then – hang him up!'[1] The wretched musician alone confessed
a crime which would give him a place in history. He did not reap the
reward promised to his infamy. Perhaps it was imagined that his death
would guarantee his silence, and that his punishment would corroborate
his defamations. The three gentlemen were condemned to be beheaded,
and the musician to be hanged.

Three days later (on 15 May) the queen and her brother were taken
before their peers in the great hall of the Tower, to which the lord mayor
and a few aldermen and citizens alone were admitted. The Duke of
Norfolk had received orders to assemble a certain number of peers to
form a court: they were twenty-six in all, and most of them enemies
of Anne and of the reformation. The Earl of Wiltshire, Anne's father,
was not of the number, as Sanders pretends. The Duke of Norfolk, the
personal enemy of the unfortunate queen, that uncle who hated her
as much as he should have loved her, had been appointed to select the
judges and to preside over the trial: a circumstance indicative of the
spirit in which it was to be conducted. Norfolk took his seat, having the
Lord Chancellor on his right and the Duke of Suffolk on his left, and
in front of him sat as deputy earl-marshal the Earl of Surrey, Norfolk's
son, an upright man, but a proud and warm supporter of Romanism.
The queen was announced: she was received in deep silence. Before her
went the governor of the Tower, behind her came Lady Kingston and
Lady Boleyn. Anne advanced with dignity, adorned with the ensigns of
royalty, and, after gracefully saluting the court, took her seat in the chair
accorded either to her weakness or her rank. She had no defender; but
the modesty of her countenance, the dignity of her manner, the peace
of her conscience, which found expression in the serenity of her look,
touched even her enemies. She appeared before the tribunal of men,
thinking only of the tribunal of God; and, relying upon her innocence,
she did not fear those whom but yesterday she had ruled as a queen. One
might have said from the calmness and nobility of her deportment, so
assured and so majestic, that she was come, not to be tried as a criminal,
but to receive the honours due to sovereigns. She was as firm, says a

[1] Godwin's *Annals,* p. 139. – Queen Elizabeth raised his son to the peerage, and four
of his grandsons were among the greatest of England's captains during the reign of
Anne Boleyn's daughter.

contemporary, as an oak that fears neither the hail nor the furious blasts of the wind.[1]

The court ordered the indictment to be read; it charged the queen with adultery, incest, and conspiracy against the king's person. Anne held up her hand and pleaded 'not guilty', and then refuted and tore to tatters, calmly yet forcibly, the accusations brought against her. Having an 'excellent quick wit', and being a ready speaker, she did not utter a word that did not strike home,[2] though full of moderation; but the tone of her voice, the calmness of her features, and the dignity of her countenance pleaded more eloquently than her words. It was impossible to look at her or to hear her, and not declare her innocent, says an eyewitness.[3] Accordingly there was a report in the Tower, and even in the city, that the queen had cleared herself by a most wise and noble speech and that she would be acquitted.

While Anne was speaking, the Duke of Northumberland, who had once loved her and whom Henry had cruelly enrolled among the number of her judges, betrayed by his uneasy movements the agitation of his bosom. Unable to endure the frightful torment any longer, he rose, pretending indisposition, and hastily left the hall before the fatal verdict was pronounced.

The king waited impatiently for the moment when he could introduce Jane Seymour into Anne Boleyn's empty apartments. Unanimity of votes was not necessary among the 'lords triers'. In England, during the sixteenth century, there was pride in the people, but servility (with few exceptions) among the great. The axe that had severed the head of the venerable Bishop of Rochester and of the ex-chancellor More had taught a fearful lesson to all who might be disposed to resist the despotic desires of the prince. The court feared to confront the queen with the musician, the only witness against her, and declared her guilty without other formality. The incomprehensible facility with which the nobility were

[1] *Histoire d'Anne de Boleyn,* by Crespin, p. 200. The last lines of this narrative are dated 2 June 1536, only seventeen days after the queen's trial and sentence. It would appear that the author, Crespin, Lord of Milherve, was an eyewitness of the scene.

[2] 'Having an excellent quick wit and being a ready speaker, she did so answer all objections.' – Harleian MSS.

[3] *Histoire d' Anne de Boleyn,* by Crespin, p. 201.

then accustomed to submit to the inflexible will of the monarch could leave no room for doubt as to the catastrophe by which this tragedy would be terminated.[1]

The Duke of Norfolk, as Lord High Steward, pronounced sentence: that the queen should be taken back to the Tower, and there on the green should be burnt or beheaded, *according to His Majesty's good pleasure*. The court, desirous of leaving a little space for Henry's compassion, left the mode of death to him: he might do the queen the favour of being only decapitated.

Anne heard this infamous doom with calmness. No change was observed in her features; the consciousness of innocence upheld her heart. Clasping her hands and raising her eyes to heaven, she cried out: 'O Father, O Creator! Thou who art the way, the truth, and the life, knowest that I have not deserved this death!' Then, turning to her cruel uncle and the other lords, she said: 'My lords, I do not say that my opinion ought to be preferred to your judgment; but if you have reasons to justify it, they must be other than those which have been produced in court, for I am wholly innocent of all the matters of which I have been accused, so that I cannot call upon God to pardon me. I have always been faithful to the king my lord; but perhaps I have not always shown to him such a perfect humility and reverence as his graciousness and courtesy deserved, and the honour he hath done me required. I confess that I have often had jealous fancies against him which I had not wisdom or strength enough to repress. But God knows that I have not otherwise trespassed against him. Do not think I say this in the hope of prolonging my life, for he who saveth from death has taught me how to die, and will strengthen my faith. Think not, however, that I am so bewildered in mind that I do not care to vindicate my innocence. I knew that it would avail me little to defend it at the last moment, if I had not maintained it all my life long, as much as ever queen did. Still the last words of my mouth shall justify my honour. As for my brother and the other gentlemen who are unjustly condemned, I would willingly die to save them; but as that is not the king's pleasure, I shall accompany them in death. And then afterwards I shall live in eternal peace and joy

---

[1] The Catholic historian, Lingard, makes this remark. Vol. iii, ch, v.

without end, where I will pray to God for the king – and for you, my lords.'

The wisdom and eloquence of this speech, aided by the queen's beauty and the touching expression of her voice, moved even her enemies. But Norfolk, determined upon carrying out his hateful task, ordered her to lay aside her royal insignia. She did so, and commending herself to all their prayers, returned to her prison.

Lord Rochford's trial had preceded that of his sister the queen. He was calm and firm, and answered every question point by point, with much clearness and decision. But it was useless for him to affirm the queen's innocence – useless to declare that he had always respected her as a sister, as an 'honoured lady': he was condemned to be beheaded and quartered.

The court broke up, and while the courtiers, who had just sealed with the blood of an innocent queen their servile submission to the most formidable of despots, were returning to their amusements and base flatteries, the lord mayor turned to a friend and said to him: 'I can only observe one thing in this trial – the fixed resolution to get rid of the queen at any price.' And that is the verdict of posterity.

The wretches who had entered into this iniquitous plot were eager to have it ended. On 17 May the gentlemen who were to be executed were brought together into a hall of the Tower. They embraced, commended each other to God, and prepared to depart. The constable of the Tower, fearing that they would speak upon the scaffold, reminded them that the honour due to the king would not permit them to doubt the justice of their sentence. When they reached the place of punishment, Lord Rochford, no longer able to keep silence, turned towards the spectators and said: 'My friends, I am going to die, as such is His Majesty's pleasure. I do not complain of my death, for I have committed many sins during my life, but *I have never injured the king*. May God grant him a long and happy life!' Then, according to the chronicler, he presented his head 'to the sharp axe which severed it at a blow.' Norris, Weston, and Brereton were beheaded after him.

The king, before putting his wife to death, desired to perform an act not less cruel: he was determined to annul his marriage with Anne, notwithstanding Northumberland's denials. Did he wish to avoid the reproach of causing his wife to perish by the hands of the executioner? or, in a fit of anger, did he desire to strike the queen on all sides at once? We cannot tell. Be that as it may, the king in his wrath did not see that he was contradicting himself; that if there was no marriage between him and Anne, there could be no adultery, and that the sentence, based on this crime, was *ex facto* null. Cranmer, the most unfortunate, but perhaps not the least guilty of all the lords who lent themselves servilely to the despotic wishes of the prince – Cranmer believed (as it appears) that the position of the queen would thus become better; that her life would be saved, if she could no longer be regarded as having been Henry's wife. This excuses, although only slightly, his great weakness. He told the unhappy lady that he was commissioned to find the means of declaring null and void the ties which united her to the king. Anne, stunned by the sentence pronounced upon her, was also of opinion that it was an expedient invented by some relics of Henry's regard, to rescue her from the bitterness of death. Her heart opened to hope, and imagining that she would only be sent into banishment, she formed a plan of returning to the Continent. 'I will go to Antwerp', she said at dinner, with an almost happy look. She knew that she would meet with Protestants in that city, who would receive her with joy. But vain hope! In the very letter wherein the governor of the Tower reports this ingenuous remark of the queen, he asks for the king's orders as to the construction of the scaffold. Henry desired personally to order the arrangement of those planks which he was about to stain with innocent blood.

About nine o'clock in the forenoon of 17 May the Lord Chancellor, the Duke of Suffolk, the Earl of Essex (Cromwell), the Earl of Sussex, with several doctors and archdeacons, entered the chapel of Lambeth. The archbishop having taken his seat, and the objections made against the marriage of Henry VIII and Anne Boleyn having been read, the proctors of the king and of the queen admitted them, and the primate declared the marriage to be null and void.

On the very day of Anne Boleyn's divorce, da Casale, the English envoy at Rome, having heard of the queen's imprisonment, hurried to the pontifical palace to inform Paul III of the good news. 'I have never ceased praying to heaven for this favour', said the pope with delight, 'and I have always hoped for it. Now His Majesty may accomplish an admirable work for the good of Christendom. Let the king become reconciled with Rome, and he will obtain from the King of France all that he can wish for. Let us be friends. I will send him a nuncio for that purpose. When the news of Cardinal Fisher's death reached Rome', he continued, recollecting that terrible bull, 'it is true I found myself driven to a measure somewhat severe ... but I never intended to follow up my words by deeds.' Thus, according to the pope and his adherents, the imprisonment of Anne Boleyn was to reconcile England and Rome. This fact points to one of the causes which made Norfolk and other Catholics enter into the conspiracy against her.

On the same day also (17 May), towards evening, the queen learnt that the sentence would assuredly be carried out. Although it was declared that she had never been the king's wife, the doom pronounced upon her for adultery must nevertheless be accomplished. This is what Henry VIII called administering justice.

Anne desired to take the Lord's Supper, and asked to be left alone. About two hours after midnight the chaplain arrived; but, before partaking of the holy rite, there was one thing she wished to do. One fault weighed heavily on her heart. She felt that she had sinned against Queen Catherine by consenting to marry the king. Her conscience reproached her with having injured the Princess Mary. It filled her with the deepest sorrow, and she was eager, before she died, to make reparation to the daughter of the woman whose place she had taken. Anne would have liked to see Mary, to fall a queen at her feet, and implore her pardon; but alas! she could not: she was only to leave the prison for the scaffold. Resolved, however, to confess her fault, she did so in a striking manner which showed all the sincerity of her repentance and her firm determination to humble herself before Catherine's daughter. She begged Lady Kingston, the wife of the constable of the Tower, who had little regard for her, to take her seat in the chair of state. When the latter objected, Anne compelled her, and kneeling before her, she said, all the while crying bitterly: 'I charge you – as you would answer before God – to go in my name to the Princess Mary, to fall down before her as I do now before you, and ask her forgiveness for all the wrongs I have done her. Until that is done', she added, 'my conscience will have no rest.' At the moment when she was about to appear before the throne of God, she wished to make reparation for a fault that weighed heavily upon her heart. 'In fact', she said, 'I wish to do what a Christian ought.' This touching incident leads us to hope that if, during life, Anne was simply an honest Protestant, trusting too much to her own works, the trial had borne fruit and had made her a true Christian. But of this she was to give a still more striking proof.

As she rose from her knees, Anne felt more calm and prepared to receive the sacrament. Before taking it, she once more declared her innocence of the crime imputed to her. The governor was present, and he did not fail to inform Cromwell of this declaration, made as it were in the presence of God. Anne had found in Christ's death new strength to endure her own: she sighed after the moment that would put an end to her sorrows. Contrary to her expectation, she was told that the execution was put off until the afternoon. 'Mr Kingston', she said, 'I hear that I am not to die this afternoon, and I am very sorry for it; for I thought by this time to be dead and past my pain.' – 'Madam', replied the governor, 'you will feel no pain, the blow will be so sharp and swift.' – 'Yes', resumed Anne, 'I have heard say that the headsman is very clever', and then she added: 'and I have but a little neck', putting her hand about it and smiling. Kingston left the room.

Meanwhile the devout adherents of the Roman primacy were full of exultation, and allowed the hopes to appear which Anne's death raised in their bosoms. 'Sire', they told the king, 'the tapers placed round the tomb of Queen Catherine suddenly burst into flame of their own accord.' They concluded, from this prodigy, that Roman Catholicism was once more about to shed its light on England.

The hour appointed for Anne's death now drew near. Protesting her innocence to the last, she determined to send to Henry a final message. It was carried to him by a member of his privy chamber. Thus she addressed him: 'Commend me to His Majesty, and tell him that he has ever been constant in his career of advancing me. From a private gentlewoman he made me a marchioness, from a marchioness a queen; and now that he has no higher degree of honour left, he gives my innocence the crown of martyrdom.'[1] The gentleman went and reported this noble farewell to his master. Even the gaoler bore testimony to the peace and joy which filled Anne Boleyn's heart at this solemn moment. 'I have seen men and also women executed', wrote Kingston to Cromwell, 'and they have been in great sorrow; but to my knowledge this lady has much joy and pleasure in death.'

Everything was arranged so that the murder should be perpetrated without publicity and without disturbance. Kingston received orders to turn all strangers out of the Tower, and readily obeyed. About eleven in the forenoon of 19 May, the dukes of Suffolk and Richmond, the Lord Chancellor, Cromwell, the lord mayor with the sheriffs and aldermen, entered the Tower, and took their stations on the green, where the instrument of punishment had been erected. The executioner, whom Henry had summoned from Calais, was there with his sword and his attendants. A cannon, mounted on the walls, was to announce both to king and people that all was over. A little before noon Anne appeared, dressed in a robe of black damask, and attended by four of her maids of honour. She walked up to the block on which she was to lay her head. Her step was firm, her looks calm; all indicated the most complete resignation. 'Never had she looked so beautiful before', says a French contemporary, then in London. Her eyes expressed a meek submission; a pleasing smile accompanied the look she turned on the spectators of this tragic scene. But just when the executioners had made the last preparations, her emotion was so keen that she nearly fainted. Gradually she recovered her strength, and her faith in the Saviour filled her with courage and hope.

It is important to know what, in this last and solemn moment, were her sentiments towards the king. She had desired that Mary should be asked to forgive her wrongs: it was her duty, if she died a Christian, also to pardon Henry's faults. She must obey her Saviour, who said: *Love your enemies, bless them that curse you.* She had pardoned everything; but it was her duty to declare it before she died, and if she was humble, she would do so without affectation. Addressing those who had been her

---

[1] 'Purposing to make her by martyrdom a saint in heaven.' – Strype, p. 437.

subjects and were then standing round her, she said: 'Good Christian people, I am not come here to justify myself; I leave my justification entirely to Christ, in whom I put my trust. I will accuse no man, nor speak anything of that whereof I am accused, as I know full well that aught that I could say in my defence doth not appertain unto you, and that I could draw no hope of life from the same. I come here only to die, according as I have been condemned. I commend my judges to the Lord's mercy. I pray God (and I beg you to do the same) to save the king and send him long to reign over you, for a gentler or more merciful prince there never was. To me he was ever a good, gentle, and sovereign lord. And thus I take my leave of the world and of you, and I heartily desire you all to pray for me. O Lord, have mercy upon me! To God I commit my soul!'

Such are the simple words in which Anne gave utterance to the feelings of peace with which her heart was filled towards her husband, at the moment when he was robbing her of life. Had she said that she forgave him, she would have called up the memory of the king's crime, and would thus have appeared to claim the merit of her generous pardon. She did nothing of the sort. During one part of their wedded life, Henry had been a 'good lord' to her. She desired to recall the good only, and buried the evil in oblivion. She did so without any thought of self; for she knew that before the gracious words could reach the king's ears, the sword would have already fallen upon her, and it would be impossible for Henry to arrest the fatal blow.

This Christian discourse could not fail to make a deep impression on all who heard her. As they looked at the unfortunate queen, they felt the tenderest compassion and the sharpest pain. The firmer her heart became, the weaker grew the spectators of the tragedy. Ere long they were unable to check the tears which the sufferer had the strength to restrain. One of the ladies of the royal victim approached her to cover her eyes; but Anne refused, saying that she was not afraid of death, and gave her as a memorial of that hour a little manuscript prayer-book that she had brought with her.

The queen then removed her white collar and took off her hood, that the action of the sword might not be impeded; this head-dress formed a queue and hung down behind. Then falling on her knees, she remained a few moments silent and motionless, praying inwardly. On rising up, she approached the fatal block, and laid her head on it: 'O Christ, into thy hands I commit my soul!' she exclaimed. The headsman, disturbed by the mild expression of her face, hesitated a few seconds, but his courage returned. Anne cried out again: 'O Jesus, receive my soul!' At this instant the sword of the executioner flashed in the air and her head fell. A cry escaped from the lips of the spectators, 'as if they had received the blow upon their own necks.' This is honourable to Anne's enemies, so that we may well believe the evidence. But immediately another sound was heard: the gunner, placed as a signal-man on the wall, had watched the different phases of the scene, holding a lighted match in his hand; scarcely had the head fallen, when he fired the gun, and the report, which was heard at a distance, bore to Henry the news of the crime which gave him Jane Seymour. The ladies of Queen Anne, though almost lifeless with terror, would not permit the noble remains of the mistress whom they had loved so much to be touched by common hands; they gathered round the body, wrapped it in a white sheet, and carried it (almost fainting as they were) to an old elm chest, which had been brought out of the arsenal and had been used for storing arrows. This rough box was the last home assigned to her who had inhabited costly palaces: not so much as a coffin had been provided for her. The ladies placed in it Anne's head and body; 'the eyes and lips were observed to move', says a document, as if her mouth was repeating the last words it had uttered. She was immediately buried in the Tower chapel.

Thus died Anne Boleyn. If the violent passions of a prince and the meanness of his courtiers brought her to an untimely death, hatred and credulity have killed her a second time. But an infamous calumny, forged by dishonest individuals, ought to be sternly rejected by all sensible men. Not in vain did Anne, at the hour of death, place her cause in the hands of God, and we willingly believe that all enlightened men, without prejudice or partiality, among Roman Catholics as among others, turn with disgust from the vile falsehoods of malicious courtiers and the deceitful fables of the papist Sanders and his followers.

On the morning of this day, Henry VIII had dressed himself in white, as for a festival, and ordered a hunting party. There was a great stir round the palace: huntsmen hurrying to and fro, dogs baying, horns sounding, nobles arriving. The troop was formed and they all set off for Epping Forest, where the sport began. At noon the hunters met to repose themselves under an oak which still bears the name of the *King's Oak*. Henry had taken his seat beneath it, surrounded by his suite and the dogs; he listened and seemed to be agitated. Suddenly a cannon shot resounded through the forest – it was the concerted signal – the queen's head had fallen. 'Ha, ha!' exclaimed the king, rising, 'the deed is done! uncouple the hounds and away.' Horns and trumpets were sounded, and dogs and horses were soon in pursuit. The wretched prince, led away by his passions, forgot that there is a God to whom he would have to render an account not only of the execution in the Tower, but of the chase in the forest; and by these cruel acts, which should have shocked the hearts even of his courtiers, he branded himself with his own hands as a great criminal. The king and his court returned to the palace before nightfall.

At last Henry was free. He had desired Jane Seymour, and everything had been invented – adultery, incest – to break the bonds that united him to the queen. The proofs of Anne's crimes failing, the ferocious acts of the king were to supply their place. Could those who witnessed the cruelty of the husband venture to doubt the guilt of the wife? Henry had become inhuman that he might not appear faithless. Now that the object was obtained, it only remained to profit by his crime. His impatience to gratify his passions made him flout all propriety. The mournful death of his queen; the Christian words that she had uttered, kissing as it were the cruel hand that struck her – nothing softened his heart. On 19 May, the day of Anne's execution, Cranmer issued a special licence to enable the king to marry again. On the 20th, Henry and Jane Seymour were betrothed, and ten days later they were married privately at York Place. It would have been difficult to say in a more striking manner: 'This is why Anne Boleyn is no more!' When we see side by side the bloodstained block on which Anne had received her death-blow, and the brilliant altar before which Henry and Jane were united, we can understand the story. The prince, at once voluptuous and cruel, liked to combine the most contrary objects in the same picture – crime and festivities, marriage and death, sensuality and hatred. He showed himself the most magnificent and most civilized monarch of Europe; but also the rival of those barbarous kings of savage hordes who take delight in cutting off the heads of those who have been their favourites and even the objects of their most passionate love. We must employ different standards in judging of the same person, when we regard him as a private and as a public individual. The Tudor prince, so guilty as a husband, father, and friend, did much good as a ruler for England. Louis XIV, as well as Henry VIII, had some of the characteristics of a great king; and his moral life was certainly not better than that of his prototype in England. He had as many, and even more mistresses than the predecessor of the Stuarts had wives; but the only advantage which the French monarch had over the English one is that he knew how to get rid of them without cutting off their heads.

The death of Anne Boleyn caused a great sensation in Europe, as that of Fisher and More had done before it. Her innocence, which Henry (it is said) acknowledged on his death-bed, was denied by some and maintained by others; but all men of principle expressed a feeling of horror when they heard of her punishment. The Protestant princes and divines of Germany had not a doubt that this cruel act was the pledge of reconciliation offered to the pope by Henry VIII, and renounced the alliance they were on the point of concluding with England. 'At last I am free from that journey', said Melanchthon, whom Anne Boleyn's death, added to that of Sir Thomas More, had rendered even less desirous of approaching the prince who had struck them. 'The queen', he continued, 'accused, rather than convicted, of adultery, has suffered the penalty of death, and that catastrophe has wrought great changes in our plans.'

Somewhat later the Protestants ascribed Anne's death especially to the pope: 'That blow came from Rome', they cried; 'in Rome all these tricks and plots are contrived.' In this I suspect there is a mistake. The plots of the Roman court against Elizabeth have caused it to be accused of similar designs against the mother of the great Protestant queen. The friends of that court in England were probably no strangers to the crime, but the great criminal was Henry.

CHAPTER ELEVEN

Catholicism versus Protestantism

(Summer 1536)

After Queen Anne's death the two parties were agitated in opposite directions. The friends of the reformation wished to show that the disgrace of that princess did not carry with it the disgrace of the cause they had at heart, and consequently believed that they ought to accelerate the reform movement. The friends of Rome and its doctrines imagining, on their part, that the queen's death had put their affairs in good train, thought they had but to redouble their activity to gain a complete victory. The latter seemed indeed to have some reasons for encouragement. If Catherine's death four months earlier reconciled Henry VIII and the emperor just when the latter was threatening England with invasion, the death of Anne Boleyn appeared as if it would reconcile the king with Paul III, who was ready to issue his terrible bull. Henry's wives played a great part in his private history, but they had also a certain importance in his relations with the powers of Europe, especially with the pope. The court of Rome was very desirous of reviving the ancient friendship which had united it to England. These desires increased rapidly.

On 20 May, when the news of the queen's prosecution arrived in Rome, both pope and cardinals were transported with joy. The frightful calumnies of which Anne was the victim served the cause of the papacy too well not to be accepted as truths, and all felt persuaded that, if she fell from the throne, the acts done at London against the Italian primacy would fall with her. When Henry's agent, da Casale, informed the pope that the queen had been sent to prison, Paul exclaimed with delight: 'I always thought, when I saw Henry endowed with *so many virtues,* that heaven would not forsake him. If he is willing to unite with me', he added, 'I shall have authority enough to enjoin the emperor and the King of France to make peace with him; and the King of England, reconciled with the church, will command the powers of Europe.' At the same time Paul III confessed that he had made a mistake in raising Fisher to the cardinalate, and wound up this pontifical effusion in the kindest of terms. Da Casale, much delighted on his part, asked whether he was to repeat these matters to the king. 'Tell him', answered the pope, 'that His Majesty may, without hesitation, expect everything from me.' Da Casale, therefore, made his report to London, and intimated that, if Henry made the least sign of reconciliation, the pope would immediately send him a nuncio. Thus Paul left not a stone unturned to win over the King of England. He extolled his virtues, promised him the foremost place in Europe, flattered his vanity as an author, and did not fear – he the infallible one – to acknowledge that he had made a mistake. Everybody at the court of Rome felt convinced that England was about to return to the bosom of the church; Cardinal Campeggio even sent his brother to London to resume possession of the bishopric of Salisbury, of which he had been deprived in 1534. Up to the end of June, the pope and the cardinals became kinder and more respectful to the English, and entertained the most flattering expectations regarding the return of England.

Would these expectations be realized? Henry VIII was not one man, but two: his domestic passions and his public acts formed two departments entirely distinct. Guided as an individual by passion, he was, as a king, sometimes led by just views. He believed that neither pope nor foreign monarch had a right to exercise the smallest jurisdiction in England. He was therefore resolved – and this saved England – to maintain the rupture with Rome. One circumstance might have taught him that in all respects it was the best thing he could do.

Rome has two modes of bringing back princes under her yoke – flattery and abuse. The pope had adopted the first: a person, at that time without influence, Reginald Pole, an Englishman, and also a relative and *protégé* of Henry, undertook the second. In 1535 he was in the north of Italy. Burning with love for the papacy and hatred for the king, his benefactor, he wrote a defence of the unity of the church, addressed to Henry VIII, and overflowing with violence. The wise and pious Contarini, to whom he showed it, begged him to soften a tone that might cause much harm. As Pole refused, Contarini entreated him at least to submit his manuscript to the pope; but the young Englishman, fearing that Paul would require him to suppress the untoward publication, declined to accede to his friend's request. His object was, not to convert the king, but to stir up the English against their lawful prince, and induce them to fall prostrate again before the Roman pontiff. The treatise, finished in the winter of 1535–36, before Anne's trial, reached London the first week in June. Tunstall, now Bishop of Durham, and Pole's friend, read the book, which contained a few truths mixed up with great errors, and then communicated it to the king. Never did haughty monarch receive so rough a lesson.

'Shall I write to you, O Prince', said the young Englishman, 'or shall I not? Observing in you the certain symptoms of the most dangerous malady, and assured as I am that I possess the remedies suitable to cure you, how can I refrain from pronouncing the word which alone can preserve your life? I love you, sire, as son never loved his father, and God perhaps will make my voice to be like that of his own Son, *whose voice even the dead hear*. O Prince, you are dealing the most deadly blow against the church that it can possibly receive; you rob it of the chief whom it possesses upon earth. Why should a king, who is the supreme head of the state, occupy a similar place in the church? If we may trust the arguments of your doctors, we must conclude that Nero was the head of the church. We should laugh, if the laughter were not to be followed by tears. There is as great a distance between the ecclesiastical and the civil power, as there is between heaven and earth. There are three estates in human society: first, the people; then the king, who is the son of the people; and lastly, the priest, who being the *spouse of the people* is consequently the *father of the king*. But you, in imitation of the pride of Lucifer, set yourself above the Vicar of Jesus Christ. ...

'What! you have rent the church, as it was never before rent in that island, you have plundered and cruelly tormented it, and you claim, in virtue of such merits, to be called its supreme head. There are two churches: if you are at the head of one, it is not the church of Christ; if you are, it is like Satan, who is the prince of the world, which he oppresses under his tyranny. ... You reign, but after the fashion of the Turks. A simple nod of your head has more power than ancient laws and rights. Sword in hand you decide religious controversies. Is not that thoroughly Turkish and barbarian? ...

'O England! if you have not forgotten your ancient liberty, what indignation ought to possess you, when you see your king plunder, condemn, murder, squander all your wealth, and leave you nothing but tears. Beware, for if you let your grievances be heard, you will be afflicted with still deeper wounds. O my country! it is in your power to change your great sorrow into greater joy. Neither Nero nor Domitian, nor – I dare affirm – Luther himself, if he had been King of England, would have wished to avenge himself by putting to death such men as Fisher and Sir Thomas More! ...

'What king has ever given more numerous signs of respect to the supreme pontiff than that Francis I who spoke of you, O Henry, in words received with applause by the whole Christian world: 'your friend even to the altar' [*i.e.* to the last extremity]? – The Emperor Charles has just subdued the pirates; but is there any pirate that is worse than you? Have you not plundered the wealth of the church, thrown the bodies of the saints into prison, and reduced men's souls to slavery? If I heard that the emperor with all his fleet was sailing for Constantinople, I would fall at his feet, and say – were it even in the straits of the Hellespont – "O Emperor, what are you thinking of? Do you not see that a much greater danger than the Turks threatens the Christian republic? Change your route. What would be the use of expelling the Turks from Europe, when new Turks are hatched among us?" Certainly the English for slighter causes have forced their kings to put off their crowns.'

After the apostrophe addressed to Charles V, Reginald Pole returns to Henry VIII, and imagining himself to be the prophet Elijah before King Ahab, he says with great boldness: 'O King, the Lord hath commanded me to curse you; but if you will patiently listen to me, he will return you good for evil. Why delay to confess your sin? Do not say that you have done everything according to the rules of Holy Scripture. Does not

the church, which gives it authority, know what is to be received and
what rejected? You have forsaken the fountain of wisdom. Return to the
church, O Prince! and all that you have lost you shall regain with more
splendour and glory.

'But if anyone hears the sound of the trumpet and does not heed
it, the sword is drawn from the scabbard, the guilty is smitten, and his
blood is upon his own head.'

We have hardly given the flower of this long tirade, written in the
style of the sixteenth century, which, divided into four books, fills one
hundred and ninety-two folio pages. It reached England at the moment
of the condemnation of the innocent Anne, which Pole unconsciously
protested against as unjust, more unjust even than the sentences of Fisher
and More. Henry did not at first read his 'pupil's' philippic through. He
saw enough, however, to regard it as an insult, a divorce which Italy had
sent him. He ordered Pole to return to England; but the latter remembered too well the fate of Fisher and Sir Thomas More to run the risk.
Bishop Tunstall, one of the enemies of the reformation, wrote, however,
to Pole, that as Christ was the head of the church, to separate it from
the pope was not to separate from its head. This refutation was short but
complete.

The king was resolved to maintain his independence of the pope.
Some have ascribed this determination to Pole's treatise, and others to
the influence of Jane Seymour. Both these circumstances may have had
some weight in Henry's mind; but the great cause, we repeat, is that he
would not suffer any master but himself in England. Gardiner replied to
Pole in a treatise which he entitled: *On True Obedience,* to which Bonner
wrote the preface.

Paul III was not the only one who descried the signal of triumph in
Anne's death: the Princess Mary believed that she would now become
heiress-presumptive to the crown. Lady Kingston, having discharged
Anne Boleyn's Christian commission, Catherine's daughter, but slightly
affected by this touching conduct, took advantage of it for her own
interest, and charged that lady with a letter addressed to Cromwell, in
which she begged him to intercede for her with the king, so that the
rank which belonged to her should be restored. Henry consented to

receive his daughter into favour, but not without conditions: 'Madam', said Norfolk, who had been sent to her by the king, 'here are the articles which require your signature.'

The daughter of the proud Catherine of Aragon was to acknowledge four points: the supremacy of the king, the imposture of the pope, the incest of her own mother, and her own illegitimacy. She refused, but as Norfolk was not to be shaken, she signed the two first articles; then laying down the pen, she exclaimed: 'As for my own shame and my mother's – never!' Cromwell threatened her, called her obstinate and unnatural, and told her that her father would abandon her: the unhappy princess signed everything. She was restored to favour, and given the means to maintain a household suitable to her rank; but she was deceived in thinking that the misfortune of her little half-sister Elizabeth would replace her on the steps of the throne.

Parliament met on 8 June, when the chancellor announced to them that the king, notwithstanding his mishaps in matrimony, *had yielded to the humble solicitations of the nobility,* and formed a new union. The two houses ratified the accomplished facts. No man desired to stir the ashes from which sparks might issue and kindle a great conflagration. At no price would they compromise the most exalted persons in the kingdom, and especially the king. All the allegations, even the most absurd, were admitted: Parliament wanted to have done with the matter. It even went further: the king was thanked for the *most excellent goodness* which had induced him to marry a lady whose brilliant youth, remarkable beauty, and purity of blood were the sure pledges of the happy issue which a marriage with her could not fail to produce; and his most respectful subjects, determined to bury the faults of their prince under flowers, compared him for beauty to Absalom, for strength to Samson, and for wisdom to Solomon. Parliament added that as the daughters of Catherine and Anne were both illegitimate, the succession had devolved upon the children of Jane Seymour. As, however, it was possible that she might not have any issue, Parliament granted Henry the privilege of naming his successor in his will: an enormous prerogative, conferred upon the most capricious of monarchs. Those who refused to take the oath required by the statute were to be declared guilty of high treason.

Parliament, having thus arranged the king's business, set about the business of the country. 'My lords', said ministers on 4 July to the upper house, 'the Bishop of Rome, whom some persons call *pope,* wishing to have the means of satisfying his love of luxury and tyranny, has obscured the word of God, excluded Jesus Christ from the soul, banished princes from their kingdoms, monopolized the mind, body, and goods of all Christians, and, in particular, extorted great sums of money from England by his worthless superstitions.' Parliament decided that the penalties of *præmunire* should be inflicted on everybody who recognized the authority of the Roman pontiff, and that every student, ecclesiastic, and civil functionary should be bound to renounce the pope in an oath made in the name of God and all his saints.[1]

This bill was the cause of great joy in England; the Protestant spirit was stirred; there was a great outburst of sarcasms, and one could see that the citizens of the capital naturally were not friends to the papacy. Man is inclined to laugh at what he has respected when he finds that he has been deceived, and then readily classes among human follies what he had once taken for the wisdom of heaven. A contest of epigrams was begun in London, similar to that which had so often taken place at Rome between Pasquin and Marforio: perhaps, however, the jokes were occasionally a little heavy. 'Do you see the stole round the priest's neck?' said one wit; 'it is nothing else but the Bishop of Rome's rope' – 'Matins, masses, and evensong are nothing but a roaring, howling, whistling, murmuring, tomring, and juggling.' – 'It is as lawful to christen a child in a tub of water at home or in a ditch by the way, as in a font-stone in the church.' – Gradually this jesting spirit made its way to the lower classes of society – 'Holy water is very useful', said one who haunted the London taverns; 'for as it is already salted, you have only to put an onion in it to make sauce for a gibbet of mutton.' – 'What is that you say?' replied some blacksmith; 'it is a very good medicine for a horse with a galled back.' But while frivolity and a desire to show one's wit, however coarse it might be, gave birth to silly jests merely provocative of laughter, the love of truth inspired the evangelical Christians with serious words which irritated the priests more than the raillery of the jesters. 'The

---

[1] 'So help me God, all saints, and the holy Evangelists.' – Act of Parliament, 28 Henry VIII, Cap. 7.

church', they said, 'is not the clergy, the church is the congregation of good men only. All ceremonies accustomed in the church and not clearly expressed in Scripture ought to be done away. When the sinner is converted, all the sins over which he sheds tears are remitted freely by the Father who is in heaven.'

Along with the words of the profane and of the pious came the words of the priests. A convocation of the clergy was summoned to meet at St Paul's on 9 June. The bishops came and took their places, and anyone might count the votes which Rome and the reformation had on the episcopal bench. For the latter there were: Archbishop Cranmer; Goodrich, Bishop of Ely; Shaxton, Bishop of Salisbury; Fox, Bishop of Hereford; Latimer, Bishop of Worcester; Hilsey, Bishop of Rochester; Barlow, Bishop of St David's; Warton, Bishop of St Asaph; and Sampson, Bishop of Chichester – nine votes in all. For Rome there were: Lee, Archbishop of York; Stokesley, Bishop of London; Tunstall, Bishop of Durham; Longland, Bishop of Lincoln; Vesey, Bishop of Exeter; Clerk, Bishop of Bath; Lee, Bishop of Lichfield; Salcot, Bishop of Bangor; and Rugge, Bishop of Norwich – nine against nine. If Gardiner had not been in France there would have been a majority against the reformation. A numerous company of priors and mitred abbots, members of the upper house, seemed to assure victory to the partisans of tradition. The clergy, who assembled under their respective banners, were divided not by shades but by glaring colours, and people asked, as they looked on this chequered group, which of the colours would carry the day. Cranmer had taken precautions that they should not leave the church without being enlightened on that point.

The Bishop of London having sung the mass of the Holy Ghost, Latimer, who had been selected by the primate to edify the assembly, went up into the pulpit. Being a man of bold and independent character, and penetrating, practical mind which would discover and point out every subterfuge, he wanted a reform more complete even than Cranmer desired. He took for his text the parable of the unjust steward (Luke 16:1-8). 'Brethren', he said, 'ye have come here today to hear of great and weighty matters. Ye look, I am assured, to hear of me such things as shall be meet for this assembly.' Then, having introduced his subject Latimer

continued: 'A faithful steward coineth no new money, but taketh it
ready coined of the good man of the house. Now, what numbers of our
bishops, abbots, prelates, and curates, despising the money of the Lord
as copper and not current, teach that now redemption purchased by
money, and devised by men is of efficacy, and not redemption purchased
by Christ.'

The whole of Latimer's sermon was in this strain. He did not stop
here; in the afternoon he preached again. 'You know the proverb', he
said – "An evil crow, an evil egg.' The devil has begotten the world, and
the world in its turn has many children. There is my Lady Pride, Dame
Gluttony, Mistress Avarice, Lady Lechery, Dame Subtlety, and others,
that now hard and scant ye may find any corner, any kind of life, where
many of his children be not. In court, in cowls, in cloisters, yea, where
shall ye not find them? Howbeit, they that be secular are not children
of the world, nor they children of light that are called spiritual and of
the clergy. No, no; as ye find among the laity many children of light,
so among the clergy ye shall find many children of the world. They do
execrate and detest the world (though indeed the world is their father)
in words and outward signs; but in heart and works they coll[1] and kiss
him. They ever say one thing and think another, and live every day as if
all their life were a shroving time [a carnival]. I see many such among the
bishops, abbots, priors, archdeacons, deans, and others of that sort, who
are met together in this convocation, to take into consideration all that
concerns the glory of Christ and the wealth of the people of England.
But it is to be feared lest, as light hath many of her children here, so the
world hath sent some of his whelps hither; amongst the which I know
there can be no concord nor unity, albeit they be in one place, in one
congregation. What have you been doing these seven years and more?
Show us what the English have gained by your long and great assemblies. Have they become even a hair's breadth better? In God's name,
what have you done? – so great fathers, so many, so long a season, so
oft assembled together – what have you done? Two things: the one that
you have burnt a dead man;[2] the other, that ye went about to burn one

---

[1] [To hang round the neck.]
[2] [William Tracy, in the year 1532. See vol. 2, p. 72.]

being alive.[1] Ye have oft sat in consultation, but what have ye done? Ye have had many things in deliberation, but what one is put forth whereby either Christ is more glorified, or else Christ's people made more holy? I appeal to your own conscience.'

Here Latimer began, as Luther had done in his *Appeal to the German Nobility*, to pass in review the abuses and errors of the clergy – the Court of Arches,[2] the episcopal consistories, saints' days, images, vows, pilgrimages, certain vigils which he called 'bacchanalia', marriage, baptism, the mass, and relics.

After this severe catalogue, the bishop exclaimed: 'If there be nothing to be amended or redressed, my lords, be ye of good cheer, be merry; and at the least, because we have nothing else to do, let us reason the matter how we may be richer. Let us fall to some pleasant communication; afterwards let us go home, even as good as we came hither, that is, right-begotten children of the world, and utterly worldlings. ... If there be nothing to be changed in our fashions, let us say as the evil servant said, 'It will be long ere my master come.' This is pleasant. Let us beat our fellows; let us eat and drink with drunkards. Surely, as oft as we do not take away the abuse of things, so oft we beat our fellows. As oft as we give not the people their true food, so oft we beat our fellows. As oft as we let them die in superstition, so oft we beat them. To be short, as oft as we blind lead them blind, so oft we beat and grievously beat our fellows. When we welter in pleasures and idleness, then we eat and drink with drunkards. But God will come, God will come. He will not tarry long away. He will come upon such a day as we nothing look for him and at such hour as we know not. He will come and cut us in pieces. He will reward us as he doth the hypocrites. He will set us where wailing shall be, my brethren; where gnashing of teeth shall be, my brethren. And let here be the end of our tragedy, if ye will. These be the delicate dishes prepared for the world's beloved children. These be the wafers and junkets provided for worldly prelates – wailing and gnashing of teeth.

'If you will not die eternally, live not worldly. Preach truly the word of God. Feed ye tenderly the flock of Christ. Love the light. Walk in the

[1] Referring to himself.

[2] [The chief and most ancient consistory court belonging to the Archbishop of Canterbury.]

light, and so be the children of light while you are in the world, that you may shine in the world to come bright as the sun, with the Father, the Son, and the Holy Ghost. Amen.'[1]

An action full of simplicity and warmth had accompanied the firm and courageous words of the reformer. The reverend members of convocation had found their man, and his sermon appeared to them more bitter than wormwood. They dared not, however, show their anger, for behind Latimer was Cranmer, and they feared lest they should find the king behind Cranmer.

Ere long the clergy received another mortification which they dared not complain of. A rumour got abroad that Cromwell would be the representative of Henry VIII in the assembly. 'What!' they cried out, 'a layman, a man who has never taken a degree in any university!' But what was the astonishment of the prelates, when they saw not Cromwell enter, but Dr William Petre, the proctor of the vicar-general, whom the primate seated by his side – a delegate of a delegate! On 21 June, Cromwell himself came down, and took his seat above all the prelates. The lay element took, with a bold step, a position from which it had been so long banished.

It was to be expected that the champions of the Middle Ages would not submit to such affronts, and particularly to such a terrible fire as Latimer's, without unmasking their batteries in return, and striving to dismantle those of the enemy. They saw that they could not maintain the supremacy of the pope and attack that of the king; but they knew that Henry adhered to transubstantiation and other superstitious doctrines of the dark ages; and accordingly they determined to attack by this breach, not only Latimer, but all the supporters of the reformation. Roman Catholicism did not intend to perish without a struggle; it resolved – in order that it might hold its ground in England – to make a vigorous onslaught. The lower house having chosen for its prolocutor one Richard Gwent, archdeacon of Bishop Stokesley and a zealous upholder of Romish doctrine, the cabal set to work, and the words of Wycliffe, of the Lollards, of the reformers, and even of the jesting citizens having been carefully recorded, Gwent proposed that the lower house should

---

[1] Latimer, *Sermons* (Parker Society), pp. 33-57.

lay before the upper house sixty-seven evil doctrines (*mala dogmata*). Nothing was forgotten, not even *the horse with the galled back*. To no purpose were they reminded that what was blamable in this catalogue were only 'the indiscreet expressions of illiterate persons'; and that the roughness of their imagination alone had caused them to utter these pointed sarcasms. In vain were they reminded that, even in horse races, the riders to be sure of reaching their goal pass beyond it. The enumeration of the *mala dogmata* was carried, without omitting a single article.

On 23 June, the prolocutor appeared with his long list before the upper house of convocation. 'There are certain errors', he said, 'which cause disturbance in the kingdom', and then he read the sixty-seven *mala dogmata*. 'They affirm', he continued, 'that no doctrine must be believed unless it be proved by Holy Scripture; that Christ, having shed his blood, has fully redeemed us, so that now we have only to say, O God, I entreat thy majesty to blot out my iniquity. They say that the sacrifice of the mass is nothing but a piece of bread; that auricular confession was invented by the priests to learn the secrets of the heart, and to put money in their purse; that purgatory is a cheat; that what is usually called the church is merely the old synagogue, and that the true church is the assembly of the just; that prayer is just as effectual in the open air as in a temple; that priests may marry. And these heresies are not only preached, but are printed in books stamped *cum privilegio* [with privilege] and the ignorant imagine that those words indicate the king's approbation.'

The two armies stood face to face, and the scholastic party had no sooner read their lengthy manifesto than the combat began. 'Oh, what tugging was here betwixt these opposite sides', says honest Fuller. They separated without coming to any decision. Men began to discuss which side they should take: 'Neither one nor the other', said those who fancied themselves the cleverest. 'When two stout and sturdy travellers meet together and both desire the way, yet neither is willing to fight for it, in their passage they so shove and shoulder one another, that they divide the way between them, and yet neither gets the same. So these two opposite parties in the convocation were fain at last in a drawn battle to part the prize between them, neither of them being conquering or conquered.'[1] Thus the church, the *pillar of truth,* was required to admit both black and white – to say Yes and No. 'A medley religion', exclaims Fuller; 'an expedient, to salve (if not the consciences) at least the credits of both sides.'

Cranmer and Cromwell determined to use the opportunity to make the balance incline to the evangelical side. They went down to convocation. While passing along the street Cromwell noticed a stranger – one Alesius, a Scotsman, who had been compelled to seek refuge in Germany for having professed the pure gospel, and there had formed a close intimacy with Melanchthon. Cranmer, as well as Cromwell, desirous of having such an evangelical man in England – one who was in perfect harmony with the Protestants of Germany, and whose native tongue was English – had invited him over to London.[2] Melanchthon had given him a letter for the king, along with which he sent a copy of his *Commentary on the Epistle to the Romans.* Henry was so charmed with the Scotsman, that he gave him the title of 'King's Scholar'. Alesius was living at the archbishop's palace in Lambeth. Cromwell, observing him so seasonably, called him and invited him to accompany them to Westminster. He thought that a man of such power might be useful to him; and it is even possible that the meeting had been prearranged. Together the Englishman and the Scotsman entered the chamber in which the bishops were sitting round a table, with a number of priests standing behind them. When the vicar-general and Alesius, who was unknown to most of them, appeared, they all rose and bowed to the king's representative. Cromwell returned the salutation, and, after seating the exile in the highest place, opposite the two archbishops, he addressed them as follows: 'His Majesty will not rest until, in harmony with convocation and Parliament, he has put an end to the controversies which have taken place, not only in this kingdom but in every country. Discuss these questions, therefore, with charity, without brawling or scolding, and decide all things by the word of God. Establish the divine and perfect truth as it is found in Scripture.'

Cromwell wanted the submission of *all* to the divine revelation; the traditional party answered him by putting forward human doctrines and

---

[1] Fuller's *Church History* (1655), p. 213.
[2] Preface to Alesius' treatise *On the Authority of the Word of God.*

human authorities. Stokesley, Bishop of London, endeavoured to prove, by certain glosses and passages, that there were seven sacraments: the Archbishop of York and others supported him by their sophistry and their shouts. 'Such disputes about words, and such cries', said Cranmer, 'are unbecoming serious men. Let us seek Christ's glory, the peace of the church, and the means by which sins are forgiven. Let us enquire how we may bring consolation to uneasy souls; how we may give the assurance of God's love to consciences troubled by the remembrance of their sins. Let us acknowledge that it is not the outward use of the sacraments that justifies a man, and that our justification proceeds solely from faith in the Saviour.' The prelate spoke admirably and in accordance with Scripture: it was necessary to back up this noble confession. Cromwell, who kept his Scotsman in reserve, now introduced him to the clergy, as the 'King's Scholar', and asked him what he thought of the discussion. Alesius, speaking in the assembly of bishops, showed that there were only *two* sacraments – Baptism and the Lord's Supper – and that no ceremony ought to be put in the same rank with them. The Bishop of London chafed with anger in his seat. Shall a mere Scotsman, driven from his country and entertained by German Protestants, presume to teach the prelates of England? He shouted out indignantly, 'All that is false!' Alesius declared himself ready to prove what he had said out of Scripture and the old Fathers. Then Fox, Bishop of Hereford, who had just returned from Wittenberg, whither he had been sent by the king, and where he had been enlightened by conversing with Luther and Melanchthon, rose up and uttered these noble sentiments: 'Christ hath so lightened the world at this time', he said, 'that the light of the gospel hath put to flight all misty darkness; and the world will no longer endure to be led astray by all that fantastic rubbish with which the priests formerly filled their imaginations and their sermons.' This was pointed at Bishop Stokesley and his friends: 'It is vain to resist the Lord; his hand drives away the clouds. The laity know the Holy Scriptures now better than many of us. The Germans have made the text of the Bible so easy, by the Hebrew and Greek tongue, that even women and children wonder at the blindness and falsehood that hath been hitherto. Consider that you make not yourselves to be laughed to scorn of all the world.

If you resist the voice of God, you will give cause for belief that there is not one spark of learning or godliness in you. All things consist not in painted eloquence and strength of authority. For truth is of so great power, strength, and efficacy, that it can neither be defended with words nor be overcome with any strength; but after she hath hidden herself long, at length she pusheth up her head and appeareth.' Such was the eloquent and Christian language with which even bishops endeavoured to bring about the triumph of that English reformation which some have been pleased to represent as 'the product of an amorous caprice'. Moved by such Christian remarks, Alesius exclaimed, 'Yes, it is the word of God that bringeth life; the word of God is the very substance and body of the sacrament. It makes us certain and sure of the will of God to save our souls: the outward ceremony is but a token of that lively inflammation which we receive through faith in the word and promise of the Lord.' At these words the Bishop of London could not contain himself. 'The word of God', he cried; 'Yes, granted! But you are far deceived if you think there is no *other* word of God but that which every souter [shoemaker] and cobbler may read in his mother-tongue.' Stokesley believed in another word of God besides the Bible; he thought, as the council of Trent did a little later, 'That we must receive *with similar respect and equal piety the Holy Scriptures and* TRADITION.'[1] As it was noon, Cromwell broke up the meeting.

The debate had been sharp. The sacerdotal, sacramental, ritualist party had been beaten; the evangelicals desired to secure their victory.

Alesius, after his return to Lambeth, began to compose a treatise; Stokesley, on the other hand, prepared to get up a conspiracy against Alesius. Next day the bishops, who arrived first at Westminster, entered into conversation about the last sitting, and were very indignant that a stranger, a Scotsman, should have been allowed to sit and speak among them. Stokesley called upon Cranmer to resist such an irregularity. The archbishop, who was always rather weak, consented, and Cromwell entering shortly after with his protégé, an archdeacon went up to the latter and told him that his presence was disagreeable to the bishops. 'It is better to give way', said Cromwell to Alesius; 'I do not want to

---

[1] Council of Trent, 4th sitting, 8 April 1546.

expose you to the hatred of the prelates. When once they take a dislike to a man, they never rest until they have got him out of the way. They have already put to death many Christians for whom the king felt great esteem.' Alesius withdrew and the debate opened. 'Are there seven sacraments or only two?' was the question. It was impossible to come to an understanding.

Convocation, an old clerical body, in which were assembled the most resolute partisans of the abuses, superstitions, and doctrines of the Middle Ages, was the real stronghold of Rome in England. To undertake to introduce the light and life of the gospel into it was a rash and impracticable enterprise. The divine Head of the church himself has declared that *'no man putteth new cloth to an old garment, neither do men put new wine into old bottles.'* There was but one thing to be done: suppress the assembly and form a new one, composed of members and ministers of the church, who acknowledge no other foundation, no other rule, than the word of God. *'New wine must be put into new bottles.'* Such a step as this would have helped powerfully to reform the Church of England really and completely. But it was not taken.

CHAPTER TWELVE

Henry Enforces 'Catholicism minus the Pope'

(Autumn 1536)

After Anne Boleyn's death, the men of the reformation had taken the initiative, and Cranmer, Cromwell, Latimer, and Alesius seemed on the point of winning the prize of the contest. The intervention of a greater personage was about to affect the situation profoundly.

Anne's disgrace and the wedding with Jane Seymour had occupied the king with far other matters than theology. Cranmer had the field free to advance the reformation. This was not what Henry intended; and as soon as he noticed it, he roused himself, as if from slumber, and hastened to put things in order. Though rejecting the authority of the pope, he remained faithful to his doctrines. He proceeded to act in his character as head of the church, and resolved to fulminate a bull, as the pontiffs had done. Reginald Pole, in the book which he had addressed to him, observed that in matters touching the pope, we must not regard either his character or his life, but only his authority; and that the lapses of a pope in morals detract nothing from his infallibility in faith. Henry understood this distinction very clearly, and showed himself a pope in every way. He did not believe that there was any incompatibility between the right he claimed of taking a new wife whenever he pleased, by means of divorce or the scaffold, and that of declaring the oracles of God on contrition, justification, and ecclesiastical rites and ceremonies. The rupture of the negotiations with the obstinate German Protestants gave him more liberty, and even caused him a little vexation. His chagrin was not unmingled with anger, and he was not grieved to show them what they stood to lose by not accepting him. In this respect

Henry was like a woman who, annoyed at being rejected by the man she prefers, gives her hand to his rival in bravado. He returned, therefore, to his theological labours. The doctors of the scholastic party spared him the pains of drawing up for himself the required articles; but he revised them and was elated at the importance of his work. 'We have in our own person taken great pain, study, labours, and travails', he said, 'over certain articles which will establish concord in our church.' Cromwell, always submissive to his master and well knowing the cost of resistance, laid this royal labour before the upper house of convocation. In religious matters Henry had never done anything so important. The doctrine of the authority of the prince over the dogmas of the church now became a fact. The king's dogmatic paper, entitled *Articles about Religion Set Out by the Convocation, and Published by the King's Authority,* bears a strong resemblance to the *Exposition and the Type of Faith,* published in the seventh century, during the monothelite controversy, by the emperors of Constantinople – Heraclius and Constans II. That prince, who in a political sense gave England a new impulse, sought his models as an ecclesiastical ruler in the Lower Empire. Everybody was eager to know what doctrines the new head of the church was going to proclaim. The partisans of Rome were doubtless quite as much surprised as the reformers, but their astonishment was that of joy; the surprise of the evangelicals was that of fear. The vicar-general read the royal oracles aloud: 'All the words contained in the whole canon of the Bible', he said, 'and in the three creeds – the Apostles', the Nicene, and the Athanasian – *according to the interpretation which the holy approved doctors in the church do defend,* shall be received and observed as the infallible words of God, so that whosoever rejects them is not a member of Christ but a member of the devil, and eternally damned.'

That was the Romish doctrine, and Bossuet, in his examination of the royal document, appears much satisfied with the article.

'The sacrament of baptism should be administered to infants, in order that they may receive the Holy Ghost and be purified of sin by its secret virtue and operation. If a man falls after baptism the sacrament of penance is necessary to his salvation; he must go to confession, ask absolution at the priest's hands, and look upon the words uttered by the confessor as the *voice of God* speaking out of heaven.'

– 'That is the whole substance of the Catholic doctrine', the partisans of Rome might urge.

'Under the form of the bread and the wine are verily, substantially, and really contained the body and very blood of the Saviour which was born of the Virgin.'

– 'That indicates most precisely the real presence of the body', say the Romish doctors.[1]

'The merits of the Saviour's passion are the only and worthy causes of our justification; but, before giving it to us, God requires of us inward contrition, perfect faith, hope, and charity, and all the other spiritual motions which must necessarily concur in the remission of our sins.'

– The council of Trent declared the same doctrine not long after.[2]

'Images ought to be preserved in the churches. Only let those who kneel before them and adore them know that such honour is not paid to the images, but to God.'

– 'To use such language', Rornan Catholics have said, 'is to approve of image-worship to the extreme.'[3]

'It is praiseworthy', continued Cromwell, 'to address prayers to our Blessed Lady, to St John the Baptist, to each of the apostles, or to any other saint, in order that they may pray for us and with us; but without believing there is more mercy in them than in Christ.'

– 'If the king looks upon this as a kind of reformation', said a Romish doctor, 'he is only making game of the word; for no Catholic addresses the saints except to have their prayers.'[4]

'As for the ceremonies, such as sprinkling with holy water, distributing the consecrated bread, prostration before the cross and kissing it, exorcisms, *etc.*, these rites and others equally praiseworthy ought to be maintained as putting us in remembrance of spiritual things.'

– 'That is precisely our idea', said the partisans of Romish tradition.[5]

'Finally, as to purgatory, the people shall be taught that Christians ought to pray for the souls of the dead, and give alms, in order that

[1] Bossuet, *Histoire des Variations,* vii, § 25.
[2] Council of Trent, sixth session, canons 9 & 11.
[3] Bossuet, *Variations,* vii, § 26.
[4] *Ibid.*
[5] *Ibid.* vii, § 27.

others may pray for them, so that their souls may be relieved of some part of their pain.'

– 'All that we teach is here approved of', said the great opponent of Protestantism.[1]

Such was the religion which the prince whom some writers call the father of the reformation desired to establish in England. If England became Protestant, it was certainly in spite of Henry VIII.

A long debate ensued in convocation and elsewhere. The decided evangelicals could see nothing in these articles but an abandonment of Scripture, a 'political daubing', in which the object was only to please certain persons and to attain certain ends. The men of the moderate party said, on the other hand, 'Ought we not to rejoice that the Scriptures and ancient creeds are re-established as rules of faith, without considering the pope?' But above these opposite opinions rose the terrible voice of the king: *Sic volo, sic jubeo:* Such is my pleasure, such are my orders. If the primate and his friends resisted, they would be set aside and the reformation lost.

It does not appear that Cranmer had any share in drawing up these articles, but he signed them. It has been said, to excuse him, that neither he, nor many of his colleagues, had at that time a distinct knowledge of such matters, and that they intended to make amendments in the articles; but these allegations are insufficient. Two facts alone explain the concessions of this pious man: the king's despotic will and the archbishop's characteristic weakness. He always bent his head; but, we must also acknowledge, it was in order to raise it again. Archbishop Lee, sixteen bishops, forty abbots or priors, and fifty archdeacons or proctors signed after Cromwell and the primate. The articles passed through convocation, because – like Anne's condemnation – *it was the king's will.* Nothing can better explain the concessions of Cranmer, Cromwell, and others in the case of Anne Boleyn, than their support of these articles, which were precisely the opposite of the scriptural doctrine whose triumph they had at heart. In both cases they had yielded slavishly to those magic words: *Le roi le veut,* the king wills it. Those four words were sufficient: that man was *loyal* who sacrificed his own will to the will of

[1] Bossuet, *Variations,* vii, § 28.

the sovereign. It was only by degrees that the free principles of Protestantism were to penetrate among the people, and give England liberty along with order. Still, that excuse is not sufficient: Cranmer would have left a more glorious name if he had suffered martyrdom under Henry VIII, and not waited for the reign of Mary.

When the king's articles were known, discontent broke out in the opposite parties. 'Be silent, you contentious preachers and you factious schoolmen', said the politicians: 'you would sooner disturb the peace of the world, than relinquish or retract one particle!' The articles were sent all over England, with orders that everyone should conform to them or incur the wrath of the king and the church.

Cranmer did not look upon the game as lost. To bend before the blast, and then rise up again and guide the reform to a good end, was his system. He first strove to prevent the evil by suggesting measures calculated to remedy it. Convocation resolved that a petition should be addressed to the king, praying him to permit his lay subjects to read the Bible in *English,* and to order a new translation of it to be made; moreover, a great number of feast days were abolished as favouring 'sloth, idleness, thieves, excesses, vagabonds, and riots'; and finally, on the last day of the session (20 July), convocation declared – to show clearly that there was no question of returning to popery – that there was nothing more pernicious than a general council; and that, consequently, they must decline to attend that which the pope intended to hold in the city of Mantua. Thereupon Parliament and convocation were dissolved, and the king did without them for three years.

Henry VIII was satisfied with his minister. Cromwell was created Lord Privy Seal, 2 July 1536, baron, and a few days later vice-gerent in ecclesiastical matters (*in rebus ecclesiasticis*). Wishing to tone down what savoured too much of the schools in the king's articles, he circulated among all the priests some instructions which were passably evangelical. 'I enjoin you', he said, 'to make your parishioners understand that they do rather apply themselves to the keeping of God's commandments and fulfilling of his works of charity, and providing for their families, than if they went about to pilgrimages. Advise parents and masters to teach their children and their servants the Lord's Prayer, the Apostles' Creed, and

the Ten Commandments, in their mother-tongue.' He even undertook
to reform the clergy. 'Deans, parsons, vicars, curates, and priests', he
said, 'are forbidden to haunt taverns, to drink or brawl after dinner or
supper, to play at cards day or night. If they have any leisure, they should
read the Scriptures, or occupy themselves with some honest exercise.'

But Cranmer and Cromwell went further than this. They wished
to circulate the Holy Scriptures. Tyndale's version was, in Cromwell's
opinion, too far compromised to be officially circulated; he had,
therefore, patronized another translation. Coverdale, who was born in
1488, in the North Riding of Yorkshire, had undertaken (as we have
seen) to translate the Bible, and had applied to Cromwell to procure him
the necessary books.[1] Tyndale was more independent, a man of firmer
and bolder character than Coverdale. He did not seek the aid of men,
and finished his work (so to say) alone with God. Coverdale, pious no
doubt like his rival, felt the need of being supported, and said, in his
letter to Cromwell, that he implored his help, 'prostrate on the knees of
his heart'.

Coverdale knew Greek, and Hebrew. He began his task about 1530;
on 4 October 1535, the book appeared, probably at Zurich, under the
title: BIBLIA, *the Bible, that is to say, the Holy Scriptures of the Old and
New Testament;* and reached England in the early part of 1536. At the
beginning of the volume was a dedication to Henry VIII, which ended
by imploring the divine blessing on the king and on his 'dearest just wife,
and most virtuous princess, Queen Anne'. Cromwell was to present this
translation to the king, and circulate it throughout the country; but
this *dearest wife,* this *most virtuous princess* had just been accused by
Henry, dragged before the tribunals, and beheaded. It was impossible to
distribute a single copy of this version without arousing the monarch's
anger. Those who desired that the ship which had come so far should
not be wrecked in the harbour had recourse to several expedients. The
decapitated queen's name was *Anne,* that of the queen-regnant was
Jeanne: there was a resemblance between them. Some copies corrected
with a pen have instead of *Queen Anne, Queen Jane;* in others the name

[1] Coverdale's *Remains* (Parker Society), p. 490. The letter is dated 1 May, but has no
year: it appears to me to be 1530 [but it may be as early as 1527].

of the queen is simply scratched out.¹ These expedients were not sufficient: a new title-page was printed and dated 1536, the current year.

It seems probable that the king gave his verbal approval to the new
translation, but that he showed no appreciation of its merits and no
enthusiasm for its circulation. Nevertheless, the reformation, taught by
pious ministers, was spreading more and more. The priests murmured
in vain: 'Not long ago', they said, 'the Lollards were put to death for
reading the gospel in English, and now we are ordered to teach it in that
language. We are robbed of our privileges, and our labours are increased.'

The king had proclaimed and laid down his Ten Articles to little
purpose: faith gave pious ministers and Christians a courage which the
great ones of the earth did not possess. John Gale, pastor of Thwaite,
in Suffolk, a quick, decided, but rather imprudent man, attacked the
royal articles from his pulpit. But he did not stop there. His church
was ornamented with images of the Virgin and saints, before which the
devout used to stick up tapers. 'Austin', said he one day to a parishioner,
'follow me'; and the two men, with great exertions, took away the iron
rods on which the worshippers used to set their tapers, and turned the
images to the wall. – 'Listen', said Dr Barret to his parishioners, 'the
lifting up of the host betokens simply that the Father has sent his Son
to suffer death for man, and the lifting up of the chalice that *the Son has
shed his blood for our salvation.*' – 'Christ', said the Prior of Dorchester,
'does not dwell in churches of stone, but in heaven above and in the
hearts of men on earth.' – The minister of Hothfield declared that: 'Our
Lady is not the queen of heaven, and has no more power than another
woman.' 'Pull him out of the pulpit', said the exasperated bailiff to the
vicar. 'I dare not', answered the latter. In fact, the congregation were
delighted at hearing their minister say of Jesus, as Peter did: *Neither
is there salvation in any other,* and that very day more than a hundred
embraced their pastor's doctrines. Jerome, Vicar of Stepney, endeavoured
to plant the pure truth of Christ in the conscience, and root out all vain
traditions, dreams, and fantasies. Being invited to preach at St Paul's
Cross, on the fourth Sunday in Lent, he said: 'There are two sorts of
people among you: the free, who are freely justified without the penance

¹ Such copies may be found at the British Museum, and in the library at Lambeth.

of the law and without meritorious works; and the slaves, who are still under the yoke of the law.' – Even a bishop, Barlow of St David's, said in a stately cathedral: 'If two or three cobblers or weavers, elect of God, meet together in the name of the Lord, they form a true church of God.'

Proceedings were commenced against those who had thus braved the king's articles. Jerome appeared before Henry VIII at Westminster. The poor fellow, intimidated by the royal majesty, tremblingly acknowledged that the sacraments were necessary for salvation; but he was burnt five years after in the cause of the gospel. Gale and others were accused of heresy and treason before the criminal court. The books were not spared. There were some, indeed, that went beyond all bounds. One, entitled *The little garden of the souls,* contained a passage in which the beheading of John the Baptist and of Anne Boleyn were ascribed to the same motive – the reproach of a criminal love uttered against two princes: one by Anne, and the other by John. Henry compared to Herod! Anne Boleyn to St John the Baptist! Tunstall denounced this audacious publication to Cromwell.

The crown-officers were to see that the doctrines of the pope were taught everywhere; but, without the pope and his authority, this system has no solid foundation. The Holy Scriptures, to which evangelical Christians appeal, is a firm foundation. The authority of the pope – a vicious principle – at least puts those who admit it in a position to know what they believe. But Catholicism with Romish doctrine and without the pope has no ground to stand on. Non-Roman Catholicism has but a treacherous support. Another system had already, in the sixteenth century, set up reason as the supreme rule; but it presents a thousand different opinions, and no absolute truth. There is but one real foundation: *Thy word is truth,* says Jesus Christ, and Jesus Christ is Lord.

CHAPTER THIRTEEN

The Pilgrimage of Grace

(October 1536)

The bastard system of a Catholicism without a pope, put forward by the king, did not enjoy great favour, and the evangelical reform gained fresh adherents every day. The more consistent popish system endeavoured to stand against it. There were still many partisans of Rome in the aristocracy and among the populations of the north. A mighty effort was about to be made to expel both Cranmer's Protestantism and the king's Catholicism, and restore the papacy to its privileges. A great revolution is rarely accomplished without the friends of the old order of things combining to resist it.

Many members of the House of Lords saw with alarm the House of Commons gaining an influence which it had never possessed before, and taking the initiative in reforms which were not (as they thought) within its sphere. Trained in the hatred of heresy, those noble lords were indignant at seeing heretics invested with the episcopal dignity, and a layman, Cromwell, presuming to direct the convocation of the clergy. Some of them formed a league, and Lord Darcy, who was at their head, had a conference on the subject with the ambassador of Charles V. That prince assured him that he would be supported. The English partisans of the pope, aided by the imperialists, would be amply sufficient, they thought, to re-establish the authority of the Roman pontiff.

There was great agitation especially among the inhabitants of the towns and villages of the north. Those of the counties of York and Lincoln, too remote from London to feel its influence, besides being ignorant and superstitious, were submissive to the priests as to the very representatives of God. The names of the reformers Luther, Melanchthon,

Œcolampadius, and Tyndale were known by the priests, who taught their flocks to detest them. Everything they saw exasperated them. If they went on a journey, the monasteries which were their ordinary hostelries existed no longer. If they worked in the fields, they saw approaching them some ragged monk, with tangled hair and beard, with haggard eye, without bread to support him, or roof to shelter him, to whom hatred still gave strength to complain and to curse. These unhappy wretches went roaming up and down the country, knocking at every door; the peasants received them like saints, seated them at their table, and starved themselves for their nourishment. 'See', said the monks, showing their rags to the people about them, 'see to what a condition the members of Jesus Christ are reduced! A schismatic and heretical prince has expelled us from the houses of the Lord. But the Holy Father has excommunicated and dethroned him: no one should henceforth obey him.' Such words produced their effect.

In the autumn of 1536, the ferment increased among the inhabitants of the rural districts who had no longer their field labours to divert them. They assembled in great numbers round the monasteries to see what the king meant to do with them. They looked on at a distance, and with angry eyes watched the commissioners who at times behaved violently, indulged in exactions, or threw down, one after another, the stones of the building which had been held for so long in reverence. Another day they saw the agent of some lord settle in the monastery with his wife, children, and servants; they heard those profane lay folks laugh and chatter as they entered the sacred doors, whose thresholds had until now been trodden only by the sandals of the silent monks. A report spread abroad that the monasteries still surviving were also about to be suppressed. Dr Makerel, formerly Prior of Barlings, disguised as a labourer, and a monk (some writers say a shoemaker) named Nicholas Melton, who received the name of 'Captain Cobbler', endeavoured to inflame men's minds and drive them to revolt. Everywhere the people listened to the agitators; and ere long the superior clergy appeared in the line of battle. 'Neither the King's Highness nor any temporal man', they said, 'may be supreme head of the church. The pope of Rome is Christ's vicar, and must alone be acknowledged as supreme head of Christendom.'

On Monday, 2 October 1536, the ecclesiastical commission was to visit the parish of Louth in Lincolnshire, and the clergy of the district were ordered to be present. Only a few days before, a neighbouring monastery had been suppressed and two of Cromwell's agents placed in it to see to the closing. The evening before the inspection (it was a Sunday) a number of the townspeople brought out a large silver cross which belonged to the parish, and shouting out, 'Follow the cross! All follow the cross! God knows if we can do so for long', marched in procession through the town, with Melton leading the way. Some went to the church, took possession of the consecrated jewels, and remained under arms all night to guard them for fear the royal commissioners should carry them off. On Monday morning one of the commissioners, who had no suspicions, quietly rode into the town, followed by a single servant. All of a sudden the alarm bell was rung, and a crowd of armed men filled the streets. The terrified commissioner ran into the church, hoping to find it an inviolable asylum; but the mob laid hold of him, dragged him out into the market-place, and pointing a sword at his breast, said to him, 'Swear fidelity to the commons or you are a dead man.' All the town took an oath to be faithful 'to God, the king, and the commons, for the wealth of holy church'. On Tuesday morning the alarm bell was rung again; the cobbler and a tailor named Big Jack marched out, followed by a crowd of men, some on foot and some on horseback. Whole parishes, headed by their priests, joined them and marched with the rest. The monks prayed aloud for the pope, and cried out that if the gentry did not join them they should all be hanged; but gentlemen and even sheriffs united with the tumultuous troops. Twenty thousand men of Lincolnshire were in arms. England, like Germany, had its peasants' revolt; but while Luther was opposed to it, the Archbishop of York, with many abbots and priests, encouraged it in England.

The insurgents did not delay proclaiming their grievances. They declared that if the monasteries were restored, men of mean birth dismissed from the council, and heretic bishops deprived, they would acknowledge the king as head of the church. The movement was instigated by the monks more than by the pope. Great disorders were committed.

The court was plunged into consternation by this revolt. The king, who had no standing army, felt his weakness, and his anger knew no bounds. 'What!' he said to the *traitors* (for such was the name he gave them) 'what! do you, the rude commons of one shire, and that one of the most *brute and beastly* [stupid] of the whole realm, presume to find fault with your king? Return to your homes, surrender to our lieutenants a hundred of your leaders, and prepare to submit to such condign punishment as we shall think you worthy of; otherwise you will expose yourselves, your wives and children, your lands and goods, not only to the indignation of God, but to utter destruction by force and violence of the sword.'

Such threats as these only served to increase the commotion. 'Christianity is going to be abolished', said the priests; 'you will soon find yourselves under the sword of *Turks!* But whoever sheds his blood with us shall inherit eternal glory.' The people crowded to them from all quarters. Lord Shrewsbury, sent by the king against the rebellion, being unable to collect more than 3,000 men, and having to contend against ten times as many, had halted at Nottingham. London already imagined the rebels were at its gates, and mighty exertions were made. Sir John Russell and the Duke of Suffolk were sent forward with forces hurriedly equipped.

The insurgents were numerically strong, but with no efficient leader or store of provisions. Two opinions arose among them: the gentlemen and farmers cried, 'Home, home!' the priests and the people shouted, 'To arms!' The party of the friends of order continued increasing, and at last prevailed. The Duke of Suffolk entered Lincoln on 17 October, and the rebels dispersed.

A still greater danger threatened the established order of things. The men of the north were more extreme than those of Lincoln. On 8 October there was a riot at Beverley, in Yorkshire. A Westminster lawyer, Robert Aske, who had passed his vacation in field sports, was returning to London, when he was stopped by the rebels and proclaimed their leader. On 15 October he marched to York and replaced the monks in possession of their monasteries. Lord Darcy, an old soldier of Ferdinand of Spain and Louis XII and a warm papal partisan, quitted his castle of

Pontefract to join the insurrection. The priests stirred up the people, and ere long, the army, which amounted to at least 30,000 men, formed a long procession, 'the *Pilgrimage of Grace*', which marched through the county of York. Each parish paraded under a captain, priests carrying the church cross in front by way of flag. A large banner, which floated in the midst of this multitude, represented on one side Christ with the five wounds on a cross, and on the other a plough, a chalice, a pix, and a hunting horn. Every pilgrim wore embroidered on his sleeve the five wounds of Christ with the name of Jesus in the midst. The insurgents had a thousand bows and as many bills, besides other arms;[1] but hardly one poor copy of the Testament of Christ. 'Ah!' said Latimer, preaching in Lincolnshire, 'I will tell you what is the true Christian man's pilgrimage. There are, the Saviour tells us, eight days' journeys.' Then he described the eight beatitudes in the most evangelical manner: the poor in spirit, those who mourn, those who are meek, those who hunger and thirst after righteousness, and the rest.[2]

Aske's pilgrimage was of another sort. Addressing the people of those parts, he said to them: 'Lords, knights, masters, and friends, evil-disposed persons have filled the king's mind with new inventions: the holy body of the church has been despoiled. We have therefore undertaken this *pilgrimage* for the reformation of what is amiss and the punishment of heretics.[3] If you will not come with us we will fight and die against you.' Bonfires were lighted on all the hills to call the people to arms. Wherever these new crusaders appeared the monks were replaced in their monasteries and the peasants constrained to join the pilgrimage, under pain of seeing their houses pulled down, their goods seized, and their bodies handed over to the mercy of the captains.

There was this notable difference between the revolt in Germany and that in the north of England. In Germany, a few nobles only joined the people and were compelled to do so. In England, almost all the nobility of the north rallied to it of their own accord. The earls of Westmorland,

---

[1] Bale, *Works* (Parker Society), p. 327.

[2] Latimer, *Sermons* (Parker Society), p. 476.

[3] Lingard says that this expedition was named jestingly 'the Pilgrimage of Grace'. He is mistaken: the rebels themselves seriously call it by this name six times in their proclamation.

Rutland, and Huntingdon, Lords Latimer, Lumley, Scrope, Conyers, and the representatives of several other great families followed the example of old Lord Darcy. One single nobleman, Percy, Earl of Northumberland, remained faithful to the king. He had been ill since the unjust sentence which had struck the loyal wife of Henry VIII – a sentence in which he had refused to join – and was now at his castle lying on a bed of pain which was soon to be the bed of death. The rebels surrounded his dwelling and summoned him to join the insurrection. He might now have avenged the crime committed by Henry VIII against Anne Boleyn, but he refused. Savage voices shouted out, 'Cut off his head, and make Sir Thomas Percy earl in his stead.' But the noble and courageous man said calmly to those around him, 'I can die but once; let them kill me, and so put an end to my sorrows.'

The king, more alarmed at this revolt than at the former one, asked with terror whether his people desired to force him to replace his neck under the detested yoke of the pope. In this crisis he displayed great activity. Being at Windsor, he wrote letter after letter to Cromwell. 'I will sell all my plate', he said. 'Go to the Tower, take as much plate as you may want, and coin it into money.' Henry displayed no less intelligence than decision. He named as commander of his little army a devoted servant, who was also the chief of the papal party at the court – the Duke of Norfolk. Once already, for the condemnation of the Protestant Anne Boleyn, Henry had selected this chief of the Romish party. This clever policy succeeded equally well for the king in both affairs.

London, Windsor, and all the south of England were in great commotion. People imagined that the papacy, borne on the lusty arms of the northern men, was about to return in triumph into the capital; that perhaps the Catholic King of the Scots, Henry's nephew, would enter with it and place England once more under the papal sceptre. The friends of the gospel were deeply agitated. 'That great captain the devil', said Latimer in the London pulpits, 'has all sorts of ordnance to shoot at Christian men. These men of the north, who wear the cross and the wounds before and behind, are marching against him who bore the cross and suffered those wounds. They have risen (they say) to support the king, and they are fighting against him. They come forward in the name of the church, and fight against the church, which is the congregation of faithful men. Let us fight with the sword of the Spirit, which is the word of God.'

The rebels, far from being calmed, showed – part of them at least – that they were animated by the vilest sentiments. A body of insurgents had invested the castle of Skipton, the only place in the county of York which still held for the king. The wife and daughters of Lord Clifford, and other ladies who inhabited it, happened to be at an abbey not far off, just when the castle was beleaguered. The insurgents caused Lord Clifford to be informed that if he did not surrender, his wife and daughters would be brought next day to the foot of the walls and be given up to the camp followers. In the middle of the night, Christopher Aske, brother of Robert, who had remained faithful, crept through the camp of the besiegers, and by unfrequented roads succeeded in bringing into the castle all those ladies, whom he thus saved from the most infamous outrages.[1]

Robert Aske, Lord Darcy, the Archbishop of York, and several other leaders had their headquarters at Pontefract Castle, where the Lancaster herald, despatched by the king, presented himself on 21 October. After passing through many troops of armed men – 'very cruel fellows', he says – he was at last introduced to the great captain. Seeing Lord Darcy and the archbishop before him – persons more important than the Westminster lawyer – the herald began to address them. Aske was offended, and rising from his seat told him haughtily that he was the person to be addressed. The messenger discharged his mission. He represented to the leaders of the rebellion that they were but a handful before the great power of His Majesty, and that the king had done nothing in regard to religion but what the clergy of York and Canterbury had acknowledged to be in conformity with the word of God. When the speech was ended, Aske, as if he did not care for the herald's words, said rudely to him, 'Show me your proclamation.' 'He behaved', wrote the envoy, 'as though he had been some great prince, with great rigour and like a tyrant.' 'Herald', said Aske, 'this proclamation shall neither be

---

[1] This fact is mentioned in one of the depositions of the trial which followed the revolt. See Christopher Aske's Examination.

read at the market-cross nor elsewhere amongst my people. We want the redress of our grievances, and we will die fighting to obtain them.' The herald asked what were their grievances. 'My followers and I', replied the chief, 'will walk in pilgrimage to London, to His Majesty, to expel from the council all the vile blood in it, and set up all the noble blood again; and also to obtain the full restitution of Christ's church.' 'Will you give me that in writing?' said the herald. Aske gave him the oath which the rebels took, and at the same time putting his hand on the paper, he said with a loud voice, 'This is my act; I will die in its defence, and all my followers will die with me.' The herald, intimidated by the authoritative tone of the chief, bent his knee before the rebel captain, for which he was brought to trial and executed in the following year. 'Give him a guard of forty men, and see him out of town', said Aske.

Forthwith 30,000 well-armed men, of whom 12,000 were mounted, set out under the orders of Aske, Lord Darcy, and other noblemen of the country. Norfolk had only a small force, which he could not trust; accordingly the rebels were convinced that when they appeared, the king's soldiers and perhaps the duke himself would join them. The rebel army arrived on the banks of the Don, on the other side of which (at Doncaster) the king's forces were stationed. Those ardent men, who were six against one, inflamed by monks who were impatient to return to their nests, proposed to pass the Don, overthrow Norfolk, enter London, dictate to the king the execution of all the partisans of the reformation, and restore the papal power in England. The rising of the water, increased by heavy rains, did not permit them to cross the river. Every hour's delay was a gain to the royal cause; the insurgents, having brought no provisions with them, were forced to disband to go in search of them elsewhere. Norfolk took advantage of this to circulate an address among the rebels. 'Unhappy men!' it said, 'what folly hath led you to make this most shameful rebellion against our most righteous king, who hath kept you in peace against all your enemies? Fye, for shame! How can you do this to one who loves you more than all his subjects? If you do not return, every man to his house, we will show you the hardest courtesy that ever was shown to men, that have loved you so well as we have done. But if you go to your homes, you shall have us most humble suitors to His Highness for you.' This proclamation was signed by Lords Norfolk, Shrewsbury, Exeter, Rutland, and Huntingdon, all Catholics, and the greatest names in England.

The insurgents thus found themselves in the most difficult position. They must attack the supporters of their own cause. If the lords who had signed the proclamation were slain, England would lose her best councillors, and her greatest generals, and the church would be deprived of the most zealous Catholics. The strength of England would be sacrificed and the country opened to her enemies. Old Lord Darcy was for attacking; young Robert Aske for negotiation. On 27 October, commissioners from both parties met on the bridge leading to Doncaster. The rebel commissioners consented to lay down their arms, provided the heresies of Luther, Wycliffe, Huss, Melanchthon, Œcolampadius, and the works of Tyndale were destroyed and nullified; that the supremacy was restored to the see of Rome; that the suppressed abbeys were re-established; that heretical bishops and lords were punished by fire or otherwise; and that a Parliament was held promptly at Nottingham or York.

There could no longer be any doubt that the object of the insurrection was to crush the reformation. The names of most of the reformers were mentioned in the articles, and fire or sword were to do justice to the most illustrious of their adherents. The same evening they handed in a letter addressed: *To the King's Royal Highness. From Doncaster, this Saturday, at eleven of the clock at night. Haste, post, haste, haste, haste!* The rebels themselves were in such haste that they waited no longer. The next day (28 October) the king's lieutenant announced at one in the afternoon that the insurgents had dispersed and were returning to their homes. Two of the rebel leaders were to carry the stipulated conditions to the king, and Norfolk was to accompany them. That zealous Catholic was not perhaps without a hope that the petition would induce Henry to become reconciled to the pope. He was greatly deceived.

It was clear that the king was rapidly gaining the upper hand. Norfolk caused the rebels to believe that their demands would be met. In the outcome, however, this was not the case. The king benefited by delay. He was able to build up his forces in the north, and early in December, in consequence of threats and promises, the rebel army finally broke up. The one formidable insurrection of Henry's reign was over.

Thus God had scattered the forces of those who had stood up against Wycliffe, Huss, and Luther. The kingdom resumed its usual tranquillity. A little later the men of the north, excited by the intrigues of the pope and Reginald Pole, now a cardinal, again took up arms; but they were defeated; seventy of them were hanged on the walls of Carlisle, and Lords Darcy and Hussey, with sundry barons, abbots, priors, and a great number of priests, were executed in different places. The scheming Archbishop of York alone escaped, it is not known how. The cottages, parsonages, and castles of the north were filled with anguish and terror. Henry, who cut off the heads of his most intimate friends and of his queen, did not think of sparing rebels. It was a terrible lesson, but not very effectual. The priests did not lose their courage; they still kept asking for the re-establishment of the pope, the death of the Lutherans, and the annihilation of the reform. An event which occurred at this time seemed likely to favour their desires. A great blow was about to be dealt against the reformation. But the ways of God are not as our ways, and from what seems destined to compromise his cause, he often makes his triumph proceed.

CHAPTER FOURTEEN

The Martyrdom of Tyndale

(From 1535 to October 1536)

Most of the reformers, Luther, Zwingli, Calvin, Knox, and others, have acquired that name by their preachings, their writings, their struggles, and their actions. It is not so with the principal reformer of England: all his activity was concentred in the Holy Scriptures. Tyndale was less prominent than the other instruments of God who were awakened to upraise the church. We might say that, knowing the weakness of man, he had retired and hidden himself to allow the word from heaven to act by itself. He had studied it, translated it, and sent it over the sea: it must now do its own work. Is it not written: *The field is the world, and the seed is the word?* But there is another characteristic, or rather another fact, which distinguishes him from them, and this we have to describe.

While Pole and the papistical party, the new adversaries of Henry VIII, were agitating on the Continent, Tyndale, the man whom the king had pursued so long without being able to catch, was in prison at Vilvorde, near Brussels. In vain was he girt around with the thick walls of that huge fortress. Tyndale was free. 'There is the captivity and bondage', he could say, 'whence Christ delivered us, redeemed and loosed us. His blood, his death, his patience in suffering rebukes and wrongs, his prayers and fastings, his meekness and fulfilling of the uttermost point of the law ... broke the bonds of Satan, wherein we were so strait bound.' Thus Tyndale was as truly free at Vilvorde, as Paul had been at Rome.

For some years before his arrest, Tyndale had been labouring hard to produce a translation of the Old Testament worthy to take its place beside his English New Testament of 1525, and in the task he had realized his need of a skilled and sympathetic assistant. At that time there lived at Antwerp, as chaplain to the English merchants in that city, a young man from the county of Warwick, named John Rogers, who had been educated at Pembroke Hall, Cambridge, and was a little more than thirty years old. Rogers was learned, but submissive to the Romish traditions. Tyndale, having made his acquaintance, asked him to help in translating the Holy Scriptures, and Rogers caught joyfully at the opportunity of employing his Greek and Hebrew. Close and constant contact with the word of God gradually effected in him that great transformation, that total renewal of the man which is the object of redemption. 'I have found the true light in the gospel', he said one day to Tyndale; 'I now see the filthiness of Rome, and I cast from my shoulders the heavy yoke it has imposed upon me.' From that hour Tyndale received from Rogers the help which he had formerly received from John Fryth, that pious martyr, whose example Rogers was to follow by enduring the punishment of fire – the first to do so under Mary. The Holy Scriptures have been written in English with the blood of martyrs – if we may so speak – the blood of Fryth, Tyndale, and Rogers: it is a crown of glory for that translation.

It is highly probable that Tyndale, before his imprisonment, had completed his Old Testament translation as far as the end of the books of Chronicles. The manuscript was left by him in the capable hands of Rogers, who pressed on so diligently with the work of printing, that a few months before Tyndale was burned, an English version of the entire Bible was in circulation in his native land. Rogers did not himself undertake the translation of the remainder of the Old Testament but made use of the version which Myles Coverdale had already published.

Doubtless, Tyndale took pleasure in his gloomy dungeon in following with his mind's eye the divine Scripture from city to city and from cottage to cottage; his imagination pictured to him the struggles it would have to go through, and also its victories. 'The word of God', he said, 'never was without persecution – no more than the sun can be without his light. By what right doth the pope forbid God to speak in the English tongue? Why should not the sermons of the apostles, preached no doubt in the mother-tongue of those who heard them, be now written in the mother-tongue of those who read them?'[1] Tyndale did not think of proving the divinity of the Bible by learned dissertations. 'Scripture derives its authority from him who sent it', he said. 'Would you know the reason why men believe in Scripture? – It is *Scripture*. – It is itself the instrument which outwardly leads men to believe, whilst inwardly, the Spirit of God himself, speaking through Scripture, gives faith to his children.'[2] We do not know for certain in what city Rogers printed the great English folio Bible but it was probably Antwerp. Extraordinary precautions were required to prevent the persecutors from entering the house where men had the boldness to print the word of God, and from breaking the printing presses. Tyndale had the great comfort of knowing that the whole Bible was going to be published, and that prophets, apostles, and Christ himself would speak by it after his death.

This man, so active, so learned, and so truly great, whose works circulated far and wide with so much power, had at the same time within him a pure and beneficent light – the love of God and of man – which shed its mild rays on all around him. The depth of his faith, the charm of his conversation, the uprightness of his conduct touched those who came near him. The gaoler liked to bring him his food, in order to talk with him, and his daughter often accompanied him and listened eagerly to the words of the pious Englishman. Tyndale spoke of Jesus Christ; it seemed to him that the riches of the divine Spirit were about to transform Christendom; that the children of God were about to be manifested, and that the Lord was about *to gather together his elect*. 'Summer is nigh', he was wont to say, 'for the trees blossom.' In truth, young shoots and even old trees, long barren, flourished within the very walls of the castle. The gaoler, his daughter, and other members of their house were converted to the gospel by Tyndale's life and doctrine. However dark the machinations of his enemies, they could not obscure the divine light kindled in his heart, and which *shone before men*. There was an invincible power in this Christian man. Full of hope in the final victory of Jesus Christ, he courageously trampled under foot tribulations, trials, and death itself. He believed in the victory of the word. 'I am bound like a malefactor', he

---

[1] Tyndale, *Doctrinal Treatises* (Parker Society), pp. 131, 161, 148.
[2] Tyndale, *Answer to More* (Parker Society), pp. 136, 139.

said, 'but the word of God is not bound.' The bitterness of his last days was changed into great peace and divine sweetness.

His friends did not forget him. Among the English merchants at Antwerp was one whose affection had often reminded him that 'friendship is the assemblage of every virtue', as a wise man of antiquity styles it. Thomas Poyntz, one of whose ancestors had come over from Normandy with William the Conqueror, had perhaps known the reformer in the house of Lady Walsh, who also belonged to this ancient family. For nearly a year the merchant had entertained the translator of the Scriptures beneath his roof, and a mutual and unlimited confidence was established between them. When Poyntz saw his friend in prison, he resolved to do everything possible to save him. Poyntz's elder brother, John, who had retired to his estate at North Ockenden, in Essex, had accompanied the king in 1520 to the Field of Cloth of Gold, and although no longer at court, he still enjoyed the favour of Henry VIII. Thomas determined to write to John. 'Brother', he said, 'William Tyndale is in prison, and likely to suffer death, unless the king should extend his gracious help to him. He has lain in my house three quarters of a year, and I know that the king has never a truer-hearted subject.[1] When the pope gave His Majesty the title of Defender of the Faith, he prophesied like Caiaphas. The papists thought our prince should be a great maintainer of their abominations; but God has entered His Grace into the right battle. The king should know that the death of this man will be one of the highest pleasures to the enemies of the gospel. If it might please His Majesty to send for this man, it might, by the means thereof, be opened to the court and council of this country [Brabant] that they would be at another point with the Bishop of Rome within a short space.'

The letter is dated 25 August, and was forwarded by John Poyntz to the vicar-general on 21 September. Meanwhile, however, having received information from other sources, Cromwell had, with the king's approval, already taken action, for by 4 September he had prepared letters to be sent to two leading members of the council of Brabant. On 10 September, 1535, a messenger arrived in Antwerp with two letters

---

[1] Robert Demaus, *William Tyndale*, pp. 401-4.

from the vicar-general – one for the marquis of Bergen-op-Zoom, and the other for Carondolet, Archbishop of Palermo and president of the council of Brabant. Alas! the marquis had started two days before for Germany, whither he was conducting the princess of Denmark. Thomas Poyntz mounted his horse, and caught up the escort about fifteen miles from Maastricht. The marquis hurriedly glanced over Cromwell's despatch. 'I have no leisure to write', he said; 'the princess is making ready to depart.' 'I will follow you to the next baiting place', answered Tyndale's indefatigable friend. 'Be it so', replied Bergen-op-Zoom.

On arriving at Maastricht, the marquis wrote to the Company of Merchant Adventurers, to Cromwell, and to his friend the archbishop, president of the council of Brabant, and gave the three letters to Poyntz. The latter presented the letters of Cromwell and of the marquis to the president, but the archbishop and the council of Brabant were opposed to Tyndale. Poyntz immediately started for London, and laid the answer of the council before Cromwell, entreating him to insist that Tyndale should be immediately set at liberty, for the danger was great. The answer was delayed a month. Poyntz handed it to the emperor's council at Brussels, and every day this true and generous friend went to the office to learn the result. 'Your request will be granted', said one of the clerks on the fourth day. Poyntz was transported with joy. Tyndale was saved.

The traitor Philips, however, who had delivered Tyndale to his enemies, was then at Louvain. He had run away from Antwerp, knowing that the English merchants were angry with him, and had sold his books with the intent of escaping to Paris. But the Louvain priests, who still needed him, reassured him, and remaining in that stronghold of Romanism, he began to translate into Latin such passages in Tyndale's writings as he thought best calculated to offend the Catholics. He was thus occupied when the news of Tyndale's approaching deliverance filled him and his friends with alarm. What was to be done? He thought the only means of preventing the liberation of the prisoner was to shut up the liberator himself. Philips went straight to the procurator-general. 'That man, Poyntz', he said, 'is as much a heretic as Tyndale.' Two sergeants-of-arms were sent to keep watch over Poyntz at his house, and for six days in succession he was examined upon a hundred different articles. At the beginning of February 1536, he learnt that he was about to be sent to prison, and knowing what would follow, he formed a prompt resolution. One night, when the sergeants-of-arms were asleep, he escaped and left the city early, just as the gates were opened. Horsemen were sent in search of him; but as Poyntz knew the country well, he escaped them, got on board a ship, and arrived safe and sound at his brother's house at North Ockenden.[1]

When Tyndale heard of this escape, he knew what it indicated; but he was not overwhelmed, and almost at the foot of the scaffold, he bravely fought many a tough battle. The Louvain doctors undertook to make him abjure his faith, and represented to him that he was condemned by the church. 'The authority of Jesus Christ', answered Tyndale, 'is independent of the authority of the church.' They called upon him to make submission to the successor of the Apostle Peter. 'Holy Scripture', he said, 'is the first of the apostles, and the *ruler* in the kingdom of Christ.'[2] The Romish doctors ineffectually attacked him in his prison: he showed them that they were entangled in vain traditions and miserable superstitions, and overthrew all their pretences.

A most interesting memento of Tyndale's confinement at Vilvorde, and the only surviving document in the reformer's own hand, has come to light in the archives of the council of Brabant. It is a letter, written in Latin, which Tyndale addressed in all probability to the governor of the prison, and is worthy of being quoted in full:

I believe, right worshipful, that you are not ignorant of what

[1] [Poyntz's efforts to obtain the release of his friend Tyndale proved very costly to him, and are worthy of the grateful remembrance of his fellow countrymen. His goods in the Netherlands he lost; his wife, Anna van Calva, a native of Antwerp, refused to join him in England; for many years he was separated from his children. After eleven years he succeeded, on his brother's death, to the family estates in Essex, but financial embarrassment, dating from his losses in 1536, seems to have been his lot until his death in 1562. His epitaph in North Ockenden church reads as follows: 'He, for faithful service to his prince and warm-hearted profession of gospel truth, suffered bonds and imprisonment beyond the sea, and would plainly have been destined to death, had he not, trusting in divine providence, saved himself in a striking manner by escaping from his prison. In this chapel he now sleeps peacefully in the Lord, 1562.']

[2] Tyndale's *Expositions* (Parker Society), pp. 195, 251.

has been determined concerning me [by the Council of Brabant]; therefore I entreat your lordship and that by the Lord Jesus, that if I am to remain here [in Vilvorde] during the winter, you will request the Commissary to be kind enough to send me from my goods which he has in his possession, a warmer cap, for I suffer extremely from cold in the head, being afflicted with a perpetual catarrh, which is considerably increased in this cell. A warmer coat also, for that which I have is very thin: also a piece of cloth to patch my leggings; my overcoat is worn out; my shirts are also worn out. He has a woollen shirt of mine, if he will be kind enough to send it. I have also with him leggings of thicker cloth for putting on above; he has also warmer night caps. I wish also his permission to have a lamp in the evening, for it is wearisome to sit alone in the dark. But above all I entreat and beseech your clemency to be urgent with the Commissary that he may kindly permit me to have my Hebrew Bible, Hebrew Grammar, and Hebrew Dictionary, that I may spend my time with that study. And in return, may you obtain your dearest wish, provided always it be consistent with the salvation of your soul. But if, before the close of the winter, a different decision be reached concerning me, I shall be patient, abiding the will of God to the glory of the grace of my Lord Jesus Christ, whose Spirit, I pray, may ever direct your heart. Amen. W. TYNDALE.

What reception this letter met with we do not know, but the noble dignity which marks its style is a tribute to the continued power of the word of the truth of the gospel in the life and witness of the illustrious prisoner. In season and out of season he bore faithful testimony to the word of divine grace, until 'death God's endless mercies sealed, and made the sacrifice complete'.

During this time Poyntz was working with all his might in England to ward off the blow by which his friend was about to be struck. John assisted Thomas, but all was useless. The king cared very little for these evangelicals. His religion consisted in rejecting the Roman pontiff and making himself pope; as for those reformers, let them be burnt in Brabant, it will save him the trouble.

All hope was not, however, lost. They had confidence in the vice-gerent, the *hammer* of the monks. On 13 April Stephen Vaughan wrote to Cromwell from Antwerp: 'If you will send me a letter for the Privy Council, I can still save Tyndale from the fire; only make haste, for if you are slack about it, it will be too late.' But there were cases in which Cromwell could do nothing without the king, and Henry was deaf. He had special motives at that time for sacrificing Tyndale: the discontent which broke out in the north of England made him desirous of conciliating the Low Countries. Charles V also, who was vigorously attacked by Francis I, prayed *his very good brother* (Henry VIII) to unite with him *for the public good of Christendom*. Queen Mary, regent of the Netherlands, wrote from Brussels to her uncle, entreating him to yield to this prayer, and the king was quite ready to abandon Tyndale to such powerful allies. Mary, a woman of upright heart but feeble character, easily yielded to outward impressions, and had at that time bad counsellors about her. 'Those animals [the monks] are all powerful at the court of Brussels', said Erasmus. 'Mary is only a puppet placed there by our nation; Montigny is the play-thing of the Franciscans; the Cardinal-Archbishop of Liège is a domineering person, and full of violence; and as for the Archbishop of Palermo, he is a mere giver of words and nothing else.'[1]

Among such personages, and under their influence, the court was formed, and the trial of the English reformer began. Tyndale refused to be represented by counsel. 'I will answer my accusers myself', he said. The doctrine for which he was tried was this: 'The man who throws off the worldly existence which he has lived far from God, and receives by a living faith the complete remission of his sins, which the death of Christ has purchased for him, is introduced by a glorious adoption into the very family of God.' This was certainly a crime for which a reformer could joyfully suffer. In August 1536, Tyndale appeared before the ecclesiastical court. 'You are charged', said his judges, 'with having infringed the imperial decree which forbids anyone to teach that faith alone justifies.' The accusation was not without truth. A new edition of Tyndale's *Wicked Mammon* had just appeared in London under the title: *Treatise of Justification by Faith Only*. Every man could read in it the crime with which he was charged.

Tyndale had his reasons when he declared he would defend himself.

[1] Letter to Cholerus. Erasmus died shortly after, on 12 July 1536.

It was not his own cause that he undertook to defend, but the cause of the Bible: a Brabant lawyer would have supported it very poorly. It was in his heart to proclaim solemnly, before he died, that while all human religions make salvation proceed from the works of man, the divine religion makes it proceed from a work of God. 'A man, whom the sense of his sins has confounded', said Tyndale, 'loses all confidence and joy. The first thing to be done to save him is, therefore, to lighten him of the heavy burden under which his conscience is bowed down. He must believe in the perfect work of Christ which reconciles him completely with God; then he has peace, and Christ imparts to him, by his Spirit, a holy regeneration. – Yes', he exclaimed, 'we believe and are at peace in our consciences, because that God who cannot lie, hath promised to forgive us for Christ's sake. ... As a child, when his father threateneth him for his fault, hath never rest till he hear the word of mercy and forgiveness of his father's mouth again; but as soon as he heareth his father say, "Go thy way, do me no more so; I forgive thee this fault!" then is his heart at rest; then runneth he to no man to make intercession for him; neither, though there come any false merchant, saying: "What wilt thou give me and I will obtain pardon of thy father for thee?" will he suffer himself to be beguiled. No, he will not buy of a *wily fox* what his father hath given him freely.'[1]

Tyndale had spoken to the consciences of his hearers, and some of them were beginning to believe that his cause was the cause of the gospel. 'Truly', exclaimed the procurator-general, as did formerly the centurion near the cross; 'truly this was a good, learned, and pious man.'[2] But the priests would not allow so costly a prey to be snatched from them. Tyndale was declared guilty of erroneous, captious, rash, ill-sounding, dangerous, scandalous, and heretical propositions, and was condemned to be solemnly degraded and then handed over to the secular power. They were eager to make him go through the ceremonial, even all the mummeries, used on such occasions: it was too good a case to allow of any curtailment. The reformer was dressed in his sacerdotal robes, the sacred vessels were placed in his hands, and he was taken before the

---

[1] Tyndale, *Doctrinal Treatises* (Parker Society), p. 294.
[2] Foxe, *Acts*, v, p. 127.

bishop. The latter, having been informed of the crime of the accused man, stripped him of the ornaments of his order, and after a barber had shaved the whole of his head, the bishop declared him deprived of the crown of the priesthood, and expelled, like an undutiful child, from the inheritance of the Lord.

One day would have been sufficient to cut off from this world the man who was its ornament, and those who walked in the darkness of fanaticism waited impatiently for the fatal hour; but the secular power hesitated for a while, and the reformer stayed nearly two months longer in prison, always full of faith, peace, and joy. 'Well', said those who came near him in the castle of Vilvorde, 'if that man is not a good Christian, we do not know of one upon earth.' Religious courage was personified in Tyndale. He had never suffered himself to be stopped by any diffi-culty, privation, or suffering; he had resolutely followed the call he had received, which was to give England the word of God. Nothing had terrified him, nothing had dispirited him; with admirable perseverance he had continued his work, and now he was going to give his life for it. Firm in his convictions, he had never sacrificed the least truth to prudence or to fear; firm in his hope, he had never doubted that the labour of his life would bear fruit, for that labour had the promises of God. A pious and intrepid man, he is one of the noblest examples of Christian heroism.

The faint hope which some of Tyndale's friends had entertained, on seeing the delay of 'justice', was soon destroyed. The imperial government prepared at last to complete the wishes of the priests. Friday, 6 October 1536, was the day that terminated the miserable but glorious life of the reformer. The gates of the prison rolled back, a procession crossed the foss and the bridge under which slept the waters of the Senne, passed the outer walls, and halted without the fortifications. Before leaving the castle, Tyndale, a grateful friend, had entrusted the gaoler with a letter intended for Poyntz; the gaoler took it himself to Antwerp not long after, but it has not come down to us. On arriving at the scene of punishment, the reformer found a numerous crowd assembled. The government had wished to show the people the punishment of a heretic, but they only witnessed the triumph of a martyr. Tyndale was calm. 'I call God to record', he could say, 'that I have never altered, against the voice of my conscience, one syllable of his word. Nor would do this day, if all the pleasures, honours, and riches of the earth might be given me.'[1] The joy of hope filled his heart: yet one painful idea took possession of him. Dying far from his country, abandoned by his king, he felt saddened at the thought of that prince, who had already persecuted so many of God's servants, and who remained obstinately rebellious against that divine light which everywhere shone around him. Tyndale would not have that soul perish through carelessness. His charity buried all the faults of the monarch: he prayed that those sins might be blotted out from before the face of God; he would have saved Henry VIII at any cost. While the executioner was fastening him to the post, the reformer exclaimed in a loud and suppliant voice: 'Lord, open the King of England's eyes!'[2] They were his last words. Instantly afterwards he was strangled, and flames consumed the martyr's body. His last cry was wafted to the British Isles, and repeated in every assembly of Christians. A great death had crowned a great life. 'Such', says the old chronicler, John Foxe, 'such is the story of that true servant and martyr of God, William Tyndale, who, for his notable pains and travail, may well be called *the Apostle of England in this our later age.*'[3]

His fellow countrymen profited by the work of his life. After the arrival in England of the first copies of Tyndale's New Testament early in 1526, edition followed rapidly upon edition. It was like a mighty river continually bearing new waters to the sea. Did the reformer's death dry them up suddenly? No. A greater work still was to be accomplished: the entire Bible (Matthew's Bible) was already circulating privately. The king had refused his consent to the circulation of Coverdale's Bible; would he not do the same with this, and with greater reason? A powerful protector alone could secure the free circulation of Scripture. Richard Grafton, the printer, went to London to ask permission openly to sell the precious volume, and with the intention of applying to Cranmer.

Would Cranmer protect it? The king and Cromwell had declared

---

[1] Foxe, *Acts,* v, p. 134.
[2] *Ibid.*, p. 127.
[3] *Ibid.*, p. 114.

against Tyndale, and the primate had looked on: that was too much his custom. His essentially prudent mind, the conviction he felt that he could do no good to the church unless he kept the place he occupied, and perhaps his love of life inclined him to yield to his master's despotic will. So long as Henry VIII was on the throne of England, Cranmer was (humanly speaking) the only possible reformer. A John the Baptist, a Knox would have been dashed to pieces at the first shock. The sceptre was then an axe; to save the head, it was necessary to bend it. The primate, therefore, bent his head frequently. He hid himself during the royal anger, but when the storm had passed he appeared again. The primate was the victim of an error. He had said that the king ought to command the church, and every time the tyrant's order was heard, he appeared to believe that God himself enjoined him to obey. Cranmer was the image of his church which, under the weight of its greatness and with many weaknesses hidden beneath its robes, has notwithstanding always had within it a mighty principle of truth and life.

Grafton, the printer, had an audience of the archbishop at Forde, in Kent: he presented the martyr's Bible, and asked him to procure its free circulation. The archbishop took the book, examined it, and was delighted with it. Fidelity, clearness, strength, simplicity, unction – all were combined in this admirable translation. Cranmer had much eagerness in proposing what he thought useful. He sent the volume to Cromwell, begging him to present it to His Majesty and obtain permission for it to be sold, 'until such time that we [the bishops]', he added, 'shall put forth a better translation – which, I think, will not be till a day after doomsday'.[1]

Henry ran over the book: Tyndale's name was not in it, and the dedication to His Majesty was very well written. The king regarding (and not without reason) Holy Scripture as the most powerful engine to destroy the papal system, and believing that this translation would help him to emancipate England from the Romish domination, came to an unexpected resolution: he authorized the sale and the reading of the Bible throughout the kingdom. The book carried the words at the foot of its title page, 'Set forth with the Kinges most gracyous lycence.' All

---

[1] Cranmer, *Letters and Remains* (Parker Society) (4 August 1537), p. 344.

Englishmen might safely buy and read it. Inconsistent and whimsical prince! at one and the same time he published and imposed all over his realm the doctrines of Romanism, and circulated without obstacle the divine word that overthrew them! We may well say that the blood of a martyr, precious in the eyes of the Supreme King, opened the gates of England to the Holy Scriptures. Cromwell having informed the archbishop of the royal decision, the latter exclaimed, 'What you have just done gives me more pleasure than if you had given me a thousand pounds. I doubt not but that hereby such fruit of good knowledge shall ensue, that it shall well appear hereafter, what high and acceptable service you have done unto God and the king, which shall so much redound to your honour that (besides God's reward) you shall obtain perpetual memory for the same.'[1]

For centuries the English people had been waiting for such a permission, even from before the time of Wycliffe; and accordingly the Bible circulated rapidly. The impetuosity with which the living waters rushed forth, carrying with them everything they met in their course, was like the sudden opening of a huge floodgate. This great event, more important than divorces, treaties, and wars, was the conquest of England by the reformation. 'It was a wonderful thing to see', says an old historian. Whoever possessed the means bought the book and read it or had it read to him by others. Aged persons learnt their letters in order to study the Holy Scriptures of God. In many places there were meetings for reading; poor people clubbed their savings together and purchased a Bible, and then in some remote corner of the church, they modestly formed a circle, and read the holy book between them. A crowd of men, women, and young folks, disgusted with the barren pomp of the altars, and with the worship of dumb images, would gather round them to taste the precious promises of the gospel. God himself spoke under the arched roofs of those old chapels or time-worn cathedrals, where for generations nothing had been heard but masses and litanies. The people wished, instead of the noisy chants of the priests, to hear the voice of Jesus Christ, of Paul and of John, of Peter and of James. The Christianity of the apostles reappeared in the church.

But with it came persecution, according to the words of the Master:

[1] *Ibid.*, p. 346.

The brother shall deliver up the brother to death, and the father the child.
A father, exasperated because his son, a mere boy, had taken part in
these holy readings, caught him by the hair, and put a cord round his
neck to hang him. In all the towns and villages of Tyndale's country the
holy pages were opened, and the delighted readers found therein those
treasures of peace and joy which the martyr had known. Many cried out
with him, 'We know that this word is from God, as we know that fire
burns; not because anyone has told us, but because a divine fire consumes
our hearts. O the brightness of the face of Moses! O the splendour of
the glory of Jesus Christ, which no veil conceals! O the inward power of
the divine word, which compels us, with so much sweetness, to love and
to do! O the temple of God within us, in which the Son of God dwells!'
Tyndale had desired to set the world on fire by his Master's word, and
that fire was kindled. The general dissemination of the Holy Scriptures
forms an important epoch in the reformation of England. It is like one
of those pillars which separate one territory from another.

BOOK THREE

Reformation, Reaction, Relief

Thomas Cranmer

CHAPTER ONE

Three Parties Divide England

(1536–1540)

There were in 1536 three distinct parties in England: the papists, the evangelicals, and the Anglican Catholics who were halting between the two extremes. It was a question which of the three would gain the upper hand.

The reformation in England was born of the power of the word of God, and did not encounter there such obstacles as were raised against it in France by a powerful clergy and by princes hostile to evangelical faith and morality. The English prelates, weakened by various circumstances, were unable to withstand an energetic attack; and the sovereign was 'the mad Henry', as Luther had called him. His whims opened the doors to religious freedom, of which the reformation was to take advantage. Thus England, which had remained in a state of rudeness and ignorance much longer than France, was early enlightened by the reformation; and the nation awakened by the gospel gave birth in the sixteenth century to such masterminds as France, though more highly civilized, failed to produce so early. Shakespeare was born in 1564, one month before the death of Calvin. The reformation placed England a century ahead of the rest of Europe. The final triumph, however, of the reformation was not reached without many conflicts; and the two adversaries more than once engaged hand to hand, before one overthrew the other.

About the middle of October 1537 an event occurred which was of great importance for the triumph of the gospel. There was at that time great rejoicing in the palace of the Tudors and in all England, for Queen Jane (Seymour), on 12 October, presented to Henry VIII the son which he had so much desired. Letters written beforehand, in the name of the queen, announced it in every place, and congratulations arrived from all quarters. This birth was called 'the most joyful news which for many years had been announced in England'. Bishop Latimer wrote: 'Here is no less joying and rejoicing in these parts for the birth of our prince, whom we hungered so long, than there was, I trow, among the neighbours at the birth of St John Baptist' (Luke 1:58). A prince born to reign! exclaimed the politicians. 'God grant him long life and abundant honours!' they wrote from the Continent. 'Our prince', Cromwell sent word to the ambassadors of England, 'our Lord be thanked, is in good health, and sucketh like a child of his puissance, which you my Lord William can declare.' It was all the more important to declare this, because the very contrary was asserted. It was even reported by some that the child was dead. As Henry feared that some attempt might be made on his son's life, he forbade that anyone should approach the cradle without an order signed by his own hand. Everything brought into the child's room was to be perfumed, and measures of precaution against poison were taken. The infant was named Edward; Archbishop Cranmer baptized him, and was one of his godfathers. A fortnight after his birth Sir Edward Seymour, his uncle by the mother's side, was created Earl of Hertford. It was alleged that a spell had been thrown upon the king to prevent his having a male child; and behold, he had now an heir in spite of the spell. His dynasty was strengthened. Henry VIII became more powerful at home, more respected abroad.

This great rejoicing was followed by a great mourning. The queen developed puerperal fever and died twelve days after the birth of her son. 'Divine Providence', wrote Henry to his fellow monarch of France, 'has mingled my joy with the bitterness of the death of her who brought me this happiness.' Certainly Henry lamented her untimely death with all sincerity.

With the birth of the young prince the hopes of the partisans of the Catholic Mary disappeared, and the friends of the reformation rejoiced at the thought that the young prince was godson of the archbishop. Many circumstances contributed to their encouragement. They witnessed the formation of unlooked-for ties between the evangelicals of England and those of Switzerland; and the pure gospel as professed by the latter began to exercise a real influence over England.

Edward, during his very short reign, was to fulfil the best hopes to which his birth had given rise, and the triumph to which his reign seemed destined was already visibly in preparation.

Simon Grynaeus, the friend of Erasmus and Melanchthon, and professor at the University of Basel, had as early as 1531 held intercourse with Henry VIII and Cranmer.[1] Afterwards Cranmer and Henry Bullinger, successor of Zwingli at Zurich, had also become acquainted with each other; and, as early as 1536, some young Englishmen of good family had betaken themselves to Zurich, that they might drink at the full fountain of Christian knowledge and life which sprang forth there. Some of them lived in the house of Pellican, others with Bullinger himself. These young men were John Butler, who had a rich patrimony in England – a sagacious man and a Christian who persevered in prayer; Nicholas Partridge, from Kent, a man of active and devoted character; Bartholomew Traheron, who had already (1527 and 1528) declared at Oxford for the reformation, and had been persecuted by Dr London; Nicholas Eliot, who had studied law in England, and who afterwards held some government office; and others besides.[2] Bullinger was strongly attached to these young Englishmen. He directed their studies and, in addition to his public teaching, he explained to them in his own house the prophet Isaiah.

There was much talk at Zurich at this time about a young French theologian, Calvin by name, who was settled at Geneva, and had published a profound and eloquent exposition of Christian doctrines. The young Englishmen eagerly longed to make his acquaintance. Butler, Partridge, Eliot, and Traheron set out for Geneva in November 1537, bearing letters of introduction from Bullinger to the reformer. The latter received them in the most kindly manner. It was more than common courtesy, they wrote to Bullinger.[3] They were delighted with his appearance and with his conversation, at once so simple and so fruitful. They felt a charm which drew them to his presence again and again. The master taught well, and the disciples listened well. The four Englishmen,

---

[1] See his letter to Henry VIII, *Original Letters Relative to the English Reformation* (Parker Society), ii, p. 554.

[2] *Ibid.*, ii, pp. 621, 316, 608, 225, 226.

[3] *Ibid.*, p. 623.

being called elsewhere, took their departure deeply saddened by the painful separation. A letter written by Butler and Traheron shortly afterwards is the first communication addressed by England to the reformer of Geneva. It runs as follows: 'We wish you the true joy in Christ. May as much happiness be appointed to us from henceforth as our going away from you has occasioned us sorrow! For although our absence, as we hope, will not be of very long continuance, yet we cannot but grieve at being deprived even for a few hours of so much suavity of disposition and delightful conversation. And this also distresses us in no small measure, lest there should be any persons who may regard us as resembling flies, which swarm everywhere in the summer, but disappear on the approach of winter. You may be assured that, if we had been able to assist you in any way, no pleasure should have called us away from you, nor should any peril have withdrawn us. This distress, indeed, which the disordered tempers of certain individuals have brought upon you, is far beyond our power to alleviate. But you have one, Christ Jesus, who can easily dispel by the beams of his consolation whatever cloud may arise upon your mind. He will restore to you a joyful tranquillity; he will scatter and put to flight your enemies; he will make you gloriously to triumph over your conquered adversaries; and we will entreat him, as earnestly as we can, to do this as speedily as possible. We have written these few lines at present, most amiable and learned Master Calvin, that you may receive a memorial of our regard towards you. Salute in our names that individual of a truly heroic spirit and singular learning and godliness, Master Farel. Salute, too, our sincere friends Master Olivetan and your brother Fontaine. Our countrymen send abundant salutations. Farewell, very dear friend.'[1]

England at this time did justice to the Genevan reformer.

Much admiration was likewise felt for Bullinger. 'We confess ourselves to be entirely yours', wrote to him the four Englishmen, 'as long as we can be our own.' The works of the Zurich doctor were much read in England, and diffused there the spirit of the gospel. Nicholas Eliot wrote to him: 'And how great weight all persons attribute to your commentaries, how greedily they embrace and admire them (to pass over

[1] *Original Letters,* ii, p. 621.

numberless other arguments), the booksellers are most ample witnesses whom by the sale of your writings alone … you see suddenly become as rich as Crœsus. May God, therefore, give you the disposition to publish all your writings as speedily as possible, whereby you will not only fill the coffers of the booksellers, but will gain over very many souls to Christ, and adorn his church with most precious jewels.'[1]

At the news that the King of England had separated from the pope, the Swiss theologians were filled with hope, and they vied with each other in speeding his progress towards the truth. Bullinger composed two works in Latin which he dedicated to Henry VIII; the first of them on *The Authority, the Certitude, the Stability and the Absolute Perfection of Holy Scripture;* the second on *The Institution and the Function of Bishops.* He forwarded copies of these works to Partridge and Eliot for presentation to the king, to Cranmer, and to Cromwell. The two young Englishmen went first to the archbishop and delivered to him the volumes intended for the king and for himself. The archbishop consented to present the book to the prince, but not till after he had read it himself, and on condition that Eliot and Partridge should be present, that they might answer any questions asked by the king. Then going to Cromwell, they gave him the copy intended for him; and the vice-gerent, more prompt than the archbishop, showed it the same day to Henry VIII, to whom Cranmer then hastened to present his own copy. The king expressed a wish that the work should be translated into English. 'Your books are wonderfully well received', wrote Eliot to Bullinger, 'not only by our king, but equally so by the Lord Cromwell, who is Keeper of the King's Privy Seal and Vicar-general of the Church of England.'

Other continental divines who held the same views as the Swiss likewise dedicated some theological writings both to the king and to Cranmer. Wolfgang Capito, who was at the time at Strasburg, dedicated to Henry VIII a book in which he treated, among other subjects, of the mass (*Responsum de Missa, etc.*). The king, as usual, handed it to two persons belonging to the two opposing parties, in order to get their opinions. He then examined their verdict, and announced his own. Cranmer wrote to Capito that the king 'could by no means digest' his

---

[1] *Ibid.*, ii, p. 620.

piece on the mass,[1] although at the same time he approved some of the other pieces. Martin Bucer, a colleague of Capito, having written a commentary on the Epistle to the Romans, dedicated it to Cranmer, and wrote to him as follows: 'It is not enough to have shaken off the yoke of the pope, and to be unwilling to take upon us the yoke of Christ; but if God be for us who can be against us? and Christianity is a warfare.'[2]

While the Swiss and the Strasburgers were seeking to enlighten England, the Roman party on the Continent and the Catholic party in England itself were striving to keep her in darkness. The pope, in sorrow and in anger, saw England lost to Rome. Nevertheless the Catholic rising in the northern counties in October 1536, allowed him still to cherish hope. The King of France and the emperor, both near neighbours of England, could if necessary strike with the sword. The pope must therefore stir up to action not only the English Catholics, but also the courts of Paris and Brussels. Whom should he select for the mission? Reginald Pole, an Englishman, a zealous Roman Catholic, and a kinsman of Henry VIII, seemed to be the man made for the occasion. It was he who had lately written these words: 'There was never a greater matter entreated, of more importance to the wealth of the realm and the whole church than this [the re-establishment of papal authority]. And this same that you go about to take away, the authority of one head in the church, was a more principal and profound cause of the loss of the Orient, to be in infidels' hands, and all true religion degenerate, than ever was the Turk's sword, as most wisest men have judged. For if they had agreed all with the Occidental Church, they had never come to that misery; and like misery, if God have not mercy on us to return to the church, is most to be feared in our realm. ... Your sweet liberty you have got, since you were delivered from the obedience papal, speaketh for itself. Whereof the rest of the realm hath such part that you be without envy of other countries, that no nation wisheth the same to have such liberty granted them.' This last assertion was doubtful.

Pole was at this time at Padua, where he had studied, and where he was resident by permission of the king. He avoided going to Rome lest

---

[1] Cranmer to Capito, *Original Letters* (Parker Society), p. 16.
[2] Bucer to Cranmer, *Ibid.*, p. 525.

he should offend Henry. But he received one day an invitation from Paul III, who summoned him to the Vatican to take part in a consultation about the general council. To comply with this summons would be to cross the Rubicon; it would make Henry VIII his irreconcilable enemy, and would expose to great danger not only himself but all his family. Pole therefore hesitated. The advice, however, of the pious Contarini, the command of the pope, and his own enthusiasm for the cause, brought him to a decision. On his arrival at Rome he gave himself up entirely; and when Christmas was drawing near, on 20 December 1536, the pope created him cardinal, together with Del Monte, afterwards Julius III; Caraffa, afterwards Paul IV; Sadoleto, Borgia, Cajetan, and four others. These proceedings were very seriously criticized in England. For the vain-glory of a red hat, said Tunstall and Stokesley, Pole is, in fact, an instrument of the pope to set forth his malice, to depose the king from his kingdom, and to stir his subjects against him. There was, however, something more in his case than a cardinal's hat; there was, we must acknowledge, a faith, doubtless fanatical but sincere, in the papacy. Not long afterwards the pope nominated him the new cardinal-legate beyond the Alps; the object of this measure being to excite men's minds. He was to induce the King of France and the emperor to enter into the views of the Roman court, to inflame the Catholics of England, and, if he should be unable to go there himself, to take up his residence in the Netherlands, and thence conspire for the overthrow of Protestantism in England.

At the beginning of Lent 1537, Pole, attended by a numerous suite, set out from Rome. The pope, who was not thoroughly sure of his new legate, had appointed as his adviser the Bishop of Verona, who was to make up for any deficiency of experience on the part of the legate, and to put him on his guard against pride. Henry VIII, on learning the nature of his young cousin's mission, was exceedingly angry. He declared Pole a rebel, set a price on his head, and promised 50,000 crowns to anyone who should kill him. Cromwell, following his master's example, exclaimed, 'I will make him eat his own heart.' This was only a figure of speech, but it was rather a strong one. No sooner had Henry VIII heard of the arrival of Pole in France than he demanded that Francis I should deliver him up, as a subject in rebellion against his king. Pole had not been long at Paris before he heard of this demand. It aroused in his heart more pride than fear. It revealed to him his own importance; and turning to his attendants he said, 'This news makes me glad; I know now that I am a cardinal.' Francis I did not concede the demand of the angry Tudor; but he did consider the mission of Pole as one of those attacks on the power of kings in which the papacy from time to time indulged. When Pole, therefore, made his appearance at the palace he was refused admission. While still only at the door, and even before he had had time to knock, he himself tells us, he was sent away. 'I am ready to weep', he added, 'to find that a king does not receive a legate of Rome.' Francis I having sent him an order to leave France, he fled to Cambrai, which at that time formed part of the Netherlands.

No sooner was he there than, under great excitement about what had occurred to him at Paris, he wrote to Cromwell, complaining bitterly that Henry VIII, in order to get him into his power, did not scruple to violate both God's law and man's, and even 'to disturb all commerce between country and country'. 'I was ashamed to hear that ... a prince of honour should desire of another prince of like honour, Betray thine own ambassador, betray the legate, and give him into my ambassador's hands to be brought to me.' The like, he says, was never heard of in Christendom. Pole had more hope of the emperor than of Francis I; but he was soon undeceived. He was not permitted to go out of the town; and a courier entrusted with his despatches was arrested by the imperialists at Valenciennes and sent back to him. He now resolved on taking a step towards opening communication with the English government; and as he did not venture to present himself to the ambassadors of Henry VIII in France, he sent to them the Bishop of Verona. But this prelate, likewise, was not received, and he was only allowed to speak to one of the secretaries. He endeavoured to convince him of the perfect innocence of Pole and of his mission. 'The cardinal-legate', he said, 'is solely charged by the pope to treat of the safety of Christendom.' This was true in the sense intended by Rome; but it is well known what this safety, in her view, required.

Fresh movements in the north of England tended to increase the anger of Henry VIII. It was not enough that Pole had been driven from

France. The king himself now wrote to Hutton, his envoy at Brussels: 'You shall deliver unto the regent [Margaret] our letters for the stay of his entry into the emperor's dominions; … you shall press them … neither to admit him to her presence, nor to suffer unto him to have any other entertainment than beseemeth the traitor and rebel of their friend and ally. … You shall in any wise cause good secret and substantial espial to be made upon him from place to place where he shall be.' Pole, on his part, spoke as a Roman legate. He summoned the queen to prove her submission to the apostolic see, and to grant him an audience; and he made use of serious menaces. 'If traitors, conspirators, rebels, and other offenders', said the English ambassador, 'might under the shadow of legacy have sure access into all places, and thereby to trouble and espy all things, that were overmuch dangerous.' This was no question of rebellion, Pole sent word to the regent by the Bishop of Verona, but of the reformation; and he was sent to refute the errors which it was spreading in England. Her opinion was that he should return, 'for that she had no commission of the emperor to intermeddle in any point of his legacy'.

Hereupon Pole went from Cambrai to Liège; but in consequence of the advice of the Bishop of Liège, he only ventured to go there in disguise. He was received into the bishop's palace, but his stay there was 'not without great fear'. He set out again on 22 August, and went to Rome. Never had any mission of a Roman pontiff so entirely failed. The ambitious projects of the pope against the reformation in England had proved abortive. But one of the secrets of Roman policy is to put a good face on a bad case. The less successful Pole had been the more necessary it was to assume an air of satisfaction with him and his embassy. In any case, was it not a victory for him to have returned safe and sound after having to do with Francis I, Henry VIII, and Charles V? It was November when he reached Rome; and he was received as generals used to be received by the ancient Romans after great victories. They carried him, so to speak, on their arms; everyone heaped upon him demonstrations of respect and joy; and his secretary, on the last day of the year 1537, wrote to the Catholics of England, to describe to them *the great triumph that was made at Rome for the safe arrival of his master*. Rome may win or lose, she always celebrates a triumph.

This mission of Reginald Pole had fatal consequences. In the following year, his brother, Henry Lord Montague, and his kinsmen, Henry the marquis of Exeter, and Sir Edward Nevil, were arrested and committed to the Tower. Some time afterwards his mother, Margaret Countess of Salisbury, the last of the Plantagenets, a woman of remarkable spirit, was likewise arrested. They were charged with aiming at the deposition of Henry and at placing Reginald on the throne. 'I do perceive', it was said, 'it should be for my Lord Montague's brother, which is beyond the sea with the Bishop of Rome, and is an arrant traitor to the King's Highness.' They were condemned and executed in January 1539. The countess was not executed till May 1541.

Paul III had been mistaken in selecting the cousin of the king to stir up Catholic Europe against him. But some other legate might have a chance of success. Henry felt the necessity of securing allies upon the Continent. Cranmer promptly availed himself of this feeling to persuade Henry to unite with the Protestants of Germany. The Elector of Saxony, the Landgrave of Hesse, and the other Protestant princes, finding that the king had resolutely broken with the pope, had suppressed the monasteries, and begun other reforms, consented to send a deputation. On 12 May 1538, Francis Burkhardt, vice-chancellor of Saxony, George von Boyneburg, doctor of law, and Frederick Myconius, superintendent of the church of Gotha – a diplomatist, a jurist, and a theologian – set out for London. The princes wished to be worthily represented, and the envoys were to live in magnificent style and keep a liberal table. The king received them with much goodwill. He thanked them that, laying aside their own affairs, they had undertaken so laborious a journey; and he especially spoke of Melanchthon in the most loving terms. But the delegates, whilst they were so honourably treated by their own princes and by the King of England, were much less so by inferior agents. They were hardly settled in the house assigned to them than they were attacked by the inhabitants, 'a multitude of rats daily and nightly running in their chambers'. In addition to this annoyance, the kitchen was adjacent to the parlour in which they were to dine, so that the house was full of smells, and all who came in were offended.

But certain bishops were to give them more trouble than the rats. Cranmer received them as friends and brethren, and endeavoured to take advantage of their presence to promote the triumph of the gospel in England; but Tunstall, Stokesley, and others left no stone unturned to render their mission abortive. The discussion took place in the archbishop's palace at Lambeth, and they did their best to protract it, obstinately defending the doctrines and the customs of the Middle Ages. They were willing, indeed, to separate from Rome; but this was in order to unite with the Greek Church, not with the evangelicals. Each of the two conflicting parties endeavoured to gain over to itself those English doctors who were still wavering. One day, Richard Sampson, Bishop of Chichester, who usually went with the scholastic party, having come to Lambeth at an early hour, Cranmer took him aside and so forcibly urged on him the necessity of abandoning tradition that the bishop, a weak man, was convinced. But Stokesley, who had doubtless noticed something in the course of the discussion, in his turn took Sampson aside into the gallery, just when the meeting was breaking up, and spoke to him very earnestly in behalf of the practices of the church. These customs are essential, said Stokesley, for they are found in the Greek Church. The Bishop of Chichester, driven in one direction by the Bishop of London and in the opposite by the Archbishop of Canterbury, was much embarrassed, and did not know which way to turn. His decision was for the last speaker. The semi-Roman doctors at this period, who sacrificed to the king the Roman rite, felt it incumbent upon them to cross all Europe for the purpose of finding in the Turkish empire the Greek rite, which was for them the gospel. England must be dressed in a Grecian garb. But Cranmer would not hear of it; and he presented to his countrymen the wedding garment of which the Saviour speaks.

The summer was now drawing to an end. The German delegates had been in London for some three months without having made any progress. Wearied with fruitless discussions, they began to think of their departure. But before setting out, about the middle of August, they forwarded to the king a document in which they argued from Holy Scripture, from the testimony of the most ancient of the Fathers, and from the practice of the primitive church, against the withdrawal of the cup from the laity, private masses, and the celibacy of priests, three errors which they looked upon as having essentially contributed to the deformation of Christendom. When Cranmer heard of their intention to leave England, he was much affected. Their departure dissipated all his hopes. Must he then renounce the hope of seeing the word of God prevail in England as it was prevailing in evangelical Germany? He summoned them to Lambeth, and entreated them earnestly and with much kindliness for the king's sake to remain. They replied 'that at the king's request they would be very well content to tarry during his pleasure, not only a month or two, but a year or two, if they were at their own liberty. But forasmuch they had been so long from their princes, and had not all this season any letters from them, it was not to be doubted but that they were daily looked for at home, and therefore they durst not tarry.' However, after renewed entreaties, they said, 'We will consult together.' They discussed with one another the question whether they ought to leave England just at the time when she was perhaps on the point of siding with the truth. Shall we refuse to sacrifice our private convenience to interests so great? They adopted the least convenient but most useful course. We will tarry, they said, for a month, 'upon hope that their tarrying should grow into some good success concerning the points of their commission', and 'trusting that the King's Majesty would write unto their princes for their excuse in thus long tarrying.' The evangelicals of Germany believed it to be their duty to tolerate certain secondary differences, but frankly to renounce those errors and abuses which were contrary to the essential doctrines of the gospel, and to unite in the great truths of the faith. This was precisely what the Catholic party and the king himself had no intention of doing. When Cranmer urged the bishops to apply themselves to the task of answering the Germans, they replied 'that the King's Grace hath taken upon himself to answer the said orators in that behalf ... and therefore they will not meddle with the abuses, lest they should write therein contrary to that the king shall write.' It was, indeed, neither pleasant nor safe to contradict Henry VIII. But in this case the king's opinion was only a convenient veil, behind which the bishops sought to conceal their ill-will and their evil doctrines. Their reply was nothing but an evasion. The book was written, not by the king, but by one of themselves, Tunstall Bishop of Durham. He ran no risk of contradicting himself. In spite of this ill-will, the Germans remained not only one month but two. Their conduct, like that of Cranmer, was upright, devoted, noble, and Christian; while the bishops of London and Durham and their friends, clever men no doubt, were souls of a lower cast, who strove to escape by chicanery from the free discussion proposed to them, and passed off their knavery as prudence.

The German doctors had now nothing more to do. They had offered the hand and it had been rejected. The vessel which was to convey them was waiting. They were exhausted with fatigue; and one of them, Myconius, whom the English climate appeared not to suit, was very ill. They set out at the beginning of October, and gave an account of their mission to their sovereigns and to Melanchthon. The latter thought that, considering the affection which the king displayed towards him, he might, if he intervened at this time, do something to incline the balance the right way. He therefore wrote to Henry VIII a remarkable letter, in which, after expressing his warm gratitude for the king's goodwill, he added: 'I commend to you, sire, the cause of the Christian religion. Your Majesty knows that the principal duty of sovereigns is to protect and propagate the heavenly doctrine, and for this reason God gives them the same name as his own, saying to them, *Ye are gods* [Psa. 82:6]. My earnest desire is to see a true agreement, so far as regards the doctrine of piety, established between all the churches which condemn Roman tyranny, an agreement which should cause the glory of God to shine forth, should induce the other nations to unite with us and maintain peace in the churches.' Melanchthon was right as to the last point; but was he right as to the office he assigned to kings? In his view it was a heroic action to take up arms for the church. But what church was it necessary to protect and extend sword in hand? Catholic princes, assuredly, drew the sword against the Protestants rather than the Protestants against the Catholics. The most heroic kings, by this rule, would be Philip II and Louis XIV. Melanchthon's principle leads by a straight road to the Inquisition. To express our whole thought on the matter – what descendant of the Huguenots could possibly acknowledge as true, as divine, a principle by virtue of which his forefathers, men of whom the world was not worthy, were stripped of everything, afflicted, tormented, scattered in the deserts, mountains, and caves of the earth, cast into prison, tortured, banished, and put to death? Conscience, which is the voice of God, is higher than all the voices of men.

CHAPTER TWO

An 'Appeal to Caesar' and Its Outcome

(1538)

The Romish party in England did not confine itself to preventing the union of Henry with the Protestants of Germany; but contended at all points against evangelical reformation, and strove to gain over the king by a display of enthusiastic devotion to his person and his ecclesiastical supremacy. This was especially the policy of Bishop Stephen Gardiner. Endowed with great acuteness of intellect, he had studied the king's character, and he put forth all his powers to secure his adoption of his own views. Henry did not esteem his character, but highly appreciated his talents, and on this account employed him. Now Gardiner was the mainstay of the scholastic doctrines and the most inflexible opponent of the reformation. He had been employed by the king and Wolsey in numerous diplomatic missions on the Continent, where his extensive knowledge of canon law gave him great advantages. He had visited the court of the emperor, and had had interviews with the Roman legate. One day, at Ratisbon, an Italian named Ludovico, a servant of the legate, while talking with one of the attendants of Sir Henry Knyvet, who was a member of the English embassy, had confided to him the statement that Gardiner had secretly been reconciled with the pope, and had entered into correspondence with him. Knyvet, exceedingly anxious to know what to think of it, had had a conference with Ludovico, and had come away convinced of the reality of the fact. No sooner did Gardiner get wind of these things, than he betook himself to Granvella, chancellor of the empire, and sharply complained to him of the calumnies of Ludovico. The chancellor ordered the Italian to be put in prison; but in spite of this measure many continued to believe that he had spoken truth. We are inclined to think that Ludovico said more than he knew. The story, however, indicates from which quarter the wind was blowing in the sphere in which Gardiner moved. He had set out for Paris on 1 October 1535; and on 28 September 1538, there was to be seen entering London a brilliant and numerous band, mules and chariots hung with draperies on which were embroidered the arms of the master, lackeys, gentlemen dressed in velvet, with many ushers and soldiers. This was Gardiner and his suite.

The three years' absence of this formidable adversary of the gospel had been marked by a slackening of the persecution, and by a more active propagation of the Holy Scriptures. His return was to be distinguished by a vigorous renewal of the struggle against the gospel. This was the main business of Gardiner. To this he consecrated all the resources of the most acute understanding and the most persistent character. He began immediately to lay snares round the king, whom in this respect it was not very hard to entrap. Two difficulties, however, arose. At first Henry VIII, by the influence of the deceased queen as some have supposed, had been somewhat softened towards the reformation. Then the rumours of the reconciliation of Gardiner with the pope might have alienated the king from him. The crafty man proceeded cleverly and killed two birds with one stone. 'The pope', he said to the king, 'is doing all he can to ruin you.' Henry, provoked at the mission of Pole, had no doubt of that. 'You ought then, sire', continued the bishop, 'to do all that is possible to conciliate the continental powers, and to place yourself in security from the treacherous designs of Rome. Now the surest means of conciliating Francis I, Charles V, and other potentates, is to proceed rigorously against heretics.' Henry agreed to the means proposed with the more readiness because he had always been a fanatic for the corporal presence, and because the Lutherans, in his view, could not take offence at seeing him burn some who denied it.

A beginning was made with the Anabaptists. These wretched people were persecuted in all European countries. Some of them had taken refuge in England. In October 1538 the king appointed a commission to examine certain people 'lately come into the kingdom, who are keeping themselves in concealment in various nooks and corners'. The commission was authorized to proceed, even supposing this should be in contravention of any statutes of the realm.

Four Anabaptists bore the faggots at St Paul's Church, and two others, a man and a woman, originally from the Netherlands, were burnt in Smithfield. Cranmer and Bonner sat on this commission, side by side with Stokesley and Sampson. This fact shows what astonishing error prevailed at the time in the minds of men. Gardiner wanted to go further; and while associating, when persecution was in hand, with such men as Cranmer, he had secret conferences with Stokesley, Bishop of London, Tunstall of Durham, Sampson of Chichester, and others who were devoted to the doctrines of the Middle Ages. They talked over the means of resisting the reforms of Cranmer and Cromwell, and of restoring Catholicism.

Bishop Sampson, one of Gardiner's allies, was a staunch friend of ancient superstitions, and attached especial importance to the requirement that God should not be addressed in a language understood by the common people. 'In all places', he said, 'both with the Latins and the Greeks, the ministers of the church sung or said their offices or prayers in the Latin or Greek grammatical tongue, and not in the vulgar. That the people prayed apart in such tongues as they would … and [he wished that] all the ministers were so well learned that they understood their offices, service, or prayers which they said in the Latin tongue.' In his view, it was not lawful to speak to God except *grammatically*.

Sampson, a weak and narrow-minded man, was swayed by prejudices and ruled by stronger men; and he had introduced in his diocese customs contrary to the orders of the king. Weak minds are often in the van when important movements are beginning; the strong ones are in the rear and urge them on. This was the case with Sampson and Gardiner. Cromwell, who had a keen and penetrating intellect, and whose glance easily searched the depths of men's hearts and pierced to the core of facts, perceived that some project was hatching against the reformation; and as he did not dare to attack the real leaders, he had Sampson arrested and committed to the Tower. The bishop was not strong-minded and trembled for a slight cause; it may, therefore, be imagined how it was with him when he found himself in the state prison. He fell into great trouble and extraordinary dejection of mind. His imagination was filled with fatal presentiments, and his soul was assailed by great terrors. To have displeased the king and Cromwell, what a crime! One might have thought that he would die of it, says a historian. He saw himself already on the scaffold of Bishop Fisher and Sir Thomas More. At this time the powerful minister summoned him to his presence. Sampson admitted the formation of an alliance between Gardiner, Stokesley, Tunstall, and himself to maintain the old religion, its traditions and rites, and to resist any innovation. He avowed the fact that his colleagues and himself stood pledged to put forth all their efforts for the restoration of degenerated Catholicism. In their opinion, nothing which the Greeks had preserved ought to be rejected in England. One day when Bishop Sampson was passing over the Thames in a barge, in company with the Bishop of Durham, to Lambeth Palace, the latter produced an old Greek book which he used to carry in his pocket, and showed Sampson several places in that book wherein matters that were then in controversy were ordained by the Greek Church. These bishops, who spoke so courageously to each other, did not speak so with the king. They feigned complete accordance with him; and for him they had nothing but flatteries. Cranmer was not strong, but at least he was never a hypocrite. Sampson, however, exhibited so much penitence and promised so much submission that he was liberated. But Cromwell now knew what to think of the matter. A conspiracy was threatening the work which he had been at so much pains to accomplish. He observed that the archbishop's influence was declining at court, and he began to have secret forebodings of calamity in which he would be himself involved.

Gardiner, in fact, energetically urged the king to re-establish all the ancient usages. Thus, although but a little while before orders had been given to place Bibles in the churches, and to preach against pilgrimages, tapers, kissing of relics, and other like practices, it was now forbidden to translate, publish, and circulate any religious works without the king's permission; and injunctions were issued for the use of holy water, for processions, for kneeling down and crawling before the cross, and for lighting of tapers before the *Corpus Christi*. Discussions about the sacrament of the Eucharist were prohibited. It was Gardiner's wish to seal these ordinances with the blood of martyrs. He proceeded therefore to strike a blow at an evangelical and esteemed Englishman, and to invest his death with a certain importance.

We have previously mentioned a certain young minister, John Nicholson, surnamed Lambert, who had been arrested and imprisoned in 1532, but afterwards released. The passing of the years only deepened his firm evangelical convictions.

In 1538, being informed one day that Dr Taylor was to preach at St Peter's Church, Cornhill, Lambert went to hear him, not only because of his well-known gifts, but also because he was not far from the gospel. He was later appointed Bishop of Lincoln under pious King Edward, and was deprived of that office under the fanatical Mary. Taylor preached that day on the real presence of Christ in the bread and the wine. Lambert also believed, indeed, in the presence of the Lord in the Supper, but this presence, he believed, was in the hearts of the faithful. After the service he went to see Taylor, and with modesty and kindliness urged various arguments against the doctrines which he had been setting forth. 'I have not time just now', said the doctor, 'to discuss the point with you, as other matters demand my attention; but oblige me by putting your thoughts in writing and call again when I am more at leisure.' Lambert applied himself to the task of writing, and against the doctrine of the presence in the *bread* he adduced ten arguments, which were, says Foxe, very powerful. It does not appear that Taylor replied to them. He was an upright man, who gave impartial consideration to these questions, and by Lambert's reasoning he seems to have been somewhat shaken. As Taylor was anxious to be enlightened himself and to try to satisfy his friendly opponent, he communicated the document to Dr Barnes. The latter, a truly evangelical Christian, was nevertheless of opinion that to put forward the doctrine of this little work would seriously injure the cause of the reformation. He therefore advised Taylor to speak to Archbishop Cranmer on the subject. Cranmer, who was of the same opinion, invited Lambert to a conference, at which Barnes, Taylor, and Latimer were also present. These four divines had not at this time abandoned the view which the ex-chaplain of Antwerp opposed; and considering the fresh revival of sacramental Catholicism, they were not inclined to do so. They strove therefore to change the opinion of the pious minister, but in vain. Finding that they unanimously condemned his views, he exclaimed: 'Well then, I appeal to the king.' This was a foolish and fatal appeal.

Gardiner did not lose a minute, but promptly took the business in hand, because he saw in it an opportunity of striking a heavy blow; and, what was an inestimable advantage, he would have on his side, he thought, Cranmer and the other three evangelical divines. He therefore 'went straight to the king', and requesting a private audience, addressed him in the most flattering terms. Then, as if the interests of the king were dearer to him than to the king himself, he respectfully pointed out that he had everywhere excited by various recent proceedings suspicion and hatred; but that at this moment a way was open for pacifying men's minds, 'if only in this matter of John Lambert, he would manifest unto the people how strictly he would resist heretics; and by this new rumour he would bring to pass not only to extinguish all other former rumours, and as it were with one nail to drive out another, but also should discharge himself of all suspicion, in that he now began to be reported to be a favourer of new sects and opinions.'

The vanity as well as the interests of Henry VIII dictated to him the same course as Gardiner advised. He determined to avail himself of this opportunity to make an ostentatious display of his own knowledge and zeal. He would make arrangements of an imposing character; it would not be enough to hold a mere conversation, but there must be a grand show. He therefore ordered invitations to be sent to a great number of nobles and bishops to attend the solemn trial at which he would appear as head of the church. He was not content with the title alone, he would show that he acted the part. One of the principal characteristics of Henry VIII was a fondness for showing off what he conceived himself to be or what he supposed himself to know, without ever suspecting that display is often the ruin of those who wish to seem more than they are.

Meanwhile Lambert, confined at Lambeth, wrote an apology for his faith which he dedicated to the king, and in which he solidly established the doctrine which he had professed.[1] He rejoiced that his request to

---

[1] This apology, entitled *A Treatise of John Lambert upon the Sacrament, Addressed to the King,* is given in Foxe, *Acts,* v, pp. 237-50.

be heard before Henry VIII had been granted. He desired that his trial might be blessed, and he indulged in the pleasing illusion that the king, once set in the presence of the truth, must needs be enlightened and would publicly proclaim it. These pleasant fancies gave him courage, and he lived and hoped.

On the appointed day, Friday, 16 November 1538, the assembly was constituted in Westminster Hall. The king, in his robes of state, sat upon the throne. On his right were the bishops, judges, and jurisconsults; on his left the lords temporal of the realm and the officers of the royal house. The guards, attired in white, were near their master, and a crowd of spectators filled the hall. The prisoner was placed at the bar. The Bishop of Chichester spoke to the following effect: That the king in this session would have all states, degrees, bishops, and all others to be admonished of his will and pleasure, that no man should conceive any sinister opinion of him, as that now, the authority and name of the Bishop of Rome being utterly abolished, he would also extinguish all religion, or give liberty unto heretics to perturb and trouble, without punishment, the churches of England, whereof he is the head. And moreover that they should not think that they were assembled at that present to make any disputation upon the heretical doctrine; but only for this purpose, that by the industry of him and other bishops the heresies of this man here present (meaning Lambert), and the heresies of all such like, should be refuted or openly condemned in the presence of them all. Henry's part then began. His look was sternly fixed on Lambert, who stood facing him; his features were contracted, his brows were knit. His whole aspect was adapted to inspire terror, and indicated a violence of anger unbecoming in a judge, and still more so in a sovereign. He rose, stood leaning on a white cushion, and looking Lambert full in the face, he said to him in a disdainful tone: 'Ho! good fellow, what is thy name?' The accused, humbly kneeling down, replied: 'My name is John Nicholson, although of many I be called Lambert.' 'What!' said the king, 'have you two names? I would not trust you, having two names, although you were my brother.' 'O Most Noble Prince', replied the accused, 'your bishops forced me of necessity to change my name.' Thereupon the king, interrupting him, commanded him to declare what he thought as touching the sacrament of the altar. 'Sire', said Lambert, 'first of all I give God thanks that you do not disdain to hear me. Many good men, in many places, are put to death, without your knowledge. But now, forasmuch as that high and eternal King of kings, in whose hands are the hearts of all princes, hath inspired and stirred up the king's mind to understand the causes of his subjects, specially whom God of his divine goodness hath so abundantly endued with so great gifts of judgment and knowledge, I do not mistrust but that God will bring some great thing to pass through him, to the setting forth of the glory of his name.' Henry, who could not bear to be praised by a heretic, rudely interrupted Lambert, and said to him in an angry tone: 'I came not hither to hear mine own praises thus painted out in my presence; but briefly go to the matter, without any more circumstance.' There was so much harshness in the king's voice that Lambert was agitated and confused. He had dreamed of something very different. He had conceived a sovereign just and elevated above the reach of clerical passions, whose noble under-standing would be struck with the beauty of the gospel. But he saw a passionate man, a servant of the priests. In astonishment and confusion he kept silence for a few minutes, questioning within himself what he ought to do in the extremity to which he was reduced.

Lambert was especially attached to the great verities of the Christian religion, and during his previous trial he made unreserved confession of them. 'Our Saviour would not have us greatly esteem our merits', said he, 'when we have done what is commanded by God, but rather reckon ourselves to be but servants unprofitable to God ... not regarding our merit, but his grace and benefit. Woe be to the life of men, said St Augustine, be they ever so holy, if thou shalt examine them, setting thy mercy aside. ... Again he says, Doth any man give what he oweth not unto thee, that thou should'st be in his debt? and hath any man aught that is not thine? ... All my hope is in the Lord's death. His death is my merit, my refuge, my health, and my resurrection. And thus', adds Lambert, 'we should serve God with hearty love as children, and not for need or dread, as unloving thralls and servants.'[1]

On this occasion the king wanted to localize the attack and to limit the examination of Lambert to the subject of the sacrament. Finding

[1] Foxe, *Acts*, v, pp. 188-89.

that the accused stood silent, the king said to him in a hasty manner with anger and vehemency:[1] 'Why standest thou still? Answer as touching the sacrament of the altar, whether dost thou say that it is the body of Christ or wilt deny it?' After uttering these words, the king lifted up his cap adorned with pearls and feathers, probably as a token of reverence for the subject under discussion. 'I answer with St Augustine', said Lambert, 'that it is the body of Christ after a certain manner.' The king replied: 'Answer me neither out of St Augustine, nor by the authority of any other; but tell me plainly whether thou sayest it is the body of Christ or no.' Lambert felt what might be the consequences of his answer, but without hesitation he said: 'Then I deny it to be the body of Christ.' 'Mark well!' exclaimed the king; 'for now thou shalt be condemned even by Christ's own word, *Hoc est corpus meum* [This is my body].'

The king then turning to Cranmer commanded him to refute the opinion of the accused. The archbishop spoke with modesty, calling Lambert 'brother', and although opposing his arguments he told him that if he proved his opinion from Holy Scripture, he (Cranmer) would willingly embrace it. Gardiner, finding that Cranmer was too weak, began to speak. Tunstall and Stokesley followed. Lambert had put forward ten arguments, and ten doctors were appointed to deal with them, each doctor to impugn one of them. Of the whole disputation the passage which made the deepest impression on the assembly was Stokesley's argument. 'It is the doctrine of the philosophers', he said, 'that a substance cannot be changed but into a substance.' Then, by the example of water boiling on the fire, he affirmed the substance of the water to pass into the substance of the air.[2] On hearing this argument, the aspect of the bishops, hitherto somewhat uneasy, suddenly changed. They were transported with joy, and considered this transmutation of the elements as giving them the victory, and they cast their looks over the whole assembly with an air of triumph. Loud shouts of applause for some time interrupted the sitting. When silence was at length restored, Lambert replied that the moistness of the water, its real essence, remained even after this transformation; that nothing was changed but

---

[1] *Ibid.*, p. 230.
[2] *Ibid.*, v, pp. 232-33.

the form; while in their system of the *corpus domini* (the body of the Lord) the substance itself was changed; and that it is impossible that the qualities and accidents of things should remain in their own nature apart from their own subject. But Lambert was not allowed to finish his refutation. The king and the bishops, indignant that he ventured to impugn an argument which had transported them with admiration, gave vent to their rage against him, so that he was forced to silence, and had to endure patiently all their insults.

The sitting had lasted from noon till five o'clock. It had been a real martyrdom for Lambert. Loaded with rebukes and insults, intimidated by the solemnity of the proceedings and by the authority of the persons with whom he had to do, alarmed by the presence of the king and by the terrible threats which were uttered against him, his body too, which was weak before, giving way under the fatigue of a session of five hours, during which, standing all the time, he had been compelled to fight a fierce battle, convinced that the clearest and most irresistible demonstrations would be smothered amidst the outcries of the bystanders, he called to mind these words of Scripture, 'Be still', and was silent. This self-restraint was regarded as defeat. Where is the knowledge so much boasted of? they said; where is his power of argumentation? The assembly had looked for great bursts of eloquence, but the accused was silent. The palm of victory was awarded to the king and the bishops by noisy and universal shouts of applause.

It was now night. The servants of the royal house appeared in the hall and lighted the torches. Henry began to find his part as head of the church somewhat wearisome. He determined to bring the business to a conclusion, and by his severity to give to the pope and to Christendom a brilliant proof of his orthodoxy. 'What sayest thou now', he said to Lambert, 'after all these great labours which thou hast taken upon thee, and all the reasons and instructions of these learned men? Art thou not yet satisfied? Wilt thou live or die? What sayest thou? Thou hast yet free choice.' Lambert answered, 'I commend my soul into the hands of God, but my body I wholly yield and submit unto your clemency.' Then said the king, 'In that case you must die, for I will not be a patron unto heretics.' Unhappy Lambert! He had committed himself to the mercy of a prince who never spared a man who offended him, were it even his closest friend. The monarch turned to his vicar-general and said, 'Cromwell, read the sentence of condemnation.' This was a cruel task to impose upon a man universally considered to be the friend of the evangelicals. But Cromwell felt the ground already trembling under his feet. He took the sentence and read it. Lambert was condemned to be burnt.

Four days afterwards, on Tuesday, 20 November, the evangelist was taken out of the prison at eight o'clock in the morning and brought to Cromwell's house. Cromwell summoned him to his room and announced that the hour of his death was come. The tidings greatly consoled and gladdened Lambert. It is stated that Cromwell added some words by way of excuse for the part which he had taken in his condemnation, and sent him into the room where the gentlemen of his household were at breakfast. He sat down and at their invitation partook of the meal with them, with all the composure of a Christian. Immediately after breakfast he was taken to Smithfield, and was there placed on the pile, which was not raised high. His legs only were burnt, and nothing remained but the stumps. He was, however, still alive; and two of the soldiers, observing that his whole body could not be consumed, thrust into him their halberds, one on each side, and raised him above the fire. The martyr, stretching towards the people his hands now burning, said, 'None but Christ! None but Christ!' At this moment the soldiers withdrew their weapons and let the pious Lambert drop into the fire, which speedily consumed him.

Henry VIII, however, was not satisfied. The hope which he had entertained of inducing Lambert to recant had been disappointed. The Anglo-Catholic party made up for this by everywhere extolling his learning and his eloquence. They praised his sayings to the skies – every one of them was an oracle; he was in very deed the defender of the faith. There was one, not belonging to that party, who wrote to Sir Thomas Wyatt, then foreign minister to the king, as follows: 'It was marvellous to see the gravity and the majestic air with which His Majesty discharged the functions of *Supreme Head of the Anglican Church;* the mildness with which he tried to convert that unhappy man; the force of reasoning with

which he opposed him. Would that the princes and potentates of Christendom could have been present at the spectacle; they would certainly
have admired the wisdom and judgment of His Majesty, and would have
said *that the king is the most excellent prince in the Christian world.'*

This writer was Cromwell himself. He suppressed at this time all the
best aspirations of his nature, believing that, as is generally thought, if
one means to retain the favour of princes, it is necessary to adapt oneself
to all their wishes. A mournful fall, which was not to be the only one of
the kind! It has been said, 'Every flatterer, whoever he may be, is always
a treacherous and hateful creature.'

CHAPTER THREE

The 'Whip of Six Strings'

(1538–1540)

While the English Catholic party were recovering their former influence over Henry's mind, some members of the Roman Catholic party were labouring to re-establish the influence of the pope. They supposed that they had found a clue by means of which the king might be brought back to the obedience of Rome. Henry who, while busy in preparing fires for the martyrs, did not forget the marriage altar, was very desirous of obtaining the hand of Christina of Denmark, Duchess of Milan and a widow. Now, it was this princess, a niece of Charles V, of whom it was thought possible to make use for gaining over the king to the pope. She was now at the court of Brussels; and it is related that to the first offer of Henry VIII she had replied with a smile: 'I have but one head; if I had two, one of them should be at the service of His Majesty.' If she did not say this, as some friends of Henry VIII have maintained, something like it was doubtless said by one of the courtiers. However this may be, the king did not meet with a refusal. Francis I, alarmed at the prospect of an alliance between Henry VIII and Charles V, sent word to Henry that the emperor was deceiving him. The king did not believe it. The queen regent of the Netherlands endeavoured to bring about this union; Spanish commissioners arrived to conduct the negotiation, and Wriothesley, the English envoy at Brussels, devoted himself zealously to the business. One of the principal officers of the court, taking supper with the latter, in June 1538, inquired of him for news about the negotiation. Wriothesley expressed his surprise 'that the emperor had been so slack therein'. His companion remarked that the only difficulty in the matter was that Henry VIII had 'married the Lady Catherine, to whom the duchess is near kinswoman', so that the marriage could not be solemnized without a dispensation from the pope.

The emperor spoke more clearly still. Wyatt was instructed to tell the king that the hand of the Duchess of Milan would be given to him, with a dowry of 100,000 crowns, and an annuity of 15,000, secured on the duchy; and that for the gift of this beautiful and accomplished young widow all they required of him was that *he should be reconciled with the Bishop of Rome*. This was fixing a high price on the hand of Christina. The princess, considering perhaps that it was a glorious task to bring back Henry VIII to the bosom of the papacy, declared her readiness to obey the emperor. The pope, on his part, was willing to grant the necessary dispensation; but the king must first make his submission. To the great regret of the Roman party nothing came of these proposals. One circumstance might have influenced the king's decision. Before the negotiations were closed, in December 1538, the pope published the bull of 1535, in which he excommunicated Henry VIII. Had the pontiff no hope of good from the matrimonial intrigue, or did he intend to catch the king by fear?

During the late summer of 1538, while these mundane negotiations were continuing, a remarkable decision had been taken on a totally different matter. It had been strangely resolved by the King's Majesty that the Bible in an English translation should be made available to all His Majesty's subjects. 'Strangely' in respect of the king's character and religious inclinations, but perhaps not so when looked at in the light of the dying Tyndale's prayer, 'Lord, open the King of England's eyes.' The royal sanction was transmitted to the nation through injunctions issued by Thomas Cromwell to all the clergy, and dated 5 September:

> In the name of God, Amen. By the authority and commission of ... Henry ... I, Thomas Lord Cromwell, Lord Privy Seal, Vice-gerent to the King's said Highness, for all his jurisdiction ecclesiastical within this realm, do for the advancement of the true honour of Almighty God, increase of virtue, and discharge of the King's Majesty, give and exhibit unto you [Parson So and so] these injunctions following:

ITEM, That ye shall provide ... one book of the whole Bible of the largest volume in English, and the same shall be set up in some convenient place within the ... church ... whereas your parishioners may most commodiously resort to the same and read it; the charge of which book shall be ratably borne between you the parson and the parishioners aforesaid, the onehalf by you and the otherhalf by them.

ITEM, That you shall discourage no man privily or apertly from the reading and hearing of the said Bible, but shall expressly provoke, stir, and exhort every person to read the same, as that which is the very lively word of God, that every Christian person is bound to embrace, believe, and follow, if they look to be saved; admonishing them nevertheless to avoid all contention and altercation therein, but to use an honest sobriety in the inquisition of the true sense of the same, and to refer the explication of obscure places to men of higher judgment in Scripture. ...

Other Items deal with the memorizing of the *Pater Noster*, the Creed, and the Ten Commandments; the turning away from objects of superstition and idolatry; a warning not to repose trust in works devised by men, such as pilgrimages, and the offering of money to images and at the shrines of relics; and the necessity for keeping a parish register of weddings, christenings, and burials.

A truly momentous series of injunctions! the first official recognition of the authority, necessity, and availability of the holy book of God! the first clear declaration of the infinite value to men's souls of God's word written!

It is remarkable that another king than Henry played a part in introducing the Bible into the churches. The emperor and Francis I, King of France, occasionally coquetted with the King of England, whom each of them was anxious to win over to his own side. Francis, knowing how sensitive Henry was on the subject of marriage, offered him his son Henry of Orleans for the Princess Mary. Cromwell, who was now giving way to the Anglo-Catholic party on many points essential to reform, was all the more desirous of holding by those which his master would really permit. Amongst these was the translation of the Bible. He saw in the offer made by Francis I an opening of which he might avail himself. An edition of the Bible, extending to 2,500 copies, published the year before by the eminent printer Richard Grafton in conjunction with Whitchurch, was now exhausted. Cromwell determined to issue a new one; and as printing was better executed at Paris than in London, the French paper also being superior, he begged the king to request permission of Francis I to have the edition printed at Paris. Francis addressed a royal letter to his beloved Grafton and Whitchurch, saying that having received credible testimonies to the effect that his very dear brother, the King of the English, whose subjects they were, had granted full and lawful liberty to print, both in Latin and in English, the Holy Bible, and to import it into his kingdom, he gave them himself his authorization so to do. Francis comforted himself with the thought that his own subjects spoke neither English nor Latin; and, besides, this book so much dreaded would be immediately exported from France.

Grafton and the pious and learned Coverdale arrived at Paris, at the end of spring 1538, to undertake this new edition of Tyndale's translation. They lodged in the house of the printer Francis Regnault, who had for some time printed missals for England. As the sale of these had very much fallen off, Regnault changed his course, and determined to print the Bible. The two Englishmen selected a fine type and the best paper to be had in France. But these were expensive, and as early as 23 June they were obliged to apply to Cromwell to furnish them with the means for carrying on *his* edition of the Bible. They were moreover beset with other difficulties. They could not make their appearance out of doors in Paris without being exposed to threats; and they were in daily expectation that their work would be interrupted. Francis I, their reputed protector, was gone to Nice. By 13 December, after six months' labour, their fears had become so serious that when Bonner, who had succeeded Gardiner as English ambassador in France, was setting out from Paris on his way to London, they begged him to take with him the portion already printed and deliver it to Cromwell. The hypocritical Bonner, not satisfied with all the benefices he now held, was grasping at the bishopric of Hereford, which he called *a great good fortune,* and which he succeeded in getting. He was at this time bent on currying favour with Cromwell, on whose influence the election depended, and therefore, hiding his face under a gracious mask, which he was ere long impudently to throw off, he had most eagerly complied with the request.

Four days later, 17 December, the officers of the French inquisitor-general entered the printing office and presented a document signed by Le Tellier, summoning Regnault and all whom it concerned to appear and make answer touching the printing of the Bible. He was at the same time enjoined to suspend the work, and forbidden to take away what was already printed. Are we to suppose that the Inquisition did not trouble itself about the royal letters of Francis I, or that the prince had changed his mind? Either of these suppositions might be entertained. In consequence of the despatch of the packet to London, there were but a few sheets to be seized, and these were condemned to be burnt in the Place Maubert. But the officer was even more greedy of gain than fanatical; and gold being offered him by the Englishmen for the property, almost all the sheets were restored to them. His compliance is perhaps partly to be explained by the consideration that this was not a common case. The proprietors of the sheets seized were the Lord Cromwell, first Secretary of State, and the King of England. The matter did not rest here; the bold Cromwell was not to be baffled. Agents sent by him to Paris got possession of the presses, the types, and even the *printers,* and took the whole away with them to London. In two months from the time of their arrival the printing was completed. On the last page appeared the statement: *The whole Bible finished in 1539;* and the grateful editors added, *To the Lord the achievement is due.* The violent proceeding of the Inquisition turned to a great gain for England. Many French printers and a large stock of type had been imported; and henceforward many and more beautiful editions of the Bible were printed in England. 'The wicked diggeth a pit and falleth into it.'

Two parties therefore existed in England, and these frequently concerned themselves more with the points on which they differed than with the great facts of their religion. In one pulpit a preacher would call for reformation of the abuses of Rome; in a neighbouring church, another preacher would advocate their maintenance at any cost. One monk of York preached against purgatory, while some of his colleagues defended the doctrine. All this gave rise to most exciting discussion amongst the hearers. In addition to the two chief parties, there were the profane, animated by a spirit of unbelief and without reverence for sacred things. While pious men were peacefully assembled for the reading of the Holy Scriptures these mockers sat in public houses over their pots of beer, uttering their sarcasms against everybody, and especially against the priests. If they spoke of those who gave only the wafer, and not the wine, they would say: 'That is because he has drunk the whole of it; the bottle is empty.' At times they undertook even to discuss, as in old times was done at Byzantium, the most difficult points in theology, and this was still worse. The king, anxious to play his part as head of the church, was desirous of bringing about a union of the two chief parties, and had no doubt that the party of the profane would then disappear. His favourite notion, like that of princes in general, was to have but one single religious opinion in his kingdom. In a royal proclamation he required that the party of reformation and the party of tradition should 'draw in one yoke', like a pair of good oxen at the plough. He did not omit, however, to read the priests a lesson. He rebuked them for busying themselves far more with the distribution of the consecrated wafer and with the sprinkling of their flocks with holy water than with teaching them what these acts meant.

When the Parliament met on 28 April 1539, the Lord Chancellor announced that the king was very anxious to see all his subjects holding one and the same opinion in religion, and required that a committee should be nominated to examine the various opinions, and to draw up articles of agreement to which everyone might give his consent. On 5 May nine commissioners were named, five of whom were rigid Catholics, and at their head was Lee, Archbishop of York. A project was presented 'for extirpating heresies among the people'. A catalogue of heresies was to be drawn up and read at all the services. The commissioners held discussion for one day, but neither of the two parties would make any concession. As the vice-gerent Cromwell and the Archbishop of Canterbury were in the ranks of the reformation party, the majority was unable to gain the ascendancy, and the commission arrived at no decision.

The king was very much dissatisfied with this result. He had been willing to leave the work of conciliation in the hands of the bishops, and now the bishops did not agree. His patience, of which he had no large stock, was exhausted. The Catholic party took advantage of his dissatisfaction, and hinted to him that if he really aimed at unity he would have to take the matter into his own hands, and settle the doctrine to which all must assent. Why should he allow his subjects the liberty of thinking for themselves? Was he not in England master and ruler of everything?

Another circumstance, of an entirely different kind, acted powerfully, about this time, upon the king's mind. The pope had just entered into an alliance with the emperor and the King of France. Invasion threatened. A fact of such importance could not fail to make a great noise in England. 'Methinks', said one of the foreign diplomatists now in England, 'that if the pope sent an interdict and excommunications, with an injunction that no merchant should trade in any way with the English, the nation would, without further trouble, bestir itself and compel the king to return to the church.' Henry, in alarm, adopted two measures of defence against this. triple alliance. He gave orders for the fortification of the ports, examination of the condition of various landing places, and reviewing of the troops; and at the same time, instead of endeavouring after a union of the two parties, he determined to throw himself entirely on the scholastic and Catholic side. He hoped thereby to satisfy the majority of his subjects, who still adhered to the Roman Church, and perhaps also to appease the powers. 'The king is determined on grounds of policy', it was said, 'that these articles should pass.'

Six articles were therefore drawn up of a reactionary character, and the Duke of Norfolk was selected to bring them forward. He did not pride himself on scriptural knowledge. 'I have never read the Holy Scriptures and I never will read them', he said; 'all that I want is that everything should be as it was of old.' But if Norfolk was not a great theologian, he was the most powerful and the most Catholic Lord of the Privy Council and of the kingdom. On 16 May, the duke rose in the upper house and spoke to the following effect: 'The commission which you had named has done nothing, and this we had clearly foreseen. We come, therefore, to present to you six articles, which, after your examination and approval, are to become binding. They are the following: 1st, if anyone allege that after consecration there remains any other substance in the sacrament of the altar than the natural body of Christ conceived of the Virgin Mary, he shall be adjudged a heretic and suffer death by burning, and shall forfeit to the king all his lands and goods, as in the case of high treason; 2nd, if anyone teach that the sacrament is to be given to laymen under both kinds; or 3rd, that any man who has taken holy orders may nevertheless marry; 4th, that any man or woman who has vowed chastity may marry; 5th, that private masses are not lawful and should not be used; or 6th, that auricular confession is not according to the law of God – any such person shall be adjudged to suffer death, and forfeit lands and goods as a felon.'

Cromwell had been obliged to sanction, and perhaps even to prepare, this document. When once the king energetically announced his will the minister bowed his head, knowing well that if he raised it in opposition he would certainly lose it. Nevertheless, that he might to some extent be justified in his own sight, he had resolved that the weapon should be two-edged, and had added an article purporting that any priest giving himself up to uncleanness should for the first offence be deprived of his benefices, his goods, and his liberty, and for the second should be *punished with death* like the others.

These articles which have been called *the Whip with six strings* and *the Bloody Statute,* were submitted to the Parliament. But none of the lords temporal, or of the commons, aware that the king was fully resolved, ventured to assail them. One man, however, rose, and this was Cranmer. 'Like a constant patron of God's cause', says the chronicler, 'he took upon him the earnest defence of the truth, oppressed in the Parliament; three days together disputing against those six wicked articles; bringing forth such allegations and authorities as might easily have helped the cause, if the majority, as is often the case, had not overthrown the better.' Cranmer spoke temperately, with respect for the sovereign, but also with fidelity and courage. 'It is not my own cause that I defend', he said, 'it is that of God Almighty.'

The Archbishop of Canterbury was not, however, alone. The bishops who belonged to the evangelical party, Latimer of Worcester, Hilsey of Rochester, Barlow of St David's, Goodrich of Ely, and Shaxton of Salisbury, likewise spoke against the articles. But the king insisted, and the act passed. These articles, said Cranmer at a later time, were 'in some things so enforced by the evil counsel of certain papists against the truth and common judgment both of divines and lawyers, that if the King's Majesty himself had not come personally into the Parliament house, those laws had never passed.' Cranmer never signed nor consented to the Six Articles.

The Parliament at the same time conferred on the king unlimited powers. A bill was carried purporting that some having by their disobedience shown that they did not well understand what a king can do by virtue of his royal power, it was decreed that every proclamation of His Majesty, even when inflicting fines and penalties, should have the same force as an act of Parliament. The act was not passed without difficulty and as soon as Henry died it was repealed. But the fact was clearly shown in 1539 that when truth was sacrificed, liberty became the next victim.

Latimer, Bishop of Worcester, immediately after the close of the Parliamentary session, received word from Cromwell that the king requested him to resign his office. His heart leaped for joy as he laid aside his episcopal vestments. 'Now I am rid of a heavy burden', he said, 'and never did my shoulders feel so light.' One of his former colleagues having expressed his surprise, he replied: 'I am resolved to be guided only by the book of God, and sooner than depart one jot from that, let me be trampled under the feet of wild horses!' It seems highly probable that, although the king must have been offended at Latimer's resistance to the Six Articles, he had not himself actually informed Cromwell that Latimer must be removed from his post. But the resignation having been tendered ('freely' says the subsequent 'writ to elect' a successor), Henry allowed it to stand, and, to show his royal displeasure, he ordered the ex-bishop to be kept in custody in the house of Sampson, Bishop of Chichester, near Chancery Lane. It seems probable that after several months he was allowed his liberty. The fact is, however, that his activities between 1540 and 1547 when the king died, are very obscure. He certainly ended this period as a prisoner in the Tower of London. Shaxton, Bishop of Salisbury, likewise resigned his see, after the Six Articles were passed. Under Queen Mary he became a violent persecutor. Many evangelical Christians quitted England, and among them especially to be noted are

John Hooper, John Rogers, and John Butler. Cranmer remained in his archiepiscopal palace at Lambeth. Historians have generally stated that he sent away his wife and children to his wife's relations in Germany, but there is no strong evidence for such a belief. Cranmer, during his trial in Mary's reign, admitted that he had kept his wife secretly during the latter years of Henry's reign and had brought her out during the reign of Edward, but no suggestion was made that her years of hiding were spent with her relations in Germany.

That Cranmer did not resign is only explicable on the ground of the efforts made by Henry VIII to retain him. On the day of the prorogation of Parliament, 28 June 1539, Henry, fearing lest the archbishop, disheartened and distrusted, should offer to him his resignation, sent for him, and, receiving him with all the graciousness of manner which he knew so well how to assume when he wished, said: 'I have heard with what force and learning you opposed the Six Articles. Pray state your arguments in writing, and deliver the statement to me.' Nor was this all that Henry did. Desirous that all men, and particularly the adherents of English Catholicism, should know the esteem which he felt for the primate, he commanded the leader of this party, the Duke of Norfolk, his brother-in-law, the Duke of Suffolk, Norfolk's rival, Lord Cromwell, and several other lords to dine the next day with the archbishop at Lambeth. You will assure him, he said, of my sincere affection, and you will add that although his arguments did not convince the Parliament, they displayed much wisdom and learning.

The company, according to the king's request, arrived at the archbishop's palace, and Cranmer gave his guests an honourable reception. The latter executed the king's commission, adding that he must not be disheartened although the Parliament had come to a decision contrary to his opinion. Cranmer replied that 'he was obliged to His Majesty for his good affection, and to the lords for the pains they had taken'. Then he added resolutely: 'I have hope in God that hereafter my allegations and authorities will take place, to the glory of God and commodity of the realm.' They sat down to table. Every guest apparently did his best to make himself agreeable to the primate. 'My Lord of Canterbury', said Cromwell, 'you are most happy of all men; for you may do and speak what you list, and, say what all men can against you, the king will never believe one word to detriment or hindrance.' The meal, however, did not pass altogether so smoothly. The king had brought together, in Cromwell and Norfolk, the most heterogeneous elements; and the feast of peace was disturbed by a sudden explosion. Cromwell, continuing his praises, instituted a parallel between Cardinal Wolsey and the Archbishop of Canterbury. 'The cardinal', he said, 'lost his friends by his haughtiness and pride; while you gain over your enemies by your kindliness and your meekness.' 'You must be well aware of that, my Lord Cromwell', said the Duke of Norfolk, 'for the cardinal was *your master.*' Cromwell, stung by these words, acknowledged the obligations under which he lay to the cardinal, but added: 'I was never so far in love with him as to have waited upon him to Rome if he had been chosen pope, as I understand, my Lord Duke, that you would have done.' Norfolk denied this. But Cromwell persisted in his assertion, and even specified a considerable sum which the duke was to receive for his services as admiral to the new pope, and for conducting him to Rome. The duke, no longer restraining himself, swore with great oaths that Cromwell was a liar. The two speakers, forgetting that they were attending a feast of peace, became more and more excited and did not spare hard words. Cranmer interposed to pacify them. But from this time these two powerful ministers of the king swore deadly hatred to each other. One or other of them must needs fall.

The king's course with respect to Cranmer is not so strange as it appears. Without Cranmer, he would have been under the necessity of choosing another primate, and what a task would that have been. Gardiner, indeed, was quite ready to take the post; but the king, although he listened to him, did not place complete confidence in him. Not only did it seem to Henry difficult to find any other man than Cranmer; but there was a further difficulty of appointing an archbishop in due form. Could it be done by the aid of the pope? Impossible. Without the pope? This too was very difficult. The priesthood would not concede such a power to the king, nor was it probable that they would accept his choice. The king foresaw troubles and conflicts without end. The best course was to keep the present primate, and this was the course adopted. Herein lay the security of the archbishop in the midst of the misfortunes and scenes of blood around him. He had made a declaration of his faith, and he did not withdraw from it. He hoped for better things, according to the advances which were made him. He believed that by keeping his post he might prevent many calamities. The Six Articles were a storm which must be allowed to blow over; and, in accordance with his character, he bowed his head while the wind blew in that direction.

It should further be remembered that, in the sixteenth century, the idea of the overriding obligation of duty to the state and the sovereign normally held the rights of the individual conscience in abeyance, whenever the two came into conflict. In modern times men feel free to resign public posts which begin to trouble their consciences. In the time of the Tudors this was rarely the case: the martyrs were exceptions. Men in office esteemed the royal power and prerogative to be so great that most of them would have considered opposition to the king's will almost tantamount to rebellion against God.

Moreover, Henry's absolutism was in practice modified by a spasmodic consideration and understanding which he showed towards servants he favoured. In certain circumstances he was prepared to permit the exercise of their private consciences. Thus, Sir Thomas More, chancellor though he was, disapproved of the king's desire for a divorce from Catherine of Aragon. Accordingly, Henry was careful not to require him to put his hand to the business. Similarly, the king exempted Archbishop Cranmer from the awful work of enforcing the penalties imposed by the 'whip of six strings'. Cranmer, therefore, continued to hold office. Never had he passed through a sadder term of years.

The 'bloody statute' was the cause of profound sorrow among the evangelical Christians. Some of them, more hasty than others, making use of the strong language of the time, asserted that the Six Articles had been written, not with Gardiner's ink, as people said, 'but with the blood of a dragon, or rather the claws of the devil'.[1] They have been spoken of, by Roman Catholics of a later age, as 'the enactments of this severe and barbarous statute'.[2] But the Catholics of that age rejoiced in them,

---

[1] Foxe, *Acts,* v, p. 359.
[2] Lingard, *Hist. of England,* v, p. 131.

and believed that it was all over with the reformation. Commissioners were immediately named to execute this cruel law, and there was always a bishop among them. These commissioners, who sat in London in Mercer's Chapel, formerly a dwelling house and reputed to be the place of Becket's birth, even exaggerated the harshness of the Six Articles. Fifteen days had not elapsed before five hundred persons were imprisoned, some for having read the Bible, others for their posture at church. The greatest zeal was displayed by Norfolk among the lords temporal, and by Stokesley, Gardiner, and Tunstall among the lords spiritual. Their aim was to get a *Book of Ceremonies,* a strange farrago of Romish superstitions, adopted as the rule of worship.

The violent thunder-clap which had suddenly pealed over England, and occasioned so much trouble, was nowhere on the Continent more unexpected, nowhere excited a greater commotion than at Wittenberg. Bucer on one side, and several refugees arriving at Hamburg on the other had made known this barbarous statute to the reformers, and had entreated the Protestants of Germany to interpose with Henry in behalf of their fellow religionists. Luther, Melanchthon, Jonas, and Bugenhagen met together, and were unanimous in their indignation. 'The king', they said, 'knows perfectly well that our doctrine concerning the sacrament, the marriage of priests, and other analogous subjects, is true. How many books he has read on the subject! How many reports have been made to him by the most competent judges! He has even had a book translated, in which the whole matter is explained, and he makes use of this book every day in his prayers. Has he not heard and approved Latimer, Cranmer, and other pious divines? He has even censured the King of France for condemning this doctrine. And now he condemns it himself more harshly than the king or the pope. He makes laws like Nebuchadnezzar, and declares that he will put to death anyone who does not observe them. Great sovereigns of our day are taking it into their heads to fashion for themselves religions which may turn to their own advantage, like Antiochus Epiphanes of old. I have power, says the King of England, to require that any one of my courtiers shall not marry so long as he intends to remain at court; for the same reason I have also power to forbid the marriage of priests. We are now entreated to address remonstrances to this prince. The Scripture certainly teaches us to endeavour to bring back the weak; but it requires that the proud who compound with their conscience should be left to go in their own way. It is clear that the King of England makes terms with conscience. He has already been warned, and has paid no attention; there is, therefore, no hope that he will listen to reason if he be warned anew. Consider, besides, what kind of men those are in whose hands he places himself. Look at Gardiner, who while exposing before all the nation his scandalous connections [*liaisons*] dares to assert that it is contrary to the law of God for a minister of God to have a lawful wife.'

Thus did the theologians of Wittenberg talk of the matter.

Calvin thought with them, and he wrote, almost on the same day, that the King of England had distinctly shown his disposition by the impious edict which he had published. On behalf of the theologians, Melanchthon wrote to Henry; and after an exordium in which he endeavoured to prepare the king's mind, he said, 'What affects and afflicts me is not only the danger of those who hold the same faith as we do; but it is to see you making yourself the instrument of the impiety and cruelty of others; the doctrine of Christ is set aside in your kingdom, superstitious rites are perpetuated, and debauchery is sanctioned; in a word, the Roman antichrist is rejoicing in his heart because you take up arms on his side and against us, and is hoping, by means of your bishops, easily to recover what by wise counsel has been taken from him.' Melanchthon then combats the several articles and refutes the sophisms of the Catholic party on the subject. 'Illustrious King', he continued, 'I am grieved at heart that you, while condemning the tyranny of the Bishop of Rome, should undertake the defence of institutions which are the very sinews of his power, You are threatening the members of Jesus Christ with the most atrocious punishments, and you are putting out the light of evangelical truth which was beginning to shine in your churches. Sire, this is not the way to put away antichrist, this is establishing him … this is confirmation of his idolatry, his errors, his cruelty, and his debaucheries.

'I implore you, therefore, to alter the decree of your bishops. Let the prayers offered up to God by so many pious souls throughout the world for the true reformation of the church, for the suppression of impious rites, and for the propagation of the gospel, move you. Do justice to those pious men who are now in prison for the Lord's sake. If you do this, your great clemency will be praised by posterity as long as learning exists. Behold how Jesus Christ wandered about from place to place. He was hungry, he was thirsty, naked, and bound; he complained of the raging of the priests, of the unjust cruelty of kings; he commands that the members of his body should not be torn in pieces, and that his gospel should be honoured. It is the duty of a pious king to receive this gospel and to watch over it. By doing so, you will be rendering to God acceptable worship.'

Had these eloquent exhortations any influence on Henry VIII? On a former occasion he had shown himself provoked rather than pleased by letters of the reformer. However, after the loud peal of thunder which had alarmed evangelical Christians in every part of Europe, the horizon cleared a little, and the future looked less threatening.

About this time a bill was passed withdrawing heretics from the juris-diction of the bishops, and subjecting them to the secular courts. The chancellor, supported by Cranmer, Cromwell, and Suffolk, and with the sanction of the king, set at liberty the five hundred persons who had been committed to prison. The thunderbolt had indeed trenched the seas, but nobody was hurt – at least for the moment.

Henry resorted to other means for the purpose of reassuring those who imagined that the pope was already re-established in England. He exhibited to the citizens of London the spectacle of one of those sea fights on which the ancient Romans used to lavish such enormous sums. Two galleys, one of them decorated with the royal ensigns, the other with the papal arms, appeared on the Thames, and a naval combat began. The two crews attacked each other; the struggle was sharp and obstinate; at length the soldiers of the king boarded the enemy and threw into the water amidst the shouts of the people an effigy of the pope and images of several cardinals. The pontifical phantom, seized by bold hands, was dragged through the streets; it was then hanged and burnt. It would have been better for the king to let alone such puerile and vulgar sports, which pleased none but the mob, and to give more serious proofs of his attachment to the gospel.

CHAPTER FOUR

A Bitter Cup for Henry VIII

(1539–1540)

A t the period which we have now reached, Henry VIII displayed to an increasingly marked degree that autocratic disposition which submits to no control. He lifted up or cast down; he crowned men with honours or sent them to the scaffold. He pronounced things white or black as suited him, and there was no other rule but his own absolute and arbitrary power. A simple and modest princess was one of the first to learn by experience that he was a despot in his family as well as in church and state.

Henry had now been a widower for two years – a widower against his will; for shortly after the death of Jane Seymour he had sought in almost all quarters for a wife, but he had failed. The two great continental sovereigns had just been reconciled with each other, and the emperor had even cast a slight upon the King of England in the affair of the Duchess of Milan. Henry was therefore now desirous of contracting a marriage which should give offence to Charles, and should at the same time win for himself allies among the enemies of that potentate. Cromwell, for his part, felt the ground tremble under his feet; Norfolk and Gardiner had confirmed their triumph by getting the Six Articles passed. The vicegerent was therefore aiming to strengthen at once his own position and that of the reformation, both of them impaired. Some have supposed it possible that his scheme was to unite the nations of the Germanic race, England, Germany, and the north, in support of the reformation against the nations of the Latin race. We do not think that Cromwell went so far as this. A young Protestant princess, Anne, daughter of the Duke of Cleves and sister-in-law of the Elector of Saxony, who consequently possessed both the religious and the political qualifications looked for by the king and his minister, was proposed to Henry by his ambassadors on the Continent, and Cromwell immediately took the matter in hand. This union would bring the King of England into intimate relations with the Protestant princes, and would ensure, he thought, the triumph of the reformation in England, for Henry's wives appeared to have great influence over him, at least so long as they were in favour. Henry was, however, seeking something more in his betrothed than diplomatic advantages. Cromwell knew this, and did not fail to make use of that argument. 'Everyone praises the beauty of this lady', he wrote to the king (18 March 1539), 'and it is said that she surpasses all other women, even the Duchess of Milan. She excels the latter both in the features of her countenance and in her whole figure as much as the golden sun excelleth the silver moon. Her portrait shall be sent you. At the same time, everyone speaks of her virtue, her chastity, her modesty, and the seriousness of her aspect.' The portrait of Anne, painted by Hans Holbein, was presented to the king, and it gave him the idea of a lady not only very beautiful, but of tall and majestic stature. He was charmed and hesitated no longer. On 16 September, the Count Palatine of the Rhine and other ambassadors of the Elector of Saxony and the Duke of Cleves arrived at Windsor. Cromwell having announced them to the king, the latter desired his minister to put all other matters out of his head, saving this only. The affair was arranged, the marriage contract signed on 14 October at Hampton Court, and the ambassadors on their departure received magnificent presents.

The princess, whose father was dead and had been succeeded by his son, left Germany towards the close of the year 1539. Her suite numbered two hundred and sixty-three persons, among them a great many *seigneurs,* thirteen trumpeters, and two hundred and twenty-eight horses. The Earl of Southampton, Lord Howard, and four hundred other noblemen and gentlemen, arrayed in damask, satin, and velvet, went a mile out of Calais to escort her. The superb cortège entered the town, and came in sight of the English vessels decorated with a hundred banners of silk and gold, and the marines all under arms. As soon as the princess appeared the trumpets sounded, volleys of cannon succeeded each other, and so dense was the smoke that the members of the suite could no longer see each other. Everyone was in admiration. After a repast provided by Southampton, there were jousts and tourneys. The progress of the princess being delayed by rough weather, Southampton, aware of the impatience of his master, felt it necessary to write to him to remember 'that neither the winds nor the seas obey the commands of men'. He added that 'the surpassing beauty of the princess did not fall short of what had been told him'. Anne was of simple character and timid disposition, and very desirous of pleasing the king; and she dreaded making her appearance at the famous and sumptuous court of Henry VIII. Southampton having called the next day to pay his respects to her, she invited him to play with her some game at cards which the king liked, with a view to her learning it and being able to play with His Majesty. The earl took his seat at the card table in company with Anne and Lord William Howard, while other courtiers stood behind the princess and taught her the game. 'I can assure Your Majesty', wrote the courtier, 'that she plays with as much grace and dignity as any noble lady that I ever saw in my life.' Anne, resolved on serving her apprenticeship to the manners of the court, begged Southampton to return to sup with her, bringing with him some of the nobles, because she was 'much desirous to see the manner and fashion of Englishmen sitting at their meat'. The earl replied that this would be contrary to English custom; but at length he yielded to her wish.

As soon as the weather appeared more promising, the princess and her suite crossed the Channel and reached Dover, whence, in the midst of a violent storm, they proceeded to Canterbury. The archbishop, accompanied by several other bishops, received Anne in his episcopal town, in a high wind and heavy rain; the princess appearing as if she might be the sun which was to disperse the fogs and the darkness of England, and to bring about there the triumph of evangelical light. Anne went on to Rochester, about half way between Canterbury and London. The king, unable to rest, eagerly longing to see his intended spouse, set out accompanied by his grand equerry, Sir Anthony Brown, and went incognito to Rochester. He was announced, and entered the room in which the princess was; but no sooner had he crossed the threshold and seen Anne, than he stopped confused and troubled. Never had any man been more deceived in his expectation. His imagination – that mistress of error and of falsehood, as it has been called – had depicted to him a beauty full of majesty and grace; and one glance had dispersed all his dreams. Anne was good and well-meaning, but rather weak-minded. Her features were coarse; her brown complexion was not at all like roses and lilies; she was very corpulent, and her manners were awkward. Henry had exquisite good taste; he could appreciate beauties and defects, especially in the figure, the bearing, and the attire of a woman. Taste is not without its corresponding distaste. Instead of love, the king felt for Anne only repugnance and aversion. Struck with astonishment and alarm, he stood before her, amazed and silent. Moreover, any conversation would have been impossible, for Anne was not acquainted with English nor Henry with German. The betrothed couple could not even speak to each other. Henry left the room, not having courage even to offer to the princess the handsome present which he brought for her. He threw himself into his bark, and returned gloomy and pensive to Greenwich. 'He was woe', he said to himself, 'that ever she came unto England.' He deliberated with himself how to break it off. How could men in their senses have made him reports so false? He was glad, he said, that 'he had kept himself from making any pact of bond with her'. He thought, however, that the matter was too far gone for him to break it off. 'It would drive the duke her brother into the emperor or French king's hands.' The inconvenience of a flattering portrait had never been so deeply felt. It is not to be doubted that if at this very moment the emperor and the King of France had not been together at Paris, Henry would have immediately sent back the unfortunate young lady.

Shortly after the king's arrival at Greenwich, Cromwell, the promoter of this unfortunate affair, presented himself to His Majesty, not without fear, and inquired how he liked the Lady Anne. The king replied: 'Nothing so well as she was spoken of. Had I known as much before as I do now, she should not have come within this realm.' Then, with a deep sigh, he exclaimed, 'What remedy?' 'I know none', said Cromwell, 'and I am very sorry therefor.' The agents of the king had given proof neither of intelligence nor of integrity in the matter. Southampton, who had had a good view of her at Calais, had spoken to the king only of her beauty. On the following day Anne arrived at Greenwich; the king conducted her to the apartment assigned to her, and then retired to his own, very melancholy and in an ill-humour. Cromwell again presented himself. 'My lord', said the king, 'say what they will, she is nothing so fair as she hath been reported ... howbeit, she is well and seemly.' 'By my faith, sir', replied Cromwell, 'ye say truth; but I think she has a queenly manner.' 'Call together the council', said Henry.

The princess made her entry into London in great pomp, and appeared at the palace. The court had heard of Henry's disappointment and was in consternation. 'Our king', they said, 'could never marry such a queen.' In default of speech, music would have been a means of communication; it speaks and moves. Henry and his courtiers were passionately fond of it; but Anne did not know a single note. She knew nothing but the ordinary occupations of women. In vain did Cromwell venture to say to his master that she had, nevertheless, a portly and fine person. Henry's only thought was how to get rid of her. The marriage ceremony was deferred for a few days. The council took into consideration the question whether certain projects of union between Anne and the son of the Duke of Lorraine did not form an obstacle to her marriage with Henry. But they found here no adequate ground of objection. 'I am not well treated', the king said to Cromwell. Many were afraid of a rupture. The divorce between Henry and Catherine, the cruelty with which he had treated the innocent Anne Boleyn, had already given rise to so much discontent in Europe that people dreaded a fresh outbreak. The cup was bitter, but he must drink it. The 6th of January was positively fixed for the fatal nuptials. The king was heard the day before murmuring in a low tone with an accent of despair, 'It must be; it must be', and presently after, 'I will put my neck under the yoke.' He determined to live in a becoming way with the queen. An insuperable antipathy filled his heart, but courteous words were on his lips. In the morning the king said to Cromwell, 'If it were not for the great preparations that my states and people have made for her, and for fear of making a ruffle in the world, and of driving her brother into the hands of the emperor and the French king's hands, being now together,

I would never have married her.' Cromwell's position had been first shaken by his quarrel with Norfolk; it sustained a second shock from the king's disappointment. Henry blamed him for his misfortune, and Cromwell in vain laid the blame on Southampton.

On 6 January the marriage ceremony was performed at Greenwich by the archbishop, with much solemnity but also with great mournfulness. Henry comforted himself for his misfortune by the thought that he should be allied with the Protestant princes against the emperor, if only they would consent somewhat to modify their doctrine. On the morrow Cromwell again asked him how he liked the queen. Worse than ever, replied the king. He continued, however, to testify to his wife the respect due to her.

It was generally anticipated that this union would be favourable to the reformation. Butler, in a letter to Bullinger at Zurich, wrote: 'The state and condition of that kingdom is much more sound and healthy since the marriage of the queen than it was before. She is an excellent woman, and one who fears God; great hopes are entertained of a very extensive propagation of the gospel by her influence.' And in another letter he says: 'There is great hope that it [the kingdom] will ere long be in a much more healthy state; and this every good man is striving for in persevering prayer to God.'[1] Religious books were publicly offered for sale, and many faithful ministers, particularly Barnes, freely preached the truth with much power, and no one troubled them.[2] These good people were under a delusion. 'The king', they said, 'who is exceedingly merciful, would willingly desire the promotion of the truth.'[3]

But the Protestantism of the King of England was displayed not so much in matters of faith as in public affairs. He showed much irritation against the emperor; and this gave rise to a characteristic conversation. Henry having instructed (January 1540) his ambassador in the Netherlands, Sir Thomas Wyatt, to make certain representations and demands on various subjects which concerned his government, '*I shall not interfere*', Charles drily replied. Wyatt having further made complaint that the

---

[1] *Original Letters Relative to the English Reformation* (Parker Society), ii, pp. 627-28, 24 Feb. and 29 March 1540.

[2] 'The word is powerfully preached by Barnes and his fellow ministers.' – *Ibid*.

[3] Partridge to Bullinger, 26 Feb. 1540. – *Ibid.*, p. 614.

English merchants in Spain were interfered with by the Inquisition, the emperor laconically answered that he knew nothing about it, and referred him to Granvella. Wyatt then having been so bold as to remark that the monarch answered him in an ungracious manner, Charles interrupted him and said that he 'abused his words toward him'. But the ambassador, who meant exactly to carry out his master's orders, did not stop, but uttered the word ingratitude. Henry considered Charles ungrateful on the ground that he had greatly obliged him on one important occasion. In fact, the Emperor Maximilian having offered to secure the empire for the King of England, the thought of encircling his brows with the crown of the Roman emperors inflamed the ardent imagination of the young prince, who was an enthusiast for the romantic traditions of the Middle Ages. But, after the death of Maximilian, the Germans decided in favour of Charles. The latter then came to England, and the two kings met. Not very much is known of what they said in their interview; but whatever it might be, Henry yielded, and he believed that to his generosity Charles was indebted for the empire. '*Ingratitude*', replied the emperor to the ambassador. 'From whom mean you to proceed that ingratitude? ... I would ye knew I am not ingrate, and if the king your master hath done me a good turn I have done him as good or better. And I take it so, that I cannot be toward him ingrate; the inferior may be ingrate to the greater. But peradventure because the language is not your natural tongue, ye may mistake the term.' 'Sir', replied Wyatt, 'I do not know that I misdo in using the term that I am commanded.' The emperor was much moved. 'Monsieur l'ambassadeur', he said, 'the king's opinions be not always the best.' 'My master', Wyatt answered, 'is a prince to give reason to God and to the world sufficient in his opinions.' 'It may be', Charles said coolly. His intentions were evidently becoming more and more aggressive. Henry VIII clearly perceived what his projects were. 'Remember', said the king the same month to the Duke of Norfolk, whom he had sent as envoy extraordinary to France, 'that Charles has it in his head to bring Christendom to a monarchy. For if he be persuaded that he is a superior to all kings, then it is not to be doubted that he will by all ways and means ... cause all those whom he so reputeth for his inferiors to acknowledge his superiority in such sort as their estates should easily be altered at his will.' These words show that Henry possessed more political good sense than was usually attributed to him; but they are not exactly a proof of his *evangelical* zeal.

He did something, however, in this direction. Representatives of the Elector of Saxony and the Landgrave of Hesse had accompanied Anne of Cleves to England. Henry received them kindly and entertained them magnificently; he succeeded so well in dazzling them by his converse and his manners, that these grave ambassadors sent word to their masters how the nuptials of His Majesty had been celebrated under joyful and sacred auspices. Nevertheless, they did not conceal from Henry VIII that the elector and the landgrave 'had been thrown into consternation, as well as many others, by an atrocious decree, the result of the artifices of certain bishops, partisans of Roman impiety'. Thereupon the king, who wished by all means to gain over the evangelical princes, declared to their representatives 'that his wisdom should soften the harshness of the decree, that he would even suspend its execution, and that there was nothing in the world that he more desired than to see the true doctrine of Christ shine in all churches, and that he was determined always to set heavenly truth before the tradition of men.' In consequence of these statements of the king the Wittenberg theologians sent to him some evangelical articles, to which they requested his adherence, and which were entirely opposed to those of Gardiner. We shall presently see how Henry proceeded to fulfil his promises.

Cromwell was anxious to take advantage of these declarations to get the gospel preached, and he knew men capable of preaching it. He relied most of all on Barnes, who had returned to England with the most flattering testimonials from the Wittenberg reformers, and even from the Elector of Saxony and the King of Denmark. Barnes had been employed by Henry in the negotiation of his marriage with Anne of Cleves, and had thus contributed to this union, a circumstance which did not greatly recommend him to the king. There were, besides, Thomas Garret, curate of All Saints' Church, in Honey Lane, of whom we have elsewhere spoken; William Jerome, Vicar of Stepney, and others. Bonner, who on his return from France was elected Bishop of London, and who was afterwards a zealous persecutor, designated these three evangelical ministers to preach at Paul's Cross during Lent in 1540. Bonner, perhaps, still wished to curry favour with Cromwell; or perhaps these preachers had been complained of, and the king wished to put them to the test. Barnes was to preach the first Sunday (14 Feb.); but Gardiner, foreboding danger, wished to prevent him, and consequently sent word to Bonner that he would himself preach that day. Barnes resigned the pulpit to this powerful prelate, who, well aware what doctrine the three evangelicals would proclaim at St Paul's, was determined to prevent them, and craftily to stir up prejudices against the innovators and their innovations. Confutation beforehand, he thought, is more useful than afterwards. It is better to be first than second; better to prevent evils than to cure them. He displayed some ingenuity and wit. Many persons were attracted by the notion that the reformation was a progress and advance. He alleged that it was the contrary; and, taking for his text the words addressed to Jesus by the tempter on the pinnacle of the temple, *Cast thyself down*, he said: 'Nowadays the devil tempteth the world and biddeth them to cast themselves backward. There is no 'forward' in the new teaching, but all backward. Now the devil teacheth, Come back from fasting, come back from praying, come back from confession, come back from weeping for thy sins; and all is backward, insomuch that men must now learn to say their *Pater Noster* backward.'[1] The Bishop of Winchester censured with especial severity the evangelical preachers, on the ground that they taught the remission of sins through faith and not by works. Of old, he said, heaven was sold at Rome for a little money; now that we have done with all that trumpery the devil hath invented another – he offers us heaven for nothing! A living faith which unites us to the Saviour was counted as nothing by Gardiner.

On a subsequent Sunday Barnes preached. The lord mayor and Gardiner, side by side, and many other *reporters,* says the chronicle, were present at the service. The preacher vigorously defended the doctrine attacked by the bishop; but unfortunately, he indulged, like him, in attempts at wit, and even in a play upon his name, complaining of the *gardener* who 'had planted such evil herbs in the garden of God's Scripture'. This punning would anywhere have been offensive; it was

[1] Gardiner's Sermon, Foxe, *Acts,* v, p. 430.

doubly offensive in the pulpit in the presence of the bishop himself. 'Punning', says one 'is the poorest kind of would-be wit.' Garret preached energetically the next Sunday; but he studiously avoided offending anyone. Lastly, Jerome preached, and taking up the passage relating to Sarah and Hagar in the Epistle of St Paul to the Galatians, maintained that all those who are born of Sarah, the lawful wife, that is, who have been regenerated by faith, are fully and positively justified.

Bishop Gardiner and his friends lost no time in complaining to the king of the 'intolerable arrogance of Barnes'. 'A prelate of the kingdom to be thus insulted at Paul's Cross!' said the former ambassador to France. Henry sent for the culprit to his cabinet. Barnes confessed that he had forgotten himself, and promised to be on his guard against such rash speeches in future. Jerome and Garret likewise were reprimanded; and the king commanded the three evangelists to read in public on the following Sunday, at the solemn Easter service celebrated in the church of St Mary's Hospital, a retractation which was delivered to them in writing. They felt bound to submit unreservedly to the commands of the king. Barnes, therefore, when the 4th of April was come, ascended the pulpit and read word for word the official paper which he had received. After this, turning to the Bishop of Winchester, who was present by order of the king, he earnestly and respectfully begged his pardon, asking him twice to lift up his hand, if he forgave him. Gardiner 'with much ado, wagged his finger a little'. Having thus discharged, as he believed, his duty, first as a subject, then as a Christian, Barnes felt bound to discharge also that of a minister of God. He therefore preached powerfully the doctrine of salvation by grace, the very doctrine for which he was persecuted. The lord mayor, who was sitting by Gardiner's side, turned to the bishop and asked him whether he should send him from the pulpit to prison for preaching so boldly contrary to his retractation. Garret and Jerome having followed the example of Barnes, the king gave orders that the three evangelists should be taken and confined in the Tower. 'Three of our best ministers', wrote Butler to Bullinger, 'are confined in the Tower of London. You may judge from this of our misfortunes.'

At the same time that Henry VIII was imprisoning the ministers of God's word, he was giving more liberty to the word itself. It must be confessed that in his conflict with the pope he did make use of the Bible. He interpreted it, indeed, in his own way; but still he used it and helped to circulate it. This was a fact of importance for the reformation in England.

The edition of the Bible sometimes called 'Cranmer's Bible' appeared at this time (April 1540). Actually it was the second edition of the Great Bible already mentioned, but as the archbishop supplied a preface to it, his name has thus been honourably linked with the word. The preface commends to the subjects of Henry the widespread reading of the Holy Scriptures, and appeals to the authority of the ancient Fathers of the church in support of the claim that the word is the sufficient rule of faith and life.

'Here may all manner of persons: men, women, young, old; learned, unlearned; rich, poor; priests, laymen; lords, ladies; officers, tenants, and mean men; virgins, wives, widows; lawyers, merchants, artificers, husbandmen; and all manner of persons, of what estate or condition so ever they be; may in this book learn all things, what they ought to believe, what they ought to do, and what they should not do, as well concerning Almighty God, as also concerning themselves, and all others … to the reading of Scripture none can be enemy. … I would advise you all, that come to the reading or hearing of this book, which is the word of God, the most precious jewel and most holy relic that remaineth upon earth, that ye bring with you the fear of God … and use not your knowledge thereof to vain-glory of frivolous disputation, but to the honour of God, increase of virtue, and edification both of yourselves and of others.'

Thus ran Cranmer's preface. In the fourth and sixth editions the title includes mention of the fact that Cuthbert Tunstall was one of the two bishops made responsible for the oversight of the work of printing and publishing. We may well conjecture whether Tunstall did this work with a willing mind: he was the Bishop of London who had refused help and permission to Tyndale to translate the word into English, and who had previously bought up copies of the Testaments in order to burn them at Paul's Cross: and the book he now helped to bring before the people was based, in part, on the work he had so vigorously opposed!

A magnificent copy on vellum was presented to the king. In the same month appeared another Bible, printed in smaller type; in July another great Bible; in November a third in folio, authorised by Henry VIII, 'supreme head of his church'. It would seem even that there was one more edition this year. The enemies of the Bible were in power. Nevertheless the Bible was gaining the victory; and the luminary which was to enlighten the world was beginning to shed abroad its light everywhere.

CHAPTER FIVE

The Disgrace and Death of Thomas Cromwell

(1540)

Eight days after the imprisonment of Barnes and his two friends (12 April 1540), Parliament opened for the first time without abbots or priors. Cromwell was thoughtful and uneasy; he saw everywhere occasions of alarm; he felt his position insecure. The statute of the Six Articles, the conviction which possessed his mind that the doctrines of the Middle Ages were regaining an indisputable ascendancy over the king, the wrath of Norfolk, and Henry's ill-will on account of the queen whom Cromwell had chosen for him – these were the dark points which threatened his future. His friends were scattered or persecuted; his enemies were gathered about the throne. Henry, however, made no sign, but secretly meditated a violent blow. He concealed the game he was playing so that others, and especially Cromwell himself, should have no perception of it. The powerful minister, therefore, appeared in Parliament, assuming a confident air, as the ever-powerful organ of the supreme will of the king. Henry VIII, the man of extremes, thought proper at this time to exhibit himself as an advocate of a middle course. The country is agitated by religious dissensions, said the vicegerent, his representative; and in his speech to the house he set forth on the one hand the rooted superstition and obstinate clinging to popery, and on the other thoughtless and impertinent and culpable rashness (referring doubtless to Barnes). He said that the king desired a union of the two parties; that he leaned to neither side; that he would equally repress the licence of heretics and that of the papists, and that he 'set the pure and sincere doctrine of Christ before his eyes'. These words of Cromwell were wise. Union in the truth is the great want of all ages.

But Henry added his comment. He refused to turn to the right or to the left. He would not himself hold, nor did he intend to permit England to hold, any other doctrine than that prescribed by his own sovereign authority, sword in hand. Cromwell did not fail to let it be known by what method the king meant to bring about this union; he insisted on penalties against all who did not submit to the Bible and against those who put upon it a wrong interpretation. Henry intended to strike right and left with his vigorous hand. To carry out the scheme of union a commission was appointed, the result of which, after two years' labours, was a confused medley of truths and errors.

Strange to say, although Cromwell was now on the brink of an abyss, the king still heaped favours upon him. He was already Chancellor of the Exchequer, First Secretary of State, Vice-gerent, and Vicar-general of England in spiritual affairs, Lord Privy Seal, and Knight of the Garter; but he was now to see fresh honours added to all these. The Earl of Essex had just died, and a week later died William, Lord Sandys of 'The Vyne', who had been Lord Chamberlain. Hereupon Henry made Cromwell, 'the blacksmith's son', whom Norfolk and the other nobles despised so heartily, Earl of Essex and Lord Chamberlain, and had his name placed at the head of the roll of peers. Wealth was no more wanting to him than honours. He received a large portion of the property of the deceased Lord Essex; the king conferred on him numerous manors taken from the suppressed monasteries; he owned great estates in eight counties; and he still continued to superintend the business of the Crown. We might well ask how it came to pass that such a profusion of favours fell to his lot just at the time when the king was angry with him as the man who had given him Anne of Cleves for a wife; when the imprisonment of Barnes, his friend and confidential agent, greatly compromised him, and when, in addition to these things, Norfolk, Gardiner, and the whole Catholic party were striving to put down this *parvenu,* who offended them and stood in their way. Two answers may be given to this question. Henry was desirous that Cromwell should make a great effort to secure the assent of Parliament to bills of a very extraordinary character but very advantageous to the king; and it was his hope that the titles under which Cromwell would appear before the houses would make success easier.

Several contemporaries, however, assigned a different cause for these royal favours. 'Some persons now suspect', wrote Hilles to Bullinger, 'that this was all an artifice, to make people conclude that he [Cromwell] must have been a most wicked traitor, and guilty of treason in every possible way; or else the king would never have executed one who was so dear to him, as was made manifest by the presents he had bestowed upon him.' Besides, was it not the custom of the ancients to crown their victims with flowers before sacrificing them?

Henry was greedy of money, and was in want of it, for he spent it prodigally. He applied to Cromwell for it. The latter was aware that in making himself the king's instrument in this matter he was estranging from himself the mind of the nation; but he considered that a great sovereign must have great resources, and he was always willing to sacrifice himself for the king, for to him he owed everything, and he loved him in spite of his faults. On 23 April, four days after receiving from the king such extraordinary favours, Cromwell proposed to the house to suppress the Knights of St John of Jerusalem, and urged that their estates, which were considerable, should be given to the king. This was agreed to by Parliament. On 3 May he demanded for His Majesty a subsidy of unparalleled character, namely, four tenths and fifteenths, in addition to ten per cent on the rents of lands and five per cent on the value of merchandise. This also he obtained. Next he went to the convocation of the clergy, and claimed from them two tenths and twenty per cent on ecclesiastical revenues for two years. Again he succeeded. By 8 May the king had obtained through Cromwell's energy all that he wished for.

On the very next day, Sunday, 9 May, Cromwell received in his palace a note from the king thus worded:

'Henry R. By the King.

Right trusty and well-beloved cousin, – We greet you well; signifying unto you our pleasure and commandment is that forthwith, and upon the receipt of these our letters, setting all other affairs apart, ye do repair unto us, for the treaty of such great and weighty matters as whereupon doth consist the surety of our person, the preservation of our honour, and the tranquillity and quietness of you, and all other our loving and faithful subjects, like as at your arrival here ye shall more plainly perceive and understand. And that ye fail not hereof, as we specially trust you.

Given under our signet, at our manor of Westminster, the 9th day of May.

What could this urgent and mysterious note mean? Cromwell could not rest after reading it. 'The surety of our person, the preservation of our honour' are in question, said the king. We may imagine the agitation of his mind, his fears as to the result of the visit, and the state of perplexity in which, without losing a minute, he went in obedience to the king's command. We have no information as to what passed at this interview. Probably the minister supposed that he had justified himself in his master's sight. On the following day, Monday, the Earl of Essex was present as usual in the House of Lords and introduced a bill. The day after, Parliament was prorogued till 25 May. What could be the reason for this? It has been supposed that Cromwell's enemies wished to gain the time needful for collecting evidence in support of the charges which they intended to bring against him. When the fifteen days had elapsed, Parliament met again, and the Earl of Essex was in his place on the first and following days. He was still in the assembly as minister of the king on 10 June, on which day, at three o'clock, there was a meeting of the Privy Council. The Duke of Norfolk, the Earl of Essex, and the other members were quietly seated round the table, when the duke rose and accused Cromwell of high treason. Cromwell understood that Norfolk was acting under the sanction of the king, and he recollected the note of 9 May. The Lord Chancellor arrested him and had him conducted to the Tower.

Norfolk was more than ever in favour, for Henry, husband of Anne of Cleves, was at this time enamoured of Norfolk's niece. He believed – and Gardiner, doubtless, did not fail to encourage the belief – that he must promptly take advantage of the extraordinary goodwill which the king testified to him to overthrow the adversary of English Catholicism, the powerful protector of the Bible and the reformation. In the judgment of this party, Cromwell was a heretic and a chief of heretics. This was the principal motive, and substantially the only motive of the attack made on the Earl of Essex. In a letter addressed at this time by the council to Sir John Wallop, ambassador at the court of France, a circular letter sent also to the principal officers and representatives of the king, the crime of which Cromwell was accused is distinctly set forth. 'The Lord Privy Seal', it was therein said, 'to whom the king's said Majesty hath been so special good and gracious lord, neither remembering his duty herein to God, nor yet to His Highness ... hath not only wrought clean contrary to this His Grace's most godly intent, secretly and indirectly advancing the one of the extremes, and leaving the mean indifferent true and virtuous way which His Majesty sought and so entirely desired; but also hath showed himself so fervently bent to the maintenance of that his outrage that he hath not spared most privily, most traitorously, to devise how to continue the same, and plainly in terms to say, as it hath been justified to his face by good witness, that if the king and all his realm would turn and vary from his opinions, he would fight in the field in his own person, with his sword in his hand, against him and all other; adding that if he lived a year or two he trusted to bring things to that frame that it should not lie in the king's power to resist or let it, if he would; binding his words with such oaths and making such gesture and demonstration with his arms, that it might well appear he had no less fixed in his heart than was uttered with his mouth. For the which apparent and most detestable treasons, and also for ... other enormities ... he is committed to the Tower of London, there to remain till it shall please His Majesty to have him thereupon tried according to the order of his laws.' It was added that the king, remembering how men wanting the knowledge of the truth would speak diversely of the matter, desired them to declare and open the whole truth.

Nothing could be more at variance with the character and the whole life of Cromwell than the foolish sayings attributed to him. Every intelligent man might see that they were mere falsehoods invented by the Catholic party to hide its own criminal conduct. But at the same time it most clearly pointed out in this letter the real motive of the blow aimed at Cromwell, the first, true, efficient cause of his fall, the object which his enemies had in view and towards which they were working. They fancied that the overthrow of Cromwell would be the overthrow of the reformation. Wallop did not fail to impart the information to the court to which he was accredited; and Henry VIII was delighted to hear of 'the friendly rejoyce of our good brother the French king, the constable and others there', on learning of the arrest of the Lord Privy Seal. This rejoicing was very natural on the part of Francis I, Montmorency, and the rest of them.

As soon as the arrest of 10 June was known, the majority of those who had most eagerly sought after the favour of Cromwell, and especially Bonner, Bishop of London, immediately turned round and declared against him. He had gained no popularity by promoting the last bills passed to the king's advantage; and the news of his imprisonment was therefore received with shouts of joy. In the midst of the general dejection, one man alone remained faithful to the prisoner – this was Cranmer. The man who had formerly undertaken the defence of Anne Boleyn now came forward in defence of Cromwell. The archbishop did not attend the Privy Council on Thursday, 10 June; but being in his place on the Friday, he heard that the Earl of Essex had been arrested as a traitor. The tidings astonished and affected him deeply. He saw in Cromwell at this time not only his personal friend, not only the prudent and devoted supporter of the reformation, but also the ablest minister and the most faithful servant of the king. He saw the danger to which he exposed himself by undertaking the defence of the prisoner; and he felt that it was his duty not recklessly to offend the king. He therefore wrote to him in a prudent manner, reminding him, nevertheless, energetically of all that Cromwell had been. His letter to the king was written the day after he heard of the fall of the minister. 'I heard yesterday in Your Grace's council', he says, 'that he [Cromwell] is a traitor; yet who cannot be sorrowful and amazed that he should be a traitor against Your Majesty, he that was so advanced by Your Majesty; he whose surety was only by Your Majesty; he who loved Your Majesty (as I ever thought) no less than God; he who studied always to set forwards whatsoever was Your Majesty's will and pleasure; he that cared for no man's displeasure to serve Your Majesty; he that was such a servant, in my judgment, in wisdom, diligence, faithfulness, and experience, as no prince in this realm ever had; he that was so vigilant to preserve Your Majesty from all treasons that few could be so secretly conceived but he detected the same in the beginning? If the noble princes of memory, King John, Henry II, and Richard II had had such a counsellor about them, I suppose that they should never have been so traitorously abandoned and overthrown as those good princes were. ... I loved him as my friend, for so I took him to be; but I chiefly loved him for the love which I thought I saw him bear ever towards Your Grace, singularly above all other. But now, if he be a traitor, I am sorry that ever I loved him or trusted him, and I am very glad that his treason is discovered in time. But yet again I am very sorrowful, for who shall Your Grace trust hereafter, if you might not trust him? Alas! I bewail and lament Your Grace's chance herein, I wot not whom Your Grace may trust. But I pray God continually night and day to send such a counsellor in his place whom Your Grace may trust, and who for all his qualities can and will serve Your Grace like to him, and that will have so much solicitude and care to preserve Your Grace from all dangers as I ever thought he had.'

Cranmer was doubtless a weak man; but assuredly it was a proof of some devotion to truth and justice, and of some boldness too, thus to plead the cause of the prisoner before a prince so absolute as Henry VIII, and even to express the wish that some efficient successor might be found. Cranmer wrote to the king *boldly*. The prince being intolerant of contradiction, this step of the archbishop was more than was needed to ruin him as well as Cromwell.

Meanwhile, the enemies of the prisoner were trying to find other grounds of accusation besides that which they had first brought forward. Indeed, it seemed to some persons a strange thing that he who, under Henry VIII, was head of the church, vice-gerent in spiritual affairs, should be a heretic and a patron of heretics; and many found in this charge an 'occasion of merriment'. They set to work, therefore, after the blow, to discover offences on the part of the accused. After taking great pains, this is what they discovered and set forth in the bill of attainder: 1. That he had set at liberty some prisoners suspected of treason; a crime indeed in the eyes of a gloomy despot, but in the judgment of righteous men an act of justice and virtue. 2. That he had granted freedom of export of corn, horses, and other articles of commerce; the crime of free trade which would be no crime now. Not a single instance can be specified in which Cromwell had received a present for such licence. 3. That he had, though a low-born man, given places and orders, saying only that he was sure that the king would approve them. On this point Cromwell might reasonably allege the multiplicity of matters entrusted to his care, and the annoyance to which it must have subjected the king, had he continually troubled him to decide the most trifling questions. 4. That he had given permission, both to the king's subjects and to foreigners, to cross the sea 'without any search'. This intelligent minister appears to have aimed at an order of things less vexatious and more liberal than that established under Henry VIII, and in this respect he stood ahead of his age. 5. That he had made a large fortune, that he had lived in great state, and had not duly honoured the nobility. There were not a few of the nobles who were far from being honourable, and this great worker had no liking for drones and idlers. With respect to his fortune, Cromwell incurred heavy expenses for the affairs of the realm. In many countries he kept well-paid agents, and the money which he had in his hands was spent more in state affairs than in satisfying his personal wishes. In all this there was evidently more to praise than to blame. But Cromwell had enemies who went further than his official accusers. The Roman Catholics gave out that he had aspired to the hand of the king's daughter, the Princess Mary.

These groundless charges were followed by the true motives for his disgrace. It was alleged that he had adopted heretical (that is to say, evangelical) opinions; that he had promoted the circulation of heretical works; that he had settled in the realm many heretical ministers; and that he had caused men accused of heresy to be set at liberty. That when anyone went to him to make complaint of detestable errors, he defended the heretics and severely censured the informers; and that in March last, persons having complained to him of the new preachers, he answered that 'their preaching was good'. For these *crimes,* the acts of a Christian, honest and beneficent man, condemnation must be pronounced. Cromwell indeed was guilty.

The conduct of the prosecution was entrusted to Richard Rich, formerly Speaker of the House of Commons, now solicitor-general and chancellor of the court of augmentations. He had already rendered service to the king in the trials of Bishop Fisher and Sir Thomas More; the same might be expected of him in the trial of Cromwell. It appears that he accused Cromwell of being connected with Throgmorton, the friend and agent of Cardinal Pole. Now the mere mention of Pole's name would put Henry out of temper. Cromwell's alliance with this friend of the pope was the pendant of his scheme of marriage with the Lady Mary; the one was as probable as the other. Cromwell wrote from his prison to the king on the subject, and stoutly denied the fable. It was not introduced into the formal pleadings; but the charge was left vaguely impending over him, and it was reasserted that he was guilty of treason. Cromwell was certainly not faultless. He was above all a politician, and political interests had too much weight with him. He was the advocate of some vexatious and unjust measures, and he acted sometimes in opposition to his own principles. But his main fault was a too servile devotion to the prince who pretended that he had been betrayed by him. His fall, in certain respects, resembles that of his earlier master, Cardinal Wolsey.

His enemies were afraid that, if the trial were conducted openly before his peers according to law, he would make his voice heard and clear himself of all their imputations. They resolved therefore to proceed against him without trial and without discussion, by the Parliamentary method, by bill of attainder; a course pronounced by Roman Catholics themselves 'a most iniquitous measure'.[1] He ought to have been tried, and he was not tried. He was, however, confronted on Friday, 11 June, the day after his arrest, with one of his accusers, and thus learnt what were the charges brought against him. Conducted again to the Tower, he became fully aware of the danger which was impending over him. The power of his enemies, Gardiner and Norfolk, the increasing disfavour of Anne of Cleves, which seemed inevitably to involve his own ruin, the proceedings instituted against Barnes and other evangelists, the anger of the king – all these things alarmed him and produced the conviction in his mind that the issue was doubtful, and that the danger was certain. He was in a state of great distress and deep melancholy; gloomy thoughts

---

[1] Lingard, *Hist. of England,* v, p. 143.

oppressed him, and his limbs trembled. The prison has been called the porch of the grave, and Cromwell indeed looked upon it as a grave. On 30 June he wrote to the king from his gloomy abode an affecting letter, 'with heavy heart and trembling hand', as he himself said.

About the end of June, the Duke of Norfolk, the Lord Chancellor, and the Lord High Admiral went to the Tower, instructed to examine Cromwell and to make various declarations to him on the part of the king. The most important of these related to the marriage of Henry VIII with Anne of Cleves. They called upon him to state all that he knew touching this marriage, 'as he might do before God on the dread day of judgment'. On 30 June Cromwell wrote to the king a letter in which he set forth what he knew on the subject; and he added: 'And this is all that I know, most gracious and most merciful sovereign lord, beseeching Almighty God … to counsel you, preserve you, maintain you, remedy you, relieve and defend you, as may be most to your honour, with prosperity, health and comfort of your heart's desire … [giving you] continuance of Nestor's years. … I am a most woeful prisoner, ready to take the death, when it shall please God and Your Majesty; and yet the frail flesh inciteth me continually to call to Your Grace for mercy and grace for mine offences: and thus Christ save, preserve, and keep you.

'Written at the Tower this Wednesday, the last day of June, with the heavy heart and trembling hand of Your Highness' most heavy and most miserable prisoner and poor slave,

'THOMAS CROMWELL.'

After having signed the letter, Cromwell, overpowered with terror at his future prospects, added: 'Most Gracious Prince, I cry for mercy, mercy, mercy.'[1]

The heads of the clerical party, impatient to be rid of an enemy whom they hated, hurried on the fatal decree. The Parliament met on Thursday, 17 June, seven days after Cromwell's imprisonment; and Cranmer, who had attended the sittings of the House of Lords on the previous days, was not present on this occasion. The Earl of Southampton, who had become Lord Keeper of the Privy Seal in Cromwell's place, entered and presented the bill of attainder against his predecessor. It was read

[1] Cromwell's Letter to Henry VIII. Burnet, *Records,* i, p. 301.

a first time. The second and third readings followed on Saturday the 19th. Cranmer, whose absence had probably been noticed, was present; and, according to his lamentable system, adapted to the despotism of his master, after having complied with the dictate of his conscience by calling to mind the merits of Cromwell, he complied with the will of the king, and by his silence acquiesced in the proceedings of the house. The bill was sent to the lower house. It appears that the commons raised some scruples or objections, for the bill remained under consideration for ten days. It was not until 29 June that the commons sent the bill back to the peers, with some amendments; and the peers, ever in haste, ordered that the three readings should take place at the same sitting. They then sent it to the king, who gave his assent to it. The man who was prosecuted had been so powerful that it was feared lest he should regain his strength and begin to advance with fresh energy.

The king, meanwhile, seems to have hesitated. He was less decided than those who at this time enjoyed his favour.

Although the Lord Chancellor, the Duke of Norfolk, and Lord Russell had come to announce to Cromwell that the bill of attainder had passed, he remained still a whole month in the Tower. The royal commissioners interrogated him at intervals on various subjects. It seems even that the king sent him relief, probably to mitigate the severities of his imprisonment. Cromwell habitually received the king's commissioners with dignity, and answered them with discretion. Whether the questions touched on temporal or ecclesiastical affairs, he ever showed himself better informed than his questioners.[1]

Henry sent word to him that he might write anything that he thought meet under his present circumstances. From this, Cromwell appears to have conceived a hope that the king would not permit his sentence to be executed. He took courage and wrote to the king. 'Most Gracious King', he said,

> your most lamentable servant and prisoner, prostrate at the feet of Your Most Excellent Majesty, have heard your pleasure ... that I should write. ... First, where I have been accused to Your Majesty of treason, to that I say, I never in all my life thought willingly to do that thing

[1] Foxe, *Acts,* v, p. 401.

that might or should displease Your Majesty. ... What labours, pains, and travails I have taken, according to my most bounden duty God also knoweth. ... If it had been or were in my power, to make Your Majesty so puissant, as all the world should be compelled to obey you, Christ he knoweth I would ... for Your Majesty hath been ... more like a dear father ... than a master. Should any faction or any affection to any point make me a traitor to Your Majesty, then all the devils in hell confound me, and the vengeance of God light upon me. ... Yet our Lord, if it be his will, can do with me as he did with Susan, who was falsely accused. ... Other hope than in God and Your Majesty I have not. ... Amongst other things, Most Gracious Sovereign, master comptroller shewed me that Your Grace shewed him that within these fourteen days ye committed a matter of great secrecy, which I did reveal. ... This I did. ... I spake privily with her [the queen's] Lord Chamberlain ... desiring him ... to find some mean that the queen might be induced to order Your Grace pleasantly in her behaviour towards you. ... If I have offended Your Majesty therein, prostrate at Your Majesty's feet I most lowly ask mercy and pardon of Your Highness. ... Written with the quaking hand and most sorrowful heart of your most sorrowful subject and most humble servant and prisoner, this Saturday at the Tower of London.

THOMAS CROMWELL.[1]

Cromwell was resigned to death; and the principal object of his concern was the fate of his son, his grandchildren, and likewise of his domestic servants. His son was in a good position, having married a sister of the queen Jane Seymour. 'Sir, upon my knees', he said, 'I most humbly beseech Your Gracious Majesty to be a good and gracious lord to my poor son, the good and virtuous woman his wife, and their poor children, and also to my servants. And this I desire of Your Grace for Christ's sake.' The unhappy father, returning to his own case, finished by saying, 'Most Gracious Prince, mercy, mercy, mercy!' Cromwell wrote twice in this manner; and the king was so much affected by the second of these letters that he 'commanded it thrice to be read to him'.

Would Cromwell then, after all, escape? Those who were ignorant of what was passing at court looked upon it as impossible that he should be

[1] Burnet, *Records,* ii, p. 214.

sacrificed so long as Anne of Cleves was Queen of England. But the very circumstances which seemed to them the guarantee of his safety were to be instead the occasion of his ruin.

Henry's dislike to his wife was ever increasing, and he was determined to get rid of her. But, as usual, he concealed beneath flowers the weapon with which he was about to strike her. In the month of March, the king gave, in honour of the queen, a grand fête with a tournament, as he had done for Anne Boleyn; and amongst the numerous combatants who took part in the jousting were Sir Thomas Seymour, the Earl of Sussex, Harry Howard, and Richard Cromwell, nephew of the Earl of Essex, and ancestor of the great Protector Oliver.

One circumstance contributed to hasten the decision of the king. There was at the court a young lady, small of stature, of a good figure and beautiful countenance, of lady-like manners, coquettish, and forward, who at this time made a deep impression on Henry. This was Catherine Howard, a niece of the Duke of Norfolk, now residing with her grand-mother, the duchess dowager, who allowed her great liberty. Catherine was in every respect a contrast to Anne of Cleves. Henry resolved to marry her, and for this purpose to get rid forthwith of his present wife. As he was desirous of being provisionally relieved of her presence, he persuaded her that a change of air would be very beneficial to her, and that it was necessary that she should make a stay in the country. On 24 June he sent the good princess, who felt grateful for his attentions, to Richmond. At the same time he despatched the Bishop of Bath to her brother, the Duke of Cleves, with a view to prepare him for the very unexpected decision which was impending over his sister, and to avert any vexatious consequences.

Cromwell, then, had no aid to look for at the hands of a queen already forsaken and ere long repudiated. He could not hope to escape death. His enemies were urgent for the execution of the bill. They professed to have discovered a correspondence which he had carried on with the Protestant princes of Germany.

Cromwell's determination to offer no opposition to the king led him to commit serious mistakes, unworthy of a Christian. Never-theless, according to documents still extant, he died like a Christian. He was not the first, nor the last, who in the presence of death, of capital punishment, has examined himself, and confessed himself a sinner. While he spurned the accusations made by his enemies, he humbled himself before the weightier and more solemn accusations of his own conscience. How often had his own will been opposed to the commandments of the divine will! But at the same time he discovered in the gospel the grace which he had but imperfectly known; and the doctrines which the catholic church of the first ages had professed became dear to him.

On 28 July 1540, Cromwell was taken to Tower Hill, the place of execution. On reaching the scaffold he said: 'I am come hither to die, and not to purge myself. ... For since the time that I have had years of discretion, I have lived a sinner and offended my Lord God, for the which I ask him heartily forgiveness. And it is not unknown to many of you that I have been a great travailler in this world, and being but of a base degree, was called to high estate; and since the time I came thereunto I have offended my prince, for the which I ask him heartily forgiveness, and beseech you all to pray to God with me, that he will forgive me. O Father, forgive me! O Son, forgive me! O Holy Ghost, forgive me! O Three Persons in one God, forgive me! ... I die in the catholic faith. ... I heartily desire you to pray for the King's Grace, that he may long live with you in health and prosperity.'

By insisting in so marked a manner on the doctrine of the Trinity, professed in the fourth century by the councils of Nicæa and Constantinople, Cromwell doubtless intended to show that this was the catholic doctrine in which he asserted that he died. But he did not omit to give evidence that his faith was that of the Scriptures.

After his confession, he knelt down, and at this solemn hour he uttered this Christian and fervent prayer:

> O Lord Jesu! which art the only health of all men living and the everlasting life of them which die in thee, I, wretched sinner, do submit myself wholly unto thy most blessed will, and being sure that the thing cannot perish which is committed unto thy mercy, willingly now I leave this frail and wicked flesh, in sure hope that thou wilt, in better wise, restore it to me again at the last day in the resurrection of the just. I beseech thee, most merciful Lord Jesus Christ! that thou wilt

by thy grace make strong my soul against all temptations, and defend me with the buckler of thy mercy against all the assaults of the devil. I see and acknowledge that there is in myself no hope of salvation, but all my confidence, hope, and trust is in thy most merciful goodness. I have no merits nor good works which I may allege before thee. Of sins and evil works, alas! I see a great heap; but yet through thy mercy I trust to be in the number of them to whom thou wilt not impute their sins; but wilt take and accept me for righteous and just, and to be the inheritor of everlasting life. Thou, merciful Lord! wast born for my sake; thou didst suffer both hunger and thirst for my sake; thou didst teach, pray, and fast for my sake; all thy holy actions and works thou wroughtest for my sake; thou sufferedst most grievous pains and torments for my sake; finally, thou gavest thy most precious body and thy blood to be shed on the cross for my sake. Now, most merciful Saviour! let all these things profit me, that thou freely hast done for me, which hast given thyself also for me. Let thy blood cleanse and wash away the spots and foulness of my sins. Let thy righteousness hide and cover my unrighteousness. Let the merits of thy passion and blood-shedding be satisfaction for my sins. Give me, Lord, thy grace, that the faith of my salvation in thy blood waver not in me, but may ever be firm and constant; that the hope of thy mercy and life everlasting never decay in me: that love wax not cold in me. Finally, that the weakness of my flesh be not overcome with the fear of death. Grant me, merciful Saviour! that when death hath shut up the eyes of my body, yet the eyes of my soul may still behold and look upon thee; and when death hath taken away the use of my tongue, yet my heart may cry and say unto thee, 'Lord! into thy hands I commend my soul; Lord Jesu! receive my spirit!' Amen.[1]

This is one of the most beautiful prayers handed down to us in Christian times.

Cromwell having finished his prayer and being now ready, a stroke of the axe severed his head from his body.

Thus died a man who, although he had risen from the lowliest to the loftiest estate, never allowed himself to be seduced by pride, nor made

---

[1] Foxe, *Acts*, v, p. 403. It is possible that the prayer may have been written in the prison.

giddy by the pomps of the world, who continued attached to his old acquaintances, and was eager to honour the meanest who had rendered him any service; a man who powerfully contributed to the establishment of Protestantism in England, although his enemies, unaware of the very different meanings of the words 'catholicism' and 'popery', took pleasure in circulating the report in Europe, after his death, that he died a Roman Catholic; a man who for eight years governed his country, the king, the Parliament, and convocation, who had the direction of all domestic as well as foreign affairs; who executed what he had advised, and who, in spite of the blots which he himself lamented, was one of the most intelligent, most active, and most influential of English ministers. It is said that the king ere long regretted him. However this may be, he protected his son and gave him proofs of his favours, doubtless in remembrance of his father.

Another nobleman, Walter, Lord Hungerford, was beheaded at the same time with Cromwell, for having endeavoured to ascertain, by 'conjuring', how long the king would live.

CHAPTER SIX

The Divorce of Anne of Cleves

(1540)

The Catholic party was triumphant. It had set aside the Protestant queen and sacrificed the Protestant minister; and it now proceeded to take measures of a less startling character, but which were a more direct attack on the very work of the reformation. It thought proper to put to death some of those zealous men who were boldly preaching the pure gospel, not only for the sake of getting rid of them, but even more for the purpose of terrifying those who were imitating them or who were willing to do so.

Of these men, Barnes, Garret, and Jerome were best known. They were in prison; but Henry had hitherto scrupled about sacrificing men who preached a doctrine opposed to the pope. The party, moreover, united all their forces to bring about the fall of Cromwell, who had been confined within the same walls. After his death, the death of the preachers followed as a matter of course; it was merely the corollary; it was a natural consequence, and needed no special demonstration; the sentence, according to the Romish party, had only to be pronounced to be evidently justified. On these principles the king's council and the Parliament proceeded; and two days after the execution of Cromwell, these three evangelists, without any public hearing, without knowing any cause of their condemnation, without receiving any communication whatsoever, were taken out of prison, 30 July 1540, to be conducted to Smithfield, where they were to be deprived, not only of their ministry, but of their lives.

Henry, however, was not free from uneasiness. He had openly asserted that he leaned neither to one side nor to the other; that he weighed both parties in a just balance; and now, while he is boasting of his impartiality, everybody persists in saying that he gives all the advantage to the papists. What is he to do in order to be just and impartial? Three papists must be found to be put to death at the same time with the evangelicals. Then nobody will venture to assert that the king does not hold the balance even. The measure shall be faultless and one of the glories of his reign. The three papists selected to be placed in the other scale bore the names of Abel, Powel, and Fetherstone. The first two were political pamphleteers who had supported the cause of Catherine of Aragon; and the third was, like them, an opponent of royal supremacy. It seems that in this matter the king also made allowance for the composition of his own council, which comprised both friends and enemies of the reformation. Amongst the former were the Archbishop of Canterbury, the Duke of Suffolk, Viscounts Beauchamp and Lisle, Russell, Paget, Sadler, and Audley. Amongst the latter were the bishops of Winchester and Durham, the Duke of Norfolk, the Earl of Southampton, Sir Anthony Browne, Paulet, Baker, Richard, and Wingfield. There was therefore a majority of one against the reformation, just enough to turn the scale. Henry, with a show of impartiality, assigned three victims to each of these parties. Preparations were made at the Tower for carrying out this equitable sentence. In the courtyard were three hurdles, of oblong shape, formed of branches of trees closely intertwined, on which the culprits were to be drawn to the place of execution. Why three only, as there were six condemned? The reason was soon to be seen. When the three prisoners of each side were brought out, they proceeded to lay one evangelical on the first hurdle, and by his side a papist, binding them properly to each other to keep them in this strange coupling. The same process was gone through with the second and the third hurdles; they then set out, and the six prisoners were drawn two and two to Smithfield. Thus, in every street through which the procession passed, Henry VIII proclaimed by this strange spectacle that his government was impartial, and condemned alike the two classes of divines and of doctrines.

The three hurdles reached Smithfield. Two and two, the prisoners were unbound, and the three evangelicals were conducted to the stake. No trial having been allowed them by the court, these upright and pious men felt it their duty to supply its place at the foot of the scaffold. The day of their death thus became for them the day of hearing. The tribunal was sitting and the assembly was large. Barnes was the first speaker. He said: 'I am come hither to be burned as a heretic. ... God I take to record, I never (to my knowledge) taught any erroneous doctrine ... and I neither moved nor gave occasion of any insurrection. ... I believe in the Holy and Blessed Trinity; ... and that this Blessed Trinity sent down the second person, Jesus Christ, into the womb of the most blessed and purest Virgin Mary. ... I believe that through his death he overcame sin, death, and hell; and that there is none other satisfaction to the Father, but this his death and passion only.' At these words Barnes, deeply moved, raised his hands to heaven, and prayed God to forgive him his sins. This profession of faith did not satisfy the sheriff. Then someone asked him what he thought of praying to the saints. 'I believe', answered Barnes, 'that they are worthy of all the honour that Scripture willeth them to have. But, I say, throughout all Scripture we are not commanded to pray to any saints. ... If saints do pray for us, then I trust to pray for you within the next half hour.' He was silent, and the sheriff said to him: 'Well, have you anything more to say?' He answered: 'Have ye any articles against me for the which I am condemned?' The sheriff answered: 'No.' Barnes then put the question to the people whether any knew wherefore he died. No one answered. Then he resumed: 'They that have been the occasion of it, I pray God forgive them, as I would be forgiven myself. And Dr Stephen, Bishop of Winchester that now is, if he have sought or wrought this my death, either by word or deed, I pray God forgive him. ... I pray that God may give [the king] prosperity, and that he may long reign among you; and after him that godly prince Edward may so reign that he may finish those things that his father hath begun.'[1] Then collecting himself, Barnes addressed three requests to the sheriff, the prayer of a dying man. The first was that the king might employ the wealth of the abbeys which had been poured into the treasury in relieving his poor subjects who were in great need of it. The second was that marriage might be respected, and that men might not live in uncleanness. The third, that the name of God might not

---

[1] Foxe, *Acts,* v, p. 435.

be taken in vain in abominable oaths. These prayers of a dying man, who was sent to the scaffold by Henry himself, ought to have produced some impression on the heart of the king. Jerome and Garret likewise addressed affecting exhortations to the people. After this, these three Christians uttered together their last prayer, shook hands with and embraced one another, and then meekly gave themselves up to the executioner. They were bound to the same stake, and breathed their last in patience and in faith.

On the same day, at the same hour, and at the same place where the three friends of the gospel were burnt, the three followers of the pope, Abel, Fetherstone, and Powel were hanged. A foreigner who was present exclaimed: 'What strange people live here? Here they hang papists, there they burn anti-papists!' The simple-minded and ignorant asked what kind of religion people should have in England, seeing that both Romanism and Protestantism led to death. A courtier exclaimed: 'Verily, henceforth I will be of the king's religion, that is to say, of none at all!'

Cromwell and these six men were not to be the only objects of the king's displeasure. Even before they had undergone their sentence, the king had caused his divorce to be pronounced. In marrying Anne of Cleves, his chief object had been to form an alliance with the Protestants against the emperor. Now these two opponents were by this time reconciled with each other. Henry, therefore, deeply irritated, no longer hesitated to rid himself of the new queen. He was influenced, moreover, by another motive. He was smitten with the charms of another woman. However, as he dreaded the raillery, the censures, and even the calamities which the divorce might bring upon him, he was anxious not to appear as the originator of it, and should the accusation be made, to be able to repel it as a foul imposture without shadow of reality. He resolved, therefore, to adopt such a course that this strange proceeding should seem to have been imposed upon him. This intention he hinted to one of the lords in whom he had full confidence; and the latter made some communications about it, on 3 July, to the Privy Council. On the 6th His Majesty's ministers pointed out to the upper house the propriety of their humbly requesting the king, in conjunction with the lower house, that the convocation of the clergy might examine into his marriage with Anne of Cleves, and see whether it were valid. The lords adopted the proposal; and a commission consisting of the Lord Chancellor, the Archbishop of Canterbury, and the dukes of Norfolk and Suffolk, presented it to the commons, who gave their assent to it. Consequently the whole House of Lords and a commission of twenty members of the lower house appeared before the king, and stated that the matter about which they had to confer with him was of such an important character that they must first request his permission to lay it before them. Henry, feigning utter ignorance of what they meant, commanded them to speak. They then said: 'We humbly pray Your Majesty to allow the validity of your marriage to be investigated by the convocation of the clergy; we attach all the more importance to this proceeding because the question bears upon the succession to the throne of Your Majesty.' It was well known that the king did not love Anne, and that he was even in love with another. This is a striking instance of the degree of meanness to which Henry VIII had reduced his Parliament; for an assembly, even if some mean souls are to be found in it, undertakes not to be despicable, and what is noblest in it usually comes to the surface. But if the shameful compliances of the Parliament astonish us, the audacious hypocrisy of Henry VIII surprises us still more. He stood up to answer as if in the presence of the Deity; and concealing his real motives he said: 'There is nothing in the world more dear to me than the glory of God, the good of England, and the declaration of the truth.' All the actors in this comedy played their parts to perfection. The king immediately sent to Richmond some of his councillors, amongst them Suffolk and Gardiner, to communicate to the queen the demand of the Parliament and to ascertain her opinion with respect to it. Without delay, Anne gave her consent to the proposal.

The next day, 7 July, the matter was brought before convocation by Gardiner, Bishop of Winchester, who was very anxious to see a Roman Catholic queen upon the throne of England. A committee was nominated for the purpose of examining the witnesses; and of this committee the bishop was a member. An autograph declaration of the king was produced, in which he dwelt strongly on the fact that he took such a dislike to Anne as soon as he saw her that he thought instantly of breaking off the match; that he never inwardly consented to the marriage, and that in fact it had never been consummated. Within two days all the witnesses were heard. Henry was impatient; and the Roman party urgently appealed to the assembly to deliver a judgment which would rid England of a Protestant queen. Cranmer, out of fear or feebleness (he had just seen Cromwell lose his head), went with the rest of them.

On 9 July, convocation, relying upon the two reasons given by the king, and upon the fact that there was something ambiguous in Anne's engagement with the son of the Duke of Lorraine, decided that His Majesty 'was at liberty to contract another marriage for the good of the realm'. None of these reasons had any validity. Nor did Henry escape the condemnation and the raillery which he had so much feared. 'It appears', said Francis I, 'that over there they are pleased to do with their women as with their geldings – bring a number of them together and make them trot, and then take the one which goes easiest.'

The Archbishop of Canterbury on 10 July reported to the upper house that convocation had declared the marriage null and void by virtue both of the law of God and of the law of England. The Bishop of Winchester read the judgment and explained at length the grounds of it, and the house declared itself satisfied. The archbishop and the bishop made the same report to the commons. On the following day – Henry did not intend that any time should be lost – the Lord Chancellor, the Duke of Norfolk, the Earl of Southampton, and the Bishop of Winchester betook themselves to Richmond again, and informed Anne, on the king's behalf, of the proceedings of Parliament and of convocation. Anne was distressed by the communication. She had supposed that the clergy would acknowledge, as it was their duty to do, the validity of her marriage. However it may be, so sharp was the stroke that she fainted away. The necessary care was bestowed on her, and she recovered, and gradually reconciled herself to the thought of submission to Henry's will. The delegates told her that the king, while requiring her to renounce the title of queen, conferred on her that of his adopted sister, and gave her precedence in rank of all the ladies of the court, immediately after the queen and the daughters of the king. Anne was modest; she did not think highly of herself, and had often felt that she was not made to be Queen of England. She therefore submitted, and the same day, 11 July, wrote to the king: 'Though this case must needs be most hard and sorrowful unto me, for the great love which I bear to your most noble person, yet having more regard to God and his truth than to any worldly affection, as it beseemed me. ... I knowledge myself hereby to accept and approve the same [determination of the clergy] wholly and entirely putting myself, for my state and condition, to Your Highness' goodness and pleasure; most humbly beseeching Your Majesty ... to take me for one of your most humble servants.' She subscribed herself 'Your Majesty's most humble sister and servant, Anne of Cleves.'

The king sent word to her that he conferred on her a pension of £4,000 a year, and the palace at Richmond. Anne wrote to him again, 16 July, to thank him for his great kindness, and at the same time sent him her ring. She preferred – and herein she showed some pride – to remain in England, rather than to go home after such a disgrace had fallen upon her. 'I account God pleased', she wrote to her brother, 'with what is done, and know myself to have suffered no wrong or injury. ... I find the King's Highness ... to be as a most kind, loving, and friendly father and brother. ... I am so well content and satisfied, that I much desire my mother, you, and other mine allies so to understand it, accept, and take it.' Seldom has a woman carried self-renunciation to such a length.

CHAPTER SEVEN

Catherine Howard, the Fifth Queen

(1540)

W ho should take the place of the repudiated queen? This was the question discussed at court and in the town. The Anglican Catholics, delighted at the dismissal of the Protestant queen, were determined to do all they possibly could to place on the throne a woman of their own party. Such a one was already found. The Bishop of Winchester, for some time past, had frequently been holding feasts and entertainments for the king. To these he invited a young lady, who though of small stature was of elegant carriage, and had handsome features and a graceful figure and manners. She was the fifth child and second daughter of Lord Edmund Howard, and niece of the Duke of Norfolk, the leader of the Catholic party. She very soon attracted the attention of the king, who took increasing pleasure in her society. This occurred before the divorce of Anne. 'It is a certain fact', says a contemporary, 'that about the same time many citizens of London saw the king very frequently in the daytime, and sometimes at midnight, pass over to her on the River Thames in a little boat. ... The citizens regarded all this not as a sign of divorcing the queen, but of adultery.'[1] Whether this supposition was well founded or not we cannot say. The king, when once he had decided on a separation from Anne of Cleves, had thought of her successor. He was quite determined, after his mischance, to be guided neither by his ministers, nor by his ambassadors, nor by political considerations, but solely by his own eyes, his own tastes, and the happiness he might hope for. Catherine pleased him very much; and his union with Anne was no sooner annulled than

[1] *Original Letters Relative to the English Reformation* (Parker Society), i, p. 202.

435

he proceeded to his fifth marriage. The nuptials were celebrated on 8 August, eleven days after the execution of Cromwell; and on the same day Catherine was presented at court as queen. The king was charmed with Catherine Howard, his pretty young wife; she was so amiable, her intercourse was so pleasant, that he believed he had, after so many more or less unfortunate attempts, found his ideal at last. Her virtuous sentiments, the good behaviour which she resolved to maintain filled him with delight; and he was ever expressing his happiness in 'having obtained such a jewel of womanhood'. He had no foreboding of the terrible blow which was soon to shatter all this happiness.

The new queen was distinguished from the former chiefly by the difference in religion, with a corresponding difference in morality. The niece of the Duke of Norfolk, Gardiner's friend, was of course an adherent of the Catholic faith; and the Catholic party hailed her as at once the symbol and the instrument of reaction. They had had plenty of Protestant queens, Anne Boleyn, Jane Seymour, and Anne of Cleves. Now that they had a Catholic queen, Catholicism – many said popery – would recover its power. Henry was so much enamoured of his new spouse that, in honour of her, he once more became a fervent Catholic. He celebrated all the saints' days, frequently received the holy sacrament, and publicly offered thanksgiving to God for this happy union which he hoped to enjoy for a long time. The conversion of Henry, for the change was nothing less, brought with it a change of policy. He now abandoned France and the German Protestants in order to ally himself with the empire; and we find him ere long busily engaged in a project for the marriage of his daughter Mary to the emperor Charles V. This project, however, came to nothing. Gardiner, Norfolk, and the other leaders of the Catholic party, rejoicing in the breeze which bore their vessel onward, set all sails to the wind. Just after the divorce of Anne of Cleves, and by way of a first boon to the Romish party, the penalties for impure living imposed on the priests and nuns were mitigated. In contempt of the authority of Holy Scripture as well as of that of Parliament itself, Henry got an act passed by virtue of which every determination concerning faith, worship, and ceremonies, adopted with the sanction of the king by a commission of archbishops, bishops, and other ecclesiastics nominated by him, was to be received, believed, and observed by the whole nation, just as if Parliament had approved every one of these articles, even if this decree were contrary to former usages and ordinances. This was a proclamation of infallibility in England, for the benefit of the pope-king, under cover of which he might found a religion to his own taste. Cranmer had established in all cathedral churches professors entrusted with the teaching of Hebrew and Greek, in order that students might become well acquainted with sacred literature, and that the church might never want ministers capable of edifying it. But the enemies of the reformation, who now enjoyed royal favour, fettered or abolished this institution and other similar ones, to the great damage both of religion and the country. On the other hand, the Catholic ceremonies, abrogated by Cranmer and Cromwell – the consecration of bread and of water, the embers with which the priest marked the foreheads of the faithful, the palm branches blessed on Palm Sunday, the tapers carried at Candlemas, and other like customs – were re-established; and penalties were imposed on those who should neglect them. A new edition of the *Institution of a Christian Man* explained to the people the king's doctrine. It treated of the seven sacraments, the mass, transubstantiation, the salutation of the Virgin, and other doctrines of the kind to which conformity was required. At length, as if with a view to ensure the permanence of this system, Bonner was made Bishop of London; and this man, who had been the most abject flatterer and servant of Cromwell during his life, turned about after his death and became the persecutor of those whom Cromwell had protected.

At the spectacle of this reaction, so marvellous in their eyes, the Anglican Catholics and even the papists broke out with joy, and awaited with impatience 'the crowning of the edifice'. England, in their view, was saved. The church was triumphant. But while there was rejoicing on the one side, there was mourning on the other. The establishment of superstitious practices, the prospect of the penalties contained in the statute of the Six Articles, penalties which had not yet been enforced but were on the point of being so, spread distress and alarm among the evangelicals. Those who did not add to their faith manly energy shut up their convictions in their own breasts, carefully abstained from conversation on religious subjects, and looked with suspicion upon every stranger, fearing that he might be one of Gardiner's spies.

Bonner was active and eager, going forward in pursuit of his object and allowing nothing to check him. Cromwell and Cranmer, to whom he used to make fair professions, believed that he was capable of being of service to the reformation, and therefore gave him promotion in ecclesiastical offices. But no sooner had Cromwell been put in prison than his signal deceitfulness showed itself. Grafton, who printed the Bible under the patronage of the vice-gerent, having met Bonner, to whom Cromwell had introduced him, exclaimed, 'How grieved I am to hear that Lord Cromwell has been sent to the Tower!' 'It would have been much better', replied Bonner, 'if he had been sent there long ago.' Shortly after, Grafton was cited before the council, and was accused of having printed, by Cromwell's order, certain suspected verses; and Bonner, for the purpose of aggravating his criminality, did not fail to report what the accused had said to him about the man who had been his own personal benefactor. The chancellor, however, a friend of Grafton, succeeded in saving the printer of the Bible. Bonner indemnified himself for this disappointment by persecuting a great many citizens of London. He vented his rage especially on a poor youth of fifteen, ignorant and uncultivated, named Richard Mekins, whom he accused of having spoken against the Eucharist and in favour of Barnes; but the grand jury found him 'not guilty'. Hereupon Bonner became furious. 'You are perjured', he said to the jury. 'The witnesses do not agree', they replied. 'The one deposed that Mekins had said the sacrament was nothing but a *ceremony;* and the other that it was nothing but a *signification.*' 'But did he not say', exclaimed the bishop, 'that Barnes died holy'? 'But we cannot find these words', said the jury, 'to be against the statute.' Upon which Bonner cursed and was in a great rage. 'Retire again', he said, 'consult together, and bring in the bill.' Mekins was condemned to die. In vain was it shown that he was a poor ignorant creature and that he had done nothing worse than repeat what he had heard, and this without even understanding it. In vain, too, did his father and mother, who were in great distress, attempt to mitigate the harsh treatment to which he was subjected in prison. The poor lad was ready to say or do anything to escape being burnt. They made him speak well of Bonner and of his great charity towards him; they made him declare that he hated all heretics, and then they burnt him. This was only the beginning, and Bonner hoped by such proceedings to prepare the way for greater triumphs.

The persecution became more general. Two hundred and two persons were prosecuted in thirty-nine London parishes. The offences were such as the following – having read the Holy Scriptures aloud in the churches; having refused to carry palm branches on Palm Sunday; having had one or other of their kinsfolk buried without the masses for the dead; having received Latimer, Barnes, Garret, or other evangelicals; having held religious meetings in their houses of an evening; having said that the holy sacrament was a good thing, but was not, as some asserted, God himself; having spoken much about the Holy Scriptures; having declared that they liked better to hear a sermon than a mass; and other like offences. Among the delinquents were some of the priests. One of these was accused of having caused suspected persons to be invited to his sermons by his beadle, without having the bells rung; another of having preached without the orders of his superior; others, of not making use of holy water, of not going in procession, and so on.[1]

The inquisition which was made at this time was so rigorous that all the prisons of London would not hold the accused. They had to place some of them in the halls of various buildings. The case was embarrassing. The Catholics of the court were not alone in instigating the king to persecution. Francis I sent word to him by Wallop, 'that it had well liked him to hear that His Majesty *was reforming* the Lutheran sect, for that he was ever of opinion that no good could come of them but much evil.' But there were other influences at court besides that of Francis I, Norfolk, and Gardiner. Lord Audley obtained the king's sanction for the release of the prisoners, who, however, had to give their promise to appear at the Star Chamber on All Souls' Day. Ultimately they were let alone.

But this does not mean that all the evangelicals were spared. Two ministers were at this time distinguished both for their high connections

---

[1] Foxe, in his *Acts,* v, pp. 443-9, gives the names of all these persons, naming also their parishes and their offences.

and for their faith and eloquence. One of these was the Scotsman, Alexander Seaton, chaplain to the Duke of Suffolk. Preaching powerfully at St Antholin's Church, in London, he said: *'Of ourselves we can do nothing,* says St Paul; *I pray thee, then, where is thy will? Art thou better than Paul, James, Peter, and all the apostles?* Hast thou any more grace than they? Tell me now if thy will be anything or nothing? ... Paul said he could do nothing. ... If you ask me when we will leave preaching only Christ, even when they do leave to preach that works do merit, and suffer Christ to be a whole satisfier and only mean to our justification.' Seaton was condemned to bear a faggot at Paul's Cross. Another minister, Dr Crome, was a learned man and a favourite of the archbishop. This did not prevent the king from commanding him to preach that the sacrifice of the mass is useful both for the living and the dead. Crome preached the gospel in its simplicity at St Paul's on the appointed day, and contented himself with reading the king's order after the sermon. He was immediately forbidden to preach.

Laymen were treated with greater severity. Bibles, it is known, had been placed in all the churches, and were fastened by chains to the pillars. A crowd of people used to gather about one of these pillars. On one occasion a young man of fine figure, possessed of great zeal, and gifted with a powerful voice, stood near the pillar holding the Bible in his hands, and reading it aloud so that all might hear him. His name was John Porter. Bonner sharply rebuked him. 'I trust I have done nothing against the law', said Porter; and this was true. But the bishop committed him to Newgate. There this young Christian was put in irons; his legs, his arms, and his head were attached to the wall by means of an iron collar. One of his kinsmen, by a gift of money, induced the gaoler to deliver him from this punishment; and the favour they accorded him was to place him in the company of thieves and murderers. Porter exhorted them to repent, and taught them the way of salvation. The unhappy man was then cast into the deepest dungeon, was cruelly treated, and loaded with irons. Eight days afterwards he died. Cries and groans had been heard in the night. Some said that he had been subjected to the torture called 'the devil on the neck', a horrible instrument by which, in three or four hours, the back and the whole body were torn in pieces.

Meanwhile, a far more formidable blow was preparing. Cromwell, the lay protector of the reformation, had already been sacrificed; its ecclesiastical protector, Cranmer, must now fall in the same way. This second blow seemed easier than the first. Since the fall of Cromwell, men of the utmost moderation thought 'there was no hope that reformed religion should any one week longer stand'. All those of feeble character sided with the opposite party. Cranmer alone, amongst the bishops and the ecclesiastical commissioners of the king, still upheld evangelical truth. This obstacle in the way of the extension of English Catholicism must be utterly overthrown.

Plot after plot was formed against him, but Cranmer's foes retired baffled. New plans were concocted. Dr London and other agents of the party which looked up to Gardiner as its head took in hand to go over the diocese of the archbishop with a view to collecting all the sayings and all the facts, true or false, which they might turn to account as weapons against him. In one place a conversation was reported to them; in another a sermon was denounced; elsewhere neglected ritual was talked about. 'Three of the preachers of the Cathedral Church', they were told, namely, Ridley, Drum, and Scory, 'are attacking the ceremonies of the church.' Some of the canons, opponents of the primate, brought various charges against him, and strove to depict his marriage in the most repulsive colours. Sir John Gostwick, whose accounts as Treasurer of War and of the court were not correct, accused Cranmer before the Parliament of being the pastor of heretics.[1] All these grievances were set forth in a memorial which was presented to the king. At the same time, the most influential members of the Privy Council declared to the king that the realm was infested with heresies; that thereby 'horrible commotions and uproars' might spring up, as had been the case in Germany; and that these calamities must be chiefly imputed to the Archbishop of Canterbury, who both by his own preaching and that of his chaplains had filled England with pernicious doctrines. 'Who is his accuser?' said the king. The lords replied: 'Forasmuch as Cranmer is a councillor, no man durst take upon him to accuse him. But if it please Your Highness to commit him to the Tower for a time, there would be accusations and

---

[1] [Probably the Parliament of 1544–45.]

proofs enough against him.' 'Well then', said the king, 'I grant you leave to commit him tomorrow to the Tower for his trial.' The enemies of the archbishop and of the reformation went away well content.

Meanwhile, Henry VIII began to reflect on the answer which he had given to his councillors. There is nothing to show that it was not made in earnest; but he foresaw that Cranmer's death would leave an awkward void. When Cranmer was gone, how should he maintain the conflict with the pope and the papists, with whom he had no mind to be reconciled? The primate's character and services came back to his memory. Time was passing. At midnight the king, unable to sleep, sent for Sir Antony Denny and said to him, 'Go to Lambeth and command the archbishop to come forthwith to the court.' Henry then, in a state of excitement, began to walk about in one of the corridors of the palace, awaiting the arrival of Cranmer. At length the primate entered and the king said to him: 'Ah, my Lord of Canterbury, I can tell you news. ... It is determined by me and the council, that you tomorrow at nine o'clock shall be committed to the Tower, for that you and your chaplains (as information is given us) have taught and preached, and thereby sown within the realm such a number of execrable heresies, that it is feared the whole realm being infected with them no small contentions and commotions will rise thereby amongst my subjects ... and therefore the council have requested me, for the trial of this matter, to suffer them to commit you to the Tower.'

The story of Cromwell was to be repeated, and this was the first step. Nevertheless, Cranmer did not utter a word of opposition or supplication. Kneeling down before the king, according to his custom, he said: 'I am content, if it please Your Grace, with all my heart to go thither at Your Highness' commandment, and I most humbly thank Your Majesty that I may come to my trial, for there be that have many ways slandered me, and now this way I hope to show myself not worthy of such a report.' The king, touched by his uprightness, said: 'Oh Lord, what manner of man be you! What simplicity is in you! ... Do you not know ... how many great enemies you have? Do you consider what an easy thing it is to procure three or four false knaves to witness against you? Think you to have better luck that way than Christ your master had? I see it, you will run headlong to your undoing, if I would suffer you. Your enemies shall not so prevail against you, for I have otherwise devised with myself to keep you out of their hands. Yet, notwithstanding, tomorrow when the council shall sit and send for you, resort unto them; and if in charging you with this matter they do commit you to the Tower, require of them … that you may have your accusers brought before them and that you may answer their accusations. … If no entreaty or reasonable request will serve, then deliver unto them this ring' – the king at the same time delivered his ring to the archbishop – 'and say unto them: If there be no remedy, my lords, but that I must needs go to the Tower, then I revoke my cause from you and appeal to the king's own person by this his token to you all. So soon as they shall see this my ring, they know it so well, that they shall understand that I have resumed the whole cause into mine own hands.' The archbishop was so much moved by the king's kindness that he 'had much ado to forbear tears'. 'Well', said the king, 'go your ways, my lord, and do as I have bidden you.' The archbishop bent his knee in expression of his gratitude, and taking leave of the king returned to Lambeth before day.

On the morrow, about eight o'clock, the council sent an usher of the palace to summon the archbishop. He set out forthwith and presented himself at the door of the council chamber. But his colleagues, glad to complete the work which they had begun by putting the vice-gerent to death, were not content with sending the primate to the scaffold; but were determined to subject Cranmer to various humiliations before the final catastrophe. The archbishop could not be let in, but was compelled to wait there among the pages, lackeys, and other serving men. Dr Butts, the king's physician, happening to pass through the room, and observing how the archbishop was treated, went to the king and said: 'My Lord of Canterbury, if it please Your Grace, is well promoted; for now he is become a lackey or a serving man, for yonder he standeth this half hour without the council chamber door amongst them.' 'It is not so', said the king, 'I trow, nor the council hath not so little discretion as to use the metropolitan of the realm in that sort, specially being one of their own number; but let them alone, and we shall hear more soon.'

At length the archbishop was admitted. He did as the king had bidden him; and when he saw that none of his statements or reasons were of any avail with the council, he presented the king's ring, appealing at the

443

same time to His Majesty. Hereupon, the whole council was struck with astonishment; and the Earl of Bedford, who was not one of Gardiner's party, with a solemn oath exclaimed: 'When you first began this matter, my lords, I told you what would come of it. Do you think that the king will suffer this man's finger to ache? Much more, I warrant you, will he defend his life against brabbling varlets. You do but cumber yourselves to hear tales and fables against him.' The members of the council immediately rose and carried the king's ring to him, thus surrendering the matter, according to the usage of the time, into his hands.

When they had all come into the presence of the king, he said to them with a severe countenance: 'Ah, my lords, I thought I had had wiser men of my council than now I find you. What discretion was this in you, thus to make the primate of the realm, and one of you in office, to wait at the council chamber door amongst serving men? … You had no such commission of me to handle him. I was content that you should try him as a councillor, and not as a mean subject. But now I well perceive that things be done against him maliciously; and if some of you might have had your minds, you would have tried him to the uttermost. But I do you all to wit, and protest, that if a prince may be beholding unto his subject' (and here Henry laid his hand solemnly upon his breast), 'by the faith I owe to God, I take this man here, my Lord of Canterbury, to be of all other a most faithful subject unto us, and one to whom we are much beholding.' The Catholic members of the council were disconcerted, confused, and unable to make any answer. One or two of them, however, took courage, made excuses, and assured the king that their object in trying the primate was to clear him of the calumnies of the world, and not to proceed against him maliciously. The king, who was not to be imposed upon by these hypocritical assertions, said: 'Well, well, my lords, take him and well use him, as he is worthy to be, and make no more ado.' All the lords then went up to Cranmer, and took him by the hand as if they had been his dearest friends. The archbishop, who was of a conciliatory disposition, forgave them. But the king sent to prison for a certain time some of the archbishop's accusers; and he sent a message to Sir John Gostwick, to the effect that he was a wicked varlet, and that unless he made his apologies to the metropolitan, he would make of him an example which should be a warning to all false accusers. These facts are creditable to Henry VIII. It was doubtless his aim to keep a certain middle course; and like many other despots he had happy intervals.

At the end of August 1541, Henry went to York, for the purpose of holding an interview with his nephew, the King of Scotland, whom he was anxious to persuade to declare himself independent of the pope. Henry made magnificent preparations for his reception; but Cardinal Beaton prevented the young prince from going. This excited the bitterest discontent in Henry's mind, and became afterwards the cause of a breach. The queen, who accompanied him, endeavoured to divert him from his vexation; and the king, more and more pleased with his marriage, after his return to London, made public thanksgiving on All Saints' Day (24 October) that God had given him so amiable and excellent a wife, and even requested the Bishop of Lincoln to join in his commendations of her. This excessive satisfaction was ere long to be interrupted.

During the king's journey, one John Lascelles, who had a married sister living in the county of Sussex, paid her a visit. This woman had formerly been in the service of the old Duchess of Norfolk, grandmother to the queen, and by whom Catherine had been brought up. In the course of conversation the brother and sister talked about this young lady, whom the sister had known well, and who had now become wife to the king. The brother, ambitious for his sister's advancement, said to her: 'You ought to ask the queen to place you among her attendants.' 'I shall certainly not do so', she answered; 'I cannot think of the queen but with sadness.' 'Why?' 'She is so frivolous in character and in life.' 'How so?' Then the woman related that Catherine had had improper intercourse with one of the officers of the ducal house of Norfolk, named Francis Derham; and that she had been very familiar with another whose name was Manox. Lascelles perceived the importance of these statements; and as he could not take upon himself the responsibility of concealing them, he determined to report them to the archbishop. The communication greatly embarrassed Cranmer. If he should keep the matter secret and it should afterwards become known, he would be ruined. Nor would he less certainly be ruined if he should divulge it, and then no proof be forthcoming. But what chiefly weighed upon his mind was the thought of the agitation which would be excited. To think of another wife of the king executed at the Tower! To think of this prince, his country, and perhaps also the work which was in process of accomplishment in England, becoming the objects of ridicule and perhaps of abhorrence! As he was unwilling to assume alone the responsibility imposed by so grave a communication, he opened his mind on the subject to the Lord Chancellor and to other members of the Privy Council, to whom the king had entrusted the despatch of business during his absence. 'They were greatly troubled and inquieted.' After having well weighed the reasons for and against, they came to the conclusion that, as this matter mainly concerned the king, Cranmer should inform him of it. This was a hard task to undertake; and the archbishop, who was deeply affected, durst not venture to make *viva voce* so frightful a communication. He therefore put down in writing the report which had been made to him, and had it laid before the king. The latter was terribly shocked; but as he tenderly loved his wife and had a high opinion of her virtue, he said that it was a calumny. However, he privately assembled in his cabinet the Lord Privy Seal, the Lord Admiral, Sir Anthony Browne, and Sir Thomas Wriothesley, a friend of the Duke of Norfolk, who had taken a leading part in the divorce of Anne of Cleves, and laid the case before them, declaring at the same time that he did not believe in it. These lords privately examined Lascelles and his sister, who persisted in their depositions; next Manox and Derham, who asserted the truth of their statements; the latter, moreover, mentioning three of the Duchess of Norfolk's women who likewise had knowledge of the facts. The members of the council made their report to the king, who, pierced with grief, remained silent for some time. At length he burst into tears, and commanded the Duke of Norfolk, the queen's uncle, the Archbishop of Canterbury, the high chamberlain, and the Bishop of Winchester, who had promoted the marriage, to go to Catherine and examine her. At first she denied everything. But when Cranmer was sent to her, on the evening of the first inquisition, the words of the primate, his admonitions, the reports which he made to her, which proved that her conduct was perfectly well known, convinced her of the uselessness of her denials, and she then made full confession, and even added some strange details. It does not appear that the queen felt it her duty to confess her offences to God, but she resolved at least to confess them to men. While making her confession she was in a state of so great agitation that the archbishop was in dread every moment of her losing her reason. He thought, according to her confessions, that she had been seduced by the infamous Derham, with the privity even of his own wife. The household of the duchess dowager of Norfolk appears to have been very disorderly. Cranmer wrote down or caused to be written this confession, and Catherine signed it.[1] He had scarcely left the unhappy woman, when she fell into a state of raving delirium.

The king was thrown into great excitement by the news of Catherine's confession of the reality of his misfortune. The very intensity of his love served to increase his trouble and his wrath; but, for all this, some feeling of pity remained in his heart. 'Return to her', he said to Cranmer, 'and first make use of the strongest expressions to give her a sense of the greatness of her offences; second, state to her what the law provides in such cases, and what she must suffer for her crime; and lastly express to her my feelings of pity and forgiveness.' Cranmer returned to Catherine and found her in a fit of agitation so violent that he never remembered – so he wrote to the king – seeing any creature in such a state. The keepers told him that this had continued from his departure from her. 'It would have pitied', said the good archbishop, 'any man's heart in the world to have looked upon her.' Indeed, she was almost in a frenzy; she was not without strength, but her strength was that of a frantic person. The archbishop had had too much experience in the cure of souls to adopt the order prescribed by the king. He saw that if he spoke first to her of the crime and its punishment, he might throw her into some dangerous ecstasy, from which she could not be rescued. He therefore began with the last part of the royal message, and told the queen that His Majesty's mercy extended to her, and that he had compassion on her misfortune. Catherine hereupon lifted up her hands, became quiet, and gave utterance to the humblest thanksgivings to the king who showed her so much mercy. She became more self-possessed; continuing, however,

---

[1] The confession is given by Burnet, *Hist. Reform.*, iii, p. 224.

to sob and weep. But 'after a little pausing, she suddenly fell into a new state of agony, much worse than she was before'.[1]

Cranmer, desirous of delivering her from this frightful delirium, said to her: 'Some new fantasy has come into your head, madam; pray open it to me.' After a time, when her passion subsided and she was capable of speech, she wept freely and said: 'Alas, my lord, that I am alive! The fear of death grieved me not so much before, as doth now the remembrance of the king's goodness. For when I remember how gracious and loving a prince I had, I cannot but sorrow; but this sudden mercy, and more than I could have looked for, showed unto me so unworthy at this time, maketh mine offences to appear before mine eyes much more heinous than they did before; and the more I consider the greatness of his mercy, the more I do sorrow in my heart that I should so misorder myself against His Majesty.' The fact that the compassion of the king touched Catherine more than the fear of a trial and of death, seemed to indicate a state of mind less wayward than one might have expected. But in vain Cranmer said to her everything calculated to pacify her; she remained for a long time 'in a great pang'; and even fell soon into another fearful state of agitation. At length, in the afternoon she came gradually to herself, and was in a quiet state till night. Cranmer, during this interval of relief, had 'good communications with her'. He rejoiced at having brought her into some quiet. She told him that there had been a marriage contract between her and Derham, only verbal indeed, she said; but that nevertheless, though never announced and acknowledged, it had been consummated. She added that she had acted under compulsion of that man. At six o'clock, she had another fit of frenzy. 'Ah', she said afterwards to Cranmer, 'when the clock struck, I remembered the time when Master Heneage was wont to bring me knowledge of His Grace.' In consequence of Cranmer's report, Henry commanded that the queen should be conducted to Sion House, where two apartments were to be assigned to her and attendants nominated by the king.

Charges against Catherine were accumulating. She had taken into her service, as queen, the wretched Derham and, employing him as secretary, had often admitted him into her private apartments; and this

[1] Cranmer, *Works* (Parker Society), ii, p. 408.

the council regarded as evidence of adultery. She had also again attached to herself one of the women implicated in her first irregularities. At length it was proved that another gentleman, one Culpepper, a kinsman of her mother, had been introduced, in the king's absence on a journey, into the queen's private apartments by Lady Rochford, at a suspicious hour and under circumstances which usually indicate crime. Culpepper confessed it.

Now began the condemnations and the executions; and Henry VIII included in the trial not only those who were guilty but also the near relatives and servants of the queen, who, though well knowing her offences, had not reported them to the king. On the 7th, the council determined that the duchess dowager of Norfolk, grandmother to the queen, her uncle, Lord William Howard, her aunts Lady Howard and Lady Bridgewater, together with Alice Wilks, Catherine Tylney, Damport, Walgrave, Malin Tilney, Mary Lascelles, Bulmer, Ashby, Anne Haward, and Margaret Benet were all guilty of not having revealed the crime of high treason, and that they should be prosecuted. On the 8th the king ordered that all these persons, Mary Lascelles excepted, should be committed to the Tower; and this was done. Lord William Howard was imprisoned on 9 December; the Duchess of Norfolk on the 10th, and Lady Bridgewater on the 13th. All of them stoutly protested their ignorance and their innocence. On 10 December 1541, Culpepper was beheaded at Tyburn; and the same day Derham was hanged, drawn, and quartered.

Meanwhile, the Duke of Norfolk had taken refuge at Kenninghall, about ninety miles from London. On 15 December, he wrote to the king, saying that by reason of the offences committed by his family he found himself in the utmost perplexity. Twice in his letter he 'prostrates himself at the king's feet'; and he expresses 'some hope that Your Highness will not conceive any displeasure in your most gentle heart against me; that, God knoweth, never did think thought which might be to your discon-tentation.' There did, however, remain something in the 'most gentle heart' of Henry VIII.

Parliament met, by the king's command, on 16 January 1542, to give its attention to this business. Thus it was to the highest national assembly that the king entrusted the regulation of his domestic interests. On 21 January, the chancellor introduced in the upper house a bill in which the king was requested not to trouble himself about the matter, considering that it might shorten his life; to declare guilty of high treason the queen and all her accomplices; and to condemn the queen and Lady Rochford to death. The bill passed both houses and received the royal assent.

On 12 February, the queen – she was only about twenty years of age – and Lady Rochford, her accomplice, were taken to Tower Hill and beheaded. The queen, while she confessed the offences which had preceded her marriage, protested to the last before God and his holy angels that she had never violated her faith to the king. But her previous offences gave credibility to those which were subsequent to her marriage. With regard to Lady Rochford, the confidant of the queen, she was universally hated. People called to mind the fact that her calumnies had been the principal cause of the death of the innocent Anne Boleyn and of her own husband; and nobody was sorry for her. The king pardoned the old Duchess of Norfolk and some others who had been prosecuted for not disclosing the crime.

These events did not call forth within the realm many remarks of a painful kind for Henry VIII; but the great example of immorality presented by the English court lessened the esteem in which it was held in Europe. There was no lack of similar licentiousness in France and elsewhere; but there a veil was thrown over it, while in England it was public talk. Opinion afterwards became severe with regard to the king; and when his conduct to three of his former wives was remembered, people said of the disgrace cast on him by Catherine Howard, that he well deserved it. As for the Catholic party, which had given Catherine to Henry and had cherished the hope that by her influence it should achieve its final triumph, it was greatly mortified. Some Catholics, referring to these offences, have since tried to lessen the abhorrence and the shame of them by saying 'that a conspiracy was hatched to bring the queen to the scaffold'. But the evidence produced against Catherine is so clear that they have been obliged to alter their tone. Catholicism assuredly has had its virtuous princesses in abundance, but it must be acknowledged that she who became its patroness in England in 1541 did not do it much honour.

The elevation of Catherine Howard to the throne had been followed by an elevation of Catholicism in England; and the fall of this unhappy woman was followed by a depression of the party to which she belonged. This is our reason for dwelling on her history. These last events appear to have given offence at Rome. Pope Paul III displayed more irritation than ever against Henry VIII. One of the king's ambassadors at Venice wrote to him at this time: 'The Bishop of Rome is earnestly at work to bring about a union of the emperor and the King of France for the ruin of Your Majesty.' The zeal and the caution of Cranmer in the affair of Catherine had greatly increased the king's liking for him. Cranmer, however, was in no haste to take advantage of this to get any bold measures passed in favour of the reformation. He knew that any such attempt would have had a contrary result. But he lost no opportunity of diffusing in England the principles of the reformation.

The convocation of the clergy met on 20 January. On Friday, 17 February, the translation of the Holy Scriptures was on the order of the day. The suppression of the English Bible was desired by the majority of the bishops, most of all by Gardiner, who, since the fall of Catherine Howard, felt more than ever the necessity of resisting reformation. As he was unable to re-establish at once the Vulgate as a whole, he endeavoured to retain what he could of it in the translation, so that the people might not understand what they read and might abandon it altogether. He proposed therefore to keep in the English translation one hundred and two Latin words 'for the sake of their native meaning and their dignity'. Among these words were *Ecclesia, pœnitentia, pontifex, holocaustum, simulacrum, episcopus, confessio, hostia,* and others. In addition to the design which he entertained of preventing the people from understanding what they read, he had still another in regard to such as might understand any part of it. If he was desirous of retaining certain words, this was for the purpose of retaining certain dogmas. 'Witness', says Fuller, 'the word *penance,* which according to *vulgar sound,* contrary to the *original sense* thereof, was a *magazine of will-worship,* and brought in much *gain* to the *priests* who were desirous to *keep* that *word,* because that *word kept them.*'[1] Cranmer gave the king warning of the matter;

---

[1] Fuller, *Church History* (1655), Book v, p. 239.

and it was agreed that the bishops should have nothing to do with the translation of the Bible. On 10 March the archbishop informed convocation that it was the king's intention to have the translation examined by the universities of Oxford and Cambridge. The bishops were greatly annoyed; but Cranmer assured them that the king's determination was to be carried out. All the prelates but two protested against this course. This decree, however, had no other object than to get rid of the bishops, for the universities were never consulted. This was obviously a blow struck at the convocation of the clergy.

The change which resulted from the disgrace of the Howards was apparent even in the case of the enemies of the reformation. Bonner, Bishop of London, a man at once violent and fickle, who after the death of Cromwell had suddenly turned against the reformation, after the death of Catherine made a show of turning in the contrary direction. He published various admonitions and injunctions for the guidance of his diocese. 'It is very expedient', he said to the laity, 'that whosoever repaireth hither [to the church] to read this book, or any such like, in any other place, he prepare himself chiefly and principally with all devotion, humility, and quietness to be edified and made the better thereby.' To the clergy he said: 'Every parson, vicar, and curate shall read over and diligently study every week one chapter of the Bible ... proceeding from chapter to chapter, from the beginning of the Gospel of Matthew, to the end of the New Testament. ... You are to instruct, teach, and bring up in learning the best ye can all such children of your parishioners as shall come to you for the same; or at the least to teach them to read English ... so that they may thereby the better learn and know how to believe, how to pray, how to live to God's pleasure.'

CHAPTER EIGHT

Cranmer Pursues His Task

(1542)

The principles of the reformation were spreading more and more, and especially among the London merchants; doubtless because they held more intercourse than other classes with foreigners. These men of business were much better informed than we in our days would suppose. One of them, Richard Hilles, had large business transactions with Strasburg and the rest of Germany; and while engaged in these he paid some attention to theological literature. He not merely read, but formed an opinion of the works which he read, and was thus at the same time merchant and critic. He read the *Ecclesiastical History* of Eusebius, as well as his *Preparation* and *Demonstration;* but he was not satisfied with *Eusebius.* He found in his writings false notions on free will and on the marriage of ministers. On the other hand he was exceedingly pleased with this author's comments on Daniel's seventy weeks. Tertullian charmed him by his simplicity, his piety, and likewise by the soundness of his judgment on the Eucharist; but he found much fault with his work on *Prescriptions against Heretics.*[1] Cyprian edified him by the fulness of his piety; but he was shocked by his overmuch severity, and by his opinions on satisfaction, which in his view were derogatory to the righteousness of Christ. Lactantius he loved as the defender of the cause of God; but he sharply criticized his opinions on the virtue of almsgiving, on the necessity of abstinence from the use of flowers and perfumes, on the method of making up for evil works by good ones, on the millennium, and many other subjects. Origen, Augustine, and

[1] Letter from Hilles to Bullinger, of 18 December 1542, the date of Catherine's trial. – *Original Letters Relative to the English Reformation* (Parker Society), i, pp. 228, 229.

Jerome were also included in the cycle of his studious labours.[1] Hilles considered it a great loss, even to a merchant, to pursue no studies. He found in them a remedy against the too strong influences of worldly affairs.

For him, however, the essential matter was the study of the word of God. He used frequently to read and expound it in the houses of evangelical Christians in London. Bishop Gardiner, when examining one of Hilles' neighbours, said to him: 'Has not Richard Hilles been every day in your house, teaching you and others like you, and poisoning my flock?' Some ecclesiastics one day called upon him, while making a collection for placing tapers before the crucifix and the sepulchre of Christ in the parish church. He refused to contribute. The priests entreated his kinsmen and friends to urge him not to set himself against a practice which had existed for five centuries. No custom, said he, can prevail against the word of Christ – *They that worship him must worship him in spirit and in truth.* The priests now increased their threatenings, and Hilles left London and went to Strasburg, keeping up at the same time his house of business in London. The reader of Tertullian, Cyprian, Origen, and Augustine, on leaving the banks of the Rhine, went to Frankfurt and to Nüremberg to sell his cloth. Moreover he made a good use of the money which he received. 'I send herewith to your piety', he wrote to Bullinger, 'ten Italian crowns, which I desire to be laid out according to your pleasure, as occasion may offer, upon the poor exiles (rich, however, in Christ), and those especially, if such there be, who are in distress among you.'

While laymen thus joined knowledge with faith, and business with teaching, Cranmer was slowly pursuing his task. When Parliament met, 22 January 1543, the archbishop introduced *a bill for the advancement of true religion.* This act at once prohibited and enjoined the reading of the Bible. Was this intentional or accidental? We are disposed to think it accidental. There were two currents of opinion in England, and both of them reappeared in the laws. Only it is to be noted that the better current was the stronger; it was the good cause which seemed ultimately to gain the ascendancy on this occasion. It was ordered that the Bibles

[1] *Original Letters Relative to the English Reformation*, pp. 234-5.

bearing Tyndale's name should be suppressed; but the printers still issued his translation with hardly any alteration, shielding it under the names of Matthew, Taverner, Cranmer, and even Tunstall and Heath. It was therefore read everywhere. The act forbade that anyone should read the Bible to others, either in any church or elsewhere, without the sanction of the king or of some bishop. But at the same time the chancellor of England, officers of the army, the king's judges, the magistrates of any town or borough, and the Speaker of the House of Commons, who were accustomed to take a passage of Scripture as the text of their discourses, were empowered to read it. Further, every person of noble rank, male or female, being head of a family, was permitted to read the Bible or to cause it to be read by one of their domestics, in their own house, their garden or orchard, to their own family. Likewise, every trader or other person being head of a household was allowed to read it in private; but apprentices, work people, and such like, were to abstain. This enactment, thus interdicting the Bible to the common people, was both impious and absurd; impious in its prohibition, but also absurd, because reading in the family was recommended, and this might be done even by the domestics. The knowledge of the Scriptures might thus reach those to whom they were proscribed.

At the same time, on the demand of Cranmer, the act of Six Articles was somewhat modified. Those who had infringed its clauses were no longer to be punished with death, if they were laymen; and priests were to incur this penalty only after the third offence. This was certainly no great gain, but the primate obtained what he could.

He also endeavoured to render as harmless as possible the book, *The Necessary Doctrine and Erudition of Any Christian Man,* which was published in 1543, and was called *The King's Book,* to distinguish it from *The Institution of a Christian Man* of 1537, which was called *The Bishops' Book.* This book of the king held a middle course between the doctrine of the pope and that of the reformation, leaning, however, towards the latter. The grace and the mercy of God were established as the principle of our justification. Some reforms were introduced with respect to the worship of images and of the saints; the article on purgatory was omitted; large rights were granted to the church of every country; the vulgar tongue was recognized as necessary to meet the religious wants of the people. Still, many obscurities and errors were to be found in this book.

An event was approaching which would draw the king more decisively to the side of the reformation. Although he had now made five successive marriages, and had experienced, undoubtedly by his own fault, only a long series of disappointments and vexations, he was once more looking for a wife. A law which had been passed after the discovery of the misconduct of Catherine Howard terrified the maidens of England, even the most innocent among them; they would have been afraid of falling victims to the unjust suspicions of Henry VIII. The new law stated that any unchaste woman marrying a king of England without informing him of her unchastity would be guilty of high treason. Henry now determined to marry a widow.

Catherine Parr, a lady of some thirty years of age, already twice widowed, was now at the court. She was a woman of good sense, of virtuous and amiable character, beautiful, and agreeable in manners. But she was wanting in that human prudence, so necessary at the court, and particularly to the wife of Henry VIII; and hereby she was exposed to great danger. The king was now in a declining state; and his bodily infirmities as well as his irritable temper made it a necessity that some gentle and very considerate wife should take care of him. He married the noble dowager on 12 July 1543; and he found in her the affection and the kind attentions of a virtuous lady. The crown was to Catherine but a poor compensation; but she discharged her duty devotedly, and shed some rays of sunshine over the last years of the king. The queen was favourable to the reformation, as was likewise her brother, who was created Earl of Essex, and her uncle, made Lord Parr of Horton. Cranmer and all those who wished for a real reformation were on the side of the new queen; while Gardiner and his party, including the new chancellor, Wriothesley (now created baron), taking alarm at this influence which was opposed to them, became more zealous than ever in the maintenance of the old doctrine. These men felt that the power which they had possessed under Catherine Howard might slip out of their hands; and they resolved to spread terror among the friends of the reformation, not excepting the queen herself, by attacking Cranmer. It was always this man at whom they aimed and struck their blows, nor was this the last time they did so.

The prebendaries of Canterbury and other priests of the same diocese, strongly attached to the Catholic doctrine, and disquieted and shocked by the reforming principles of the archbishop, came to an under-standing with Gardiner, held a great many meetings among themselves, and collected a large number of reports hostile to the archbishop. They accused him of having removed images and prohibited the partisans of the old doctrines from preaching; and the rumour was soon everywhere current that 'the Bishop of Winchester had bent his bow to shoot at some of the head deer'. The long list of charges brought against the primate was forwarded to the king. Amongst the accusers were found some members of Cranmer's church, magistrates whom he had laid under obligation to him, and men who almost daily sat at his table. Henry was pained and irritated; he loved Cranmer, but these numerous accusations disturbed him. Taking the document with him, he went out, as if going to take a walk alone on the banks of the Thames. He entered his bark. 'To Lambeth', he said to his boatmen. Some of the domestics of the archbishop saw the boat approaching: they recognized the king, and gave information to their master, who immediately came down to pay his respects to His Majesty. Henry invited him to enter the bark; and when they were seated together, the boatmen being at a distance, the king began to lament the growth of heresy, and the debates which would inevitably result from it, and declared that he was determined to find out who was the principal promoter of these false doctrines and to make an example of him. 'What think you of it?' he added. 'Sir', replied Cranmer, 'it is a good resolution; but I entreat you to consider well what heresy is, and not to condemn those as heretics who stand for the word of God against human inventions.' After further explanations, the king said to him: 'You are the man who, as I am informed, is the chief encourager of heresy.' The king then handed to him the articles of accusation collected by his opponents. Cranmer took the papers and read them. When he had finished, he begged the king to appoint a commission to investigate these grievances, and frankly explained to him his own view of the case. The king, touched by his simplicity and candour, disclosed to him the conspiracy, and promised to nominate a commission; insisting, however, that the primate should be the chief member and that he should proceed against his accusers. Cranmer refused to do this. The commission was nominated, but as some of its members secretly favoured the cause of Cranmer's opponents, it made little progress during the six long weeks of its sittings. At this point the king's favourite physician, and an influential gentleman of the chamber intervened. In consequence, Sir (Dr) Thomas Legh, a layman of York, who had acquired a reputation for energy and thoroughness during the visitation of the monasteries was introduced into the commission. He made diligent inquiry, and found that men to whom Cranmer had rendered great services were in the number of the conspirators. Cranmer bore himself with great meekness towards them. He declined to confound and put them to shame as the king had required him to do; and the result was that, instead of condemning Cranmer, every one of them acknowledged that he was the first to practise the virtues which he preached to others, and thus showed himself to be a true bishop and a worthy reformer.

As Gardiner and his colleagues had failed in their attempt to bring down the head deer, they determined to indemnify themselves by attacking lesser game. A society of friends of the gospel had been formed at Oxford, the members of which were leading lowly and quiet lives, but at the same time were making courageous confession of the truth. Fourteen of them were apprehended by Dr London, supported by the Bishop of Winchester. The persecutors chiefly directed their attack against three of these men. Robert Testwood, famed for his musical attainments and attached as a 'singing man' to the chapel of Windsor College, used to speak with respect of Luther, ventured to read the Holy Scriptures, and exhorted his acquaintances not to bow down before dumb images, but to worship only the true and living God. Henry Filmer, a church-warden, could not endure the fooleries which the priests retailed in the pulpit; and the latter, greatly stung by his criticism, accused him of being so thoroughly corrupted by heresy that he alone would suffice to poison the whole nation. Antony Peerson, a priest, preached with so much faith and eloquence, that the people flocked in crowds to hear him, both at Oxford and in the surrounding country places.

A fourth culprit at length appeared before the council. He was a poor man, simple-minded, and of mean appearance. Some loose sheets of a book lay upon the table in front of the Bishop of Winchester. 'John Marbeck', said the bishop, 'dost thou know wherefore thou art sent for?' 'No, my lord', he replied. The bishop, taking up some of the sheets said to him: 'Understandest thou the Latin tongue?' 'No, my lord', he answered, 'but simply.' Gardiner then stated to the council that the book he held in his hand was a concordance, and that it was translated word for word from the original compiled for the use of preachers. He asserted 'that if such a book should go forth in English, it would destroy the Latin tongue'. Two days later Gardiner again sent for Marbeck. 'Marbeck', said the bishop, 'what a devil made thee to meddle with the Scriptures?[1] Thy vocation was another way ... why the devil didst thou not hold thee there? ... What helpers hadst thou in setting forth thy book?' 'Forsooth, my lord', answered Marbeck, 'none.' 'It is not possible that thou should'st do it without help', exclaimed the bishop. Then addressing one of his chaplains: 'Here is a marvellous thing; this fellow hath taken upon him to set out the concordance in English, which book, when it was set out in Latin, was not done without the help and diligence of a dozen learned men at least, and yet will he bear me in hand that he hath done it alone.' Then, addressing Marbeck, he said: 'Say what thou wilt, except God himself would come down from heaven and tell me so, I will not believe it.' Marbeck was taken back to prison, and was placed in close confinement, with irons on his hands and feet. He was five times examined; and on the fifth occasion a new charge was brought against him; he had written out with his own hand a letter of John Calvin. This was worse than spending his time over the Bible.

Gardiner exerted himself to the utmost to secure the condemnation of this man to death, in company with Testwood, Filmer, and Peerson. His efforts met with success. These three Christians were burnt alive; and they met death with so much humility, patience, and devotion to Jesus, their only refuge, that some of the bystanders declared that they would willingly have died with them and like them. But the persecutors

[1] Foxe, who relates these circumstances, adds in a note, 'Christ saith – Search the Scriptures; and Winchester saith – The devil makes men to meddle with the Scriptures.' *Acts,* v, p. 478.

failed in their attempt with respect to Marbeck. Cranmer was able to convince the king that the making of a concordance to the Bible ought not to be visited with death. It is well known that Henry VIII attached much importance to the Holy Scriptures, which he considered the most powerful weapon against the pope. Marbeck, therefore, was spared.

It is, moreover, no wonder that there should still have been martyrs. The queen, indeed, was friendly to their cause; but political circumstances were not favourable. After forty years' intermittent friendship with France, Henry VIII was about to declare war against that kingdom. The pretexts for this course were many. The first was the alliance of the King of France with the Turks, 'who are daily advancing to destroy and ruin our holy faith and religion, to the great regret of all good Christians', said the Privy Council. A second pretext was that the sums of money which France was bound to pay annually to the king had fallen into arrears for nine years; there was also the question of the subsidies granted by France to Scotland during the war between Henry VIII and the Scots in 1542; the reception and protection of English rebels by Francis I; and the detention in French ports of faithful subjects of the king, merchants and others, with their ships and merchandise. In the despatch which we have just cited, the king also declared that, if within twenty days the grievances set forth were not redressed, he should claim the kingdom of France unjustly held by Francis I. The French ambassador replied in a conciliatory manner. Diplomacy made no reference to other grounds of complaint of a more private character, which perhaps throw light upon those which occasioned the rupture. Francis I had jested about the way in which Henry VIII dealt with his wives. Henry had sought the hand of French princesses, and they had no mind for this foreign husband; and lastly, Francis did not fulfil the promise which he had made to separate from Rome. There were many other pretexts besides, more or less reasonable, which determined the king to invade France.

While withdrawing from alliance with Francis I, Henry could not but at the same time enter into closer relation with Charles V. This reconciliation seemed natural, for the King of England was really, in respect to religion, more in harmony with the emperor than with the Protestants of Germany, whose alliance he had for some time desired.

But Charles required first of all that the legitimacy and the rights of his cousin, the Princess Mary, should be acknowledged; and this Henry refused to do, because it would have involved an acknowledgment of his injustice to Catherine of Aragon. A solution which satisfied the emperor was ultimately devised. It was provided by act of Parliament that if Prince Edward should die without children, 'the crown should go to the Lady Mary'.[1] But in this act no mention was made of her legitimacy. The result of the concession of this point to Charles V was to bring on England a five years' bloody persecution, and to give her people Philip II of Spain for their king. In default of any issue of Mary, Elizabeth was to succeed to the throne. This matter being arranged, the emperor Charles V and Henry concluded a treaty of alliance in February 1543, agreeing to attack France jointly within the next two years.

The war which Henry VIII, 'King of England, *France,* and Ireland', said the Parliament, now carried on against Francis I has little to do with the history of the reformation. The king, having named the queen regent of his kingdom, embarked for Calais on 14 July 1544, on a vessel hung with cloth of gold. He was now feeble and corpulent and he suffered from an open ulcer in his leg, but his vanity and love of display were always conspicuous, even when setting out for a war. He arrived on the frontier of France at the head of a considerable force, but he himself did not take active control. The emperor, who had got the start of him, was already within two days' march of Paris; and the city was in alarm at the approach of the Germans. 'I cannot prevent my people of Paris from being afraid', said Francis, 'but I will prevent them from suffering injury.' Charles paid little respect to his engagement with Henry VIII, and now treated separately with Francis at Crépy, near Laon, 19 September, and left the King of England to get out of the affair as well as he could. Henry captured Boulogne, but this was all that he had of his kingdom of France. On 30 September he returned to London.

The war, however, continued until 1546. England, abandoned by the emperor, found sympathy in a quarter where it might least have been expected – in Italy. Some of the Italians, who were conscious of the evils brought on their own land by the papacy, were filled with admiration for

[1] Act of Succession, 35 Henry VIII, c. 1.

the prince and the nation which had cast off its yoke. Edmund Harvel, ambassador of Henry VIII in Italy, being at this time at Venice, was continually receiving visits from captains of high reputation, who came to offer their services. Among these was Ercole Visconti of Milan, a man of high birth, a great captain, and one who, having extensive connections in Italy, might render great service to the king. The French were now making an attempt to retake Boulogne; but the Italian soldiers who were serving in their army were constantly going over to the English, at the rate of thirty per day. The Italian companies were thus so largely reduced that the captains requested permission to leave the camp for want of soldiers to command; and permission was given them. In this matter the pope was involved in difficulty. He had undertaken to furnish Francis I with a body of 4,000 men; but as the king was afraid that these Roman soldiers would pass over to the English army, he requested Paul III to substitute for these auxiliaries a monthly subsidy of 16,000 crowns. 'As the Italian nation', added the English ambassador optimistically in his letter to Henry VIII, 'is alienate from the French king, so the same is more and more inclined to Your Majesty.'

But if in Italy there were many supporters of Protestantism, in England its opponents were still more numerous. The fanatical party had attempted in 1543 to expel the reformed party from the town of Windsor by means of martyrdom. But the account was not settled; it still remained to purify the castle. It was known that Testwood, Filmer, Peerson, and Marbeck himself had had patrons in Sir Thomas and Lady Cardine, Sir Philip and Lady Hobby, Dr Haynes, Dean of Exeter, and other persons at the court. Dr London, who was always on the look-out for heretics, and a pleader named Simons, sent to Gardiner one Robert Ockam, a secretary, with letters, accusations, and secret documents as to the way in which they intended to proceed. But one of the queen's servants reached the court before him and gave notice of the scheme. Ockam, on his arrival, was arrested, all the papers were examined, and evidence was discovered in them of an actual conspiracy against many persons at the court. This aroused great indignation in the king's mind. It is highly probable that these gentlemen and their wives owed their safety to the influence of the queen and of Cranmer. London and

Simons, unaware that their letters and documents had fallen into the hands of their judges, denied the plot, and this even upon oath. Their own writings were now produced, it was proved that they were guilty of perjury, and they were condemned to ignominious punishment. London, that great slayer of heretics, and his colleague were conducted on horseback, facing backwards, with the name of perjurer on their foreheads, through the streets of Windsor, Reading, and Newbury, the king being now at the last-named town. They were afterwards set in the pillory, and then taken back to prison. London died there of distress caused by this public disgrace. It was well that the wind should change, and that persecutors should be punished instead of the persecuted; but the manners of the time subjected these wretches to shocking sufferings which it would have been better to spare them.

CHAPTER NINE

The Last Martyrs of Henry's Reign

(1545)

Henry VIII, sick and fretful, was easily drawn first to one side, then to the other. He was a victim of indecision, of violent excitement, and of irresolution. His brother-in-law, the Duke of Suffolk, who of all the members of the Privy Council was the most determined supporter of the reformation, had died in August 1545, and that body was thenceforward impelled in an opposite direction, and carried the king along with it.

Shaxton, having resigned his see of Salisbury after the publication of the Six Articles, had been put in prison, and had long rejected all proposals of recantation addressed to him. Having aggravated his offence while in prison by asserting that the natural body of Christ was not in the sacrament, he was condemned to be burnt. The bishops of London and Worcester, sent by the king, visited him in the prison and strove to convince him. This weak unfortunate man readily professed himself persuaded, and thanked the king 'for that he had delivered him at the same time from the temporal and from the everlasting fire'. On 13 July 1546, he was set at liberty. As he grew old his understanding became still weaker; and in Mary's reign the unhappy man was one of the most eager to burn those whom he had called his brethren.

While there were men like Shaxton, whose fall was decisive and final, others were to be met with who, although in their own hearts decided for the truth, were alarmed when they found themselves in danger of death, and subscribed the Catholic declarations which were offered to them. But after having thus plunged into the abyss, they lifted up their heads as soon as possible and again confessed the truth. One of this class was Dr Edward Crome, who, at this period, gave way on two occasions, but recovered himself.

Many other blemishes were visible in the general state of the Anglican Church; and the obstinacy of the king, in particular, in maintaining in his kingdom, side by side, two things in opposition to each other, the Catholic doctrines and the reading of the Bible, subjected the sacred volume to strange honours. The king in person prorogued the Parliament on 24 December, and on this occasion made his last speech to the highest body in the state. He spoke as *vicar of God,* and gave a lecture to the ministers and the members of the church. It was his taste; he believed that he was born for this position, and there was in his nature as much of the preceptor as of the king. Moreover, there was nothing which offended him so much as the attempt to address a lecture to himself. Anyone who did so risked his own life. But while he was easily hurt, he did not shrink from hurting the feelings of others. He handled the rod more easily than the sceptre. The Speaker of the House of Commons having delivered an address to the king in which he extolled his virtues, Henry replied as follows: 'Whereas you … have both praised and extolled me for the notable qualities you have conceived to be in me, I most heartily thank you all that you put me in remembrance of my duty, which is to endeavour myself to obtain and get such excellent qualities and necessary virtues. … No prince in the world more favoureth his subjects than I do you, nor any subjects or commons more love and obey their sovereign lord than I perceive you do me. Yet, although I with you, and you with me, be in this perfect love and concord, this friendly amity cannot continue except you, my lords temporal, and you, my lords spiritual, and you, my loving subjects, study and take pains to amend one thing, which is surely amiss and far out of order, … which is, that charity and concord is not among you; but discord and dissension beareth rule in every place. St Paul saith to the Corinthians, in the thirteenth chapter, "Charity is gentle, charity is not envious, charity is not proud", and so forth. Behold then what love and charity is amongst you when one calleth the other heretic and anabaptist; and he calleth him again papist, hypocrite, and Pharisee. Be these things tokens of charity amongst you? Are these the signs of fraternal love between you? No, no, I assure you that this lack of charity amongst yourselves will be the hindrance and assuaging of the fervent love between us, except this wound be salved and clearly made whole. I must needs judge the fault and occasion of this discord to be partly by the negligence of you, the fathers and preachers of the spiritualty. ... I see and hear daily that you of the clergy preach one against another, ... and few or none do preach truly and sincerely the word of God. ... Alas! how can the poor souls live in concord when you preachers sow amongst them, in your sermons, debate and discord? Of you they look for light, and you bring them to darkness. Amend these crimes, I exhort you, and set forth God's word, both by true preaching and good example-giving; or else I, whom God hath appointed his vicar and high minister here, will see these divisions extinct. ... Although (as I say) the spiritual men be in some fault ... yet you of the temporalty be not clean and unspotted of malice and envy; for you rail on bishops, speak slanderously of priests, and rebuke and taunt preachers. ... Although you be permitted to read Holy Scripture, and to have the word of God in your mother-tongue, you must understand that it is licensed you so to do, only to inform your own conscience, and to instruct your children and family; not to dispute and make Scripture a railing and a taunting stock against priests and preachers, as many light persons do. I am very sorry to know and hear how unreverently that most precious jewel, the word of God, is disputed, rhymed, sung, and jangled in every alehouse and tavern, contrary to the true meaning and doctrine of the same. ... Be in charity one with another, ... to the which I, as your supreme head and sovereign lord, exhort and require you; and then I doubt not but that love and league, which I spake of in the beginning, shall never be dissolved or broken between us.'[1]

The schoolmaster had not spoken amiss. The Parliament did not make the retort, 'Physician, heal thyself', though it might have been applicable. One of the measures by which the king manifested his *sweet charity* proves that, if he were not, like some old schoolmasters, a tyrant of words and syllables, he tyrannized over the peace and the lives of his people.

---

[1] Foxe, *Acts*, v, p. 534.

There were at the court a certain number of ladies of the highest rank who loved the gospel – the Duchess of Suffolk, the Countess of Sussex, the Countess of Hertford, Lady Denny, Lady Fitzwilliam, and above all the queen. Associated with these was a pious, lively, and beautiful young lady, of great intelligence and amiable disposition, whose fine qualities had been improved by education. Her name was Anne Askew.[1] She was the second daughter of Sir William Askew, member of a very ancient Lincolnshire family. She had two brothers and two sisters. Her brother Edward was a member of the king's bodyguard. The queen frequently received Anne and other Christian women in her private apartments; and there prayer was made and the word of God expounded by an evangelical minister. The king, indeed, was aware of these secret meetings, but he feigned ignorance. Anne was at this time in great need of the consolations of the gospel. Her father, Sir William, had a rich neighbour named Thomas Kyme, with whom he was intimate; and being anxious that his eldest daughter, Martha, should marry a rich man, he arranged with Kyme that she should wed his eldest son. The young lady died before the nuptials took place; and Sir William, reluctant to let slip so good a chance, compelled his second daughter Anne to marry the betrothed of her sister, and by him she became the mother of two children. The Holy Scriptures in the English version attracted Anne's attention, and ere long she became so attached to them that she meditated on them day and night. Led by them to a living faith in Jesus Christ, she renounced Romish superstitions. The priests, who were greatly annoyed, stirred up her young husband against her: being a rough man and a staunch papist, he 'violently drove her out of his house'. Anne said, 'Since, according to the Scripture, *if the unbelieving depart, let him depart. A brother or a sister is not under bondage in such cases* – I claim my divorce.' She went to London to take the necessary proceedings; and either through her brother, or otherwise, made the acquaintance of the pious ladies of the court and of the queen herself.

It was a great vexation to the enemies of the reformation to see persons of the highest rank almost openly professing the evangelical faith. As they did not dare to attack them, they determined to make

[1] [Sometimes spelt 'Ascue.']

a beginning with Anne Askew, and thereby to terrify the rest. She had said one day, 'I would sooner read five lines in the Bible than hear five masses in the church.' On another occasion she had denied the corporeal presence of the Saviour in the sacrament. She was sent to prison. When she was taken to Sadler's Hall, the judge, Christopher Dare, asked her, 'Do you not believe that the sacrament hanging over the altar is the very body of Christ really?' Anne replied, 'Wherefore was St Stephen stoned to death?' Dare, doubtless, remembered that Stephen had said, 'I see the Son of Man sitting *at the right hand of God.*' From this it followed that he was not in the sacrament. He preferred to answer, 'I cannot tell.' It is possible, however, that his ignorance was not feigned. 'No more', said Anne, 'will I solve your vain question.' Anne was afterwards taken before the lord mayor, Sir Martin Bowes, a passionate bigot. He was Under-Treasurer of the Mint, and in 1550 obtained the king's pardon for all the false money which he had coined. The magistrate gravely asked her whether a mouse, eating the host, received God or no? 'I made no answer, but smiled', says Anne. The bishop's chancellor, who was present, sharply said to her, 'St Paul forbade women to speak or to talk of the word of God.' 'How many women', said she in reply, 'have you seen go into the pulpit and preach?' 'Never any', he said. 'You ought not to find fault in poor women, except they have offended the law.' She was unlawfully committed to prison, and for eleven days no one was allowed to see her. At this time she was about twenty-five years of age.

One of her cousins, named Brittayne, was admitted to see her. He immediately did everything he could to get Anne released on bail. The lord mayor bade him apply to the chancellor of the Bishop of London. The chancellor replied to him, 'Apply to the bishop.' The bishop said, 'I will give order for her to appear before me tomorrow at three o'clock in the afternoon.' He then subjected her to a long examination. He asked her, amongst other things, 'Do you not think that private masses help the souls departed?' 'It is great idolatry', she replied, 'to believe more in private masses than in the healthsome death of the dear Son of God.' 'What kind of answer is this?' said the Bishop of London. 'It is a mean one', replied Anne, 'but good enough for your question.' After the examination, at which Anne made clear and brief replies, Bonner wrote down a certain number of articles of faith, and required that Anne should set her hand to them. She wrote, 'I believe so much thereof as the Holy Scripture doth agree unto.' This was not what Bonner wanted. The bishop pressed the point, and said, 'Sign this document.' Anne then wrote, 'I, Anne Askew, do believe all manner of things contained in the faith of the catholic church.' The bishop, well knowing what Anne meant by this word, hurried away into an adjoining room in a great rage. Her cousin Brittayne followed him and implored him to treat his kinswoman kindly. 'She is a woman', exclaimed the bishop, 'and I am nothing deceived in her.' 'Take her as a woman', said Brittayne, 'and do not set her weak woman's wit to your lordship's great wisdom.' At length, Anne's two sureties, to wit, Brittayne and Master Spilman of Grays Inn, were on the following day accepted, and she was set at liberty. These events took place in the year 1545.

Anne having continued to profess the gospel and to have meetings with her friends, she was again arrested three months later, and was brought before the Privy Council at Greenwich. On the opening of the examination she refused to go into the matter before the council, and said, 'If it be the king's pleasure to hear me, I will show him the truth.' 'It is not meet', they replied, 'for the king to be troubled with you.' She answered, 'Solomon was reckoned the wisest king that ever lived, yet misliked he not to hear two poor common women; much more His Grace a single woman and his faithful subject.' 'Tell me your opinion on the sacrament', said the Lord Chancellor. 'I believe', she said, 'that so oft as I, in a Christian congregation, do receive the bread in remembrance of Christ's death, and with thanksgiving ... I receive therewith the fruits also of his most glorious passion.' 'Make a direct answer to the question', said Gardiner. 'I will not sing a new song of the Lord', she said, 'in a strange land.' 'You speak in parables', said Gardiner. 'It is best for you', she answered; 'for if I show the open truth, ye will not accept it.' 'You are a parrot', said the incensed bishop. She replied, 'I am ready to suffer all things at your hands, not only your rebukes, but all that shall follow besides, yea, and all that gladly.'

The next day Anne once more appeared before the council. They began the examination on the subject of transubstantiation. Seeing

Lord Parr, uncle to the queen, and Lord Lisle, she said to them, 'It is a great shame for you to counsel contrary to your knowledge.' 'We would gladly', they answered, 'all things were well.' Gardiner wished to speak privately with her, but this she refused. Wriothesley, the Lord Chancellor, then began to examine her again. 'How long', said Anne, 'will you halt on both sides?' 'Where do you find that saying?' said he. 'In the Scripture', replied Anne. 'You shall be burnt', said the Bishop of London. She replied, 'I have searched all the Scriptures, yet could I never find that either Christ or his apostles put any creature to death.'

Anne was sent back to prison. She was very ill, and believed herself to be near death. Never had she had to endure such attacks. She requested leave to see Latimer, friend and comforter of evangelicals; but this consolation was not allowed her. Resting firmly, as she did, on scriptural grounds, she did not suffer herself to swerve. To her constitutional resolution she added that which was the fruit of communion with God; and she was thus placed by faith above the attacks which she experienced. Having a good foundation, she resolutely defended the freedom of her conscience and her full trust in Christ; and not only did she encounter her enemies without wavering, but she spoke to them with a power sufficient to awe them, and gave home-thrusts which threw them into confusion. Nevertheless she was only a weak woman, and her bodily strength began to fail. In Newgate she said, 'In all my life afore I was never in such pain. The Lord strengthen us in the truth. Pray, pray, pray.' She composed while in prison some stanzas which have been pronounced extraordinary, not only for simple beauty and sublime sentiment, but also for the noble structure and music of the verse:

> Like as the armèd knight
> Appointed to the field,
> With this world will I fight,
> And faith shall be my shield.

> Faith is that weapon strong
> Which will not fail at need;
> My foes therefore among
> Therewith will I proceed.

I now rejoice in heart,
  And hope bids me do so,
For Christ will take my part,
  And ease me of my woe.

Thou saidst, Lord, whoso knock,
  To him wilt Thou attend;
Undo therefore the lock,
  And Thy strong power send.

More enemies now I have
  Than hairs upon my head,
Let them not me deprave
  But fight Thou in my stead.

On Thee my care I cast,
  For all their cruel spite
I set not by their haste,
  For Thou art my delight.

I am not she that list
  My anchor to let fall
For every drizzling mist;
  My ship's substantial.

Not oft use I to write
  In prose nor yet in rhyme,
Yet will I shew one sight
  That I saw in my time.

I saw a royal throne
  Where justice should have sit,
But in her stead was one
  Of moody cruel wit;

Absorpt was righteousness,
  As by the raging flood;
Satan, in his excess,
  Suck'd up the guiltless blood.

Then thought I, Jesus Lord!
　When Thou shalt judge us all,
Hard is it to record
　On these men what will fall.

Yet, Lord, I Thee desire,
　For that they do to me,
Let them not taste the hire
　Of their iniquity.

By law, Anne had a right to be tried by jury; but on 28 June 1546, she was condemned by the Lord Chancellor and the council, without further process, to be burnt, for having denied the corporeal presence of Christ in the sacrament. 'They would needs know', said Anne, 'whether the bread in the box were God, or no; I said "God is a Spirit and will be worshipped in spirit and truth."' They asked her whether she wished for a priest; she smiled and said she would confess her faults unto God, for she was sure that he would hear her with favour. She added: 'I think his grace shall well perceive me to be weighed in an uneven pair of balances. … Here I take heaven and earth to record that I shall die in mine innocency.'

It was proved that Anne had derived her faith from the Holy Scriptures. Gardiner and his partisans therefore prevailed upon the government, eight days before the death of this young Christian, to draw up a proclamation purporting 'that from henceforth no man, woman, or person of what estate, condition, or degree soever he or they be [consequently including the ladies and gentlemen of the court as well as others], shall, after the last day of August next ensuing, receive, have, take, or keep in their possession the text of the New Testament, of Tyndale's or Coverdale's translation in English, nor any other than is permitted by the act of Parliament; … nor after the said day shall receive, have, take, or keep in his or their possession any manner of books printed or written in the English tongue which be or shall be set forth in the names of Fryth, Tyndale, Wycliffe, … Barnes, Coverdale, … or by any of them; …' and it was required that all such books should be delivered to the mayor, bailiff, or chief constable of the town to be openly burned. (Proclamation of 8 July 1546.)

This was a remarkable proceeding on the part of Henry VIII. But events were stronger than the proclamation, and it remained a dead letter.

Anne's sentence was pronounced before the issue of the proclamation. The trial was over, and there was to be no further inquiry. But her death was not enough to satisfy Rich, Wriothesley, and their friends. They had other designs, and were about to perpetrate the most shameful and cruel acts. The object which these men now proposed to themselves was to obtain such evidence as would warrant them in taking proceedings against those ladies of the court who were friends of the gospel. They went (13 July) to the Tower, where Anne was still confined, and questioned her about her accomplices, naming the duchess dowager of Suffolk, the Countess of Sussex, and several others. Anne answered, 'If I should pronounce anything against them, I should not be able to prove it.' They next asked her whether there were no members of the royal council who gave her their support. She said, none. The king is informed, they replied, that if you choose you can name a great many persons who are members of your sect. She answered that 'the king was as well deceived in that behalf as dissembled with in other matters'. The only effect of these denials was to irritate Wriothesley and his colleague; and, determined at any cost to obtain information against influential persons at the court, they ordered the rack to be applied to the young woman. This torture lasted a long time; but Anne gave no hint, nor even uttered a cry. The Lord Chancellor, more and more provoked, said to Sir Antony Knyvet, lieutenant of the Tower, 'Strain her on the rack again.' The latter refused to do this. It was to no purpose that Wriothesley threatened him if he would not obey. Rich, a member of the Privy Council, had frequently given proof of his baseness. Wriothesley was ambitious, inflated with self-conceit, haughty, and easily angered if his advice was not taken. These two men now forgot themselves; and the spectacle was presented of the Lord Chancellor of England and a privy councillor of the king turned into executioners. They set their own hands to the horrible instrument, and so severely applied the torture to the innocent young woman, that she was almost broken upon it and quite dislocated. She fainted away and was well-nigh dead.[1] 'Then the lieutenant caused me to be loosed; incontinently I swooned, and then they recovered me again. After that I sat two long hours, reasoning with my Lord Chancellor on the bare floor, where he, with many flattering words, persuaded me to leave my opinion. But my Lord God (I thank his everlasting goodness) gave me grace to persevere and will do, I hope, to the very end.' Henry VIII himself censured Wriothesley for his cruelty, and excused the lieutenant of the Tower. 'Then was I brought to a house', says Anne, 'and laid in a bed, with as weary and painful bones as ever had patient Job.' The chancellor sent word to her that if she renounced her faith she would be pardoned and should want for nothing, but that otherwise she should be burnt. She answered, 'I will sooner die than break my faith.' At the same time she fell on her knees in the dungeon and said: 'O Lord, I have more enemies now than there be hairs on my head; yet, Lord, let them never overcome me with vain words, but fight thou, Lord, in my stead, for on thee I cast my care. With all the spite they can imagine, they fall upon me, who am thy poor creature. Yet, sweet Lord, let me not set by them that are against me; for in thee is my whole delight. And Lord, I heartily desire of thee, that thou wilt of thy most merciful goodness forgive them that violence which they do, and have done, unto me. Open also thou their blind hearts, that they may hereafter do that thing in thy sight, which is only acceptable before thee, and to set forth thy verity aright, without all vain fantasies of sinful men. So be it, O Lord, so be it.'[2]

The 16th of July, the day fixed for the last scene of this tragedy, had arrived; everything was ready for the burning of Anne at Smithfield. The execution was to take place not in the morning, the usual time, but at nightfall, to make it the more terrible. It was thus, in every sense, a deed of darkness. They were obliged to carry Anne to the place of execution,

---

[1] 'My Lord Chancellor and Master Rich took pains to rack me in their own hands, *till I was nigh dead.*' Bale's *Works* (Parker Society), p. 224. Foxe, *Acts*, v, p. 547. Burnet also relates the fact and adds some details: 'The Lord Chancellor, throwing off his gown, drew the rack so severely that he almost tore her body asunder.' But Burnet is inclined to doubt the fact. The evidence of Anne Askew is positive. Burnet's doubt means nothing more than a bishop's respect for a Lord Chancellor.

[2] Bale's *Works* (Parker Society), p. 238. Foxe, *Acts*, v, p. 549.

for in her state at that time she was unable to walk. When she reached the pile, she was bound to the post by her waist, with a chain which prevented her from sinking down. The wretched Shaxton, nominated for the purpose, then completed his apostasy by delivering a sermon on the sacrament of the altar, a sermon abounding in errors. He had visited Anne in prison and advised her to recant as he had done. She had replied that it had been better for him if he had never been born. In reply to his sermon, Anne, who was in full possession of her faculties, contented herself with saying, 'He misseth, and speaketh without the book.' Three other evangelical Christians were to die at the same time with her: Nicholas Belenian, a priest of Shropshire; John Lacels (Lascelles), of the king's household, probably the man who had revealed the incontinence of Catherine Howard, a deed for which the Roman party hated him; and one John Adams, a Colchester tailor. 'Now, with quietness', said Lacels, 'I commit the whole world to their pastor and herdsman Jesus Christ, the only Saviour and true Messias.' The letter from which we quote is subscribed, 'John Lacels, late servant to the king, and now I trust to serve the everlasting King, with the testimony of my blood in Smithfield.'

There was an immense gathering of the people. On a platform erected in front of St Bartholomew's Church were seated, as presidents at the execution, Wriothesley, Lord Chancellor of England, the old Duke of Norfolk, the old Earl of Bedford, the lord mayor Sir Martin Bowes, and various other notables. When the fire was about to be lighted, the chancellor sent a messenger to Anne Askew, instructed to offer her the king's pardon if she would recant. She answered, 'I am not come hither to deny my Lord and Master.' The same pardon was offered to the other martyrs, but they refused to accept it and turned away their heads. Then stood up the ignorant and fanatical Bowes, and exclaimed with a loud voice, *'Fiat Justitia'* (Let justice be done). Anne was soon wrapt in the flames; and this noble victim who freely offered herself a sacrifice to God, gave up her soul in peace. Her companions did likewise.[1]

These four persons were the last victims of the reign of Henry VIII. The enemies of the reformation were especially annoyed at this time to see women of the first families of England embrace the faith

---

[1] Foxe, *Acts,* v, pp. 550-52.

which they hated. On a woman of most superior mind, but young and weak, fell the last blow levelled against the gospel by the *defender of the faith*. Anne Askew fell; but the great doctrines which she had so courageously professed were soon to be triumphant in the midst of her fellow countrymen.

CHAPTER TEN

Death Casts Its Shadow over Catherine Parr

(1546)

I t might be asked how it came to pass that the queen did not put a
stop to these cruel executions. The answer is easy – she was herself
in danger. The enemies of the reformation, perceiving her influence
over the king, bethought themselves that the execution of Anne Askew
and of her companions did not advance their cause; that to make it
triumphant the death of the queen was necessary; and that if Catherine
were ruined, the reformation would fall with her. Shortly after the
king's return from France, these men approached him and cautiously
insinuated that the queen had made large use of her liberty during his
absence; that she diligently read and studied the Holy Scriptures; that
she chose to have about her only women who shared her opinions; that
she had engaged certain would-be wise and pious persons to assist her
in attaining a thorough knowledge of the sacred writings; that she held
private conferences with them on spiritual subjects all the year round,
and that 'in Lent every day in the afternoon, for the space of an hour,
one of her said chaplains, in her privy chamber', expounded the word of
God to the queen, to the ladies of her court and of her bedchamber, and
others who were disposed to hear these expositions; that the minister
frequently attacked what he called the abuses of the existing church;
that the queen read heretical books proscribed by royal ordinances;
further, that she, the Queen of England, employed her leisure hours in
translating religious works, and in composing books of devotion; and
that she had turned some of the Psalms into verse, and had made a
collection entitled *Prayers or Meditations*. The king had always ignored
these meetings, determined not to see what was nevertheless clear, that

the queen was an evangelical Christian like Anne Askew who had lately been burnt.

Catherine was encouraged by this consideration on the part of the king. She professed her faith in the gospel unreservedly, and boldly took up the cause of the evangelicals. Her one desire was to make known the truth to the king, and to bring him to the feet of Jesus Christ to find forgiveness for the errors of his life. Without regard to consequences she allowed her overflowing zeal to have free and unrestricted course. She longed to transform not the king alone, but England also. She often exhorted the king 'that as he had, to the glory of God and his eternal fame, begun a good and a godly work in banishing that monstrous idol of Rome, so he would thoroughly perfect and finish the same, cleansing and purging his Church of England clean from the dregs thereof, wherein as yet remained great superstition.'

Was the passionate Henry going to act rigorously towards this queen as he had towards the others? Catherine's blameless conduct, the affection which she testified for him, her respectful bearing, her unwearied endeavour to please him, the attentions which she lavished on him had so much endeared her to him that he allowed her the privilege of being freespoken; and had it not been for the active opposition of its enemies, she might have propagated the gospel throughout the kingdom. As these determined enemies of the reformation were beginning to fear the total ruin of their party, they strove to rekindle the evil inclinations of Henry VIII, and to excite his anger against Catherine. In their view it seemed that the boldness of her opinions must inevitably involve her ruin.

But the matter was more difficult than they thought. The king not only loved his wife, but he also liked discussion, especially on theological subjects; and he had too much confidence in his own cleverness and knowledge to dread the arguments of the queen. The latter therefore continued her petty warfare, and in respectful terms advanced good scriptural proofs in support of her faith. Henry used to smile and take it all in good part, or at least never appeared to be offended. Gardiner, Wriothesley, and others who heard these discussions were alarmed at them. They were almost ready to give up all for lost; and trembling for themselves, they renounced their project. Not one of them ventured to breathe a word against the queen either before the king or in his absence. At length, they found an unexpected auxiliary.

The ulcer burst in the king's leg, and gave him acute pain which constantly increased. Henry had led a sensual life, and had now become so corpulent, that it was exceedingly difficult to move him from one room to another. He insisted that no one should take notice of his failing powers; and those about him hardly dared to speak of the fact in a whisper. His condition made him peevish; he was restless, and thought that his end was not far off. The least thing irritated him; gloomy and passionate, he had frequent fits of rage. To approach and attend to him had become a difficult task; but Catherine, far from avoiding it, was all the more zealous. Since his illness Henry had given up coming into the queen's apartments, but he invited her to come to see him; and she frequently went of her own accord, after dinner, or after supper, or at any other favourable opportunity. The thought that Henry was gradually drawing near to the grave filled her heart with the deepest emotion; and she availed herself of every opportunity of bringing him to a decision in favour of evangelical truth. Her endeavours for this end may sometimes have been made with too much urgency. One evening when Wriothesley and Gardiner, the two leaders of the Catholic party, were with the king, Catherine, who ought to have been on her guard, carried away by the ardour of her faith, endeavoured to prevail upon Henry to undertake the reformation of the church. The king was hurt. His notion that the queen was lecturing him as a pupil in the presence of the Lord Chancellor and the Bishop of Winchester, increased his vexation. He roughly 'brake off that matter and took occasion to enter into other talk'. This he had never before done; and Catherine was surprised and perplexed. Henry, however, did not reproach her, but spoke affectionately, which was certainly on his part the mark of real love. The queen having risen to retire, he said to her as usual, 'Farewell! sweetheart.' Catherine meanwhile was disquieted, and felt that keen distress of mind which seizes upon a refined and susceptible woman when she has acted imprudently.

The chancellor and the bishop remained with the king. Gardiner had observed the king's breaking off the conversation; and he thought, says a contemporary, 'that he must strike while the iron was hot'; that he must take advantage of Henry's ill-humour, and by a skilful effort get rid of Catherine and put an end to her proselytism. It was a beaten track; the king had already in one way or another rid himself of four of his queens, and it would be an easy matter to do as much with a fifth.

Henry furnished them with the wished-for opportunity. Annoyed at having been humiliated in the presence of the two lords, he said to them in an ironical tone: 'A good hearing it is when women become such clerks; and a thing much to my comfort, to come in mine old days to be taught by my wife.' The bishop adroitly availed himself of this opening, and put forth all his powers and all his malice to increase the anger of the king. He urged that it was lamentable that the queen 'should so much forget herself as to take upon her to stand in any argument with His Majesty'; he praised the king to his face 'for his rare virtues, and especially for his learned judgment in matters of religion, above not only princes of that and other ages, but also above doctors professed in theology.' He said 'that it was an unseemly thing for any of His Majesty's subjects to reason and argue with him so malapertly', and that it was 'grievous to him [Gardiner] for his part, and other of His Majesty's counsellors and servants to hear the same'. He added 'that they all by proof knew his wisdom to be such, that it was not needful for any to put him in mind of any such matters; inferring, moreover, how dangerous and perilous a matter it is … for a prince to suffer such insolent words at his subjects' hands, who, as they take boldness to contrary their sovereign in words, so want they no will, but only power and strength, to overthwart him in deeds. Besides this, that the religion by the queen so stiffly maintained did not only disallow and dissolve the policy and politic government of princes, but also taught the people that all things ought to be in common.' The bishop went on to assert that 'whosoever (saving the reverence due to her for His Majesty's sake) should defend the principles maintained by the queen, deserved death.' He did not, however, dare, he said, to speak of the queen, unless he were sure that His Majesty would be his buckler. But with His Majesty's consent his faithful counsellors would soon tear off the hypocritical mask of heresy and would disclose treasons so horrible that His Majesty would no longer cherish a serpent in his own bosom.

The Lord Chancellor spoke in his turn; and the two conspirators did everything they could to stir up the anger of the king against the queen. They filled his head with a variety of tales, both about herself and about some of her lady attendants; they told him that they had been favourable to Anne Askew; that they had in their possession heretical books; and that they were guilty of treason as well as of heresy. Suspicion and distrust, to which the king's disposition was too naturally inclined, took possession of him, and he required his two councillors to ascertain whether any articles of law could be brought forward against the queen, even at the risk of her life. They quitted the king's presence, promising to make very good use of the commission entrusted to them.

The bishop and the chancellor set to work immediately. They resorted to means of every kind – tricks, intrigues, secret correspondence – for the purpose of making out an appearance of guilt on the part of the queen. By bribing some of her domestics they were enabled to get a catalogue of the books which she had in her cabinet. Taking counsel with some of their accomplices, it occurred to them that if they began by attacking the queen, this step would excite almost universal reprobation. They determined, therefore, to prepare men's minds by making a beginning with the ladies who enjoyed her confidence, and particularly with those of her own kindred – Lady Herbert, afterwards Countess of Pembroke, the queen's sister, and first lady of her court; Lady Lane, her cousin-german; and Lady Tyrwhitt, who by her virtues had gained her entire confidence. Their plan was to examine these three ladies on the Six Articles; to institute a rigorous search in their houses with a view to finding some ground of accusation against Queen Catherine; and, in case they should succeed, to arrest the queen herself and carry her off *by night, in a barge,* to the Tower. The further they proceeded with their work of darkness, the more they encouraged and cheered each other on; they considered themselves quite strong enough to strike at once the great blow, and they resolved to make the first attack on the queen. They therefore drew up against her a bill of indictment, which purported especially that she had contravened the Six Articles, had violated the royal proclamation by reading prohibited books, and, in short, had openly maintained heretical doctrine. Nothing was wanting but to get the king's signature to the bill; for if, without the sanction of this signature, they should cast suspicions on the queen, they would expose themselves to a charge of high treason.

Henry VIII was now at Whitehall; and in consequence of the state of his health he very seldom left his private apartments. But few of his councillors, and these only by special order, were allowed to see him. Gardiner and Wriothesley alone came to the palace more frequently than usual to confer with him on the mission which he had entrusted to them. Taking with them their hateful indictment, they went to the palace, were admitted to the king's presence, and after a suitable introduction they laid before him the fatal document, requesting him to sign it. Henry read it, and took careful note of its contents; then asked for writing materials, and notwithstanding his feebleness he signed it. This was a great victory for the bishop, the chancellor, and the Catholic party; and it was a great defeat for the reformation party, apparently the signal for its ruin. Nothing was now wanting but a writ of arrest, and the chancellor of England would send the queen to the Tower. Once there, her situation would be hopeless.

So cleverly had the plot been managed, that during the whole time the queen had neither known nor suspected anything; she paid her usual visits to the king, and had gradually allowed herself to speak to him on religion as she used to do. The king permitted this without gainsaying her; he did not choose to enter into explanations with her. He was, however, ill at ease. The burden was oppressive; and one evening, just after the queen left him, he opened his mind to one of his physicians – his name appears to have been Thomas Wendy – in whom he placed full confidence, and said: 'I do not like the queen's religion, and I do not intend to be much longer worried by the discourses of this *doctoress.*' He likewise revealed to the physician the project formed by some of his councillors, but forbade him, upon pain of death, to say a word about it to any living soul. Apparently forgetting the wives whom he had already sacrificed, Henry was thus coolly preparing, at the very time when he was himself about to go down to the grave, to add another victim to the hecatomb.

The queen, although encompassed with deadly enemies who were contriving her ruin, was in a state of perfect calmness, when suddenly there burst upon her one of those heavy squalls which so unexpectedly dash the most powerful vessels against the rocks. The chancellor, contented with his triumph, but at the same time agitated, snatched up the paper which, now bearing the king's signature, ensured the ruin of the queen. Vehement passions sometimes distract men and produce absence of mind. In this case it appears that Wriothesley carelessly thrust the paper into his bosom, and dropped it while crossing one of the apartments of the palace. A pious woman of the court, happening to pass that way shortly afterwards, saw the paper and picked it up. Perceiving at the first glance its importance she took it immediately to the queen. Catherine opened it, read the articles with fear and trembling, and as soon as she saw Henry's signature, was struck as by a thunderbolt, and fell into a frightful agony. Her features were completely changed: she uttered loud cries, and seemed to be in her death-struggle. She too, then, was to lay down her life on the scaffold. All her attentions, all her devotion to the king had availed nothing; she must undergo the common lot of the wives of Henry VIII. She bewailed her fate, and struggled against it. At other times she had glimpses of her own faults and uttered reproaches against herself, and then her distress and her lamentations increased. Those of her ladies who were present could hardly bear the sight of so woeful a state; and, trembling themselves, and supposing that the queen was about to be put to death, they were unable to offer her consolation. The remembrance of this harrowing scene was never effaced from their minds.[1]

Someone brought word to the king that the queen was in terrible distress, and that her life seemed to be in danger. A feeling of compassion was awakened in him, and he sent to her immediately the physicians who were with him. They, finding Catherine in this extremity, endeavoured to bring her to herself, and gradually she recovered her senses. The physician to whom Henry had revealed Gardiner's project, discovering from some words uttered by the queen that the conspiracy was the cause of her anxiety, requested leave to speak to her in private. He told her that he was risking his life by thus speaking to her, but that his conscience would not allow him to take part in the shedding of innocent blood.

[1] Foxe, *Acts,* v, p. 558.

He therefore confirmed the foreboding of danger which was impending over her; but added that if she henceforward endeavoured to behave with humble submission to His Majesty, she would regain, he did not doubt, his pardon and his favour.

These words were not enough to deliver Catherine from her disquietude. Her danger was not concealed from the king; and, unable to endure the thought that she might die of grief, he had himself carried into her room. At the sight of the king Catherine rallied sufficiently to explain to him the despair into which she was thrown by the belief that he had totally abandoned her. Henry then spoke to her as an affectionate husband, and comforted her with gentle words; and this poor heart, till then agitated like a stormy sea, gradually became calm again.

The king could now forget the faults of the queen; but the queen herself did not forget them. She understood that she had habitually assumed a higher position than belonged to a wife, and that the king was entitled to an assurance that this state of things should be changed. After supper the next evening, therefore, Catherine rose and, taking with her only her sister, Lady Herbert, on whom she leaned, and Lady Jane Grey, who carried a candle before her, went to the king's bedchamber. When the three ladies were introduced, Henry was seated and speaking with several gentlemen who stood round him. He received the queen very courteously, and of his own accord, contrary to his usual practice, began to talk with her about religion, as if there was one point on which he wished for further information from the queen. She replied discreetly and as the circumstances required. She then added meekly and in a serious and respectful tone: 'Your Majesty doth right well know, neither I myself am ignorant, what great imperfection and weakness by our first creation is allotted unto us women, to be ordained and appointed as inferior and subject unto man as our head; from which head all our direction ought to proceed. And that as God made man in his own shape and likeness, whereby he being endued with more special gifts of perfection, might rather be stirred to the contemplation of heavenly things and to the earnest endeavour to obey his commandments, even so also made he woman of man, of whom and by whom she is to be governed, commanded and directed. ... Your Majesty being so excellent in gifts and ornaments of wisdom, and I a silly poor woman, so much inferior in all respects of nature unto you, how then cometh it now to pass that Your Majesty in such diffuse causes of religion will seem to require my judgment? Which when I have uttered and said what I can, yet must I, will I, refer my judgment … to Your Majesty's wisdom, as my only anchor, supreme head and governor here in earth, next under God, to lean unto.' 'Not so' said the king; 'you are become a doctor, Kate, to instruct us (as we take it), and not to be instructed or directed by us.' 'If Your Majesty take it so', replied the queen, 'then hath Your Majesty very much mistaken me, who have ever been of the opinion, to think it very unseemly and preposterous for the woman to take upon her the office of an instructor or teacher to her lord and husband, but rather to learn of her husband and be taught by him. And whereas I have, with Your Majesty's leave, heretofore been bold to hold talk with Your Majesty, wherein sometimes in opinions there hath seemed some difference, I have not done it so much to maintain opinion, as I did it rather to minister talk, not only to the end Your Majesty might with less grief pass over this painful time of your infirmity, being attentive to our talk, and hoping that Your Majesty should reap some ease thereby; but also that I, hearing Your Majesty's learned discourse, might receive to myself some profit thereby; wherein I assure Your Majesty, I have not missed any part of my desire in that behalf, always referring myself in all such matters unto Your Majesty, as by ordinance of nature it is convenient for me to do.' 'And is it even so, sweetheart?' answered the king; 'and tended your arguments to no worse end? Then perfect friends we are now again, as ever at any time heretofore.' Then, as if to seal this promise, Henry, who was sitting in his chair, embraced the queen and kissed her. He added: 'It does me more good at this time to hear the words of your mouth, than if I had heard present news that a hundred thousand pounds in money had fallen unto me.' Lavishing on Catherine tokens of his affection and his happiness, he promised her that such misapprehensions with regard to her should never arise again. Then, resuming general conversation, he talked on various interesting subjects with the queen and with the lords who were present, until the night was advanced; when he gave the signal for their departure. There may possibly have been somewhat of exaggeration in Catherine's words. She had not been altogether so submissive a learner as she said; but she felt the imperative necessity of entirely dispersing the clouds which the ill-will of her enemies had gathered over the king's mind, and it is not to be doubted that in saying what she did she uttered her inmost thought.

Meanwhile, the queen's enemies, who had no suspicion of the turn things were taking, gave their orders and made their preparations for the great work of the morrow, which was to confine Catherine in the Tower. The day was fine, and the king, wishing to take an airing, went in the afternoon into the park, accompanied only by two of the gentlemen of his bedchamber. He sent an invitation to the queen to bear him company; and Catherine immediately arrived, attended by her three favourite ladies in waiting. Conversation began, but they did not talk of theology. Never had the king appeared more amiable; and his good humour inspired the rest with cheerfulness. In his conversation there was all the liveliness of a frank communicative disposition, and the mirth, it seems, was even noisy. Suddenly, forty halberds were seen gleaming through the park trees. The Lord Chancellor was at the head of the men, and forty bodyguards followed him. He was coming to arrest the queen and her three ladies and to conduct them to the Tower. The king, breaking off the conversation which entertained him so pleasantly, glanced sternly at the chancellor, and stepping a little aside called him to him. The chancellor knelt down and addressed to the king, in a low voice, some words which Catherine could not understand. She heard only that Henry replied to him in insulting terms, 'Fool, beast, arrant knave!' At the same time he commanded the chancellor to be gone. Wriothesley and his followers disappeared. Such was the end of the conspiracy formed against the king's Protestant wife by Wriothesley, Gardiner, and their friends. Henry then rejoined the queen. His features still reflected his excitement and anger; but as he approached her he tried to assume an air of serenity. She had not clearly understood what was the subject of conversation between the king and the chancellor; but the king's words had startled her. She received him gracefully and sought to excuse Wriothesley, saying: 'Albeit I know not what just cause Your Majesty has at this time to be offended with him, yet I think that ignorance, not will, was the cause of his error; and so I beseech Your Majesty (if the cause be not very heinous), at my humble suit to take it.' 'Ah, poor soul!' said the king, 'thou little knowest how evil he deserveth this grace at thy hands. On my word, sweetheart, he hath been to thee a very knave.' Says Foxe: 'Thus departed the Lord Chancellor out of the king's presence as he came, with all his train: the whole mould of all his device being utterly broken.'

CHAPTER ELEVEN

The Last Days of Henry VIII

(1546–January 1547)

Weighty consequences followed the miscarriage of the conspiracy formed against the queen. It had been aimed at the queen and the reformation; but it turned against Roman Catholicism and its leaders. The proverb was again fulfilled – *whoso diggeth a pit shall fall therein.* The wind changed; Romanism suffered an eclipse, it was no longer illumined by the sun of royalty. The first to fall into disgrace with Henry VIII was, as we have seen, Wriothesley. The king displayed his coolness in various ways. The chancellor, disquieted and alarmed for his own pecuniary interests, was annoyed to see preparations for establishing a new court of augmentations, by which his privileges and emoluments would be lessened. He earnestly entreated the king that it might not be established in his time. 'I shall have cause', he wrote on 16 October, 'to be sorry in my heart during my life, if the favour of my gracious master shall so fail, that partly in respect of his poor servant he do not somewhat of his clemency temper it. Thus I make an end, praying God long to preserve His Majesty.' In spite of all his efforts, he lost the royal favour, and the new court which he so much dreaded was erected.

A still heavier blow fell upon Gardiner. After the reconciliation between Henry and Catherine, he was obliged to abstain from making his appearance at the court. On 2 December, he wrote to the king: 'I am so bold to molest Your Majesty with these very letters, which be only to desire Your Highness, of your accustomed goodness and clemency, to be my good and gracious lord, and to continue such opinion of me as I have ever trusted and, by manifold benefits, certainly known Your Majesty to have had of me … declare mine inward rejoice of Your Highness' favour, and that I would not willingly offend Your Majesty for no worldly thing.' This man, at other times so strong, now saw before him nothing but disgrace and became excessively fearful. He might be overtaken by a long series of penalties. Who could tell whether Henry, like Ahasuerus of old, would not inflict upon the accuser the fate which he had designed for the accused? The bishop, restless, wrote to Paget, Secretary of State: 'I hear no specialty of the King's Majesty's miscontentment in this matter of lands, but confusedly that my doings should not be well taken.' No answer to either of these two letters is extant. Towards the end of December, the king excluded Gardiner from the number of his executors and from the council of regency under his successor, Edward; and this involved a heavy loss of honour, money, and influence. Henry felt that for the guardianship of his son and of his realm, he must make his choice between Cranmer and Gardiner. Cranmer was selected. It was in vain that Sir Anthony Browne appealed to him, and requested him to reinstate the Bishop of Winchester in this office. 'If he be left among you', said the king, 'he would only sow trouble and division. Do not speak of it.' The conspiracy against the queen was not the sole, although probably it was the determining cause of Gardiner's disgrace.

This, however, was but the beginning of the storm. The first lord of the realm and his family were about to be attacked. If Henry no longer struck to the right, he struck to the left; but he dealt his blows without intermission; in one thing he was ever consistent, cruelty.

In addition to the suffering caused by his disease, the king was oppressed by anxiety at the thought of the ambition and rebellion which might snatch the crown from his son and create disturbances in the kingdom after his death. The court was at this time divided into two parties. One of these was headed by the Duke of Norfolk, who, owing to his position as chief of the ancient family of the Howards, allied even to the blood royal, was next to the king the most influential man in England. He had been Lord Treasurer for twenty-five years, and had rendered signal services to the Crown. Opposed to this party was that of the Seymours, who had not hitherto played any great part, but who now, as uncles to the young prince, found themselves continually advancing in esteem and authority. Norfolk was the chief of the Catholic party; and a great number of evangelical Christians had been burnt while his influence was dominant. His son, Henry, the Earl of Surrey, was likewise attached to the doctrines of the Middle Ages, and was even suspected of having associated in Italy with Cardinal Pole. The Seymours, on the other hand, had always shown themselves friendly to the reformation; and while Norfolk supported Gardiner, they supported Cranmer. It appeared inevitable that, after the king's death, war would break out between these chiefs, and what would happen then? The more Henry's strength declined, the more numerous became the partisans of the Seymours. The sun was rising for the uncles of the young prince, and was setting for Norfolk. The duke, perceiving this, made advances to the Seymours. He would have liked his son to marry the daughter of Edward Seymour, Earl of Hertford, and his daughter, widow of the Duke of Richmond, the natural son of the king, to marry Sir Thomas Seymour, Hertford's brother. But neither Surrey nor the duchess were disposed to the match. There was therefore nothing to expect but a vigorous conflict; and the king chose that the victory of the one party and the defeat of the other should be determined in his lifetime and through his intervention. To which of the two parties would the king give the preference? He had always leaned for support upon Norfolk, and the religious views of this old servant were his own. Would he separate from him at this critical moment? After having from the first resisted the reformation, would he, on the brink of the grave, give it the victory? The past had belonged to Roman Catholicism; should the future belong to the gospel preached by the party of reform? Should his death belie his whole life? The infamous conspiracy formed against the queen by the Catholic party would not have been enough in itself to induce the king to adopt so strange a resolution. A circumstance of another kind occurred to determine his course.

At the beginning of December 1546, Sir Richard Southwell, who had been one of Cromwell's men, and was afterwards a member of the Privy Council under Queen Mary, gave the king a warning that the powerful family of the Howards would expose his son to great danger. Before the birth of Edward, Norfolk had been designated as one of the claimants of the crown. His eldest son was a young man of great intelligence, high spirit, and indomitable courage, and excelled in military exercises. To these qualifications he added the polish of a courtier, fine taste, and an ardent love for the fine arts; his contemporaries were charmed by his poems; and he was looked upon as the flower of the English nobility. These brilliant endowments formed a snare for him. 'His head', people said to the king, 'is filled with ambitious projects.' He had borne the arms of Edward the Confessor in the first quarter, which the king alone had the right to do; if, it was added, he has refused the hand of the daughter of the Earl of Hertford, it is because he aspires to that of the Princess Mary; and if he should marry her after the death of the king, Prince Edward will lose the crown.

The king ordered his chancellor to investigate the charges against the Duke of Norfolk and his son, the Earl of Surrey; and Wriothesley ere long presented to him a paper, in the form of questions, in his (Wriothesley's) own handwriting. The king read it attentively, pen in hand, hardly able to repress his anger, and underlined with a trembling hand those passages which appeared to him the most important. The following sentences are specimens of what he read:

'If a man coming *of the collateral line to the heir of the crown,* who ought not to bear the arms of England but on the second quarter … *do presume* … to bear them in the first quarter, … *how this man's intent is to be judged.* …

'If a man compassing *with himself to govern the realm do actually go about to rule the king,* and should for that purpose advise his daughter or sister to become the king's harlot, thinking thereby to bring it to pass … what this importeth.

'If a man say these words – "If the king die, who should have the rule of the prince but my father or I?" what it importeth.'[1]

On Saturday, 12 December, the duke and the earl were separately arrested and taken to the Tower, one by land, the other by the river, neither of them being aware that the other was suffering the same fate. The king had often shown himself very hasty in a matter of this kind; but in this case he was more so than usual. He had not long to live, and

---

[1] The words underlined by the king are here printed in italics.

he desired that these two great lords should go before him to the grave. The same evening the king sent Sir Richard Southwell, Sir John Gate, and Wymound Carew to Kenninghall, in Norfolk, a principal seat of the family, about ninety miles from London. They travelled as swiftly as they could, and arrived at the mansion by daybreak on Tuesday. They had orders to examine the members of the family, and to affix seals to the effects.

The Howard family, unhappily for itself, was deeply divided. Elizabeth, Duchess of Norfolk, daughter of the Duke of Buckingham, an irritable and passionate woman, had been separated from her husband since 1533, and apparently not without reason. She said of one of the ladies who were in attendance on her, Elizabeth Holland, 'This woman is the cause of all my unhappiness.' There was a certain coolness between the Earl of Surrey and his sister, the Duchess of Richmond, probably because the latter leaned to the side of the reformation. Surrey had also had a quarrel with his father, and he was hardly yet reconciled to him. A house divided against itself will not stand. The members of the family, therefore, accused one another; the duchess, it may be believed, did not spare her husband, and the duke called his son a fool. When Sir Richard Southwell and his two companions arrived at Kenninghall on Tuesday morning, they caused all the doors to be securely closed so that no one might escape; and after having taken some evidence of the almoner, they requested to see the Duchess of Richmond, the only member of the family then at the mansion, and Mistress Elizabeth Holland, who passed for the duke's favourite. These ladies had only just risen from their beds, and were not ready to make their appearance. However, when they heard that the king's envoys requested to see them, they betook themselves as quickly as possible to the dining room. Sir John Gate and his friends informed them that the duke and the earl had just been committed to the Tower. The duchess, deeply moved at this startling news, trembled and almost fainted away. She gradually recovered herself, and kneeling down humbled herself as though she were in the king's presence. She said: 'Although nature constrains me sore to love my father, whom I have ever thought to be a true and faithful subject, and also to desire the well-doing of his son my natural brother, whom I note to be a rash man, yet for my part I would nor will hide or conceal anything from His Majesty's knowledge, specially if it be of weight.' The king's agent searched the house of the Duchess of Richmond, inspected her cabinets and her coffers, but they found nothing tending to compromise her. They found no jewels, for she had parted with her own to pay her debts. Next, they visited Elizabeth Holland's room, where they found much gold, many pearls, rings, and precious stones; and of these they sent a list to the king. They laid aside the books and manuscripts of the duke; and the next day by their direction the Duchess of Richmond and Mistress Holland set out for London, where they were to be examined.

Mistress Holland was examined first. She deposed that the duke had said to her 'that the king was sickly, and could not long endure; and the realm like to be in an ill case through diversity of opinions'. The Duchess of Richmond deposed 'that the duke her father would have had her marry Sir Thomas Seymour, brother to the Earl of Hertford, which her brother also desired, wishing her withal to endear herself so into the king's favour, as she might the better rule here as others had done; and that she refused.' The deposition appears to corroborate one of the charges brought against Norfolk by the chancellor. Nevertheless, the supposition that a father, from ambitious motives, could urge his daughter to consent to incestuous intercourse is so revolting, that one can hardly help asking whether there really was anything more in the case than an exercise of the natural influence of a daughter-in-law over her father-in-law. The duchess corroborated the accusation touching the royal arms borne by Surrey, his hatred of the Seymours, and the ill which he meditated doing them after the king's death; and she added that he had urged her not to carry too far the reading of the Holy Scriptures.

Various other depositions having been taken, the duke and his son were declared guilty of high treason (7 January). On the 13th, Surrey was tried before a jury at Guildhall. He defended himself with much spirit; but he was condemned to death, after a special message from the king had settled the mind of the hesitant jury. This young nobleman, only about thirty years of age, the idol of his countrymen, was executed on Tower Hill. Public feeling was shocked by this act of cruelty, and everyone extolled the high qualities of the earl. His sister, the Duchess of

Richmond, took charge of his five children, and admirably fulfilled her duty as their aunt, appointing as their tutor John Foxe, author of the *Acts and Monuments of the Martyrs*.

The king was now dangerously ill, but he showed no signs of tenderness. People said that he had never hated or ruined anyone by halves; and he was determined, after the death of the eldest son, to sacrifice the father. Norfolk was very much surprised to find himself a prisoner in the Tower, to which he had consigned so many prisoners. He wrote to the lords to let him have some books, for he said that unless he could read he fell asleep. He asked also for a confessor, as he was desirous of receiving his Creator; and for permission to hear mass and to walk outside his apartment in the daytime. At the age of seventy-three, after having taken the lead in the most cruel measures of the reign of Henry VIII, from the death of Anne Boleyn to the death of Anne Askew, he now found that the day of terror was approaching for himself. His heart was agitated, and fear chilled him. He knew the king too well to have any hope that the great and numerous services which he had rendered to him would avail to arrest the sword already suspended over his head. Meanwhile the prospect of death alarmed him; and in his distress he wrote from his prison in the Tower to his royal master: 'Most gracious and merciful sovereign lord, I your most humble subject prostrate at your foot, do most humbly beseech you to be my good and gracious lord. … In all my life I never thought one untrue thought against you or your succession, nor can no more judge or cast in my mind what should be laid to my charge than the child that was born this night. … I know not that I have offended any man … unless it were such as are angry with me for being quick against such as have been accused for sacramentaries.' And fancying that he detected the secret motive of his trial, he added: 'Let me recover your gracious favour, with taking of me all the lands and goods I have, or as much thereof as pleaseth Your Highness.'

The charges brought against Norfolk and Surrey were mere pretexts. No notice having been taken of the letter just cited, the old man, who was anxious by any means to save his life, determined to humble himself still further. On 12 January, nine days before the death of Surrey, in the hope of satisfying the king, he made, in the presence of the members of the

Privy Council, the following confession: 'I, Thomas, Duke of Norfolk do confess and acknowledge myself ... to have offended the King's Most Excellent Majesty, in the disclosing ... of his privy and secret counsel ... to the great peril of His Highness. ... That I have concealed high treason, in keeping secret the false and traitorous act ... committed by my son ... against the King's Majesty ... in the putting and using the arms of Edward the Confessor, ... in his scutcheon or arms. ... Also, that to the peril, slander, and disinherison of the King's Majesty and his noble son, Prince Edward, I have ... borne in the first quarter of my arms ... the arms of England. ... Although I be not worthy to have ... the king's clemency and mercy to be extended to me, ... yet with a most sorrowful and repentant heart do beseech His Highness to have mercy, pity, and compassion on me.'

All was fruitless; Norfolk must die like the best servants and friends of the king, like Fisher, Sir Thomas More, and Cromwell. But the duke, the chief nobleman of the land, could not be tried as was his son. The king assembled the Parliament; a bill of attainder was presented to the House of Lords, and the three readings were hurried through on 18, 19, and 20 January. The bill, sent down to the commons, was passed by them, and was sent back on the 24th. Although it was customary to reserve the final step to the close of the session, the king, who was in haste, gave his assent on Thursday the 27th, and the execution of Norfolk was fixed for the morning of the next day. All the preparations for this last act were made during the night; and but a few moments were to intervene before this once powerful man was to be led to the scaffold.

Two victims were now awaiting the remorseless scythe of destiny. Death was approaching at the same time the threshold of the palace and that of the prison. Two men who had filled the world with their renown, who during their lifetime had been closely united, and were the foremost personages of the realm, were about to pass the inexorable gates and to be bound with those bonds which God alone can burst. The only question was which of the two would be the first to receive the final stroke. The general expectation was, no doubt, that Norfolk would be the first, for the executioner was already sharpening the axe which was to smite him.

While the duke, still full of vigorous life, was awaiting in his dungeon the cruel death which he had striven so much to avert, Henry VIII was prostrate on his sick bed at Whitehall. Although everything showed that his last hour was at hand, his physicians did not venture to inform him of it, as it was against the law for anyone to speak of the death of the king. One might almost have said that he was determined to have himself declared immortal by act of Parliament. At length, however, Sir Antony Denny, chief gentleman of the chamber, who hardly ever left him, took courage and, approaching the bedside of the dying monarch, cautiously told him that all hope, humanly speaking, was lost, and entreated him to prepare for death. The king, conscious of his failing strength, accused himself of various offences, but added that the grace of God could forgive him all his sins. It has been asserted that he did really repent of his errors. 'Several English gentlemen', says Thevet, 'assured me that he was truly repentant, and among other things, on account of the injury and crime committed against the said queen [Anne Boleyn].' This is not certain; but we know that Denny, glad to hear him speak of his sins, asked him whether he did not wish to see some ecclesiastic. 'If I see anyone', said Henry, 'it must be Archbishop Cranmer.' 'Shall I send for him?' said Denny. The king replied: 'I will first take a little sleep, and then, as I feel myself, I will advise upon the matter.' An hour or two later the king awoke, and finding that he was now weaker, he asked for Cranmer. The archbishop was at Croydon; and when he arrived the dying man was unable to speak, and was almost unconscious. However, when he saw the primate, he stretched out his hand, but could not utter a word. The archbishop exhorted him to put all his trust in Christ and to implore his mercy. 'Give some token with your eyes or hand', he said, 'that you trust in the Lord.' The king wrung Cranmer's hand as hard as he could, and soon after breathed his last. He died at two o'clock in the morning, Friday, 28 January 1547.

By Henry's death Norfolk's life was saved. The new government declined to begin the new reign by putting to death the foremost peer of England. Norfolk lived for eight years longer. He spent, indeed, the greater part of it in prison; but for more than a year he was at liberty, and died at last at Kenninghall.

Henry died at the age of fifty-six years. It is no easy task to sketch the character of a prince whose principal feature was inconsistency. Moreover, as Lord Herbert of Cherbury said, his history is his best portrait. The epoch in which he lived was that of a resurrection of the human mind. Literature and the arts, political liberty, and evangelical faith were now coming forth from the tomb and returning to life. The human mind, since the outburst of bright light which then illumined it, has sometimes given itself up, it must be confessed, to strange errors; but it has never again fallen into its old sleep. There were some kings, such as Henry VIII and Francis I, who took an interest in the revival of letters; but the greater number were alarmed at the revival of freedom and of faith, and instead of welcoming tried to stifle them. Some authors, and particularly Foxe, the martyrologist, have asserted that if death had not prevented him, Henry VIII would have so securely established the reformation as not to leave a single mass in the kingdom. This is nothing more than a hypothesis, and it appears to us a very doubtful one. The king had made his will some two years before his death, when he was setting out for the war with France. In it, his chief object was to regulate the order of succession and the composition of the council of regency; but at the same time it contains positive signs of scholastic Catholicism. In this document the king says: 'We do instantly desire and require the blessed Virgin Mary his mother, with all the holy company of heaven, continually to pray for us and with us while we live in this world, and in time of passing out of the same.'

Moreover, he ordained that the dean and canons of the Chapel Royal, Windsor, and their successors for ever, should have two priests to say masses at the altar. The will was rewritten on 13 December 1546; and the members of the Privy Council signed it as witnesses. But the only change which the king introduced was the omission of Gardiner's name among the members of the council of regency. The passages respecting the Virgin and masses for his soul were retained.

Henry had brought into the world with him remarkable capacities, and these had been improved by education. He has been praised for his application to the business of the state, for his wonderful cleverness, his rare eloquence, his high courage. His abilities certainly give him a place above the average of kings. He regularly attended the council, corresponded with his ambassadors, and took much pains. In politics he had some clear views; he caused the Bible to be printed; but the moral sentiment is shocked when he is held up as a model. The two most conspicuous features of his character were pride and sensuality; and by these vices he was driven to most blameworthy actions, and even to crimes. Pride led him to make himself head of the church, to claim the right to regulate the faith of his subjects, and to punish cruelly those who had the audacity to hold any other opinions on matters of religion than his own. The reformation of which he is assumed to be the author was hardly a pseudo-reform; we might rather see in it another species of deformation. Claiming autocracy in matters of faith, he naturally claimed the same in matters of state. All the duties of his subjects were summed up by him in the one word *obedience;* and those who refused to bow the head to his despotic rule were almost sure to lose it. He was covetous, prodigal, capricious, suspicious; not only was he fickle in his friendships, but on many occasions he did not hesitate to take his victims from amongst his best friends. His treatment of his wives, and especially of Anne Boleyn, condemns him as a man; his bloody persecutions of the evangelicals condemn him as a Christian; the scandalous servility which he endeavoured, and not unsuccessfully, to engraft in the nobles, the bishops, the House of Commons, and the people, condemn him as a king.

INDEX

[The page references for Volume Two are shown in bold type. The Italic *n*. indicates reference in footnotes.]

503

The Banner of Truth Trust originated in 1957 in London. The founders believed that much of the best literature of historic Christianity had been allowed to fall into oblivion and that, under God, its recovery could well lead not only to a strengthening of the church, but to true revival.

Interdenominational in vision, this publishing work is now international, and our lists include a number of contemporary authors along with classics from the past. The translation of these books into many languages is encouraged.

A monthly magazine, *The Banner of Truth,* is also published. More information about this and all our publications can be found on our website or supplied by either of the offices below.

THE BANNER OF TRUTH TRUST

<table>
<tr><td>3 Murrayfield Road
Edinburgh, EH12 6EL
UK</td><td></td><td>PO Box 621, Carlisle,
Pennsylvania 17013,
USA</td></tr>
</table>

www.banneroftruth.org

THE ENDVR
WORDE ET
OF & FOR
LORDE EVER

SVPERSTICION

IDOLATRY

POIS

ALL FLESHE
IS GRASSE

FEYNED
HOLINES

The Reformation
in England

Volume One

History should be made to live with its own proper life.
God is this life. God must be acknowledged—
God proclaimed—in history.

J. H. MERLE D'AUBIGNÉ

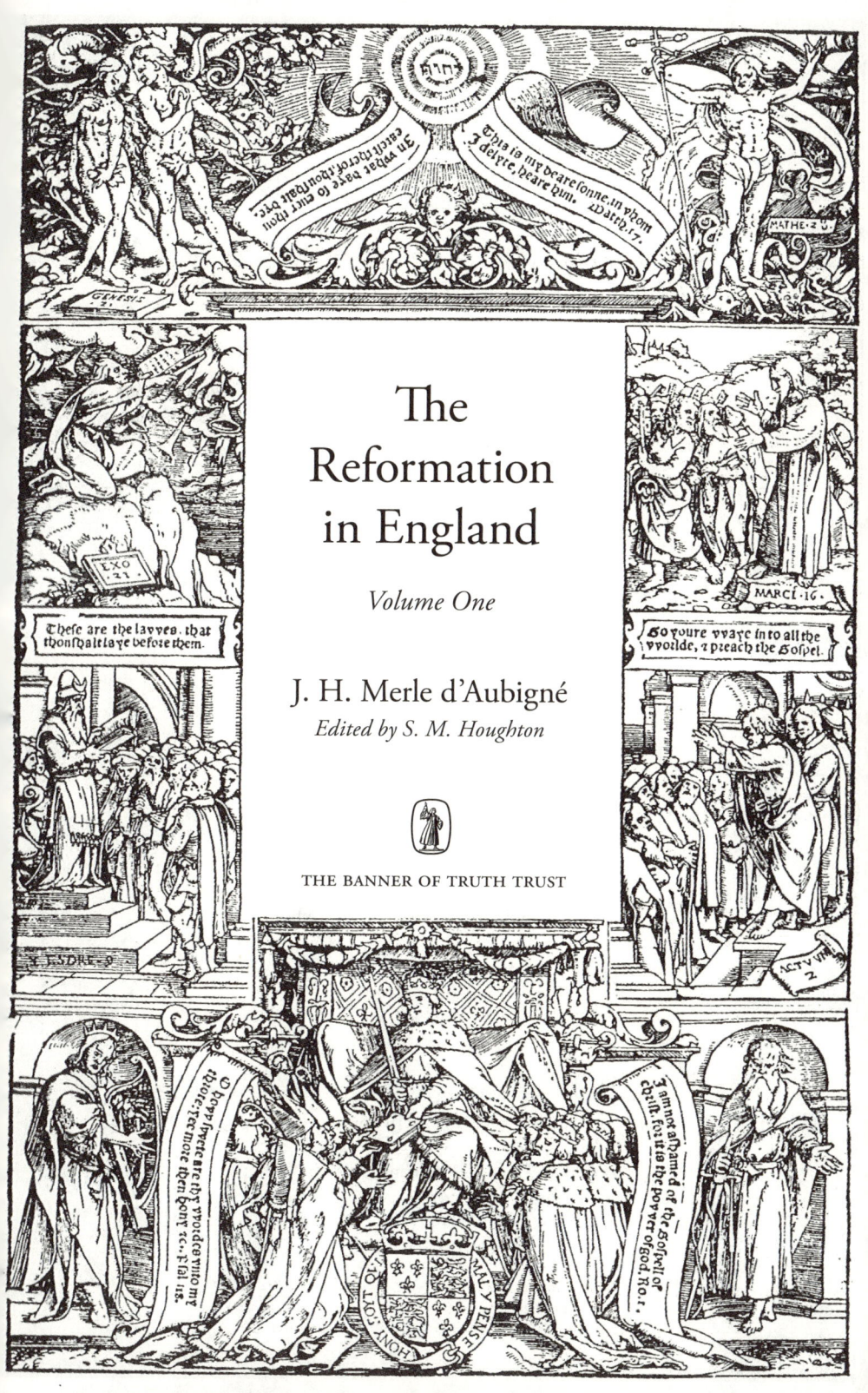

The
Reformation
in England

Volume One

J. H. Merle d'Aubigné

Edited by S. M. Houghton

THE BANNER OF TRUTH TRUST

THE BANNER OF TRUTH TRUST

Head Office
3 Murrayfield Road
Edinburgh
EH12 6EL
UK

North America Office
PO Box 621
Carlisle
PA 17013
USA

banneroftruth.org

First published in 1853 as Vol. V of
The History of the Reformation of the Sixteenth Century
Translated by H. White, M.A., Ph.D,
and carefully revised by the author.

First Banner of Truth Trust edition 1962
Reprinted 1971, 1977, 1985, 1994
This revised and re-typeset edition 2015

*

ISBN
Print: 978 1 84871 643 8
Epub: 978 1 84871 644 5
Kindle: 978 1 84871 645 2

2-Volume Set: 978 1 84871 650 6

*

Typeset in 10.5/13.5 Adobe Garamond Pro
at The Banner of Truth Trust, Edinburgh

Printed in the USA by
Versa Press Inc.,
East Peoria, IL.

Title page illustration: Taken from the title page of the Coverdale Bible,
reproduced with permission. © The British Library Board, G.12208.

Endpaper image: 'The English People Reading Wycliffe's Bible'
(detail from a larger painting), ol painting by George Clausen.
Used with permission. © Parliamentary Art Collection WOA 2603.
www.parliament.uk/art

Contents

CHAPTER SEVEN

LIGHT STREAMS FROM LUTTERWORTH

(c. 1329–1380)

CHAPTER EIGHT

THE MORNING STAR OF THE REFORMATION

(1380–1384)

CHAPTER NINE

THE LOLLARD BURNINGS

(15th Century)

CHAPTER TEN

THE NEW LEARNING AND THE NEW DYNASTY

(c. 1485–1512)

BOOK TWO
The Revival of the Church

CHAPTER TWO

The Greek Testament Awakens the Dead

(1516–1525)

CHAPTER THREE

Persecution and Intrigue

(1518–1520)

CHAPTER FOUR

A Storm at Sodbury Hall

(1522–1523)

CHAPTER FIVE

The Onslaught on Luther

(1517–1521)

BOOK THREE
The English New Testament and the Court of Rome

CHAPTER SIX

ANNE BOLEYN

(1522–1527)

CHAPTER SEVEN

BILNEY IN STRENGTH AND WEAKNESS

(1527)

CHAPTER EIGHT

THE CAMPAIGN FOR HENRY'S DIVORCE

(1527)

CHAPTER NINE

THE DILEMMA AND DUPLICITY OF CLEMENT VII

(1527–1528)

CHAPTER TWO
Scripture and the Spreading Revival
(1527–1529)

CHAPTER THREE
Campeggio Arrives in England
(July to November 1528)

CHAPTER FOUR
The Search for William Tyndale
(1528–1530)

CHAPTER FIVE
The Pope Burns His Bull
(November 1528)

CHAPTER TEN

'Tyndale' Received in a King's Palace

(1529)

CHAPTER ELEVEN

Wolsey Alone and Facing Ruin

(Summer 1529)

CHAPTER TWELVE

To Introduce Thomas Cranmer

(1489–1529)

CHAPTER SIXTEEN
Wolsey Falls like Lucifer
(1530)

Introduction

Merle d'Aubigné, whose work on the reformation in England is here reprinted, was the most popular of Church historians of the nineteenth century. His *History of the Reformation* enjoyed an enormous sale. It took Protestant England by storm, and, of its kind, it must have been one of the best-sellers of the Victorian era.

Jean Henri Merle d'Aubigné was born in 1794, in the canton of Geneva, the scion of a celebrated French family. When Louis XIV revoked the Edict of Nantes (which gave protection to Protestants) in 1685, and thousands of Huguenots were driven from France, his paternal great-grandfather, Jean Louis Merle, had moved from Nîmes to Geneva. In the middle of the next century, Francis, the son of Jean Merle, married Elizabeth d'Aubigné, a descendant of the famous poet and historian, Theodore Agrippa d'Aubigné. Elizabeth's children retained her maiden name, and were all known as Merle d'Aubigné. Aime Robert, the son of Francis and Elizabeth, and the father of our historian, undertook a commercial mission to Constantinople during the troubled years following the French Revolution of 1789. Returning to Geneva by way of Vienna, he was met on the road near Zurich by a company of Russian soldiers who had recently been defeated by the French General Masséna, and cruelly murdered. At that time his second son, Jean Henri, was but five years of age. The widow survived for almost half a century longer.

Jean Henri soon displayed a liking for academic pursuits, entered the Academy of his native city (later called the University of Geneva), completed what would now be called an Arts Course, and then entered the Faculty of Theology. Unhappily the professors of the faculty were strongly biased towards Unitarianism, and evangelical doctrine had been largely abandoned. The year was about 1816. Frédéric Monod, who was a fellow student of Merle d'Aubigné, has left it on record that 'Unitarianism, with all its chilling influence, and all its soul-destroying appendages, was the only doctrine taught us by our professors.' 'For myself', he adds, 'during the four years I attended the Theological Faculty of Geneva, I did not, as part of my studies, read one single chapter of the word of God, except a few psalms and chapters, exclusively with a view to learning Hebrew, and I did not receive one single lesson of exegesis of the Old or New Testaments.'

Happily for Geneva, and, it may be added, happily too for France, there came a Scotsman to plough and sow the barren field. In 1816, as an instrument specially chosen of God for the work, there reached Geneva, without invitation from the faculty, a theological teacher whose doctrine was identical with that of John Calvin himself. Robert Haldane, though born in London, was of Scottish descent, and in every respect a true 'Scots worthy'. The impact he made on the city of Geneva was so remarkable that Merle d'Aubigné in later years used to point to the apartments Haldane occupied (looking down the Lake towards Savoy and the Alps) saying, 'There is the cradle of the second Genevan reformation.'

Some twenty or thirty divinity students, one of whom was d'Aubigné, responded to Haldane's invitation to meet him in his apartments, in which he had arranged chairs on both sides of a long table covered with copies of the Scriptures in French, English, German, and other modern languages, besides the Greek and Hebrew Testaments. One of the professors made it his business to pace up and down under the shady trees of the avenue at the time the students were assembling, making clear his high displeasure at their attendance, and noting their names in his pocket book.

Haldane's exposition of the word made an ineffaceable impression on Monod, later the chief founder of the Free Churches of France, who thus records his experience: 'What struck me most, and what struck us all, was Mr Haldane's solemnity of manner. It was evident he was in earnest about our souls, and the souls of those who might be placed under our pastoral care, and such feelings were new to us. Then his meekness, the unwearying patience with which he listened to our sophisms, our ignorant objections, our attempts now and then to embarrass him by difficulties invented for the purpose, and his answers to each and all of us! But what astonished me, and made me reflect more than anything else, was his ready knowledge of the word of God and implicit faith in its divine authority ... We had never seen anything like this. Even after this lapse of years, I still see presented to my mind's eye his tall and manly figure, surrounded by the students; his English Bible in his hand, wielding as his only weapon that word which is the sword of the Spirit; satisfying every objection, removing every difficulty, answering every question by a prompt reference to various passages, by which objections, difficulties, and questions were all fairly met and conclusively answered. He never wasted his time in arguing against our so-called reasonings, but at once pointed with his finger to the Bible, adding the simple words, "Look here – how readest thou?" "There it stands written with the finger of God." He was, in the full sense of the word, a living concordance ... He expounded to us the Epistle to the Romans which several of us had probably never read, and which none of us understood ... I reckon it as one of my greatest privileges to have been his interpreter ... being almost the only one who knew English well enough to be thus honoured and employed.'

Merle d'Aubigné was as deeply impressed as Monod by what he heard. 'I met Robert Haldane', he said to a friend, 'and heard him read from an English Bible a chapter from Romans about the natural corruption of man, a doctrine of which I had never before heard. In fact I was quite astonished to hear of man being corrupt by nature. I remember saying to Mr Haldane, "Now I see that doctrine in the Bible." "Yes", he replied, "but do you see it in your heart?" That was but a simple question, yet it came home to my conscience. It was the sword of the Spirit: and from that time I saw that my heart was corrupted, and knew from the word of God that I can be saved by grace alone. So that, if Geneva gave something to Scotland at the time of the reformation, if she communicated light to John Knox, Geneva has received something from Scotland in return in the blessed exertions of Robert Haldane.'[1]

[1] The whole matter is of deep interest and should be read in Alex. Haldane's *Lives of Robert and James Haldane*, pp. 398-407.

Having completed his academic course at Geneva, Merle d'Aubigné continued his studies at the Universities of Leipzig and Berlin. In the latter city he 'sat at the feet' of Neander – son of a Jewish pedlar – Christian theologian and church historian, whose lectures made a deep impression on the maturing student. Unlike the historians whose interest lay chiefly in institutions, Neander's chief interest lay in persons, and he made it his aim in his study of church history to discover in it 'the interpenetration of human life by the Divine'. It cannot be doubted that d'Aubigné's own particular genius as a historian derived from this source. The interest in persons rather than institutions which dominates the volumes of his *History* here reprinted is proof that he had been Neander's apt learner.

Even before d'Aubigné had reached Berlin, however, he had formed the project of writing the history of the reformation. His journey from Geneva to Berlin took him through the Luther country, and he had visited Eisenach and the Castle of Wartburg, famous in the life story of the German reformer. This visit proved a life-long inspiration: and the subsequent training under Neander only confirmed the resolution to let all men know the things that God had wrought during sixteenth-century days. His study of the great reformers which now commenced did not cease until, after half a century of labour, he bequeathed to his generation and to posterity the thirteen volumes which form a major contribution to the understanding of the age of Luther, Calvin, Cranmer, and Knox.

Merle d'Aubigné's ministerial labours appropriately commenced in the Protestant Church which had been planted in Hamburg by French Huguenots fleeing from their homeland during the persecution of Louis XIV. After spending five years in the German city he was invited by William, King of the United Netherlands, to become pastor of a newly-formed French Church in Brussels. This post he held until the Revolution of 1830 which led to the separation of Belgium from Holland. Refusing an invitation to take up a tutorial post in the family of the Dutch king, and having experienced, as a friend of the king, threats against his life at the hands of irate Belgians, he felt constrained to return to Geneva where he assisted in the formation of a seminary for the training of pastors and teachers of the word. In this he became professor of church history, and was shortly joined by Louis Gaussen, another member of the Haldane group of 1816, later famous as the author of an excellent treatise on the plenary inspiration of Holy Scripture. Gaussen, in 1834, became professor of systematic theology. The college prospered and fulfilled a similar purpose to that in Calvin's day by sending out able, trained teachers of the Reformed faith into a wide field of service.

Merle d'Aubigné held his post until his death in 1872. He had ample opportunity to acquaint himself not only with the main thoroughfares of reformation history, but also with its byways. His visits to the chief libraries of Central and Western Europe led to his acquisition of a vast knowledge of the sixteenth century. Such became his fame as a historian that he was given the freedom of the city of Edinburgh and the degree of doctor of civil law of the University of Oxford. He frequently visited England, being held in high honour by English evangelicals. Not a few Scotsmen would like to have secured him for a post in one of their theological colleges. On a visit to Britain in May 1862, when he was desired by Queen Victoria to preach in the Royal Chapel of St James, he also visited the Metropolitan Tabernacle. C. H. Spurgeon purposely shortened his own discourse to allow time for d'Aubigné to speak to the vast congregation. The address was completely typical of the man, as was the story he narrated towards its close, so typical indeed that it is worthy of quotation.

'There was', he said, 'in the latter part of the sixteenth century, a man in Italy who was a child of God, taught by the Spirit. His name was Aonio Paleario. He had written a book called *The Benefit of Christ's Death*. That book was destroyed in Italy, and for three centuries it was not possible to find a copy; but two or three years ago an Italian copy was found, I believe, in one of your libraries at Cambridge or Oxford, and it has been printed again. It is perhaps singular, but this man did not leave the Romish Church, as he ought to have done, but his whole heart was given to Christ. He was brought before the judge in Rome, by order of the pope. The judge said, "We will put to him three questions: we will ask him what is the first cause of salvation, then what is the second cause of salvation, then what is the third cause of salvation." They thought that, in putting these three questions, he would at last be made to say something which should be to the glory of the Church of Rome. So they asked him, "What is the first cause of salvation?" and he answered, "CHRIST." Then they asked him, "What is the second cause of salvation?" and he answered, "CHRIST." Then they asked him, "What is the third cause of salvation?" and he answered, "CHRIST." They thought he would have said, first, Christ; secondly, the word; thirdly, the church; but no, he said, "CHRIST." The first cause, Christ; the second, Christ; the third, Christ; and for that confession, which he made in Rome, he was condemned to be put to death as a martyr. My dear friends, let us think and speak like that man; let every one of us say, "The first cause of my salvation is Christ; the second is Christ; the third is Christ. Christ and his atoning blood; Christ and his regenerating Spirit; Christ and his eternal electing grace. Christ is my only salvation. I know of nothing else.'"

It may be fitting to add that, some months earlier, Spurgeon had, by invitation of d'Aubigné, visited Geneva, and had preached to his great joy in Calvin's pulpit (robed in the black Genevan gown). After the service he 'spent a very delightful evening with the most noted preachers of Switzerland, talking about our common Lord, and of the progress of his work in England and on the Continent.' 'When they bade me "Goodbye"', adds Spurgeon, 'every one of those ministers – a hundred and fifty or perhaps two hundred of them – kissed me on both cheeks. It was rather an ordeal for me ...'

Merle d'Aubigné's *History of the Reformation in the Sixteenth Century* was published in Paris in five volumes between the years 1835 and 1853. This was followed by *The History of the Reformation in Europe in the Time of Calvin*, a work which appeared in eight volumes between 1863 and 1878. His *History of the Reformation in England* is contained in various sections within these thirteen volumes. They have been extracted from the whole and are here printed together under the new title, *The Reformation in England*. Volume one of this edition[2] covers the period until the death of Cardinal Wolsey in 1530; the second volume[3] ends with the death of Henry VIII in 1547. Unhappily the work remained incomplete on account of the author's sudden and unexpected death in 1872.

[2] First published as vol. 5 of *The History of the Reformation in the Sixteenth Century.*
[3] Taken from vols. 4, 5, and 8 of *The History of the Reformation in Europe in the Time of Calvin.*

The immense popularity of Merle d'Aubigné's *History* in his own day was largely due to the fact that it was written by an expert in the field, not for fellow experts but for the ordinary Christian public. He judged that public interest could best be stirred, not by erudite disquisitions on the intricacies of canon law and on Church institutions, but by continual stress on the personal factor in history, the emotions of the human soul, the mental strains and stresses occasioned by the impact of ancient and yet newborn truth upon minds long in bondage to Roman Catholicism, and the tortures experienced by the human spirit when the moment came for decisive action. It was this aspect of the reformation which d'Aubigné's pen portrayed with a skill hitherto lacking in Church historians. Undue concentration on the merely legislative and political aspects of religious history leaves the human soul unmoved, whereas the graphic portrayal of souls stirred to the depths by the force of divine truth, of souls agonized by the awful tensions that can and do result from an experience of new birth in an intensely hostile ecclesiastical, not to say domestic, environment – this it was, as described by a writer able to weep with those who wept, which stirred the soul of Victorian England, and made d'Aubigné's work a potent factor in holding thousands to Protestantism and biblical truth at a time when Rome was making a fresh effort to repair the ravages of centuries. As did Foxe the martyrologist, he wrote not so much for the scholar and the collegiate world, but for the person of scanty knowledge and non-academic bent. But his depth of scholarship enabled him to rise far above the level of a mere popularizer of knowledge. A superficial reader might at times suppose that the history was itself superficial, and that, being 'popular', it could not be at the same time scholarly and critical. In this, however, he would deceive himself. Normally the scholar is not the popularizer, but in d'Aubigné the two roles are combined. 'Art consists in concealing art' runs the ancient saying, and of this particular skill d'Aubigné was the humble master. His knowledge, based on the most extensive and prolonged research, was immense, but with it he never overloads his narrative. His terse racy style never becomes bogged in a morass of mere factual information.

That a historian should be a popularizer of his theme is liable, in the eyes of the more academic type of historian, to be an unforgivable offence against all good scholarship. But it was not only in this respect that d'Aubigné departed from the generally accepted canons of historical writing. As the basis of his *History* there are two principles which are generally regarded by almost all members of the historical fraternity as forming no part of serious history. The first is the conviction that the divine element in human history is essential to its true understanding and his refusal to hide from his readers his own personal faith and heart convictions. In the Modern Age it has become almost an axiom of the historian that he must treat his subject 'scientifically', and above all impersonally, concealing to the last degree his own personal convictions, if perchance he possesses any, and writing as if possessed of neither conscience (except for the establishment of cold historical truth) nor faith. As a strictly academic exercise this method may possess its merits, but as a vehicle for the stimulation of interest in the mind of the average reader, it conspicuously fails. History, to live, must pulsate with the life of the historian. He must himself be stirred by the events on which he chooses to dilate. And it is here that d'Aubigné achieves his greatest success. He is no mere spectator from afar, dissecting, as it were, the dry bones of men of the bygone years. He lives in the age he depicts. He shares the agonies of sixteenth-century martyrs. His heart throbs and aches as he walks with confessors of the faith on the highroads of the Tudor Age. He is present at their trials. He feels the heat of the flames as those who have 'opened their mouths to the Lord and who cannot go back' yield themselves to fiery death. In this respect he recaptures the 'living spirit' of the Tudor Age, and becomes the John Foxe of the nineteenth century. 'I write the history of the reformation in its own spirit', is his claim.

The other principle likely to be held against him by secular historians is his unceasing insistence on the ever-present divine element in man's history. It might almost seem a truism to say that reformation history cannot be understood without such insistence, but writers who fail to perceive and own the presence and work of the Spirit of God are plentiful. Sir Maurice Powicke's *Reformation in England*, first published in 1940, says, for example, that the 'one definite thing which can be said about the reformation in England is that it was an act of state'. It may almost be assumed that to call it an act of God would be accounted rank historical heresy. Much historical writing is deliberately coldly factual and non-interpretative. But d'Aubigné belongs to the school of the prophets. His writing is 'pregnant with celestial fire'. It is his primary object to show the divine hand at work in human affairs, and this not only in respect of the spiritual movements of his period, but equally so in respect of political and ecclesiastical movements. God ruling, God overruling, God hiding his power, God openly intervening in the affairs of states and of individuals – this, to Merle d'Aubigné, is the essential stuff of history, the principal thread needful for the weaving of his tapestry. He is careful to render this point as clear as words can make it. Thus, in his preface to his first *History* he says, 'History should be made to live with its own proper life. God is this life. God must be acknowledged – God proclaimed – in history. The history of the world should purport to be annals of the government of the supreme King … Strange! this inter-position of God in human affairs, which even pagans have recognized, men reared amid the grand ideas of Christianity treat as superstition … The short-sighted wisdom of our boasted days is far below those heights of pagan wisdom. History has been robbed of her divine parent, and now an illegitimate child, a bold adventurer, she roams the world, not knowing whence she comes or whither she goes.'

While Merle d'Aubigné laments the blindness of the secular historian, that blindness does not cause him surprise. He finds in it but the fulfilment of the apostolic word that 'the natural man receiveth not the things of the Spirit of God'. If the historian is but a 'natural man', the spiritual interpretation of history will obviously be foolishness to him, not so much because he will not see but rather because he cannot see.

It will be well to hear d'Aubigné himself speaking on this matter, and at a time anterior to the actual beginning of his life-work as a historian. In 1832 he delivered at Geneva a discourse on 'the History of Christi-anity', with the history of the reformation particularly in view. 'There are two histories', he said; 'there is what we may call "The History of the Church", that is, of human institutions, forms, doctrines, and actions; and "The History of Christianity" which has brought into the world, and still preserves, a new life, a life divine, the history of the government of that King who has said, "the words which I speak unto you are spirit and life". ... Most historians have hitherto presented only the barren history of the external church, because they themselves were only the outward man and had scarcely even imagined the life of the spiritual man ... The "old man" sees in the field of the Church but dry bones; the "new man" there discerns that Spirit which blows from the four winds, and creates for the Eternal "an exceeding great army".'

The reader may expect, then, from d'Aubigné's pen a history different in quality from that of the detached secular historian, a history which seeks to show God as his own interpreter, and which (to use a Lutheran phrase) aims at bringing the conscience of the reader into captivity to the word of God. At the same time d'Aubigné knew the potency of vivid portraiture and picturesque narration in winning the interest and the sympathy of the human mind, and his *History* acquired its reputation, in part, because of its fine literary qualities. In this connection the words of Principal Rainy of Edinburgh are noteworthy. They were written in 1879: 'The great quality which sustains the popularity of d'Aubigné's *History* is this – that it is vivid. It reproduces with great power the tide of human life in which the events took shape; it sets before us the convictions, the passions, the interests that drove men on, uttered in the language and clothed in the colours of the time. This is not done, as has been insidiously imputed, by efforts of idle fancy or rhetorical amplification. It is effected by a minute study of the physiognomy of the time, as it may be discovered in individual men, and in specific instances; and by a sympathetic appreciation and reproduction of it, so as to bring the reader face to face with that forgotten past. This is no cheap and vulgar way of becoming popular. It is a great form of historical success.' And again (after speaking of the Romanism, the humanism, and the politics of the reformation period), 'All these things d'Aubigné conceives after the manner of a very intelligent man who has spent a thousand times more pains on the period than his readers have done, and who knows all its elements correctly and well. But one great element he knows by a perfect sympathy, an entire conviction, an unvarying attraction. He conceives it *from the inside*; it is alive for him wherever he meets it; and all his powers are spontaneously ready to reproduce it in its original truth and force.'

As a historian of the reformation, Merle d'Aubigné had the great advantage of seeing it in its full continental setting, and of having access to the multitudinous documents scattered throughout the libraries of Europe. His handling of the English story benefits from this wealth and breadth of scholarship. The *History*, as here reprinted, is not furnished with all the numerous references supplied in footnotes in the original editions. A selection has been retained, particularly those which apply to books still readily accessible – for example, the volumes of the Parker Society and Foxe's *Acts and Monuments*. The four chief nineteenth-century editions of Foxe's work are in eight volumes, and, very conveniently, they have the same paging, so that reference to any one edition is an easy matter. Readers who desire to track down the authority for any particular statement outside the range of the references given in the reprint should obtain access to the nineteenth-century editions of the *History* which contain full references.

In view of the fact that d'Aubigné makes extensive use of Foxe's *Acts and Monuments*, lest any readers should regard Foxe merely as an unreliable propagandist of Protestantism, it may be helpful here to state the present position about his degree of usefulness as a historian, and, for many of the events he narrates, a contemporary historian. Until the fourth decade of the nineteenth century, Foxe was held in high repute in all non-Romanist quarters. From 1837 onwards a school of historians, headed by S. R. Maitland, librarian at Lambeth Palace, began to pour scorn on the martyrology, declaring it to be both untrustworthy and in many places plainly dishonest. In such criticisms Maitland was followed by his two 'able lieutenants', J. S. Brewer and James Gairdner, and later (though in milder fashion) by Sidney Lee in the *Dictionary of National Biography*. So violent and sustained was the attack on Foxe that not a few later historians were inclined to accept the new school's charges as proven, and they came to regard Foxe as a purveyor of unreliabilities. But the 'debunking' process is now over and will in all probability shortly be forgotten. In 1940 there appeared *John Foxe and His Book* by J. F. Mozley, which subjected the book in all its aspects to a thorough reinvestigation. In the outcome Foxe re-emerges as a writer of undoubted integrity and of immense value for his own particular century; sharing, indeed, in the weaknesses of his contemporaries as historians of earlier ages, but unrivalled in his understanding of the Tudor scene and in his portrayal of the reformation story.

The testimony of C. S. Lewis, given in his *English Literature in the Sixteenth Century* (Oxford University Press, 1954) runs thus: 'Maitland had many successors, and the nineteenth-century tradition represents Foxe as an unscrupulous propagandist who records what he knows to be false, suppresses what he knows to be true, and claims to have seen documents he has not seen. In 1940, however, Mr J. F. Mozley reopened the whole question and defended Foxe's integrity, as it seems to me, with complete success. From his examination Foxe emerges, not indeed as a great historian, but as an honest man. For early Church history he relies on the obvious authorities and is of very mediocre value. For the Marian persecution his sources are usually the narratives of eyewitnesses … There seems no evidence that Foxe ever accepted what he did not himself believe or ever refused to correct what he had written in the light of fresh evidence. The most horrible of all his stories, the Guernsey martyrdoms, was never refuted, though violently assailed; in some ways the defence may be thought scarcely less damaging than the charge. And in one respect – in his hatred of cruelty – Foxe was impartial to a degree hardly paralleled in that age.'

To what extent, the reader may ask, is the present reprint an exact reproduction of Merle d'Aubigné's work? In answer, it must be remarked that the work is little short of a century old, and it would be unkind to reader and author alike to reproduce, as originally written, any statement which has been proved by later researchers to go beyond or fall short of truth. Historical research has made substantial progress since d'Aubigné's day, and this has necessitated a careful reappraisal of all that he wrote. Substantially, of course, the work remains unchanged, but needful amendments have been introduced wherever warranted by later findings. Footnotes inside square brackets are supplied by the reviser, and attention is occasionally drawn to books of recent days. As far as practicable, quotations have been checked against the original sources, and occasionally clarified. At times, the author quotes the sense rather than the exact words, and such quotations have normally been allowed to stand. In sundry places, where it was judged that a more extensive quotation from an original document than that given would enlighten the reader, this has been supplied. It is d'Aubigné's method roughly to alternate chapters of political history (to which he gives adequate attention) with chapters on the more spiritual aspects of his story. No attempt has been made to interfere with this arrangement: but one short political chapter has been omitted in its entirety, as unnecessary to the elucidation of the reformation and as rendered somewhat obsolete by later historical writing.

It is not merely the pleasurable quality and readability of d'Aubigné's work which has led the Banner of Truth Trust to republish his account of the reformation. Its 'apologia' for so doing is that the present state of religion in England renders knowledge of the reformation of vast spiritual importance to our people, a plain necessity for the preacher, and a highly desirable acquirement for the Christian public at large. It is granted that most people can and do live quite happily without such knowledge. It is conceded, too, that knowledge of reformation history is not for one moment to be equated with the knowledge of the word of God itself. At the same time, however, few would dispute the claim that knowledge of more than the word itself is good for the soul. Much of the stuff of life, spiritual as well as temporal, meets us day by day in historical garb. Controversies which still rend asunder the professing church of Jesus Christ are only understandable in their historic setting. It was a saying of one of the most famous and respectable of ancient philosophers that 'not to know what has happened in the past is always to remain a child'; and ignorance of the reformation story tends to weaken our grasp of the spiritual verities for which the times demand unrelenting contention.

Some knowledge of history is accounted an essential part of a sound education even in the secular sphere, and Scripture certainly lends strong support to the claim that certain aspects of history at least have pronounced spiritual value. Much of the divine word is itself history, and not written merely for purposes of factual record. God's ways with men are to be vindicated. Man must be told what are the thoughts toward him of 'the God of knowledge by whom actions are weighed'. The word is the critic of the thoughts and intents of the heart, and herein lies the supreme value of Bible history: it glows with divine comment. Far from being mere chronicle, it is divine judgment pronounced on the human story, so that man may be forewarned as to what will one day happen on an infinitely vaster scale at the judgment seat of God. God will judge the world in righteousness by the one whom he has ordained and raised from the dead. Of that trial and verdict Bible history is a preview and a foreshadowing.

Merle d'Aubigné, as has already been stated, was called of God to take up our national story at a period of particular spiritual importance, and to present it to view, not as a mere 'act of state' but as a movement on a great scale of the Spirit of God, a work of divine initiative, a testimony of the Spirit to the truth as exemplified in the lives and deaths of many sixteenth-century men and women. Twentieth-century believers, living in days of luxury and ease, may learn in d'Aubigné's pages the story of their forerunners in the faith who loved not their lives to the death, but accounted it honour to jeopardize them, for the Son of Man's sake, in the high places of the field.

Somewhat strangely, some Christians have shown a curious unwillingness to give attention to matters historical, claiming that they possess little relevance for the Christian life. In their desire to re-establish first-century Christianity, which in itself cannot but be commended, they overleap the centuries and regard the lessons of history as unworthy of their notice. They forget that some of their choicest liberties were purchased by believers who, in the age of the reformation, sealed their testimony with their blood: and such blood still cries to us from the ground. We are unworthy of our heritage if we turn a deaf ear to its voice.

Among our liberties is the willingness of the state to allow us to 'contend earnestly for the faith once delivered to the saints', and still to claim that 'the Bishop of Rome hath no jurisdiction in this realm of England'. Maybe we do not care to use the downright words of the Geneva Bible beloved of many Elizabethan Christians, and to assert that 'the pope hath his power out of hell, and cometh thence', but we are certainly in grave danger of seeking compromise with a system which openly claims to be unchanged since days out of mind. We are prone to forget that believers of the Tudor Age warned us against Romanism's 'blasphemous fables and dangerous deceits'. The fact is that Englishmen of today, in their easy-going attitude to all things religious, need such words to shake them out of their deep spiritual slumber and to remind them of certain things in heaven and earth which have no place in their philosophy of tolerance. That the state should not intervene in matters of religious belief, and bring no manner of pressure upon the human conscience, is a right founded on a true conception of the functions of the state; but if it is claimed, as frequently is the case, that as individuals we are to hold that one religious profession is as good as another, and that all are facets of eternal truth, no claim could be more fundamentally false. If error exists it must be opposed by truth. The two are bound to be in conflict. If masses are 'dangerous deceits', the system which embodies them must be attacked by the word of God. The sword is spiritual. If people are duped by 'blasphemous fables', all right endeavours to disillusion them must be used. This is not exclusively the task of those set apart to the ministry of the word. All true Christians are to be ministers for such a purpose. If, said Luther, a place is found to be on fire, it is not the duty of one class of citizen alone to give the alarm, but the plain responsibility of all and sundry. Thus should every Christian act according to his knowledge, opportunity, and capacity; thus should he seek to do good to his neighbour. And the aptitude of a man thus to serve the interests of the kingdom of God is augmented by his knowledge of God's acts which constitute history.

Merle d'Aubigné's stress on the content of history as something much more than 'past politics' has already been mentioned. It is his glory as a historian to share with John Foxe the conviction that the rank and file of God's elect make history just as surely as those whose names have become household words: and with this is linked an evaluation of events which may startle the secular historian. At times d'Aubigné may seem to wear the mantle of the prophet, or at least to trespass into the domain of the preacher. He would have delighted in the pulpit saying of C. H. Spurgeon that 'when John Knox went upstairs to plead (with God) for Scotland, it was the greatest event in Scottish history', and would certainly have us believe that the voice of history was the voice of

God, a silver thread which might well be intertwined with the golden cord of the inspired word itself.

That witness after the d'Aubigné pattern is vital today few ardent believers will doubt. The times are out of joint. Rome imitates in its character the unchangeableness of the word of God. Unrepentant, intolerant where it holds the upper hand, it remains the chief advocate of an ancient unscriptural doctrine in a predominantly secular and materialistic age. An archbishop pays his compliments, and a cordial visit, to its chief representative. An ecumenical movement of considerable size, but with very insecure doctrinal foundations, if foundations they can be called, seeks Rome's co-operation and approval and membership. A national church plays into Rome's hands by the illegal reintroduction of masses, and, on the part of those who look wistfully towards the Vatican, by secretly believing and in some cases openly confessing that the reformation was a tremendous mistake, the prime cause of the divisions of Christendom. John Bunyan in his day could say of the pope: 'He is, by reason of age, and also of the many shrewd brushes that he met with in his younger days, grown so crazy and stiff in his joints, that he can now do little more than sit in his cave's mouth, grinning at pilgrims as they go by, and biting his nails because he cannot come at them.' Separated by three hundred years from Bunyan's day, we feel that the description is no longer valid. The papacy is an intensely active institution. One of its dearest ambitions is the re-conquest of England. It pursues its aims in the language of affection. It dangles its antiquity, its eminence, its powers, its catholicity, in the sight of restless seeking souls. It promises soul-security through the efficacy of its priesthood. The public press carries its advertisements on which it lavishes considerable wealth. Its chief functionary proclaims not only his holiness, by means of his title, but also the ancient and modern love of his church for the island kingdom. He longs to Romanize its throne. The glamour of colourful pageantry, and the claim to hold sway in this world and in the world to come, still exercise their influences on souls uninstructed in the word and without knowledge of the past. Let the answer to 'the lie' be given in the first place from Scripture and in scriptural terms – there can be no substitute for that – but let the testimony of history too be heard. The past has a voice. History is the voice of the centuries speaking against the delusive voice of the hour. Events of the sixteenth century have lessons for us today. reformation history is much more than a plaintive rendering of 'old unhappy things and battles long ago' which have no relevance to modern life. The voices which call to us across four centuries, warning us against 'blasphemous fables and dangerous deceits', and recalling us to the testimony of Scripture, are the voices of holy men of God. Let us hear their bold and faithful witness, for it has been wisely declared that 'a nation which does not know its history is destined to repeat it'.

The Banner of Truth Trust is confident that the present reprint deserves a wide public. It will, under God, help to stem the rising tide of Romanism, and to assist the believer to avoid the 'shallows and miseries' of a Protestantism falsely so called. It is hoped that it will be a major contribution to the religious needs of the present age, and that it will lead to the strengthening of the foundations of a wonderful God-given heritage of truth.

S. M. HOUGHTON
Rhyl, North Wales
15 November 1961

BOOK ONE

England before the Reformation

John Wycliffe

CHAPTER ONE

Christ Mightier than Druid Altars and Roman Swords

(From 2nd to 6th Century)

T hose heavenly powers which had lain dormant in the church since the first ages of Christianity, awoke from their slumber in the sixteenth century, and this awakening called the modern times into existence. The church was created anew, and from that regeneration flowed great developments of literature and science, of morality, liberty, and industry. None of these things would have existed without the reformation. Whenever society enters upon a new era, it requires the baptism of faith. In the sixteenth century God gave to man this consecration from on high by leading him back from mere outward profession and the mechanism of works to an inward and lively faith.

This transformation was not effected without struggles – struggles which presented at first a remarkable unity. On the day of battle one and the same feeling animated every bosom: after the victory they became divided. Unity of faith indeed remained, but the difference of nationalities brought into the church a diversity of forms. Of this we are about to witness a striking example. The reformation, which had begun its triumphal march in Germany, Switzerland, France, and several other parts of the Continent, was destined to receive new strength by the conversion of a celebrated country long known as the *Isle of Saints*. This island was to add its banner to the trophy of Protestantism, but that banner preserved its distinctive colours. When England became Reformed, a puissant individualism joined its might to the great unity.

If we search for the characteristics of the British reformation, we shall find that, beyond any other, they were social, national, and truly human. There is no people among whom the reformation has produced to the same degree that morality and order, that liberty, public spirit, and activity, which are the very essence of a nation's greatness. Just as the papacy has degraded the Spanish peninsula, the gospel has exalted the British islands. Hence the study upon which we are entering possesses an interest peculiar to itself.

In order that this study may be useful, it should have a character of universality. To confine the history of a people within the space of a few years, or even of a century, would deprive that history of both truth and life. We might indeed have traditions, chronicles, and legends, but there would be no history. History is a wonderful organization, no part of which can be retrenched. To understand the present, we must know the past. Society, like man himself, has its infancy, youth, maturity, and old age. Ancient or pagan society, which had spent its infancy in the East in the midst of the non-Hellenic races, had its youth in the animated epoch of the Greeks, its manhood in the stern period of Roman greatness, and its old age under the decline of the Empire. Modern society has passed through analogous stages: at the time of the reformation it attained that of the full-grown man.

We shall now proceed to trace the destinies of the church in England, from the earliest times of Christianity. These long and distant preparations are one of the distinctive characteristics of its reformation. Before the sixteenth century this church had passed through two great phases.

The first was that of its formation, when Britain came within the orbit of the worldwide gospel preaching which commenced at Jerusalem in the days of the apostles. The second phase is the story of the church's corruption and decline through its connection with Rome and the papacy. Then came the phase of the church's regeneration known to history as the reformation.

* * * * *

In the second century of the Christian era vessels were frequently sailing to the savage shores of Britain from the ports of Asia Minor, Greece, Alexandria, or the Greek colonies in Gaul. Among the merchants busied in calculating the profits they could make upon the produce of the East with which their ships were laden, would occasionally be found a few pious men from the Roman province of Asia, conversing peacefully with one another about the birth, life, death, and resurrection of Jesus of Nazareth, and rejoicing at the prospect of saving by these glad tidings the pagans towards whom they were steering. It would appear that some British prisoners of war, having learnt to know Christ during their captivity, bore also to their fellow countrymen the knowledge of this Saviour. It may be, too, that some Christian soldiers, the Corneliuses of those imperial armies whose advanced posts reached the southern parts of Scotland, desirous of more lasting conquests, may have read to the people whom they had subdued, the writings of Matthew, John, and Paul. It is of little consequence to know whether one of these first converts was, according to tradition, a prince named Lucius. It is probable that the tidings of the Son of man, crucified and raised again during the reign of the emperor Tiberius, later spread through these islands more rapidly than the dominion of the emperors, and that before the end of the second century, Christ was worshipped by not a few beyond the wall of Hadrian. It was about A.D. 200 that Tertullian wrote thus: 'Parts of Britain were inaccessible to the Romans but have yielded to Christ.' In those mountains, forests, and western isles, which for centuries past the Druids had filled with their mysteries and their sacrifices, and on which the Roman eagles had never swooped, even there the name of Christ was known and honoured.

Towards the end of the third century came the savage Diocletian persecution, which may have caused some British Christians to flee into the remote and all but inaccessible lands of the north, where, doubtless, they strengthened the hands of the few disciples already located there. The names of three of the Diocletian martyrs have survived – Alban of Verulam (St Albans), who was executed in all probability on the hill where the abbey church of the same name now stands; Aaron, an otherwise unknown Christian; and Julius of Caerleon. We know nothing in detail about these honoured disciples of the Lord. In A.D. 305, Constantius Chlorus succeeded Diocletian in the throne of the Caesars, and shortly the persecution ended. In the fourth century, representatives of the church in Britain attended councils on the Continent, and it is more than likely that British Christians accepted as truth the Creed of Athanasius which combated the heresies of the period. It is clear that the

Christian faith was firmly rooted in Roman Britain before the departure of the legions early in the fifth century, but information about Christian communities beyond the Roman frontiers is scanty in the extreme.

After the extraordinary manifestations of the Holy Ghost, which had produced and distinguished the apostolic age, the church had been left to the inward power of the word and of the Comforter. But Christians did not generally comprehend the spiritual life to which they were called. God had been pleased to give them a Divine religion; and this they gradually assimilated more and more to the religions of human origin. Instead of saying, in the spirit of the gospel, the word of God first, and through it the doctrine and the life – the doctrine and the life, and through them the forms; they said, forms first, and salvation by these forms. They began to ascribe to bishops a power which belongs only to holy Scripture. Instead of ministers of the word, they desired to have priests; instead of an inward sacrifice, a sacrifice offered on the altar; and costly temples instead of a living church. They began to seek in men, in ceremonies, and in holy places, what they could find only in the word and in the lively faith of the children of God. In this manner evangelical religion gradually gave place to Catholicism, and by gradual degeneration in after-years Catholicism gave birth to popery.

This grievous transformation took place more particularly in the East, in Africa, and in Italy. Britain was at first comparatively exempt. At the very time that the savage Picts and Scots, rushing from their heathen homes, were devastating the country, spreading terror on all sides, and reducing the people to slavery, we discover here and there some humble Christian receiving salvation not by a clerical sacramentalism, but by the work of the Holy Ghost in the heart. At the end of the fourth century we meet with an illustrious example of such conversions.

At this period, in the Christian village of Bannavern,[1] a little boy, of tender heart, lively temperament, and indefatigable activity, passed the

[1] [The locality of Bannavern has been much debated. The claim that it was Kilpatrick on the Clyde is now maintained by few. Some favour the shores of the Bristol Channel. The latest conjecture, that of the Celticist Paul Grosjean, is Ravenglass in Cumberland. Professor Margaret Deanesly, in her *Pre-Conquest Church in England*, 1961, p. 37, argues that he was born in the province of Bernicia, more probably south of the wall than in the land of the southern Picts.]

earlier days of his life. He was born about the year A.D. 385, of a British family, and was named Succat. His father was Calpurnius, deacon of the Church of Bannavern, a simple-hearted pious man. Doubtless his parents endeavoured to instil into his heart the doctrines of Christianity; but Succat did not understand them. He was fond of pleasure, and delighted to be the leader of his youthful companions.

Then a terrible calamity befell him. One day as he was playing near the seashore with two of his sisters, some Irish pirates, commanded by O'Neal, carried them all three off to their boats, and sold them in Ireland to the petty chieftain of some pagan clan. Succat was sent into the fields to keep swine. It was while alone in these solitary pastures, without priest and without temple, that the young slave called to mind the Divine lessons which his pious parents had so often read to him. The faults which he had committed pressed heavily night and day upon his soul: he groaned in heart, and wept. He turned repenting towards that meek Saviour of whom his parents had so often spoken; he fell at his knees in that heathen land, and imagined he felt the arms of a father uplifting the prodigal son. Succat was then born from on high, but by an agent so spiritual and unseen that he knew not 'whence it cometh or whither it goeth'. The gospel was written with the finger of God on the tablets of his heart. 'I was sixteen years old', said he, 'and knew not the true God; but in that strange land the Lord opened my unbelieving eyes, and, although late, I called my sins to mind, and was converted with my whole heart to the Lord my God, who regarded my low estate, had pity on my youth and ignorance, and consoled me as a father consoles his children.'

Such words as these from the lips of a swineherd in the green pastures of Ireland set clearly before us the Christianity which in the fourth and fifth centuries converted many souls in the British Isles. In after-years, Rome established the dominion of the priest and salvation by forms, independently of the dispositions of the heart; but the primitive religion of these celebrated islands was that living Christianity whose substance is the grace of Jesus Christ, and whose power is the grace of the Holy Ghost. The herdsman from Bannavern was then undergoing those experiences which so many evangelical Christians in Britain have subsequently undergone. 'The love of God increased more and more in me', said he, 'with faith and the fear of his name. The Spirit urged me to such a degree that I poured forth as many as a hundred prayers in one day. And even during the night, in the forests and on the mountains where I kept my herd, the rain, and snow, and frost, and sufferings which I endured, excited me to seek after God. At that time, I felt not the indifference which now I feel: the Spirit fermented in my heart.' Evangelical faith even then existed in the British islands in the person of this slave, and of some few Christians born again, like him, from on high.

Twice a captive and twice rescued, Succat, after returning to his family, felt an irresistible appeal in his heart. It was his duty to carry the gospel to those Irish pagans among whom he had found Jesus Christ. His parents and his friends endeavoured in vain to detain him; the same ardent desire pursued him in his dreams. During the silent watches of the night he fancied he heard voices calling to him from the dark forests of Erin: 'Come, holy child, and walk once more among us.' He awoke in tears, his breast filled with the keenest emotion. He tore himself from the arms of his parents, and rushed forth – not as heretofore with his playfellows, when he would climb the summit of some lofty hill – but with a heart full of charity in Christ. He departed: 'It was not done of my own strength', said he; 'it was God who overcame all.'

Succat, afterwards known as St Patrick, and to which name, as to that of St Peter and other servants of God, many superstitions have been attached, returned to Ireland, but without visiting Rome, as an historian of the twelfth century has asserted. Ever active, prompt, and ingenious, he collected the pagan tribes in the fields by beat of drum, and then narrated to them in their own tongue the history of the Son of God. Ere long his simple recitals exercised a divine power over their rough hearts, and many souls were converted, not by external sacraments or by the worship of images, but by the preaching of the word of God. The son of a chieftain, whom Patrick calls Benignus, learnt from him to proclaim the gospel, and was destined to succeed him. The court bard, Dubrach Mac Valubair, no longer sang druidical hymns, but canticles addressed to Jesus Christ. Patrick was not entirely free from the errors of the time; perhaps he believed in pious miracles; but generally speaking we meet with nothing but the gospel in the earlier days of the British Church.

Shortly before the evangelization of Patrick in Ireland, a Briton named Pelagius, having visited Italy, Africa, and Palestine, began to teach a strange doctrine. Desirous of making head against the moral indifference into which most of the Christians in those countries had fallen, and which would appear to have been in strong contrast with the British austerity, he denied the doctrine of original sin, extolled free will, and maintained that, if man made use of all the powers of his nature, he would attain perfection. We do not find that he taught these opinions in his own country; but from the Continent, where he disseminated them, they soon reached Britain. The British churches refused to receive this 'perverse doctrine', their historian (Bede) tells us, 'and to blaspheme the grace of Jesus Christ'. They do not appear to have held the strict doctrine of St Augustine: they believed indeed that man has need of an inward change, and that this the Divine power alone can effect; but they seem to have conceded something to our natural strength in the work of conversion; and Pelagius, with a good intention it would appear, went still further. However that may be, these churches, strangers to the controversy, were unacquainted with all its subtleties. Two Gaulish bishops, Germanus of Auxerre and Lupus of Troyes, came to their aid, and appear to have silenced the heretics at St Albans.

Shortly after this, events of great importance took place in Great Britain, and the light of faith disappeared in profound night. In 449, Hengist and Horsa, with their Saxon followers, being invited by the wretched inhabitants to aid them against the cruel ravages of the Picts and Scots, soon turned their swords against the people they had come to assist. Christianity was driven back with the Britons into the mountains of Wales and the wild moors of Cumberland and Cornwall. Many British families remained in the midst of the conquerors, but without exercising any religious influence over them. While the conquering races settled at Paris, Ravenna, or Toledo, and gradually laid aside their paganism and savage manners, the barbarous customs of the Saxons prevailed unmoderated throughout the kingdoms of the Heptarchy, and in every quarter temples to Thor rose above the churches in which Jesus Christ had been worshipped. Gaul and the south of Europe, which still exhibited to the eyes of the barbarians the last vestiges of Roman grandeur, alone had the power of inspiring some degree of respect in the formidable invaders, and of transforming their faith. From this period, the Greeks and Latins, and even the converted Goths, looked at this island with unutterable dread. The soil, said they, is covered with serpents; the air is thick with deadly exhalations; the souls of the departed are transported thither at midnight from the shores of Gaul. Ferrymen, sons of Erebus and Night, admit these invisible shades into their boats, and listen, with a shudder, to their mysterious whisperings. England, whence light was one day to be shed over the habitable globe, was then the trysting-place of the dead. And yet the Christianity of the British Isles was not to be annihilated by these barbarian invasions; it possessed a strength which rendered it capable of energetic resistance.

In one of the churches formed by Succat's preaching, there arose about two centuries after him a pious man named Columba, son of Feidlimyd, the son of Fergus. Valuing the cross of Christ more highly than the royal blood that flowed in his veins, he resolved to devote himself to the King of Heaven. 'I will go', said he, 'and preach the word of God in Scotland'; for the word of God and not an ecclesiastical hierarchism was then the converting agency. The grandson of Fergus communicated the zeal which animated him to the hearts of several fellow Christians. They repaired to the seashore, and cutting down the pliant branches of the osier, constructed a frail bark, which they covered with the skins of beasts. In this rough boat they embarked about the year 563, and after being driven to and fro on the ocean, the little missionary band reached the waters of the Hebrides. Columba landed near the barren rocks of Mull, to the south of the basaltic caverns of Staffa, and fixed his abode in a small island, afterwards known as Iona or Icolmkill, 'the island of Columba's cell'. Some Christian Culdees, driven out by the dissensions of the Picts and Scots, had already found a refuge in the same retired spot. Here the missionaries erected a chapel, whose walls, it is said, still exist among the stately ruins of a later age. Some authors have placed Columba in the first rank after the apostles. True, we do not find in him the faith of a Paul or a John; but he lived as in the sight of God; he mortified the flesh, and slept on the ground with a stone for his pillow. Amid this solemn scenery, and among customs so rough, the form of the missionary, illumined by a light from heaven, shone with love, and manifested the joy and serenity of his heart. Although subject to the same passions as ourselves, he wrestled against his weakness, and would not have one moment lost for the glory of God. He prayed and read, he wrote and taught, he preached and redeemed the time. With indefatigable activity he went from house to house, and from kingdom to kingdom. Brude, the King of the Picts, was converted, as were also many of his people; precious manuscripts were conveyed to Iona; a school of theology was founded there, in which the word was studied; and many received through faith the salvation which is in Christ Jesus. Erelong a missionary spirit breathed over this ocean rock, so justly named 'the light of the Western world'.

The Judaical sacerdotalism which was beginning to extend in the Christian church found no support in Iona. They had forms, but not to them did they look for life. It was the Holy Ghost, Columba maintained, that made a servant of God. When the youth of Caledonia assembled around the elders on these savage shores, or in their humble chapel, these ministers of the Lord would say to them: 'The holy Scriptures are the only rule of faith. Throw aside all merit of works, and look for salvation to the grace of God alone. Beware of a religion which consists of outward observances: it is better to keep your heart pure before God than to abstain from meats. One alone is your head, Jesus Christ. Bishops and presbyters are equal; they should be the husbands of one wife, and have their children in subjection.'

The sages of Iona knew nothing of transubstantiation or of the withdrawal of the cup in the Lord's Supper, or of auricular confession, or of prayers to the dead, or tapers, or incense; they celebrated Easter on a different day from Rome; synodal assemblies regulated the affairs of the church, and the papal supremacy was unknown. The sun of the gospel shone upon these wild and distant shores. In after-years, it was the privilege of Great Britain to recover with a purer lustre the same sun and the same gospel.

Iona, governed by a simple elder, had become a missionary college. It has been sometimes called a monastery, but the dwelling of the grandson of Fergus in no wise resembled the popish houses. When its youthful inmates desired to spread the knowledge of Jesus Christ, they thought not of going elsewhere in quest of episcopal ordination. Kneeling in the chapel of Icolmkill, they were set apart by the laying-on of the hands of the elders: they were called bishops, but remained obedient to the elder or presbyter of Iona. They even consecrated other bishops: thus Finan laid hands upon Diuma, Bishop of Middlesex. These British Christians attached great importance to the ministry; but not to one form in preference to another. Presbytery and episcopacy were with them, as with the primitive church, almost identical.[2] The religious and moral element that belongs to Christianity still predominated; the sacerdotal element, which characterizes human religions, whether among the Brahmins or elsewhere, was beginning to show itself, but in Great Britain at least it held a very subordinate station. Christianity was still a religion and not a caste. They did not require of the servant of God, as a warrant of his capacity, a long list of names succeeding one another like the beads of a rosary; they entertained serious, noble, and holy ideas of the ministry; its authority proceeded wholly from Jesus Christ its head.

The missionary fire, which Columba had kindled in a solitary island, soon spread over Great Britain. Not in Iona alone, but at Bangor (County Down) and other places, the spirit of evangelization burst out. A fondness for travelling had already become a second nature in this people. Men of God, burning with zeal, resolved to carry the evangelical torch to the Continent – to the vast wilderness sprinkled here and there with barbarous and heathen tribes. They did not set forth as antagonists of Rome, for at that epoch there was no place for such antagonism; but Iona and Bangor, less illustrious than Rome in the history of nations, possessed a more lively faith than the city of the Caesars; and that faith – unerring sign of the presence of Jesus Christ – gave those whom it inspired a right to evangelize the world, which Rome could not gainsay.

The missionary bishops of Britain accordingly set forth and traversed the Low Countries, Gaul, Switzerland, Germany, and even Italy. The free church of the Scots and Britons did more for the conversion of

---

[2] Somewhat later we find that neither the venerable Bede, nor Lanfranc, nor Anselm – the two last were archbishops of Canterbury – made any objection to the ordination of British bishops by plain presbyters. Bishop Munter makes this remark in his dissertation *On the Ancient British Church*, about the primitive identity of bishops and priests, and episcopal consecration. *Stud. und Krit.* an. 1833.

central Europe than the half-enslaved Church of the Romans. These missionaries were not haughty and insolent like the priests of Italy; but supported themselves by the work of their hands. Columbanus (whom we must not confound with Columba) 'feeling in his heart the burning of the fire which the Lord had kindled upon earth', quitted Bangor about 590 with twelve other missionaries, and carried the gospel to the Burgundians, Franks, and Swiss. He continued to preach it amidst frequent persecutions, left his disciple Gall in Helvetia, and retired to Bobbio, where he died, honouring Christian Rome, but placing the church of Jerusalem above it – exhorting it to beware of corruption, and declaring that the power would remain with it so long only as it retained the true doctrine (*recta ratio*). Thus was Britain faithful in planting the standard of Christ in the heart of Europe. We might almost imagine this unknown people to be a new Israel, and Icolmkill and Bangor to have inherited the virtues of Zion.

Yet they should have done more: they should have preached – not only to the Continental heathens, to those in the north of Scotland and the distant Ireland, but also to the still pagan Saxons of England. It is true that they made several attempts; but while the Britons considered their conquerors as the enemies of God and man, and shuddered while they pronounced their name, the Saxons refused to be converted by the voice of their slaves. By neglecting this field, the Britons left room for other workmen, and thus it was that England yielded to a foreign power, beneath whose heavy yoke it long groaned in vain.

CHAPTER TWO

Iona versus Rome

(6th & 7th Centuries)

I t is matter of fact that the spiritual life had waned in Italian Catholicism; and in proportion as the heavenly spirit had become weak, the lust of dominion had grown strong. The Roman metropolitans and their delegates soon became impatient to mould all Christendom to their peculiar forms.

About the end of the sixth century an eminent man filled the see of Rome. Gregory was born of senatorial family, and already on the high road to honour, when he suddenly renounced the world, and transformed the palace of his fathers into a monastery. But his ambition had only changed its object. In his view, the whole church should submit to the ecclesiastical jurisdiction of Rome. True, he rejected the title of *universal bishop* assumed by the patriarch of Constantinople; but if he desired not the name, he was not the less eager for the substance. On the borders of the West, in the island of Britain, was a Christian church independent of Rome: this must be conquered, and a favourable opportunity soon occurred.

Before his elevation to the primacy, and while he was as yet only the monk Gregory, he chanced one day to cross a market in Rome where certain foreign dealers were exposing their wares for sale. Among them he perceived some fair-haired youthful slaves, whose noble bearing attracted his attention. On drawing near them, he learned that the Anglo-Saxon nation to which they belonged had refused to receive the gospel from the Britons. When he afterwards became Bishop of Rome, this crafty and energetic pontiff, 'the last of the good and the first of the bad', as he has been called, determined to convert these proud conquerors, and make use of them in subduing the British Church to the papacy, as he had already made use of the Frankish monarchs to reduce the Gauls. Rome has often shown herself more eager to bring Christians rather than idolaters to the pope. Was it thus with Gregory? We must leave the question unanswered.

Æthelbert, King of Kent, having married a Christian princess of Frankish descent, the Roman bishop thought the conjuncture favourable for his design, and in 596 despatched a mission under the direction of one of his friends named Augustine, the Prior of St Andrew's monastery at Rome. At first the missionaries recoiled from the task appointed them; but Gregory was firm. Desirous of gaining the assistance of the Frankish kings, Theodoric and Theodebert, he affected to consider them as the lords paramount of England, and commended to them the conversion of *their subjects*. Nor was this all. He claimed also the support of the powerful Brunhilda, grandmother of these two kings, and equally notorious for her treachery, her irregularities, and her crimes; and did not scruple to extol the *good works* and *godly fear* of this sixth-century Jezebel. Under such auspices the Romish mission arrived in England. The pope had made a skilful choice of his delegate. Augustine possessed even to a greater extent than Gregory himself a mixture of ambition and devotedness, of superstition and piety, of cunning and zeal. He thought that faith and holiness were less essential to the church than authority and power; and that its prerogative was not so much to save souls as to collect all the human race under the sceptre of Rome. Gregory himself was distressed at Augustine's spiritual pride, and often exhorted him to humility.

Success of that kind which popery desires soon crowned the labours of its servants. The forty-one missionaries having landed in the Isle of Thanet, in the summer of 597, the King of Kent consented to receive them, but in the open air, for fear of magic. They drew up in such a manner as to produce an effect on the rough islanders. The procession was opened by a monk bearing a huge cross on which the figure of Christ was represented: his colleagues followed chanting their Latin hymns, and thus they approached the oak appointed for the place of conference. They inspired sufficient confidence in Æthelbert to gain permission to celebrate their worship in an old ruinous chapel at Durovernum

(Canterbury) where British Christians had in former times adored the Saviour Christ. The king and thousands of his subjects received not long after, with certain forms, and certain Christian doctrines, the errors of the Roman pontiffs – as purgatory, for instance, which Gregory was advocating with the aid of the most absurd fables. Augustine reported the baptism of more than ten thousand pagans in one day. As yet Rome had only set her foot in Great Britain; she did not fail erelong to establish her kingdom there.

We do not wish to undervalue the religious element now placed before the Anglo-Saxons, and we can readily believe that many of the missionaries sent from Italy desired to work a Christian work. We think, too, that the Middle Ages ought to be appreciated with more equitable sentiments than have always been found in the persons who have written on that period. Man's conscience lived, spoke, and groaned during the long dominion of popery; and like a plant growing among thorns, it often succeeded in forcing a passage through the obstacles of tradition-alism and hierarchy, to blossom in the quickening sun of God's grace. The Christian element is even strongly marked in some of the most eminent men of the theocracy – in Anselm for instance.

Yet as it is our task to relate the history of the struggles which took place between primitive Christianity and Roman Catholicism, we cannot forbear pointing out the superiority of the former in a religious light, while we acknowledge the superiority of the latter in a political point of view. We believe (and we shall presently have a proof of it)[1] that a visit to Iona would have taught the Anglo-Saxons much more than their frequent pilgrimages to the banks of the Tiber. Doubtless, as has been remarked, these pilgrims contemplated at Rome 'the noble monuments of antiquity', but there existed at that time in the British Islands – and it has been too often overlooked – a Christianity which, if not perfectly pure, was at least better than that of popery. The British Church, which at the beginning of the seventh century carried faith and civilization into Burgundy, the Vosges mountains, and Switzerland, might well have spread them both over Britain. The influence of the arts, whose civilizing influence we are far from depreciating, would have come later.

[1] In the history of Oswald, King of Northumbria.

But so far was the Christianity of the Britons from converting the Saxon kingdoms, that it was, alas! the Romanism of those kingdoms which was destined to conquer Britain. These struggles between the Roman and British Churches, which fill all the seventh century, are of the highest importance to the English Church, for they establish clearly its primitive liberty. They possess also great interest for the other churches of the West, as showing in the most striking characters the usurping acts by which the papacy eventually reduced them beneath its yoke.

Augustine, appointed archbishop not only of the Saxons, but of the free Britons, was settled by papal ordinance at Canterbury although it was probably intended to transfer his seat to London at the first suitable opportunity. Being at the head of a hierarchy composed of twelve bishops, he soon attempted to bring all the Christians of Britain under the Roman jurisdiction. At that time there existed at Bangor Iscoed, in North Wales about twenty-five miles south of Chester, a large Christian society, amounting to nearly three thousand individuals, collected together to work with their own hands, to study, and to pray, and from whose bosom numerous missionaries had from time to time gone forth. The president of this church was Dionoth, a faithful teacher, ready to serve all men in charity, yet firmly convinced that no one should have supremacy in the Lord's vineyard. Although one of the most influential men in the British Church, he was somewhat timid and hesitating; he would yield to a certain point for the love of peace; but would never flinch from his duty. He was another apostle John, full of mildness, and yet condemning the Diotrephes, *who love to have pre-eminence among the brethren*. Augustine thus addressed him: 'Acknowledge the authority of the Bishop of Rome.' These are the first words of the papacy to the ancient Christians of Britain. 'We desire to love all men', meekly replied the venerable Briton; 'and what we do for you, we will do for him also whom you call the pope. But he is not entitled to call himself the *Father of fathers*, and the only submission we can render him is that which we owe to every Christian.' This was not what Augustine asked.

He was not discouraged by this first check. Proud of the pallium which Rome had sent him, and relying on the swords of the Anglo-Saxons, he convoked in 601 a general assembly of British and Saxon bishops. The meeting took place in the open air, beneath a venerable oak, near Wigornia (Worcester, or perhaps Hereford) and here occurred the second Romish aggression. Dionoth resisted with firmness the extravagant pretensions of Augustine, who again summoned him to recognize the authority of Rome. Another Briton protested against the presumption of the Romans, who ascribed to their consecration a virtue which they refused to that of Iona or of the Eastern Churches. The Britons, exclaimed a third, 'cannot submit either to the haughtiness of the Romans or the tyranny of the Saxons'. To no purpose did the archbishop lavish his arguments, prayers, censures, and miracles even; the Britons were firm. Some of them who had eaten with the Saxons while they were as yet heathens, refused to do so now that they had submitted to the pope. The Scots were particularly inflexible; for one of their number, by name Dagam, would not only take no food at the same table with the Romans, but not even under the same roof. Thus did Augustine fail a second time, and the independence of the British Church appeared secure.

And yet the formidable power of the popes, aided by the sword of the conquerors, alarmed the Britons. They imagined they saw a mysterious decree once more yoking the nations of the earth to the triumphal car of Rome, and many left Wigornia uneasy and sad at heart. How is it possible to save a cause, when even its defenders begin to despair? It was not long before they were summoned to a new council. 'What is to be done?' they exclaimed with sorrowful forebodings. Popery was not yet thoroughly known: it was hardly formed. The half-enlightened consciences of these believers were a prey to the most violent agitation. They asked themselves whether, in rejecting this new power, they might not be rejecting God himself. A pious Christian, who led a solitary life, had acquired a great reputation in the surrounding district. Some of the Britons visited him, and inquired whether they should resist Augustine or follow him. 'If he is a man of God, follow him', replied the hermit. – 'And how shall we know that?' – 'If he is meek and humble of heart, he bears Christ's yoke; but if he is violent and proud, he is not of God.' – 'What sign shall we have of his humility?' – 'If he rises from his seat when you enter the room.' Thus spoke the oracle of Britain: it would have been better to have consulted the holy Scriptures.

But humility is not a virtue that flourishes among Romish pontiffs and legates: they love to remain seated while others court and worship them. The British bishops entered the council hall, and the archbishop, desirous of indicating his superiority, proudly kept his seat. Astonished at this sight, the Britons would hear no more of the authority of Rome. For the third time they said No – they knew *no other master but Christ*. Augustine, who expected to see these bishops prostrate their churches at his feet, was surprised and indignant. He had reckoned on the immediate submission of Britain, and the pope had now to learn that his missionary had deceived him. Animated by that insolent spirit which is found too often in the ministers of the Romish Church, Augustine exclaimed: 'If you will not receive brethren who bring you peace, you shall receive enemies who will bring you war. If you will not unite with us in showing the Saxons the way of life, you shall receive from them the stroke of death.' Having thus spoken, the haughty archbishop withdrew, and occupied his last days in preparing the accomplishment of his ill-omened prophecy. Argument had failed: now for the sword!

Shortly after the death of Augustine, Æthelfrith, one of the Anglo-Saxon kings, and who was still a heathen, made war against Solomon, son of Cynan, King of Powys, the country between the Upper Severn and the Dee, and advanced towards Bangor Iscoed, the centre of British Christianity. The magnitude of the danger seemed to recall the Britons to their pristine piety: not to men, but to the Lord himself will they turn their thoughts. Twelve hundred and fifty servants of the living God, calling to mind what are the arms of Christian warfare, after preparing themselves by fasting, met together in a retired spot to send up their prayers to God. A British chief, named Brocmail, moved by tender compassion, stationed himself near them with a few soldiers; but the cruel Æthelfrith, observing from a distance this band of kneeling Christians, demanded: 'Who are these people, and what are they doing?' On being informed, he added: 'They are fighting then against us, although unarmed'; and immediately he ordered his soldiers to fall upon the prostrate crowd. Almost all of them were slain. They prayed and they died. The Saxons forthwith proceeded to Bangor, the chief seat of Christian learning, and razed it to the ground. Romanism was triumphant in

England. The news of these massacres filled the country *with weeping and great mourning*; but the priests of Romish consecration (and the venerable Bede, who narrates the massacre, shared their sentiments) beheld in this cruel slaughter the accomplishment of the prophecy of 'the *holy pontiff* Augustine';[2] and a national tradition among the Welsh for many ages pointed to him as the instigator of this cowardly butchery.

But while the Saxon sword appeared to have swept everything from before the papacy, the ground trembled under its feet, and seemed about to swallow it up. The hierarchical rather than Christian conversions effected by the priests of Rome were so unreal that a vast number of the new converts suddenly returned to the worship of their idols. Eadbald, King of Kent, was himself among them. Such reversions to paganism are not infrequent in the history of the Romish missions. The bishops fled into Gaul: Mellitus of London and Justus of Rochester had already reached the Continent in safety, and Laurentius, Augustine's successor, was about to follow them. While lying in the church where he had desired to pass the night before leaving England, he groaned in spirit as he saw the work founded by Augustine perishing in his hands. He saved it, says Bede, by a miracle. The next morning he presented himself before the king with his clothes all disordered and his body covered with wounds. 'St Peter', he said, 'appeared to me during the night and scourged me severely because I was about to forsake his flock.' The *scourge* was a means of moral persuasion which Peter had forgotten in his Epistles. Did Laurentius cause these blows to be inflicted by others – or did he inflict them himself – or is the whole account an idle dream? We should prefer adopting the last hypothesis. The superstitious prince, excited at the news of this supernatural intervention, eagerly acknowledged the authority of the pope, the vicar of an apostle who so mercilessly scourged those who had the misfortune to displease him. If the dominion of Rome had then disappeared from England, it is probable that the Britons, regaining their courage, and favoured in other respects by the wants which would have been felt by the Saxons, would have recovered from their defeat, and would have imparted their free Christianity to their conquerors. Now, however, the Roman bishop

---

[2] *Bede's Ecclesiastical History of England*, Book II, Chapter 2.

seemed to remain master of England, and the faith of the Britons to be crushed for ever. But it was not so. A young man, sprung from the energetic race of the Anglo-Saxon conquerors, was about to become the champion of truth and liberty, and to cause almost the whole island to be freed from the Roman yoke.

Oswald, King of Northumbria, son of the heathen and cruel Æthelfrith, had been compelled by family reverses to take refuge in Scotland, when very young, accompanied by his brother Oswiu and several other youthful chiefs. He acquired the language of the country, was instructed in the truths of holy writ, converted by the grace of God, and baptized into the Scottish Church. He loved to sit at the feet of the elders of Iona and listen to their words. They showed him Jesus Christ going from place to place doing good, and he desired to do likewise; they told him that Christ was the only head of the church, and he promised never to acknowledge any other. Being a single-hearted, generous man, he was especially animated with tender compassion towards the poor, and would take off his own cloak to cover the nakedness of one of his brethren. Often, while mingling in the quiet assemblies of the Scottish Christians, he had desired to go as a missionary to the Anglo-Saxons. It was not long before he conceived the bold design of leading the people of Northumbria to the Saviour; but being a prince as well as a Christian, he determined to begin by reconquering the throne of his fathers. There was in this young Englishman the love of a disciple and the courage of a hero. At the head of an army, small indeed, but strong by faith in Christ, he entered Northumbria, knelt with his troops in prayer on the field of battle, and gained a signal victory over Cadwallon, King of Gwynedd, A.D. 633.

To recover the kingdom of his ancestors was only a part of his task. Oswald desired to give his people the benefits of the true faith. The Christianity taught in 625 to King Edwin and the Northumbrians by preachers from York had disappeared amidst the ravages of pagan armies. Oswald requested a missionary from the Scots who had given him asylum, and they accordingly sent one of the brethren named Corman, a pious but uncultivated and austere man. He soon returned dispirited to Iona: 'The people to whom you sent me', he told the elders of that island, 'are so obstinate that we must renounce all idea of changing their manners.' As Aidan, one of their number, listened to this report, he said to himself: 'If thy love had been preached to this people, oh, my Saviour, many hearts would have been touched! ... I will go and make thee known – thee who breakest not the bruised reed!' Then, turning to the missionary with a look of mild reproach, he added: 'Brother, you have been too severe towards hearers so dull of heart. You should have given them spiritual milk to drink until they were able to receive more solid food.' All eyes were fixed on the man who spoke so wisely. 'Aidan is worthy of the episcopate', exclaimed the brethren of Iona; and, like Timothy, he was consecrated by the laying on of the hands of the company of elders.

Oswald received Aidan as an angel from heaven and, as the missionary was ignorant of the Saxon language, the king accompanied him every-where, standing by his side, and interpreting his gentle discourses. The people crowded joyfully around Oswald, Aidan, and other missionaries from Scotland and Ireland, listening eagerly to the *word of God*. The king preached by his works still more than by his words. One day during Easter, as he was about to take his seat at table, he was informed that a crowd of his subjects, driven by hunger, had collected before his palace gates. Instantly he ordered the food prepared for himself to be carried out and distributed among them; and taking the silver vessels which stood before him, he broke them in pieces and commanded his servants to divide them among the poor. He also introduced the knowledge of the Saviour to the people of Wessex, whither as overlord of all the English kingdoms south of the Humber, he had gone to marry the king's daughter. After a reign of nine years, he died at the head of his army while repelling an invasion of the idolatrous Mercians, headed by the cruel Penda (5 August 642). As he fell he exclaimed: 'Lord, have mercy on the souls of my people!' This youthful prince has left a name dear to the churches of Great Britain.

His death did not interrupt the labours of the missionaries. Their meekness and the recollection of Oswald endeared them to all. As soon as the villagers caught sight of one on the high road, they would throng round him, begging him to teach them the *word of life*. The faith which the terrible Æthelfrith thought he had washed away in the blood of the worshippers of God, was reappearing in every direction; and Rome, which once already in the days of Honorius, in the first part of the fifth century, had been forced to leave Britain, might be perhaps a second time compelled to flee to its ships from before the face of a people who asserted their liberty.

CHAPTER THREE

Rome 'Converts' Britain

(7th Century)

Then uprose the papacy. If victory remained with the Britons, their church, becoming entirely free, might even in these early times head a strong opposition against the papal dominion. If, on the contrary, the last champions of liberty were defeated, centuries of slavery awaited the Christian church. We shall have to witness the struggle that took place erelong in the very palace of the Northumbrian kings.

Oswald was succeeded in Bernicia (the northern section of Northumbria) by his brother Oswiu, a prince instructed in the free doctrine of the Britons, but whose religion was all external. His heart overflowed with ambition, and he shrank from no crime that might increase his power. The throne of Deira (the southern section of Northumbria) was filled by his relation, Oswine, an amiable king, much beloved by his people. Oswiu, conceiving a deadly jealousy towards him, marched against him at the head of an army, and Oswine, desirous of avoiding bloodshed, took shelter with a chief whom he had loaded with favours. But the latter offered to lead Oswiu's soldiers to his hiding place; and at dead of night the fugitive king was basely assassinated, one only of his servants fighting in his defence. The gentle Aidan died of sorrow at his cruel fate. Such was the first exploit of that monarch who surrendered England to the papacy. Various circumstances tended to draw Oswiu nearer Rome. He looked upon the Christian religion as a means of combining the Christian princes against the heathen Penda, and such a religion, in which expediency predominated, was not very unlike popery. And further, Oswiu's wife, Eanfled, was of the Romish communion.

The private chaplain of this princess was a priest named Romanus, a man worthy of the name. He zealously maintained the rites of the Latin Church, and accordingly the festival of Easter was celebrated at court twice in the year; for while the king, following the Eastern rule, was joyfully commemorating the resurrection of our Lord, the queen, who adopted the Roman ritual, was keeping Palm Sunday with fasting and humiliation. Eanfled and Romanus would often converse together on the means of winning over Northumbria to the papacy. But the first step was to increase the number of its partisans, and the opportunity soon occurred.

A young Northumbrian, named Wilfrid, was one day admitted to an audience of the queen. He was a comely man, of extensive knowledge, keen wit, and enterprising character, of indefatigable activity, and insatiable ambition. In this interview he remarked to Eanfled: 'The way which the Scots teach us is not perfect; I will go to Rome and learn in the very temples of the apostles.' She approved of his project, and with her assistance and directions he set out for Italy. Alas! he was destined at no very distant day to chain the whole British Church to the Roman see. After a stay of three years at Lyons, where the bishop, delighted at his talents, would have desired to keep him, he arrived at Rome, and immediately became on the most friendly footing with Archdeacon Boniface, the pope's favourite councillor. He soon discovered that the priests of France and Italy possessed more power both in ecclesiastical and secular matters than the humble missionaries of Iona; and his thirst for honours was inflamed at the court of the pontiffs. If he should succeed in making England submit to the papacy, there was no dignity to which he might not aspire. Henceforward this was his only thought, and he had hardly returned to Northumbria before Eanfled eagerly summoned him to court. A fanatical queen, from whom he might hope everything; a king with no religious convictions, and enslaved by political interests; a pious and zealous prince, Alfred, the king's son, who was desirous of imitating his noble uncle Oswald and converting the pagans, but who had neither the discernment nor the piety of the illustrious disciple of Iona – such were the materials Wilfrid had to work upon. He saw clearly that if Rome had gained her first victory by the sword of Æthelfrith, she could only expect to gain a second by craft and management. He came to an understanding on the subject with the queen and Romanus, and having been placed about the person of the young prince, by adroit flattery he soon gained over Alfred's mind. Then finding himself secure of two members of the royal family, he turned all his attention to Oswiu.

The elders of Iona could not shut their eyes to the dangers which threatened Northumbria. They had sent Finan to supply Aidan's place, and this bishop, consecrated by the presbyters of Iona, had witnessed the progress of popery at the court: at first humble and inoffensive, and then increasing year by year in ambition and audacity. He had openly opposed the pontiff's agents, and his frequent contests had confirmed him in the truth. He was dead, and the presbyters of the Western Isles, seeing more clearly than ever the wants of Northumbria, had sent thither Bishop Colman, a simple-minded but stout-hearted man, one determined to oppose a front of adamant to the wiles of the seducers.

Yet Eanfled, Wilfrid, and Romanus were skilfully digging the mine that was to destroy the apostolic church of Britain. At first Wilfrid prepared his attack by adroit insinuations; and next declared himself openly in the king's presence. If Oswiu withdrew into his domestic circle, he there found the bigoted Eanfled, who zealously continued the work of the Roman missionary. No opportunities were neglected: in the midst of the diversions of the court, at table, and even during the chase, discussions were perpetually raised on the controverted doctrines. Men's minds became excited: the Romanists already assumed the air of conquerors; and the Britons often withdrew full of anxiety and fear. The king, placed between his wife and his faith, and wearied by these disputes, inclined first to one side, and then to the other, as if he would soon fall altogether.

The papacy had more powerful motives than ever for coveting Northumbria. Oswiu had not only usurped the throne of Deira, but after the death of the cruel Penda, who fell in battle near Leeds in 654, he had conquered his states with the exception of a portion governed by his son-in-law Peada, the son of Penda. But Peada himself having fallen in a conspiracy said to have been made by his wife, the daughter of Oswiu, the latter completed the conquest of Mercia, and thus united most of England under his sceptre. Kent alone at that time acknowledged the jurisdiction of Rome: in every other province, free ministers, protected by the kings of Northumbria, preached the gospel. This wonderfully simplified the question. If Rome gained over Oswiu, she would gain England: if she failed, she must sooner or later leave that island altogether.

This was not all. The blood of Oswine, the premature death of Aidan, and other things besides, troubled the king's breast. He desired to appease the Deity he had offended and, not knowing that *Christ is the door*, as holy Scripture tells us, he sought among men for a *doorkeeper* who would open to him the kingdom of heaven. He was far from being the last of those kings whom the necessity of expiating their crimes impelled towards Romish practices. The crafty Wilfrid, keeping alive both the hopes and fears of the prince, often spoke to him of Rome, and of the grace to be found there. He thought that the fruit was ripe, and that now he had only to shake the tree. 'We must have a public disputation, in which the question may be settled once for all', said the queen and her advisers; 'but Rome must take her part in it with as much pomp as her adversaries. Let us oppose bishop to bishop.' A Saxon bishop named Agilbert, a friend of Wilfrid's, who had won the affection of the young Prince Alfred, was invited by Eanfled to the conference and he duly arrived in Northumbria. Alas! poor British Church, the earthen vessel is about to be dashed against the vase of iron. Britain must yield before the invading march of Rome.

On the coast of Yorkshire, at the farther extremity of a quiet bay, was situated the monastery of Streanaeshalch, or Whitby, of which Hilda, a descendant of the Northumbrian royal line, was abbess. She, too, was desirous of seeing a termination of the violent disputes which had agitated the church since Wilfrid's return. On the shores of the North Sea the struggle was to be decided between Britain and Rome, between the East and the West, or, as they said then, between St John and St Peter. It was not a mere question about Easter, or certain rules of discipline, but of the great doctrine of the freedom of the church under Jesus Christ, or its enslavement under the papacy. Rome, ever domineering, desired for the second time to hold England in its grasp, not by means of the sword, but by her dogmas. With her usual cunning she concealed her enormous pretensions under secondary questions, and many superficial thinkers were deceived by this manoeuvre.

The meeting took place in the monastery of Whitby. The king and his son entered first; then, on the one side, Colman, with the bishops and elders of the Britons; and, on the other, Bishop Agilbert, Agatho, Wilfrid, Romanus, a deacon named James, and several other priests of the Latin confession. Last of all came Hilda with her attendants, among whom was an English bishop named Cedda, one of the most active missionaries of the age. He had at first preached the gospel in the Midland districts, whence he turned his footsteps towards the Anglo-Saxons of the East and, after converting a great number of these pagans, he had returned to Finan, and, although an Englishman, had received episcopal consecration from a bishop, who had been himself ordained by the elders of Iona. An indefatigable evangelist, he founded churches and appointed elders and deacons wherever he went. By birth an Englishman, by ordination a Scotsman, everywhere treated with respect and consideration, he appeared to be set apart as mediator in this solemn conference. His intervention could not, however, retard the victory of Rome. Alas! the primitive evangelism had gradually given way to an ecclesiasticism, coarse and rude in one place, subtle and insinuating in another. Whenever the priests were called upon to justify certain doctrines or ceremonies, instead of referring solely to the word of God as the fountain of all light, they maintained that thus St James did at Jerusalem, St Mark at Alexandria, St John at Ephesus, or St Peter at Rome. They gave the name of *apostolical canons* to rules which the apostles had never known. They went even further than this: at Rome and in the East, ecclesiasticism represented itself to be a law of God. Some marks of this error were already beginning to appear in the Christianity of the Britons.

King Oswiu was the first to speak: 'As servants of one and the same God, we hope all to enjoy the same inheritance in heaven; why then should we not have the same rule of life here below? Let us inquire which is the true one, and follow it.'

'Those who sent me hither as bishop', said Colman, 'and who gave me the rule which I observe, are the beloved of God. Let us beware how we despise their teaching, for it is the teaching of Columba, of the blessed Evangelist John, and of the churches over which that apostle presided.'

'As for us', boldly rejoined Wilfrid, for to him as to the most skilful had Bishop Agilbert entrusted the defence of their cause, 'our custom is that of Rome, where the holy apostles Peter and Paul taught; we find it in Italy and Gaul, nay, it is spread over every nation. Shall the Picts and Britons, cast on these two islands on the very confines of the ocean, dare to contend against the whole world? However holy your Columba may have been, will you prefer him to the prince of the apostles, to whom Christ said, *Thou art Peter, and I will give unto thee the keys of the kingdom of heaven?*'

Wilfrid spoke with animation, and his words being skilfully adapted to his audience, began to make them waver. He had artfully substituted Columba for the apostle John, from whom the British Church claimed descent, and opposed to St Peter a plain elder of Iona. Oswiu, whose idol was power, could not hesitate between paltry bishops and that pope of Rome who commanded the whole world. Already imagining he saw Peter at the gates of paradise, with the keys in his hand, he exclaimed with emotion: 'Is it true, Colman, that these words were addressed by our Lord to St Peter?' – 'It is true.' 'Can you prove that similar powers were given to your Columba?' – The bishop replied, 'We cannot'; but he might have told the king: 'John, whose doctrine we follow, and indeed every disciple, has received in the same sense as St Peter the power to remit sins, to bind and to loose on earth and in heaven.'[1] But the knowledge of the holy Scriptures was fading away in Iona, and the unsuspecting Colman had not observed Wilfrid's stratagem in substituting Columba for St John. Upon this Oswiu, delighted to yield to the continual solicitations of the queen and, above all, to find someone who would admit him into the kingdom of heaven, exclaimed: 'Peter is the doorkeeper, I will obey him, lest when I appear at the gate there should be no one to open it to me.' The spectators, carried away by this royal confession, hastened to give in their submission to the Vicar of St Peter.

Thus did Rome triumph at the Whitby conference. Oswiu forgot that the Lord had said: *I am he that openeth, and no man shutteth; and shutteth, and no man openeth.*[2] It was by ascribing to Peter the servant what belongs to Jesus Christ the master, that the papacy reduced Britain. Oswiu stretched out his hands, Rome riveted the chains, and the liberty which Oswald had given his church seemed at the last gasp.

[1] John 20:23; Matt. 18:18.
[2] John 10:9; Rev. 3:7.

Colman saw with grief and consternation Oswiu and his subjects bending their knees before the foreign priests. He did not, however, despair of the ultimate triumph of the truth. The apostolic faith could still find shelter in the old sanctuaries of the British Church in Scotland and Ireland. Immovable in the doctrine he had received, and resolute to uphold Christian liberty, Colman withdrew with those who would not bend beneath the yoke of Rome, and returned to Scotland. Thirty Anglo-Saxons, and a great number of Britons, shook off the dust of their feet against the tents of the Romish priests. The hatred of popery became intensified among the remainder of the Britons. Determined to repel its erroneous dogmas and its illegitimate dominion, they maintained their communion with the Eastern Church, which was more ancient than that of Rome. They ascribed their misfortunes to a horrible conspiracy planned by the iniquitous ambition of the foreign monks, and the bards in their chants cursed the negligent ministers who defended not the flock of the Lord against the wolves of Rome. But vain were their lamentations!

The Romish priests, aided by the queen, lost no time. Wilfrid, whom Oswiu desired to reward for his triumph, was named Bishop of Northumbria, and he immediately visited Gaul to receive episcopal consecration, at Compiègne, in due form. He soon returned, and proceeded with singular activity to establish the Romish doctrine in all the churches. Bishop of a diocese extending from Edinburgh to Northampton, enriched with the goods which had belonged to divers monasteries, surrounded by a numerous train, served upon gold and silver plate, Wilfrid congratulated himself on having espoused the cause of the papacy; he offended everyone who approached him by his insolence, and taught England how wide was the difference between the humble ministers of Iona and a Romish priest. At the same time Oswiu, coming to an understanding with the King of Kent, sent another priest, named Wighard, to Rome to learn the pope's intentions respecting the church in England, and to receive consecration as Archbishop of Canterbury. There was no episcopal ordination in England worthy of a priest! In the meanwhile Oswiu, with all the zeal of a new convert, ceased not to repeat that 'the Roman Church was the Catholic and Apostolic Church', and thought night and day on the means of converting his subjects, hoping thus (says a pope) to redeem his own soul.

The arrival of this news at Rome created a great sensation. Vitalian, who then filled the papal chair, and was as insolent to his bishops as he was fawning and servile to the emperor, exclaimed with transport: 'Who would not be overjoyed! A king converted to the true apostolic faith, a people that believes at last in Christ the Almighty God!' For many long years this people had believed in Christ, but they were now beginning to believe in the pope, and the pope would soon make them forget Jesus the Saviour. Vitalian wrote to Oswiu, and sent him – not copies of the holy Scriptures (which were already becoming scarce at Rome) but – relics of the Saints Peter, John, Laurentius, Gregory, and Pancratius; and being in an especial manner desirous of rewarding Queen Eanfled, to whom with Wilfrid belonged the glory of this work, he offered her a cross, made, as he assured her, out of the chains of St Peter and St Paul. 'Delay not', said the pope in conclusion, 'to reduce all your island under Jesus Christ', – or in other words, under the Bishop of Rome.

The essential thing, however, was to send an archbishop from Rome to Britain; but Wighard was dead, and no one seemed willing to undertake so long a journey. There was not much zeal in the city of the pontiffs: and the pope was compelled to look out for a stranger. There happened at that time to be in Rome a man of great reputation for learning, who had come from the East, and adopted the rites and doctrines of the Latins in exchange for the knowledge he had brought them. He was pointed out to Vitalian as well qualified to be the metropolitan of England. Theodore, for such was his name, belonging by birth to the churches of Asia Minor, would be listened to by the Britons in preference to any other, when he solicited them to abandon their Eastern customs. The Roman pontiff, however, fearful perhaps that he might yet entertain some leaven of his former Greek doctrines, gave him as companion, or rather as overseer, a zealous African monk named Hadrian.

Theodore began the great crusade against British Christianity, and endeavouring to show the sincerity of his conversion by his zeal, he traversed all England in company with Hadrian, everywhere imposing on the people the ecclesiastical supremacy of Rome. The superiority of character which distinguished St Peter, Theodore transformed into a superiority of office. For the jurisdiction of Christ and his word, he substituted that of the Bishop of Rome and of his decrees. He insisted on the necessity of ordination by bishops who, in an unbroken chain, could trace back their authority to the apostles themselves. The British still maintained the validity of their consecration; but the number was small of those who understood that pretended successors of the apostles, who sometimes carry Satan in their hearts, are not true ministers of Christ. It was forgotten that the one thing needful for the church is the word of God and the presence of the Holy Spirit, and that just as the apostles themselves had been members only by faith in Christ, so must their successors manifest the same faith and possess the same Divine Comforter.

The grand defection now began: the best were sometimes the first to yield. When Theodore met Cedda, who had been consecrated by a bishop who had himself received ordination from the elders of Iona, he said to him: 'You have not been regularly ordained.' Cedda, instead of standing up boldly for the truth, gave way in a carnal modesty, and replied: 'I never thought myself worthy of the episcopate, and am ready to lay it down.' – 'No', said Theodore, 'you shall remain a bishop, but I will consecrate you anew according to the Catholic ritual.' The British minister submitted. Rome triumphant felt herself strong enough to deny the imposition of hands of the elders of Iona, which she had hitherto recognized. The most steadfast believers took refuge in Scotland.

In this manner a church in some respects deficient, but still a church in which the spiritual element held the foremost place, was succeeded by another in which the clerical element predominated. This was soon apparent: questions of authority and precedence, hitherto unknown among the British Christians, were now of daily occurrence. Wilfrid, who had fixed his residence at York, thought that no one deserved better than he to be primate of all England; and Theodore on his part was irritated at the haughty tone assumed by this bishop. During the life of Oswiu, peace was maintained, for Wilfrid was his favourite; but erelong that prince fell ill; and, terrified by the near approach of death, he vowed that if he recovered he would make a pilgrimage to Rome and there end his days. 'If you will be my guide to the city of the apostles', he said to Wilfrid, 'I will give you a large sum of money.' But his vow was of no avail: Oswiu died in the spring of the year 670, and his youngest brother Ecgfrith was raised to the throne. The new monarch, who had often been offended by Wilfrid's insolence, denounced this haughty prelate to the archbishop. Nothing could be more agreeable to Theodore. He assembled a council at Hertford in September 672, before which the chief of his converts were first summoned and, presenting to them not the holy Scripture but the *canons of the Romish Church*, he received their solemn oaths: such was the religion then taught in England. But this was not all. 'The diocese of our brother Wilfrid is so extensive', said the primate, 'that there is room in it for four bishops.' They were appointed accordingly. Wilfrid indignantly appealed from the primate and the king to the pope. 'Who converted England, who, if not I? … and it is thus I am rewarded!' … Not allowing himself to be checked by the difficulties of the journey, he set out for Rome, attended by a few monks and, Pope Agatho assembling a council (679), the Englishman presented his complaint, and the pontiff declared the destitution to be illegal. Wilfrid immediately returned to England, and haughtily presented the pope's decree to the king. But Ecgfrith, who was not of a disposition to tolerate these transalpine manners, far from restoring the see, cast the prelate into prison, and did not release him until the end of the year, and then only on condition that he would immediately quit Northumbria.

Wilfrid – for we must follow even to the end of his life that remarkable man, who exercised so great an influence over the destinies of the English Church – was determined to be a bishop at any cost. The kingdom of Sussex was still pagan; and the deposed prelate, whose indefatigable activity we cannot but acknowledge, formed the resolution of winning a bishopric, as other men plan the conquest of a kingdom. He arrived in Sussex during a period of famine, and having brought with him a number of nets, he taught the people the art of fishing, and thus gained their affections. Their king Æthelwalh was baptized, his subjects followed his example, and Wilfrid was placed at the head of the church.

In 685 King Ecgfrith died, and was succeeded by his brother Alfred, whom Wilfrid had brought up, a prince fond of learning and religion, and ambitious to serve his people. The ambitious Wilfrid now hastened to claim his see of York, by acquiescing in the partition imposed by the

Council of Hertford; it was restored to him, and he forthwith began to plunder others to enrich himself. A council begged him to submit to the decrees of the Church of England; he refused and, having lost the esteem of the king, his former pupil, he undertook, notwithstanding his advanced years, a third journey to Rome. Knowing how popes are won, he threw himself at the pontiff's feet, exclaiming that 'the suppliant bishop Wilfrid, the humble slave of the servant of God, implored the favour of our most blessed lord, the pope universal'. But Wilfrid was not restored to his see and spent the short remainder of his life in the midst of the riches his cupidity had so unworthily accumulated.[3]

Yet he had accomplished the task of his life: all England was subservient to the papacy. The names of *Oswiu* and of *Wilfrid* should be inscribed in letters of mourning in the annals of Great Britain. Posterity has erred in permitting them to sink into oblivion; for they were two of the most influential and energetic men that ever flourished in England. Still this very forgetfulness is not wanting in generosity. The grave in which the liberty of the church lay buried for nine centuries is the only monument – a mournful one indeed – that should perpetuate their memory.

But Scotland was still free and, to secure the definitive triumph of Rome, it was necessary to invade that virgin soil, over which the standard of the faith had floated for so many years.

Adamnan (known in Ireland as St Eunan) was then at the head of the church of Iona, the first elder of that religious house. He was virtuous and learned, but weak and somewhat vain, and his religion had little spirituality. To gain him was in the eyes of Rome to gain Scotland. A singular circumstance favoured the plans of those who desired to draw him into the papal communion. One day during a violent tempest, a ship coming from the Holy Land, and on board of which was a Gaulish bishop named Arculf, was wrecked in the neighbourhood of Iona. Arculf sought asylum among the pious inhabitants of that island. Adamnan never grew tired of hearing the stranger's descriptions of Bethlehem, Jerusalem, and Golgotha, of the sun-burnt plains over which our Lord

---

[3] [The course of events that followed Wilfrid's last visit to the pope is far from clear. Ultimately he was restored to church office in the Ripon and Hexham areas, about four years before he died in the Mercian monastery of Oundle.]

had wandered, and the cleft stone which still lay before the door of the sepulchre. The elder of Iona, who prided himself on his learning, noted down Arculf's conversation, and from it composed a description of the Holy Land. As soon as his book was completed, the desire of making these wondrous things more widely known, combined with a little vanity, and perhaps other motives, urged him to visit the court of Northumbria, where he presented his work to the pious King Alfred, who, being fond of learning and of the Christian traditions, caused a number of copies of it to be made.

Nor was this all: the Romish clergy perceived the advantage they might derive from this imprudent journey. They crowded round the elder; they showed him all the pomp of their worship, and said to him: 'Will you and your friends, who live at the very extremity of the world, set yourselves in opposition to the observances of the universal church?' The nobles of the court flattered the author's self-love, and invited him to their festivities, while the king loaded him with presents. The free presbyter of Britain became a priest of Rome, and Adamnan returned to Iona to betray his church to his new masters. But it was all to no purpose: Iona would not give way. He then went to hide his shame in Ireland, where having brought a few individuals to the Romish uniformity, he took courage and revisited Scotland. But that country, still inflexible, repelled him with indignation.

When Rome found herself unable to conquer by the priest, she had recourse to the prince, and her eyes were turned to Naitam, King of the Picts. 'How much more glorious it would be for you', urged the Latin priests, 'to belong to the powerful church of the universal pontiff of Rome, than to a congregation superintended by miserable elders! The Romish Church is a monarchy, and ought to be the church of every monarch. The Roman ceremonial accords with the pomp of royalty, and its temples are palaces.' The prince was convinced by the last argument. He despatched messengers to Abbot Ceolfrith of Wearmouth, begging him to send him *architects* capable of building a church *after the Roman pattern* – of stone and not of wood. Architects, majestic porches, lofty columns, vaulted roofs, gilded altars, have often proved the most influential of Rome's missionaries. The builder's art, though in its earliest and simplest days, was more powerful than the Bible. Naitam, who, by submitting to the pope, thought himself the equal of Clovis and Clotaire, kings of the Franks, assembled the nobles of his court and the pastors of his church, and thus addressed them: 'I recommend all the clergy of my kingdom to receive the tonsure of St Peter.' Then without delay (as Bede informs us) this important revolution was accomplished by royal authority. He sent agents and letters into every province, and caused all the ministers and monks to receive the circular tonsure according to the Roman fashion. It was the mark that popery stamped, not on the forehead, but on the crown. A royal proclamation and a few clips of the scissors placed the Scots, like a flock of sheep, beneath the crook of the shepherd of the Tiber.

Iona still held out. The orders of the Pictish king, the example of his subjects, the sight of that Italian power which was devouring the earth, had shaken some few minds; but the church still resisted the innovation. Iona was the last citadel of liberty in the western world, and popery was filled with anger at that miserable band which in its remote corner refused to bend before it. Human means appeared insufficient to conquer this rock: something more was needed, visions and miracles for example; and these Rome always finds when she wants them. One day towards the end of the seventh century, an English monk named Egbert, arriving from Ireland, appeared before the elders of Iona, who received him with their accustomed hospitality. He was a man in whom enthusiastic devotion was combined with great gentleness of heart, and he soon captured the minds of these simple believers. He spoke to them of an external unity, urging that a universality manifested under different forms was unsuited to the church of Christ. He advocated the special form of Rome and, for the truly catholic element which the Christians of Iona had thus far possessed, substituted a sectarian element. He attacked the traditions of the British Church, and lavishly distributing the rich presents confided to him by the lords of Ireland and of England, he soon had reason to acknowledge the truth of the saying of the wise man: *A gift is as a precious stone in the eyes of him that hath it: whithersoever it turneth it prospereth.*

Some pious souls, however, still held out in Iona. The enthusiast Egbert – for such he appears to have been rather than an impostor – had recourse to other means. He represented himself to be a messenger from heaven: the saints themselves, said he, have commissioned me to convert Iona; and then he told the following history to the elders who stood round him. 'About thirty years ago I entered the monastery of Rathmelfig in Ireland, when a terrible pestilence fell upon it, and of all the brethren the monk Eelhun and myself were left alone. Attacked by the plague, and fearing my last hour was come, I rose from my bed and crept into the chapel. There my whole body trembled at the recollection of my sins, and my face was bathed with tears. "O God," I exclaimed, "suffer me not to die until I have redeemed my debt to thee by an abundance of good works." I returned staggering to the infirmary, got into bed, and fell asleep. When I awoke, I saw Eelhun with his eyes fixed on mine. "Brother Egbert," said he, "it has been revealed to me in a vision that thou shalt receive what thou hast asked." On the following night Eelhun died and I recovered.

'Many years passed away: my repentance and my vigils did not satisfy me and, wishing to pay my debt, I resolved to go with a company of monks and preach the blessings of the gospel to the heathens of Germany. But during the night a blessed saint from heaven appeared to one of the brethren and said: "Tell Egbert that he must go to the monasteries of Columba, for their ploughs do not plough straight, and he must put them into the right furrow." I forbade this brother to speak of his vision, and went on board a ship bound for Germany. We were waiting for a favourable wind, when, of a sudden, in the middle of the night, a frightful tempest burst upon the vessel, and drove us on the shoals. "For my sake this tempest is upon us," I exclaimed in terror; "God speaks to me as he did to Jonah"; and I ran to take refuge in my cell. At last I determined to obey the command which the holy man had brought me. I left Ireland, and came among you, in order to pay my debt by converting you. And now', continued Egbert, 'make answer to the voice of heaven, and submit to Rome.'

A ship thrown on shore by a storm was a frequent occurrence on those coasts, and the dream of a monk, absorbed in the plans of his brother, was nothing very unnatural. But in those times of darkness, everything appeared miraculous; phantoms and apparitions had more weight than the word of God. Instead of detecting the emptiness of these visions by the falseness of the religion they were brought to support, the elders of

Iona listened seriously to Egbert's narrative. The primitive faith planted on the rock of Icolmkill was now like a pine-tree tossed by the winds: but one gust, and it would be uprooted and blown into the sea. Egbert, perceiving the elders to be shaken, redoubled his prayers, and even had recourse to threats. 'All the West', said he, 'bends the knee to Rome: alone against all, what can you do?' The Scots still resisted: obscure and unknown, the last British Christians contended in behalf of expiring liberty. At length bewildered – they stumbled and fell. The scissors were brought; they received the Latin tonsure – they were the pope's.

Thus fell Scotland. Yet there still remained some sparks of grace, and the mountains of Caledonia long concealed the hidden fire which after many ages burst forth with such power and might. Here and there a few independent spirits were to be found who testified against the tyranny of Rome. In the time of Bede they might be seen 'halting in their paths' (to use the words of the Romish historian), refusing to join in the holidays of the pontifical adherents, and pushing away the hands that were eager to shave their crowns. But the leaders of the state and of the church had laid down their arms. The contest was over, after lasting more than a century. British Christianity had in some degree prepared its own fall, by substituting too often the form for the faith. The foreign superstition took advantage of this weakness, and triumphed in these islands by means of royal decrees, church ornaments, monkish phantoms, and conventual apparitions. At the beginning of the eighth century the British Church became the serf of Rome; but an internal struggle was commencing, which did not cease until the period of the reformation.

CHAPTER FOUR

The Conflict with Papal Supremacy

(7th to 11th Century)

The independent Christians of Scotland, who subordinated the authority of man to that of God, were filled with sorrow as they beheld these backslidings: and it was this no doubt which induced many to leave their homes and fight in the very heart of Europe on behalf of that Christian liberty which had just expired among themselves.

At the commencement of the eighth century a great idea took possession of a pious doctor of the Scottish Church named Clement. The *work of God* is the very essence of Christianity, thought he, and this work must be defended against all the encroachments of man. To human traditionalism he opposed the sole authority of the word of God; to clerical materialism, a church which is the assembly of the saints; and to Pelagianism, the sovereignty of grace. He was a man of decided character and firm faith, but without fanaticism; his heart was open to the holiest emotions of our nature; he was a husband and a father. He quitted Scotland and travelled among the Franks, everywhere scattering the seeds of the faith. It happened unfortunately that a man of kindred energy, Winifrid or Boniface of Wessex (680–754), was planting the pontifical Christianity in the same regions. This great missionary, who possessed in an essential degree the faculty of organization, aimed at external unity above all things and, when he had taken the oath of fidelity to Gregory II, he had received from that pope a collection of the Roman laws. Boniface, henceforth a docile disciple or rather a fanatical champion of Rome, supported on the one hand by the pontiff, and on the other by Charles Martel, ruler of the Franks, had preached to the people of Germany, among some undoubted Christian truths, the doctrine of tithes and of papal supremacy. The Englishman and the Scotsman, representatives of two great systems, were about to engage in deadly combat in the heart of Europe – in a combat whose consequences might be incalculable.

Alarmed at the progress made by Clement's evangelical doctrines, Boniface, Archbishop of the German churches, undertook to oppose them. At first he confronted the Scotsman with the laws of the Roman Church; but the latter denied the authority of these ecclesiastical canons, and refuted their contents. Boniface then put forward the decisions of various councils; but Clement replied that if the decisions of the councils were contrary to holy Scripture, they had no authority over Christians. The archbishop, astonished at such audacity, next had recourse to the writings of the most illustrious Fathers of the Latin Church, quoting Jerome, Augustine, and Gregory; but the Scotsman told him that, instead of submitting to the word of men, he would obey the word of God alone. Boniface with indignation now introduced the Catholic Church which, by its priests and bishops, all united to the pope, formed an invincible unity; but to his great surprise his opponent maintained that there only, where the Holy Spirit dwells, can be found the spouse of Jesus Christ. Vainly did the archbishop express his horror; Clement was not to be turned aside from his great idea, either by the clamours of the followers of Rome, or by the imprudent attacks made on the papacy by other Christian ministers.

Rome had, indeed, other adversaries. A Gallic bishop named Adalbert, with whom Boniface affected to associate Clement, one day saw the archbishop complacently exhibiting to the people some relics of St Peter which he had brought from Rome; and being desirous of showing the ridiculous character of these Romish practices, he distributed among the bystanders his own hair and nails, praying them to pay these the same honours as Boniface claimed for the relics of the papacy. Clement smiled, like many others, at Adalbert's singular argument; but it was not with such arms that he was wont to fight. Gifted with profound discernment, he had remarked that the authority of man substituted for the authority of God was the source of all the errors of Romanism.

At the same time he maintained on predestination what the archbishop called 'horrible doctrines, contrary to the Catholic faith'. Clement's character inclines us to believe that he was favourable to the doctrine of predestination. A century later the pious Gottschalk was persecuted by one of Boniface's successors for holding this very doctrine of Augustine's. Thus then did a Scotsman, the representative of the ancient faith of his country, withstand almost unaided in the centre of Europe the invasion of the Romans. But he was not long alone: the nobility especially, more enlightened than the common people, thronged around him. If Clement had succeeded, a Christian church would have been founded on the Continent independent of the papacy.

Boniface was confounded. He wished to do in central Europe what his fellow countryman Wilfrid had done in England; and, at the very moment he fancied he was advancing from triumph to triumph, victory escaped from his hands. He turned against this new enemy and, applying to Charles Martel's sons, Pepin and Carloman, he obtained their consent to the assembling of a council before which he summoned Clement to appear.

The bishops, counts, and other notabilities having met at Soissons on 2 March 744, Boniface accused the Scotsman of despising the laws of Rome, the councils, and the Fathers; attacked his marriage, which he called an adulterous union; and called in question some secondary points of doctrine. Clement was accordingly excommunicated by Boniface, at once his adversary, accuser, and judge, and thrown into prison, with the approbation of the pope and the King of the Franks.

The Scotsman's cause was everywhere taken up; accusations were brought against the German primate, his persecuting spirit was severely condemned, and his exertions for the triumph of the papacy were resisted. Carloman yielded to this unanimous movement. The prison doors were opened, and Clement had hardly crossed the threshold before he began to protest boldly against human authority in matters of faith: the word of God is the only rule. Upon this Boniface applied to Rome for the heretic's condemnation, and accompanied his request by a silver cup and a garment of delicate texture. The pope decided in synod that if Clement did not retract his errors, he should be delivered up to everlasting damnation; he then requested Boniface to send him to Rome under a sure guard. We here lose all traces of the Scotsman, but it is easy to conjecture what must have been his fate.

Clement was not the only Briton who became distinguished in this contest. Two fellow countrymen, Sampson and Virgil, who preached in central Europe, were in like manner persecuted by the Church of Rome. Virgil, one of the most learned men of his age, anticipating Galileo, and believing in the existence of the Antipodes, dared maintain that there were other men and another world beneath our feet. He was denounced by Boniface for this *heresy*, and condemned by the pope, as were other Britons for the apostolical simplicity of their lives. In 813, certain Scotsmen who called themselves bishops, says a canon, having appeared before a council of the Roman Church at Châlons, were rejected by the French prelates, because, like St Paul, *they worked with their own hands*. Those enlightened and faithful men were superior to their time: Boniface and his ecclesiastical materialism were better fitted for an age in which clerical forms were regarded as the substance of religion!

Even Britain, although its light was not so pure, was not altogether plunged in darkness. The Anglo-Saxons imprinted on their church certain characteristics which distinguished it from that of Rome; several books of the Bible were translated into their tongue, and daring spirits on the one hand, with some pious souls on the other, laboured in a direction hostile to popery.

At first we see the dawning of that philosophic rationalism, which gives out a certain degree of brightness, but which can neither conquer error nor still less establish truth. In the ninth century there was a learned scholar in Ireland, who afterwards settled at the court of Charles the Bald. He was a strange mysterious man, of profound thought, and as much raised above the doctors of his age by the boldness of his ideas, as Charlemagne above the princes of his day by the force of his will. John Scot Erigena – that is, 'born in the Isle of Saints' (Ireland) – was a meteor in the theological heavens. With a great philosophic genius he combined a cheerful jesting disposition. One day, while seated at table opposite to Charles the Bald, the latter archly inquired of him: 'What is the distance between a *Scot* and a *sot*?' 'The width of the table', was his ready answer, which drew a smile from the king. While the doctrine of Bede, Boniface, and even Alcuin was traditional, servile, and, in one word, Romanist, that of Scot was mystical, philosophic, free, and daring. He sought for the truth not in the word or in the church, but in himself: – 'The knowledge of ourselves is the true source of religious wisdom. Every creature is a theophany – a manifestation of God; since revelation presupposes the existence of truth, it is this truth, which is above revelation, with which man must set himself in immediate relation, leaving him at liberty to show afterwards its harmony with Scripture and the other theophanies. We must first employ reason, and then authority. Authority proceeds from reason, and not reason from authority.' Yet this bold thinker, when on his knees, could give way to aspirations full of piety: 'O Lord Jesus', exclaimed he, 'I ask no other happiness of thee, but to understand, unmixed with deceitful theories, the word that thou hast inspired by thy Holy Spirit! Show thyself to those who ask for thee alone!' But while Scot rejected on the one hand certain traditional errors, and in particular the doctrine of transubstantiation which was creeping into the church, he was near falling as regards God and the world into other errors savouring of pantheism. The philosophic rationalism of this contemporary of Charles the Bald – the strange product of one of the obscurest periods of history (850) – was destined after the lapse of many centuries to be taught once more in Britain as a modern invention of the most enlightened age.

While Scot was thus plumbing the depths of philosophy, others were examining their Bibles; and if thick darkness had not spread over these first glimpses of the dawn, perhaps the Church of Britain might even then have begun to labour for the regeneration of Christendom. A youthful prince, thirsting for intellectual enjoyments, for domestic happiness, and for the word of God, and who sought, by frequent prayer, for deliverance from the bondage of sin, had ascended the throne of Wessex, in the year 871. Alfred being convinced that Christianity alone could rightly mould a nation, assembled round him the most learned men from all parts of Europe, and was anxious that the English, like the Hebrews, Greeks, and Latins, should possess the holy Scripture in their own language. He is the real patron of the biblical work, which indeed constitutes one of his chief titles to fame. After having fought numerous campaigns and battles by land and sea, he died while translating the Psalms of David for his subjects.[1]

After this gleam of light thick darkness once more settled upon Britain. Nine Anglo-Saxon kings ended their days in monasteries; there was a seminary in Rome from which every year fresh scholars bore to England the new forms of popery; the celibacy of priests, that cement of the Romish hierarchy, was reaffirmed by a bull about the close of the tenth century; convents were multiplied, considerable possessions were bestowed on the church, and the tax of *Peter's pence*, laid at the pontiff's feet, proclaimed the triumph of the papal system. But a reaction took place: England collected her forces for a war against the papacy – a war at one time secular and at another spiritual. William of Normandy, Edward III, Wycliffe, and the reformation, are the four ascending steps of Protestantism in England.

William of Normandy, a proud, enterprising, and far-sighted prince, the illegitimate son of a peasant girl of Falaise and Robert the Devil, Duke of Normandy, began a contest with the papacy which lasted until the reformation. After defeating the Saxons at Hastings in 1066, he took possession of England, under the benediction of the Roman pontiff. But the conquered country was destined to conquer its master. William, who had invaded England in the pope's name, had no sooner touched the soil of his new kingdom, than he learned to resist Rome, as if the ancient liberty of the British Church had revived in him. Being firmly resolved to allow no foreign prince or prelate to possess in his dominions a jurisdiction independent of his own, he made preparations for a conquest far more difficult than that of the Anglo-Saxon kingdom. The papacy itself furnished him with weapons. The Roman legates prevailed on the king to dispossess the English episcopacy in a Mass, and this was exactly what he wished. To resist the papacy, William desired to be sure of the submission of the priests of England. Stigand, Archbishop of Canterbury, was removed, and Lanfranc of Pavia, who had been summoned from Bec in Normandy to fill his place, was commissioned

[1] [An Anglo-Saxon version of the first fifty psalms has been attributed to Alfred. There is no absolute proof that the work is his but the ascription is reasonably certain.]

by the Conqueror to bend the clergy to obedience. This prelate, who was regular in his life, abundant in almsgiving, a learned disputant, a prudent politician, and a skilful mediator, finding that he had to choose between his master King William and his friend the pontiff Hildebrand, gave the prince the preference. He refused to go to Rome, notwithstanding the threats of the pope, and applied himself resolutely to the work the king had entrusted to him. The Saxons sometimes resisted the Normans, as the Britons had resisted the Saxons; but the second struggle was less glorious than the first. A synod at which the king was present having met in the abbey of Westminster, William commanded Wulfstan, Bishop of Worcester, to give up his crosier to him. The old man rose and animatedly cried: 'O king, from a better man than you I received it, and to him only will I return it.' Unhappily this 'better man' was not Jesus Christ. Then, approaching the tomb of Edward the Confessor, and addressing the deceased monarch, he continued: 'O my master, it was you who compelled me to assume this office; but now behold a new king and a new primate who promulgate new laws. Not unto them, O Master, but unto you, do I resign my crosier and the care of my flock.' With these words Wulfstan laid his pastoral staff on Edward's tomb. On the sepulchre of the Confessor perished the liberty of the Anglo-Saxon hierarchy. The deprived Saxon bishops were consigned to fortresses or shut up in monasteries.

The Conqueror, being thus assured of the obedience of the bishops, put forward the supremacy of the sword in opposition to that of the pope. He nominated directly to all vacant ecclesiastical offices, filled his treasury with the riches of the churches, required that all priests should make oath to him, forbade them to excommunicate his officers without his consent, not even for incest, and declared that all synodal decisions must be countersigned by him. 'I claim', said he to the archbishop one day, raising his arm towards heaven, 'I claim to hold in this hand all the pastoral staffs in my kingdom.' Lanfranc was astonished at this daring speech, but prudently kept silent, for a time at least. Episcopacy connived at the royal pretensions.

Would Hildebrand (Gregory VII), the most inflexible of popes, bend before William? The king was earnest in his desire to enslave the church to the state; the pope to enslave the state to the church: the collision of these two mighty champions threatened to be terrible. But the haughtiest of pontiffs was seen to yield as soon as he felt the mail-clad hand of the Conqueror, and to shrink unresistingly before it. The pope filled all Christendom with confusion, that he might deprive princes of the right of investiture to ecclesiastical dignities: William would not permit him to interfere with that question in England, and Hildebrand submitted. The king went even farther: the pope, wishing to enslave the clergy, deprived the priests of their lawful wives; William got a decree passed by the Council of Winchester in 1076 to the effect that the married priests living in castles and towns should not be compelled to put away their wives. This was too much: Hildebrand summoned Lanfranc to Rome, but William forbade him to go. 'Never did king, not even a pagan', exclaimed Gregory, 'attempt against the holy see what this man does not fear to carry out!' To console himself, he demanded payment of the *Peter's pence*, and an oath of fidelity. William sent the money, but refused the homage; and when Hildebrand saw the tribute which the king had paid, he said bitterly: 'What value can I set on money which is contributed with so little honour!' William forbade his clergy to recognize a pope, or to publish a bull without the royal approbation, which did not prevent Hildebrand from styling him 'the pearl of princes'. 'It is true', said he to his legate, 'that the English king does not behave in certain matters so religiously as we could desire ... Yet beware of exasperating him ... We shall win him over to God and St Peter more surely by mildness and reason than by strictness or severity.' In this manner the pope acted like the archbishop – *siluit*: he was silent. It is for feeble governments that Rome reserves her energies.

The Norman kings, desirous of strengthening their work, constructed Gothic cathedrals in the place of wooden churches, in which they installed their soldier-bishops, as if they were strong fortresses. Instead of the moral power and the humble crook of the shepherd, they gave them secular power and a staff. The religious episcopate was succeeded by a political one. William Rufus went to even greater lengths than his father. Taking advantage of the schism which divided the papacy, he did without a pope for ten years, leaving abbeys, bishoprics, and even Canterbury vacant, and scandalously squandering their revenues. Caesaropapia (which transforms a king into a pope) having thus attained its greatest excess, a sacerdotal reaction could not fail to take place.

CHAPTER FIVE

The Iron Age of Spiritual Slavery

(11th to 13th Century)

We are now entering upon a new phase of history. Romanism was on the point of triumphing by the exertions of learned men, energetic prelates, and princes in whom extreme imprudence was joined with extreme servility. This was the era of the dominion of popery, and we shall see it unscrupulously employing the despotism by which it is characterized.

A malady having occasioned some degree of remorse in William Rufus, he consented to fill up the vacancy in the archiepiscopal see. And now Anselm first appears in England. He was born in an Alpine valley, at the town of Aosta in Piedmont. Imbibing the instructions of his pious mother Ermenberga, and believing that God's throne was placed on the summit of the gigantic mountains he saw rising around him, the child Anselm climbed them in his dreams, and received the bread of heaven from the hands of the Lord. Unhappily in after-years he recognized another throne in the church of Christ, and bowed his head before the chair of St Peter. In 1078 he became Abbot of Bec in Normandy. This was the man whom William II summoned in 1093 to fill the primacy of Canterbury. Anselm, who was then sixty years old, refused at first: the character of Rufus terrified him. 'The Church of England', said he, 'is a plough that ought to be drawn by two oxen of equal strength. How can you yoke together an old and timid sheep like me and that wild bull?' At length he accepted and, concealing a mind of great power under an appearance of humility, he had hardly arrived in England before he recognized Pope Urban II (against the imperial Anti-Pope Wibert whom the king supported), demanded the estates of his see which the treasury had seized upon, refused to pay the king the sums he demanded, contested the right of investiture against Henry I, forbade all ecclesiastics to take the feudal oath, and determined that the priests should forthwith put away their wives. Scholasticism,[1] of which Anselm was one of the earlier representatives, freed the church from the yoke of royalty, but only to chain it to the papal chair. The fetters were about to be riveted by a still more energetic hand; and what this great theologian had begun, a great worldling was to carry on.

At the hunting parties of Henry II a man attracted the attention of his sovereign by his air of frankness, agreeable manners, witty conversation, and exuberant vivacity. This was Thomas Becket, born in 1118 of middle-class Norman parents. Being both priest and soldier, he was appointed at the same time by the king prebend of Hastings and governor of the Tower. When nominated chancellor of England in 1155, he showed himself no less expert than Wilfrid in misappropriating the wealth of the minors in his charge, and of the abbeys and bishoprics, and indulged in the most extravagant luxury. Henry, the first of the Plantagenets, a young inexperienced king of twenty-two, having noticed Becket's zeal in upholding the prerogatives of the Crown, in 1162 appointed him Archbishop of Canterbury. 'Now, sire', remarked the primate, with a smile, 'when I shall have to choose between God's favour and yours, remember it is yours that I shall sacrifice.'

Becket, who, as Keeper of the Seals, had been the most magnificent of courtiers, affected as archbishop to be the most venerable of saints. He resigned the chancellorship, assumed the robe of a monk, wore sackcloth filled with vermin, lived on the plainest food, every day knelt down to wash the feet of the poor, paced the cloisters of his cathedral with tearful eyes, and spent hours in prayer before the altar. As champion of the priests, even in their crimes, he took under his protection one who to the crime of seduction had added the murder of his victim's father.

The judges having represented to Henry that during the first eight years of his reign a hundred murders had been committed by ecclesiastics, the king in 1164 summoned a council at Clarendon, in which

---

[1] [Scholasticism, a form of Medievalism, was a method of systematizing and expounding religious doctrines according to the rules of logic laid down by Aristotle.]

certain regulations or *constitutions* were drawn up, with the object of preventing the encroachments of the hierarchy. Becket at first refused to sign them, but at length consented, and then withdrew into solitary retirement to mourn over his fault. Pope Alexander III released him from his oath of consent; and then began a fierce and long struggle between the king and the primate. Finally, four knights of the court, catching up a hasty expression of their master's, barbarously murdered the archbishop at the foot of the altar in his own cathedral church in the afternoon of 27 December 1170. The people looked upon Becket as a saint: immense crowds came to pray at his tomb, at which it was said that many miracles were worked. 'Even from his grave', said Becket's partisans, 'he renders his testimony in behalf of the papacy.'

Henry now passed from one extreme to the other. He entered Canterbury barefooted, and prostrated himself before the martyr's tomb: the bishops, priests, and monks, to the number of eighty, passed before him, each bearing a scourge, and struck three or five blows according to their rank on the naked shoulders of the king. In former ages, so the priestly fable ran, St Peter had scourged an Archbishop of Canterbury: now Rome in sober reality scourges the back of royalty, and nothing can henceforward check her victorious career. A Plantagenet surrendered England to the pope, and the pope gave him authority to subdue Ireland.

Rome, who had set her foot on the neck of a king, was destined under one of the sons of Henry II to set it on the neck of England. King John being unwilling to acknowledge an Archbishop of Canterbury illegally nominated by Pope Innocent III, the latter, more daring than Hildebrand, laid the kingdom under an interdict (1208). Many of the higher clergy fled from England to escape the king's wrath. Five years later, as John still remained obdurate, the pope moved Philip Augustus, King of France, to invade and rule England. John thereupon decided to submit. On 15 May 1213, he laid his crown at the papal legate's feet, declared that he surrendered his kingdom of England to the pope, and made oath to him as to his lord paramount.

Shortly a national protest boldly claimed the ancient liberties of the people. Forty-five mounted barons, armed in complete mail, and accompanied by some two thousand knights, besides a large number of men-at-arms and infantry, met at Brackley during the festival of Easter in 1215, and sent a deputation to the king. 'Here', they said, 'is the charter which consecrates the liberties confirmed by Henry I, and which you also have solemnly sworn to observe.' 'Why do they not demand my crown also?' said the king in a furious passion, and then with an oath, he added: 'I will not grant them liberties which will make me a slave.' But the nation was firmer still in its resolve to avoid enslavement. The barons occupied London, and on 15 June 1215, the king signed the famous *Magna Carta* at Runnymede. The political Protestantism of the thirteenth century would have done but little, however, for the greatness of the nation, without the religious Protestantism of the sixteenth.

This was the first time that the papacy came into collision with modern liberty. It shuddered in alarm, and the shock was violent. Innocent swore (as was his custom) and then declared the Great Charter null and void, forbade the king under pain of anathema to respect the liberties which he had confirmed, ascribed the conduct of the barons to the instigation of Satan, and ordered them to make apology to the king, and to send a deputation to Rome to learn from the mouth of the pope himself what should be the government of England. This was the way in which the papacy welcomed the first manifestations of liberty among the nations, and made known the model system under which it claimed to govern the whole world.

The priests of England supported the anathemas pronounced by their chief. They indulged in a thousand jeers and sarcasms against John about the charter he had accepted: – 'This is the twenty-fifth King of England – not a king, not even a kingling – but the disgrace of kings – a king without a kingdom – the fifth wheel of a wagon – the last of kings, and the disgrace of his people! – I would not give a straw for him … *Fuisti rex, nunc fex* (Once a king, but now a clown).' John, unable to support his disgrace, groaned and gnashed his teeth and rolled his eyes, tore sticks from the hedges and gnawed them like a maniac, or dashed them into fragments on the ground.

The barons, unmoved alike by the insolence of the pope and the despair of the king, replied that they would maintain the charter. Innocent excommunicated them. 'Is it the pope's business to regulate temporal matters?' asked they. 'By what right do vile usurers and foul simoniacs domineer over our country and excommunicate the whole world?'

The pope soon triumphed throughout England. His vassal John, having hired some bands of adventurers from the Continent, traversed at their head the whole country from the Channel to the Forth. These mercenaries carried desolation in their track: they extorted money, made prisoners, burnt the barons" castles, laid waste their parks, and dishonoured their wives and daughters. The king would sleep in a house, and the next morning set fire to it. Blood-stained assassins scoured the country during the night, the sword in one hand and the torch in the other, marking their progress by murder and conflagration. Such was the enthronement of popery in England. At this sight the barons, overcome by emotion, denounced both the king and the pope: 'Alas! poor country!' they exclaimed. 'Wretched England! ... And thou, O pope, a curse light upon thee!'

The curse was not long delayed. As the king was returning from some more than usually successful foray, and as the royal wagons were crossing the sands of the Wash, the tide rose and all sank in the abyss. This accident filled John with terror: it seemed to him that the earth was about to open and swallow him up. Stricken with dysentery which, finally, was aggravated by a surfeit of peaches and new cider, John reached Newark and died.

Such was the end of the pope's vassal – of his armed missionary in Britain. Never had so vile a prince been the involuntary occasion to his people of such great benefits. From his reign England may date her enthusiasm for liberty and her dread of popery.

During this time a great transformation had been accomplished. Magnificent churches and the marvels of religious art, with ceremonies and a multitude of prayers and chantings, dazzled the eyes, charmed the ears, and captivated the senses; but testified also to the absence of every strong moral and Christian disposition, and the predominance of worldliness in the church. At the same time the adoration of images and relics, saints, angels, and Mary the mother of God – the worships of *latria*, *doulia, and hyperdoulia*[2] – at once indicated and kept up among the people that ignorance of truth and absence of grace which characterize popery. All these errors tended to bring about a reaction: and in fact the march of the reformation may now be said to begin.

England had been brought low by the papacy: it rose up again by resisting Rome. Grosseteste, Bradwardine, and Edward III prepared the way for Wycliffe, and Wycliffe for the reformation.

---

[2] The Romish Church distinguishes three kinds of worship: *latria*, that paid to God; *doulia*, to saints; and *hyperdoulia*, to the Virgin Mary.

CHAPTER SIX

Grosseteste and Bradwardine

(13th & 14th Centuries)

In the reign of Henry III, son of John, while the king was conniving at the usurpations of Rome, and the pope ridiculing the complaints of the barons, a pious and energetic man, of comprehensive understanding, was occupied in the study of the holy Scriptures in their original languages, and bowing to their sovereign authority. Robert Grosseteste was born of poor parents at Stradbroke in Suffolk, and being raised to the see of Lincoln in 1235, when he was about sixty years of age, he boldly undertook to reform his diocese, one of the largest in England. Nor was this all. At the very time when the Roman pontiff, who had hitherto been content to be called the Vicar of St Peter, proclaimed himself the Vicar of God, and was ordering the English bishops to find benefices for *three hundred Romans*, Grosseteste was declaring that 'to follow a pope who rebels against the will of Christ, is to separate from Christ and his body; and if ever the time should come when all men follow an erring pontiff, then will be the great apostasy. Then will true Christians refuse to obey, and Rome will be the cause of an unprecedented schism.' Thus did he predict the reformation. Disgusted at the avarice of the monks and priests, he visited Rome to demand a reform. 'Brother', said Innocent IV to him with some irritation, '*Is thine eye evil, because I am good?*' The English bishop exclaimed with a sigh: 'O money, money! how great is thy power – especially in this court of Rome!'

A year had scarcely elapsed before Innocent commanded the bishop to give a canonry in Lincoln Cathedral to his infant nephew. Grosseteste replied: 'After the sin of Lucifer there is none more opposed to the gospel than that which ruins souls by giving them a faithless minister.

Bad pastors are the cause of unbelief, heresy, and disorder. Those who introduce them into the church are little better than antichrists, and their culpability is in proportion to their dignity. Although the chief of the angels should order me to commit such a sin, I would refuse. My obedience forbids me to obey; and therefore I rebel.'

Such was the bishop's response to the papal requirement: his obedience to the word of God forbade him to obey the pope. This was the principle of the reformation. 'Who is this old driveller that in his dotage dares to judge of my conduct?' exclaimed Innocent, whose wrath was appeased by the intervention of certain cardinals. Grosseteste on his dying bed – he died in 1253 – professed still more clearly the principles of the reformers; he declared that a heresy was 'an opinion conceived by carnal motives, *contrary to Scripture*, openly taught and obstinately defended', thus asserting the authority of Scripture instead of the authority of the church. He died in peace, and the public voice proclaimed him 'a searcher of the Scriptures, an adversary of the pope, and despiser of the Romans'. Innocent, desiring to take vengeance on his bones, meditated the exhumation of his body, when one night (says the mediaeval chronicler, Matthew of Paris) the bishop appeared before him. Drawing near the pontiff's bed, he struck him with his crosier, and thus addressed him with terrible voice and threatening look: 'Wretch! the Lord doth not permit thee to have any power over me. Woe be to thee!' The vision disappeared, and the pope, uttering a cry as if he had been struck by some sharp weapon, lay senseless on his couch. Never after did he pass a quiet night, and pursued by the phantoms of his troubled imagination, the year after Grosseteste's death he also expired while the palace re-echoed with his lamentable groans.

Grosseteste was not alone in his opposition to the pope. Sewal, Archbishop of York, did the same, and 'the more the pope cursed him, the more the people blessed him'. – 'Moderate your tyranny', said the archbishop to the pontiff, 'for the Lord said to Peter, *Feed* my sheep, and not *shear them, flay them, or devour them.*' The pope smiled and let the bishop speak, because the king allowed the pope to act. The power of England, which was constantly increasing, was soon able to give more force to these protests.

The nation was indeed growing in greatness. The madness of John, which had caused the English people to lose their Continental possessions, had given them more unity and power. The Angevin kings, being compelled to renounce entirely the country which had been their cradle, had at length made up their minds to look upon England as their home. The two races, so long hostile, melted one into the other. Free institutions were formed; the laws were studied; and colleges were founded. The language began to assume a regular form, and the ships of England were already formidable at sea. For more than a century the most brilliant victories attended the British armies. A king of France was brought captive to London: an English king was crowned at Paris. Even Spain and Italy felt the valour of these proud islanders. The English people took their station in the foremost rank. Now the character of a nation is never raised by halves. When the mighty ones of the earth were seen to fall before her, England could no longer crawl at the feet of an Italian priest.

At no period did her laws attack the papacy with so much energy. At the beginning of the fourteenth century an Englishman having brought to London one of the pope's bulls – a bull of an entirely spiritual character, it was an excommunication – was prosecuted as a traitor to the Crown, and would have been hanged, had not the sentence, at the chancellor's intercession, been changed to perpetual banishment. The *common law* was the weapon the government then opposed to the papal bulls. Shortly afterwards, in 1307, King Edward ordered the sheriffs to resist the arrogant pretensions of the Romish agents. But it is to two great men in the fourteenth century, equally illustrious, the one in the state, and the other in the church, that England is indebted for the development of the Protestant element in the country.

In 1346, an English army, about 15,000 strong, met face to face at Crécy a French army of much greater size. Two individuals of very different characters were in the English host. One of them was King Edward III, a brave and ambitious prince, who, being resolved to recover for the royal authority all its power, and for England all her glory, had undertaken the conquest of France. The other was his chaplain Thomas Bradwardine, a native of Chichester, a man of so humble a character that his meekness was often taken for stupidity. And thus it was that on his receiving the pallium at Avignon from the hands of the pope on his elevation to the see of Canterbury, a jester mounted on an ass rode into the hall and petitioned the pontiff to make him *primate* instead of that imbecile priest.

Bradwardine was one of the most pious men of the age, and to his prayers his sovereign's victories were ascribed. He was also one of the greatest geniuses of his time, and occupied the first rank among astronomers, philosophers, and mathematicians. The pride of science had at first alienated him from the doctrine of the cross. But one day while in the house of God and listening to the reading of the holy Scriptures, these words struck his ear: *It is not of him that willeth, nor of him that runneth, but of God that showeth mercy.* His ungrateful heart, he tells us, at first rejected this humiliating doctrine with aversion. Yet the word of God had laid its powerful hold upon him; he was converted to the truths he had despised, and immediately began to set forth the doctrines of eternal grace at Merton College, Oxford. He drank so deep at the fountain of Scripture that the traditions of men concerned him but little, and he was so absorbed in adoration in spirit and in truth, that he remarked not outward superstitions. His lectures were eagerly listened to and circulated through all Europe. The grace of God was their very essence, as it was of the reformation. With sorrow Bradwardine beheld Pelagianism everywhere substituting a mere religion of externals for inward Christianity, and on his knees he struggled for the salvation of the church. 'As in the times of old four hundred and fifty prophets of Baal strove against a single prophet of God; so now, O Lord', he exclaimed, 'the number of those who strive with Pelagius against thy free grace cannot be counted. They pretend not to receive grace freely, but to buy it. The will of men (they say) should precede, and thine should follow: theirs is the mistress, and thine the servant ... Alas! nearly the whole world is walking in error in the steps of Pelagius. Arise, O Lord, and judge thy cause.'[1] And the Lord did arise, but not until after the death of this pious archbishop – in the days of Wycliffe, who matriculated at Oxford probably shortly after Bradwardine's departure – and

---

[1] *Concerning the Cause of God against Pelagius*, Book 3, ed. H. Savile (London, 1618).

especially in the days of Luther and of Calvin. His contemporaries gave him the name of the *profound doctor.*

If Bradwardine walked truthfully in the path of faith, his illustrious patron Edward III advanced triumphantly in the field of policy. Pope Clement IV having decreed that the first two vacancies in the Anglican Church should be conferred on two of his cardinals: 'France is becoming *English*', said the courtiers to the king; 'and by way of compensation, England is becoming *Italian.*' Edward, desirous of guaranteeing the religious liberties of England, passed with the consent of Parliament in 1350 the Statute of *Provisors*, which made void every ecclesiastical appointment contrary to the rights of the king, the chapters, or the patrons. Thus the privileges of the chapters and the liberty of the English Catholics, as well as the independence of the Crown, were protected against the invasion of foreigners; and imprisonment or banishment for life was pronounced upon all offenders against the law.

This bold step alarmed the pontiff. Accordingly, three years after, the king having nominated one of his secretaries to the see of Durham – a man without any of the qualities becoming a bishop – the pope readily confirmed the appointment. When someone expressed his astonishment at this, the pope made answer: 'If the King of England had nominated *an ass*, I would have accepted him.' Thus the pope withdrew his pretensions. 'Empires have their term', observes the quaint Thomas Fuller in his *Church History of Britain*, at this place; 'when once they have reached it, they halt, they go back, they fall.'

The term seemed to be drawing nearer every day. In the reign of Edward III, between 1343 and 1353, again in 1364, and finally under Richard II in 1393, those stringent laws were passed which interdicted all appeal to the court of Rome, all bulls from the Roman bishop, all excommunications, in a word, every act infringing on the rights of the Crown; and declared that whoever should bring such documents into England, or receive, publish, or execute them, should be put out of the king's protection, deprived of their property, arrested, and brought before the king in council to undergo their trial according to the terms of the act. Such was the Statute of Præmunire.

Great was the indignation of the Romans at the news of this law: 'If the Statute of Mortmain put the pope into a sweat', says Fuller, 'this of Præmunire gave him a fit of fever.' One pope called it an 'execrable statute' – 'a horrible crime'. Such are the terms applied by the pontiffs to all that thwarts their ambitions.

Of the two wars carried on by Edward – the one against the King of France, and the other against popery – the latter was the more righteous and important. The benefits which this prince had hoped to derive from his brilliant victories at Crécy and Poitiers dwindled away almost entirely before his death; while his struggles with the papacy, founded as they were on truth, have exerted even to our own days an indisputable influence on the destinies of Great Britain. Yet the prayers and the conquests of Bradwardine, who proclaimed in that fallen age the doctrine of grace, produced effects still greater, not only for the salvation of many souls, but for the liberty, moral force, and greatness of England.

CHAPTER SEVEN

Light Streams from Lutterworth

(c. 1329–1380)

Thus in the first half of the fourteenth century, nearly two hundred years before the reformation, England appeared weary of the yoke of Rome. Bradwardine died in 1349; but a greater than he was about to succeed him, and without attaining to the highest functions, to exhibit in his person the past and future tendencies of the church of Christ in Britain. The English reformation did not begin with Henry VIII: the revival of the sixteenth century is but a link in the chain commencing with the apostles and reaching to us.

The resistance of Edward III to the papacy without had not suppressed the papacy *within*. The mendicant friars, and particularly the Franciscans, those fanatical soldiers of the pope, were endeavouring by pious frauds to monopolize the wealth of the country. 'Every year', said they, 'St Francis descends from heaven to purgatory, and delivers the souls of all those who were buried in the dress of his order.' These friars were said to kidnap children from their parents and shut them up in monasteries. They affected to be poor and, with a wallet on their back, begged with a piteous air from both high and low; but at the same time they dwelt in palaces, heaped up treasures, dressed in costly garments and wasted their time in luxurious entertainments.[1] The least of them looked upon themselves as *lords*, and those who wore the doctor's cap considered themselves *kings*. While they diverted themselves, eating and drinking at their well-spread tables, they used to send ignorant uneducated persons

---

[1] 'When they have overmuch riches, both in great waste houses and precious clothes, in great feasts and many jewels and treasures.' Wycliffe's *Tracts and Treatises*, edited by the Wycliffe Society, p. 224.

in their place to preach fables and legends to amuse and plunder the people. If any rich man talked of giving alms to the poor and not to the church, they exclaimed loudly against such impiety, and declared with threatening voice: 'If you do so we will leave the country, and return accompanied by a legion of glittering helmets.' Public indignation was at its height. 'The monks and priests of Rome', was the cry, 'are eating us away like a cancer. God must deliver us or the people will perish … Woe be to them! the cup of wrath will run over. Men of holy church shall be despised as carrion, as dogs shall they be cast out in open places.'[2]

The arrogance of Rome made the cup run over. Pope Urban V, heedless of the laurels won by the conqueror at Crécy and Poitiers, summoned Edward III to recognize him as legitimate sovereign of England, and to pay as feudal tribute the annual sum of one thousand marks. In case of refusal the king was to appear before him at Rome. For thirty-three years the popes had never mentioned the tribute accorded by John to Innocent III, and which had always been paid very irregularly. The conqueror of the Valois was irritated by this insolence on the part of an Italian bishop, and called on God to avenge England. From Oxford came forth the avenger.

John Wycliffe, born about 1329 near Richmond, in Yorkshire, probably arrived in Oxford as a student shortly after the departure of the pious Bradwardine from Merton College. He quickly acquired a great reputation for learning and came to be known as 'flos Oxonie' (the flower, or pride, of Oxford). In 1348, a terrible pestilence, which is said to have carried off half the human race, appeared in England after successively devastating Asia and the continent of Europe. This visitation of the Almighty sounded like the trumpet of the judgment day in the heart of Wycliffe. Alarmed at the thoughts of eternity, the young man – for he was then a mere youth – passed days and nights in his cell groaning and sighing, and calling upon God to show him the path he ought to follow. He found it in the holy Scriptures, and resolved to make it known to others. He commenced with prudence; but being elected in 1360 Master of Balliol, and about 1365 Warden of Canterbury Hall (later incorporated in Christ Church), he began to set forth the doctrine of faith in a more energetic manner. His biblical and

[2] Wycliffe, *The Last Age of the Church.*

philosophical studies, his knowledge of theology, his penetrating mind, the purity of his manners, and his unbending courage, rendered him the object of general admiration. A profound teacher, like Bradwardine, and an eloquent preacher, he demonstrated to the learned during the course of the week what he intended to preach, and on Sunday he preached to the people what he had previously demonstrated. His disputations gave strength to his sermons, and his sermons shed light upon his disputations. He accused the clergy of having banished the holy Scriptures, and required that the authority of the word of God should be re-established in the church. Loud acclamations crowned these discussions, and the crowd of vulgar minds trembled with indignation when they heard these shouts of applause.

Wycliffe was in middle life when the papal arrogance stirred England to its depths. Being at once an able politician and a fervent Christian, he vigorously defended the rights of the Crown against the Romish aggression, and by his arguments not only enlightened his fellow countrymen generally, but stirred up the zeal of several members of both houses of Parliament.

The Parliament assembled, and never perhaps had it been summoned on a question which excited to so high a degree the emotions of England, and indeed of Christendom. The debates in the House of Lords were especially remarkable: all the arguments of Wycliffe were reproduced. 'Feudal *tribute* is due', said one, 'only to him who can grant feudal *protection* in return. Now how can the pope wage war to protect his fiefs?' – 'Is it as vassal of the Crown or as feudal superior', asked another, 'that the pope demands part of our property? Urban V will not accept the first of these titles … Well and good! but the English people will not acknowledge the second.' – 'Why', said a third, 'was this tribute originally granted? To pay the pope for absolving John … His demand, then, is mere simony, a kind of clerical swindling, which the lords spiritual and temporal should indignantly oppose.' – 'No', said another speaker, 'England belongs not to the pope. The pope is but a man, subject to sin; but Christ is the Lord of lords, and this kingdom is held directly and solely of Christ alone.' Thus spoke the lords inspired by Wycliffe. Parliament decided unanimously that no prince had the right to alienate the sovereignty of the kingdom without the consent of the other two estates, and that if the pontiff should attempt to proceed against the King of England as his vassal, the nation should rise in a body to maintain the independence of the Crown.

To no purpose did this generous resolution excite the wrath of the partisans of Rome; to no purpose did they assert that, by the canon law, the king ought to be deprived of his fief, and that England now belonged to the pope: 'No', replied Wycliffe, 'the canon law has no force when it is opposed to the word of God.' Edward III made Wycliffe one of his chaplains, and the papacy has ceased from that hour to lay claim – in explicit terms at least – to the sovereignty of England.

When the pope gave up his temporal, he was desirous, at the very least, of keeping up his ecclesiastical pretensions, and to procure the repeal of the Statutes of Præmunire and Provisors. It was accordingly resolved to hold a conference at Bruges to treat of this question, and Wycliffe, who had been created doctor of divinity two years before, proceeded thither with the other commissioners in July 1374, although he only remained with them two or three months. The decision of the conference was that the king should bind himself to repeal the penalties denounced against the pontifical agents, and that the pope should confirm the king's ecclesiastical presentations. But the nation was not pleased with this compromise. 'The clerks sent from Rome', said the commons, 'are more dangerous for the kingdom than Jews or Saracens: every papal agent resident in England, and every Englishman living at the court of Rome, should be punished with death.' Such was the language of the *Good Parliament* (1376). In the fourteenth century the English nation called a Parliament good which did not yield to the papacy.

Wycliffe, immediately prior to his visit to Bruges, had been presented by the king to the rectory of Lutterworth, and from that time a practical activity was added to his academic influence. At Oxford he spoke as a master to the young theologians; in his parish he addressed the people as a preacher and as a pastor. 'The gospel', said he, 'is the only source of religion. The Roman pontiff is a mere cutpurse, and, far from having the right to reprimand the whole world, he may be lawfully reproved by his inferiors, and even by laymen.'

The papacy grew alarmed. Courtenay, fourth son of the Earl of Devon, an imperious but grave priest, and full of zeal for what he believed to be the truth, had recently been appointed to the see of London. In Parliament he had resisted Wycliffe's patron, John of Gaunt, Duke of Lancaster, third son of Edward III, and head of the house of that name. The bishop, observing that the doctrines of the reformer were spreading among the people, both high and low, charged him with heresy, and summoned him to appear before the convocation assembled in St Paul's Cathedral.

On the 19th February, 1377, an immense crowd, heated with fanaticism, thronged the approaches to the church and filled its aisles, while the citizens favourable to the reform remained concealed in their houses. Wycliffe moved forward, preceded by Lord Percy, marshal of England, and supported by the Duke of Lancaster, who defended him from purely political motives. He was followed by four doctors of divinity, his counsel, and passed through the hostile multitude who looked upon Lancaster as the enemy of their liberties, and upon himself as the enemy of the church. 'Let not the sight of these bishops make you shrink a hair's-breadth in your profession of faith', said the prince to the doctor. 'They are unlearned; and as for this concourse of people, fear nothing, we are here to defend you.' When the reformer had crossed the threshold of the cathedral, the crowd within appeared like a solid wall; and, notwithstanding the efforts of the earl-marshal, Wycliffe and Lancaster could not advance. The people swayed to and fro, hands were raised in violence, and loud hootings re-echoed through the building. At length Percy made an opening in the dense multitude, and Wycliffe passed on.

The haughty Courtenay, who had been commissioned by the archbishop to preside over the assembly, watched these strange movements with anxiety, and beheld with displeasure the learned doctor accompanied by the two most powerful men in England. He said nothing to the Duke of Lancaster, who at that time administered the kingdom, but turning towards Percy observed sharply: 'If I had known, my lord, that you claimed to be master in this church, I would have taken measures to prevent your entrance.' Lancaster coldly rejoined: 'He shall keep such mastery here, though you say nay.' Percy now turned to Wycliffe, who had remained standing, and said: 'Sit down and rest yourself.' At this Courtenay gave way to his anger, and exclaimed in a loud tone: 'It is unreasonable that one, cited to appear before a bishop, should sit down during his answer. He must and shall stand.' Lancaster, indignant that a learned doctor of England should be refused a favour to which his age alone entitled him (for he was approaching fifty years) made answer to the bishop: 'My lord, you are very arrogant; take care … or I may bring down your pride, and not yours only, but that of all the prelacy in England.' – 'Do your worst, sir', was Courtenay's reply. The prince rejoined with some emotion: 'You are insolent, my lord. You think, no doubt, you can trust on your family … but your relations will have trouble enough to protect themselves.' To this the bishop nobly replied: 'My confidence is not in my parents nor in any man; but only in God, in whom I trust, and by whose assistance I will be bold to speak the truth.' Lancaster, who saw hypocrisy only in these words, turned to one of his attendants, and whispered in his ear, but so loud as to be heard by the bystanders: 'I would rather pluck the bishop by the hair of his head out of the church, than take this at his hands.' Every impartial reader must confess that the prelate spoke with greater dignity than the prince. Lancaster had hardly uttered these imprudent words before the bishop's partisans fell upon him and Percy, and even upon Wycliffe, who alone had remained calm. The two noblemen resisted, their friends and servants defended them, the uproar became extreme, and there was no hope of restoring tranquillity. The two lords escaped with difficulty, taking Wycliffe with them, and the assembly broke up in great confusion.

On the following day the earl-marshal having called upon Parliament to apprehend the disturbers of the public peace, the clerical party uniting with the enemies of Lancaster filled the streets with their clamour; and while the duke and the earl escaped by the Thames, the mob collected before Percy's house, broke down the doors, searched every chamber, and thrust their swords into every dark corner. When they found that he had escaped, the rioters, imagining that he was concealed in Lancaster's palace, rushed to the Savoy, at that time the most magnificent building in the kingdom. They killed a priest who endeavoured to stay them, tore down the ducal arms, and hung them up reversed, in Cheapside, like those of a traitor. They would have gone still farther if the bishop had not very opportunely reminded them that they were *in Lent*. As for Wycliffe, he was dismissed with an injunction against preaching his doctrines.

But this decision of the priests was not ratified by the people of England. Public opinion declared in favour of Wycliffe. 'If he is guilty', said they, 'why is he not punished? If he is innocent, why is he ordered to be silent? If he is the weakest in power, he is the strongest in truth!' And so indeed he was, and never had he spoken with such energy. He openly attacked the pretended apostolical chair, and declared that the two antipopes who sat at Rome and Avignon – for this was the period when there were rival popes, each imprecating curses on the other – together made *one* Antichrist. Being now in opposition to the pope, Wycliffe was soon to confess that Christ alone was king of the church; and that it is not possible for a man to be excommunicated, unless first and principally he be excommunicated by himself.

Rome could not close her ears. Wycliffe's enemies sent thither nineteen propositions which they ascribed to him, and in the month of June 1377, just as Richard II, son of the Black Prince, a child ten years old, was ascending the throne, three letters from Gregory XI, addressed to the king, the Archbishop of Canterbury, and the University of Oxford, denounced Wycliffe as a heretic, and called upon them to proceed against him as against a common thief. The archbishop issued the citation: the Crown and the university were silent.

On the appointed day, Wycliffe, unaccompanied by either Lancaster or Percy, proceeded to the archiepiscopal chapel at Lambeth. 'Men expected he should be devoured', says an historian, 'being brought into the lion's den.' But the burgesses had taken the prince's place. The assault of Rome had aroused the friends of liberty and truth in England. 'The pope's briefs', said they, 'ought to have no effect in the realm without the king's consent. Every man is master in his own house.'

The archbishop had scarcely opened the sitting, when Sir Louis Clifford entered the chapel, and forbade the court, on the part of the widowed princess of Wales (the mother of Richard II) to proceed against the reformer. The bishops were struck with a panic-fear: 'they bent their heads', says a Roman Catholic historian, 'like a reed before the wind'. Wycliffe retired after handing in a protest. 'In the first place', said he, 'I resolve with my whole heart, and by the grace of God, to be a sincere Christian; and, while my life shall last, to profess and defend the law of Christ so far as I have power.' Wycliffe's enemies attacked this protest, and one of them eagerly maintained that whatever the pope ordered should be looked upon as right. 'What!' answered the reformer; 'the pope may then exclude from the canon of the Scriptures any book that displeases him, and alter the Bible at pleasure?' Wycliffe thought that Rome, unsettling the grounds of infallibility, had transferred it from the Scriptures to the pope. He was desirous of restoring it to its true place, and re-establishing authority in the church on a truly Divine foundation.

A great change was now taking place in the reformer. Busying himself less about the kingdom of England, he occupied himself more about the kingdom of Christ. In him the political phase was followed by the religious. To carry the glad tidings of the gospel into the remotest hamlets, was now the great idea which possessed Wycliffe. If begging friars (said he) stroll over the country, preaching the legends of saints and the history of the Trojan War, we must do for God's glory what they do to fill their wallets, and form a vast itinerant evangelization to convert souls to Jesus Christ. Turning to the most pious of his disciples, he said to them: 'Go and preach, it is the sublimest work; but imitate not the priests whom we see after the sermon sitting in the ale-houses, or at the gaming-table, or wasting their time in hunting. After your sermon is ended, do you visit the sick, the aged, the poor, the blind, and the lame, and succour them according to your ability.' Such was the new practical theology which Wycliffe inaugurated – it was that of Christ himself.

The 'poor priests', as they were called, set off barefoot, a staff in their hands, clothed in a coarse robe, living on alms, and satisfied with the plainest food. They stopped in the fields near villages, in the church-yards, in the market-places of the towns, and sometimes in the churches themselves. The people, among whom they were favourites, thronged around them, as the men of Northumbria had done at Aidan's preaching. They spoke with a popular eloquence that entirely won over those who listened to them. Of these missionaries none was more beloved than John Aston, a Fellow of Merton College, Oxford. He might be seen wandering over the country in every direction, or seated at some cottage hearth, or alone in some retired crossway, preaching to an attentive crowd. Missions of this kind have constantly revived in England at the great epochs of the church.

The 'poor priests' were not content with mere disputings against Rome: they preached the great mystery of godliness. 'An angel could have made no propitiation for man', one day exclaimed their master Wycliffe, 'for the nature which has sinned is not that of the angels. The mediator must needs be a man; but every man being indebted to God for everything that he is able to do, this man must needs have infinite merit, and be at the same time God.'

The clergy became alarmed, and a law was passed commanding every king's officer to commit the preachers and their followers to prison. In consequence of this, as soon as the humble missionary began to preach, the monks set themselves in motion. They watched him from the windows of their cells, at the street-corners, or from behind a hedge, and then hastened off to procure assistance. But when the constables approached, a body of stout bold men stood forth, with arms in their hands, who surrounded the preacher, and zealously protected him against the attacks of the clergy. Carnal weapons were thus mingled with the preachings of the word of peace. The poor priests returned to their master: Wycliffe comforted them, advised them, and then they departed once more. Every day this evangelization reached some new spot, and the light was thus penetrating into every quarter of England, when the reformer was suddenly stopped in his work.

Wycliffe was at Oxford in the year 1379, busied in the discharge of his duties as professor of divinity, when he fell dangerously ill. His was not a strong constitution; and work, age, and above all persecution had weakened him. Great was the joy in the monasteries; but for that joy to be complete, the *heretic* must recant. Every effort was made to bring this about in his last moments.

Representatives of the four religious orders, accompanied by four aldermen, hastened to the bedside of the dying man, hoping to frighten him by threatening him with the vengeance of heaven. They found him calm and serene. 'You have death on your lips', said they; 'be touched by your faults, and retract in our presence all that you have said to our injury.' Wycliffe remained silent, and the visitors flattered themselves with an easy victory. But the nearer the reformer approached eternity, the greater was his horror of their evil doctrine. The consolation he had found in Jesus Christ had given him fresh energy. He begged his servant to raise him on his couch. Then feeble and pale, and scarcely able to support himself, he turned towards the friars, who were waiting for his recantation and, opening his livid lips, and fixing on them a piercing look, he said with emphasis: 'I shall not die but live, and again declare the evil deeds of the friars.' We might almost picture to ourselves the spirit of Elijah threatening the priests of Baal. The visitors looked at one another with astonishment. They left the room in confusion, and the reformer recovered to put the finishing touch to the most important of his works against false religion and against the pope.

CHAPTER EIGHT

The Morning Star of the Reformation

(1380–1384)

Wycliffe's ministry had followed a progressive course. At first he had attacked the papacy; next he preached the gospel to the poor; he could take one more step and put the people in permanent possession of the word of God. This was the third phase of his activity.

Scholasticism had banished the Scriptures into a mysterious obscurity. It is true that Bede had translated the Gospel of St John; that the learned men at Alfred's court had translated the four Evangelists; that Ælfric in the reign of Ethelred II had translated some books of the Old Testament; that an Anglo-Norman priest had paraphrased the Gospels and the Acts; that Richard Rolle, 'the hermit of Hampole' (near Doncaster), and some pious clerks in the fourteenth century, had produced a version of the Psalms, the Gospels, and Epistles – but these rare volumes were hidden, like theological curiosities, in the libraries of a few monasteries. It was then a maxim that the reading of the Bible was injurious to the laity; and accordingly the priests forbade it, just as the Brahmins forbid the Shastras to the Hindus. Oral tradition alone preserved among the people the histories of the holy Scriptures, mingled with legends of the saints. The time appeared ripe for the publication of a Bible. The increase of population, the attention the English were beginning to devote to their own language, the development which the system of representative government had received, the awakening of the human mind – all these circumstances favoured the reformer's design.

Wycliffe was ignorant indeed of Greek and Hebrew; but was it nothing to shake off the dust which for ages had covered the Latin Bible, and to translate it into English? He was a good Latin scholar, of sound understanding and great penetration; but above all he loved the Bible, he understood it, and desired to communicate this treasure to others. Let us imagine him in his quiet study: on his table is the Vulgate text, corrected after the best manuscripts; and lying open around him are the commentaries of the doctors of the church, especially those of St Jerome and Nicholas of Lyra. Between ten and fifteen years he steadily prosecuted his task; learned men aided him with their advice, and one of them, Nicholas of Hereford, a Fellow of Queen's College, Oxford, appears to have translated a few chapters for him.[1] At last, some time between 1380 and 1384, it was completed. This was a great event in the religious history of England; outstripping the nations on the Continent, she took her station in the foremost rank in the great work of disseminating the Scriptures.

As soon as the translation was finished, the labour of the copyists began, and the Bible was erelong widely circulated either wholly or in portions. The reception of the work surpassed all expectations. The holy Scriptures exercised a reviving influence over men's hearts; minds were enlightened; souls were converted; the voices of the 'poor priests' had done little in comparison with this voice; something new had entered into the world. Citizens, soldiers, and the lower classes welcomed this new era with acclamations; the highborn curiously examined the unknown book; and even Anne of Bohemia, wife of Richard II, prompted perhaps by the popular interest, began to read the Gospels diligently. She did more than this: she made them known to Thomas Arundel, Archbishop of York and chancellor, and afterwards a persecutor, but who now, struck by the sight of a foreign lady – of a queen, humbly devoting her leisure to the study of 'such virtuous books', commenced reading them himself, and rebuked the prelates who neglected this holy pursuit. 'You could not meet two persons on the highway', says a contemporary writer, 'but one of them was Wycliffe's disciple.'

[1] [Since these words were written the whole question has been several times investigated. Some modern scholars are inclined to doubt whether Wycliffe was himself the author of the translation which bears his name. F. F. Bruce discusses the matter in *The English Bible* (1961), pp. 13-20. It may at least be claimed that the traditional view, though called in question, has not been satisfactorily disproved.]

Yet all in England did not equally rejoice: the lower clergy opposed this enthusiasm with complaints and maledictions. 'Master John Wycliffe, by translating the gospel into English', said the monks, 'has rendered it more acceptable and more intelligible to laymen and even to women, than it has hitherto been to learned and intelligent clerks! ... The gospel pearl is everywhere cast out and trodden under foot of swine.' New contests arose for the reformer. Wherever he bent his steps, he was violently attacked. 'It is heresy', cried the monks, 'to speak of holy Scripture in English.' – 'Since the church has approved of the four Gospels, she would have been just as able to reject them and admit others! The church sanctions and condemns what she pleases ... Learn to believe in the church rather than in the gospel.' These clamours did not alarm Wycliffe. 'Many nations have had the Bible in their own language. The Bible is the faith of the church. Though the pope and all his clerks should disappear from the face of the earth', said he, 'our faith would not fail, for it is founded on Jesus alone, our Master and our God.' But Wycliffe did not stand alone: in the palace as in the cottage, and even in Parliament, the rights of holy Scripture found defenders. A motion having been made in the Upper House (1390) to seize all the copies of the Bible, the Duke of Lancaster exclaimed: 'Are we then the very dregs of humanity, that we cannot possess the laws of our religion in our own tongue?'

Having given his fellow countrymen the Bible, Wycliffe began to reflect on its contents. This was a new step in his onward path. There comes a moment when the Christian, saved by a lively faith, feels the need of giving an account to himself of this faith, and this originates the science of theology. This is a natural movement: if the child, who at first possesses sensations and affections only, feels the want, as he grows up, of reflection and knowledge, why should it not be the same with the Christian? Politics – home missions – holy Scripture – had engaged Wycliffe in succession; theology had its turn, and this was the fourth phase of his life.

It is clear that up to the year 1378 Wycliffe was a firm believer in the doctrine of transubstantiation, which stands at the very centre of the Roman Catholic system, the belief that when at the Mass, the 'words of consecration' are pronounced by the 'priest', the bread and wine are miraculously changed into the very body and blood of the Lord. It is equally clear, however – it might even be claimed that it is clearer still – that three years later Wycliffe denied this doctrine with tremendous energy. Indeed he was now asserting that there never had been a heresy more cunningly smuggled into the church than transubstantiation. The reasons for his complete change of front are clear: he denounced it as contrary to Scripture (both Gospels and Epistles), as unsupported by early church tradition,[2] as plainly opposed to the testimony of the senses, and as based upon false reasoning.[3] He proclaimed furthermore, with immense vigour, that the doctrine was essentially idolatrous, and productive of arrogant priestly claims without warrant in Scripture. In sum, the doctrine of the Mass was to Wycliffe in the closing years of his life a 'blasphemous deceit', or, to use his exact language, 'a veritable abomination of desolation in the holy place'.

When Wycliffe's enemies heard these propositions, they appeared horror-stricken, and yet in secret they were delighted at the prospect of destroying him. They met together, examined twelve theses he had published, and pronounced against him suspension from all teaching, imprisonment, and the greater excommunication.[4] At the same time his friends became alarmed, their zeal cooled, and many of them forsook him. The Duke of Lancaster, in particular, could not follow him into this new sphere. That prince had no objection to an ecclesiastical opposition which might aid the political power, and for that purpose he had tried to enlist the reformer's talents and courage; but he feared a dogmatic opposition that might compromise him. The sky was heavy with clouds; Wycliffe was alone.

---

[2] [Nor had the Anglo-Saxon Church professed this doctrine. 'The host is the body of Christ, not bodily but spiritually', said Aelfric in the tenth century in a letter addressed to the Archbishop of York. Berengar of Tours in the eleventh century had written a treatise denying the possibility of material change in the elements, and refuting Lanfranc, Archbishop of Canterbury, who had taught England that at the word of a priest God quitted heaven and descended on the altar.]

[3] [Lechler's *Wycliffe and His English Precursors*, pp. 340-51, should be consulted on all these points.]

[4] [The 'greater' excommunication, as distinguished from the 'less', deprived a man of the right to administer or receive the sacraments, and of all intercourse, public or private, with his fellow Christians.]

The storm soon burst upon him. One day, while he was seated in his doctoral chair in Oxford, and calmly explaining the nature of the Lord's Supper, an officer entered the hall, and read the sentence of condemnation. It was the design of his enemies to humble the professor in the eyes of his disciples. Lancaster immediately became alarmed and, hastening to his old friend, begged him – ordered him, even – to trouble himself no more about this matter. Attacked on every side, Wycliffe for a time remained silent. Shall he sacrifice the truth to save his reputation – his repose – perhaps his life? Shall expediency get the better of faith? Shall Lancaster prevail over Wycliffe? No: his courage was invincible. 'Since the year of our Lord 1000', said he, 'all the doctors have been in error about the Sacrament of the Altar – except, perhaps, it may be Berengar of Tours. How canst thou, O priest, who art but a man, make thy Maker? What! the thing that groweth in the fields – that ear which thou pluckest today, shall be God tomorrow! … As you cannot make the works which he made, how shall ye make him who made the works? Woe to the adulterous generation that believeth the testimony of Innocent rather than of the gospel.' Wycliffe called upon his adversaries to refute the opinions they had condemned and, finding that they threatened him with a civil penalty (imprisonment), he appealed to the king.

The time was not favourable for such an appeal. A fatal circumstance increased Wycliffe's danger. Wat Tyler and a dissolute priest named Ball, taking advantage of the ill-will excited by the rapacity and brutality of the royal tax-gatherers, had occupied London with a tremendous company of supporters. John Ball kept up the spirits of the insurgents, not by expositions of the gospel, like Wycliffe's *poor priests*, but by fiery comments on the distich they had chosen for their device –

> When Adam delved and Eve span,
> Who was then the gentleman?

There were many who felt no scruple in ascribing these disorders to the reformer, who was quite innocent of them; and Courtenay, Bishop of London, having been translated to the see of Canterbury, lost no time in convoking a synod to pronounce on this matter. They met in the middle of May, about two o'clock in the afternoon, and were proceeding to pronounce sentence on Wycliffe when a severe earthquake shook the city of London and so alarmed the members of the council that they unanimously demanded the adjournment of a decision which appeared so manifestly rebuked by God. But the archbishop skilfully turned this strange phenomenon to his own purposes: 'Know you not', said he, 'that the noxious vapours which catch fire in the bosom of the earth, and give rise to these phenomena which alarm you, lose all their force when they burst forth? Well, in like manner, by rejecting the wicked from our community, we shall put an end to the convulsions of the church.' The bishops regained their courage; and one of the primate's officers read ten propositions, said to be Wycliffe's, but ascribing to him certain errors of which he was quite innocent. The following most excited the anger of the priests: 'God must obey the devil ... After Urban VI we must receive no one as pope, but live according to the manner of the Greeks.' The ten propositions were condemned as heretical, and the archbishop enjoined all persons to shun, as they would a venomous serpent, all who should preach the aforesaid errors. 'If we permit this heretic to appeal continually to the passions of the people', said the primate to the king, 'our destruction is inevitable. We must silence these *lollards* – these psalm-singers.'[5] The king gave authority 'to confine in the prisons of the state any who should maintain the condemned propositions'.

Day by day the circle contracted around Wycliffe. Some of his chief supporters, the prudent Philip Repingdon, the learned Nicholas of Hereford, and even the eloquent John Aston, the firmest of the three, departed from him. The veteran champion of the truth which had once gathered a whole nation round it, had reached the days when 'strong men shall bow themselves', and now, when harassed by persecution, he found himself alone. But boldly he uplifted his hoary head and exclaimed: 'The doctrine of the gospel shall never perish; and if the earth once quaked, it was because they condemned Jesus Christ.'

He did not stop here. In proportion as his physical strength decreased, his moral strength increased. Instead of parrying the blows aimed at him, he resolved on dealing more terrible ones still. He knew that if the king and the nobility were for the priests, the Lower House and the

---

[5] [The origin of the term 'lollards' is uncertain. Some derive it from the old Dutch 'lollen', to sing or to chant; others from the Latin 'lolium', tares (mingled with the Catholic wheat).]

citizens were for liberty and truth. He therefore presented a bold petition to the commons in the month of November 1382. 'Since Jesus Christ shed his blood to free his church, I demand its freedom. I demand that everyone may leave those gloomy walls (the monasteries) within which a tyrannical law prevails, and embrace a simple and peaceful life under the open vault of heaven. I demand that the poor inhabitants of our towns and villages be not constrained to furnish a worldly priest, often a vicious man and a heretic, with the means of satisfying his ostentation, his gluttony, and his licentiousness – of buying a showy horse, costly saddles, bridles with tinkling bells, rich garments, and soft furs, while they see their wives, children, and neighbours, dying of hunger.'[6] The House of Commons, recollecting that they had not given their consent to the persecuting statute drawn up by the clergy and approved by the king and the lords, demanded its repeal. Was the reformation about to begin by the will of the people?

Courtenay, indignant at this intervention of the commons, and ever stimulated by a zeal for his church, which would have been better directed towards the word of God, visited Oxford in November 1382, and having gathered round him a number of bishops, doctors, priests, students, and laymen, summoned Wycliffe before him. A generation ago the reformer had come up to the university: Oxford had become his home … and now it was turning against him! Weakened by labours, by trials, by that ardent soul which preyed upon his feeble body, he might have refused to appear. But Wycliffe, who never feared the face of man, came before them with a good conscience. We may conjecture that there were among the crowd some disciples who felt their hearts burn at the sight of their master; but no outward sign indicated their emotion. The solemn silence of a court of justice had succeeded the shouts of enthusiastic youths. Yet Wycliffe did not despair: he raised his venerable head, and turned to Courtenay with that confident look which had in earlier days made his opponents shrink away. Growing wroth against the *priests of Baal*, he reproached them with disseminating error in order to sell their masses. Then he stopped, and uttered these simple and energetic

---

[6] A complaint of John Wycliffe. *Tracts and Treatises*, edited by the Wycliffe Society, p. 268.

words: 'The truth shall prevail!' Having thus spoken he prepared to leave the court: his enemies dared not say a word; and, like his Divine Master at Nazareth, he passed through the midst of them, and no man ventured to stop him. He then withdrew to his parish of Lutterworth.

He had not yet reached the harbour. He was living peacefully among his books and his parishioners, and the priests seemed inclined to leave him alone, when another blow was aimed at him. A papal brief summoned him to Rome, to appear before that tribunal which had so often shed the blood of its adversaries. His bodily infirmities convinced him that he could not obey this summons. But if Wycliffe refused to hear Urban, Urban could not choose but hear Wycliffe. The church was at that time divided between two chiefs: France, Scotland, Savoy, Lorraine, Castile, and Aragon acknowledged Clement VII; while Italy, England, Germany, Sweden, Poland, and Hungary acknowledged Urban VI. Wycliffe shall tell us who is the true head of the church universal. And while the two popes were excommunicating and abusing each other, and, selling heaven and earth for their own gain, the reformer was confessing that incorruptible word, which establishes real unity in the church. 'I believe', said he, 'that the gospel of Christ is the whole body of God's law. I believe that Christ, who gave it to us, is very God and very man, and by this it passes all other laws. I believe that the Bishop of Rome is bound more than all other men to submit to it, for greatness among Christ's disciples did not consist in worldly dignity or honours, but in the exact following of Christ in his life and manners. No faithful man ought to follow the pope, but in such points as he hath followed Jesus Christ. The pope ought to leave unto the secular power all temporal dominion and rule; and thereunto effectually more and more exhort his whole clergy ... If I could labour according to my desire in mine own person, I would surely present myself before the Bishop of Rome, but the Lord hath otherwise visited me to the contrary, and hath taught me rather to obey God than men.'

Urban, who at that moment chanced to be very busied in his contest with Clement, did not think it prudent to begin another with Wycliffe and so let the matter rest there. From this time the doctor passed the remainder of his days in peace in the company of three personages, two of whom were his particular friends and the third his constant adversary: these were *Aletheia*, *Phronesis*, and *Pseudes*. *Aletheia* (truth) proposed questions; *Pseudes* (falsehood) urged objections; and *Phronesis* (understanding) laid down the sound doctrine. These three characters carried on a conversation (*trialogue*) in which great truths were boldly professed. The opposition between the pope and Christ – between the canons of Romanism and the Bible – was painted in striking colours. This is one of the primary truths which the church must never forget. 'The church has fallen', said one of the interlocutors in the work in question, 'because she has abandoned the gospel, and preferred the laws of the pope. Although there should be a hundred popes in the world at once, and all the friars living should be transformed into cardinals, we must withhold our confidence from them in the matter of faith except so far as their teachings are those of the Scriptures.'

These words were the last flicker of the torch. Wycliffe looked upon his end as near, and entertained no idea that it would come in peace. A dungeon on one of the seven hills, or a burning pile in London, was all he expected. 'Why do you talk of seeking the crown of martyrdom afar?' asked he. 'Preach the gospel of Christ to haughty prelates, and martyrdom will not fail you. What! I should live and be silent? … never! Let the blow fall, I await its coming.'

The stroke was spared him. The war between two wicked priests, Urban and Clement, left the disciples of our Lord in peace. And besides, was it worth while cutting short a life that was drawing to a close? Wycliffe, therefore, continued tranquilly to preach Jesus Christ; and on 29 December 1384, as he was in his church at Lutterworth, in the midst of his flock, he was suddenly stricken with paralysis. He was carried to his house by the affectionate friends around him, and, after lingering forty-eight hours, resigned his soul to God on the last day of the year.

Thus was removed from the church one of the boldest witnesses to the truth. The seriousness of his language, the holiness of his life, and the energy of his faith, had intimidated the popedom. Travellers relate that if a lion is met in the desert, it is sufficient to look steadily at him, and the beast turns away roaring from the eye of man. Wycliffe had fixed the eye of a Christian on the papacy, and the affrighted papacy had left him in peace. Hunted down unceasingly while living, he died in quiet, in life and death a faithful witness to the truth of the word of God. A glorious end to a glorious life.

The reformation of England had begun.

Wycliffe is the greatest of English reformers: he was in truth the first reformer of Christendom, and to him, under God, Britain is indebted for the honour of being the foremost in the attack upon the theocratic system of Gregory VII. The work of the Waldenses, excellent as it was, cannot be compared to his. If Luther and Calvin are the fathers of the reformation, Wycliffe is its grandfather.

Wycliffe, like most great men, possessed qualities which are not generally found together. While his understanding was eminently speculative – his treatise entitled *De universalibus realibus* (*On the Reality of Universal Ideas*) made a sensation in philosophy – he possessed that practical and active mind which characterizes the Anglo-Saxon race. As a divine, he was at once scriptural and spiritual, soundly orthodox, and possessed of an inward and lively faith. With a boldness that impelled him to rush into the midst of danger, he combined a logical and consistent mind, which constantly led him forward in knowledge, and caused him to maintain with perseverance the truths he had once proclaimed. First of all, as a Christian, he had devoted his strength to the cause of the church; but he was at the same time a citizen, and the realm, his nation, and his king, had also a great share in his unwearied activity. He was a man complete.

If the man is admirable, his teaching is no less so. Scripture, which is the rule of truth, should be (according to his views) the rule of reformation, and we must reject every doctrine and every precept which does not rest on that foundation. He declared that to believe in the power of man in the work of regeneration is the great heresy of Rome, and from that error has come the ruin of the church. Conversion proceeds from the grace of God alone, and the system which ascribes it partly to man and partly to God is worse than Pelagianism. Christ is everything in Christianity; whosoever abandons that fountain which is ever ready to impart life, and turns to muddy and stagnant waters, is a madman. Faith is a gift of God; it puts aside all merit, and should banish all fear from the mind. The one thing needful in the Christian life and in the Lord's Supper is not a vain formalism and superstitious rites, but communion with Christ according to the power of the spiritual life. Let Christians submit not to the word of a priest but to the word of God. In the primitive church there were but two orders, the deacon and the presbyter: the presbyter and the bishop were one. The sublimest calling which man can attain on earth is that of preaching the word of God. The true church is the assembly of the righteous for whom Christ shed his blood. So long as Christ is in heaven, in him the church possesses the best pope. It is possible for a pope to be condemned at the last day because of his sins. Should men compel us to recognize as our head 'a devil of hell'? Such were the essential points of Wycliffe's doctrine. It was the echo of the doctrine of the apostles – the prelude to that of the reformers.[7]

---

[7] [Professor Gotthard Lechler's *John Wycliffe and His English Precursors* (described by Prof. Lorimer, who translated it from the German, as 'a preliminary history of the reformation') should be consulted by all who desire to reach an understanding of Wycliffe's doctrine. Discussing Wycliffe's doctrine of the church, he writes as follows: 'There is one peculiar feature of his fundamental idea of the church. Not that this peculiarity was anything new, or belonged only to Wycliffe (he has it, as he was well aware, in common with Augustine), but it is one of very great importance, and runs like a scarlet thread through the whole system of Wycliffe's thinking – we mean the thought that the church is nothing else than *the whole number of the elect* ... According to Wycliffe, the eternal ground or basis of the church lies in the *Divine election* ... he places himself in deliberate opposition to the idea of the church which prevailed in his time ... according to which men took the church to mean the *visible* Catholic Church – the organized communion of the hierarchy. Wycliffe, on the contrary, seeks the church's centre of gravity in the past eternity, in the invisible world above ... A soul is incorporated with Christ, or betrothed to Christ, not by any act of man, not by any earthly means and visible signs, but by the decree of God, according to his eternal election and foreordination. The church, therefore, has in the visible world only its manifestation, its temporary pilgrimage; it has its home and its origin, as also its end, in the invisible world, in eternity. Every individual devout Christian owes all that he possesses in his inner life to the regeneration which is the fruit of election. It is only by virtue of the gracious election of God that the individual belongs to the number of the saved ... Further, as Wycliffe carries back conversion, salvation, and membership of the church to the election of grace, *i.e.* to the eternal and free decree of God in Christ, he, at the same time, is far removed from the assumption, which up to that time was universal, that participation in salvation and the hope of heaven were conditioned exclusively by a man's connection

In many respects Wycliffe is the Luther of England; but the times of revival had not yet come, and the English reformer could not gain such striking victories over Rome as the German reformer. While Luther was surrounded by an ever-increasing number of scholars and princes who confessed the same faith as himself, Wycliffe shone almost alone in the firmament of the church. The boldness with which he substituted a living spirituality for a superstitious formalism, caused those to shrink back in affright who had gone with him against friars, priests, and popes. Erelong the Roman pontiff ordered him to be thrown into prison, and the monks threatened his life; but God protected him, and he remained calm amidst the machinations of his adversaries. 'Antichrist', said he, 'can only kill the body.' Having one foot in the grave already, he foretold that, from the very bosom of monkery, would some day proceed the regeneration of the church. 'If the friars, whom God condescends to teach, shall be converted to the primitive religion of Christ', said he, 'we shall see them abandoning their unbelief, returning freely, with or without the permission of Antichrist, to the primitive religion of the Lord, and building up the church, as did St Paul.'

Thus did Wycliffe's piercing glance discover, at the distance of nearly a century and a half, the young monk Luther in the Augustine convent at Erfurt, converted by the Epistle to the Romans, and returning to the spirit of St Paul and the religion of Jesus Christ. Time was hastening on to the fulfilment of this prophecy. 'The morning star of the reformation', for so has Wycliffe been called, had appeared above the horizon, and its beams were no more to be extinguished. In vain will thick clouds veil it at times; the distant hilltops of central Europe will soon reflect its rays;[8] and its piercing light, increasing in brightness, will pour over all the world, at the hour of the church's renovation, floods of knowledge and of life.

---

with the official Church, and were dependent entirely upon the mediation of the priesthood. There is thus included in Wycliffe's idea of the church the recognition of the free and immediate access of believers to the grace of God in Christ; in other words, of the general priesthood of believers.' (R.T.S. edition, revised by Lorimer, pp. 288-90.)]

[8] John Huss in Bohemia.

CHAPTER NINE

The Lollard Burnings

(15th Century)

Wycliffe's death manifested the power of his teaching. The master being removed, his disciples set their hands to the plough, and England was almost won over to the reformer's doctrines. The Wycliffites recognized a ministry independent of Rome, and deriving authority from the word of God alone. 'Every minister', said they, 'can administer the sacraments and attend to the cure of souls as well as the pope.' To the licentious wealth of the clergy they opposed a Christian poverty, and to the degenerate asceticism of the mendicant orders, a spiritual and free life. The townsfolk crowded around these humble preachers; the soldiers listened to them, armed with sword and buckler to defend them; the nobility took down the images from their baronial chapels; and even the royal family was partly won over to the reformation. England was like a tree cut down to the ground, from whose roots fresh buds were shooting out on every side, erelong to cover all the earth beneath their shade.

This augmented the courage of Wycliffe's disciples, and in many places the people took the initiative in the reform. The walls of St Paul's and other cathedrals were hung with placards aimed at the priests and friars, and the abuses of which they were the defenders; and in 1395 the friends of the gospel petitioned Parliament for a general reform. 'The essence of the worship which comes from Rome', said they, 'consists in signs and ceremonies, and not in the effectual ministry of the Holy Ghost: and therefore it is not that which Christ has ordained. Temporal things are distinct from spiritual things: a king and a bishop ought not to be one and the same person.' And then, from not clearly understanding the principle of the separation of the functions which they proclaimed, they called upon Parliament to 'abolish celibacy, transubstantiation, prayers for the dead, offerings to images, auricular confession, war, the arts unnecessary to life, the practice of blessing oil, salt, wax, incense, stones, mitres, and pilgrims' staffs. All these pertain to necromancy and not to theology.' Emboldened by the absence of the king in Ireland, they fixed their *Twelve Conclusions* on the gates of St Paul's and Westminster Abbey. This became the signal for persecution.

As soon as Arundel, Archbishop of York, and Braybrooke, Bishop of London, had read these propositions, they hastily crossed St George's Channel, and conjured the king to return to England. He did so. Richard, during childhood and youth, had been committed in succession to the charge of several guardians, and like children (says an historian) whose nurses have been often changed, he thrived none the better for it. He did good or evil, according to the influence of those around him, and, after the death of his pious wife, Anne of Bohemia, in 1394, he had no decided inclinations except for ostentation and licentiousness. The clergy were not mistaken in calculating on such a prince. On his return to London he forbade the Parliament to take the Wycliffite petition into consideration; and having summoned before him the most distinguished of its supporters, such as Story, Clifford, Latimer, and Montacute, he threatened them with death if they continued to defend their abominable opinions. Thus was the work of the reformer about to be destroyed.

But Richard had hardly withdrawn his hand from the gospel, when God (says Foxe the annalist) withdrew his hand from him. His cousin, Henry Bolingbroke, son of the famous Duke of Lancaster, and who had been banished from England, suddenly sailed from the Continent, landed in Yorkshire, gathered all the malcontents around him, and was acknowledged king. The unhappy Richard, after being formally deposed, was confined in Pontefract Castle, where his earthly career was soon terminated.

The son of Wycliffe's old defender was now king with the title of Henry IV: a reform of the church seemed imminent; but the primate Arundel had foreseen the danger. This cunning priest and skilful politician had observed which way the wind blew, and deserted Richard in good time.

Taking Lancaster by the hand, he put the crown on his head, saying to him: 'To consolidate your throne, conciliate the clergy, and sacrifice the Lollards.' – 'I will be the protector of the church', replied Henry IV, and from that hour the power of the priests was greater than the power of the nobility. Rome has ever been adroit in profiting by revolutions.

Henry ascended the throne in the late summer of 1399. In 1401 the famous act for the burning of heretics, *De Haeretico Comburendo*, was passed by Parliament. The church claimed that the act was in accord with a well-established principle, and to provide evidence that this was so, they hurried through the burning of a Lollard martyr in March 1401. The act was passed some eight days later.

Protestantism's proto-martyr was a pious priest named William Sawtre who had presumed to say: 'Instead of adoring the cross on which Christ suffered, I adore Christ who suffered on it.' He was dragged to St Paul's; his hair was shaved off; a layman's cap was placed on his head; and the primate handed him over to the *mercy* of the earl-marshal of England. This mercy was shown him – he was burnt alive at Smithfield, the first of a 'noble army' in England who loved not their lives unto the death.

Encouraged by this act of faith – this *auto da fé* – the clergy drew up the articles known as the 'Constitutions of Arundel', which forbade the translation and reading of the Bible without the permission of the ordinary (*i.e.* a bishop or similar high officer of the church) and styled the pope, 'not a mere man, but a true God.' The Lollards' Tower, in the archiepiscopal palace of Lambeth, was soon filled with pretended heretics, many of whom carved on the walls of their dungeons the expression of their sorrow and their hopes: *Jesus amor meus*, (Jesus is my love), wrote one of them. The words are still to be read in the tower.

To crush the lowly was not enough: the gospel must be driven from the more exalted stations. The priests, who were sincere in their belief, regarded those noblemen as misleaders, who set the word of God above the laws of Rome; and accordingly they girded themselves for the work. A few miles from Rochester stood Cowling Castle, in the midst of the fertile pastures watered by the Medway,

> The fair Medway that, with wanton pride,
> Forms silver mazes with her crooked tide!

In the beginning of the fifteenth century it was inhabited by Sir John Oldcastle, who became by his marriage, Lord Cobham, a man in high favour with the king.[1] The 'poor priests' thronged to Cowling in quest of Wycliffe's writings, of which Cobham had caused numerous copies to be made, and whence they were circulated through the dioceses of Canterbury, Rochester, London, and Hertford. Cobham attended their preaching and, if any enemies ventured to interrupt them, he threatened them with his sword. 'I would sooner risk my life', said he, 'than submit to such unjust decrees as dishonour the everlasting Testament.' The king would not permit the clergy to lay hands on his favourite.

But Henry V having succeeded his father in 1413, and passed from the houses of ill-fame he had hitherto frequented to the foot of the altars and the head of the armies, the archbishop immediately denounced Cobham to him, and he was summoned to appear before the king. Sir John had understood Wycliffe's doctrine, and experienced in his own person the might of the Divine word. 'As touching the pope and his spirituality', he said to the king, 'I owe them neither suit nor service, forasmuch as I know him by the Scriptures to be the great Antichrist.' Henry thrust aside Cobham's hand as he presented his confession of faith: 'I will not receive this paper; lay it before your judges.' When he saw his profession refused, Cobham had recourse to the only arm which he knew of out of the gospel. The differences which we now settle by pamphlets were then very commonly settled by the sword – 'I offer in defence of my faith to fight for life or death with any man living, Christian or pagan, always excepting Your Majesty.' Cobham was led to the Tower.

On 23 September 1413, he was taken before the ecclesiastical tribunal then sitting at St Paul's. 'We must believe', said the primate to him, 'what the holy Church of Rome teaches, without demanding Christ's authority.' – 'Believe!' shouted the priests, 'believe!' – 'I am willing to believe all that God desires', said Sir John; 'but that the pope should have authority to teach what is contrary to Scripture – that I can never believe.' He was led back to the Tower. The word of God was to have its martyr.

---

[1] [It is highly probable that he had been the close friend and companion of the youthful Henry V in the days of that prince's 'riotous living'. As such he is said to have been the basis of Shakespeare's Falstaff.]

On Monday, 25 September, a crowd of priests, canons, friars, clerks, and indulgence-sellers, thronged the large hall of the Dominican convent, and attacked Lord Cobham with abusive language. These insults, the importance of the moment for the reformation of England, the catastrophe that must needs close the scene: all agitated his soul to its very depths. When the archbishop called upon him to confess his offence, he fell on his knees and, lifting up his hands to heaven, exclaimed: 'I confess to thee, O God! and acknowledge that in my frail youth I seriously offended thee by my pride, anger, intemperance, and impurity: for these offences I implore thy mercy!' Then standing up, his face still wet with tears, he said: 'I ask not your absolution: it is God's only that I need.' The clergy did not despair, however, of reducing this high-spirited gentleman: they knew that spiritual strength is not always conjoined with bodily vigour, and they hoped to vanquish by priestly sophisms the man who dared challenge the papal champions to single combat. 'Sir John', said the primate at last, 'you have said some very strange things; we have spent much time in endeavours to convince you, but all to no effect. The day passeth away: you must either submit yourself to the ordinance of the most holy church or …' 'I will none otherwise believe than what I have told you. Do with me what you will.' – 'Well then, we must needs do the law', the archbishop made answer.

Arundel stood up; all the priests and people rose with him and uncovered their heads. Then holding the sentence of death in his hand, he read it with a loud clear voice. 'It is well', said Sir John; 'though you condemn my body, you can do no harm to my soul, by the grace of my eternal God.' He was again led back to the Tower, and given forty days in which to recant. But one night before that period ended Lord Cobham escaped, and took refuge in Wales. He was retaken in December 1417, carried to London, dragged on a hurdle to St Giles' fields, and there suspended by chains over a slow fire, and cruelly burned to death. Thus died a Christian, illustrious after the fashion of his age – a champion of the word of God. Shortly the London prisons were filled with Wycliffites, and it was decreed that they should be hanged on the king's account, and burnt for God's.

The intimidated Lollards were compelled to hide themselves in the humblest ranks of the people, and to hold their meetings in secret. The work of redemption was proceeding noiselessly among the elect of God. Of these Lollards, there were many who were doubtless true disciples of Jesus Christ; but in general they knew not, to the same extent as the evangelical Christians of the sixteenth century, the quickening and justifying power of faith. They were plain, meek, and often timid folks, attracted by the word of God, affected at the condemnation it pronounces against the errors of Rome, and desirous of living according to its commandments. God had assigned them a part – and an important part too – in the great transformation of Christianity. Their humble piety, their passive resistance, the shameful treatment which they bore with resignation, the penitent's robes with which they were covered, the tapers they were compelled to hold at the church door – all these things betrayed the pride of the priests, and filled the most generous minds with doubts and vague desires. By a baptism of suffering, God was then preparing the way to a glorious reformation.

CHAPTER TEN

The New Learning and the New Divinity

(c. 1485–1512)

This reformation was to be the result of two distinct forces – the revival of learning and the resurrection of the word of God. The latter was the principal cause, but the former was necessary as a means. Without it the living waters of the gospel would probably have traversed the age, like summer streams which soon dry up, such as those which had burst forth here and there during the Middle Ages; it would not have become that majestic river, which, by its inundations, fertilized all the earth. It was necessary to discover and examine the original fountains, and for this end the study of Greek and Hebrew was indispensable. Lollardism and humanism (the study of the classics) were the two laboratories of the reform. Having seen the preparations of the one, we must now trace the commencement of the other; and as we have discovered the light in the lowly valleys, we shall discern it also on the lofty mountain tops.

About the end of the fifteenth century, several young Englishmen chanced to be at Florence, attracted thither by the literary glory which environed the city of the Medici. Cosmo had collected together a great number of works of antiquity, and his palace was thronged with learned men. William Sellyng, a young English ecclesiastic, afterwards distinguished at Canterbury by his zeal in collecting valuable manuscripts; his fellow countrymen, William Grocyn, William Lilly, and William Latimer 'more bashful than a maiden'; and, above all, Thomas Linacre, whom Erasmus ranked before all the scholars of Italy – used to meet in the delightful villa of the Medici with Politian, Chalcondyles, and other men of learning; and there, in the calm evenings of summer, under that glorious Tuscan sky, they dreamt romantic visions of the Platonic philosophy. When they returned to England, these learned men laid before the youth of Oxford the marvellous treasures of the Greek language. Some Italians even, attracted by the desire to enlighten the barbarians, and a little, it may be, by the brilliant offers made them, quitted their beloved country for the distant Britain. Cornelio Vitelli taught at Oxford, and Caius Amberino at Cambridge. Caxton imported the art of printing from Germany, and the nation hailed with enthusiasm the brilliant dawn which was breaking at last in their cloudy sky.

While learning was reviving in England, a new dynasty succeeded to the throne, bringing with it that energy of character which of itself is able to effect great revolutions; the Tudors succeeded the Plantagenets. That inflexible intrepidity by which the reformers of Germany, Switzerland, France, and Scotland were distinguished, did not exist so generally in those of England; but it was found in the character of her kings, who often stretched it even to violence. It may be that to this preponderance of energy in its rulers, the church owes the preponderance of the state in its affairs.

Henry Tudor, the Louis XI of England, was a clever prince, of decided but suspicious character, avaricious and narrow-minded. Being descended from a Welsh family, he belonged to that ancient race of Celts, who had so long contended against the papacy. Henry extinguished faction at home, and taught foreign nations to respect his power. A good genius seemed to exercise a salutary influence over his court as well as over himself: this was his mother, the Countess Richmond. From her chamber, where she consecrated the first five hours of the day to reading, meditation, and prayer, she moved to another part of the palace to dress the wounds of some of the lowest mendicants; thence she passed into the carefree saloons, where she would converse with the scholars, whom she encouraged by her munificence. This noble lady's passion for study, of which her son inherited but little, was not without its influence in her family. Arthur and Henry, the king's sons, trembled in their father's presence; but, captivated by the affection of their pious grandmother, they began to find a pleasure in the society of learned men. An important circumstance gave a new impulse to one of them.

Among the countess's friends was William Blount, Lord Mountjoy, who had known Erasmus at Paris, and heard his cutting sarcasms upon the schoolmen and friars. He invited the illustrious Dutchman to England, and Erasmus, who was fearful of catching the plague, gladly accepted the invitation, and set out for what he believed to be the kingdom of darkness. But he had not been long in England before he discovered unexpected light.

Shortly after his arrival, happening to dine with the Lord Mayor of London, Erasmus noticed on the other side of the table a young man of nineteen, slender, fresh-coloured, with blue eyes, coarse hands, and the right shoulder somewhat higher than the other. His features indicated affability and gaiety, and pleasant jests were continually dropping from his lips. If he could not find a joke in English, he would in French, and even in Latin or Greek. A literary contest soon ensued between Erasmus and the English youth. The former, astonished at meeting with anyone that could hold his own against him, exclaimed: *Aut tu es Morus aut nullus!* (you are either More or nobody); and his companion, who had not learnt the stranger's name, quickly replied: *Aut tu es Erasmus aut diabolus!* (you are either the devil or Erasmus). More flung himself into the arms of Erasmus, and they became inseparable friends. More was continually joking, even with women, teasing the sprightly, and making fun of the dull, though without any tinge of ill-nature in his jests. But under this sportive exterior he concealed a deep understanding. He was at that time lecturing on Augustine's *City of God* before a numerous audience composed of priests and aged men. The thought of eternity had seized him; and being ignorant of that internal discipline of the Holy Ghost, which is the only true discipline, he had recourse to the scourge every Friday. Thomas More is the ideal of the Catholicism of this period. He had, like the Romish system, two poles – worldliness and asceticism; which, although contrary, often meet together. In fact, asceticism makes a sacrifice of *self*, only to preserve it; just as a traveller attacked by robbers will readily give up a portion of his treasures to save the rest. This was the case with More, if we rightly understand his character. He sacrificed the accessories of his fallen nature to save that same nature. He submitted to fasts and vigils, wore a shirt of hair-cloth, mortified his body by small chains next his skin – in a word, he immolated everything in order to preserve that *self* which a real regeneration alone can sacrifice.

From London Erasmus went to Oxford, where he met with John Colet, a friend of More's, but older, and of very dissimilar character. Colet, the scion of an ancient family, was a very portly man, of imposing aspect, great fortune, and elegance of manners, to which Erasmus had not been accustomed. Order, cleanliness, and decorum prevailed in his person and in his house. He kept an excellent table, which was open to all the friends of learning, and at which the Dutchman, no great admirer of the colleges of Paris with their sour wine and stale eggs, was glad to take a seat. He there met also most of the classical scholars of England, especially Grocyn, Linacre, Thomas Wolsey, bursar of Magdalen College, Halsey, and some others. 'I cannot tell you how I am delighted with your England', he wrote to Lord Mountjoy from Oxford. 'With such men I could willingly live in the farthest coasts of Scythia.'

But if Erasmus on the banks of the Thames found a Maecenas in Lord Mountjoy, a Labeo and perhaps a Virgil in More, he nowhere found an Augustus. One day as he was expressing his regrets and his fears to More, the latter said: 'Come, let us go to Eltham, perhaps we shall find there what you are looking for.' They set out, More jesting all the way, inwardly resolving to expiate his merriment by a severe scourging at night. On their arrival they were heartily welcomed by Lord and Lady Mountjoy, the governor and governess of the king's children. As the two friends entered the hall, a pleasing and unexpected sight greeted Erasmus. The whole of the family were assembled, and they found themselves surrounded not only by some of the royal household, but by the domestics of Lord Mountjoy also. On the right stood the Princess Margaret, a girl of eleven years, whose great-grandson under the name of Stuart was to continue the Tudor line in England; on the left was Mary, a child four years of age; Edmund was in his nurse's arms; and in the middle of the circle, between his two sisters, stood a boy, at that time only nine years old, whose handsome features, royal carriage, intelligent eye, and exquisite courtesy, had an extraordinary charm for Erasmus. That boy was Henry, Duke of York, the king's second son, born on 28 June 1491. More, advancing towards the young prince, presented to him some piece of his own writing; and from that hour Erasmus kept up a friendly intercourse with Henry, which in all probability exercised a certain influence over the destinies of England. The scholar of Rotterdam was delighted to see the prince excel in all the manly sports of the day. He sat his horse with perfect grace and rare intrepidity, could hurl a javelin farther than any of his companions, and having an excellent taste for music, he was already a performer on several instruments. The king took care that he should receive a learned education – it may have been the case that he destined him to fill the see of Canterbury – and the illustrious Erasmus, noticing his aptitude for everything he undertook, did his best to cut and polish this English diamond that it might glitter with the greater brilliancy. 'He will begin nothing that he will not finish', said the scholar. And it is but too true that this prince always attained his end, even if it were necessary to tread on the bleeding bodies of those he had loved. Flattered by the attentions of the young Henry, attracted by his winning grace, charmed by his wit, Erasmus on his return to the Continent everywhere proclaimed that England at last had found its Octavius.

As for Henry VII he thought of everything but Virgil or Augustus. Avarice and ambition were his predominant tastes, which he gratified by the marriage of his eldest son Arthur in 1501. Burgundy, Artois, Provence, and Brittany having been recently united to France, the European powers felt the necessity of combining against that encroaching state. It was in consequence of this that Ferdinand of Aragon had given his daughter Joanna to Philip of Austria, and that Henry VII asked the hand of his daughter Catherine, then in her sixteenth year and the richest princess in Europe, for Arthur, Prince of Wales, a youth about ten months younger. The Catholic king attached one condition to the marriage of his daughter. Warwick, the last of the Plantagenets and a pretender to the crown, was confined in the Tower. Ferdinand, to secure the certainty that Catherine would really ascend the English throne, required that the unhappy prince should be put to death. Nor did this alone satisfy the King of Spain. Henry VII, who was not a cruel man, might conceal Warwick, and say that he was no more. Ferdinand demanded that the chancellor of Castile should be present at the execution. The blood of

Warwick was shed; his head rolled duly on the scaffold; the Castilian chancellor verified and registered the murder, and on 14 November the marriage was solemnized at St Paul's. At midnight the prince and princess were conducted with great pomp to the bridal chamber. These were ill-omened nuptials – fated to set the kings and nations of Christendom in battle against one another, and to serve as a pretext for the external and political discussions of the English reformation. The marriage of Catherine the Catholic was a marriage of blood.

In the early part of 1502 Prince Arthur fell ill, and on 2 April he died. The necessary time was taken to be sure that Catherine had no hope of becoming a mother, after which the friend of Erasmus, the youthful Henry, was declared heir to the crown, to the great joy of all the learned. This prince did not forsake his studies: he spoke and wrote in French, German, and Spanish with the facility of a native; and England hoped to behold one day the most learned of Christian kings upon the throne of Alfred the Great.

A very different question, however, filled the mind of the covetous Henry VII. Must he restore to Spain the one hundred thousand crowns which formed the half of Catherine's dowry already paid, and forfeit his claims to the half as yet unpaid? Should this rich heiress be permitted to marry some rival of England? To prevent so great a misfortune the king conceived the project of uniting Henry to Arthur's widow. The most serious objections were urged against it. 'It is not only inconsistent with propriety', said Warham, the primate, 'but the will of God himself is against it. It is declared in his law that *if a man shall take his brother's wife, it is an unclean thing* (Lev. 20:21); and in the Gospel John Baptist says to Herod: *It is not lawful for thee to have thy brother's wife'* (Mark 6:18). Fox, Bishop of Winchester, suggested that a dispensation might be procured from the pope, and in December 1503 Julius II granted a bull[1] declaring that for the sake of preserving union between the Catholic princes he authorized Catherine's marriage with the brother of her first husband, *accedente forsan copula carnali*. These four words, it is said, were inserted in the bull at the express desire of the princess. All these details will be of

---

[1] [The Papal Bull dated 26 December 1503 is extant, but it seems that Henry VII did not receive it at that time, for months later he was in correspondence with the pope complaining that it had not been received in England.]

importance in the course of our history. The two parties were betrothed, but not married in consideration of the youth of the Prince of Wales.

The second marriage projected by Henry VII was ushered in with auspices still less promising than the first. The king having fallen sick and lost his queen, looked upon these visitations as a Divine judgment. The nation murmured, and demanded whether it was in the pope's power to permit what God had forbidden. The young prince, being informed of his father's scruples and of the people's discontent, declared, on the eve of his fourteenth birthday (27 June 1505) in the presence of the Bishop of Winchester and several royal counsellors, that he protested against the engagement entered into during his minority, and that he would never make Catherine his wife.

His father's death, which made him free, made him also recall this virtuous decision. In 1509, the hopes of the learned seemed about to be realized. On 9 May, a hearse decorated with regal pomp, bearing on a rich pall of cloth of gold the mortal remains of Henry VII, with his sceptre and his crown, entered London from Richmond, followed by a long procession. The great officers of state, assembled round the coffin, broke their staves and cast them into the vault, and the heralds cried with a loud voice: 'God send the noble King Henry VIII long life.' Such a cry perhaps had never on any previous occasion been so joyfully repeated by the people. The young king gratified the wishes of the nation by ordering the arrest of Empson and Dudley, who were charged with extortion; and he conformed to the enlightened counsels of his grandmother, by choosing the most able ministers, and placing the Archbishop of Canterbury as Lord Chancellor at their head. Warham was a man of great capacity. The day was not too short for him to hear Mass, receive ambassadors, consult with the king in the royal chamber, entertain as many as two hundred guests at his table, take his seat on the woolsack, and find time for his private devotions. The joy of the learned surpassed that of the people. The old king wanted none of their praises or congratulations, for fear he should have to pay for them; but now they could give free course to their enthusiasm.

Mountjoy pronounced the young king 'divine'; the Venetian ambassador likened his bearing to Apollo's, and his noble chest to the torso of Mars; he was lauded both in Greek and Latin; he was hailed as the founder of a new era; and Henry seemed desirous of meriting these eulogiums. Far from permitting himself to be intoxicated by so much adulation, he said to Mountjoy: 'Ah! how I should like to be a scholar!' – 'Sire', replied the courtier, 'it is enough that you show your regard for those who possess the learning you desire for yourself.' – 'How can I do otherwise?' he replied with earnestness; 'without them we hardly exist!' Mountjoy immediately communicated this to Erasmus.

Erasmus! – Erasmus! – the walls of Eltham, Oxford, and London resounded with the name. The king could not live without the learned; nor the learned without Erasmus. This scholar, who was an enthusiast for the young king, was not long in answering to the call. When Richard Pace, the king's secretary, and one of the most accomplished men of that age, met the learned Dutchman at Ferrara, the latter took from his pocket a little box which he always carried with him: 'You do not know', he said, 'what a treasure you have in England: I will just show you'; and he took from the box a letter of Henry's expressing in Latin of considerable purity the tenderest regard for his correspondent. Immediately after the coronation Mountjoy wrote to Erasmus: 'Our Henry *Octavus*, or rather *Octavius*, is on the throne. Come and behold the new star. The heavens smile, the earth leaps for joy, and all is flowing with milk, nectar, and honey. Avarice has fled away, liberality has descended, scattering on every side with gracious hand her bounteous largesses. Our king desires not gold or precious stones, but virtue, glory, and immortality.'

In such glowing terms was the young king described by a man who had seen him closely. Erasmus could resist no longer: he bade the pope farewell, and hastened to London, where he met with a hearty welcome from Henry. Knowledge and power embraced each other: England was about to have its Medici; and the friends of learning no longer doubted of the regeneration of Britain.

Julius II, who had permitted Erasmus to exchange the white frock of the monks for the black dress of the seculars, allowed him to depart without much regret. This pontiff had little taste for letters, but was fond of war, hunting, and the pleasures of the table. The English sent him a dish to his taste in exchange for the scholar. Sometime after Erasmus had left, as the pope was one day reposing from the fatigues of the chase, he heard voices near him singing a strange song. He asked with surprise what it meant. 'It is some Englishmen', was the answer, and three foreigners entered the room, each bearing a closely-covered jar, which the youngest presented on his knees. This was Thomas Cromwell, who appears here for the first time on the historic scene. He was the son of a blacksmith of Putney; but he possessed a mind so penetrating, a judgment so sound, a heart so bold, ability so consummate, such easy elocution, such an accurate memory, such great activity, and so able a pen, that the most brilliant career awaited him. At about eighteen years of age he left England, being desirous to see the world, and after a period in Italy he began life as a trader in the English factory at Antwerp. Shortly after this two fellow countrymen from Boston came to him in their embarrassment. 'What do you want?' he asked them. 'Our townsmen have sent us to the pope', they told him, 'to get the renewal of the *greater* and *lesser pardons*, whose term is nearly run, and which are necessary for the repair of our harbour. But we do not know how to appear before him.' Cromwell, prompt to undertake everything, and knowing a little Italian, replied, 'I will go with you.' Then slapping his forehead he muttered to himself: 'What fish can I throw out as a bait to these greedy cormorants?' A friend informed him that the pope was very fond of dainties. Cromwell immediately ordered some exquisite jelly to be prepared, after the English fashion, and set out for Italy with his provisions and his two companions.

This was the man who appeared before Julius after his return from the chase. 'Kings and princes alone eat of this preserve in England', said Cromwell to the pope. One cardinal, who was a greedier 'cormorant' than his master, eagerly tasted the delicacy. 'Try it', he exclaimed, and the pope, relishing this new confectionery, immediately signed the pardons, on condition however that the recipe for the jelly should be left with him. 'And thus were the *jelly pardons* obtained', says the annalist. It was Cromwell's first exploit, and the man who began his busy career by presenting jars of confectionery to the pope was also the man destined to separate England from Rome.

The court of the pontiff was not the only one in Europe devoted to gaiety. Hunting parties were as common in London as at Rome. The young king and his companions were at that time absorbed in balls, banquets, and the other festivities inseparable from a new reign. He recollected however that he must give a queen to his people: Catherine of Aragon was still in England, and the council recommended her for his wife. He admired her piety without caring to imitate it; he was pleased with her love for literature, and even felt some inclination towards her. His advisers represented to him that 'Catherine, daughter of the illustrious Isabella of Castile, was the image of her mother; that, like her, she possessed that wisdom and greatness of mind which win the respect of nations; and that if she carried to any of his rivals her marriage-portion and the Spanish alliance, the long-contested crown of England would soon fall from his head ... We have the pope's dispensation: will you be more scrupulous than he is?' The Archbishop of Canterbury opposed in vain: Henry gave way, and on 11 June, about seven weeks after his father's death, the nuptials were privately celebrated at Greenwich. On the 23rd the king and queen went in state through the city, the bride wearing a white satin dress with her hair hanging down her back nearly to her feet. On the next day they were crowned at Westminster with great magnificence.

Then followed a series of expensive entertainments. The treasures which the nobility had long concealed from fear of the old king, were now brought out; the ladies glittered with gold and diamonds; and the king and queen, whom the people never grew tired of admiring, amused themselves like children with the splendour of their royal robes. Henry VIII was the forerunner of Louis XIV. Naturally inclined to pomp and pleasure, the idol of his people, a devoted admirer of female beauty, and the husband of almost as many wives as Louis had adulterous mistresses, he made the court of England what the son of Anne of Austria made the court of France – one constant scene of amusements. He thought he could never get to the end of the riches amassed by his prudent father. His youth – for he was only eighteen – the gaiety of his disposition, the grace he displayed in all bodily exercises, the tales of chivalry in which he delighted, and which even the clergy recommended to their high-born hearers, the flattery of his courtiers – all these combined to set his young imagination in a ferment. Wherever he appeared, all were filled with admiration of his handsome countenance and graceful figure: such is the portrait bequeathed to us by the Jesuit, Nicholas Sander, his greatest enemy. 'His brow was made to wear the crown, and his majestic port the kingly mantle', adds Noryson.

Henry resolved to realize without delay the chivalrous combats and fabulous splendours of the heroes of the round table, as if to prepare himself for those more real struggles which he would one day have to maintain against the papacy. At the sound of the trumpet the youthful monarch would enter the lists, clad in costly armour, and wearing a plume that fell gracefully down to the saddle of his vigorous courser; 'like an untamed bull', says an historian, 'which breaks away from its yoke and rushes into the arena'. On one occasion, at the celebration of the queen's churching, Catherine with her ladies was seated in a tent of purple and gold, in the midst of an artificial forest, strewn with rocks and variegated with flowers. On a sudden a monk stepped forward, wearing a long brown robe, and kneeling before her, begged permission to run a course. It was granted, and rising up he threw aside his coarse frock, and appeared gorgeously armed for the tourney. He was Charles Brandon, afterwards Duke of Suffolk, one of the handsomest and strongest men in the kingdom, and the first after Henry in military exercises. He was followed by a number of others dressed in black velvet, with wide-brimmed hats on their heads, staffs in their hands, and scarfs across their shoulders ornamented with cockle shells, like pilgrims from St James of Compostella. These also threw off their disguise, and stood forth in complete armour. At their head was Sir Thomas Boleyn, whose daughter was destined to surpass in beauty, greatness, and misfortune, all the women of England. The tournament began. Henry, who has been compared to Amadis in boldness, to the lion-hearted Richard in courage, and to Edward III in courtesy, did not always escape danger in these chivalrous contests. One day the king had forgotten to lower his vizor, and Brandon, his opponent, setting off at full gallop, the spectators noticed the oversight, and cried out in alarm. But nothing could stop their horses: the two cavaliers met. Suffolk's lance was shivered against Henry, and the fragments struck him in the face. Everyone thought the king was dead, and some were running to arrest Brandon, when Henry, recovering from the blow which had fallen on his helmet, recommended the combat, and ran six new courses amid the admiring cries of his subjects. This intrepid courage changed, as he grew older, into unsparing cruelty; and it was this young tiger, whose movements were then so graceful, that at no distant day tore with his blood-red fangs the mother of his children.

CHAPTER ELEVEN

War, Marriage, and Preaching

(1513–1515)

A message from the pope stopped Henry in the midst of these amusements. In Scotland, Spain, France, and Italy, the young king had nothing but friends; a harmony which the papacy was intent on disturbing. One day, immediately after High Mass had been celebrated, the Archbishop of Canterbury, on behalf of Julius II, laid at his feet a golden rose, which had been blessed by the pope, anointed with holy oil, and perfumed with musk. It was accompanied by a letter saluting him as head of the Italian league. The warlike pontiff having reduced the Venetians, desired to humble France, and to employ Henry as the instrument of his vengeance. Henry, only a short time before, had renewed his alliance with Louis XII; but the pope was not to be baffled by such a trifle as that, and the young king soon began to dream of rivalling the glories of Crécy, Poitiers, and Agincourt. To no purpose did his wisest councillors represent to him that England, in the most favourable times, had never been able to hold her ground in France, and that the sea was the true field open to her conquests. Julius, knowing his vanity, had promised to deprive Louis of the title of Most Christian King, and confer it upon him. 'His Holiness hopes that Your Grace will utterly exterminate the King of France', wrote the king's agent. Henry saw nothing objectionable in this very unapostolic mission, and decided on substituting the terrible game of war for the gentler sports of peace.

After some unsuccessful attempts by his generals, Henry determined to invade France in person. He was in the midst of his preparations when the festival of Easter arrived. Dean Colet had been appointed to preach before Henry on Good Friday, and in the course of his sermon he showed more courage than could have been expected in a scholar, for a spark of the Christian spirit was glowing in his bosom. He chose for the subject of his discourse Christ's victory over death and the grave. 'Whoever takes up arms from ambition', said he, 'fights not under the standard of Christ, but of Satan. If you desire to contend against your enemies, follow Jesus Christ as your prince and captain, rather than Caesar or Alexander.' His hearers looked at each other with astonishment; the friends of polite literature became alarmed; and the priests, who were getting uneasy at the uprising of the human mind, hoped to profit by this opportunity of inflicting a deadly blow on their antagonists. There were among them men whose opinions we must condemn, while we cannot forbear respecting the zeal for what they believed to be the truth: of this number were Bricot, Fitzjames, and above all Standish. Their zeal, however, went a little too far on this occasion: they even talked of *burning* the dean.[1] After the sermon, Colet was informed that the king requested his attendance in the garden of the Franciscan monastery, and immediately the priests and monks crowded round the gate, hoping to see their adversary led forth as a criminal. 'Let us be alone', said Henry; 'put on your cap, Mr Dean, and we will take a walk. Cheer up', he continued, 'you have nothing to fear. You have spoken admirably of Christian charity, and have almost reconciled me to the King of France; yet, as the contest is not one of choice, but of necessity, I must beg of you in some future sermon to explain this to my people. Unless you do so, I fear my soldiers may misunderstand your meaning.' Colet was not a John Baptist, and, affected by the king's condescension, he gave the required explanation. The king was satisfied, and exclaimed: 'Let every man have his doctor as he pleases; this man is my doctor, and I will drink his health!' Henry was then young: very different was the fashion with which in after-years he treated those who opposed him.

At heart the king cared little more about the victories of Alexander than of Jesus Christ. Having fitted out his army, he embarked at the end of June 1513, accompanied by his almoner, Wolsey, who was rising into favour, and set out for the war as if for a tournament. Shortly after this,

---

[1] Dr Colet was in trouble and should have been burnt, if God had not turned the king's heart to the contrary. *Latimer's Sermons* (Parker Society), p. 440.

he went, all glittering with jewels, to meet the emperor Maximilian, who received him in a plain doublet and cloak of black serge. After his victory at the battle of the Spurs, Henry, instead of pressing forward to the conquest of France, returned to the siege of Thérouanne, wasted his time in jousts and entertainments, conferred on Wolsey the bishopric of Tournai which he had just captured, and then returned to England, delighted at having made so pleasant an excursion.

Louis XII was a widower in his 53rd year, and bowed down by the infirmities of a premature old age; but being desirous of preventing, at any cost, the renewal of the war, he sought the hand of Henry's sister, the Princess Mary, then in her 18th year. Her affections were already fixed on Charles Brandon, and for him she would have sacrificed the splendour of a throne. But reasons of state opposed their union. 'The princess', remarked Wolsey, 'will soon return to England a widow with a royal dowry.' This decided the question. The disconsolate Mary, who was an object of universal pity, embarked at Dover with a numerous train, and from Boulogne, where she was received by the Duke of Angoulême, she was conducted to the king, who was elated at the idea of marrying the handsomest princess in Europe.

Among Mary's attendants was the youthful Anne Boleyn. Her father, Sir Thomas Boleyn, had been charged by Henry, conjointly with the Bishop of Ely, with the diplomatic negotiations preliminary to this marriage. Anne had passed her childhood at Hever Castle, Kent, surrounded by all that could heat the imagination. Her maternal grandfather, the Earl of Surrey, whose eldest son had married the sister of Henry VII's queen, had filled, as did his sons also, the most important offices of state. When summoned by her father to court, she wrote him the following letter in French, which appears to refer to her departure for France:

> Sir – I find by your letter that you wish me to appear at court in a manner becoming a respectable female, and likewise that the queen will condescend to enter into conversation with me; at this I rejoice, as I do to think that conversing with so sensible and elegant a princess will make me even more desirous of continuing to speak and to write good French; the more as it is by your earnest advice, which (I

acquaint you by this present writing) I shall follow to the best of my ability ... As to myself, rest assured that I shall not ungratefully look upon this fatherly office as one that might be dispensed with; nor will it tend to diminish my affection, quest [wish], and deliberation to lead as holy a life as you may please to desire of me; indeed my love for you is founded on so firm a basis that it can never be impaired. I put an end to this my lucubration after having very humbly craved your goodwill and affection. Written at Hever, by

Your very humble and obedient daughter,

Anna de Boullan.

Such were the feelings under which this young and interesting lady, so calumniated by papistical writers, appeared at court.

The marriage which took place by proxy in London, on 18 August 1514, was formally proclaimed and celebrated at Abbeville on 9 October, and, after a sumptuous banquet, the King of France distributed his royal largesses among the English lords, who were charmed by his courtesy. But the morrow was a day of trial to the young queen. Louis XII had dismissed the numerous train which had accompanied her, and even Lady Guildford, to whom Henry had specially confided her. Three only were left – of whom the youthful Anne Boleyn was one. At this separation, Mary gave way to the keenest sorrow. To cheer her spirits, Louis proclaimed a grand tournament. Brandon hastened to France at its first announcement, and carried off all the prizes, while the king, languidly reclining on a couch, could with difficulty look upon the brilliant spectacle over which his queen presided, sick at heart yet radiant with youth and beauty. Mary was unable to conceal her emotion, and Louisa of Savoy, who was watching her, divined her secret. But Louis, if he experienced the tortures of jealousy, did not feel them long, for his death took place on 1 January 1515.

Even before her husband's funeral was over, Mary's heart beat high with hope. The new French monarch, Francis I, impatient to see her wedded to some unimportant political personage, encouraged her love for Brandon. The latter, who had been commissioned by Henry to convey to her his letters of condolence, feared his master's anger if he should dare aspire to the hand of the princess. But the widowed queen, who was resolved to brave everything, told her lover: 'Either you marry me in four days or you see me no more.' The choice the king had made of his ambassador announced that he would not behave very harshly. The marriage was celebrated in the abbey of Clugny, and Henry pardoned them, but only on the payment of a heavy fine by both parties.

While Mary returned to England, as Wolsey had predicted, Anne Boleyn remained in France. Her father, desiring his daughter to become an accomplished woman, entrusted her to the care of the virtuous Claude of France, *the good queen*, at whose court the daughters of the first families of the kingdom were trained. Margaret, Duchess of Alençon, the sister of Francis, and afterwards Queen of Navarre, often charmed the queen's circle by her lively conversation. She soon became deeply attached to the young Englishwoman, and on the death of Claude took her into her own family. Anne Boleyn was destined at no very remote period to be at the court of London a reflection of the graceful Margaret, and her relations with that princess were not without influence on the English reformation.

And indeed the literary movement which had passed from Italy into France appeared at that time as if it would cross from France into Britain. Oxford exercises over England as great an influence as the metropolis; and it is almost always within its walls that a movement commences whether for good or evil. At this period of our history, enthusiastic youth hailed with joy the first beams of the new sun, and attacked with their sarcasms the idleness of the monks, the immorality of the clergy, and the superstition of the people. Disgusted with the priestcraft of the Middle Ages, and captivated by the writers of antiquity and the purity of the gospel, Oxford boldly called for a reform which should burst the bonds of clerical domination and emancipate the human mind. Men of letters thought for a while that they had found in the most powerful man in England, Thomas Wolsey, the ally that would give them the victory. He possessed little taste for learning, but seeing the wind of public favour blow in that direction, he readily spread his sails before it. He got the reputation of a profound divine, by quoting a few words of Thomas Aquinas, and the fame of a Mæcenas and a Ptolemy, by inviting the learned to his gorgeous entertainments. 'O happy cardinal', exclaimed Erasmus, 'who can surround his table with such torches!'

At that time the king felt the same ambition as his minister, and, having tasted in turn the pleasures of war and diplomacy, he now bent his mind to literature. He desired Wolsey to present Sir Thomas More to him. – 'What shall I do at court?' replied the latter. 'I shall be as awkward as a man that never rode sitteth in a saddle.' Happy in his family circle, where his father, mother, and children, gathering round the same table, formed a pleasing group, which the pencil of Holbein has transmitted to us, More had no desire to leave it. But Henry was not a man to put up with a refusal; he employed force almost to draw More from his retirement, and in a short time he could not live without the society of the man of letters. On calm and starlight nights they would walk together upon the leads at the top of the palace, discoursing on the motions of the heavenly bodies. If More did not appear at court, Henry would go to Chelsea and share the frugal dinner of the family with some of their simple neighbours. 'Where', asked Erasmus, 'where is the Athens, the Porch, or the Academy, that can be compared with the court of England? ... It is a seat of the muses rather than a palace ... The golden age is reviving, and I congratulate the world.'

But the friends of classical learning were not content with the cardinal's banquets or the king's favours. They wanted victories, and their keenest darts were aimed at the cloisters, those strong fortresses of the hierarchy and of uncleanness. The Abbot of St Albans, having taken a married woman for his concubine, and placed her at the head of a nunnery, his monks had followed his example, and indulged in the most scandalous debauchery. Public indignation was so far aroused, that Wolsey himself – Wolsey, the father of several illegitimate children, and who was suffering the penalty of his irregularities – was carried away by the spirit of the age, and demanded of the pope a general reform of manners. When they heard of this request, the priests and friars were loud in their outcries.

'What are you about?' said they to Wolsey. 'You are giving the victory to the enemies of the church, and your only reward will be the hatred of the whole world.' As this was not the cardinal's game, he abandoned his project, and conceived one more easily executed. Wishing to deserve the name of 'Ptolemy' conferred on him by Erasmus, he undertook to build two large colleges, one at Ipswich, his native town, the other at Oxford, and found it convenient to take the money necessary for their endowment, not from his own purse, but from the purses of the monks. He pointed out to the pope twenty-two monasteries in which (he said) vice and impiety had taken up their abode. The pope granted their secularization, and Wolsey having thus procured a revenue of £2,000 sterling, laid the foundations of his college, traced out various courts, and constructed spacious kitchens. He fell into disgrace before he had completed his work, which led Gualter to say with a sneer: 'He began a college and built a cook's shop.' But a great example had been set: the monasteries had been attacked, and the first breach made in them by a cardinal. Cromwell, Wolsey's secretary, took note how his master had set about his work, and in after-years profited by the lesson.

It was fortunate for learning that it had sincerer friends in London than Wolsey. Of these were Colet, Dean of St Paul's, whose house was the centre of the literary movement which preceded the reformation, and his friend and guest Erasmus. The latter was the hardy pioneer who opened the road of antiquity to modern Europe. One day he would entertain Colet's guests with the account of a new manuscript; on another, with a discussion on the forms of ancient literature; and at other times he would attack the schoolmen and monks, when Colet would take the same side. The only antagonist who dared measure his strength with him was Sir Thomas More, who, although a layman, stoutly defended the ordinances of the church.

But mere table-talk could not satisfy the dean: a numerous audience attended his sermons at St Paul's. The spirituality of Christ's words, the authority which characterizes them, their admirable simplicity and mysterious depth had deeply charmed him: 'I admire the writings of the apostles', he would say, 'but I forget them almost, when I contemplate the wonderful majesty of Jesus Christ.' Setting aside the texts prescribed by the church, he explained, like Zwingli, the Gospel of St Matthew. Nor did he stop here. Taking advantage of the convocation, he delivered a sermon on *conformation and reformation*, which was one of the numerous forerunners of the great reform of the sixteenth century. 'We see strange and heretical ideas appear in our days, and no wonder', said he. 'But you must know there is no heresy more dangerous to the church than the vicious lives of its priests. A reformation is needed; and that reformation must begin with the bishops and be extended to the priests. The clergy once reformed, we shall proceed to the reformation of the people.' Thus spoke Colet, while the citizens of London listened to him with rapture, and called him a new St Paul.

Such discourses could not be allowed to pass unpunished. Richard Fitzjames, Bishop of London, was a superstitious obstinate old man of eighty, fond of money, excessively irritable, a poor theologian, and a slave to Duns Scotus, the *subtle doctor*. Calling to his aid two other bishops as zealous as himself for the preservation of abuses, namely, Bricot and Standish, he denounced the Dean of St Paul's to Warham. The archbishop having inquired what he had done: 'What has he done?' rejoined the Bishop of London. 'He teaches that we must not worship images; he translates the Lord's Prayer into English; he pretends that the text *Feed my sheep*, does not include the temporal supplies the clergy draw from their flock. And besides all this', he continued with some embarrassment, 'he has spoken against those who carry their manuscripts into the pulpit and read their sermons!' As this was the bishop's practice, the primate could not refrain from smiling; and since Colet refused to justify himself, Warham did so for him.

From that time Colet laboured with fresh zeal to scatter the darkness. He devoted the larger portion of his fortune to found the celebrated school of St Paul, of which the learned William Lilly was the first master. Two parties, the *Greeks* and the *Trojans*, entered the lists, not to contend with sword and spear, as in the ancient epic, but with the tongue, the pen, and sometimes the fist. If the Trojans (the obscurants) were defeated in the public disputations, they had their revenge in the secret of the confessional. *Cave a Græcis ne fias hereticus* (Beware of the Greeks, lest you should become a heretic) was the watchword of the priests – their daily lesson to the youths under their care. They looked on the school founded by Colet as the monstrous horse of the perjured Sinon, and announced that from its bosom would inevitably issue the destruction of the people. Colet and Erasmus replied to the monks by inflicting fresh blows. Linacre, a thorough literary enthusiast – Grocyn, a man of sarcastic humour but generous heart – and many others, reinforced the *Grecian* phalanx. Henry himself used to take one of them with him during his journeys, and if any hostile *Trojan* ventured in his presence to attack the tongue of Plato and of St Paul, the young king would set his Hellenian on him. Not more numerous were the contests witnessed in times of yore on the classic banks of Xanthus and Simois.

CHAPTER TWELVE

Wolsey's Rise to Power

(1507–1518)

Just as everything seemed tending to a reformation, a powerful priest rendered the way more difficult.

One of the most striking personages of the age was then making his appearance on the stage of the world. It was the destiny of that man, in the reign of Henry VIII, to combine extreme ability with notorious immorality; and to be a new and striking example of the wholesome truth that immorality is more effectual to destroy a man than ability to save him. Wolsey was the last high priest of Rome in England, and when his fall startled the nation, it was the signal of a still more striking fall – the fall of popery.

Thomas Wolsey, the son of a wealthy butcher and innkeeper of Ipswich, according to the common story, which is sanctioned by high authority, had attained under Henry VII the post of a royal chaplain, at the recommendation of Sir Richard Nanfan, deputy lieutenant of Calais and an old patron of his. But Wolsey was not at all desirous of passing his life in saying Mass. As soon as he had discharged the regular duties of his office, instead of spending the rest of the day in idleness, as his colleagues did, he strove to win the good graces of the persons round the king.

Fox, Bishop of Winchester, Keeper of the Privy Seal under Henry VII, uneasy at the growing powers of the Earl of Surrey, looked about for a man to counterbalance them. He thought he had found such a one in Wolsey. It was doubtless to oppose the Surreys, the grandfather and uncles of Anne Boleyn, that the son of the Ipswich butcher was drawn from his obscurity. Fox began to praise Wolsey in the king's hearing, and at the same time he encouraged him to give himself to public affairs. The latter was not deaf to the call, and soon found an opportunity of winning his sovereign's favour.

The king, having business of importance with the emperor Maximilian, who was then in Flanders, sent for Wolsey, explained his wishes, and ordered him to prepare to set out. The chaplain determined to show Henry VII how capable he was of serving him. It was about noon when he took leave of the king at Richmond – by four o'clock he was in London, by seven at Gravesend. By travelling all night he reached Dover just as a boat carrying passengers was about to sail. After a passage of three hours he reached Calais, whence he travelled post, and the same evening appeared before Maximilian. Having obtained what he desired, he set off again by night, and on the next day but one reached Richmond, three days and some few hours after his departure. The king, catching sight of him just as he was going to Mass, sharply inquired why he had not set out. 'Sire, I am just returned', answered Wolsey, placing the emperor's letters in his master's hands. Henry was delighted, and Wolsey saw that his fortune was made.[1] Shortly Henry VII died and his only surviving son ascended the throne.

The courtiers hoped at first that Wolsey, like an inexperienced pilot, would run his vessel on some hidden rock; but never did helmsman manage his ship with more skill. Although twenty years older than Henry VIII, the almoner (for such he had now been appointed) danced, and sang, and laughed with the prince's companions, and amused his new master with tales of scandal and quotations from Thomas Aquinas; and while Henry's councillors were entreating him to leave his pleasures and attend to business, Wolsey was continually reminding him that he ought to devote his youth to learning and amusement, and leave the toils of government to others. Wolsey was created Bishop of Tournai during Henry's campaign in Flanders, and on his return to England, was raised to the sees of Lincoln and of York. Three mitres had been placed on his head in one year. He found at last the vein he so ardently sought for.

[1] [The story of the speedy journey is narrated in *The Life of Wolsey* by George Cavendish, Wolsey's gentleman-usher. Some modern historians give it little credence, but there are no sound reasons for rejecting it.]

And yet he was not satisfied. The Archbishop of Canterbury had insisted, as primate, that the cross of York should be lowered to his. Wolsey was not of a disposition to concede this, and, when he found that Warham was not content with being his equal, he resolved to make him his inferior. He wrote to Paris and to Rome. Francis I, who desired to conciliate England, demanded the purple for Wolsey, and the Archbishop of York received the title of Cardinal St Cecilia beyond the Tiber. In November 1515, the red hat was brought by the envoy of the pope: 'It would have been better to have given him a Tyburn tippet', said some indignant Englishmen; 'these Romish hats never brought good into England'[2] – a saying that has become proverbial.

This was not enough for Wolsey: he desired secular greatness above all things. Warham, tired of contending with so arrogant a rival, resigned the seals of the lord-chancellorship, and the king immediately transferred them to the cardinal. At length a bull appointed him legate *a latere* of the holy see, and placed under his jurisdiction all the colleges, monasteries, spiritual courts, and bishops (1518). Over the primate himself Wolsey now believed himself to have precedence.[3] From that time, as Lord Chancellor of England and papal legate, Wolsey administered almost everything in church and state. He filled his coffers with money procured both at home and from abroad, and yielded without restraint to his dominant vices, ostentation and pride. Whenever he appeared in public, two priests, the tallest and comeliest that could be found, carried before him two huge silver crosses, one to mark his dignity as archbishop, the other as papal legate. Chamberlains, gentlemen, pages, sergeants, chaplains, choristers, clerks, cupbearers, cooks, and other domestics, to the number of more than 500, among whom were nine or ten lords and the stateliest yeomen of the country, filled his palace. He generally wore a dress of scarlet velvet and silk, with hat and gloves of the same colour. His shoes were embroidered with gold and silver, inlaid with pearls and precious stones. A kind of papacy was thus forming in England; for wherever pride flourishes there popery is developed.

---

[2] *Latimer's Sermons* (Parker Society), p. 119.

[3] Warham outlived Wolsey by two years and retained the office of primate to the end. Hence Wolsey never became Archbishop of Canterbury.

One thing occupied Wolsey more than all the pomp with which he was surrounded – his desire to captivate the king. For this purpose, says Tyndale, he cast Henry's nativity, and procured an amulet which he wore constantly, in order to charm his master by its magic properties.[4] Then having recourse to a still more effectual form of bewitchment, he selected from among the licentious companions of the young monarch those of the keenest discernment and most ambitious character; and after binding them to him by a solemn oath, he placed them at court to be as eyes and ears to him. Accordingly not a word was said in the presence of the monarch, particularly against Wolsey, of which he was not informed an hour afterwards. If the culprit was not in favour, he was expelled without mercy; in the contrary case, the minister sent him on some distant mission. The queen's ladies, the king's chaplains, and even their confessors, were the cardinal's spies. He pretended to omnipresence, as the pope to infallibility.

Wolsey was not devoid of certain showy virtues, for he was liberal to the poor even to affectation. As chancellor he was inexorable to every kind of irregularity, and strove particularly to make the rich and high-born bend beneath his power. Men of learning alone obtained from him some little attention, and hence Erasmus calls him 'the Achates of a new Æneas'. But the nation was not to be carried away by the eulogies of a few scholars. Wolsey – a man of more than suspected morals, double-hearted, faithless to his promises, ostentatious to the last degree, and exceedingly arrogant – Wolsey soon became hated by the people of England.

The elevation of a prince of the Roman Church could not be favourable to the reformation. The priests, encouraged by it, determined to make a stand against the triple attack of the learned, the reformers, and the state; and they soon had an opportunity of trying their strength. Holy orders had become during the Middle Ages a warrant for every sort of crime. Parliament, desirous of correcting this abuse and checking the encroachments of the church, declared in the year 1513 that any ecclesiastic accused of theft or murder, should be tried before the secular

---

[4] 'He calked [calculated] the king's nativity ... he made by craft of necromancy graven imagery to bear upon him, wherewith he bewitched the king's mind.' Tyndale's *Expositions* (Parker Society), p. 308.

tribunals. Exceptions, however, were made in favour of bishops, priests, and deacons – that is to say, nearly all the clergy. Notwithstanding this timid precaution, Richard Kidderminster, an insolent clerk, the Abbot of Wynchcombe, began the battle by exclaiming in a sermon at St Paul's: '*Touch not mine anointed, said the Lord.*' At the same time Wolsey, accompanied by a long train of priests and prelates, had an audience of the king, at which he said with hands upraised to heaven: 'Sire, to try a clerk is a violation of God's laws.' This time, however, Henry did not give way. 'By God's will, we are King of England', he replied, 'and the kings of England in times past had never any superior but God only. Therefore know you well that we will maintain the right of our crown.' He saw distinctly that to put the clergy above the laws was to put them above the throne. The priests were defeated, but not disheartened: perseverance is a characteristic feature of every hierarchical order. Not walking by faith, they walk all the more by sight; and skilful combinations supply the place of the holy aspirations of the Christian. Humble disciples of the gospel were soon to experience this, for the clergy by a few isolated attacks were about to flesh their swords for the great struggles of the reformation.

CHAPTER THIRTEEN

The Need for Reformation

(1514–1517)

I t is occasionally necessary to soften down the somewhat exaggerated colours in which contemporary writers describe the Romish clergy; but there are certain appellations which history is bound to accept. The *wolves*, for so the priests were called, by attacking the lords and commons had attempted a work beyond their reach. They turned their wrath on others. There were many shepherds endeavouring to gather together the sheep of the Lord beside the peaceful waters: these must be frightened, and the sheep driven into the howling wilderness. 'The wolves' determined to fall upon the Lollards.

There lived in London a prosperous merchant-tailor of good reputation named Richard Hunne, one of those witnesses of the truth who, sincere though unenlightened, have been often found in the bosom of Catholicism. It was his practice to retire to his chamber and spend a portion of each day in the study of the Bible. At the death of one of his children, the priest required of him an exorbitant mortuary fee, which Hunne refused to pay, and for which he was summoned before the legate's court. He felt indignant that an Englishman should be cited before a foreign tribunal, and laid an information against the priest and his counsel under the Act of Præmunire. Such boldness – most extraordinary at that time – exasperated the clergy beyond all bounds. 'If these proud citizens are allowed to have their way', exclaimed the clerics, 'every layman will dare to resist a priest.'

Exertions were accordingly made to snare the pretended rebel in the trap of heresy; he was thrown into the Lollards' Tower at St Paul's, and an iron collar was fastened round his neck, attached to which was a chain so heavy that neither man nor beast (says Foxe) would have been able to bear it long. When taken before his judges, they could not convict him of heresy, and it was observed with astonishment 'that he had his beads in prison with him'. They would have set him at liberty, after inflicting on him perhaps some trifling penance – but then, what a bad example it would be, and who could stop the reformers, if it was so easy to resist the papacy? Unable to triumph by justice, certain fanatics resolved to triumph by crime.

At midnight on 2 December – the day of his examination – three men stealthily ascended the stairs of the Lollards' Tower: the bell-ringer went first carrying a torch; the jailer, Charles Joseph, followed, and last came the bishop's chancellor, Dr Horsey. Having entered the cell, they went up to the bed on which Hunne was lying and, finding that he was asleep, the chancellor said: 'Lay hands on the thief.' Charles Joseph and the bell-ringer fell upon the prisoner, who, awaking with a start, saw at a glance what this midnight visit meant. He resisted the assassins at first, but was soon overpowered and strangled. Charles Joseph then fixed the dead man's belt round his neck, the bell-ringer helped to raise his lifeless body, and the chancellor slipped the other end of the belt through a ring fixed in the wall. They then placed his cap on his head, and hastily quitted the cell. Immediately after, the conscience-stricken Charles Joseph got on horseback and rode from the city; the bell-ringer left the cathedral and hid himself: the crime dispersed the criminals. The chancellor alone kept his ground, and he was at prayers when the news was brought him that the turnkey had found Hunne hanging. 'He must have killed himself in despair', said the hypocrite. But everyone knew poor Hunne's Christian feelings. 'It is the priests who have murdered him', was the general cry in London, and an inquest was ordered to be held on his body.

On Tuesday, 5 December, Thomas Barnwell the city coroner, the two sheriffs, and twenty-four jurymen proceeded to the Lollards' Tower. They remarked that the belt was so short that the head could not be got out of it, and that consequently it had never been placed in it voluntarily, and hence the jury concluded that the suspension was an afterthought of some other persons. Moreover they found that the ring was too high for the poor victim to reach it – that the body bore marks of violence – and that traces of blood were to be seen in the cell: 'Wherefore all we find by God and all our consciences [runs the verdict] that Richard Hunne was murdered. Also we acquit the said Richard Hunne of his own death.'

It was but too true, and the criminals themselves confessed it. The miserable Charles Joseph having returned home on the evening of 6 December, said to his maidservant: 'If you will swear to keep my secret, I will tell you all.' – 'Yes, master', she replied, 'if it is neither felony nor treason.' – Joseph took a book, swore the girl on it, and then said to her: 'I have killed Richard Hunne!' – 'O master! how? he was called a worthy man.' – 'I would lever [rather] than a hundred pounds it were not done', he made answer; 'but what is done cannot be undone.' He then rushed out of the house.

The clergy foresaw what a serious blow this unhappy affair would be to them, and to justify themselves they examined Hunne's Bible (it was Wycliffe's version) and, having read in the preface that 'poor men and idiots [simple folks] have the truth of the holy Scriptures more than a thousand prelates and religious men and clerks of the school', and further, that 'the pope ought to be called Antichrist', the Bishop of London, assisted by the bishops of Durham and Lincoln, declared Hunne guilty of heresy, and on 20 December his dead body was burnt at Smithfield. 'Hunne's bones have been burnt, and therefore he was a heretic', said the priests; 'he was a heretic, and therefore he committed suicide.'

The triumph of the clergy was of short duration; for almost at the same time William Horsey, the bishop's chancellor, Charles Joseph, and John Spalding the bell-ringer, were convicted of the murder. Strenuous ecclesiastical pressure led to the dropping of the charge against Horsey, but he only escaped justice by paying a fine of £600 and suffering exile from London. By royal letter, the confiscated property of Hunne was restored to his children.[1] – 'If the clerical theocracy should gain the mastery of the state', was the general remark in London, 'it would not only be a very great lie, but the most frightful tyranny!' England

---

[1] [Foxe in his *Book of Martyrs* produces extremely strong evidence to prove that Hunne was murdered. Thomas More in his *Dialogue Concerning Heresies* attempts an unconvincing defence of Horsey which is clearly 'special pleading'.]

has never gone back since that time, and a theocratic rule has always inspired the sound portion of the nation with a just and insurmountable antipathy. Such were the events taking place in England shortly before the reformation. This was not all.

The clergy had not been fortunate in Hunne's affair, but they were not for that reason unwilling to attempt a new one.

In the spring of 1517 – the year in which Luther posted up his *theses* – a priest, whose manners announced a man swollen with pride, happened to be on board the passage-boat from London to Gravesend with an intelligent and pious Christian of Ashford, by name John Browne. The passengers, as they floated down the stream, were amusing themselves by watching the banks glide away from them, when the priest, turning towards Browne, said to him insolently: 'You are too near me, you are sitting on my clothes, get farther off. Do you know who I am?' – 'No, sir', answered Browne. – 'Well then, you must know that I am a priest.' – 'Indeed, sir; are you a parson, or vicar, or a lady's chaplain?' – 'No; I am a *soul-priest*', he haughtily replied; 'I sing Mass to save souls.' – 'Do you, sir', replied Browne somewhat ironically, 'that is well done; and can you tell me where you find the soul when you begin the Mass?' – 'I cannot', said the priest. – 'And where you leave it when the Mass is ended?' – 'I do not know.' – 'What!' continued Browne with marks of astonishment, 'you do not know where you find the soul or where you leave it ... and yet you say that you save it!' – 'Go thy ways', said the priest angrily, 'thou art a heretic, and I will be even with thee.' Thenceforward the priest and his neighbour conversed no more together. At last they reached Gravesend and the boat anchored.

As soon as the priest had landed, he hastened to two of his friends, Walter and William More, and all three mounting their horses set off for Canterbury, and denounced Browne to the archbishop.

In the meantime John Browne had reached home. Three days later, his wife, Elizabeth, who had just left her chamber, went to church, dressed all in white, to return thanks to God for delivering her in the perils of childbirth. Her husband, assisted by her daughter Alice and the maidservant, were preparing for their friends the feast usual on such occasions, and they had all of them taken their seats at table, joy beaming on every face, when the street-door was abruptly opened, and Chilton, the constable, a cruel and savage man, accompanied by several of the archbishop's servants, seized upon the worthy townsman. All sprang from their seats in alarm; Elizabeth and Alice uttered the most heart-rending cries; but the primate's officers, without showing any emotion, pulled Browne out of the house, and placed him on horseback, tying his feet under the animal's belly. It is a serious matter to jest with a priest. The cavalcade rode off quickly, and Browne was thrown into prison, and there left forty days.

At the end of this time, the Archbishop of Canterbury and the Bishop of Rochester called before them the impudent fellow who doubted whether a priest's Mass could save souls, and required him to retract this 'blasphemy'. But Browne, if he did not believe in the Mass, believed in the gospel: 'Christ was once offered', he said, 'to take away the sins of many. It is by this sacrifice we are saved, and not by the repetitions of the priests.' At this reply the archbishop made a sign to the executioners, one of whom took off the shoes and stockings of this pious Christian, while the other brought in a pan of burning coals, upon which they set the martyr's feet. The English laws in truth forbade torture to be inflicted on any subject of the Crown, but the clergy thought themselves above the laws. 'Confess the efficacy of the Mass', cried the two bishops to Browne. 'If I deny my Lord upon earth', he replied, 'he will deny me before his Father in heaven.' The flesh was burnt off the soles of the feet even to the bones, and still John Browne remained unshaken. The bishops therefore ordered him to be given over to the secular arm that he might be burnt alive.

On the Saturday preceding the festival of Pentecost, in the year 1517, the martyr was led back to Ashford, where he arrived just as the day was drawing to a close. A number of idle persons were collected in the street, and among them was Browne's maidservant, who ran off crying to the house, and told her mistress: 'I have seen him! ... He was bound, and they were taking him to prison.' Elizabeth hastened to her husband and found him sitting with his feet in the stocks, his features changed by suffering, and expecting to be burnt alive on the morrow. The poor woman sat down beside him, weeping most bitterly, while he, being hindered by his chains, could not so much as bend towards her. 'I cannot set my feet to the ground', said he, 'for bishops have burnt them to the bones; but they could not burn my tongue and prevent my confessing the Lord ... O Elizabeth! ... continue to love him for he is good; and bring up our children in his fear.'

On the following morning – it was Whitsunday – the brutal Chilton and his assistants led Browne to the place of execution, and fastened him to the stake. Elizabeth and Alice, with his other children and his friends, desirous of receiving his last sigh, surrounded the pile, uttering cries of anguish. The faggots were set on fire, while Browne, calm and collected, and full of confidence in the blood of the Saviour, clasped his hands, and repeated this hymn, which Foxe has preserved:[2]

> O Lord, I yield me to Thy grace,
> Grant me mercy for my trespass;
> Let never the fiend my soul chase.
> Lord, I will bow, and Thou shalt beat,
> Let never my soul come in hell-heat.

The martyr was silent: the flames had consumed their victim. Then redoubled cries of anguish rent the air. His wife and daughter seemed as if they would lose their senses. The bystanders showed them the tenderest compassion, and turned with a movement of indignation towards the executioners. The brutal Chilton perceiving this, cried out: 'Come along; let us toss the heretic's children into the flames, lest they should one day spring from their father's ashes.'[3] He rushed towards Alice, and was about to lay hold of her, when the maiden shrank back screaming with horror. To the end of her life, she recollected the fearful moment, and to her we are indebted for the particulars. The fury of the monster was checked. Such were the scenes passing in England shortly before the reformation.

The priests were not yet satisfied, for the scholars still remained in England: if they could not be burnt, they could at least be banished. They set to work accordingly. Standish, Bishop of St Asaph, a sincere man, as it would seem, but fanatical, was inveterate in his hatred of

[2] Foxe, *Acts and Monuments*, edited by Josiah Pratt (London, 1838), iv, p. 132.
[3] Bade cast in his children also, for they would spring of his ashes. *Ibid.*

Erasmus, who had irritated him by an idle sarcasm. When speaking of
St Asaph's it was very common to abbreviate it into *St As'*; and as Standish
was a theologian of no great learning, Erasmus, in his jesting way, would
sometimes call him *Episcopus a Sancto Asino*. As the bishop could not
destroy Colet, the disciple, he flattered himself that he should triumph
over the master.

Erasmus knew Standish's intentions. Should he commence in
England that struggle with the papacy which Luther was about to begin
in Germany? It was no longer possible to steer a middle course: he must
either fight or leave. The Dutchman was faithful to his nature – we may
even say, to his vocation: he left the country.

Erasmus was, in his time, the head of the great literary community.
By means of his connections and his correspondence, which extended
over all Europe, he established between those countries where learning
was reviving, an interchange of ideas and manuscripts. The pioneer of
antiquity, an eminent critic, a witty satirist, the advocate of correct taste,
and a restorer of literature, one only glory was wanting: he had not the
creative spirit, the heroic soul of a Luther. He calculated with no little
skill, could detect the smile on the lips or the knitting of the brows; but
he had not that self-abandonment, that enthusiasm for the truth, that
firm confidence in God, without which nothing great can be done in the
world, and least of all in the church. 'Erasmus *had* much, but *was* little',
said one of his biographers.

In the year 1517 a crisis had arrived: the period of the revival was
over, that of the reformation was beginning. The restoration of letters
was succeeded by the regeneration of religion: the days of criticism and
neutrality by those of courage and action. Erasmus was then only about
fifty years old; but he had finished his career. From being first, he must
now be second: the monk of Wittenberg dethroned him. He looked
around himself in vain: placed in a new country, he had lost his road. A
hero was needed to inaugurate the greatest movement of modern times:
Erasmus was a mere man of letters.

When attacked by Standish in 1516, the literary king determined
to quit the court of England, and take refuge in a printing office. But
before laying down his sceptre at the foot of a Saxon monk, he signalled

the end of his reign by the most brilliant of his publications. The epoch of 1516–17, memorable for the theses of Luther, was destined to be equally remarkable by a work which was to imprint on the new times their essential character. What distinguishes the reformation from all anterior revivals is the union of learning with piety, and a faith more profound, more enlightened, and based on the word of God. Christians were then emancipated from the tutelage of the schools and the popes, and their charter of enfranchisement was the Bible. The sixteenth century did more than its predecessors: it went straight to the fountain (the holy Scriptures), cleared it of weeds and brambles, plumbed its depths, and caused its abundant streams to pour forth on all around. The reformation age studied the Greek Testament, which the clerical age had almost forgotten – and this is its greatest glory. One of the first explorers of this Divine source was Erasmus. When attacked by the hierarchy, the leader of the schools withdrew from the splendid halls of Henry VIII. It seemed to him that the new era which he had announced to the world was rudely interrupted: he could do nothing more by his conversation for the country of the Tudors. But he carried with him those precious leaves, the fruit of his labours – a book which would do more than he desired. He hastened to Basle, and took up his quarters in Johann Froben's printing office, where he not only laboured himself; but made others labour. England was soon to receive the seed of the new life, and the reformation was about to begin.

BOOK TWO

The Revival of the Church

William Tyndale

CHAPTER ONE

The Origin of the English Reformation

(1516–1519)

I t was within the province of four powers in the sixteenth century to effect a reformation of the church: these were the papacy, the episcopate, the monarchy, and holy Scripture. The reformation in England was essentially the work of Scripture.

The only true reformation is that which emanates from the word of God. The holy Scriptures, by bearing witness to the incarnation, death, and resurrection of the Son of God, create in man by the Holy Ghost a faith which justifies him. That faith which produces in him a new life, unites him to Christ, without his requiring a chain of bishops or a Roman mediator, who would separate him from the Saviour instead of drawing him nearer. This reformation by the word restores that spiritual Christianity which the outward and hierarchical religion destroys; and from the regeneration of individuals naturally results the regeneration of the church.

The reformation of England, perhaps to a greater extent than that of the Continent, was effected by the word of God. This statement may appear paradoxical, but it is not the less true. Those great personages we meet with in Germany, Switzerland, and France – men like Luther, Zwingli, and Calvin – do not appear in England; but holy Scripture is widely circulated. What brought light into the British Isles subsequent to the year 1517, and on a more extended scale after the year 1526, was the word – the invisible power of the invisible God. The religion of the Anglo-Saxon race – a race called more than any other to circulate the oracles of God throughout the world – is particularly distinguished by its biblical character.

The reformation of England could not be papal. No reform can be expected from that which ought to be not only reformed but abolished; and besides, no monarch dethrones himself. We may even affirm that the popedom has always felt a peculiar affection for its conquests in Britain, and that they would have been the last it would have renounced. A Carthusian prior had declared in the middle of the fifteenth century: 'A reform is neither in the will nor in the power of the popes.'

The reformation of England was not episcopal. Roman hierarchism will never be abolished by Roman bishops. An episcopal assembly may perhaps, as at Constance, depose three competing popes, but then it will be to save the papacy. And if the bishops could not abolish the papacy, still less could they reform themselves. The then-existing episcopal power being at enmity with the word of God, and the slave of its own abuses, was incapable of renovating the church. On the contrary, it exerted all its influence to prevent such a renovation.

The reformation in England was not royal. Samuel, David, and Josiah were able to do something for the raising up of the church, when God again turned his face towards it; but a king cannot rob his people of their religion, and still less can he give them one. It has often been repeated that 'the English reformation derives its origin from the monarch'; but the assertion is incorrect. The work of God, here as elsewhere, cannot be put in comparison with the work of the king; and if the latter was infinitely surpassed in importance, it was also preceded in time by many years. The monarch was still keeping up a vigorous resistance behind his entrenchments, when God had already decided the victory along the whole line of operations.

Shall we be told that a reform effected by any other principle than the established authorities, both in *church* and *state*, would have been a revolution? But has God, the lawful sovereign of the church, forbidden all *revolution* in a sinful world? A revolution is not a revolt. The fall of the first man was a great revolution: the restoration of man by Jesus Christ was a counter-revolution. The corruption occasioned by popery was allied to the fall: the reformation accomplished in the sixteenth century was connected therefore with the restoration. There will no doubt be other interventions of the Deity, which will be revolutions in the same direction as the reformation. When God creates a new heaven and a new earth, will not that be one of the most glorious of revolutions? The reformation by the word alone gives truth, alone gives unity; but more than that, it alone bears the marks of true *legitimacy*; for the church belongs not unto men, even though they be priests. God alone is its lawful sovereign.

And yet the human elements which we have enumerated were not wholly foreign to the work that was accomplishing in England. Besides the word of God, other principles were in operation, and although less radical and less primitive, they still retain the sympathy of eminent men of that nation.

And in the first place, the intervention of the king's authority was necessary to a certain point. Since the supremacy of Rome had been established in England by several usages which had the force of law, the intervention of the temporal power was necessary to break the bonds which it had previously sanctioned. But it was requisite for the monarchy, while adopting a negative and political action, to leave the positive, doctrinal, and creative action to the word of God.

Besides the reformation *in the name of the Scriptures*, there was then in England another *in the name of the king*. The word of God began, the kingly power followed; and ever since, these two forces have sometimes gone together against the authority of the Roman pontiffs – sometimes in opposition to each other, like those troops which march side by side in the same army, against the same enemy, and which have occasionally been seen, even on the field of battle, to turn their swords against each other.

Finally, the episcopate, which had begun by opposing the reformation, was compelled to accept it in despite of its convictions. The majority of the bishops were opposed to it; but the better portion were found to incline, some to the side of outward reform, of which separation from the papacy was the very essence, and others to the side of internal reform, whose mainspring was union with Jesus Christ. At last, the episcopate took up its ground on its own account, and soon two great parties alone existed in England: the scriptural party and the clerical party.

These two parties have survived even to our days, and their colours are still distinguishable in the river of the church, like the muddy River Arve and the limpid Rhone after their confluence. The royal supremacy, from which many Christians, preferring the paths of independence, have withdrawn since the end of the sixteenth century, is recognized by both parties in the Establishment, with some few exceptions. But whilst the high church is essentially hierarchical, the low church is essentially biblical. In the one, the church is above and the word below; in the other, the church is below and the word above. These two principles, evangelicalism and hierarchism, are found in the Christianity of the first centuries, but with a signal difference. Hierarchism then almost entirely effaced evangelicalism; in the age of Protestantism, on the contrary, evangelicalism continued to exist by the side of hierarchism, and it has remained *de jure*, if not always *de facto*, the only legitimate opinion of the church.

Thus there is in England a complication of influences and contests, which render the work more difficult to describe; but it is on that very account more worthy the attention of the philosopher and the Christian.

* * * * *

Great events had just occurred in Europe. Francis I had crossed the Alps, gained a signal victory at Marignano, and conquered the north of Italy. The affrighted Maximilian knew of none who could save him but Henry VIII. 'I will adopt you; you shall be my successor in the Empire', he intimated to him in May 1516. 'Your army shall invade France; and then we will march together to Rome, where the sovereign pontiff shall crown you King of the Romans.' The King of France, anxious to effect a diversion, had formed a league with Denmark and Scotland, and had made preparations for invading England to place on the throne the 'white rose'; at least he had offered the pretender Richard Pole, heir to the claims of the house of York, the services of 12,000 German mercenaries for that purpose. Henry now showed his prudence; he declined Maximilian's offer, and turned his whole attention to the security of his kingdom. But while he refused to bear arms in France and Italy, a war of quite another kind broke out in England.

The great work of the sixteenth century was about to begin. A volume fresh from the presses of Basle had just crossed the Channel. Being transmitted to London, Oxford, and Cambridge, this book, the fruit of Erasmus' vigils, soon found its way wherever there were friends of learning. It was the *New Testament* of our Lord Jesus Christ, published for the first time in Greek with a new Latin translation – an event more important for the world than would have been the landing of the Yorkist pretender in England, or the appearance of the chief of the Tudors in Italy. This book, in which God has deposited for man's salvation the seeds of life, was about to effect alone, without patrons and without interpreters, the most astonishing revolution which had ever taken place in Britain.

When Erasmus published this work, at the dawn, so to say, of modern times, he did not see all its scope. Had he foreseen it, he would perhaps have recoiled in alarm. He saw indeed that there was a great work to be done, but he believed that all good men would unite to do it with common accord. 'A spiritual temple must be raised in desolated Christendom', said he. 'The mighty of this world will contribute towards it their marble, their ivory, and their gold; I who am poor and humble offer the foundation-stone', and he laid down before the world his edition of the Greek Testament. Then glancing disdainfully at the traditions of men, he said: 'It is not from human reservoirs, fetid with stagnant waters, that we should draw the doctrine of salvation; but from the pure and abundant streams that flow from the heart of God.' And when some of his suspicious friends spoke to him of the difficulties of the times, he replied: 'If the ship of the church is to be saved from being swallowed up by the tempest, there is only one anchor that can save it: it is the heavenly word, which, issuing from the bosom of the Father, lives, speaks, and works still in the gospel.' These noble sentiments served as an introduction to those blessed pages which were to reform England. Erasmus, like Caiaphas, prophesied without being aware of it.

The New Testament in Greek and Latin had hardly appeared when it was received by all men of upright mind with unprecedented enthusiasm. Never had any book produced such a sensation. It was in every hand: men struggled to procure it, read it eagerly, and would even kiss it. The words it contained enlightened every heart. But a reaction soon took place. Traditional Catholicism uttered a cry from the depths of its noisome pools (to use Erasmus' figure). Franciscans and Dominicans, priests and bishops, not daring to attack the educated and well-born, went among the ignorant populace, and endeavoured by their tales and clamours to stir up susceptible women and credulous men. 'Here are horrible heresies', they exclaimed, 'here are frightful antichrists! If this book be tolerated it will be the death of the papacy!' – 'We must drive this man from the university', said one. 'We must turn him out of the church', added another. 'The public places re-echoed with their howlings', said Erasmus. The firebrands tossed by their furious hands were raising fires in every quarter; and the flames kindled in a few obscure monasteries threatened to spread over the whole country.

This irritation was not without a cause. The book, indeed, contained nothing but Latin and Greek; but this first step seemed to augur another – the translation of the Bible into the vulgar tongue. Erasmus loudly called for it. 'Perhaps it may be necessary to conceal the secrets of kings', he remarked, 'but we must publish the mysteries of Christ. The holy Scriptures, translated into all languages, should be read not only by the Scottish and Irish, but even by Turks and Saracens. The husbandman should sing them as he holds the handle of his plough, the weaver repeat them as he plies his shuttle, and the wearied traveller, halting on his journey, refresh himself under some shady tree by these godly narratives.' These words prefigured a golden age after the iron age of popery. A number of Christian families in Britain and on the Continent were soon to realize these evangelical predictions, and England after three centuries was to endeavour to carry them out for the benefit of all the nations on the face of the earth.

The priests saw the danger and, by a skilful manoeuvre, instead of finding fault with the Greek Testament, attacked the Latin translation and the translator. 'He has corrected the Vulgate', they said, 'and puts himself in the place of St Jerome. He sets aside a work authorized by the consent of ages and inspired by the Holy Ghost. What audacity!' And then, turning over the pages, they pointed out the most odious passages: 'Look here! this book calls upon men to *repent*, instead of requiring them, as the Vulgate does, *to do penance!*' (Matt. 4:17.) The priests thundered against him from their pulpits: 'This man has committed the unpardonable sin', they asserted, 'for he maintains that there is nothing in common between the Holy Ghost and the monks – that they are logs rather than men!' These simple remarks were received with a general laugh; but the priests, in no wise disconcerted, cried out all the louder: 'He's a heretic, an heresiarch, a forger! He's a goose ... what do I say? He's a very Antichrist!'

It was not sufficient for the papal janissaries to make war in the plain: they must carry it to the higher ground. Was not the king a friend of Erasmus? If he should declare himself a patron of the Greek and Latin Testament, what an awful calamity! ... After having agitated the cloisters, towns, and universities, they resolved to protest against it boldly, even in Henry's presence. They thought: 'If he is won, all is won.' It happened one day that a certain theologian (whose name is unknown) having to preach in his turn before the king, he declaimed violently against the *Greek* language and its new interpreters. Pace, the king's secretary, was present, and turning his eyes on Henry, observed him smiling good-humouredly. On leaving the church everyone began to exclaim against the preacher. 'Bring the priest to me', said the king; and then turning to Thomas More, he added: 'You shall defend the Greek cause against him, and I will listen to the disputation.' The literary tribunal was soon formed, but the sovereign's order had taken away all the priest's courage. He came forward trembling, fell on his knees, and with clasped hands exclaimed: 'I know not what spirit impelled me.' – 'A spirit of madness', said the king, 'and not the spirit of Jesus Christ.' He then added: 'Have you ever read Erasmus?' – 'No, sire.' – 'Away with you then, you are a blockhead.' – 'And yet', said the preacher in confusion, 'I remember to have read something about *Moria*' (Erasmus' treatise on *Folly*). – 'A subject, Your Majesty, that ought to be very familiar to him', wickedly interrupted Pace. The *obscurant* could say nothing in his justification. 'I am not altogether opposed to the Greek', he added at last, 'seeing that it is derived from the Hebrew.' This was greeted with a general laugh, and the king impatiently ordered the monk to leave the room, and never appear before him again.

Erasmus was astonished at these discussions. He had imagined the season to be most favourable. 'Everything looks peaceful', he had said to himself; 'now is the time to launch my Greek Testament into the learned world.' As well might the sun rise upon the earth, and no one see it! At that very hour God was raising up a monk at Wittenberg who would lift the trumpet to his lips, and proclaim the new day. 'Wretch that I am!' exclaimed the timid scholar, beating his breast, 'who could have foreseen this horrible tempest!'

Nothing was more important at the dawn of the reformation than the publication of the Testament of Jesus Christ in the original language. Never had Erasmus worked so carefully. 'If I told what sweat it cost me, no one would believe me.' He had collated the Greek manuscripts of the New Testament then available to him, and was surrounded by all the commentaries and translations, by the writings of Origen, Cyprian, Ambrose, Basil, Chrysostom, Cyril, Jerome, and Augustine. *Hic sum in campo meo!* (Here I am in my field of action!) he exclaimed as he sat in the midst of his books. He had investigated the texts according to the principles of sacred criticism. When a knowledge of Hebrew was necessary, he had consulted Capito and more particularly Œcolampadius. *Nothing without Theseus*, said he of the latter, making use of a Greek proverb. He had corrected the ambiguities, obscurities, Hebraisms, and barbarisms of the Vulgate; and had caused a list to be printed of the errors in that version.

'We must restore the pure text of the word of God', he had said; and when he heard the maledictions of the priests, he had exclaimed: 'I call God to witness I thought I was doing a work acceptable to the Lord and necessary to the cause of Christ.' Nor in this was he deceived.

At the head of his adversaries was Edward Lee, successively king's almoner, archdeacon of Colchester, and Archbishop of York. Lee, at that time but little known, was a man of talent and activity, but also vain and loquacious, and determined to make his way at any cost. Even when a schoolboy he looked down on all his companions. As child, youth, man, and in mature years, he was always the same, Erasmus tells us; that is to say, vain, envious, jealous, boastful, passionate, and revengeful. We must bear in mind, however, that when Erasmus describes the character of his opponents, he is far from being an impartial judge. In the bosom of Roman Catholicism, there have always existed well-meaning, though ill-informed men, who, not knowing the inward power of the word of God, have thought that if its authority were substituted for that of the Romish Church, the only foundation of truth and of Christian society would be shaken. Yet while we judge Lee less severely than Erasmus does, we cannot close our eyes to his faults. His memory was richly furnished, but his heart was a stranger to Divine truth: he was a schoolman and not a believer. He wanted the people to obey the church and not trouble themselves about the Scriptures. He was the Dr Eck of England, but with more of outward appearance and morality than Luther's adversary. Yet he was by no means a rigid moralist. On one occasion, when preaching at the palace, he introduced ballads into his sermon, one of which began thus: 'Pass time with good company.' And the other: 'I love unloved.' We are indebted to Secretary Pace for this characteristic trait.[1]

During Erasmus' stay in England, Lee, observing his influence, had sought his friendship, and Erasmus, with his usual courtesy, had solicited his advice upon his work. But Lee, jealous of his great reputation, only waited for an opportunity to injure it, which he seized upon as soon as it occurred. The New Testament had not been long published, when Lee turned round abruptly, and from being Erasmus' friend became his implacable adversary. 'If we do not stop this leak', said he, when he heard of the New Testament, 'it will sink the ship.' Nothing terrifies the defenders of human traditions so much as the word of God.

Lee immediately leagued himself with all those in England who abhorred the study of Scripture, says Erasmus. Although exceedingly conceited, he showed himself the most amiable of men, in order to accomplish his designs. He invited Englishmen to his house, welcomed strangers, and gained many recruits by the excellence of his dinners. While seated at table among his guests, he hinted perfidious charges against Erasmus, and his company left him (so Erasmus claims in his letters) 'loaded with lies'. – 'In this New Testament', said he, 'there are three hundred dangerous, frightful passages … three hundred did I say? … there are more than a thousand!' Not satisfied with using his tongue,

---

[1] State Papers, Henry VIII, *etc.* (edition of 1830), i, p. 10.

Lee wrote scores of letters, and employed several secretaries. Was there any monastery in the odour of sanctity, he 'forwarded to it instantly wine, choice viands, and other presents'. To each one he assigned his part, and over all England they were rehearsing what Erasmus calls Lee's tragedy. In this manner they were preparing the catastrophe: a prison for Erasmus, the fire for the holy Scriptures.

When all was arranged, Lee issued his manifesto. Although a poor Greek scholar, he drew up some *Annotations* on Erasmus' book, which the latter called 'mere abuse and blasphemy'; but which the members of the league regarded as *oracles*. They passed them secretly from hand to hand, and these obscure sheets, by many indirect channels, found their way into every part of England, and met with numerous readers. There was to be no publication – such was the watchword; Lee was too much afraid. 'Why did you not publish your work?' asked Erasmus, with cutting irony. 'Who knows whether the Holy Father, appointing you the Aristarchus of letters, might not have sent you a birch to keep the whole world in order!'[2]

The *Annotations* having triumphed in the monasteries, the conspiracy took a new flight. In every place of public resort, at fairs and markets, at the dinner table and in the council chamber, in shops, and taverns, and houses of ill-fame, in churches and in the universities, in cottages and in palaces, the league prated against Erasmus and the Greek Testament. Carmelites, Dominicans, and Sophists, invoked heaven and conjured hell. What need was there of Scripture? Had they not the apostolical succession of the clergy? No hostile landing in England could, in their eyes, be more fatal than that of the New Testament. The whole nation must rise to repel this impudent invasion. There is, perhaps, no country in Europe where the reformation encountered so unexpected a storm.

[2] [The author, in this section of his work, frequently quotes from the letters of Erasmus. A complete collection of these letters has been edited by P. S. Allen, 1906–47.]

CHAPTER TWO

The Greek Testament Awakens the Dead

(1516–1521)

While this rude blast was rushing over England, and roaring in the long galleries of its monasteries, the still small voice of the word was making its way into the peaceful homes of praying men and into the ancient halls of Oxford and Cambridge. In private chambers, in the lecture rooms and refectories, students, and even masters of arts, were to be seen reading the Greek and Latin Testament. Animated groups were discussing the principles of the reformation. When Christ came on earth (said some) he gave the word, and when he ascended up into heaven he gave the Holy Spirit. These are the two forces which created the church, and these are the forces that must regenerate it. – No (replied the partisans of Rome), it was the teaching of the apostles at first, and it is the teaching of the priests now. – The apostles (rejoined the friends of the Testament of Erasmus) – yes, it is true – the apostles were during their ministry a living scripture; but their oral teaching would most certainly have been altered by passing from mouth to mouth. God willed, therefore, that these precious lessons should be preserved to us in their writings, and thus become the ever-undefiled source of truth and salvation. To set the Scriptures in the foremost place, as your pretended reformers are doing (replied the schoolmen of Oxford and Cambridge) is to propagate heresy! And what are the reformers doing (asked their defenders) but what Christ did before them? The sayings of the prophets existed in the time of Jesus only as Scripture, and it was to this written word that our Lord appealed when he founded his kingdom.[1] And now in like manner the teaching of

[1] Matt. 22:29; 26:24, 54; Mark 14:49; Luke 18:31; 24:27, 44, 45; John 5:39, 46; 10:35; 17:12, *etc.*

the apostles exists only as *Scripture*, and it is to this written word that we appeal in order to re-establish the kingdom of our Lord in its primitive condition. The night is far spent, the day is at hand; all is in motion – in the lofty halls of our colleges, in the mansions of the rich and noble, and in the lowly dwellings of the poor. If we want to scatter the darkness, must we light the shrivelled wick of some old lamp? Ought we not rather to open the doors and shutters and admit freely into the house the great light which God has placed in the heavens?

There was in Trinity Hall, Cambridge, a young student of the canon law, of serious turn of mind and bashful disposition, and whose tender conscience strove, although ineffectually, to fulfil the commandments of God. Anxious about his salvation, Thomas Bilney applied to the priests, whom he looked upon as physicians of the soul. Kneeling before his confessor, with humble look and pale face, he told him all his sins, and even those of which he doubted. The priest prescribed at one time fasting, at another prolonged vigils, and then masses and indulgences which cost him dearly. Bilney went through all these practices with great devotion, but found no consolation in them. Being weak and slender, his body wasted away by degrees; his understanding grew weaker, his imagination faded, and his purse became empty. 'Alas!' said he with anguish, 'my last state is worse than the first.' From time to time an idea crossed his mind: 'May not the priests be seeking their own gain, and not the salvation of my soul?' But immediately rejecting the rash doubt, he fell back under the iron hand of the clergy.

One day Bilney heard his friends talking about a new book: it was the Greek Testament printed with a translation which was highly praised for its elegant Latinity. Attracted by the beauty of the style rather than by the divinity of the subject, he stretched out his hand; but just as he was going to take the volume, fear came upon him and he withdrew it hastily. In fact the confessors strictly prohibited Greek and Hebrew books, 'the sources of all heresies'; and Erasmus' Testament was particularly forbidden. Yet Bilney regretted so great a sacrifice; was it not the Testament of Jesus Christ? Might not God have placed therein some word which perhaps might heal his soul? He stepped forward, and then again shrank back. At last he took courage. Urged, said he, by the hand of God, he walked out of the college, slipped into the house where the volume was sold in secret, bought it with fear and trembling, and then hastened back and shut himself up in his room.

He opened it – his eyes caught these words: *This is a faithful saying, and worthy of all acceptation, that Christ Jesus came into the world to save sinners; of whom I am chief.*[2] He laid down the book, and meditated on the astonishing declaration. 'What! St Paul the chief of sinners, and yet St Paul is sure of being saved!' He read the verse again and again. 'O assertion of St Paul, how sweet art thou to my soul!' he exclaimed. This declaration continually haunted him, and in this manner God instructed him in the secret of his heart. He could not tell what had happened to him; it seemed as if a refreshing wind were blowing over his soul, or as if a rich treasure had been placed in his hands. The Holy Spirit took what was Christ's, and announced it to him. 'I also am like Paul', exclaimed he with emotion, 'and more than Paul, the greatest of sinners! ... But Christ saves sinners. At last I have heard of Jesus.'

His doubts were ended – he was saved. Then took place in him a wonderful transformation. An unknown joy pervaded him; his conscience until then sore with the wounds of sin was healed; instead of despair he felt an inward peace passing all understanding. 'Jesus Christ', exclaimed he. 'Yes, Jesus Christ saves!' – Such is the character of the reformation: it is Jesus Christ who saves and not the church. 'I see it all', said Bilney; 'my vigils, my fasts, my pilgrimages, my purchase of masses and indulgences were destroying instead of saving me. All these efforts were, as St Augustine says, a hasty running out of the right way.'

Bilney never grew tired of reading his New Testament. He no longer lent an attentive ear to the teaching of the schoolmen; he heard Jesus at Capernaum, Peter in the temple, Paul on Mars' hill, and felt within himself that Christ possesses the words of eternal life. A witness to Jesus Christ had just been born by the same power which had transformed Paul, Apollos, and Timothy. The reformation in England was beginning. Bilney was united to the Son of God, not by a remote succession, but by an immediate generation. Leaving to the disciples of the pope the entangled chain of their imaginary succession, whose links it is

[2] 1 Tim. 1:15.

impossible to disengage, he found himself closely attached to Christ. The word of the first century gave birth to the work of reformation in the sixteenth. Protestantism does not descend from the gospel in the fiftieth generation like the Romish Church of the Council of Trent: it is the direct legitimate son – the son of the Master.

God's action was not limited to one spot. The first rays of the sun from on high gilded with their fires at once the gothic colleges of Oxford and the ancient schools of Cambridge.

Along the banks of the Severn extends a picturesque country, bounded by the Forest of Dean, and sprinkled with villages, steeples, and ancient castles. In the sixteenth century it was particularly admired by priests and friars, and a familiar oath among them was: 'As sure as God's in Glo'ster!' The papal birds of prey had swooped upon it. For the fifty years commencing in 1484, four Italian bishops, placed in succession over the diocese, had surrendered it to the pope, to the monks, and to immorality.³ Thieves in particular were the objects of the tenderest favours of the hierarchy. John de Giglis, collector of the apostolical chamber, had received from the sovereign pontiff authority to pardon murder and theft, on condition that the criminal shared his profits with the pontifical commissioners.

It was in this county of Gloucester, and probably between the years 1490 and 1494, William Tyndale was born. Whether his childhood was passed amid the 'breezy beauties' of the Western Cotswolds or beside the 'rushy-fringed banks' of the Lower Severn, it cannot certainly be said, but it is on record that 'Tyndale was brought up from a child in the University of Oxford', a pointer to the child's linguistic skill which was shortly dedicated to the service of the word of God. In the university city he learnt grammar and philosophy in Magdalen Hall, adjoining the college of that name. He made rapid progress, particularly in languages, under the finest classical scholars in England – Grocyn, William Latimer, and Linacre – and took his degrees. A more excellent master than these doctors – the Holy Spirit speaking in Scripture – was soon to teach him a science which it is not in the power of man to impart.

³ [After 1512 and until the appointment of Hugh Latimer in 1535 there was no resident Bishop of Worcester.]

Oxford, where Erasmus had so many friends, was the city in which his New Testament met with the warmest welcome. The young Gloucestershire student, inwardly impelled towards the study of sacred literature, read the celebrated book which was then attracting the attention of Christendom. At first he regarded it only as a work of learning, or at most as a manual of piety, whose beauties were calculated to excite religious feelings; but erelong he found it to be something more. The more he read it, the more was he struck by the truth and energy of the word. This strange book spoke to him of God, of Christ, and of regeneration, with a simplicity and authority which completely subdued him. William had found a Master whom he had not sought at Oxford – this was God himself. The pages he held in his hand were the Divine revelation so long mislaid. Possessing a noble soul, a bold spirit, and indefatigable activity, he did not keep this treasure to himself. He uttered that cry, more suited to a Christian than to Archimedes: εὑρηκα, *I have found it!* It was not long before several of the younger members of the university, attracted by the purity of his life and the charm of his conversation, gathered round him, and read with him the Greek and Latin Gospels of Erasmus. 'A certain well-informed young man', wrote Erasmus in a letter wherein he speaks of the publication of his New Testament, 'began to lecture with success on Greek literature at Oxford.' He was probably speaking of Tyndale.

The monks took the alarm. '*A barbarian*', continues Erasmus, 'entered the pulpit and violently abused the Greek language.' – 'These folk', said Tyndale, 'wished to extinguish the light which exposed their trickery, and they have been laying their plans these dozen years.'[4] This observation was made in 1531, and refers doubtless to the proceedings of 1517. Germany and England were beginning the struggle at nearly the same time, and Oxford perhaps before Wittenberg. Tyndale, bearing in mind the injunction: 'When they persecute you in one city, flee ye into another', left Oxford and proceeded to Cambridge. It must needs be that souls whom God has brought to his knowledge should meet and enlighten one another: live coals, when separated, go out; when gathered together, they brighten up, so as even to purify silver and gold.

---

[4] Tyndale's *Expositions* (Parker Society), p. 225.

The Romish hierarchy, not knowing what they did, were collecting the scattered brands of the reformation.

Bilney had not been inactive at Cambridge. Not long had the 'sublime lesson of Jesus Christ' filled him with joy, before he fell on his knees and exclaimed: 'O thou who art the truth, give me strength that I may teach it; and convert the ungodly by means of one who has been ungodly himself.' After this prayer his eyes gleamed with new fire; he had assembled his friends and, opening Erasmus' Testament, had placed his finger on the words that had reached his soul, and these words had touched many. The arrival of Tyndale gave him fresh courage, and the light burnt brighter in Cambridge.

John Fryth, a young man of eighteen, the son of an innkeeper of Westerham in Kent, was distinguished among the students of King's College, by the promptitude of his understanding and the integrity of his life. He was as deeply read in mathematics as Tyndale in the classics, and Bilney in canon law. Although of an exact turn of mind, yet his soul was elevated, and he recognized in holy Scripture a learning of a new kind. 'These things are not demonstrated like a proposition of Euclid', he said; 'mere study is sufficient to impress the theories of mathematics on our minds; but this science of God meets with a resistance in man that necessitates the intervention of a Divine power. Christianity is a regeneration.' 'Through Tyndale's instructions', says John Foxe, 'he first received with his heart the seed of the gospel and sincere godliness.'

These three young scholars set to work with enthusiasm. They declared that neither priestly absolution nor any other religious rite could give remission of sins; that the assurance of pardon is obtained by faith alone; and that faith purifies the heart. Then they addressed to all men that saying of Christ's at which the monks were so greatly offended: *Repent and be converted!*

Ideas so new produced a great clamour. A famous orator undertook one day at Cambridge to show that it was useless to preach conversion to the sinner. 'Thou, who, for sixty years past', said he, 'hast wallowed in thy lusts, like a sow in her mire, dost thou think that thou canst in one year take as many steps towards heaven, and that in thine age, as thou hast done towards hell?' Bilney left the church with indignation.

'Is that preaching repentance in the name of Jesus?' he asked. 'Does not this priest tell us: Christ will not save thee? Alas! for so many years that this deadly doctrine has been taught in Christendom, not one man has dared open his mouth against it!' Many of the Cambridge Fellows were scandalized at Bilney's language: was not the preacher whose teaching he condemned duly *ordained* by the bishop? He replied: 'What would be the use of being a hundred times consecrated, were it even by a thousand papal bulls, if the inward calling is wanting?[5] To no purpose hath the bishop breathed on our heads if we have never felt the breath of the Holy Ghost in our hearts.' Thus, at the very beginning of the reformation, England, rejecting the Romish superstitions, discerned with extreme nicety what constitutes the essence of consecration to the service of the Lord.

After pronouncing these noble words, Bilney, who longed for an outpouring of the Holy Ghost, shut himself up in his room, fell on his knees, and called upon God to come to the assistance of his church. Then rising up, he exclaimed, as if animated by a prophetic spirit: 'A new time is beginning. The Christian assembly is about to be renewed … Someone is coming unto us, I see him, I hear him – it is Jesus Christ … He is the king, and it is he who will call the true ministers commissioned to evangelize his people.'

Tyndale, full of the same hopes as Bilney, left Cambridge, probably at the close of 1521.

Thus the English reformation began independently of those of Luther and Zwingli – deriving its origin from God alone. In every province of Christendom there was a simultaneous action of the Divine word. The principle of the reformation at Oxford, Cambridge, and London was the *Greek New Testament*, published by Erasmus. England in course of time learnt to be proud of this origin of its reformation.

---

[5] Without this inward calling it helpeth nothing before God to be a hundred times elect and consecrated. Foxe, *Acts* iv, 638.

CHAPTER THREE

Persecution and Intrigue

(1518–1520)

T he Divine work of revival caused great alarm throughout the Roman hierarchy. Content with the baptism they adminis- tered, they feared the baptism of the Holy Ghost perfected by faith in the word of God. Some of the clergy, who were full of zeal, but of zeal without knowledge, prepared for the struggle, and the cries raised by the prelates were repeated by all the inferior orders.

The first blows did not fall on the members of the universities, but on those humble Christians, the relics of Wycliffe's ministry, to whom the reform movement among the learned had imparted a new life. The awakening of the fourteenth century was about to be succeeded by that of the sixteenth, and the last gleams of the closing day were almost lost in the first rays of that which was commencing. The young scholars of Oxford and Cambridge aroused the attention of the agitated hierarchy, and attracted their eyes to the humble disciples of the Lord, who here and there still recalled the days of Wycliffe.

An artisan named Thomas Man, sometimes called Dr Man, from his knowledge of holy Scripture, and his bold testimony to the truth as it is in Jesus, had been imprisoned for his faith in the monastery of Osney, near Oxford (1511). Tormented by the remembrance of a recantation which had been extorted from him, he had escaped from Oxford and fled into the eastern parts of England, where he had preached the word, supplying his daily wants by the labour of his hands. This 'champion of God' afterwards drew near the capital, and assisted by his wife, the new Priscilla of this new Aquila, he proclaimed the doctrine of Christ to the crowd collected around him in some 'upper chamber' of London, or in some lonely meadow watered by the Thames, or under the aged oaks of Windsor Forest. He thought with Chrysostom of old, that 'all priests are not saints, but all saints are priests'.[1] 'He that receiveth the word of God', said he, 'receiveth God himself: that is the true *real presence*. The vendors of masses are not the high-priests of this mystery; but the men whom God hath *anointed with his Spirit* to be kings and priests.' From six to seven hundred persons were converted by his preaching.

The monks who dared not as yet attack the universities, resolved to fall upon those preachers who made their temple on the banks of the Thames, or in some remote corner of the city. Man was seized, condemned, and burnt alive on 29 March 1518, at Smithfield.

And this was not all. There lived at Coventry a little band of serious Christians – four shoemakers, a glover, a hosier, and a widow named Smith – who gave their children a pious education. The Franciscans were annoyed that *laymen*, and even a *woman*, should dare meddle with religious instruction. On Ash Wednesday (1519) Simon Mourton, the bishop's summoner, apprehended them all, men, women, and children. On the following Friday, the parents were taken to the abbey of Mackstock, about six miles from Coventry, and the children to the Grey Friars' convent. 'Let us see what heresies you have been taught', said Friar Stafford to the intimidated little ones. The poor children confessed they had been taught in English the Lord's Prayer, the Apostles' Creed, and the Ten Commandments. On hearing this, Stafford told them angrily: 'I forbid you (unless you wish to be burnt as your parents will be) to have anything to do with the *Pater*, the *Credo*, or the Ten Commandments in *English*.'

Five weeks after this, the men were condemned to be burnt alive, but the judges had compassion on the widow, because of her young family (for she was their only support) and let her go. It was night: Mourton offered to see Dame Smith home; he took her arm, and they threaded the dark and narrow streets of Coventry. 'Eh, eh!' said the summoner on a sudden, 'what have we here?' He heard in fact the rattling of a scroll within her sleeve. 'What have you got there?' he continued, putting his hand up her sleeve, from which he drew out a parchment. Approaching

---

[1] Chrysostom, 43 Homily on Matt.

a window whence issued the faint rays of a lamp, he examined the mysterious scroll, and found it to contain the Lord's Prayer, certain articles of
faith, and the Ten Commandments in *English*. 'Oh, oh! sirrah!' said he;
'come along. As good now as another time!' Then seizing the poor widow
by the arm, he dragged her before the bishop. Sentence of death was
immediately pronounced on her, and on 4 April, Dame Smith, Robert
Hatchets, Archer, Hawkins, Thomas Bond, Wrigsham, and Landsdale,
were burnt alive at Coventry in the Little Park, for the crime of teaching
their children the Lord's Prayer, the Apostles' Creed, and the commandments of God.

But what availed it to silence these obscure lips, so long as the
Testament of Erasmus could speak? Lee's conspiracy must be revived.
Henry Standish, Bishop of St Asaph, was a narrow-minded man, rather
fanatical, but probably sincere, of great courage, and not without some
degree of piety. This prelate, being determined to preach a crusade
against the New Testament, began at London, in St Paul's Cathedral,
before the mayor and corporation. 'Away with these new translations',
he said, 'or else the religion of Jesus Christ is threatened with utter
ruin.' But Standish was deficient in tact, and instead of confining
himself to general statements, like most of his party, he endeavoured to
show how far Erasmus had corrupted the gospel, and continued thus:
'Must I who for so many years have been a doctor of the holy Scriptures, and who have always read in my Bible: *In principio erat* VERBUM
– must I now be obliged to read: *In principio erat* SERMO' – for thus
had Erasmus translated the opening words of St John's Gospel. 'Let us
restrain our laughter', whispered one to another, when they heard this
puerile charge. 'My lord', proceeded the bishop, turning to the mayor,
'magistrates of the city, and citizens all, fly to the succour of religion!'
Standish continued his pathetic appeals, but his oratory was all in vain;
some stood unmoved, others shrugged their shoulders, and others grew
impatient. The citizens of London seemed determined to support liberty
and the Bible.

Seeing the failure of his attack in the city, Standish sighed and
groaned and prayed, and repeated Mass against the so much dreaded
book. But he also made up his mind to do more. One day, during the

rejoicings at court for the betrothal of the Princess Mary, then two years old, with a French prince who was an infant in arms, St Asaph, eaten up with zeal, decided upon a bold step. Suddenly he made his way through the crowd, and threw himself at the feet of the king and queen. All were thunderstruck, and asked one another what the old bishop could mean. 'Great king', said he, 'your ancestors who have reigned over this island – and yours, O great queen, who have governed Aragon, were always distinguished by their zeal for the church. Show yourselves worthy of your forefathers. Times full of danger are come upon us; a book has just appeared, and been published too, by Erasmus! It is such a book that, if you close not your kingdom against it, it is all over with the religion of Christ among us.'

The bishop ceased, and a dead silence ensued. The devout Standish, fearing lest Henry's well-known love of learning should cause his prayer to be rejected, raised his eyes and his hands toward heaven and, kneeling in the midst of the courtly assembly, exclaimed in a sorrowful tone: 'O Christ! O Son of God! save thy spouse! … for no man cometh to her help.'

Having thus spoken, the prelate, whose courage was worthy of a better cause, rose up and waited. Everyone strove to guess at the king's thoughts. Sir Thomas More was present, and he could not forsake his friend Erasmus. 'What are the heresies this book is likely to engender?' he inquired. After the sublime came the ridiculous. With the forefinger of his right hand, touching successively the fingers of his left, Standish replied: 'First, this book destroys *the resurrection*; secondly, it annuls the *Sacrament of Marriage*; thirdly, it abolishes *the Mass*.' Then uplifting his thumb and two fingers, he showed them to the assembly with a look of triumph. The bigoted Catherine shuddered as she saw these unusual signs of the three heresies of Erasmus; and Henry himself, an admirer of Aquinas, was embarrassed. It was a critical moment: the Greek Testament was on the point of being banished from England. 'The proof, the proof?' exclaimed the friends of literature. – 'I will give it', rejoined the impetuous Standish, and then once more touching his left thumb: 'Firstly', he said … But he brought forward such foolish reasons that even the women and the unlearned were ashamed of them. The more he endeavoured to justify his assertions, the more confused he became: he affirmed among other things that the Epistles of St Paul were written in *Hebrew*. 'There is not a schoolboy that does not know that Paul's Epistles were written in *Greek*', said a doctor of divinity kneeling before the king. Henry, blushing for the bishop, turned the conversation, and Standish, ashamed at having made a Greek write to the Greeks in Hebrew, would have withdrawn unobserved. 'The beetle must not attack the eagle', was whispered in his ear. Thus did the book of God remain in England the standard of a faithful band, who found in its pages the motto which the Church of Rome had usurped: *The truth is in me alone.*

A more formidable adversary than Standish aspired to combat the reformation, not only in England, but in all the West. One of those ambitious designs, which easily germinate in the human heart, developed itself in the soul of the chief minister of Henry VIII; and if this project succeeded, it promised to secure for ever the empire of the papacy on the banks of the Thames, and perhaps in the whole of Christendom.

Wolsey, as chancellor and legate, governed both in state and in church, and could, without an untruth, utter his famous *Ego et rex meus*. Having reached so great a height, he desired to soar still higher. The favourite of Henry VIII, almost his master, treated as a brother by the emperor, by the King of France, and by other crowned heads, invested occasionally with the title of majesty, the peculiar property of sovereigns, the cardinal, sincere in his faith in the popedom, aspired to fill the throne of the pontiffs, and thus become *Deus in terris*. He thought that if God permitted a Luther to appear in the world, it was because he had a Wolsey to oppose to him.

It would be difficult to fix the precise moment when this immoderate desire entered his mind: it was about the end of 1518 that it began to show itself. The Bishop of Ely, ambassador at the court of Francis I, being in conference with that prince on 18 December in that year, said to him mysteriously: 'The cardinal has an idea in his mind ... on which he can unbosom himself to nobody ... except it be to Your Majesty.' Francis understood him.

An event occurred to facilitate the cardinal's plans. If Wolsey desired to be the first priest, Henry desired to be the first king. The imperial crown, vacant by the death of Maximilian in 1519, was sought by two princes – by Charles of Spain, a cold and calculating man, caring little about the pleasures and even the pomp of power, but forming great designs, and knowing how to pursue them with energy; and by Francis I of France, a man of less penetrating glance and less indefatigable activity, but more daring and impetuous. At the same time, Henry VIII, several years older than these Continental kings, passionate, capricious, and selfish, thought himself strong enough to contend with them and secretly strove to win 'the monarchy of all Christendom'. Wolsey flattered himself that, hidden under the cloak of his master's ambition, he might satisfy his own. If he procured the crown of the Caesars for Henry, he might easily obtain the tiara of the popes for himself; if he failed, the least that could be done to compensate England for the loss of the Empire, would be to give the sovereignty of the church to her prime minister.

Henry first sounded the King of France. Sir Thomas Boleyn appeared one day before Francis I just as the latter was returning from Mass. The king, desirous to anticipate a confidence that might be embarrassing, took the ambassador aside to the window and whispered to him: 'Some of the electors have offered me the Empire; I hope your master will be favourable to me.' Sir Thomas, in confusion, made some vague reply, and the chivalrous king, following up his idea, took the ambassador firmly by one hand and, laying the other on his breast, exclaimed: 'By my faith, if I become emperor, in three years I shall be in Constantinople, or I shall die on the road!' This was not what Henry wanted; but, dissembling his wishes, he took care to inform Francis that he would support his candidature. Upon hearing this Francis raised his hat and exclaimed: 'I desire to see the King of England; I will see him, I tell you, even if I go to London with only one page and one lackey.'

Francis was well aware that if he threatened the king's ambition, he must flatter the minister's and, recollecting the hint given by the Bishop of Ely, he said one day to Boleyn: 'It seems to me that my brother of England and I could do, indeed ought to do … something for the cardinal. He was prepared by God for the good of Christendom … one of the greatest men in the church … and on the word of a king, if he consents, I will do it.' A few minutes after he continued: 'Write and tell the cardinal that if he aspires to be the head of the church and, if anything should happen to the reigning pope, I will promise him fourteen cardinals on my part. Let us only act in concert, your master and me, and I promise you, Mr Ambassador, that neither pope nor emperor shall be created in Europe without our consent.'

But Henry did not act in concert with the King of France. At Wolsey's instigation he supported three candidates at once: at Paris he was for Francis I; at Madrid for Charles V; and at Frankfurt for himself. The kings of France and England failed, and on the 10th August, Dr Pace, Henry's envoy at Frankfurt, having returned to England, desired to console the king by mentioning the sums of money which Charles had spent, totalling, so Pace reckoned, no less than 1,500,000 gold florins. Henry congratulated himself on not having obtained the crown at so dear a rate.

Charles had scarcely ascended the imperial throne, in despite of the King of France, when these two princes swore eternal hatred of each other, and each was anxious to win over Henry VIII. At one time Charles, under the pretence of seeing his uncle and aunt, visited England; at another, Francis had an interview with the king in the neighbourhood of Calais. Cardinal Wolsey shared in the flattering attentions of the two monarchs. 'It is easy for the King of Spain, who has become the head of the Empire, to raise whomsoever he pleases to the supreme pontificate', said the young emperor to him; and at these words the ambitious cardinal surrendered himself to Maximilian's successor. But erelong Francis I flattered him in his turn, and Wolsey replied also to his advances. The King of France gave Henry tournaments and banquets of Asiatic luxury; and Wolsey, whose countenance yet bore the marks of the graceful smile with which he had taken leave of Charles, smiled also on Francis, and sang Mass in his honour. He engaged the hand of the Princess Mary to the Dauphin of France and to Charles V, leaving the care of unravelling the matter to futurity. Then proud of his skilful practices he returned to London full of hope. By walking in falsehood he hoped to attain the tiara: and if it was yet too far above him, there were certain *gospellers* in England who might serve as a ladder to reach it. Murder might serve as the complement to fraud.

CHAPTER FOUR

A Storm at Sodbury Hall

(1522–1523)

Whilst the ambitious prelate was thinking of nothing but his own glory and the means necessary to acquire the Roman pontificate, a great desire, but of a very different nature, was springing up in the heart of one of the humble 'gospellers' of England. If Wolsey had his eyes fixed on the throne of the popedom in order to seat himself there, Tyndale thought of raising up the true throne of the church by re-establishing the legitimate sovereignty of the word of God. The Greek Testament of Erasmus had been one step; and it now became necessary to place before the simple what the king of the schools had given to the learned. This idea, which pursued the young Oxford scholar everywhere, was to be the mighty mainspring of the English reformation.

On a south-western slope of the Cotswolds there stood a plain but large mansion, the manor house of Little Sodbury, commanding an extensive view over the beautiful vale of the Severn where Tyndale was born. It was inhabited by a family of gentle birth: Sir John Walsh had shone in the tournaments of the court, and by this means conciliated the favour of his prince. He kept open table; and gentlemen, deans, abbots, archdeacons, doctors of divinity, and rectors, charmed by Sir John's cordial welcome and by his good table, were ever at his house. The former brother-at-arms of Henry VIII felt an interest in the questions then discussing throughout Christendom. Lady Walsh herself, a sensible and generous woman, lost not a word of the animated conversation of her guests, and discreetly tried to incline the balance to the side of truth.

Tyndale after leaving Oxford and Cambridge had returned to the home of his fathers. Sir John had requested him to educate his children, and he had accepted the trust. Then in the prime of life (he was about thirty) and well instructed in Scripture, Tyndale was full of desire to show forth the light which God had given him. Opportunities were not wanting. Seated at table with all the clerics welcomed by Sir John, Tyndale entered into conversation with them. They talked of the learned men of the day – of Erasmus much, and sometimes of Luther, who was beginning to astonish England. They discussed questions touching the holy Scriptures, and sundry points of theology. Tyndale expressed his convictions with admirable clearness, supported them with great learning, and kept his ground against all with unbending courage. These animated conversations in the vale of the Severn are one of the essential features of the picture presented by the reformation in this country. The historians of antiquity invented the speeches which they have put into the mouths of their heroes. In our times history, without such inventions, should make us acquainted with the sentiments of the persons of whom it treats. It is sufficient to read Tyndale's works to form some idea of these conversations. It is from his writings that the following discussion has been drawn.

In the dining room of the old hall a varied group was assembled round the hospitable table. There were Sir John and Lady Walsh, a few gentlemen of the neighbourhood, with several abbots, deans, monks, and doctors, in their respective costumes. Tyndale occupied the humblest place, and kept Erasmus' New Testament within reach in order to prove what he advanced.[1] Numerous domestics were moving about engaged in waiting on the guests. At length the conversation, after wandering a little, took a more precise direction. The priests grew impatient when they saw the terrible volume appear. 'Your Scriptures only serve to make heretics', they exclaimed. 'On the contrary', replied Tyndale, 'the source of all heresies is pride; now the word of God strips man of everything, and leaves him as bare as Job.' – '*The word of God!* why even we don't understand it; how then can the common people understand it?' – 'You do not understand it', rejoined Tyndale, 'because you look into it only for foolish questions, as you would into *our Lady's Matins* or *Merlin's*

---

[1] When they at any time did vary from Tyndale in opinions and judgment, he would show them in the book. Foxe, *Acts*, v, p. 115.

Prophecies.[2] Now the Scriptures are a clue which we must follow, without turning aside, until we arrive at Christ; for Christ is the end.' – 'And I tell you', shouted out a priest, 'that the Scriptures are a Dædalian labyrinth, rather than Ariadne's clue – a conjuring book wherein everybody finds what he wants.' – 'Alas!' replied Tyndale; 'you read them without Jesus Christ; that is why they are an obscure book to you, a thicket of thorns where you only escape from the briers to be caught by the brambles.'[3] 'No!' exclaimed another clerk, heedless of contradicting his colleague, 'nothing is obscure to us; it is we who give the Scriptures, and we who explain them to you.' – 'You would lose both your time and your trouble', said Tyndale; 'do you know who taught the eagles to spy out their prey? Well, that same God teaches his hungry children to spy out their Father in his word. Christ's elect spy out their Lord, and trace out the paths of his feet, and follow; yea, though he go upon the plain and liquid water, which will receive no step, yet there they find out his foot. His elect know him, but the world knows him not.[4] And as for you, far from having given us the Scriptures, it is you who have hidden them from us; it is you who burn those who teach them and, if you could, you would burn the Scriptures themselves.'

Tyndale was not satisfied with merely laying down the great principles of faith: he always sought after what he calls 'the sweet marrow within'; but to the Divine unction he added no little humour, and unmercifully ridiculed the superstitions of his adversaries. 'You set candles before images', he said to them; 'and since you give them *light*, why don't you give them *food*. Why don't you make their bellies hollow, and put victuals and drink inside. To serve God by such mummeries is treating him like a spoilt child, whom you pacify with a toy or with a horse made of a stick.'

But Tyndale soon returned to more serious thoughts; and when his adversaries extolled the papacy as the power that would save the church in the tempest, he replied: 'Let us only take on board our ship the anchor of faith in Christ's blood; let us secure it by the cable of love; and when the storm bursts upon us, let us boldly cast the anchor into the sea; then

---

[2] Tyndale, *Expositions*, p. 141.

[3] A grave of briers; if thou loose thyself in one place thou art caught in another. *Ibid.*, p. 5.

[4] Tyndale, *Answer to More* (Parker Society), p. 49.

you may be sure the ship will remain safe on the great waters.' And, in fine, if his opponents rejected any doctrine of the truth, Tyndale (says the chronicler) opening his Testament would set his finger on the verse which refuted the Romish error, and exclaim: 'Look and read.'

The beginnings of the English reformation are not to be found, as we have seen, in a material ecclesiasticism, which has been decorated with the name of *English Catholicism*: they are essentially spiritual. The Divine word, the creator of the new life in the individual, is also the founder and reformer of the church. The Reformed churches, and particularly the Reformed churches of Great Britain, are the fruit of the word of the gospel.

The contemplation of God's works refreshed Tyndale after the discussions he had to maintain at his patron's table. He would often ramble to the top of Sodbury Hill, where Queen Margaret of Anjou halted during the War of the Roses; and here too rested Edward IV, who pursued her, before the fatal battle of Tewkesbury, which caused this princess to fall into the hands of the Yorkists. But Tyndale meditated upon other battles, which were to restore liberty and truth to Christendom, battles not against flesh and blood but against the rulers of the darkness of the world, and against spiritual wickedness in high places.

Behind the mansion stood a little church, overshadowed by two large yew trees, and dedicated to St Adeline. On Sundays Tyndale used to preach there, Sir John and Lady Walsh, with the older children, occupying the manorial pew. This humble sanctuary was filled by their household and tenantry, listening attentively to the words of their teacher, which fell from his lips like *the waters of Shiloah that go softly*. Tyndale was very lively in conversation; but he explained the Scriptures with so much unction, says the chronicler, 'that his hearers thought they heard St John himself'. If he resembled John in the mildness of his language, he resembled Paul in the strength of his doctrine. The pope, he said, 'turneth the roots of the trees upward. He makes the goodness of God the branches and our goodness the roots. We must be first good, says he, and move God to be good to us for our goodness' sake: so must God's goodness spring out of our goodness. Nay verily; God's goodness is the root of all goodness; and our goodness, if we have any, springs out of his goodness.'⁵ … 'As the husband marrieth the wife, before he can have any lawful children by her; even so faith justifieth us to make us fruitful in good works.⁶ But neither the one nor the other should remain barren. Faith is the holy candle wherewith you must bless yourselves at the last hour; without it, you will go astray in the valley of the shadow of death, though you had a thousand tapers about you, a hundred tons of holy water, a shipful of pardons, a cloth-sack full of friars' coats, and all the ceremonies of the world, and all the good works, deservings, and merits of all the men in the world, be they, or were they, never so holy. God's word only lasteth for ever; and that which he hath sworn doth abide when all other things perish.'⁷

The priests, irritated at such observations, determined to ruin Tyndale, and some of them invited Sir John and his lady to an enter-tainment, at which he was not present. During dinner, they so abused the young scholar and his New Testament that his patrons retired greatly annoyed that their tutor should have made so many enemies. They told him all they had heard, and Tyndale successfully refuted his adversaries' arguments. 'What!' exclaimed Lady Walsh, 'there are some of these doctors worth one hundred, some two hundred, and some three hundred pounds … and were it reason, think you, Master William, that we should believe you before them?' Tyndale thought it wise to give her no answer at the time, but as weeks passed by, she and her husband were alike convinced that their children's tutor was imparting to them nothing less than the plain truth of the gospel of God.

Before long the manor house and St Adeline's Church became too narrow for Tyndale's zeal. He preached every Sunday, sometimes in a village, sometimes in a town. The inhabitants of Bristol assembled to hear him in a large meadow, called St Austin's Green. But no sooner had he preached in any place than the priests hastened thither, tore up what he had planted, called him a heretic, and threatened to expel from the church everyone who dared listen to him. When Tyndale returned he found the field laid waste by the enemy; and looking sadly upon it,

⁵ Antichrist turneth the roots of the trees upward. Tyndale, *Doctrinal Treatises* (Parker Society), p. 295.

⁶ Tyndale, *Parable of the Wicked Mammon. Ibid.*, p. 126.

⁷ *Ibid.*, p. 48.

as the husbandman who sees his corn beaten down by the hail, and his rich furrows turned into a barren waste, he exclaimed: 'What is to be done? While I am sowing in one place, the enemy ravages the field I have just left. I cannot be everywhere. Oh! if Christians possessed the holy Scriptures in their own tongue, they could of themselves withstand these sophists. Without the Bible it is impossible to establish the laity in the truth.'

Then a great idea sprang up in Tyndale's heart: 'It was in the language of Israel', said he, 'that the Psalms were sung in the temple of Jehovah; and shall not the gospel speak the language of England among us? ... Ought the church to have less light at noonday than at the dawn? ... Christians must read the New Testament in their mother-tongue.' Tyndale believed that this idea proceeded from God. The new sun would lead to the discovery of a new world, and the infallible rule would make all human diversities give way to a Divine unity. 'One holdeth this doctor, another that', said Tyndale, 'one followeth Duns Scotus, another St Thomas Aquinas, another Bonaventure, Alexander of Hales, Raymond de Pennaforti, Nicholas de Lyra, Hugh de Sancto Victore, and so many others besides ... Now, each of these authors contradicts the other. How then can we distinguish him who says right from him who says wrong? ... How? ... Verily, by God's word. Nay, say they, the Scripture is so hard that we could not understand it but by the help of the doctors. But that is to measure the measuring rod by the cloth. Here be twenty cloths of divers lengths and of divers breadths: how shall I be sure of the length of the meteyard by them? I suppose, rather, I must be first sure of the length of the meteyard, and thereby measure and judge of the cloths. If I must first believe the doctor, then is the doctor first true and the truth of the Scripture is dependent on his truth: and so the truth of God springs out of the truth of man. Thus Antichrist turns the roots of the trees upward.'[8] Tyndale hesitated no longer. While Wolsey sought to win the papal tiara, the humble tutor of Sodbury undertook to place the torch of heaven in the midst of his fellow countrymen. The translation of the Bible must be the chief work of his life.

[8] Tyndale, *Doctrinal Treatises*, pp. 149-54.

The first triumph of the word was a revolution in the manor house. In proportion as Sir John and Lady Walsh acquired a taste for the gospel, they became disgusted with the priests. The clergy were not so often invited to Sodbury, nor did they meet with the same welcome. 'Neither', says Foxe, 'had they the cheer and countenance when they came, as before they had.' They soon discontinued their visits, and thought of nothing but how they could drive Tyndale from the mansion and from the diocese.

Unwilling to compromise themselves in this warfare, they sent forward some of those light troops which the church has always at her disposal. Mendicant friars and poor curates, who could hardly understand their missal, and the most learned of whom made *Albertus de secretis mulierum*[9] their habitual study, fell upon Tyndale like a pack of hungry hounds. They trooped to the alehouses and, calling for a jug of beer, took their seats, one at one table, another at another. They invited the peasantry to drink with them and, entering into conversation with them, poured forth a thousand curses upon the daring reformer: 'He's a hypocrite', said one; 'He's a heretic', said another. The most skilful among them would mount upon a stool and, turning the tavern into a temple, deliver, for the first time in his life, an extemporaneous discourse. They reported words that Tyndale had never uttered, and actions that he had never committed. Rushing upon the poor tutor (he himself informs us) 'like unclean swine that follow their carnal lusts', they tore his good name to very tatters, and shared the spoil among them; while the audience, excited by their calumnies and heated by the beer, departed overflowing with rage and hatred against the heretic of Sodbury.

After the friars came the dignitaries. The deans and abbots, Sir John's former guests, accused Tyndale to the chancellor of the diocese, and the storm which had begun in the tavern burst forth in the episcopal palace.

The titular Bishop of Worcester (an appanage of the Italian prelates) was Julio de Medici, a learned man, great politician, and crafty priest, who already governed the popedom without being pope, and who later, as Pope Clement VII, was appealed to in the question of the divorce of Henry VIII. Wolsey, who administered the diocese for his

---

[9] Treatise *On the Secrets of Wives*, by Albertus Magnus.

absent colleague, had appointed Dr Thomas Parker chancellor, a man devoted to the Roman Church. It was to him the churchmen made their complaint. A judicial inquiry had its difficulties; the king's companion-at-arms was the employer and patron of the pretended heretic, and Sir Anthony Poyntz, Lady Walsh's brother, was sheriff of the county. The chancellor was therefore content to convoke a general conference of the clergy. Tyndale obeyed the summons, but foreseeing what awaited him, he cried heartily to God, as he pursued his way up the banks of the Severn, 'to give him strength to stand fast in the truth of his word.'

When they were assembled, the abbots and deans, and other ecclesiastics of the diocese, with haughty heads and threatening looks, crowded round the humble but unbending Tyndale. When his turn arrived, he stood forward, and the chancellor administered him a severe reprimand, to which he made a calm reply. This so exasperated the chancellor, that, giving way to his passion, he treated Tyndale as if he had been a dog.[10] 'Where are your witnesses?' demanded the latter. 'Let them come forward, and I will answer them.' Not one of them dared support the charge – they looked another way. The chancellor waited, one witness at least he must have, but he could not get that. Annoyed at this desertion of the priests, the representative of the Medici became more equitable, and let the accusation drop. Tyndale quietly returned to Sodbury, blessing God who had saved him from the cruel hands of his adversaries,[11] and entertaining nothing but the tenderest charity towards them. 'Take away my goods', he said to them one day, 'take away my good name! yet so long as Christ dwelleth in my heart, so long shall I love you not a whit the less.'[12] Here indeed is the St John to whom Tyndale has been compared.

In this violent warfare, however, he could not fail to receive some heavy blows; and where could he find consolation? Fryth and Bilney were far from him. Tyndale recollected an *aged doctor*, formerly chancellor to a bishop, who lived near Sodbury and who had shown him great affection. He went to see him, and opened his heart to him. The old

[10] He threatened me grievously and reviled me, and rated me as though I had been a dog. Tyndale, *Doctrinal Treatises*, p. 395.

[11] Escaping out of their hands. Foxe, *Acts*, v, p. 116.

[12] Tyndale, *Doctrinal Treatises*, p. 298.

man looked at him for a while as if he hesitated to disclose some great mystery. 'Do you not know', said he, lowering his voice 'that *the pope is the very Antichrist* whom the Scripture speaketh of? ... But beware what you say. ... That knowledge may cost you your life.' This doctrine of Antichrist, which Luther was at that moment enunciating so boldly, struck Tyndale. Strengthened by it, as was the Saxon reformer, he felt fresh energy in his heart, and the aged doctor was to him what the aged friar had been to Luther.

When the priests saw that their plot had failed, they commissioned a celebrated divine to undertake his conversion. The reformer replied with his Greek Testament to the schoolman's arguments. The theologian was speechless: at last he exclaimed: 'Well then! it were better to be without God's laws than the pope's.' Tyndale, who did not expect so plain and blasphemous a confession, made answer: 'I defy the pope and all his laws!' and then, as if unable to keep his secret, he added: 'If God spares my life, ere many years I will take care that a ploughboy shall know more of the Scriptures than you do.'

All his thoughts were now directed to the means of carrying out his plans; and desirous of avoiding conversations that might compromise them, he thenceforth passed the greater portion of his time in the library. He prayed, he read, he began his translation of the Bible, and in all probability communicated portions of it to Sir John and Lady Walsh.

All his precautions were useless: the scholastic divine had betrayed him, and the priests had sworn to stop him in his translation of the Bible. One day he fell in with a troop of monks and curates, who abused him in the grossest manner. 'It's the favour of the gentry of the county that makes you so proud', said they; 'but notwithstanding your patrons, there will be a talk about you before long, and in a pretty fashion too! ... You shall not always live in a manor house!' – 'Banish me to the obscurest corner of England', replied Tyndale; 'provided you will permit me to teach children and preach the gospel, and give me ten pounds a year for my support. ... I shall be satisfied!' The priests left him, but with the intention of preparing him a very different fate.

Tyndale indulged in his pleasant dreams no longer. He saw that he was on the point of being arrested, condemned, and interrupted in his great work. He must seek a retreat where he could discharge in peace the task God had allotted him. 'You cannot save me from the hands of the priests', said he to Sir John, 'and God knows to what troubles you would expose yourself by keeping me in your family. Permit me to leave you.' Having said this, he gathered up his papers, took his Testament, pressed the hands of his benefactors, kissed the children, and then descending the hill, bade farewell to the smiling banks of the Severn, and departed alone – alone with his faith. What shall he do? What will become of him? Where shall he go? He went forth like Abraham, one thing alone engrossing his mind – the Scriptures must be translated into the language of the people, and deposited as the oracles of God in the midst of his countrymen.[13]

[13] [An excellent biography of Tyndale was produced by R. Demaus in 1872, and subsequently republished as revised by Richard Lovett. A more recent biography by J. F. Mozley, supplementing but not superseding that by Demaus, was published by the S.P.C.K. in 1937. See also David Daniel's *William Tyndale: A Biography* (New Haven & London: Yale University Press, 1994).]

CHAPTER FIVE

The Onslaught on Luther

(1517–1521)

W hilst a plain minister was commencing the reformation in a tranquil valley in the west of England, powerful reinforcements were landing on the shores of Kent. The writings and actions of Luther excited a lively sensation in Great Britain. His appearance before the Diet of Worms was a common subject of conversation. Ships from the harbours of the Low Countries brought his books to London, and the German printers had made answer to the nuncio Aleander, who was prohibiting the Lutheran works in the Empire: 'Very well! we shall send them to *England!*' One might almost say that England was destined to be the asylum of truth. And in fact, the *theses* of 1517, the *Explanation of the Lord's Prayer, the books against Emser, against the papacy of Rome, against the bull of Antichrist, the Commentary on the Epistle to the Galatians, the Appeal to the German nobility,* and above all, the *Babylonish Captivity of the Church* – all crossed the sea, were translated, and circulated throughout the kingdom. The German and English nations, having a common origin, and being sufficiently alike at that time in character and civilization, the works intended for one might be read by the other with advantage. The monk in his cell, the country gentleman in his hall, the doctor in his college, the tradesman in his shop, and even the bishop in his palace, studied these extraordinary writings. The laity in particular, who had been prepared by Wycliffe and disgusted by the avarice and disorderly lives of the priests, read with enthusiasm the eloquent pages of the Saxon monk. They strengthened all hearts.

The papacy was not inactive in presence of all these efforts. The times of Gregory VII and of Innocent III, it is true, had passed; and weakness and irresolution had succeeded to the former energy and activity of the Roman pontificate. The spiritual power had resigned the dominion of Europe to the secular powers, and it was doubtful whether faith in the papacy could be found in the papacy itself. Yet a German (Dr Eck) by the most indefatigable exertions had extorted a bull from the profane Leo X, and this bull had just reached England. The pope himself sent it to Henry, calling upon him to extirpate the Lutheran heresy. The king handed it to Wolsey, and the latter transmitted it to the bishops, who, after reading *the heretic's* books, met together to discuss the matter. There was more Romish faith in London than in the Vatican. 'This false friar', exclaimed Wolsey, 'attacks submission to the clergy – that fountain of all virtues.' The humanist prelates were the most annoyed; the road they had taken ended in an abyss, and they shrank back in alarm. Tunstall, the friend of Erasmus, afterwards Bishop of London, and who had just returned from his embassy to Germany where Luther had been painted to him in the darkest colours, was particularly violent: 'This monk is a *Proteus* ... I mean an *atheist*. If you allow the heresies to grow up which he is scattering with both hands, they will choke the faith and the church will perish. Have we not enough of the Wycliffites – here are new legions of the same kind! ... Today Luther calls for the abolition of the Mass; tomorrow he will ask for the abolition of Jesus Christ. He rejects everything, and puts nothing in its place. What? if barbarians plunder our frontiers, we punish them ... and shall we bear with heretics who plunder our altars? ... No! by the mortal agony that Christ endured, I entreat you ... What am I saying? the whole church conjures you to combat against this devouring dragon ... to punish this *hell-dog*, to silence his sinister howlings, and to drive him shamefully back into his den.' Thus spoke the eloquent Tunstall. Nor was Wolsey far behind him. The only attachment at all respectable in this man was that which he entertained for the church; it may perhaps be called respectable, for it was the only one that did not exclusively regard himself. On 14 May 1521, this English pope, in imitation of the Italian pope, issued his bull against Luther.

It was read (probably on the first Sunday in June) in all the churches during High Mass, when the congregation was most numerous. A priest exclaimed: 'For every book of Martin Luther's found in your possession within fifteen days after this injunction, you will incur the greater excommunication.' Then a public notary, holding the pope's bull in his hand, with a description of Luther's *perverse opinions*, proceeded towards the principal door of the church and fastened up the document. The people gathered round it; the most competent person read it aloud, while the rest listened. The following are some of the Lutheran 'heresies' which, by the pope's order, resounded in the porches of all the cathedral, conventual, collegiate, and parish churches of every county in England, and were the subjects of papal condemnation:

11. Sins are not pardoned to any, unless, the priest remitting them, he believe they are remitted to him.

13. If by reason of some impossibility, the *contrite* be not confessed, or the priest absolve him, not in earnest, but in jest; yet if he believe that he is absolved, he is most truly absolved.

14. In the Sacrament of *Penance* and the remission of a fault, the pope or bishop doth not more than the lowest priest; yea, where there is not a priest, then any Christian will do; yea, if it were a woman or a child.

26. The pope, the successor of Peter, is not Christ's vicar.

28. It is not at all in the hand of the church or the pope to decree articles of faith, no, nor to decree the laws of manners or of good works.

The cardinal-legate, accompanied by the nuncio, by the ambassador of Charles V, and by several bishops, proceeded in great pomp to St Paul's, where the Bishop of Rochester preached, and Wolsey burnt Luther's books. But they were hardly reduced to ashes, before sarcasms and jests were heard in every direction. '*Fire* is not a theological argument', said one. 'The papists, who accuse Martin Luther of slaying and murdering Christians', added another, 'are like the pickpocket, who began to cry *stop thief*, as soon as he saw himself in danger of being caught.' – 'The Bishop of Rochester', said a third, 'concludes that because Luther has thrown the pope's decretals into the fire, he would throw in the pope himself. ... We may hence deduce another syllogism, quite as sound: Rochester and his brethren have burnt the New Testament, an evident sign, verily, that they would have burnt Christ himself also, if they had had him!'[1] These sayings were rapidly circulated from mouth to mouth. It was not enough that Luther's writings were in England, they must needs be known, and the priests took upon themselves to advertise them. The reformation was advancing, and Rome herself pushed behind the car.

The cardinal saw that something more was required than these paper *autos-da-fé*, and the activity he displayed may indicate what he would have done in Europe, if ever he had reached the pontifical chair. 'The spirit of Satan left him no repose', says the papist Sanders. Some action out of the ordinary course is needful, thought Wolsey. Kings have hitherto been the enemies of the popes: a king shall now undertake their defence. Princes are not very anxious about learning: a prince shall publish a book! ... 'Sire', said he to the king, to get Henry in the vein, 'you ought to write to the princes of Germany on the subject of this heresy.' He did so. Writing to the Archduke Palatine, he said: 'This fire, which has been kindled by Luther, and fanned by the arts of the devil, is raging everywhere. If Luther does not repent, deliver him and his audacious treatises to the flames. I offer you my royal co-operation, and even, if necessary, my life.'[2] This was the first time Henry showed that cruel thirst, which was in after days to be quenched in the blood of his wives and friends.

The king having taken the first step, it was not difficult for Wolsey to induce him to take another. To defend the honour of Thomas Aquinas, to stand forward as the champion of the church, and to obtain from the pope a title equivalent to that of *Christianissimus*, Most Christian King, were more than sufficient motives to induce Henry to break a lance with Luther. 'I will combat with the pen this Cerberus, sprung from the depths of hell', said he, 'and if he refuses to retract, the fire shall consume the heretic and his heresies together.'

The king shut himself up in his library: all the scholastic tastes with which his youth had been imbued were revived; he worked as if he were Archbishop of Canterbury, and not King of England; with the pope's permission he read Luther's writings; he ransacked Thomas Aquinas;

---

[1] They would have burnt Christ himself. Tyndale, *Doctrinal Treatises*, p. 221.

[2] [An excellent recent work on Henry's letters against Luther is, Erwin Doernberg, *Henry VIII and Luther* (Barrie and Rockliff).]

forged, with infinite labour, the arrows with which he hoped to pierce the heretic; called several learned men to his aid; and at last published his book. His first words were a cry of alarm. 'Beware of the track of this serpent', said he to his Christian readers; 'walk on tiptoe; fear the thickets and caves in which he lies concealed, and whence he will dart his poison on you. If he licks you, be careful! the cunning viper caresses only that he may bite!' After that Henry sounded a charge: 'Be of good cheer! Filled with the same valour that you would display against Turks, Saracens, and other infidels, march now against this *little friar* – a fellow apparently weak, but more formidable through the spirit that animates him than all infidels, Saracens, and Turks put together.' Thus did Henry VIII, the *Peter the Hermit* of the sixteenth century, preach a crusade against Luther, in order to save the papacy.

He had skilfully chosen the ground on which he gave battle: sacramentalism and tradition are in fact the two essential features of the papal religion; just as a lively faith and holy Scripture are of the religion of the gospel. Henry did a service to the reformation, by pointing out the principles it would mainly have to combat; and by furnishing Luther with an opportunity of establishing the authority of the Bible, he made him take a most important step in the path of reform. 'If a teaching is opposed to Scripture', said the reformer, 'whatever be its origin – traditions, custom, kings, Thomists, sophists, Satan, or even an angel from heaven – all from whom it proceeds must be accursed. *Nothing can exist contrary to Scripture*, and everything must exist for it.'

Henry's book having been finished by the aid of the Bishop of Rochester, the king showed it to Sir Thomas More, who begged him to pronounce less decidedly in favour of the papal supremacy. 'I will not change a word', replied the king, full of servile devotion to the popedom. 'Besides, I have my reasons', and he whispered them in More's ear.

Dr Clarke, ambassador from England at the court of Rome, was commissioned to present the pope with a magnificently bound copy of the king's work. 'The glory of England', said he, 'is to be in the foremost rank among the nations in obedience to the papacy.' Happily Britain was erelong to know a glory of a very different kind. The ambassador added that his master, after having refuted Luther's errors with the *pen*,

was ready to combat his adherents with the *sword*. The pope, touched
with this offer, gave him his foot, and then his cheek to kiss, and said to
him: 'I will do for your master's book as much as the church has done
for the works of St Jerome and St Augustine.'

The enfeebled papacy had neither the power of intelligence nor
even of fanaticism. It still maintained its pretensions and its pomp,
but it resembled the corpses of the mighty ones of the earth that lie in
state, clad in their most magnificent robes: splendour above, death and
corruption below. The thunderbolts of a Hildebrand ceasing to produce
their effect, Rome gratefully accepted the defence of laymen, such as
Henry VIII and Sir Thomas More, without disdaining their judicial
sentences and their scaffolds. 'We must honour those noble champions',
said the pope to his cardinals, 'who show themselves prepared to cut off
with the sword the rotten members of Jesus Christ. What title shall we
give to the virtuous King of England?' – *Protector of the Roman Church*,
suggested one; *Apostolic King*, said another; and finally, but not without
some opposition, Henry VIII was proclaimed *Defender of the Faith*. At
the same time the pope promised ten years' indulgence to all readers of
the king's book. This was a lure after the fashion of the Middle Ages,
and which never failed in its effect. The clergy compared its author to
the wisest of kings; and the book, of which many thousand copies were
printed, filled the Christian world (Cochlæus tells us) with admiration
and delight.

Nothing could equal Henry's joy. 'His Majesty', said the Vicar of
Croydon, 'would not exchange that name for all London and twenty
miles round.' According to a tradition preserved by Thomas Fuller, the
king's fool, entering the room just as his master had received the title,
asked him the cause of his transports. 'The pope has just named me
Defender of the Faith!' – 'Ho! ho! good Harry', replied the fool, 'let you
and me defend one another; but ... take my word for it ... *let the faith
alone to defend itself*.' In the midst of the general intoxication, the fool
was the only sensible person. But Henry could listen to nothing. Seated
on an elevated throne, with the cardinal at his right hand, he caused the
pope's letter to be read in public. The trumpets sounded: Wolsey said
Mass; the king and his court took their seats around a sumptuous table,

and the heralds-at-arms proclaimed: *Henricus Dei gratia Rex Angliæ et Franciæ, Defensor Fidei et Dominus Hiberniæ!*[3]

Thus did it appear that the pope of Rome and the King of England were united firmly in their resolve to maintain the doctrine of the Romish Church. Henry VIII had, as it were, thrown down the gauntlet. He aimed at warning all English followers of the German reformer that in his kingdom they might expect to encounter the utmost opposition of the law (which was little more than the expression of the royal will) and the use of that material sword in which the papacy so much delighted.

---

[3] ['Henry by the grace of God King of England and France, Defender of the Faith, and Lord of Ireland!' It may seem strange that, long after the Middle Ages, kings of England should still lay claim to the title of King of France. Such was the case, however, until 1802, when George III relinquished it. The title is retained in the Address to James I, often printed with the Authorised Version of 1611.]

CHAPTER SIX

Early Martyrs in Lincolnshire

(1521–1522)

Henry had now to justify the title conferred on him by the pope; Wolsey desired to gain the popedom; and both could satisfy their desires by hunting down heretics. Thus it was not long before persecution again broke out against the disciples of the word of God.

In the county of Lincoln on the shores of the North Sea, along the fertile banks of the Humber, Trent, and Witham, and on the slopes of the smiling hills, dwelt many peaceful Christians – labourers, artificers, and shepherds – who spent their days in toil, in keeping their flocks, in doing good, and in reading (says Foxe) 'a few English books such as they could get in corners'. The more the gospel light increased in England, the greater was the increase in the number of these children of peace. These 'just men', as they were called, were possessed of little human knowledge, but they thirsted for the knowledge of God. Thinking they were alone the true disciples of the Lord, they married only among themselves. They appeared occasionally at church; but instead of repeating their prayers like the rest, they sat, said their enemies, 'mum like beasts', and especially so when the elevation of the host took place. On Sundays and holidays, they assembled in each other's houses, and sometimes passed a whole night in reading a portion of Scripture. If there chanced to be few books among them, one of the brethren, who had learnt by heart the Epistle of St James, the beginning of St Luke's Gospel, the Sermon on the Mount, or an Epistle of St Paul's, would recite a few verses in a loud and calm voice; then all would piously converse about the holy truths of the faith, and exhort one another to put them in practice.

But if any person joined their meetings who did not belong to their body, they would all keep silent. Speaking much among each other, they were speechless before those from without: fear of the priests and of the faggot made them dumb. There was no family rejoicing without the Scriptures. At the marriage of a daughter of the aged Durdant, one of their patriarchs, the wedding party met secretly in a barn, and read the whole of one of St Paul's Epistles. Marriages are rarely celebrated with such pastimes as this!

Although they were dumb before enemies or suspected persons, these poor people did not keep silence in the presence of the humble: a glowing proselytism characterized them all. 'Come to my house', said the pious Agnes Ashford to James Morden, 'and I will teach you some verses of Scripture.' Agnes was an educated woman; she could read; Morden came, and the poor woman's chamber was transformed into a school of theology. Agnes began: 'We be the salt of the earth', and then recited the following verses. 'If it be putrefied and vanished away, it is nothing worth. A city set upon a hill may not be hid. Teen ye not a candle, and put it under a bushel but set it on a candlestick that it may give a light to all in the house. So shine your light before men, as they may see your works, and glorify the Father that is in heaven. No tittle nor letter of the law shall pass over till all things be done.' Five times did Morden return to Agnes before he had well learned his lesson. 'We are spread like salt over the various parts of the kingdom', said this Christian woman to the neophyte, 'in order that we may check the progress of superstition by our doctrine and our life. But', added she in alarm, 'keep this secret in your heart, as a man would keep a thief in prison.'[1] Then again, Agnes taught him to say this lesson: 'Blessed be the poor men in spirit, for the kingdom of heaven is theirs. Blessed be mild men for they shall weld the earth.' Twice he came to her to learn these words.

As books were rare these pious Christians had established a kind of itinerant library, and one John Scrivener was continually engaged in carrying the precious volumes from one to another. But at times, as he was proceeding along the banks of the river or through the forest

---

[1] [Foxe records that when apprehended and questioned, 'Agnes was bid to recite before six bishops who straightway enjoined and commanded her that she should teach these lessons no more to any man, and specially not to her children.']

glades, he observed that he was followed. He would quicken his pace and run into some barn where the friendly peasants promptly hid him beneath the straw, or, like the spies of Israel, under the stalks of flax. The bloodhounds arrived, sought and found nothing; and more than once those who so generously harboured these evangelists cruelly expiated the crime of charity.

The disappointed officers had scarcely retired from the neighbourhood when these friends of the word of God came out of their hiding place, and profited by the moment of liberty to assemble the brethren. The persecutions they suffered irritated them against the priests. They worshipped God, read, and sang with a low voice; but when the conversation became general, they gave free course to their indignation. 'Would you know the use of the pope's pardons?' said one of them; 'they are to blind the eyes and empty the purse.' – 'True pilgrimages', said the tailor Geoffrey of Uxbridge, 'consist in visiting the poor, the weak, and the sick – barefoot, if so it please you – for these are the little ones that are God's true image.' – 'Money spent in pilgrimages', added a third, 'serves only to maintain thieves and harlots.' The women were often the most animated in the controversy. 'What need is there to go to the *feet*', said Agnes Ward, who disbelieved in saints, 'when we may go to the *head*?' – 'The clergy of the good old times', said the wife of David Lewis, 'used to lead the people as a hen leadeth her chickens; but now if our priests lead their flocks anywhere, it is to the devil assuredly.'

Erelong there was a general panic throughout this district. The king's confessor, John Longland, was Bishop of Lincoln. This fanatic priest, Wolsey's creature, took advantage of his position to petition Henry for a severe persecution: this was the ordinary use in England, France, and elsewhere, of the confessors of princes. It was unfortunate that among these pious disciples of the word, men of a cynical turn were now and then met with, whose biting sarcasms went beyond all bounds. Wolsey and Longland knew how to employ these expressions in arousing the king's anger. 'As one of these fellows', they said, 'was busy beating out his corn in his barn, a man chanced to pass by. "Good morrow, neighbour," (said the latter) "you are hard at it!" – "Yes," replied the old heretic, thinking of transubstantiation, "I am thrashing the corn out of which the priests make God Almighty."' Henry hesitated no longer.

On 20 October 1521, nine days after the bull on the *Defender of the Faith* had been signed at Rome, the king, who was at Windsor, summoned his secretary, and dictated an order commanding all his subjects to assist the Bishop of Lincoln against the heretics. 'You disobey it at the peril of your lives', added he. The order was transmitted to Longland, and the bishop immediately issued his warrants, and his officers spread terror far and wide. When they beheld them, these peaceful but timid Christians were troubled. Isabella Bartlet, hearing them approach her cottage, cried out to her husband: 'You are a lost man! and I am a dead woman!' This cry was re-echoed in many of the cottages of Lincolnshire. The bishop, on his judgment seat, skilfully played upon the fears of these poor unhappy beings to make them accuse one another. Alas! according to the ancient prophecy: 'the brother delivered up the brother to death'. Robert Bartlet deposed against his brother Richard and his own wife; Jane Bernard accused her own father, and Thomas Tredway his mother, who had taught him that he should not worship the images of saints. It was not until after the most cruel anguish that these poor creatures were driven to such frightful extremities; but the bishop and the threat of death terrified them: a small number alone remained firm. As regards heroism, Wycliffe's reformation brought but a feeble aid to the refor- mation of the sixteenth century; still, if it did not furnish many heroes, it prepared the English people to love God's word above all things. Of these humble people, some were condemned to do penance in different monasteries; others to carry a faggot on their shoulders thrice round the market-place, and then to stand some time exposed to the jeers of the populace; others were fastened to a post while an official branded them on the cheek with a red-hot iron. They also had their martyrs. Wycliffe's revival had never been without them. Four of these brethren were chosen to be put to death, and among them the pious evangelical *colporteur* John Scrivener. By burning him to ashes, the clergy desired to make sure that he would no longer circulate the word of God; and by a horrible refinement of cruelty his children were compelled to set fire to the pile that was to consume their father, 'the example of which cruelty', says Foxe, 'as it is contrary both to God and nature, so it hath not been seen or heard of in the memory of the heathen'. But it is easier to burn the limbs of Christians than to quench the Spirit of heaven. These cruel fires could not destroy among the Lincolnshire peasantry that love of the Bible which in all ages has been England's strength, far more than the wisdom of her senators or the bravery of her generals.

Having by these exploits gained indisputable claims to the papal tiara, Wolsey turned his efforts towards Rome. Leo X died on the first day of December 1521. The cardinal sent Dr Pace to Rome, instructing him to 'Represent to the cardinals that by choosing a partisan of Charles or Francis, they will incur the enmity of one or the other of these princes, and that if they elect some feeble Italian priest, the apostolical see must become the prey of the strongest. Luther's revolt and the emperor's ambition endanger the papacy. There is only one means of preventing the threatening dangers. ... It is to choose me. ... Now go and exert yourself.' The conclave opened at Rome on 27 December, and Wolsey was proposed; but the cardinals were not generally favourable to his election. 'He is too young', said one. – 'Too firm', said another. – 'He will fix the seat of the papacy in England and not in Rome', urged many. He received insufficient votes; as few as seven, says one account, nineteen says another. 'The cardinals', wrote the English ambassador, 'snarled and quarrelled with each other; and their bad faith and hatred increased every day.' Finally, to enable the cardinals to reach a decision, their food supplies were drastically restricted; and then in despair they chose Adrian, who had been tutor to the emperor, and the cry was raised: *Papam habemus!* (We have a pope!)

During all this time Wolsey was in London, consumed by ambition, and counting the days and hours. At length a despatch from Ghent, dated 22 January, reached him with these words: 'On the 9th of January, the Cardinal of Tortosa was elected!' Wolsey was almost distracted. To gain Charles, he had sacrificed the alliance of Francis I; there was no stratagem that he had not employed, and yet Charles, in spite of his engagements, had procured the election of his tutor! The emperor knew what must be the cardinal's anger, and endeavoured to appease it: 'The new pope', he wrote, 'is old and sickly; he cannot hold his office long. ... Beg the Cardinal of York for my sake to *take great care of his health.*'

Charles did more than this: he visited London in person, under pretence of his betrothal with Mary of England, and, on 19 June 1522, in the treaty then drawn up, he consented to the insertion of an article by virtue of which Henry VIII and the mighty emperor bound themselves, if either should infringe the treaty, to appear before Wolsey and to submit to his decisions. The cardinal, gratified by such condescension, grew calm; and at the same time he was soothed with the most flattering hopes. 'Charles' imbecile preceptor', they told him, 'has arrived at the Vatican, attended only by his female cook; you shall soon make your entrance there surrounded by all your grandeur.' To be certain of his game, Wolsey made secret approaches to Francis I, and then waited for the death of the pope.

CHAPTER SEVEN

All England Closed to Tyndale

(1523–1524)

W hile the cardinal was intriguing to attain his selfish ends, Tyndale was humbly carrying out the great idea of giving the Scriptures of God to England.

After bidding a sad farewell to the manor house of Sodbury, the learned tutor had departed for London. This probably occurred during the summer of 1523. He had left the university – he had forsaken the house of his protector; his wandering career was about to commence, but a thick veil hid from him all its sorrows. Tyndale, a man simple in his habits, sober, daring, and generous, fearing neither fatigue nor danger, inflexible in his duty, anointed with the Spirit of God, overflowing with love for his brethren, emancipated from human traditions, the servant of God alone, and loving nought but Jesus Christ, imaginative, quick at repartee, and of touching eloquence – such a man might have shone in the foremost ranks; but he preferred a retired life in some poor corner, provided he could give his countrymen the Scriptures of God. Where could he find this calm retreat? Such was the question he doubtless put to himself as he was making his solitary way to London. The metropolitan see was then filled by Cuthbert Tunstall, who was more of a statesman and a scholar than of a churchman, 'the first of Englishmen in Greek and Latin literature', said Erasmus. This eulogy pronounced by the learned Dutchman occurred to Tyndale's memory. It was the Greek Testament of Erasmus that led me to Christ, said he to himself; why should not the house of Erasmus' friend offer me a shelter that I may translate it. … At last he reached London, and, a stranger in that crowded city, he wandered along the streets, a prey by turns to hope and fear.

Being recommended by Sir John Walsh to Sir Harry Guildford, controller of the royal household, and by him to several priests, Tyndale began to preach almost immediately, especially at St Dunstan's-in-the-West, and bore into the heart of the capital the truth which had been banished from the banks of the Severn. The *word* of God was with him the basis of salvation, and the *grace* of God its essence. His inventive mind presented the truths he proclaimed in a striking manner. He said on one occasion: 'It is the blood of Christ that opens the gates of heaven, and not thy works. I am wrong. ... Yes, if thou wilt have it so, by thy good works shalt thou be saved. Yet, understand me well, not by those which thou hast done, but by those which Christ has done for thee. Christ is in thee and thou in him, knit together inseparably. Thou canst not be damned, except Christ be damned with thee; neither can Christ be saved except thou be saved with him.' This lucid view of justification by faith places Tyndale among the reformers. He did not take his seat on a bishop's throne, or wear a silken cope; but he mounted the scaffold, and was clothed with a garment of flames. In the service of a crucified Saviour this latter distinction is higher than the former.

Yet the translation was his chief business; he spoke to his acquaintances about it, and some of them opposed his project. 'The teachings of the doctors', said some of the city tradesmen, 'can alone make us understand Scripture.' To this Tyndale replied: 'Whatsoever opinions every man findeth with his doctor, that is his gospel, and that only is true with him: and that holdeth he all his life long. And every man, to maintain his doctor withal, corrupteth the Scripture and fashioneth it after his own imagination, as a potter doth his clay. Of what text thou provest hell will another prove purgatory, and another limbo ... and of what text the grey friar proveth our lady was without original sin, of the same will the black friar prove that she was conceived in original sin ... and all this with false similitudes and likenesses, and with arguments and persuasions of man's wisdom. ... Happy are they which search the testimonies of the Lord.'

Desirous of carrying out his project, Tyndale aspired to become the bishop's chaplain; his ambition was more modest than Wolsey's. The Hellenist possessed qualities which could not fail to please the most learned of Englishmen in Greek literature: Tunstall and Tyndale both liked and read the same authors. The ex-tutor determined to plead his cause through the elegant and harmonious disciple of Radicus and Gorgias: 'Here is one of Isocrates' orations that I have translated into Latin', said he to Sir Harry Guildford; 'I should be pleased to become chaplain to his lordship the Bishop of London; will you beg him to accept this trifle. Isocrates ought to be an excellent recommendation to a scholar; will you be good enough to add yours?' Guildford spoke to the bishop, placed the translation in his hands, and Tunstall replied with that benevolence which he showed to everyone. 'Your business is in a fair way', said the controller to Tyndale; 'write a letter to his lordship, and deliver it yourself.'

Tyndale's hopes now began to be raised. He wrote his letter in the best style, and then, commending himself to God, proceeded to the episcopal palace. He fortunately knew one of the bishop's officers, William Hebilthwayte, to whom he gave the letter. Hebilthwayte carried it to his lordship, while Tyndale waited. His heart throbbed with anxiety: would he find at last the long-hoped-for asylum? The bishop's answer might decide the whole course of his life. If the door were to be opened, if the translator of the Scriptures should be settled in the episcopal palace, why should not his London patron receive the truth like his patron at Sodbury? and, in that case, what a future for the church and for the kingdom! ... The reformation was knocking at the door of the hierarchy of England, and the latter was about to utter its yea or its nay. After a few moments' absence Hebilthwayte returned: 'I am going to conduct you to his lordship.' Tyndale fancied himself that he had attained his wishes.

The bishop was too courteous to refuse an audience to a man who called upon him with the triple recommendation of Isocrates, of the controller, and of the king's old companion-in-arms. He received Tyndale with cool politeness, as if he were a man whose acquaintanceship might compromise him. Tyndale having made known his wishes, the bishop hastened to reply: 'Alas! my house is full; I have now more people than I can employ.'[1] Tyndale was discomfited by this answer. The Bishop of

---

[1] Tyndale, *Doctrinal Treatises*, p. 395.

London was a learned man, but wanting in courage and consistency; he gave his right hand to the friends of letters and of the gospel, and his left hand to the friends of the priests; and then endeavoured to walk with both. But when he had to choose between the two parties, clerical interests prevailed. There was no lack of bishops, priests, and laymen about him, who intimidated him by their clamours. After taking a few steps forward, he suddenly recoiled. Still Tyndale ventured to hazard a word; but the prelate was cold as before. The humanists, who laughed at the ignorance of the monks, hesitated to touch an ecclesiastical system which lavished on them such rich sinecures. They accepted the new ideas in theory, but not in practice. They were very willing to discuss them at table, but not to proclaim them from the pulpit; and covering the Greek Testament with applause, they tore it in pieces when rendered into the vulgar tongue. 'If you will look well about London', said Tunstall coldly to the poor priest, 'you will not fail to meet with some suitable employment.' This was all Tyndale could obtain. He departed from the bishop's presence sad and desponding.

His expectations were disappointed. Driven from the banks of the Severn, without a home in the capital, what would become of the translation of the Scriptures? 'Alas!' he said; 'I was deceived ... there is nothing to be looked for from the bishops ... Christ was smitten on the cheek before the bishop, Paul was buffeted before the bishop ... and a bishop has just turned me away.' His dejection did not last long: there was an elastic principle in his soul. 'I hunger for the word of God', said he, 'I will translate it, whatever they may say or do. God will not suffer me to perish. He never made a mouth but he made food for it, nor a body, but he made raiment also.'

This trustfulness was not misplaced. It was the privilege of a layman to give what the bishop refused. Among Tyndale's hearers at St Dunstan's was a wealthy cloth-merchant named Humphrey Monmouth, who had visited Jerusalem and Rome, and to whom (as well as to his companions) the pope had been so kind as to give certain Roman curiosities, such as indulgences, *a culpâ et a pœnâ*. Ships laden with his manufactures every year quitted London for foreign countries. He had formerly attended Colet's preaching at St Paul's, and from the year 1515 he had known

the word of God.[2] He was one of the gentlest and most obliging men
in England; he kept open house for the friends of learning and of the
gospel, and his library contained the newest publications. In putting on
Jesus Christ, Monmouth had particularly striven to put on his character;
he helped generously with his purse both priests and men of letters; he
gave forty pounds sterling to the chaplain of the Bishop of London, the
same to the king's, to the provincial of the Augustines, and to others
besides. Hugh Latimer, who sometimes dined with him, once related in
the pulpit an anecdote characteristic of the friends of the reformation
in England. Among the regular guests at Monmouth's table was one
of his poorest neighbours, a zealous Romanist, to whom his generous
host often used to lend money. One day when the pious merchant was
extolling Scripture and blaming popery, his neighbour turned pale, rose
from the table, and left the room. 'I will never set foot in his house
again', he said to his friends, 'and I will never borrow another shilling
of him.' He next went to the bishop and laid an information against
his benefactor. Monmouth forgave him, and tried to bring him back;
but the neighbour constantly turned out of his way. Once, however,
they met in a street so narrow that he could not escape. 'I will pass by
without looking at him', said the Romanist turning away his head. But
Monmouth went straight to him, took him by the hand, and said affectionately: 'Neighbour, what wrong have I done you?' and he continued
to speak to him with so much love, that the poor man fell on his knees,
burst into tears, and begged his forgiveness. Such was the spirit which,
at the very outset, animated the work of the reformation in England: it
was acceptable to God, and found favour with the people.

Monmouth, being edified by Tyndale's sermons, inquired into his
means of living. 'I have none', replied he, 'but I hope to enter into the
bishop's service.' This was before his visit to Tunstall. When Tyndale saw
all his hopes frustrated, he went to Monmouth and told him everything.
'Come and live with me', said the wealthy merchant, 'and there labour.'
God did to Tyndale according to his faith. Simple, frugal, devoted to
work, he studied night and day; and wishing to guard his mind against

---

[2] The rich man began to be a Scripture man. Latimer's *Sermons* (Parker Society),
p. 440.

'being overcharged with surfeiting', he refused the delicacies of his patron's table, and would take nothing but sodden meat and small beer. It would even seem that he carried simplicity in dress almost too far. By his conversation and his works, he shed over the house of his patron the mild light of the Christian virtues, so that Monmouth's love for him steadily increased.

Tyndale was advancing in his work when John Fryth, the mathematician of King's College, Cambridge, arrived in London. It is probable that Tyndale, feeling the want of an associate, had invited him. United like Luther and Melanchthon, the two friends held many precious conversations together. 'I will consecrate my life wholly to the church of Jesus Christ', said Fryth. 'To be a good man, you must give a great part of yourself to your parents, a greater part to your country; but the greatest part of all to the church of the Lord.' – 'The people should know the word of God', they unitedly said. 'The interpretation of the gospel, without the intervention of councils or popes, is sufficient to create a saving faith in the heart.' They shut themselves up in the little room in Monmouth's house, and translated chapter after chapter from the Greek into plain English. The Bishop of London knew nothing of the work going on a few yards from him, and everything was succeeding to Tyndale's wishes when it was interrupted by an unforeseen circumstance.

Bishop Longland, the persecutor of the Lincolnshire Christians, did not confine his activity within the limits of his diocese; he besieged the king, the cardinal, and the queen with his cruel importunities, using Wolsey's influence with Henry, and Henry's with Wolsey. 'His Majesty', he wrote to the cardinal, 'shows in this holy dispute as much goodness as zeal … yet, be pleased to urge him to overthrow God's enemies.' And then turning to the king, the confessor said, to spur him on: 'The cardinal is about to fulminate the greater excommunication against all who possess Luther's works or hold his opinions, and to make the booksellers sign a bond before the magistrates, not to sell *heretical* books.' 'Wonderful!' replied Henry with a sneer, 'they will fear the *magisterial* bond, I think, more than the *clerical* excommunication.' And yet the consequences of the 'clerical' excommunication were to be very positive; whosoever persevered in his offence was to be pursued by the law *ad ignem*, even to the fire. At last the confessor applied to the queen: 'We cannot be sure of restraining the press', he said to her. 'These wretched books come to us from Germany, France, and the Low Countries; and are even printed in the very midst of us. Madam, we must train and prepare skilful men, such as are able to discuss the controverted points, so that the laity, struck on the one hand by well-developed arguments, and frightened by the fear of punishment on the other, may be kept in obedience.' In the bishop's system, 'fire' was to be the complement of Roman learning. The essential idea of Jesuitism is already visible in this conception of Henry VIII's confessor. That system is the natural development of Romanism.

Tunstall, urged forward by Longland, and desirous of showing himself as holy a churchman as he had once been a skilful statesman and elegant scholar – Tunstall, the friend of Erasmus, began to persecute. Like Longland, he would have feared to shed blood; but there are measures which torture the mind and not the body, and which the most moderate men fear not to make use of. John Higgins, Henry Chambers, Thomas Eglestone, a priest named Edmund Spilman, and some other Christians in London, used to meet and read portions of the Bible in English; they even asserted publicly that 'Luther had more learning in his little finger than all the doctors in England in their whole bodies.' The bishop ordered these rebels to be arrested: he flattered and alarmed them, threatening them with a cruel death (which he would hardly have inflicted on them), and by these skilful practices reduced them to silence.

Tyndale, who witnessed this persecution, feared lest the stake should interrupt his labour. If those who read a few fragments of Scripture were threatened with death, what would he not have to endure who was translating the whole? His friends entreated him to withdraw from the bishop's pursuit. 'Alas!' he exclaimed, 'is there then no place where I can translate the Bible? ... It is not the bishop's house alone that is closed against me, but all England.'[3]

He then made a great sacrifice. Since there is no place in his own country where he can translate the word of God, he will go and seek one among the nations of the Continent. It is true the people are unknown to him; he is without resources; perhaps persecution and even death await him there. ... It matters not! Some time must elapse before it is

---

[3] But also that there was no place to do it in all England. Tyndale, *Doctrinal Treatises*, p. 396.

known what he is doing, and perhaps he will have been able to translate the Bible. He turned his eyes towards Germany. 'God does not destine us to a quiet life here below', he said.[4] 'If he calls us to peace on the part of Jesus Christ, he calls us to war on the part of the world.'

There lay at that moment in the river Thames a vessel loading for Hamburg. Monmouth gave Tyndale ten pounds sterling for his voyage, and other friends contributed a like amount. He left the half of this sum in the hands of his benefactor to provide for his future wants, and prepared to quit London, where he had spent a year. Rejected by his fellow countrymen, persecuted by the clergy, and carrying with him only his New Testament and his ten pounds, he went on board the ship, shaking off the dust of his feet, according to his Master's precept, and that dust fell back on the priests of England. He was indignant (says the chronicler) against those coarse monks, covetous priests, and pompous prelates, who were waging an impious war against God. 'What a trade is that of the priests!' he said in one of his later writings; 'they want money for everything: money for baptism, money for churchings, for weddings, for buryings, for images, brotherhoods, penances, soul-masses, bells, organs, chalices, copes, surplices, ewers, censers, and all manner of ornaments. Poor sheep! The parson shears, the vicar shaves, the parish priest polls, the friar scrapes, the indulgence seller pares ... we lack but a butcher to pull off the skin. He will not leave you long. Why are the prelates dressed in red? To signify that they are ready every hour to suffer martyrdom for the testimony of God's word. But what a false sign is this, when because of them no man dares once open his mouth to ask a question concerning God's word; if he does so they are ready to burn him.' Scourge of states, devastators of kingdoms, the priests take away not only holy Scripture, but also prosperity and peace; but of their councils is no layman; reigning over all, they obey nobody; and making all concur to their own greatness, they conspire against every kingdom.'

No kingdom was to be more familiar than England with the conspiracies of the papacy of which Tyndale spoke; and yet none was to free itself more irrevocably from the power of Rome.

---

[4] We be not called to a soft living. Tyndale, *Practice of Prelates, Works*, ii, p. 28.

Yet Tyndale was leaving the shores of his native land, and as he turned his eyes towards the new countries, hope revived in his heart. He was going to be free, and he would use his liberty to deliver the word of God, so long held captive. 'The priests', he said one day, 'when they had slain Christ, set pole-axes[5] to keep him in his sepulchre, that he should not rise again; even so have our priests buried the testament of God, and all their study is to keep it down, that it rise not again. But the hour of the Lord is come, and nothing can hinder the word of God, as nothing could hinder Jesus Christ of old from issuing from the tomb.'

And so Tyndale left England and sailed for Germany. A poor man in material things, he was soon to send back to his countrymen, even from the banks of the Elbe, the book which was to lead many of them to become 'rich in faith and heirs of the kingdom which God has promised to them that love him.' With what greater boon can a man bless his native land?

The lines which appear beneath Tyndale's portrait preserved in Hertford College, Oxford, aptly describe the reformer's courage and purpose:

> *Hac ut luce tuas dispergam Roma tenebras*
> *Sponte ex terris ero sponte sacrificium.*[6]

---

[5] [An allusion to the pole-axes which were carried before papal legates *a latere*.]
[6] That light o'er all thy darkness, Rome,
  In triumph might arise,
  An exile freely I become,
  Freely a sacrifice.

CHAPTER EIGHT

Bluff Hugh Latimer

(1485–1524)

This ship did not bear away all the hopes of England. A society of
Christians had been formed at Cambridge, of which Bilney was
the centre. He now knew no other canon law than Scripture,
and had found a new master, 'the Holy Spirit of Christ', says an historian.
Although he was naturally timid, and often suffered from the exhaustion
brought on by his fasts and vigils, there was in his language a life,
liberty, and strength, strikingly in contrast with his sickly appearance.
He desired to draw to the knowledge of God, all who came nigh him;
and by degrees, the rays of the gospel sun, which was then rising in the
firmament of Christendom, pierced the ancient windows of the colleges,
and illuminated the solitary chambers of certain of the Masters and
Fellows. Master Thomas Arthur, Master Thistle of Pembroke Hall, and
Master Stafford, were among the first to join Bilney. George Stafford,
professor of divinity, was a man of deep learning and holy life, clear
and precise in his teaching. He was admired by everyone in Cambridge,
so that his conversion, like that of his friends, spread alarm among the
partisans of the schoolmen. But a conversion still more striking than this
was destined to give the English reformation a champion more illustrious than either Stafford or Bilney.

There was in Cambridge, at that time, a priest notorious for his ardent
fanaticism. In the processions, amidst the pomp, prayers, and chanting
of the train, none could fail to notice a master of arts, about thirty years
of age, who, with erect head, carried proudly the university cross. Hugh
Latimer, for such was his name, combined a biting humour with an
impetuous disposition and indefatigable zeal, and was very quick in

ridiculing the faults of his adversaries. There was more wit and raillery in his fanaticism than can often be found in such characters. He followed the friends of the word of God into the colleges and houses where they used to meet, debated with them, and pressed them to abandon their faith. He was a second Saul, and was soon to resemble the apostle of the Gentiles in another respect.

He first saw light about the year 1485, at Thurcaston in the county of Leicester. Hugh's father was an honest yeoman; and, accompanied by one of his six sisters, the little boy had often tended in the pastures the five score sheep belonging to the farm, or driven home to his mother the thirty cows it was her business to milk.[1] In 1497, the Cornish rebels, under Lord Audley, having encamped at Blackheath, our farmer had donned his rusty armour, and, mounting his horse, responded to the summons of the Crown. Hugh was present at his departure, and, as if he had wished to take his little part in the battle, he had buckled the straps of his father's armour.[2] Fifty-two years afterwards he recalled this circumstance to mind in a sermon preached before King Edward VI. His father's house was always open to the neighbours; and no poor man ever turned away from the door without having received alms. The old man brought up his family in the love of men and in the fear of God and, having remarked with joy the precocious understanding of his son, he had him educated in the country schools, and then sent to Cambridge. This was in 1506, shortly after Luther entered the Augustine monastery of Erfurt.

The son of the Leicestershire yeoman was lively, fond of pleasure, and of cheerful conversation, and mingled frequently in the amusements of his fellow students. One day, as they were dining together, one of the party exclaimed: *Nil melius quam lætari et facere bene!* – 'There is nothing better than to be merry and to do well.'[3] – 'A vengeance on that *bene!*' replied a monk of impudent mien; 'I wish it were beyond the sea;[4] it mars all the rest. I like to be merry, and I like to do, but I love not to do well.' Young Latimer was much surprised at the remark: 'I understand it

[1] Latimer's *Sermons* (Parker Society), p. 101.
[2] I can remember that I buckled his harness. *Ibid.*
[3] Eccles. 3:12.
[4] Latimer's *Sermons*, p. 153.

now', said he; 'that will be a heavy *bene* to these monks when they have
to render God an account of their lives.'

Latimer, having become more serious, threw himself heart and
soul into the practices of superstition, and a very bigoted old cousin
undertook to instruct him in them. One day, when one of their relations
lay dead, she said to him: 'Now we must drive out the devil. Take this
holy taper, my child, and pass it over the body, first longways and then
athwart, so as always to make the sign of the cross.'

But the scholar performing this exorcism very awkwardly, his aged
cousin snatched the candle from his hand, exclaiming angrily: 'It's a
great pity your father spends so much money on your studies: he will
never make anything of you.'

This prophecy was not fulfilled. While still an undergraduate he
became Fellow of Clare Hall in 1510, and took his Master's degree in
1514. His classical studies being ended, he began to study divinity.
Duns Scotus, Aquinas, and Hugo de Sancto Victore were his favourite
authors. The practical side of things, however, engaged him more than
the speculative; and he was more distinguished in Cambridge for his
asceticism and enthusiasm than for his learning. He attached importance to the merest trifles. As the missal directs that water should be
mingled with the sacramental wine, often while saying Mass he would
be troubled in his conscience for fear he had not put in sufficient water.
This remorse never left him a moment's tranquillity during the service.
In him, as in many others, attachment to puerile ordinances occupied in
his heart the place of faith in the great truths. With him, the cause of the
church was the cause of God, and he respected Thomas Becket at least
as much as St Paul. 'I was then', said he, 'as obstinate a papist as any in
England.' Luther said a similar thing of himself.

The fervent Latimer soon observed that everybody around him was
not equally zealous with himself for the ceremonies of the church. He
watched with surprise certain young members of the university who,
forsaking the doctors of the school, met daily to read and search into
the holy Scriptures. People sneered at them in Cambridge: 'It is only the
sophists', was the cry; but raillery was not enough for Latimer. One day
he entered the room where these *sophists* were assembled, and begged

them to cease studying the Bible. All his entreaties were useless. Can we be astonished at it? said Latimer to himself. Don't we see even the tutors setting an example to these stray sheep? There is Master Stafford, the most illustrious professor in English universities, devoting his time *ad Biblia*, like Luther at Wittenberg, and explaining the Scriptures according to the Hebrew and Greek texts! while the delighted students celebrate in bad verse the doctor,

Qui Paulum explicuit rite et evangelium.[5]

That young people should occupy themselves with these new doctrines was conceivable, but that a doctor of divinity should do so – what a disgrace! Latimer therefore determined to attack Stafford. He insulted him;[6] he entreated the youth of Cambridge to abandon the professor and his heretical teaching; he attended the hall in which the doctor taught, made signs of impatience during the lesson, and cavilled at it after leaving the school. He even preached in public against the learned doctor. But it seemed to him that Cambridge and England were struck blind: true, the clergy approved of Latimer's proceedings – nay, praised them; and yet they did nothing. To console him, however, he was named cross-bearer to the university, and we have already seen him discharging this duty.

Latimer desired to show himself worthy of such an honour. He had left the students to attack Stafford; and he now left Stafford for a more illustrious adversary. But this attack led him to someone *that was stronger than he.* In 1524 on the occasion of receiving the degree of bachelor of theology he had to deliver a Latin discourse in the presence of the university; Latimer chose for his subject *Philip Melanchthon and his doctrines.* Had not this daring heretic presumed to say quite recently that the fathers of the church have altered the sense of Scripture? Had he not asserted that, like those rocks whose various colours are imparted to the polypus which clings to them, so the doctors of the church give each their own opinion in the passages they explain? And finally had he not discovered a new touchstone (it is thus he styles the holy Scripture) by which we must test the sentences even of St Thomas Aquinas?

[5] Who has explained to us the true sense of St Paul and of the gospel. Strype's *Eccles. Memorials*, i, p. 74.

[6] Most spitefully railing against him. Foxe, *Acts*, vii, p. 437.

Latimer's discourse made a great impression. At last (said his hearers) England, nay Cambridge, will furnish a champion for the church that will confront the Wittenberg doctors, and save the vessel of our Lord. But very different was to be the result. There was among the hearers one man almost hidden through his small stature: it was Bilney. For some time he had been watching Latimer's movements, and his zeal interested him, though it was a zeal without knowledge. Bilney's energy was not great, but he possessed a delicate tact, a skilful discernment of character which enabled him to distinguish error, and to select the fittest method for combating it. Accordingly, a chronicler styles him 'a trier-out of Satan's subtleties, called of God to detect the bad money that the enemy was circulating through the church'.[7] Bilney easily detected Latimer's sophisms, but at the same time loved his person, and conceived the design of winning him to the gospel. But how to manage it? The prejudiced Latimer would not even listen to the evangelical Bilney. The latter reflected, prayed, and at last planned a very candid and very strange plot, which led to one of the most astonishing conversions recorded in history.

He went to the college where Latimer resided. 'For the love of God', he said to him, 'be pleased to hear my confession.'[8] The *heretic* prayed to make confession to the *Catholic*: what a singular fact! My discourse against Melanchthon has no doubt converted him, said Latimer to himself. Was he not once among the number of the most pious zealots? His pale face, his wasted frame, and his humble look are clear signs that he ought to belong to the ascetics of Catholicism. If he turns back, all will turn back with him, and the reaction will be complete at Cambridge. The ardent Latimer eagerly yielded to Bilney's request, and the latter, kneeling before the cross-bearer, related to him with touching simplicity the anguish he had once felt in his soul, the efforts he had made to remove it; their unprofitableness so long as he determined to follow the precepts of the church and, lastly, the peace he had felt when he believed that Jesus Christ is *the Lamb of God that taketh away the sin of the world*. He described to Latimer the spirit of adoption he had

---

[7] Foxe, *Acts*, vii, p. 438.
[8] Latimer's *Sermons* (Parker Society), p. 334.

received, and the happiness he experienced in being able now to call God his Father. ... Latimer, who expected to receive a confession, listened without mistrust. His heart was opened, and the voice of the pious Bilney penetrated it without obstacle. From time to time the confessor would have chased away the new thoughts which came crowding into his bosom; but the penitent continued. His language, at once so simple and so lively, entered like a two-edged sword. Bilney was not without assistance in his work. A new, a strange witness – the Holy Ghost[9] – was speaking in Latimer's soul. He learned from God to know God: he received a new heart. At length grace prevailed: the penitent rose up, but Latimer remained seated, absorbed in thought. The strong cross-bearer contended in vain against the words of the feeble Bilney. Like Saul on the way to Damascus, he was conquered, and his conversion, like the apostle's, was instantaneous. He stammered out a few words; Bilney drew near him with love, and God scattered the darkness which still obscured his mind. He saw Jesus Christ as the only Saviour given to man: he contemplated and adored him. 'I learnt more by this confession', he said afterwards, 'than in many years before. From that time forward I began to smell the word of God, and forsook the doctors of the schools and such fooleries.'[10] It was not the penitent but the confessor who received absolution. Latimer viewed with horror the obstinate war he had waged against God; he wept bitterly; but Bilney consoled him. 'Brother', said he, 'though your sins be as scarlet, they shall be white as snow.' These two young men, then locked in their solitary chamber at Cambridge, were one day to mount the scaffold for that Divine Master whose Spirit was teaching them. But one of them before going to the stake was first to sit on an episcopal throne.

Latimer was changed. The energy of his character was tempered by a Divine unction. Becoming a believer, he ceased to be superstitious. Instead of persecuting Jesus Christ, he became a zealous seeker after him.[11] Instead of cavilling and railing, he showed himself meek and

[9] He was through the good Spirit of God so touched. Foxe, *Acts*, vii, p. 438.
[10] Latimer's *Sermons*, pp. 334-5.
[11] Whereas before he was an enemy and almost a persecutor of Christ, he was now a zealous seeker after him. Foxe, *Acts*, vii, p. 438.

gentle;[12] instead of frequenting company, he sought solitude, studying the Scriptures and advancing in true theology. He threw off the old man and put on the new. He waited upon Stafford, begged forgiveness for the insult he had offered him, and then regularly attended his lectures, being subjugated more by this doctor's angelic conversation[13] than by his learning. But it was Bilney's society Latimer cultivated most. They conversed together daily, took frequent walks together into the country, and occasionally rested at a place long known as 'the Heretics' Hill'.[14]

So striking a conversion gave fresh vigour to the evangelical movement. Hitherto Bilney and Latimer had been the most zealous champions of the two opposite causes; the one despised, the other honoured; the weak man had conquered the strong. This action of the Spirit of God was not thrown away upon Cambridge. Latimer's conversion, as of old the miracles of the apostles, struck men's minds; and was it not in truth a miracle? All the youth of the university ran to hear Bilney preach. He proclaimed 'Jesus Christ as he who, having tasted death, has delivered his people from the penalty of sin.' While the doctors of the schools (even the most pious of them) laid most stress upon *man's* part in the work of redemption, Bilney on the contrary emphasized the other term, namely, *God's* part. This doctrine of grace, said his adversaries, annuls the sacraments, and contradicts baptismal regeneration. The selfishness which forms the essence of fallen humanity rejected the evangelical doctrine, and felt that to accept it was to be lost. 'Many listened with the *left ear*', to use an expression of Bilney's; 'like Malchus, having their *right ear* cut off'; and they filled the university with their complaints.

But Bilney did not allow himself to be stopped. The idea of eternity had seized on his mind, and perhaps he still retained some feeble relics of the exaggerations of asceticism. He condemned every kind of recreation, even when innocent. Music in the churches seemed to him a mockery of God; and when Thurlby, who was afterwards a bishop, and who as a scholar lived at Cambridge in the room below his, used to begin playing on the recorder, Bilney would fall on his knees and pour out his soul in

[12] *Ibid.*

[13] A man of a very perfect life and angelic conversation. Becon's *Works* (Parker Society), p. 425.

[14] Foxe, *Acts*, vii, p. 452.

prayer: to him prayer was the sweetest melody. He prayed that the lively faith of the children of God might in all England be substituted for the vanity and pride of the priests. He believed – he prayed – he waited. His waiting was not to be in vain.

Latimer trod in his footsteps: the transformation of his soul was going on; and the more fanaticism he had shown for the sacerdotal system, which places salvation in the hands of the priest, the more zeal he now showed for the evangelical system, which places it in the hands of Christ. He saw that if the churches must needs have ministers, it is not because they require a human mediation, but from the necessity of a regular preaching of the word and a steady direction of the flock; and accordingly he would have wished to call the servant of the Lord *minister* (ὑπηρέτης or διάκονος τοῦ λόγου), and not *priest* (ἱερεύς or *sacerdos*). In his view, it was not the imposition of hands by the bishop that gave grace, but grace which authorized the imposition of hands. He considered activity to be one of the essential features of the gospel ministry. 'It is commonly seen', he said, 'that fishers and hunters be very painful people both: they spare no labour to catch their game. ... Therefore our Saviour chose fishers, because of these properties, that they should be painful and spare no labour: and then that they should be greedy to catch men, and to take them with the net of God's word, to turn the people from wickedness to God. Ye see by daily experience what pain fishers and hunters take; how the fisher watcheth the day and night at his net, and is ever ready to take all such fishes that he can get, and that come in his way. So likewise the hunter runneth hither and thither after his game: leapeth over hedges, and creepeth through rough bushes; and all this labour he esteemeth for nothing because he is so desirous to obtain his prey and catch his venison. So all our prelates, bishops, and curates, parsons and vicars, should be as painful and greedy in casting their nets: that is to say, in preaching God's word; in shewing unto the people the way to everlasting life; in exhorting them to leave their sins and wickedness ... such a charge they have. But the most of them set aside this fishing; they put away this net; they take other business in hand; they will rather be surveyors or receivers, or clerks in the kitchen, than to cast out this net: they have the living of fishers, but

they fish not, they are otherways occupied.'[15] He regarded all confidence
in human strength as a remnant of paganism. 'Let us not do', he said, 'as
the haughty Ajax, who said to his father as he went to battle: Without
the help of God I am able to fight, and I will get the victory with mine
own strength.'

The reformation had gained in Latimer a very different man from
Bilney. He had not so much discernment and prudence perhaps, but he
had more energy and eloquence. What Tyndale was to be for England by
his writings, Latimer was to be by his discourses. The tenderness of his
conscience, the warmth of his zeal, and the vivacity of his understanding,
were enlisted in the service of Jesus Christ; and, if at times he was carried
too far by the liveliness of his wit, it only shows that the reformers were
not *saints*, but sanctified men. 'He was one of the first', says an historian,
'who, in the days of King Henry VIII, set himself to preach the gospel
in the truth and simplicity of it.' He preached in Latin to the clergy, and
in English to the people. He boldly placed the law with its curses before
his hearers, and then conjured them to flee to the Saviour of the world.
The same zeal which he had employed in saying Mass, he now employed
in preaching the true sacrifice of Christ. He said one day: 'If one man
had committed all the sins since Adam, you may be sure he should be
punished with the same horror of death, in such a sort as all men in the
world should have suffered. ... Such was the pain Christ endured. ... If
our Saviour had committed all the sins of the world; all that I for my
part have done, all that you for your part have done, and that any man
else hath done; if he had done all this himself, his agony that he suffered
should have been no greater nor grievouser than it was. ... Believe in
Jesus Christ, and you shall overcome death. ... But, alas!' said he at
another time, 'the devil, by the help of that Italian bishop yonder, his
chaplain, has laboured by all means that he might frustrate the death of
Christ and the merits of his passion.'

Thus began in British Christendom the preaching of the cross. The
reformation was not the substitution of the Catholicism of the First Ages
for the popery of the Middle Ages: it was a revival of the preaching of St
Paul, and thus it was that on hearing Latimer everyone exclaimed with
rapture: 'Of a *Saul*, God has made him a very *Paul*.'

---

[15] A sermon on Matt. 4:18-20.

To the inward power of faith, the Cambridge evangelists added the outward power of a godly life. Saul become Paul, the strong, the ardent Latimer, had need of action; and Bilney, the weak and humble Bilney, in delicate health, observing a severe diet, taking ordinarily but one meal a day, and never sleeping more than four hours, absorbed in prayer and in the study of the word, displayed at that time all the energy of charity. These two friends devoted themselves not merely to the easy labours of Christian beneficence; but caring little for that formal Christianity so often met with among the comfortable classes, they explored the gloomy cells of the madhouse to bear the sweet and subtle voice of the gospel to the infuriate maniacs. They visited the miserable lazar houses outside the city, in which poor lepers and other diseased persons were dwelling; they carefully tended them, wrapped them in clean sheets, and wooed them to be converted to Christ. The gates of the jail at Cambridge were opened to them, and they announced to the poor prisoners that word which gives liberty. Some were converted by it. One such is mentioned by Latimer in his Fifth Sermon preached long afterwards before King Edward VI: 'This woman, when she came to prison, was all on her beads, and nothing else, a popish woman, and savoured not of Jesus Christ. In process (of time) she tasted that the Lord is gracious. She had such a savour, such a sweetness and feeling that she thought it long to the day of execution. She was with Christ already, as touching faith, longing to depart and to be with him. The word of God had so wrought in her.'

Thus commenced the evangelical ministry of Hugh Latimer, afterwards Bishop of Worcester, one of the finest types of the reformation in England! But he had many adversaries. In the front rank were the priests, who spared no endeavours to retain souls in bondage. 'Beware', said Latimer to the new converts, 'lest robbers overtake you, and plunge you into the pope's prison of purgatory.' After these came the sons and favourites of the aristocracy, worldly and frivolous students, who felt little disposition to listen to the gospel. 'By yeomen's sons the faith of Christ is and hath been chiefly maintained in the church',[16] said Latimer. 'Is this realm taught by rich men's sons? No, no; read the chronicles; ye shall find sometime noblemen's sons which have been unpreaching

---

[16] Latimer's *Sermons*, p. 102.

bishops and prelates, but ye shall find none of them learned men.' He would have desired a mode of election which placed in the Christian pulpit, not the richest and most fashionable men, but the ablest and most pious. This important reform was reserved for other days. Lastly, the evangelists of Cambridge came into collision with the *brutality* of many, to use Latimer's own expression. 'What need have we of universities and schools?' said the members of this class. The Holy Ghost 'will give us always what to say'. – 'We must trust in the Holy Ghost', replied Latimer, 'but not presume on the Holy Ghost. If you will not maintain schools and universities, you shall have a *brutality*. Preaching must not be allowed to decay: for surely, if preaching decay, ignorance and brutishness will enter again.'[17] In this manner the reformation restored to Cambridge gravity and knowledge, along with truth and charity.

Yet Bilney and Latimer often turned their eyes towards Oxford, and wondered how the light would be able to penetrate there. Wolsey provided for that. A Cambridge master of arts, John Clark, a conscientious man, of tender heart, great prudence, and unbounded devotion to his duty, had been enlightened by the word of God. Wolsey, who since 1523 had been seeking everywhere for distinguished scholars to adorn his new college, invited Clark among the first. This doctor, desirous of bearing to Oxford the light which God had given Cambridge, immediately began to deliver a course of divinity lectures, to hold conferences, and to preach in his eloquent manner. He taught every day. Among the graduates and students who followed him was Anthony Dalaber, a young man of simple but profound feeling, who while listening to him had experienced in his heart the regenerating power of the gospel. Overflowing with the happiness which the knowledge of Jesus Christ imparted to him, he went to the cardinal's college, knocked at Clark's door, and said: 'Father, allow me never to quit you more!' The teacher, beholding the young disciple's enthusiasm, loved him, but thought it his duty to try him: 'Anthony', said he, 'you know not what you ask. My teaching is now pleasant to you, but the time will come when God will lay the cross of persecution on you; you will be dragged before bishops; your name will be covered with shame in the world, and all who love

---

[17] *Ibid.*, p. 269.

you will be heartbroken on account of you. … Then, my friend, you will regret that you ever knew me.'

Anthony believing himself rejected, and unable to bear the idea of returning to the barren instructions of the priests, fell on his knees, and weeping bitterly, exclaimed: 'For the tender mercy of God, turn me not away.' Touched by his sorrow, Clark folded him in his arms, kissed him, and with flowing tears exclaimed: 'The Lord Almighty give thee what thou askest! … Take me for thy father, I take thee for my son in Christ.' From that hour Anthony, all joy, was like Timothy at the feet of Paul. He united a quick understanding with tender affections. When any of the students had not attended Clark's conferences, the master commissioned his disciple to visit them weekly, to inquire into their doubts, and to impart to them his instructions. 'This exercise did me much good', said Dalaber, 'and I made great progress in the understanding of Scripture.'

Thus the kingdom of God, which consists not in forms, but in the power of the Spirit, was set up in Cambridge and Oxford. The Lord Christ was building his church on himself the Rock. His work was being set at nought of the foolish builders of the age, the worthlessness of whose hay, wood, and stubble was being daily revealed. The truth which is mighty, and must prevail over every lie, gigantic though that lie may be, was becoming the theme of attraction. The yeoman and the scholar were alike being drawn to the only true God and Jesus Christ whom he had sent. The centres of learning, the palaces of the bishops, the seats of the mighty, were being compelled to hear the trumpet blasts of the Divine word. It was as though the hosts of the Lord were marching around the all-but-impregnable walls of Antichrist's citadel, bearing in their van the ark of truth. Certainly the adversaries were many and strong, but the Lord mighty in battle was about to do, yea was already doing, great things. The Lord Omnipotent was with his Israel, and the shout of a king was among them. Clouds and darkness might be round about him, but judgment and truth were the habitation of his throne. Evil had been arraigned and challenged in England as on the continent of Europe. In the womb of the unknown morrow lay the church of the free.

CHAPTER NINE

Wolsey's Hopes and Fears

(1523–1525)

Adrian VI died on 14 September 1523, before the end of the second year of his pontificate. Wolsey thought himself pope. At length he would no longer be the favourite only, but the arbiter of the kings of the earth; and his genius, for which England was too narrow, would have Europe and the world for its stage. Already revolving gigantic projects in his mind, the future pope dreamt of the destruction of heresy in the West, and in the East the cessation of the Greek schism, and new crusades to replant the cross on the walls of Constantinople. There is nothing that Wolsey would not have dared undertake when once seated on the throne of Catholicism, and the pontificates of Gregory VII and Innocent III would have been eclipsed by that of the Ipswich butcher's son. The cardinal reminded Henry of his promise, and the very next day the king signed a letter addressed to the emperor Charles V, the nephew of Catherine, Queen of England.

Believing himself sure of the emperor, Wolsey turned all his exertions to the side of Rome. 'The legate of England', said Henry's ambassadors to the cardinals, 'is the very man for the present time. He is the only one thoroughly acquainted with the interests and wants of Christendom, and strong enough to provide for them. He is all kindness, and will share his dignities and wealth among all the prelates who support him.'

But Julio de Medici, the titular Bishop of Worcester, himself aspired to the papacy and, as eighteen cardinals were devoted to him, the election could not take place without his support. 'Rather than yield', said he in the conclave, 'I would die in this prison.' A month passed away, and nothing was done. New intrigues were then resorted to: there were cabals for Wolsey, cabals for Medici. The cardinals were besieged:

> Into their midst, by many a secret path,
> Creeps sly intrigue.

At length, on 18 November 1523, the people collected under their windows, shouting: 'No foreign pope.' After forty-nine days of debating, Julio was elected and, according to his own expression, 'bent his head beneath the yoke of apostolic servitude'. He took the name of Clement VII.

Wolsey was exasperated. It was in vain that he presented himself before St Peter's chair at each vacancy: a more active or more fortunate rival always reached it before him. Master of England, and the most influential of European diplomatists, he saw men preferred to him who were his inferiors. This election was an event which favoured the reformation in England. Wolsey as pope would, humanly speaking, have tightened the cords which already bound England so closely to Rome; but Wolsey, rejected, could hardly fail to throw himself into tortuous paths which would perhaps contribute to the emancipation of the church. He became more crafty than ever; declared to Henry that the new election was quite in conformity with his wishes,[1] and hastened to congratulate the new pope. He wrote to Dr Pace at Rome: 'This election, I assure you, is as much to the king's and my rejoicing, consolation, and gladness, as possibly may be devised or imagined. ... Ye shall show unto His Holiness what joy, comfort, and gladness it is both to the King's Highness and me to perceive that once in our lives it hath pleased God of his great goodness to provide such a pastor unto his church, as His Grace and I have long inwardly desired; who for his virtue, wisdom, and other high and notable qualities, we have always reputed the most able and worthy person to be called to that dignity.' But the pope, divining his competitor's vexation, sent the king a golden rose, and a ring to Wolsey. 'I am sorry', he said as he drew it from his finger, 'that I cannot present it to His Eminence in person.' Clement moreover conferred on him the quality of legate *for life* – an office which had hitherto been temporary only. Thus the popedom and England embraced each other, and nothing appeared more distant than that Christian revolution which was destined very shortly to emancipate Britain from the tutelage of the Vatican.

---

[1] I take God to witness, I am more joyous thereof, than if it had fortuned upon my person. Wolsey to Henry VIII. Burnet, Records (Lond. 1841), p. cccxxviii.

Wolsey's disappointed ambition made him suspend the proceedings of the clergy at Cambridge. He had revenge in his heart, and cared not to persecute his fellow countrymen merely to please his rival; and besides, like several popes, he had a certain fondness for learning. To send a few Lollards to prison was a matter of no difficulty; but learned doctors ... this required a closer examination. Hence he gave Rome a sign of independence. And yet it was not specially against the pope that he began to entertain sinister designs: Clement had been more fortunate than himself; but that was no reason why he should be angry with him. ... Charles V was the offender, and Wolsey swore a deadly hatred against him. Resolved to strike, he sought only the place where he could inflict the severest blow. To obtain his end, he resolved to dissemble his passion, and to distil drop by drop into Henry's mind that mortal hatred against Charles, which gave fresh energy to his activity.

Charles discovered the indignation that lay hid under Wolsey's apparent mildness and, wishing to retain Henry's alliance, he made more pressing advances to the king. Having deprived the minister of a tiara, he resolved to offer the king a crown: this was, indeed, a noble compensation! 'You are King of France', the emperor said, 'and I undertake to win your kingdom for you. Only send an ambassador to Italy to negotiate the matter.' Wolsey, who could hardly contain his vexation, was forced to comply, in appearance at least, with the emperor's views. The king, indeed, seemed to think of nothing but his arrival at St Germain's, and commissioned Pace to visit Italy for this important business. Wolsey hoped that he would be unable to execute his commission; it was impossible to cross the Alps, for the French troops blockaded every passage. But Pace, who was one of those adventurous characters whom nothing can stop, spurred on by the thought that the king himself had sent him, determined to cross the *Col di Tenda*. On 27 July 1524 he entered the mountains, traversed precipitous passes, sometimes climbing them on all-fours, and often falling during the descent. In some places he could ride on horseback; 'but in the most part thereof I durst not either turn my horse traverse [he wrote to the king] for all the worldly riches, nor in manner look on my left hand, for the steep slope and deepness to the valley.' After this passage, which lasted six days, Pace arrived in Italy worn out by fatigue. 'If the King of England will enter France immediately by way of Normandy', said the Constable of Bourbon to him, 'I will give him leave to pluck out both my eyes if he is not master of Paris before All Saints; and when Paris is taken, he will be master of the whole kingdom.' But Wolsey, to whom these remarks were transmitted by the ambassador, slighted them, delayed furnishing the subsidies, and required certain conditions which were calculated to thwart the project. Pace, who was ardent and ever imprudent, but plain and straightforward, forgot himself, and in a moment of vexation wrote to Wolsey: 'To speak frankly, if you do not attend to these things, I shall impute to Your Grace the loss of the crown of France.' These words ruined Henry's envoy in the cardinal's mind. Was this man, who owed everything to him, trying to supplant him? … Pace in vain assured Wolsey that he should not take seriously what he had said, but the bolt had hit. Pace was associated with Charles in the cruel enmity of the minister, and he was one day to feel its terrible effects. It was not long before Wolsey was able to satisfy himself that the service Charles had desired to render the King of England was beyond the emperor's strength.

No sooner at ease on one side, than Wolsey found himself attacked on another. This man, the most powerful among king's favourites, felt at this time the first breath of disfavour blow over him. On the pontifical throne, he would no doubt have attempted a reform after the manner of Sixtus V; and wishing to rehearse on a smaller stage, and regenerate after his own fashion the Catholic Church in England, he submitted the monasteries to a strict inquisition, patronized the instruction of youth, and was the first to set a great example, by suppressing certain religious houses whose revenues he applied to his college in Oxford.[2] Thomas Cromwell, his right-hand man, displayed much skill and industry in this business, and thus, under the orders of a cardinal of the Roman Church, made his first campaign in a war of which he was in later days to hold the chief command. Wolsey and Cromwell, by their reforms, drew down the hatred of certain monks, priests, and noblemen, always the very humble servants of the clerical party. The latter accused the cardinal of not having estimated the monasteries at their just value, and

---

[2] [Cardinal College: afterwards renamed Christ Church.]

of having, in certain cases, encroached on the royal jurisdiction. Henry, whom the loss of the crown of France had put in a bad humour, resolved, for the first time, not to spare his minister: 'There are loud murmurs throughout this kingdom', he said to him; 'it is asserted that your new college at Oxford is only a convenient cloak to hide your malversations.' – 'God forbid', replied the cardinal, 'that this virtuous foundation at Oxford, undertaken for the good of my poor soul, should be raised *ex rapinis*! [out of plunderings]. But, above all, God forbid that I should ever encroach upon your royal authority.' He then cunningly insinuated, that by his will he left all his property to the king. Henry was satisfied: he had a share in the business.

Events of very different importance drew the king's attention to another quarter. The two armies, of the Empire and of France, were met for battle before Pavia, in the Plain of Lombardy. Wolsey, who openly gave his right hand to Charles V, and secretly his left to Francis, repeated to his master: 'If the emperor gains the victory, are you not his ally? and if Francis, am I not in secret communication with him?' 'Thus', added the cardinal, 'whatever happens, Your Highness will have great cause to give thanks to Almighty God.'

On 24 February 1525 the battle of Pavia was fought. The army of Francis I was utterly routed. The king himself was taken prisoner to Madrid. 'Of all things', he wrote to his mother, 'nothing remains to me but honour and life.' Charles V, who celebrated his twenty-fifth birthday on the day of the battle, was virtually emperor of the West. England apart, he was supreme over all. Henry and Wolsey had in every sense been playing a double game. Professing friendship for Charles, and bound to support his cause by the Treaty of Windsor of August 1522, they had at the same time been negotiating with Charles' enemy, Francis I of France. The agent employed in the negotiations was Giovanni Giovacchino di Passano, known to the English court as John Joachim, who passed for a merchant of Bologna and lived in concealment at Blackfriars. In fact, he was a Genoese attached to the household of Louise, mother of the French king and, after Pavia, regent of France until the release of her son from custody at Madrid. De Praet, the imperial ambassador in London, had secret knowledge of Joachim's presence in the city, and his master was not unaware that Henry and Wolsey were not to be trusted. He was indeed much too knowledgeable of the diplomatic situation to be deceived by them. When, after Pavia, Wolsey urged upon him a joint invasion of France, as a reward for which Henry was to become its king, Charles bluntly refused to consider the proposal, and for the rest of the year ignored English suggestions. Wisely so, for meanwhile Wolsey re-opened negotiations with Louise, accepted her secret present for himself of 100,000 crowns, and concluded a treaty of peace between the two countries. In March 1526, Charles released his royal prisoner, after obtaining his assent to onerous treaty terms, at the same time requiring him to surrender to him his two sons as hostages for his future good faith. To Louise Wolsey expressed the hope that Francis would feel free to repudiate his solemn promises at the first convenient opportunity. Feeling certain that Charles had obstructed his accession to the popedom, Wolsey hoped to prove to him by such actions that it was dangerous to thwart the ambitions of a cardinal and chancellor.

While diplomatic moves of great intricacy and delicacy thus occupied Wolsey's attention, he met with difficulties in home affairs, particularly in matters of finance. Foreign policy, to be effective, must be backed by adequate expenditure on armed forces. In 1523, the chancellor had himself visited the House of Commons to demand four shillings in the pound of every man's land and goods. The commons administered to him a humiliating rebuff, and voted a much smaller sum. In 1525, he demanded no less than one-sixth of the movables and incomes of the laity, and more still from the clergy. 'You desire to conquer France', said Wolsey; 'you are right. Give me then for that purpose the sixth part of your property; that is a trifle to gratify so noble an inclination.' England did not think so; this illegal demand aroused universal complaint. 'We are English and not French, freemen and not slaves', was the universal cry. Wolsey might tyrannize over the court, but not lay hands on the property of the king's subjects.

The eastern counties rose in insurrection: four thousand men were under arms in a moment; and Henry was guarded in his own palace by only a few servants. It was necessary to break down the bridges to stop the insurgents. The courtiers complained to the king; the king threw the blame on the cardinal; the cardinal laid it on the clergy, some of whom had encouraged him to impose this tax by quoting to him the example of Joseph demanding of the Egyptians the fifth part of their goods; and the clergy in their turn ascribed the insurrection to the gospellers, who (said they) were stirring up a peasant war in England, as they had done in Germany. Reformation produces revolution: this is the favourite text of the followers of the pope. Violent hands must be laid upon the heretics. *Non pluit Deus, duc ad christianos.*[3]

The charge of the priests was absurd; but the people are blind whenever the gospel is concerned, and occasionally the governors are blind also. Serious reasoning was not necessary to confute this invention. 'Here, by the way, I will tell you a merry toy', said Latimer one day in the pulpit. 'Master More was once sent in commission into Kent to help to try out, if it might be, what was the cause of Goodwin Sands and the shelf that stopped up Sandwich haven. He calleth the country afore him, such as were thought to be men of experience, and among others came in an old man with a white head, and one that was thought to be little less than a hundred years old. So Master More called the old aged man unto him, and said: Father, tell me if you can, what is the cause of this great arising of the sands and shelves hereabout, that stop up Sandwich haven? Forsooth, sir, (quoth he) I am an old man, for I am well nigh an hundred, and I think that Tenterden steeple is the cause of the Goodwin Sands. For I am an old man, sir, and I may remember the building of Tenterden steeple, and before that steeple was in building, there was no manner of flats or sands.' After relating this anecdote, Latimer slyly added: 'Even so, to my purpose, is preaching of God's word the cause of rebellion, as Tenterden steeple was the cause Sandwich haven is decayed.'[4]

There was no persecution for the present, as there were other things to be done. Wolsey, still smarting at his failure to reach the pontifical throne, could only think of how he might repay Charles and obstruct his ambitions. But during this time Tyndale also was pursuing his aim; and the year 1525, memorable for the battle of Pavia, was destined to be no less so in the British Isles, for a still more important victory.

---

[3] 'God sends no rain: lead us against the Christians.' A cry ascribed by Augustine to the pagans of the First Ages.
[4] Latimer's *Sermons*, p. 251.

CHAPTER TEN

An Exile's Toil for a Nation's Life

(1524–1526)

T he ship carrying Tyndale and his manuscripts cast anchor in the busy mercantile city of Hamburg, where the gospel had counted numerous friends. Encouraged by the presence of his brethren, the Oxford scholar had taken a quiet lodging in one of the narrow winding streets of that old city, and had immediately resumed his task. A secretary, whom he terms his 'faithful companion', aided him in collating texts; but it was not long before this brother, whose name is unknown to us, thinking himself called to preach Christ in places where he had as yet never been proclaimed, left Tyndale. A former friar-observant of the Franciscan order at Greenwich, having abandoned the cloister, and being at this time without resources, offered his services to the translator. William Roye was one of those men (and they are always pretty numerous) whom impatience of the yoke alienates from Rome without their being attracted by the Spirit of God to Christ. Acute, insinuating, crafty, and yet of pleasing manners, he charmed all those who had mere casual relations with him. Tyndale, banished to the distant shores of the Elbe, surrounded by strange customs, and hearing only a foreign tongue, often thought of England, and was impatient that his country should enjoy the result of his labours: he accepted Roye's aid. The Gospels of Matthew and Mark, translated at Hamburg, became, it would seem, the firstfruits to England of his great task.

It is not possible from the evidence available to be completely certain about Tyndale's changes of residence during the period 1524–25. In all probability he and his assistant moved from Hamburg to Wittenberg in the late spring of 1524, and remained there until the spring of 1525.

That Tyndale came into direct contact with Luther at Wittenberg is tolerably certain.[1] Could he be in the reformer's own neighbourhood and not desire to see him and speak with him? He did not need the Saxon Valiant-for-the-Truth, either to teach him the gospel which he had already known at Oxford, or to instruct him in the translation of the Scriptures. But did not all evangelical foreigners flock to Luther's city? The strong personality of the German reformer, his lectures, his table-talk, would doubtless be potent sources of encouragement to the fugitive Englishman. Above all he would be spurred on with his work of Bible translation.

It may be the case that the two Gospels already translated into English were printed at Wittenberg. Hamburg itself seems to have had no resident printer at that time. During the period 1524–25 also, Tyndale must have worked with uncommon energy at his translation of the remainder of the New Testament. The work done, he probably moved with Roye to the Rhineland.

There were at Cologne some celebrated printers well known in England, and among others, Peter Quentel and Arnold and Francis Byrckmann. Francis Byrckmann had warehouses in St Paul's churchyard in London – a circumstance that might facilitate the introduction and sale of the Testament printed on the banks of the Rhine. This providential circumstance probably decided Tyndale in favour of Cologne, and thither he repaired with Roye and his manuscripts. In the gloomy streets of the city of Agrippina, he contemplated its innumerable churches, and above all its ancient cathedral re-echoing to the voices

[1] Not all historians believe that Tyndale and Luther met. We can understand how Luther, at that time busily engaged in his dispute with Carlstadt, does not mention Tyndale's visit in his letters. But, besides Foxe, there are other contemporary authorities in favour of this fact. Cochlæus, a German well informed on all the movements of the reformers, and whom we shall presently see on Tyndale's traces, says of him and Roye, that they had been to Wittenberg. And Sir Thomas More, having said that Tyndale had gone to see Luther, Tyndale was content to reply: 'When Mr More saith Tyndale was confederate with Luther, that is not truth.' *Answer to Sir Thos. More's Dialogue* (Parker Soc.), p. 147. He denied the confederation, but not the visit. If Tyndale had not *seen* Luther, he would have been more explicit, and would probably have said that he had never even met him. [J. F. Mozley in his *William Tyndale*, 1937, claims that the university registers of Wittenberg for 1524 bear unmistakable proof of our reformer's visit to that city, pp. 52-3.]

of its canons, and was oppressed with sorrow as he beheld the priests and monks and mendicants and pilgrims who, from all parts of Europe, poured in to adore the pretended relics of the *three wise men* and of the *eleven thousand virgins*. And then Tyndale asked himself whether it was really in this superstitious city that the New Testament was to be printed in English. This was not all. The reform movement then at work in Germany had broken out at Cologne during the feast of Whitsuntide, and the archbishop had just forbidden all evangelical worship. Yet Tyndale persevered and, submitting to the most minute precautions so as not to compromise his work, he took an obscure lodging where he kept himself closely hidden.

Soon however, trusting in God, he called on the printer, presented his manuscripts to him, and ordered three thousand copies. The printing went on. The work was to appear as a quarto, with prologue and marginal notes and references. One sheet followed another. Gradually the gospel unfolded its mysteries in the English tongue, and Tyndale could not contain himself for very joy. He saw in his mind's eye the triumphs of the Scriptures over all the kingdom, and exclaimed with great delight: 'Whether the king wills it or not, ere long all the people of England, enlightened by the New Testament, will obey the gospel.'

But on a sudden that sun whose earliest beams he had hailed with songs of joy was hidden by thick clouds. One day, just as the tenth sheet (making 80 quarto pages in all) had been thrown off, the printer hastened to Tyndale, and informed him that the senate of Cologne forbade him to continue the work. Everything was discovered then. No doubt Henry VIII, who had burnt Luther's books, wished to burn the New Testament also, to destroy Tyndale's manuscripts, and deliver him up to death. Who had betrayed him? He was lost in unavailing conjectures, and one thing only appeared certain: alas! his vessel, which was moving onwards in full sail, had struck upon a reef! The following is the explanation of this unexpected setback.

One of the most violent enemies of the reformation – we mean John Cochlæus – had arrived in Cologne. The wave of popular agitation which had stirred this city during the Whitsuntide holidays, had previously swept over Frankfurt during the festival of Easter, and the Romish clergy had been threatened with violence. Cochlæus, the Dean of Nôtre

Dame, taking advantage of a moment when the gates of the city were open, had escaped a few minutes before the burghers entered his house to arrest him. On arriving at Cologne, where he hoped to live unknown under the shadow of the powerful elector, he had gone to lodge with George Lauer, a canon in the Church of the Apostles.

By a singular destiny the two most opposite men, Tyndale and Cochlæus, were in hiding in the same city; they could not long remain there without coming into collision.

On the right bank of the Rhine, and opposite Cologne, stood the monastery of Deutz, one of whose abbots, Rupert, who lived in the twelfth century, had said: 'To be ignorant of Scripture is to be ignorant of Jesus Christ. This is *the scripture of nations!* This book of God, which is not pompous in words and poor in meaning like Plato, ought to be set before every people, and to proclaim aloud to the whole world the salvation of all.' One day, when Cochlæus and his host were talking of Rupert, the canon informed the dean that the *heretic* Osiander of Nuremberg was in treaty with the Abbot of Deutz about publishing the writings of this ancient doctor. Cochlæus guessed that Osiander was desirous of bringing forward the contemporary of St Bernard as a witness in defence of the reformation. Hastening to the monastery he alarmed the abbot: 'Intrust to me the manuscripts of your celebrated predecessor', he said; 'I will undertake to print them and prove that he was one of us.' The monks placed them in his hands, stipulating for an early publication, from which they expected no little renown. Cochlæus immediately went to Peter Quentel and Arnold Byrckmann to make the necessary arrangements. They were Tyndale's printers.

There Cochlæus made a more important discovery than that of Rupert's manuscripts. Byrckmann and Quentel having invited him one day to meet several of their colleagues at dinner, a printer, somewhat elevated by wine, declared in his cups (to borrow the words of Cochlæus): 'Whether the king and the Cardinal of York wish it or not, all England will soon be Lutheran.' Cochlæus listened and grew alarmed; he made inquiry; and was informed that *two Englishmen*, learned men and skilled in the languages, were concealed at Cologne. But all his efforts to discover more proved unavailing.

There was no more repose for the Dean of Frankfurt; his imagination fermented, his mind became alarmed. 'What', said he, 'shall England, that faithful servant of the popedom, be perverted like Germany? Shall the English, the most religious people of Christendom, and whose king once ennobled himself by writing against Luther – shall they be invaded by heresy? ... Shall the mighty cardinal-legate of York be compelled to flee from his palace, as I was from Frankfurt?' Cochlæus continued his search; he paid frequent visits to the printers, spoke to them in a friendly tone, flattered them, invited them to visit him at the canon's; but as yet he dared not hazard the important question; it was sufficient for the moment to have won the good graces of the depositaries of the secret. He soon took a new step; he was careful not to question them before one another; but he procured a private interview with one of them, and supplied him plentifully with Rhenish wine – he himself is our informant. Artful questions embarrassed the unwary printer, and at last the secret was disclosed. 'The New Testament', Cochlæus learnt, 'is translated into English; three thousand copies are in the press; fourscore pages in quarto are ready; the expense is fully supplied by English merchants, who are secretly to convey the work when printed, and to disperse it widely through all England, before the king or the cardinal can discover or prohibit it. ... Thus will Britain be converted to the opinions of Luther.'

The surprise of Cochlæus equalled his alarm; he dissembled; he wished to learn, however, where the two Englishmen lay concealed; but all his exertions proved ineffectual, and he returned to his lodgings filled with emotion. The danger was very great. A stranger and an exile, what can he do to oppose this impious undertaking? Where shall he find a friend to England, prepared to show his zeal in warding off the threatened blow? ... He was bewildered.

A flash of light suddenly dispelled the darkness. A person of some consequence at Cologne, Herman Rincke, a knight and an imperial councillor, had years before been sent on important business by the emperor Maximilian to Henry VII, and from that time he had always shown a great attachment to England. Cochlæus determined to reveal the fatal secret to him; but, being still alarmed by the scenes at Frankfurt, he was afraid to conspire openly against the reformation. He had left an aged mother and a little niece at home, and was unwilling to do anything which might compromise them. He therefore crept stealthily towards Rincke's house (as he tells us himself), slipped in secretly, and unfolded the whole matter to him. Rincke could not believe that the New Testament in English was printing at Cologne; however, he sent a confidential person to make inquiries, who reported to him that Cochlæus' information was correct, and that he had found in the printing office a large supply of paper intended for the edition. The knight immediately proceeded to the senate, and spoke of Wolsey, of Henry VIII, and of the preservation of the Romish Church in England; and that body which, under the influence of the archbishop, had long since forgotten the rights of liberty, forbade the printer to continue the work. Thus then there were to be no New Testaments for England! A practised hand had warded off the blow aimed at Roman Catholicism; Tyndale would perhaps be thrown into prison, and Cochlæus enjoy a complete triumph.

Tyndale was at first confounded. Were so many months of toil lost, then, for ever? His trial seemed beyond his strength. 'They are ravening wolves', he exclaimed; 'they preach to others, Steal not, and yet they have robbed the soul of man of the bread of life, and fed her with the shales [husks] and cods of the hope in their merits and confidence in their good works.'[2] Yet Tyndale did not long remain cast down; for his faith was of that kind which removes mountains. Is it not the word of God that is imperilled? Did God ever abandon those who trusted in him? He must anticipate the senate of Cologne. Daring and prompt in all his movements, Tyndale bade Roye follow him, hastened to the printing office, collected the sheets, jumped into a boat, and rapidly ascended the river, carrying with him the hope of England.

When Cochlæus and Rincke, accompanied by the officers of the senate, reached the printing office, they were surprised beyond measure. The apostate had secured the abominable papers! ... Their enemy had escaped like a bird from the snare of the fowler. Where was he to be found now? He would no doubt go and place himself under the protection of

---

[2] Tyndale, *Expositions* (Parker Society), p. 123.

some *Lutheran* prince, whither Cochlæus would take good care not to pursue him; but there was one resource left. These English books can do no harm in Germany; they must be prevented from reaching London. He wrote to Henry VIII, to Wolsey, and to the Bishop of Rochester. 'Two Englishmen', said he to the king, 'like the two eunuchs who desired to lay hands on Ahasuerus, are plotting wickedly against the peace of your kingdom; but I, like the faithful Mordecai, will lay open their designs to you. They wish to send the New Testament in English to your people. Give orders at every seaport to prevent the introduction of this most baneful merchandise.' Such was the name given by this zealous follower of the pope to the word of God. An unexpected ally soon restored peace to the soul of Cochlæus. The celebrated Dr Eck, a champion of popery far more formidable than he was, had arrived at Cologne on his way to London, and he undertook to arouse the anger of the bishops and of the king. The eyes of the greatest opponents of the reformation seemed now to be fixed on England. Eck, who boasted of having gained the most signal triumphs over Luther, would easily get the better of the humble tutor and his English New Testament.

Unhappily for Cochlæus, he does not appear to have received the material reward which he expected his startling news to have called forth. His 'superlative merit' was recognized in words, but, as he himself lamented, 'he was left like Mordecai at the gate without any substantial recompense for his disclosure of a plot as dangerous as that against the life of Ahasuerus'.

His presence in Cologne thus disclosed, Tyndale had once more to resume his journeyings, and guarding his precious bales he ascended the rapid waters of the Rhine as quickly, and doubtless as secretly, as he could.

He passed the ancient cities and the smiling villages scattered along the banks amidst scenes of picturesque beauty. The mountains, glens, and rocks, the dark forests, the ruined fortresses, the gothic churches, the boats that passed and repassed each other, the birds of prey that soared over his head, as if they bore a mission from Cochlæus – nothing could turn his eyes from the treasure he was carrying with him. At last, after a voyage of five or six days, and probably in October 1525, he reached

Worms, where Luther, four years before, had exclaimed: 'Here I stand, I can do no other; so help me God!' These words of the German reformer, so well known to Tyndale, were the star that had guided him to Worms. He knew that the gospel was preached in that ancient city. 'The citizens are subject to fits of Lutheranism', said Cochlæus. Tyndale arrived there, not as Luther did, surrounded by an immense crowd, but unknown, and imagining himself pursued by the myrmidons of Charles and of Henry. As he landed from the boat he cast an uneasy glance around him, and laid down his precious burden on the bank of the river.

He had had time to reflect on the dangers which threatened his work. As his enemies would have details of the edition, some few sheets of it having fallen into their hands, he took steps to mislead the inquisitors and began a new edition, striking out the prologue and the notes, and substituting the more portable *octavo* form for the original *quarto*. Peter Schiffer, the grandson of Faust, one of the inventors of printing, lent his presses for this important work. The two editions were quietly completed about the end of the year 1525 or early in 1526.

Thus were the wicked deceived: they would have deprived the English people of the oracles of God, and *two* editions were now ready to enter England. 'Give diligence', said Tyndale to his fellow countrymen, as he sent from Worms the Testament he had just translated, 'unto the words of eternal life, by the which, if we repent and believe them, we are born anew, created afresh, and enjoy the fruits of the blood of Christ.' About March 1526, these books crossed the sea by way of Antwerp or Rotterdam. Tyndale was happy; but he knew that the unction of the Holy Ghost alone could enable the people of England to understand these sacred pages; and accordingly he followed them night and day with his prayers. 'The scribes and Pharisees', said he, 'had thrust up the sword of the word of God in a scabbard or sheath of glosses, and therein had knit it fast, so that it could neither pierce nor cut. ... Now, O God, draw this sharp sword from the scabbard. Strike, wound, cut asunder the soul and the flesh, so that man being divided in two, and set at variance with himself, may be in peace with thee to all eternity!'

CHAPTER ELEVEN

The Awakening in Cambridge

(1524–1525)

While these works were accomplishing at Cologne and Worms, others were going on at Cambridge and Oxford. On the banks of the Rhine they were preparing the seed; in England they were drawing the furrows to receive it. The gospel produced a great agitation at Cambridge. Bilney, whom we may call the father of the English reformation, since, being the first converted by the New Testament, he had brought to the knowledge of God the energetic Latimer, and so many other witnesses of the truth – Bilney did not at that time put himself forward, like many of those who had listened to him: his vocation was prayer. Timid before men, he was full of boldness before God, and day and night called upon him for souls. But while he was kneeling in his chamber, others were at work in the world. Among these Stafford was particularly remarkable. 'Paul is risen from the dead', said many as they heard him. And in fact Stafford explained with so much life the true meaning of the words of the apostle and of the four Evangelists, that these holy men, whose faces had been so long hidden under the dense traditions of the schools, reappeared before the youth of the university such as the apostolic times had beheld them. But it was not only their *persons* (for that would have been a trifling matter), it was their *doctrine* which Stafford laid before his hearers. While the schoolmen of Cambridge were declaring to their pupils a reconciliation which was not yet worked out, and telling them that pardon must be purchased by the works prescribed by the church, Stafford taught that redemption was *accomplished*, that the satisfaction offered by Jesus Christ was *perfect*; and he added that, popery having revived the *kingdom of the law*, God, by the reformation, was now reviving the *kingdom of grace*. The Cambridge students, charmed by their master's teaching, greeted him with applause, and, indulging a little too far in their enthusiasm, said to one another as they left the lecture room: 'Which is the most indebted to the other? Stafford to Paul, who left him the Holy Epistles; or Paul to Stafford, who has resuscitated that apostle and his holy doctrines, which the Middle Ages have obscured?'

Above Bilney and Stafford rose Latimer, who, by the power of the Holy Ghost, transfused into other hearts the learned lessons of his master.[1] Being informed of the work that Tyndale was preparing, he maintained from the Cambridge pulpits that the Bible ought to be read in the vulgar tongue.[2] 'The author of holy Scripture', said he, 'is the Mighty One, the Everlasting ... *God himself!* ... and this Scripture partakes of the might and eternity of its author. There is neither king nor emperor that is not bound to obey it. Let us beware of those bypaths of human tradition, filled of stones, brambles, and uprooted trees. Let us follow the straight road of the word. It does not concern us what the Fathers have done, but what they should have done.'

A numerous congregation crowded to Latimer's preaching, and his hearers hung listening to his lips. One in particular attracted attention. He was a Norfolk youth, sixteen years of age, whose features were lighted up with understanding and piety. This poor scholar had received with eagerness the truth announced by the former cross-bearer. He did not miss one of his sermons; with a sheet of paper on his knees, and a pencil in his hand, he took down part of the discourse, trusting the remainder to his memory.[3] This was Thomas Becon, afterwards chaplain to Thomas Cranmer, Archbishop of Canterbury. 'If I possess the knowledge of God', said he, 'I owe it (under God) to Latimer.'

Latimer had hearers of many sorts. By the side of those who gave way to their enthusiasm stood men 'swelling, blown full, and puffed up like unto Æsop's frog, with envy and malice against him', said Becon;

---

[1] A private instructor to the rest of his brethren within the university by the space of three years. Foxe, *Acts*, vii, p. 438.

[2] He proved in his sermons that the holy Scriptures ought to be read in the English tongue of all Christian people. Becon's *Works* (Parker Society), ii, p. 424.

[3] A poor scholar of Cambridge ... but a child of sixteen years. *Ibid.*

these were the partisans of traditional Catholicism, whom curiosity had attracted, or whom their evangelical friends had dragged to the church. But as Latimer spoke a marvellous transformation was worked in them; by degrees their angry features relaxed, their fierce looks grew softer; and, if these friends of the priests were asked, after their return home, what they thought of the heretic preacher, they replied, in the exaggeration of their surprise and rapture: '*Nunquam sic locutus est homo, sicut hic homo!*' (John 7:46.)

When he hastened from the pulpit, Latimer hastened to practise what he had taught. He visited the narrow chambers of the poor scholars, and the dark rooms of the working classes: 'he watered with good deeds whatsoever he had before planted with godly words',[4] said the student who collected his discourses. The disciples conversed together with joy and simplicity of heart; everywhere the breath of a new life was felt; as yet no external reforms had been effected, and yet the spiritual church of the gospel and of the reformation was already there. And thus the recollection of these happy times was long commemorated in the adage:

> When Master Stafford read,
> And Master Latimer preached,
> Then was Cambridge blessed.[5]

The priests could not remain inactive: they heard speak of grace and liberty, and would have nothing to do with either. If *grace* is tolerated, will it not take from the hands of the clergy the manipulation of salvation, indulgences, penance, and all the rubrics of the canon law? If *liberty* is conceded, will not the hierarchy, with all its degrees, pomps, violence, and scaffolds, be shaken? Rome desires no other liberty than that of free will, which, exalting the natural strength of fallen man, dries up as regards mankind the springs of Divine life, withers Christianity, and changes that heavenly religion into a human moralism and legal observances.

The friends of popery, therefore, collected their forces to oppose the new religion. 'Satan, who never sleeps', says the simple chronicler, 'called up his familiar spirits, and sent them forth against the reformers.'

---

[4] *Ibid.*, p. 425.
[5] *Ibid.*

Meetings were held in the convents, but particularly in that belonging to the Greyfriars. They mustered all their forces. *An eye for an eye, and a tooth for a tooth*, said they. Latimer extols in his sermons the *blessings* of Scripture; we must deliver a sermon also to show its *dangers*. But where was the orator to be found who could cope with him? This was a very embarrassing question to the clerical party. Among the Dominicans there was a friar, adroit and skilful in little matters: it was the prior Bockenham. No one had shown more hatred against the evangelical Christians, and no one was in truth a greater stranger to the gospel. This was the man commissioned to set forth the dangers of the word of God. He was by no means familiar with the New Testament; he opened it however, picked out a few passages here and there which seemed to favour his thesis; and then, arrayed in his costliest robes, with head erect and solemn step, already sure of victory, he went into the pulpit, combated the heretic, and with pompous voice stormed against the reading of the Bible; it was in his eyes the fountain of all heresies and misfortunes. 'Scripture', he said, 'is full of figurative language which the laity will be certain to misinterpret to their own ruin. If that heresy should prevail', he exclaimed, 'there will be an end of everything useful among us. The ploughman, reading in the gospel that *no man having put his hand to the plough should look back*, would soon lay aside his labour. ... The baker, reading that *a little leaven leaveneth the whole lump*, will in future make us nothing but very insipid bread; and the simple man finding himself commanded *to pluck out the right eye and cast it from thee*, England, after a few years, will be a frightful spectacle; it will be little better than a nation of blind and one-eyed men, sadly begging their bread from door to door.'

This discourse moved that part of the audience for which it was intended. 'The heretic is silenced', said the monks and clerks; but sensible people smiled, and Latimer was delighted that they had given him such an adversary. Being of a lively disposition and inclined to irony, he resolved to lash the platitudes of the pompous friar. There are some absurdities, he thought, which can only be refuted by showing how foolish they are. Does not even the grave Tertullian speak of things which are only to be laughed at, for fear of giving them importance by a serious refutation? 'Next Sunday I will reply to him', said Latimer.

The church was crowded when Bockenham, with the hood of St Francis on his shoulders and with a vain-glorious air, took his place solemnly in front of the preacher. Latimer began by recapitulating the least weak of his adversary's arguments; then taking them up one by one, he turned them over and over, and pointed out all their absurdity with so much wit, that the poor prior was buried in his own nonsense. Then turning towards the listening crowd, he exclaimed with warmth: 'This is how your skilful guides abuse your understanding. They look upon you as children that must be for ever kept in leading-strings. Now, the hour of your majority has arrived; boldly examine the Scriptures, and you will easily discover the absurdity of the teaching of your doctors.' And then desirous, as Solomon has it, of *answering a fool according to his folly*, he added: 'As for the comparisons drawn from the *plough*, the *leaven*, and the *eye*, of which the reverend prior has made so singular a use, is it necessary to justify these passages of Scripture? Must I tell you what *plough*, what *leaven*, what *eye* is here meant? Is not our Lord's teaching distinguished by those expressions which, under a popular form, conceal a spiritual and profound meaning? Do not we know that in all languages and in all speeches, it is not on the *image* that we must fix our eyes, but on the *thing* which the image represents? ... For instance', he continued, and as he said these words he cast a piercing glance on the prior, 'if we see a fox painted preaching in a friar's hood, nobody imagines that a fox is meant, but that craft and hypocrisy are described, which are so often found disguised in that garb.' At these words the prior, on whom the eyes of all the congregation were turned, rose and left the church hastily, and went off to hide his rage and confusion among his brethren. The monks and their creatures uttered loud cries against Latimer. It was unpardonable (they said) to have been thus wanting in respect to the cowl of St Francis. But his friends replied: 'Do we not whip children? and he who treats Scripture worse than a child, does he not deserve to be well flogged?'

The Romish party did not consider themselves beaten. The heads of colleges and the priests held frequent conferences. The professors were desired to watch carefully over their pupils, and to lead them back to the teaching of the church by flattery and by threats. 'We are putting our lance in rest', they told the students; 'if you become evangelicals, your advancement is at an end.' But these open-hearted generous youths loved rather to be poor with Christ, than rich with the priests. Stafford continued to teach, Latimer to preach, and Bilney to visit the poor: the doctrine of Christ ceased not to be spread abroad, and souls to be converted.

It was difficult, if not impossible, to silence a preacher so popular with the ordinary people as Latimer. A plan to do so had been in contemplation a considerable time before the encounter with Bockenham just recorded. The aid of the bishops was sought. Dr West, Bishop of Ely, was ordinary of Cambridge; in response to an urgent request for his intervention, he ordered one of the doctors to inform him the next time Latimer was to preach; 'but', added he, 'do not say a word to anyone. I wish to come without being expected'.

One day as Latimer was preaching in Latin *ad clerum* (to the clergy), the bishop suddenly entered the University Church, attended by a number of priests. Latimer stopped, waiting respectfully until West and his train had taken their places. 'A new audience', he adroitly remarked, 'and moreover, an audience of such rank calls for a new theme. Leaving, therefore, the subject I had proposed, I will take up one that relates to the episcopal charge, and will preach on these words: *Christus existens Pontifex futurorum bonorum.*' (Heb. 9:11.) Then describing Jesus Christ, Latimer represented him as the 'true and perfect pattern unto all other bishops'. There was not a single virtue pointed out in the divine bishop that did not correspond with some defect in the Romish bishops. Latimer's caustic wit had a free course at their expense; but there was so much gravity in his sallies, and so lively a Christianity in his descriptions, that everyone must have felt them to be the cries of a Christian conscience rather than the sarcasms of an ill-natured disposition. Never had bishop been taught by one of his priests like this man. 'Alas!' said many, 'our bishops are not of that breed: they are descended from Annas and Caiaphas.' West was not more at his ease than Bockenham had been formerly. He stifled his anger, however; and after the sermon, said to Latimer with a gracious accent: 'You have excellent talents, and if you would do one thing I should be ready to kiss your feet.' ... What humility in a bishop! ... 'Preach in this same church', continued West, 'a sermon ... against Martin Luther. That is the best way of checking heresy.' Latimer understood the prelate's meaning, and replied calmly: 'If Luther preaches the word of God, I cannot oppose him. If he teaches the contrary, I am ready to attack him. But, my lord, by command of my Cardinal of York, we are prohibited from reading Luther's works: therefore it were but a vain thing for me to attempt to refute them.' – 'Well, well, Master Latimer', exclaimed the bishop, 'I perceive that you smell somewhat of the pan. ... One day or another you will repent of this gear.'

West having left Cambridge in great irritation against that rebellious clerk, hastened to convoke his chapter, and forbade Latimer to preach either in the university or in the diocese. 'All that will live godly shall suffer persecution', St Paul had said; Latimer was now experiencing the truth of the saying. It was not enough that the name of heretic had been given him by the priests and their friends, and that the passers-by insulted him in the streets ... the work of God was violently checked. 'Behold then', he exclaimed with a bitter sigh, 'the use of the episcopal office ... to hinder the preaching of Jesus Christ!' Some few years later he sketched, with his usual caustic irony, the portrait of a certain bishop, of whom Luther also used frequently to speak: 'Do you know', said Latimer, 'who is the most diligent bishop and prelate in all England? ... I see you listening and hearkening that I should name him. ... I will tell you. ... It is the devil. He is never out of his diocese; ye shall never find him out of the way; call for him when you will, he's ever at home. He is ever at his plough. Ye shall never find him idle, I warrant you. Where the devil is resident – there away with books and up with candles; away with Bibles and up with beads; away with the light of the gospel and up with the light of candles, yea at noondays; down with Christ's cross, up with purgatory pickpurse; away with clothing the naked, the poor, and impotent, up with decking of images and gay garnishing of stocks and stones; down with God's traditions and his most holy word. ... Oh! that our prelates would be as diligent to sow the corn of good doctrine as Satan is to sow cockle and darnel!' Truly may it be said, 'There was never such a preacher in England as he is.'

The reformer was not satisfied with merely speaking: he acted. 'Neither the menacing words of his adversaries nor their cruel imprison-ments', says one of his contemporaries, 'could hinder him from proclaiming God's truth.' Forbidden to preach in the churches, he went about from house to house. He longed for a pulpit, however, and this he obtained. A haughty prelate had in vain interdicted his preaching; Jesus Christ, who is above all bishops, is able, when one door is shut, to open another. Instead of one great preacher there were soon two at Cambridge.

An Augustine monk named Robert Barnes, a native of the county of Norfolk, and a great scholar, had gone to Louvain to prosecute his studies. Here he received the degree of doctor of divinity and, having returned to Cambridge, was nominated prior of his monastery in 1523. It was his fortune to reconcile learning and the gospel in the university; but by leaning too much to learning he diminished the force of the word of God. A great crowd collected every day in the Augustine lecture hall, to hear him discourse upon Terence and Plautus, and in particular upon Cicero. Many of those who were offended by the simple Christianity of Bilney and Latimer, were attracted by this reformer of another kind. Coleman, Coverdale, Field, Cambridge, Barley, and many other young men of the university, gathered round Barnes and proclaimed him 'the restorer of letters'.[6]

But the classics were only a preparatory teaching. The masterpieces of antiquity having aided Barnes to clear the soil, he opened before his class the Epistles of St Paul. He did not understand their Divine depth, like Stafford; he was not, like him, anointed with the Holy Ghost; he differed from him on several of the apostle's doctrines, on justification by faith, and on the new creature; but Barnes was an enlightened and liberal man, not without some degree of piety, and desirous, like Stafford, of substituting the teaching of Scripture for the barren disputations of the schools. But they soon came into collision, and Cambridge long remembered that celebrated discussion in which Barnes and Stafford contended with so much renown, employing no other weapons than the word of God, to the great astonishment of the blind doctors, and the great joy of the clear-sighted, says the chronicler.

[6] The great restorer of good learning. Strype, i, p. 568; Foxe, *Acts*, v, p. 415. [An excellent account of Barnes' teaching is in D. B. Knox, *The Doctrine of Faith* (James Clarke, 1961), pp. 63-69. This is the best modern treatment of the theology of the early English reformers.]

Barnes was not as yet thoroughly enlightened, and the friends of the gospel were astonished that a man, a stranger to the truth, should deal such heavy blows against error. Bilney, whom we continually meet with when any secret work, a work of irresistible charity, is in hand – Bilney, who had converted Latimer, undertook to convert Barnes; and Stafford, Arthur, Thistel of Pembroke College, and Fooke of Benet's[7] earnestly prayed God to grant his assistance. The experiment was difficult: Barnes had reached that *juste milieu,* that 'golden mean' of the humanists, that intoxication of learning and glory, which render conversion more difficult. Besides, could a man like Bilney really dare to instruct the restorer of antiquity? But the humble bachelor of arts, so simple in appearance, knew, like David of old, a secret power by which the Goliath of the university might be vanquished. He passed days and nights in prayer; and then urged Barnes openly to manifest his convictions without fearing the reproaches of the world. After many conversations and prayers, Barnes was converted to the gospel of Jesus Christ.[8] Still, the prior retained something undecided in his character, and only half relinquished that middle state with which he had begun. For instance, he appears to have always believed in the efficacy of sacerdotal consecration to transform the bread and wine into the body and blood of Christ. His eye was not single, and his mind was often agitated and driven to and fro by contrary thoughts: 'Alas!' said this divided character one day, 'I confess that my cogitations be innumerable.'

Barnes, having come to a knowledge of the truth, immediately displayed a zeal that was somewhat imprudent. Men of the least decided character, and even those who are destined to make a signal fall, are often those who begin their course with the greatest ardour. Barnes seemed prepared at this time to withstand all England. Being now united to Latimer by a tender Christian affection, he was indignant that the powerful voice of his friend should be lost to the church. 'The bishop has forbidden you to preach', he said to him, 'but my monastery is not under episcopal jurisdiction. You can preach there.' Latimer went into the pulpit at the Augustine's, and the church could not contain the crowd that flocked to it. At Cambridge, as at Wittenberg, the chapel of

---

[7] [St Benedict's, later renamed Corpus Christi.]

[8] Bilney converted Dr Barnes to the gospel of Jesus Christ. Foxe, *Acts,* iv, p. 620.

the Augustine monks was used for the first struggles of the gospel. It was here that Latimer delivered some of his best sermons.

A very different man from Latimer, and particularly from Barnes, was daily growing in influence among the English reformers: this was Fryth.[9] No one was more humble than he, and on that very account no one was stronger. He was less brilliant than Barnes, but more solid. He might have penetrated into the highest departments of science, but he was drawn away by the deep mysteries of God's word; the call of conscience prevailed over that of the understanding. He did not devote the energy of his soul to difficult questions; he thirsted for God, for his truth, and for his love. Instead of propagating his particular opinions and forming divisions, he clung only to the faith which saves, and advanced the dominion of true unity. This is the mark of the great servants of God. Humble before the Lord, mild before men, and even in appearance somewhat timid, Fryth in the face of danger displayed an intrepid courage. 'My learning is small', he said, 'but the little I have I am determined to give to Jesus Christ for the building of his temple.'

Latimer's sermons, Barnes' ardour, and Fryth's firmness, excited fresh zeal at Cambridge. They knew what was going on in Germany and Switzerland; shall the English, ever in front, now remain in the rear? Shall not Latimer, Bilney, Stafford, Barnes, and Fryth do what the servants of God are doing in other places?

A secret ferment announced an approaching crisis: everyone expected some change for better or for worse. The evangelicals, confident in the truth, and thinking themselves sure of victory, resolved to fall upon the enemy simultaneously on several points. The Sunday before Christmas, in the year 1525, was chosen for this great attack. While Latimer should address the crowds that continued to fill the Augustine chapel, and others were preaching in a variety of places, Barnes was to deliver a sermon in one of the churches in the town. But nothing compromises the gospel so much as a disposition turned towards outward things. God, who grants his blessing only to undivided hearts, permitted this general assault, of which Barnes was to be the hero, to be marked by a defeat. The prior, as he went into the pulpit, thought only of Wolsey. As

[9] [For Fryth's teaching see Knox, *op. cit.*, pp. 43-51.]

the representative of the popedom in England, the cardinal was the great obstacle to the reformation. Barnes preached from the epistle for the day: Rejoice in the Lord always.[10] But instead of announcing Christ and the joy of the Christian, he imprudently declaimed against the luxury, pride, and diversions of the churchmen, and everybody understood that he aimed at the cardinal. He described those magnificent palaces, that brilliant suite, those scarlet robes, and pearls, and gold, and precious stones, and all the prelate's ostentation, so little in keeping (said he) with the stable of Bethlehem. Two Fellows of King's College, Robert Ridley and Walter Preston, relations of Tunstall, Bishop of London, who were intentionally among the congregation, noted down in their books the prior's imprudent expressions.

The sermon was scarcely over when the storm broke out. 'These people are not satisfied with propagating monstrous heresies', exclaimed their enemies, 'but they must find fault with the powers that be. Today they attack the cardinal, tomorrow they will attack the king!' Ridley, Preston, and others, accused Barnes to the vice-chancellor. All Cambridge was in commotion. What! Barnes the Augustine prior, the restorer of letters, accused as a Wycliffite! … The gospel was threatened with a danger more formidable than a prison or a scaffold. The friends of the priests, knowing Barnes' weakness, and even his vanity, hoped to obtain of him a disavowal that would cover the evangelical party with shame. 'What!' said these dangerous counsellors to him, 'the noblest career was open to you, and would you close it? … Do, pray, explain away your sermon.' They alarmed, they flattered him; and the poor prior was near yielding to their solicitations. 'Next Sunday you will read this declaration', they said to him. Barnes ran over the paper put into his hands, and saw no great harm in it. However, he desired to show it to Bilney and Stafford. 'Beware of such weakness', said these faithful men. Barnes then recalled his promise, and for a season the enemies of the gospel were silent.

Its friends worked with increased energy. The fall from which one of their companions had so narrowly escaped inspired them with fresh zeal. The more indecision and weakness Barnes had shown, the more did his brethren flee to God for courage and firmness. It was reported,

[10] Philippians 4:4-7.

moreover, that a powerful ally was coming across the sea, and that the holy Scriptures, translated into the vulgar tongue, were at last to be given to the people. Whenever the word was preached, there the congregation was largest. It was the seed-time of the church; all were busy in the fields to prepare the soil and trace the furrows. Seven colleges at least were in full ferment: Pembroke, St John's, Queens', King's, Caius, Benet's, and Peterhouse. The gospel was preached at the Augustine's, at St Mary's (the University Church) and in other places, and when the bells rang to prayers, the streets were alive with students issuing from the colleges, and hastening to the sermon.

There was at Cambridge a house called the White Horse, so situated as to permit the most timid members of King's, Queens', and St John's Colleges, to enter at the rear without being perceived. In every age Nicodemus has had his followers. Here those persons used to assemble who desired to read the Bible and the works of the German reformers. The priests, looking upon Wittenberg as the focus of the reformation, named this house Germany: the people will always have their bywords. At first the frequenters of the White Horse were called sophists; and now, whenever a group of 'Fellows' was seen walking in that direction, the cry was, 'There are the Germans going to Germany.' – 'We are not Germans', was the reply, 'neither are we Romans.' The Greek New Testament had made them Christians. The gospel meetings had never been more fervent. Some attended them to communicate the new life they possessed; others to receive what God had given to the more advanced brethren. The Holy Spirit united them all, and thus, by the fellowship of the saints, were real churches created. To these young Christians the word of God was the source of so much light, that they imagined themselves transported to that heavenly city of which the Scriptures speak, *which had no need of the sun, for the glory of God did lighten it.* 'So oft as I was in the company of these brethren', said a youthful student of St John's, 'methought I was quietly placed in the new glorious Jerusalem.'[11]

Similar things were taking place at Oxford. In 1524 and 1525, Wolsey had successively invited thither several Cambridge Fellows, and although only seeking the most able, he found that he had taken some of the

---

[11] Becon (Parker Society), ii, p. 426.

most pious. Besides John Clark, there were Richard Cox, John Fryer, Godfrey Harman, W. Betts, Henry Sumner, W. Baily, Michael Drumm, Th. Lawny, and, lastly, the excellent John Fryth. These Christians, associating with Clark, with his faithful Dalaber, and with other evangelicals of Oxford, held meetings, like their Cambridge brethren, at which God manifested his presence. The bishops made war upon the gospel; the king supported them with all his power; but the word had gained the victory; there was no longer any doubt. The church was born again in England.

The great movement of the sixteenth century had begun more particularly among the younger doctors and students at Oxford and Cambridge. From them it was necessary that it should be extended to the people, and for that end the New Testament, hitherto read in Latin and in Greek, must be circulated in English. The voices of these youthful evangelists were heard, indeed, in London and in the provinces; but their exhortations would have been insufficient, if the mighty hand which directs all things had not made this Christian activity coincide with that holy work for which it had set Tyndale apart. While all was agitation in England, the waves of ocean were bearing from the Continent to the banks of the Thames those Scriptures of God, which, three centuries later, multiplied by thousands and by millions, and translated into an ever-increasing number of tongues, were to be wafted from the same banks to the ends of the world. If in the fifteenth century, and even in the early years of the sixteenth, the English New Testament had been brought to London, it would only have fallen into the hands of a few Lollards. Now, in every place, in the parsonages, the universities, and the palaces, as well as in the cottages of the husbandmen and the shops of the tradesmen, there was an ardent desire to possess the holy Scriptures. The *fiat lux* was about to be uttered over the chaos of the church, and light to be separated from darkness by the word of God.

BOOK THREE

The English New Testament and the Court of Rome

Anne Boleyn

CHAPTER ONE

The Year of Grace

(1526)

The church and the state are essentially distinct. They both receive their task from God, but that task is different in each. The task of the church is to lead men to God; the task of the state is to secure the earthly development of a people in conformity with its peculiar character. There are certain bounds, traced by the particular spirit of each nation, within which the state should confine itself; while the church, whose limits are co-extensive with the human race, has a universal character, which raises it above all national differences. These two distinctive features should be maintained. A state which aims at universality loses itself; a church whose mind and aim are sectarian falls away. Nevertheless, the church and the state, the two poles of social life, while they are in many respects opposed to each other, are far from excluding each other absolutely. The church has need of that justice, order, and liberty, which the state is bound to maintain; but the state has especial need of the church. If Jesus can do without kings to establish his kingdom, kings cannot do without Jesus, if they would have their kingdoms prosper. Justice, which is the fundamental principle of the state, is continually fettered in its progress by the internal power of sin; and as force can do nothing against this power, the state requires the gospel in order to overcome it. That country will always be the most prosperous where the church is the most evangelical. These two communities having thus need one of the other, we must be prepared, whenever a great religious manifestation takes place in the world, to witness the appearance on the scene not only of the little ones, but of the great ones also, of the state. We must not then be surprised to meet with Henry VIII, but let us endeavour to appreciate accurately the part he played.

If the reformation, particularly in England, happened necessarily to be mixed up with the state, with the world even, it originated neither in the state nor in the world. There was much worldliness in the age of Henry VIII, passions, violence, festivities, a trial, a divorce; and some historians call that *the history of the reformation in England*. We shall not pass by in silence these manifestations of the worldly life; opposed as they are to the Christian life, they are in history, and it is not our business to tear them out. But most assuredly they are not the reformation. From a very different quarter proceeded the Divine light which then rose upon the human race.

To say that Henry VIII was the reformer of his people is to betray ignorance of history. The kingly power in England by turns opposed and favoured the reform in the church; but it opposed before it favoured, and much more than it favoured. This great transformation was begun and extended by its own strength, by the Spirit from on high.

When the church has lost the life that is peculiar to it, it must again put itself in communication with its creative principle, that is, with the word of God. Just as the buckets of a wheel employed in irrigating the meadows have no sooner discharged their reviving waters, than they dip again into the stream to be refilled, so every generation, void of the Spirit of Christ, must return to the Divine source for renewal. The primitive words which created the church have been preserved for us in the Gospels, the Acts, and the Epistles; and the humble reading of these Divine writings will create in every age the communion of saints. God was the father of the reformation, not Henry VIII. The visible world which then glittered with such brightness, those princes and sports, those noblemen, and trials and laws, far from effecting a reform, were calculated to stifle it. But the light and the warmth came from heaven, and the new creation was completed.

In the reign of Henry VIII a great number of citizens, priests, and noblemen possessed that degree of cultivation which favours the action of the holy books. It was sufficient for this Divine seed to be scattered on the well-prepared soil for the work of germination to be accomplished.

A time not less important was also approaching – that in which the action of the popedom was to come to an end. The hour had not yet struck. God was first creating within by his word a spiritual church, before he broke without by his dispensations the bonds which had so long fastened England to the power of Rome. It was his good pleasure first to give truth and life, and then liberty. It has been said that if the pope had consented to a reform of abuses and doctrines, on condition of his keeping his position, the religious revolution would not have been satisfied at that price and that, after demanding reform, the next demand would have been for liberty. The only reproach that can be made to this assertion is that it is superabundantly true. Liberty was an integral part of the reformation, and one of the changes imperatively required was to withdraw religious authority from the pope, and acknowledge it as belonging to the word of God. In the sixteenth century there was a great outpouring of the Christian life in France, Italy, and Spain; it is attested by martyrs without number, and history shows that to transform these three great nations, all that the gospel wanted was liberty. 'If we had set to work two months later', said a grand inquisitor of Spain who had dyed himself in the blood of the saints, 'it would have been too late: Spain would have been lost to the Roman Church.' We may therefore believe that if Italy, France, and Spain had had some generous king to check the myrmidons of the pope, those three countries, carried along by the renovating power of the gospel, would have entered upon an era of liberty and faith.

The struggles of England with the popedom began shortly after the dissemination of the English New Testament by Tyndale. The epoch at which we are arrived accordingly brings in one view before our eyes both the Testament of Jesus Christ and the court of Rome. We can thus study the men – the reformers and the Romanists – and the works they produce, and arrive at a just valuation of the two great principles which dispute the possession of authority in the church.

* * * * *

It was probably in the early spring of 1526 that the English New Testaments were crossing the sea; pious Hanseatic merchants had taken charge of the books. Captivated by the holy Scriptures they had taken them on board their ships, hidden them among their merchandise; and then made sail from Antwerp for London.

Thus those precious pages were approaching England which were to become its light and the source of its greatness. The merchants, whose zeal unhappily cost them dear, were not without alarm. Had not Cochlæus caused orders to be sent to every port to prevent the entrance of the precious cargo they were bringing to England? They arrived and cast anchor; they lowered the boat to reach the shore; what were they likely to meet there? Tunstall's agents, no doubt, and Wolsey's, and Henry's, ready to take away their New Testaments! They landed and soon again returned to the ship; boats passed to and fro, and the vessel was unloaded. No enemy appeared; and no one seemed to imagine that these ships contained so great a treasure.

Just at the time this invaluable cargo was ascending the river, an invisible hand had dispersed the preventive guard. Tunstall, Bishop of London, had been sent as ambassador to Spain; Henry and Wolsey were occupied in political combinations with Scotland, France, and the Empire. God, if we may so speak, had sent his angel to remove or otherwise occupy the guards.

Seeing nothing that could stop them, the merchants, whose establishment was at the Steelyard in Thames Street, hastened to conceal their precious charge in their warehouses. But who will receive them? Who will undertake to distribute these holy Scriptures in London, Oxford, Cambridge, and all England? It is a little matter that they have crossed the sea. The principal instrument God was about to use for their dissemination was an humble servant of Christ.

In Honey Lane, a narrow thoroughfare adjoining Cheapside, stood the old Church of All Hallows, of which Dr Robert Forman was rector. His curate was a plain man of lively imagination, delicate conscience, and timid disposition, but rendered bold by his faith, to which he was to become a martyr. Thomas Garret, for that was his name, having believed in the gospel, earnestly called his hearers to repentance; he urged upon them that works, however good they might be in appearance, were by no means capable of justifying the sinner, and that faith alone could save him. He maintained that every man had the right to preach the word of

God; and called those bishops pharisees, who persecuted Christian men. Garret's discourses, at once so quickening and so gentle, attracted great crowds; and to many of his hearers, the street in which he preached was rightly named Honey Lane, for there they found the *honey out of the rock*.[1] But Garret was about to commit a fault still more heinous in the eyes of the priests than preaching faith. The Hanse merchants were seeking some sure place where they might store up the New Testaments and other books sent from Germany; the curate offered his house, stealthily transported the holy deposit thither, hid them in the most secret corners, and kept a faithful watch over this sacred library. He did not confine himself to this. Night and day he studied the holy books; he held gospel meetings, read the word, and explained its doctrines to the citizens of London. At last, not satisfied with being at once student, librarian, and preacher, he became a trader, and sold the New Testament to laymen, and even to priests and monks, so that the holy Scriptures were dispersed over the whole realm.[2] Others, of whom we know nothing, must have given him their powerful, but secret, assistance.

And thus the word of God, presented by Erasmus to the learned in 1516, was given to the people by Tyndale in 1526. In the parsonages and in the monastic cells, but particularly in shops and cottages, a crowd of persons were studying the New Testament. The clearness of the holy Scriptures struck each reader. None of the systematic or aphoristic forms of the school were to be found there: it was the language of human life which they discovered in those Divine writings: here a conversation, there a discourse; here a narrative, and there a comparison; here a command, and there an argument; here a parable, and there a prayer. It was not all doctrine or all history; but these two elements mingled together made an admirable whole. Above all, the life of our Saviour, so Divine and so human, had an inexpressible charm which captivated the simple. One work of Jesus Christ explained another, and the great facts of the redemption, birth, death, and resurrection of the Son of God, and the sending of the Holy Ghost, followed and completed each other. The authority of Christ's teaching, so strongly contrasting with the doubts

[1] Psalm 31:16.

[2] Dispersing abroad of the said books within this realm. Foxe, *Acts*, v, p. 428. See also Strype, *Cranmer's Mem.*, p. 81.

of the schools, increased the clearness of his discourses to his readers; for the more certain a truth is, the more distinctly it strikes the mind. Academical explanations were not necessary to those noblemen, farmers, and citizens. It is to me, for me, and of me that this book speaks, said each one. It is whom all these promises and teachings concern. This *fall* and this *restoration* ... they are mine. That old *death* and this new *life* ... have passed through them. That *flesh* and that *spirit* ... I know them. This *law* and this *grace*, this *faith*, these *works*, this *slavery*, this *glory*, this *Christ* and this *Belial* ... all are familiar to me. It is my own history that I find in this book. Thus by the aid of the Holy Ghost each one had in his own experience a key to the mysteries of the Bible. To understand certain authors and certain philosophers, the intellectual life of the reader must be in harmony with theirs; so must there be an intimate affinity with the holy books to penetrate their mysteries. 'The man that has not the Spirit of God', said Martin Luther, 'does not understand one jot or tittle of the Scripture.' Now that this condition was fulfilled, the Spirit of God moved upon the face of the waters.

Such at that period were the hermeneutics of England. Tyndale had set the example himself by explaining many of the words which might stop the reader. 'The *New Testament!*' we may suppose some farmer saying, as he took up the book; 'what *Testament* is that?' – 'Christ', replied Tyndale in his prologue, 'commanded his disciples before his death to publish over all the world *his last will*, which is to give all his goods unto all that repent and believe. He bequeaths them his righteousness to blot out their sins – his salvation to overcome their condemnation; and this is why that document is called the *Testament* of Jesus Christ.'

'The *law* and the *gospel*', says a citizen of London, in his shop; 'what is that?' – 'They are two *keys*', answered Tyndale. 'The *law* is the key which shuts up all men under condemnation, and the *gospel* is the key which opens the door and lets them out. Or, if you like it, they are two salves. The law, sharp and biting, driveth out the disease and killeth it; while the gospel, soothing and soft, softens the wound and brings life.' Everyone understood and read, or rather devoured the inspired pages; and the hearts of the elect (to use Tyndale's words), warmed by the love of Jesus Christ, began to melt like wax.

This transformation was observed to take place even in the most Catholic families. William Roper, More's son-in-law, having read the New Testament, received the truth. 'I have no more need', said he, 'of auricular confession, of vigils, or of the invocation of saints. The ears of God are always open to hear us. Faith alone is necessary to salvation. I believe ... and I am saved. ... Nothing can deprive me of God's favour.'[3]

The amiable and zealous young man desired to do more. 'Father', said he one day to Sir Thomas, 'procure for me from the king, who is very fond of you, a licence to preach. God hath sent me to instruct the world.' More was uneasy. Must this new doctrine, which he detested, spread even to his children? He exerted all his authority to destroy the work begun in Roper's heart. 'What', said he with a smile, 'is it not sufficient that we that are your friends should know that you are a fool, but you would proclaim your folly to the world? Hold your tongue: I will debate with you no longer.' The young man's imagination had been struck, but his heart had not been changed. The discussions having ceased, the father's authority being restored, Roper became less fervent in his faith, and gradually he returned to popery, of which he was afterwards a zealous champion.

As for Thomas Garret, the humble curate of All Hallows, having sold the New Testament to persons living in London and its neighbourhood, and to many pious men who would carry it to the farthest parts of England, he formed the resolution to introduce it into the University of Oxford, that citadel of traditional Catholicism. It was there he had studied, and he felt towards that school the affection which a son bears to his mother: he set out with his books. Terror occasionally seized him, for he knew that the word of God had many deadly enemies at Oxford; but his inexhaustible zeal overcame his timidity. In concert with Anthony Dalaber, he stealthily offered the mysterious book for sale; many students bought it, and Garret carefully entered their names in his account book. This was sometime during 1526.

It was not only the New Testament and such doctrinal works as Luther's *Bondage of the Will* which Garret and others were quietly selling that men were starting to read. Another sort of literature was also beginning to circulate and before long it added its testimony to the truth even within the walls of the royal palace. One morning when Edmund Moddis, one of Henry's valets-de-chambre, was in attendance on his master, the king, who was much attached to him, spoke to him of the new books come from beyond the sea. 'If Your Grace', said Moddis, 'would promise to pardon me and certain individuals, I would present you a wonderful book which is dedicated to Your Majesty.' – 'Who is the author?' – 'A lawyer of Gray's Inn named Simon Fish, at present on the Continent.' 'What is he doing there?' – 'About three years ago, Mr Row, a fellow student of Gray's Inn, composed for a private theatre a drama against my lord the cardinal.' The king smiled; when his minister was attacked, his own yoke seemed lighter. 'As no one was willing to represent the character employed to give the cardinal his lesson', continued the valet, 'Master Fish boldly accepted it. The piece produced a great effect; and my lord, being informed of this impertinence, sent the police one night to arrest Fish. But he managed to escape, crossed the sea, joined one Tyndale, the author of some of the books so much talked of; and, carried away by his friend's example, he composed the book of which I was speaking to Your Grace.' – 'What's the name of it?' – '*A Supplication for the Beggars.*'[4] – 'Where did you see it?' – 'At two of your tradespeople's, George Elyot and George Robinson; if Your Grace desires it, they shall bring it you.' The king appointed the day and the hour.

The book was written for the king, and everybody read it but the king himself. At the appointed day Moddis appeared with Elyot and Robinson, who were not entirely without fear, as they might be accused of proselytism even in the royal palace.

The king received them in his private apartments. 'What do you want?' he said to them. 'Sir', replied one of the merchants, 'we are come about an extraordinary book that is addressed to you.' – 'Can one of you read it to me?' – 'Yes, if it so please Your Grace', replied Elyot. 'You may repeat the contents from memory', rejoined the king … 'but no, read it all; that will be better. I am ready.' Elyot began,

---

[4] Published about 1529.

A SUPPLICATION FOR THE BEGGARS

To the King our Sovereign Lord –

Most lamentably complaineth of their woeful misery, unto Your Highness, your poor daily bedesmen,[5] the wretched hideous monsters, on whom scarcely, for horror, any eye dare look; the foul unhappy sort of lepers and other sore people, needy, impotent, blind, lame, and sick, that live only by alms; how that their number is daily sore increased, that all the alms of all the well-disposed people of this your realm are not half enough to sustain them, but that for very constraint they die for hunger.

And this most pestilent mischief is come upon your said poor bedesmen, by the reason that there hath, in the time of your noble predecessors, craftily crept into this your realm, another sort, not of impotent, but of strong, puissant, and counterfeit, holy and idle beggars and vagabonds, who by all the craft and wiliness of Satan are now increased not only into a great number, but also into a kingdom.

Henry was very attentive; Elyot continued:

These are not the shepherds, but the ravenous wolves going in shepherd's clothing, devouring the flock: bishops, abbots, priors, deacons, archdeacons, suffragans, priests, monks, canons, friars, pardoners, and summoners. … The goodliest lordships, manors, lands, and territories are theirs. Besides this, they have the tenth part of all the corn, meadow, pasture, grass, wood, colts, calves, lambs, pigs, geese, and chickens. Over and besides, the tenth part of every servant's wages, the tenth part of wool, milk, honey, wax, cheese, and butter. The poor wives must be accountable to them for every tenth egg, or else she getteth not her rights [*i.e.* absolution] at Easter. … Finally what get they in a year? Summa totalis: £430,333, 6s. 8d. sterling, whereof not four hundred years past they had not a penny. …

What subjects shall be able to help their prince, that be after this fashion yearly polled? What good Christian people can be able to succour us poor lepers, blind, sore, and lame, that be thus yearly oppressed? … The ancient Romans had never been able to have put all the whole world under their obeisance, if they had had at home such an idle sort of cormorants.

[5] A bedesman was a pensioner bound to pray for a benefactor.

No subject could have been found more likely to captivate the king's attention. 'And what doth all this greedy sort of sturdy idle holy thieves with their yearly exactions that they take of the people? Truly nothing, but translate all rule, power, lordship, authority, obedience, and dignity from Your Grace unto them. Nothing, but that all your subjects should fall into disobedience and rebellion. ... Priests and doves make foul houses; and if you will ruin a state, set up in it the pope with his monks and clergy. ... Send these sturdy loobies [louts] abroad in the world to take them wives of their own, instead of meddling with other men's wives, and to get their living with their labour in the sweat of their faces. ... Then shall your commons increase in riches; then shall matrimony be much better kept; then shall not your sword, power, crown, dignity, and obedience of your people be translated from you.'

When Elyot had finished reading, the king was silent, sunk in thought. The true cause of the ruin of the state had been laid before him; but Henry's mind was not ripe for these important truths. At last he said, with an uneasy manner: 'If a man who desires to pull down an old wall, begins at the bottom, I fear the upper part may chance to fall on his head.' Thus then, in the king's eyes, Fish by attacking the priests was disturbing the foundations of religion and society. It was imperative that the mischievous book should be withstood.

Of the Roman Church in England at this period, Sir Thomas More was the literary champion. Already famous as the author of *Utopia*, he now produced *The Supplications of the Souls in Purgatory*. 'Suppress', said they, 'the pious stipends paid to the monks, and then Luther's gospel will come in, Tyndale's Testament will be read, heresy will be preached, fasts will be neglected, the saints will be blasphemed, God will be offended, virtue will be mocked at, vice will run riot, and England will be peopled with beggars and thieves.' The *Souls in Purgatory* then call the author of the *Beggars' Supplication* 'a goose, an ass, a mad dog'. Thus did superstition degrade More's noble genius. Notwithstanding the abuse of the *Souls in Purgatory*, the New Testament was daily read more and more in England.

CHAPTER TWO

Oxford's Baptism of Suffering

(1526–1528)

W e have already seen how Tyndale's New Testament had entered England by surprise early in 1526, and how in parsonages and monastic cells, shops and private houses, its startling message was entering the souls of men. Great were the fears of the bishops. They saw in the circulation of the 'heretical' book the greatest threat to their power which had appeared in a thousand years. The gospellers who presumed to emancipate man from the priests, and put him in absolute dependence on God, were thereby undermining the very foundations of the papal system. What must be done?

Wolsey, as the greatest of the church dignitaries, hastened to assemble the bishops, and these, particularly Warham of Canterbury and Tunstall of London, gave immediate and diligent attention to the problem. With Wolsey they believed that the authority of the pope and of the clergy was a dogma to which all others were subordinate. They saw in the reform an uprising of the human mind, a desire in men to think for themselves, and to judge freely the doctrines and institutions which the nations had hitherto received humbly from the hands of the priests. The new teachers justified their attempt at enfranchisement by substituting a new authority for the old. It was the New Testament that compromised the absolute power of Rome. It must be seized and destroyed, said the bishops. London, Oxford, and, above all, Cambridge, those three haunts of heresy, must be carefully searched. Definitive orders were issued in February 1528, and the work began immediately.

The first visit of the inquisitors was to Honey Lane, to the house of the curate of All Hallows. They did not find Garret; they sought after him at Monmouth's, and throughout the city, but he could not be met with. 'He is gone to Oxford to sell his detestable wares', the inquisitors were informed, and they set off after him immediately, determined to burn the evangelist and his books; 'so burning hot', says an historian, 'was the charity of these holy fathers'.

Early in February,[1] Garret was quietly selling his books at Oxford and carefully noting down his sales in his record, when two of his friends came to him exclaiming, 'Fly! or else you will be taken before the cardinal, and thence ... to the Tower.' The poor curate was greatly agitated. 'From whom did you learn that?' – 'From Master Cole, the clerk of the assembly, who is deep in the cardinal's favour.' Garret, who saw at once that the affair was serious, hastened to Anthony Dalaber, who held the stock of the holy Scriptures at Oxford; others followed him; the news had spread rapidly, and those who had bought the book were seized with alarm, for they knew by the history of the Lollards what the Romish clergy could do. They took counsel together. The brethren, 'for so did we not only call one another, but were in deed one to another', says Dalaber, decided that Garret should change his name; that Dalaber should give him a letter for his brother, the rector of Stalbridge, in Dorsetshire, who was in want of a curate; and that, once in this parish, he should seek the first opportunity of crossing the sea. The rector was in truth a 'rank papist', says Dalaber, 'afterwards the most mortal enemy that ever I had, for the gospel's sake'; but that did not alter their resolution. They knew of no other resource. Anthony wrote to him hurriedly; and Garret immediately left Oxford without being observed.

Having provided for Garret's safety, Dalaber next thought of his own. He carefully concealed in a secret recess of his chamber, at St Alban's Hall, Tyndale's Testament, and the works of Luther, Œcolampadius, and others, on the word of God. Then, disgusted with the scholastic sophisms which he heard in that college, he took with him the New Testament and the *Commentary on the Gospel of St Luke*, by Lambert of Avignon, the second edition of which had just been published at

---

[1] [Foxe, *Acts*, v, p. 421, gives the date of these happenings as '1526, or thereabout'. The true date, however, verifiable from sources not available to Foxe, is 1528. Additional documents relative to Garret are printed in Josiah Pratt's edition of the *Acts and Monuments*, Appendix to vol. v.]

Strasburg, and went to Gloucester College, where he intended to study the civil law, not caring to have anything more to do with the church.

During this time, poor Garret was making his way into Dorsetshire. His conscience could not bear the idea of being, although for a short time only, the curate of a bigoted priest – of concealing his faith, his desires, and even his name. He felt more wretched, although at liberty, than he could have been in Wolsey's prisons. It is better, he said within himself, to confess Christ before the judgment seat, than to seem to approve of the superstitious practices I detest. He went forward a little, then stopped – and then resumed his course. There was a fierce struggle between his fears and his conscience. At length, after a day and a half spent in doubt, his conscience prevailed; unable to endure any longer the anguish that he felt, he retraced his steps, returned to Oxford, which he entered on a Friday evening, and lay down calmly in his bed. It was barely past midnight when Wolsey's agents, who had received information of his return, arrived, and dragged him from his bed, and delivered him up to Dr Cottisford, the commissary of the university. The latter locked him up in one of his rooms, while London, Warden of New College, and Higdon, Dean of Frideswide, 'two arch papists' (as the chronicler terms them), announced this important capture to the cardinal. They thought popery was saved, because a poor curate had been taken.

Dalaber, engaged in preparing his new room at Gloucester College, knew nothing of all this. On Saturday, at noon, having finished his arrangements, he double-locked his door, and began to read the Gospel according to St Luke. All of a sudden he hears a knock. Dalaber made no reply; it is no doubt the commissary's officers. A louder knock was given; but he still remained silent. Immediately after, there was a third knock, as if the door would be beaten in. 'Perhaps somebody needs me', thought Dalaber. He laid his book aside, opened the door, and to his great surprise saw Garret, who, with alarm in every feature, exclaimed, 'I am a lost man! They have caught me!' Dalaber, who thought his friend was with his brother at Stalbridge, could not conceal his astonishment, and at the same time he cast an uneasy glance on a stranger who accompanied Garret. He was one of the college servants who had led the fugitive curate to Dalaber's new room. As soon as this man had gone away, Garret told Anthony everything: 'Observing that Dr Cottisford and his household had gone to prayers, I put back the bolt of the lock with my finger ... and here I am.' – 'Alas! Master Garret', replied Dalaber, 'the imprudence you committed in speaking to me before that young man has ruined us both!' At these words, Garret, whose fear of the priests had returned, now that his conscience was satisfied, exclaimed with a voice interrupted by sighs and tears: 'For mercy's sake, help me! Save me!' Without waiting for an answer, he threw off his gown and hood, begged Anthony to give him a sleeved coat and, thus disguised, he said: 'I will escape into Wales, and from there, if possible, to Germany.'

Garret checked himself; there was something to be done before he left. The two friends fell on their knees and prayed together; they called upon God to lead his servant to a secure retreat. That done, they embraced each other, their faces bathed with tears, and unable to utter a word.

Silent on the threshold of his door, Dalaber followed both with eyes and ears his friend's retreating footsteps. Having heard him reach the bottom of the stairs, he returned to his room, locked the door, took out his New Testament and, placing it before him, read on his knees the tenth chapter of the Gospel of St Matthew, breathing many a heavy sigh: *Ye shall be brought before governors and kings for my sake ... but fear them not; the very hairs of your head are all numbered.* This reading having revived his courage, Anthony, still on his knees, prayed fervently for the fugitive and for all his brethren: 'O God, by thy Holy Spirit endue with heavenly strength this tender and new-born little flock in Oxford. Christ's heavy cross is about to be laid on the weak shoulders of thy poor sheep. Grant that they may bear it with godly patience and unflinching zeal!'

Rising from his knees, Dalaber put away his book, folded up Garret's hood and gown, placed them among his own clothes, locked his room door, and proceeded to the cardinal's college (now Christ Church) to tell Clark and the other brethren what had happened. They were in chapel: the evening service had begun; the dean and canons, in full costume, were chanting in the choir. Dalaber stopped at the door listening to the majestic sounds of the organ at which Taverner presided, and to the harmonious strains of the choristers. They were singing the *Magnificat: My soul doth magnify the Lord ... He hath holpen his servant Israel.* It seemed to Dalaber that they were singing Garret's deliverance. But his voice could not join in their song of praise. 'Alas!' he exclaimed, 'all my singing and music is turned into sighing and musing.'

As he listened, leaning against the entrance into the choir, Dr Cottisford, the university commissary, arrived with hasty step, 'bare headed, and as pale as ashes'. He passed Anthony without noticing him, and going straight to the dean appeared to announce some important and unpleasant news. 'I know well the cause of his sorrow', thought Dalaber as he watched every gesture. The commissary had scarcely finished his report when the dean arose, and both left the choir with undisguised confusion. They had only reached the middle of the anti-chapel when Dr London came in, 'puffing, blustering, and blowing, like a hungry and greedy lion seeking his prey'. All three stopped, questioned one another, and deplored their misfortune. Their rapid and eager movements indicated the liveliest emotion; London above all could not restrain himself. He attacked the commissary, and blamed him for his negligence, so that at last Cottisford burst into tears. 'Deeds, not tears', said the fanatical London; and forthwith they despatched officers and spies along every road.

Anthony having left the chapel hurried to Clark's to tell him of the escape of his friend. 'We are walking in the midst of wolves and tigers', replied Clark; 'prepare for persecution. *Prudentia serpentina et simplicitas columbina* (the wisdom of serpents and the harmlessness of doves) must be our motto. O God, give us the courage these evil times require.' All in the little flock were delighted at Garret's deliverance. Sumner and Betts, who had come in, ran off to tell it to the other brethren in the college, and Dalaber hastened to Corpus Christi. All these pious young men felt themselves to be soldiers in the same army, travellers in the same company, brothers in the same family. Fraternal love nowhere shone so brightly in the days of the reformation as among the Christians of Great Britain. This is a feature worthy of notice.

Fitzjames, Udal, and Diet were met together in the rooms of the last-named, at Corpus Christi College, when Dalaber arrived. They ate their frugal meal with downcast eyes and broken voices, conversing of Oxford, of England, and of the perils hanging over them. Then rising from table they fell on their knees, called upon God for aid, and separated, Fitzjames taking Dalaber with him to St Alban's Hall. They were afraid that the servant of Gloucester College had betrayed him.

The disciples of the gospel at Oxford passed the night in great anxiety. Garret's flight, the rage of the priests, the dangers of the rising church, the roaring of a storm that filled the air and re-echoed through the long cloisters – all filled them with the liveliest apprehensions. The Lord's Day came. Dalaber, who was stirring at five in the morning, set out for his room in Gloucester College. Finding the gates shut, he walked up and down beneath the walls in the mud, for it had rained heavily. As he paced to and fro along the solitary street in the obscure dawn, a thousand thoughts alarmed his mind. It was known, he said to himself, that he had assisted Garret's flight; he would be arrested, and his friend's escape would be revenged on him. He was weighed down by sorrow and alarm; he sighed heavily; he imagined he saw Wolsey's commissioners demanding the names of his accomplices, and pretending to draw up a proscription list at his dictation; he recollected that on more than one occasion cruel priests had extorted from the Lollards the names of their brethren and, terrified at the possibility of such a crime, he exclaimed; 'O God, I swear to thee that I will accuse no man. ... I will tell nothing but what is perfectly well known.'

At last, after an hour of anguish, he was able to enter the college. He hastened in, but when he tried to open his door, he found that the lock had been tampered with. The door gave way to a strong push, and what a sight met his eyes! his bedstead overturned, the blankets scattered on the floor, his clothes all confusion in his wardrobe, his study broken into and left open. He doubted not that Garret's dress had betrayed him; and he was gazing at this sad spectacle in alarm, when a monk who occupied the adjoining rooms came and told him what had taken place: 'The commissary and two proctors, armed with swords and bills, broke open your door in the middle of the night. They pierced your bed-straw through and through to make sure Garret was not hidden there; they carefully searched every nook and corner, but were not able to discover any traces of the fugitive.' At these words Dalaber breathed again ... but the monk had not ended. 'I have orders', he added, 'to send you to the prior.' Anthony Dunstan, the prior, was a fanatical and avaricious monk; and the confusion into which this message threw Dalaber was so great, that he went just as he was, all bespattered with mud, to the rooms of his superior.

The prior, who was standing with his face towards the door, looked at Dalaber from head to foot as he came in. 'Where did you pass the night?' he asked. – 'At St Alban's Hall with Fitzjames.' The prior with a gesture of incredulity continued: 'Was not Master Garret with you yesterday?' – 'Yes.' – 'Where is he now?' – 'I do not know.' During this examination, the prior had noticed a large double-gilt silver ring on Anthony's finger, with the initials A.D. 'Show me that', said the prior. Dalaber gave him the ring and the prior, believing it to be of solid gold, put it on his own finger, adding with a cunning leer: 'This ring is mine: it bears my name. A is for *Anthony*, and D for *Dunstan*.' – 'Would to God', thought Dalaber, 'that I were as well delivered from his company, as I am sure of being delivered of my ring.'

At this moment the chief beadle, with two or three of the commissary's men, entered and conducted Dalaber to the chapel of Lincoln College, where three ill-omened figures were standing beside the altar: they were Cottisford, London, and Higdon. 'Where is Garret?' asked London; and pointing to his disordered dress, he continued: 'Your shoes and garments covered with mud prove that you have been out all night with him. If you do not say where you have taken him, you will be sent to the Tower.' – 'Yes', added Higdon, 'to *Little-ease* [one of the most horrible dungeons in the prison], and you will be put to the torture, do you hear?' Then the three doctors spent two hours attempting to shake the young man by flattering promises and frightful threats; but all was useless. The commissary then gave a sign, the officers stepped forward, and the judges ascended a narrow staircase leading to a large room situated above the commissary's chamber. Here Dalaber was deprived of his purse and girdle, and his legs were placed in the stocks, so that his feet were almost as high as his head. When that was done, the three doctors devoutly went to Mass.

Left alone in this frightful position, Dalaber recollected the warning Clark had given him two years before. He groaned heavily and cried to God: 'O Father! grant that my suffering may be for thy glory, and for the consolation of my brethren! Happen what may, I will never accuse one of them.' After this noble protest, Anthony felt an increase of peace in his heart; but a new sorrow was reserved for him.

Garret, who had directed his course south-westwards, was caught at Bedminster, near Bristol. He was brought back, and thrown into the dungeon in which Dalaber had been placed after the torture. Their gloomy presentiments were to be more than fulfilled.

In fact Wolsey was deeply irritated at seeing the college [Christ Church], which he had intended should be 'the most glorious in the world', made the haunt of heresy, and the young men, whom he had so carefully chosen, become distributors of the New Testament. By favouring literature, he had had in view the triumph of the clergy, and literature had on the contrary served to the triumph of the gospel. He issued his orders without delay, and the university was filled with terror. John Clark, John Fryth, Henry Sumner, William Betts, Richard Taverner, Richard Cox, Michael Drumm, Godfrey Harman, Thomas Lawney, Radley, and others besides of Cardinal College; Udal, Diet, and others of Corpus Christi; Eden and several of his friends of Magdalen; Goodman, William Bayley, Robert Ferrar, John Salisbury of Gloucester, Barnard, and St Mary's Colleges; were seized and thrown into prison. Wolsey had promised them glory; he gave them a dungeon, hoping in this manner to save the power of the priests, and to repress that awakening of truth and liberty which was spreading from the Continent to England.

Under Cardinal College there was a deep cellar sunk in the earth, in which the butler kept his salt fish. Into this hole these young men, the choice of England, were thrust. The dampness of this cave, the corrupted air they breathed, the horrible smell given out by the fish, seriously affected the prisoners, already weakened by study. Their hearts were bursting with groans, their faith was shaken, and the most mournful scenes followed one another in this foul dungeon. The wretched captives gazed on one another, wept, and prayed. This trial was destined to be a salutary one to them: 'Alas!' said Fryth on a subsequent occasion, 'I see that besides the word of God, there is indeed a second purgatory ... but it is not that invented by Rome; it is the cross of tribulation to which God has nailed us.'

At last the prisoners were taken out one by one and brought before their judges; two only were released. The first was Betts, afterwards chaplain to Anne Boleyn: they had not been able to find any prohibited books in his room, and he pleaded his cause with great talent. The other was Taverner; he had hidden Clark's books under his school-room floor, where they had been discovered; but his love for the arts saved him: 'Pshaw! he is only a musician', said the cardinal.

All the rest were condemned. A great fire was kindled at the top of Carfax, in the centre of Oxford, a long procession was marshalled, and these unfortunate men were led out, each bearing a faggot. When they came near the fire, they were compelled to throw into it the heretical books that had been found in their rooms, after which they were taken back to their noisome prison. There seemed to be a barbarous pleasure in treating these young and generous men so vilely. In other countries also, Rome was preparing to stifle in the flames the noblest geniuses of France, Spain, and Italy. Such was the reception letters and the gospel met with from popery in the sixteenth century. Every plant of God's must be beaten by the wind, even at the risk of its being uprooted; if it receives only the gentle rays of the sun, there is reason to fear that it will dry up and wither before it produces fruit. *Except a corn of wheat fall into the ground and die, it abideth alone.* There was to arise one day a true church in England; persecution was but the prelude to its appearing.

But we must now turn to give attention to the lot of confessors of the faith in another university city.

CHAPTER THREE

The Severities of Popery

(1526–1528)

Oxford and Cambridge, which alike shared the glories of the 'new learning' in early Tudor days, and which were both deeply stirred by reformation teaching, were alike also in their experience of persecution. It was in 1526 that the party of reform in the city on the Cam received its baptism of suffering.

Early in February in that year, two of Wolsey's agents, Dr Capon, one of his chaplains, and Gibson, a sergeant-at-arms, notorious for his arrogance, left London for Cambridge. Submission was the password of popery. 'Yes, submission', was responded from every part of Christendom by men of sincere piety and profound understanding; 'submission to the legitimate authority against which Roman Catholicism has rebelled.' According to their views the traditionalism and pelagianism of the Romish Church had set up the supremacy of fallen reason in opposition to the Divine supremacy of the word and of grace. The external and apparent sacrifice of self which Roman Catholicism imposes – obedience to a confessor or to the pope, arbitrary penance, ascetic practices, and celibacy – only served to create, and so to strengthen and perpetuate, a delusion as to the egotistic preservation of a sinful personality. When the reformation proclaimed liberty, so far as regarded ordinances of human invention, it was with the view of bringing man's heart and life into subjection to their real Sovereign. The reign of God was commencing; that of the priests must needs come to an end. No man can serve two masters. Such were the important truths which gradually dawned upon the world, and which Wolsey and countless others thought it necessary to extinguish without delay.

On the day after their arrival in Cambridge, Capon and Gibson went to the convocation house, where several of the doctors were talking together. Their appearance caused some anxiety among the spectators, who looked upon the strangers with distrust. On a sudden Gibson moved forward, put his hand on Barnes, and arrested him in the presence of his friends. The latter were frightened, and this was what the sergeant wanted. 'What!' said they, 'the Prior of the Augustines, the restorer of letters in Cambridge, arrested by a sergeant!' This was not all. Wolsey's agents were to seize the books come from Germany, and their owners; Bilney, Latimer, Stafford, Arthur, and their friends, were all to be imprisoned, for they possessed the New Testament. Thirty members of the university were pointed out as suspected; and some miserable wretches, who had been bribed by the inquisitors, offered to show the place in every room where the prohibited books were hidden. But while the necessary preparations were making for this search, Bilney, Latimer, and their colleagues, being warned in time, got the books removed; they were taken away not only by the doors but by the windows, even by the roofs, and anxious inquiry was made for sure places in which they could be concealed.

This work was hardly ended, when the vice-chancellor of the university, the sergeant-at-arms, Wolsey's chaplain, the proctors, and the informers began their rounds. They opened the first room, entered, searched, and found nothing. They passed on to the second, there was nothing. The sergeant was astonished, and grew angry. On reaching the third room, he ran directly to the place that had been pointed out – still there was nothing. The same thing occurred everywhere; never was inquisitor more mortified. He dared not lay hands on the persons of the evangelical doctors; his orders read that he was to seize the books and *their owners*. But as no books were found, there could be no prisoners. However, there was one man (the Prior of the Augustines) against whom there were particular charges. The sergeant promised to compensate himself at Barnes' expense for his useless labours.

The next day Gibson and Capon set out for London with Barnes. During this mournful journey the prior, in great agitation, at one time determined to brave all England, and at another trembled like a leaf. At last their journey was ended; the chaplain left his prisoner at Parnell's house, close by the stocks. Three students (Coverdale, Goodwin, and Field) had followed their master to cheer him with their tender affection.

On Thursday (8 February) the sergeant conducted Barnes to the cardinal's palace at Westminster; the wretched prior, whose enthusiasm had given way to dejection, waited all day before he could be admitted. What a day! Will no one come to his assistance? Doctor Gardiner, Wolsey's secretary, and Fox, his steward, both old friends of Barnes, passed through the gallery in the evening, and went up to the prisoner, who begged them to procure him an audience with the cardinal. These officers agreed to introduce the prior into the room where their master was sitting, and Barnes, as was customary, fell on his knees before him. 'Is this the Doctor Barnes who is accused of heresy?' asked Wolsey, in a haughty tone, of Fox and Gardiner. They replied in the affirmative. The cardinal then turning to Barnes, who was still kneeling, said to him ironically, and not without reason: 'What, Master Doctor, had you not sufficient scope in the Scriptures to teach the people; but my golden shoes, my pole-axes, my pillars, my golden cushions, my crosses, did so sore offend you, that you must make us a laughing-stock, *ridiculum caput*, amongst the people? We were jollily that day laughed to scorn. Verily it was a sermon more fit to be preached on a stage than in a pulpit; for at the last you said I wore a pair of *red* gloves. … Eh! what think you, Master Doctor?' Barnes, wishing to elude these embarrassing questions, answered vaguely: 'I spoke nothing but the truth out of the Scriptures, according to my conscience and according to the old doctors.' He then presented to the cardinal a statement of his teaching.

Wolsey received the papers with a smile: 'Oh, ho!' said he, as he counted the six sheets, 'I perceive you intend to stand to your articles and to show your learning.' – 'By the grace of God', said Barnes. Wolsey then began to read them, and stopped at the sixth article, which ran thus: 'I will never believe that one man may, by the law of God, be bishop of two or three cities, yea, of a whole country, for it is contrary to St Paul, who saith: *I have left thee behind, to set in every city a bishop.*' Barnes did not quote correctly, for the apostle says: '*to ordain elders in every city*'.[1] Wolsey was displeased at this thesis: 'Ah! this touches me', he said: 'Do you think it wrong (seeing the ordinance of the church) that

---

[1] Titus 1:5.

one bishop should have so many cities underneath him?' – 'I know of no ordinance of the church', Barnes replied, 'as concerning this thing, but Paul's saying only.'

Although this controversy interested the cardinal, the personal attack of which he had to complain touched him more keenly. 'Good', said Wolsey; and then with a condescension hardly to be expected from so proud a man, he deigned almost to justify himself. 'You charge me with displaying a royal pomp; but do you not understand that, being called to represent His Majesty, I must strive by these means to strike terror into the wicked?' – 'It is not your pomp or your pole-axes', Barnes courageously answered, 'that will save the king's person. ... God will save him, who said: *Per me reges regnant.*' (By me kings reign.) Barnes, instead of profiting by the cardinal's kindness to present an humble justification, as Dean Colet had formerly done to Henry VIII, dared preach him a second sermon to his face. Wolsey felt the colour mount to his cheeks. 'Well, gentlemen', said he, turning to Fox and Gardiner, 'you hear him! Is this the wise and learned man of whom you spoke to me?'

At these words both steward and secretary fell on their knees, saying: 'We desire Your Grace to be good unto him, for he will be reformable.' – 'Do you not know', said Wolsey to Barnes, 'that I am *legatus de latere*, and that I am able to dispense in all matters concerning religion within this realm, as much as the pope may?' Barnes replied, 'I know it to be so.' – 'Will you then be ruled by us, and we will do all things for your good, and for the good of the university.' He answered: 'I thank Your Grace for your goodwill; I will stick to the holy Scripture, and to God's book, according to the simple talent that God hath lent me.' – 'Well', replied Wolsey, 'thou shalt have thy learning tried to the utmost, and thou shalt have the law.' Orders were then given that he should be taken to the Tower, but Gardiner and Fox offered to become his sureties, and Wolsey permitted him to pass the night at the house of a Master Parnell. He spent most of the night in writing, and did not sleep. The next day he was taken into the chapter house at Westminster and re-examined before Islip, Abbot of Westminster, and sundry bishops. His judges laid before him a long statement, and said to him: 'Promise to read this paper in public, without omitting or adding a single word.' It was then read to him. 'I would die first', was his reply. 'Will you abjure or be burnt alive?' said his judges; 'take your choice.' The alternative was dreadful. A prey to the deepest agony, Barnes shrank at the thought of the stake; then, suddenly his courage revived, and he exclaimed: 'I would rather be burnt than abjure.' Gardiner and Fox did all they could to persuade him. 'Listen to reason', said they craftily: 'your articles are true; that is not the question. We want to know whether by your death you will let error triumph, or whether you would rather remain to defend the truth, when better days may come.'

They entreated him; they put forward the most plausible motives; from time to time they uttered the terrible words, *burnt alive!* His blood froze in his veins; he knew not what he said or did ... they placed a paper before him – they put a pen in his hand – his head was bewildered, he signed his name with a deep sigh. This unhappy man was destined at a later period to be a faithful martyr of Jesus Christ; but he had not yet learnt to 'resist even unto blood'. Barnes had fallen.

On the following Sunday morning a solemn spectacle was preparing at St Paul's. Before daybreak, all were astir in the prison of the unhappy prior; and at eight o'clock, the knight-marshal with his tipstaves, and the warden of the Fleet prison, with his billmen, conducted Barnes to St Paul's, along with four of the Hanse merchants who had first brought to London the New Testament of Jesus Christ in English. The fifth of these pious merchants held an immense taper, five pounds in weight, in his hands. A persevering search had discovered that it was these men to whom England was indebted for the so much dreaded book; their warehouses were surrounded and their persons arrested. On the top of St Paul's steps was a platform, and on the platform a throne, and on the throne the cardinal, dressed in purple. On his head glittered the mitre of which Barnes had spoken so ill; around him were thirty-six bishops, abbots, priors, and all his doctors, dressed in damask and satin; the cathedral held a vast congregation. The Bishop of Rochester having gone into a pulpit placed at the top of the steps, Barnes and the merchants, each bearing a faggot, were compelled to kneel and listen to a sermon intended to cure these poor creatures of that taste for insurrection against popery which was beginning to spread in every quarter. The sermon ended, Dr Barnes was then required to declare that he was more charitably handled than he deserved, and to ask pardon for his heresies. All this done, the cardinal took his station under a magnificent canopy, moved with his escort of bishops to the cathedral gate, mounted his mule, and rode off. After this Barnes and his five companions walked three times round a fire lighted before the cross at the north gate of the cathedral. The dejected prior, with downcast head, dragged himself along, rather than walked. After the third turn, the prisoners threw their faggots into the flames; some 'heretical' books also were flung in; and the Bishop of Rochester having given absolution to the six penitents, they were led back to prison to be kept there during the lord cardinal's pleasure. Barnes could not weep now; the thought of his relapse, and of the effects so guilty an example might produce, had deprived him of all moral energy. In the month of August, he was led out of prison and confined in the Augustine monastery.

Barnes was not the only man at Cambridge upon whom the blow had fallen. Since the year 1520, a monk named Richard Bayfield had been an inmate of the abbey of Bury St Edmunds. His affability delighted every traveller. One day, when engaged as chamberlain in receiving Barnes, who had come to visit Doctor Ruffam, his fellow student at Louvain, two men entered the monastery. They were pious persons, and of great consideration in London, where they carried on the occupation of brick-making, and had risen to be wardens of their guild. Their names were Maxwell and Stacy, men 'well grafted in the doctrine of Christ', says the historian, who had led many to the Saviour by their conversation and exemplary life. Being accustomed to travel once a year through the counties to visit their brethren, and extend a knowledge of the gospel, they used to lodge, according to the usages of the time, in the monasteries and abbeys. A conversation soon arose between Barnes, Stacy, and Maxwell, which struck the lay-brother. Barnes, who had observed his attention, gave him, as he was leaving the monastery, a New Testament in Latin, and the two brick-makers added a New Testament in English, with *The Wicked Mammon* and *The Obedience of a Christian Man*. The lay-brother ran and hid the books in his cell, and for two years read them constantly. At last he was discovered, and reprimanded; but he boldly confessed his faith. Upon this the monks threw him into prison, set him in the stocks, put a gag in his mouth, and cruelly whipped him, to prevent his speaking of grace. The unhappy Bayfield remained nine months in this condition.

When Barnes repeated his visit to Bury at a later period, he did not find the amiable chamberlain at the gates of the abbey. Upon inquiry he learnt his condition, and immediately took steps to procure his deliverance. Dr Ruffam came to his aid: 'Give him to me', said Barnes, 'I will take him to Cambridge.' The Prior of the Augustines was at that time held in high esteem; his request was granted, in the hope that he would lead back Bayfield to the doctrines of the church. But the very reverse took place: intercourse with the Cambridge brethren strengthened the young monk's faith. On a sudden his happiness vanished. Barnes, his friend and benefactor, was carried to London, and the monks of Bury St Edmunds, alarmed at the noise this affair created, summoned him to return to the abbey. But Bayfield, resolving to submit to their yoke no longer, went to London, and lay concealed with Maxwell and Stacy. One day, having left his hiding place, he was crossing Lombard Street, when he met a priest named Pierson and two other members of his order, with whom he entered into a conversation which greatly scandalized them. 'You must depart forthwith', said Maxwell and Stacy to him on his return. Bayfield received a small sum of money from them, went on board a ship and, as soon as he reached the Continent, hastened to find Tyndale.

During this time scenes of a very different nature from those which had taken place at Cambridge, but not less heart-rending, were passing at Oxford. The storm of persecution was raging there with more violence than at Cambridge. Clark and the other confessors of the name of Christ were still confined in their underground prison. The air they breathed, the food they took (and they were given nothing but salt fish), the burning thirst this created, the thoughts by which they were agitated, all together combined to crush these noble-hearted men. Their bodies wasted day by day; they wandered like spectres up and down their gloomy cellar. Those animated discussions in which the deep questions then convulsing Christendom were so eloquently debated were at an end; they were like shadow meeting shadow. Their hollow eyes cast a vague and haggard glance on one another and, after gazing for a moment, they passed on without speaking. Clark, Sumner, Bayley, and Goodman, consumed by fever, feebly crawled along, leaning against their dungeon walls. The first, who was also the eldest, could not walk without the support of one of his fellow prisoners. Soon he was quite unable to move, and lay stretched upon the damp floor. The brethren gathered round him, sought to discover in his features whether death was not about to cut short the days of him who had brought many of them to the knowledge of Christ. They repeated to him slowly the words of Scripture, and then knelt down by his side and uttered a fervent prayer.

Clark, feeling his end draw near, asked for the communion. The jailers conveyed his request to their master; the noise of the bolts was soon heard, and a turnkey, stepping into the midst of the disconsolate band, pronounced a cruel no! On hearing this, Clark looked towards heaven, and exclaimed with a father of the church: *Crede et manducasti* (Believe and thou hast eaten). He was lost in thought: he contemplated the crucified Son of God; by faith he ate and drank the flesh and blood of Christ, and experienced in his inner life the strengthening action of the Redeemer. Men might refuse him the host, but Jesus had given him his body; and from that hour he felt strengthened by a living union with the king of heaven.

Not alone did Clark descend into the shadowy valley: Sumner, Bayley, and Goodman were sinking rapidly. Death, the gloomy inhabitant of this foul prison, had taken possession of these four friends. Their brethren addressed fresh solicitations to the cardinal, at that time closely occupied in negotiations with France, Rome, and Venice. He found means, however, to give a moment to the Oxford martyrs; and just as these Christians were praying over their four dying companions, the commissioner came and informed them, that 'his lordship, of his great goodness, permitted the sick persons to be removed to their own chambers'. Litters were brought, on which the dying men were placed and carried to their rooms; the doors were closed again upon those whose lives this frightful dungeon had not yet attacked.

It was the middle of August 1528. The wretched men who had passed six months in the cellar were transported in vain to their chambers and their beds; several members of the university ineffectually tried by their cares and their tender charity to recall them to life. It was too late. The severities of popery had killed these noble witnesses. The approach of death soon betrayed itself; their blood grew cold, their limbs stiff, and their bedimmed eyes sought only Jesus Christ, their everlasting hope. Clark, Sumner, and Bayley died in the same week. Goodman followed close upon them.

This unexpected catastrophe softened Wolsey. He was cruel only as far as his interest and the safety of the church required. He feared that the death of so many young men would raise public opinion against him, or that these catastrophes would damage his college; perhaps even some sentiment of humanity may have touched his heart. 'Set the rest at liberty', he wrote to his agents, 'but upon condition that they do not go above ten miles from Oxford.' The university beheld these young men issue from their living tomb pale, wasted, weak, and with faltering steps. At that time they were not men of mark; it was their youth that touched the spectators' hearts; but in after-years they all occupied an important place in the church. They were Cox, who became Bishop of Ely, and tutor to Edward the Prince Royal; Drumm, who under Cranmer became one of the six preachers at Canterbury; Udal, afterwards master of Westminster and Eton schools; Salisbury, Dean of Norwich, and then Bishop of Sodor and Man, who in all his wealth and greatness often recalled his frightful prison at Oxford as a title to glory; Ferrar, afterwards Cranmer's chaplain, Bishop of St David's, and a martyr even unto death, after an interval of thirty years; Fryth, Tyndale's friend, to whom this deliverance proved only a delay; and several others. When they came forth from their terrible dungeon, their friends ran up to them, supported their faltering steps, and embraced them amidst floods of tears. Fryth quitted the university not long after and went to Flanders. Thus was the tempest stayed which had so fearfully ravaged Oxford. But the calm was of no long duration; an unexpected circumstance became perilous to the cause of the reformation.

CHAPTER FOUR

The Tempest against the Truth

(1526)

I
n 1526 the peace of mind of Henry, King of England, was disturbed,
not only by the circulation of unauthorized New Testaments from
the Continent, but by the reception of a communication from
Martin Luther. The letter which, at the advice of Christian II, King
of Denmark, this reformer had written to him in September 1525, had
miscarried. The Wittenberg doctor hearing nothing of it, had boldly
printed it, and sent a copy to the king. 'I am informed', said Luther,
'that Your Majesty is beginning to favour the gospel, and to be disgusted
with the perverse race that fights against it in your noble kingdom. ...
It is true that, according to Scripture, *the kings of the earth take counsel
together against the Lord*, and we cannot, consequently, expect to see
them favourable to the truth. How fervently do I wish that this miracle
may be accomplished in the person of Your Majesty.'

We may imagine Henry's wrath as he read this letter. 'What!' said
he, 'does this apostate monk dare print a letter addressed to us, without
having even sent it, or at the least without knowing if we have ever
received it? ... And as if that were not enough, he insinuates that we are
among his partisans. ... He wins over also one or two wretches, born in
our kingdom, and engages them to translate the New Testament into
English, adding thereto certain prefaces and poisonous glosses.' Thus
spoke Henry. The idea that his name should be associated with that of
the Wittenberg monk called all the blood into his face. He will reply
right royally to such unblushing impudence. He summoned Wolsey
forthwith. 'Here!' said he, pointing to a passage concerning the prelate,
'here! read what is said of you!' And then he read aloud: "'*Illud monstrum*

et publicum odium Dei et hominum, cardinalis Eboracensis, pestis illa regni tui." You see, my lord, you are a monster, an object of hatred both to God and man, the *plague* of my kingdom!' The king had hitherto allowed the bishops to do as they pleased, and observed a sort of neutrality. He now determined to lay it aside and begin a crusade against the gospel of Jesus Christ, but he must first answer this impertinent letter. He consulted Sir Thomas More, shut himself in his chamber, and dictated to his secretary a reply to the reformer: 'You are ashamed of the book you have written against me', he said; 'I would counsel you to be ashamed of all that you have written. They are full of disgusting errors and frantic heresies; and are supported by the most audacious obstinacy. Your venomous pen mocks the church, insults the Fathers, abuses the saints, despises the apostles, dishonours the holy Virgin, and blasphemes God, by making him the author of evil. ... And after all that, you claim to be an author whose like does not exist in the world!

'You offer to publish a book in my praise. ... I thank you! ... You will praise me most by abusing me; you will dishonour me beyond measure if you praise me. I say with Seneca: "Let it be as disgraceful to you to be praised by the vile, as if you were praised for vile deeds."'

This letter, written by the king of the English to the *king of the heretics*, was immediately circulated throughout England bound up with Luther's epistle.[1] Henry, by publishing it, put his subjects on their guard against the *unfaithful* translations of the New Testament, which were besides about to be burnt everywhere. 'The grapes seem beautiful', he said, 'but beware how you wet your lips with the wine made from them, for the adversary hath mingled poison with it.'

Luther, agitated by this rude lesson, tried to excuse himself. 'I said to myself, *There are twelve hours in the day.* Who knows? perhaps I may find one favourable hour to gain the King of England. I therefore laid my humble epistle at his feet; but alas! the swine have torn it. I am willing to be silent ... but as regards my doctrine, I cannot impose silence on it. It must cry aloud, it must bite. If any king imagines he can make me retract my faith, he is a dreamer. So long as one drop of blood remains in my body, I shall say *No.* Emperors, kings, the devil, and even the

---

[1] [The date of publication appears to have been February 1527.]

whole universe, cannot frighten me when faith is concerned. I claim to be proud, very proud, exceedingly proud. If my doctrine had no other enemies than the King of England, Duke George, the pope, and their allies, all these soap-bubbles ... one little prayer would long ago have worsted them all. Where are Pilate, Herod, and Caiaphas now? Where are Nero, Domitian, and Maximilian? Where are Arius, Pelagius, and Manes? – Where are they? ... Where all our scribes and all our tyrants will soon be. – But Christ? Christ is the same always.

'For a thousand years the holy Scriptures have not shone in the world with so much brightness as now. I wait in peace for my last hour; I have done what I could. O princes, my hands are clean from your blood; it will fall on your own heads.'

Bowing before the supreme royalty of Jesus Christ, Luther spoke thus boldly to King Henry, who contested the rights of the word of God.

A letter written against the reformer was not enough for the bishops. Profiting by the wound Luther had inflicted on Henry's self-esteem, they urged him to put down this revolt of the human understanding, which threatened (as they averred) both the popedom and the monarchy. They commenced the persecution. Latimer was summoned before Wolsey, but his learning and presence of mind procured his dismissal. Bilney also, who had been ordered to London, received an injunction not to preach *Luther's doctrines*. 'I will not preach Luther's doctrines, if there are any peculiar to him', he said; 'but I can and I must preach the doctrine of Jesus Christ, although Luther should preach it too.' And finally Garret, led into the presence of his judges, was seized with terror, and fell before the cruel threats of the bishop. When restored to liberty, he fled from place to place, endeavouring to hide his sorrow, and to escape from the despotism of the priests, awaiting the moment when he should give his life for Jesus Christ.

The adversaries of the reformation were not yet satisfied. The New Testament continued to circulate, and depots were formed in several monasteries. Barnes, a prisoner in the Augustine monastery in London, had regained his courage, and loved his Bible more and more. One day about the end of September, as three or four friends were reading in his chamber, two simple peasants, John Tyball and Thomas Hilles, natives of Bumpstead in Essex, came in. 'How did you come to a knowledge of the truth?' asked Barnes. They drew from their pockets some old volumes containing the Gospels, and a few of the Epistles in English. Barnes returned them with a smile. 'They are nothing', he told them, 'in comparison with the new edition of the New Testament', a copy of which the two peasants bought for three shillings and twopence. 'Hide it carefully', said Barnes. When this came to the ears of the clergy, Barnes was removed to Northampton to be burnt at the stake; but he managed to escape; his friends reported that he was drowned; and while strict search was making for him during a whole week along the sea-coast, he secretly went on board a ship, and was carried to Germany. 'The cardinal will catch him even now', said the Bishop of London, 'whatever amount of money it may cost him.' When Barnes was told of this, he remarked: 'I am a poor simple wretch, not worth the tenth penny they will give for me. Besides, if they burn me, what will they gain by it? … The sun and the moon, fire and water, the stars and the elements – yea, and also stones shall defend this cause against them, *rather than the truth should perish*.' Faith had returned to Barnes' feeble heart.

His escape added fuel to the wrath of the clergy. They proclaimed, throughout the length and breadth of England, that the English translations of the holy Scriptures contained an *infectious poison*, and ordered a general search after the word of God. On 24 October 1526, the Bishop of London enjoined on his archdeacons to seize all translations of the New Testament in English with or without glosses; and, a few days later, the Archbishop of Canterbury issued a mandate against all the books which should contain 'any particle of the New Testament'. The primate remembered that a spark was sufficient to kindle a large fire.

On hearing of this order, William Roye, a sarcastic writer, published a violent satire, in which figured *Judas* (Standish), *Pilate* (Wolsey), and *Caiaphas* (Tunstall). The author exclaimed with energy:

> God, of his goodness, grudged not to die,
> Man to deliver from deadly damnation;
> Whose will is, that we should know perfectly
> What He here hath done for our salvation.

> O cruel Caiaphas! full of crafty conspiration,
> How durst thou give them false judgment
> To burn God's word – the Holy Testament.

The efforts of Caiaphas and his colleagues were indeed useless: the priests were undertaking a work beyond their strength. If by some terrible revolution all social forms should be destroyed in the world, the living church of the elect, a Divine institution in the midst of human institutions, would still exist by the power of God, like a rock in the midst of the tempest, and would transmit to future generations the seeds of Christian life and civilization. It is the same with the word, the creative principle of the church. It cannot perish here below. The priests of England had something to learn on this matter.

While the agents of the clergy were carrying out the archiepiscopal mandate, and a merciless search was made everywhere for the New Testaments from Worms, a new edition was discovered, fresh from the press, of a smaller and more portable, and consequently more dangerous, size. It was printed by Christopher Eyndhoven of Antwerp, who had consigned it to his correspondents in London. The annoyance of the priests was extreme, and Hackett, the agent of Henry VIII in the Low Countries, immediately received orders to get this man punished. 'We cannot deliver judgment without inquiry into the matter', said the lords of Antwerp; 'we will therefore have the book translated into Flemish.' – 'God forbid', said Hackett in alarm; 'What! would you also on your side of the ocean translate this book into the language of the people?' – 'Well then', said one of the judges, less conscientious than his colleagues, 'let the King of England send us a copy of each of the books he has burnt, and we will burn them likewise.' Hackett wrote to Wolsey for them, and as soon as they arrived the court met again. Eyndhoven's counsel called upon the prosecutor to point out the *heresies* contained in the volume. The margrave (an officer of the imperial government) shrank from the task, and said to Hackett, 'I give up the business!' The charge against Eyndhoven was dismissed.

Thus did the reformation awaken in Europe the slumbering spirit of law and liberty. By enfranchising thought from the yoke of popery, it prepared the way for other enfranchisements; and by restoring the authority of the word of God, it brought back the reign of the law among nations long the prey of turbulent passions and arbitrary power. Then, as at all times, religious society forestalled civil society, and gave it those two great principles of order and liberty, which popery compromises or annuls. It was not in vain that the magistrates of a Flemish city, enlightened by the first dawn of the reformation, set so noble an example; the English, who were very numerous in the Hanse towns, thus recovered that civil and religious liberty which is the time-honoured right of England, and of which they were in after-years to give other nations the so much needed lessons.

'Well then', said Hackett, who was annoyed at their setting the law above his master's will, 'I will go and buy all these books, and send them to the cardinal, that he may burn them.' With these words he left the court. But his anger evaporating, he set off for Malines to complain to the regent and her council of the Antwerp decision. 'What!' said he, 'you punish those who circulate false money, and you will not punish still more severely the man who coins it? – in this case, he is the printer.' – 'But that is just the point in dispute', they replied; 'we are not sure the money is *false*.' – 'How can it be otherwise', answered Henry's agent, 'since the bishops of England have declared it so?' The imperial government, which was not very favourably disposed towards England, ratified Eyndhoven's acquittal, but permitted Hackett to burn all the copies of the New Testament he could seize. He hastened to profit by this concession, and began hunting after the holy Scriptures, while the priests eagerly came to his assistance. In their view, as well as in that of their English colleagues, the supreme decision in matters of faith rested not with the word of God but with the pope; and the best means of securing this privilege to the pontiff was to reduce the Bible to ashes.

Notwithstanding these trials, the year 1526 was a memorable one for England. The English New Testament had been circulated from the shores of the Channel to the borders of Scotland, and the reformation had begun in that island by the word of God. The revival of the sixteenth century was in no country less than in England the outcome of a royal mandate. But God, who had disseminated the Scriptures over Britain, in defiance of the rulers of the nation, was about to make use of their passions to remove the difficulties which opposed the final triumph of his plans. We here enter upon a new phase in the history of the reformation; and, having studied the work of God in the faith of the little ones, we proceed to contemplate the work of man in the intrigues of the great ones of the earth.

CHAPTER FIVE

The Divorce Question Opens

(1526–1527)

W olsey, mortified at not being able to obtain the pontifical throne, to which he had so ardently aspired, and being especially irritated by the ill-will of Charles V, meditated a plan which, entirely unsuspected by him, was to lead to the enfranchisement of England from the papal yoke. 'They laugh at me, and thrust me into the second rank', he had exclaimed. 'So be it! I will create such a confusion in the world as has not been seen for ages. ... I will do it, even should England be swallowed up in the tempest!' Desirous of exciting imperishable hatred between Henry VIII and Charles V, he had undertaken to break the marriage which Henry VII and Ferdinand the Catholic had planned to unite for ever their families and their crowns. His hatred of Charles was not his only motive. Catherine had reproached him for his dissolute life, and he had sworn to be revenged. There can be no doubt about Wolsey's share in the matter.[1] 'The *first terms* of the divorce were put forward by me', he told the French ambassador. 'I did it', he added, 'to cause a lasting separation between the houses of England and Burgundy.' The best-informed writers of the sixteenth century, men of the most opposite parties, Pole, Polydore Virgil, Tyndale, Meteren, Pallavicini, Sanders, and Roper, More's son-in-law, all agree in pointing

---

[1] [Merle d'Aubigné presents a reasoned case for regarding Wolsey as the originator of the divorce proposal, but some modern historians do not agree with his views and conclusions. One of them fitly says that almost the only statement about the question which one can make without fear of contradiction from some quarter is that Henry VIII, shortly after his accession, married Catherine of Aragon, his brother's widow. Readers who wish to explore the matter further will have no difficulty in finding histories, ancient and modern, which present widely-contrasted views.]

to Wolsey as the instigator of that divorce, which has become so famous. He desired to go still farther and, after inducing the king to put away his queen, he hoped to prevail on the pope to depose the emperor. It was not the king's passion for Anne Boleyn, as so many of the Romish fabulists have repeated; but the passion of a cardinal for the triple crown which gave the signal of England's emancipation. Offended pride is one of the most active principles of human nature.

Wolsey's design was a strange one, and difficult of execution, but not impossible. Henry was living apparently on the best terms with Catherine; on more than one occasion Erasmus had spoken of the royal family of England as the pattern of the domestic virtues. But the most ardent of Henry's desires was not satisfied; he had no son; those whom the queen had borne him had died in their infancy, and Mary alone survived. The deaths of these little children, at all times so heart-rending, were particularly so in the palace of Greenwich. It appeared to Catherine that the shade of the last Plantagenet, immolated on her marriage altar, came forth to seize one after another the heirs she gave to the throne of England, and to carry them away to his tomb.[2] The queen shed tears almost unceasingly, and implored the Divine mercy, while the king cursed his unhappy fate. The people seemed to share in the royal sorrow; and men of learning and piety (Longland was among their number) declared against the validity of the marriage. They said that 'the papal dispensations had no force when in opposition to the law of God'. Yet hitherto Henry had rejected every idea of a divorce.

The times had changed since 1509. The king appears genuinely to have loved Catherine: her reserve, mildness, and dignity, had charmed him. Greedy of pleasure and applause, he was delighted to see his wife content to be the quiet witness of his joys and of his triumphs. But gradually the queen had grown older, her Spanish gravity had increased, her devout practices were multiplied, and her infirmities, become more frequent, had left the king no hope of having a son to succeed him on the throne. From that hour, even while continuing to praise her virtues, Henry grew cold towards her person, and his love by degrees changed into repugnance. And then he thought that the death of his children

---

[2] [The reference is to the death of Warwick, *cf.* pp. 95-96.]

might be a sign of God's anger. This idea had taken hold of him, and induced him to occupy apartments separate from the queen's.

Wolsey judged the moment favourable for beginning the attack. It was in the latter months of 1526, when calling Longland, Bishop of Lincoln and the king's confessor, to him, and concealing his principal motive, he said: 'You know His Majesty's anguish. The stability of his crown and his everlasting salvation seem to be compromised alike. To whom can I unbosom myself, if not to you, who must know the inmost secrets of his soul?' The two bishops resolved to awaken Henry to the perils incurred by his union with Catherine; but Longland insisted that Wolsey should take the first steps.

The cardinal waited upon the king, and reminded him of his scruples before the betrothal; he exaggerated those entertained by the nation and, speaking with unusual warmth, he entreated the king to remain no longer in such danger: 'The holiness of your life and the legitimacy of your succession are at stake.' – 'My good father', said Henry, 'you would do well to consider the weight of the stone that you have undertaken to move. The queen is a woman of such exemplary life that I have no motive for separating from her.'

The cardinal did not consider himself beaten; three days later he appeared before the king accompanied by the Bishop of Lincoln. 'Most mighty prince', said the confessor, who felt bold enough to speak after the cardinal, 'you cannot, like Herod, have your brother's wife. I exhort and conjure you, as having the care of your soul, to submit the matter to competent judges.' Henry consented, and perhaps not unwillingly.

It was not enough for Wolsey to separate Henry from the emperor; he must, for greater security, unite him to Francis I. The King of England shall repudiate the aunt of Charles V, and then marry the sister of the French king. Proud of the success he had obtained in the first part of his plan, Wolsey entered upon the second. 'There is a princess', he told the king, 'whose birth, graces, and talents charm all Europe. Margaret of Valois, sister of King Francis, is superior to all of her sex, and no one is worthier of your alliance.' Henry made answer that it was a serious matter, requiring deliberate examination. Wolsey, however, placed in the king's hands a portrait of Margaret, and it has been imagined that he even privily caused her sentiments to be sounded. Be that as it may, the sister of Francis I having learnt that she was pointed at as the future Queen of England, rebelled at the idea of taking from an innocent woman a crown she had worn so nobly. 'The French king's sister knows too much of Christ to consent unto such wickedness', said Tyndale. Margaret of Valois replied: 'Let me hear no more of a marriage that can be effected only at the expense of Catherine of Aragon's happiness and life.' Shortly after this, on 24 January 1527, the sister of Francis I married Henry d'Albret, King of Navarre.

Henry VIII, desirous of information with regard to his favourite's suggestion, commissioned Fox, his almoner, Pace, Dean of St Paul's, and Wakefield, professor of Hebrew at Oxford, to study the passages of Leviticus and Deuteronomy which related to marriage with a brother's wife. Wakefield, who had no wish to commit himself, asked whether Henry was *for* or *against* the divorce. Pace replied to this servile Hebraist that the king wanted nothing but the truth.

But who would take the first public step in an undertaking so hazardous? Everyone shrank back; the terrible emperor alarmed them all. It was a French bishop that hazarded the step; bishops meet us at every turn in this affair of the divorce, with which bishops have so violently reproached the reformation. Henry, desirous of excusing Wolsey, pretended afterwards that the objections of the French prelate had preceded those of Longland and the cardinal. In February 1527, Francis I had sent an embassy to London, at the head of which was Gabriel de Grammont, Bishop of Tarbes, with the intention to procure the hand of Mary of England. Henry's ministers having inquired whether the engagement of Francis with the queen dowager of Portugal did not oppose the commission with which the French bishop was charged, the latter answered: 'I will ask you in turn what has been done to remove the impediments which opposed the marriage of which the Princess Mary is issue.' They laid before the ambassador the dispensation of Julius II, which he returned, saying, that the bull was not *sufficient*, seeing that such a marriage was forbidden *jure divino*; and he added: 'Have you English a different gospel from ours?'

The king, when he heard these words (as he informs us himself) was filled with fear and horror. Three of the most respected bishops of

Christendom united to accuse him of incest! He began to speak of it to certain individuals: 'The scruples of my conscience have been terribly increased (he said) since the bishop spoke of this matter before my council in exceedingly plain words.' There is no reason to believe that these *terrible* troubles of which the king speaks were a mere invention on his part. A disputed succession might again plunge England into civil war. Even if no pretenders should spring up, might they not see a rival house, a French prince for instance, wedded to Henry's daughter, reigning over England? The king, in his anxiety, had recourse to his favourite author, Thomas Aquinas, and this *angel of the schools* declared his marriage unlawful. Henry next opened the Bible, and found this threat against the man who took his brother's wife: 'He shall be *childless*!' The denunciation increased his trouble, for he had no heir. In the midst of this darkness a new perspective opened before him. His conscience might be unbound; his desire to have a younger wife might be gratified; he might have a son! ... The king resolved to lay the matter before a commission of lawyers, and this commission soon wrote volumes.

During all this time Catherine, suspecting no evil, was occupied in her devotions. Her heart, bruised by the death of her children and by the king's coldness, sought consolation in prayer both privately and in the royal chapel. She would rise at midnight and kneel down upon the cold stones, and never missed any of the canonical services. But one day (probably in May or June 1527) some officious person informed her of the rumours circulating in the city and at court. Bursting with anger and alarm, and all in tears, she hastened to the king, and addressed him with the bitterest complaints. Henry was content to calm her by vague assurances; but the unfeeling Wolsey, troubling himself still less than his master about Catherine's emotion, called it, with a smile, 'a short tragedy'.

The offended wife lost no time: it was necessary that the emperor should be informed promptly, surely, and accurately of this unpreced-ented insult. A letter would be insufficient, even were it not intercepted. Catherine therefore determined to send her servant Francis Philip, a Spaniard, to her nephew; and to conceal the object of his journey, they proceeded, after the *tragedy*, to play a *comedy* in the Spanish style. 'My mother is sick and desires to see me', said Philip. Catherine begged the king to refuse her servant's prayer; and Henry, divining the stratagem, resolved to employ trick against trick. 'Philip's request is very proper', he made answer; and Catherine, *from regard to her husband*, consented to his departure. Henry meantime had given orders that, 'notwithstanding any safe conduct, the said Philip should be arrested and detained at Calais, in such a manner, however, that no one should know whence the stoppage proceeded'.

It was to no purpose that the queen indulged in a culpable dissimulation; a poisoned arrow had pierced her heart, and her words, her manners, her complaints, her tears, the numerous messages she sent, now to one and now to another, betrayed the secret which the king wished still to conceal. Her friends blamed her for this publicity; men wondered what Charles would say when he heard of his aunt's distress; they feared that peace would be broken; but Catherine, whose heart was 'rent in twain', was not to be moved by diplomatic considerations. Her sorrow did not check Henry; with the two motives which made him eager for a divorce – the scruples of his conscience and the desire of an heir – was now combined a third still more forcible. A woman was about to play an important part in the destinies of England.

CHAPTER SIX

Anne Boleyn

(1522–1527)

bout the year 1522, or possibly a little earlier, Anne Boleyn had
returned from the court of France. It is probable that she was
little more than fifteen years of age.[1] Historians hold widely
differing views about her charms, but when she appeared in the English
court an unfriendly contemporary was compelled to own that she
eclipsed her companions 'by her excellent gesture and behaviour'. Her
chief attractiveness appears to have been in her eyes, which are described
as 'black and beautiful and of great effect'. Cranmer, some ten years
later, found her appearance very impressive as she 'sat in her hair' (it
seems that on great occasions she appeared with her hair falling over her
shoulders) upon a horse litter, richly apparelled at her coronation.

Anne Boleyn brought to the English court the polished manners
and deportment of the court of France. But more important, as later
events were to show, she also brought home something of the influence
which reached her through Margaret of Angoulême, the sister of the
French king. This gracious woman became renowned for the support
and protection she afforded to advocates and preachers of reformation
doctrine and practice. It is probable that, before Anne left France, she

---

[1] [The date of Anne Boleyn's birth is uncertain. 1501 and 1507 have both been
claimed. The place of her birth was probably Blickling Hall, Norfolk. At a later
date she lived at Hever Castle, Kent. Her father permitted her to accompany Mary
Tudor, Henry VIII's sister, to France, on the marriage of that princess to Louis XII
in 1514. Remaining at the French court after the death of Louis in 1515, she served
Queen Claude, the wife of Francis I, for several years, and thus came into contact
with Margaret of Valois, better known as Margaret of Angoulême, or Margaret of
Navarre.]

had begun to read, without thoroughly understanding it, the holy book in which Margaret found consolation and repose, and to direct a few light and passing thoughts to that 'mild Emmanuel' to whom the latter addressed such beautiful verses.

Among the young noblemen in the cardinal's household was Lord Percy, eldest son of the Earl of Northumberland. While Wolsey was in conference with the king, Percy was accustomed to resort to the queen's apartments, where he passed the time among her ladies. He soon felt a sincere passion for Anne, and the young maid of honour, who had been cold to the addresses of the gentlemen at the court of Francis, replied to the affections of the heir of Northumberland. The two young people already indulged in day-dreams of a quiet, elegant, and happy life in their noble castles of the north; but such dreams were fated to be of short duration.

Wolsey hated the Norfolks, and consequently the Boleyns. It was to counterbalance their influence that he had been first introduced at court. He became angry, therefore, when he saw one of his household suing for the hand of the daughter and niece of his enemies. Besides, certain partisans of the clergy accused Anne of being friendly to the reformation. One day, therefore, when Percy was in attendance upon the cardinal, the latter rudely addressed him: 'I marvel at your folly, that you should attempt to contract yourself with that girl without your father's or the king's consent. I command you to break with her.' Percy burst into tears, and besought the cardinal to plead his cause. 'I charge you to resort no more into her company', was Wolsey's cold reply, after which he rose up and left the room.[2] Anne received an order at the same time to leave

[2] [On the evidence of Cavendish's *Life of Wolsey* (written between 1554 and 1557) it was long believed that as early as 1523 Wolsey had discovered Henry's eyes turned complacently on the young maid of honour, and that this induced him to thwart Percy's love, but it has now been conclusively shown that Henry had quite different motives. Thomas Boleyn, father to Anne, had a claim to certain Irish estates through his mother, but was strongly opposed in this matter by a member of the Butler family living in Ireland. It suited Henry's schemes to seek for a reconciliation between the rival families, and this, he thought, could best be effected by a marriage between Anne and Sir James Butler. She would in time become Lady Ormonde and live in Kilkenny Castle. But the marriage never came about; perhaps Anne herself refused to be drawn into it.]

the court. Proud and bold, and ascribing her misfortune to Wolsey's hatred, she exclaimed as she quitted the palace, 'I will be revenged for this insult.' But she had scarcely taken up her abode in the gothic halls of Hever Castle, when news still more distressing overwhelmed her. Percy was married to Lady Mary Talbot. She wept long and bitterly, and vowed against the young nobleman who had deserted her a contempt equal to her hatred of the cardinal. Anne was reserved for a more illustrious, but more unhappy, fate.

While life at the court of Henry VIII was thus perturbed by these seemingly small and comparatively unimportant affairs, a strange report filled all England with surprise. It was reported that the imperialist soldiers of Charles V had taken Rome by assault, and that the pope was a prisoner in his own city.

Shortly, the captive pope and cardinals wrote letters 'filled with tears and groans'. Full of zeal for the papacy, Wolsey ordered a public fast. 'The emperor will never release the pope, unless he be compelled', he told the king. 'Sir, God has made you *Defender of the Faith*; save the church and its head!' – 'My lord', answered the king with a smile, 'I assure you that this war between the emperor and the pope is not for the faith, but for temporal possessions and dominions.'

But Wolsey would not be discouraged; and, on 3 July, he passed through the streets of London, riding a richly caparisoned mule, and resting his feet on gilt stirrups, while nine hundred gentlemen accompanied him on horseback. He was going to entreat Francis to aid his master in saving Clement VII. He had found no difficulty in prevailing upon Henry; Charles talked of carrying the pope to Spain, and of permanently establishing the apostolic see in that country.[3] Now, how could they obtain the divorce from a *Spanish* pope? During the procession, Wolsey seemed oppressed with grief, and even shed tears; but he soon raised his head and exclaimed: 'My heart is inflamed, and I wish it may be said of the pope *per secula sempiterna*,[4]

Rediit Henrici octavi virtute serena.[5]

[3] The see apostolic should remain in Spain. State Papers, i, p. 227.
[4] [Latin: 'through eternal ages'.]
[5] [Latin: 'He returned with the calm courage of Henry VIII.]

Desirous of forming a close union between France and England for the accomplishment of his designs, he had cast his eyes on the Princess Renée, daughter of Louis XII, and sister-in-law to Francis I, as a possible future wife of Henry VIII. A treaty of alliance between the two crowns was signed at Amiens on 18 August (1527), after which Francis, with his mother and the cardinal, proceeded to Compiègne, and there Wolsey, styling Charles the most obstinate defender of Lutheranism, promising 'perpetual *conjunction* on the one hand [between France and England], and perpetual *disjunction* on the other' [between England and Germany], sought to discover whether the French saw advantages in a marriage between Renée and King Henry. Staffileo, Dean of Rota, affirmed that the pope had been able to permit the marriage between Henry and Catherine only by an error of the keys of St Peter. This avowal, so remarkable on the part of the dean of one of the first juris-dictions of Rome, induced Francis' mother to listen favourably to the cardinal's demand. But whether this proposal was displeasing to Renée, who was destined on a future day to profess the pure faith of the gospel with greater earnestness than Margaret of Valois, or whether Francis was not over-anxious for a union that would have given Henry rights over the Duchy of Brittany, she was promised to the son of the Duke of Ferrara. It was a check to the cardinal; but it was his ill-fortune to receive one still more severe on his return to England.

The daughter of Sir Thomas Boleyn (who had been created Viscount Rochford in 1525) was constantly at court, 'where she flourished in great estimation and favour', says Cavendish, 'having always a private indignation against the cardinal for breaking off the pre-contract made between Lord Percy and her'. Her beauty, her graceful carriage, her black hair, oval face, and bright eyes, her sweet voice in singing, her skill and dignity in the dance, her desire to please which was not entirely devoid of coquetry, her sprightliness, the readiness of her repartees, and above all the amiability of her character, won every heart. Every day (it was reported) she invented a new style of dress, and set the fashion in England. But to all these qualities, she added modesty, and even imposed it on others by her example. The ladies of the court, who had hitherto adopted a different fashion (says her greatest enemy), covered the neck and bosom as she did; and the malicious, unable to appreciate Anne's motives, ascribed this modesty on the young lady's part to a desire to hide a secret deformity. Numerous admirers once more crowded round Anne Boleyn, and among others, one of the most illustrious noblemen and poets of England, Sir Thomas Wyatt, a follower of Wycliffe. He, however, was not the man destined to replace the son of the Percys.

Henry, absorbed in anxiety about his divorce from Catherine, had become low-spirited and melancholy. The laughter, songs, repartees, and beauty of Anne Boleyn struck and captivated him, and his eyes were soon fixed complacently on the young maid of honour. Catherine was more than forty years old, and it was hardly to be expected that so susceptible a man as Henry would have made, as Job says, *a covenant with his eyes not to think upon a maid*. Desirous of showing his admiration, he presented Anne, according to usage, with a costly jewel; she accepted and wore it, and continued to dance, laugh, and chatter as before, without attaching particular importance to the royal present. Henry's attentions became more continuous; and he took advantage of a moment when he found Anne alone to declare his sentiments. With mingled emotion and alarm, the young lady fell trembling at the king's feet, and exclaimed, bursting into tears: 'I think, most noble and worthy king, Your Majesty speaks these words in mirth to prove me. … I will rather lose my life than my virtue.' Henry gracefully replied that he should at least continue to hope. But Anne, rising up, proudly made answer: 'I understand not, most mighty king, how you should retain any such hope; your wife I cannot be, both in respect of mine own unworthiness, and also because you have a queen already. Your mistress I will not be.' Anne kept her word. She continued to show the king, even after this interview, all the respect that was due to him; but on several occasions she proudly, violently even, repelled his advances. In this age of gallantry, we find her resisting for nearly six years all the seductions Henry scattered round her. Such an example is not often met with in the history of courts. The books she had read in Margaret's palace gave her a secret strength. All looked upon her with respect; and even the queen treated her with politeness. Catherine showed, however, that she had remarked the king's preference. One day, as she was playing at cards with her maid of honour, while Henry was in the room, Anne frequently holding the *king*, she said: 'My Lady Anne, you have good hap to stop ever at a *king*; but you are not like others, you will have all or none.' Anne blushed: from that moment Henry's attentions acquired more importance; she resolved to withdraw from them, and quitted the court with Lady Rochford.

The king, who was not accustomed to resistance, was extremely grieved; and having learnt that Anne would not return to the court either with or without her mother, sent a courier to Hever with a message and a letter for her. If we recollect the manners of the age of Henry VIII, and how far the men, in their relations with the gentler sex, were strangers to that reserve which society now imposes upon them, we cannot but be struck by the king's respectful tone; he writes thus in French:

> As the time seems to me very long since I heard from you or concerning your health, the great love I have for you has constrained me to send this bearer to be better informed both of your health and pleasure; particularly, because since my last parting with you, I have been told that you have entirely changed the mind in which I left you, and that you neither mean to come to court with your mother nor any other way; which report, if true, I cannot enough marvel at, being persuaded in my own mind that I have never committed any offence against you; and it seems hard, in return for the great love I bear you, to be kept at a distance from the person and presence of the woman in the world that I value the most. And if you love me with as much affection as I hope you do, I am sure the distance of our two persons would be equally irksome to you, though this does not belong so much to the mistress as to the servant.
>
> Consider well, my mistress, how greatly your absence afflicts me. I hope it is not your will that it should be so; but if I heard for certain that you yourself desired it, I could but mourn my ill-fortune, and strive by degrees to abate of my great folly.
>
> And so for lack of time I make an end of this rude letter, beseeching you to give the bearer credence in all he will tell you from me. Written by the hand of your entire servant,
>
> H. R.[6]

[6] It is difficult to fix the order and chronology of Henry's letters to Anne Boleyn. This is the second in the Vatican Collection, but it appears to us to be of older date.

The word *servant* (serviteur) employed in this letter explains the sense in which Henry used the word *mistress*. In the language of chivalry, the latter term expressed a person to whom the lover had surrendered his heart.

It would seem that Anne's reply to this letter was the same she had made to the king from the very first; and Cardinal Pole mentions more than once her obstinate refusal of an adulterous love. At last Henry understood Anne's virtue; but he was far from *abating of his great folly*, as he had promised. That tyrannical selfishness, which the prince often displayed in his life, was shown particularly in his amours. Seeing that he could not attain his end by illegitimate means, he determined to break, as quickly as possible, the bonds which united him to the queen. Anne's virtue was the third cause of Henry's divorce.

His resolution being once taken, it must needs be carried out. Henry, having succeeded in bringing Anne back to court, procured a private interview with her, offered her his crown, and, seizing her hand, took off one of her rings. But Anne, who would not be the king's mistress, refused also to be his wife. The glory of a crown could not dazzle her, said Wyatt, and two motives in particular counterbalanced all the prospects of greatness which were set before her eyes. The first was her respect for the queen: 'How could I injure a princess of such great virtue?' she exclaimed. The second was the fear that a union with 'one that was her lord and her king', would not give her that freedom of heart and that liberty which she would enjoy by marrying a man of the same rank with herself.

Yet the noblemen and ladies of Henry's court whispered to one another that Anne would certainly become Queen of England. Some were tormented by jealousy; others, her friends, were delighted at the prospect of a rapid advancement. Wolsey's enemies in particular were charmed at the thought of ruining the favourite. It was at the very moment when all these emotions were so variously agitating the court that the cardinal, returning from his embassy to Francis, reappeared in London, where an unexpected blow struck him.

It is considered as written in May 1528; we are inclined to place it in the autumn of 1527. The originals of these letters, chiefly in old French, are still preserved in the Vatican, having been stolen from Anne's cabinet and conveyed thither.

Wolsey was expressing his grief to Henry at having failed in obtaining either Margaret or Renée for him, when the king interrupted him: 'Console yourself, I shall marry Anne Boleyn.' The cardinal remained speechless for a moment. What would become of him, if the king placed the crown of England on the head of the daughter and niece of his greatest enemies? What would become of the church, if a second Anne of Bohemia should ascend the throne? Wolsey threw himself at the feet of his master, and entreated him to renounce so fatal a project. It was then no doubt that he remained (as he afterwards said) *an hour or two* on his knees before the king in his privy chamber, but without prevailing on Henry to give up his design. Wolsey, persuaded that if he continued openly to oppose Henry's will, he would for ever lose his confidence, dissembled his vexation, waiting an opportunity to get rid of this unfortunate rival by some intrigue. He began by writing to the pope, informing him that a young lady, brought up by the Queen of Navarre, and consequently tainted by the Lutheran heresy, had captivated the king's heart; and from that hour Anne Boleyn became the object of the hatred and calumnies of Rome. But at the same time, to conceal his intentions, Wolsey received Henry at a series of splendid entertainments, at which Anne outshone all the ladies of the court.

CHAPTER SEVEN

Bilney in Strength and Weakness

(1527)

W hile these passions were agitating Henry's palace, the most moving scenes, produced by Christian faith, were stirring the nation. Bilney, animated by that courage which God sometimes gives to the weakest men, seemed to have lost his natural timidity, and preached for a time with an energy quite apostolic. He taught that all men should first acknowledge their sins and condemn them, and then hunger and thirst after that righteousness which Jesus Christ gives. To this testimony borne to the truth, he added his testimony against error. 'These five hundred years', he added, 'there hath been no good pope ... for they have neither preached nor lived well, nor conformably to their dignity; wherefore, unto this day, they have borne the keys of simony.'

As soon as he descended from the pulpit, this pious scholar, with his friend, Thomas Arthur, visited the neighbouring towns and villages. 'The Jews and Saracens would long ago have become believers', he once said at Wilsdon, 'had it not been for the idolatry of Christian men in offering candles, wax, and money to stocks and stones.' One day when he visited Ipswich, where there was a Franciscan monastery, he exclaimed: 'The cowl of St Francis wrapped round a dead body hath no power to take away sins. ... *Ecce agnus Dei qui tollit peccata mundi*.' (John 1:29.) The monks, who were little versed in Scripture, had recourse to the *Almanac* to convict the *Bible* of error. 'St Paul did rightly affirm', said Friar John Brusierd, 'that there is but one mediator of God and man, because as yet there was no *saint* canonized or put into the calendar.' – 'Let us ask of the Father in the name of the Son', rejoined Bilney, 'and he will give unto us. He says not, whatsoever ye shall ask of the Father in the name of St Peter, St Paul, or other saints, but in my name.' – 'You are always speaking of the Father and never of the *saints*', replied the friar; 'you are like a man who has been looking so long upon the sun, that he can see nothing else.' As he uttered these words the monk seemed bursting with anger. 'If I did not believe and know that God and all his saints would take everlasting vengeance upon you, I would surely with these nails of mine be your death.' Twice in fact did two monks pull him out of his pulpit. He was arrested and taken to London.

Arthur, instead of fleeing, began to visit the flocks which his friend had converted. 'Good people', said he, 'if I should suffer persecution for the preaching of the gospel, there are seven thousand more that would preach it as I do now. Therefore, good people! good people!' (and he repeated these words several times in a sorrowful voice) 'think not that if these tyrants and persecutors put a man to death, the preaching of the gospel therefore is to be forsaken. Every Christian man, yea every layman, is a priest. Let our adversaries preach by the authority of the cardinal; others by the authority of the university; others by the pope's; we will preach by the authority of God. It is not the man who brings the word that saves the soul, but the word which the man brings. Neither bishops nor popes have the right to forbid any man to preach the gospel; and if they kill him he is not a heretic but a martyr.' The priests were horrified at such doctrines. In their opinion, there was no God out of their church, no salvation out of their sacrifices. Arthur was thrown into the same prison as Bilney.

On 27 November 1527 the cardinal and the Archbishop of Canterbury, with a great number of bishops, divines, and lawyers, met in the chapter house of Westminster, when Bilney and Arthur were brought before them. But the king's prime minister thought it beneath his dignity to occupy his time with miserable heretics. Wolsey had hardly commenced the examination, when he rose, saying: 'The affairs of the realm call me away; all such as are found guilty, you will compel them to abjure, and those who rebel you will deliver over to the secular power.' After a few questions proposed by the Bishop of London, the two accused men were led back to prison.

Abjuration or death – that was Wolsey's order. But the conduct of the trial was confided to Tunstall; Bilney conceived some hope. 'Is it possible', he said to himself, 'that the Bishop of London, the friend of Erasmus, will gratify the monks? ... I must tell him that it was the Greek Testament of his learned master that led me to the faith.' Upon which the humble evangelist, having obtained paper and ink, set about writing to the bishop from his gloomy prison those admirable letters which have been transmitted to posterity. Tunstall, who was not a cruel man, was deeply moved, and then a strange struggle took place: a judge wishing to save the prisoner, the prisoner desiring to give up his life. Tunstall, by acquitting Bilney, had no desire to compromise himself. 'Submit to the church', said the bishop, 'for God speaks only through it.' But Bilney, who knew that God speaks in the Scriptures, remained inflexible. 'Very well, then', said Tunstall, taking up the prisoner's eloquent letters, 'in discharge of my conscience I shall lay these letters before the court.' He hoped, perhaps, that they would touch his colleagues, but he was deceived. He determined, therefore, to make a fresh attempt. On 4 December, Bilney was brought again before the court. 'Abjure your errors', said Tunstall. Bilney refusing by a shake of the head, the bishop continued: 'Retire into the next room and consider.' Bilney withdrew, and when he returned shortly after with joy beaming in his eyes, Tunstall thought he had gained the victory. 'You will return to the church, then?' said he. ... Bilney answered calmly: 'Let judgment be done in the name of the Lord.' – 'Be quick', continued the bishop, 'this is the last moment, and you will be condemned.' – 'This is the day which the Lord hath made', answered Bilney, 'we will rejoice and be glad in it.' Upon this Tunstall took off his cap, and said: 'In the name of the Father and of the Son and of the Holy Ghost ... let God arise and let his enemies be scattered.' Then making the sign of the cross on his forehead and on his breast, he gave judgment: 'Thomas Bilney, I pronounce thee convicted of heresy.' He was about to name the penalty ... a last hope restrained him; he stopped: 'For the rest of the sentence we take deliberation until tomorrow.' Thus was the struggle prolonged between two men, one of whom desired to walk to the stake, the other to bar the way as it were with his own body.

'Will you return to the unity of the church?' asked Tunstall the next day. 'I hope I was never separated from the church', answered Bilney. 'Go and consult with some of your friends', said the bishop, who was resolved to save his life; 'I will give you till one o'clock in the afternoon.' In the afternoon Bilney made the same answer. 'I will give you two nights' respite to deliberate', said the bishop; 'on Saturday at nine o'clock in the forenoon, the court will expect a plain definitive answer.' Tunstall reckoned on the night with its dreams, its anguish, and its terrors, to bring about Bilney's recantation.

This extraordinary struggle occupied many minds both in court and city. Anne Boleyn and Henry VIII watched with interest the various phases of this tragic history. What will happen? was the general question. Will he give way? Shall we see him live or die? One day and two nights still remained; everything was tried to shake the Cambridge doctor. His friends crowded to his prison; he was overwhelmed with arguments and examples; but an inward struggle, far more terrible than those without, agitated the pious Bilney. 'Whoever will save his soul shall lose it', Christ had said. That selfish love of his soul, which is found even in the advanced Christian – that self, which, after his conversion had been not absorbed, but overruled by the Spirit of God, gradually recovered strength in his heart, in the presence of disgrace and death. His friends who wished to save him, not understanding that the fallen Bilney would be Bilney no longer, conjured him with tears to have pity on himself; and by these means his firmness was overcome. The bishop pressed him, and Bilney asked himself: 'Can a young soldier like me know the rules of war better than an old soldier like Tunstall? Or can a poor silly sheep know his way to the fold better than the chief pastor of London?' His friends quitted him neither night nor day and, entangled by their fatal affection, he believed at last that he had found a compromise which would set his conscience at rest. 'I will preserve my life', he said, 'to dedicate it to the Lord.' This delusion had scarcely laid hold of his mind before his views were confused, his faith was veiled, the Holy Ghost departed from him, God gave him over to his carnal thoughts and, under the pretext of being useful to Jesus Christ for many years, Bilney disobeyed him at the present moment. Being led before the bishops on the morning of Saturday, 7 December, at nine o'clock, he fell … (Arthur had fallen before him), and whilst the false friends who had misled him hardly dared raise their eyes, the living church of Christ in England uttered a cry of anguish. 'If ever you come in danger, in durance, in prison', said Latimer, 'for God's quarrel, I would advise you, above all things, to abjure all your friends, all your friendships; leave not one unabjured. It is they that shall undo you, and not your enemies. It was his very friends that brought Bilney to it.'[1]

On the following day (Sunday, 8 December) Bilney was placed at the head of a procession, and the fallen disciple, bareheaded, with a faggot on his shoulders, stood in front of St Paul's Cross, while a priest from the pulpit exhorted him to repentance; after which he was led back to prison.

What a solitude for the wretched man! At one time the cold darkness of his cell appeared to him as a burning fire; at another he fancied he heard accusing voices crying to him in the silence of the night. Death, the very enemy he had wished to avoid, fixed his icy glance upon him and filled him with fear. He strove to escape from the horrible spectre, but in vain. Then the friends who had dragged him into this abyss, crowded round and endeavoured to console him; but if they gave utterance to any of Christ's gentle promises, Bilney started back with affright and shrank to the farthest part of the dungeon, with a cry 'as though a man had run him through the heart with a sword'.[2] Having denied the word of God, he could no longer endure to hear it. The curse of the Apocalypse: *Ye mountains, hide me from the wrath of the Lamb!* was the only passage of Scripture in harmony with his soul. His mind wandered, the blood froze in his veins, he sank under his terrors; he lost all sense, and almost his life, and lay motionless in the arms of his astonished friends. 'God', exclaimed those unhappy individuals who had caused his fall, 'God, by a just judgment, delivers up to the tempests of their conscience all who deny his truth.'

This was not the only sorrow of the church. As soon as Richard Bayfield, the late chamberlain of St Edmunds' Bury, had joined Tyndale

---

[1] Latimer's *Sermons* (Parker Society), p. 222.
[2] *Ibid.*

and Fryth, he said to them: 'I am at your disposal; you shall be my head and I will be your hand; I will sell your books and those of the German reformers in the Low Countries, France, and England.' It was not long indeed before he returned to London. But Pierson, the priest whom he had formerly met in Lombard Street, found him again, and accused him to the bishop. The unhappy man was brought before Tunstall. 'You are charged', said the prelate, 'with having asserted that praise is due to God alone, and not to saints or creatures.' Bayfield acknowledged the charge to be true. 'You are accused of maintaining that every priest may preach the word of God by the authority of the gospel without the licence of the pope or cardinals.' This also Bayfield acknowledged. A penance was imposed on him; and then he was sent back to his monastery with orders to show himself there on 25 April. But he crossed the sea once more, and hastened to join Tyndale.

The New Testaments, however, sold by him and others remained in England. At that time the bishops subscribed to suppress the Scriptures, as so many persons have since done to circulate them; and, accordingly, a great number of the copies brought over by Bayfield and his friends were bought up. A scarcity of food was erelong added to the scarcity of the word of God; for as the cardinal was endeavouring to foment a war between Henry and the emperor, the Flemish ships ceased to enter the English ports. It was in consequence of this that the Lord Mayor and Aldermen of London hastened to express their apprehensions to Wolsey almost before he had recovered from the fatigues of his return from France. 'Fear nothing', he told them; 'the King of France assured me, that if he had three bushels of wheat, England should have two of them.' But none arrived, and the people were on the point of breaking out into violence, when a fleet of ships suddenly appeared off the mouth of the Thames. They were German and Flemish vessels laden with corn, in which the worthy people of the Low Countries had also concealed the New Testament. An Antwerp bookseller, named John Raimond or Ruremond, from his birthplace, had printed a fourth edition more beautiful than the previous ones. It was enriched with references and engravings on wood, and each page bordered with red lines. Raimond himself had embarked on board one of the ships with five hundred copies of his New Testament. About Christmas 1527, the book of God was circulated in England along with the bread that nourishes the body. But certain priests and monks, having discovered the Scriptures among the sacks of corn, carried several copies to the Bishop of London, who threw Raimond into prison. The greater part, however, of the new edition escaped him. The New Testament was read everywhere, and even the court did not escape the contagion. Anne Boleyn, notwithstanding her smiling face, often withdrew to her rooms at Greenwich or at Hampton Court, to study the gospel. Frank, courageous, and proud, she did not conceal the pleasure she found in such reading; her boldness astonished the courtiers, and exasperated the clergy. In the city things went still further: the New Testament was explained in frequent conventicles, particularly in the house of one Russell, and great was the joy among the faithful. 'It is sufficient only to enter London', said the priests, 'to become a heretic!' The reformation was taking root among the people before it arrived at the upper classes.

CHAPTER EIGHT

The Campaign for Henry's Divorce

(1527)

The sun of the word of God, which daily grew brighter in the sky of the sixteenth century, was sufficient to scatter all the darkness in England; but popery, like an immense wall, intercepted its rays. Britain had hardly received the Scriptures in Greek and Latin, and then in English, before the priests began to make war upon them with indefatigable zeal. It was necessary that the wall should be thrown down in order that the sun might penetrate freely among the Anglo-Saxon people. And now events were ripening in England, destined to make a great breach in popery. The negotiations of Henry VIII with Clement VII play an important part in the reformation. By showing up the court of Rome, they destroyed the respect which the people felt for it; they took away that *power and strength*, as Scripture says, which the monarchy had given it; and the throne of the pope once fallen in England, Jesus Christ uplifted and strengthened his own.

Henry, ardently desiring an heir, and thinking that he had found the woman that would ensure his own and England's happiness, conceived the design of severing the ties that united him to the queen, and with this view he consulted his most favourite councillors about the divorce. There was one in particular whose approval he coveted: this was Sir Thomas More. One day as Erasmus' friend was walking with his master in the beautiful gallery at Hampton Court, giving him an account of a mission he had just executed on the Continent, the king suddenly interrupted him: 'My marriage with the queen', he said, 'is contrary to the laws of God, of the church, and of nature.' He then took up the Bible, and pointed out the passages in his favour. 'I am not a theologian', said

More, somewhat embarrassed; 'Your Majesty should consult a council of doctors.'

Accordingly, by Henry's order, Warham assembled the most learned canonists at Hampton Court; but weeks passed away before they could agree. Most of them quoted in the king's favour those passages in Leviticus (28:16; 20:21), which forbid a man to take *his brother's wife*. But Fisher, Bishop of Rochester, and the other opponents of the divorce, replied that, according to Deuteronomy (25:5), when a woman is left a widow without children, her brother-in-law ought to take her to wife, to perpetuate his brother's name in Israel. 'This law concerned the Jews only', replied the partisans of the divorce; they added that its object was 'to maintain the inheritances distinct, and the genealogies intact, until the coming of Christ. The Judaical dispensation has passed away; but the law of Leviticus, which is a moral law, is binding upon all men in all ages.'

To free themselves from their embarrassment, the bishops demanded that the most eminent universities should be consulted; and commissioners were forthwith despatched to Oxford, Cambridge, Paris, Orleans, Toulouse, Louvain, Padua, and Bologna, furnished with money to reward the foreign doctors for the time and trouble this question would cost them. This caused some little delay, and every means was now to be tried to divert the king from his purpose.

Wolsey, who was the first to suggest the idea of a divorce, was now thoroughly alarmed. It appeared to him that a nod from the daughter of the Boleyns would hurl him from the post he had so laboriously won, and this made him vent his ill-humour on all about him, at one time threatening Warham, and at another persecuting Pace. But fearing to oppose Henry openly, he summoned from Paris, Clarke, Bishop of Bath and Wells, at that time ambassador to the French court. The latter entered into his views, and after cautiously preparing the way, he ventured to say to the king: 'The progress of the inquiry will be so slow, Your Majesty, that it will take more than seven years to bring it to an end!' – 'Since my patience has already held out for *eighteen* years', the king replied coldly, 'I am willing to wait *four* or *five* more.'

As the political party had failed, the clerical party set in motion a scheme of another kind. A young woman, Elizabeth Barton, known as the *holy maid of Kent*, had been subject from childhood to epileptic fits. The priest of her parish, named Masters, had persuaded her that she was inspired of God and, confederating with one Bocking, a monk of Canterbury, he turned the weakness of the prophetess to account. Elizabeth wandered over the country, passing from house to house, and from convent to convent; on a sudden her limbs would become rigid, her features distorted; violent convulsions shook her body, and strange unintelligible sounds fell from her lips, which the amazed bystanders received as revelations from the Virgin and the saints. Fisher, Bishop of Rochester, Abel, the queen's ecclesiastical agent, and even Sir Thomas More, were among the number of Elizabeth's partisans. Rumours of the divorce having reached the maid's ears, an angel commanded her to appear before the cardinal. As soon as she stood in his presence, the colour fled from her cheeks, her limbs trembled, and falling into an ecstasy, she exclaimed: 'Cardinal of York, God has placed three swords in your hand: the spiritual sword, to range the church under the authority of the pope; the civil sword, to govern the realm; and the sword of justice, to prevent the divorce of the king. ... If you do not wield these three swords faithfully, God will lay it sore to your charge.' After these words the prophetess withdrew.

But other influences were then dividing Wolsey's breast: hatred, which induced him to oppose the divorce; and ambition, which foreboded his ruin in this opposition. At last ambition prevailed, and he resolved to make his objections forgotten by the energy of his zeal.

Henry hastened to profit by this change. 'Declare the divorce yourself', said he to Wolsey; 'has not the pope named you his vicar-general?' The cardinal was not anxious to raise himself so high. 'If I were to decide the affair', said he, 'the queen would appeal to the pope; we must therefore either apply to the Holy Father for special powers, or persuade the queen to retire to a nunnery. And if we fail in either of these expedients, we will obey the voice of conscience, even in despite of the pope.' It was arranged to begin with the more regular attempt, and Gregory da Casale, Secretary Knight, and the prothonotary[1] Gambara, were appointed to an extraordinary mission at the pontifical court. Da Casale was Wolsey's man, and Knight was Henry's. Wolsey told the

---

[1] [A chief clerk in certain courts of law.]

envoys: 'You will demand of the pope: *firstly*, a *commission* authorizing me to inquire into this matter; *secondly*, his promise to pronounce the nullity of Catherine's marriage with Henry, if we should find that her marriage with Arthur was consummated; and *thirdly*, a *dispensation* permitting the king to marry again.' In this manner Wolsey hoped to make sure of the divorce without damaging the papal authority. It was insinuated that false representations, with regard to the consummation of the first marriage, had been sent from England to Julius II, which had induced the pontiff to permit the second. The pope being deceived as to the *fact*, his infallibility was untouched. Wolsey desired something more; knowing that no confidence could be put in the good faith of the pontiff, he demanded a fourth instrument by which the pope should bind himself never to recall the other three; he only forgot to take precautions in case Clement should withdraw *the fourth*. 'With these four snares, skilfully combined', said the cardinal, 'I shall catch the hare; if he escapes from one, he will fall into the other.' The courtiers anticipated a speedy termination of the affair. Was not the emperor the declared enemy of the pontiff? Had not Henry, on the contrary, made himself *protector of the Clementine league*? Could Clement hesitate, when called upon, to choose between his jailer and his benefactor?

Indeed, Charles V, at this moment, was in a very embarrassing position. It is true, his guards were posted at the gates of the Castle of St Angelo, where Clement was a prisoner, and people in Rome said to one another with a smile: 'Now indeed it is true, *Papa non potest errare*.'[2] But it was not possible to keep the pope a prisoner in Rome; and then what was to be done with him? The viceroy of Naples proposed to Alercon, the governor of St Angelo, to remove Clement to Gæta; but the affrighted colonel exclaimed: 'Heaven forbid that I should drag after me the very body of God!' Charles thought at one time of transporting the pontiff to Spain; but might not an enemy's fleet carry him off the road? The pope in prison was far more embarrassing to Charles than the pope at liberty.

It was at this critical time that Francis Philip, Queen Catherine's servant, having escaped the snares laid by Henry VIII and Wolsey, arrived at Madrid, where he passed a whole day in conference with

[2] The pope cannot err – a play upon the double meaning of the word *errare*.

Charles V. This prince was at first astonished, shocked even, by the designs of the King of England. The curse of God seemed to hang over his house. Charles' mother was a lunatic; his sister of Denmark expelled from her dominions; his sister of Hungary made a widow by the battle of Mohacz; the Turks were encroaching upon his territories; Lautrec was victorious in Italy, and the Catholics, irritated by the pope's captivity, detested his ambition. This was not enough. Henry VIII was striving to divorce his aunt, and the pope would naturally give his aid to this criminal design. Charles must choose between the pontiff and the king. The friendship of the King of England might aid him in breaking the league formed to expel him from Italy, and by sacrificing Catherine he would be sure to obtain his support; but placed between reasons of state and his aunt's honour, the emperor did not hesitate; he even renounced certain projects of reform that he had at heart. He suddenly decided for the pope, and from that very hour followed a new course.

Charles, who possessed great discernment, had understood his age; he had seen that concessions were called for by the movement of the human mind, and would have desired to carry out the change from the Middle Ages to modern times by a carefully-managed transition. He had consequently demanded a council to reform the church and weaken the Romish dominion in Europe. But very different was the result. If Charles turned away from Henry, he was obliged to turn towards Clement; and after having compelled the head of the church to enter a prison, it was necessary to place him once more upon the throne. Charles V sacrificed the interests of Christian society to the interests of his own family. This divorce, which in England has been looked upon as the ruin of the popedom, was what saved it in continental Europe.

But how could the emperor win the heart of the pontiff, filled as it was with bitterness and anger? He selected for this difficult mission a friar of great ability, de Angelis, general of the Spanish Observance, and ordered him to proceed to the Castle of St Angelo under the pretext of negotiating the liberation of the Holy Father. The cordelier was conducted to the strongest part of the fortress, called the Rock, where Clement was lodged; and the two priests brought all their craft to bear on each other. The monk, assisted by the artful Moncade, adroitly mingled together the pope's deliverance and Catherine's marriage. He affirmed that the emperor wished to open the gates of the pontiff's prison, and had already given the order; and then he added immediately: 'The emperor is determined to maintain the rights of his aunt, and will never consent to the divorce.' – 'If you are a *good shepherd* to me', wrote Charles to the pope with his own hand on 22 November 1527, 'I will be a *good sheep* to you.' Clement smiled as he read these words; he understood his position; the emperor had need of the priest, Charles was at his captive's feet; Clement was saved! The divorce was a rope fallen from the skies which could not fail to drag him out of the pit; he had only to cling to it quietly to reascend his throne. Accordingly from that hour Clement appeared less eager to quit the castle than Charles to liberate him. 'So long as the divorce is in suspense', thought the crafty de Medici, 'I have two great friends; but as soon as I declare for one, I shall have a mortal enemy in the other.' He promised the monk to come to no decision in the matter without informing the emperor.

Meantime Knight, the envoy of the impatient monarch, having heard, as he crossed the Alps, that the pope was at liberty, hastened on to Parma, where he met Gambara: 'He is not free yet', replied the prothonotary; 'but the general of the Franciscans hopes to terminate his captivity in a few days. Continue your journey', he added. Knight could not do so without great danger. He was told at Foligno, sixty miles from the metropolis, that if he had not a safe-conduct he could not reach Rome without exposing his life; Knight halted. Just then a messenger from Henry brought him despatches more pressing than ever; Knight started again with one servant and a guide. At Monte Rotondo he was nearly murdered by the inhabitants; but on the next day (25 November), protected by a violent storm of wind and rain, Henry's envoy entered Rome at ten o'clock without being observed, and kept himself concealed.

It was impossible to speak with Clement, for the emperor's orders were positive. Knight, therefore, began to practise upon the cardinals; he gained over the Cardinal of Pisa, by whose means his despatches were laid before the pontiff. Clement after reading them laid them down with a smile of satisfaction. 'Good!' said he, 'here is *the other* coming to me now!' But night had hardly closed in before the Cardinal of Pisa's secretary hastened to Knight and told him: 'Don Alercon is informed of your arrival; and the pope entreats you to depart immediately.' This officer had scarcely left him, when the prothonotary Gambara arrived in great agitation: 'His Holiness presses you to leave; as soon as he is at liberty, he will attend to your master's request.' Two hours after this, two hundred Spanish soldiers arrived, surrounded the house in which Knight had concealed himself, and searched it from top to bottom, but to no purpose; the English agent had escaped.

Knight's safety was not the true motive which induced Clement to urge his departure. The very day on which the pope received the message from the King of England, he signed a treaty with Charles V, restoring him, under certain conditions, to both his powers. At the same time the pontiff, for greater security, pressed the French general Lautrec to hasten his march to Rome in order to save him from the hands of the emperor. Clement, a disciple of Machiavelli, thus gave the right hand to Charles and the left to Francis; and as he had not another for Henry, he made him the most positive promises. Each of the three princes could reckon on the pope's friendship, and on the same grounds.

The 10th of December (1527) was the day on which Clement's imprisonment would terminate; but he preferred to owe his freedom to intrigue rather than to the emperor's generosity. He therefore procured the dress of a tradesman, and, on the evening before the day fixed for his deliverance, his ward being already much relaxed, he escaped from the castle, and, accompanied only by Louis of Gonzago in his flight, he made his way to Orvieto.[3]

---

[3] [The vacillations of Pope Clement VII (1523–34) are noteworthy. He was distressed by the long rivalry between the Houses of Hapsburg (Spain and the Empire) and Valois (France). At length he decided to side with Francis I of France, but that king's crushing defeat at Pavia (1525) caused him to come to terms with Charles, only to depart from him again by joining a League of Freedom which aimed at asserting the independence of Italy from foreign powers. On the failure of this movement, Clement again submitted to Charles the emperor, but a year later he absolved Francis from his oath to submit to Charles (entered into at Madrid after a long captivity), and helped to form the Holy League of Cognac, by which he, France, and the leading Italian states, bound themselves to resist the ambitions of Charles. Then followed the Imperial invasion of Italy to break the League, and the sack of Rome (May 1527) which horrified the West. Clement remained Charles' prisoner from June to

While Clement was experiencing all the joy of a man just escaped from prison, Henry was a prey to the most violent agitation. Having ceased to love Catherine, he persuaded himself that he was the victim of his father's ambition, a martyr to duty, and the champion of conjugal sanctity. His very gait betrayed his vexation and, even among the gay conversation of the court, deep sighs would escape from his bosom. He had frequent interviews with Wolsey. 'I regard the safety of my soul above all things', he said; 'but I am concerned also for the peace of my kingdom. For a long while an unceasing remorse has been gnawing at my conscience, and my thoughts dwell upon my marriage with unutterable sorrow. God, in his wrath, has taken away my sons, and if I persevere in this unlawful union, he will visit me with still more terrible chastisements. My only hope is in the Holy Father.' Wolsey replied with a low bow: 'Please Your Majesty, I am occupied with this business, as if it were my only means of winning heaven.'

And indeed he redoubled his exertions. He wrote to Sir Gregory da Casale on 5 December (1527): 'You will procure an audience of the pope at any price. Disguise yourself, appear before him as the servant of some nobleman, or as a messenger from the Duke of Ferrara. Scatter money plentifully; sacrifice everything, provided you procure a secret interview with His Holiness; ten thousand ducats are at your disposal. You will explain to Clement the king's scruples, and the necessity of providing for the continuance of his house and the peace of his kingdom. You will tell him that in order to restore him to liberty, the king is ready to declare war against the emperor, and thus show himself to all the world to be a true son of the church.'

Wolsey saw clearly that it was essential to represent the divorce to Clement VII as a means likely to secure the safety of the popedom. The cardinal, therefore, wrote again to da Casale on 6 December: 'Night and day, I revolve in my mind the actual condition of the church, and

---

December 1527. In 1528 Francis once more made war in Italy, but eventually Charles again proved victorious, and for several years Clement VII became dependent upon him. This dependence had important bearings on the English divorce question, for Clement would not nullify the marriage between Henry and Catherine while he was in the power of Charles, the nephew of Catherine. Hence Wolsey could make no real progress in his suit.]

seek the means best calculated to extricate the pope from the gulf into which he has fallen. While I was turning these thoughts over in my mind during a sleepless night ... one way suddenly occurred to me. I said to myself, the king must be prevailed upon to undertake the defence of the Holy Father. This was no easy matter, for His Majesty is strongly attached to the emperor; however, I set about my task. I told the king that His Holiness was ready to satisfy him; I staked my honour; I succeeded. ... To save the pope, my master will sacrifice his treasures, subjects, kingdom, and even his life. ... I therefore conjure His Holiness to entertain our just demand.'

Never before had such pressing entreaties been made to a pope by the government of England.

CHAPTER NINE

The Dilemma and Duplicity of Clement VII

(1527–1528)

The envoys of the King of England appeared in the character of the saviours of Rome. This was doubtless no stratagem; and Wolsey probably regarded that thought as coming from heaven, which had visited him during the weary sleepless night. The zeal of his agents increased. The pope was hardly set at liberty, before Knight and da Casale appeared at the foot of the precipitous rock on which Orvieto is built, and demanded to be introduced to Clement VII. Nothing could be more compromising to the pontiff than such a visit. How could he appear on good terms with England, when Rome and all his states were still in the hands of Catherine's nephew? The pope's mind was utterly bewildered by the demand of the two envoys. He recovered however; to reject the powerful hand extended to him by England, was not without its danger; and as he knew well how to bring a difficult negotiation to a successful conclusion, Clement regained confidence in his skill, and gave orders to introduce Henry's ambassadors.

Their discourse was not without eloquence. 'Never was the church in a more critical position', said they. 'The unmeasured ambition of the kings who claim to dispose of spiritual affairs at their own pleasure (this was aimed at Charles V) holds the apostolical bark suspended over an abyss. The only port open to it in the tempest is the favour of the august prince whom we represent, and who has always been the shield of the faith. But, alas! this monarch, the impregnable bulwark of Your Holiness, is himself the prey of tribulations almost equal to your own. His conscience torn by remorse, his crown without an heir, his kingdom without security, his people exposed once more to perpetual disorders.

... Nay, the whole Christian world given up to the most cruel discord. ... Such are the consequences of a fatal union which God has marked with his displeasure. ... There are also', they added in a lower tone, 'certain things of which His Majesty cannot speak in his letter ... certain incurable disorders under which the queen suffers, which will never permit the king to look upon her again as his wife. If Your Holiness puts an end to such wretchedness by annulling his unlawful marriage, you will attach His Majesty by an indissoluble bond. Assistance, riches, armies, crown, and even life – the king our master is ready to employ all in the service of Rome. He stretches out his hand to you, Most Holy Father ... stretch out yours to him; by your union the church will be saved, and Europe will be saved with it.'

Clement was cruelly embarrassed. His policy consisted in holding the balance between the two princes, and he was now called upon to decide in favour of one of them. He began to regret that he had ever received Henry's ambassadors. 'Consider my position', he said to them, 'and entreat the king to wait until more favourable events leave me at liberty to act.' – 'What!' replied Knight proudly, 'has not Your Holiness promised to consider His Majesty's prayer? If you fail in your promise now, how can I persuade the king that you will keep it some future day?' Da Casale thought the time had come to strike a decisive blow. 'What evils', he exclaimed, 'what inevitable misfortunes your refusal will create! ... The emperor thinks only of depriving the church of its power, and the King of England alone has sworn to maintain it.' Then speaking lower, more slowly, and dwelling upon every word, he continued: 'We fear that His Majesty, reduced to such extremities ... of the two evils will choose the *least*, and supported by the purity of his intentions, will do *of his own authority* ... what he now so respectfully demands. ... What should we see then? ... I shudder at the thought. ... Let not Your Holiness indulge in a false security which will inevitably drag you into the abyss. ... Read all ... remark all ... divine all ... take note of all. ... Most Holy Father, this is a question of life and death.' And da Casale's tone said more than his words.

Clement understood that a positive refusal would expose him to lose England. Placed between Henry and Charles, as between the hammer and the anvil, he resolved to gain time. 'Well then', he said to Knight and da Casale, 'I will do what you ask; but I am not familiar with the *forms* these dispensations require. ... I will consult the cardinal sanctorum quatuor on the subject ... and then will inform you.'

Knight and da Casale, wishing to anticipate Clement VII, hastened to Lorenzo Pucci, cardinal sanctorum quatuor, and intimated to him that their master would know how to be grateful. The cardinal assured the deputies of his affection for Henry VIII, and they, in the fulness of their gratitude, laid before him the four documents which they were anxious to get executed. But the cardinal had hardly looked at the first – the proposal that Wolsey should decide the matter of the divorce in England – when he exclaimed: 'Impossible! ... a bull in such terms would cover with eternal disgrace not only His Holiness and the king, but even the Cardinal of York himself.' The deputies were confounded, for Wolsey had ordered them to ask the pope for nothing but his signature. Recovering themselves, they rejoined: 'All that we require is a competent commission.' On his part, the pope wrote Henry a letter, in which he managed to say nothing.

Of the four required documents there were two on whose immediate despatch Knight and da Casale insisted: these were the *commission* to pronounce the divorce, and the *dispensation* to contract a second marriage. The *dispensation* without the *commission* was of no value; this the pope knew well; accordingly he resolved to give the *dispensation* only. It was as if Charles had granted Clement when in prison permission to visit his cardinals, but denied him liberty to leave the Castle of St Angelo. It is in such a manner as this that a religious system transformed into a political system has recourse, when it is without power, to stratagem. 'The *commission*', said the artful Medici to Knight, 'must be corrected according to the style of our court; but here is the *dispensation*.' Knight took the document; it was addressed to Henry VIII and ran thus: 'We accord to you, in case your marriage with Catherine shall be declared null, free liberty to take another wife, provided she have not been the wife of your brother. ...' The Englishman was duped by the Italian. 'In my poor judgment', he said, 'this document will be of use to us.' After this Clement appeared to concern himself solely about Knight's health, and suddenly manifested the greatest interest for him: 'It is proper that you should hasten your departure', said he, 'for it is necessary that you should travel *at your ease*. Gambara will follow you post, and bring the commission.' Knight thus mystified, took leave of the pope, who got rid of da Casale and Gambara in a similar manner. He then began to breathe once more. There was no diplomacy in Europe which Rome, even in its greatest weakness, could not easily dupe.

It had now become necessary to elude the commission. While the king's envoys were departing in good spirits, reckoning on the document that was to follow them, the general of the Spanish Observance reiterated to the pontiff in every tone: 'Be careful to give no document authorizing the divorce and, above all, do not permit this affair to be judged in Henry's realm.' The cardinals drew up the document under the influence of de Angelis, and made it a masterpiece of insignificance. If good theology ennobles the heart, bad theology, so fertile in subtleties, imparts to the mind a skill by no means common; and hence the most celebrated diplomatists have often been churchmen. The act being thus drawn up, the pope despatched three copies, to Knight, to da Casale, and to Gambara. Knight was near Bologna when the courier overtook him. He was stupefied, and taking post-horses returned with all haste to Orvieto. Gambara proceeded through France to England with the useless *dispensation* which the pope had granted.

Knight had thought to meet with more good faith at the court of the pope than with kings, and he had been outwitted. What would Wolsey and Henry say of his folly? His wounded self-esteem began to make him believe all that Tyndale and Luther said of the popedom. The former had just published the *Obedience of a Christian Man*, and the *Parable of the Wicked Mammon*, in which he represented Rome as one of the transformations of Antichrist. 'Antichrist', said he in the latter treatise, 'is not a man that should suddenly appear with wonders; he is a spiritual thing, who was in the Old Testament and also in the time of Christ and the apostles, and is now and shall (I doubt not) endure till the world's end. His nature is (when he is overcome with the word of God) to go out of the play for a season, and to disguise himself, and then to come in again with a new name and new raiment. The scribes and Pharisees in the gospel were very antichrists; popes, cardinals, and bishops have gotten their new names, but the thing is all one. Even so now, when we have uttered [vanquished] him, *he will change himself once more*, and turn himself into an angel of light. Already *the beast*, seeing himself now to be sought for, roareth and seeketh new holes to hide himself in, and changeth himself into a thousand fashions with all manner of wiliness, falsehood, subtlety, and craft.'[1] This idea, paradoxical at first, gradually made its way into men's minds. The Romans, by their practices, familiarized the English to the somewhat coarse descriptions of the reformers. England was to have many such lessons, and thus by degrees learn to set Rome aside for the sake of her own glory and prosperity.

Knight and da Casale reached Orvieto about the same time. Clement replied with sighs: 'Alas! I am the emperor's prisoner. The imperialists are every day pillaging towns and castles in our neighbourhood. ... Wretch that I am! I have not a friend except the king your master, and he is far away. ... If I should do anything now to displease Charles, I am a lost man. ... To sign the commission would be to sign an eternal rupture with him.' But Knight and da Casale pleaded so effectually with cardinal sanctorum quatuor, and so pressed Clement, that the pontiff, without the knowledge of the Spaniard de Angelis, gave them a more satisfactory document, but not such as Wolsey required. 'In giving you this commission', said the pope, 'I am giving away my liberty, and perhaps my life. I listen not to the voice of prudence, but to that of affection only. I confide in the generosity of the King of England: he is the master of my destiny.' He then began to weep, and seemed ready to faint. Knight, forgetting his vexation, promised Clement that the king would do everything to save him. – 'Ah!' said the pope, 'there is one effectual means.' – 'What is that?' inquired Henry's agents. – 'M. Lautrec, who says daily that he will come, but never does', replied Clement, 'has only to bring the French army promptly before the gates of Orvieto; then I could excuse myself by saying that he constrained me to sign the commission.' – 'Nothing is easier', replied the envoys, 'we will go and hasten his arrival.'

Clement was not even now at ease. The safety of the Roman Church troubled him not less than his own. ... Charles might discover the trick and make the popedom suffer for it. There was danger on all sides. If the

[1] Tyndale, *Doctrinal Treatises*, pp. 42, 43.

English spoke of *independence*, did not the emperor threaten a *reform*?
… The Catholic princes, said the papal councillors, are capable, without
perhaps a single exception, of supporting the cause of Luther to gratify
a criminal ambition. The pope reflected and, withdrawing his word,
promised to give the commission when Lautrec was under the walls
of Orvieto; but the English agents insisted on having it immediately.
To conciliate all, it was agreed that the pope should give the required
document at once, but as soon as the French army arrived, he should
send another copy bearing the date of the day on which he saw Lautrec.
'Beseech the king to keep secret the commission I give you', said Clement
VII to Knight; 'if he begins the process immediately he receives it, I am
undone for ever.' The pope thus gave permission to act, on condition of
not acting at all. Knight took leave on 1 January 1528; he promised all the
pontiff desired, and then, as if fearing some fresh difficulty, he departed
the same day. Da Casale, on his side, after having offered the cardinal
sanctorum quatuor a gift of 4,000 crowns, which he refused, repaired to
Lautrec, to beg him to *constrain* the pope to sign a document which was
already on its way to England.

But while the business seemed to be clearing at Rome, it was
becoming more complicated in London. The king's project got wind,
and Catherine gave way to the liveliest sorrow. 'I shall protest', said she,
'against the commission given to the Cardinal of York. Is he not the
king's subject, the vile flatterer of his pleasures?' Catherine did not resist
alone; the people, who hated the cardinal, could not with pleasure see
him invested with such authority. To obviate this inconvenience, Henry
resolved to ask the pope for another cardinal, who should be empowered
to terminate the affair in London with or without Wolsey.

The latter agreed to the measure: it is even possible that he was the
first to suggest it, for he feared to bear alone the responsibility of so
hateful an inquiry. Accordingly, on 27 December, he wrote to the king's
agents at Rome: 'Procure the envoy of a legate, and particularly of an
able, easy, *manageable* legate … desirous of meriting the king's favour,
Campeggio for instance. You will earnestly request the cardinal who may
be selected, to travel with all diligence, and you will assure him that the
king will behave liberally towards him.'

Knight reached Asti in Savoy on 10 January, where he found letters with fresh orders. This was another check: at one time it is the pope who compels him to retrace his steps, at another it is the king. Henry's unlucky valetudinarian secretary, a man very susceptible to fatigue, and already wearied and exhausted by ten painful journeys, was in a very bad humour. He determined to permit Gambara to carry the two documents to England; to commission da Casale, who had not left the pope's neighbourhood, to solicit the despatch of the legate; and as regarded himself, to go and wait for further orders at Turin: – 'If it be thought good unto the king's Highness that I do return unto Orvieto, I shall do as much as *my poor carcass* may endure.'

When da Casale reached Bologna, he pressed Lautrec to go and constrain the pontiff to sign the act which Gambara was already bearing to England. On receiving the new despatches he returned in all haste to Orvieto, and the pope was very much alarmed when he heard of his arrival. He had feared to grant a simple paper, destined to remain secret; and now he is required to send a prince of the church! Will Henry never be satisfied? 'The mission you desire would be full of dangers', he replied; 'but we have discovered another means, alone calculated to finish this business. Mind you do not say that I pointed it out to you', added the pope in a mysterious tone, 'but that it was suggested by cardinal sanctorum quatuor and Simonetta.' Da Casale was all attention. 'There is not a doctor in the world who can better decide on this matter, and on its most private circumstances, than the king himself. If therefore he sincerely believes that Catherine had really become his brother's wife, let him empower the Cardinal of York to pronounce the divorce, and let him take another wife without any further ceremony; he can then afterwards demand the confirmation of the consistory. The affair being concluded in this way, I will take the rest upon myself.' – 'But', said da Casale, somewhat dissatisfied with this new intrigue, 'I must fulfil my mission, and the king demands a legate.' – 'And whom shall I send?' asked Clement. 'Da Monte? he cannot move. De Cæsis? he is at Naples. Ara Cœli? he has the gout. Piccolomini? he is of the imperial party. ... Campeggio would be the best, but he is at Rome, where he supplies my place, and cannot leave without peril to the church.' ... And then with some emotion he added, 'I throw myself into His Majesty's arms. The emperor will never forgive what I am doing. If he hears of it he will summon me before his *council*; I shall have no rest until he has deprived me of my throne and my life.'

Da Casale hastened to forward to London the result of the conference. Clement, being unable to untie the knot, requested Henry to cut it. Will this prince hesitate to employ so easy a means, the pope (Clement declared it himself) being willing to ratify everything?

Here closes Henry's first campaign in the territories of the popedom. We shall now see the results of so many efforts.

CHAPTER TEN

Royal Threats Counter Papal Cunning

(January to March 1528)

N ever was disappointment more complete than that felt by Henry and Wolsey after the arrival of Gambara with the commission; the king was angry, the cardinal vexed. What Clement called the *sacrifice of his life* was in reality but a sheet of paper fit only to be thrown into the fire. 'This commission is of no value', said Wolsey. – 'And even to put it into execution', added Henry, 'we must wait until the imperialists have quitted Italy! The pope is putting us off to the Greek calends.'[1] – 'His Holiness', observed the cardinal, 'does not bind himself to pronounce the divorce; the queen will therefore appeal from our judgment.' – 'And even if the pope had bound himself', added the king, 'it would be sufficient for the emperor to smile upon him, to make him retract what he had promised.' – 'It is all a cheat and a mockery', concluded both king and minister.

What was to be done next? The only way to make Clement ours, thought Wolsey, is to get rid of Charles; it is time his pride was brought down. Accordingly, on 22 January 1528, Clarencieux,[2] being sent to France with instructions which had not been revealed to Henry VIII or to his council, made a formal proclamation of hostilities against Charles. The King of France acted likewise. When Charles heard of this proceeding he exclaimed: 'I know the hand that has flung the torch of war into the midst of Europe. My crime is not having placed the Cardinal of York on St Peter's throne.'

---

[1] [Greek calends: a point or time that does not or will not exist.]

[2] [Clarencieux is the second king-of-arms in England. He is so named after the Duke of Clarence, son of Edward III.]

A mere declaration of hostilities was not enough for Wolsey; the Bishop of Bayonne, ambassador from France, seeing him one day somewhat excited, whispered in his ear: 'In former times popes have deposed emperors for smaller offences.' The deposition of Charles would have delivered the King of France from a troublesome rival; but Du Bellay, fearing to take the initiative in so bold an enterprise, suggested the idea to the cardinal. Wolsey reflected: such a thought had never before occurred to him. Taking the ambassador aside to a window, he there swore *stoutly*, said Du Bellay, that he should be delighted to use all his influence to get Charles deposed by the pope. 'No one is more likely than yourself', replied the bishop, 'to induce Clement to do it.' – 'I will use all my credit', rejoined Wolsey, and the two priests separated. This bright idea the cardinal never forgot. Charles had robbed him of the tiara; he would retaliate by depriving Charles of his crown. *An eye for an eye, and a tooth for a tooth.* Staffileo, Dean of the Rota, was then in London, and still burning with resentment against the author of the sack of Rome, he favourably received the suggestions Wolsey made to him; and, finally, the envoy from John Zapolyai, king-elect of Hungary, supported the project. But the kings of France and England were not so easily induced to put the thrones of kings at the disposal of the priests. It appears, however, that the pope was sounded on the subject; and if the emperor had been beaten in Italy, it is probable that the bull would have been fulminated against him. His sword preserved his crown, and the plot of the two bishops failed.

The king's councillors began to seek for less heroic means. 'We must prosecute the affair at *Rome*', said some. – 'No', said others, 'in England. The pope is too much afraid of the emperor to pronounce the divorce in person.' – 'If the pope fears the emperor more than the King of *England*', exclaimed the proud Tudor, 'we shall find some other way to set him at ease.' Thus, at the first contradiction, Henry placed his hand on his sword, and threatened to sever the ties which bound his kingdom to the throne of the Italian pontiff.

'I have hit it!' said Wolsey at length; 'we must combine the two plans – judge the affair in London, and at the same time bind the pontiff at Rome.' And then the able cardinal proposed the draft of a bull, by which the pope, delegating his authority to two legates, should declare that the acts of that delegation should have a perpetual effect, notwithstanding any contrary decrees that might subsequently emanate from his infallible authority. A new mission was decided upon for the accomplishment of this bold design.

Wolsey, annoyed by the weakness of Knight and his colleagues, desired men of another stamp. He therefore cast his eyes on his own secretary, Stephen Gardiner, an active man, intelligent, supple, and crafty, a learned canonist, desirous of the king's favour, and, above all, a good Romanist, which at Rome was not without its advantage. Gardiner was in miniature the living image of his master; and hence the cardinal sometimes styled him *the half of himself.* Edward Fox, the chief almoner, was joined with him – a moderate, influential man, a particular friend of Henry's, and a zealous advocate of the divorce. Fox was named first in the commission; but it was agreed that Gardiner should be the real head of the embassy. 'Repeat without ceasing', Wolsey told them, 'that His Majesty cannot do otherwise than separate from the queen. Attack each one on his weak side. Declare to the pope that the king promises to defend him against the emperor; and to the cardinals that their services will be nobly rewarded. If that does not suffice, let the energy of your words be such as to excite a wholesome fear in the pontiff.'

Fox and Gardiner, after a gracious reception at Paris (23 February) by Francis I, arrived at Orvieto on 21 March, after many perils, and with their dress in such disorder on account of foul weather, that no one could have taken them for the ambassadors of Henry VIII. 'What a city!' they exclaimed, as they passed through its streets; 'what ruins, what misery! It is indeed truly called Orvieto [the aged city]!' The state of the town gave them no very grand idea of the state of the popedom, and they imagined that with a pontiff so poorly lodged, their negotiation could not be otherwise than easy. 'I give you my house', said da Casale, to whom they went, 'my room and my own bed'; and as they made some objections, he added: 'It is not possible to lodge you elsewhere; I have even been forced to borrow what was necessary to receive you.' Da Casale pressing them to change their clothes, which were still dripping (they had just crossed a river on their mules) they replied that being obliged to travel post, they had not been able to bring a change of raiment. 'Alas!' said da Casale, 'what is to be done? There are few persons in Orvieto who have more garments than one; even the shopkeepers have no cloth for sale; this town is quite a prison. People say the pope is at liberty here. A pretty liberty indeed! Want, impure air, wretched lodging, and a thousand other inconveniences keep the Holy Father closer than when he was in the Castle of St Angelo. Accordingly, he told me the other day, it was better to be in captivity at Rome than at liberty here.'[3]

Shortly, however, they managed to procure some new clothing; and being now in a condition to show themselves, Henry's agents were admitted to an after-dinner audience on Monday 25 March (1528).

Da Casale conducted them to an old building in ruins. 'This is where His Holiness lives', he said. They looked at one another with astonishment and, crossing the rubbish lying about, passed through three chambers whose ceilings had fallen in, whose windows were curtainless, and in which thirty persons '*riff-raff* were standing against the bare walls for a garnishment'. This was the pope's court.

At length the ambassadors reached the pontiff's room, and placed Henry's letters in his hands. 'Your Holiness', said Gardiner, 'when sending the king a dispensation, was pleased to add, that if this document were not sufficient, you would willingly give a better. It is that favour the king now desires.' The pope with embarrassment strove to soften his refusal. 'I am informed', he said, 'that the king is led on in this affair by a secret inclination, and that the lady he loves is far from being worthy of him.' Gardiner replied with firmness: 'The king truly desires to marry again after the divorce, that he may have an heir to the crown; but the woman he proposes to take is animated by the noblest sentiments; the Cardinal of York and all England do homage to her virtues.' The pope appeared convinced. 'Besides', continued Gardiner, 'the king has written a book on the motives of his divorce.' – 'Good! come and read it to me tomorrow', rejoined Clement.

The next day the English envoys had hardly appeared, before Clement took Henry's book, ran over it as he walked up and down the room, and then seating himself on a long bench covered with an old carpet, 'not worth twenty pence', says an annalist, he read the book aloud. He counted the number of arguments, made objections as if Henry were present, and piled them one upon another without waiting for an answer.

[3] State Papers, vii, p. 63.

'The marriages forbidden in Leviticus', said he, in a short and quick tone of voice, 'are permitted in Deuteronomy; now Deuteronomy coming after Leviticus, we are bound by the latter. The honour of Catherine and the emperor is at stake, and the divorce would give rise to a terrible war.' The pope continued speaking, and whenever the Englishmen attempted to reply, he bade them be silent, and kept on reading. 'It is an excellent book', said he, however, in a courteous tone, when he had ended; 'I shall keep it to read over again at my leisure.' Gardiner then presenting a draft of the commission which Henry required, Clement made answer: 'It is too late to look at it now; leave it with me.' – 'But we are in haste', added Gardiner. – 'Yes, yes, I know it', said the pope. All his efforts tended to protract the business.

On 28 March, the ambassadors were conducted to the room in which the pope slept; the cardinals sanctorum quatuor and de Monte, as well as the councillor of the Rota, Simonetta, were then with him. Chairs were arranged in a semicircle. 'Be seated', said Clement, who stood in the middle. 'Master Gardiner, now tell me what you want.' – 'There is no question between us but one of *time*', said Gardiner. 'You promised to ratify the divorce, as soon as it was pronounced; and we require you to do *before* what you engage to do *after*. What is right on one day, must be right on another.' Then, raising his voice, the Englishman added: 'If His Majesty perceives that no more respect is paid to him than to a common man, he will have recourse to a *remedy* which I will not name, but which will not fail in its effect.'

The pope and his councillors looked at one another in silence; they had understood him. The imperious Gardiner, remarking the effect which he had produced, then added in an absolute tone: 'We have our instructions, and are determined to keep to them.' – 'I am ready to do everything compatible with my honour', exclaimed Clement, in alarm. – 'What Your Honour would not permit you to grant', said the proud ambassador, 'the honour of the king, my master, would not permit him to ask.' Gardiner's language became more imperative every minute. 'Well, then', said Clement, driven to extremity, 'I will do what the king demands, and if the emperor is angry, I cannot help it.' The interview, which had commenced with a storm, finished with a gleam of sunshine.

That bright gleam soon disappeared: Clement, who imagined he saw in Henry a Hannibal at war with Rome, wished to play the temporizer, the *Fabius Cunctator* [Fabius the Delayer.] 'He gives twice who gives quickly', said Gardiner sharply, who observed this manoeuvre. – 'It is a question of law', replied the pope, 'and as I am very ignorant in these matters, I must give the doctors of the canon law the necessary time to make it all clear.' – 'By his delays Fabius Maximus saved Rome', rejoined Gardiner; 'you will destroy it by yours.' – 'Alas!' exclaimed the pope, 'if I say the king is right, I shall have to go back to prison.' – 'When truth is concerned', said the ambassador, 'of what consequence are the opinions of men?' Gardiner was speaking at his ease, but Clement found that the Castle of St Angelo was not without weight in the balance. 'You may be sure that I shall do everything for the best', replied the modern Fabius. With these words the conference terminated.

Such were the struggles of England with the popedom – struggles which were to end in a definitive rupture. Gardiner knew that he had a skilful adversary to deal with; too cunning to allow himself to be irritated, he coolly resolved to frighten the pontiff: that was in his instructions. On the Friday before Palm Sunday, he was ushered into the pope's private room; there he found Clement attended by de Monte, Sanctorum Quatuor, Simonetta, Staffileo, Paul, auditor of the Rota, and Gambara. 'It is impossible', said the cardinals, 'to grant a decretal commission in which the pope pronounces *de jure* in favour of the divorce, with a promise of confirmation *de facto*.' Gardiner insisted; but no persuasion, 'neither *dulce* nor *poynante*',[4] could move the pontiff. The envoy judged the moment had come to discharge his strongest battery. 'O perverse race', said he to the pontiff's ministers, 'instead of being harmless as doves, you are as full of dissimulation and malice as serpents; promising everything but performing nothing. England will be driven to believe that God has taken from you the key of knowledge, and that the laws of the popes, ambiguous to the popes themselves, are only fit to be cast into the fire. The king has hitherto restrained his people, impatient of the Romish yoke; but he will now give them the rein.' A long and gloomy silence followed. Then the Englishman, suddenly changing his

---

[4] [dulce = sweet; poynante = stinging, harsh.]

tone, softly approached Clement, who had left his seat, and conjured him in a low voice to consider carefully what justice required of him. 'Alas!' replied Clement, 'I tell you again, I am ignorant in these matters. According to the maxims of the canon law *the pope carries all laws in the tablets of his heart*, but unfortunately God has never given me the key that opens them.' As he could not escape by silence, Clement retreated under cover of a jest, and heedlessly pronounced the condemnation of the popedom. If he had never received the famous key, there was no reason why other pontiffs should have possessed it. The next day he found another loophole; for when the ambassadors told him that the king would carry on the matter without him, he sighed, drew out his handkerchief, and said, as he wiped his eyes: 'Would to God that I were dead!' Clement employed tears as a political engine.

'We shall not get the *decretal* commission [that which pronounced the divorce]', said Fox and Gardiner after this, 'and it is not really necessary. Let us demand the *general* commission [authorizing the legates to pronounce it] and exact a promise that shall supply the place of the act which is denied us.' Clement, who was ready to make all the promises in the world, agreed to ratify the sentence of the legates without delay. Fox and Gardiner then presented to Simonetta a draft of the act required. The dean, after reading it, returned it to the envoys, saying, 'It is very well, I think, except *the end*; show it to sanctorum quatuor.' The next morning they carried the draft to that cardinal: 'How long has it been the rule for the patient to write the prescription? I always thought it was the physician's business.' – 'No one knows the disease so well as the patient', replied Gardiner; 'and this disease may be of such a nature that the doctor cannot prescribe the remedy without taking the patient's advice.' Sanctorum quatuor read the prescription, and then returned it, saying: 'It is not bad, with the exception of *the beginning*. Take the draft to de Monte and the other councillors.' The latter liked neither beginning, middle, nor end. 'We will send for you this evening', said de Monte.

Three or four days having elapsed, Henry's envoys again waited on the pope, who showed them the draft prepared by his councillors. Gardiner, remarking in it additions, retrenchments, and corrections, threw it disdainfully from him, and said coldly: 'Your Holiness is deceiving us;

you have selected these men to be the instruments of your duplicity.' Clement, in alarm, sent for Simonetta; and after a warm discussion, the envoys, more discontented than ever, quitted the pope at one in the morning.

The night brings wisdom. 'I only desire two little words more in the commission', said Gardiner the next day to Clement and Simonetta. The pope requested Simonetta to wait upon the cardinals immediately; the latter sent word that they were at dinner, and adjourned the business until the morrow.

When Gardiner heard of this epicurean message, he thought the time had come for striking a decisive blow. A new tragedy began. 'We are deceived', exclaimed he, 'you are laughing at us. This is not the way to gain the favour of princes. Water mixed with wine spoils it; your corrections nullify our document. These ignorant and suspicious priests have spelled over our draft as if a scorpion was hidden under every word. – You made us come to Italy', said he to Staffileo and Gambara, 'like hawks which the fowler lures by holding out to them a piece of meat; and now that we are here, the bait has disappeared, and, instead of giving us what we sought, you pretend to lull us to sleep by the sweet voice of the sirens.' Then, turning to Clement, the English envoy added, 'Your Holiness will have to answer for this.' The pope sighed and wiped away his tears. 'It was God's pleasure', continued Gardiner, whose tone became more threatening every minute, 'that we should see with our own eyes the disposition of the people here. It is time to have done. Henry is not an ordinary prince – bear in mind that you are insulting *the Defender of the Faith.* ... You are going to lose the favour of the only monarch who protects you, and the apostolical chair, already tottering, will fall into dust, and disappear entirely amidst the applause of all Christendom.'

Gardiner paused. The pope was moved. The state of Italy seemed to confirm but too strongly the sinister predictions of the envoy of Henry VIII. The imperial troops, terrified and pursued by Lautrec, had abandoned Rome and retired on Naples. The French general was following up this wretched army of Charles V, decimated by pestilence and debauchery; Andrea Doria, at the head of his galleys, had destroyed the Spanish fleet; Gæta and Naples only were left to the imperialists;

and Lautrec, who was besieging the latter place, wrote to Henry on 26 August that all would soon be over. The timid Clement VII had attentively watched all these catastrophes. Accordingly, Gardiner had hardly spoken of the danger which threatened the popedom, before he turned pale with affright, rose from his seat, stretched out his arms in terror, as if he had desired to repel some monster ready to devour him, and exclaimed, 'Write, write! Insert whatever words you please.' As he said this, he paced up and down the room, raising his hands to heaven and sighing deeply, while Fox and Gardiner, standing motionless, looked on in silence. A tempestuous wind seemed to be stirring the depths of the abyss; the ambassadors waited until the storm was abated. At last Clement recovered himself, made a few trivial excuses, and dismissed Henry's ministers. It was an hour past midnight.

It was neither morality, nor religion, nor even the laws of the church which led Clement to refuse the divorce; ambition and fear were his only motives. He would have desired that Henry should first constrain the emperor to restore him his territories. But the King of England, who felt himself unable to protect the pope against Charles, required, however, this unhappy pontiff to provoke the emperor's anger. Clement reaped the fruits of that fatal system which had transformed the church of Jesus Christ into a pitiful combination of policy and cunning.

On the next day, the tempest having thoroughly abated, *sanctorum quatuor* corrected the commission. It was signed, completed by a leaden seal attached to a piece of string, and then handed to Gardiner, who read it. The bull was addressed to Wolsey, and 'authorized him, in case he should acknowledge the nullity of Henry's marriage, to pronounce judicially the sentence of divorce, but without noise or display of judgment; for that purpose he might take any English bishop for his colleague.' – 'All that we can do, you can do', said the pope. 'We are very doubtful', said the importunate Gardiner after reading the bull, 'whether this commission, without the clauses of *confirmation and revocation*, will satisfy His Majesty; but we will do all in our power to get him to accept it.' – 'Above all, do not speak of our altercations', said the pope. Gardiner, like a discreet diplomatist, did not scruple to note down every particular in cipher in the letters whence these details are procured. 'Tell the king', continued the pontiff, 'that this commission is on my part a declaration of war against the emperor, and that I now place myself under His Majesty's protection.' The chief almoner of England departed for London with the precious document.

But one storm followed close upon another. Fox had not long quitted Orvieto when new letters arrived from Wolsey, demanding the fourth of the acts previously requested, namely, the *engagement* to ratify at Rome whatever the commissioners might decide in England. Gardiner was to set about it *in season and out of season*; the verbal promise of the pope counted for nothing; this document must be had, whether the pope was ill, dying, or dead. '*Ego et Rex meus*, His Majesty and I command you', said Wolsey; 'this divorce is of more consequence to us than twenty popedoms.' The English envoy renewed his demand. 'Since you refuse the decretal', he said, 'there is the greater reason why you should not refuse *the engagement*.' This application led to fresh discussion and fresh tears. Clement gave way once more; but the Italians, more crafty than Gardiner, reserved a loophole in the document through which the pontiff might escape. The messenger Thaddeus carried it to London; and Gardiner left Orvieto for Rome to confer with Campeggio.

Clement was a man of penetrating mind and, although he knew as well as any how to deliver a clever speech, he was irresolute and timid; and accordingly the commission had not long been despatched before he repented. Full of distress, he paced the ruined chambers of his old palace, and imagined he saw hanging over his head that terrible sword of Charles V, whose edge he had already felt. 'Wretch that I am', said he; 'cruel wolves surround me; they open their jaws to swallow me up. ... I see none but enemies around me. At their head is the emperor. ... What will he do? Alas! I have yielded that fatal commission which the general of the Spanish Observance had enjoined me to refuse. Behind Charles come the Venetians, the Florentines, the Duke of Ferrara. ... They have cast lots upon my vesture. ... Next comes the King of France, who promises nothing, but looks on with folded arms; or rather, what perfidy! calls upon me at this critical moment to deprive Charles V of his crown. ... And last, but not least, Henry VIII, *the Defender of the Faith*, indulges in frightful menaces against me. ... The emperor desires to maintain the queen on the throne of England; the latter, to put her away. … Would to God that Catherine were in her grave! But, alas! she lives … to be the apple of discord dividing the two greatest monarchies, and the inevitable cause of the ruin of the popedom. … Wretched man that I am! how cruel is my perplexity, and around me I can see nothing but horrible confusion.'

CHAPTER ELEVEN

Wolsey's Desperate Demands

(April to July 1528)

D uring this time Fox was making his way to England. On 27 April (1528) he reached Paris; on 2 May he landed at Sandwich, and hastened to Greenwich, where he arrived the next day at five in the evening, just as Wolsey had left for London. Fox's arrival was an event of great importance. 'Let him go to Lady Anne's apartments', said the king, 'and wait for me there.' Fox told Anne Boleyn of his and Gardiner's exertions, and the success of their mission, at which she expressed her very great satisfaction. It is clear that she no longer resisted Henry's project for divorce. 'Mistress Anne always called me Master Stephen', wrote Fox to Gardiner, 'her thoughts were so full of you.' The king appeared and Anne withdrew.

'Tell me as briefly as possible what you have done', said Henry. Fox placed in the king's hands the pope's insignificant letter, which he bade his almoner read; then that from Staffileo, which was put on one side; and lastly Gardiner's letter, which Henry took hastily and read himself. 'The pope has promised us', said Fox, as he terminated his report, 'to confirm the sentence of the divorce, as soon as it has been pronounced by the commissioners.' – 'Excellent!' exclaimed Henry; and then he ordered Anne to be called in. 'Repeat before this lady', he said to Fox, 'what you have just told me.' The almoner did so. 'The pope is convinced of the justice of your cause', he said in conclusion, 'and the cardinal's letter has convinced him that my lady is worthy of the throne of England.' – 'Make your report to Wolsey this very night', said the king.

It was ten o'clock when the chief almoner reached the cardinal's palace; he had gone to bed, but immediate orders were given that Fox should be conducted to his room. Being a churchman, Wolsey could understand the pope's artifices better than Henry; accordingly, as soon as he learnt that Fox had brought the commission only, he became alarmed at the task imposed upon him. 'What a misfortune!' he exclaimed; 'your commission is no better than Gambara's. ... However, go and rest yourself; I will examine these papers tomorrow.' Fox withdrew in confusion. 'It is not bad', said Wolsey the next day, 'but the whole business still falls on me alone! – Never mind, I must wear a contented look, or else. ...' In the afternoon he summoned into his chamber Fox, Dr Bell, and Viscount Rochford: 'Master Gardiner has surpassed himself', said the crafty supple cardinal; 'What a man! what an inestimable treasure! what a jewel in our kingdom!'

He did not mean a word he was saying. Wolsey was dissatisfied with everything – with the refusal of the *decretal*, and with the drawing up of the *commission*, as well as of the *engagement* (which arrived soon after in good condition, so far as the outside was concerned). But the king's ill-humour would infallibly recoil on Wolsey; so putting a good face on a bad matter, he ruminated in secret on the means of obtaining what had been refused him. 'Write to Gardiner', said he to Fox, 'that everything makes me desire the pope's *decretal* – the need of unburdening my conscience, of being able to reply to the calumniators who will attack my judgment, and the thought of the accidents to which the life of man is exposed. Let His Holiness, then, pronounce the divorce himself; we engage on our part to keep his resolution secret. But order Master Stephen to employ every kind of persuasion that his *rhetoric* can imagine.' In case the pope should positively refuse the decretal, Wolsey required that at least Campeggio should share the responsibility of the divorce with him.

This was not all: while reading the engagement, Wolsey discovered the loophole which had escaped Gardiner, and this is what he contrived: 'The *engagement* which the pope has sent us', he wrote to Gardiner, 'is drawn up in such terms that he can retract it at pleasure; we must therefore find some *good way* to obtain another. You may do it under this pretence. You will appear before His Holiness with a dejected air, and tell him that the courier, to whom the conveyance of the said engagement was entrusted, fell into the water with his despatches, so that the rescripts were totally defaced and illegible; that I have not dared deliver it into the king's hands, and unless His Holiness will grant you a duplicate, some notable blame will be imputed unto you for not taking better care in its transmission. And further, you will continue: I remember the expressions of the former document, and to save Your Holiness trouble, I will dictate them to your secretary. Then', added Wolsey, 'while the secretary is writing, you will find means to introduce, without its being perceived, as many *fat, pregnant,* and available words as possible, to bind the pope and enlarge my powers, the politic handling of which the king's Highness and I commit unto your good discretion.'

Such was the expedient invented by Wolsey. The papal secretary, imagining he was making a fresh copy of the original document (which was, by the way, in perfect condition), was at the dictation of the ambassador to draw up another of a different tenor. The 'politic handling' of the cardinal-legate, which was not very unlike forgery, throws a disgraceful light on the policy of the sixteenth century.

Wolsey read this letter to the chief almoner; and then, to set his conscience at rest, he added piously: 'In an affair of such high importance, on which depends the glory or the ruin of the realm – my honour or my disgrace – the condemnation of my soul or my everlasting merit – I will listen solely to the voice of my conscience, and I shall act in such a manner as to be able to render an account to God without fear.'

Wolsey did more; it seems that the boldness of his declarations reassured him with regard to the baseness of his works. Being at Greenwich on the following Sunday, he said to the king in the presence of Fox, Bell, Wolman, and Tuke: 'I am bound to your royal person more than any subject was ever bound to his prince. I am ready to sacrifice my goods, my blood, my life for you. ... But my obligations towards God are greater still. For that cause, rather than act against his will, I would endure the extremest evils. I would suffer your royal indignation, and, if necessary, deliver my body to the executioners that they might cut it in pieces.' What could be the spirit then impelling Wolsey? Was it blindness or impudence? He may have been sincere in the words he addressed to Henry; at the bottom of his heart he may have desired to set the pope above the king, and the Church of Rome above the kingdom of England; and this desire may have appeared to him a sublime virtue, such as would hide a multitude of sins. What the public conscience would have called treason was heroism to the Romish priest. This zeal for the papacy is sometimes met with in conjunction with the most flagrant immorality. If Wolsey deceived the pope, it was to save popery in the realm of England. Fox, Bell, Wolman, and Tuke listened to him with astonishment. Henry, who thought he knew his man, received these holy declarations without alarm, and the cardinal, having thus eased his conscience, proceeded boldly in his iniquities. It seems, however, that the inward reproaches which he silenced in public, had their revenge in secret. One of his officers, entering his private room shortly afterwards, presented a letter addressed to Campeggio for his signature. It ended thus: 'I hope all things shall be done according to the will of God, the desire of the king, the quiet of the kingdom, and to our honour *with a good conscience.*' The cardinal, having read the letter, dashed out the last four words. Conscience has a sting from which none can escape, not even a Wolsey.

However, Gardiner lost no time in Italy. When he met Campeggio (to whom Henry VIII had given a palace at Rome, and a bishopric in England) he entreated him to go to London and pronounce the divorce. This prelate, who was to be empowered in 1530 with authority to crush Protestantism in Germany, seemed bound to undertake a mission that would save Romanism in Britain. But proud of his position at Rome, where he acted as the pope's representative, he cared not for a charge that would undoubtedly draw upon him either Henry's hatred or the emperor's anger. He begged to be excused. The pope spoke in a similar tone. When he was informed of this, the terrible Tudor, beginning to believe that Clement desired to entangle him, as the hunter entangles the lion in his toils, gave vent to his anger on Tuke, Fox, and Gardiner, but particularly on Wolsey. Nor were reasons wanting for this explosion. The cardinal, perceiving that his hatred against Charles had carried him too far, pretended that it was without his orders that Clarencieux, bribed by France, had combined with the French ambassador to declare war against the emperor; and added that he would have the English king-at-arms put to death as he passed through Calais. This was an infallible means of preventing disagreeable revelations. But the herald, who had been forewarned, crossed by way of Boulogne, and, without the cardinal's knowledge, obtained an interview with Henry, before whom he placed the *orders* he had received from Wolsey in *three* consecutive letters. The king was astonished at his minister's impudence. With an oath he exclaimed: 'The man in whom I had most confidence told me quite the contrary.' He then summoned Wolsey before him, and reproached him severely for his falsehoods. The wretched man shook like a leaf. Henry appeared to pardon him, but the season of his favour had passed away. Henceforward he kept the cardinal as one of those instruments we make use of for a time, and then throw away when we have no further need of them.

The king's anger against the pope far exceeded that against Wolsey; he trembled from head to foot, rose from his seat, then sat down again, and vented his wrath in the most violent language: 'What!' he exclaimed, 'I shall exhaust my political combinations, empty my treasury, make war upon my friends, consume my forces ... and for whom? ... for a heartless priest who, considering neither the exigencies of my honour, nor the peace of my conscience, nor the prosperity of my kingdom, nor the numerous benefits which I have lavished on him, refuses me a favour, which he ought, as the common father of the faithful, to grant even to an enemy. ... Hypocrite! ... You cover yourself with the cloak of friendship, you flatter us by crafty practices, but you give us only a bastard document, and you say like Pilate: It matters little to me if this king perishes, and all his kingdom with him; take him and judge him according to your law! ... I understand you ... you wish to entangle us in the briers, to catch us in a trap, to lure us into a pitfall. ... But we have discovered the snare; we shall escape from your ambuscade, and brave your power.'

Such was the language then heard at the court of England, says John Strype, the historian. The monks and priests began to grow alarmed, while the more enlightened minds already saw in the distance the first gleams of religious liberty. One day, at a time when Henry was proving himself a zealous follower of the Romish doctrines, Sir Thomas More was sitting in the midst of his family, when his son-in-law, William Roper, now become a warm papist, exclaimed: 'Happy kingdom of England, where no heretic dares show his face!' – 'That is true, son Roper', said More; 'we seem to sit now upon the mountains, treading the heretics under our feet like ants; but I pray God that some of us do not live to see the day when we gladly would wish to be at league with them, to suffer them to have their churches quietly to themselves, so that they would be content to let us have ours peaceably to ourselves.' Roper angrily replied: 'By my word, sir, that is very desperately spoken!' More, however, was in the right; genius is sometimes a great diviner. The reformation was on the point of inaugurating religious liberty, and by that means placing civil liberty on an immovable foundation.

Henry himself grew wiser by degrees. He began to have doubts about the Roman hierarchy, and to ask himself whether a priest-king, embarrassed in all the political complications of Europe, could be the head of the church of Jesus Christ. Pious individuals in his kingdom recognized in Scripture and in conscience a law superior to the law of Rome, and refused to sacrifice at the command of the church their moral convictions, sanctioned by the revelation of God. The hierarchical system, which claims to absorb man in the papacy, had oppressed the consciences of Christians for centuries. When the Romish Church had required from such as Berengarius, John Huss, Savonarola, John Wesel, and Martin Luther the denial of their consciences enlightened by the word, that is to say, by the voice of God, it had shown most clearly how great is the iniquity of its claim to substitute papal domination for the sovereignty of Almighty God. 'If the Christian consents to this enormous demand of the hierarchy', said the most enlightened men; 'if he renounces his own notions of good and evil in favour of the clergy; if he reserves not his right to obey God, who speaks to him in the Bible, rather than men, even if their agreement is universal; if Henry VIII, for instance, should silence his conscience, which condemns his union with his brother's widow, to obey the clerical voice which approves of it; by that very act he renounces truth, duty, and even God himself.' But we must add, that if the rights of conscience were beginning to be understood in England, it was not about such holy matters as these that the pope and Henry were contending. They were both intriguers – both dissatisfied, the one desirous of love, the other of power.

Be that as it may, a feeling of disgust for Rome then took root in the king's heart, and nothing could afterwards eradicate it. He immediately made every exertion to attract Erasmus to London. Indeed, if Henry separated from the pope, his old friends, the humanists, must be his auxiliaries, and not the heretical doctors. But Erasmus, in a letter dated 1 June, alleged the weak state of his health, the robbers who infested the roads, the wars and rumours of wars then afloat. 'Our destiny leads us', he said; 'let us yield to it.' It is a fortunate thing for England that Erasmus was not its reformer.

Wolsey noted this movement of his master's, and resolved to make a strenuous effort to reconcile Clement and Henry; his own safety was at stake. He wrote to the pope, to Campeggio, to da Casale, to all Italy. He declared that if he was ruined, the popedom would be ruined too, so far at least as England was concerned: 'I would obtain the *decretal* bull with my own blood, if possible', he added. 'Assure the Holy Father on my life that no mortal eye shall see it.' Finally, he ordered the chief almoner to write to Gardiner: 'If Campeggio does not come, *you shall never return* to England'; an infallible means of stimulating the secretary's zeal.

This was the last effort of Henry VIII. The Duke of Bourbon and the Prince of Orange had not employed more zeal a year before in scaling the walls of Rome. Wolsey's fire had inflamed his agents; they argued, entreated, stormed, and threatened. The alarmed cardinals and theologians, assembling at the pope's call, discussed the matter, mixing political interests with the affairs of the church. At last they understood what Wolsey now communicated to them. 'Henry is the most energetic defender of the faith', they said. 'It is only by acceding to his demand that we can preserve the kingdom of England to the popedom. The army of Charles is in full flight, and that of Francis triumphs.' The last of these arguments decided the question; the pope suddenly felt a great sympathy for Wolsey and for the English Church; the emperor was beaten; therefore he was wrong. Clement granted everything.

First, Campeggio was desired to go to London. The pontiff knew that he might reckon on his intelligence and inflexible adhesion to the interests of the hierarchy; even the cardinal's gout was of use, for it might help to innumerable delays. Next, on 8 June, the pope, then at

Viterbo, gave a new commission, by which he conferred on Wolsey and Campeggio the power to declare null and void the marriage between Henry and Catherine, with liberty for the king and queen to form new matrimonial ties. A few days later he signed the famous *decretal* by which he himself annulled the marriage between Henry and Catherine; but instead of entrusting it to Gardiner, he gave it to Campeggio, with orders not to let it go out of his hands. Clement was not sure of the course of events: if Charles should decidedly lose his power, the bull would be published in the face of Christendom; if he should recover it, the bull would be burnt. In fact the flames did actually consume some time afterwards this decree which Clement had wetted with his tears as he put his name to it. Finally, on 23 July, the pope signed a valid engagement, by which he declared beforehand that all retraction of these acts should be *null and void*. Campeggio and Gardiner departed. Charles' defeat was as complete at Rome as at Naples; the justice of his cause had vanished with his army.

Nothing, therefore, was wanting to Henry's desires. He had Campeggio, the commission, the decretal bull of divorce signed by the pope, and the engagement giving an irrevocable value to all these acts. Wolsey was conqueror – the conqueror of Clement! ... He had often wished to mount the restive courser of the popedom and to guide it at his will, but each time the unruly steed had thrown him from the saddle. Now he was firm in his seat, and held the horse in hand. Thanks to Charles' reverses, he was master at Rome. The popedom, whether it was pleased or not, must take the road he had chosen, and before which it had so long recoiled. The king's joy was unbounded, and equalled only by Wolsey's. The cardinal, in the fulness of his heart, wishing to show his gratitude to the officers of the Roman court, made them presents of carpets, horses, and vessels of gold. All near Henry felt the effects of his good humour. Anne smiled; the court indulged in amusements; the *great affair* was about to be accomplished. The union between England and the popedom appeared confirmed for ever, and the victory which Rome seemed about to gain in the British Isles might secure her triumph in the West. Vain omens! Far different were the events in the womb of the future.

BOOK FOUR

The Two Divorces

Cardinal Wolsey

CHAPTER ONE

'A Thousand Wolseys for One Anne Boleyn'

(1528)

While England seemed binding herself to the court of Rome, the general course of the church and of the world gave stronger presage every day of the approaching emancipation of Christendom. The respect which for so many centuries had hedged in the Roman pontiff was everywhere shaken; the Reform, already firmly established in several states of Germany and Switzerland, was extending in France, the Low Countries, and Hungary, and beginning in Sweden, Denmark, and Scotland. The south of Europe appeared indeed submissive to the Romish Church; but Spain, at heart, cared little for the pontifical infallibility; and even Italy began to inquire whether the papal dominion was not an obstacle to her prosperity. England, notwithstanding appearances, was also going to throw off the yoke of the bishops of the Tiber, and many faithful voices might already be heard demanding that the word of God should be acknowledged the supreme authority in the church.

The conquest of Christian Britain by the papacy occupied all the seventh century, as we have seen. The sixteenth was the counterpart of the seventh. The struggle which England then had to sustain, in order to free herself from the power that had enslaved her during nine hundred years, was full of sudden changes; like those of the times of Augustine and Oswiu. This struggle indeed took place in each of the countries where the church was reformed; but nowhere can it be traced in all its diverse phases so distinctly as in Great Britain. The positive work of the reformation – that which consisted in recovering the truth and life so long lost – was nearly the same everywhere; but as regards the negative work – the struggle with the popedom – we might almost say that other nations committed to England the task by which they were all to profit. An unenlightened piety may perhaps look upon the relations of the court of London with the court of Rome, at the period of the reformation, as void of interest to the faith; but history will not think the same. It has been too often forgotten that the main point in this contest was not the divorce (which was only the occasion) but the contest itself and its important consequences. The divorce of Henry Tudor and Catherine of Aragon is a secondary event; but the divorce of England and the popedom is a primary event, one of the great watersheds of history, a creative act (so to speak) which still exercises a profound influence over the destinies of mankind. And accordingly everything connected with it is full of instruction for us. Already a great number of pious men had attached themselves to the authority of God; but the king and that part of the nation who were strangers to the evangelical faith, clung to Rome, which Henry had so valiantly defended. The word of God had spiritually separated England from the papacy; the *great matter* separated it materially. There is a close relationship between these two divorces, which gives extreme importance to the process between Henry and Catherine. When a great revolution is to be effected in the bosom of a people (we have the reformation particularly in view), God instructs the minority by the holy Scriptures, and the majority by the dispensations of the Divine government. Facts undertake to push forward those whom the more spiritual voice of the word leaves behind. England, profiting by this great teaching of facts, has thought it her duty ever since[1] to avoid all contact with a power that had deceived her; she has thought that popery could not have the dominion over a people without infringing on its vitality, and that it was only by emancipating themselves from this priestly dictatorship that modern nations could advance safely in the paths of liberty, order, and greatness.

For more than a year, as Henry's complaints testify, Anne hesitated to give Henry encouragement in his love-suit. She seems to have halted between two opinions. The despairing king saw that he must set other

---

[1] [Readers will remember that these words were written in the middle of the nineteenth century.]

springs to work and, taking Lord Rochford aside, he unfolded his plans to him. The ambitious father promised to do all in his power to influence his daughter. 'The divorce is a settled thing', he said to her; 'you have no control over it. The only question is, whether it shall be you or another who shall give an heir to the crown. Bear in mind that terrible revolutions threaten England, if the king has no son.' Thus did everything combine to weaken Anne's resolution. The voice of her father, the interests of her country, the king's love, and doubtless some secret ambition, influenced her to grasp the proffered sceptre. These thoughts haunted her in society, in solitude, and even in her dreams. At one time she imagined herself on the throne, distributing to the people her charities and the word of God; at another, in some obscure exile, leading a useless life, in tears and ignominy. When, in the sports of her imagination, the crown of England appeared all glittering before her, she at first rejected it; but afterwards that regal ornament seemed so beautiful, and the power it conferred so enviable, that she repelled it less energetically. Anne still refused, however, to give the so ardently solicited assent.

Henry, troubled by her hesitation, wrote to her frequently, and usually in French. As the court of Rome makes use of these letters, which are kept in the Vatican, to abuse the reformation, we think it our duty to quote them.[2] The theft committed by a cardinal has preserved them for us; and we shall see that, far from supporting the calumnies that have been spread abroad, they tend, on the contrary, to refute them. We are far from approving their contents as a whole; but we cannot deny to the young lady, to whom they are addressed, the possession of noble and generous sentiments.

Henry, unable to support the anguish caused by Anne's refusal, wrote to her, as it is generally supposed, in May 1528:

> By revolving in my mind the contents of your last letters, I have put myself into great agony, not knowing how to interpret them, whether to my disadvantage, as I understand some passages, or not, as I conclude from others. I beseech you earnestly to let me know your real mind as to the love between us two. It is needful for me to obtain

---

[2] [The *Love-letters of Henry VIII*, reprinted from the Harleian Miscellany, with an introduction by Ladbroke Black, were reprinted by the Blandford Press in 1933.]

this answer of you, having been for a whole year wounded with the dart of love, and not yet assured whether I shall succeed in finding a place in your heart and affection. This uncertainty has hindered me of late from declaring you my mistress, lest it should prove that you only entertain for me an ordinary affection. But if you please to do the duty of a true and loyal mistress, and to give up yourself, body and heart to me, ... I promise you that not only the name shall be given to you, but also that I will take you for my mistress, casting off all others that are in competition with you, out of my thoughts, and affection, and serving you only. I beg you to give an entire answer to this my rude letter, that I may know on what and how far I may depend. But if it does not please you to answer me in writing, let me know some place where I may have it by word of mouth, and I will go thither with all my heart. No more for fear of tiring you. Written by the hand of him who would willingly remain yours,

H. REX.

Such were the affectionate, and we may add (if we think of the time and the man) the respectful terms employed by Henry in writing to Anne Boleyn. The latter, without making any promises, betrayed some little affection for the king, and added to her reply an emblematical jewel, representing 'a solitary damsel in a boat tossed by the tempest', wishing thus to make the prince understand the dangers to which his love exposed her. Henry was delighted and immediately replied:

For a present so valuable, that nothing could be more (considering the whole of it), I return you my most hearty thanks, not only on account of the costly diamond, and the ship in which the solitary damsel is tossed about, but chiefly for the fine interpretation, and the too humble submission which your goodness hath made to me. Your favour I will always seek to preserve, and this is my firm intention and hope, according to the matter, *aut illic aut nullibi* [either here or nowhere].

The demonstrations of your affections are such, the fine thoughts of your letter so cordially expressed, that they oblige me for ever to honour, love, and serve you sincerely. I beseech you to continue in the same firm and constant purpose, and assuring you that, on my part, I will not only make you a suitable return, but outdo you, so great is the loyalty of the heart that desires to please you. I desire, also, that if, at any time before this, I have in any way offended you, that you would give me the same absolution that you ask, assuring you, that hereafter my heart shall be dedicated to you alone. ... God can do it, if he pleases, *to whom I pray once a day* for that end, hoping that at length *my prayers will be heard*. I wish the time may be short, but I shall think it long till we see one another. Written by the hand of that secretary, who in heart, body, and will, is

Your loyal and most faithful Servant,
H. T. REX.[3]

Henry was a passionate lover, and history is not called upon to vindicate that cruel prince; but in the preceding letter we cannot discover the language of a seducer. It is impossible to imagine the king praying to God *once a day* for anything but a lawful union. These daily prayers seem to present the matter in a different light from that which Romanist writers have imagined.

Henry thought himself more advanced than he really was. Anne then shrank back; embarrassed by the position she held at court, she begged for one less elevated. The king submitted, although very vexed at first:

Nevertheless that it belongeth not to a gentleman, to put *his mistress* in the situation of a *servant*, yet, by following your wishes, I would willingly concede it, if by that means you are less uncomfortable in the place you shall choose than in that where you have been placed by me. I thank you most cordially that you are pleased still to bear me in your remembrance.

H. T.

[3] After the signature comes the following device:

Nulle autre que A B *ne cherche H. T.*

(Henry seeks Anne Boleyn, no other.)

Anne having retired in May to Hever Castle, her father's residence, the king wrote to her as follows:

My Mistress and my Friend,

My heart and I surrender ourselves into your hands, and we supplicate to be commended to your good graces, and that by absence your affections may not be diminished to us. For that would be to augment our pain, which would be a great pity, which absence alone does sufficiently, and more than I could ever have thought. This brings to my mind a fact in astronomy, which is, that the farther off is the sun, yet the more scorching is his heat. Thus is it with our love; absence has placed distance between us, nevertheless fervour increases, at least on my part. I hope the same from you, assuring you that in my case the anguish of absence is so great that it would be intolerable were it not for the firm hope I have of your indissoluble affection towards me. In order to remind you of it, and because I cannot in person be in your presence, I send you the thing which comes nearest that is possible, that is to say, my picture, … set in bracelets; wishing myself in their place when it pleases you. This is from the hand of

Your Servant and Friend,

H. T. REX.

Pressed by her father, her uncles, and by Henry, Anne's firmness was shaken. That crow, rejected by Renée and by Margaret, dazzled the young Englishwoman; every day she found some new charm in it; and gradually familiarizing herself with her new future, she said at last: 'If the king becomes free, I shall be willing to marry him.' This was a great fault; but Henry was at the height of joy.

The courtiers watched with observant eyes these developments of the king's affection, and were already preparing the homage which they proposed to lay at Anne Boleyn's feet. But there was one man at court whom Henry's resolution filled with sorrow; this was Wolsey. He had been the first to suggest to the king the idea of separating from Catherine; but if Anne is to succeed her, there must be no divorce. He had first alienated Catherine's party; he was now going to irritate that of the Boleyns; accordingly he began to fear that whatever might be the issue of this affair, it would cause his ruin. He took frequent walks in his park at Hampton Court, accompanied by the French ambassador, John

Du Bellay, the confidant of his sorrows: 'I would willingly lose one of my fingers', he said, 'if I could only have two hours' conversation with the King of France.' At another time, fancying all England was pursuing him, he said with alarm, 'The king my master and all his subjects will cry murder against me; they will fall upon me more fiercely than on a Turk, and all Christendom will rise against me!' The next day Wolsey, to gain the French ambassador, gave him a long history of what he had done for France *against the wishes of all England*: 'I need much dexterity in my affairs', he added, 'and must use a terrible *alchemy*.' But alchemy could not save him. Rarely has so much anguish been veiled beneath such grandeur. Du Bellay was moved with pity at the sight of the unhappy man's sufferings. 'When he gives way', he wrote to Montmorency, 'it lasts a day together – he is continually sighing. – You have never seen a man in such anguish of mind.'

In truth Wolsey's reason was tottering. That fatal idea of the divorce was the cause of all his woes, and to be able to recall it, he would have given, not a *finger* only, but an arm, and perhaps more. It was too late; Henry had started his car down the steep, and whoever attempted to stop it must needs be crushed beneath its wheels. However, the cardinal tried to obtain something. Francis I had intercepted a letter from Charles V in which the emperor spoke of the divorce as likely to raise the English nation in revolt. Wolsey caused this letter to be read to the king, in the hope that it would excite his serious apprehensions; but Henry only *frowned*, and Du Bellay, to whom the monarch ascribed the report on these troubles foreboded by Charles, received a 'gentle lash'. This was the sole result of the manoeuvre.

Wolsey now resolved to broach this important subject in a straight-forward manner. The step might prove his ruin; but if he succeeded he was saved and the popedom with him. Accordingly one day (shortly before the sweating sickness broke out, says Du Bellay, probably in June 1528) Wolsey openly prayed the king to renounce his design; his own reputation, he told him, the prosperity of England, the peace of Europe, the safety of the church – all required it; besides, the pope would never grant the divorce. While the cardinal was speaking, Henry's face grew black; and before he had concluded the king's anger broke out. 'The king used terrible words', said Du Bellay. He would have given a thousand

Wolseys for one Anne Boleyn. 'No other than God shall take her from me', was his most decided resolution.

Wolsey, now no longer doubting of his disgrace, began to take his measures accordingly. He commenced building in several places, in order to win the affections of the common people; he took great care of his bishoprics, in order that they might ensure him an easy retreat; he was affable to the courtiers; and thus covered the earth with flowers to deaden his fall. Then he would sigh as if he were disgusted with honours, and would celebrate the charms of solitude. He did more than this. Seeing plainly that the best way of recovering the king's favour would be to conciliate Anne Boleyn, he made her the most handsome presents, and assured her that all his efforts would now be directed to raise her to the throne of England. Anne, believing these declarations, replied that she would help him in her turn, 'as long as any breath was in her body'. Even Henry had no doubt that the cardinal had profited by his lesson.

Thus were all parties restless and uneasy – Henry desiring to marry Lady Anne, the courtiers to get rid of Wolsey, and the latter to remain in power – when a serious event appeared to put everyone in harmony with his neighbour. About the middle of June, the terrible sweating sickness (*sudor anglicus*) broke out in England. The citizens of London, 'thick as flies', said Du Bellay, suddenly feeling pains in the head and heart, rushed from the streets or shops to their chambers, began to sweat, and took to their beds. The disease made frightful and rapid progress, a burning heat preyed on their limbs; if they chanced to uncover themselves, the perspiration ceased, delirium came on, and in four hours the victim was dead and 'stiff as a wall', says the French ambassador. Every family was in mourning. Sir Thomas More, kneeling by his daughter's bedside, burst into tears, and called upon God to save his beloved Margaret. Wolsey, who was at Hampton Court, suspecting nothing amiss, arrived in London as usual to preside in the Court of Chancery; but he ordered his horses to be saddled again immediately and rode back. In four days, 2,000 persons died in London.

The court was at first safe from the contagion; but on the fourth day one of Anne Boleyn's ladies was attacked; it was as if a thunderbolt had fallen on the palace. The king removed with all haste, and stayed at a place twelve miles off, for he was not prepared to die. He ordered Anne

to return to her father, invited the queen to join him, and took up his
residence at Waltham. His real conscience awoke only in the presence
of death. Four of his attendants and a friar, Anne's confessor, as it would
appear, falling ill, the king departed for Hunsdon. He had been there
two days only when Powis, Carew, Carton, and others of his court, were
carried off in two or three hours. Henry had met an enemy whom he
could not vanquish. He quitted the place attacked by the disease; he
removed to another quarter; and when the sickness laid hold of any of
his attendants in his new retreat, he again left that for a new asylum.
Terror froze his blood; he wandered about pursued by that terrible
scythe whose sweep might perhaps reach him; he cut off all communication, even with his servants; shut himself up in a room at the top of an
isolated tower; ate all alone, and would see no one but his physician; he
prayed, fasted, confessed, became reconciled with the queen; took the
Sacrament every Sunday and feast day; received *his Maker*, to use the
words of a gentleman of his chamber; and the queen and Wolsey did the
same. Nor was that all: his councillor, Sir Brian Tuke, was sick in Essex;
but that mattered not; the king ordered him to come to him, even in his
litter; and on 10 June, Henry after hearing three masses (he had never
done so much before in one day) said to Tuke: 'I want you to write *my
will*.' He was not the only one who took that precaution. 'There were *a
hundred thousand* made', says Du Bellay.

During this time, Anne in her retirement at Hever was calm and
collected; she prayed much, particularly for the king and for Wolsey. But
Henry, far less submissive, was very anxious. 'The uneasiness my doubts
about your health gave me', he wrote to her, 'disturbed and frightened
me exceedingly; but now, since you have as yet felt nothing, I hope it
is with you as it is with us. ... I beg you, my entirely beloved, not to
frighten yourself, or be too uneasy at our absence, for wherever I am, I
am yours. And yet we must sometimes submit to our misfortunes, for
whoever will struggle against fate, is generally but so much the farther
from gaining his end. Wherefore, comfort yourself and take courage,
and make this misfortune as easy to you as you can.'

As he received no news, Henry's uneasiness increased; he sent to
Anne a messenger and a letter: 'To acquit myself of the duty of a true

servant, I send you this letter, beseeching you to apprise me of your welfare, which I pray may continue as long as I desire mine own.'

Henry's fears were well founded; the malady became more severe; in four hours eighteen persons died at the Archbishop of Canterbury's; Anne Boleyn herself and her brother also caught the infection. The king was exceedingly agitated; Anne alone appeared calm; the strength of her character raised her above exaggerated fears; but her enemies ascribed her calmness to other motives. 'Her ambition is stronger than death', they said. 'The king, queen, and cardinal tremble for their lives, but she … she would die content if she died a queen.' Henry once more changed his residence. All the gentlemen of his privy chamber were attacked with one exception; 'he remained alone, keeping himself apart', says Du Bellay, and confessed every day. He wrote again to Anne, sending her his physician, Dr Butts: 'The most displeasing news that could occur came to me suddenly at night. On three accounts I must lament it. One, to hear of the illness of my mistress, whom I esteem more than all the world, and whose health I desire as I do my own. I would willingly bear half of what you suffer to cure you. The second, from the fear that I shall have to endure my wearisome absence much longer, which has hitherto given me all the vexation that was possible; and when gloomy thoughts fill my mind, then I pray God to remove far from me such troublesome and rebellious ideas. The third, because my physician, in whom I have most confidence, is absent. Yet, from the want of him, I send you my second, and hope that he will soon make you well. I shall then love him more than ever. I beseech you to be guided by his advice in your illness. By your doing this, I hope soon to see you again, which will be to me a greater comfort than all the precious jewels in the world.'

The pestilence soon broke out with more violence around Henry; he fled in alarm to Hatfield, taking with him only the gentlemen of his chamber; he next quitted this place for Tittenhanger, a house belonging to Wolsey, whence he commanded 'general processions' throughout the kingdom in order to avert this scourge of God. At the same time he wrote to Wolsey: 'As soon as anyone falls ill in the place where you are, fly to another; and go thus from place to place.' The poor cardinal was still more alarmed than Henry. As soon as he felt the slightest perspiration, he fancied himself a dead man. 'I entreat Your Highness', he wrote trembling to the king on 5 July, 'to show yourself full of pity for my soul; these are perhaps the last words I shall address to you ... the whole world will see by my last testament that you have not bestowed your favour upon an ungrateful man.' The king, perceiving that Wolsey's mind was affected, bade him 'put apart fear and fantasies', and wear a cheerful humour in the midst of death.

At last the sickness began to diminish, and immediately the desire to see Anne revived in Henry's bosom. On 18 August she reappeared at court, and all the king's thoughts were now bent on the divorce.

But this business seemed to proceed in inverse ratio to his desires. There was no news of Campeggio; was he lost in the Alps or at sea? Did his gout detain him in some village, or was the announcement of his departure only a feint? Anne Boleyn herself was uneasy, for she attached great importance to Campeggio's coming. If the church annulled the king's marriage, Anne, seeing the principal obstacle removed, thought she might accept Henry's hand. She therefore wrote to Wolsey: 'I long to hear from you news of the legate, for I do hope (an' they come from you) they shall be very good.' The king added in a postscript: 'The not hearing of the legate's arrival in France causeth us somewhat to muse. Notwithstanding we trust by your diligence and vigilancy (with the assistance of Almighty God) shortly to be eased out of that trouble.'

But still there was no news. While waiting for the long-desired ambassador, everyone at the English court played his part as well as he could. Anne, whether from conscience, prudence, or modesty, refused the honours which the king would have showered upon her, and never approached Catherine but with marks of profound respect. Wolsey appeared to desire the divorce, while in reality he dreaded it, as fated to cause his ruin and that of the popedom. Henry strove to conceal the motives which impelled him to separate from the queen; to the bishops, he spoke of his *conscience*, to the nobility *of an heir*, and to all of the sad obligation which compelled him to put away so justly beloved a princess. In the meanwhile, he seemed to live on the best terms with her, from what Du Bellay says. But Catherine was the one who best dissembled her sentiments; she lived with the king as during their happiest days, treated

Anne with every kindness, adopted an elegant costume, encouraged music and dancing in her apartments, often appeared in public, and seemed desirous of captivating by her gracious smiles the goodwill of England. This was a mournful comedy, destined to end in tragedy full of tears and agony.

CHAPTER TWO

Scripture and the Spreading Revival

(1527–1529)

While these scenes were acting in the royal palaces, far different discussions were going on among the people. After having dwelt for some time on the agitations of the court, we gladly return to the lowly disciples of the Divine word. The reformation in England (and this is its characteristic) brings before us by turns the king upon his throne, and the laborious artisan in his humble cottage; and between these two extremes we meet with the doctor in his college, and the priest in his pulpit.

Among the young men trained at Cambridge under Barnes' instruction, and who had aided him at the time of his trial, was Miles Coverdale, afterwards Bishop of Exeter, a man distinguished by his zeal for the gospel of Jesus Christ. Some time after the prior's fall, on Easter Eve, 1527, Coverdale and Cromwell met at the house of Sir Thomas More, when Cromwell exhorted the Cambridge student to apply himself to the study of sacred learning.[1] The lapse of his unhappy master had alarmed Coverdale, and he felt the necessity of withdrawing from that outward activity which had proved so fatal to Barnes. He therefore turned to the Scriptures, read them again and again, and perceived, like Tyndale, that the reformation of the church must be effected by the word of God. The inspiration of that word, the only foundation of its sovereign authority, had struck Coverdale. 'Wherever the Scripture is known it reformeth all things, and setteth everything in order. And why? Because it is given *by*

---

[1] *Coverdale's Remains* (Parker Society), p. 490. The editor of the *Remains* dates this letter to Cromwell, 1 May 1527. Others assign it to a later period.

the inspiration of God.[2] This fundamental principle of the reformation in England must, in every age, be that of the church.

Coverdale found happiness in his studies: 'Now', he said, 'I begin to taste of holy Scriptures! Now, honour be to God! I am set to the most sweet smell of holy letters.'[3] He did not stop there, but thought it his duty to attempt in England the work which Tyndale was prosecuting in Germany. The Bible was so important in the eyes of these Christians, that two translations were undertaken simultaneously. 'Why should other nations', said Coverdale, 'be more plenteously provided for with the Scriptures in their mother tongue than we?'[4] – 'Beware of translating the Bible!' exclaimed the partisans of the schoolmen; 'your labour will only make divisions in the faith and in the people of God.'[5] – 'God has now given his church', replied Coverdale, 'the gifts of translating and of printing; we must improve them.' And if any friends spoke of Tyndale's translation, he answered: 'Do not you know that when many are shooting together, everyone doth his best to be nighest the mark?'[6] – 'But Scripture ought to exist in Latin only', objected the priests. – 'No', replied Coverdale again, 'the Holy Ghost is as much the author of it in the Hebrew, Greek, French, Dutch, and English, as in Latin. ... The word of God is of like worthiness and authority, in what language soever the Holy Ghost speaketh it.'[7] This does not mean that translations of holy Scripture are inspired, but that the word of God, faithfully translated, always possesses a Divine authority.

Coverdale determined therefore to translate the Bible, and, to procure the necessary books, he wrote to Cromwell, who, during his travels, had made a collection of these precious writings. 'Nothing in the world I desire but books, as concerning my learning', he wrote; 'like Jacob, you have drunk of the dew of heaven. ... I ask to drink of your waters.'[8] Cromwell did not refuse Coverdale his treasures. 'Since the Holy Ghost

[2] *Coverdale's Remains*, p. 10.
[3] *Ibid.*, p. 490.
[4] *Ibid.*, p. 12.
[5] *Ibid.*
[6] *Ibid.*, p. 14.
[7] *Ibid.*, p. 26.
[8] *Ibid.*, p. 491.

has moved other men to bear the cost of this work', exclaimed the latter, 'God gives me boldness to labour in the same.'[9] He commenced without delay, saying: 'Whosoever believeth not the Scripture, believeth not Christ; and whoso refuseth it, refuseth God also.'[10] Such were the foundations of the Reformed Church in England.

Coverdale did not undertake to translate the Scriptures as a mere literary task: the Spirit which had moved him spoke to his heart; and tasting their life-giving promises, he expressed his happiness in pious songs:

> Be glad now, all ye christen men,
>   And let us rejoyce unfaynedly.
> The kyndnesse cannot be written with penne,
>   That we have receaved of God's mercy;
> Whose love towarde us hath never ende:
> He hath done for us as a frende;
>   Now let us thanke him hartely.
>
> These lovynge wordes he spake to me:
>   I wyll delyver thy soule from payne;
> I am desposed to do for thee,
>   And to myne owne selfe thee to retayne.
> Thou shalt be with me, for thou art myne;
> And I with thee, for I am thyne;
>   Soch is my love, I can not layne.
>
> They wyll shed out my precyous bloude,
>   And take away my lyfe also;
> Which I wyll suffre all for thy good:
>   Beleve this sure, where ever thou go.
> For I wyll yet ryse up agayne;
> Thy synnes I beare, though it be payne,
>   To make thee safe and free from wo.

Coverdale did not remain long in the solitude he desired. The study of the Bible, which had attracted him to it, soon drew him out

---

[9] *Coverdale's Remains*, p. 10.
[10] *Ibid.*, p. 19.

of it. A revival was going on in Essex; John Tyball, an inhabitant of Bumpstead, having learnt to find in Jesus Christ the *true bread from heaven*, did not stop there. One day as he was reading the First Epistle to the Corinthians, these words: 'eat of this *bread*', and 'drink of this *cup*', repeated four times within a few verses, convinced him that there was no transubstantiation. 'A priest has no power to create the body of the Lord', said he; 'Christ truly is present in the Eucharist, but he is there only *for him that believeth*, and by a spiritual presence and action only.' Tyball, disgusted with the Romish clergy and worship, and convinced that Christians are called to a universal priesthood, soon thought that men could do without a special ministry and, without denying the offices mentioned in Scripture, as some Christians have done since, he attached no importance to them. 'Priesthood is not necessary', he said: 'every layman may administer the sacraments as well as a priest.' The minister of Bumpstead, one Richard Foxe, and next a greyfriar of Colchester named Meadow, were successively converted by Tyball's energetic preaching.

Coverdale, who was living not far from these parts, having heard speak of this religious revival, came to Bumpstead, and went into the pulpit on 29 March 1528, to proclaim the treasures contained in Scripture. Among his hearers was an Augustine monk, named Topley, who was supplying Foxe's place during his absence. This monk, while staying at the parsonage, had found a copy of Wycliffe's *Wicket*, which he read eagerly. His conscience was wounded by it, and all seemed to totter about him. He had gone to church full of doubt, and after Divine service he waited upon the preacher, exclaiming: 'O my sins, my sins!' – 'Confess yourself to God', said Coverdale, 'and not to a priest. God accepteth the confession which cometh from the heart, and blotteth out all your sins.'[11] The monk believed in the forgiveness of God, and became a zealous evangelist for the surrounding country.

The Divine word had hardly lighted one torch, before that kindled another. At Colchester, in the same county, a worthy man named Pykas, had received a copy of the Epistles of St Paul from his mother, with this advice: 'My son, live according to these writings, and not according to

[11] *Coverdale's Remains*, p. 481.

the teaching of the clergy.' Some time after, Pykas having bought a New Testament, and 'read it thoroughly many times', a total change took place in him. 'We must be baptized by the Holy Ghost', he said, and these words passed like a breath of life over his simple-minded hearers. One day, Pykas having learnt that Bilney, the first of the Cambridge doctors who had known the power of God's word, was preaching at Ipswich, he proceeded thither, for he never refused to listen to a priest, when that priest proclaimed the truth. 'O, what a sermon! how full of the Holy Ghost!' exclaimed Pykas.

From that period meetings of the brothers in Christ (for thus they were called) increased in number. They read the New Testament, and each imparted to the others what he had received for the instruction of all. One day when the twenty-fourth chapter of Matthew had been read, Pykas, who was sometimes wrong in the spiritual interpretation of Scripture, remarked: 'When the Lord declares that *not one stone of the temple shall be left upon another*, he speaks of those haughty priests who persecute those whom they call heretics, and who pretend to be the temple of God. God will destroy them all.' After protesting against the priest, he protested against the host: 'The real body of Jesus Christ is in the word', he said; 'God is in the word, the word is in God. God and the word cannot be separated. Christ is the living Word that nourishes the soul.' These humble preachers increased. Even women knew the Epistles and Gospels by heart; Marion Matthew, Dorothy Long, Catherine Swain, Alice Gardiner, and, above all, Gyrling's wife, who had been in service with a priest lately burnt for heresy, took part in these gospel meetings. And it was not in cottages only that the glad tidings were then proclaimed; Bower Hall, the residence of the squires of Bumpstead, was open to Foxe, Topley, and Tyball, who often read the holy Scriptures in the great hall of the mansion, in the presence of the master and all their household: a humble reformation more real than that effected by Henry VIII.

There was, however, some diversity of opinion among these brethren. 'All who have begun to believe', said Tyball, Pykas, and others, 'ought to meet together to hear the word and increase in faith. We pray in common ... and that constitutes a church.' Coverdale, Bilney, and

Latimer willingly recognized these incomplete societies, in which the members met simply as *disciples*; they believed them necessary at a period when the church was forming. These societies (in the reformers' views) proved that organization has not the priority in the Christian church, as Rome maintains, and that this priority belongs to the faith and the life. But this imperfect form they also regarded as provisional. To prevent numerous dangers, it was necessary that this society should be succeeded by another, the church of the New Testament, with its elders or bishops, and deacons. The word, they thought, rendered a ministry of the word necessary; and for its proper exercise not only piety was required, but a knowledge of the sacred languages, the gift of eloquence, its exercise and perfection. However, there was no division among these Christians upon primary matters.

For some time the Bishop of London watched this movement with uneasiness. He caused Hacker to be arrested, who, for six years past, had gone from house to house reading the Bible in London and Essex; examined and threatened him, inquired carefully after the names of those who had shown him hospitality; and the poor man in alarm had given up about forty of his brethren. Sebastian Harris, priest of Kensington, Forman, rector of All Hallows, John and William Pykas, and many others, were summoned before the bishop. They were taken to prison; they were led before the judges; they were put in the stocks; they were tormented in a thousand ways. Their minds became confused; their thoughts wandered; and many made the confessions required by their persecutors.

The adversaries of the gospel, proud of this success, now desired a more glorious victory. If they could not reach Tyndale, had they not in London the patron of his work, Monmouth, the most influential of the merchants, and a follower of the true faith? The clergy had made religion their business, and the reformation was restoring it to the people. Nothing offended the priests so much, as that laymen should claim the right to believe without their intervention, and even to propagate the faith. Sir Thomas More, one of the most amiable men of the sixteenth century, participated in their hatred. He wrote to Cochlæus: 'Germany now daily bringeth forth monsters more deadly than what Africa was wont to do';[12] 'But, alas! she is not alone. Numbers of Englishmen, who would not a few years ago even hear Luther's name mentioned, are now publishing his praises! England is now like the sea, which swells and heaves before a great storm, without any wind stirring it.'[13] More felt particularly irritated, because the boldness of the gospellers had succeeded to the timidity of the Lollards. 'The heretics', he said, 'have put off hypocrisy, and put on impudence.' He therefore resolved to set his hand to the work.

On 24 May 1529, Monmouth was in his shop, when an usher came and summoned him to appear before Sir John Dauncies, one of the Privy Council. The pious merchant obeyed, striving to persuade himself that he was wanted on some matter of business; but in this he was deceived, as he soon found out. On arrival he was interrogated by Sir Thomas More, who, with Sir William Kingston, was Sir John's colleague. 'What letters and books have you lately received from abroad?' asked Sir Thomas More, with some severity. – 'None', replied Monmouth. – 'What aid have you given to any persons living on the Continent?' – 'None, for these last three years. William Tyndale abode with me six months', he continued, 'and his life was what a good priest's ought to be. I gave him ten pounds at the period of his departure, but nothing since. Besides, he is not the only one I have helped; the Bishop of London's chaplain, for instance, has received of me more than £50.' – 'What books have you in your possession?' The merchant named the New Testament and some other works. 'All these books have lain more than two years on my table, and I never heard that either priests, friars, or laymen learnt any great errors from them.' More tossed his head. 'It is a hard matter', he used to say, 'to put a dry stick in the fire without its burning, or to nourish a snake in our bosom and not be stung by it.[14] – That is enough', he continued, 'we shall go and search your house.' Not a paper escaped their curiosity; but they found nothing to compromise Monmouth; he was however sent to the Tower.

After some interval the merchant was again brought before his judges. 'You are accused', said More, 'of having bought Martin Luther's tracts;

[12] *More's Life*, p. 82.
[13] *Ibid.*, p. 117.
[14] *Ibid.*, p. 116.

of maintaining those who are translating the Scriptures into English; of subscribing to get the New Testament printed in English, with or without glosses; of having imported it into the kingdom; and, lastly, of having said that faith alone is sufficient to save a man.'

Here was matter enough to burn several men. Monmouth, feeling convinced that Wolsey alone had power to deliver him, resolved to apply to him. 'What will become of my poor workmen in London and in the country during my imprisonment?' he wrote to the cardinal. 'They must have their money every week; who will give it them? ... Besides, I make considerable sales in foreign countries, which bring large returns to His Majesty's customs. If I remain in prison, this commerce is stopped, and of course all the proceeds for the exchequer.' Wolsey, who was as much a statesman as a churchman, began to melt; on the eve of a struggle with the pope and the emperor, he feared, besides, to make the people discontented. Monmouth was released from prison. As alderman, and then as sheriff of London, he was faithful until death, and ordered in his last will that thirty sermons should be preached by the most evangelical ministers in England, 'to make known the holy word of Jesus Christ'. – 'That is better', he thought, 'than founding masses.' The reformation showed, in the sixteenth century, that great activity in commerce might be allied to great piety.

CHAPTER THREE

Campeggio Arrives in England

(July to November 1528)

While these persecutions were agitating the fields and the capital of England, all had changed in the ecclesiastical world, because all had changed in the political. The pope, pressed by Henry VIII and intimidated by the armies of Francis I, had granted the decretal and despatched Campeggio. But, on a sudden, there was a new development; a change of events brought a change of counsels. Doria had gone over to the emperor; his fleet had restored abundance to Naples; the army of Francis I, ravaged by famine and pestilence, had capitulated, and Charles V, triumphant in Italy, had said proudly to the pope: 'We are determined to defend the Queen of England against King Henry's injustice.'

Charles having recovered his superiority, the affrighted pope opened his eyes to the justice of Catherine's cause. 'Send four messengers after Campeggio', said he to his officers; 'and let each take a different road; bid them travel with all speed and deliver our despatches to him.' They overtook the legate, who opened the pope's letters. 'In the first place', said Clement VII to him, 'protract your journey. In the second place, when you reach England, use every endeavour to reconcile the king and queen. In the third place, if you do not succeed, persuade the queen to take the veil. And in the last place, if she refuses, do not pronounce any sentence favourable to the divorce without a new and express order from me. This is the essential: *Summum et maximum mandatum.*'[1] The ambassador of the sovereign pontiff had a mission to do nothing. This instruction is sometimes as effective as any.

---

[1] The chief and greatest commandment.

Campeggio, the youngest of the cardinals, was the most intelligent and the slowest; and this slowness caused his selection by the pope. He understood his master. If Wolsey was Henry's spur to urge on Campeggio, the latter was Clement's bridle to check Wolsey.[2] One of the judges of the divorce was about to pull forwards, the other backwards; thus the business stood a chance of not advancing at all, which was just what the pope required.

The legate, very eager to relax his speed, spent three months on his journey from Italy to England. He should have embarked for France on 23 July; but the end of August was approaching, and no one knew in that country what had become of him.[3] At length they learnt that he had reached Lyons on 22 August. The English ambassador in France sent his horses, carriages, plate, and money, in order to hasten his progress; the legate complained of the gout, and Gardiner found the greatest difficulty in getting him to move. Henry wrote every day to Anne Boleyn, complaining of the slow progress of the nuncio. 'He arrived in Paris last Sunday or Monday', he says at the beginning of September; 'Monday next we shall hear of his arrival in Calais, and then I shall obtain what I have so longed for, to God's pleasure and both our comforts.'

At the same time this impatient prince sent message after message to accelerate the legate's rate of travelling. Anne began to desire a future which surpassed all that her youthful imagination had conceived, and her agitated heart expanded to the breath of hope. She wrote to Wolsey:

> This shall be to give unto Your Grace, as I am most bound, my humble thanks for the great pain and travail that Your Grace doth take in studying, by your wisdom and great diligence, how to bring to pass honourably the greatest wealth [well-being] that is possible to come to any creature living; and in especial remembering how wretched and unworthy I am in comparison to His Highness. ... Now, good my lord, your discretion may consider as yet how little it is in my power to recompense you but alonely [only] with my goodwill; the which I assure you, look what thing in this world I can imagine to do you pleasure in, you shall find me the gladdest woman in the world to do it.

[2] Fuller, *Church History of Britain* (1655), Book v, p. 172.
[3] State Papers, vii, pp. 91, 92.

But the impatience of the King of England and of Anne seemed as if it would never be satisfied. Campeggio, on his way through Paris, told Francis I that the divorce would never take place, and that he should soon go to *Spain* to see Charles V. ... This was significative. 'The King of England ought to know', said the indignant Francis to the Duke of Suffolk, 'that Campeggio is *imperialist* at heart, and that his mission in England will be a mere mockery.'[4]

In truth, the Spanish and Roman factions tried every manoeuvre to prevent a union they detested. Anne Boleyn, Queen of England, signified not only Catherine humbled, but Charles offended; the clerical party weakened, perhaps destroyed, and the evangelical party probably strengthened. The Romish faction found accomplices even in Anne's own family. Her brother George's wife, a proud and passionate woman, and a rigid Roman Catholic, had sworn an implacable hatred against her young sister. By this means wounds might be inflicted, even in the domestic sanctuary, which would not be the less deep because they were the work of her own kindred. One day we are told that Anne found in her chamber a book of pretended prophecies, in which was a picture representing a king, a queen shedding tears, and at their feet a young lady headless. Anne turned away her eyes with disgust. She desired, however, to know what this emblem signified, and officious friends brought to her one of those pretended wise men, so numerous at all times, who abuse the credulity of the ignorant by professing to interpret such mysteries. 'This prophetic picture', he said, 'represents the history of the king and his wife.' Anne was not credulous, but she understood what her enemies meant to insinuate, and dismissed the mock interpreter without betraying any signs of fear; then turning to her favourite attendant, Anne Saville, 'Come hither, Nan', said she, 'look at this book of prophecies; this is the king, this is the queen wringing her hands and mourning, and this [putting her finger on the bleeding body] is *myself*, with my head cut off.' – The young lady answered with a shudder: 'If I thought it were true, I would not myself have him were he an emperor.' – 'Tut, Nan', replied Anne Boleyn with a smile, 'I think the

---

[4] 'The cardinal intended not that Your Grace's matter should take effect, but only to use dissimulation with Your Grace, for he is entirely imperial.' Suffolk to Henry, State Papers, vii, p. 183.

book a bauble, and am resolved to have him, that my issue may be royal, whatever may become of me.' This story is based on good authority, and there were so many predictions of this kind afloat that it was very possible one of them might come true; people afterwards recollected only the prophecies confirmed by the events. But, be that as it may, this young lady, so severely chastised in afterdays, found in her God an abundant consolation.

At length Campeggio embarked at Calais on 29 September, and unfortunately for him he had an excellent passage across the Channel. A storm to drive him back to the French coast would have suited him admirably. But on 1 October he was at Canterbury, whence he announced his arrival to the king. At this news, Henry forgot all the delays which had so irritated him. 'His Majesty can never be sufficiently grateful to Your Holiness for so great a favour', wrote Wolsey to the pope; 'but he will employ his riches, his kingdom, his life even, and deserve the name of *Restorer of the Church* as justly as he has gained that of *Defender of the Faith.*' This zeal alarmed Campeggio, for the pope wrote to him that any proceeding which might irritate Charles would inevitably cause the ruin of the church. The nuncio became more dilatory than ever, and although he reached Canterbury on 1 October, he did not arrive at Dartford until the 5th, thus taking four days for a journey of about thirty miles.

Meanwhile preparations were making to receive him in London. Wolsey, feeling contempt for the poverty of the Roman cardinals, and very uneasy about the equipage with which his colleague was likely to make his entrance into the capital, sent a number of showy chests, rich carpets, litters hung with drapery, and harnessed mules. On the other hand Campeggio, whose secret mission was to keep in the background, and above all to do nothing, feared these banners, and trappings, and all the parade of a triumphal entry. Alleging therefore an attack of gout in order to escape from the pomps his colleague had prepared for him, he quietly took a boat, and thus reached the palace of the Bishop of Bath, where he was to lodge.

While the nuncio was thus proceeding unnoticed up the Thames, the equipages sent by Wolsey entered London through the midst of a gaping crowd, who looked on them with curiosity as if they had come from the banks of the Tiber. Some of the mules however took fright and ran away, the coffers fell off and burst open, when there was a general rush to see their contents; but to the surprise of all they were empty. This was an excellent jest for the citizens of London. 'Fine outside, empty inside; a just emblem of the popedom, its embassy, and foolish pomps', they said; 'a sham legate, a procession of masks, and the whole a farce!'

Campeggio was come at last, and now what he dreaded most was an audience. 'I cannot move', he said, 'or endure the motion of a litter.' Never had an attack of gout been more seasonable. Wolsey, who paid him frequent visits, soon found him to be his equal in cunning. To no purpose did he treat him with every mark of respect, shaking his hand and making much of him; it was labour lost, the Roman nuncio would say nothing, and Wolsey began to despair. The king, on the contrary, was full of hope, and fancied he already had the Act of Divorce in his portfolio, because he had the nuncio in his kingdom.

The greatest effect of the nuncio's arrival was the putting an end to Anne Boleyn's indecision. She had several relapses: the trials which she foresaw, and the grief Catherine must necessarily feel, had agitated her imagination and disturbed her mind. But when she saw the church and her own enemies prepared to pronounce the king's divorce, her doubts were removed, and she regarded as legitimate the position that was offered her. The king, who suffered from her scruples, was delighted at this change. 'I desire to inform you', he wrote to her in English, 'what joy it is to me to understand of your conformableness with reason, and of the suppressing of your inutile and vain thoughts and fantasies with the bridle of reason. I assure you all the greatness of this world could not counterpoise for my satisfaction the knowledge and certainty thereof … The unfeigned sickness of this well-willing legate doth somewhat retard his access to your person.' It was therefore the determination of the pope that made Anne Boleyn resolve to accept Henry's hand; this is an important lesson for which we are indebted to the *Vatican letters*. We should be grateful to the papacy for having so carefully preserved them.

But the more Henry rejoiced, the more Wolsey despaired; he would have desired to penetrate into Pope Clement's thoughts, but could not succeed. Imagining that de Angelis, the general of the Spanish

Observance, knew all the secrets of the pope and of the emperor, he conceived the plan of kidnapping him. 'If he goes to Spain by sea', said he to Du Bellay, 'a good brigantine or two would do the business; and if by land, it will be easier still.' Du Bellay failed not (as he informs us himself) 'to tell him plainly that by such proceedings he would entirely forfeit the pope's goodwill.' – 'What matter?' replied Wolsey; 'I have nothing to lose.' As he said this, tears started to his eyes. At last he made up his mind to remain ignorant of the pontiff's designs, and wiped his eyes, awaiting, not without fear, the interview between Henry and Campeggio.

On 22 October, a month after his arrival, the nuncio, borne in a sedan chair of red velvet, was carried to court. He was placed on the right of the throne, and his secretary in his name delivered a high-sounding speech, saluting Henry with the name of Saviour of Rome, *Liberator urbis*. 'His Majesty', replied Fox in the king's name, 'has only performed the duties incumbent on a Christian prince, and he hopes that the holy see will bear them in mind.' – 'Well attacked, well defended', said Du Bellay. For the moment, a few Latin declamations got the papal nuncio out of his difficulties.

Campeggio did not deceive himself: if the divorce were refused, he foresaw the reformation of England. Yet he hoped still, for he was assured that Catherine would submit to the judgment of the church; and being fully persuaded that the queen would refuse the Holy Father nothing, the nuncio began 'his approaches', as Du Bellay calls them. On 22 October, and again on the 27th, the two cardinals waited on Catherine, and in flattering terms insinuated that she might prevent the blow which threatened her by voluntary retirement into a convent. And, then, to end all indecision in the queen's mind, Campeggio put on a severe look and exclaimed: 'How is it, madam, explain the mystery to us? From the moment the Holy Father appointed us to examine the question of your divorce, you have been seen not only at court, but in public, wearing the most magnificent ornaments, participating with an appearance of gaiety and satisfaction at amusements and festivities which you had never tolerated before. ... The church is in the most cruel embarrassment with regard to you; the king, your husband, is in

the greatest perplexity; the princess, your daughter, is taken from you …
and instead of shedding tears, you give yourself up to vanity. Renounce
the world, madam; enter a nunnery. Our Holy Father himself requires
this of you.'

The agitated queen was almost fainting; stifling her emotion, however,
she said mildly but firmly: 'Alas! my lords, is it now a question whether I
am the king's lawful wife or not, when I have been married to him almost
twenty years and no objection raised before? … Divers prelates and lords
are yet alive who then adjudged our marriage good and lawful – and
now to say it is detestable! this is a great marvel to me, especially when
I consider what a wise prince the king's father was, and also the natural
love and affection my father, King Ferdinand, bare unto me. I think that
neither of these illustrious princes would have made me contract an illicit
union.' At these words, Catherine's emotion compelled her to stop – 'If I
weep, my lords', she continued almost immediately, 'it is not for myself,
it is for a person dearer to me than my life. What! I should consent to
an act which deprives my daughter of a crown? No, I will not sacrifice
my child. I know what dangers threaten me. I am only a weak woman,
a stranger, without learning, advisers or friends … and my enemies are
skilful, learned in the laws, and desirous to merit their master's favour
… and more than that, even my judges are my enemies. Can I receive
as such', she said as she looked at Campeggio, 'a man extorted from the
pope by manifest lying? … And as for you', added she, turning haughtily
to Wolsey, 'having failed in attaining the tiara, you have sworn to revenge
yourself on my nephew the emperor … and you have kept him true
promise; for of all his wars and vexations, he may only thank you. One
victim was not enough for you. Forging abominable suppositions, you
desire to plunge his aunt into a frightful abyss. … But my cause is just,
and I trust it in the Lord's hand.' After this bold language, the unhappy
Catherine withdrew to her apartments. The imminence of the danger
effected a salutary revolution in her; she laid aside her brilliant ornaments,
assumed the sober garments in which she is usually represented, and
passed days and nights in mourning and in tears.

Thus Campeggio saw his hopes deceived; he had thought to find a
nun, and had met a queen and a mother. He now proceeded to set every

imaginable spring at work; as Catherine would not renounce Henry, he must try to prevail upon Henry to renounce his idea of separating from the queen. The Roman legate therefore changed his batteries, and turned them against the king.

Henry, always impatient, went one day unannounced to Campeggio's lodging, accompanied by Wolsey only: 'As we are without witnesses', he said, taking his seat familiarly between the two cardinals, 'let us speak freely of our affairs. – How shall you proceed?' But to his great astonishment and grief, the nuncio prayed him, with all imaginable delicacy, to renounce the divorce. At these words the fiery Tudor burst out: 'Is this how the pope keeps his word? He sends me an ambassador to annul my marriage, but in reality to confirm it.' He made a pause. Campeggio knew not what to say. Henry and Catherine being equally persuaded of the justice of their cause, the nuncio was in a dilemma. Wolsey himself suffered a martyrdom. The king's anger grew fiercer; he had thought the legate would hasten to withdraw an imprudent expression, but Campeggio was dumb. 'I see that you have chosen your part', said Henry to the nuncio; 'mine, you may be sure, will soon be taken also. Let the pope only persevere in this way of acting, and the apostolical see, covered with perpetual infamy, will be visited with a frightful destruction.' The lion had thrown off the lamb's skin which he had momentarily assumed. Campeggio felt that he must appease the monarch. 'Craft and delay' were his orders from Rome; and with that view the pope had provided him with the necessary arms. He hastened to produce the famous *decretal* which pronounced the divorce. 'The Holy Father', he told the king, 'ardently desires that this matter should be terminated by a happy reconciliation between you and the queen; but if that is impossible, you shall judge yourself whether or not His Holiness can keep his promises.' He then read the bull, and even showed it to Henry, without permitting it, however, to leave his hands. This exhibition produced the desired effect: Henry grew calm. 'Now I am at ease again', he said; 'this miraculous talisman revives all my courage. This decretal is the efficacious remedy that will restore peace to my oppressed conscience, and joy to my bruised heart. Write to His Holiness, that this immense benefit binds me to him so closely, that he may expect from me more than his imagination can conceive.'

And yet a few clouds gathered shortly after in the king's mind.

Campeggio having shown the bull had hastened to lock it up again. Would he presume to keep it in his own hands? Henry and Wolsey will leave no means untried to get possession of it; that point gained, and victory is theirs.

Wolsey having returned to the nuncio, he asked him for the decretal with an air of candour as if it was the most natural thing in the world. He desired, he said, to show it to the king's privy councillors. 'The pope', replied Campeggio, 'has granted this bull, not to be used, but to be kept secret; he simply desired to show the king the good feeling by which he was animated.' Wolsey having failed, Henry tried his skill. 'Have the goodness to hand me the bull which you showed me', said he. The nuncio respectfully refused. 'For a single moment', he said. Campeggio still refused. The haughty Tudor retired, stifling his anger. Then Wolsey made another attempt, and founded his demand on justice. 'Like you, I am delegated by His Holiness to decide this affair', he said, 'and I wish to study the important document which is to regulate our proceedings.' – This was met by a new refusal. 'What!' exclaimed the minister of Henry VIII, 'am I not, like you, a cardinal? … like you, a judge? your colleague?' It mattered not, the nuncio would not, by any means, let the decretal go. Clement was not deceived in the choice he had made of Campeggio; the ambassador was worthy of his master.

It was evident that the pope in granting the bull had been acting a part: this trick revolted the king. It was no longer anger that he felt, but disgust. Wolsey knew that Henry's contempt was more to be feared than his wrath. He grew alarmed, and paid the nuncio another visit. 'The *general* commission', he said, 'is insufficient, the *decretal* commission alone can be of service, and you do not permit us to read a word of it. … The king and I place the greatest confidence in the good intentions of His Holiness, and yet we find our expectations frustrated. Where is that paternal affection with which we had flattered ourselves? What prince has ever been trifled with as the King of England is now? If this is the way in which the *Defender of the Faith* is rewarded, Christendom will know what those who serve Rome will have to expect from her, and every power will withdraw its support. Do not deceive yourselves: the foundation on which the holy see is placed is so very insecure that the least movement will suffice to precipitate it into everlasting ruin. What a sad futurity! … what inexpressible torture! … whether I wake or sleep, gloomy thoughts continually pursue me like a frightful nightmare.' This time Wolsey spoke the truth.

But all his eloquence was useless; Campeggio refused to give up the so much desired bull. When sending him, Rome had told him: 'Above all, do not succeed!' This means having failed, there remained for Wolsey one other way of effecting the divorce. 'Well then', he said to Campeggio, 'let us pronounce it ourselves.' – 'Far be it from us', replied the nuncio; 'the anger of the emperor will be so great, that the peace of Europe will be broken for ever.' – 'I know how to arrange all that', replied the English cardinal, 'in political matters you may trust to me.' The nuncio then took another tone and, proudly wrapping himself up in his morality, he said: 'I shall follow the voice of my conscience; if I see that the divorce is possible, I shall leap the ditch; if otherwise, I shall not.' – 'Your conscience! that may be easily satisfied', rejoined Wolsey. 'Holy Scripture forbids a man to marry his brother's widow; now no pope can grant what is forbidden by the law of God.' – 'The Lord preserve us from such a principle', exclaimed the Roman prelate; 'the power of the pope is unlimited.' – The nuncio had hardly put his conscience forward, before it stumbled; it bound him to Rome and not to heaven. But for that matter, neither public opinion nor Campeggio's own friends had any great idea of his morality; they thought that to make him *leap the ditch*, it was only requisite to know the price at which he might be bought. The Bishop of Bayonne wrote to Montmorency: 'Put at the close of a letter which I can show Campeggio something *promissory*, that he shall have *benefices*. … That will cost you nothing, and may serve in this matter of the marriage; for I know that he is longing for something of the sort.' – 'What is to be done then?' said Wolsey at last, astonished at meeting with a resistance to which he was unaccustomed. 'I shall inform the pope of what I have seen and heard', replied Campeggio, 'and I shall wait for his instructions.' Henry was forced to consent to this new course, for the nuncio hinted that if it were opposed he would go in person to Rome to ask the pontiff's orders, and he never would have returned. By this means several months were gained.

During this time men's minds were troubled. The prospect of a divorce between the king and queen had stirred the nation; and the majority, particularly among the women, declared against the king. 'Whatever may be done', the people said boldly, 'whoever marries the Princess Mary will be King of England.' Wolsey's spies informed him that Catherine and Charles V had many devoted partisans even at the court. He wished to make sure of this. 'It is pretended', he said one day in an indifferent tone, 'that the emperor has boasted that he will get the king driven from his realm, and that by His Majesty's own subjects. ... What do you think of it, my lords?' – 'Tough against the spur', says Du Bellay, the lords remained silent. At length, however, one of them more imprudent than the rest, exclaimed: 'Such a boast will make the emperor lose more than a hundred thousand Englishmen.' This was enough for Wolsey. To *lose* them, he thought, Charles must *have* them. If Catherine thought of levying war against her husband, following the example of former queens of England, she would have, then, a party ready to support her; this became dangerous.

The king and the cardinal immediately took their measures. More than 15,000 of Charles' subjects were ordered to leave London; the arms of the citizens were seized, 'in order that they might have no worse weapon than the tongue'; the Flemish councillors accorded to Catherine were dismissed, after they had been heard by the king and Campeggio, 'for they had no commission to speak to *the other* [Wolsey]' – and finally, they kept 'a great and constant watch' upon the country. Men feared an invasion of England, and Henry was not of a humour to subject his kingdom to the pope.

This was not enough; the alarmed king thought it his duty to come to an explanation with his people; and having summoned the lords spiritual and temporal, the judges, the members of the Privy Council, the mayor and aldermen of the city, and many of the gentry, to meet him at his palace of Bridewell on 13 November, he said to them with a very condescending air: 'You know, my lords and gentlemen, that for these twenty years past Divine Providence has granted our country such prosperity as it has never known before. But in the midst of all the glory that surrounds me, the thought of my last hour often occurs to me, and

I fear that if I should die without an heir, my death would cause more damage to my people than my life has done them good. God forbid that for want of a legitimate king England should be again plunged into the horrors of civil war!' Then calling to mind the illegalities invalidating his marriage with Catherine, the king continued: 'These thoughts have filled my mind with anxiety, and are continually pricking my conscience. This is the only motive, and God is my witness, which has made me lay this matter before the pontiff. As touching the queen, she is a woman incomparable in gentleness, humility, and buxomness, as I these twenty years have had experiment of; so that if I were to marry again, if the marriage might be good, I would surely choose her above all other women. But if it be determined by judgment that our marriage was against God's law, and surely void, then I shall not only sorrow in departing from so good a lady and loving companion, but much more lament and bewail my unfortunate chance, that I have so long lived in adultery, to God's great displeasure, and have no true heir of my body to inherit this realm. ... Therefore I require of you all to pray with us that the very truth may be known, for the discharging of our conscience and the saving of our soul.' These words, though wanting in sincerity, were well calculated to soothe men's minds. Unfortunately, it appears that after this *speech from the Crown*, the official copy of which has been preserved, Henry added a few words of his own. 'If however', he said, according to Du Bellay, casting a threatening glance around him, 'there should be any man whatsoever who speaks of his prince in other than becoming terms, I will show him that I am the master, and there is no head so high that I will not roll it from his shoulders.' This was a speech in Henry's style; but we cannot give unlimited credit to Du Bellay's assertions, this diplomatist being very fond, like others of his class, of 'seasoning' his despatches. But whatever may be the fact as regards the postscript, the speech on the divorce produced an effect. From that time there were no more jests, not even on the part of the Boleyns' enemies. Some supported the king, others were content to pity the queen in secret; the majority prepared to take advantage of a court revolution which everyone foresaw. 'The king so *plainly* gave them to understand his pleasure', says the French ambassador, 'that they speak more soberly than they have done hitherto.'

Henry, wishing to silence the clamours of the people, and to allay the fears felt by the higher classes, gave several magnificent entertainments, at one time in London, at another at Greenwich, now at Hampton Court, and then at Richmond. The queen accompanied him, but Anne generally remained 'in a very handsome lodging which Henry had furnished for her', says Du Bellay. The cardinal, following his master's example, gave representations of French plays with great magnificence. All his hope was in France. 'I desire nothing in England, neither in word nor in deed, which is not French', he said to the Bishop of Bayonne. At length Anne Boleyn had accepted the brilliant position she had at first refused, and every day her stately mansion (Suffolk House) was filled with a numerous court – 'more than ever had crowded to the queen.' – 'Yes, yes', said Du Bellay, as he saw the crowd turning towards the *rising sun*, 'they wish by these *little* things to accustom the people to endure her, that when *great* ones are attempted, they may not be found so strange.'

In the midst of these festivities the grand business did not slumber. When the French ambassador solicited the subsidy intended for the ransom of the sons of Francis I, the cardinal required of him in exchange a paper proving that the marriage had never been valid. Du Bellay excused himself on the grounds of his age and want of learning; but being given to understand that he could not have the subsidy without it, he wrote the memoir in a single day. The enraptured cardinal and king entreated him to speak with Campeggio. The ambassador consented, and succeeded beyond all expectation. The nuncio, fully aware that a bow too much bent will break, made Henry by turns become the sport of hope and fear. 'Take care how you assert that the pope had not the right to grant a dispensation to the king', said he to the French bishop; 'this would be denying *his power, which is infinite*. But', added he in a mysterious tone, 'I will point out a road that will infallibly lead you to the mark. Show that the Holy Father has been deceived by false information. *Push me hard on that*', he continued, 'so as to force me to declare that the dispensation was granted on erroneous grounds.' Thus did the legate himself reveal the breach by which the fortress might be surprised. 'Victory!' exclaimed Henry, as he entered Anne's apartments all beaming with joy.

But this confidence on the part of Campeggio was only a new trick. 'There is a great rumour at court', wrote Du Bellay soon after, 'that the emperor and the King of France are coming together, and leaving Henry alone, so that all will fall on his shoulders.' Wolsey, finding that the intrigues of diplomacy had failed, thought it his duty to put fresh springs in motion, 'and by all good and honest means to gain the pope's favour'. He saw, besides, to his great sorrow, the new catholicity then forming in the world, and uniting, by the closest bonds, the Christians of England to those of the Continent. To strike down one of the leaders of this evangelical movement might incline the court of Rome in Henry's favour. The cardinal undertook, therefore, to persecute Tyndale; and this resolution will now transport us to Germany.

CHAPTER FOUR

The Search for William Tyndale

(1528–1530)

The residence of Tyndale and his friends in foreign countries, and the connections there formed with pious Christians, testify to the fraternal spirit which the reformation then restored to the church. It is in Protestantism that true catholicity is to be found. The Romish Church is not a catholic church. Separated from the churches of the East, which are the oldest in Christendom, and from the reformed churches, which are the purest, it is nothing but a sect, and that a degenerate one. A church which should profess to believe in an episcopal unity, but which kept itself separate from the episcopacy of Rome and of the East, and from the evangelical churches, would be no longer a catholic church; it would be a sect more sectarian still than that of the Vatican, a fragment of a fragment. The church of the Saviour requires a truer, a diviner unity than that of priests, who condemn one another. It was the reformers, and particularly Tyndale, who proclaimed throughout Christendom the existence of a *body of Christ*, of which all the children of God are members. The disciples of the reformation are the true Catholics.

It was a catholicity of another sort that Wolsey desired to uphold. He did not reject certain reforms in the church, particularly such as brought him any profit; but, before all, he wished to preserve for the hierarchy their privileges and uniformity. The Romish Church in England was then personified in him, and if he fell, its ruin would be near. His political talents and multiplied relations with the Continent, caused him to discern more clearly than others the dangers which threatened the popedom. The publication of the Scriptures of God in English appeared to some a cloud without importance, which would soon disappear from the horizon; but to the foreseeing glance of Wolsey, it betokened a mighty tempest. Besides, he loved not the fraternal relations then forming between the evangelical Christians of Great Britain and of other nations. Annoyed by this spiritual catholicity, he resolved to procure the arrest of Tyndale, who was its principal organ.[1]

Already had Hackett, Henry's envoy to the Low Countries, caused the imprisonment of Harman, an Antwerp merchant, one of the principal supporters of the English reformer. But Hackett had in vain asked Wolsey for such documents as would convict him of *treason* (for the crime of loving the Bible was not sufficient to procure Harman's condemnation in Brabant); the envoy had remained without letters from England, and the last term fixed by the law having expired, Harman and his wife were liberated after seven months' imprisonment.

And yet Wolsey had not been inactive. The cardinal hoped to find elsewhere the co-operation which Margaret of Austria refused. It was Tyndale that he wanted, and everything seemed to indicate that he was then hidden at Cologne or in its neighbourhood. Wolsey, recollecting Senator Rincke and the services he had already performed, determined to send to him one John West, a friar of the Franciscan house at Greenwich. West, a somewhat narrow-minded but energetic man, was very desirous of distinguishing himself, and he had already gained some notoriety in England among the adversaries of the reformation. Flattered by his mission, this vain monk immediately set off for Antwerp, accompanied by another friar, in order to seize Tyndale, and even Roye, once his colleague at Greenwich, and against whom he had there ineffectually contended in argument.

While these men were conspiring his ruin, Tyndale composed several works, got them printed, and sent to England, and prayed God night and day to enlighten his fellow countrymen. 'Why do you give yourself so much trouble?' said some of his friends. 'They will burn your books as they have burnt the gospel.' 'They will only do what I expect', replied he, 'if they burn me also.' Already he beheld his own burning pile in the distance; but it was a sight which only served to increase his zeal.

[1] [In this work Wolsey did not himself take the initiative. Rather was his name and authority used by other leaders of the church in England who pressed on with the persecutions.]

Hidden, like Luther at the Wartburg, not however in a castle, but in a humble lodging, Tyndale, like the Saxon reformer, spent his days and nights translating the Bible. But not having an Elector of Saxony to protect him, he was forced to change his residence from time to time.

Before the close of 1528, Fryth, who had escaped from the prisons of Oxford, rejoined Tyndale, and the sweetness of friendship softened the bitterness of their exile. Tyndale having finished the New Testament, and begun the translation of the Old, the learned Fryth was of great use to him. The more they studied the word of God, the more they admired it. During 1529 they were busily occupied in seeing through the press the translation of the Five Books of Moses on which Tyndale had been engaged since the completion of his work on the New Testament. Early in 1530 this first instalment of the Old Testament was in circulation. Addressing his fellow countrymen in his Prologue to the Book of Genesis, Tyndale said: 'As thou readest, think that every syllable pertaineth to thine own self, and suck out the pith of the Scripture.'[2] Then denying that visible signs naturally impart grace, as the schoolmen had pretended, Tyndale maintained that the sacraments are effectual only when the Holy Ghost sheds his influence upon them. 'The ceremonies of the law', he wrote in his Prologue to Leviticus, 'stood the Israelites in the same stead as the sacraments do us. We are saved not by the power of the sacrifice or the deed itself, but by virtue of *faith in the promise*, whereof the sacrifice or ceremony was a token or sign. The Holy Ghost is no dumb God, no God that goeth a mumming. Wherever the word is proclaimed, this inward witness worketh. If baptism preach me the washing in Christ's blood, so doth the Holy Ghost accompany it; and that deed of preaching through faith doth put away my sins. The ark of Noah saved them in the water through faith.'[3]

The man who dared address England in language so contrary to the teaching of the Middle Ages must be imprisoned. John West, who had been sent with this object, arrived at Antwerp; Hackett procured for him as interpreter a friar of English descent, made him assume a secular dress, and gave him 'three pounds' on the cardinal's account; the less attention

[2] Prologue to the Book of Genesis (*Doctrinal Treatises*), pp. 398-403.
[3] Prologue to the Book of Leviticus (*Doctrinal Treatises*), pp. 421-8.

the embassy attracted, the more likely it would be to succeed. But great was West's vexation, on reaching Cologne, to learn that Rincke was at Frankfurt. But that mattered not; the Greenwich monk could search for Tyndale at Cologne, and desire Rincke to do the same at Frankfurt; thus there would be two searches instead of one. West procured a 'swift' messenger (he too was a monk) and gave him the letter Wolsey had addressed to Rincke.

It was fair time at Frankfurt, and the city was filled with merchants and their wares. As soon as Rincke had finished reading Wolsey's letter, he hastened to the burgomasters, and required them to confiscate the English translations of the Scriptures, and, above all, to seize 'the heretic who was troubling England as Luther troubled Germany'. – 'Tyndale and his friends have not appeared in our fairs since the month of March 1528', replied the magistrates, 'and we know not whether they are dead or alive.'

Rincke was not discouraged. John Schott of Strasburg, who was said to have printed Tyndale's books, and who cared less about the works he published than the money he drew from them, happened to be at Frankfurt. 'Where is Tyndale?' Rincke asked him. 'I do not know', replied the printer; but he confessed that he had printed a thousand volumes at the request of Tyndale and Roye. 'Bring them to me', continued the senator of Cologne – 'If a fair price is paid me, I will give them up to you.' Rincke paid all that was demanded.

Wolsey would now be gratified, for the New Testament annoyed him almost as much as the divorce; this book, so dangerous in his eyes, seemed on the point of raising a conflagration which would infallibly consume the edifice of Roman traditionalism. Rincke, who participated in his patron's fear, impatiently opened the volumes made over to him; but there was a sad mistake: they were not the New Testament, not even a work of Tyndale's, but one written by William Roye, a changeable and violent man, whom the reformer had employed for some time at Hamburg, and who had followed him to Cologne, but with whom he had soon become disgusted. 'I bade him farewell for our two lives', said Tyndale, 'and a day longer.' Roye, on quitting the reformer, had gone to Strasburg, where he boasted of his relations with him, and had got a satire in that city printed against Wolsey and the monastic orders, entitled *The Burial of the Mass*: this was the book delivered to Rincke. The monk's sarcastic spirit had exceeded the legitimate bounds of controversy, and the senator accordingly dared not send the volumes to England. He did not however discontinue his inquiries, but searched every place where he thought he could discover the New Testament and, having seized all the suspected volumes, set off for Cologne.

Yet he was not satisfied. He wanted Tyndale, and went about asking everyone if they knew where to find him. But the reformer, whom he was seeking in so many places, and especially at Frankfurt and Cologne, chanced to be residing at about equal distance from these two towns, so that Rincke, while travelling from one to the other, might have met him face to face, as Ahab's messenger met Elijah. Tyndale was at Marburg, whither he had been drawn by several motives. Prince Philip the Magnanimous, of Hesse-Kassel, was the great protector of the evangelical doctrines. The university had attracted attention in the Reform by the paradoxes of Lambert of Avignon. Here a young Scotsman named Hamilton, afterwards illustrious as a martyr, had studied shortly before, and here too the celebrated printer, John Luft, had his presses. In this city Tyndale and Fryth had taken up their abode, in September 1528, and, hidden on the quiet banks of the Lahn, were translating the Old Testament. If Rincke had searched this place he could not have failed to discover them. But either he thought not of it, or was afraid of the terrible landgrave. The direct road by the Rhine was that which he followed, and Tyndale escaped.

When he arrived at Cologne, Rincke had an immediate interview with West. Their investigations having failed, they must have recourse to more vigorous measures. The senator, therefore, sent the monk back to England, accompanied by his son Hermann, charging them to tell Wolsey: 'To seize Tyndale we require fuller powers, ratified by the emperor. The traitors who conspire against the life of the King of England are not tolerated in the Empire, much less Tyndale and all those who conspire against Christendom. He must be put to death; nothing but some striking example can check the Lutheran heresy. – And as to ourselves', they were told to add, 'by the favour of God there may possibly be an opportunity for His Royal Highness and Your Grace to recompense us.' Rincke had not forgotten the subsidy of ten thousand pounds which he had received from Henry VII for the Turkish war, when he had gone to London as Maximilian's envoy.

West returned to England sorely vexed that he had failed in his mission. What would they say at court and in his monastery? A fresh humiliation was in reserve for him. Roye, whom West had gone to look for on the banks of the Rhine, had paid a visit to his mother on the banks of the Thames; and to crown all, the new doctrines had penetrated into his own house. The warden, Father Robinson, had embraced them, and night and day the Greenwich monks read that New Testament which West had gone to Cologne to burn. The Antwerp friar, who had accompanied him on his journey, was the only person to whom he could confide his sorrows; but the Franciscans sent him back again to the Continent, and then amused themselves at poor West's expense. If he desired to tell of his adventures on the banks of the Rhine, he was laughed at; if he boasted of the names of Wolsey and Henry VIII, they jeered at him still more. He desired to speak to Roye's mother, hoping to gain some useful information from her; this the monks prevented. 'It is in my commission', he said. They ridiculed him more and more. Robinson, perceiving that the commission made West assume unbecoming airs of independence, requested Wolsey to withdraw it; and West, fancying he was about to be thrown into prison, exclaimed in alarm: 'I am weary of my life!' and conjured a friend whom he had at court to procure him before Christmas an *obedience* under his lordship's hand and seal, enabling him to leave the monastery; 'What you pay him for it', he added, 'I shall see you be reimbursed.' Thus did West expiate the fanatical zeal which had urged him to pursue the translator of the oracles of God. What became of him, we know not: he is never heard of more.

At that time Wolsey had other matters to engage him than this 'obedience'. While West's complaints were going to London, those of the king were travelling to Rome. The great business in the cardinal's eyes was to maintain harmony between Henry and the church. There was no more thought about investigations in Germany, and for a time Tyndale was saved.

CHAPTER FIVE

The Pope Burns His Bull

(November 1528)

The king and a part of his people still adhered to the popedom, and so long as these bonds were not broken the word of God could not have free course. But to induce England to renounce Rome, there must indeed be powerful motives: and these were not wanting.

Wolsey had never given such pressing orders to any of Henry's ambassadors: 'The king', he wrote to da Casale on 1 November 1528, 'commits this business to your prudence, dexterity, and fidelity; and I conjure you to employ all the powers of your genius, and even to surpass them. Be very sure that you have done nothing and can do nothing that will be more agreeable to the king, more desirable by me, and more useful and glorious for you and your family.'

Da Casale possessed a tenacity which justified the cardinal's confidence, and an active excitable mind: trembling at the thought of seeing Rome lose England, he immediately requested an audience of Clement VII. 'What!' said he to the pope, 'just as it was proposed to go on with the divorce, your nuncio endeavours to dissuade the king! ... There is no hope that Catherine of Aragon will ever give an heir to the crown. Holy Father, there must be an end of this. Order Campeggio to place the *decretal* in His Majesty's hands.' – 'What say you?' exclaimed the pope. 'I would gladly lose one of my fingers to recover it again, and you ask me to make it public ... it would be my ruin.' Da Casale insisted: 'We have a duty to perform', he said; 'we remind you at this last hour of the perils threatening the relations which unite Rome and England. The crisis is at hand. We knock at your door, we cry, we urge, we entreat, we lay before you the present and future dangers which threaten the papacy. ... The world shall know that the king at least has fulfilled the duty of a devoted son of the church. If Your Holiness desires to keep England in St Peter's fold, I repeat ... now is the time ... now is the time.' At these words, da Casale, unable to restrain his emotion, fell down at the pope's feet, and begged him to save the church in Great Britain. The pope was moved. 'Rise', said he, with marks of unwonted grief, 'I grant you all that is in my power; I am willing to confirm the judgment which the legates may think it their duty to pass; but I acquit myself of all responsibility as to the untold evils which this matter may bring with it. ... If the king, after having defended the faith and the church, desires to ruin both, on him alone will rest the responsibility of so great a disaster.' Clement granted nothing. Da Casale withdrew disheartened, and feeling convinced that the pontiff was about to treat with Charles V.

Wolsey desired to save the popedom; but the popedom resisted. Clement VII was about to lose that island which Gregory the Great had won with such difficulty. The pope was in the most cruel position. The English envoy had hardly left the palace before the emperor's ambassador entered breathing threats. The unhappy pontiff escaped the assaults of Henry only to be exposed to those of Charles; he was thrown backwards and forwards like a ball. 'I shall assemble a general council', said the emperor through his ambassador, 'and if you are found to have infringed the canons of the church in any point, you shall be proceeded against with every rigour. Do not forget', added his agent in a low tone, 'that your birth is *illegitimate*, and consequently excludes you from the pontificate.' The timid Clement, imagining that he saw the tiara falling from his head, swore to refuse Henry everything. 'Alas!' he said to one of his dearest confidants, 'I repent in dust and ashes that I ever granted this decretal bull. If the King of England so earnestly desires it to be given him, certainly it cannot be merely to know its contents. He is but too familiar with them. It is only to tie my hands in this matter of the divorce; I would rather die a thousand deaths.' Clement, to calm his agitation, sent one of his ablest gentlemen of the bed chamber, Francis Campana, apparently to feed the king with fresh promises, but in reality to cut the only thread on which Henry's hopes still hung. 'We embrace

Your Majesty', wrote the pope in the letter given to Campana, 'with the paternal love your numerous merits deserve.' Now Campana was sent to England to burn clandestinely the famous decretal; Clement concealed his blows by an embrace. Rome had granted many divorces not so well founded as that of Henry VIII; but a very different matter from a divorce was in question here; the pope, desirous of upraising in Italy his shattered power, was about to sacrifice the Tudor, and to prepare the triumph of the reformation. Rome was separating herself from England.

All Clement's fear was that Campana would arrive too late to burn the bull; he was soon reassured; a dead calm prevented the *great matter* from advancing. Campeggio, who took care to be in no hurry about his mission, gave himself up, like a skilful diplomatist, to his worldly tastes; and when he could not, due respect being had to the state of his legs, indulge in the chase, of which he was very fond, he passed his time in gambling, to which he was much addicted. Respectable historians assert that he indulged in still more illicit pleasures. But this could not last for ever, and the nuncio sought some new means of delay, which offered itself in the most unexpected manner. One day an officer of the queen presented to the Roman legate a *brief* of Julius II, bearing the same date as the *bull* of dispensation, signed too, like that, by the secretary Sigismond, and in which the pope expressed himself in such a manner, that Henry's objections fell of themselves. 'The emperor', said Catherine's messenger, 'has discovered this brief among the papers of Puebla, the Spanish ambassador in England at the time of the marriage.' – 'It is impossible to go on', said Campeggio to Wolsey; 'all your reasoning is now cut from under you. *We must wait for fresh instructions.*' This was the cardinal's conclusion at every new incident, and the journey from London to the Vatican being very long (without reckoning the Roman dilatoriness), the expedient was infallible.

Thus there existed two acts of the same pope, signed on the same day – the one secret, the other public, in contradiction to each other. Henry determined to send a new mission to Rome. Anne proposed for this embassy one of the most accomplished gentlemen of the court, her cousin, Sir Francis Bryan. With him was joined an Italian, Peter Vannes, Henry's Latin secretary. 'You will search all the registers of the time of Julius II', said

Wolsey to them; 'you will study the handwriting of Secretary Sigismond, and you will attentively examine the ring of the fisherman used by that pontiff. – Moreover you will inform the pope that it is proposed to set a certain greyfriar, named de Angelis, in his place, to whom Charles would give the *spiritual* authority, reserving the temporal for himself. You will manage so that Clement takes alarm at the project, and you will then offer him a presidy (guard) of 2,000 men to protect him. You will ask whether, in case the queen should desire to embrace a religious life, on condition of the king's doing the same, and Henry should yield to this wish, he could have the assurance that the pope would afterwards release him from his vows. And, finally, you will inquire whether, in case the queen should refuse to enter a convent, the pope would permit the king to have *two wives*, as we see in the Old Testament.' This idea, which brought so much reproach on the Landgrave of Hesse, was not a new one; the honour of it belongs to a cardinal and legate of Rome, whatever Bossuet may say. 'Lastly', continued Wolsey, 'as the pope is of a timid disposition, you will not fail to season your remonstrances with threats. You, Peter, will take him aside and tell him that, as an Italian, having more at heart than anyone the glory of the holy see, it is your duty to warn him that, if he persists, the king, his realm, and many other princes, will for ever separate from the papacy.'

It was not on the mind of the pope alone that it was necessary to act; the rumour that the emperor and the King of France were treating together disturbed Henry. Wolsey had vainly tried to sound Du Bellay; these two priests tried craft against craft. Besides, the Frenchman was not always seasonably informed by his court, letters taking *ten days* to come from Paris to London. Henry resolved to have a conference with the ambassador. He began by speaking to him of *his matter*, says Du Bellay, 'and I promise you', he added, 'that he needs no advocate, he under-stands the whole business so well'. Henry next touched upon the *wrongs* of Francis I, 'recalling so many things that the envoy knew not what to say'. – 'I pray you, Master Ambassador', said Henry in conclusion, 'to beg the king, my brother, to give up a little of his amusements during a year only for the prompt despatch of his affairs. Warn those whom it concerns.' Having given this spur to the King of France, Henry turned his thoughts towards Rome.

In truth, the fatal brief from Spain tormented him day and night, and the cardinal tortured his mind to find proofs of its non-authenticity; if he could do so, he would acquit the papacy of the charge of duplicity, and accuse the emperor of forgery. At last he thought he had succeeded. 'In the first place', he said to the king, 'the brief has the same date as the bull. Now, if the errors in the latter had been found out on the day it was drawn up, it would have been more natural to make another than to append a brief pointing out the errors. What! the same pope, the same day, at the petition of the same persons, give out two rescripts for one effect,[1] one of which contradicts the other! Either the bull was good, and then, why the brief? Or the bull was bad, and then, why deceive princes by a worthless bull? Certain names are found in the brief incorrectly spelt, and these are faults which the pontifical secretary, whose accuracy is so well known, could not have committed.[2] Lastly, no one in England ever heard mention of this brief; and yet it is here that it ought to be found.' Henry charged Knight, his principal secretary, to join the other envoys with all speed, in order to prove to the pope the supposititious character of the document.

This important paper revived the irritation felt in England against Charles V, and it was resolved to come to extremities. Everyone discontented with Austria took refuge in London, particularly the Hungarians. The ambassador from Hungary proposed to Wolsey to adjudge the imperial crown of Germany to the Elector of Saxony or the Landgrave of Hesse, the two chiefs of Protestantism. Wolsey exclaimed in alarm: 'It will be an inconvenience to Christendom, *they are so Lutheran.*' But the Hungarian ambassador so satisfied him that in the end he did not find the matter quite so inconvenient. These schemes were prospering in London, when suddenly a new metamorphosis took place under the eyes of Du Bellay. The king, the cardinal, and the ministers appeared in strange consternation. Vincent da Casale had just arrived from Rome with a letter from his cousin the prothonotary, informing Henry that the pope, seeing the triumph of Charles V, the indecision of Francis I,

---

[1] State Papers, vii, p. 130.

[2] Queen *Isabella* was called *Elizabeth* in the brief; but I have seen a document from the court of Madrid in which Queen Elizabeth of England was called Isabella; it is not therefore an error without a parallel.

the isolation of the King of England, and the distress of his cardinal, had flung himself into the arms of the emperor. At Rome they went so far as to jest about Wolsey, and to say that since he could not be St Peter they would make him St Paul.

While they were ridiculing Wolsey at Rome, at St Germain's they were joking about Henry. 'I will make him get rid of the notions he has in his head', said Francis; and the Flemings, who were again sent out of the country, said as they left London, 'that this year they would carry on the war so vigorously, that it would be really a sight worth seeing.'

Besides these public griefs, Wolsey had his private ones. Anne Boleyn, who had already begun to use her influence on behalf of the despotic cardinal's victims, gave herself no rest until Cheyney, a courtier disgraced by Wolsey, had been restored to the king's favour. Anne even gave utterance to several biting sarcasms against the cardinal, and the Duke of Norfolk and his party began 'to speak big', says Du Bellay. At the moment when the pope, scared by Charles V, was separating from England, Wolsey himself was tottering. Who shall uphold the papacy? ... After Wolsey, nobody! Rome was on the point of losing the power which for nine centuries she had exercised in the bosom of this illustrious nation. The cardinal's anguish cannot be described; unceasingly pursued by gloomy images, he saw Anne on the throne causing the triumph of the reformation: this nightmare was stifling him. 'His Grace, the legate, is in great trouble', wrote the Bishop of Bayonne. 'However ... he is more cunning than they are.'

To still the tempest Wolsey had only one resource left: this was to render Clement favourable to his master's designs. The crafty Campana, who had burnt the decretal, conjured him not to believe all the reports transmitted to him concerning Rome. 'To satisfy the king', said he to the cardinal, 'the Holy Father will, if necessary, descend from the pontifical throne.' Wolsey therefore resolved to send to Rome a more energetic agent than Vannes, Bryan, or Knight, and cast his eyes on Gardiner. His courage began to revive, when an unexpected event fanned once more his loftiest hopes.

CHAPTER SIX

Wolsey between Scylla and Charybdis

(1529)

On 11 January 1529, just as the pope was performing Mass, he was attacked by a sudden illness; he was taken to his room, apparently in a dying state. When this news reached London, the cardinal resolved to hasten to abandon England, where the soil trembled under his feet, and to climb boldly to the throne of the pontiffs. Bryan and Vannes, then at Florence, hurried on to Rome through roads infested with robbers. At Orvieto they were informed the pope was better; at Viterbo, no one knew whether he was alive or dead; at Ronciglione, they were assured that he had expired; and, finally, when they reached the metropolis of the popedom, they learnt that Clement could not survive, and that the imperialists, supported by the Colonnas, were striving to have a pope devoted to Charles V.

But great as might be the agitation at Rome, it was greater still at Whitehall. If God caused Clement to descend from the pontifical throne, it could only be, thought Wolsey, to make him mount it. 'It is expedient to have such a pope as may save the realm', said he to Gardiner. 'And although it cannot but be incommodious to me in this mine old age to be the common father, yet, when all things be well pondered, the qualities of all the cardinals well considered, I am the only one, without boasting, that can and will remedy the king's secret matter. And were it not for the re-integration of the state of the church, and especially to relieve the king and his realm from their calamities, all the riches and honour of the world should not cause me to accept the said dignity.[1] Nevertheless I conform myself to the necessities of the times, and am

[1] [Foxe caustically comments: 'You may long say so, before we will believe you.']

379

content to apply all my wit and study, and to set forth all means and ways for the attaining of the said dignity. ... Wherefore, Master Stephen, that this matter may succeed, I pray you to apply all your ingenuity, spare neither money nor labour. I give you the amplest powers, without restriction or limitation.'[2] Gardiner departed to win for his master the coveted tiara.

Henry VIII and Wolsey, who could hardly restrain their impatience, soon heard of the pontiff's death from different quarters. 'The emperor has taken away Clement's life', said Wolsey, blinded by hatred. 'Charles', rejoined the king, 'will endeavour to obtain by force or fraud a pope according to his desires.' – 'Yes, to make him his chaplain', replied Wolsey, 'and to put an end by degrees both to pope and popedom.' – 'We must fly to the defence of the church', resumed Henry, 'and with that view, my lord, make up your mind to be pope.' – 'That alone', answered the cardinal, 'can bring Your Majesty's weighty matter to a happy termination, and by saving you, save the church ... and myself also', he thought in his heart. – 'Let us see, let us count the voters.'

Henry and his minister then wrote down on a strip of parchment the names of all the cardinals, marking with the letter A those who were on the side of the kings of England and France, and with the letter B all who favoured the emperor. 'There was no C', says a chronicler sarcastically, 'to signify any on *Christ's* side.' The letter N designated the neutrals. 'The cardinals present', said Wolsey, 'will not exceed thirty-nine, and we must have two-thirds, that is, twenty-six. Now, there are twenty upon whom we can reckon; we must therefore, at any price, gain six of the neutrals.'

Wolsey, deeply sensible of the importance of an election that would decide whether England was to be reformed or not, carefully drew up the instructions, which Henry signed, and which history must register. 'We desire and ordain', the ambassadors were informed in them,

> that you secure the election of the Cardinal of York; not forgetting that next to the salvation of his own soul, there is nothing the king desires more earnestly.
>
> To gain over the neutral cardinals you will employ two methods in particular. The first is, the cardinals being present, and having God

[2] Foxe, *Acts*, iv, pp. 600–1.

and the Holy Ghost before them, you shall remind them that the Cardinal of York alone can save Christendom.

The second is, because human fragility suffereth not all things to be pondered and weighed in a just balance, it appertaineth in matter of so high importance, to the comfort and relief of all Christendom, to succour the infirmity that may chance ... not for corruption, you will understand ... but rather to help the lacks and defaults of human nature. And, therefore, it shall be expedient that you promise spiritual offices, dignities, rewards of money, or other things which shall seem meet to the purpose.

Then shall you, with good dexterity, combine and knit those favourable to us in a perfect fastness and indissoluble knot. And that they may be the better animated to finish the election to the king's desire, you shall offer them a guard of 2,000 or 3,000 men from the kings of England and France, from the viscount of Turin, and the republic of Venice.

If, notwithstanding all your exertions, the election should fail, then the cardinals of the king shall repair to some sure place, and there proceed to such an election as may be to God's pleasure.

And to win more friends for the king, you shall promise, on the one hand, to the Cardinal de Medici and his party our special favour; and the Florentines, on the other hand, you shall put in comfort of the exclusion of the said family de Medici.

Likewise you shall put the cardinals in perfect hope of recovering the patrimony of the church; and you shall contain the Venetians in good trust of a reasonable way to be taken for Cervia and Ravenna [which formed part of the patrimony] to their contentment.

Such were the means by which the cardinal hoped to win the papal throne. To the right he said *yes*, to the left he said *no*. What would it matter that these perfidies were one day discovered, provided it were after the election. Christendom might be very certain that the choice of the future pontiff would be the work of the Holy Ghost. Alexander VI had been a poisoner; Julius II had given way to ambition, anger, and vice; the liberal Leo X had passed his life in worldly pursuits; the unhappy Clement VII had lived on stratagems and lies; Wolsey would be their worthy successor: 'All the seven deadly sins have worn the triple crown.'

Wolsey found his excuse in the thought that if he succeeded, the divorce was secured, and England enslaved for ever to the court of Rome.

Success at first appeared probable. Many cardinals spoke openly in favour of the English prelate; one of them asked for a detailed account of his life, in order to present it as a model to the church; another worshipped him (so he said) as a divinity. Among the gods and popes adored at Rome there were some no better than he. But ere long alarming news reached England. What grief! the pope was getting better. 'Conceal your instructions', wrote the cardinal.

Wolsey not having obtained the tiara, it was necessary at least to gain the divorce. 'God declares', said the English ambassadors to the pope, '*except the Lord build the house, they labour in vain that build it.*[3] Therefore, the king, taking God alone for his guide, requests of you, in the first place, an engagement to pronounce the divorce in the space of three months, and in the second the avocation to Rome.' – 'The promise first, and only after that the avocation', Wolsey had said; 'for I fear that if the pope begins with the avocation, he will never pronounce the divorce.' – 'Besides', added the envoys, 'the king's second marriage admits of no refusal, whatever bulls or briefs there may be. The only issue of this matter is the divorce; the divorce in one way or another must be procured.'

Wolsey had instructed his envoys to pronounce these words with a certain air of familiarity, and at the same time with a gravity calculated to produce an effect. His expectations were deceived: Clement was colder than ever. He had determined to abandon England in order that he might secure the states of the church, of which Charles was then master, thus sacrificing the spiritual to the temporal. 'The pope will not do the least thing for Your Majesty', wrote Bryan to the king; 'your matter may well be in his *Pater noster*, but it certainly is not in his *Credo*.' – 'Increase in importunity', answered the king; 'the Cardinal of Verona should remain about the pope's person and counterbalance the influence

---

[3] Where Christ is not the foundation, surely no building can be of good work. State Papers, vii, p. 122.

of de Angelis and the Archbishop of Capua. I would rather lose my two crowns than be beaten by these two friars.'

Thus was the struggle about to become keener than ever, when Clement's relapse once more threw doubt on everything. He was always between life and death; and this perpetual alternation agitated the king and the impatient cardinal in every way. The latter considered that the pope had need of *merits* to enter the kingdom of heaven. 'Procure an interview with the pope', he wrote to the envoys, 'even though he be in the very agony of death;[4] and represent to him that nothing will be more likely *to save his soul* than the bill of divorce.' Henry's commissioners were not admitted; but towards the end of March, the deputies appearing in a body, the pope promised to examine the letter from Spain. Vannes began to fear this document; he represented that those who had fabricated it would have been able to give it an appearance of authenticity. 'Rather declare immediately that this brief is not a brief'; said he to the pope. 'The King of England, who is Your Holiness's son, is not so like the rest of the world. We cannot put the same shoe on every foot.' This rather vulgar argument did not touch Clement. 'If to content your master in this business', said he, 'I cannot employ my head, at least I will my finger.' – 'Be pleased to explain yourself', replied Vannes, who found the *finger* a very little matter. – 'I mean', resumed the pontiff, 'that I shall employ every means, provided they are *honourable.*' Vannes withdrew disheartened.

He immediately conferred with his colleagues, and all together, alarmed at the idea of Henry's anger, returned to the pontiff; they thrust aside the lackeys, who endeavoured to stop them, and made their way into his bed chamber. Clement opposed them with that resistance of inertia by which the popedom has gained its greatest victories: *siluit*, he remained silent. Of what consequence to the pontiff were Tudor, his island, and his church, when Charles of Austria was threatening him with his armies? Clement, less proud than Hildebrand, submitted willingly to the emperor's power, provided the emperor would protect him. 'I had rather', he said, 'be Caesar's servant, not only in a temple, but in a stable if necessary, than be exposed to the insults of rebels and

---

[4] Burnet's *Reformation*, i, p. 49.

vagabonds.' At the same time he wrote to Campeggio: 'Do not irritate the king, but spin out this matter as much as possible; the Spanish brief gives us the means.'

In fact, Charles V had twice shown Lee, Henry's ambassador, the original document, and Wolsey, after this report, began to believe that it was not Charles who had forged the brief, but that Pope Julius II had really given two contradictory documents on the same day. Accordingly the cardinal now feared to see this letter in the pontiff's hands. 'Do all you can to dissuade the pope from seeking the original in Spain', wrote he to one of his ambassadors; 'it may exasperate the emperor.' We know how cautious the cardinal was towards Charles. Intrigue attained its highest point at this epoch, and Englishmen and Romans encountered craft with craft. 'In such ticklish negotiations', says Burnet (who had had some little experience in diplomacy), 'ministers must say and unsay as they are instructed, which goes of course as a part of their business.' Henry's envoys to the pope intercepted the letters sent from Rome, and had Campeggio's seized. On his part the pope indulged in flattering smiles and perfidious equivocations. Bryan wrote to Henry VIII: 'Always Your Grace hath done for him in deeds, and he hath recompensed you with fair words and fair *writings*, of which both I think Your Grace shall lack none; but as for the *deeds*, I never believe to see them, and especially at this time.' Bryan had comprehended the court of Rome better perhaps than many politicians. Finally, Clement himself, wishing to prepare the king for the blow he was about to inflict, wrote to him: 'We have been able to find nothing that would satisfy your ambassadors.'

Henry thought he knew what this message meant: that he had found nothing, and would find nothing; and accordingly this prince, who, if we may believe Wolsey, had hitherto shown incredible patience and gentleness, gave way to all his violence. 'Very well then', said he; 'my lords and I well know how to withdraw ourselves from the authority of the Roman see.' Wolsey turned pale, and conjured his master not to rush into that fearful abyss; Campeggio, too, endeavoured to revive the king's hopes. But it was all of no use. Henry recalled his ambassadors.

Henry, it is true, had not yet reached the age when violent characters become inflexible from the habit they have encouraged of yielding to their passions. But the cardinal, who knew his master, knew also that his inflexibility did not depend upon the number of his years; he thought Rome's power in England was lost, and placed between Henry and Clement, he exclaimed: 'How shall I avoid Scylla, and not fall into Charybdis?' He begged the king to make one last effort by sending Dr Bennet to the pope with orders to support the avocation to Rome, and he gave him a letter in which he displayed all the resources of his eloquence. 'How can it be imagined', he wrote, 'that the persuasions of sense urge the king to break a union in which the ardent years of his youth were passed with such purity? ... The matter is very different. I am on the spot, I know the state of men's minds. ... Pray, believe me. ... The divorce is the secondary question; the primary one is *the fidelity of this realm* to the papal see. The nobility, gentry, and citizens all exclaim with indignation: Must our fortunes, and even our lives, depend upon the nod of a foreigner? We must abolish, or at the very least diminish, the authority of the Roman pontiff. ... Most Holy Father, we cannot mention such things without a shudder.' ... This new attempt was also unavailing. The pope demanded of Henry how he could doubt his goodwill, seeing that the King of England had done so much for the apostolic see. This appeared a cruel irony to Tudor; the king requested a favour of the pope, and the pope replied by calling to mind those which the papacy had received from his hands. 'Is this the way', men asked in England, 'in which Rome pays her debts?'

Wolsey had not reached the end of his misfortunes. Gardiner and Bryan had just returned to London: they declared that to demand an avocation to Rome was to lose their cause. Accordingly Wolsey, who turned to every wind, ordered da Casale, in case Clement should pronounce the avocation, to appeal from the pope, the false head of the church, *to the true vicar of Jesus Christ.*[5] This was almost in Luther's style. Who was this true vicar? Probably a pope nominated by the influence of England.

But this proceeding did not assure the cardinal: he was losing his judgment. A short time before this, Du Bellay, who had just returned

---

[5] State Papers, vii, p. 191.

from Paris, whither he had gone to retain France on the side of England, had been invited to Richmond by Wolsey. As the two prelates were walking in the park, on that hill whence the eye ranges over the fertile and undulating fields through which the winding Thames pours its tranquil waters, the unhappy cardinal observed to the bishop: 'My trouble is the greatest that ever was! … I have excited and carried on this matter of the divorce, to dissolve the union between the two houses of Spain and England, by sowing misunderstanding between them, as if I had no part in it. You know it was in the interest of France; I therefore entreat the king your master and Her Majesty to do everything that may forward the divorce. I shall esteem such a favour more than if they made me pope; but if they refuse me, my ruin is inevitable.' And then giving way to despair, he exclaimed: 'Alas! would that I were going to be buried tomorrow!'

The wretched man was drinking the bitter cup his perfidies had prepared for him. All seemed to conspire against Henry, and Bennet was recalled shortly after. It was said at court and in the city: 'Since the pope sacrifices us to the emperor, let us sacrifice the pope.' Clement VII, intimidated by the threats of Charles V, and tottering upon his throne, madly repelled with his foot the bark of England. Europe was all attention, and began to think that the proud vessel of Albion, cutting the cable that bound her to the pontiffs, would boldly spread her canvas to the winds, and ever after sail the sea alone, wafted onwards by the breeze that comes from heaven.

The influence of Rome over Europe is in great measure political. It loses a kingdom by a royal quarrel, and might in this same way lose ten.

CHAPTER SEVEN

More and Tyndale: A Theological Duel

(1528–1529)

O ther circumstances from day to day rendered the emancipation of the church more necessary. If behind these political debates there had not been found a Christian people, resolved never to temporize with error, it is probable that England, after a few years of independence, would have fallen back into the bosom of Rome. The affair of the divorce was not the only one agitating men's minds; the religious controversies, which for some years filled the Continent, were always more animated at Oxford and Cambridge. The *evangelicals* and the *Catholics* (not very 'catholic' indeed) warmly discussed the great questions which the progress of events brought before the world. The former maintained that the primitive church of the apostles and the actual church of the papacy were not identical; the latter affirmed, on the contrary, the identity of popery and apostolic Christianity. Other Romish doctors in later times, finding this position somewhat embarrassing, have asserted that catholicism existed only *in the germ* in the apostolic church, and had subsequently developed itself. But a thousand abuses, a thousand errors may creep into a church under cover of this theory. A plant springs from the seed and grows up in accordance with immutable laws; whilst a doctrine cannot be transformed in the mind of man without falling under the influence of sin. It is true that the disciples of popery have supposed a constant action of the Divine Spirit in the Catholic Church, which excludes every influence of error. To stamp on the development of the church the character of truth, they have stamped on the church itself the character of infallibility; *quod erat demonstrandum.* Their reasoning is a mere begging of the question. To know whether the Romish development is identical with the gospel, we must examine it by Scripture.

It was not university men alone who occupied themselves with Christian truth. The separation which has been remarked in other times between the opinions of the people and of the learned, did not now exist. What the doctors taught, the citizens practised; Oxford and London embraced each other. The theologians knew that learning has need of life, and the citizens believed that life has need of that learning which derives the doctrine from the wells of the Scriptures of God. It was the harmony between these two elements, the one theological, the other practical, which constituted the strength of the English reformation.

The evangelical life in the capital alarmed the clergy more than the evangelical doctrine in the colleges. Since Monmouth had escaped, they must strike another. Among the London merchants was John Tewkesbury, one of the oldest friends of the Scriptures in England. As early as 1512 he had become possessor of a manuscript copy of the Bible, and had attentively studied it; when Tyndale's New Testament appeared, he read it with avidity; and, finally, *The Wicked Mammon* had completed the work of his conversion. Being a man of heart and understanding, clever in all he undertook, a ready and fluent speaker, and liking to get to the bottom of everything, Tewkesbury, like Monmouth, became very influential in the city, and one of the most learned in Scripture of any of the evangelicals. These generous Christians, being determined to consecrate to God the good things they had received from him, were the first among that long series of laymen who were destined to be more useful to the truth than many ministers and bishops. They found time to interest themselves about the most trifling details of the kingdom of God; and in the history of the reformation in Britain their names should be inscribed beside those of Latimer and Tyndale.

The activity of these laymen could not escape the cardinal's notice. Clement VII was abandoning England: it was necessary for the English bishops, by crushing the heretics, to show that they would not abandon the popedom. We can understand the zeal of these prelates and, without excusing their persecutions, we are disposed to extenuate their crime. The bishops determined to ruin Tewkesbury. One day in April 1529, as he was busy among his peltries, the officers entered his warehouse, arrested him, and led him away to the Bishop of London's chapel, where, besides the ordinary (Tunstall) the bishops of Ely, St Asaph, Bath, and Lincoln, with the Abbot of Westminster, were on the bench. The composition of this tribunal indicated the importance of his case. The emancipation of the laity, thought these judges, is perhaps a more dangerous heresy than justification by faith.

'John Tewkesbury', said the Bishop of London, 'I exhort you to trust less to your own wit and learning, and more unto the doctrine of the holy mother the church.' Tewkesbury made answer that in his judgment he held no other doctrine than that of the church of Christ. Tunstall then broached the principal charge, that of having read *The Wicked Mammon*, and after quoting several passages, he exclaimed: 'Renounce these errors.' – 'I find no fault in the book', replied Tewkesbury. 'It has enlightened my conscience and consoled my heart. But it is not my gospel. I have studied the holy Scriptures these seventeen years and, as a man sees the spots of his face in a glass, so by reading them I have learnt the faults of my soul. If there is a disagreement between you and the New Testament, put yourselves in harmony with it, rather than desire to put that in accord with you.' The bishops were surprised that a leather seller should speak so well, and quote Scripture so happily that they were unable to resist him. Annoyed at being catechized by a layman, the bishops of Bath, St Asaph, and Lincoln thought they could conquer him more easily by the rack than by their arguments. He was taken to the Tower, where they ordered him to be put to the torture. His limbs were crushed, which was contrary to the laws of England, and the violence of the rack tore from him a cry of agony to which the priests replied by a shout of exultation. The inflexible merchant had promised at last to renounce Tyndale's *Wicked Mammon*. Tewkesbury left the Tower 'almost a cripple', and returned to his house to lament the fatal word which the question had extorted from him, and to prepare in the silence of faith to confess in the burning pile the precious name of Christ Jesus.

We must, however, acknowledge that the 'question' was not Rome's only argument. The gospel had two classes of opponents in the sixteenth century, as in the first ages of the church. Some attacked it with the torture, others with their writings. Sir Thomas More, a few years later, was to have recourse to the first of these arguments; but for the moment he took up his pen. He had first studied the writings of the fathers of the church and of the reformers, but rather as an advocate than as a theologian; and then, armed at all points, he rushed into the arena of polemics, and in his attacks dealt those 'technical convictions and that malevolent subtlety', says one of his greatest admirers, 'from which the honestest men of his profession are not free'. Jests and sarcasms had fallen from his pen in his discussion with Tyndale, as in his controversy with Luther. In 1528 there appeared *A Dialogue of Sir Thomas More, Knt., touching the pestilent Sect of Luther and Tyndale, by the one begun in Saxony, and by the other laboured to be brought into England.*[1]

Tyndale soon became informed of More's publication, and a remarkable combat ensued between these two representatives of the two doctrines that were destined to divide Christendom – Tyndale the champion of Scripture,[2] and More the champion of the church. More having called his book a *Dialogue*, Tyndale adopted this form in his reply, and the two combatants valiantly crossed their swords, though wide seas lay between them.

This theological duel is not without importance in the history of the reformation. The struggles of diplomacy, of sacerdotalism, and of royalty were not enough; there must be struggles of doctrine. Rome had set the hierarchy above the faith; the reformation was to restore faith to its place above the hierarchy.

---

[1] [Sir Thomas More, regarded by his church as the greatest English scholar of his time, was invited by Tunstall to read the works of the reformers in order that he might use his pen to refute them. The *Dialogue* was the outcome. It was intended to be a popular work, intermingling 'merry tales' with somewhat shallow theological disquisitions. C. S. Lewis, in his *English Literature in the Sixteenth Century*, speaks of it as a weak defence of Romanism but as 'great Platonic dialogue, perhaps the best specimen of that form ever produced in English' (p. 172).]

[2] The *Dialogue* consisted of 250 pages, and was printed by Rastell, More's brother-in-law. Tyndale's answer did not appear until later; we have thought it best to introduce it here. [Tyndale's *Answer to Sir Thomas More's Dialogue* roots the Christian faith firmly in Scripture, and is to be found in the Parker Society Publications.]

MORE. Christ said not, the Holy Ghost shall *write*, but shall *teach*. Whatsoever the church says, it is the word of God, though it be not in Scripture.

TYNDALE. It is not the custom of Scripture to say the Holy Ghost writeth but inspireth the writer ... and it is manifest that ... love compelled the apostles to leave nothing unwritten that should be necessarily required, and that, if it were left out, should hurt the soul. ... *These are written, says St John, that ye may believe and through belief have life.* (1 John 2:1; Rom. 15:4; Matt. 22:29.)

MORE. The apostles have taught by *mouth* many things they did not *write*, because they should not come into the hands of the heathen for mocking.

TYNDALE. I pray you what thing more to be mocked by the heathen could they teach than the resurrection; and that Christ was God and man, and died between two thieves? And yet all these things the apostles *wrote*. And again, purgatory, penance, and satisfaction for sin, and praying to saints, are marvellous agreeable unto the superstition of the heathen people, so that they needed not to abstain from writing of them for fear lest the heathen should have mocked them.

MORE. We must not examine the teaching of the church by Scripture, but understand Scripture by means of what the church says.

TYNDALE. What! Does the air give light to the sun, or the sun to the air? Is the church before the gospel, or the gospel before the church? Is not the father older than the son? *God begat us with his own will, with the word of truth*, says St James (1:18.) If he who begetteth is before him who is begotten, the *word* is before the *church*, or, to speak more correctly, before the *congregation*.

MORE. Why do you say *congregation* and not *church*?

TYNDALE. Because by that word *church*, you understand nothing but a multitude of shaven, shorn, and oiled, which we now call the spiritualty or clergy; while the word of right is common unto all the congregation of them that believe in Christ.

MORE. The church is the pope and his sect or followers.

TYNDALE. The pope teacheth us to trust in holy works for salvation, as penance, saints' merits, and friars' coats. Now, he that hath no faith to be saved through Christ, is not of Christ's church.

MORE. The Romish Church from which the Lutherans came out, was before them, and therefore is the right one.

TYNDALE. In like manner you may say, the church of the Pharisees, whence Christ and his apostles came out, was before them, and was therefore the right church, and consequently Christ and his disciples are heretics.

MORE. No: the apostles came out from the church of the Pharisees because they found not Christ there; but your priests in Germany and elsewhere, have come out of our church, because they wanted wives.

TYNDALE. Wrong … these priests were at first attached to what you call *heresies*, and then they took wives; but yours were first attached to the *holy* doctrine of the pope, and then they took harlots.

MORE. Luther's books be open, if ye will not believe us.

TYNDALE. Nay, ye have shut them up, and have even burnt them. …

MORE. I marvel that you deny *purgatory*, Sir William, except it be a plain point with you to go straight to hell.

TYNDALE. I know no other purging but faith in the cross of Christ; while you, for a groat or a sixpence, buy some secret pills [indulgences] which you take to purge yourselves of your sins.

MORE. Faith, then, is your purgatory, you say; there is no need, therefore, of works – a most immoral doctrine!

TYNDALE. It is faith *alone* that saves us, but not a *bare faith*. When a horse beareth a saddle and a man thereon, we may well say that the horse only and alone beareth the saddle, but we do not mean the saddle empty, and no man thereon.

In this manner did the Catholic and the evangelical carry on the discussion. According to Tyndale, what constitutes the true church is the work of the Holy Ghost within; according to More, the constitution of the papacy without. The spiritual character of the gospel is thus put in opposition to the formalist character of the Roman Church. The reformation restored to our belief the solid foundation of the word of

God; for the sand it substituted the rock.[3] In the discussion to which we have just been listening, the advantage remained not with the Catholic. Erasmus, a friend of More, embarrassed by the course the latter was taking, wrote to Tunstall: 'I cannot heartily congratulate More.'

Henry interrupted the celebrated knight in these contests to send him to Cambrai, where a peace was negotiating between France and the

---

[3] [The latest Roman Catholic historian of the reformation in England (*The Reformation in England*, vol. i. 'The King's Proceedings' by Philip Hughes, 1950) necessarily devotes considerable attention to Tyndale's attack on the Roman Church. While he classes Tyndale as 'the greatest English light in the heretical firmament in these first years, and the most powerful solvent in English Catholicism since Wycliffe (p. 133, 4th ed.), he strangely states that 'Tyndale can hardly be reckoned a religious thinker of any real importance. The ideas he puts forth are none of them his own.' In this respect, says Hughes, all other English reformers of the period are like Tyndale: 'all are derivative'. The verdict is not justified. It is easy to claim originality for a pioneer and to deny it to those who follow. The fact is that, although Tyndale was thoroughly well acquainted with Luther's writings – their influence certainly appears in his treatises – his doctrine came, not from Luther, but from his own independent study of the Scriptures. Hughes rightly links Tyndale's recalling of his countrymen to the word with the following: 'The whole Catholic conception of sacraments, of the sacramental sacrifice and the sacramentally qualified and endowed priesthood that offered it, was violently rejected. The Mass was idolatry, an abomination. And all the elaborately wrought system of the mediaeval and patristic theologians was swept aside also.' (p. 135.) Exactly so! That Luther and Tyndale put forth the same teachings is proof, not that the one was the mere copyist of the other, but that both alike, illumined by the same Holy Spirit, had drunk deeply of the enlightening word.

The best that Hughes can say of Tyndale reads as follows: 'But Tyndale's passion and his skill in languages is another matter: and of his own language he showed himself a master indeed. His fiery zeal, and burning hate; the vicious bite of his attack; the unfailing, simple, clear style; the real eloquence when indignation drives him, or the thought of all that the "gospel" will one day accomplish, or the thought of God's saving love; it is the rhetorician who is powerful, who will convert men and hold them to his school.' (p. 138.)

That Tyndale often used words of 'bitterest hatred' in denouncing a delusive Romanism is undeniable. Romanism was, in his eyes, the 'abomination that made the land desolate of truth'. But equally strong terms were used of Tyndale by his adversaries. And if an apostle was moved by the Spirit of God to anathematize teachers in Galatia who, though nominally Christian, desired to add man's works and ceremonies to faith as the instrument of justification before God, it is not surprising that Tyndale and his fellow reformers used the strongest expressions to denounce a system which departed so grievously from the plain 'truth as it is in Jesus'.]

Empire. Wolsey would have been pleased to go himself; but his enemies suggested to the king, 'that it was only that he might not expedite the matter of the divorce'. Henry, therefore, despatched More, Knight, and Tunstall; but Wolsey had created so many delays that they did not arrive until after the conclusion of the *Ladies' Peace* (August 1529). The king's vexation was extreme. Du Bellay had in vain helped him to spend a *good preparatory July* to make him *swallow the dose*. Henry was angry with Wolsey, Wolsey threw the blame on the ambassador, and the ambassador defended himself, he tells us, 'with tooth and nail'.

By way of compensation, the English envoys concluded with the emperor a treaty prohibiting on both sides the printing and sale of 'any Lutheran books'. Some of them could have wished for a good persecution, for a few burning piles, it may be. A singular opportunity occurred. In the spring of 1529, Tyndale and Fryth had left Marburg for Antwerp, and were thus in the vicinity of the English envoys. What West had been unable to effect, it was thought the two most intelligent men in Britain could not fail to accomplish. 'Tyndale must be captured', said More and Tunstall. – 'You do not know what sort of a country you are in', replied Hackett. 'Will you believe that on 7 April, Harman arrested me at Antwerp for damages caused by his imprisonment? If you can lay anything to my charge as a private individual, I said to the officer, I am ready to answer for myself; but if you arrest me *as ambassador*, I know no judge but the emperor. Upon which the procurator had the audacity to reply, that I was arrested as ambassador; and the lords of Antwerp only set me at liberty on condition that I should appear again at the first summons. These merchants are so proud of their franchises, that they would resist even Charles himself.' This anecdote was not at all calculated to encourage More; and not caring about a pursuit, which promised to be of little use, he returned to England. But the Bishop of London, who was left behind, persisted in the project, and repaired to Antwerp to put it in execution.

Tyndale was at that time greatly embarrassed; considerable debts, incurred with his printers, compelled him to suspend his labours. Nor was this all: the prelate who had spurned him so harshly in London, had just arrived in the very city where he lay concealed. ... What would become of him? ... A merchant, named Augustin Packington, a clever man, but somewhat inclined to dissimulation, happening to be at Antwerp on business, hastened to pay his respects to the bishop. The latter observed, in the course of conversation: 'I should like to get hold of the books with which England is poisoned.' – 'I can perhaps serve you in that matter', replied the merchant. 'I know the Flemings, who have bought Tyndale's books; so that if your lordship will be pleased to pay for them, I will make sure of them all.' – 'Oh, oh!' thought the bishop; 'Now, as the proverb says, I shall have God by the toe. Gentle Master Packington', he added in a flattering tone, 'I will pay for them whatsoever they cost you. I intend to burn them at St Paul's Cross.' The bishop, having his hand already on Tyndale's Testaments, fancied himself on the point of seizing Tyndale himself.

Packington, being one of those men who love to conciliate all parties, ran off to Tyndale, with whom he was intimate, and said: 'William, I know you are a poor man, and have a heap of New Testaments and books by you, for which you have beggared yourself; and I have now found a merchant who will buy them all, and with ready money too.' – 'Who is the merchant?' said Tyndale. – 'The Bishop of London.' – 'Tunstall? ... If he buys my books, it can only be to burn them.' – 'No doubt', answered Packington; 'but what will he gain by it? The whole world will cry out against the priest who burns God's word, and the eyes of many will be opened. Come, make up your mind, William; the bishop shall have the books, you the money, and I the thanks.' ... Tyndale resisted the proposal; Packington became more pressing. 'The question comes to this', he said; 'shall the bishop pay for the books or shall he not? for, make up your mind ... he will have them.' – 'I consent', said the reformer at last; 'I shall pay my debts, and bring out a new and more correct edition of the Testament.' The bargain was made.

Ere long the danger thickened around Tyndale. Placards, posted at Antwerp and throughout the province, announced that the emperor, in conformity with the treaty of Cambrai, was about to proceed against the reformers and their writings. Not an officer of justice appeared in the street but Tyndale's friends trembled for his liberty. Under such circumstances, how could he print his translations? It appears probable that he made up his mind about the end of August to go to Hamburg, and took his passage in a vessel loading for that port. Embarking with his books, his manuscripts, and the rest of his money, he glided down the Scheldt, and soon found himself afloat on the German ocean.

But one danger followed close upon another. He had scarcely passed the mouth of the Meuse when a tempest burst upon him, and his ship, like that of old which bore St Paul, was almost swallowed up by the waves. – 'Satan, envying the happy course and success of the gospel', says a chronicler, 'set to his might how to hinder the blessed labours of this man.' The seamen toiled, Tyndale prayed, all hope was lost. The reformer alone was full of courage, not doubting that God would preserve him for the accomplishment of his work. All the exertions of the crew proved useless; the vessel was dashed on the coast, and the passengers escaped with their lives. Tyndale gazed with sorrow upon that ocean which had swallowed up his beloved books and precious manuscripts, and deprived him of his resources. What labours, what perils! banishment, poverty, thirst, insults, watchings, persecution, imprisonment, the stake! ... Like Paul, he was in perils by his own countrymen, in perils among strange people, in perils in the city, in perils in the sea. Recovering his spirits, however, he went on board another ship, entered the Elbe, and at last reached Hamburg.[4]

Great joy was in store for him in that city. Coverdale, Foxe informs us, was waiting there to confer with him, and to help him in his labours. It has been supposed that Coverdale went to Hamburg to invite Tyndale, in Cromwell's name, to return to England; but it is merely a conjecture, lacking confirmation. As early as 1527, Coverdale had made known to Cromwell his desire to translate the Scriptures.[5] It was natural that, meeting with difficulties in this undertaking, he should desire to converse with Tyndale. The two friends lodged with a pious woman named Margaret van Emmersen, and spent some time together in the autumn of 1529, undisturbed by the sweating sickness which was making such cruel havoc all around them. Coverdale returned to England shortly

---

[4] [A number of historians have seen fit to cast doubt on this part of Tyndale's history, which is narrated by Foxe alone. J. F. Mozley however, in his *William Tyndale*, 1937, gives substantial reasons for accepting it.]

[5] This is the date assigned in *Coverdale's Remains* (Parker Society), p. 490.

after; the two reformers had, no doubt, discovered that it was better for each of them to translate the Scriptures separately.

Before Coverdale's return, Tunstall had gone back to London, exulting at carrying with him the books he had bought so dearly. But when he reached the capital, he thought he had better defer the meditated *auto da fé* until some striking event should give it increased importance. And besides, just at that moment, very different matters were engaging public attention on the banks of the Thames, and the liveliest emotions agitated every mind.

CHAPTER EIGHT

A Queen's Pleadings Convict a Court

(1529)

Affairs had changed in England during the absence of Tunstall and More; and even before their departure, events of a certain importance had occurred. Henry, finding there was nothing more to hope from Rome, had turned to Wolsey and Campeggio. The Roman nuncio had succeeded in deceiving the king. 'Campeggio is very different from what he is reported', said Henry to his friends; 'he is not for the emperor, as I was told; I have said somewhat to him which has changed his mind.' No doubt he had made some brilliant promise.

Henry therefore, imagining himself sure of his two legates, desired them to proceed with the matter of the divorce without delay. There was no time to lose, for the king was informed that the pope was on the point of recalling the commission given to the two cardinals; and as early as 19 March, Salviati, the pope's uncle and Secretary of State, wrote to Campeggio about it. Henry's process, once in the Court of the Pontifical Chancery, it would have been long before it got out again. Accordingly, on 31 May, the king, by a warrant under the great seal, gave the legates *leave* to execute their commission, 'without any regard to his own person, and having the fear of God only before their eyes'. The legates themselves had suggested this formula to the king.

On the same day the commission was opened; but to begin the process was not to end it. Every letter which the nuncio received forbade him to do so in the most positive manner. 'Advance slowly and never finish', were Clement's instructions. The trial was to be a farce, played by a pope and two cardinals.

The ecclesiastical court met in the Great Hall of the Blackfriars, commonly called the 'Parliament chamber'. The two legates, having successively taken the commission in their hands, devoutly declared that they were resolved to execute it (they should have said, to elude it), made the required oaths, and ordered a peremptory citation of the king and queen to appear on 18 June at nine in the morning. Campeggio was eager to proceed *slowly*; the session was adjourned for three weeks. The citation caused a great stir among the people. 'What!' said they, 'a king and a queen constrained to appear, in their own realm, before their own subjects.' The papacy set an example which was to be strictly followed in after-years both in England and in France.

On 18 June, Catherine appeared before the commission in the Parliament chamber and, stepping forward with dignity, said with a firm voice: 'I protest against the legates as incompetent judges, and appeal to the pope.' This proceeding of the queen, her pride and firmness, troubled her enemies, and in their vexation they grew exasperated against her. 'Instead of praying God to bring this matter to a good conclusion', they said, 'she endeavours to turn away the people's affections from the king. Instead of showing Henry the love of a youthful wife, she keeps away from him night and day. There is even cause to fear', they added, 'that she is in concert with certain individuals who have formed the horrible design of killing the king and the cardinal.' But persons of generous heart, seeing only a queen, a wife, and a mother, attacked in her dearest affections, showed themselves full of sympathy for her.

On 21 June, the day to which the court adjourned, the two legates entered the Parliament chamber with all the pomp belonging to their station, and took their seats on a raised platform. Near them sat the bishops of Bath and Lincoln, the Abbot of Westminster, and Doctor Taylor, master of the rolls, whom they had added to their commission. Below them were the secretaries, among whom the skilful Stephen Gardiner held the chief rank. On the right beneath a canopy of cloth of gold sat the king surrounded by his officers; and on the left, a little lower, and under a similar canopy, was the queen, attended by her ladies. The Archbishop of Canterbury and the bishops were seated between the legates and Henry VIII, and on both sides of the throne were stationed the counsellors of the king and queen – Fisher, Bishop of Rochester, Standish of St Asaph, West of Ely, and Dr Ridley. The people, when they

saw this procession pass before them, were far from being dazzled by
the pomp. 'Less show and more virtue', they said, 'would better become
such judges.'

The pontifical commission having been read, the legates declared that
they would judge without fear or favour, and would admit of neither
recusation nor appeal. Then the usher cried: 'Henry, King of England,
come into court.' The king, cited in his own capital to accept as judges
two priests, his subjects, repressed the throbbing of his proud heart,
and replied, in the hope that this strange trial would have a favourable
issue, 'Here I am.' The usher continued: 'Catherine, Queen of England,
come into court.' The queen handed the cardinals a paper in which she
protested against the legality of the court, as the judges were the subjects
of her opponent, and appealed to Rome. The cardinals declared they
could not admit this paper, and consequently Catherine was again called
into court. After the king and Wolsey had in turn briefly spoken, the
queen devoutly crossed herself, made the circuit of the court to where
the king sat, bending with dignity as she passed in front of the legates,
and fell on her knees before her husband. Every eye was turned upon her.
Then speaking in English, but with a Spanish accent, which by recalling
the distance she was from her native home, pleaded eloquently for her,
Catherine said with tears in her eyes, and in a tone at once dignified and
impassioned:

> Sir – I beseech you, for all the love that hath been between us, and for
> the love of God, let me have justice and right; take some pity on me,
> for I am a poor woman and a stranger, born out of your dominions.
> I have here no assured friend, much less impartial counsel, and I flee
> to you as to the head of justice within this realm. Alas! sir, wherein
> have I offended you, or what occasion given you of displeasure, that
> you should wish to put me from you? I take God and all the world to
> witness, that I have been to you a true, humble, and obedient wife,
> ever conformable to your will and pleasure. Never have I said or done
> aught contrary thereto, being always well pleased and content with all
> things wherein you had delight; neither did I ever grudge in word or
> countenance, or show a visage or spark of discontent. I loved all those
> whom you loved, only for your sake. This twenty years I have been
> your true wife, and by me ye have had divers children, although it

hath pleased God to call them out of this world, which yet hath been no default in me.

The judges, and even the most servile of the courtiers, were touched when they heard these simple and eloquent words, and the queen's sorrow moved them almost to tears. Catherine continued:

Sir – When ye married me at the first, I take God to be my judge I was a true maid; and whether it be true or not, I put it to your conscience. ... If there be any just cause that ye can allege against me, I am contented to depart from your kingdom, albeit to my great shame and dishonour; and if there be none, then let me remain in my former estate until death. Who united us? The king, your father, who was called the second Solomon; and my father, Ferdinand, who was esteemed one of the wisest princes that, for many years before, had reigned in Spain. It is not, therefore, to be doubted that the marriage between you and me is good and lawful. Who are my judges? Is not one the man that has put sorrow between you and me? ... a judge whom I refuse and abhor! – Who are the counsellors assigned me? Are they not officers of the Crown, who have made oath to you in your own council? ... Sir, I conjure you not to call me before a court so formed. Yet, if you refuse me this favour ... your will be done ... I shall be silent, I shall repress the emotions of my soul and remit my just cause to the hands of God.

Thus spoke Catherine through her tears; humbly bending, she seemed to embrace Henry's knees. She rose and made a low obeisance to the king. It was expected that she would return to her seat; but leaning on the arm of Master Griffiths, her receiver-general, she moved towards the door. The king, observing this, ordered her to be recalled; and the usher following her, thrice cried aloud: 'Catherine, Queen of England, come into court.' – 'Madam', said Griffiths, 'you are called back.' – 'I hear it well enough', replied the queen, 'but go you on, for this is no court wherein I can have justice: let us proceed.' Catherine returned to the palace, and never again appeared before the court either by proxy or in person.

She had gained her cause in the minds of many. The dignity of her person, the quaint simplicity of her speech, the propriety with which, relying upon her innocence, she had spoken of the most delicate subjects, and the tears which betrayed her emotion, had created a deep impression. But 'the sting in her speech', as an historian says, was her appeal to the king's conscience, and to the judgment of Almighty God, on the capital point in the cause. 'How could a person so modest, so sober in her language', said many, 'dare utter such a falsehood? Besides, the king did not contradict her.'

Henry was greatly embarrassed: Catherine's words had moved him. Catherine's defence, one of the most touching in history, had gained over the accuser himself. He therefore felt constrained to render this testimony to the accused: 'Since the queen has withdrawn, I will, in her absence, declare to you all present, that she has been to me as true and obedient a wife as I could desire. She has all the virtues and good qualities that belong to a woman. She is as noble in character as in birth.'

But Wolsey was the most embarrassed of all. When the queen had said, without naming him, that one of her judges was the cause of all her misfortunes, looks of indignation were turned upon him. He was unwilling to remain under the weight of this accusation. As soon as the king had finished speaking, he said: 'Sir, I humbly beg Your Majesty to declare before this audience, whether I was the first or chief mover in this business, for I am greatly suspected of all men herein.' Wolsey had formerly boasted to Du Bellay, 'that the first project of the divorce was set on foot by himself, to create a perpetual separation between the houses of England and Spain'; but now it suited him to affirm the contrary. The king, who needed his services, took care not to contradict him. 'My lord cardinal', he said, 'I can well excuse you herein. Marry, so far from being a mover, ye have been rather against me in attempting thereof. It was the Bishop of Tarbes, the French ambassador, who begot the first scruples in my conscience by his doubts on the legitimacy of the Princess Mary.' This was not correct. The Bishop of Tarbes was not in England before the year 1527, and we have proof that the king was meditating a divorce in 1526.[1] 'From that hour', he continued. 'I was much troubled, and thought myself in danger of God's heavy displeasure, who, wishing to punish my incestuous marriage, had taken away all the sons my wife had

---

[1] See Pace's letter to Henry in 1526. Pace there shows that it is incorrect to say: *Deuteronomium abrogare Leviticum* (Deuteronomy abrogates Leviticus), so far as concerns the prohibition to take the wife of a deceased brother.

borne me. I laid my grief before you, my Lord of Lincoln, then being my spiritual father; and by your advice I asked counsel of the rest of the bishops, and you all informed me under your seals, that you shared in my scruples.' – 'That is the truth', said the Archbishop of Canterbury. – 'No, sir, not so, under correction', quoth the Bishop of Rochester, 'you have not my hand and seal.' – 'No?' exclaimed the king, showing him a paper which he held in his hand; 'is not this your hand and seal?' – 'No, forsooth', he answered. Henry's surprise increased, and turning with a frown to the Archbishop of Canterbury, he asked him: 'What say you to that?' – 'Sir, it is his hand and seal', replied Warham. – 'It is not', rejoined Rochester; 'I told you I would never consent to any such act.' – 'You say the truth', responded the archbishop, 'but you were fully resolved at the last, that I should subscribe your name and put your seal.' – 'All which is untrue', added Rochester, in a passion. The bishop was not very respectful to his primate. 'Well, well', said the king, wishing to end the dispute, 'we will not stand in argument with you; for you are but one man.' The court adjourned. The day had been better for Catherine than for the prelates.

In proportion as the first sitting had been pathetic, so the discussions in the second between the lawyers and bishops were calculated to revolt a delicate mind. The advocates of the two parties vigorously debated *pro* and *con* respecting the consummation of Arthur's marriage with Catherine. 'It is a very difficult question', said one of the counsel; 'none can know the truth.' – 'But I know it', replied the Bishop of Rochester. – 'What do you mean?' asked Wolsey. – 'My lord', he answered, 'he was the very Truth who said: *What God hath joined together, let not man put asunder*: that is enough for me.' – 'So everybody thinks', rejoined Wolsey; 'but whether it was God who united Henry of England and Catherine of Aragon, *hoc restat probandum* (that remains to be proved). The king's council decides that the marriage is unlawful, and consequently it was not *God who joined them together*.' The two bishops then exchanged a few words less edifying than those of the preceding day. Several of the hearers expressed a sentiment of disgust. 'It is a disgrace to the court', said Dr Ridley with no little indignation, 'that you dare discuss questions which fill every right-minded man with horror.' This sharp reprimand put an end to the debate.

The agitations of the court spread to the religious houses; priests, monks, and nuns were everywhere in commotion. It was not long before astonishing revelations began to circulate through the cloisters. There was no talk then of an old portrait of the Virgin that winked its eyes; but other miracles were invented. 'An angel', it was rumoured, 'has appeared to Elizabeth Barton, the maid of Kent, as he did formerly to Adam, to the patriarchs, and to Jesus Christ.' At the epochs of the creation and of the redemption, and in the times which lead from one to the other, miracles are natural; God then appeared, and his coming without any signs of power would be as surprising as the rising of the sun unattended by its rays of light. But the Romish Church does not stop there; it claims in every age, for its saints, the privilege of miraculous powers, and the miracles are multiplied in proportion to the ignorance of the people. And accordingly the angel said to the epileptic maid of Kent: 'Go to the unfaithful King of England, and tell him there are three things he desires, which I forbid now and forever. The first is the power of the pope; the second the new doctrine; the third Anne Boleyn. If he takes her for his wife, God will visit him.' The vision-seeing maid delivered the message to the king, whom nothing could now stop.

On the contrary, he began to find out that Wolsey proceeded too slowly, and the idea sometimes crossed his mind that he was betrayed by this minister. One fine summer's morning, Henry, as soon as he rose, summoned the cardinal to him at Bridewell. Wolsey hastened thither, and remained closeted with the king from eleven till twelve. The latter gave way to all the fury of his passion and the violence of his despotism. 'We must finish this matter promptly', he said, 'we must positively.' Wolsey retired very uneasy, and returned by the Thames to Westminster. The sun darted his bright rays on the water. The Bishop of Carlisle, who sat by the cardinal's side, said as he wiped his forehead: 'A very warm day, my lord.' – 'Yes', replied the unhappy Wolsey, 'if you had been *chafed* for an hour as I have been, you would say it was a *hot* day.' When he reached his palace, the cardinal lay down on his bed to seek repose; he was not quiet long.

Catherine had grown in Henry's eyes, as well as in those of the nation. The king shrank from a judgment; he even began to doubt of his success. He wished that the queen would consent to a separation. This idea occurred to his mind after Wolsey's departure, and the cardinal had hardly closed his eyes before the Earl of Wiltshire (Anne Boleyn's father) was announced to him with a message from the king. 'It is His Majesty's pleasure', said Wiltshire, 'that you represent to the queen the shame that will accrue to her from a judicial condemnation, and persuade her to confide in his wisdom.' Wolsey, commissioned to execute a task he knew to be impossible, exclaimed: 'Why do you put such fancies in the king's head?' and then he spoke so reproachfully that Wiltshire, with tears in his eyes, fell on his knees beside the cardinal's bed. Boleyn, desirous of seeing his daughter Queen of England, feared perhaps that he had taken a wrong course. 'It is well', said the cardinal, recollecting that the message came from Henry VIII, 'I am ready to do everything to please His Majesty.' He rose, went to Bath Place to fetch Campeggio, and together they waited on the queen.

The two legates found Catherine quietly at work with her maids of honour. Wolsey addressed the queen in Latin: 'Nay, my lord', she said, 'speak to me in English; I wish all the world could hear you.' – 'We desire, madam, to communicate to you alone our counsel and opinion.' – 'My lord', said the queen, 'you are come to speak of things beyond my capacity'; and then, with noble simplicity, showing a skein of white thread hanging about her neck, she continued: 'These are my occupations and all that I am capable of. I am a poor woman, without friends in this foreign country and lacking wit to answer persons of wisdom as ye be; and yet, my lords, to please you, let us go to my withdrawing room.'

At these words the queen rose, and Wolsey gave her his hand. Catherine earnestly maintained her rights as a woman and a queen. 'We who were in the outer chamber', says Cavendish, 'from time to time could hear the queen speaking very loud, but could not understand what she said.' Catherine, instead of justifying herself, boldly accused her judge. 'I know, Sir Cardinal', she said with noble candour, 'I know who has given the king the advice he is following: it is you. I have not ministered to your pride – I have blamed your conduct – I have complained of your tyranny, and my nephew the emperor has not made you pope. ... Hence all my misfortunes. To revenge yourself you have kindled a war in Europe and have stirred up against me this most wicked matter. God will be my judge … and yours!' Wolsey would have replied, but Catherine haughtily refused to hear him and, while treating Campeggio with great civility, declared that she would not acknowledge either of them as her judge. The cardinals withdrew, Wolsey full of vexation and Campeggio beaming with joy, for the business was getting more complicated. Every hope of accommodation was lost: nothing remained now but to proceed judicially.

CHAPTER NINE

The Trial Ends in Farce

(July 1529)

The trial was resumed. The Bishop of Bath and Wells waited upon the queen at Greenwich and peremptorily summoned her to appear in the Parliament chamber. On the day appointed Catherine limited herself to sending an appeal to the pope. She was declared contumacious, and the legates proceeded with the cause.

Twelve articles were prepared, which were to serve for the examination of the witnesses and the summary of which was that the marriage of Henry with Catherine, being forbidden both by the law of God and of the church, was null and void.

The hearing of the witnesses began, and Dr Taylor, archdeacon of Buckingham, conducted the examination.[1] The Duke of Norfolk, high-treasurer of England, the Duke of Suffolk, Maurice St John, gentleman-carver to Prince Arthur, the Viscount Fitzwalter and Anthony Willoughby, his cup-bearers, testified to their being present on the morrow of the wedding at the breakfast of the prince, then in sound health, and reported the conversation that took place. The old Duchess of Norfolk, the Earl of Shrewsbury, and the marquis of Dorset, confirmed these declarations, which proved that Arthur and Catherine were really married. It was also called to mind that, at the time of Arthur's death, Henry was not permitted to take the title of Prince of Wales, because Catherine hoped to give an heir to the crown of England.

'If Arthur and Catherine were really married', said the king's counsellors after these extraordinary depositions, 'the marriage of this

---

[1] The evidence is to be found recorded in Lord Herbert of Cherbury's *History of Henry VIII* (first published in 1649).

princess with Henry, Arthur's brother, was forbidden by the Divine law, by an express command of God contained in Leviticus, and no dispensation could permit what God had forbidden.' Campeggio would never concede this argument, which limited the right of the popes; it was necessary therefore to abandon the *Divine right* (which was in reality to lose the cause) and to seek in the bull of Julius II and in his famous brief for flaws that would invalidate them both; and this the king's counsel did, although they did not conceal the weakness of their position. 'The motive alleged in the dispensation', they said, 'is the necessity of preserving a cordial relation between Spain and England; now, there was nothing that threatened their harmony. Moreover, it is said in this document that the pope grants it at the prayer of Henry, Prince of Wales. Now as this prince was only thirteen years old, he was not of age to make such a request. As for the brief, it is found neither in England nor in Rome; we cannot therefore admit its authenticity.' It was not difficult for Catherine's friends to invalidate these objections. 'Besides', they added, 'a union that has lasted twenty years sufficiently establishes its own lawfulness. And will you declare the Princess Mary illegitimate, to the great injury of this realm?'

The king's advocates then changed their course. Was not the Roman legate provided with a decretal pronouncing the divorce, in case it should be proved that Arthur's marriage had been really consummated? Now, this fact had been proved by the depositions. 'This is the moment for delivering judgment', said Henry and his counsellors to Campeggio. 'Publish the pope's decretal.' But the pope feared the sword of Charles V, then hanging over his head; and accordingly, whenever the king advanced one step, the Romish prelate took several in an opposite direction. 'I will deliver judgment in *five* days', said he; and when the five days were expired, he bound himself to deliver it in six. 'Restore peace to my troubled conscience', exclaimed Henry. The legate replied in courtly phrase; he had gained a few days' delay, and that was all he desired.

Such conduct on the part of the Roman legate produced an unfavourable effect in England, and a change took place in the public mind. The first movement had been for Catherine; the second was for Henry. Clement's endless delays and Campeggio's stratagems exasperated the nation. The king's argument was simple and popular: 'The pope cannot dispense with the laws of God'; while the queen, by appealing to the authority of the Roman pontiff, displeased both high and low. 'No precedent', said the lawyers, 'can justify the king's marriage with his brother's widow.'

There were, however, some evangelical Christians who thought Henry was 'troubled' more by his passions than by his conscience; and they asked how it happened that a prince, who represented himself to be so disturbed by the possible transgression of a law of doubtful inter-pretation, could desire, after twenty years, to violate the indisputable law which forbade the divorce? ... On the 21st of July, the day fixed *ad concludendum*, the cause was adjourned until the Friday following, and no one doubted that the matter would then be terminated.

All prepared for this important day. The king ordered the dukes of Norfolk and Suffolk to be present at the sitting of the court; and, being himself impatient to hear the so much coveted judgment, he stole into a gallery of the Parliament chamber facing the judges.

The legates of the holy see having taken their seats, the attorney-general signified to them, 'that everything necessary for the information of their conscience having been judicially laid before them, that day had been fixed for the conclusion of the trial'. There was a pause; everyone, feeling the importance of this judgment, waited for it with impatience. 'Either the papacy pronounces my divorce from Catherine', the king had said, 'or I shall divorce myself from the papacy.' That was the way Henry put the question. All eyes, and particularly the king's, were turned on the judges; Campeggio could not retreat; he must now say yes or no. For some time he was silent. He knew for certain that the queen's appeal had been admitted by Clement VII, and that the latter had concluded an alliance with the emperor. It was no longer in his power to grant the king's request. Clearly foreseeing that a no would perhaps forfeit the power of Rome in England, while a yes might put an end to the plans of religious emancipation which alarmed him so much, he could not make up his mind to say either *yes* or *no*.

At last the nuncio rose slowly from his chair, and all the assembly listened with emotion to the oracular decision which for so many years the powerful King of England had sought from the Roman pontiff. 'The general vacation of the harvest and vintage', he said, 'being observed every year by the court of Rome, dating from tomorrow the 24th of July, the beginning of the dog-days, we adjourn, to some future period, the conclusion of these pleadings.'

The auditors were thunderstruck. 'What! because the *malaria* renders the air of Rome dangerous at the end of July, and compels the Romans to close their courts, must a trial be broken off on the banks of the Thames, when its conclusion is looked for so impatiently?' The people hoped for a judicial sentence, and they were answered with a jest; it was thus Rome made sport of Christendom. Campeggio, to disarm Henry's wrath, gave utterance to some noble sentiments; but his whole line of conduct raises legitimate doubts as to his sincerity. 'The queen', he said, 'denies the competency of the court; I must therefore make my report to the pope, who is the source of life and honour, and wait his sovereign orders. I have not come so far to please any man, be he king or subject. I am an old man, feeble and sickly, and fear none but the Supreme Judge, before whom I must soon appear. I therefore adjourn this court until the 1st of October.' It was evident that this adjournment was only a formality intended to signify the definitive rejection of Henry's demand.

The king, who from his place of concealment had heard Campeggio's speech, could scarcely control his indignation. He wanted a regular judgment; he clung to forms; he desired that his cause should pass successfully through all the windings of ecclesiastical procedure, and yet here it is wrecked upon the vacations of the Romish court. Henry was silent, however, either from prudence, or because surprise deprived him of the power of speech, and he hastily left the gallery.

Norfolk, Suffolk, and the other courtiers, did not follow him. The king and his ministers, the peers and the people, and even the clergy, were almost unanimous, and yet the pope pronounced his *veto*. He humbled the Defender of the Faith to flatter the author of the sack of Rome. This was too much. The impetuous Suffolk started from his seat, struck his hand violently on the table in front of him, cast a threatening look upon the judges and exclaimed: 'By the Mass, the old saying is confirmed today, that no cardinal has ever brought good to England.' – 'Sir, of all men in this realm', replied Wolsey, 'you have the least cause to disparage cardinals, for if I, poor cardinal, had not been, you would not have a head on your shoulders.' It would seem that Wolsey pacified Henry at the time of the duke's marriage with the Princess Mary. 'I cannot pronounce sentence', continued Wolsey, 'without knowing the good pleasure of His Holiness.' The two dukes and the other noblemen left the hall in anger, and hastened to the palace. The legates, remaining with the officers, looked at each other for a few moments. At last Campeggio, who alone had remained calm during this scene of violence, arose, and the audience dispersed.

Henry did not allow himself to be crushed by this blow. Rome, by her strange proceedings, aroused in him that suspicious and despotic spirit, of which he gave such tragic proofs in after-years. The papacy was making sport of him. Clement and Wolsey tossed his divorce from one to the other like a ball which, now at Rome and now at London, seemed fated to remain perpetually in the air. The king thought he had been long enough the plaything of His Holiness and of the crafty cardinal; his patience was exhausted, and he resolved to show his adversaries that Henry VIII was more than a match for these bishops. We shall find him seizing this favourable opportunity, and giving an unexpected solution to the matter.

Wolsey sorrowfully hung his head; by taking part with the nuncio and the pope, he had signed the warrant of his own destruction. So long as Henry had a single ray of hope, he thought proper still to dissemble with Clement VII; but he might vent all his anger on Wolsey. From the period of the *Roman Vacations* the cardinal was ruined in his master's mind. Wolsey's enemies, seeing his favour decline, hastened to attack him. Suffolk and Norfolk in particular, impatient to get rid of an insolent priest who had so long chafed their pride, told Henry that Wolsey had been continually playing false; they went over all his negotiations month by month and day by day, and drew the most overwhelming conclusions from them. Sir William Kingston and Lord Manners laid before the king one of the cardinal's letters which Sir Francis Bryan had obtained from the papal archives. In it the cardinal desired Clement to spin out the divorce question, and finally to oppose it, seeing (he added) that if

Henry was separated from Catherine, a friend to the reformers would become Queen of England. This letter clearly expressed Wolsey's inmost thoughts: Rome at any price ... and perish England and Henry rather than the popedom! We can imagine the king's anger.

Anne Boleyn's friends were not working alone. There was not a person at court whom Wolsey's haughtiness and tyranny had not offended; no one in the king's council in whom his continual intrigues had not raised serious suspicions. He had, they said, betrayed in France the cause of England; kept up in time of peace and war secret intelligence with madam, mother of Francis I; received great presents from her; oppressed the nation, and trodden under foot the laws of the kingdom. The people called him *Frenchman* and *traitor*, and all England seemed to vie in throwing burning brands at the superb edifice which the pride of this prelate had so laboriously erected.

Wolsey was too clear sighted not to discern the signs of his approaching fall. 'Both the rising and the setting sun [for thus an historian calls Anne Boleyn and Catherine of Aragon] frowned upon him',[2] and the sky, growing darker around him, gave token of the storm that was to overwhelm him. If the cause failed, Wolsey incurred the vengeance of the king; if it succeeded, he would be delivered up to the vengeance of the Boleyns, without speaking of Catherine's, the emperor's, and the pope's. Happy Campeggio! thought the cardinal, he has nothing to fear. If Henry's favour is withdrawn from him, Charles and Clement will make him compensation. But Wolsey lost everything when he lost the king's good graces. Detested by his fellow citizens, despised and hated by all Europe, he saw to whatever side he turned nothing but the just reward of his avarice and falseness. He strove in vain, as on other occasions, to lean on the ambassador of France; Du Bellay was solicited on the other side. 'I am exposed here to such a heavy and continual fire that I am half dead', exclaimed the French ambassador; and the cardinal met with an unusual reserve in his former confidant.

Yet the crisis approached. Like a skilful but affrighted pilot, Wolsey cast his eyes around him to discover a port in which he could take refuge. He could find none but his see of York. He therefore began once more

[2] Thomas Fuller's *Church History of Britain* (1655), v, p. 176.

to complain of the fatigues of power, of the weariness of the diplomatic career, and to extol the sweetness of an episcopal life. On a sudden he felt a great interest about the flock of whom he had never thought before. Those around him shook their heads, well knowing that such a retreat would be to Wolsey the bitterest of disgraces. One single idea supported him; if he fell, it would be because he had clung more to the pope than to the king: he would be the martyr of his faith. – What a faith! what a martyr!

CHAPTER TEN

'Tyndale' Received in a King's Palace

(1529)

While these things were taking place Anne was living at Hever Castle in retirement and sadness. Scruples from time to time still alarmed her conscience. It is true, the king represented to her unceasingly that his salvation and the safety of his people demanded the dissolution of a union condemned by the Divine law, and that what he solicited several popes had granted. Had not Alexander VI annulled, after ten years, the marriage of Ladislaus and Beatrice of Naples? Had not Louis XII, the father of his people, been divorced from Joan of France? Nothing was more common, he said, than to see the divorce of a prince authorized by a pope; the security of the state must be provided for before everything else. Carried away by these arguments and dazzled by the splendour of a throne, Anne Boleyn consented to usurp at Henry's side the rank belonging to another. Yet, if she was imprudent and ambitious, she was feeling and generous, and the misfortunes of a queen whom she respected soon made her reject with terror the idea of taking her place. The fertile pastures of Kent and the gothic halls of Hever Castle were by turns the witnesses of the mental conflicts this young lady experienced. The fear she entertained of seeing the queen again, and the idea that the two cardinals, her enemies, were plotting her ruin, made her adopt the resolution of not returning to court, and she shut herself up in her solitary chamber.

Anne had neither the deep piety of a Bilney, nor the somewhat vague and mystic spirituality observable in Margaret of Valois; it was not feeling which prevailed in her religion, it was knowledge, and a horror of superstition and pharisaism. Her mind required light and activity, and at that time she sought in reading the consolations so necessary to her position.

One day she opened one of the books prohibited in England, which a friend of the reformation had given her: *The Obedience of a Christian Man*. Its author was William Tyndale, that invisible man whom Wolsey's agents were hunting for in Brabant and Germany, and this was a recommendation to Anne. 'If thou believe the promises', she read, 'then God's truth justifieth thee; that is, forgiveth thy sins and sealeth thee with his Holy Spirit. If thou have true faith, so seest thou the exceeding and infinite love and mercy which God hath shown thee freely in Christ: then must thou needs love again: and love cannot but compel thee to work. If when tyrants oppose thee thou hast power to confess, then art thou sure that thou art safe. If thou be fallen from the way of truth, come thereto again and thou art safe. Yea, Christ shall save thee, and the angels of heaven shall rejoice at thy coming.' These words did not change Anne's heart, but she marked with her nail, as was her custom, other passages which struck her more, and which she desired to point out to the king if as she hoped, she was ever to meet him again. She believed that the truth was there, and took a lively interest in those whom Wolsey, Henry, and the pope were at that time persecuting.

Anne was soon dragged from these pious lessons, and launched into the midst of a world full of dangers. Henry, convinced that he had nothing to expect henceforward from Campeggio, neglected those proprieties which he had hitherto observed, and immediately after the adjournment required Anne Boleyn to return to court; he restored her to the place she had formerly occupied, and even surrounded her with increased splendour. Everyone saw that Anne, in the king's mind, was Queen of England; and a powerful party was formed around her, which proposed to accomplish the definitive ruin of the cardinal.

After her return to court, Anne read much less frequently the *Obedience of a Christian Man* and the *Testament of Jesus Christ*. Henry's homage, her friends' intrigues, and the whirl of festivities, bade fair to stifle the thoughts which solitude had aroused in her heart. One day having left Tyndale's book in a window, Miss Gainsford, a fair young gentlewoman attached to her person, took it up and read it. A gentleman of handsome mien, cheerful temper, and extreme mildness, named

George Zouch, also belonging to Anne's household, and betrothed to Miss Gainsford, profiting by the liberty his position gave him, indulged sometimes in 'love tricks'. On one occasion when George desired to have a little talk with her, he was annoyed to find her absorbed by a book of whose contents he knew nothing; and taking advantage of a moment when the young lady had turned away her head, he laughingly snatched it from her. Miss Gainsford ran after Zouch to recover her book; but just at that moment she heard her mistress calling her, and she left George, threatening him with her finger.

As she did not return immediately, George withdrew to his room, and opened the volume; it was the *Obedience of a Christian Man*. He glanced over a few lines, then a few pages, and at last read the book through more than once. He seemed to hear the voice of God. 'I feel the Spirit of God', he said, 'speaking in my heart as he has spoken in the heart of him who wrote the book.' The words which had only made a temporary impression on the preoccupied mind of Anne Boleyn, penetrated to the heart of her equerry and converted him. Miss Gainsford, fearing that Anne would ask for her book, entreated George to restore it to her; but he positively refused, and even the young lady's tears failed to make him give up a volume in which he had found the life of his soul. Becoming more serious, he no longer jested as before; and when Miss Gainsford peremptorily demanded the book, he was, says the chronicler, 'ready to weep himself'.

Zouch, finding in this volume an edification which empty forms and ceremonies could not give, used to carry it with him to the king's chapel. Dr Sampson, the dean, generally officiated; and while the choir chanted the service, George would be absorbed in his book, where he read: 'If when thou seest the celebration of the Sacrament of the Lord's Supper, thou believest in this promise of Christ: *This is my body that is broken for you*, and if thou have this promise fast in thine heart, thou art saved and justified thereby; thou eatest his body and drinkest his blood. If not, so helpeth it thee not, though thou hearest a thousand masses in a day: no more than it should help thee in a dead thirst to behold a bush at a tavern door, if thou knowest not thereby that there was wine within to be sold.' The young man dwelt upon these words: by faith he ate the body and drank the blood of the Son of God. This was what was passing in the palaces of Henry VIII; there were saints in the household of Caesar.

Wolsey, desirous of removing from the court everything that might favour the reformation, had recommended extreme vigilance to Dr Sampson so as to prevent the circulation of the innovating books. Accordingly, one day when George was in the chapel absorbed in his book, the dean, who, even while officiating, had not lost sight of the young man, called him to him after the service and, rudely taking the book from his hands, demanded: 'What is your name, and in whose service are you?' Zouch having replied, the dean withdrew with a very angry look, and carried his prey to the cardinal.

When Miss Gainsford heard of this mishap, her grief was extreme; she trembled at the thought that the *Obedience of a Christian Man* was in Wolsey's hands. Not long after this, Anne having asked for her book, the young lady fell on her knees, confessed all, and begged to be forgiven. Anne uttered not a word of reproach; her quick mind saw immediately the advantage she might derive from this affair. 'Well', said she, 'it shall be the dearest book to them that ever the dean or cardinal took away.'

'The noble lady', as the chronicler styles her, immediately demanded an interview of the king, and on reaching his presence she fell at his feet, and begged his assistance. 'What is the matter, Anne?' said the astonished monarch. She told him what had happened, and Henry promised that the book should not remain in Wolsey's hands.

Anne had scarcely quitted the royal apartments when the cardinal arrived with the famous volume, with the intention of complaining to Henry of certain passages which he knew could not fail to irritate him, and of taking advantage of it even to attack Anne, if the king should be offended. Henry's icy reception closed his mouth; the king confined himself to taking the book, and bowing out the cardinal. This was precisely what Anne had hoped for. She begged the king to read the book, which he promised to do.

And Henry accordingly shut himself up in his chamber, and read the *Obedience of a Christian Man*. There were few works better calculated to enlighten him, and none, after the Bible, that had more influence upon the reformation in England.

Tyndale treated of *obedience*, 'the essential principle', as he terms it, 'of every political or religious community'. He declaimed against the unlawful power of the popes, who usurped the lawful authority of Christ and of his word. He professed political doctrines too favourable doubtless to absolute power, but calculated to show that the reformers were not, as had been asserted, instigators of rebellion. Henry read as follows:

> The king is in the room of God in this world. He that resisteth the king, resisteth God; he that judgeth the king, judgeth God. He is the minister of God to defend thee from a thousand inconveniences; though he be the greatest tyrant in the world, yet is he unto thee a great benefit of God; for it is better to pay the tenth than to lose all, and to suffer wrong of one man than of every man. It is better to have a tyrant as king than a shadow ... for a tyrant, though he do wrong unto the good, yet he punisheth the evil, and makes all men obey, neither suffers any man to exact taxes but himself. A king that is soft as silk is much more grievous unto the realm than a right tyrant. Read the chronicles and thou shalt find it ever so.[1]

These are indeed strange doctrines for *rebels* to hold, thought the king; and he read further:

> Let kings, if they had lever [rather] be Christians in deed than so to be called, give themselves altogether to the wealth [well being] of their realms after the example of Jesus Christ; remembering that the people are God's, and not theirs; yea, are Christ's inheritance, bought with his blood. The most despised person in his realm (if he is a Christian) is equal with him in the kingdom of God and of Christ. Let the king put off all pride, and become a brother to the poorest of his subjects.

We may surmise that these words were less satisfactory to the king. He kept on reading:

> The emperor and kings are nothing nowadays, but even hangmen unto the pope and bishops, to kill whomsoever they condemn, as Pilate was unto the scribes and Pharisees and high bishops to hang Christ.

---

[1] *Tyndale's Works*, edited by Russell, i, p. 212.

This seemed to Henry rather strong language.

> The pope hath received no other authority of Christ than to preach
> God's word. Now, this word should rule only, and not bishops' decrees
> or the pope's pleasure. *In præsentia majoris cessat potestas minoris*: in the
> presence of the greater, the lesser hath no power. The pope, against all
> the doctrine of Christ, which saith, *My kingdom is not of this world*,
> hath usurped the right of the emperor. Kings must make account
> of their doings only to God. No person may be exempt from this
> ordinance of God; neither can the profession of monks and friars, or
> anything that the popes or bishops can lay for themselves, except them
> from the sword of the emperor or king, if they break the laws. For it
> is written (Rom. 13), Let every soul submit himself unto the authority
> of the higher powers.

'What excellent reading!' exclaimed Henry, when he had finished; 'this is truly a book for all kings to read, and for me particularly.'

Captivated by Tyndale's work, the king began to converse with Anne about the church and the pope; and she who had seen Margaret of Valois unassumingly endeavour to instruct Francis I, strove in like manner to enlighten Henry VIII. She did not possess the influence over him she desired; this unhappy prince was, to the very end of his life, opposed to the evangelical reformation; Protestants and Catholics have been equally mistaken when they have regarded him as being favourable to it. 'In a short time', says the annalist quoted by Strype at the end of his narrative, 'the king, by the help of this virtuous lady, had his eyes opened to the truth. He learned to seek after that truth, to advance God's religion and glory, to detest the pope's doctrine, his lies, his pomp, and pride, and to deliver his subjects from the Egyptian darkness and Babylonian bonds that the pope had brought him and his subjects under. Despising the rebellions of his subjects and the rage of so many mighty potentates abroad, he set forward a religious reformation, which, beginning with the triple-crowned head, came down to all the members of the hierarchy.' History has rarely delivered a more erroneous judgment. Henry's eyes were never opened to the truth, and it was not he who made the reformation. It was accomplished first of all by Scripture, and then by the ministry of simple and faithful men baptized of the Holy Ghost.

Yet Tyndale's book and the conduct of the legates had given rise in the king's mind to new thoughts which he sought time to mature. He desired also to conceal his anger from Wolsey and Campeggio, and dissipate his *spleen*, says the historian Collyer; he therefore gave orders to remove the court to the palace of Woodstock. The magnificent park attached to this royal residence, in which was the celebrated bower constructed (it is said) by Henry II to conceal the fair Rosamond, offered all the charms of the promenade, the chase, and solitude.[2] From here he could easily travel to Langley, Grafton, and other country seats. It was not long before the entertainments, horse races, and other rural sports began. The world with its pleasures and its grandeur, were at the bottom the idols of Anne Boleyn's heart; but yet she felt a certain attraction for the new doctrine, which was confounded in her mind with the great cause of all knowledge, perhaps even with her own. More enlightened than the generality of women, she was distinguished by the superiority of her understanding not only over her own sex, but even over many of the gentlemen of the court. While Catherine, a member of the third order of St Francis, indulged in trifling practices, the more intelligent, if not more pious Anne, cared but little for amulets which the friars had blessed, for apparitions, or visions of angels. Woodstock furnished her with an opportunity of curing Henry VIII of the superstitious ideas natural to him. There was a place in the forest said to be haunted by evil spirits; not a priest or a courtier dared approach it. A tradition ran that if a king ventured to cross the boundary, he would fall dead. Anne resolved to take Henry there. Accordingly, one morning she led the way in the direction of the place where these mysterious powers manifested their presence (as it was said) by strange apparitions; they entered the wood; they arrived at the so much dreaded spot; all hesitated; but Anne's calmness reassured her companions; they advanced; they found ... nothing but trees and turf, and, laughing at their former terrors, they explored every corner of this mysterious resort of the evil spirits. Anne returned to the palace, congratulating herself on the triumph Henry had gained over his imaginary fears.

[2] The letters from the king's secretaries Gardiner and Tuke to Wolsey, dated from Woodstock, run from 4 August to 8 September. State Papers, i, pp. 335-47.

CHAPTER ELEVEN

Wolsey Alone and Facing Ruin

(Summer 1529)

W hile the court was thus taking its pleasure at Woodstock, Wolsey remained in London, a prey to the acutest anguish. 'This calling of the case to Rome', wrote he to Gregory da Casale, 'will not only completely alienate the king and his realm from the apostolic see, but will ruin me utterly.' This message had hardly reached the pope, before the imperial ambassadors handed to him the queen's protest, and added in a very significant tone: 'If Your Holiness does not call this cause before you, the emperor, who is determined to bring it to an end, will have recourse to *other arguments*.' The same perplexity always agitated Clement: which of the two must be sacrificed, Henry or Charles? Anthony de Leyva, who commanded the imperial forces, having routed the French army, the pope no longer doubted that Charles was the elect of heaven. It was not Europe alone which acknowledged this prince's authority; a new world had just laid its power and its gold at his feet. The formidable priest-king of the Aztecs had been unable to withstand Cortez; could the priest-king of Rome withstand Charles V? Cortez had returned from Mexico, bringing with him Mexican chiefs in all their barbarous splendour, with thousands of pesos, with gold and silver and emeralds of extraordinary size, with magnificent tissues and birds of brilliant plumage. He had accompanied Charles, who was then going to Italy, to the place of embarkation, and had sent to Clement VII costly gifts of the precious metals, valuable jewels, and a troop of Mexican dancers, buffoons, and jugglers, who charmed the pope and the cardinal above all things.

Clement, even while refusing Henry's prayer, had not as yet granted the emperor's. He thought he could now resist no longer the star of a monarch victorious over two worlds, and hastened to enter into negotiations with him. Sudden terrors still assailed him from time to time: My refusal (he said to himself) may perhaps cause me to lose England. But Charles, holding him in his powerful grasp, compelled him to submit. Henry's antecedents were rather encouraging to the pontiff. How could he imagine that a prince, who alone of all the monarchs of Europe had once contended against the great German reformer, would now separate from the popedom? On 6 July Clement declared to the English envoys that he *avoked to Rome* the cause between Henry VIII and Catherine of Aragon. In other words, this was refusing the divorce. 'There are twenty-three points in this case', said the courtiers, 'and the debate on the first has lasted a year; before the end of the trial, the king will be not only past marrying but past living.'

When he learned that the fatal blow had been struck, Dr William Bennett, one of Henry's envoys, in a tone of sadness exclaimed: 'Alas! Most Holy Father, by this act the church in England will be utterly destroyed; the king declared it to me with tears in his eyes.' – 'Why is it my fortune to live in such evil days?' replied the pope, who, in his turn, began to weep; 'but I am encircled by the emperor's forces, and, if I were to please the king, I should draw a fearful ruin upon myself and upon the church. … God will be my judge.'

On 15 July da Casale sent the fatal news to the English minister. The king was cited before the pope and, in case of refusal, condemned to a fine of 10,000 ducats. On 18 July peace was proclaimed at Rome between the pontiff and the emperor, and on the next day (these dates are important) Clement, wishing still to make one more attempt to ward off the blow with which the papacy was threatened, wrote to Cardinal Wolsey: 'My dear son, how can I describe to you my affliction? Show in this matter the prudence which so distinguishes you, and preserve the king in those kindly feelings which he has ever manifested towards me.' A useless attempt! Far from saving the papacy, Wolsey was to be wrecked along with it.

Wolsey was thunderstruck. At the very time he was assuring Henry of the attachment of Clement and Francis, both were deserting him. The 'politic handling' failed, which the cardinal had thought so skilful, and which had been so tortuous. Henry now had none but enemies on the continent of Europe, and the reformation was daily spreading over his kingdom. Wolsey's anguish cannot be described. His power, his pomp, his palaces were all threatened; who could tell whether he would even preserve his liberty and his life. – A just reward for so much duplicity.

But the king's wrath was to be greater than even the minister's alarm. His terrified servants wondered how they should announce the pontiff's decision. Gardiner, who, after his return from Rome, had been named Secretary of State, went down to Langley, Northamptonshire, on 3 August to communicate it to him. What news for the proud Tudor! The decision on the divorce was forbidden in England; the cause avoked to Rome, there to be buried and unjustly lost; Francis I treating with the emperor; Charles and Clement on the point of exchanging at Bologna the most striking signs of their unchangeable alliance; the services rendered by the king to the popedom repaid with the blackest ingratitude; his hope of giving an heir to the crown disgracefully frustrated; and last, but not least, Henry VIII, the proudest monarch of Christendom, summoned to Rome to appear before an ecclesiastical tribunal – it was too much for Henry. His wrath, a moment restrained, burst forth like a clap of thunder, and all trembled around him. 'Do they presume', he exclaimed, 'to try my cause elsewhere than in my own dominions? I, the King of England, summoned before an Italian tribunal! ... Yes, ... I will go to Rome, but it shall be with such a mighty army that the pope, and his priests, and all Italy shall be struck with terror. – I forbid the letters of citation to be executed', he continued; 'I forbid the commission to consider its functions at an end.' Henry would have desired to tear off Campeggio's purple robes, and throw this prince of the Roman Church into prison, in order to frighten Clement; but the very magnitude of the insult compelled him to restrain himself. He feared above all things to appear humbled in the eyes of England, and he hoped, by showing moderation, to hide the affront he had received. 'Let everything be done', he told Gardiner, 'to conceal from my subjects these letters of citation, which are so hurtful to my glory. Write to Wolsey that I have the greatest confidence in his dexterity, and that he ought, by good handling, to win over Campeggio and the queen's counsellors, and, above all, prevail upon them at any price not to serve these citatory letters on me.' But Henry had hardly given his instructions when the insult of which he had been the object recurred to his imagination; the thought of Clement haunted him night and day, and he swore to exact a striking vengeance from the pontiff. Rome desires to have no more to do with England … England in her turn will cast off Rome. Henry will sacrifice Wolsey, Clement, and the church; nothing shall stop his fury. The crafty pontiff has concealed his game, the king shall beat him openly; and from age to age the popedom shall shed tears over the imprudent folly of a Medici.

Thus after insupportable delays which had fatigued the nation, a thunderbolt fell upon England. Court, clergy, and people, from whom it was impossible to conceal these great events, were deeply stirred, and the whole kingdom was in commotion. Wolsey, still hoping to ward off the ruin impending over both himself and the papacy, immediately put in play all that dexterity which Henry had spoken of; he so far prevailed that the letters citatorial were not served on the king, but only the brief addressed to Wolsey by Clement VII. The cardinal, gratified by this trivial success, and desirous of profiting by it to raise his credit, resolved to accompany Campeggio, who was going down to Grafton to take leave of the king. When the coming of the two legates was heard of at court, the agitation was very great. The dukes of Norfolk and Suffolk regarded this proceeding as the last effort of their enemy, and entreated Henry not to receive him. 'The king will receive him', said some. 'The king will not receive him', answered others. At length one Sunday morning it was announced that the prelates were at the gates of the mansion. Wolsey looked round with an anxious eye for the great officers who were accustomed to introduce him. They appeared, and desired Campeggio to follow them. When the legate had been taken to his apartments, Wolsey waited his turn; but great was his consternation on being informed that there was no chamber appointed for him in the palace. Sir Henry Norris, groom of the stole, offered Wolsey the use of his own room, and the cardinal followed him, almost sinking beneath the humiliation he had undergone. He made ready to appear before the king and, summoning up his courage, proceeded to the presence-chamber.

The lords of the council were standing in a row according to their rank; Wolsey, taking off his hat, passed along saluting each of them with affected civility. A great number of courtiers arrived, impatient to see how Henry would receive his old favourite; and most of them were already exulting in the striking disgrace of which they hoped to be witnesses. At last the king was announced.

Henry stood under the cloth of state; and Wolsey advanced and knelt before him. Deep silence prevailed throughout the chamber. ... To the surprise of all, Henry stooped down and raised him up with both hands. ... Then, with a pleasing smile, he took Wolsey to the window, desired him to put on his hat, and talked familiarly with him. 'Then', says Cavendish, the cardinal's gentleman usher, 'it would have made you smile to behold the countenances of those who had laid wagers that the king would not speak with him.'

But this was the last ray of evening which then lighted up the darkening fortunes of Wolsey: the star of his favour was about to set for ever. ... The silence continued, for everyone desired to catch a few words of the conversation. The king seemed to be accusing Wolsey, and Wolsey to be justifying himself. On a sudden Henry pulled a letter out of his bosom and, showing it to the cardinal, said in a loud voice: 'How can that be? Is not this your hand?' It was no doubt the letter which Bryan had intercepted. Wolsey replied in an undertone, and seemed to have appeased his master. The dinner hour having arrived, the king left the room telling Wolsey that he would not fail to see him again; the courtiers were eager to make their profoundest reverences to the cardinal, but he haughtily traversed the chamber, and the dukes hastened to carry to Anne Boleyn the news of this astonishing reception.

Wolsey, Campeggio, and the lords of the council sat down to dinner. The cardinal, well aware that the terrible letter would be his utter ruin, and that Henry's good graces had no other object than to prepare his fall, began to hint at his retirement. 'Truly', said he with a devout air, 'the king would do well to send his bishops and chaplains home to their cures and benefices.' The company looked at one another with aston-ishment. 'Yea, marry', said the Duke of Norfolk somewhat rudely, 'and so it were meet for you to do also.' – 'I should be very well contented therewith', answered Wolsey, 'if it were the king's pleasure to license me with leave to go to my cure at Winchester.' – 'Nay, to your benefice at York, where your greatest honour and charge is', replied Norfolk, who was not willing that Wolsey should be living so near Henry. – 'Even as it shall please the king', added Wolsey, and changed the subject of conversation.

Henry had caused himself to be announced to Anne Boleyn, who (says Cavendish) 'kept state at Grafton more like a queen than a simple maid'. Professing extreme sensibility, and an ardent imagination, Anne, who felt the slightest insult with all the sensibility of her woman's heart, was very dissatisfied with the king after the report of the dukes. Accordingly, heedless of the presence of the attendants, she said to him: 'Sir, is it not a marvellous thing to see into what great danger the cardinal hath brought you with all your subjects?' – 'How so, sweetheart?' asked Henry. Anne continued: 'Are you ignorant of the hatred his exactions have drawn upon you? There is not a man in your whole realm of England worth one hundred pounds, but he hath made you his debtor.' Anne here alluded to the loan the king had raised among his subjects. 'Well, well', said Henry, who was not pleased with these remarks, 'I know that matter better than you.' – 'If my Lord of Norfolk, my Lord of Suffolk, my uncle, or my father had done much less than the cardinal hath done', continued Anne, 'they would have lost their heads ere this.' – 'Then I perceive', said Henry, 'you are none of his friends.' – 'No, sir, I have no cause, nor any that love you', she replied. The dinner was ended; the king, without appearing at all touched, proceeded to the presence-chamber where Wolsey expected him.

After a long conversation, carried on in a low tone, the king took Wolsey by the hand and led him into his private chamber. The courtiers awaited impatiently the termination of an interview which might decide the fate of England; they walked up and down the gallery, often passing before the door of the chamber, in the hope of catching from Wolsey's looks, when he opened it, the result of this secret conference; but one quarter of an hour followed another, these became hours, and still the cardinal did not appear. Henry, having resolved that this conversation should be the last, was no doubt collecting from his minister all the information necessary to him. But the courtiers imagined he was returning into his master's favour; Norfolk, Suffolk, Wiltshire, and the other enemies of the prime minister, began to grow alarmed, and hastened off to Anne Boleyn, who was their last hope.

It was night when the king and Wolsey quitted the royal chamber; the former appeared gracious, the latter satisfied; it was always Henry's custom to smile on those he intended to sacrifice. 'I shall see you in the morning', he said to the cardinal with a friendly air. Wolsey made a low bow, and, turning round to the courtiers, saw the king's smile reflected on their faces. Wiltshire, Tuke, and even Suffolk, were full of civility. 'Well', thought he, 'the motion of such weathercocks as these shows me from what quarter the wind of favour is blowing.'

But a moment after the wind began to change. Men with torches waited for the cardinal at the gates of the palace to conduct him to the place where he would have to pass the night. Thus he was not to sleep beneath the same roof as Henry. He was to lie at Euston, one of Empson's houses, about three miles off. Wolsey, repressing his vexation, mounted his horse and, after an hour's riding along very bad roads, he reached the lodging assigned him.

He had sat down to supper, to which some of his most intimate friends had been invited, when suddenly Gardiner was announced. Gardiner owed everything to the cardinal, and yet he had not appeared before him since his return from Rome. He comes no doubt to play the hypocrite and the spy, thought Wolsey. But as soon as the secretary entered, Wolsey rose, made him a graceful compliment, and prayed him to take a seat. 'Master Secretary', he asked, 'where have you been since your return from Rome?' – 'I have been following the court from place to place.' – 'You have been hunting, then? Have you any dogs?' asked the cardinal, who knew very well what Gardiner had been doing in the king's chamber. 'A few', replied Gardiner. Wolsey thought that even the secretary was a bloodhound on his track. And yet after supper he took Gardiner aside, and conversed with him until midnight. He thought it prudent to neglect nothing that might clear up his position; and Wolsey sounded Gardiner, just as he himself had been sounded by Henry not long before.

The same night at Grafton the king gave Campeggio a farewell audience, and treated him very kindly, 'by giving him presents and other matters', says Du Bellay. Henry then returned to Anne Boleyn. The dukes had pointed out to her the importance of the present moment; she therefore asked and obtained of Henry, without any great difficulty, his promise never to speak to his minister again. The insults of the papacy had exasperated the King of England, and, as he could not punish Clement, he took his revenge on the cardinal.

The next morning, Wolsey, impatient to have the interview which Henry had promised, rode back early to Grafton. But as he came near, he met a numerous train of servants and packhorses; and shortly afterwards Henry, with Anne Boleyn and many lords and ladies of the court, came riding up. 'What does all this mean?' thought the cardinal in dismay. 'My lord', said the king, as he drew near, 'I cannot stay with you now. You will return to London with Cardinal Campeggio.' Then striking the spurs into his horse, Henry galloped off with a friendly salutation. After him came Anne Boleyn, who rode past Wolsey with head erect, and casting on him a proud look. The court proceeded to Hartwell Park, where Anne had determined to keep the king all day. Wolsey was confounded. There was no room for doubt; his disgrace was certain. His head swam, he remained immovable for an instant, and then recovered himself; but the blow he had received had not been unobserved by the courtiers, and the cardinal's fall became the general topic of conversation.

After dinner, the legates departed, and on the second day reached Moor Park, a mansion built by Archbishop Neville, one of Wolsey's predecessors, who for high treason had been first imprisoned at Calais, and afterwards at Ham. These recollections were by no means agreeable to Wolsey. The next morning the two cardinals separated, Campeggio proceeded to Dover and Wolsey to London.

Campeggio was impatient to get out of England, and great was his annoyance, on reaching Dover, to find that the wind was contrary. But a still greater vexation was in reserve. He had hardly lain down to rest himself, before his door was opened, and a band of sergeants entered the room. The cardinal, who knew what scenes of this kind meant in Italy, thought he was a dead man, and fell trembling at his chaplain's feet begging for absolution. Meantime the officers opened his luggage, broke into his chests, scattered his property about the floor, and even shook out his clothes.

Henry's tranquillity had not been of long duration. 'Campeggio is the bearer of letters from Wolsey to Rome', whispered some of the

courtiers; 'who knows but they contain treasonable matter?' – 'There
is, too, among his papers the famous *decretal* pronouncing the divorce',
said one; 'if we had but that document it would finish the business.'
Another affirmed that Campeggio 'had large treasure with him of my
lord's [Wolsey's] to be conveyed in great tuns to Rome', whither it
was surmised the Cardinal of York would escape to enjoy the fruits of
his treason. 'It is certain', added a third, 'that Campeggio, assisted by
Wolsey, has been able to procure Your Majesty's correspondence with
Anne Boleyn, and is carrying it away with him.' Henry, therefore, sent
a messenger after the nuncio, with orders that his baggage should be
thoroughly searched.

Nothing was found, neither letters, nor bull, nor treasures. The bull
had been destroyed; the treasures Wolsey had never thought of entrusting
to his colleague; and the letters of Anne and Henry, Campeggio had sent
on before by his son Rodolph, and the pope was stretching out his hands
to receive them, proud, like his successors, of the robbery committed by
two of his legates.

Campeggio being reassured, and seeing that he was neither to be
killed nor robbed, made a great noise at this act of violence, and at the
insulting remarks which had given rise to it. 'I will not leave England',
he caused Henry to be informed, 'until I have received satisfaction.'
'My lord forgets that he is legate no longer', replied the king, 'since
the pope has withdrawn his powers; he forgets, besides, that, as Bishop
of Salisbury, he is my subject; as for the remarks against him and the
Cardinal of York, it is a liberty the people of England are accustomed
to take, and which I cannot put down.' Campeggio, anxious to reach
France, was satisfied with these reasons, and soon forgot all his sorrows
at the sumptuous table of Cardinal Duprat.

Wolsey was not so fortunate. He had seen Campeggio go away, and
remained like a wrecked seaman thrown on a desert isle, who has seen
depart the only friends capable of giving him any help. His necromancy
had forewarned him that this would be a fatal year. The angel of the
maid of Kent had said: 'Go to the cardinal and announce his fall,
because he has not done what you have commanded him to do.' Other
voices besides hers made themselves heard: the hatred of the nation,
the contempt of Europe, and, above all, Henry's anger, told him that

his hour was come. It was true the pope said that he would do all in his power to save him; but Clement's good offices would only accelerate his ruin. Du Bellay, whom the people believed to be the cardinal's accomplice, bore witness to the change that had taken place in men's minds. While passing on foot through the streets of the capital, followed by two valets, 'his ears were so filled with coarse jests as he went along', he said, 'that he knew not which way to turn.' – 'The cardinal is utterly undone', he wrote, 'and I see not how he can escape.' The idea occurred to Wolsey, from time to time, to pronounce the divorce himself; but it was too late. He was even told that his life was in danger. Fortune, blind and bald, her foot on the wheel, fled rapidly from him, nor was it in his power to stop her. And this was not all: after him (he thought) there was no one who could uphold the church of the pontiffs in England. The ship of Rome was sailing on a stormy sea among rocks and shoals; Wolsey at the helm looked in vain for a port of refuge; the vessel leaked on every side; it was rapidly sinking, and the cardinal uttered a cry of distress. Alas! he had desired to save Rome, but Rome would not have it so.

CHAPTER TWELVE

To Introduce Thomas Cranmer

(1489–1529)

As Wolsey's star was disappearing in the midst of stormy clouds, another was rising in the sky, to point out the way to save Britain. Men, like stars, appear on the horizon at the command of God.

On his return from Woodstock to Greenwich, Henry stopped full of anxiety at Waltham in Essex. His attendants were lodged in the houses of the neighbourhood. Fox, the almoner, and Secretary Gardiner, were quartered on a gentleman named Cressy, at Waltham Abbey. When supper was announced, Gardiner and Fox were surprised to see an old friend enter the room. It was Thomas Cranmer, a Cambridge doctor of divinity. 'What! is it you?' they said, 'and how came you here?' – 'Our host's wife is my relation', replied Cranmer, 'and as the epidemic is raging at Cambridge, I brought home my friend's sons, who are under my care.' As this new personage is destined to play an important part in the history of the reformation, it may be worth our while to interrupt our narrative, and give a particular account of him.

Cranmer was descended from an ancient family, which came into England, as is generally believed, with the Conqueror. He was born at Aslacton in Nottinghamshire on 2 July 1489, six years after Luther. His early education had been very much neglected; his tutor, an ignorant and severe priest, had taught him little else than patiently to endure severe chastisement – a knowledge destined to be very useful to him in after life. His father was an honest country gentleman, who cared for little besides hunting, racing, and military sports. At this school, the son learnt to ride, to handle the bow and the sword, to fish, and to hawk; and he never entirely neglected these exercises, which he thought essential to his health. Thomas Cranmer was fond of walking, of the charms of nature, and of solitary meditations; and a hill, near his father's mansion, used often to be shown where he was wont to sit, gazing on the fertile country at his feet, fixing his eyes on the distant spires, listening with melancholy pleasure to the chime of the bells, and indulging in sweet contemplations. About 1504, he was sent to Cambridge, where 'barbarism still prevailed', says an historian. His plain, noble, and modest air conciliated the affections of many, and, in 1510 or 1511, he was elected Fellow of Jesus College. Possessing a tender heart, he became attached, at the age of twenty-three, to a young person of good birth (says Foxe) or of inferior rank, as other writers assert. Cranmer was unwilling to imitate the disorderly lives of his fellow students, and, although marriage would necessarily close the career of honours, he married the young lady, known as 'Black Joan', resigned his fellowship (in conformity with the regulations), and took a modest lodging at the Dolphin Inn. He then began to study earnestly the most remarkable writings of the times, polishing, it has been said, his old asperity on the productions of Erasmus, of Lefèvre of Etaples, and other great authors; every day his crude understanding received new brilliancy. He then began to lecture in Buckingham (afterwards Magdalene) College, and thus provided for his wants.

His lessons excited the admiration of enlightened men, and the anger of obscure ones, who disdainfully called him (because of the inn at which he lodged) the *hostler*. 'This name became him well', said Fuller, 'for in his lessons he roughly rubbed the backs of the friars, and famously curried the hides of the lazy priests.' His wife dying a year after his marriage, Cranmer was re-elected Fellow of his old college, and the first writing of Luther's having appeared, he said: 'I must know on which side the truth lies. There is only one infallible source, the Scriptures; in them I will seek for God's truth.' And for three years he constantly studied the holy books, without commentary, without human theology, and hence he gained the name of the *Scripturist*. At last his eyes were opened; he saw the mysterious bond which unites all biblical revelations, and understood the completeness of God's design. Then without forsaking the Scriptures, he studied all kinds of authors. He was a slow reader, but a close observer; he never opened a book without having a pen in his hand. He did not take up with any particular party or age; but possessing a free and philosophic mind, he weighed all opinions in the balance of his judgment, taking the Bible for his standard.

Honours soon came upon him; he was made successively doctor of divinity, professor, university preacher, and examiner. He used to say to the candidates for the ministry: 'Christ sendeth his hearers to the Scriptures, and not to the church.' – 'But', replied the monks, 'they are so difficult.' – 'Explain the obscure passages by those which are clear', rejoined the professor, 'Scripture by Scripture. Seek, pray, *and he who has the key of David* will open them to you.' The monks, affrighted at this task, withdrew bursting with anger; and ere long Cranmer's name was a name of dread in every monastery. Some, however, submitted to the labour, and one of them, Dr Barrett, blessed God that the examiner had turned him back; 'for', said he, 'I found the knowledge of God in the holy book he compelled me to study.' Cranmer toiled at the same work as Latimer, Stafford, and Bilney.

Fox and Gardiner having renewed acquaintance with their old friend at Waltham Abbey, they sat down to table, and both the almoner and the secretary asked the doctor what he thought of the divorce. It was the usual topic of conversation, and not long before, Cranmer had been named member of a commission appointed to give their opinion on this affair. 'You are not in the right path', said Cranmer to his friends; 'you should not cling to the decisions of the church. There is a surer and a shorter way which alone can give peace to the king's conscience.' – 'What is that?' they both asked. – 'The true question is this', replied Cranmer: '*What says the word of God?* If God has declared a marriage of this nature bad, the pope cannot make it *good*. Discontinue these interminable Roman negotiations. When God has spoken man must obey.' – 'But how shall we know what God has said?' – 'Consult the universities; they will discern it more surely than Rome.'

This was a new view. The idea of consulting the universities had been acted upon before; but then their own opinions only had been demanded; now, the question was simply to know *what God says in his word*. 'The word of God is above the church', was the principle laid down by Cranmer, and in that principle consisted the whole of the reformation. The conversation at the supper table of Waltham was destined to be one of those secret springs which an invisible Hand sets in motion for the accomplishment of his great designs. The Cambridge doctor, suddenly transported from his study to the foot of the throne, was on the point of becoming one of the principal instruments of Divine Wisdom.

The day after this conversation, Fox and Gardiner arrived at Greenwich, and the king summoned them into his presence the same evening. 'Well, gentlemen', he said to them, 'our holidays are over; what shall we do now? If we still have recourse to Rome, God knows when we shall see the end of this matter.' – 'It will not be necessary to take so long a journey', said Fox; 'we know a shorter and surer way.' – 'What is it?' asked the king eagerly. – 'Dr Cranmer, whom we met yesterday at Waltham, thinks that the Bible should be the sole judge in your cause.' Gardiner, vexed at his colleague's frankness, desired to claim all the honour of this luminous idea for himself; but Henry did not listen to him. 'Where is Dr Cranmer?' said he, much affected. 'Send, and fetch him immediately. Mother of God! (this was his customary oath) this man has the right sow by the ear. If this had only been suggested to me two years ago, what expense and trouble I should have been spared.'

Cranmer had gone into Nottinghamshire; a messenger followed and brought him back. 'Why have you entangled me in this affair?' he said to Fox and Gardiner. 'Pray make my excuses to the king.' Gardiner, who wished for nothing better, promised to do all he could; but it was of no use. 'I will have no excuses', said Henry. The wily courtier was obliged to make up his mind to introduce the ingenuous and upright man, to whom that station, which he himself had so coveted, was one day to belong. Cranmer and Gardiner went down to Greenwich, both alike dissatisfied.

Cranmer was then forty years of age, with pleasing features, and mild and winning eyes, in which the candour of his soul seemed to be reflected. Sensible to the pains as well as to the pleasures of the heart, he was destined to be more exposed than other men to anxieties and falls; a peaceful life in some remote parsonage would have been more to his taste than the court of Henry VIII. Blessed with a generous mind, unhappily he did not possess the firmness necessary in a public man; a little stone sufficed to make him stumble. His excellent understanding showed him the better way; but his great timidity made him fear the more dangerous. He was rather too fond of relying upon the power of men, and made them unhappy concessions with too great facility. If the king had questioned him, he would never have dared advise so bold a course as that he had pointed out; the advice had slipped from him at table during the intimacy of familiar conversation. Yet he was sincere, and after doing everything to escape from the consequences of his frankness, he was ready to maintain the opinion he had given.

Henry, perceiving Cranmer's timidity, graciously approached him. 'What is your name?' said the king, endeavouring to put him at his ease. 'Did you not meet my secretary and my almoner at Waltham?' And then he added: 'Did you not speak to them of my great affair?' – repeating the words ascribed to Cranmer. The latter could not retreat: 'Sir, it is true, I did say so.' – 'I see', replied the king with animation, 'that you have found the breach through which we must storm the fortress. Now, sir doctor, I beg you, and as you are my subject I command you, to lay aside every other occupation, and to bring my cause to a conclusion in conformity with the ideas you have put forth. All that I desire to know is, whether my marriage is contrary to the laws of God or not. Employ all your skill in investigating the subject, and thus bring comfort to my conscience as well as to the queen's.'

Cranmer was confounded; he recoiled from the idea of deciding an affair on which depended, it might be, the destinies of the nation, and sighed after the lonely fields of Aslacton. But grasped by the vigorous hand of Henry, he was compelled to advance. 'Sir', said he, 'pray entrust this matter to doctors more learned than I am.' – 'I am very willing', answered the king, 'but I desire that you will also give me your opinion in writing.' And then summoning the Earl of Wiltshire to his presence, he said to him: 'My lord, you will receive Dr Cranmer into your house at Durham Place, and let him have all necessary quiet to compose a report for which I have asked him.' After this precise command, which admitted of no refusal, Henry withdrew.

In this manner was Cranmer introduced by the king to Anne Boleyn's father, and not, as some Romanist authors have asserted, by Sir Thomas Boleyn to the king.[1] Wiltshire conducted Cranmer to Durham House

---

[1] *E.g.*, Lingard, vol. vi, chap. iii. Compare Foxe, *Acts*, viii, p. 8.

(now the Adelphi in the Strand) and the pious doctor on whom Henry had imposed these quarters, soon contracted a close friendship with Anne and her father, and took advantage of it to teach them the value of the Divine word, as *the pearl of great price*. Henry, while profiting by the skill of a Wolsey and a Gardiner, paid little regard to the men; but he respected Cranmer, even when opposed to him in opinion, and until his death placed the learned doctor above all his courtiers and all his clerks. The pious man often succeeds better, even with the great ones of this world, than the ambitious and the intriguing.

CHAPTER THIRTEEN

The Dethronement of Cardinal Wolsey

(October 1529)

While Cranmer was rising notwithstanding his humility, Wolsey was falling in despite of his stratagems. The cardinal still governed the kingdom, gave instructions to ambassadors, negotiated with princes, and filled his sumptuous palaces with his haughtiness. The king could not make up his mind to turn him off; the force of habit, the need he had of him, the recollection of the services Henry had received from him, pleaded in his favour. Wolsey without the seals appeared almost as inconceivable as the king without his crown. Yet the fall of one of the most powerful favourites recorded in history was inevitably approaching, and we must now describe it.

On 9 October, after the Michaelmas vacation, Wolsey, desirous of showing a bold face, went and opened the High Court of Chancery with his accustomed pomp; but he noticed, with uneasiness, that none of the king's servants walked before him, as they had been accustomed to do. He presided on the bench with an inexpressible depression of spirits, and the various members of the court sat before him with an absent air; there was something gloomy and solemn in this sitting, as if all were taking part in a funeral: it was destined indeed to be the last act of the cardinal's power. Some days before (Foxe says on 1 October) the dukes of Norfolk and Suffolk, with other lords of the Privy Council, had gone down to Windsor, and denounced to the king Wolsey's unconstitutional relations with the pope, his usurpations, 'his robberies, and the discords sown by his means between Christian princes'. Such motives would not have sufficed; but Henry had stronger. Wolsey had not kept any of his promises in the matter of the divorce; it would even appear that he had advised the pope to excommunicate the king, and thus raise his people against him. This enormity was not at that time known by the prince; it is even probable that it did not take place until later. But Henry knew enough, and he gave his attorney-general, Sir Christopher Hales, orders to prosecute Wolsey.

Whilst the heartbroken cardinal was displaying his authority for the last time in the Court of Chancery, the attorney-general was accusing him in the king's bench for having obtained papal bulls conferring on him a jurisdiction which encroached on the royal power, and calling for the application of the penalties of Præmunire. The two dukes received orders to demand the seals from Wolsey; and the latter, informed of what had taken place, did not quit his palace on the 10th, expecting every moment the arrival of the messengers of the king's anger; but no one appeared.

The next day the two dukes arrived: 'It is the king's good pleasure', said they to the cardinal, who remained seated in his armchair, 'that you give up the broad seal to us and retire to Esher' (a country seat near Hampton Court). Wolsey, whose presence of mind never failed him, demanded to see the commission under which they were acting. 'We have our orders from His Majesty's mouth', said they. – 'That may be sufficient for you', replied the cardinal, 'but not for me. The great seal of England was delivered to me by the hands of my sovereign; I may not deliver it at the simple word of any lord, unless you can show me your commission.' Suffolk broke out into a passion, but Wolsey remained calm, and the two dukes returned to Windsor. This was the cardinal's last triumph.

The rumour of his disgrace created an immense sensation at court, in the city, and among the foreign ambassadors. Du Bellay hastened to York Place (Whitehall) to contemplate this great ruin and console his unhappy friend. He found Wolsey, with dejected countenance and lustreless eyes, 'shrunk to half his wonted size', wrote the ambassador to Montmorency, 'the greatest example of fortune which was ever beheld'. Wolsey desired 'to set forth his case' to him; but his thoughts were confused, his language broken, 'for heart and tongue both failed him entirely'; he burst into tears. The ambassador regarded him with compassion: 'Alas!' thought he, 'his enemies cannot but feel pity for him.' At last the unhappy cardinal recovered his speech, but only to give way to despair. 'I desire no more authority', he exclaimed, 'nor the pope's legation, nor the broad seal of England. ... I am ready to give up everything, even to my shirt. ... I can live in a hermitage, provided the king does not hold me in disgrace.' The ambassador 'did all he could to comfort him', when Wolsey, catching at the plank thrown out to him, exclaimed: 'Would that the King of France and madam might pray the king to moderate his anger against me. But above all', he added in alarm, 'take care the king never knows that I have solicited this of you.' Du Bellay wrote indeed to France that the king and madam alone could 'withdraw their affectionate servant from the gates of hell', and Wolsey being informed of these despatches, his hopes recovered a little. But this bright gleam did not last long.

On Sunday, 17 October, Norfolk and Suffolk reappeared at Whitehall, accompanied by Fitzwilliam, Taylor, and Gardiner, Wolsey's former dependant. It was six in the evening; they found the cardinal in an upper chamber, near the great gallery, and presented the king's orders to him. Having read them he said: 'I am happy to obey His Majesty's commands'; then having ordered the great seal to be brought him, he took it out of the white leather case in which he kept it, and handed it to the dukes, who placed it in a box, covered with crimson velvet, and ornamented with the arms of England, ordered Gardiner to seal it up with red wax, and gave it to Taylor to convey to the king.

Wolsey was thunderstruck; he was to drink the bitter cup even to the dregs: he was ordered to leave his palace forthwith, taking with him neither clothes, linen, nor plate; the dukes had feared that he would convey away his treasures. Wolsey comprehended the greatness of his misery; he found strength however to say: 'Since it is the king's good pleasure to take my house and all it contains, I am content to retire to Esher.' The dukes left him.

Wolsey remained alone. This astonishing man, who had risen from a butcher's shop to the summit of earthly greatness – who, for a word that displeased him, sent his master's most faithful servants (Pace for instance) to the Tower – and who had governed England as if he had been its monarch, and even more, for he had governed without a Parliament, was driven out, and thrown, as it were, upon a dunghill.

A sudden hope flashed like lightning through his mind; perhaps the magnificence of the spoils would appease Henry. Was not Esau pacified by Jacob's present? Wolsey summoned his officers: 'Set tables in the great gallery', he said to them, 'and place on them all I have entrusted to your care, in order to render me an account.' These orders were executed immediately. The tables were covered with an immense quantity of rich stuffs, silks and velvets of all colours, costly furs, rich copes, and other ecclesiastical vestures; the walls were hung with cloth of gold and silver, and webs of a valuable stuff named baudykin, from the looms of Damascus, and with tapestry, representing scriptural subjects or stories from the old romances of chivalry. The gilt chamber and the council chamber, adjoining the gallery, were both filled with plate, in which the gold and silver were set with pearls and precious stones: these articles of luxury were so abundant that basketfuls of costly plate which had fallen out of fashion were stowed away under the tables. On every table was an exact list of the treasures with which it was loaded, for the most perfect order and regularity prevailed in the cardinal's household. Wolsey cast a glance of hope upon this wealth, and ordered his officers to deliver the whole to His Majesty.

He then prepared to leave his magnificent palace. That moment of itself so sad, was made sadder still by an act of affectionate indiscretion. 'Ah, my lord', said his treasurer, Sir William Gascoigne, moved even to tears, 'Your Grace will be sent to the Tower.' This was too much for Wolsey: to go and join his victims! ... He grew angry, and exclaimed: 'Is this the best comfort you can give your master in adversity? I would have you and all such blasphemous reporters know that it is untrue.'

It was necessary to depart; he put round his neck a chain of gold, from which hung a pretended relic of the true cross; this was all he took. 'Would to God', he exclaimed, as he placed it on, 'that I had never had any other.' This he said alluding to the legate's cross which used to be carried before him with so much pomp. He descended the back stairs, followed by his servants, some silent and dejected, others weeping bitterly, and proceeded to the river's brink, where a barge awaited him. But, alas! it was not alone. The Thames was covered with innumerable boats full of men and women. The inhabitants of London, expecting to see the cardinal led to the Tower, desired to be present at his humiliation, and prepared to accompany him. Cries of joy hailing his fall were heard from every side; nor were the cruellest sarcasms wanting. 'The butcher's dog will bite no more', said some; 'look, how he hangs his head.' In truth, the unhappy man, distressed by a sight so new to him, lowered those eyes which were once so proud, but now were filled with bitter tears. This man, who had made all England tremble, was then like a withered leaf carried along the stream. All his servants were moved; even his fool, William Patch, sobbed like the rest. 'O, wavering and newfangled multitude!' exclaimed Cavendish, his gentleman usher. The hopes of the citizens were disappointed; the barge, instead of descending the river, proceeded upwards in the direction of Hampton Court; gradually the shouts died away, and the flotilla dispersed.

The silence of the river permitted Wolsey to indulge in less bitter thoughts; but it seemed as if invisible furies were pursuing him, now that the people had left him. He left his barge at Putney and, mounting his mule, though with difficulty, proceeded slowly with downcast looks. Shortly after, upon lifting his eyes, he saw a horseman riding rapidly down the hill towards them. 'Whom do you think it can be?' he asked of his attendants. 'My lord', replied one of them, 'I think it is Sir Henry Norris.' A flash of joy passed through Wolsey's heart. Was it not Norris, who, of all the king's officers, had shown him the most respect during his visit to Grafton? Norris came up with them, saluted him respectfully, and said: 'The king bids me declare that he still entertains the same kindly feelings towards you, and sends you this ring as a token of his confidence.' Wolsey received it with a trembling hand: it was that which the king was in the habit of sending on important occasions. The cardinal immediately alighted from his mule and, kneeling down in the road, raised his hands to heaven with an indescribable expression of happiness. The fallen man would have pulled off his velvet under-cap, but unable to undo the strings, he broke them, and threw it on the ground. He remained on his knees bareheaded praying fervently amidst profound silence. God's forgiveness had never caused Wolsey so much pleasure as Henry's.

Having finished his prayer, the cardinal put on his cap, and remounted his mule. 'Gentle Norris', said he to the king's messenger, 'if I were lord of a kingdom, the half of it would scarcely be enough to reward you for your happy tidings; but I have nothing left except the clothes on my back.' Then taking off his gold chain: 'Take this', he said, 'it contains a piece of the true cross. In my happier days I would not have parted with it for a thousand pounds.' The cardinal and Norris separated: but Wolsey soon stopped, and the whole troop halted on the heath. The thought troubled him greatly that he had nothing to send to the king; he called Norris back, and looking round saw mounted on a sorry horse poor William Patch, who had lost all his gaiety since his master's misfortune. 'Present this poor jester to the king from me', said Wolsey to Norris; 'his buffooneries are a pleasure fit for a prince; he is worth a thousand pounds.'

At last they reached Esher. What a residence compared with Whitehall! It was little more than four bare walls. The most urgent necessaries were procured from the neighbouring houses, but Wolsey could not adapt himself to this cruel contrast. Besides, he knew Henry VIII; he knew that he might send Norris one day with a gold ring, and the executioner the next with a rope. Gloomy and dejected, he remained seated in his lonely apartments. On a sudden he would rise from his seat, walk hurriedly up and down, speak aloud to himself and then, falling back in his chair, he would weep like a child. This man who formerly had shaken kingdoms, had been brought into desolation as in a moment, and was now atoning for his perfidies in humiliation and terror – a striking example of God's judgment.

CHAPTER FOURTEEN

New Leaders and a New Policy

(October & November 1529)

D
uring all this time everybody was in commotion at court.
Norfolk and Suffolk, at the head of the council, had informed
the Star Chamber of the cardinal's disgrace. Henry knew not
how to supply his place. Some suggested the Archbishop of Canterbury;
the king would not hear of him. 'Wolsey', says a French writer, 'had
disgusted the king and all England with those subjects of two masters
who, almost always, sold one to the other. They preferred a lay minister.'
– 'I verily believe the priests will never more obtain it', wrote Du Bellay.
The name of Sir Thomas More was pronounced. He was a layman, and
that quality, which a few years before would, perhaps, have excluded
him, was now a recommendation. A breath of Protestantism wafted
to the summit of honours one of its greatest enemies. Henry thought
that More, placed between the pope and his sovereign, would decide
in favour of the interests of the throne, and of the independence of
England. His choice was made.

More knew that the cardinal had been thrown aside because he was
not a sufficiently docile instrument in the matter of the divorce. The
work required of him was contrary to his convictions; but the honour
conferred on him was almost unprecedented – seldom indeed had the
seals been entrusted to a mere knight.[1] He followed the path of ambition
and not of duty; he showed, however, in after-days that his ambition
was of no common sort. It is even probable that, foreseeing the dangers
which threatened to destroy the papal power in England, More wished

---

[1] It has been often asserted that Sir Thomas More was the first layman to whom
the office of chancellor was entrusted. This is incorrect, for several laymen were
appointed to the office between 1371 and 1386.

to make an effort to save it. Norfolk installed the new chancellor in the Star Chamber.

'His Majesty', said the duke, 'has not cast his eyes upon the nobility of the blood, but on the worth of the person. He desires to show by this choice that there are among the laity and gentlemen of England, men worthy to fill the highest offices in the kingdom, to which, until this hour, bishops and noblemen alone think they have a right.'[2] The reformation which restored religion to the general body of the church, took away at the same time political power from the clergy. The priests had deprived the people of Christian activity, and the governments of power; the gospel restored to both what the priests had usurped. This result could not but be favourable to the interests of religion; the less cause kings and their subjects have to fear the intrusion of clerical power into the affairs of the world, the more will they yield themselves to the vivifying influence of faith.

More lost no time; never had Lord Chancellor displayed such activity. He rapidly cleared off the cases which were in arrear, and having been installed on 26 October he called on Wolsey's cause on the 28th or 29th. 'The crown of England', said the attorney-general, 'has never acknowledged any superior but God.[3] Now, the said Thomas Wolsey, legate *a latere*, has obtained from the pope certain bulls, by virtue of which he has exercised since 28 August 1523 an authority derogatory to His Majesty's power, and to the rights of his courts of justice. The crown of England cannot be put under the pope; and we therefore accuse the said legate of having incurred the penalties of Præmunire.'

There can be no doubt that Henry had other reasons for Wolsey's disgrace than those pointed out by the attorney-general; but England had convictions of a higher nature than her sovereign's. Wolsey was regarded as the pope's accomplice, and this was the cause of the great severity of the public officer and of the people. The cardinal is generally excused by alleging that both king and Parliament had ratified the unconstitutional authority with which Rome had invested him; but

[2] *More's Life*, p. 172.

[3] The crown of England, free at all times, has been in no earthly subjection, but immediately subject to God in all things. Herbert of Cherbury, p. 251.

had not the powers conferred on him by the pope produced unjusti-
fiable results in a constitutional monarchy? Wolsey, as papal legate, had
governed England without a Parliament; and, as if the nation had gone
back to the reign of John, he had substituted *de facto*, if not in theory,
the monstrous system of the famous bull *Unam Sanctam*[4] for the institution of *Magna Charta*. The king, and even the lords and commons,
had connived in vain at these illegalities; the rights of the constitution
of England remained not the less inviolable, and the best of the people
had protested against their infringement. And hence it was that Wolsey,
conscious of his crime, 'put himself wholly to the mercy and grace of
the king', and his counsel declared his ignorance of the statutes he was
said to have infringed. We cannot here allege, as some have done, the
prostration of Wolsey's moral powers; he could, even after his fall, reply
with energy to Henry VIII. When, for instance, the king sent to demand
for the Crown his palace of Whitehall, which belonged to the see of
York, the cardinal answered: 'Show His Majesty from me that I must
desire him to call to his most gracious remembrance that there is both a
heaven and a hell'; and when other charges besides those of complicity
with the papal aggression were brought against him, he defended himself
courageously, as will be afterwards seen. If therefore the cardinal did not
attempt to justify himself for infringing the rights of the Crown, it was
because his conscience bade him be silent. He had committed one of the
gravest faults of which a statesman can be guilty. Those who have sought
to excuse him have not sufficiently borne in mind that, since the Great
Charter, opposition to Romish aggression has always characterized the
constitution and government of England. Wolsey perfectly recollected
this; and this explanation is more honourable to him than that which
ascribes his silence to weakness or to cunning.

The cardinal was pronounced guilty, and the court passed judgment
that by the Statute of Præmunire his property was forfeited, and that
he might be taken before the king in council. England, by sacrificing
a churchman who had placed himself above kings, gave a memorable

[4] This famous bull, issued by Pope Boniface VIII in 1302, declared that the 'temporal
sword' and the 'spiritual sword' were alike committed to the church, implying that
the pope had supreme power in state as well as in church.

example of her inflexible opposition to the encroachments of the papacy. Wolsey was confounded, and his troubled imagination conjured up nothing but perils on every side.

While More was lending himself to the condemnation of his predecessor, whose friend he had been, another layman of still humbler origin was preparing to defend the cardinal, and by that very act to become the appointed instrument to throw down the monasteries in England, and to shatter the secular bonds which united this country to the Roman pontiff.

On 1 November, two days after Wolsey's condemnation, Thomas Cromwell, one of his officers, with a prayer-book in his hand, was leaning against the window in the great hall, apparently absorbed in his devotions. 'Good-morrow', said Cavendish as he passed him, on his way to the cardinal for his usual morning duties. The person thus addressed raised his head, and the gentleman-usher, seeing that his eyes were filled with tears, asked him: 'Master Cromwell, is my lord in any danger?' – 'I think not', replied Cromwell, 'but it is hard to lose in a moment the labour of a life.' In his master's fall Cromwell foreboded his own. Cavendish endeavoured to console him. 'God willing, this is my resolution', replied Wolsey's ambitious solicitor; 'I intend this afternoon, as soon as my lord has dined, to ride to London, and so go to court, where I will either make or mar before I come back again.' At this moment Cavendish was summoned, and he entered the cardinal's chamber.

Cromwell, devoured by ambition, had clung to Wolsey's robe in order to attain power. He had served under the cardinal for about nine years, and had conducted most of his legal business. But Wolsey had fallen, and the solicitor, dragged along with him, strove to reach by other means the object of his desires. Cromwell was one of those earnest and vigorous men whom God prepares for critical times. Blessed with a solid judgment and intrepid firmness, he possessed a quality rare in every age, and particularly under Henry VIII – fidelity in misfortune. The ability by which he was distinguished was not at all times without reproach: success seems to have been his first thought.

After dinner Cromwell followed Wolsey into his private room: 'My lord, permit me to go to London, I will endeavour to save you.' A gleam passed over the cardinal's saddened features – 'Leave the room', he said to his attendants. He then had a long private conversation with Cromwell, at the end of which the latter mounted his horse and set out for the capital. He did not hide from himself that it would be difficult to procure access to the king, for certain ecclesiastics, jealous of Wolsey, had spoken against his solicitor at the time of the secularization of the monasteries, and Henry could not endure him. But Cromwell knew that fortune favours the bold, and, carried away by his ambitious dreams, he galloped on, saying to himself: 'One foot in the stirrup, and my fortune is made!'

It appears to have been through the good offices of Sir Christopher Hales, master of the rolls, that the name of Cromwell was commended to the king. Probably Henry was, at the outset, strongly prejudiced against him. Was he not Wolsey's chief assistant? But other considerations prevailed, and ere long an interview given by the king to Cromwell convinced him that the secretary-lawyer was a man after his own heart.

'Sir', said Cromwell to His Majesty, 'the pope refuses your divorce. … But why do you ask his consent? Every Englishman is master in his own house, and why should not you be so in England? Ought a foreign prelate to share your power with you? It is true, the bishops make oath to Your Majesty, but they make another to the pope immediately after, which absolves them from the former. Sir, you are but half a king, and we are but half your subjects. This kingdom is a two-headed monster. Will you bear with such an anomaly any longer? What! are you not living in an age when Frederick the Wise and other German princes have thrown off the yoke of Rome? Do likewise; become once more a king; govern your kingdom in concert with your lords and commons. Henceforward let Englishmen alone have anything to say in England; let not your subjects' money be cast any more into the yawning gulf of the Tiber; instead of imposing new taxes on the nation, convert to the general good those treasures which have hitherto only served to fatten proud priests and lazy friars. Now is the moment for action. Rely upon your Parliament; proclaim yourself the head of the church in England. Then shall you see an increase of glory to your name, and of prosperity to your people.'

Never before had such language been addressed to a King of England. It was not only on account of the divorce that it was necessary to break with Rome; it was, in Cromwell's view, on account of the independence, glory, and prosperity of the monarchy. These considerations appeared more important to Henry than those which had hitherto been laid before him; none of the kings of England had been so well placed as he was to understand them. When a Tudor had succeeded to the Saxon, Norman, and Plantagenet kings, a man of the free race of the Celts had taken on the throne of England the place of princes submissive to the Roman pontiffs. The ancient British Church, independent of the papacy, was about to rise again with this new dynasty, and the Celtic race, after eleven centuries of humiliation, to recover its ancient heritage. Undoubtedly, Henry had no recollections of this kind; but he worked in conformity with the peculiar character of his race, without being aware of the instinct which compelled him to act. He felt that a sovereign who submits to the pope becomes, like King John, his vassal; and now, after having been the second in his realm, he desired to be the first.

The king reflected on what Cromwell had said. Astonished and surprised, he sought to understand the new position which his bold adviser had made for him. 'Your proposal pleases me much', he said; 'but can you prove what you assert?' – 'Certainly', replied this able politician; 'I have with me a copy of the oath the bishops make to the Roman pontiff.' With these words he drew a paper from his pocket, and placed the oath before the king's eyes. Henry, jealous of his authority even to despotism, was filled with indignation, and felt the necessity of bringing down that foreign authority which dared dispute the power with him, even in his own kingdom. He drew off his ring and gave it to Cromwell, declaring that he took him into his service, and soon after made him a member of his Privy Council. England, we may say, was now virtually emancipated from the papacy.

Cromwell had laid the first foundations of his greatness. He had observed the path his master had followed, and which had led to his ruin – complicity with the pope; and he hoped to succeed by following the contrary course, namely, by opposing the papacy. He had the king's support, but he wanted more. Possessing a clear and easy style of eloquence, he saw what influence a seat in the great council of the nation would give him. It was somewhat late, for the session began on the next day (3 November) but to Cromwell nothing was impossible. The son of his friend, Sir Thomas Rush, had been returned to Parliament; but the young member vacated his seat, and Cromwell was elected in his place.

Parliament had not met for seven years, the kingdom having been governed by a prince of the Roman Church. The reformation of the church, whose regenerating influence began to be felt already, was about to restore to the nation those ancient liberties of which a cardinal had robbed it; and Henry, being on the point of taking very important resolutions, felt the necessity of drawing nearer to his people. Everything betokened that a good feeling would prevail between the Parliament and the Crown, and that 'the priests would have a terrible fright.'

While Henry was preparing to attack the Roman Church in the papal supremacy, the commons were getting ready to war against the numerous abuses with which it had covered England. 'Some even thought', says Tyndale, 'that this assembly would reform the church, and that the golden age would come again.' But it was not from acts of Parliament that the reformation was destined to proceed, but solely from the word of God. And yet the commons, without touching upon doctrine, were going to do their duty manfully in things within their province, and the Parliament of 1529 may be regarded as the first Protestant Parliament of England. 'The bishops require excessive fines for the probates of wills', said Tyndale's old friend, Sir Henry Guildford. 'As testamentary executor to Sir William Compton I had to pay a thousand marks sterling.' – 'The spiritual men', said another member, 'would rather see the poor orphans die of hunger than give them even the lean cow, the only thing their father left them.' – 'Priests', said another, 'have farms, tanneries, and warehouses, all over the country. In short, the clerks take everything from their flocks, and not only give them nothing, but even deny them the word of God.'

The clergy were in utter consternation. The power of the nation seemed to awaken in this Parliament for the sole purpose of attacking the power of the priest. It was important to ward off these blows. The convocation of the province of Canterbury, assembling at Westminster on 5 November, thought it their duty, in self-defence, to reform the most crying abuses. It was therefore decreed, on 12 November, that the priests should no longer keep shops or taverns, play at dice or other forbidden games, pass the night in suspected places, be present at disreputable shows, go about with sporting dogs, or with hawks, falcons, or other birds of prey, on their fist; or, finally, hold suspicious intercourse with women. Penalties were denounced against these various disorders; they were doubled in case of adultery; and still further increased in the case of more abominable impurities. Such were the laws rendered necessary by the manners of the clergy.

These measures did not satisfy the commons. Three bills were introduced having reference to the fees on the probate of wills, mortuaries, pluralities, non-residence, and the exercise of secular professions. 'The destruction of the church is aimed at', exclaimed Bishop Fisher, when these bills were carried to the lords, 'and if the church falls, the glory of the kingdom will perish. Lutheranism is making great progress amongst us, and the savage cry that has already echoed in Bohemia, *Down with the church*, is now uttered by the commons. ... How does that come about? Solely from want of faith. – My lords, save your country! save the church!' Sir Thomas Audley, the Speaker of the House of Commons, with a deputation of thirty members, immediately went to Whitehall. 'Sir', they said to the king, 'we are accused of being without faith, and of being almost as bad as the Turks. We demand an apology for such offensive language.' Fisher pretended that he only meant to speak of the Bohemians; and the commons, by no means satisfied, zealously went on with their reforms.

These the king was resolved to concede; but he determined to take advantage of them to present a bill making over to him all the money borrowed of his subjects. John Petit, one of the members for the city, boldly opposed this demand. 'I do not know other persons' affairs', he said, 'and I cannot give what does not belong to me. But as regards myself personally, I give without reserve all that I have lent the king.' The royal bill passed, and the satisfied Henry gave his consent to the bills of the commons. Every dispensation coming from Rome, which might be contrary to the statutes, was strictly forbidden. The bishops exclaimed that the commons were becoming schismatical; disturbances were excited by certain priests; but the clerical agitators were punished, and the people, when they heard of it, were delighted beyond measure.

CHAPTER FIFTEEN

'They that Will Live Godly in Christ Jesus...'

(1529–1531)

The moment when Henry aimed his first blows at Rome was also that in which he began to shed the blood of the disciples of the gospel. Although ready to throw off the authority of the pope, he would not recognize the authority of Christ: obedience to the Scriptures is, however, the very soul of the reformation.

The king's contest with Rome had filled the friends of Scripture with hope. The artisans and tradesmen, particularly those who lived near the sea, were almost wholly won over to the gospel. 'The king is one of us', they used to boast; 'he wishes his subjects to read the New Testament. Our faith, which is the true one, will circulate through the kingdom, and by Michaelmas next those who believe as we do will be more numerous than those of a contrary opinion. We are ready, if needs be, to die in the struggle.' This was indeed to be the fate of many.

Language such as this aroused the clergy: 'The last hour has come', said John Stokesley, who had been raised to the see of London after Tunstall's translation to Durham; 'if we would not have Luther's heresy pervade the whole of England, we must hasten to throw it in the sea.' Henry was fully disposed to do so; but, as he was not on very good terms with the clergy, a man was wanted to serve as mediator between him and the bishops. He was soon found.

Sir Thomas More's noble understanding was then passing from ascetic practices to fanaticism, and the humanist turning into an inquisitor. In his opinion, the burning of heretics was just and necessary.[1] He has even been reproached with binding evangelical Christians to a tree in

---

[1] More's *Works, A Dialogue Concerning Heresies*, p. 274.

his garden, which he called 'the tree of truth', and with having flogged them with his own hand.[2] More has declared that he never gave 'stripe nor stroke, nor so much as a fillip on the forehead', to any of his religious adversaries;[3] and we willingly credit his denial. All must be pleased to think that if the author of the *Utopia* was a severe judge, the hand which held one of the most famous pens of the sixteenth century never discharged the duties of an executioner.

The bishops led the attack. 'We must clear the Lord's field of the thorns which choke it', said the Archbishop of Canterbury to convocation on 29 November 1529; immediately after which the Bishop of Bath read to his colleagues the list of books that he desired to have condemned. There were a number of works by Tyndale, Luther, Melanchthon, Zwingli, Œcolampadius, Pomeranus, Brentius, Bucer, Jonas, Francis Lambert, Fryth, and Fish. The Bible in particular was set down. 'It is impossible to translate the Scripture into English', said one of the prelates. – 'It is not lawful for the laity to read it in their mother-tongue', said another. – 'If you tolerate the Bible', added a third, 'you will make us all heretics.' – 'By circulating the Scriptures', exclaimed several, 'you will raise up the nation against the king.' Sir Thomas More laid the bishops' petition before the king, and, some time after, Henry gave orders by proclamation, that 'no one should preach, or write any book, or keep any school without his bishop's licence – that no one should keep any heretical book in his house – that the bishops should detain the offenders in prison at their discretion, and then proceed to the punishment of the guilty – and, finally, that the chancellor, the justices of the peace, and other magistrates, should aid and assist the bishops.' Such was the cruel proclamation of Henry VIII, 'the *father* of the English reformation'.

The clergy were not yet satisfied. The blind and octogenarian Bishop of Norwich, being more ardent than the youngest of his priests, recommenced his complaints. 'My diocese is *accumbered* with such as read the Bible', said he to the Archbishop of Canterbury, 'and there is not a clerk from Cambridge but *savoureth of the frying pan*. If this continues any

---

[2] Strype's *Mem.*, i, p. 315; Foxe, iv, p. 698.
[3] *Apology*, ch. xxxvi, pp. 901-2.

time, they will undo us all. We must have greater authority to punish them than we have.'

Consequently, on 24 May 1530, More, Warham, Tunstall, and Gardiner having been admitted into St Edward's chamber at Westminster to make a report to the king concerning heresy, they proposed forbidding, in the most positive manner, the New Testament and certain other books in which the following doctrines were taught: 'That Christ has shed his blood for our iniquities, as a sacrifice to the Father. – Faith only doth justify us. – Faith without good works is no little or weak faith, it is no faith. – Labouring in good works to come to heaven, thou dost shame Christ's blood.'

Whilst nearly everyone in the audience chamber supported the prayer of the petition, there were three or four doctors who kept silence. At last one of them – it was Latimer – opposed the proposition. Bilney's friend was more decided than ever to listen to no other voice than God's. 'Christ's sheep hear no man's voice but Christ's', he answered Dr Redman, who had called upon him to submit to the church; 'trouble me no more from the talking with the Lord my God.'[4] The church, in Latimer's opinion, presumed to set up its own voice in the place of Christ's, and the reformation did the contrary; this was his abridgement of the controversy. Being called upon to preach during Christmas-tide, he had censured his hearers because they celebrated that festival by playing at cards, like mere worldlings, and then proceeded to lay before their eyes Christ's *cards*, that is to say, his laws.[5] Being placed on the Cambridge commission to examine into the question of the king's marriage, he had won the esteem of Henry's deputy, Dr Butts, the court physician, who had presented him to his master, by whose orders he preached at Windsor.

Henry felt disposed at first to yield something to Latimer. 'Many of my subjects', said he to the prelates assembled in St Edward's hall, 'think that it is my duty to cause the Scriptures to be translated and given to the people.' The discussion immediately began between the two parties; and Latimer concluded by asking 'that the Bible should be permitted to

[4] Latimer's *Remains*, p. 297.
[5] Latimer's *Sermons*, p. 8.

circulate freely in English'. – 'But the most part overcame the better', he tells us.[6] Henry declared that the teaching of the priests was sufficient for the people, and was content to add, 'that he would give the Bible to his subjects when they renounced the arrogant pretension of interpreting it according to their own fancies'. – 'Shun these books', cried the priests from the pulpit, 'detest them, keep them not in your hands, deliver them up to your superiors. Or, if you do not, your prince, who has received from God the sword of justice, will use it to punish you.' Rome had every reason to be satisfied with Henry VIII. Tunstall, who still kept under lock and key the Testaments purchased at Antwerp through Packington's assistance, had them carried to St Paul's churchyard, where they were publicly burnt. The spectators retired shaking their heads, and saying: 'The teaching of the priests and of the Scriptures must be in contradiction to each other, since the priests destroy them.' Latimer did more: 'You have promised us the word of God', he wrote courageously to the king; 'perform your promise now rather than tomorrow! God will have the faith defended, not by man or man's power, but by his word only, by the which He hath evermore defended it, and that by a way far above man's power or reason, as all the stories of the Bible make mention. … The day is at hand when you shall give an account of your office, and of the blood that hath been shed with your sword.'[7] Latimer well knew that by such language he hazarded his life; but that he was ready to sacrifice, as he tells us himself.

Persecution soon came. Just as the sun appeared to be rising on the reformation, the storm burst forth. 'There was not a stone the bishops left unremoved', says the chronicler, 'any corner unsearched, for the diligent execution of the king's proclamation; whereupon ensued a grievous persecution and slaughter of the faithful.'

Thomas Hitton, a poor and pious minister of Kent, used to go frequently to Antwerp to purchase New Testaments. As he was returning from one of these expeditions, in 1529, Fisher, Bishop of Rochester, caused him to be arrested at Gravesend, and put him to the most cruel tortures, to make him deny his faith. But the martyr repeated with holy

---

[6] Latimer's *Remains*, p. 305.

[7] Latimer's *Remains*, pp. 297–309: *A letter written to the King for restoring again the liberty of reading the holy Scriptures*, 1 Dec. 1530.

enthusiasm: 'Salvation cometh by faith and not by works, and Christ giveth it to whomsoever he willeth.' On 10 February 1530, in Maidstone, he was tied to the stake and there burnt to death.

Scarcely were Hitton's sufferings ended for bringing the Scriptures into England, when a vessel laden with New Testaments arrived at Colchester. The indefatigable Richard Bayfield, who accompanied these books, sold them in London, went back to the Continent, and returned to England in November; but this time the Scriptures fell into the hands of Sir Thomas More. Bayfield, undismayed, again visited the Low Countries, and soon reappeared, bringing with him the New Testament and the works of almost all the reformers. 'How cometh it that there are so many New Testaments from abroad?' asked Tunstall of Packington; 'you promised me that you would buy them all.' – 'They have printed more since', replied the wily merchant; 'and it will never be better so long as they have letters and stamps [type and dies]. My lord, you had better buy the stamps too, and so you shall be sure.'

Instead of the stamps, the priests sought after Bayfield. The Bishop of London could not endure this godly man. Having one day asked Bainham (who afterwards suffered martyrdom) whether he knew *a single individual* who, since the days of the apostles, had lived according to the true faith in Jesus Christ, the latter answered: 'Yes, I know Bayfield.' Being tracked from place to place, he fled from the house of his pious hostess, and hid himself at the binder's, where he was discovered, and thrown into the Lollards' Tower.

As he entered the prison, Bayfield noticed a priest named Patmore, pale, weakened by suffering, and ready to sink under the ill-treatment of his jailers. Patmore, won over by Bayfield's piety, soon opened his heart to him. When rector of Much Hadham, in Hertfordshire, he had found the truth in Wycliffe's writings. 'They have burnt his bones', he said, 'but from his ashes have burst forth a well-spring of life.' Delighting in good works, he used to fill his granaries with wheat and, when the markets were high, he would send his corn to them in such abundance as to bring down the prices. 'It is contrary to the law of God to burn heretics', he said; and, growing bolder, he added: 'I care no more for the pope's curse than for a bundle of hay.'

His curate, Simon Smith, unwilling to imitate the disorderly lives of the priests, and finding Joan Bennore, the rector's servant, to be a discreet and pious person, desired to marry her. 'God', said Patmore, 'has declared marriage lawful *for all men*; and accordingly it is permitted to the priests in foreign parts.' The rector alluded to Wittenberg, where he had visited Luther. After his marriage Smith and his wife quitted England for a season, and Patmore accompanied them as far as London.

The news of this marriage of a priest – a fact without precedent in England – made Stokesley throw Patmore into the Lollards' Tower, and although he was ill, neither fire, light, nor any other comfort was granted him. The bishop and his vicar-general visited him alone in his prison, and endeavoured by their threats to make him deny his faith.

It was during these circumstances that Bayfield was thrust into the tower. By his Christian words he revived Patmore's languishing faith, and the latter complained to the king that the Bishop of London prevented his feeding the flock which God had committed to his charge. Stokesley, comprehending whence Patmore derived his new courage, removed Bayfield from the Lollards' Tower and shut him up in the coal house, where he was fastened upright to the wall by the neck, middle, and legs. The unfortunate gospeller passed his time in continual darkness, never lying down, never seated, but nailed as it were to the wall, and never hearing the sound of human voice. We shall see him hereafter issuing from this horrible prison to die on the scaffold. As for Patmore, he remained in prison three years before he was released.

Patmore was not the only one in his family who suffered persecution; he had in London a brother named Thomas, a friend of John Tyndale, the younger brother of the celebrated reformer. Thomas had said that the truth of Scripture was at last reappearing in the world, after being hidden for many ages; and John Tyndale had sent five marks to his brother William, and received letters from him. Moreover, the two friends (who were both tradesmen) had distributed a great number of Testaments and other works. But their faith was not deeply rooted, and it was more out of sympathy for their brothers that they had believed; accordingly, Stokesley so completely entangled them that they confessed their 'crime'. More, acting through the Star Chamber, delighted at the opportunity which offered to cover the name of Tyndale with shame, was not satisfied with condemning the two friends to pay a fine of £100 each; he invented a new disgrace. He fastened to their dress some of the New Testaments which they had circulated, placed the two penitents on horseback with their faces towards the tail, and thus paraded them through the streets of London, exposed to the jeers and laughter of the populace. In this, More succeeded better than in his refutation of the reformer's writings.

From that time the persecution became more violent. Husbandmen, artists, tradespeople, and even noblemen, felt the cruel fangs of the clergy and of Sir Thomas More. They sent to jail a pious musician, Robert Lambe, who used to wander from town to town, singing to his harp a hymn in commendation of Martin Luther. A painter, named Edward Freese, a young man of ready wit, having been engaged to paint some hangings in a house in Colchester, wrote on the borders certain sentences of the Scripture. For this he was seized and taken to the Bishop of London's palace at Fulham, and there imprisoned, where his chief nourishment was bread made mostly out of sawdust. His poor wife, who was pregnant, went down to Fulham to see her husband; but the bishop's porter had orders to admit no one, and the brute gave her so violent a kick, as to kill her unborn infant, and cause the mother's death not long after. The unhappy Freese was removed to the Lollards' Tower, where he was put into chains, his hands only being left free. With these he took a piece of coal, and wrote some pious sentences on the wall: upon this he was manacled; but his wrists were so severely pinched that the flesh grew up higher than the irons. His intellect became disturbed; his hair in wild disorder soon covered his face, through which his eyes glared fierce and haggard. The want of proper food, bad treatment, his wife's death, and his lengthened imprisonment, entirely undermined his reason. When brought to St Paul's, he was kept three days without food; and when he appeared before the consistory the poor prisoner, silent and scarce able to stand, looked around and gazed upon the spectators, 'like a wild man'. The examination was begun, but to every question put to him Freese made the same answer: 'My Lord is a good man.' They could get nothing from him but this affecting reply. Alas! the light shone no more upon his understanding, but the love of Jesus was still in his heart. He did not fully recover his reason to his dying day. His brother, Valentine Freese, and his wife, gave their lives at one stake in York, for the testimony of Jesus Christ.

Terror began to spread far and wide. The most active evangelists had been compelled to flee to a foreign land; some of the most godly were in prison; and among those in high station there were many, and perhaps Latimer was one, who seemed willing to shelter themselves under an exaggerated moderation. But just as the persecution in London had succeeded in silencing the most timid, other voices more courageous were raised in the provinces. The city of Exeter was at that time in great agitation; placards had been discovered on the gates of the cathedral containing some of the principles of 'the new doctrine.' While the mayor and his officers were seeking after the author of these 'blasphemies', the bishop and all his doctors, 'as hot as coals', says the chronicler, 'and enkindled as though they had been stung with a sort of wasps', were preaching in the most fiery style. On the following Sunday, during the sermon, two men who had been the busiest of all the city in searching for the author of the bills, were struck by the appearance of a person seated near them. 'Surely, this fellow is the heretic', they said. But their neighbour's devotion, for he did not take his eyes off his book, quite put them out; they did not perceive that he was reading the New Testament in Latin.

This man, Thomas Bennet, was indeed the offender. Being converted at Cambridge by the preaching of Bilney, whose friend he was, he had gone to Torrington in Devonshire for fear of the persecution, and thence to Exeter and, after marrying to avoid unchastity (as he says) he became schoolmaster. Quiet, humble, courteous to everybody, and somewhat timid, Bennet had lived six years in that city without his faith being discovered. At last his conscience being awakened he resolved to fasten by night to the cathedral gates certain evangelical placards. 'Everybody will read the writing', he thought, 'and nobody will know the writer.' He did as he had proposed.

Not long after the Sunday on which he had been so nearly discovered, the priests prepared a great pageant, and made ready to pronounce against the unknown heretic the great curse 'with book, bell, and candle'. The cathedral was crowded, and Bennet himself was among the spectators. In the middle stood a great cross on which lighted tapers were placed, and around it were gathered all the Franciscans and Dominicans of Exeter. One of the priests having delivered a sermon on the words: *There is an accursed thing in the midst of thee, O Israel*, the bishop drew near the cross and pronounced the curse against the offender. He took one of the tapers and said: 'Let the soul of the unknown heretic, if he be dead already, be quenched this night in the pains of hell-fire, as this candle is now quenched and put out'; and with that he put out the candle. Then, taking off a second, he continued: 'and let us pray to God, if he be yet alive, that his eyes be put out, and that all the senses of his body may fail him, as now the light of this candle is gone', extinguishing the second candle. After this, one of the priests went up to the cross to take it away. It fell, however, and the noise it made in falling re-echoing along the roof so frightened the spectators that they uttered a shriek of terror, and held up their hands to heaven, as if to pray that the Divine curse might not fall on them. Bennet, a witness of this comedy, could not forbear smiling. 'What are you laughing at?' asked his neighbours; 'here is the heretic, here is the heretic, hold him fast.' This created great confusion among the crowd, some shouting, some clapping their hands, others running to and fro, but, owing to the tumult, Bennet succeeded in making his escape.

The excommunication did but increase his desire to attack the Romish superstitions; and accordingly, before five o'clock the next morning (it was in the month of October 1530) his servant boy fastened up again by his orders on the cathedral gates some placards similar to those which had been torn down. It chanced that a citizen going to early Mass saw the boy and, running up to him, caught hold of him and pulled down the papers; and then, dragging the boy with one hand and with the placards in the other, he went to the mayor of the city. Bennet's servant was recognized; his master was immediately arrested, and put in the stocks, and in strong irons, 'with as much favour as a dog would find', says Foxe.

Exeter seemed determined to make itself the champion of sacerdotalism in England. For a whole week, not only the bishop, but all the priests and friars of the city, visited Bennet night and day. But they tried in vain to prove to him that the Roman Church was the true one. 'God has given me grace to be of a better church', he said. – 'Do you not know that ours is built upon St Peter?' – 'The church that is built upon a man', he replied, 'is the devil's church and not God's.' His cell was continually thronged with visitors; and, in default of arguments, the most ignorant of the friars called the prisoner a heretic, and spat upon him. At length they brought to him a learned doctor of theology, who, they supposed, would infallibly convert him. 'Our ways are God's ways', said the doctor gravely. But he soon discovered that theologians can do nothing against the word of the Lord. 'He only is my way', replied Bennet, 'who saith, *I am the way, the truth, and the life*. In his *way* will I walk; – his *truth* will I embrace – his everlasting *life* will I seek.'

He was condemned to be burnt; and More having transmitted the order *de comburendo* with the utmost speed, the priests placed Bennet in the hands of the sheriff on 15 January 1531, by whom he was conducted to the Livery-dole, a field outside the city, where the stake was prepared. When Bennet arrived at the place of execution, he briefly exhorted the people, but with such unction, that the sheriff's clerk, as he heard him, exclaimed: 'Truly this is a servant of God.' Two persons, however, seemed unmoved: they were Thomas Carew and John Barnehouse, both holding the station of gentlemen. Going up to the martyr, they exclaimed in a threatening voice: 'Say, *Precor sanctam Mariam et omnes sanctos Dei*.'[8] – 'I know no other advocate but Jesus Christ', replied Bennet. Barnehouse was so enraged at these words, that he took a furze-bush upon a pike and, setting it on fire, thrust it into the martyr's face, exclaiming: 'Accursed heretic, pray to our Lady, or I will make you do it.' – 'Alas!' replied Bennet patiently, 'trouble me not'; and then holding up his hands, he prayed: 'Father, forgive them!' The executioners immediately set fire to the wood, and the most fanatical of the spectators, both men and women, seized with an indescribable fury, tore up stakes and bushes, and whatever they could lay their hands on, and flung them all into the flames to increase their violence. Bennet, lifting up his eyes to heaven, exclaimed: 'Lord, receive my spirit.' Thus died, in the sixteenth century, the disciples of the reformation sacrificed by Henry VIII.

[8] I pray to holy Mary and all the saints of God.

The priests, thanks to the king's sword, began to count on victory; yet schoolmasters, musicians, tradesmen, and even ecclesiastics, were not enough for them. They wanted nobler victims, and these were to be looked for in London. More himself, accompanied by the lieutenant of the Tower, searched many of the suspected houses. Few citizens were more esteemed in London than John Petit, the same who, in the House of Commons, had so nobly resisted the king's demand about the loan. Petit was learned in history and in Latin literature: he spoke with eloquence, and for twenty years had worthily represented the city. Whenever any important affair was debated in Parliament, the king, feeling uneasy, was in the habit of inquiring which side he took. This political independence, very rare in Henry's parliaments, gave umbrage to the king and his ministers. Petit, the friend of Bilney, Fryth, and Tyndale, had been one of the first in England to taste the sweetness of God's word, and had immediately manifested that beautiful characteristic by which the gospel faith makes itself known, namely, charity. He abounded in almsgiving, supported a great number of poor preachers of the gospel in his own country and beyond the seas; and whenever he noted down these generous aids in his books, he wrote merely the words: 'Lent unto Christ.' He, moreover, forbade his testamentary executors to call in these debts.

Petit was tranquilly enjoying the sweets of domestic life in his modest home in the society of his wife and two daughters, Blanche and Audrey, when he received an unexpected visit. One day, as he was praying in his chamber, a loud knock was heard at the street door. His wife opened it, but seeing Lord Chancellor More, she returned hurriedly to her husband, and told him that the Lord Chancellor wanted him. More, who followed her, entered the chamber, and with inquisitive eye ran over the shelves of the library, but could find nothing suspicious. Presently he made as if he would retire, and Petit accompanied him. The chancellor stopped at the door and said to him: 'You assert that you have none of these new books?' – 'You have seen my library', replied Petit. – 'I am informed, however', replied More, 'that you not only read them, but pay for the printing.' And then he added in a severe tone: 'Follow the lieutenant.' In spite of the tears of his wife and daughters this independent member of Parliament was conducted to the Tower, and shut up in a damp dungeon where he had nothing but straw to lie upon. His wife went thither each day in vain, asking, with tears, permission to see him, or at least to send him a bed. The jailers refused her everything; and it was only when Petit fell dangerously ill that the latter favour was granted him. This took place in 1530; sentence was passed in 1531; we shall see Petit again in his prison. He left it, indeed, but only to sink under the cruel treatment he had there experienced.

Thus were the witnesses to the truth struck down by the priests, by Sir Thomas More, and by Henry VIII. A new victim was to be the cause of many tears. A meek and humble man, one dear to all the friends of the gospel, and whom we may regard as the spiritual father of the reformation in England, was on the point of mounting the burning pile raised by his persecutors. Some time prior to Petit's appearance before his judges, which took place in 1531, an unusual noise was heard in the cell above him; it was Thomas Bilney whom they were conducting to the Tower. We left him at the end of 1528, after his fall. Bilney had returned to Cambridge tormented by remorse; his friends in vain crowded round him by night and by day; they could not console him, and even the Scriptures seemed to utter no voice but that of condemnation. Fear made him tremble constantly, and he could scarcely eat or drink. At length a heavenly and unexpected light dawned in the heart of the fallen disciple; a witness whom he had vexed – the Holy Spirit – spoke once more in his heart. Bilney fell at the foot of the cross, shedding floods of tears, and there he found peace. But the more God comforted him, the greater seemed his crime. One only thought possessed him, that of giving his life for the truth. He had shrunk from before the burning pile; its flames must now consume him. Neither the weakness of his body, which his long anguish had much increased, nor the cruelty of his enemies, nor his natural timidity, nothing could stop him: he strove for the martyr's crown. At ten o'clock one night, when every person in Trinity Hall was retiring to rest, Bilney called his friends round him, reminded them of his fall, and added: 'You shall see me no more. ... Do not stay me: my decision is formed, and I shall carry it out. My face is set to go to Jerusalem.' Bilney repeated the words used by the Evangelist, when he describes Jesus going up to the city where he was to be put to death. Having shaken hands with his brethren, this venerable man, the foremost of the evangelists of England in order of time, left Cambridge under cover of the night, and proceeded to Norfolk, to confirm in the faith those who had believed, and to invite the ignorant multitude to the Saviour. We shall not follow him in this last and solemn ministry; these facts and others of the same kind belong to a later date. Before the year 1531 closed in, Bilney, Bainham, Bayfield, Tewkesbury, and many others, struck by Henry's sword, sealed by their blood the testimony rendered by them to the perfect grace of Christ.

CHAPTER SIXTEEN

Wolsey Falls like Lucifer

(1530)

While many pious Christians were languishing in the prisons of England, the great antagonist of the reformation was disappearing from the stage of this world. We must return to Wolsey, who was still detained at Esher.

The cardinal, fallen from the summit of honours, was seized with those panic-terrors usually felt after their disgrace by those who have made a whole nation tremble, and he fancied an assassin lay hid behind every door. 'This very night', he wrote to Cromwell on one occasion, 'I was as one that should have died. If I might, I would not fail to come on foot to you, rather than this my speaking with you shall be put over and delayed. If the displeasure of my Lady Anne be somewhat assuaged, as I pray God the same may be, then I pray you exert all possible means of attaining her favour.'

In consequence of this, Cromwell hastened down to Esher two or three days after taking his seat in Parliament, and Wolsey, all trembling, recounted his fears to him. 'Norfolk, Suffolk, and Lady Anne perhaps, desire my death. Did not Thomas Becket, an archbishop like me, stain the altar with his blood?' … Cromwell reassured him, and, moved by the old man's fears, asked and obtained of Henry an order of protection.

Wolsey's enemies most certainly desired his death; but it was from the justice of the three estates, and not by the assassin's dagger that they sought it. The House of Peers authorized Sir Thomas More, the dukes of Norfolk and Suffolk, and fourteen other lords, to prepare a bill of attainder against the cardinal-legate. They forgot nothing: that haughty formula, *Ego et rex meus*, I and my king, which Wolsey had often employed; his infringement of the laws of the kingdom; his monopolizing the church revenues; the crying injustice of which he had been guilty – as, for instance, in the case of Sir John Stanley, who was sent to prison until he gave up a lease to the son of a woman who had borne the cardinal two children; many families ruined to satisfy his avarice; treaties concluded with foreign powers without the king's order; his exactions, which had impoverished England; and the foul diseases and infectious breath with which he had polluted His Majesty's presence. These were some of the forty-four grievances presented by the peers to the king, and which Henry sent down to the Lower House for their consideration.

It was at first thought that nobody in the commons would undertake Wolsey's defence, and it was generally expected that he would be given up to the vengeance of the law (as the bill of attainder prayed) or, in other words, to the axe of the executioner. But one man stood up and prepared, though alone, to defend the cardinal: this was Cromwell. The members asked of each other who the unknown man was; he soon made himself known. His knowledge of facts, his familiarity with the laws, the force of his eloquence, and the moderation of his language, surprised the House. Wolsey's adversaries had hardly aimed a blow before the defender had already parried it. If any charge was brought forward to which he could not reply, he proposed an adjournment until the next day, departed for Esher at the end of the sitting, conferred with Wolsey, returned during the night, and next morning reappeared in the commons with fresh arms. Cromwell carried the House with him; the attainder failed, and Wolsey's defender took his station among the statesmen of England. This victory, one of the greatest triumphs of parliamentary eloquence at that period, satisfied both the ambition and the gratitude of Cromwell. He was now firmly fixed in the king's favour, esteemed by the commons, and admired by the people: circumstances which furnished him with the means of bringing to a favourable conclusion the emancipation of the Church of England.

The ministry, composed of Wolsey's enemies, was annoyed at the decision of the Lower House, and appointed a commission to examine into the matter. When the cardinal was informed of this he fell into new terrors. He lost all appetite and desire of sleep, and a fever attacked him at Christmas. 'The cardinal will be dead in four days', said his physician to Henry, 'if he receives no comfort shortly from you and Lady Anne.' – 'I would not lose him for twenty thousand pounds', exclaimed the king. He desired to preserve Wolsey in case his old minister's consummate ability should become necessary, which was by no means unlikely. Henry gave the doctor his portrait in a ring, and Anne, at the king's desire, added the tablet of gold that hung at her girdle. The delighted cardinal placed the presents on his bed and, as he gazed on them, he felt his strength return. He was removed from his miserable dwelling at Esher to the royal palace at Richmond; and before long he was able to go into the park, where every night he read his breviary.

Ambition and hope returned with life. If the king desired to destroy the papal power in England, could not the proud cardinal preserve it? Might not Thomas Wolsey do under Henry VIII what Thomas Becket had done under Henry II? His see of York, the ignorance of the priests, the superstition of the people, the discontent of the great – all would be of service to him; and indeed, six years later, 40,000 men were under arms in a moment in Yorkshire to defend the cause of Rome. Wolsey, strong in England by the support of the nation (such at least was his opinion), aided without by the pope and the Continental powers, might give the law to Henry and crush the reformation.

The king having permitted him to go to York, which he had never yet visited although he had been Archbishop of York since 1514, Wolsey prayed for an increase to his archiepiscopal revenues, which amounted, however, to four thousand pounds sterling. Henry granted him a thousand marks, and the cardinal, shortly before Easter, 1530, departed with a train of 160 persons. He thought it was the beginning of his triumph.

Wolsey took up his abode at Cawood Castle, Yorkshire, one of his archiepiscopal residences, and strove to win the affections of the people. This prelate, once 'the haughtiest of men', says George Cavendish, the man who knew him and served him best, became quite a pattern of affability. He kept an open table, distributed bounteous alms at his gate, said Mass in the village churches, went and dined with the neighbouring gentry, gave splendid entertainments, and wrote to several princes imploring their help. It is even asserted by Edward Hall, a chronicler who was a contemporary of Wolsey, that he requested the pope to excommunicate Henry VIII. All being thus prepared, he thought he might make his solemn entry into York, preparatory to his enthronement, which was fixed for Monday 7 November.

Every movement of his was known at court; every action was canvassed, and its importance exaggerated. 'We thought we had brought him down', some said, 'and here he is rising up again.' Henry himself was alarmed. 'The cardinal, by his detestable intrigues', he said, 'is conspiring against my crown, and plotting both at home and abroad.' Wolsey's destruction was resolved upon.

The morning after All Saints' day (Friday, 4 November 1530) the Earl of Northumberland, attended by a numerous escort, arrived at Cawood, where the cardinal was still residing. He was the same Percy whose affection for Anne Boleyn had been thwarted by Wolsey; and there may have been design in Henry's choice. The cardinal eagerly moved forward to meet this unexpected guest, and, impatient to know the object of his mission, took him into his bedchamber, under the pretence of changing his travelling dress. They both remained some time standing at a window without uttering a word; the earl looked confused and agitated, whilst Wolsey endeavoured to repress his emotion. But at last, with a strong effort, Northumberland laid his hand upon the arm of his former master, and with a low voice said: 'My lord, I arrest you for high treason.' The cardinal remained speechless, as if stunned. He was kept a prisoner in his room.

It is doubtful whether Wolsey was guilty of the crime with which he was charged. We may believe that he entertained the idea of some day bringing about the triumph of the popedom in England, even should it cause Henry's ruin; but perhaps this was all. But an idea is not a conspiracy, although it may rapidly expand into one.

More than three thousand persons (attracted, not by hatred, like the Londoners, when Wolsey departed from Whitehall, but by enthusiasm) collected the next day before the castle to salute the cardinal. 'God save Your Grace!' they shouted on every side, and a numerous crowd

escorted him at night; some carried torches in their hands, and all made
the air re-echo with their cries. The unhappy prelate was conducted to
Sheffield Park, the residence of the Earl of Shrewsbury. Some days after
his arrival, the faithful Cavendish ran to him, exclaiming: 'Good news,
my lord! Sir William Kingston and twenty-four of the guard are come to
escort you to His Majesty.' – 'Kingston!' exclaimed the cardinal, turning
pale, 'Kingston!' and then, slapping his hand on his thigh, he heaved a
deep sigh. This news had crushed his mind. One day a fortune-teller,
whom he consulted, had told him: '*You shall have your end at Kingston*';
and from that time the cardinal had carefully avoided the town of
Kingston-on-Thames. But now he thought he understood the prophecy.
… Kingston, Constable of the Tower, was about to cause his death. They
left Sheffield Park; but fright had given Wolsey his death-blow. Several
times he was near falling from his mule, and on the third day, when they
reached Leicester Abbey, he said as he entered: 'Father abbot, I am come
hither to leave my bones among you'; and immediately took to his bed.
This was on Saturday, 26 November.

On Monday morning, tormented by gloomy forebodings, Wolsey
asked what was the time of day. 'Past eight o'clock', replied Cavendish.
– 'That cannot be', said the cardinal, 'eight o'clock. … No! for by eight
o'clock you shall lose your master.' At six on Tuesday, Kingston having
come to inquire about his health, Wolsey said to him: 'I shall not live
long.' – 'Be of good cheer', rejoined the governor of the Tower. – 'Alas,
Master Kingston', exclaimed the cardinal, 'if I had served God as
diligently as I have served the king, he would not have given me over in
my grey hairs!' and then he added with downcast head: 'This is my just
reward.' What a judgment upon his own life!

On the very threshold of eternity (for he had but a few minutes to
live) the cardinal summoned up all his hatred against the reformation,
and made a last effort. The persecution was too slow to please him:
'Master Kingston', he said, 'attend to my last request: tell the king
that I conjure him in God's name to destroy this new pernicious sect
of Lutherans.' And then, with astonishing presence of mind in this his
last hour, Wolsey described the misfortunes which the Hussites had, in
his opinion, brought upon Bohemia; and then, coming to England, he

recalled the times of Wycliffe and Sir John Oldcastle. He grew animated; his dying eyes yet shot forth fiery glances. He trembled lest Henry VIII, unfaithful to the pope, should hold out his hand to the reformers. 'Master Kingston', said he, in conclusion, 'the king should know that if he tolerates heresy, God will take away his power, and we shall then have mischief upon mischief ... barrenness, scarcity, and disorder to the utter destruction of this realm.'

Wolsey was exhausted by the effort. After a momentary silence, he resumed with a dying voice: 'Master Kingston, farewell! My time draweth on fast. Forget not what I have said and charged you withal; for when I am dead ye shall peradventure remember my words better.' It was with difficulty he uttered these words; his tongue began to falter, his eyes became fixed, his sight failed him; he breathed his last. At the same minute the clock struck *eight*, and the attendants standing round his bed looked at each other in affright. It was 29 November 1530.

Thus died the man once so much feared. Power had been his idol: to obtain it in the state, he had sacrificed the liberties of England; and to win it or to preserve it in the church, he had fought against the reformation. If he encouraged the nobility in the luxuries and pleasures of life, it was only to render them more supple and more servile; if he supported learning, it was only that he might have a clergy fitted to keep the laity in their leading-strings. Ambitious, intriguing, and impure of life, he had been as zealous for the sacerdotal prerogative as the austere Becket; and by a singular contrast, a shirt of hair was found on the body of this voluptuous man. The aim of his life had been to raise the papal power higher than it had ever been before, at the very moment when the reformation was attempting to bring it down; and to take his seat on the pontifical throne with more than the authority of a Hildebrand. Wolsey, as pope, would have been the man of his age; and in the political world he would have done for the Roman primacy what the celebrated Loyola did for it soon after by his fanaticism. Obliged to renounce this idea, worthy only of the Middle Ages, he had desired at least to save the popedom in his own country; but here again he had failed. The pilot who had stood in England at the helm of the Romish Church was thrown overboard, and the ship, left to itself, was about to founder.

And yet, even in death, he did not lose his courage. The last throbs of his heart had called for victims; the last words from his failing lips, the last message to his master, his last testament had been – *Persecution!* This testament was to be only too faithfully executed.

* * * * *

The epoch of the fall and death of Cardinal Wolsey, which is the point at which we halt, was not only important because it ended the life of a man who had presided over the destinies of England, and had endeavoured to grasp the sceptre of the world, but it is of especial consequence because then three movements were accomplished, from which the great transformation of the sixteenth century was to proceed. Each of these movements has its characteristic result.

The first is represented by Cromwell. The supremacy of the pope in England was about to be wrested from him, as it was in all the Reformed churches. But a step further was taken in England. That supremacy was transferred to the person of the king. Wolsey had exercised as vicar-general a power till then unknown. Unable to become pope at the Vatican, he had made himself a pope at Whitehall. Henry had permitted his minister to raise this hierarchical throne by the side of his own. But he had soon discovered that there ought not to be two thrones in England, or at least not two kings. He had dethroned Wolsey; and, resolutely seating himself in his place, he was about to assume at Whitehall that tiara which the ambitious prelate had prepared for himself. Some persons, when they saw this, exclaimed that if the papal supremacy were abolished, that of the word of God ought alone to be substituted. And, indeed, the true reformation is not to be found in this first movement.

The second, which was essential to the renewal of the church, was represented by Cranmer, and consisted particularly in re-establishing the authority of holy Scripture. Wolsey did not fall alone, nor did Cranmer rise alone: each of these two men carried with him the system he represented. The fabric of Roman traditions fell with the first; the foundations of the holy Scriptures were laid by the second; and yet, while we render all justice to the sincerity of the Cambridge doctor, we must not be blind to his weaknesses, his subserviency, and even a certain degree of negligence, which, by allowing parasitical plants to shoot up here and there, permitted them to spread over the living rock of God's word. Not in this movement, then, was found the reformation with all its energy and all its purity.

The third movement was represented by the martyrs. When the church takes a new life, it is fertilized by the blood of its confessors; and being continually exposed to corruption, it has constant need to be purified by suffering. Not in the palaces of Henry VIII, nor even in the councils where the question of throwing off the papal supremacy was discussed, must we look for the true children of the reformation; we must go to the Tower of London, to the Lollards' Towers of St Paul's and of Lambeth, to the other prisons of England, to the bishops' cellars, to the fetters, the stocks, the rack, and the stake. The godly men who invoked the sole intercession of Christ Jesus, the only Head of his people, who wandered up and down, deprived of everything, gagged, scoffed at, scourged, and tortured, and who, in the midst of all their tribulations, preserved their Christian patience, and turned, like their Master, the eyes of their faith towards Jerusalem – these were the disciples of the reformation in England. The purest church is the church under the cross.

The father of this church in England was not Henry VIII. When the king cast into prison or gave to the flames men like Hitton, Bennet, Patmore, Petit, Bayfield, Bilney, and many others, he was not 'the father of the reformation of England', as some have so falsely asserted; he was its executioner.

The Church of England was foredoomed to be in its renovation a church of martyrs; and the true father of this church is our Father which is in heaven.

[An Index will be found at the end of Volume Two]

The Banner of Truth Trust originated in 1957 in London. The founders believed that much of the best literature of historic Christianity had been allowed to fall into oblivion and that, under God, its recovery could well lead not only to a strengthening of the church, but to true revival.

Inter-denominational in vision, this publishing work is now international, and our lists include a number of contemporary authors along with classics from the past. The translation of these books into many languages is encouraged.

A monthly magazine, *The Banner of Truth*, is also published. More information about this and all our publications can be found on our website or supplied by either of the offices below.

THE BANNER OF TRUTH TRUST

3 Murrayfield Road
Edinburgh, EH12 6EL
U.K.

PO Box 621, Carlisle,
Pennsylvania 17013,
U.S.A.

www.banneroftruth.org